Encyclopedia of Women & Islamic Cultures

VOLUME II

Family, Law and Politics

Encyclopedia of Women & Islamic Cultures

VOLUME II

Family, Law and Politics

General Editor
Suad Joseph

Associate Editors
Afsaneh Najmabadi
Julie Peteet
Seteney Shami
Jacqueline Siapno
Jane I. Smith

BRILL
LEIDEN – BOSTON
2005

ISBN 90 04 12818 2 (Vol. II)
ISBN 90 04 13247 3 (Set)

This book is printed on acid-free paper.

Cover design: BEELDVORM, Pijnacker

PRINTED IN THE NETHERLANDS

For author's template, see:
http://www.brill.nl
http://www.sjoseph.ucdavis.edu/ewic

Contents

List of Contributors

Dono Abdurazakova, Ph.D. (history)
Rula Abisaab, McGill University, Quebec
Lila Abu-Lughod, Columbia University, New York
Lama Abu-Odeh, Georgetown University Law Center, Washington, D.C.
Madelaine Adelman, Arizona State University
Najwa Adra, Independent Scholar
Fawzia Afzal-Khan, Montclair State University, New Jersey
Nausheen Ahmad, Shirkat Gah, Women's Resource Centre, Karachi, and South Asian Research Network on Gender, Law and Governance, Warwick, UK
Jale Ahmadi, Independent Scholar
Kristine Ajrouch, Eastern Michigan University
Muhamad Ali, Syarif Hidayatullah State Islamic University, Jakarta, Indonesia
Ousseina Alidou, Rutgers University, New Jersey
Dinara Alimdjanova, DSSP/UNDP, Uzbekistan
Lori A. Allen, University of Chicago
Özlem Altan, New York University
Ayşe Gül Altınay, Sabanci University, Turkey
Sajeda Amin, Population Council, New York
Valérie Amiraux, CNRS/CURAPP, Université Jules Verne of Picardie, France
B. Lacey Andrews, Brown University, Providence, Rhode Island
Sarah Ansari, Royal Holloway, University of London
Etin Anwar, Hamilton College, Clinton, New York
Ghazala Anwar, University of Canterbury, UK
Yeşim Arat, Bogaziçi University, Turkey
Cânân Arin, Co-founder of Purple Roof Women's Shelter Foundation, Co-founder of Association for Support and Training Women Candidates, Co-founder of Istanbul Bar Association Women's Enforcement Center, Turkey
Febe Armanios, Middlebury College, Middlebury, Vermont
Omar Ashour, McGill University, Quebec
Barbara C. Aswad, Wayne State University, Detroit, Michigan
Ayşe Ayata, Middle East Technical University, Turkey
Nodira Azimova, Sharh va Tavsiya Sociology Center, Tashkent, Uzbekistan
Shaheen Hussain Azmi, Independent Scholar
Irina Babich, Russian Academy of Sciences
Aydın Babuna, Bogaziçi University, Turkey
Jasna Bakšić Muftić, University of Sarajevo
Paula Banerjee, University of Calcutta
Jamila Bargach, School of Architecture, Rabat, Morocco
Beth Baron, City University of New York
Arpita Basuroy, Maulana Abul Kalam Azad Institute of Asian Studies, India
Asma Beatrix, City University of Hong Kong
Vida Behnam, Independent Scholar
Houri Berberian, California State University, Long Beach
Fatmagül Berktay, Istanbul University
Zarina Bhatty, Indian Asssociation of Women's Studies, New Delhi and Centre of Women's Studies, New Delhi
Laura Bier, New York University
Hande A. Birkalan-Gedik, Yeditepe University, Istanbul
Elizabeth Bishop, The University of Texas, Austin

Isa Blumi, Trinity College, Hartford, Connecticut
Michel Boivin, Centre d'Etudes de l'Inde et de l'Asie du Sud (EHESS/CNRS), Paris
Bill Bowring, London Metropolitan University
Jean Boyd, School of Oriental and African Studies, University of London
Mirjam de Bruijn, African Studies Centre, Leiden
Beth Anne Buggenhagen, University of Chicago
Katherine Bullock, University of Toronto
Amila Buturovic, York University, Toronto
Ömer Çaha, Fatih University, Istanbul
Serpil Çakır, University of Istanbul
Barbara Callaway, University of Connecticut
Mark Cammack, Southwestern University School of Law, Texas
Murat Çemrek, Selcuk University, Konya, Turkey
Jocelyne Cesari, Centre National de la Recherche Scientifique, Paris and Harvard University
Indrani Chatterjee, Rutgers University, New Jersey
Mary Ellen Chatwin, Tblisi State University, Republic of Georgia
Amrita Chhachhi, Institute of Social Studies, The Hague
Maliha Chishti, OISE/University of Toronto
Allan Christelow, Idaho State University
Oya Çitçi, Türkiye ve Orta Doğu Amme Idaresi Ensititüsü, Ankara
Dan Connell, Simmons College, Boston, Massachusetts
Lucy Creevey, University of Connecticut
Igor Cusack, University of Bristol, UK
Susanne Dahlgren, University of Helsinki
Ahmad Dallal, Georgetown University, Washington, D.C.
Mary-Catherine Daly, College of St. Catherine, St. Paul, Minnesota
Manijeh Daneshpour, St. Cloud State University, Minnesota
Suleman E. Dangor, University of Kwazulu-Natal
Shamita Das Dasgupta, Manavi, Inc., New Jersey
Jennifer L. De Maio, University of California, Los Angeles
Claudia Derichs, University of Duisburg-Essen
Theresa W. Devasahayam, Asia Research Institute, the National University of Singapore
Robert Dowd, University of Notre Dame, Indiana
Džamna Duman, University of Sarajevo
Susī Dwī Harījantī, Padjadjaran University, Indonesia
Mina Elfira, Universitas Indonesia
Noraida Endut, Universiti Sains Malaysia
Haleh Esfandiari, Woodrow Wilson International Center for Scholars, Washington, D.C.
Katherine Ewing, Duke University, North Carolina
Nadia Fadil, Catholic University of Leuven, Belgium, Research Assistant for the Fund for Scientific Research (FWO-Vlaanderen)
Elizabeth Anne Faier, University of Richmond, Virginia
Muneer Fareed, Wayne State University, Detroit, Michigan
Farideh Farhi, University of Hawaii at Manoa
Lindsey Fauss, The Queen Zein Al Sharaf Institute for Development (ZENID), Jordan
Nasreen Fazalbhoy, University of Mumbai
Carolyn Fluehr-Lobban, Rhode Island College
Emily Frank, Indiana University
Elizabeth Frierson, University of Cincinnati
Annalisa Frisina, University of Padova, Italy
Nancy Gallagher, University of California, Santa Barbara
Geetanjali Gangoli, University of Bristol, UK
Ann Gardner, Applied Social Anthropologist
Pauline van Gelder, Radboud University Nijmegen, The Netherlands
Rehana Ghadially, Indian Institute of Technology, Mumbai

Farha Ghannam, Swarthmore College, Pennsylvania
Andrea Giacomuzzi, University of Arizona, Tucson
Avner Giladi, University of Haifa
Iris Glosemeyer, Stiftung Wissenschaft und Politik, Berlin
Nasrine Gross, University of Kabul
Marie-Carin von Gumppenberg, Policy Studies Central Asia, Munich
Fakhri Haghani, Georgia State University
Sondra Hale, University of California, Los Angeles
Colette Harris, Virginia Tech
Zoya Hasan, Jawaharlal Nehru University, New Delhi
Nadia Hashmi, Formerly of European University Institute, Florence
Amir Hassanpour, University of Toronto
Mervat F. Hatem, Howard University, Washington, D.C.
Mary Elaine Hegland, Santa Clara University, California
Marcia Hermansen, Loyola University, Chicago
Hanna Herzog, Tel Aviv University and Harvard University
Leila Hessini, Ipas, USA
Farideh Heyat, School of Oriental and African Studies, University of London
Valerie Hoffman, University of Illinois at Urbana-Champaign
Paula Holmes-Eber, University of Washington
Homa Hoodfar, Concordia University, Quebec
Shareda Hosein, Hartford Seminary, Connecticut
Nadirsyah Hosen, The State University of Islamic Studies (UIN) Syarif Hidayatullah, Jakarta
Leila Hudson, University of Arizona
Jamila Hussain, University of Technology, Sydney
Sabiha Hussain, Centre for Women's Development Studies, New Delhi
Pinar Ilkkaracan, Independent scholar, Women for Women's Human Rights – New Ways, Turkey
E. Olcay Imamoğlu, Middle East Technical University, Ankara
Alia Imtoual, Gender Studies, University of Adelaide
Nilüfer A. İsvan, Channing Bete Company, Inc., South Deerfield, Massachusetts
Rounaq Jahan, Columbia University, New York
Jajang Jahroni, State Islamic University Syarif Hidayatullah, Jakarta, Indonesia
Ayesha Jalal, Tufts University, Massachusetts
Amaney Jamal, Princeton University, New Jersey
Uzma Jamil, McGill University, Quebec
Willy Jansen, Radboud University Nijmegen, The Netherlands
Haifaa Jawad, University of Birmingham, UK
Laura D. Jenkins, University of Cincinnati
Anne M. Jennings, Independent Scholar
Penny Johnson, Institute of Women's Studies, Birzeit University
Christina Jones-Pauly, Harvard University and University of London
Almaz Kadirova, Women's Resource Centre, Tashkent
Palwasha Kakar, Harvard University
Ratna Kapur, Centre for Feminist Legal Research, and Indian Society for International Law, New Delhi
Mehrangiz Kar, Harvard University
Ayfer Karakaya-Stump, Harvard University
Azza M. Karam, Regional Bureau for Arab States, United Nations Development Programme
Niaz Kasravi, Amnesty International USA (Ph.D. University of California, Irvine)
Sofia Kasymova, Academy of Sciences, Dushanbe, Republic of Tajikistan
Nursyahbani Katjasungkana, Indonesian Women's Association for Justice
Masoud Kazemzadeh, Utah Valley State College
Patricia L. Kelly Spurles, Mount Allison University, New Brunswick
Burçak Keskin-Kozat, University of Michigan
Mohammad Mohabbat Khan, University of Dhaka
Mana Kia, Harvard University

Azadeh Kian-Thiébaut, University of Paris VIII and Monde Iranien, CNRS
Diane E. King, American University of Beirut
Gritt Klinkhammer, University of Bremen
Dicle Kogacioglu, Sabanci University, Istanbul
Nita Kumar, University of Michigan and Centre for Postcolonial Education, India
Lilia Labidi, University of Tunis
Siobhan Lambert-Hurley, Nottingham Trent University, UK
Felicity Lancaster, Orkney
William Lancaster, Orkney
Kjersti Larsen, University of Oslo
Shahida Lateef, Independent Scholar
Pranee Liamputtong, La Trobe University, Melbourne
Kathryn Libal, University of Connecticut
Mandana Limbert, Queens College, City University of New York
Erika Loeffler Friedl, Western Michigan University
Scott London, Randolph-Macon College, Ashland, Virginia
Patricia M. E. Lorcin, University of Minnesota, Twin Cities
Mark David Luce, University of Chicago
Ranto Lukito, State Islamic University Sunan Kalijaga Yogyakarta, Indonesia and Faculty of Law, McGill University, Quebec
Pute Rahimah Makol-Abdul, International Islamic University, Malaysia
Helena Malikyar, New York University
Susan Stiles Maneck, Jackson State University, Mississippi
Manzurul Mannan, Independent University, Bangladesh
Julie Marcus, Charles Sturt University, New South Wales
Ingrid Mattson, Hartford Seminary, Connecticut
Katayun Mazdapour, Institute for Humanities and Cultural Studies, Tehran
Rubya Mehdi, University of Copenhagen
Anne Meneley, Trent University, Canada
Margaret L. Meriwether, Denison University, Ohio
Gwendolyn Mikell, Georgetown University, Washington, D.C.
Margaret A. Mills, Ohio State University
Qudsia Mirza, School of Law, University of East London, UK
Valentine M. Moghadam, Illinois State University and UNESCO
Haideh Moghissi, York University, Toronto
Shahzrad Mojab, University of Toronto
Erin Patrice Moore, University of Southern California
Kathleen M. Moore, University of California, Santa Barbara
Annelies Moors, University of Amsterdam/ISIM
Negar Mottahedeh, Duke University, North Carolina
Tazeen Mahnaz Murshid, Université Libre de Bruxelles and School of Oriental and African Studies, University of London
Nadira Mustapha, McGill University, Quebec
Mechthild Nagel, State University of New York at Cortland
Nima Naghibi, University of Winnipeg
Afsaneh Najmabadi, Harvard University
Senzil Nawid, Independent Scholar
Norma T. Nemeh, School for International Training, Academic Director, Jordan Program
Leyla Neyzi, Sabanci University, Turkey
Karin van Nieuwkerk, Radboud University Nijmegen, The Netherlands
Mohamed Nimer, Council on American-Islamic Relations
Isis Nusair, Saint Mary's College, Notre Dame, Indiana
Leslye Amede Obiora, University of Arizona College of Law
Ahmet Yaşar Ocak, Hacettepe Üniversitesi, Turkey
Tomoki Okawara, Tohoku University, Sendai, Japan

Ferhunde Özbay, Bogaziçi University, Turkey
Aylin Özman, Hacettepe University, Ankara, Turkey
Archana Parashar, Macquarie University, New South Wales
Ayşe Parla, New York University
Leslie Peirce, University of California, Berkeley
Alisa Perkins, University of Texas, Austin
Svetlana Peshkova, Syracuse University, New York
Maurita Poole, Independent Scholar
Sara Pursley, City University of New York
Annika Rabo, University of Stockholm
Mitra Raheb, Independent Analyst, St. Thomas University, Miami
Saodah Abdul Rahman, International Islamic University, Malaysia
Aparna Rao, University of Cologne
Sudha Ratan, Augusta State University, Georgia
Margaret J. Rausch, University of Kansas
Marleen Renders, University of Ghent
Susanna G. Rizzo, University of Wollongong, New South Wales
Kathryn Robinson, Australian National University
Elsbeth Robson, Keele University, UK
Mina Roces, The University of New South Wales
Elaheh Rostami Povey, School of Oriental and African Studies, University of London
Jasamin Rostam-Kolayi, California State Univeristy, San Marcos
Celia E. Rothenberg, McMaster University, Ontario
Alain Roussillon, Centre National de la Recherche Scientifique, Paris
Avi Rubin, Harvard University
Amalia Sa'ar, University of Haifa
Rima Sabban, Independent Researcher
Fatima Sadiqi, Sidi Mohamed Ben Abdellah University, Fes, Morocco
Chantal Saint-Blancat, University of Padova, Italy
Ayşe Saktanber, Middle East Technical University, Ankara, Turkey
Frank A. Salamone, Iona College, New Rochelle, New York
José C. M. van Santen, Leiden University
Chiara De Santi, European University Institute, Florence, Italy
Ingrid Schindlbeck, Ethnologisches Museum, Berlin
Asghar Schirazi, Free University, Berlin
Irene Schneider, University of Göttingen I
Dorothea Schulz, Free University, Berlin
Anna J. Secor, University of Kentucky
Huda A. Seif, Founder and Director: Alternative World: Partnership for Equitable Development and Social Justice, New York
Elyse Semerdjian, Whitman College, Washington
Lorelle Denise Semley, Wesleyan University, Middletown, Connecticut
Julie Shackford-Bradley, California State University, Monterey Bay
Jack G. Shaheen, Southern Illinois University, Edwardsville
Hammed Shahidian, University of Illinois at Springfield
Seteney Shami, Social Science Research Council, New York
Elora Shehabuddin, Rice University, Houston, Texas
Kim Shively, Kutztown University, Pennsylvania
Paul Silverstein, Reed College, Portland, Oregon
Rachel Simon, Princeton University, New Jersey
Kathryn Spellman, University of London and Syracuse University and Huron International University, London
Erin E. Stiles, California State University, Sacramento
Maila Stivens, University of Melbourne
Nancy L. Stockdale, University of Central Florida

Sevil Sümer, University of Bergen, Norway
Anara Tabyshalieva, Institute for Regional Studies, Kyrgyzstan
Liyakat Takim, University of Denver, Colorado
Elizabeth F. Thompson, University of Virginia
Marfua Tokhtakhodjaeva, Women's Resource Centre, Tashkent
Şule Toktaş, European University Institute, Florence, Italy
Aili Mari Tripp, University of Wisconsin, Madison
Mzia Tsereteli, Tbilisi State University, Republic of Georgia
Vicki Tsianakas, La Trobe University, Melbourne
Kari Vogt, University of Oslo
Earle Waugh, University of Alberta
Vivienne Wee, City University of Hong Kong
Lynn Welchman, School of Oriental and African Studies, University of London
Pnina Werbner, Keele University
Saskia Wieringa, University of Amsterdam
Adrien Katherine Wing, University of Iowa College of Law
Anna Würth, Free University, Berlin
Scott M. Youngstedt, Saginaw Valley State University, Michigan
Amberin Zaman, Turkey Correspondent, *Economist* (UK)
Habiba Zaman, Simon Fraser University, British Columbia
Madeline C. Zilfi, College Park, University of Maryland
Sherifa Zuhur, Strategic Studies Institute, U.S. Army War College, Pennsylvania
Feride Zurikashvili, Tbilisi State University, Republic of Georgia

List of Illustrations

The illustrations can be found between pages 428 and 429.

Family Law: Modern Family Law, 1800–Present: Gulf, Saudi Arabia, and Yemen (*Susanne Dahlgren*):
[*See page 467*]
Figure 1. Adeni family court judge in her court with her assistant, early 1990s. After Yemeni unification, women were no longer allowed to head a family court or to train as judges. Photo Susanne Dahlgren.

National Insignia, Signs, and Monuments: Iran (*Afsaneh Najmabadi*):
[*See page 524*]
Figure 2. Narinjistan, Shiraz, Qājār period building.
Figure 3. Official State Emblem of Iran, early 1970s.

Political-Social Movements: Revolutionary: South Yemen and Dhofar (*Susanne Dahlgren*):
[*See page 657–8*]
Figure 4. A factory worker in the Leather Shoe Factory, Aden. During the early years of the People's Democratic Republic of Yemen, literacy was a requirement to enter factory work. The photo is from 1989. Photo Susanne Dahlgren.
Figure 5. Participants of a literacy class run by a local club of the General Union of Yemeni Women during the late years of the People's Democratic Republic of Yemen. Photo Susanne Dahlgren.

Women's Rights: Male Advocacy: Overview (*Elizabeth Frierson*):
[*See page 781*]
Figure 6. *Khayāl al-ẓill* (Cairo n.d.), vol. 2, no. 62, Sunday, 23 August 1925, p. 16. Photo Credit: Near East Collections of the Princeton University Library.

Acknowledgments

As we send Volume II of *The Encyclopedia of Women and Islamic Cultures* to press, we take the time to respectfully and gratefully acknowledge those who have contributed to its ongoing production. We continue to be indebted to Brill for its investment in what has turned out to be a much larger and longer-lived project than any of us anticipated when EWIC was first conceived in 1994. Sam Bruinsma, the Business Unit Manager for History and Olaf Köndgen, the Islamic Studies Editor at Brill, have gone out of their way to provide support for EWIC, including adding the staff support services of Ingrid Heijckers who has significantly improved the efficiency of EWIC production. Isabella Gerritsen has loyally worked as EWIC's traffic director at Brill since 2001, managing correspondence and the flow of articles between authors, editors, and Brill. Margaret Owen has done a magnificent job as Copy Editor.

At the University of California, Davis, Dean of Social Sciences Steven Sheffrin offered EWIC and my other research projects a new server for our web work and web page (http://sjoseph.ucdavis.edu/ewic). Dean of Graduate Studies Jeffrey Gibeling kindly committed a new three-year work study grant for the EWIC research assistant. Vice Chancellor for Research Barry Klein was helpful in processing the new Ford Foundation grant, as was the Director of Sponsored Programs, Ahmad Hakim-Elahi. M. R. C. Greenwood, University of California Provost and Senior Vice President, and her staff played a vital role in working through contract details of the Ford Foundation grant. Much of the grant development could not have proceeded without the incredible efficiency and diligence of Leanna Sweha, UC Davis Contracts and Grants Officer, who worked through contract and subcontract details, and Matt Nguyen who stepped in when Leanna was away from the office. I am also indebted to Sandy Nixon and Kathy Haas in Accounting for processing the larger budget and reporting issues.

The computer expertise of Minh Nguyen from the Dean's office and the support of Assistant Dean Steven Roth and Lissa Torfi were important at crucial moments. In the Anthropology Department at UC Davis, Nancy McLaughlin, the Managerial Staff Officer, has worked hard to supervise my EWIC grants and the EWIC office, assisted valiantly by Candy Cayne Clark, the Anthropology Department Grants Officer, and the Anthropology Staff: Peggy Slaven, Barbara Raney, Royce McClellan, Eddie Ng, Tim Gilbert and Lisa Dietz. Their help has been most necessary for the continued work of EWIC.

Tracy Smith completed three years as EWIC Research Assistant in the Spring of 2004 with outstanding dedication. Bettina Schneider stepped in as EWIC Research Assistant most effectively in the fall of 2004. Jerry Lee trouble shot all our computer problems for over a year until he graduated in the Spring of 2004 when Andrey Dub took on that critical role. The number of undergraduate students working as Interns on the Scholars and Scholarship Project, to be published in a future EWIC volume, has increased. Nancy Wan, Monica Garcia, Fatima Naseem Malek, Rhyen Coombs and Tony Beukers – all of whom began working between January and Fall of 2002 – were joined by Marya Osucha, Emily Rostel, Monique Salas and Michelle Sandhoff in the Winter of 2003. Paulina Medeiros Tederer, Andrea McNees, Cristeta Shope, and Eva Brown joined in the Spring of 2004 followed, in the Summer of 2004, by Megan Fowler and Mary Beth Lansom. Fifteen undergraduates making a commitment of up to three years of work to ascertain all the Ph.D. dissertations carried out on topics related to women and Islamic cultures and to do a detailed analysis of the topics and researchers is rather unusual and quite admirable. I have been impressed and humbled by their energy and commitment.

Each of the Associate Editors have been supported by their institutions and paid assistants. Julie Peteet had the assistance of Leslie French, Whitney Gifford and Maryam Mirriahi who helped with her editorial work. Peteet is grateful for the support of the University of Louisville College of Arts and Sciences and Sharon O'Bryan, her support staff.

Seteney Shami would particularly like to thank Laleh Behbehanian and Tina Harris for research and administrative assistance, particularly in setting up systems to manage the flow of information and email traffic. Mary Ann Riad and Elissa Klein then joined the project. Shami is particularly grateful for the work of Laura Bier in diversifying the pool of invited authors, tracking authors and even reading some entries. Maria Todorova and Lucine Taminian were most helpful in suggesting authors.

Mohammed Tabishat assisted in translation. Shami also most gratefully acknowledges the Social Science Research Council for accommodating her engagement in the EWIC project, for financial assistance of project funds, and for providing facilities and logistical means for her and her research assistants.

Afsaneh Najmabadi gratefully acknowledges student assistants Avi Rubin and Tanya Zakrevskaya. She would, in very special terms, like to thank student assistant Loretta Kim whose incredible research and administrative skills and commitment made it possible for Najmabadi to persist in the hard work of editorial productivity. She is also grateful for the contributions of distinguished scholars whom she continually consulted – Yeşim Arat, Nodira Azimova, Nilüfer İsvan, Margaret Mills, Shahrzad Mojab, and Nayereh Tohidi. Najmabadi would like to recognize the contribution of Rose Glickman for translations from Russian and French and editorial work and Farideh Farhi for translations from Persian. Cory Paulsen, Harvard University History Department financial officer, was particularly helpful in processing the EWIC grants. Harvard University has been remarkably supportive during her work as Associate Editor.

Jane I. Smith would like to acknowledge the support of the Hartford Seminary, and especially Alice Horner, an independent researcher in Washington, D.C., who worked with her as Editorial Assistant for Sub-Saharan Africa to locate authors. Nathal Dessing of ISIM in Holland helped Smith with Western European sources and authors and Sheila McDonough, Nadia Wardeh, and Celine Leduc helped with sources and authors on Canada.

Similarly, Jacqueline Siapno had the support of the staff and administration at the University of Melbourne. She would also like to thank her hardworking, brilliant, and dedicated Research Assistant, Dina Afrianty, affiliated with the State Islamic Institute in Jakarta. International Advisory Board Editor Virginia Matheson Hooker was particularly helpful for South East Asia consultations.

The Editors of EWIC express their gratitude to the 42 members of the International Advisory Editorial Board. They came from all disciplines and all regions of the world. Many contributed entries to EWIC, many helped us find authors for entries, and all lent their good names to this project.

We are most grateful to the Ford Foundation for awarding EWIC a supplementary grant which was even more generous than the original grant. Without the funding from the Ford Foundation, much of the work and growth of EWIC would not have been possible. Constance Buchanan and her assistants, Maxine Gaddis and Irene Korenfield, shepherded the grant through the Foundation and elicited the joint contributions and support of Ford Foundation regional offices, including: Emma Playfair (Cairo), Ganesan Balachander (New Delhi), Omotade Aina (Nairobi), Gerry Salole (Johannesburg), Suzanne Siskel (Indonesia), and Adhiambo Odaga (Lagos). In addition contributions came from the central New York offices: Constance Buchanan and Janice Petrovich (Education, Knowledge, and Religion Program). The Ford Foundation grant allowed us to fund research assistants, buy out time, and fund Editorial Board meetings, supplies, and equipment. The grant made it possible for the Editorial Board to come closer to reaching our standards of encyclopedic knowledge production. We are greatly indebted to Constance Buchanan and all the New York City and Regional Program Officers who participated in this funding.

My personal gratitude to EWIC's Associate Editors, Afsaneh Najmabadi, Julie Peteet, Seteney Shami, Jacqueline Siapno, and Jane I. Smith and Editorial Assistant Alice Horner is profound. They have made sacrifices for EWIC at a level none of us could have anticipated when we began working together in the Spring of 1999. They have brilliantly conjoined their diverse intellectual trajectories into a interdisciplinary, cross-cultural, transhistorical, collaborative, feminist project from which and through which we have all learned and grown. They have given from their hearts and souls, and I, more than any, have benefited from their insights, guidance, and wisdom. Our five years of working together, with a few more years to go, has yielded not only a harvest of scholarship, but a bounty of friendship.

Many others have contributed and will contribute to EWIC. Hopefully, we will be able to acknowledge as many as possible in these pages of future volumes of EWIC. Volume III is nearing completing of author solicitation as I write, with Volumes IV–VI slated for completing of author solicitations in the coming few months. We encourage and invite authors who are interested in contributing to contact us. Our author database has nearly 2,000 self-volunteered writers and potential contributors to EWIC from all over the world, giving new meaning to the idea of a global project. Nevertheless, we are certain there are scholars, graduate students, and practitioners whom we have not reached and urgent them to contact us (sjoseph@ucdavis.edu or ewic@ucdavis). You may also fill out a potential author template directly on our web page http://sjoseph.ucdavis.edu/ewic. From those who submitted potential author templates and have not yet been contacted, I request patience with our labor-intensive process and urge you to contact us again if you have submitted a template, are interested in contributing, and have not heard from us. It is especially important to us to continue to develop our potential author database, as we plan to publish an online edition of EWIC which will allow for ongoing updates. On behalf of the Editors and Brill, I express my deepest gratitude to all contributors, past and future.

I would like also to express appreciation to authors who tried very hard to meet our deadlines and were not able to. We extended deadlines a number of times, but as with any publication, some final cut-off date must be set. All the entries that were accepted for publication but that did not meet our final deadline for Volume II will be published in the online edition of EWIC, on which we hope to begin work in 2006.

Finally, my daughter, Sara Rose Joseph, continued to sacrifice and bear witness to this project with which she has lived most of her life. Now she admonishes me, from her college dorm room, for the hours spent on EWIC, all the while pleased that we have produced this most marvelous contribution to feminist scholarship.

Suad Joseph,
General Editor, EWIC
Davis, California
October 2004

Preface

VOLUME II, EWIC

With Volume II, EWIC launches the first of four volumes dedicated to substantive topics of relevance to women and Islamic cultures globally. These four volumes, Volumes II–V (Volume VI is the cumulative index), are unusual in that each volume is topically organized. Within each volume, we maintain the conventional alphabetical listing of entries. Volume II brings together over 360 entries on women, family, law, politics, and Islamic cultures around the world. The Editors solicited entries on these topics in relationship to each other because of the historical and contemporary interweaving of these issues in Islamic cultures. Family is always a subject of law and politics in any state level society. States are always invested in what is defined as family and in the regulation of the activities of families as collectivities and of the persons ensconced within families. In many regions of the world, especially in the Middle East, family is defined as the basic unit of society (rather than the individualized citizen) and state actors mediate their relationships to state citizens through family structures, family relations, family idioms, and family moralities. State projects and state visions of the family as an idea and concrete family relationships are often translated into and transported through law and legal practices. In many Muslim majority countries, and even in some Muslim minority countries (such as India), the arena of family law that covers marriage, divorce, child custody, and inheritance is assigned to religious courts. The delegation of family law to religious courts in these states does not mean that the state is not interested in family or family law. In some of these states, religious clerics are salaried by the state or serve under the supervision of the state. In some cases where state law is promulgated, state family law may be influenced by Islamic law (Iraq, Egypt). Regardless of the specific articulations, however, states rarely ignore family structure and ideology. Law rarely is indifferent to the reality that most people live within families. And families and persons are rarely unaware or completely oblivious to the operations of law and politics in their lives. The topics covered in this volume do not exhaust the range of issues which intertwine family, law, and politics as many of these topics (labor, health, education, work, environment, and the like) are taken up in other volumes. What we set out to do in Volume II, then, is to bring together the core matters of state functioning, especially through law, in relation to family.

We began with a list of 109 topics. Of these, just under three dozen were originally defined as overviews on large topics. Some of the overviews were the single entry on a large topic, such as the overviews of apostasy and milk kinship. Other overviews were structured as introductions to a series of regional entries on those topics, such as the overviews of civil society and honor. During the development of Volume II, some overviews were changed and others added as we faced the constraints of author solicitations.

The non-overview topics of the original 109 were designed to generate a series of entries for each region of the world. How many such entries each topic generated and how those entries were defined by country or groups of countries was left to the Associate Editors responsible for each region. The Associate Editors faced enormous hurdles in finding authors for each of the remaining 75 topics. They had to decide what countries to group together for specific topics, which topics to do country by country, and which topics to cover on a larger regional basis. For some topics, the geographic divisions seemed, to some degree, self-evident, while others were not at all clear. On many topics, how countries were grouped together depended almost entirely on finding authors who had the expertise (and time) to write. Entry boundaries were at times driven by author expertise as much as they were by country boundaries. A degree of unevenness and inconsistency in the the geographical content of entries resulted which was unavoidable. This inconsistency is productive in many ways, as it reminds us that geographical boundaries are not "natural," but the outcomes of historical and political processes which may not be congruent with social and cultural processes.

Another unavoidable inconsistency is the regional/country gaps in coverage from one topic to another. In all cases, the Associate Editors made every effort to cover all regions for all topics. We realized this grand ambition could not be achieved for a number of reasons. Research simply does not exist on some topics for some regions. Where research does exist, we were not always able to find the appropriate authors. At times, authors were overloaded and were not able to commit to writing the entries for EWIC in the time frame which we were able to afford them (typically we invited authors to return entries within three months of their acceptance).

Some authors tried, but were not able to complete their entries in time for inclusion in the print edition of Volume II. We have over 130 entries for Volume II which were still being written or revised, or had been revised but did not arrive in time for inclusion. While we regret not being able to hold the publication of Volume II for all these entries, we are committed to publishing those which were accepted in the online edition of EWIC.

With the limitations of our capacities as Editors, the limitations of the fields covered, and the limitations of this ambitious globally defined project, we have produced an incomparable volume of entries on subjects critical to understanding women, family, law, politics, and Islamic cultures. The entries provide a basis for critical comparative research. More importantly, Volume II sets the stage for innovative rethinking of the basis for comparative and interdisciplinary research on women and Islamic cultures which will be continued in Volumes III–VI and in the online edition of EWIC.

Suad Joseph,
General Editor, EWIC
Davis, California
October 2004

Adoption and Fostering

Overview

Across cultures, adoption and fostering take different forms. In the Arabic language, adoption (*tabannā*) signifies the creation of a fictive relationship of parent to child, by naming the child as one's own and by endowing him or her with rights and duties identical to those of a biological child. Fostering (*kafāla*) is the act of assuming partial or complete responsibility for a child whose parents are temporarily or permanently unable to care for him or her. Adoption in the former sense is forbidden in Islam, while fostering is highly recommended. Nevertheless, it would be incorrect to say that "Islam forbids adoption," since some forms of adoption, like "open adoptions," which are becoming more popular in Western societies, are similar to Islamic foster arrangements. In addition, some societies use the term "partial adoption" to signify the Islamically validated foster relationship. At the same time, in examining the practice of adoption in Muslim societies, it must be recognized that legal norms are not definitive in influencing social practice. Extra-legal practices like secret adoptions and various accommodations leading to ambiguous foster relationships can be found in diverse Muslim societies.

The primary textual reference prohibiting the creation of fictive biological relationships, including adoption and the practice known as *ẓihār*, by which a man divorces his wife by calling her his "mother," is Qur'ān 4:5. Before the implementation of this prohibition, early Muslims continued the pre-Islamic form of adoption that could entail "an erasure of natal identity" (Bargach 2002, 27). References to this practice indicate that adoptees were usually, if not always, male. In Arab tribal society, dominance was achieved by being able to martial large numbers of fighting men. The adoption of male children and even adults was one way to increase this number, in addition to fathering large numbers of children by multiple wives and concubines, or acquiring male slaves. In many cases, adoption was closely linked to enslavement, which gave captors the power to strip captives of their natal identities and appropriate them into their own families.

Children in pre-Islamic Arabia were also adopted for typical emotional reasons, such as pity for a needy child or because of an inability to bear children. Before the Qur'ānic verse prohibiting adoption was revealed, the Prophet Muḥammad himself freed and adopted a slave boy given to him by his wife, calling him "the son of (*ibn*) Muḥammad." After the revelation, Zayd took the name of his biological father, and was henceforth known as "Zayd ibn Ḥāritha." There are reports that this change took place in connection with Zayd's divorce of his wife, whom the Prophet then married. This action emphasized the difference between real parenthood and adoption, since marriage to a woman who has ever been married to one's son is forbidden by Qur'ān 4:22–4. Nevertheless, as Bargach argues, the prohibition on adoption cannot be linked to an isolated event in the Prophet's life, since it was clearly necessitated by the importance placed on lineage (*nasab*) in the Islamic revelation (Bargach 2002, 56–62).

Fostering is an important theme in the biography of the Prophet. Since his father died before his birth, the Prophet's grandfather assumed guardianship (*walāya*) over him. When ʿAbd al-Muṭṭālib died, the Prophet's uncle, Abū Ṭālib, became his guardian. A custom in pre-Islamic Arabia, Islam made it a legal obligation for male relatives to provide maintenance (*nafaqa*) and protection for orphaned children. A fatherless child is considered an "orphan" (*yatīm*) even if his or her mother is still living. The duty to care for orphans is a significant theme of the Qur'ānic and Prophetic sayings. Oft-cited is the Prophetic saying, "I and the sponsor (*kafīl*) of an orphan will be like this in Paradise (and he held up two fingers close together)" (Bukhārī 1997, viii, 34).

In most schools of Islamic law, a needy orphan has the right to maintenance from a male relative even if the mother retains custody (*ḥaḍāna*) of the child (Nasir 1990, 173–89 197–200). It is not uncommon for the brother of a man who has died leaving children to marry his brother's widow in order to provide the kind of support and supervision for his nephews and nieces that he would for his own children. In traditional societies, if such a man is already married, a polygamous marriage is usually the result. As polygamy becomes less common in modern societies, the uncle's support may be limited to financial assistance.

Children whose fathers are poverty-stricken or unable to adequately care for them also have a right to support from legally designated relatives. Sometimes the child is temporarily placed in the custody of these relatives, to ensure regular maintenance and supervision (as is reported about the Prophet Muḥammad, who brought his young cousin ʿAlī into his household). In some cases, this fostering arrangement is carried a step further, and poor parents give their children away to relatives for adoption. In most Muslim societies, it is understood that Islamic law gives every person the right to know and benefit from his or her true natal identity. Nevertheless, some children are not told about their biological parents until they reach adolescence. In this case, the arrangement might best be described as temporary adoption, since the child grows up initially unaware of his different status within the family.

Fostering and adoption by relatives is also a means for dealing with infertility in many Muslim societies. A childless couple may be given a child by a relative – usually a brother or sister – who has more than one child. Sometimes this is done with the goal of stimulating conception, since there are reports in many societies, Muslim and non-Muslim, of previously childless women conceiving after adoption. In most cases, the main goal is to allow a childless couple to share in the joy of raising a child. This is usually done out of a sense of empathy for the couple, but in some traditional cultures, for example, among the Chinese Kazakhs, this is more of an obligation (Svanberg 1994, 241). Among the Kazakhs, it is also traditionally understood that grandparents have a right to adopt their eldest grandchild, so they will not be lonely in a house without small children. The emotional impact on the child has not been well studied, but there are suggestions that there are few problems in traditional societies in which group identity is paramount. However, in modern societies, in which the nuclear family is idealized and individuality is cultivated, youths may be emotionally devastated when they learn that they were given away as children in such an arrangement.

Due to Islamic restrictions on interaction between unrelated members of the opposite sex, it is less common for Muslims to assume custody of unrelated children than related children. Islamic law prohibits a man from being alone with a woman unless he is her *maḥram*, and requires women to wear *ḥijāb* in front of non-*maḥram* men. These regulations do not generally apply to children, but would affect a foster child who has reached puberty. Breastfeeding an unrelated child is a means of removing these barriers. In Islamic law, suckling (*raḍāʿa*) establishes a biological relationship that results in the same marriage prohibitions (*taḥrīmāt*) that entail from a birth relationship. Consequently, not only the foster mother, but also her sister or other close female relatives, can suckle a child to establish a relationship of *taḥrīm* among them. In modern times, women have been able to use lactation drugs to stimulate their ability to feed a foster child. Legal schools differ about the number of feedings needed to establish this relationship; five or ten feedings is the average. Most legal schools also require that the child be under a certain age, usually two years, for a nursing relationship to have legal effect. There is a *ḥadīth*, however, that the Prophet allowed this to be done for older, even post-pubescent children (Muslim 1929, x, 31–3).

Although suckling establishes a biological relationship, it does not establish maintenance and inheritance rights. Foster children, therefore, have no share in the inheritance designated for children in the Qurʾān (4:7–12). However, any Muslim can will up to one-third of his or her estate to a person who does not have a right to inherit, and foster children often benefit from this (Glander 2001, 118). In addition, during their lifetimes, Muslims may freely gift their property to any party or interest. The family trust (*waqf*) has traditionally been used in Muslim societies to ensure a stable income (and sometimes social status) for vulnerable family members, including daughters, handicapped children, freed slaves, and foster children.

The severe negative social and legal consequences for extra-marital sexual activity among Muslims have traditionally been a major deterrent to the acknowledgment and legitimization of any child born out of wedlock. Abortion, although generally prohibited in Islamic law, has always been available in Muslim societies, and certainly is used to prevent the birth of illegitimate children (Musallam 1983). Illegitimate children are sometimes abandoned anonymously, although abandonment can also be due to dire poverty. Islamic law gives the finder the right to guardianship of the foundling (*laqīṭ*), unless he or she is unfit for this responsibility (Nasir 1990, 168–9). To protect the child from living with the stigma of illegitimate birth, guardians and authorities often create respectable identities for the child. For example, guardians may claim that a child is the offspring of distant relatives who have died. In some cases, women who are expecting to take custody of an abandoned or illegitimate child fake a pregnancy before bringing the child home (Rugh 1995, 134). These "secret adoptions" are always motivated by a desire to avoid shame: the shame of being an illegitimate child, the shame of an illicit pregnancy, or the shame of infertility.

Compared with medieval Europe, orphanages have never been common in traditional Muslim societies. With changing social norms and the weakening of the extended family under the pressures of modernity, however, orphanages have been established in greater numbers in Muslim societies. It is also possible that the establishment of orphanages, like the establishment of public schools, hospitals, and other modern state institutions, was a factor that led to the weakening of the traditional extended family in Muslim societies, and subverted widespread informal arrangements for the care of children. Increased regulation of adoption and fostering arrangements has had similar results. For example, in 1993, after there was a highly publicized case of a center for abandoned babies allegedly selling them, Morocco made it a crime to abandon a child, and set up a special procedure that a woman must follow to give up her child. Obviously, few women feel comfortable meeting with a state bureaucrat to discuss their need to abandon a child because of poverty or an illicit relationship. Consequently, more Moroccan women have resorted to infanticide, abortions, or secret adoptions since this law was established (Bargach 2002, 38–41). Additionally, poor people often find it difficult to negotiate the bureaucratic procedures necessary to adopt a child, and some states permit only married couples to adopt. In Morocco, for example, unmarried women have not been permitted to adopt individually, but can only work as state appointed "mothers" to groups of orphaned children in the internationally affiliated SOS Children's Villages (Bargach 2002, 41, Glander 2001, 97).

In modern times, the establishment of orphanages has increasingly been considered an appropriate solution to the problem of large numbers of children displaced or orphaned by war. Many Muslim countries reject international adoption as a way to provide homes for these children, arguing that they have a right to be under the guardianship of individuals who share their culture and religion. Over the two decades of conflict in Afghanistan, for example, all Afghan leaders rejected international adoption, but accepted foreign aid to provide better services within their communities for needy children. Increasingly, Islamic charitable organizations operating internationally have adopted Western-style sponsorships for the support of poor or orphaned children.

Bibliography

J. Bargach, *Orphans of Islam. Family, abandonment, and secret adoption in Morocco*, Lanham, Md. 2002.

Muḥammad ibn Ismāʿīl al-Bukhārī, *Ṣaḥīḥ al-Bukhārī*, trans. M. M. Khan, 9 vols., Riyadh 1997.

J. Chelhod, Radaʿ, in *EI*², viii, 361–2.

G. Djuric, Muslims and the law of adoption in Yugoslavia, in *Islamic and Comparative Law Quarterly* 1 (1981), 39–50.

A. Giladi, *Infants, parents and wet nurses. Medieval Islamic views on breastfeeding and their social implications*, Leiden 1999.

A. Glander, *The Oriental child not born in wedlock. A study of the anthropological parameters, religious motivations and sociological phenomena of child care in Islam and Judaism*, Frankfurt am Main 2001.

D. Latifi, Adoption and the Muslim law, in *Journal of the Indian Law Institute*, 16 (1974), 118–22.

A. Laylish, Bequests as an instrument for accommodating inheritance rules. Israel as a case study, in *Islamic Law and Society* 2:3 (1995), 282–319.

——, The family waqf and the *Sharīʿa* law of succession in modern times, in *Islamic Law and Society* 4:3 (1997), 352–88.

B. F. Musallam, *Sex and society in Islam*, Cambridge 1983.

J. J. Nasir, *The Islamic law of personal status*, London 1986, 1990².

A. B. Rugh, Orphanages in Egypt. Contradiction or affirmation in a family-oriented society, in E. W. Fernea (ed.), *Children in the Muslim Middle East*, Austin, Tex. 1995, 124–41.

Ṣaḥīḥ Muslim bi-sharḥ al-Nawawī, 18 vols., Beirut 1929.

A. E. Sonbol, Adoption in Islamic society. A historical survey, in E. W. Fernea (ed.), *Children in the Muslim Middle East*, Austin, Tex. 1995, 45–67.

I. Svanberg, Xinjiang Kazak adoption practices, in *Central Asiatic Journal* 38:2 (1994), 235–43.

Ingrid Mattson

Central Asia and the Caucasus

The attitude to adoption and fostering varies according to the historical moment. During the Islamic period, the act of adoption was equated with *savab*, an act of generosity that would be rewarded by God. In periods of wars and natural disasters, this attitude is reinforced. During the Soviet period there was a solicitous attitude toward children abandoned or left without parents. This is exemplified by the celebrated case of the Uzbek family of Shoahman and Bahry Somjuradov who adopted 14 children of different nationalities during the Second World War. As the male population was away from home fighting during the war, the basic responsibility for fostering during this period lay on women's shoulders. Many families adopted or gave temporary shelter to children during the postwar period in the Soviet Union.

In the republics of Central Asia and the Caucasus, women's participation in decision-making about adoption and custodianship has taken new forms during the post-Soviet period. An increase in divorce and demographic and gender imbalance in the postwar period led to a reduction of the number of families with both husband and wife and an increase in the number of single women; for many of them creating a family was only possible through adoption or fostering of children from large families of close relatives, and in rare cases from children's homes (no statistical data available).

During the modern period, the process of adoption and fostering in the countries of Central Asia and the Caucasus has been regulated by law; the family and civil codes have corresponding chapters and articles, reflecting the order of adoption and guardianship and the rights of adopters and trustees, as well as the rights of potentially adopted children. In all the post-Soviet countries there are bureaus that regulate the legal order of adoption, fostering, and trusteeship. Although under the legislation the relative rights of men and women in the family to guardianship or adoption are not specified, the material and economic status of adopters influences the decisions of the Commission for Adoption and Fostering. Thus in Muslim families where in most cases the sole bread winner is the man, the woman has no independent means to maintain a child and consequently cannot apply for adoption or custodianship independently.

In secular states, children who are left without parental care are handed over for education to a family for adoption, trusteeship, or guardianship. If no such family is available, children are placed in an institution (educational or medical establishments, establishments for the population's social protection).

Under the family legislation, both spouses have the right to adopt. "Upon the adoption of a child by one of spouses the consent of the other spouse to adoption is required unless the child is adopted by both spouses. The consent of the spouse is not required if this spouse has discontinued family relations, has not lived with the family for more than a year, and the residence of the spouse is not known" (*Family Code of the Republic Uzbekistan*, Section IV, Chapter 19, 157).

Adopters can be adult citizens of either sex. The difference in the age between the adopter and the adoptee varies within the limits of 15 and 16 years, except in cases of adoption by a stepfather or a stepmother.

BIBLIOGRAPHY

The family code of the Republic of Uzbekistan [in Russian], 1996.

The family code of the Republic of Azerbaijan [in Azerbaijani], 2000.

Law of the Republic of Kazakhstan on marriage and family [in Russian], 1998.

V. Nalivkin and M. Nalivkina, *A sketch of the domestic life of women in a settled local population of Ferghana* [in Russian], Kazan 1886.

G. Rakhimova and J. Nuriev, *A Turkmen family. Traditions, customs, and rites* [in Russian], Ashgabat 1988.

MARFUA TOKHTAKHODJAEVA
AND ALMAZ KADIROVA

North Africa

There is a consensus in formal Islamic jurisprudence that adoption is prohibited. Adoption here means the canceling of birth affiliation and the creation of fictive kinship by a non-related party where name, succession, and inheritance rights of the child are legally created as though the non-related party were a biological parent. It is the absence of the biological bond with such a child that makes this practice dangerous, as explained in Sunnī rites; it alienates these legal heirs, it may lead to incest, and it may also cause havoc to the structure of the family. Islam as a religion, as a source of legislation, and as an ethos advocates and protects the rights of orphans because they are bereft of the protective net that a family and a clan give to their individual members. Islamic jurisprudence is, however, quite clear about not mixing between registers: orphans, children born out of wedlock, and foundlings (*laqīṭ*) cannot be adopted by a family, but can only be the recipient of the gift of care (*kafāla*) and good deeds.

This position finds its root in the episode commonly known in the Sharīʿa as that of Zayd b. Ḥāritha, formally known as Zayd b. Muḥammad after the Prophet adopted him in keeping with pre-Islamic traditions. The Prophet married Zaynab, Zayd's former wife, a marriage that was considered incestuous by the standards of the time and that thus constituted symbolically a definite rupture with pre-existing beliefs. Today in most nation-states where family laws are inspired or influenced by the Sharīʿa, there is a prohibition on adoption. In North Africa, with the exception of Tunisia where secular family law (*majalla*) gives full legal status to adoption, family codes (*mudawwana* for Morocco and *qānūn al-usra* for Algeria) only recognize affiliation within legally established marriages, though they do offer the possibility of *kafāla* to foundlings.

In this patriarchal social order, it is formally the name of the father and the father's affiliation that are considered to be legally important while women's agency is viewed as instrumental and not important in and of itself. Although adoption is officially prohibited in North Africa, there are extensive and culturally legitimized forms of secret adoptions, fostering practices, intra- and extra-family exchange of children, swapping of children, or entrusting them to individuals/families, the majority of which take place outside, and are at times contrary to, the legal norms in place. Such practices are a common heritage and shared by all social strata. The institutional codes come into play only in dire cases of inheritance or larger family conflicts while, generally speaking, what constitutes a family in the cultural imaginary transcends those legally delimited relations.

Research shows that it is women who are the primary instigators and actors in these other forms of adoptive transactions. The reasons for this can be explained through educational and practical terms; first, girls' education and socializing processes still emphasize, and at times exclusively maintain, that the ideal role for the woman is that of the procreating mother. Marriage is therefore merely instrumental for begetting offspring and families bereft of children are considered abnormal and sterility is viewed as a curse; *kafāla* and other alternative forms of adoption endow a woman with a *raison d'être* in terms of the role she and her culture have created for her. Second, birthing, nurturing, and rearing of newborns occur in largely circumscribed female spaces and hence circulation of information is simple and informal transactions are easily carried through. Most women prefer to adopt girls rather than boys as little girls are seen as allies and as potential household support and worthwhile emotional investment by their putative mothers; girls are, therefore, a scarcity in most centers for abandoned babies in the three countries.

In Morocco and Algeria legal *kafāla* is state controlled and obeys institutional norms, and the same is true for open adoption in Tunisia. Abandoned babies are usually born in or brought to centers where they are taken care of until they are chosen by a family or an individual. Those babies who are not selected are sent to orphanages (either state owned or run by philanthropists) at different age limits. In each country, a number of administrative steps need to be fulfilled prior to a child being taken home by a family (or individual) because, in Morocco and Algeria, children are considered wards of the state and are only entrusted to families for their upkeep; legally the *kafāla* party cannot be considered a parent. In Tunisia the name of the adoptive party is given to the adopted child; in Morocco and Algeria names differ as they are markers of paternal affiliation, which can officially only be the outcome of birth within a legal marriage. Outside the legal frame, however, and when women contract a secret adoption with the approval of their husbands, or swap children with neighbors or other family members, they create a family unit that emulates the biological one and there are no legal constraints on parenting. In the cases of secret adoptions, families pretend the child has been legally born while in other cases various means of agreement may be worked out to the benefit of all parties concerned. Young women who give birth outside marriage, a terrible crime in societies where the code of honor and shame still structure women's lives, often give up their newborn in public spaces, to intermediaries, to other women and individuals for their own survival. This practice is widespread although it is difficult to track such traffic empirically as it is not only illegal but a highly taboo topic. Some non-governmental organizations in Morocco and Algeria have started working with young mothers who refuse to abandon their newborns as the shared belief is that only a biological family can be an ideal environment for any child. This is especially true for the case of children born out of wedlock given that the larger social environment brands them with as bastards, a violent stigma and a means of exclusion that can at least be tempered by the mother's presence.

Bibliography

J. Bargach, *Orphans of Islam. Family, abandonment, and secret adoption in Morocco*, New York 2002.

A. Gilʿadi, *Children of Islam. Concepts of childhood in medieval Muslim society*, London 1992.

L. Lamber, *Children in changing families. A study of adoption and illegitimacy*, London 1980.

A. Rugh, *Within the circle. Parents and children in an Arab* village, New York 1997.

Jamila Bargach

Turkey

Ancient Turkic tribes had different motives and practices regarding adoption. Among Yakut Turks adoption was made for humane reasons, while wealthier Uygur Turks utilized it for servitude and slavery. But whatever the purpose was, the adopted child's rights of inheritance were equal to those of biological children and the prohibition of marriage with family members was equally applied to them. Only men had the right to adopt children, and they could adopt both sexes.

The custom of adoption existed in Arabian communities until the revelation of the Qurʾānic verse saying that adopted children could not bear the father's name and that there would be no prohibition of marriage with them abolished adoption in Islamic law (Qurʾān 33). Nevertheless, the care of orphans, and rearing and marrying them, came to be regarded as a pious act (*sevap*). Polygamy is a recommended means to protect girl orphans from deprivation. Islamic law suggests foster-family and marriage institutions instead of legal adoption, although adoption as a term still exists.

The term *evlatlık* (adopted child) referred to fostering in Turkey. It was also used to categorize the stepchildren of the husband. Wives did not have the right to accept a stepchild as *evlatlık*. Different words, such as *ahiretlik, besleme*, and *yanaşma* were strictly related to the Islamic tradition of fostering, and socially degraded the child's status. However, ironically, as these children's actual position declined in households, the term *evlatlık* gained more common use.

Muslim households overwhelmingly preferred girls for fostering in Turkey. Since the fostered boy would have the status of a stranger, the women in the household would have to be careful regarding their veiling. This was one of the reasons why mainly girls were chosen. They were used for domestic labor as they learned their gender role. Moreover, they were semi-legitimate sexual objects for the male members of the household, as in the case of domestic slaves. The potential of the fostered girl has been the subject of numerous novels, short stories, and diaries in Turkey.

The practice of fostering children spread with the waves of mass migration and wars in Ottoman society. The critical date for this was 1864, when over a million Caucasian migrants entered Ottoman territory and started to sell their girls and women as slaves. In order to restrict the slave trade, the government distributed unprotected girls and women to Muslim middle-class families as *evlatlıks*. This official arrangement redefined and in consequence degraded the status of *evlatlıks*. Very often they were treated like domestic slaves or servants. This policy formed an example for later governments. During the succession of wars from 1911 to 1922, internal conflicts and mass migration resulted in the emergence of thousands of orphans in need of protection. While boys were sent to boarding schools, the military, or to workshops as apprentices, girls were made servants to urban Muslim families where they would be called *evlatlık*.

The republican government abolished Islamic law and promulgated an adjusted Swiss Civil Code in 1926. The new order allowed individuals who did not have children and were over age 40 to legally adopt any person who was at least 18 years younger than themselves. Adoption contracts had to be made in state courts. Adopted children had all the rights and duties of biological children.

Legal adoption conflicted with the ongoing practice of having *evlatlıks* as well as with Islamic law. The new law therefore permitted the adopter to prepare an additional official contract to restrain the inheritance rights of the adopted child. Moreover, if he wanted to marry his adopted child, he could repress his adopter status, again through a court decision. The adopted child had the right to inherit from her/his biological parents as well. These items aimed to avoid religious dispute on legal adoption.

The Civil Code did not ban the tradition of having *evlatlıks*. For years poverty and misery urged peasants to give away or sell their daughters of ages six to seven to urban families. But with the prohibition of slavery and slavery-like practices in 1964, the tradition of having *evlatlıks* faded away. Although girl child labor in domestic work is still present, they are no longer described as *evlatlıks*.

The foster-family program, which was established in 1949, aims to provide temporary homes for unprotected children until age 18. The government pays the expenses of fostered children to the families, and supervises them periodically. It never became popular, partly because officials had to be very strict with the families to end the exploitation of girls embedded in cultural practices.

In 2001, a different civil law was enacted in Turkey. Legal adoption rules became milder. The minimum age limit for the adopter was lowered to 30, and this was disregarded for couples with five years of marriage. Legal adoption is becoming increasingly popular in Turkey. There are thousands of families on the government waiting list. Girls under age two are preferred, although gender balance exists among the children already adopted.

Bibliography

A. Caferoğlu, Türk taamül hukukunda evlatlık müessesi (Adoption institute in Turkish customary law), in *Türk Hukuk ve İktisat Tarihi Mecmuası* 2 (1939), 97–113.

M. Emre, *İslam'da kadın ve aile* (Women and family in Islam), Istanbul 1981.

Y. S. Karakışla, Savaş yetimleri ve kimsesiz çocuklar. Ermeni mi Türk mü? (War orphans and unprotected children. Were they Armenian or Turkish?), in *Toplumsal Tarih* 46 (1999), 46–55.

F. Özbay, *Evlatlıklar* (Adopted children), Iletişim (forthcoming).

I. Parlatır, *Tanzimat edebiyatında kölelik* (Slavery in nineteenth-century renovation fiction), Istanbul 1992.

F. H. Saymen, *Türk medeni hukuku. Umumi prensipler* (Turkish civil law. General principles), Istanbul 1948.

Ö. Şen, 19. Yüzyılda Osmanlı devleti'ndeki köle ticaretinde Kafkasya göçmenlerinin rolü (The role of Caucasian migrants in the slave trade of the Ottoman Empire in the nineteenth century, in *Dünü ve Bugünüyle Toplum ve Ekonomi* 6 (1994), 171–92.

Ferhunde Özbay

Apostasy

Overview

Radical Islamists have often filed charges of apostasy and blasphemy against secular Muslim intellectuals. Early in the twentieth century, for example, the charge of apostasy was brought against prominent intellectuals such as Tāhā Ḥusayn and ʿAlī ʿAbd al-Rāziq. It was not, however, used against Muslim women activists until 1989, the year of the apostasy suit against Salman Rushdie, when Jordanian Islamists filed a suit for apostasy against an outspoken Jordanian television talk-show host, Tūjān al-Fayṣal. Since then the charge has become almost routine. In 1990, during the build-up to the Gulf War, the charge of apostasy was used against Saudi women who illegally drove their cars in protest against the ban on women driving. The women drivers were suspended from their jobs and required to pay substantial fines. The charge of apostasy was also used in an attempt to discredit feminist activists in Morocco. In 1992, it was brought against the Bangladeshi author Taslima Nasreen who went into exile for her safety. In 1996, Islamist lawyers sued Naṣr Abū Zayd, professor of Arabic at Cairo University, for apostasy. A court found him guilty and he and his wife left Egypt to avoid being forcibly divorced. In 2001, a lawyer accused the Egyptian physician, writer, and feminist activist Nawāl al-Saʿdāwī of apostasy and argued that she be divorced from her husband. In 2002, religious conservatives charged the interim Afghan government's minister for women's affairs, Sima Samar, with blasphemy for allegedly saying in an interview with a Persian newspaper in Canada that she did not believe in Sharīʿa law, which she insisted she did not say. On 25 June 2002, Afghanistan's supreme court dropped the blasphemy charge citing lack of evidence, but Afghan President Hamid Karzai did not reappoint Samar minister for women's affairs. Many of these charges would appear to be politically motivated. What is the legal justification for the charges?

Takfīr (pronouncement of unbelief against someone) is a rather imprecise term, which is often translated as "accusation of apostasy." The terms *ridda* or *irtidād* (renunciation of faith), *kufr*, (disbelief), and *bidʿa* (non-Sharīʿa innovation) do not readily correspond to their English translations and are often used almost synonymously. The principle sources of Sharīʿa (Islamic law), Qurʾān, *sunna* (the tradition of the Prophet), *ijmā* (scholarly consensus), and *qiyās* (analogy to other legal principles), offer contradictory views on the question of apostasy. The Qurʾān does not give a penalty for apostasy and contains frequently quoted passages that call for freedom of religion. For example, "No compulsion is there in religion. Rectitude has become clear from error. So whosoever disbelieves in idols and believes in God, has laid hold of the most firm handle, unbreaking; God is All-hearing, All-knowing" (2:256); "Say: 'The truth is from your Lord; so let whosever will believe, and let whosoever will disbelieve'" (18:30). On the other hand, many other passages indicate that apostates will meet a harsh fate. For example, "Those that believe not in the signs of God God will not guide; there awaits them a painful chastisement. They only forge falsehood, who believe not in the signs of God, and those – they are the liars. Whoso disbelieves in God, after he has believed – excepting him who has been compelled, and his heart is still at rest in his belief – but whosever's breast is expanded in unbelief, upon them shall rest anger from God, and there awaits them a mighty chastisement" (16:107).

The *sunna* contains more unequivocal condemnations of apostasy than does the Qurʾān. Among the most commonly cited *ḥadīth* on apostasy are: "The blood of a fellow Muslim should never be shed except in three cases: that of the adulterer, the murderer, and whoever forsakes the religion of Islam" (Bukharī), and, "Whosoever changes his religion, kill him" (Bukharī). The four law schools agree that the penalty for apostasy is death, but there are many conditions and qualifications preceding such a judgment. An apostate (*murtadd*) must associate other gods alongside Allah, defame the Prophet, treat the Qurʾān with contempt, or deny fundamental beliefs such as the existence of the Day of Judgment. Typically two adult witnesses must testify as to the apostasy of the accused who may deny the charges, proclaim his or her faith, and/or repent and return to Islam. Usually a period of three days is given for the accused to reconsider and repent. There are contradictory views as to whether women apostates should be killed or imprisoned and beaten. Both men and women convicted of apostasy lose their property rights and must be divorced from their Muslim spouses.

Few if any of the individuals accused of apostasy in recent times considered themselves to be apostates. Indeed many took pains to state their adherence to Islam, which should invalidate the apostasy suits. The legality of apostasy charges is also unclear since most Muslim states do not have a law of apostasy. Law codes are typically based on several sources: British or French colonial law, Sharīʿa, customary law, and in some cases, tribal law. Most Muslim states have retained Sharīʿa law only pertaining to marriage, divorce, child custody, and inheritance. Governments from North Africa to Southeast Asia, however, in response to pressure from religious conservatives, have been trying to strengthen Sharīʿa law. At the same time these governments have been facing pressure from international and local advocates of Muslim women's human rights for the liberalization of Sharīʿa based personal status laws. The apostasy suits against Tūjān al-Fayṣal and Nawāl al-Saʿdāwī, because they resulted in extensive international attention and legal and political reforms, will serve to illustrate this clash of legal and social standards.

In 1989, Tūjān al-Fayṣal, the Jordanian talk-show host, was among twelve women who ran for parliament. As an opening salvo to her campaign, al-Fayṣal published an article entitled "Yushtimūnanā wa-nantakhibūhum," (They curse us and we elect them) in *al-Raʾy*, a government-owned newspaper. In her article, she ridiculed the Islamists who subscribed to a well-known *ḥadīth* that "woman by nature is deficient in intellect and religion" and who believed that "women were predictable and guided by their emotions, legal minors who need a male guardian to run their affairs." She sarcastically remarked that since the Islamists believe that "women are limited by their reproductive functions the best women must be those who are not mothers." She complained that they sugar-coat their views on women's deficiencies by praising women's femininity and decency, but when women demand their freedom and equal rights they accuse them of wanting to "abandon tradition."

Three weeks after the publication of this article, she received a subpoena to appear at the south Amman Islamic court on Tuesday, 17 October 1989. The two plaintiffs were an assistant mufti and a private in Jordan's armed forces. The charge was apostasy from Islam. Jordan, however, had no apostasy law and several Islamic courts refused to accept the case. Finally, the Islamic court in Wihdat, south Amman, agreed to hear it. The plaintiffs' lawyer accused al-Fayṣal of apostasy, heresy, and ridiculing the Qurʾān, the *ḥadīth*, and the Sharīʿa. He added, "Men of religion had tried to warn her of the danger of her words and had asked her to write an article asking for forgiveness and expressing her repentance, but that she had persisted in her infidelity." He asked the court "to declare her an apostate, to divorce her from her husband, to refuse her repentance, to ban her articles, to prevent the media from dealing with her, and to grant permission to spill her blood." The two plaintiffs then signed a document, submitted it to the court and their *wakīl* had a copy presented to al-Fayṣal's lawyer.

The charge that al-Fayṣal had called for four husbands per woman caused a sensation. At various election rallies she had asked, "If men can have four wives why not women four husbands?" The fact that she repeatedly insisted that she was trying to point out that men should not have four wives any more than women should have four husbands made no difference to her accusers. In her response to the charges, she responded, "I am a Muslim and I say that God is one and Muḥammad is the Prophet of God. So they have no ground for their case in Islam, because only God can judge if a person is sincere." She said they attacked her because she drew on Islamic laws to defend women's rights and had threatened them in their own domain. In Jordan, women's rights are embodied in the laws of personal status governing marriage, divorce, child custody, alimony, and inheritance, which are weighted against women, but, as al-Fayṣal pointed out, Article 6:22–23 of the 1946 Jordanian constitution, grants women "political, economic, and social equality." In addition, Jordan signed the 1948 Universal Declaration of Human Rights, which reaffirms the equality of men and women. The personal status laws therefore contradict the constitution and the UDHR. Al-Fayṣal effectively made the case against her a violation of her constitutional and human rights.

In the elections, all twelve women candidates lost while the Islamists and their allies made substantial gains in parliament. The day after the election, the judge ruled that the Islamic court did not have the competence to decide al-Fayṣal's case. The plaintiffs, however, did not give up. In January 1990, al-Fayṣal received another summons. A court of appeal had agreed to hear the part of the case concerning divorce from her husband because of her alleged apostasy, which it said was within its competence. This time al-Fayṣal went to court supported by a large and vocal crowd of local and international activists and by prior arrangement, simply repeated the *shahāda* before the *qāḍī*. She neither rescinded nor apologized for her views. After hearing al-Fayṣal's statement, the court found no proof of apostasy and declared her innocent of all charges.

The international response was even greater when Nawāl al-Saʿdāwī was charged with apostasy. In 2001, al-Saʿdāwī was the best known of the Arab feminist or women activists, the international women's human rights movement was burgeoning, and the Internet had become a major tool of communication. The case began when a lawyer asked the prosecutor-general to put her on trial for "deriding Islam and ridiculing its fundamental principles." He said he was motivated by an interview published in the independent weekly, *al-Midan*, in early March, 2001, in which al-Saʿdāwī stated, as she often has, that the veil was not obligatory. He alleged that she had claimed that the Islamic pilgrimage was a vestige of pagan practices and that the Islamic inheritance law, which gives males twice the share of females, should be abolished due to the fact that up to 35 percent of families in Egypt are currently dependent on the income of a woman. Nawāl al-Saʿdāwī issued a statement on 18 May 2001 that was immediately posted on her website and read around the world. She argued that the case was an attempt to make scapegoats of two intellectuals, herself and her husband, Sharīf Ḥatāta, who had both been active in the struggle for democracy and human rights. She insisted that she had only said that caring for the poor was more important than religious rituals and that kissing the Black Stone in the Kaʿba was considered by some Islamic scholars to be a "historical vestige of paganism adopted by the Prophet with the aim of rallying the tribes of Mecca under the banner of Islam." Al-Saʿdāwī cited Article 40 of the Egyptian constitution: "that all citizens are considered equal before the law, that they have the same obligations and enjoy equal rights, that they should not be discriminated against for reasons of gender, race, language or belief." As al-Fayṣal had done a dozen years earlier, al-Saʿdāwī argued that the Islamists were using religion to further their struggles for political power.

Like Jordan, Egypt has both secular and Sharīʿa laws and no law of apostasy. Article Two of its amended constitution, however, states, "Islamic Sharīʿa is the basis of legislation." Unlike Jordan, *ḥisba*, regulation of public morality, is legal in Egypt, which loosely follows the Ḥanafī law school. *Ḥisba* traditionally allowed any Muslim to sue another for beliefs that may harm society, but because of recent abuses it had been amended so that a private citizen must request the state prosecutor to bring suit.

In May 2001, the prosecutor-general's office dismissed the *ḥisba* case, but the Cairo personal status court decided to consider al-Saʿdāwī's forced separation from her husband. Journalists, lawyers, human rights activists, and private citizens from Egypt, the Arab world, Europe, and North America rallied to her defense. After several postponements, on 30 July, the court rejected the forcible divorce case and ruled that no individual can petition a court to forcibly divorce another person.

Both of these cases were sensationalized in the international media and were major embarrassments for their respective governments. Both lawsuits were apparently more political than religious in intent, both were well outside the boundaries of traditional Sharīʿa law, and the presiding judges eventually dropped both of them. Nevertheless their legal importance should not be underestimated. Taken together the lawsuits illustrate the intense and ongoing confrontation between advocates of Sharīʿa law and advocates of secular constitutional and international human rights law over the freedom of women activists to call for political and social reform.

Bibliography

C. J. Adams, Kufr, in J. L. Esposito (ed.), *The Oxford encyclopedia of the modern Islamic world*, New York 1995, ii, 439–43.

A. A. An-Na'im, The Islamic law of apostasy and its modern applicability. A case from the Sudan, in *Religion* 16 (1986), 197–224.

A. J. Arberry, *The Koran interpreted*, New York 1970.

M. Cook, *Commanding right and forbidding wrong in Islamic thought*, New York 2000.

C. W. Ernst, Blasphemy. Islamic concept, in M. Eliade (ed.), *The encyclopedia of religion*, New York 1987, 242–5.

N. Gallagher, Human rights on trial in Jordan. The triumph of Toujan al-Faisal, in M. Afkhami (ed.), *Faith and freedom. Women's rights in the Muslim world*, Syracuse, N.Y. 1995, 209–31.

M. H. Kamali, *Freedom of expression in Islam*, Cambridge 1997.

I. A. Karawan, Takfir, in *The Oxford encyclopedia of the modern Islamic world*, New York 1995, iv, 178–9.

I. Zaman, Bidʿah, in *The Oxford encyclopedia of the modern Islamic world*, New York 1995, v, 1, 215–16.

Nancy Gallagher

Armenian Women

Overview

Any discussion of Armenian women must take into consideration that they have been part of a large minority dispersed in the Ottoman Empire and Iran, concentrated in Anatolia, Iranian Azerbaijan, and Isfahan, and after the First World War in Arab lands. The study of Armenian women is fairly new and therefore limited, suffering from unevenness in scholarship and leading at times to generalizations, especially but not exclusively about the premodern period. While these communities share much with each other and the Muslim majority populations, attention must be paid to historical and regional variations when discussing women in Armenian religious doctrine and practices and Armenian women's lives within the larger Muslim communities.

The Armenian Apostolic Church does not allow the ecclesiastical ministry of women, yet there have been throughout history expressions of lay spirituality in the form of women saints and martyred virgins, scribes, members of women's guilds, parish councils, and diocesan delegations as well as nuns and deaconesses. According to church history, saints such as the fourth-century Sandukht, Gayane, and Hripsime (whose martyrdom ultimately led to the conversion of the Armenian king in the early fourth century) were among the first Armenian martyrs. Scribes, some of whom were virgins, while others such as the seventeenth-century Margarit were "the captive soul beset by sin, tossed about by life and perishing in the depths of iniquity, full of evil in spirit" (Oghlukian 1994, 27), have been responsible in small or large part for the preservation of several dozen manuscripts (Tsovakan 1954, 133–5).

Nuns and deaconesses

Nuns within the Armenian church existed throughout the medieval period up to the twentieth century in places such as Jerusalem, New Julfa, and Istanbul (Ervine 1999, 129). The history of the female deaconate goes at least as far back as the tenth century, possibly earlier. In the nineteenth century, deaconesses were present in Armenian convents such as St. Catherine's convent in New Julfa and the Galfayan convent in Istanbul, with the last deaconess being ordained in 1982. St. Catherine's convent is a great example of the strong social consciousness of women's lay activity in seeing to orphanages, hospitals, and so forth (Arat 2000, 153–89). Although canonical books of the fourth to the eight centuries remark on women, direct mention of deaconesses is made only in manuscript ritual books (*mashtots*) from the ninth to the eleventh centuries; after the twelfth century, ritual and other books appear with ordination rights for deaconesses (Arat 2000, 90–1, 98, 100–1, Thomson 2000, 278). Based on eighteenth- and nineteenth-century sources, it becomes clear that the duties of the deaconess were limited to conducting the liturgy of hours in the convent, proclaiming the Gospel, singing, bringing the chalice, and using incense during Holy Mass (Arat 2000, 110). Some medieval clerical writers rejected the female deaconate altogether, even prohibiting the testimony in court of women and "crushing grapes for the production of wine for the Holy Mass" (Arat 2000, 106). The opposition of medieval clerics seems to draw its justification from the conviction that women were "impure" (Arat 2000, 107, Oghlukian 1994, 42).

Use of Muslim courts

Medieval "*de-scriptive* and *pre-scriptive* texts" (Thomson 2000, 15) such as the *Lawcode* of Mkhitar Gosh, whose main purpose was to prevent Christian Armenians from resorting to Muslim courts, shed light on ecclesiastical laws regulating women's behavior in marriage and divorce as well as providing a view into the social lives of medieval Armenian women (Thomson 2000, 47, 52). The issue of the use of Muslim courts is an interesting one; recent studies show that non-Muslim minorities, including women, used Sharīʿa courts in almost all cities of the Ottoman Empire, including Damascus and Istanbul (al-Qattan 1999, 429). According to eighteenth-century court records of the Galata region of Istanbul, a large number of Armenian and Greek women resorted to the courts because of their dissatisfaction with their communities' inheritance practices (Göçek and Baer 1996, 57). Similarily, in Damascus, while minorities at times appeared at courts out of necessity, most often they went to seek the court's favor in cases involving marriage, divorce, child custody, and inheritance (al-Qattan 1999, 430). Sharīʿa courts provided not only efficiency, enforceability, and registry, but also better served the interests of claimants. Christian women, for example, sought divorce in these courts, where wife-instigated divorce was available and more likely to be granted. Moreover, "by availing themselves of the courts in pursuit of personal interests, they demonstrated an impressive knowledge of Islamic legal practice, an acceptance of shared cultural-legal norms, and a pragmatic outlook on marital and familial issues" (al-Qattan 1999, 433–4).

Male-female relationships

The laws regarding male and female relationships clearly placed men over women by allowing far greater rights for divorce and remarriage. For example, while the husband could remarry after divorce from an adulterous wife, the woman could not. In fact, the woman had no right to leave an adulterous husband permanently (Thomson 2000, 133–4). She could also not instigate divorce if the husband were impotent, in the same way that the husband could not leave her if she were barren (Thomson 2000, 129, 196, 221–2, 241; see also chapter 11). It seems that the latter custom survived into the eighteenth and nineteenth centuries Ottoman-Armenian communities (Villa and Matossian 1982, 91). Furthermore, a woman could not remarry for seven years after abandonment or the disappearance of her husband and could be brought back by force if she abandoned him (Thomson 2000, 136, 242). It seems the only possible reasons for the allowance of wife-instigated divorce was if the husband had a "passion for sodomy or bestiality" (Thomson 2000, 135, 222–3), or apostasy (Thomson 2000, 139), or "pollution with foreigners" (here meaning Muslims) (Thomson 2000, 135). In all cases, reconciliation was preferred and encouraged.

Regional variations and similarities

While there are regional variations, some distinct similarities or patterns emerge for eighteenth- and nineteenth-century Armenian communities in different parts of Anatolia, from Van in the east, to Bursa in the west, Amasya to the north, and Kessab and Zeytun to the south, and Iranian-Armenian communities in northwestern Iran, specifically the Azerbaijan province and Isfahan, both places having large Armenian populations.

Dress

Armenian women as members of a religious and ethnic minority retained their cultural distinctiveness far more than Armenian men who were much more likely to come into contact with the dominant group of Muslims. For instance, Armenian women in Iran retained their distinctive dress well into the first quarter of the twentieth century while men by that time had some elements of Iranian clothing (Berberian 2000, 74). Like that of Ottoman-Armenian women, Iranian-Armenian women's dress generally consisted of several layers of undergarments, shirts, long skirts, aprons, ornaments of beads and silver coins, head and mouth covers, usually in white (Berberian 2000, 74; for Anatolia, see A. Poghosyan 2001, 182, Villa and Matossian 1982, 60). While Armenian women in western Anatolia often wore an apron falling over the dress, eastern Armenian women wore no apron. Some women wore baggy trousers (Villa and Matossian 1982, 59–60). Eastern Armenian women's costume included a partial, undecorated face cover to hide the mouth, and sometimes the tip of the nose, and a white kerchief for younger women and black for older women and widows. Married women tended to cover the head and part of the face with scarves (A. Poghosyan 2001, 180). Similarily in Iran, younger girls wore a distinct headcover; unmarried older girls did not have a nose or mouth cover while new brides covered both with a white cloth. Middle-aged women dressed more simply, in darker colors, sometimes mixed with white, and wore no ornaments, while elderly women dressed even more simply and wore a white head cover and often did not cover their noses or mouths (Berberian 2000, 75). Not surprisingly, the costumes of Iranian-Armenian women resembled to a great extent those of Caucasian Armenian women in the region of Zangezur and those of the Ottoman-Armenian women of Ardahan and Van. In some cases, they were also very much like those of the Muslim tribal women of Lorestan and Kordestan, with some variations. The same could be said of other minority women in the Middle East whose dress and other social customs were often not distinguishable from those of Muslim women. In addition, the dress of Isfahan's Armenian women seemed to be much more ornamental and studded with more jewels and coins than those to the north, signifying perhaps the greater prosperity of that community (Berberian 2000, 74–5).

Marriage

Both Ottoman- and Iranian-Armenian women married between the ages of 14 and 17. Like the grooms, they had little say in whom they married and a couple may not even have seen each other until the wedding ceremony, although it seems this was more common in Iran (Villa and Matossian

1982, 72, 75, Berberian 2000, 75). The marriage of prepubescent girls in Anatolia was not unheard of as the "more physically or politically insecure the villagers felt, the younger the age of marriage" (Villa and Matossian 1982, 73). This is despite the prohibition of marriage before maturity (Thomson 2000, 238). The new bride, whose mouth was covered, could not speak or eat in the presence of her husband's family. She could speak only to and through children. The rule against speaking was often relaxed after the first child was born, but even then she spoke only when spoken to (Villa and Matossian 1982, 92, Wallis 1923, 582–3). Women's dress and behavior, including segregation during mealtimes and church services, remained basically unchanged in the rural Iranian-Armenian communities until the mid-twentieth century although here, as with other aspects of women's lives, regional and even familial variations existed (Berberian 2000, 75, Villa and Matossian 1982, 93–5).

The importance placed on the virginity of the bride is evidenced in certain regions of Anatolia by the ritual of the showing of the bloody sheet from the marriage bed as well as the prohibitions against slandering women with accusations of non-virginity and the punishment for rape in the form of a fine paid to the father or the forced marriage of the rapist to the victim, if acceptable to the victim's family. All this, of course, reaffirms the patriarchal system and the belief that women are custodians of family honor (Villa and Matossian 1982, 85, Thomson 2000, 145, Berberian 2000, 87).

Thus women did not merely physically reproduce their children, but as mothers who were the major influence in the lives of their children, they were also the socializers of children, reproducing the culture through dress, behavior, and use of language as well as culinary and other customs (Berberian 2000, 75).

Women's activities

In terms of family standing, the wife of the senior male was the matriarch (Villa and Matossian 1982, 27). In addition to the chores related to household maintenance and food preparation, women were also involved in the textile arts and crafts, combing, spinning wool, linen, flax, cotton, and making textiles, carpets, lace, embroideries (Villa and Matossian 1982, 71, Kasparian 1983, 25). Women were taught embroidery and needlelace in church schools, convents, and monasteries as well as in workshops and homes, starting as early as age 5, beginning to master techniques at 10, and learning to spin the wheel and loom by 15 (Kasparian 1983, 27, Sharambeyan 2001, 165, A. Poghosyan 2001, 156, Villa and Matossian 1982, 117). These skills provided them with a form of subsistence in economically difficult times and a voice: "needlework was one of the few forms of self-expression open to a woman in a society where she was largely without rights or prestige. A woman's skill and virtuosity in the fabric arts stood in direct opposition to her traditional role in the society, which demanded constraint and humility" (Sharambeyan 2001, 165). Some Armenian women in Iranian Azerbaijan also participated and controlled the wine trade, largely because alcohol could not be sold openly, thus making the home the site of transaction (Berberian 2000, 74).

Women's education

Girls' duties began to differentiate from those of boys at about age seven as girls began to take on household chores and later care for younger siblings (Villa and Matossian 1982, 117). For the twentieth century, indications are that certain things remained unchanged (Wallis 1923, 582–4). Differences in rights, responsibilities, and expectations between the genders continued throughout life as evidenced by inheritance customs, according to which although in principle unmarried daughters were required to receive the same share as sons, in reality they often received half that share (Thomson 2000, 182, 183, Villa and Matossian 1982, 28). Variations, of course, existed and they were due not only to regional and cultural distinctions but also to family belief systems deeply affected by education and contact with Westernizing elements such as missionaries.

Missionaries

American missionaries were first to offer secondary education to women in the Ottoman Empire by the establishment of a secondary school in 1845 in Istanbul with the primary goal of training teachers, although graduates were more likely to marry than choose a teaching career. The first girls' school in Iran was established in 1838. Communities were at first reluctant to accept or objected outright to single female teachers. The process of acceptance took at least a few decades (Merguerian 1990–1, 110, 111, Merguerian 1990, 47). Like their counterparts in Iran, missionary girls' schools in the Ottoman Empire, beginning with Istanbul but then spreading to other areas like Aintab a couple of decades later, provided instruction in modern vernacular Armenian, reading with the Bible as the main text, writing, hygiene, housekeeping, and sewing (Merguerian 1990–1, 115, 116, Merguerian 1990, 31, 47, Berberian 2000, 77–84).

Armenian schools

Education of girls often depended on availability of schools and fear for the safety of girls who might have to travel long distances to the nearest school, but also on the family's or community's belief system, which often ran counter to efforts to educate women, charging that education corrupted them (Villa and Matossian 1982, 71). Armenian schools opened soon after missionary schools in an effort to offset the influence of missionaries and assimilation or acculturation; these were experienced especially by communities where, as in the case of Iranian-Armenians in Urmieh, many Armenians communicated with each other only in Turkish or Kurdish rather than Armenian (Berberian 2000, 78–9). Proponents of education placed their arguments in the context of national progress, emphasizing that women's education would better serve the Armenian people or nation (Berberian 2000, 82–3).

A major force behind the expansion of the education of both boys and girls were Ottoman- and Iranian-Armenian women who formed charitable organizations, helped to establish new schools and often provided students with tuition, clothing, and school supplies (Berberian 2000, 83–5, Kalaidjian 2000, 165, Adanalyan 1979, 255–9).

Women in theater

Women also began to make appearances on stage starting in the late nineteenth century in Iranian and Ottoman cities (Berberian 2000, 86). In Istanbul, women's roles may have been played by women actors possibly earlier in the Aramian Theater, established in 1846, and later the Eastern Theater or Armenian Theater Society, established in 1861 (Navasargian 1999, 33, 35). Starting in the 1880s, women also began to establish their own theatrical groups, traveling and performing in Istanbul and parts of Iran and Egypt (Navasargian 1999, 43).

Armenian diaspora: feminist issues

The twentieth century saw the influx of Armenian refugees from Ottoman Anatolia into Arab lands and Iran. We have little insight into the everyday lives of women in the newer diasporas. Much of the very limited studies on Armenian women in the twentieth century focuses on women victims of the genocidal process of the First World War and on women's feminist and nationalist writings. Women's activism extended to nationalist and feminist spheres as they became involved in political activity, in membership or even as founders of political parties, in the case of Maro Vardanian, in support of the nationalist movement.

During the Iranian Constitutional Revolution, 1905–11, Iranian-Armenian women of the upper-middle and upper classes began to be involved in the women's movement in Iran, especially in the attempt to bring women's issues to the attention of Iranian women and raise their consciousness. Their organizations tried to educate women in politics, Ottoman and Iranian constitutionalism, as well as inheritance rights, hygiene, and so forth (Berberian 2000, 91). Similar organizations existed among Ottoman-Armenian women (Adanalyan 1979, 255–9). Especially significant were feminist writers Srpuhi Dussap, Sibyl (Zabel Asatur), and Zabel Esayian, whose writings promoted justice and equity for women in the public and private spheres and educational and employment opportunities (Rowe 2000, 69). Beginning in the late nineteenth century and later in the twentieth century, women's journals, some with a feminist agenda, began to appear in Istanbul, Cairo, and Beirut. Journals such as Marie Beylerian's *Artemis*, which appeared in Cairo in 1901–3, Hayganush Topuzian-Toshigian's *Dzaghig Ganants* (Women's flower), published in Istanbul in 1905–7, and *Hay Guin* (Armenian woman), published in Istanbul in 1919–32, focused on women's issues and concerns. They encouraged girls' education and women's full participation in public life as a crucial part of national development. Of the women's journals, Seza's (Siran Zarifian-Kupelian) *Yeridasart Hayuhi* (Young Armenian woman), which appeared in Beirut intermittently from 1932 to 1968, made an especially important contribution as a proponent of women's rights, education, and empowerment (Zeitlian 2000, 119–41).

Conclusion

A large segment of Ottoman- and Iranian-Armenian women began to be educated and politicized in the late nineteenth and early twentieth centuries, although the majority of both populations shared similar status, roles, and customs and remained traditional in interpersonal relations, social structure, and world-view. Their lives were not very much different from those of Muslim women. While the influence of religion cannot be denied, class and exposure to Westernization, especially through missionaries and Caucasian Armenian immigrants in the case of Iran, were more significant than religion in determining these women's lives.

The twentieth century witnessed major economic, political, and social transformations in the Middle East. The formation of new nation-states, policies of radical nationalism, homogenization, and centralization in Arab countries, Turkey, and Iran as well as more recently Islamist movements and governments such as that of Iran, political instability, civil wars, and so forth, had and continue to have special implications for women. This is especially true but not exclusively so in regard to the reforms and policies that directly targeted women's status and roles in society. It is very likely that such transformations also affected Armenian women; however, with the lack of primary and secondary literature on the impact of such changes on minority women, in particular Armenian women, it is at this point in the history of the field difficult to draw conclusions and provide a cogent analysis. This dearth and the significance of the impact of twentieth-century developments does, however, point to great possibilities in terms of future directions for research.

Bibliography

L. Abrahamian and N. Sweezy (eds.), *Folk arts, culture, and identity*, Bloomington, Ind. 2001.
M. L. Adanalyan, Patriotic Armenian women's society [in Armenian], in *Patma-banasirakan handes* 4:87 (1979), 255–9.
G. Aivazian, Saintly and profane women in classical texts. Rhipsimé and Parandzem, in B. J. Merguerian and J. Renjilian-Burgy (eds.), *Voices of Armenian women*, Belmont, Mass. 2000, 67–85.
L. P. Alishan, Sacred archetypes and the Armenian woman, in *Journal of the Society for Armenian Studies* 4 (1988–9), 77–103.
K. M. Arat, Die Diakonissen der armenischen Kirche in kanonischer Sicht, in *Handes amsorya* 1–12 (1987), 153–89.
——, The deaconess in the Armenian church, in B. J. Merguerian and J. Renjilian-Burgy (eds.), *Voices of Armenian women*, Belmont, Mass. 2000, 86–118.
L. Bakar, The Armenian woman as a governing force in society, in B. J. Merguerian and J. Renjilian-Burgy (eds.), *Voices of Armenian women*, Belmont, Mass. 2000, 269–77.
H. Berberian, Armenian women in turn-of-the-century Iran. Education and activity, in R. Matthee and B. Baron (eds.), *Iran and beyond. Essays in Middle Eastern history in honor of Nikki R. Keddie*, Costa Mesa 2000, 70–98.
R. Ervine, Women who left the world. The Armenian nuns of Jerusalem, in T. Hummel, K. Hintlian, and U. Carmesund (eds.), *Patterns of the past, prospects for the future. The Christian heritage in the Holy Land*, London 1999, 124–34.
A. Giulkhandanian, *Revolutionary Armenian women* [in Armenian], Paris 1939.
F. M. Göçek and M. D. Baer, Social boundaries of Ottoman women's experience in eighteenth-century Galata court records, in M. C. Zilfi (ed.), *Women in the Ottoman Empire*, Leiden 1996, 48–65.
A. S. Kalaidjian, Serpuhi Vahanian Dussap. Defining a new role for women, in B. J. Merguerian and J. Renjilian-Burgy (eds.), *Voices of Armenian women*, Belmont, Mass. 2000, 162–78.
A. O. Kasparian, *Armenian needlelace and embroidery. A preservation of some of history's oldest and finest needlework*, McLean, Va. 1983.
G. Lazian, The Armenian woman and the Armenian revolution [in Armenian], Cairo 1959.
B. J. Merguerian, Mt. Holyoke Seminary in Bitlis. Providing an American education for Armenian women, in *Armenian Review* 43:1/169 (Spring 1990), 103–24.
——, The beginnings of secondary education for Armenian women. The Armenian female seminary in Constantinople, in *Journal of the Society for Armenian Studies* 5 (1990–1), 31-65.
B. J. Merguerian and J. Renjilian-Burgy (eds.), *Voices of Armenian women*, Belmont, Mass. 2000.
Fr. A. Oghlukian, *The deaconess in the Armenian Church. A brief survey*, trans. S. P. Cowe, New Rochelle, N.Y. 1994.
A. Navasargian, *Armenian women of the stage*, Glendale, Calif. 1999.
A. Poghosyan, Carpets, in L. Abrahamian and N. Sweezy (eds.), *Armenian folk arts, culture, and identity*, Bloomington, Ind. 2001, 150–64.
S. Poghosyan, Costume, in L. Abrahamian and N. Sweezy (eds.), *Armenian folk arts, culture, and identity*, Bloomington, Ind. 2001, 177–94.
N. al-Qattan, *Dhimmīs* in the the Muslim court. Legal autonomy and religious discrimination, in *International Journal of Middle East Studies* 31 (1999), 429–44.
V. Rowe, The "new Armenian woman." Armenian women's writings in the Ottoman Empire, 1880–1915, Ph.D. diss., University of Toronto 2000.
E. Sanasarian, *Religious minorities in Iran*, Cambridge 2000.
A. Sharambeyan, Needle arts, in L. Abrahamian and N. Sweezy (eds.), *Armenian folk arts, culture, and identity*, Bloomington, Ind. 2001, 165–76.
R. W. Thomson (trans), *The lawcode [Datastanagirk'] of Mxit'ar Goš*, Amsterdam 2000.
N. Y. Tsovakan, Female scribes [in Armenian], in *Sion* 4–5 (April–May 1954), 133–5.
S. H. Villa and M. K. Matossian, *Armenian village life before 1914*, Detroit 1982.
W. D. Wallis, Brief communications. Some phases of Armenian social life, in *American Anthropologist* (October–December 1923), 582–4.
S. Zeitlian, The role of the Armenian woman in the Armenian revolutionary movement [in Armenian], Los Angeles 1992.
——, Pioneers of women's journalism in the western Armenian media, 1862–1968, in B. J. Merguerian and J. Renjilian-Burgy (eds.), *Voices of Armenian women*, Belmont, Mass. 2000, 119–41.

Houri Berberian

Bahāʾī Women

Overview

The Bahāʾī Faith grew out of nineteenth-century Shīʿī messianic expectations much as Christianity grew out of similar expectations within Judaism. The Bahāʾī Faith's founders (the Bāb and Bahāʾu'l-lāh), in claiming to be the latest messengers from God with new divinely revealed laws, irremediably divorced the new religion from its Islamic background. Among the distinguishing principles promulgated in the Bahāʾī writings was the equality of women and men. More important than this principle was the fact that it expressed itself in behavior strikingly different from the Islamic milieu from which it emerged. This equality does not refer solely to the spiritual plane; Bahāʾī scriptures explicitly state that education for women and men should be identical and that women should be active in political affairs and hence the public sphere. Representation of women in top Bahāʾī administrative positions is quite high compared to percentages of women observed in other religious organizations, comprising a third to half of the Bahāʾī leadership. They are, however, excluded from membership of the highest administrative body, the Universal House of Justice.

Women in the Bābī period

One of the prominent followers of Sayyid ʿAlī Muḥammad al-Bāb, who in 1844 secretly revealed himself to be the Qāʾīm, the messianic figure expected by the Shīʿī Muslims was a woman, Fāṭimih Bigum Baraghānī, later known as Ṭāhirih (Ṭāhirah Qurrat al-ʿAyn). The Bahāʾī Faith would emerge out of the Bābī movement when Bahāʾu'llāh assumed the leadership around 1863, claiming to be the fulfillment of the Bāb's prophecy regarding the coming of He Whom God would make manifest. Ṭāhirih provides one of the key models of womanhood within the Bahāʾī community.

The daughter of the leading clerical family of Qazvīn, Ṭāhirih received an excellent education from her mother and her father, both of whom were *mujtahids* in Qazvīn. Her maternal relatives belonged to the Shaykhī sect of Shīʿī Islam whereas her paternal relatives were staunchly *ʾusūlī*. Though married to her paternal uncle's son, she herself followed in her mother's footsteps, moving to Karbala, and taking up residence in the home of the late Shaykhī leader, Sayyid Kāẓim, at the behest of his widow. She became the leader of those Shaykhīs in Karbala who subsequently took up the Bābī cause.

Ṭāhirih's activities created controversy within the Bābī community, through her insistence that Islamic law was no longer binding upon Bābīs. During Muḥarram, Ṭāhirih deliberately provoked the *ʿulamāʾ* by dressing in gay colors and appearing unveiled to celebrate the birthday of the Bāb instead of donning mourning clothes to commemorate the martyrdom of Imām Ḥusayn. To prevent violence, the governor intervened and arrested Ṭāhirih, eventually sending her back to Iran.

On her arrival in Qazvīn, she refused to take up residence with her estranged husand, Mullā Muḥammad, and divorced him, taking the initiative of pronouncing the *ṭalāq* herself. No doubt this estrangement grew out of their religious differences, for her father-in-law, Muḥammad Taqī, virulently opposed both the Bābīs and the Shaykhīs, and incited mob violence against them. A Bābī sympathizer retaliated by fatally stabbing the mullā. Though the assassin insisted he acted alone, Ṭāhirih's husband implicated her and executed several Bābīs. Ṭāhirih escaped with the assistance of Bahāʾu'llāh, who hid her in his home in Tehran.

Sometime later, the Bābī leaders met in Badasht, Khurasan to discuss the future direction of the Bābī community in the face of growing persecution. Tension developed between Ṭāhirih, who advocated a complete break with Islam and a militant defense of their community, and the more conservative Quddūs, who initially advocated policies aimed at the rejuvenation of Islam. As she had in Karbala, Ṭāhirih appeared before the assembled believers unveiled. One shocked believer slit his own throat and fled. Unperturbed, Ṭāhirih declared, "I am the Word which the Qāʾim is to utter, the Word which shall put to flight the chiefs and nobles of the earth!" (Shoghi Effendi 1944, 32–3).

Eventually Quddūs conceded that Islamic law had been abrogated. So complete was his reconciliation with Ṭāhirih that the two departed from Badasht riding in the same howdah. When they neared the village of Nīyālā, the local mullā, outraged at seeing an unveiled woman sitting next to a man and chanting poems aloud, led a mob against them. A deadly clash resulted and the Bābīs dispersed in different directions. Pitched battles raged between the Bābīs and government forces between 1848 and 1850 in the Iranian province of Māzandarān and in the cities of Zanjān and Nayrīz. Ṭāhirih remained in hiding, moving from village to village until she was captured in 1848. She was sent to Tehran where she was imprisoned in the house of the chief of police. Here as elsewhere, she was able to hold meetings with the leading women of the city. Among them was Shams-i Fitnih, a Qājār princess and the granddaughter of Fatḥ ʿAlī Shāh, who became an ardent Bābī and later one of the earliest Bahāʾīs (Māzandarani 1969, 6:412–14).

In 1852, following an abortive attempt on the life of the Shah, a general massacre of Bābīs ensued in which Ṭāhirih fell victim. While male Bābī leaders were executed publicly in a brutal manner, Ṭāhirih was taken in secret to a garden and strangled. Bahāʾī sources quote her last words to have been: "You can kill me as soon as you like, but you cannot stop the emancipation of women" (Shoghi Effendi 1944, 75).

Women in the Writings of Bahāʾuʾllāh

The writings of Bahāʾuʾllāh proclaim, "In this Day the Hand of divine grace hath removed all distinction. The Servants of God and His handmaidens are regarded on the same plane." He states that differences between the sexes are the result of "vain imaginings" and "idle fancies," which his revelation dispels (1986, 2). However, like the Qurʾān, the *Kitāb-i-Aqdas*, containing Bahāʾī sacred law, is written in Arabic, a language that uses the male gender for the collective, and most of its laws are written as if addressed to men. This androcentric view, which a cursory reading of the text gives, is not, it should be recognized, the manner in which Bahāʾīs have understood the greater part of the *Aqdas*. Whereas the *Aqdas* appeared to allow bigamy, ʿAbduʾl-Bāhā, Bahāʾuʾllāh's successor, insisted that conditions of equity could not be met for two wives; therefore monogamy alone was permissible (*Aqdas*, 209). Shoghi Effendi, who led the Bahāʾī community as Guardian between 1921 and 1957, stated that in most cases the laws in the *Aqdas* applied equally to men and women except when context made this impossible. Only in the case of membership in the Universal House of Justice has the male oriented language been taken literally.

When read within the context of nineteenth-century Iran, the *Kitāb-i Aqdas* presents some startling contrasts to the norms of male-female relations. The concept of ritual uncleanliness is absent, and it is optional for women to perform the usual obligatory prayers or fast during their menses. While chastity is enjoined on men and women alike, no special attention is given to controlling the sexuality of women. In contrast to the harsher penalties for adultery found in both Judaism and Islam, adulterers are subject to a fine (*Aqdas*, 47).

While Bahāʾuʾllāh's Arabic writings necessitated the use of the male gender when referring to God, those in Persian have no gender. However, thus far, references to God have been translated using the male gender regardless of the original language. Perhaps more interesting concerning the issue of gender in the Bahāʾuʾllāh's writings is the symbol of the Heavenly Maiden or the *ḥūrī*. In the Qurʾānic vision of paradise, black-eyed damsels or *ḥūrī*s are thought to serve its inmates. Within the Bahāʾī context of fulfilled eschatology, the *ḥūrī* comes to symbolize the Holy Spirit, the personification of Bahāʾuʾllāh's revelation and the vehicle through which he receives it. His initial revelation in the dungeon of the Sīyāh Chāl consisted of a vision of this maiden who informed him of his divine mission. She appears frequently in Bahāʾuʾllāh's later, mystical works where this feminine theophany has a symbiotic relationship with Bahāʾuʾllāh and is ultimately inseparable from him (Walbridge 1996, 158–65).

From East to West

When the Bahāʾī Faith was introduced to America after 1893, women played a prominent role, outnumbering male converts by two to one. Bahāʾī administrative institutions initially included women. However, when Iranian Bahāʾī teachers arranged for the election of the Chicago House of Justice, they insisted that only men were eligible. When Corinne True wrote to ʿAbduʾl-Bahā asking for clarification ʿAbduʾl-Bahā replied that the House of Justice, "according to the explicit text of the Law of God, is confined to men, this for a wisdom of the Lord God's, which will ere long be made manifest as clearly as the sun at high noon." Seven years later ʿAbduʾl-Bahā ruled that this exclusion applied only to the as yet unformed Universal House of Justice and allowed women in America to serve on local bodies (Maneck 1994, 223–5).

From West to East

The introduction of the Bahāʾī Faith to America had a profound effect on the position of Bahāʾī women in Iran, through correspondence, through Western Bahāʾīs who traveled to Iran, and through receiving talks given by ʿAbduʾl-Bahā in America.

One Iranian Bahā'ī woman influenced by this development was Ta'irih Tihrani (1861–1911), born ʿIsmat Khanum. Ta'irih's husband served as a bodyguard to the Shah and often imprisoned Bahā'īs in his home. Ta'irih embraced the Bahā'ī Faith after her marriage, and attempted to show every kindness to Bahā'ī prisoners. For this she was often beaten until she bled. After her husband died, Ta'irih played an active part in the Bahā'ī community. She cropped her hair and received Western Bahā'ī visitors into her home, urging Iranian Bahā'ī women (with limited success) to remove their veils and mix freely with men as Western women did. Eventually she established a girls' school and published articles on women's emancipation (Najmabadi 1997, 146–95).

At the behest of ʿAbdu'l-Bahā many American Bahā'ī women came to Iran. Their presence helped transform gender relations within the Iranian Bahā'ī community. Dr. Susan Moody arrived from Chicago to assist Iranian Bahā'ī doctors in establishing a hospital. Elizabeth Stewart, a nurse, Dr. Sarah Clock, and Lillian Kappes, a teacher, later joined her, becoming instrumental in establishing one of the country's finest girls' preparatory schools. Iranian Bahā'ī women also traveled to America for study (Armstrong-Ingram 1986, 181–210).

ʿAbdu'l-Bahā explicitly promoted women's rights as an aspect of Bahā'ī teachings during his trip to the United States in 1912. He stressed the need for women's education, deeming the education of mothers so essential to the proper upbringing of children that he insisted that the education of daughters take precedence over that of sons. Despite the linkage of motherhood and education, ʿAbdu'l-Bahā did not restrict women's proper sphere to the home. He urged women to excel in arts and science. He held that their participation in the political sphere would prove to be a prerequisite for peace. The only fields where ʿAbdu'l-Bahā would not extend full and equal participation was in military endeavors and membership in the House of Justice.

Copies of ʿAbdu'l-Bahā's talks were distributed throughout Iran, and, along with the influence of American Bahā'īs residing in Iran, these awakened Iranian Bahā'ī women to possibilities unthought of in previous generations. Some began to advocate immediate abolishment of the veil and to agitate for women's full participation on Bahā'ī administrative bodies. ʿAbdu'l-Bahā felt that actions such as discarding the veil would bring on needless persecution in an already volatile situation. ʿAbdu'l-Bahā pleaded with the women not to do anything "contrary to wisdom." Women's assemblages at this time should be confined to educational matters so that "differences will, day by day, be entirely wiped out, not that, God forbid, it will end in argumentation between men and women." ʿAbdu'l-Bahā stated that he himself would in time ensure that women would achieve full equality; in the meantime they ought not to agitate (1986, 5–6).

Women were not permitted to serve on Bahā'ī institutions in Iran until 1954 but by 1981, when the members of the National Spiritual Assembly of the Bahā'īs of Iran were arrested and executed, the chairperson was a woman, Zhinus Maḥmūdi, Iran's leading chemist (Maneck 1994, 227)

Recent developments

Since the late 1960s and the 1970s the Bahā'ī Faith has seen its largest growth in areas such as India, Latin America, and Africa. While women have played a significant, and sometimes leading, role in the propagation efforts, the numbers of male enrollments in those countries has vastly exceeded those of females. Realizing that this discrepancy does not augur well for the future, some Bahā'ī communities have established institutes aimed at raising the literacy rate of rural women and providing then with basic vocational skills. It is not yet known whether these have impacted the demography of the community.

There exists no single theory of Bahā'ī feminism, but Bahā'īs, men and women alike, are agreed on one principle: hierarchical systems that place men above women in a divinely ordained order have no sanction within the Bahā'ī scriptures.

Bibliography

ʿAbdu'l-Bahā, *The promulgation of universal peace*, 1922, Wilmette 1982².

S. ʿAla'i and C. Dawes (ed.), *The role of women in an advancing civilization*, Willetton, Western Australia 1989.

R. J. Armstrong-Ingram, American Bahā'ī women and the education of girls in Tehran, 1909–1934, in P. Smith (ed.), *In Iran*, Los Angeles 1986, 181–210.

Bahā'u'llāh, *Compilation on women*, Oakham , Ill. 1986.

——, *Kitāb-i Aqdas*, Haifa 1992.

P. Caton (ed.), *Equal circles. Women and men in Bahā'ī communities*, Los Angeles 1987.

T. Culhane, *I beheld a maiden. The Baha'i Faith and the life of the spirit*, Los Angeles 2001.

J. Khan and P. Khan, *Advancement of women*, Wilmette 1999.

B. Maʿani, The interdependence of Bahā'ī communities services of North American Bahā'ī women in Iran, in *Journal of Bahā'ī studies* 4:1 (1991), 19–46.

S. Maneck, Tahirih. A religious paradigm of womanhood, in *Journal of Bahā'ī studies* 2:2 (1989), 39–54.

——, Women in the Bahā'ī Faith, in A. Sharma (ed.), *Religion and women*, Albany, N.Y. 1994, 211–27.

F. Māzandarānī, *Tarīkh-i zuhūr*, 4 vols., Tehran 1969.

A. Najmabadi (ed.), Namih-ha va nivishtih-ha va āsh'ar in "Recasting women and feminity in Qajar Iran," in *Nemeye digar* 2:3 (1997), 146–95.

Shoghi Effendi, *God passes by*, Wilmette, Ill. 1944.
J. Walbridge, *Sacred acts, sacred space, sacred time*, Oxford 1996.
Women, Compilation issued by the Universal House of Justice, Oakham, Ill. 1986.

Susan Stiles Maneck

Citizenship

The Caucasus and Central Asia

Caucasian and Central Asian women are currently in a process of constant negotiation and renegotiation of their womanness, finding themselves between a revival of Muslim norms and traditions, a Western capitalist influence, and a recent Soviet history, all with completely different standards of what it means to be both a woman and a citizen.

Soviet times

From the earliest days of rule, the Soviet Communists regarded the inclusion of Central Asian and Caucasian women in their very concept of citizenship as a strategic priority. Equating the treatment of women in these traditional societies with slavery, they identified women as the "surrogate proletariat" to engage in the class war and to wage war against religion. The Soviets tried to make women into fully-fledged citizens mainly by introducing legal reforms and social allowances for women. They provided women with rights equal to those of men by revising the existing legal system and abolishing *ʿāda* and Sharīʿa practices such as polygamy, payment of *kalym*, and marriage without consent of the bride. To draw women into socialized production, they granted them free and high level education, access to work in traditionally male dominated fields (for example, engineering), and multiple social allowances such as paid lengthy maternity leave and state-sponsored childcare. By establishing women's sections (*zhenotdely*) within the Communist Party and introducing a quota for women of 30 percent of the seats in parliaments and governing bodies, the Soviets pushed for female presence in all spheres of public life.

Despite the very real improvements in facilities and range of choices, and the greater visibility of women in public life, the women's conception of themselves as citizens did not really change. In the private sphere older patterns of behavior continued to dominate gender relations. The Communists' women's liberation campaign failed because it was perceived as the emasculation of men and the defeminization of women. To give an example, the mass unveiling of Uzbek women in 1927, known as the *khudzhum* (the attack), symbolized for Uzbek men a defeat and a brutal rape. The honor and dignity of the whole community was suddenly and monstrously violated. For the Communists, the success of the *khudzhum* was an ideological victory. To them, the *parandzha*, the veil of horsehair, symbolized everything that they were fighting to eradicate: oppression, ignorance, injustice, and human degradation. For Central Asians, the veil was a protection against unwanted contact with strangers and against the physical grime of the environment (Akiner 1997).

In response to the forced modernization, strong cultural barriers were erected, behind which sedentary and nomad traditions were frozen, to guard against Soviet encroachments. Women did not assume the role of a revolutionary force to destroy traditional society. Rather, they colluded in its preservation. By accommodating external pressures through the adoption of additional identities, appropriate to the public sphere, they deflected intrusions into the private domain, thereby protecting the integrity of the older disposition of family roles and religious practices. Cut off from the formal, male dominated teachings of Islam, women became the primary transmitter of religious knowledge to the younger generation in the home. In Uzbekistan, *otyns*, female mullahs with no spiritual education, preserved knowledge of women's role in rituals connected with the major life cycle ceremonies (male circumcision, burial rites, marriage), and semi-Islamic practices such as visits to the graves of revered individuals (Olcott 1991).

Post-Soviet times

After independence, women were caught between conflicting concepts of citizenship: they longed for the Soviet lifestyle with its high social security standards, at the same time feeling the need to return to their "authentic" roots, with a renewed emphasis on traditional domestic obligations, and continuing along the road to greater personal independence and freedom of choice.

In the Caucasus, nationalistic sentiments, fueled by war, dominated the gender discourse. Confronted with war, displacement, and destruction, women chose to subordinate gender issues to nationalist goals, constructing and perceiving their role as auxiliary to the primary nationalist task. Especially in Armenia, women felt constrained, being the guardians of the nation and bastions of resistance against assimilation. Here, a revived discourse of genocide (harking back to the large-scale 1915 slaughter of Armenians in the Ottoman Empire) and ongoing threats to Armenian survival appealed to women to remain home, maintain the family economically and morally, inspire their men with patriotism, and give birth to future soldiers (Dudwick 1997).

In Central Asia, however, nationalist sentiments could not mobilize masses. The Soviet Union's collapse was greeted with ambivalence and reluctance. Here, top-down nationalism played a major role in defining women's concepts of citizenship. Presidents functioned as primary narrators of gendered nation-building, nationalism, and national identity-forming. Reasserting their authority through the symbolic identification of the head of state as the "Father of the Nation," they a reinstated patriarchal values. Campaigning that women were supposed to be the "guardians of home and hearth," they perpetuated a fertility cult aimed at increasing their ethnic groups' populations and thence their power both within their state and in the region as a whole. At the same time, the fixed quota representation practiced under the Soviet system was removed. Politics became a "men's business," dominated by clan interests and tribal resource allocation. Women withdrew from politics, identifying political action with "masculine behavior, power struggles, private property disputes, corruption and hypocrisy" (LaFont 2001).

The post-Soviet nation-building process was accompanied by a revival of Muslim norms, idioms, and practices, also defining women's post-Soviet concepts of citizenship. Freedom of worship allowed the pilgrimage to holy places, *mazār*s, the opening of *madrasa*s and Islamic cultural centers as well as the establishment of women's non-governmental organizations (NGOs) that aimed at revitalizing Muslim traditions. This Islamic revival evoked a call for legalization of old, semi-Islamic Central Asian and Caucasian traditions such as payment of *kalym*, bride kidnapping, and polygamy. Though officially debated and widely practiced, these traditions were never legalized. Ruling elites as well as the better part of the population rejected the agenda of conservative Islamists who pressed for enforced sex segregation, compulsory veiling, and the restoration of Sharīʿa in family law. The strict implementation of Muslim norms and law in countries such as Taliban-led Afghanistan or Wahhābī Saudi Arabia figured as deterring rather than as attracting examples for the overwhelmingly secular societies in Central Asia and Caucasus.

Despite the emergence of nationalist and Muslim identities, secular, pro-Western concepts of citizenship predominate in the identity-building process currently underway, leading to the break-up of long-standing borders and boundaries and a considerable reversal of new gender roles in public and private life. This process is accelerated by the deterioration of social welfare and the collapse of the economic system. Women and men are more and more forced to make compromises with dominant gender identities and to make adjustments, often as part of desperate strategies to survive the new situation. Men see their ability to support their families remarkably reduced. Women feel impelled to seek for cash contributions to the household. As the traditional sexual division of labor is changing, relations of authority and responsibility between men and women are destabilizing. The extended family is transforming into a broken family, a single-parent family, or even a polygamous family. Violence against women, female slavery, prostitution, trafficking in women, and rapes have become widespread phenomena, radically challenging the concept of women as citizens equal to men, which women favor, formerly imposed by the Soviets and propagated by Western societies.

In post-Soviet Caucasus and Central Asia, women find themselves in a dilemma, caught between different concepts of citizenship. Socially and economically they are encouraged to seek emancipation while ethnically and religiously they are supposed to return to old behavioral norms where the functions of bearing and caring for children, looking after their husbands, and fulfilling their household duties are their sole lot (Tabyshalieva 2002). Despite awareness of this dilemma, there is no discussion underway focusing on women's contribution to the construction of citizenship in the Caucasian and Central Asian societies. Although women have taken the opportunity to become involved in society by establishing political parties and NGOs, they have so far refrained from launching a broad women's movement. None of the women-led NGOs has an explicit feminist agenda, and only a few take up the issue of women's rights at all. The majority of women's organizations have devoted themselves to channeling assistance to single mothers, families with many children, and disabled and handicapped persons. While several small women's parties have formed, women figure in very insignificant numbers in larger political parties, none of which has shown interest in women's issues. In consequence of this feminist disengagement, women do not take an active part in the construction of post-Soviet citizenship. The degree of women's future success in moving beyond the boundaries dictated by conservative nationalists and Islamists depends on state gender policies, the strength of civil society, especially women's NGOs, and the legal establishment of human rights at a general level.

BIBLIOGRAPHY

F. Acar and A. Güneş-Ayata (eds.), *Gender and identity construction. Women of Central Asia, the Caucasus and Turkey*, Leiden 2000.

S. Akiner, Between tradition and modernity. The dilemma facing contemporary Central Asian women, in M. Buckley (ed.), *Post-Soviet women. From the Baltic to Central Asia*, Cambridge 1997, 261–304.

M. Buckley (ed.), *Post-Soviet women. From the Baltic to Central Asia*, Cambridge 1997.

N. Dudwick, Out of the kitchen into the crossfire. Women in independent Armenia, in M. Buckley (ed.), *Post-Soviet women. From the Baltic to Central Asia*, Cambridge 1997, 235–49.

L. M. Handrahan, Gender and ethnicity in the "transitional democracy" of Kyrgyzstan, in *Central Asian Survey* 20 (2001), 467–96.

S. LaFont, One step forward, two steps back. Women in post-communist states, in *Communist and Post-Communist Studies* 34 (2001), 203–20.

M. B. Olcott, Women and society in Central Asia, in W. Fierman (ed.), *Soviet Central Asia. The failed transformation*, Boulder, Colo. 1991, 235–56.

A. Tabyshalieva, Central Asia. Increasing gender inequity, in A. Strasser et al. (eds.), *Central Asia and Islam*, Hamburg 2002, 150–8.

MARIE-CARIN VON GUMPPENBERG

Egypt, Sudan and Arab States

Globalization and democratization have catapulted issues of citizenship to international and national prominence. Discussions abound on the rights of citizens vis-à-vis the state, the quality of relations between the state and civil society, the status of immigrants, and the rights of women. In Arab states, tackling the problem of women's second-class citizenship has acquired urgency, chiefly because of the demands of women's movements. Constructions of citizenship are gendered and inscribed in state policies and legal frameworks (for example, constitutions, family laws, labor laws, and socioeconomic policies), in religio-cultural institutions and practices (for example, Islamic laws and norms), and in popular discourses. Laws, norms, and discourses often cast "authentic citizenship" as adherence to Islam and the state, while the media, schools, and religious institutions also reproduce images of "the ideal Muslim woman." Constructions of citizenship usually differentiate between nationals and non-nationals, women and men, and Muslim and non-Muslim citizens. Civil, political, and social rights are generally circumscribed, but nationals, men, and Muslims have more citizenship rights than non-nationals, women, and non-Muslims. Disparities between women and men are captured in indicators of citizenship such as educational attainment, access to employment and income, control over the body and fertility, and political participation.

The growing literature on Arab women's citizenship (Shehadeh 1998, Botman 1999, Hammami and Johnson 1999, Joseph 2000, Charrad 2001, Moghadam 2002, 2003b) draws attention to constructions of women's citizenship and campaigns for equality and empowerment. Empirical studies show that many Arab women are cognizant of their second-class citizenship and desire expanded rights and equality. One study found that refugee and low-income women in the West Bank cited the following desired rights: education, work, and freedom of movement; and the right to take one's inheritance, choose a marriage partner, and be free from domestic violence (Rubenberg 2001, 123). These aspirations are common throughout the Arab region, where women's organizations seek the reform of family laws, the criminalization of domestic violence (including "honor killings"), enhanced nationality rights, and greater political and economic participation.

ASPECTS OF WOMEN'S SECOND-CLASS CITIZENSHIP

Sharīʿa-based family laws or civil codes – which govern marriage, divorce, maintenance, paternity, and custody of children – place women in a disadvantaged position in the family and the society, designating them as wives, mothers, and daughters, and conferring greater privileges on men. Since the early 1980s, and in a more concerted fashion since the early 1990s, feminists and women's organizations have prioritized legal reforms to expand their citizenship rights. Feminist research, advocacy, and lobbying efforts are directed at governments, clergy, the media, international organizations, and the transnational public sphere. Women have deployed secular, universal, and Islamic discourses to disseminate their ideas and achieve their goals (Moghadam 2003a).

Reform of family law is important for several reasons: it is a central element in the modernization of religious institutions and norms in Muslim societies; it establishes women's human rights and their equality within the family and vis-à-vis male kin; it has implications for women's wider citizenship rights and their social participation, including economic citizenship; and it brings the Arab states in line with international norms and codes as enshrined in such conventions as the Universal Declaration on Human Rights, the Convention on the Elimination of All Forms of Discrimination against Women (CEDAW), the International Covenant on Civil and Political Rights, the International Covenant on Economic, Social, and Cultural Rights, and the Beijing Declaration and Platform for Action.

The content of family law varies to some degree across countries, depending on the legal school in place and, over time, change has occurred. The former People's Democratic Republic of Yemen (then known as "the Cuba of the Middle East") adopted an audaciously egalitarian family law in the late 1960s, but it was abrogated after the country merged with North Yemen in 1990. Some constitutions stipulate equality of all citizens (for example, that of Egypt), but this is contradicted by the family law, which confers different rights and obligations on women and men. Saudi Arabia, which has no modern constitution, refers to the Qur'ān as its basic law, and has institutionalized a patriarchal interpretation of Islamic precepts governing marriage and the status of women in the family and society.

What is common across Arab countries is that religious law is elevated to civil status, and religious affiliation is a requirement of citizenship. This often places women, secular Muslims, and non-Muslims in a disadvantaged position. In Sudan, where a long civil war has engaged the predominantly Arab and Muslim north against the black and non-Muslim south, the Sudanese state constructs the "authentic" citizen as a Muslim. Any abandoned or foundling children may be adopted by Muslims only, and raised as Muslims (Hale 2000, 95).

Male guardianship is usually inscribed in the family laws, and thus the father or other male kin may permit "a virgin" to marry. The Islamic marriage contract does require the consent of the wife, and in some countries women may insert stipulations into the contract, such as the condition that she be the only wife (An-Naim 2002). Marriage, however, remains largely an agreement between two families rather than two individuals with equal rights and obligations. Moreover, marriage gives the husband the right of access to his wife's body, marital rape is not recognized, and a wife is required to obey her husband (Shehadeh 1998, Welchman 2001). Children acquire citizenship and religious status through their fathers, not their mothers. Muslim women are not permitted to marry non-Muslim men. Under Islamic family law, males inherit more family wealth than do females, and non-Muslim widows cannot inherit from Muslim husbands. A husband may divorce without reason, and some countries allow repudiation, but a woman can divorce – or request that she be divorced – only upon specific conditions. Because Islamic family law operates on the principle of patrilineality, fathers or their male agnates are given automatic custody of children upon divorce. Muslim family law also permits the practice of polygamy by men.

Under Islamic family law and attendant civil codes, women are required to obtain the permission of father, husband, or other male guardian to seek employment, start a business, travel, or open a bank account for a child. In Jordan and Sudan, a father or husband has the legal right to forbid his wife or daughter to seek employment or continue in a job. In Sudan, a woman cannot claim her spouse as a dependent; only a man can do so, and only he can receive family allowances. An employed woman cannot receive any residential plot that may be allocated to those in public service if her husband already has one (Hale 2000, 94). The implication of guardianship is that women are seen as incapable of entering contracts on their own. Wives who are educated or politically aware may stipulate the condition that they be allowed to work in their marriage contracts, but others make no such stipulations, and courts have been known to side with the husband when the issue is contested (Sonbol 2003, 89–99). In constructing women as dependents of men and minors within the family, Arab legal codes have strengthened the male breadwinner/female homemaker ideal – or "the patriarchal gender contract" (Moghadam 1998) – which in turn has reinforced women's second-class citizenship in economic and political domains.

Socioeconomic implications

Muslim family law mandates a sum of money from the groom to the bride, the *mahr*, which is sometimes paid in full and sometimes deferred until the event of divorce. The marriage contract stipulates the amount, which is usually agreed to by both families. A husband is obligated to provide for his wife and children, and non-maintenance by the husband is grounds for divorce. A wife is under no obligation to share her wealth or any earnings with her husband, contribute to the family economy, or even perform household labor. In return for maintenance (*nafaqa*) by the husband, the wife is obligated to obey her husband, provide sexual services, and bear children. In the case of divorce, however, she may lose her claim to the *mahr* if she is seen to be at fault or if she initiates the divorce.

Sons inherit twice as much as daughters, and they are also expected to look after their parents in old age. (However, in many Arab countries, due to male out-migration among other reasons, it is the daughters who are increasingly looking after aged parents.) A deceased man's inheritance and his pension are divided among his widows, children, and other relatives that he may have been supporting. As a result, many widows receive insignificant pensions.

For these reasons, Arab feminists insist on reform of family laws. *Mahr, nafaqa*, and unequal inheritance rights reinforce gender difference and women's economic dependence. Legal frameworks, and especially the family laws, cast women as daughters, mothers, and wives, while men are the guardians and breadwinners. Women's association with the private sphere of the family has also resulted in relatively low rates of female participation in the political domain – a situation that Arab feminists have been seeking to change.

Recent campaigns and achievements

In Egypt, women's rights activists succeeded in having reforms adopted that ease the restrictions on women's capacity to divorce, partly through the introduction of a new marriage contract that stipulates the rights of the wife. In 1999, they secured the reversal of Article 291, which exonerated rapists who married their victims. Egyptian feminists and public health activists have also formed or worked with coalitions against female circumcision. In both Iran and Egypt, activists have made their case in an Islamic idiom – arguing that patriarchal cultural norms rather than egalitarian and emancipatory Islam are responsible for the legal status and social positions of women – but they have also appealed to the international women's rights agenda and the relevant conventions.

In Jordan, the criminalization of honor killings of daughters and sisters has become a major social issue for feminist lawyers and journalists, concerned members of the Jordanian royal family, and others. The state was initially timid before the tribe and kin-based social structure, but women's groups and the Royal Commission for Human Rights pushed for legal reforms. In December 2001 the Jordanian cabinet approved several amendments to the Civil Status Law. The legal age for marriage was raised from 15 for women and 16 for men to 18 for both, and Jordanian women were given legal recourse to divorce. New restrictions on polygamy require a man to inform his first wife of plans to marry again and to submit evidence of his financial ability to support more than one wife. As a result of an amendment to the penal code, perpetrators of honor crimes are no longer exempt from the death penalty – though judges are still allowed to commute the sentences of the convicted.

In Lebanon, feminists formed the Women's Court: The Permanent Arab Court to Resist Violence against Women, which launched highly visible campaigns in 1995, 1998, and 2000, and a Feminine Rights Campaign to focus on gender equality in divorce. In a country where communal traditions hold sway, the state is weak, and there are 15 family codes for the 18 legally recognized religious sects, many feminists nonetheless are in favor of civil codes that supersede sectarian authority (Joseph 2000, Shehadeh 1998). Secularists, feminists, and democrats in an array of civil society organizations encouraged President Hrawi to propose an optional civil marriage, but it was defeated by entrenched religious forces, especially among the Sunnīs (Saadeh 1999).

In Yemen, a woman was appointed state minister for human rights in 2001, and a successful campaign was launched against the "house of obedience" law, or the forced return of a woman to the matrimonial home. Yet much remains to be done. Feminists and human rights activists seek to insert an equality clause into the constitution, to criminalize honor killings (the penal code currently exonerates a husband's killing of his adulterous wife), to decriminalize sexual misconduct by women (90 percent of women prisoners are charged with adultery or similar sexual misconduct), and to change the electoral laws to allow for quotas for women candidates.

Enhancing women's participation in governance is a major aim, and an achievement was the appointment in 2003 of government spokeswomen in Syria and Jordan. That year, the first female judge was approved in Egypt, while in Qatar, a woman candidate ran for political office. The growing proportion of women university students in many Arab states heralds greater social participation.

Reforms have come about because of internal factors and forces (such as new governments and socio-demographic changes in the female population), but the global women's rights agenda fostered by the United Nations has helped to expand the political opportunity structure within which Arab women can make claims for enhanced citizenship rights.

Bibliography

A. An-Naim, *Islamic family law in a changing world*, London 2002.
S. Botman, *Engendering citizenship in Egypt*, New York 1999.

M. Charrad, *States and women's rights. The making of postcolonial Tunisia, Algeria, and Morocco*, Berkeley 2001.
S. Hale, The Islamic state and gendered citizenship in Sudan, in S. Joseph (ed.), *Gender and citizenship in the Middle East*, Syracuse, N.Y. 2000, 88–104.
R. Hammami and P. Johnson, Equality with a difference. Gender and citizenship in transitional Palestine, in *Social Forces* 6:3 (Fall 1999), 314–43.
S. Joseph (ed.), *Gender and citizenship in the Middle East*, Syracuse, N.Y. 2000.
V. Moghadam, *Women, work, and economic reform in the Middle East and North Africa*, Boulder, Colo. 1998.
——, Citizenship, civil society, and women in the Arab region, in *al-Raida* 19:97/98 (Spring/Summer 2002), 12–21.
——, *Modernizing women. Gender and social change in the Middle East*, Boulder, Colo. 1993, 2003²a.
——, Engendering citizenship, feminizing civil society. The case of the Middle East and North Africa, in *Women and Politics* 25:1/2 (2003b), 63–88.
C. Rubenberg, *Palestinian women. Patriarchy and resistance in the West Bank*, Boulder, Colo. 2001.
S. Saadeh, The political repercussions of President Hrawi's optional civil marriage (1998), paper presented at the 33rd annual meeting of the Middle East Studies Association, Washington, D.C. 19–22 November 1999.
L. Shehadeh, The legal status of married women in Lebanon, in *International Journal of Middle East Studies* 30:4 (1998), 501–19.
A. E. Sonbol, *Women of Jordan. Islam, labor, and the law*, Syracuse, N.Y. 2003.
L. Welchman, Jordan. Capacity, consent and under-age marriage in Muslim family law, in International Society on Family Law, *The international survey of family law. 2001 edition*, ed. A. Bainham, The Hague 2001, 243–63.

VALENTINE M. MOGHADAM

The Gulf and Yemen

Citizenship in the Arab Gulf States and Yemen is constructed on a kin-tribal basis. Within this patrilineal, patriarchal social structure, state rulers – the male heads of tribes – grant citizenship to members of society on the basis of family and tribal lineage. This differs from the universally dominant discourse of citizenship and contractual civil rights practiced in liberal democracies (Joseph 2000). Understanding this difference eases the mapping of a gendered citizenship in Gulf countries, where women are assumed to be under the guardianship of male members in society.

In the Gulf states, a *khulāṣa qā'id usra muwāṭin* (family citizenship record) or a "national certificate," officially used in some states, is the main record of citizenship. The term may differ slightly from one state to another, yet the meaning remains the same. Embedded in this construction is the inability of a national woman to extend citizenship rights to her husband and children if married to a non-national, a non-Gulf Cooperation Council national, or a non-Muslim. It is only in the exceptional case of an unknown, deceased, or absconding father that a national woman in the Gulf region can extend citizenship to her children, although she cannot have a separate family record. In the case where she does, she cannot register her children in this record. With the inability to sustain family lineage, the woman's family record will cease to exist upon her death.

The national certificate is the main document upon which nationality is issued. It defines the citizen's ranking and, in turn, the state benefits to which he or she is entitled. A woman follows her guardian's grade. Nationality is not granted on an equal basis; it varies from full nationality by descent to nationality by naturalization. When a non-national woman is granted citizenship as a result of marrying a full national, hers is considered full nationality, but is still treated as that of a dependent. The woman may lose it in case of early divorce (the period is defined differently among Gulf states) or second marriage to a non-national.

A non-national woman is not granted automatic citizenship through marriage. She must first apply for it, and then wait for a period that may vary from three years (United Arab Emirates) to five years (Saudi Arabia) to fifteen years (Kuwait). None of the Gulf States allow dual citizenship. Anyone (male and female) taking up citizenship in the Gulf region must forsake their previous citizenship and submit their old passport to the authorities in the respective Gulf state. The practice of specifying the status of women as the "daughter of" or "wife of" in all identification documents such as driving licenses, passports, and bank accounts, has been challenged and is expected to recede following complaints by women against it.

Despite the fact that all Gulf countries are signatories to the CEDAW (Convention on the Elimination of All Forms of Discrimination against Women) discrimination continues. Kin-based citizenship necessarily results in discrimination against women in the region. However, this should not obscure some of the positive elements enjoyed by women in the Gulf region. As oil states, with the exception of Yemen, Gulf countries built their legitimacy on a state welfare system that provides citizens with rights to free education, employment, housing, and health services, as well as other grants and state subsidies. Since women are by definition members of the family, they are considered beneficiaries of these rights as long as they do not conflict with their primary responsibilities to their families.

Women's progress in the field of education within a short period serves as a showcase. The United

Arab Emirates state federation, established in 1971, was able during the 1990s to make impressive inroads in women's education on a global scale (UNDP 1995). This led, in all oil-producing Gulf States, to uneven development and a situation where women are highly educated yet still denied political rights in the United Arab Emirates, Kuwait, and Saudi Arabia.

Until 1998, with the exception of Kuwait and Yemen, no Gulf state provided any of its citizens with electoral rights. Male members of legislative councils were appointed by the ruling families and acted only as consultative bodies. Bahrain has, since the turn of the millennium, led the Gulf states in terms of political rights, followed by Qatar and Oman. These states have modified their constitutions, and legislated equal gender rights. Women in these countries are making daily advancements in administrative and political offices. The United Arab Emirates grants more socioeconomic rights, but falls behind on the political, while Saudi Arabia continues to fall behind on all counts. A woman in Saudi Arabia may hold a Ph.D., or even be a global figure, yet she is still unable to drive or travel without prior male guardian approval and the escort of a *maḥram* male (kin whom she cannot marry).

Despite their uneasiness, living in such contradiction in comparison with each other across state regional borders and with women globally, women in the Gulf region believe in their relative bargaining power in the very structure of the family and tribe. In a system where rules are broken on the basis of personal contacts and direct relationships, exceptions to stated rules are sometimes available.

Bibliography

A. Abdulla (ed.), *Gulf strategic report 2002–2003*, Sharja 2003.

S. Adams, *The basic right of citizenship. A comparative study*, Center for Immigration Studies in Washington, D.C., September 1993, <http://www.cis.org/articles/1993/back793.html>.

S. Altorki, The concept and practice of citizenship in Saudi Arabia, in S. Joseph (ed.), *Gender and citizenship in the Middle East*, Syracuse, N.Y. 2000, 215–36.

S. Carapico and A. Wuerth, Passports and passage, in S. Joseph (ed.), *Gender and citizenship in the Middle East*, Syracuse, N.Y. 2000, 261–71.

Constitutions (Bahrain, Kuwait, Oman, Saudi Arabia, United Arab Emirates, United Arab Emirates, Yemen), <http://cofinder.richmond.edu>.

S. Joseph, Civic myths, citizenship and gender in Lebanon, in S. Joseph (ed.), *Gender and citizenship in the Middle East*, Syracuse, N.Y. 2000, 107–36.

Markaz dirasāt al-Khalīj, *al-Khalīj fī ʿām* 2003, Dubai 2004.

H. al-Mughni and M. A. Tetreault, Citizenship, gender, and the politics of quasi states, in S. Joseph (ed.), *Gender and citizenship in the Middle East*, Syracuse, N.Y. 2000, 237–60.

R. Sabban, al-Marʾa wa-al-qānūn fī al-Imārāt al-ʿArabiyya al-Muttaḥida. Ruʾya ijtimāʿiyya, in *al-Tashrīʿāt al-ijtimāʿiyya fī al-Imārāt*, Sharja 1997.

A. Sayad (ed.), *al-Marʾa al-Yamaniyya wa-taḥaddiyāt al-ʿaṣriyya*, Syria 1995.

United Nations, Division for the Advancement of Women, *Women 2000 and beyond. Women, nationality and citizenship*, June 2003, <http://www.un.org/womenwatch/daw/public/>.

UNDP (United Nations Development Programme), Human development report 1995, Gender and human development, <http://www.undp.org/hdro/hdrs/1995/english/95.htm>.

Rima Sabban

Southeast Asia

The Southeast Asian cultural matrix

Islam reached Southeast Asia many centuries later after it had reached China.[1] The exact time of its arrival in Southeast Asia is still debated, with dates ranging from 1100 to the 1300s (Reid 1993a, Ricklefs 1981). Despite its relatively late arrival, as compared with China, it was in Southeast Asia that Islamic sultanates emerged – for example, Pasai in north Sumatra (ca. 1297), Melaka on the west coast of Malaya (ca. 1400), Demak in west Java (ca. 1478), and many others (Milligan 2003, Federspiel 2002). Islam was thus a political force in the region long before modern nation-states emerged there.

Islam came into a region dominated by bilateral kinship patterns, in which both sexes have relative equality.[2] This indigenous egalitarianism was altered by the arrival of Hinduism and Buddhism, which inspired the formation of states ruled by god-kings who mediated between heaven and earth. The political hierarchy was believed to mirror a hierarchy of unequal souls – an idea legitimated by the concept of karma (Wolters 1982).

The Southeast Asian sultanates that subsequently emerged were transformations of these earlier "Indianized" kingdoms. Consequently, the Islamic rulers needed to reconcile the implicit egalitarianism of Islam with the Indic hierarchical conception of the god-king (Milner 1988). Islam thus came as an equalizing force which impacted on an earlier Indic hierarchy but resonated with an even earlier indigenous egalitarianism between the sexes.

The implicit egalitarianism of Islam is shared with other monotheisms in that all believers are supposedly equal before God. With this as a point of departure, Islam has been variously adapted and adopted, particularly in relation to the different schools of thought that came to the region, including schools that favor gender equality, as well as those that do not. Muslim women in Southeast Asia are thus part of an Islam that is plural and dynamic.

Southeast Asian adaptations of Islam and their gender implications

Conversion to Islam in Southeast Asia was gradual. While conversion tended to occur among certain ruling elites in port cities, peasants and tribals tended to retain earlier religious traditions. Even among converts, it was (and still is) common to find religious syncretism fusing Islam with other beliefs (Bentley and Ziegler 2003).

Islam came in the context of an Islamicate civilization brought by mystics and merchants. The former are associated with Sufi Islam and the latter with a more ritualistic, Sharīʿa-based Islam of the Sunnī Shāfiʿī school of jurisprudence (Lapidus 1991). Sufi Islam accommodated pre-Islamic practices, as well as indigenous ideas of gender equality. But even Sharīʿa-based Shāfiʿī Islam did not entrench patriarchy.

As a result, Muslim women in Southeast Asia have always enjoyed a relatively high status. Historically, among many Muslim populations in the region, women have owned property and dominated local markets as traders (Reid 1988, 146–64). Culturally, the Muslim Minangkabau people of West Sumatra continue to be matrilineal up to this day (Blackwood 1997, 1999, NationMaster.com 2004).

Religion was (and in Indonesia, still is) no hindrance to marriage between Muslim women and men of other religions. The fifteenth-century Arab navigator, Aḥmad Ibn Majīd, observed the following practices among Southeast Asian Muslims: "The infidel marries Muslim women while the Muslim takes a pagan to wife" (Ibn Majid 1462, 206, Pires 1515, 268, quoted in Reid 1988, 155).

Women's political leadership in Southeast Asia further indicates relative gender equality. The sultanates of Patani (in the Isthmus of Kra) in 1584 and Aceh (in north Sumatra) in 1641 came to be ruled by *sulṭāna*s (female rulers). Their reign lasted a century in Patani and 58 years in Aceh. During the reign of the third queen of Aceh, the *ʿulamāʾ* (theologians) mounted a campaign against her after obtaining a fatwa (legal pronouncement) from Mecca declaring women's rule illegitimate (Reid 1993b, 265–6).

Despite the controversy over female political leadership, the *sulṭāna*s' relatively long reign shows that women's right to rule was accepted to a significant degree. There are different interpretations in Islam about women's right to govern. Although tradition states that a ruler is an imam and that no man should pray behind a female as an imam, there is nevertheless a sect that declares that any capable woman who can fight the enemy can become an imam and lead the *umma* (congregation of believers).[3]

More recently, at the end of the nineteenth century, the Riau sultanate was also ruled by a self-described "Sultan Fatimah," who eventually bequeathed her throne to her son (Wee 1985). Women's right to rule continues to be a contested issue among Muslims three centuries later, as exemplified by Indonesia's President Megawati Sukarnoputri, who became the country's first female president in 2001, after initial Muslim opposition to her appointment (Mahmood 1 January 2004). Megawati is the daughter of Sukarno, the first president of Indonesia, and her case implies a persisting belief in an older right – that of a son or daughter to inherit the father's position.

The postcolonial modern nation-state

In Southeast Asia, the transition from premodern kingdoms to modern nation-states was mediated through European colonialization. Southeast Asian nation-states did not evolve through a metamorphosis of indigenous systems. Instead, the postcolonial Asian nation-state has been superimposed on at least four layers of earlier political history – that is, colonial states, Islamic sultanates (and their equivalents), Indianized kingdoms, and indigenous tribalism. None of these has completely supplanted previous layers.

The result is a dynamic plurality of different social realities, which may be complementary, competitive, or conflicting. For example, the nation-state and the *umma* may coexist in complementarity, or they may compete with each other for the allegiance of their citizens/members, or they may conflict with each other in what they demand of their citizens/members. Muslim women (and also men) thus have to negotiate their way through a complex situation of multiple interacting realities.

A historical example of the complementarity of nationalism and Islam is Sarekat Islam (Islamic Union), a reformist movement that arose in Java in 1911, regarded as Indonesia's first nationalist movement (McVey 1965). Sarekat Islam and other such movements promoted women's political participation as equal members of a modern Islamic nation (Petrus Blumberger 1931). Another such movement in Indonesia, Muhammadiyah, set up in 1914 a separate women's organization called Aisyiyah (after an influential wife of the Prophet) and built women's mosques (allegedly unique to the Indonesian archipelago), kindergartens, and women's Islamic schools, thereby encouraging women to be active agents of change (Overview of world religions). Women's political participation in modern nation-building thus began in the context of these Islamic reformist movements.

Sharīʿa, *adat*, and civil law

Many Muslims in Southeast Asia are subject to three bodies of law – Sharīʿa (Islamic law), *adat* (customary law), and secular civil law. Under British indirect rule, the sultans were allowed to administer only Sharīʿa and *adat*. This divided jurisdiction was formalized in the Treaty of Pangkor in 1874 (Wee 2003) and continues in contemporary Malaysia, where Sharīʿa and *adat* are still administered separately by the local governments of the nine sultanates (now called states). The result is "a lack of uniformity of laws among [the Malaysian] states" (ADB 2002, 62).

Sharīʿa and *adat* differ in that the former is administered formally through the Sharīʿa court, while *adat* is administered informally through social practice. In some cases, Sharīʿa takes precedence, while in other cases, *adat* prevails. For example, in the Malaysian states of Negeri Sembilan and Melaka, local Muslims follow matrilineal *adat* laws in matters of inheritance and divorce, even when these contradict Sharīʿa injunctions (Hooker 1984, Kamali 1998, 158–79).

Although Muslims in Southeast Asia are subject to three bodies of laws, they come under the jurisdiction of only two courts, Sharīʿa and civil courts. Dual jurisdiction for Muslim citizens applies not only to Malaysia with its surviving sultanates and the Brunei sultanate, but also to Singapore, Thailand, and the Philippines, where Muslims constitute minorities. The Sharīʿa court usually has jurisdiction only over cases related to marriage, divorce, betrothal, nullity of marriage, judicial separation, division of property on divorce, payment of bride-price, maintenance, compensation for a divorced wife, and inheritance (Chandrasegar 2000).

Dual jurisdiction has gendered consequences, because the status of women differs in civil law and in Islamic law. Muslim women subject to dual jurisdiction tend to be less than equal to Muslim men and to non-Muslim citizens. For example, in Malaysia and Singapore, a Muslim man is legally permitted to have up to four wives, whereas a Muslim woman can have only one husband. In contrast, non-Muslims in Malaysia and Singapore are guaranteed monogamous marriages by the civil law of the state, with polygamy deemed a crime (ADB 2002, 62).

The limitation of the Sharīʿa to family law in Malaysia and Singapore was inherited from colonial administrative practice, where criminal law and civil law, apart from family law, came under the purview of British common law (Jayasankaran 1999, *Economist* 1993, Ong 1999, Hor 2001). The Islamic state government of Kelantan in Malaysia enlarged the scope of the Sharīʿa on 25 November 1993, when it enacted the Syariah Criminal Code (II) Enactment 1993. This expanded scope covers *ḥudūd* and *qiṣāṣ* offences. *Ḥudūd* law deals with mandatory punishment for theft, robbery, illicit sex, alcohol consumption, and apostasy, with such punishment being mostly corporal in nature, while *qiṣāṣ* (law of retaliation) deals with bodily injury or loss of life, where the punishment is death or imprisonment, but with the proviso that financial compensation can be given if the victim's guardian forgives the offender.

However, the federal government of Malaysia has stated that criminal law comes under its jurisdiction. Not only has it refused to ratify these locally adopted *ḥudūd* and *qiṣāṣ* laws, the federal government has also warned that legal action will be taken should any state government implement local laws that contravene federal laws (Aljazeera.net 28 October 2003). As a result, despite the Syariah Criminal Code (II) Enactment 1993 in Kelantan, no Muslim criminal law has ever been implemented there (or elsewhere in Southeast Asia).

In countries with a single jurisdiction, such as China and Australia, civil law applies to Muslim and non-Muslim citizens alike. However, under both single and dual jurisdictions, Muslim women find themselves in a bind. If they seek to be full citizens, subject only to civic law, other Muslims may consider them as being un-Islamic in their behavior, even if the outcome of this is relative gender equality. On the contrary, if they seek to be subject to Islamic law, thereby demonstrating their Islamic identity, they may find their status reduced by certain gendered injunctions of the Sharīʿa. To transcend this bind, feminist Muslims promote a vision of Islam that upholds "equality, justice and freedom," to quote the Malaysian group called Sisters in Islam (SIS).

Women's "citizenship" in Kelantan – heartland of a proposed "Islamic state"

The Islamic Party (Parti Islam SeMalaysia or PAS) of Malaysia has formed the state government of Kelantan since 1990. PAS has long been known to have an agenda to establish an Islamic state in Malaysia (Beatrix 1994). PAS released its Islamic State Document on 12 November 2003 (PAS 2003), which has a section called "Policy on Women," declaring the following objectives:

1. To empower women in accordance to their nature and potentials [sic];
2. To present a comprehensive policy on Women Development [sic];
3. To encourage healthy competition of women alongside men within the limits of the Shari'ah;
4. To eliminate the exploitation of women in all aspects of life;
5. To prepare a new strategic plan for women in the new millennium;
6. To encourage cross-cultural women integration irregardless [sic] of race and religion (PAS 2003).

The Democratic Action Party, an opposition party, criticized this Islamic State Document, asking what constitutes the "limits of the Shari'ah" for women (Lim 2003). It is worth investigating what women's "citizenship" means in PAS-ruled Kelantan. In the 1990s, the PAS state government introduced certain Islamic policies, such as the following:

1. compulsory *ḥijāb* (Islamic dress code) for all Muslim women and all working women in the state, including non-Muslims: this entails covering the head with a headscarf;
2. banning of all forms of public entertainment, including traditional performing arts, as well as modern forms of entertainment, such as discos and fun fairs;
3. banning of liquor and gambling;
4. sex-segregated check-out lanes at supermarkets;
5. cinemas to keep the lights on during screenings.

Tourists and visitors (Philion 22 March 2000), and the queen (that is, the wife of the sultan of Kelantan) are exempted from the compulsory Islamic dress code. However, PAS leaders frequently criticize the wife of former Prime Minister Mahathir Mohamad and top women officials because they do not wear headscarves.

No woman with uncovered head is allowed to enter the office of the chief minister of the Kelantan state government. Yet a portrait of the non-veiled queen hangs in his office. In 1992, when Asma Beatrix interviewed the chief minister about hierarchy and equality in his vision of the Islamic state, he admitted that the royalty has "a very special place." This implies the persistence of an Indic hierarchy that exempts the queen as royal ruler from the compulsory Islamic dress code to which lower-ranking women are subjected (Beatrix 1999).

Apart from the compulsory covering of their heads, there has been no evident withdrawal of women from public space. The street markets of Kelantan continue to be dominated by women traders. While they too wear headscarves, they take care to choose bright colors and to match them with appropriate long dresses and make-up.

What is more significant is the political participation of Kelantan women in electoral politics. Like other women in Malaysia, Kelantan women enjoy universal suffrage. While PAS had no women candidates in the 1999 general elections, it fielded ten women candidates in the 2004 general elections, with two of them winning a parliamentary seat at the federal level and a state seat (Koshy 25 March 2004). Their wins are particularly notable, since PAS lost disastrously overall in the 2004 elections.[4]

Therefore, despite the imposition of Islamic policies and the proposal of an Islamic state, as long as all citizens are able to participate freely in political life and to vote for their representatives, women can continue to shape their political future through the ballot box. They can choose to seek in Islamic parties a sense of belonging that is akin to family ties and a position from which to resist secular dominance; they can affirm their citizenship in non-religious terms; or they can blend Islamic identity with citizenship, as feminist Muslims are trying to do.

Notes

1. The earliest country in the Asia-Pacific region to have contact with Islam was China during the Tang dynasty (618–907). 'Uthmān b. 'Affān, the third Caliph, is said to have sent a delegation to China in the year 650 – that is, 29 A.H. or 18 years after the death of the Prophet Muḥammad (peace be upon him). The head of the delegation was Sayyid Waqqās, a maternal uncle of the Prophet.

2. While matriliny is found in some Southeast Asian societies, there is an absence of patriliny except among certain migrant groups from India and China (Andaya 1994, 99–116).

3. This view is associated with a sect known in Muslim historiography as the Shabībiyya, adherents of the Khārijī Shabīb al-Najrānī (c. 100/718 also known as Shabīb b. Yazīd), who had fought, along with his mother and wife, against the reigning caliph at the beginning of the eighth century. Even in contemporary theocratic Iran, there are some clerics who promote the right of women to run for presidential elections, though such advocates are still marginal (Zan-e Ruz, no. 1440, 12/25/93, 14–17, cited in Keddie 2000, 422).

4. Seats held by PAS at the national level fell from 27 to just 7. It lost control of the Trengganu state legislature, winning only 2 of the 32 seats in the state assembly. It retained control over the Kelantan state legislature by a margin of only 4 seats over the opposition's 20 seats (Pereira 2004, *Bernama* 2004).

BIBLIOGRAPHY

ADB (Asian Development Bank), Sociolegal status of women in Indonesia, Malaysia, Philippines and Thailand, Manila 2002, <http://www.adb.org/Documents/Studies/Sociolegal_Status_Women/default.asp>.

Aljazeera.net, Mahathir rejects Islamic law, 28 October 2003, <http://www.drmahathirmohamad.com/news/007.htm>.

B. W. Andaya, The changing religious role of women in pre-modern South East Asia, in *South East Asia Research* 2:2 (September 1994), 99–116.

A. L. Beatrix, Behind the veil. Islam in Malaysia and Tunisia, in H. Buchholt and G. Stauth (eds.), *Investigating the South-South dimension of modernity and Islam*, Hamburg 1999, 41–55.

——, The Muslim state. Pursuing a mirage?, in N. Othman (ed.), *Shari'a law and the modern nation-state*, Kuala Lumpur 1994, 33–44.

J. H. Bentley and H. F. Ziegler, *Traditions and encounters. A global perspective on the past*, Boston 2003.

Bernama, Being too ambitious proved costly for PAS, Kuala Lumpur, 24 March 2004, 1.

E. Blackwood, Women, land, and labor. Negotiating clientage and kinship in a Minangkabau peasant community, in *Ethnology* 36:4 (Fall 1997), 277–91.

——, Big house and small houses. Doing matriliny in West Sumatra, in *Ethnos. Journal of Anthropology* 64:1 (March 1999), 32–57.

C. Chandrasegar, Singapore legal system, October 2000, <http://www.tpclaw.com.sg/ sls/sls.htm>.

Economist, Islam in Asia. For God and growth in Malaysia, 27 November 1993, 39.

H. M. Federspiel, Modernist Islam in Southeast Asia. A new examination, in *Muslim World* 92:3/4 (Fall 2002), 371–87.

M. B. Hooker, *Islamic law in South-East Asia*, Singapore 1984.

M. Hor, Singapore's innovations to due process, in *Criminal Law Forum* 12:1 (2001), 25–40.

S. Jayasankaran, Caught in the act, in *Far Eastern Economic Review* (28 October 1999), 60–2.

M. H. Kamali, Islamic law in Malaysia. Issues and developments, in E. Cotran and C. Mallat (eds.), *Yearbook of Islamic and Middle Eastern law*, iv, London 1998, 158–79.

N. R. Keddie, Women in Iran since 1979, in *Social Research* 67:2 (Summer 2000), 422.

S. Koshy, More women elected but will they speak up?, 25 March 2004, <http:// thestar.com.my/election2004/story.asp?file=/2004/3/25/e2004_news/7619560&sec=e2004_news>.

I. M. Lapidus, *A history of Islamic societies*, Cambridge 1991.

K. S. Lim, Five questions on the incompatibility of the PAS Islamic State blueprint with democracy, human rights, women rights and pluralism, 16 November 2003, <http://www.malaysia.net/dap/lks2748.htm>.

K. Mahmood, Megawati picks Islamic leader as running mate, 1 January 2004, <http://www.islamonline.net/English/News/2004–05/06/article05.shtml>.

R. T. McVey, *The rise of Indonesian communism*, Ithaca, N.Y. 1965.

J. A. Milligan, Teaching between the cross and the crescent moon. Islamic identity, postcoloniality, and public education in the Southern Philippines, in *Comparative Education Review* 47:4 (November 2003), 468–92.

A. C. Milner, Islam and the Muslim state, in M. B. Hooker (ed.), *Islam in South-East Asia*, Leiden 1983, 1988[2], 23–49.

NationMaster.com, Encyclopaedia. Minangkabau, 2004, <http://www.nationmaster.com/encyclopedia/Minangkabau>.

D. S. L. Ong, The Singapore family court. Family law in practice, in *International Journal of Law, Policy and the Family* 13:3 (December 1999), 328–49.

Overview of world religions, Muhammadiyah, <http://philtar.ucsm.ac.uk/ encyclopedia/indon/muham.html>.

PAS (Parti Islam SeMalaysia), The Islamic state document, 2003, <http:// www.wluml.org/english/news/pas-islamic-state-2003.pdf>.

B. Pereira, PAS dicing with bitter harvest, in *New Straits Times*, 9 April 2004, 10.

J. T. Petrus Blumberger, *De Nationalistische Beweging in Nederlandsch-Indië*, Haarlem 1931.

S. E. Philion, Malaysian state asks women to cover up (fwd), PEN-L mailing list archive, 22 March 2000, <http://archives.econ.utah.edu/archives/pen-/2000m03.4/msg00051.htm>.

A. Reid, *Southeast Asia in the age of commerce*, i, New Haven, Conn. 1988, 146–64.

——, Islamization and Christianization in Southeast Asia. The critical phase, 1550–1650, in A. Reid (ed.), *Southeast Asia in the early modern era. Trade, power, and belief*, Ithaca, N.Y. 1993a, 151–79.

——, *Southeast Asia in the age of commerce, 1450–1680*, New Haven, Conn. 1993b, 265–6.

M. C. Ricklefs, *A history of modern Indonesia, c. 1300 to the present*, Bloomington, Ind. 1981, 316.

SIS (Sisters in Islam, 2000–2004, <http://www.sistersinislam.org.my/home_mission.htm>.

V. Wee, Melayu. Hierarchies of being in Riau, Ph.D. thesis, Australian National University, Canberra 1985.

——, The quest for an Islamic state as a response to the secular state, in *Ex/Change* 7 (June 2003), 10–16.

O. W. Wolters, *History, culture and region in Southeast Asian perspectives*, Singapore 1982.

VIVIENNE WEE AND ASMA BEATRIX

Western Europe

As Westerners, and whether we like it or not, we are henceforth, as Nathan Glazer (1997) has stated, all multicultural, a point we must surely acknowledge. The multicultural nature of Europe's national communities is a recent phenomenon connected with the sedentarization of those waves of immigrants who settled in Europe following the Second World War, and who all shared the common characteristic of coming from non-European, mainly Islamic, cultures.

Postcolonial immigrants in Europe live on the fringes of their respective societies, victims of racism and discrimination. For those who oppose it, multiculturalism intends merely to excuse the fact that integration has failed, and, at the same time, the fact that the principle of equality has been defeated. Opponents of multiculturalism are keen to point out that "praise of difference" is at the heart of racist discourse (Malik 2001, 31). The debate is far from over between the following two viewpoints: a first position states that policies on multiculturalism function to sustain social inequality; a second holds that such policies promote change within the norms and values that are the very foundations of democracies by incorporating certain elements of the immigrants' cultures.

Both positions hold some truth. For a critical perspective of ethnic minorities and multiculturalism, we must note that the majority of policies that are put into action are based on a confusion between race and culture, a fact explained by their direct link with the settling of immigrants "of color." Those European countries such as the United Kingdom or the Netherlands that are often held up as examples of successful multicultural countries actually became multicultural through a reactive process. Such reactive multiculturalism is a response to the economic and social difficulties generated by the sedentarization of immigrants of color in traditionally assimilationist countries, even though such countries may not have been ethnically homogeneous. This has been the predominant situation in Europe since the Second World War, where immigrants could no longer be effortlessly assimilated given that the material potential for integration had been eroded. At the same time, the shock waves sent out by the Second World War and decolonization weakened the notion of a dominant culture. In this respect, it is revealing that in countries where regional differences have been preserved, such as is the case in the United Kingdom, Belgium, and the Netherlands, systems put into place to help new immigrants adapt are specific to each situation, borrowing very little from the historically-acquired wisdom on the incorporation of ethnic groups with cultural and linguistic differences. This happens to such a degree that the term "ethnic minority" is often made to be synonymous with "immigrant group." Britain, for example, never fully completed cultural integration, meaning that British culture is far from being homogeneous, despite the fact that political narratives still orchestrate a sense of Britishness. However, the settlement of immigrants in no way benefited from this history of diversity management. As early as 1958, with the riots of Nottingham and Notting Hill which involved immigrants, the illusion of a tolerant British society was quickly shattered. Unemployment was almost nonexistent at the time and consequently explanations put forward immediately evoked immigrants' skin color and the problems of racial conflict. The multicultural structures and systems introduced since 1968 have primarily been a response to a need to create conditions that will usher in interracial harmony.

There are, in general, many misunderstandings and false perceptions regarding the rights and privileges accorded to ethnic groups. A cursory glance at the situation in Europe reveals that, far from the often fantasized perceptions of privileges bestowed on specific communities or ethnic groups, the policies that are put into place are, for the most part, measures taken in order to prevent and fight against inequality and discrimination linked to race or ethnicity. Even in an officially assimilationist country like France, the use of such policies will be found. In addition to this element of the battle against inequalities, there is also in general what Audrey Kobayashi calls "red boot" multiculturalism (1993, 205–31), that is, the financing of various cultural events such as, for example, a festival of Berber music, a rap concert, or an exhibition of African art. What is known as multiculturalism, then, consists in a partial assimilation with the dominant public culture, and a preservation of individual cultures within the private sphere (which includes not just the family, but the neighborhood and the world of volunteer organizations). The arrival of Islam within European societies brings into question this dominant approach, and engenders a debate on what public culture actually "contains," explicitly laying down as a principle the coexistence of several cultures.

In all countries that promote them, multicultural systems and structures are far from being unanimously accepted. The common denominator of different critical accounts highlights the ineffectiveness of multiculturalism, which, far from reducing inequalities, tends, in certain cases, to exacerbate them by ethnicizing and racializing social and economic issues, and by making ethnic groups more dependent in view of their public financing. Criticism also focuses on the way that the culture that forms the foundations of public policies is conceived. From this point of view, it is in Sweden that the denunciation of "ethnic business" and the "ethnic Tower of Babel" resounds with the greatest clarity. Alund and Shierup do not baulk at the term "cultural racism" when describing the manner in which immigrants' cultures are trapped by essentialism and exoticism. In a move to respect cultural differences, the Other's culture all too often becomes an artifact disconnected from the living culture. It is perceived by most people as a homogeneous entity, fixed and imported, which the new immigrants can decide to preserve or replace. It is thus the dominant groups who define the Other's culture, as well as the place assigned to it within the public sphere. Islam very often becomes a disembodied object of knowledge in whose name public policies are put into place (such as the teaching of Arabic, or religious instruction) without immigrant populations having been consulted as to their real needs (Alund and Schierup 1991).

The most controversial aspects of acknowledging Muslim minorities are less connected with cultural differences (and respect for them), and are more strictly located within the domain of religion. The political problem does not reside in the conflict between the rights of the citizen and collective rights; rather it concerns the internal restrictions as related to common law that are laid claim to by a specific group. In other words, is one group, whatever this group may be, within its rights to ask the state to intervene in order to guarantee practices that might oppress the individual? It is within such circumstances that the status of Islam is often considered to be problematic, whether in relation to dress code, marriage, divorce, work, or social life. The cultural reality of Western female Muslims is, in fact, much more complex insofar as they are experiencing an Islamic law that has adapted to the secular and pluralistic context.

Implicit acknowledgment of civil Islamic law under Western law

It is an unprecedented situation that often receives no attention: Islamic legal norms are being reconstructed in the West as a function of the principles of dominant European law. Within the dominant scenario of the majority of Muslims who accept the legal and institutional framework of the country where they live, an adaptation of Islam to the national law is indeed in progress. Astonishingly, this adaptation is, in most cases, passive. In fact, this adjustment does not emanate from legal experts of Muslim theologians, but from European and American judges. The consequence is the slow and "invisible" construction of a new form of Islam, of an Islam that has been adjusted to Western law (Cesari 2004). The contours of this evolution are more or less clear depending on the country and the Islamic group concerned. In the case of England, Pearl and Menski (1998) call this hybrid legal system "Angrezi Shariʿa." "While English Law is clearly the official law, Muslim Law in Britain today has become part of the sphere of unofficial law. This analytical paradigm indicates that Muslims continue to feel bound by the framework of the *Shariʿa* and value it more than Western concepts . . . Thus, rather than adjusting to English law by abandoning certain facets of their *Shariʿa*, South Asian Muslims in Britain appear to have built the requirements of English Law into their own traditional legal structures" (Pearl and Menski 1998, 75). This emergent hybrid product is marked with the seal of Western individualist culture, that is, it is marked as being compatible with the principle of individual freedom. The recognition (even implicit) of such a principle is currently redefining Islamic regulations with regard to the status of the individual and the family, the two main areas where discord arises between the norms of Western law on individuals' rights and the legal norms of Muslim countries. It proves to be beneficial to the status of women and to their empowerment.

Islamic precepts regarding the family and the individual have been profoundly altered by life in the West. In matters of family law, most Muslim countries privilege a system of norms that accredits polygamy, gives priority to the husband throughout divorce proceedings, and does not recognize civil or inter-religious marriages. Usually, conflicts arise within international law on individuals' rights when the legal prescriptions of certain foreign countries contradict basic human rights in matters such as marriage or divorce.

It is within the domain of repudiation that arbitration or attempts at reconciliation between religious law and civil judgments are often necessary. Repudiation is everywhere prohibited by current Western laws. When a minority group is more organized, judges can take into account recommendations made by religious decision-makers. In England, a reconciliation body has been set up, the Shariah Council, in order to settle disputes that may occur over forms of religious and civil marriage. Concerning polyamy, when a husband refuses to consent to his wife's plea for divorce, the wife can resort to the Shariah Council, which then summons the two parties and tries to offer a form of arbitration. However, it seems that in the future legal conflicts centered on polygamy will continue to decline in number since this practice is practically no longer followed by those individuals socialized in the context of Western society. Certain female law experts are currently emerging, arguing that the Qurʾānic norms in matters of marriage are actually those of monogamy. Other conflictual aspects of Islamic family life concern the religion of children and child custody, notably in cases of inter-religious marriages. In Islam, the father transmits his name and his religion to his children. He is thus legally entitled to custody of the children in the event of divorce from a non-Muslim woman. In general, Western courts do not recognize such a principle except if it is in the best interest of the child.

A new set of Islamic norms is thus currently being

forged in the European and American courts of justice. As a general rule, negotiation is suitable in all aspects of family life. The recognition of individual freedom and the taking into account of each party's best interest leads to compromises that change not only the letter but also the spirit of the Islamic norms, stripping them of the meanings they have in Islamic societies. One example of this transformation, which sheds light on how a Muslim can be "acclimatized" to the norms of Western law, concerns the length of the commonly accepted period of viduity. The traditional law on the required amount of time that must elapse before remarriage cannot be followed to the letter in European societies. Inheritance rules offer another example of the way practices translated for the new context demonstrate flexibility. Once again, Islamic precepts (two parts for each son compared to one part per daughter) cannot always be strictly adhered to, especially within those legal systems influenced by Roman law (Roman law ensures that each descendant is equally respected under the law). It is in matters of repudiation that the changes are the most profound, but also the most difficult to identify. Even though repudiation can still officially take place in the eyes of the religious group, it may have been unofficially initiated by the wife herself. Moreover, repudiation is increasingly discussed by both partners. The fact that man and wife may respect traditional Islamic law cannot therefore predetermine a situation of oppression or inequality within the marriage. The decline of polygamy and negotiation in matters of repudiation are thus the two main elements of transformation within Muslim law within the context of democracy.

Individual freedoms undermined?

Finally, the risk often associated with the incorporation of Islam into Western society is that of a breech of individual freedoms, especially for women. The dilemma between individual freedom and the rights of minorities (which has solidified the opposition between liberals and communitarists) often serves as a reference framework for controversy. For the liberals, the highest of political values resides in individual freedom; they thus applaud the individual emancipation in all prescribed and inherited statutes. On the contrary, communitarists denounce the conception of the autonomous individual as mere fiction, and emphasize the importance of social determinisms and power relationships. Either the group is produced by individual practices, or the individual is produced by group practices: such are the alternatives that subtend the opposition between the two viewpoints. However, concrete observation of ethnic needs/demands, including those made in the name of Islam, reveal that most groups attempt on a daily basis to reconcile regard for individual freedom with the acknowledgment of specific cultures. The famous opposition between individual rights and collective rights thus appears more of a theoretical question than one based in social reality. What we are witnessing is more of an attempt at integration that also preserves religious, cultural, or ethnic differences. The debate on forced marriages in the British context illustrates the ethnic resistance to the recognition of individual freedom that is covered by Islamic arguments and denounced by some Muslims. The relevant question is thus how the protection of specific subcultures can favor individual emancipation instead of stifling it.

As we have seen, acknowledgment of Islam's specific characteristics within Western societies does not resemble, by far, a structured program for recognition of a Muslim minority endowed with special rights, but occurs in fragments within two main sectors: organization of worship and family life. The vast majority of Muslims have adapted to this situation as is shown, for example, by the lack of demand that Sharīʿa be applied. Moreover, these same Muslims are engaged in a vast process of theological and philosophical legitimization of their condition as a minority. This could be experienced as a limitation, but is, in fact, perceived as emancipatory. On the other hand, whole sections of Western societies consider inappropriate, even scandalous, certain positions or requests which could quite easily be met within the framework of existing common law. This is, for example, the case with the headscarf in the French secular context. The *ḥijāb* worn in public schools is seen as a sign of the oppression of the female while some Muslim women claim that any law that bans it violates their right to religious expression. This divergence between Muslims and non-Muslims is affecting the process of recognition of Islam in secular European societies.

Bibliography

A. Alund and K.-U. Schierup, *Paradoxes of multiculturalism. Essays on Swedish society*, Aldershot, Hants., England 1991.

J. Cesari, *When Islam and democracy meet. Muslims in Europe and the United States*, New York 2004.

N. Glazer, *We are all multicultural now*, Cambridge 1997.

M. Kenan, The perils of pluralism. A re-examination of

the terms of engagement between races and cultures, and a plea for equality, in *Diversity Factor* 9:3 (Spring 2001), 31–4.

A. Kobayashi, Multiculturalism. Representing a Canadian institution, in J. Duncan and D. Ley (eds.), *Place/culture/representation*, London 1993, 205–31.

D. Pearl and W. Menski, *Muslim family law*, London 1998, 74.

JOCELYNE CESARI

Civil Society

Overview

Recent research on Muslim women's lives outside the home and harem has called into question accepted truths about the nature of their seclusion. An important branch of this scholarship has focused on Muslim women as citizens in civil society. Scholars have engaged the prevailing liberal model of civil society, defined as an arena of public discourse and action separate from political, economic, and domestic spheres (Cohen and Arato 1992, Butenschon 2000, Norton 1995). The collective impact of this engagement constitutes a revisionist literature that rejects strict divisions of public and private as Eurocentric and that instead emphasizes the fluidity of power networks and the negotiated nature of boundaries between state, market, and family in many postcolonial and Islamic societies. Many of these scholars have found evidence of civil society where liberal thinkers have found only absence: in the medieval era, in the Ottoman Empire, and under military dictatorships today. They have also exposed the gendered process by which civil society has been historically constructed, challenging essentialist views of Islam as synonymous with patriarchy and antithetical to democracy. By focusing on the importance of intermediary groups in the creation of political discourses and structures, this literature challenges easy equivalences between Islam, women's oppression, and dictatorship.

Early and medieval Islamic societies

Scholars of Islam's earliest centuries have reexamined legal discourses that appear to have marginalized women in communal and political affairs. Mernissi (1991) has argued that the Prophet established at Medina the principle that all believers are equal before God through a revolutionary conflation of public and private spheres: he situated his wives' apartments adjacent to the first mosque and took them along to battlefields so that they might participate fully in communal affairs. Stowasser (1994) has similarly observed that seventh-century Medinan women took public oaths of allegiance and service to the community. However, she argues that the Prophet's later revelations explicitly defined a private family sphere for women and children that was off-limits to strangers, especially men. The intent was not, however, to cut women off from politics. Stowasser and other scholars use the term segregation rather than seclusion to emphasize women's separate but nonetheless important Qur'ānic role in what may be called the earliest Islamic civil society. Scholars generally agree, however, that this egalitarian ideal was corrupted after the Prophet's death, when Persian and Byzantine patriarchal values influenced Muslim legal scholars' readings of scripture. As Spellberg (1994) has shown, Sunnī and Shīʿī scholars used *ḥadīth* concerning the Prophet's favorite wife, ʿĀ'isha, to ban women from politics altogether. In ninth-century legal discourse, women's segregation became seclusion.

This portrait of legal isolation from political and communal affairs has been challenged, however, by late medievalists who have had greater access to historical sources that suggest how Muslim women actually lived. From the eleventh century, a new, Islamic civil society appears to have emerged outside Arabia. A new patrician class of scholar-merchant families reordered urban life around distinctively Islamic institutions that had varying degrees of autonomy from the state (Bulliet 1972, Lapidus 1988). In Arab lands, Goldberg (1993) has argued, scholar-merchant elites actively protected their autonomy from monarchy through their mobility and their control of legal interpretation. He and other scholars have challenged old views that there was no "public" life in medieval and early modern Islamic cities simply because they did not exhibit the formal and autonomous institutions or mental divisions between public and private that characterized the European world (Reynolds 2001). Recent research on the Ottoman eighteenth century, for example, suggests that the devolution of political power from Istanbul did not produce a chaos of private fiefdoms, but rather new, dense networks of fiscal, cultural, and political influence that bound public and private interests across the empire (Salzmann 1993).

Within the robust urbanism of merchants' bazaars, *waqf* foundations for families and charities, private *madrasa* colleges, and Sufi mystical brotherhoods, women were surprisingly active. In Mamluk Cairo, for instance, elite women routinely owned residential and other properties and expended family wealth to fund schools and charities, while poorer women worked outside the home in a variety of occupations as peddlars, bathhouse attendants, medical and spiritual advisors, and domestic servants. Women played similar roles in early modern Istanbul and Aleppo. In imperial capitals and provincial seats alike, they built mosques, libraries, and clinics for the poor, and they participated in political revolts and religious movements (Keddie and Baron 1991, Sonbol 1996, Marcus 1989, Hambly 1998). In West Africa, Muslim Hausa women remained active in public and retained authority in the local religious tradition of Bori through the eighteenth century (Callaway and Creevey 1994). And in eighteenth-century India, elite Muslim women used their seclusion as a political resource in resisting British interference in their regions (Barnett 1998). Elite women's activities should not be understood as simply extensions of state power. As Faroqhi (2000), Babayan (1998), and others have shown, art, architecture, and charity were activities embedded in urban social networks.

The precise nature of pre-nineteenth-century civil society – and the extent of women's participation in it – remains unclear. Current research on the Islamic past also lacks clarity on how the gendering of civil society changed over time and space. Certainly, the nature of the state regime was a major factor. A comparison of seventeenth-century Isfahan and Shahjahanabad, for example, shows that the poorer but more homogeneously Muslim Iranian capital permitted a greater role in architectural patronage for non-imperial women while the heterogeneous Mughal capital relaxed norms of seclusion and permitted a greater public role for royal women (Blake 1998). And scholars of the Ottoman Tulip Period in the early eighteenth century have demonstrated how the state deliberately altered gender boundaries as part of a broader cultural policy, and how it had to negotiate with other interests in order to do so (Zarinebaf-Shahr 1998). Indeed, class played an important role in gendering civil society. Ascendant military and scholarly families appear to have imposed class-based definitions of male and female space to mark their status as Petry (1991), Khouri (1996), and Zilfi (1996), among others, have shown.

Colonial-era reforms

From the late nineteenth century, civil societies in Islamic countries clearly underwent a substantial transformation. Shifting trade routes, new technologies of transportation and communication, European intervention, and state reforms combined to alter society and the nature of public life. By 1900, cityscapes had been transformed to include new forms of public spaces in governmental centers, parks and gardens, theaters, and even retail shops. Educational, cultural, political, and charitable associations mushroomed as elite classes mobilized around various programs of social and political reform. A vibrant press thrived in varying degrees of autonomy from the state. Meanwhile, workers began to form unions independent of their artisanal masters and often in defiance of state regulation.

Women's participation in the new civil societies took on new, more institutionalized forms that would coalesce into formal women's movements in the early twentieth century. By 1900, elite Egyptian women had founded journals, schools, and charity organizations that carved a newly public sphere of social and cultural reform, autonomous from the British-controlled state. Like women reformers in Tunisia, the Levant, Turkey, Iran, India, and Indonesia, they reconceived the household and housewife as part of – not apart from – the nation and society, and as principal sites of modernization and progress. Calls to educate mothers of citizens spread across the Islamic world, signaling this expansion of women's role in civil society. Women in Indonesia, for example, established groups in every major town to promote women's education and social reform (Lochar-Scholten 2000). In 1928 they held their first national congress, the same year that Lebanese and Syrian women federated their groups. Elites were not alone in promoting social change. Before the First World War, women peasant migrants returned to Mount Lebanon from the Americas to promote new gender roles in Lebanese family and society (Khater 2001).

Modernization did not necessarily mean liberation – or liberalism. In Islamic countries as in European ones, women's emergence into new urban public arenas was fraught with conflict. Men were rankled by the intrusion of women into spaces formerly reserved for them. Male writers expressed fear that educated women would no longer obey their husbands. These common gender anxieties took on forms distinctive from Europe when they reflected not only the discursive repertoire of Islam, but also the different trajectory of social and political development in countries built upon different social structures and shaped by European industrial capitalism and colonization. First, new forms of association may have reflected social changes common to those in Europe, but they also coexisted, and competed, with older social networks and Islamic institutions such as Sufi brotherhoods and charitable institutions. Second, modern civil societies formed in Western Europe as arenas for the emergent capitalist bourgeoisie, and were therefore distinct from the state. Outside Europe, modern civil societies were most often products of state reforms, and so were located not separately from the state but at the intersection of the political and social spheres. They also reflected the conditions of the economic periphery. Modernization in most Islamic countries did not come with the prosperity and liberty experienced in Europe: rather, it came as the tool of intrusive governments and foreign colonizers. These factors combined to make the new civil societies sites of tremendous tension that often focused on issues of gender. Indeed, women often became a principal site upon which political and social cleavages opened. This contentiously gendered origin of modern civil societies would have profound effects upon women's strategies of mobilization and their futures as citizens.

Scholars have studied the gendering of civil society in modern Islamic societies primarily from two perspectives, that of discourse and that of institutional structure. Ahmed (1992), Abu-Lughod (1998), and others locate the origins of Muslim women's marginalization as citizens in the binary gendered discourse in the colonial era. Typical was the notoriously anti-suffragist British ruler of Egypt, Lord Cromer, who pronounced Egypt doomed to backwardness as long as its women remained veiled. Elites replicated that public-private, modern-traditional dichotomy in books like Qāsim Amīn's *Taḥrīr al-mar'a* (The liberation of women, 1899), which argued that Egypt's path to modernity lay in the unveiling and education of its women. This modernist argument provoked a reactionary politics of authenticity by nationalists and Islamists who urged women to stay home and protect indigenous family values. This colonial binarism ultimately worked against women who fought for an equal voice in civil society, Ahmed argues, because it forced them to choose between their liberation and their patriotism, a choice eventually symbolized by their decision of whether or not to veil: "And therefore, ironically, it is Western discourse that in the first place determined the new meanings of the veil and gave rise to its emergence as a symbol of resistance" (Ahmed 1992, 164).

Even where Europeans did not directly rule, anxious discourses about Islam and gender identity in civil society exploded, as in the Constitutional Revolutions in Iran (1905–11) and the Ottoman Empire (1908–12). As Brummett (2000), Afary (1996), and others have shown in studies of the revolutionary press, gender became a touchstone of debates about democracy, Islam, and modernity. Erstwhile revolutionary allies, secular nationalists, and Islamic reformers soon split bitterly around the issues of women's education, suffrage, and even dress. After the First World War, Göle (1996) argues, Turkish Kemalists made the unveiling of women and the abolition of Islamic laws central to what became an authoritarian, Westernizing project. Kemalists' destruction of gender segregation was an all-out attack on the Islamic social order. Paidar (1995) argues that the Iranian Constitutional Revolution produced a dominant discourse of modernization under the Pahlavī dynasty (to 1979) that emphasized women's education and unveiling but left women firmly under religious law and male authority at home.

In the contentious discursive field that shaped public life, women sought to avoid the traps that would cast them as either anti-Islamic or anti-modern. It was a struggle simply to make their voices heard in public, as opponents employing a hardened Islamic discourse or patriarchal nationalism silenced women teachers and writers in early twentieth-century Iran, intimidated women writers and speakers and thus closed down women's journals in Syria and Lebanon, and harassed even the great Egyptian singer, Umm Kulthum (Milani 1992, Thompson 2000, Danielson 1999). Some women bridged secular-Islamic cleavages of public-private by mobilizing under the banner of religion. In India, Muslim women found space to mobilize within the broader Islamic revival; they advocated health reforms to assure the biological future of their community and wrote in Urdu-language journals (Ali 2000). In Algeria they used desert Sufi *ribāṭs* as bases of influence (Clancy-Smith 1991). In Egypt, women triangulated nationalist and Islamist discourses in various ways. The Muslim Sisters and other populist Islamic women's movements advocated women's reforms within an Islamic framework while biographies of famous Muslim women inspired women to public action (Booth 2001, Badran 1991). But there was a danger in pushing religious reform too far. For example, in Beirut in 1928, Nazira Zayn al-Din published a book, *Veiling and Unveiling*, that reinterpreted scripture to call for a return to the basic egalitarian principles of Islam and to remove the veils of medieval tradition that bound women. It unleashed a tide of condemnation from conservative clerics that effectively silenced her (Thompson 2000).

Locher-Scholten (2000) argues that Indonesian women adopted a particularly successful strategy under Dutch rule, in contrast to the paralyzing power of binary discourses in the Middle East. Local culture and economic practice kept the line between public and private far more fluid in

Indonesian society than in many other Islamic societies, and nationalists did not restrict women to a domestic sphere protected from the colonial state, as in the Middle East and India. This fluidity permitted wider women's mobilization and more political options. Rather than confront the fateful choice between patriotism or liberation, Indonesian women adopted Islamic modernist discourses opposed to colonial modernism. Unlike most Middle Eastern women, they obtained suffrage from their colonial government.

Other scholars have emphasized the power of state and social structure, in addition to discourse, in marginalizing women in civil society. Frierson (1996) argues that Muslim Ottoman women who founded charities, published journals, opened shops, and ventured into the new public arena were careful not to stray too far from official Islamic norms, for they recognized that Abdülhamid II's state had staked the Ottoman future upon a Islamized equivalent of European national identity and civil society (see also Deringil 1998). Even in Arab provinces like Beirut, the Ottoman state intervened vigorously to regulate morality, including gender relations, in new forms of public space (Hanssen 2001). During the First World War, however, states in both the Middle East and Europe encouraged women's mobilization. Women's organizations mushroomed to meet the needs of the wounded and poor, to build girls' schools, and publish consciousness-raising journals, laying the groundwork for the formal movements of the interwar period.

But while wartime policies may have promoted the growth of women's movements, postwar structures of colonial rule often reinforced male dominance. As Thompson (2000) has shown, Syrian and Lebanese women living under the French Mandate confronted colonial alliances that bound civil society to the patriarchal power of tribal chiefs, religious patriarchs, and large landowners. This predisposed opposition groups to overcome their class differences by also agreeing to exclude women from civil society. These political pacts reinforced religious laws that guaranteed men's power over wives and daughters, and continued to weaken the women's movement's ability to mobilize long after independence. In Egypt, not only Cromer's ideology, but also British support of the monarchy and landowning class subverted the constitutional government established in the 1920s, and so marginalized women and the poor in politics. The weakness of the British mandatory state in Palestine contributed to the absolute breakdown of civil society there; as a result, Fleischmann (2003) argues, feminist and class politics were submerged into the violent nationalist conflict between Arabs and Zionists.

The effect of colonial policy on Islamic societies of West Africa is debated. Callaway and Creevey (1994) argue, for example, that France's more interventionist rule in Senegal created greater space for women's mobilization than did British policy in Nigeria, where the state granted greater autonomy to Muslim religious leaders. Cooper (1998), on the other hand, argues that women's oppression was not merely the result of unfettered Islam: Both French and British policies toward separate Hausa populations in Niger and Nigeria undermined women's prestige as scholars and their access to farmland, which were the critical prerequisites to their growing seclusion in the twentieth century.

Other scholars dispute the primacy of state structure in determining women's participation in civil society. Charrad, in her study of North Africa (2001), proposes kinship structure as the more important factor. She argues that the strength of tribes in Algeria and Morocco forced the French to cooperate with them in policies that encouraged a paternalistic conservatism toward women's status. Only in Tunisia, because of its weaker tribal power and precolonial legacy of bureaucratic centralization, were the French able to enact legal reforms that would strengthen women's status in civil society. In her study of South Asia, Jalal (1991) privileges class interest over either state or kin structure. She argues that Muslim women in colonial India were not passive victims of male nationalists' heightened cultural protectiveness; rather, elite women were complicit in efforts to maintain seclusion as a marker of their class and religious status. They began attending formal schools primarily as a defense against the influence of Christian missionary schools, not as a step toward autonomy and participation in a liberal civil society.

The contemporary period

Colonial-era legacies of binary discourse, identity conflict, and political structure inform research on Muslim women in contemporary civil societies. In postcolonial Lebanon, Algeria, and Pakistan, for example, scholars have found that postcolonial anxiety over religious identity and communal boundaries has intensified pressure to exclude women from civil society. Joseph (2000), for example, argues that communal bargaining in Lebanon since independence has produced pacts between the state and religious leaders that have reinforced kinship ties and undercut women's individual rights. Similarly, in Algeria, Cheriet (1996) argues, the weak independent state adopted populist policies that gendered civil society by buying men's loyalty in exchange for preservation of patriarchal practices that limited women's authority and independence both in and out of the home. In Pakistan, Haeri (1999) argues that civil society emerged not alongside or outside older kin structures, but rather intertwined with them. This historical reality, she maintains, explains the new phenomenon of political rape, where groups dishonor their political foes through the violation of female relatives – a practice apparently rooted in Pakistani soldiers' rapes of Bengali women during the civil war in 1971. The effect of these rapes has been to intensify protectiveness and seclusion of women, and so their exclusion from civil affairs.

These and other scholars of the contemporary Islamic world have thus sought to explain the error of Frantz Fanon's prediction in *A Dying Colonialism* (1967) that decolonization struggles would equalize male and female citizens. Revolutionary regimes did improve women's access to public resources and office during the 1960s and 1970s (Hatem 2000, Joseph 1991, Molyneux 1991, Kandiyoti 1991). However, as under the authoritarian, interwar regimes in Turkey and Iran, women's benefits were often only partial and won at the price of lost autonomy from the state. Revolutions, moreover, did not generally void the colonial era's patriarchal pacts and dichotomous discourses. In Egypt and South Yemen, for example, socialist revolution produced a backlash centered upon the restoration of Islamic norms regarding women's status. Likewise, weak revolutionary regimes in the Palestinian entity and in Azerbaijan rolled back reforms in the 1990s as they caved to pressure from Islamic interests (Asfaruddin 1999). Meanwhile, liberal theorists had hoped that non-socialist polities might prove more egalitarian as a wave of liberalization and the reinvigoration of civil society were heralded in the late 1980s (Butenschon 2000, Norton 1995, Schwedler 1995). Brand's comparative study (1998), however, pessimistically concluded that emergent civil societies in the Arab world, as in Eastern Europe, have often become the domains of religious movements that explicitly exclude women's participation.

Three groups of scholars offer more optimistic visions, through non-liberal frameworks of inquiry. Some demonstrate that women have adopted ingenious strategies to overcome colonial binarism. Göle (1996) argues that women's reveiling in contemporary Turkey is an effort by Turks to take back their historical agency after its enslavement to European models of modernization. Ahmed (1992) similarly argues that Egyptian women's reveiling is not a withdrawal from the public sphere but rather an attempt to supersede colonial binarism. Despite Islamist pressure and state dictatorship, Egyptian women continue to mobilize in a diverse array of groups where religious and secular agendas often converge (Al-Ali 2000). Most striking, the vibrancy of debate and resilience of civil society in post-revolutionary Iran have defied earlier predictions of women's exclusion from public life, and instead fostered new forms of Islamic modernity that permit women's participation (Paidar 1995, Mir-Hosseini 1999). And in both Bangladesh and Pakistan, where Islamic politics have polarized civil society, women's groups have flourished, especially to protect women's legal rights and to provide them with jobs (Shaheed 1998). According to Shehabuddin (1999), rural Muslim women in Bangladesh do not feel compelled to follow Islamist parties whose agendas conflict with women's practical needs.

A second group of scholars has confronted the inadequacy of liberal frameworks by experimenting with feminist and communitarian models of citizenship (Joseph 1993 and 2000, Yuval-Davis and Werbner 1999, Benhabib 1998). They identify processes that sustain gender inequality in civil society, as well as strengths women have as citizens embedded in subnational communities. A third group has turned its focus away from the formal women's organizations that have emerged over the past century to study the endurance of women's informal networks. Hale, for example, argues that Sudanese women's organizations established as wings of male parties (Islamic and socialist) were not only accessories to men's domination but also obstacles to the more promising power of women's informal networks. Women's networks defy public-private dichotomies by mobilizing connections within families, workplaces, and neighborhoods not only to amass significant economic and cultural resources, but also to assert political influence at a grassroots level (White 2002, Singerman 1995, Hale 1996). However, the populism of "vernacular politics" in Turkey, White argues, masks the economic foundations of women's political weakness. Her concerns echo those of MacLeod (1992) and Ahmed (1992), who worry that women's use of Islamic symbols may ultimately play into the hands of the authoritarian Islamic elite. The debates about the relationship of Islam to women's status as citizens in civil society have only begun in this fruitful, emergent field of inquiry.

Bibliography

L. Abu-Lughod, *Remaking women. Feminism and modernity in the Middle East*, Princeton, N.J. 1998.

J. Afary, *The Iranian constitutional revolution, 1906–1911. Grassroots democracy, social democracy and the origins of feminism*, New York 1996.
A. Afsaruddin (ed.), *Hermeneutics and honor. Negotiating female "public" space in Islamic/ate societies*, Cambridge, Mass. 1999.
L. Ahmed, *Women and gender in Islam. Historical roots of a modern debate*, New Haven, Conn. 1992.
N. Al-Ali, *Secularism, gender and the state in the Middle East. The Egyptian women's movement*, New York 2000.
A. Ali, *The emergence of feminism among Indian Muslim women, 1920–1947*, Karachi 2000.
Q. Amin, *The liberation of women. A document in the history of Egyptian feminism*, trans. S. S. Peterson, Cairo 1992.
K. Babayan, The "ʿaqāid al-nisāʾa." A glimpse at Safavid women in local Isfahani culture, in G. Hambly (ed.), *Women in the medieval Islamic world*, New York 1998, 349–82.
M. Badran, Competing agenda. Feminists, Islam and the state in nineteenth and twentieth-century Egypt, in D. Kandiyoti (ed.), *Women, Islam, and the state*, Philadelphia 1991, 201–36.
R. Barnett, Embattled begums. Women as power brokers in early modern India, in G. Hambly (ed.), *Women in the medieval Islamic world*, New York 1998, 521–36.
B. Baron, *The women's awakening in Egypt. Culture, society, and the press*, New Haven, Conn. 1994.
S. Benhabib, Models of public space. Hannah Arendt, the liberal tradition, and Jurgen Habermas, in J. B. Landes (ed.), *Feminism, the public and the private*, New York 1998, 65–99.
S. Blake, Contributors to the urban landscape. Women builders in Safavid Isfahan and Mughal Shajahanabad, in G. Hambly (ed.), *Women in the medieval Islamic world*, New York 1998, 407–28.
H. Bodman and N. Tohidi (eds.), *Women in Muslim societies. Diversity within unity*, Boulder, Colo. 1998.
M. Booth, *May her likes be multiplied. Biography and gender politics in Egypt*, Berkeley 2001.
L. Brand, *Women, the state, and political liberalization. Middle Eastern and North African experiences*, New York 1998.
P. Brummett, *Image and imperialism in the Ottoman revolutionary press, 1908–1911*, Albany, N.Y. 2000.
R. W. Bulliet, *The patricians of Nishapur. A study in medieval Islamic social history*, Cambridge, Mass. 1972.
N. A. Butenschon et al. (eds.), *Citizenship and the state in the Middle East*, Syracuse, N.Y. 2000.
B. Callaway and L. Creevey, *The heritage of Islam. Women, religion and politics in West Africa*, Boulder, Colo. 1994.
M. Charrad, *States and women's rights. The making of postcolonial Tunisia, Algeria, and Morocco*, Berkeley 2001.
B. Cheriet, Gender, civil society and citizenship in Algeria, in *Middle East Report* 26:1 (January–March 1996), 22–6.
J. Clancy-Smith, The house of Zainab. Female authority and saintly succession, in N. Keddie and B. Baron (eds.), *Women in Middle Eastern history. Shifting boundaries in sex and gender*, New Haven, Conn. 1991, 254–74.
J. L. Cohen and A. Arato, *Civil society and political theory*, Cambridge, Mass. 1992.
B. M. Cooper, Gender and religion in Hausaland. Variations in Islamic practice in Niger and Nigeria, in H. Bodman and N. Tohidi (eds.), *Women in Muslim societies. Diversity within unity*, Boulder, Colo. 1998, 21–38.
V. Danielson, Moving toward public space. Women and musical performance in twentieth-century Egypt, in A. Afsaruddin (ed.), *Hermeneutics and honor. Negotiating female "public" space in Islamic/ate societies*, New Haven, Conn. 1999, 116–39.
S. Deringil, *The well-protected domains. Ideology and the legitimation of power in the Ottoman Empire, 1876–1909*, New York 1998.
F. Fanon, *A dying colonialism*, trans. H. Chevalier, New York 1967.
S. Faroqhi, *Subjects of the sultan. Culture and daily life in the Ottoman Empire*, New York 2000.
E. Fleischmann, *The nation and its "new" women. The Palestinian women's movement 1920–1948*, Berkeley 2003.
E. Frierson, Unimagined communities. State, press, and gender in the Hamidian era, Ph.D. diss., Princeton University 1996.
E. Goldberg, Private good, public wrongs, and civil society in some medieval theory and practice, in E. Goldberg, R. Kasaba, and J. Migdal (eds.), *Rules and rights in the Middle East. Democracy, law and society*, Seattle 1993, 248–71.
N. Göle, *The forbidden modern. Civilization and veiling*, Ann Arbor 1996.
S. Haeri, Women's body, nation's honor. Rape in Pakistan, in A. Afsaruddin (ed.), *Hermeneutics and honor. Negotiating female "public" space in Islamic/ate societies*, New Haven, Conn. 1999, 55–69.
S. Hale, *Gender politics in Sudan. Islamism, socialism, and the state*, Boulder, Colo. 1996.
G. R. G. Hambly (ed.), *Women in the medieval Islamic world*, New York 1998.
J. Hanssen, Public morality and marginality in *fin-de-siècle* Beirut, in E. Rogan (ed.), *Outside in. On the margins of the modern Middle East*, New York 2001, 183–211.
M. Hatem, The pitfalls of nationalist discourses on citizenship in Egypt, in S. Joseph (ed.), *Gender and citizenship in the Middle East*, Syracuse, N.Y. 2000, 33–57.
A. Jalal, The convenience of subservience. Women and the State of Pakistan, in D. Kandiyoti (ed.), *Women, Islam and the state*, Philadelphia 1991, 77–114.
S. Joseph, Elite strategies for state building. Women, family, religion and the state in Iraq and Lebanon, in D. Kandiyoti (ed.), *Women, Islam and the state*, Philadelphia, 1991, 176–200.
——, Gender and civil society, in *Middle East Report* 23:4 (July–August 1993), 22–26.
—— (ed.), *Citizenship and gender in the Middle East*, Syracuse, N.Y. 2000.
D. Kandiyoti (ed.), *Women, Islam and the state*, Philadelphia 1991.
N. Keddie and B. Baron (eds.), *Women in Middle Eastern history. Shifting boundaries in sex and gender*, New Haven, Conn. 1991.
A. Khater, *Inventing home. Emigration, gender, and the middle class in Lebanon, 1870–1920*, Berkeley 2001.
D. R. Khouri, Drawing boundaries and defining spaces. Women and space in Ottoman Iraq, in A. E. Sonbol (ed.), *Women, the family, and divorce laws in Islamic history*, Syracuse, N.Y. 1996, 173–90.
M. Lapidus, *A history of Islamic societies*, New York 1988, 2002 (rev. ed.).
E. Locher-Scholten, *Women and the colonial state. Essays on gender and modernity in the Netherlands Indies 1900–1942*, Amsterdam 2000.

A. E. MacLeod, *Accommodating protest. Working women, the new veiling, and change in Cairo*, Cairo 1992.
A. Marcus, *The Middle East on the eve of modernity. Aleppo in the eighteenth century*, New York 1989.
F. Mernissi, *The veil and the male elite. A feminist interpretation of women's rights in Islam*, trans. M. J. Lakeland, Reading, Mass. 1991.
F. Milani, *Veils and words. The emerging voices of Iranian women writers*, Syracuse, N.Y. 1992.
Z. Mir-Hosseini, *Islam and gender. The religious debate in contemporary Iran*, Princeton, N.J. 1999.
M. Molyneux, The law, the state and socialist policies with regard to women. The case of the People's Democratic Republic of Yemen 1967–1990, in D. Kandiyoti (ed.), *Women, Islam and the state*, Philadelphia, 1991, 237–71.
A. R. Norton (ed.), *Civil society in the Middle East*, 2 vols., Leiden 1995.
P. Paidar, *Women and the political process in twentieth-century Iran*, New York 1995.
C. Petry, Women as custodians of property in medieval Egypt, in N. Keddie and B. Baron (eds.), *Women in Middle Eastern history. Shifting boundaries in sex and gender*, New Haven, Conn. 1991, 122–42
D. Reynolds (ed.), *Interpreting the self. Autobiography in the Arabic literary tradition*, Berkeley 2001.
A. Salzmann, An ancien regime revisited. Privatization and political economy in the eighteenth-century Ottoman Empire, in *Politics and Society* 21:4 (December 1993), 393–423.
——, *Tocqueville in the Ottoman Empire*, Leiden 2003.
J. Schwedler (ed.), *Toward civil society in the Middle East? A primer*, Boulder, Colo. 1995.
F. Shaheed et al., *Women in politics. Participation and representation in Pakistan (with update 1993–1997)*, Lahore 1998.
E. Shehabuddin, Beware the bed of fire, Gender, democracy and the Jama'at-i Islami in Bangladesh, in *Journal of Women's History* 10:4 (Winter 1999), 148–71.
D. Singerman, *Avenues of participation. Family, politics, and networks in urban quarters of Cairo*, Princeton, N.J. 1995.
A. E.. Sonbol (ed.), *Women, the family, and divorce laws in Islamic history*, Syracuse, N.Y. 1996.
D. A. Spellberg, *Politics, gender and the Islamic past. The legacy of ʿA'isha bint Abi Bakr*, New York 1994.
B. F. Stowasser, *Women in the Qur'an. Traditions and interpretation*, Oxford 1994.
E.F. Thompson, *Colonial citizens. Republican rights, paternal privilege, and gender in French Syria and Lebanon*, New York 2000.
J. B. White, *Islamist mobilization in Turkey. A study in vernacular politics*, Seattle 2002.
N. Yuval-Davis and P. Werbner (eds.), *Women, citizenship and difference*, New York 1999.
F. Zarinebaf-Shahr, Women and the public eye in eighteenth-century Istanbul, in G. Hambly (ed.), *Women in the medieval Islamic world*, New York 1998, 301–24.
M. C. Zilfi, Women and society in the Tulip Era 1718–1730, in A. E. Sonbol (ed.), *Women, the family, and divorce laws in Islamic history*, Syracuse, N.Y. 1996, 290–306.

Elizabeth F. Thompson

Afghanistan

The Afghan women's movement in the twentieth century had a major impact on gender issues. In 1964 Afghan women participated in the drafting of the constitution and won the right to vote. In the 1960s and 1970s they had a strong presence in many institutions: education, health, engineering, the civil service, and parliament. However, the struggle between the Soviet Union and the United States to control the flow of regional oil and natural resources and their support for their chosen warlords, combined with the growth of extremist Islam and tribalism, led to war and violent conflicts and eroded any chance of achievements of women in urban centers being extended to rural or poor women (Rashid 2000, 41–54, Mehta and Mamoor 2002).

Continuous war and violent conflict from the late 1970s led to the collapse of state and other institutions. Civil society was devastated and social capital was eroded. Individuals and communities were unable to achieve their objectives as the war culture replaced all rules, norms, obligations, trust, and reciprocity in social relations and social structures. Millions were disabled or injured, or died. Millions became refugees; the majority of them lived in Iran and Pakistan, many of them with female heads of household (Shah 2000, Shakib 2002).

Despite long years of war and violent conflict women proved their strength by pulling themselves from the depths of seclusion and oppression in order to reach a free space of agency. They played a pivotal role in constructing the future civil society organizations through grassroots solidarity movements both at home and in exile. Under the Taliban, many women risked their lives by turning their homes into an underground network of schools for girls and young women. After the fall of the Taliban, they realized the importance of their underground organizations and activities. In 2001, women activists in the Literacy Corps identified 2,000 girls and female students in Kabul alone who were awarded certificates for the skills they had acquired under the Taliban years in women's secret schools (Rostami Povey 2003).

The Revolutionary Association of the Women of Afghanistan (RAWA) played a particularly crucial role by creating cohesion and solidarity in their community. RAWA was established in 1977 to struggle for democracy, women's rights, and human rights and published *Payām-e Zan* (Woman's message), a quarterly political magazine. Meena Keshwar Kamal, the founding member of RAWA, was assassinated in 1987. However, RAWA's activities continued in Afghanistan, Pakistan, and in the West (Brodsky 2003, 80–1).

Many professional women remained in Afghanistan or returned there to form networks and solidarity groups with poorer women. These networks and groups became mechanisms for women's empowerment. Amongst these women are: Suraya Parlika, a leading member of the National Union of Women of Afghanistan; Seddighe Balkhi, the head of the Islamic Center for Political and Cultural Activities of Afghan Women; Shafigha Habibi, a leading member of the Women's Association of Afghanistan; and Shafiqa Moaber, the director of the Women's Vocational Training Center.

Their secret organizations laid the foundation for the building of social capital, which was crucial for the process of reconstruction. Following the fall of the Taliban, they actively participated in rebuilding their organizations, regrouping their members and creating opportunities for women's participation in the process of transition from war to peace. Women journalists also became active. In Kabul they set up the *Cultural Journal of Afghanistan Women* (Rostami Povey 2003). In 2002–3 other women's daily, weekly, and monthly magazines appeared. In Kabul, Shukkria Barekzai Dawi published *Aeeneh Zan* (Women's mirror); Lilema Ahmadi published *Rooz* (Day); Mary Nabard published *Seerat* (Nature); Hawa Norastani published *Ershad-al Neswan* (Women's guidance); Jamila Mojahed published *Malali*; Fouzia Morady published *Zan va Ghanon* (Women and law); and in Jalalabad Arian Yon published *Nahid* (Globe).

Education was at the heart of women's struggle. In 1996 when Kabul was conquered by the Taliban, Kabul University female professors went to Bamiyan and set up a university until Bamiyan fell into the hands of the Taliban forces in 1998 (Rashid 2000, 68–9).

Women lawyers also continued their activities under extreme forms of oppression. Suraya Paikan established the Afghan Women Lawyers and Professional Association in 1998 in Mazari-i-Sharif. The organization had 400 active members. They were forced to leave Afghanistan by the Taliban but they continued their work in Peshawar and in 2001 they returned to Kabul. In 2003, despite resistance to women's legal and constitutional rights with the re-emergence of extremist Islamists, 200 women lawyers worked in Kabul as judges, prosecutors, and teachers.

After the fall of the Taliban, Afghan women emerged as a force not to be ignored. In 2000, 200 women participated in the 1,550-member Loya Jirga, the traditional grand assembly. Mahbobeh Hoghoghmal, a lawyer, was one of the 21 people chosen by the United Nations out of 1,000 names to decide how the Loya Jirga should convene and how the transitional government should be formed.

In 2001, three women delegates (Sima Wali, Sima Samar, and Suhaila Seddiqi) participated in the UN-sponsored Bonn negotiations to form an Afghan interim government. They demanded the creation of a ministry of women's affairs and the appointment of Sima Samar as deputy prime minister and Suhaila Seddiqi as the minister for public health. However, in 2002, Sharīʿa Islamic law, under the guise of the al-Amr bi-al-maʿrūf wa-al-nahy ʿan al-munkar (Ministry for the enforcement of virtue and suppression of vice), which had terrorized the people under the Taliban, was reinstated (Mehta and Mamoor 2002, 21, Brodsky 2003, 270–2). Sima Samar was forced out of her job for objecting to the continued role of warlords in the government confirmed by the Loya Jirga (Steele 2002, Viner 2002). Nevertheless, Afghan women continued their struggle for the establishment of civil society to contend with the patriarchal movements and institutions. Habiba Soraby replaced Sima Samar and published the magazine *Mermon* (Women) in Pashto; Sima Samar became the Director of the Human Rights Commission, and Mahbobeh Hoghoghmal became the adviser to Habiba Soraby.

Outside Afghanistan, Afghan women intensified their activities. In 2001, Women for Afghan Women (WAW) held their conference in New York under the leadership of Sima Wali, Sara Amiryar, Fahima Vorgetts, and Rita Amiri to promote women's rights issues (Mehta 2002).

In 2003, Liza Ghobar was appointed a member of the Loya Jirga to work with Afghan women refugees and the diaspora community in Iran, in order to identify the needs of Afghan women to be included in the new Afghan constitution.

Bibliography

A. E. Brodsky, *With all our strength. The Revolutionary Association of the Women of Afghanistan*, New York 2003.

S. Mehta and H. Mamoor, Building community across difference, in S. Mehta (ed.), *Women for Afghan women. Shattering myths and claiming the future*, New York 2002, 15–26.

A. Rashid, *Taliban. Islam, oil and the new great game in Central Asia*, London 2000.

E. Rostami Povey, Women in Afghanistan. Passive victims of the borga or active social participants? in *Development in Practice* 13:2–3 (May 2003), 266–77.

S. Shah, *Where do I belong?*, London 2000.

S. Shakib, *Afghanistan. Where God only came to weep*, London 2002.

J. Steele, Women lead protests as Afghan warlords muscle in on power, in *Guardian* (London), 13 June 2002.

K. Viner, Feminism as imperialism, in *Guardian* (London), 21 September 2002.

Elaheh Rostami Povey

The Balkans

This analysis of civil society with the focus on women and gender issues relates to the situation in the successor states of former Yugoslavia, with particular emphasis on Bosnia-Herzegovina. In addition to the factors common to all the states, the communist heritage, the process of transition, the experience of armed conflict, postwar state-building, and the reconstitution of society, Bosnia-Herzegovina is distinguished by the role and influence of the international community and the high proportion of members of the Islamic community in the region.

In the second half of the twentieth society, the Communist Party (later to be known as the Communist League) controlled every feature of society, from the economy to creativity. Party ideology thus became the framework within which everything worked: labor unions, the media, the academic community, youth organizations, religious communities, professional associations – every element of civil society. Civil society was subject to ideological stigma. For example, the *Encyclopaedia* published by the Zagreb Lexicographic Institute (1976) contained no entries for civil society, civism, or the bourgeoisie, and the *Sociological Lexicon* (Belgrade 1982) dedicated a mere six half-lines to these entries – the same column-centimeters as those for the entries on gangsterism, pilgrimage, and rogues/rascals (Pokrovac 1991). When feminist critique first made its appearance in the late 1970s, it came up against ideological condemnation from the party elite. Women's activism was endorsed within existing organizations.

The transition to civil society in the successor states of former Yugoslavia is hampered by subservience to the political culture and the weaknesses of civil initiatives. To this must be added the non-democratic way the state institutions worked, poor control mechanisms in regard to the authorities, ethnocentrism, and manifestations of political and religious exclusivity, all of them among the products of the violent dissolution of the Yugoslav union of states.

The break-up of Yugoslavia was accompanied by wars in Slovenia, Croatia, and Bosnia-Herzegovina, and by conflicts in Kosovo and Macedonia. The last decade has thus been marked by post-conflict transition and attempts to strengthen civil society as an alternative model to the authoritarian socialist heritage. The process includes efforts to establish the rule of law and democratic, responsible governance with the enactment of laws creating an environment designed to enhance the autonomy of society in relation to the state. Attempts are being made to increase the autonomy of corporations, labor unions, universities, the media, and civic associations. The role of civil society is to be a socially integrative factor and advocate of democracy. The process of reconciliation should take place within civil society (non-governmental organizations' activities associated with the truth and reconciliation process, working within local communities to restore inter-ethnic relations and reconciliation) to institute a culture of peace and tolerance (NGOs concerned with peace education and those engaged in inter-religious dialogue); to promote a culture of democracy (alternative movements, youth associations, training for the youth groups of various political parties, education in civism); to develop environmental awareness (work on the protection of the environment); and to promote a culture of values (associations engaged in the protection of the cultural heritage, intercultural exchanges).

The first women's organizations were civic peace groups, humanitarian organizations concerned with psychosocial support for women who had been raped and abused, refugees, displaced persons, and war widows, and women's rights advocacy groups. Following the first free pre-war elections, women effectively vanished from the official scene, from political electoral bodies and the executive authorities in all the successor states of former Yugoslavia. Faced with political marginalization, subject to violence, importuning for the rights they had gained under socialism (economic, social, and cultural as well as reproductive rights), women became the leading actors in civil society and NGOs. The constant work of women's NGOs can be monitored. Organizations that began work during the war with rape victims and abused women continued working on ways to protect women from violence in the family, combating trafficking in women, and providing protection for abused women. Organizations that advocated women's rights in political and public life are still active in this field, promoting women in politics and political education, conducting campaigns for women politicians and NGOs to work together. Organizations that began by providing psychosocial aid are now focusing on women's health, reproductive rights, aid for disabled women and for elderly, helpless women. Women's groups promoting women's rights are still active in this field, with education and training programs, organizing women's studies and advocating the right to sexual orientation and human rights in general.

The pluralism of women's interests and the way they organize can also be observed in religious matters. Faith-based women's organizations have emerged, concerned with education and promoting religious values and lifestyle. In Bosnia-Herzegovina, Muslim women's organizations have been set up, concerned with education, humanitarian aid, the promotion of Islamic values and the Islamic way of life, and defending the right to dress in an Islamic way. The present women's NGO scene reflects the country's religious, political, and cultural pluralism.

The international community has an important part to play in the activities and development, but also in the frailties of civil society, with its aid programs and focus on specific issues. Given that civil society is still undeveloped, has not achieved financial independence, has failed to introduce internal organizational structures, and lacks experience in the field, it is subject to the influence of international donors. Analyses indicate that local organizations are subordinate to international organizations and donors. The activities of local NGOs derive from foreign projects, missions in the region, and the goals they aim to achieve. The absence of coordination between donors, and the imbalance between the needs of beneficiaries and donors, make it harder to achieve genuine results in the operations of civil society. It seems as though the entire process of developing civil society, including the work of women's organizations, is taking place top-down and from outside the country. Top-down development means that project leadership is in the hands of people who are not from this region, and development outside the country means that the needs, aims, and resources required to carry them out are determined in different circles. Paradoxically, civil society has been accorded a responsible role but the opportunities available for it to develop are limited.

Bibliography

Primary Sources

G. O. Csepeli, A. Scheppele, and K. Lane, Acquired Immune Deficiency Syndrome in social science in Eastern Europe. The colonisation of East European science, in Social Research, 22 June 1996, <http://www.c3.hu/scripta/scriptao/replika/honlap/english/01/12ecsep.htm>.

International Crisis Group, Denied justice. Individuals lost in a legal maze, Balkans Report 85, 23 February 2000, <http://www.crisisweb.org/home/ index.cfm?id=1525&l=1>.

D. D. Lakičević, *"Archipelago Balkan." Political authoritarian regimes and xenophobia in new Balkan states* [in Serbian], Belgrade 2002.

M. Ottaway and T. Carothers (eds.), *Funding virtue. Civil society aid and democracy promotion*, Washington, D.C. 2000.

Z. Pokrovac, The difference between civil society-state and new government [in Croatian], Zagreb 1991.

S. Sali Terzić, International support policies to SEE countries. Lessons (not) learned in Bosnia-Herzegovina, in S. Terzić, *Civil society* [in Bosnian], Sarajevo 2001, 136–54.

F. Sero and M. Mrđa, *Study of local non-governmental organisations in Bosnia-Herzegovina. Problems, analyses and recommendations* [in Bosnian], Sarajevo 1998.

——, Overview of the current situation and the level of development of the non-government sector in Bosnia-Herzegovina in civil society and local democracy [in Bosnian], Center for Promotion of Civil Society, Sarajevo 2001, <www.cpcd.net/-72k>.

Secondary Sources

Activities of Belgrade non-governmental organizations. Civil society and political culture the Balkan way. Recommendations for the road to Europe, in *Diary* (Novi Sad) [in Serbian], 5 February 2004.

CARE, Role of civil society in northeast European countries [in Croatian], <http://www.carecro.org/care/dok/civilno_drustvo.doc>.

Helsinki Committee for Human Rights in Serbia, <http://www.helsinki.org.yu/>. http://www.yungo.org/yucom>.

M. Matulović, Nationalism, cosmopolitanism, and the problem of the political responsibilities of an individual [in Croatian], <www.cedet.org.yu/disc_doc/ Miomir%Matulovic%20–Nacio%20 i20ljprava2.doc>.

B. Stojković, Debate. Culture and civil society – non-governmental organizations as factors of culture policy [in Serbian], November 2001, <www.zaprokul.orgxu/debate/debata_20011122html>.

Jasna Bakšić Muftić

Iran

Contemporary debates about gender, Islam, and civil society in Iran have been greatly influenced by the Islamic Revolution of 1979 and the policies promulgated immediately after the revolution. The tensions created by the formal affirmation of women's rights to political participation and education in the post-revolutionary constitution in the face of actual negation of women's individual rights, particularly in the area of family law and in the differential treatment of men and women in criminal law, opened a fissure through which a vibrant debate about the treatment and role of women in Islamic civil societies gradually entered the Iranian public discourse. Following the presidential election of 1997, the concept of civil society and the need for its expansion was introduced as a campaign platform by the winning candidate, Mohammad Khatami, and women, along with youth and intellectuals, became publicly identified as harbingers of civil society activism and enlargement.

Debates about how women's status in society can be enhanced in an Islamic society such as Iran are not new. The pre-revolutionary state attempted to approach the question by identifying itself as indispensable to the securing of women's rights in Iran through such policies as making the veil illegal as early as 1936 and instituting legal changes in the arena of family rights in the 1960s and 1970s. In this pre-revolutionary formulation, however, autocratic modernization, secularism, and women's rights were intertwined in such a way as to foreclose the possibility of civil society activism on the part of the majority of women in Iran's Islamic and modernizing society. Women's rights were mostly conceptualized as a necessity to be promoted by the modernizing elite sectors in the face of opposition from the societal forces associated with tradition and religion.

In the post-revolutionary political discourse, in contrast, discussions about women's rights and civil society activism have been the inevitable outcome of a political system that has pursued misogynous policies in the arena of women's individual rights while insisting on an Islamic rhetoric that nominally promotes the equality and dignity of men and women in the political, economic, and spiritual arenas. This tension has allowed women's civil society activism to be framed as a struggle for a more egalitarian and democratic interpretation of Islamic commands and precepts and not a rejection of Islam and Iran's native culture. Given the essentially equal rights orientation of women's activism in Iran, the question of its relationship to feminism, a movement generally identified as anti-Islamic and in the service of foreign powers in the Iranian public discourse, has naturally come to the fore. While many women involved in agitation for equal rights have resisted the term Islamic feminism, it has slowly become part of the public discourse thanks to pioneering feminist journals such as *Zanān*, which began operating in early 1990s with an explicit commitment to both feminism and Islam.

The idea of agitation for reform in women-related laws within an Islamic framework has also brought forth questions about the relationship between women's civil society activism and the broader movement to expand the civil society and democratize/reform the Iranian Islamic state. One set of questions has focused on whether there is a distinct Woman Question in Iran. Many male intellectuals associated with the reform movement, in a forum held in *Zanān* magazine in the mid-to-late 1990s, reasoned that the Woman Question was part and parcel of the democracy question in Iran. By implication they argued that civil society activism centering on women's issues takes or should take a back seat to the more inclusive struggle for democracy and human rights. Many women activists and thinkers explicitly rejected this formulation. The least this debate, still unresolved, showed was that the women who were concerned with the reform of Islam and the Iranian state had a different understanding of the issue from that of their male counterparts.

Another set of questions that has come to the fore more recently deals with the question of whether women's civil society activism constitutes a movement at all, with some arguing that at best it is a proto-movement. Others have conceptualized the character of women's civil society activism in Iran as essentially leaderless, decentralized, and yet widespread. Still others have seen these types of questions as attempts to devalue women's activism; that is, attempts to portray women's struggle to bring about change as less organized and hence less effective or important than the movement for political reform and democracy.

Given the important strides women have made in the areas of education and employment, women's civil society involvement and debates about it are bound to expand in Iran, particularly now that the international community has acknowledged the importance of women's struggles in Iran by granting the 2003 Nobel Peace Prize to one of the country's premier women civil society activists, the lawyer Shirin Ebadi.

Bibliography

F. Farhi, Religious intellectuals, the Woman Question, and the struggle for the creation of a democratic public sphere in Iran, in *International Journal of Politics, Culture and Society* 15:2 (Winter 2001), 315–37.

E. Gheytanchi, Civil society in Iran. Politics of motherhood and the public sphere, in *International Sociology* 16:4 (2001) 557–76.

H. Jalaeipour, "Mas'ala-yi" ijtimāʿyi na "junbish-i" ijtimāʿyi, in *Yas-e-No*, 1 November 2003, 7 and 9.

Z. Mir-Hosseini, *Islam and gender. The religious debate in contemporary Iran*, Princeton, N.J. 1999.

A. Najmabadi, Feminism in an Islamic republic. Years of hardship, years of growth, in Y. Y. Haddad and J. L. Esposito (eds.), *Women, gender, and social change in the Muslim world*, New York 1998, 59–84.

P. Paidar, *Women and the political process in twentieth-century Iran*, Cambridge 1995.

Zanān, various issues.

Farideh Farhi

Israel

The liberal definition of civil society as an "independent social sphere of the state, the market, and family" where citizens act voluntarily and individually, is at odds with the equivalent feminist and postcolonial definition of civil society. This perceives these categories as fluid, socially negotiated, and shaped by the relationship of convergence and separation, a result of the political and cultural construction of reality carried by various social forces in a particular historical period. From this perspective, civil society offers alternative options for inclusive equal citizenship.

Though geographically in the Middle East, and surrounded by Islamic countries, Israel is, in many senses, a Western nation. A liberal democratic state, with an 18 percent Palestinian minority, Israel grants equal rights to all citizens regardless of sex, religion, or race. However, ethnic, national, and gender inequality are deeply woven into the cultural and structural landscape. Five basic components have produced a culture of exclusion and inclusion of women in Israel: (1) the myth of equality; (2) a binary gendered perception of the world; (3) patriarchal cultural and structural arrangements of Jewish and Palestinian society; (4) the lack of separation between state and religion, which supports patriarchy; and (5) the protracted Israeli-Arab conflict, which emphasizes military and militarism as a male domain and the family as female domain. In both Jewish and Arab Palestinian society women embrace familial roles, which, though they marginalize them, include them as signifiers of the collective boundaries and national solidarity (Kanaaneh 2002, Hasan 2002, Herzog 1998, Yuval-Davis 1987). These components subordinate women's roles and status to the state, and neutralize female power in institutionalized politics. Women's forums, which often define themselves as feminist, challenge the predominantly patriarchal culture by suggesting alternatives to the dominant structures.

Israel's highly segregated society is represented in the history of Jewish and Palestinian civil activity; each traveled three major stages in its history.

Jewish society

1. Under Ottoman and British colonial rule, Jewish social activities occurred mainly at the civil society level. The predominant historiography of this period is narrated from a male perspective and stresses the construction of governmental institutions and economic infrastructure. Until recently, it neglected women's roles entirely. Women were extremely active in the suffrage struggle, and in their contributions to the establishment of schools, health services, and clinics for women and infants, and organized social work (Shilo 2001). Most of these endeavors were eventually co-opted by and institutionalized within a national framework. With the centralization of political power and bureaucratization, however, women were marginalized.

2. Ruled by the hegemony of the Labor Party in the first three decades of the state – from 1948 until the late 1970s – state and civil society merged (Ben Eliezer 1998). Women's organizations, as most other organizations, were forced to adjust to the dominant political agenda of the period – one that gave priority to a gender biased nation-state (Fogiel-Bijaoui 1992, Izraeli 1999, Herzog 2004).

3. Since the late 1970s, feminist organizing has flourished in Israel, extending civil society, and becoming particularly strong in the 1990s. The emergence of feminist organizations in Israel was part of an international trend cemented by the United Nation's Declaration of the Decade For Women in 1975, the extension of non-governmental organizations (NGOs) (Yishai 1998), and the decentralization of the state (Ben Eliezer 2003). In 1981, the Law of Associations (NGOs, in Hebrew *amutot*) was brought into force and new organizations were required to register with the ministry of the interior. This was part of the state's effort to monitor the flood of organizational activity. In 1982, there were 12,000 Jewish and Palestinian-Israeli NGOs. In 2000 that number reached 27,000 (Jaffe 2002). Nearly a quarter of these organizations are women's organizations and women are very active in all the organizations.

Many women's organizations focus on a single issue, for example, working to end violence and sexual assault, protecting reproductive and marital rights, advocating for one-parent families and lesbian rights, or addressing offensive advertising, sexism, racism, ethnic inequality, and religious discrimination. Some also work to enhance the political agenda. Many of the latter used ideas of womanhood and motherhood as their banner, for example, mothers of soldiers, Women in Black, Women in Green (of the Right), Woman to Woman (for Jewish and Palestinian co-existence) (Helman 1997, El-Or 1995).

Most of the women's organizations are small, somewhat marginal, and often isolated from each other. In spite of the weak ties between organizations the growth of feminism has had a cumulative effect in the political sphere. Proposals for feminist legislation and a Women's Status Committee have resulted from grassroots activity and the diffuse and decentralized character of women's activity within civil society. This activity is slowly transforming the political culture of Israel by suggesting alternative visions of gender relations and women's social status.

Palestinian civil society in Israel

1. In the Mandate period, Palestinian society developed social and political organizations as part of its internal dynamics, the broader Arab national movement, and the anticolonial movement (Kimmerling 1993). With urbanization and the development of the middle class, women's organizations – some of them explicitly feminist – began emerging in Jaffa, Jerusalem, and other major cities (Peteet 1991, Fleischmann 2003). The war of 1948 led to the collapse of the social structure of Palestinian society and the women's organizations that were a part of that structure.

2. From1948 to 1966 Palestinian citizens of Israel were under military rule. During this period, Palestinian civil society was almost non-existent. The only women's organizations were branches of the Communist Party, Israeli parties, and church-related charity groups run by women.

3. From the mid-1970s, and especially in the 1990s, Palestinian NGOs in Israel grew in numbers and their sphere of activities expanded (Payes 2004). Since 1980, nearly 1,000 Israeli-Palestinian organizations have registered as *amutot*. Many of them work for equal citizenship and social equality; 5 percent of these NGOs are women's organizations. Palestinian women are proportionally more involved in civil society organizations than in the formal Arab political parties in Israel (Abu Baker 1998). Palestinian women's associations advocate for welfare, health, and education reform (Mar'i 1991) and work to protect victims of domestic violence and women who have been threatened with honor killings by their families (Hasan 2002). These groups have also been active in peace organizations (Sharoni 1995, Cockburn 1998, Herzog 1999, Peteet 1991). Feminist activists stress the link between national and feminist causes, arguing that the oppression of Palestinian women in Israel results not only from the oppression perpetuated by Palestinian society, but from patriarchal patterns that are often inextricably linked to official policies (Payes 2004, Rabinowitz 2002).

The "national solidarity" demanded of Palestinian and Jewish women acts as an obstacle to an understanding that women of both national groups share similar concerns and might benefit from cooperation and coalitions that work toward protecting women's rights and freedoms. The increasing strength of the feminist movement has revealed the connection between nationalism and women's status. In the 1990s, this approach spawned numerous women's peace movements and coalition building between Israeli-Jewish and Israeli-Palestinian women (Emmett 1996, Sharoni 1995, Pope 1993). The fragile nature of such coalitions has been exacerbated by the fragility and difficulty of the peace process.

Bibliography

K. Abu Baker, *A rocky road. Arab women as political leaders in Israel* [in Hebrew], Ra'ananna 1999.

U. Ben Eliezer, State versus civil society. A non-binary model of domination through the example of Israel, in *Journal of Historical Sociology* 11:3 (1998), 370–96.

——, New Associations or new politics? The significance of Israeli-style post-materialism, in *Hagar. International Social Science Review* 4 (2003), 5–34.

C. Cockburn, *The space between us. Negotiating gender and national identities in conflict*, London 1998.

T. El-Or and G. Aran, Giving birth to settlement maternal thinking and political action of Jewish women on the West Bank, in *Gender and Society* 9:1 (1995), 60–78.

A. Emmett, *Our sisters' promised land. Women, politics, and Israeli-Palestinian coexistence*, Ann Arbor 1996.

E. Fleischmann, *The nation and its "new" women. The Palestinian women's movement, 1920–1948*, Berkeley 2003.

S. Fogiel-Bijaoui, Feminine organizations in Israel. Current situation [in Hebrew], in *International Problems, Society and Politics* 31 (1992), 65–76.

M. Hasan, The politics of honor. Patriarchy, the state and the murder of women in the name of the family honor, in *Journal of Israeli History* 21:2 (2002), 1–37.

S. Helman and T. Rapoport, Women in Black. Challenging Israel's gender and socio-political orders, in *British Journal of Sociology* 48:4 (1997), 682–700.

H. Herzog, Homefront and battlefront and the status of Jewish and Palestinian women in Israel, in *Israeli Studies* 3:1 (1998), 61–84.

——, A space of their own. Social-civil discourses among Palestinian Israeli women in peace organizations, in *Social Politics. International Studies of Gender, State and Society* 6:3 (1999), 344–69.

——, Women in Israeli society, in U. Rebhun and C. I. Waxman (eds.), *Jews in Israel. Contemporary social and cultural patterns*, Hanover, N.H. 2004, 195–220.

D. Izraeli, A. Friedman, H. Dahan-Kalev, S. Fogiel-Bijoui, H. Herzog, M. Hasan, and H. Naveh, *Sex, gender, politics. Women in Israel* [in Hebrew], Tel Aviv 1999.

E. D. Jaffe, *Giving wisely. The internet directory of Israeli nonprofit and philanthropic organizations*, 2002, <http://givingwisely.org.il/Copyright.htm>.

R. A. Kanaaneh, *Birthing the nation. Strategies of Palestinian women in Israel*, Berkeley 2002.

B. Kimmerling and J. Migdal, *The Palestinian*, New York 1993.

M. M. Mar'i and S. K. Mar'i, The role of women as change agent in Arab society in Israel, in B. Swirski and M. P. Safir, *Calling the equality bluff. Women in Israel*, New York 1991, 213–21.

S. Payes, *Palestinian NGOs in Israel. The politics of civil society*, I. B. Tauris (forthcoming).

J. M. Peteet, *Gender in crisis. Women and the Palestinian resistance movement*, New York 1991.

J. Pope, The emergence of a joint Israeli-Palestinian women's peace movement during the intifada, in H. Afshar (ed.), *Women in the Middle East. Perceptions, realities and struggles for liberation*, London 1993, 172–83.

D. Rabinowitz and K. Abu Baker, *The stand tall generation. The Palestinian citizens of Israel today* [in Hebrew], Jerusalem 2002.

M. Shilo, R. Kark, and G. Hasan-Rokem (eds.), *Jewish*

women in the Yishuv and Zionism. A gender perspective [in Hebrew], Jerusalem 2001.
Y. Yishai, Civil society in transition. Interest politics in Israel, in *Annals of the American Academy of Political and Social Science* 555 (1998), 147–62.
N. Yuval-Davis, Woman/nation/state. The demographic race and national reproduction in Israel, in *Radical America* 21 (1987): 37–59.

HANNA HERZOG

Sub-Saharan Africa

While it is generally true that the voices of women, and Muslim women in particular, have been conspicuously absent from the political discourse conducted in postcolonial Sub-Saharan Africa, there is variation within the region. In light of this variation, this entry addresses three questions: (1) Where have Sub-Saharan African Muslim women been most organized, politically active, and openly supportive of the development of civil society? (2) Why have Muslim women been more organized, politically active, and openly supportive of democracy in some countries of Sub-Saharan Africa than in others? (3) How might democratization itself affect the political influence of Muslim women in Sub-Saharan Africa?

Of the Sub-Saharan African countries with a significant Muslim presence, it is Nigeria where Muslim women have been most organized, politically active, and openly supportive of democracy. This does not mean that Muslim women have always and everywhere enjoyed more social freedoms and political rights in Nigeria than in other countries. In fact, unlike Muslim women in other countries of West Africa, such as Mali, Niger, and Senegal, Muslim women in many predominantly Muslim areas of northern Nigeria were not given the right to vote at independence. In some parts of northern Nigeria, women were not granted the right to vote until 1976. At the dawn of the twenty-first century, Muslim women in certain parts of northern Nigeria continue to live in domestic seclusion. However, in other parts of Nigeria, especially western Nigeria, Muslim women have played a more public and influential political role, even if it has been less public and politically influential than that played by men and non-Muslim women.

In Nigeria, organizations such as the Federation of Muslim Women's Associations of Nigeria (FOMWAN) and Women Living Under Muslim Laws (WLUML) were founded during the 1980s and became forces for social and political change during the 1990s (Callaway and Creevey 1994, Quinn and Quinn 2003). These organizations have been founded and/or led by relatively educated and charismatic Muslim women, such as Haja Bilkisu and Latifa Okunna of FOMWAN, and Ayesha Imam of WLUML. FOMWAN and WLUML have been dedicated to educating Muslim women about their rights under Islamic law, encouraging faithfulness to that law in Muslim communities, and promoting Islamic principles of justice and protection of the weak in the wider society (Dunbar 2000). FOMWAN became one of the major sponsors of the Muslim League for Accountability (MULAC), which was founded to fight corruption and to promote responsive government in Nigeria (Quinn and Quinn 2003). Of the Muslim women's organizations in Nigeria, FOMWAN has been especially important. Evidence of FOMWAN's importance includes the size and scope of the organization and the attention and support it receives from the Muslim establishment.

In Kenya, South Africa, Sudan, and Tanzania, Muslim women have also been relatively organized and politically active (Strobel 1979, Mirza and Strobel 1989, Hale 1996, Geiger 1997, Oded 2000, Quinn and Quinn 2003). During the 1980s and 1990s, Muslim women became openly supportive of democracy in these countries. In Kenya, the voices of Muslim women were amplified during the 1990s through organizations with political agendas that include both men and women, such as the Supreme Council of Kenya Muslims (SUPKEM), the Muslim Students' Association at the University of Nairobi and the Young Muslim Association in Nairobi. SUPKEM included a Department of Women's Affairs, which, during the run-up to national elections, conducted seminars in order to promote political participation by Muslim women and to educate Muslim women as to their rights as citizens (Oded 2000). The Muslim Students' Association and the Young Muslim Association in Nairobi have included many young and educated Muslim women who have been dedicated to promoting participation in and support for Kenya's fledgling civil society. In South Africa, Muslim women played an active part in organizations intended to end apartheid and, during the 1990s, women have added their voices to those of their male counterparts in the Muslim Youth Movement, calling for greater governmental transparency (Quinn and Quinn 2003). In Sudan, the Sudanese Women's Union (WU), under the leadership of Fāṭima Aḥmad Ibrāhīm, was influential through the 1980s. During the 1980s, women became increasingly involved and openly vocal in the National Islamic Front (NIF), an Islamist party that took control of government in 1989 (Hale 1996). Throughout the

1990s, Muslim women in Tanzania have been active in politics and have formed non-governmental organizations intended to promote political awareness among Muslim women (Dunbar 2000).

Typically, Muslim women have been more politically organized and openly supportive of democracy in Sub-Saharan African countries which are not overwhelmingly Muslim (Nigeria, Kenya, South Africa, Sudan, and Tanzania – Kenya and South Africa are predominantly Christian), than in countries that are overwhelmingly Muslim (Mali, Niger, and Senegal). One possible reason that Muslim women have become more engaged in these developing civil societies is that more Muslim women have been exposed to and inspired by non-Muslim women's movements in countries that are pluralistic. It is also possible that more Muslim women have been politically active in countries that do not have Islamic majorities because more of them have had the opportunity to be formally educated, often in Christian schools. This implies that Islam itself sometimes prevents women from participating in politics and openly supporting democracy. It implies that only exposure to non-Islamic, Western ideas, secular values, feminist discourses and the idea of universal human rights can explain why Muslim women have been more politically active and openly supportive of democracy in some settings than in others. However, this does not appear to be the case. In the Sub-Saharan African countries where Muslim women have become most organized, politically active, and openly supportive of democracy, they have typically appealed to Islam and religious values, not Western ideas, secular values, feminist discourses, or universal human rights. For example, FOMWAN and WLUML have called for greater fidelity to Islamic law and democracy. Thus, the question is, why might Islam inspire political participation and vocal support for democracy by women in some settings more than others? The answer to this question is certainly complex.

One possible explanation has to do with religious competition. Sub-Saharan Africa is one of the world's most religiously competitive regions (Barrett 2001). Islam has competed with a myriad of Christian churches, both mainline and independent, for converts and influence over the wider society for more than a hundred years (Hansen and Twaddle 1995, Haynes 1996, Gifford 1998). This competition burst out into the open with the breakdown of authoritarian regimes and the advent of multiparty elections in Sub-Saharan Africa during the 1990s, and has been especially intense in the most religiously plural settings, settings where a significant number of Muslims and Christians are present. In religiously competitive settings, particularly during periods of political transition, when constitutions are revised or created and the relationship between the state and religious institutions may be renegotiated, it becomes very important for religious leaders to ensure that the voice of the religious institution they lead is heard. In religiously competitive and democratizing settings, there is good reason to expect that Muslim leaders will be most encouraging of political participation by Muslim women, since including Muslim women more than doubles the Muslim voting population and increases the leverage of the Muslim community vis-à-vis the state.

Thus, women become an important political resource for Muslim leaders in the most religiously competitive settings. This does not necessarily mean that Muslim women will simply do the bidding of their religious leaders, who, at the dawn of the twenty-first century, are mostly men. As Muslim women come to recognize that they are a valuable political resource, they are likely to become more organized and effective at promoting change, within the Islamic community and in the wider society, as they did in Nigeria, Kenya, South Africa, Sudan, and Tanzania during the 1990s. In these countries, Muslim women are likely to use newly found social and political leverage to address issues of importance to them, including education and domestic violence, as well as inheritance and property rights.

The consolidation of democracy is far from inevitable in contemporary Sub-Saharan Africa. Poverty, disease, political corruption, and global inequities, among other factors, threaten the prospects that fledgling democratic institutions will be strengthened in the region. However, assuming that democratization continues and that elections become increasingly free, fair, and regular, it is likely that the social and political leverage of Muslim women will increase, within the Muslim communities and in the wider society, particularly in the most religiously plural and competitive national settings of Sub-Saharan Africa.

Bibliography

D. Barrett (ed.), *World Christian encyclopedia. A comparative survey of churches and religions in the modern world*, Oxford 2001.

B. Callaway and L. Creevey, *The heritage of Islam. Islam, women, religion and politics in West Africa*, Boulder, Colo. 1994.

R. A. Dunbar, Muslim women in African history, in N. Levtzion and R. L. Pouwels (eds.), *The history of Islam in Africa*, Athens, Ohio 2000, 397–418.

J. Esposito and J. Voll, *Islam and democracy*, New York 1996.

S. Geiger, *TANU Women. Gender and culture in the making of Tanganyikan nationalism (1955–1965)*, Portsmouth, N.H. 1997.
P. Gifford, *African Christianity. Its public role*, Bloomington, Ind. 1998.
S. Hale, *Gender politics in Sudan. Islamism, socialism and the state*, Boulder, Colo. 1996.
H. B. Hansen and M. Twaddle (eds.), *Religion and politics in East Africa*, Athens, Ohio 1995.
J. Haynes, *Religion and politics in Africa*, London 1996.
A. Imam and J. Ibrahim, Democratic processes in Africa. Problems and prospects, in *Review of African Political Economy* 54 (1992), 102–5.
I. M. Lewis (ed.), *Islam in tropical Africa*, London 1980.
S. Mirza and M. Strobel, *Three Swahili Women. Life histories from Mombasa, Kenya*, Bloomington, Ind. 1989.
A. Oded, *Islam and politics in Kenya*, Boulder, Colo. 2000.
C. Quinn and F. Quinn, *Pride, faith, and fear. Islam in Sub-Saharan Africa*, New York 2003.
M. Strobel, *Muslim women in Mombasa (1890–1975)*, New Haven, Conn. 1979.

ROBERT A. DOWD

Civil Society and Democracy Ideologies

Central Asia and the Caucasus

The Muslim states of Central Asia and the Caucasus (Kazakhstan, Kyrgyzstan, Uzbekistan, Tajikistan, Turkmenistan, and Azerbaijan) have many common features in their cultures and histories, but have taken different ways in their transition to democracy. An overwhelming majority of the population of Central Asia are Muslims. In Azerbaijan and several republics of the Russian Federation, Daghestan, Ingushetia, and Chechnya, all indigenous peoples identify themselves as Muslim as well. Except for some groups of Shīʿīs in Azerbaijan and the Ismāʿīlīs in Tajikistan, the majority of Muslims in Central Asia and the Caucasus are Ḥanafī Sunnīs.

Before the 1917 October Revolution, all these countries were part of the Russian Empire. They organized several holy wars, *gazavat*, against what was seen as Orthodox Christian rule. In the nineteenth century and at the beginning of the twentieth, Jadidism (from *uṣūl-i jadīd*, the new method) spread among the Muslim population of the Russian Empire, including Crimea, Volga, Central Asia, and the Muslim Caucasus. Led by Ismail Bey Gasprinsky, this movement for Islamic modernization proposed to elevate the status of women in society. Jadidism advocated equality and secular education for women, and condemned polygamy and the poor treatment of women. Jadidists believed that Islam grants women the right to knowledge and participation in a new enlightened Muslim society. However, after the takeover of Central Asia and the Caucasus by the Soviet government, Jadidism as an Islamic political and cultural movement was uprooted and the idea that emancipation of Muslim women was an important element for modernization and national progress was forgotten.

During the Soviet era (1917–91), the Communist Party aimed to suppress Islam as an ideology and paid great attention to gender relationship and the status of women in Muslim republics of the Caucasus and Central Asia. A Soviet campaign, the *khudzhum*, forcing and encouraging women to discard their veils and be integrated in political and economic life led to numerous deaths of women and their relatives; it also drastically changed gender relations in Muslim societies. *Ḥijāb* and veiling were strongly suppressed by Soviet authorities as a sign of ideological backwardness. With open practice of Islam discouraged, a substantial proportion of women continued to worship at the holy places (*mazārs*). Modernization, women's emancipation campaigns, the abolishment of Sharīʿa law and introduction of secular Soviet law, mass education, and participation in elections and the public sector all had great impact on the status of women. The active participation of well-educated women in public life in post-Soviet Central Asia and the Caucasus is a consequence of the Soviet policies.

In 1991, Central Asia and the Caucasus gained independence. After *perestroika* and the collapse of the Soviet Union, a remarkable process of re-Islamization spread across the area. Thousands of mosques and tens of *madrasas* were established, and millions of people began to openly practice Islam. Women set up non-governmental organizations (NGOs) that support local cultural and Muslim traditions and modernity. In Kazakhstan, for instance, a league of Muslim women has several branches across the country.

In all Muslim countries of Central Asia and the Caucasus, political leadership has imposed strict state control to prevent the spread of fundamentalism and Islamic militancy. In Uzbekistan, after a short period of *perestroika*, a Soviet-style attitude to religious believers has been restored: men and women suspected of participation in Islamic movements are persecuted; the government discourages women from wearing the *ḥijāb*. The establishment of political parties based on religion is forbidden everywhere except in Tajikistan. After the civil war in 1992–7, the Islamic Renaissance Party actively participates in political life and has its representatives in the government.

The countries of Central Asia and the Caucasus signed the United Nations Convention on the Elimination of All Forms of Discrimination against Women (CEDAW). However, on the whole, this has had little impact on the improvement of women's status in society. Women's representation in national governments and parliaments is significant compared to many other countries. In Turkmenistan under authoritarian rule women form 26 percent of the parliament and in Kyrgyzstan with its more liberal regime they form only 6.7 percent, figures that do not show the real process of democratization and women's access to political power in either country.

Table 1. Seats in parliament held by women in the Muslim countries of Central Asia and the Caucasus.

Country	Percentage
Azerbaijan	10.5
Kazakhstan	11.2
Kyrgyzstan	6.7
Tajikistan	12.4
Turkmenistan	26.0
Uzbekistan	7.2

Source: *Human Development Report, 2002. Deepening democracy in a fragmented world*, published for the United Nations Development Programme (UNDP), New York 2002, 227–8.

Some women's NGOs and movements advocate a restoration of the quota system as a way of ensuring women's political participation, even though the Soviet case clearly illustrates the ineffectiveness of such an approach. Token participation of women in political life supported by a 30 percent quota system did not lead to the real political empowerment of women. Current efforts by women's NGOs concerning the restoration of a quota have had limited support among both women and men. In Uzbekistan, the president issued a decree to appoint a woman as a deputy governor. Some Uzbek women's NGOs commented that this decision was a signal to block the access of women to positions of governor (*ḥākim*) and other higher posts. In Kyrgyzstan, reminiscent of the Soviet-style women's committees, a pro-governmental women's party was organized. In general, although there are several female leaders of political parties in Azerbaijan, Kyrgyzstan, and Kazakhstan, women in the Caucasus and Central Asia are more active and powerful in NGOs than in political parties. In a transition that led to mass unemployment, women were the first to lose their jobs in both the private and public sectors, so some women moved to the non-governmental sector. Women are alienated from political life in all countries; often they express their concerns by joining dissident forces, as editors of newspapers, journalists, scholars, and activists in political parties and NGOs.

Reforms involving political liberalization and the strengthening of civil society are most successful in Kyrgyzstan, Kazakhstan, Azerbaijan, and Tajikistan. Women in these countries are thus better able to discuss civil society issues and the role of Islam in transition to democracy and the market economy. They can be heard and express their own interests publicly in the media, whereas the leaderships in Uzbekistan and Turkmenistan still maintain a Soviet-style governance and control over civil society that impedes women from openly expressing their concerns and discussing democracy ideologies. Despite these differences between the states, in the non-governmental sectors in all countries of Central Asia and the Caucasus women's NGOs are the most numerous and well organized thanks to the enthusiasm of women themselves and the support of international organizations and Western donors.

After the collapse of the Soviet Union, as a result of numerous missions from Muslim countries, the first women in *ḥijāb* appeared on the streets of cities and villages in all Muslim states of Central Asia and the Caucasus. A number of Muslim leaders and politicians began to restore discriminatory interpretations of the Qur'ān and some Muslim families brought back traditions humiliating to women. Polygamy, under-age marriage, and seclusion of women, especially in rural areas, are seen by some politicians and families as the fair restoration of ancestors' traditions. Despite progressive written law protecting women's rights, a significant number of families practice customary law, mainly in rural areas. Predominance of customary law in inheritance, access of women to land and their tenure rights are little discussed in society. Many women regret losing the previous Soviet system with its safety net of free health care, protection of mothers, children, and retired people, and employment opportunities; the transition to a market economy involved increasing poverty accompanied by de-emancipation of women, and the inability of the states to maintain social allowances and support for women and children.

At the same time, leaders of the newly independent Muslim countries in search of national ideology have promoted the veneration of medieval figures. Building national ideology through nationalism and praise of wartime rulers contradict commitments of the leadership of all these countries to pursue democratization and stability in the region. Unfortunately, the voice of women leaders in NGOs, the media, and political parties aiming to prevent a spread of these ideas is not heard well. The majority of NGOs and political parties and the media rarely debate gender issues linked to the revival of Islam and male-dominated interpretations of the Qur'ān and national histories.

Since the late 1990s, Hizb ut-Tahrir (Party of Liberation), a transnational Islamic party, has called for non-violent establishment of a caliphate including Central Asia and the Caucasus. Both men and women, inspired by ideas of social equity and justice, and frustrated by current economic and political crises, rampant corruption, and ideological vacuum, have joined this party. Participation in such radical Islamic movements needs to be seen as an outlet for the expression of social and political dissatisfaction and de-Russification (anticolonial) feelings among dissident people. The low resistance of the younger generation to religious extremism is partly explained by the weakness of official clergy, who face financial and ideological problems in their actions and who are severely restricted by state authorities.

In general, an intensive process of re-Islamization and democratization in the countries of Central Asia and the Caucasus has led to a critique of the Soviet ideological legacy and to a search for new democratic ideologies combined with Islamic values and a high status of women in society.

BIBLIOGRAPHY

F. Acar and A. Güneş-Ayata (eds.), *Gender and identity construction. Women of Central Asia, the Caucasus and Turkey*, Leiden 2000.

M. Buckley (ed.), *Post-Soviet women. From the Baltic to Central Asia*, Cambridge 1997.

U. Ikramova and K. McConnel, Women's NGOs in Central Asia's evolving societies, in M. Ruffin and D. Waugh (eds.), *Civil society in Central Asia*, Seattle 1999, 198–213.

A. Khalid, *The politics of Muslim cultural reform. Jadidism in Central Asia*, Berkeley 1998.

G. Massell, *The surrogate proletariat. Moslem women and revolutionary strategies in Soviet Central Asia, 1924–1929*, Princeton, N.J. 1974.

OSCE/ODIHR, NGOs in the Caucasus and Central Asia. Development and co-operation with the OSCE, Human Dimension Implementation meeting background paper 2000/1, Warsaw 2000.

A. Tabyshalieva, Central Asia. Increasing gender inequality, in A. Strasser, A. Haas, G. Mangott, and V. Heuberger (eds.), *Central Asia and Islam*, Hamburg 2002, 151–8.

ANARA TABYSHALIEVA

South Asia

Approximately half of the world's 1.1 billion Muslims live in three countries of South Asia: 145 million and 130 million in Muslim-majority Pakistan and Bangladesh respectively, and 125 million in Hindu-majority India. Yet, the global discourse on Muslim women in civil society and democracy is shaped largely by the experiences of the Middle East where only 172 million Muslims live.

The Western media generally portray Muslim women as veiled and excluded from the public sphere. This is not so for South Asian Muslim women. They are rarely veiled and they are active in civil society as leaders as well as members of organizations. Similarly, South Asian Muslim women participate in local and national politics as voters and as people's representatives. Since the return of democratically elected governments in the 1990s, Pakistan and Bangladesh have been ruled by women leaders.

In Pakistan, Benazir Bhutto was elected head of government from 1988 to 1990 and again from 1993 to 1996. She was forcibly ousted from power because of her differences with the civil-military elite that dominated Pakistan. Two elected women prime ministers have governed Bangladesh since 1991: Khaleda Zia, 1991 to 1996 and 2001 to the present, and Sheikh Hasina from 1996 to 2001. Khaleda and Hasina have led the two major political parties of Bangladesh since the early 1980s. They also led the movement that finally toppled the military regimes that ruled for two decades.

Detractors argue that these women entered politics through dynastic connections. Benazir and Hasina inherited the political mantels of their assassinated fathers and Khaleda that of her assassinated husband. But the very fact that these women led their male-dominated political organizations for nearly three decades and enjoyed personal popularity with the voters demonstrates that women are acceptable as leaders in Muslim societies. Even the fundamentalist Islamist parties in South Asia, such as Jamaat-e-Islami in Pakistan and Bangladesh, accepted women in leadership positions when they entered into electoral alliances with the mainstream parties headed by women.

The Muslim world is not homogeneous. The countries and regions have different social, cultural, and political traditions. These differences explain the varying levels of women's participation in the public sphere. For example, in contrast to the Middle East where most countries are still ruled by authoritarian regimes that strictly control civil society, South Asia has a long tradition of Western-style liberal democracy. Here the nationalist movements against colonialism embraced visions of a democratic polity. After independence all three South Asian states opted for democratic parliamentary government, though Pakistan and Bangladesh were later ruled by military regimes for long periods of time. South Asia's cultural tradition is characterized by a mild observance of purdah. As a result, South Asian Muslim women have been able to participate in civil society and political organizations for nearly a century.

The pattern of women's engagement in civil society, politics, and governance has changed over the years. During the first half of the twentieth century South Asian women, mainly aristocratic and upper-middle-class, became involved in social welfare organizations. The nationalist movements recruited a few of these female leaders to mobilize support of female voters. The last three decades, however, have seen a sea change in women's involvement in social and political organizations. Beginning in the 1970s, following the United Nations declaration of the International Women's Decade (1976–85), hundreds of women's organizations and non-governmental organizations (NGOs) have emerged. Some of these organizations provide services such as education, health, credit, and employment, while others advocate women's human rights. They have mobilized grassroots women into economic, social, and political activities; the leadership is no longer exclusively upper-middle-class women.

Women's organizations now go beyond the traditional role of simply mobilizing women's votes for political parties. Increasingly they are pressing political parties to explicitly address women's issues in their platforms and to ensure a critical mass of women representatives in national parliaments and local governments.

Predictably, the growing visibility of women in the public arena has elicited a backlash from the religious extremists. In Pakistan, the Islamist forces succeeded in introducing new Islamic laws curtailing women's equal rights. In Bangladesh, they exerted pressure through fatwas that violated the existing laws of the land. In India, they successfully reversed the government's decision to introduce uniform civil family laws for all religious communities. However, women's organizations continue to resist the religious extremist forces and have been in the forefront of citizens' movements for secularism, human rights, and democracy.

Begum Rokeya Sakhawat Hossain (1880–1932) was a pioneer in the emergence of Muslim women's participation in public space in South Asia. She established the first Muslim Girls' school (later a college) in 1911 in Calcutta and founded the Anjuman-i-Khawatin-i-Islam Bangla (Bengali Muslim Women's Association) in 1916. From 1903 she was a vanguard feminist author with articles on the oppression of Muslim women. She strongly criticized the role of mullahs and their misuse of religion. Her best-known book, *Sultana's Dream* (published in English in 1905) describes a feminist utopia (Hossain 1988). Her writing demonstrates the long-standing indigenous feminism in South Asia.

PAKISTAN

In the 1920s and 1930s several elite Muslim women entered the public sphere in five major areas: education, health care, social reform, literary culture, and political work (Asghar Ali 2000). The influx of refugee women and children after the partition of India and the creation of Pakistan in 1947 impelled many middle-class women to become involved in charity and volunteer organizations. The All Pakistan Women's Association (APWA) established branches all over the country. Though closely tied to the government, APWA launched a campaign in 1955 against the prime minister's polygamous second marriage. APWA successfully lobbied to create the Family Laws Commission, which drafted the Family Laws ordinance in 1961. It set a minimum age for marriage, made second marriage and divorce difficult for men, and facilitated divorce for women (Hussain 1991).

In the early 1970s in Pakistan the popularly elected government of Zulfikar Ali Bhutto (1971–7) supported women's advancement by appointing women to high level government positions and by establishing a National Commission on the Status of Women. Several women's organizations, such as Aurat and Shirkat Gah, emerged during this period. However, the military regime of General Zia ul-Haq (1977–88) which overthrew Bhutto in 1977 imposed a dress code in offices and schools, introduced Islamic punishments through the Hudood Ordinance (1979), and established Sharīʿa courts. Women's organizations protested against these restrictions. In 1981, the Women's Action Forum (WAF) was formed with branches in all four major cities of Pakistan. WAF was the first organization to publicly protest against the actions of the military regime. In the 1980s and 1990s several NGOs and women's organizations emerged, some with grassroots connections. Women (Asma Jahangir, Hina Zilani) assumed leadership of mainstream human rights organizations. They succeeded in making violence against women, like honor killings, major issues in the human rights discourse nationally and internationally.

Women led by the mother and daughter team of Nusrat and Benazir Bhutto were active in the pro-democracy movement of the 1980s in Pakistan. After the return of a democratically elected government (1988–99) several women were elected to parliament, though their numbers remained small. In the current parliament in Pakistan, elected in 2002, a system of women's reserved seats (elected indirectly) has created a 21 percent representation of women in the lower house and a 17 percent representation in the upper house of parliament.

BANGLADESH

Compared to Pakistan, women in Bangladesh have participated even more in social and political movements; they participated in the various people's movements against Pakistan's government, such as the language movement of 1952 and the student movement of the 1960s. Women cultural activists were in the forefront of the resistance to the assault on Bengali culture. The country's leading female poet – Begum Sufia Kamal – was the conscience and leader of civil society, protesting against autocratic military rule and demanding a secular and democratic polity. In the 1954 provincial assembly election women were directly elected to seven reserved seats in the assembly. Several women gained prominence as top ranking leaders of political parties. In 1966, Anwara Khatun led the main Bengali nationalist party, the Awami League, when its male leadership was imprisoned.

During the 1950s and 1960s, several women's voluntary neighborhood associations emerged promoting literacy and skill training for women. In 1969, the country's largest women's organization, the Mahila Parishad, was established to advocate for the release of political prisoners. The Mahila Parishad is now a multi-faceted organization for women's rights with more than 100,000 members throughout Bangladesh. Following the birth of Bangladesh in 1971, thousands of NGO women fieldworkers went to villages to mobilize millions of rural women to access education, health care, credit, and employment. Though the majority of women involved in NGO activities are either fieldworkers or "beneficiaries," women lead some prominent NGOs such as Nijera Kori, Ain o Salish Kendra, and the Preep Trust.

Many NGOs emphasize women's issues (Jahan 1995). Over 500 women's organizations are registered with the women's ministry. Some, like Women for Women and Nari Pokkho, focus on feminist research, advocacy, and training. Others, like Bangladesh Mahila Ainjibi Samity, focus on women's rights. Some work in specific sectors, for example, garment workers, commercial sex workers, and migrant labor. Others, such as Sammalito Nari Samaj and the National Committee on Beijing, are umbrella organizations, lobbying for specific policy and action.

In the three decades since independence, gender issues have certainly entered the mainstream discourse. Beginning with issues of "women in development" (WID), women's rights activists have expanded the feminist discourse to include sexuality, violence, human rights, and political participation. They have also built alliances with a broad array of civil society organizations headed by men. Civil society protests around issues of violence against women draw widespread participation of men.

Women's increasing participation in civil society organizations is accompanied by increasing participation in politics. At the time of independence, there were no women directly elected by the citizens to the national parliament. The 1973 constitution provided for 300 general and 15 reserved women's seats to be elected by the general members of the parliament. Later the number of women's reserved seats increased to 30. Similarly a 30 percent quota for women was reserved in local councils, again indirectly elected. In the early 1980s, the two major mainstream political parties of the country chose two female leaders, Sheikh Hasina (the Awami League) and Khaleda Zia (Bangladesh Nationalist Party) as party presidents in order to hold the various feuding factions together. In the last quarter century these two women not only maintained their hold on the party but also led pro-democracy movements and ruled the country after winning three successive democratic elections.

While Hasina and Khaleda owe their leadership positions primarily to dynastic connections (Jahan 1987), several women (Motia Chowdhury and Sajeda Chowdhury in the Awami League) have emerged as top ranking leaders without any familial ties. As prominent figures in civil society, some women led political movements that had major social and political impact. For example, in the late 1980s and early 1990s Jahanara Imam, a literary figure, led the Ghatak Dalal Nirmal Committee (committee to eliminate killers and collaborators), which mobilized public opinion against the post-1975 military government's policy of rehabilitating collaborators with the Pakistanis.

With the return of democratic elections, women's organizations started a public advocacy campaign in favor of direct elections for 30 percent of women's reserved seats in the national parliament and local bodies. In 1997 direct elections were introduced in local elections, but not for the national parliament. Since the expiration of the women's quota system in 2001, women hold just 2 percent of the parliamentary seats; however 9 percent of cabinet posts are held by women. Women's voting percentage has also steadily increased and at present they vote in higher numbers than do men. Many observers have argued that in 1996 election results were determined by the women's swing vote, when they voted in favor of the Awami League to resist the rising strength of the officially sponsored Islamist forces.

INDIA

In contrast to Pakistan and Bangladesh the Muslims in India had the disadvantage of being a minority community. Muslim women were doubly disadvantaged. Lacking national or visionary leadership, the voices and experiences of Muslim women are represented by male Muslims claiming to represent the entire community. The restrictive agendas of Islamist organizations like Jamiat-e-Ulema Hind and Jamaat-e-Islami, which focus on retention of Sharīʿa laws, have limited Indian governments' capacity to take legislative measures to end discrimination in personal laws for Muslim women. Sharīʿa laws became a major contested issue in the late 1980s when the Supreme Court passed a judgment in favor of women. It was supported by women's organizations but rejected by the Islamist parties. The 1990s, however, saw the emergence of Muslim civil society organizations such as the Muslim Intelligentsia Forum that questioned the authority of Muslim political and religious leaders. The National Commission for Women held a series of public hearings on Muslim women to highlight the economic problems faced by them. Several Muslim women also started to discuss specific reforms in Muslim personal laws. These efforts symbolize Muslims' determination to challenge existing Sharīʿa laws and renegotiate ideas on women's rights.

CONCLUSION

What are the challenges for Muslim women's civic and political engagement in South Asia? First, for the majority of Muslim women, poverty, illiteracy, lack of education, employment, and income still remain the major constraints. Upper-middle-class women dominate among activists and leaders. Second, the gradual erosion of the elite's commitment to secular ideology and the ascendance of religious extremists since the 1980s pose another threat. In Pakistan and Bangladesh the power of Islamist forces has gradually increased under the patronage of military regimes supported by the United States. The democratically elected governments in the 1990s did not vigorously defend secular ideology, as did the founding fathers. Finally, increasing corruption of electoral politics (for example, the dominant role of black money and muscle men to capture votes) deters women's participation in democratic parties (Jahan 1994).

Women's organizations pursue multiple strategies to address these challenges. They consistently demand greater investment in social sectors to reduce gender gaps in human development. Many NGOs also address these issues. Often women's organizations are the lone voices protesting at the extremist religious organizations. However, the women's organizations have yet to devise effective strategies to counter political corruption, which has excluded the majority of women from participating in electoral democracies.

BIBLIOGRAPHY

A. A. Ali, *The emergence of feminism among Indian Muslim women 1920–1947*, New York 2000.
N. Hoodbhoy, The women's movement in Pakistan, in R. dos Tempos (ed.), *Alternative women's visions and movements*, ii, Rio de Janeiro 1991, 247–54.
R. S. Hossain, *Sultana's Dream*, New York 1988.
N. Hussain, Military rule, fundamentalism, and the women's movement in Pakistan, in R. dos Tempos (ed.), *Alternatives. Women's visions and movements*, ii, 1991, Rio de Janeiro 1991, 211–28.
R. Jahan, Women in South-Asian Politics, in *Third World Quarterly* 9:3 (July 1987), 848–70.
——, Why women, what politics?, in R. Jimenez-David (ed.), *Proceedings of the first Asia-Pacific congress of women in politics, 21–23 June, 1994*, Manila, Philippines 1994, 7–15.
——, Men in seclusion, women in public. Rokeya's dream and women's struggles in Bangladesh, in A. Basu (ed.), *The challenge of local feminism. Women's movements in global perspective*, Oxford 1995, 87–109.
P. Jeffery and A. Basu (eds.), *Appropriating gender. Women's activism and politicized religion in South Asia*, New York 1998.

ROUNAQ JAHAN

Turkey

It is widely argued that civil society flourished in Turkey in the 1980s. Social scientists estimate that there were approximately 60,000 associations by the late 1990s and that women's organizations constituted 0.3 percent of all non-governmental organizations (NGOs) (Kalaycıoğlu 2002, Pusch 2003). In 2000, there were 179 registered women's NGOs (Pusch 2000, 483). Women's activism in the public realm contributed to the democratization process in the country, particularly through its resonance in public discourse, regardless of ideological stand or numerical strength. If democracy is self-rule, women contributed to democratization in the country by challenging the state and demanding that state institutions respond to women's needs as women defined these needs themselves. In a context with a strong state tradition where state defined what the best interests of its citizens were, such a challenge was a significant step in self-rule. At another level, women's activism within civil society contributed to the process of democratization by helping liberalize the polity. A liberal context where individual, civil, or sociopolitical rights are respected is a necessary condition of a democratic polity. Communal norms, which have disregarded individual rights, have long been causes of women's discrimination as women themselves have argued. Working through civil society and women's organizations that prioritize respect for individual rights, women expanded the opportunities they could have as individuals and defended their rights of public expression, and/or religion, thereby contributing to the liberalization of the polity.

Despite their cross-cutting cleavages and blurred boundaries, it is possible to plot a division between secular and Islamist women based on their self-identification. Secular groups in search of rights and opportunities included different socialist, radical, Kemalist or unidentified feminists, Kurdish women and/or feminists, and mothers who organized to protest at the loss of relatives. Islamist groups organized primarily in defense of their right to wear headscarves in universities, though there were some organized to promote Islamic life and dispense charity.

Secular feminists as members of civil society

Women who called themselves feminists emerged in the early 1980s and formed what they later recognized as consciousness-raising groups. Şirin Tekeli, Stella Ovadia, and Şule Torun were the foremost feminist women in this early stage. In 1984, the short-lived Kadın Çevresi (Women's circle) a book club that aimed to translate feminist works and serve as a medium of feminist communication, was formed. In 1986, Şirin Tekeli initiated a petition campaign in which 4,000 signatures were collected to have the 1985 United Nations Convention on the Elimination of All Forms of Discrimination against Women (CEDAW) implemented by government. In 1987 feminist women organized a march and later a festival to protest against domestic violence. They drew attention for the first time in Turkey's history to this widespread problem, which cut across class lines. The mobilizing spirit of the campaign against domestic violence prompted the emergence of feminist publications – called *feminist* (sic) and *Kaktüs* – that allowed the crystallization of radical feminist and socialist feminist ideas respectively. Feminists institutionalized their demands for expansion of women's opportunities by establishing the Women's Library and Information Center and the Purple Roof Women's Shelter Foundation in 1990 in Istanbul. In 1991, the Women's Solidarity Foundation was established in Ankara and in 1993 this group opened the Altındağ women's shelter. On the issue of domestic violence, Kurdish women established the center KA-MER (Kadın Merkezi) in Diyarbakır in 1997. Meanwhile, other women's associations, platforms, initiatives, and organizations arose to promote women's rights, including many beyond the major cities of the country and others among university students (Bora and Günal 2002). The journal *Pazartesi* published between April 1995 and March 2002 became an organ of feminist dialogue and perspective. An award-winning woman's interest group was Kadının İnsan Hakları Projesi (Women for women's human rights), established in 1993 to work toward the realization of women's human rights. KADER, the Association to Support and Educate Women Candidates was initiated by some feminists in 1997 and supported by a large coalition of women to promote women into parliament.

As this feminist activism surged, a group of women, some of whom called themselves Kemalist feminists, emerged in reaction to Islamist activism that spread. They established a foundation in 1989 called Çağdaş Yaşamı Destekleme Derneği (Association to promote contemporary life) to promote secular (that is, Kemalist) education and spread Westward-looking official ideology to counter the demands of the Islamists. They generated income and scholarships to educate women in less developed regions of the country and the peripheral areas of capital cities.

Meanwhile, feminism penetrated the state, and public universities began opening women's studies centers and programs. Istanbul University Women's Research Center coordinated a petition campaign in 1993, which about 119,000 women joined, to have the Civil Code amended. The Civil Code, which was adapted from the Swiss Code in 1926, had inegalitarian clauses where the husband was recognized as the head of the family and its representative and the wife as his helper. The campaign for the amendment of the Civil Code was endorsed by a large coalition of feminists and women's groups. The association of Turkish women jurists drafted the amendment. Although international pressures were an important factor precipitating change, the diverse feminist groups succeeded in having the Law for the Protection of Family passed in 1998 to protect women against domestic violence and the Civil Code amended by the end of 2001. The new Civil Code abolished the supremacy of the husband in the marriage union and, in cases of divorce, allowed women to share the property acquired during marriage.

Besides those who organized to promote their

rights, women, mostly mothers whose sons "disappeared" in police custody, also expanded the parameters of democratic participation and civil rights. They gathered regularly every Saturday in a central meeting place in the heart of Istanbul, from May 1995 for more than three years, to protest at the lack of information on more than 300 lost sons or relatives. The Saturday Mothers, as they were commonly known, assumed a political role as mothers to make their individual claims against the state. They did not merely challenge the realm in which mothers could define their predicament but they also defied the statist understanding of "the common good" by redefining their own interests in their own words.

Independently of Turkish women and feminists, Kurdish women made their mark on civil society in Turkey with their journals *Yaşamda Özgür Kadın* (Free women in life, January 1998–March 2000), the feminist *Roza* (March 1996–2000), and *Jujin*, brought out by feminists who split from *Roza* (December 1996–March 2000). *Yaşamda Özgür Kadın* focused on women's place in the Kurdish nationalist struggle, while the latter two adopted a Kurdish feminist posture analyzing problems of Kurdish women in relation to Kurdish men as well as Turkish feminists. In these feminist journals, questions of assimilation, the prohibition of Kurdish as a public language, and the relationship of Kurdish women to the Turkish state and its population control policies were widely discussed (Açık 2002). Kurdish women, though they might have been few in numbers, were critical in challenging the discourse of homogeneous Turkish nationalism and Turkish feminism in defense of their democratic rights.

Islamist feminists as members of civil society

Perhaps the most visible and active group of women who had their voices heard in defense of their rights in opposition to the state were the Islamist women. Even though women who gathered informally and mostly spontaneously to seek their right to attend universities wearing headscarves, as they claimed Islam dictated, were most visible, there were other Islamist women's organizations dispensing charity or promoting an Islamic way of life. The latter were mostly organized around three coalitions founded in the mid-1990s that were quite short-lived and rather amorphous: the Gökkuşağı Istanbul Kadın Platformu (Istanbul women's rainbow platform), the Başkent Kadın Platformu (Capital city women's platform), and the Güneydoğu Kadın ve Kültür Platformu (Platform of women and culture of the Southeast) organized in Diyarbakır.

Women who organized spontaneously or as part of human rights associations such as Mazlum Der (Headscarf commission), to protest the ban on headscarves in universities constituted a radical challenge to state secularism. The Turkish state had secular laws and the women who covered their heads did so in obedience to Islamic law. The women who protested the ban on headscarves challenged the nature and boundaries of state secularism in defense of their rights of religious observance. Even though the ban remains in force, the nature and limits of Turkish secularism is keenly disputed.

Conclusion

Women of diverse ideological positions who came together in formal associations, foundations, or informal groups and initiatives expanded the boundaries of a democratic society in Turkey. Not only did these groups bring to public debate diverse issues that radically challenged the principles on which Turkish democracy was expected to be built, but they also allowed those women who became members of civil society to empower themselves as individuals whether they espoused an Islamist or a secular feminist ideology. The unprecedented issues they brought to public debate and the individualism they cultivated promoted a culture of liberalism that could nurture a democracy respectful of difference and coexistence.

Bibliography

N. Açık, Ulusal mücade, kadın mitosu ve kadınların hareket geçirilmesi. Türkiye'deki çağdaş Kürt kadın dergilerinin bir analizi, in A. Bora and A. Günal (eds.), *90'larda Türkiye'de feminizm*, Istanbul 2002, 279–306.

Y. Arat, Toward a democratic society. The women's movement in Turkey in the 1980s, in *Women's Studies International Forum* 17 (1994), 241–8.

——, *Political Islam in Turkey and women's organizations*, Istanbul 1999.

——, Democracy and women in Turkey. In defense of liberalism, in *Social Politics* 6:3 (Fall 1999), 370–87.

A. Bora and A. Günal (eds.), *90'larda Türkiye'de feminizm*, Istanbul 2002.

K. Çayır, Islamist civil associations. The case of the Rainbow Istanbul Women's Platform, unpublished M.A. thesis, Boğaziçi University 1997.

E. Kalaycıoğlu, State and civil society in Turkey. Democracy, development and protest, in A. B. Sajoo (ed.), *Civil society in the Muslim world. Contemporary perspectives*, London 2002, 247–72.

B. Pusch, Stepping into the public sphere. The rise of Islamist and religious conservative women's non-governmental organizations, in S. Yerasimos et al. (eds.), *Civil society in the grip of nationalism*, Istanbul 2000, 475–505.

N. Sirman, Feminism in Turkey. A short history, in *New Perspectives on Turkey* 3 (1989), 1–34.

Ş. Tekeli, Emergence of the feminist movement in Turkey, in D. Dahlerup (ed.), *The new women's movement. Feminism and political power in Europe and the USA*, London 1986, 179–99.

Yeşim Arat

Colonialism and Imperialism

British Colonial Domains of South Asia

British colonial rule was imposed on most regions of South Asia (with the notable exception of present-day Afghanistan) from 1757 under the auspices of the East India Company, though it was not formalized until a century later when official Mughal sovereignty was dissolved in favor of direct rule by the British crown after the Indian rebellion of 1857. As early as 1826, however, the centrality of the Woman Question to Britain's "civilizing mission" in India was established when James Mill decreed in his influential *History of British India*: "Among rude people, the women are generally degraded; among civilized people they are exalted." From his limited reading about Indian religions and society, he concluded, "nothing can exceed the habitual contempt which the Hindus entertain for their women." As this quotation indicates, it was those customs defined specifically as "Hindu" that were considered most objectionable by the British in the course of the nineteenth century. Hence, the colonial government introduced legislation (often at the explicit encouragement of Indian reformers) to prohibit *sati* or widow burning (1829), enable Hindu widows to remarry (1856), and raise the age of consent from the age of ten to twelve years (1891). It was not until the early twentieth century that the government of India responded to calls within the Muslim community (consisting of approximately 20 percent of India's population in the colonial period) by passing a number of acts intended to augment Muslim women's legal rights.

The first of these acts was the Waqf Validating Act of 1913, which sought to reinstate those endowments (*awqāf*) that benefited surviving members of a donor's family (as opposed to funding religious or charitable projects). By virtue of ties of kinship, needy Muslim women were to receive support. The second was the Shariat Application Act of 1937. As the title suggests, it aimed to replace customary law in India with Muslim personal law, which was deemed to be more advantageous to women, though it had little actual effect after compromises were made on the issue of inheritance. More influential was the Muslim Dissolution of Marriage Act of 1939, which permitted women to initiate divorce proceedings, primarily on grounds accepted by the Mālikī school of Islamic jurisprudence. The act that caused the greatest upheaval among Muslims, however, was one that applied to all religious communities, namely, the Child Marriage Restraint Act of 1929. Raising the minimum age of marriage to 14 for girls and 18 for boys, it brought Muslim women into conflict with men of their community as never before when they vigorously endorsed it through women's organizations, while leading male reformers, politicians, and *ʿulamāʾ* denounced it as irrelevant or "un-Islamic" on account of its failure to recognize the jurisdiction of Muslim judges.

Beyond this legislation, colonial rule in South Asia had its most dramatic effects on women by inspiring a process of self-examination within the Muslim community itself. Having experienced a loss of political power, Indian Muslims were forced to recognize that the Islamic world had fallen behind Europe in terms of intellectual, technological, and material development. The question arose as to how they could maintain their cultural identity in the face of European encroachment and the numerical dominance of the Hindu community. By the late nineteenth century, a response had come in the form of socioreligious reform movements that sprang up across India to restore a "pure" Islam that was free of cultural accretions. A number of variations existed, but, in general terms, this process was understood to mean a return to scriptural sources, including the Qur'ān and *ḥadīth*, and early Islamic history.

Early Muslim reformers, such as Sayyid Aḥmad Khān (1817–98), highlighted the significance of women to this project of reform by dictating that the real strength of Islam lay in a "private" domestic sphere that was outside the purview of the British government. As women were responsible for maintaining the home as an oasis of tradition and passing on religious knowledge to their children, they were deemed to have a vital role to play in the maintenance of Islamic culture. Yet, when these male reformers turned their attention to women, they discovered that many of them were ignorant of scriptural Islam and even the basic tenets of their religion. A particular complaint was that they were dedicated to rituals and customs that were expensive and unrelated to their faith, including exorcism, vows to spirits, idol worship, and life-cycle ceremonies. Their response was to advocate a changed role for women to be achieved through specific moral and practical education. This reformist program represented male intrusion into a segregated female world over which women had previously exercised a substantial degree of autonomy.

In order to spread their message, Muslim reformers utilized the new print technology which had been introduced to India by the British, publishing a range of short tracts, journals, manuals, and novels. Despite a shared agenda, two main strands may be identified within this genre of literature. The first encompassed traditional Muslim scholars (*ʿulamāʾ*) who devised a program of reform largely independently of European influence. With regard to gender, this approach meant that no distinction was made between the moral and intellectual capabilities of men and women. A key example of this type of text was *Bihishti Zewar* (Heavenly ornaments) by the Deobandi scholar, Mawlana Ashraf ʿAlī Thānawī (1864–1943). It advocated that both sexes should follow the example of the Prophet and read religious texts in Arabic (though girls were expected to begin their training in the vernacular). The second strand included social reformers, known as Islamic modernists, who were motivated by their encounter with the colonial power to take example from European prototypes. In particular, they were inspired by Victorian notions of bourgeois domesticity to argue that women had special moral and spiritual qualities that prepared them for an exalted role within the home. Representative authors of this type of literature included Nazir Aḥmad (1833?–1912) and Alṭāf Ḥusayn Ḥālī (1837–1914).

Other Muslim reformers took practical steps to found private schools for girls from the 1880s. Prominent early examples included the Nampalli Girls School in Hyderabad (founded 1890), the Victoria Girls High School in Lahore (founded 1906), the Zenana Madrasa in Aligarh (founded 1906), and the Muslim Girls School in Lucknow (founded 1912). The key aim of these institutions was to prepare girls to better fulfill their future roles as wives and mothers of the Muslim community. In doing so, their achievements should not be overstated; by the time of the 1931 census, only 1.2 percent of Indian Muslim women (as compared to 1.9 percent of Indian women as a whole) were literate. Yet female education did have a number of unforeseen and often paradoxical effects as well. The institutionalization of certain customary practices, such as purdah, in girls schools, for instance, stimulated a demand for segregated medical and educational facilities to be staffed by Muslim female professionals, including teachers, doctors, and nurses. School attendance also fostered women's interest in social service organizations and Urdu journalism, while cultivating broader networks of female communication. The result was a burgeoning of Muslim women's activism in the Indian subcontinent in the early decades of the twentieth century. Like prior efforts by male reformers, it sought to introduce incremental change to society by building on Islamic norms.

The first stage in this process was the establishment of women's journals to which Muslim women themselves contributed. Some of the first were *Tahzib un-niswan* (founded 1898, Lahore), *Khatun* (founded 1904, Aligarh) and *ʿIsmat* (founded 1908, Delhi), though a large number of other titles soon proliferated across India in Urdu and other regional languages. These journals provided reading material to newly educated women on topics as diverse as female education, women's rights in Islam, health, nutrition, home economics, and gardening. By the 1920s, they also began to take up more explicitly feminist issues, including female suffrage, legislative reform, economic independence, "love" marriages, and the relaxation of purdah, while also reporting on contemporary politics and travel. Certain Indian Muslim women also wrote longer pieces, including novels, manuals, and reformist tracts. At the forefront of this movement were pioneering figures, such as Muhammadi Begam (1878?–1908) and Rokeya Sakhawat Hossain (1880–1932), who introduced a distinctly feminine sensibility to Urdu literature for women. It was to be developed by a later generation of female authors, including Nazr Sajjad Hyder (1894–1967) and Ismat Chughtai (1911–91).

Other Muslim women took practical steps for women's education and emancipation by establishing schools, health programs, and women's organizations. Leading figures in this field were the Nawab Begams of Bhopal, Sikandar (1816–68), Shah Jahan (1838–1901), and Sultan Jahan (1858–1930), who used their semi-autonomous state in central India as a testing ground for women's reform. Specific projects included schools for elite and less privileged girls (the best known being the Sultania Girls School, founded 1903), a purdah women's hospital (founded 1891), and a women's social club (founded 1909). The last Begam of Bhopal also sought to lay the foundations of an autonomous women's movement in India in which

Muslim women would play an active role by inaugurating the Anjuman-i-Khawatin-i-Islam (All-India Muslim Ladies Conference) in 1914 and the All-India Ladies Association in 1918. Furthermore, she and other Muslim women participated in the three main women's organizations at the national level, namely, the Women's Indian Association (WIA, founded 1917), the National Council of Women in India (NCWI, founded 1925) and the All India Women's Conference (AIWC, founded 1927). Their involvement in these bodies represented a willingness to establish an alliance with women of other communities over the issues of female education, social uplift, and legislative reform.

Despite these activities, Muslim women failed to become involved in the Indian women's movement in large numbers. What proved to be more influential in stimulating their involvement in mass movements in the colonial period were causes related to their Muslim identity. The first evidence of this may be seen in connection with political activities in India following the Balkan wars when women-only meetings were held by the Anjuman-i-Khuddam-i-Ka'aba (founded 1913) to raise funds for the defense of the *khalīfa* and the holy places of Islam. During the Khilafat movement in the early 1920s, Indian Muslim women were mobilized in even greater numbers to attend mass rallies with speeches by women leaders, such as Abadi Banu Begam (known as Bi Amman, 1852–1924). In particular, they were called upon to build on their traditional roles as defenders of their family's faith by donating gold ornaments, wearing only handspun (*swadeshi*) cloth, and taking up the nationalist ritual of spinning. The depiction of women's political activities as an extension of their domestic role enabled them to gain social acceptance for an expanded role in society in a way that would not have been possible otherwise.

This statement gains even greater credence when applied to Muslim women's activities in the 1930s and 1940s. As part of the resuscitation of the All-India Muslim League under the leadership of Mohammad Ali Jinnah, a separate Women's Central Sub-Committee was established in 1938. It stimulated unprecedented numbers of women to attend the league's meetings, including the annual session in Lahore in 1940 at which the demand for Pakistan was articulated. From this point, street politics became an accepted pastime for veiled Muslim women, who organized mass processions, public meetings, and fundraising campaigns across India in support of the Muslim League. Indeed, the decisive victory of this party in the elections of 1946 may be attributed in large part to the campaigning efforts of female activists who convinced *burqaʿ*-clad women in urban constituencies to come to the polling stations to vote. Yet women's involvement in the Pakistan movement was too brief to bring any qualitative change to their social status in the long term. Rather, the intertwining of religion with politics has meant that Muslim women's relationship with the state has been fraught with difficulties in the postcolonial era.

Bibliography

A. A. Ali, *The emergence of feminism among Indian Muslim women 1920–1947*, Karachi 2000.

S. N. Amin, *The world of Muslim women in colonial Bengal, 1876–1939*, Leiden 1996.

A. Basu and B. Ray, *Women's struggle. A history of the All India Women's Conference 1927–1990*, New Delhi 1990.

G. Forbes, *Women in modern India*, Cambridge 1996.

S. Ikramullah, *From purdah to parliament*, London 1963, repr. Karachi 1998.

A. Jalal, The convenience of subservience. Women and the state of Pakistan, in D. Kandiyoti (ed.), *Women, Islam and the state*, London 1991, 77–104.

S. Lambert-Hurley, Contesting seclusion. The political emergence of Muslim women in Bhopal, 1901–1930, Ph.D. thesis, University of London 1998.

B. D. Metcalf, *Perfecting women. Mawlana Ashraf ʿAli Thanawi's Bihishti Zewar*, Berkeley 1990.

——, Reading and writing about Muslim women in British India, in Z. Hasan (ed.), *Forging identities. Gender, communities, and the state*, New Delhi 1994, 6–14.

G. Minault, *Secluded scholars. Women's education and Muslim social reform in colonial India*, Delhi 1998.

—— (ed.), *The extended family. Women and political participation in India and Pakistan*, Columbia, Mo. 1981.

—— (trans.), *Voices of silence. English translation of Khwaja Altaf Hussain Hali's Majalis un-nissa and Chup ki dad*, Delhi 1986.

S. H. Mirza, *Muslim women's role in the Pakistan movement*, Lahore 1969.

Q. A. Rasul, *From purdah to parliament. The memoirs of a Muslim woman in Indian politics*, Delhi 2001.

D. Saiyid, *Muslim women of the British Punjab. From seclusion to politics*, London 1998.

J. Shahnawaz, *Father and daughter. A political autobiography*, Lahore 1971, repr. Karachi 2002.

R. F. Woodsmall, *Moslem women enter a new world*, Lahore 1936.

Siobhan Lambert-Hurley

East Asia, Southeast Asia, Australia and Oceania

Introduction

It's queer how out of touch with truth women are. They live in a world of their own, and there had never been anything like it, and never can be (Conrad 1995, 28).

Conrad's words in *Heart of Darkness* (1902) clearly reveal how in colonial narratives the representations of colonized peoples and women tended to coincide or mirror each other. Women were associated with notions of "darkness" and "savage" as opposed to "light" and "civilized"; they represented a potential destabilizing Dionysian or chthonian force, which had to be tamed and controlled to protect the Apollonian, urianian entity of the imperial state. The Nietzschean undertows of imperial images and perceptions are indicative of the aggressively fearful nature of the enterprise. Women, native and non, along with the colonized males embodied the devastating forces of nature, of esoteric and exotic obscurity, primitive, as Mille and Delmaison describe in their novel *La femme et l'homme nu*, in being simultaneously "slave[s] of dominant forces" and sources of the "unleashing of forces" (1924, 118, cf. Ridley 1983, 90–1).

In perusing the literature on colonialism and imperialism in East Asia, Southeast Asia, and Australia/Oceania, one cannot fail to notice the scarce attention paid to the effects that these phenomena have had on shaping the image and role of both migrant and native women in colonial settings. Female agency appears conspicuously absent from the narratives and historiographies of both colonial and nation-building enterprises and when it does appear, it plays an instrumental or structural-functional role in the construction of both the colony and the empire, a function that persisted during the decolonization and nation-building era. Women's bodies were disposed of in a way that served male interests. In the masculine context of the colony both European and native women, as bearers of life and of the imprint of ethnicity, became "instrumental" in the structuring of the foundational ethnic and social differences and relations within the empire (Yuval-Davis and Anthias 1989). As Summers (2002) effectively summarizes, in colonial settings women were "categorized" as either "damned whores" or "God's police." That colonialism and its cognate imperialism were gendered phenomena, giving rise to masculine categories of dominance, appears clear from the metalanguage by and in which the enterprise came to be articulated, which inherently posed as the metaphor and metonymy of masculine dominance over the feminine "other." They were the product or systemic arrangements of masculine discourses, practices, and policies by which colonized peoples were subdued and power relations were structured. The regimentation of the relations between the colonizer and the colonized was deemed essential in order to avoid the entropy brought about by miscegenation and the annihilation of difference and, consequently, of identity.

Exploring the *Status Quaestionis*

At the outset of an analysis of the effects of colonial policies and practices on colonized populations and in particular on women, it is necessary to draw attention to some of the main issues connected to the topic in the geographical setting under examination. First, it must be postulated that colonial policies were framed with reference to the interests of the colonial power, which produced particular practices, as well as discourses, in colonial settings. In East Asia, Southeast Asia, and Australia/Oceania, colonial policies concerning women were designed to structure and systemize the boundaries and the power relations between Europeans and native populations in order to protect the economic and political interests of power groups.

In a vast region in which the discourses of Primitivism and Orientalism often overlap and which is characterized by the presence of several European powers (Great Britain, The Netherlands, France, Portugal, and Spain, the last replaced after 1898 by the United States) and by cultural and religious heterogeneity, the task of analyzing and defining the effects of colonial policies and practices on colonized people proves to be elusive, if not daunting. Notwithstanding the universal approach adopted by the colonial powers in the application and implementation of policies in colonial settlements, which were not tailored to fit specific local realities, these did not produce homogeneous effects. The local culture and religiousness acted, in fact, as a filter or reagent precipitating particular analyses and syntheses *in loco*. As Furnivall states, it is superfluous to argue that the Western powers that colonized the territories in Asia and Oceania have a "fundamental" unity since they share a common "civilization" derived from Greece and Rome and reinterpreted in the light of Christianity (1956, 3). Differences between the policies implemented by colonial governments stemmed from the particularist interests they were pursuing and the fundamental principles informing particular practices. Considering the two major colonial powers in Southeast Asia during the nineteenth century, Great Britain and The Netherlands, the differences appear evident: British colonial policy was based on the principles of the rule of law and economic freedom, whereas the Dutch aimed at "imposing restraints on economic forces by strengthening personal authority and by conserving the influence of custom" (Furnivall 1956, 3). Consequently, while colonial policies appear to be homogeneous, colonial practices come to differ. The analysis of the latter therefore becomes the main focus for understanding the effects that the former had on the structuring of social roles and functions of individual categories.

A second question that must be considered in the context of the study of the effects of colonial policies and practices on the local populace is that colonial partitions brought about the breaking up of cultural areas which were demarcated by the presence of specific values and norms derived from the spread and acceptance of religious beliefs based on either a historical revelation or theophany (Islam, Christianity, and, to a certain extent, Buddhism) or on a philosophical-gnomic system (Confucianism). Although these often were either influenced by or incorporated local customs in the domain of ritual, overall they continued to preserve their intrinsic structural semantics. Disregarding completely the contours of colonial partitions and of modern political geography in this region, in fact, it is possible to distinguish four areas defined by the prominence of a particular religion: the Theravada Buddhist nations of continental Southeast Asia (Thailand, Burma, Vietnam, Laos, Cambodia); the Muslim countries of archipelagic Southeast Asia (Malaysia, Indonesia); the Christian areas of Oceania (Australia, New Guinea, and the Pacific); and the Confucian and Shinto areas of China and Japan respectively. The borders of these areas are not sharp but rather blur and overlap current state borders so that religious enclaves may be found beyond colonial and, later, national boundaries. The implementation of colonial policies, however, notwithstanding the cultural-religious-ethnic heterogeneity of the regions in question, was homogeneous and uniform. Colonial governments considered colonial peoples as a shapeless mass or entity and as a mere "territorial" extension of the colonial power. The policies of the mother country were extended indiscriminately to the colonial periphery.

Women in colonial settings came to epitomize the "colonized mass" as a whole. Since reproduction was the means of perpetuation and transmission of genetic/ethnic markers, it was necessary to control those considered to be the bearers of racial features, namely women. Policies were designed to target the maintenance of ethnic boundaries and perpetuate European dominance. By controlling women, both native and European, through laws regulating mixed marriages, prostitution, and education, it was possible to draw and maintain distinctive ethnic boundaries between the colonizer and the colonized, which constituted the basis for the structuring of political and social relations of dominance and dependency.

The absence of policies discriminating among the heterogeneity of local cultural realities, although indicating the instrumental function of women in colonial settings, makes the task of defining the effects of those policies, particularly on native women, extremely difficult. While European women continued to live within the boundaries of their autochthonous cultural-religious templates even in colonial settings, the status and role of native women presumably underwent radical changes. The analysis of precolonial narratives and of socioeconomic and political patterns in the areas in question reveals that women played an important participatory role in society that complemented that of their male counterparts. Buddhism, Islam, Confucianism, and Animism all acknowledged the important social and economic function of women (Furnivall 1956, 13). It follows that the policies enacted by the Christian colonizers profoundly altered the precolonial balance and complementarity underlying gender relations.

Strange Bedfellows: Religion and Colonial/Imperial Policies and Practices

Religion and religious institutions have been regarded by scholars of all times as playing a functional role in the creation of colonies and empires. The expansion of and conversion to the religion of the colonizer were deemed or envisaged as means to facilitate and foster the stability of colonial rule. Such an approach, however, has been unable to account for the ideological discontinuities and persisting dialectics that characterized colonial settings. As a matter of fact, religious beliefs, values, and norms, sanctioned and transmitted by ritual repetition informed the actions of both colonizers and colonized, shaping particular socioeconomic and political organizations and engendering perceptions of difference and epistemological misunderstandings. If one assumes religion to be the constantly changing product of continuous processes of adaptation to a particular ecosystem, which in turn prompt parallel processes of internal group integration through the linkages of language and the conceptions of time and space, in other words as a system of survival and perpetuation, it appears that religion plays a foundational, rather than functional role in patterning and structuring cultural, political, and socioeconomic templates. Religious motives were not only adduced to justify the colonial/imperial enterprise, but informed the drawing of policies and practices in colonial possessions.

The role and function of women in colonized societies was strongly influenced by religious beliefs and institutions. The spread and acceptance of monotheistic religions (Islam and Christianity) brought about the domestication or social segregation of women. Women's morality became the tool to shape discourses of male dominance and superiority and to preserve cultural and ethnic integrity (Lerner 1986) in the clash/encounter between institutionalized historical religions.

Historians have devoted little attention to the effect colonial policies had on the Muslim women in what can be referred to as the "Muslim Basin" of Southeast Asia, the Indo-Malaysian archipelago. The cause may be attributed to the scarce archival information on women, in particular on those who did not engage in some activity under colonial government control, such as prostitution. The silence of the archives is, however, indicative of the discontinuity characterizing the social history of these regions but also of the subjugation of women in the colonial system. This is not the place to enter the debate regarding the hermeneutics of Islamic law on women and the structuring of their asymmetric position in Islamic society vis-à-vis their male counterparts (Ahmed 1992, Mernissi 1991). It suffices to state that in areas outside the original birthplace of Islam, Muslim religious norms and customs tended to fuse with local popular religiousness. It follows that it is possible that women who lived in the fold of Islam continued to maintain their original pre-Islamic status and role in society. The homogenizing effect, however, of European colonial policies, which aimed at homologating subjected populations, overruled local customs and divested the markers of religious boundaries of their social significance.

It is possible, however, to infer that the policies prompted radical changes in the status, role, and function of Muslim women. On the basis of Islamic law, in fact, women were endowed with a certain degree of freedom. The Qur'ān states that women may inherit and own property (4:6) and are recognized to have rights similar to those exercised against them by their male counterparts, although it is stated that men have a "status above" or precedence over (*daraja*) women (2:226). Although it appears that *daraja* occurs in the context of matters regarding divorce (4:34–8), it is stated that men have, however, *qawwām*, that is authority, over women since they have an obligation or moral duty to protect and support them (Bowker 1999, 1043). In Muslim societies and communities of the Indo-Malay archipelago the norms of Islam regulating gender relations were generally applied matching the role of women under local *adat*.

Colonial policies brought about the abrogation of many precolonial norms and practices. In Malaysia, in stark contrast with the policy of non-interference in matters affecting Malay custom and religion declared in the 1874 Pangkor Treaty, the British enacted policies that gradually contributed to weaken the Islamic factor in the life of the Malays (Cowan 1961). In the courts civil servants tended to refer to British statutory law practices in preference to those of Sharīʿa or *adat* (Sadka 1968, 156). For instance in the cases of Muslim children who were declared illegitimate by Islamic courts, British judges made them legitimate, overruling also the granting of custody to the father (Ahmad 1973). It follows that colonial practices weakened the position of women in Islamic communities and in colonial settings as a whole, inaugurating a trend that would continue during the decolonization and nation-building phase.

As stated earlier, women in colonial settings were listed under the categories of either "damned whores" or "God's police." The former was mainly the reserve of native women who became concubines of European settlers or prostitutes in brothels to serve the needs of European men; the latter encompassed the European women who came to the colonies to protect and police male morality and genetic integrity. The extension of the 1864 Contagious Disease Act to British colonial possessions led to the registration of prostitutes and the definition of women's roles and responsibilities. The act was designed not to abolish prostitution but to place sex work in the hands of the male state (McClintock 1995, 288–9). The Dutch implemented an analogous policy in their Indonesian possessions at the turn of the twentieth century in an attempt to curtail the negative effects of concubinage (Ming 1983) and prostitution (Hesselink 1987), which, if left unchecked, posed a serious threat to white male fertility and the propagation and perpetuation of the white race in colonial contexts. The policies coincided with the arrival of European women in the colonies, as wives of settlers and officials, who had been instructed in the mother country before departure in regard to their role in the colony (Stoler 1991).

The regulation of sex relations and the enactment of eugenic policies were deemed essential, if not vital, by European colonial governments in order to establish effective and stable rule. European motherhood, consequently, came to be placed at the center of the programs of empire-building as a means to regiment male morality as well as to provide an example to native women of a civilized and morally appropriate way of life. Wives of missionaries, for instance, who worked side by side with their spouses in colonial settlements, were regarded as having a "gracious influence of wise and thoughtful womanhood" on local women (Langmore 1989, 165–84). White women, as the bearers and breeders of ethnic markers, consequently had to be protected. In 1926 in British New Guinea the White Women's Protection Ordinance was issued to protect white women, and indirectly whiteness, from the "black peril." In Indonesia, although in 1901 the Dutch enacted the so-called Ethical Policy, which called for consideration of native *adat*, this was accompanied by the simultaneous enactment of welfare programs concerning parents and parenting, servants, orphanages, nurse maids, and nurseries (Stoler 2002, 1996). In 1898, the Mixed Marriage Law, which called for the abrogation of polygamy had been issued (Stoler 2002, 101–6). The motive adduced to its promulgation was that it aimed at protecting native men's rights. In reality it went to correct the 1848 Civil Code, which, ruling that marriage partners of European and native standing were subject to European law, allowed European men living in concubinage with native women (*nyai*) to legalize their union and legitimate their mestizo children. Policies regulating marriage arrangements were also implemented in British Malaya, in particular in regard to child marriage. The Age of Consent Act of 1891 raised the age of consent to sexual relations for girls from 10 to 12 and the Child Marriage Restraint Act of 1929 forbade marriages of girls below the age of 14. In the Dutch East Indies laws of this kind were never promulgated: child marriages took place in the form of betrothal to be followed later by marriage. Muslim women maintained a certain degree of freedom in particular in matters regarding divorce and property (Keddie 1990, Locher-Scholten 2000, 193–6).

During the 1930s, amendments introduced to the law in order to protect European women who married Indo-Malay men generated a debate within the Muslim community instigated by local Muslim women and religious authorities in both Indonesia (Locher-Scholten 2000, 187–209) and Malaysia (Manderson 1980, 17–18, 22–4), which brought about its withdrawal. Muslim Indonesians argued that such a law subverted the issue of marriage and gender relations in Islam (Locher-Scholten 2000, 187–8) since women and family law play an essential role in the preservation of Islamic unity and identity (Eickelman and Piscatori 1996, 83–94). The colonial government argued that the law inherently aimed at protecting European women against Muslim practices in inter-religious and inter-ethnic marriages. In reality it acted as a means for preventing European properties from falling into the hands of Muslim subjects, which would have led to a change in European practices of inheritance and property ownership. The law, however, encroached upon the structural semantics of Islamic *ḥadīth* (tradition) and consequently its application was strongly resisted, generating widespread calls for its abrogation. What emerges from the dynamics and dialectics of the debate is that the categories of race, gender, and class came to intersect with those of religion (Locher-Scholten 2000, 209–10), placing the latter at the center of the structuring of inter-ethnic relations and later of nationalist ideologies.

Conclusions

Colonial policies and practices prompted cultural and social change in the autochthonous templates of colonized populations. These changes are evident when comparing precolonial cultural templates with the programs of nation-building and state-crafting implemented during the decolonization era. The hiatus that exists between the two periods not only indicates the deep transformations that took place during colonial rule but also calls for a re-examination of the dynamics and dialectics of anti-colonial struggles and resistance. Colonized populations, in a frenzy to shake off the yoke of European dominance, did not completely reverse the practices that generated particular gender relations. Women's bodies continued to represent the *tabula* on which to draw nationalist ideologies and policies. The control of the reproductive function of women was vital to the reproduction and perpetuation of the nation and to the legitimacy of claims of nationhood. Presumably the veiling of women in Islamic societies was prompted by the need to preserve community, and later national, integrity and unity: the discussion regarding the asymmetric position of women in Islam vis-à-vis their male counterparts should, therefore, be set in the particular context and regarded as a legacy of the effects of colonial practices and policies.

Bibliography

I. Ahmad, The administration of Islamic law in Southeast Asia, in *Islamic Culture* 57 (1973), 37–55.
L. Ahmed, *Women and gender in Islam. Historical roots of a modern debate*, New Haven, Conn. 1992.
J. Bowker (ed.), *The Oxford dictionary of word religions*, Oxford 1999.

J. Conrad, *Heart of darkness*, London 1995.
C. D. Cowan and O. W. Wolters, *Nineteenth century Malaya. Origins of British political control*, London 1961.
D. Eickelman and J. Piscatori (eds.), *Muslim politics*, Princeton, N.J. 1996.
J. S. Furnivall, *Colonial policy and practice. A comparative study of Burma and Netherlands India*, New York 1956.
L. Hesselink, Prostitution, a necessary evil particularly in the colonies. Views on prostitution in the Netherlands Indies, in E. Locher-Scholten and A. Niehof (eds.), *Indonesian women in focus. Past and present notions*, Dordrecht 1987, 205–24.
E. Keddie, The past and present of women in the Muslim world, in *World History* 1 (1990), 77–108.
D. Langmore, *Missionary lives. Papua, 1874–1914*, Honolulu 1989.
G. Lerner, *The origins of patriarchy*, New York 1986.
E. Locher-Scholten, *Women and the colonial state*, Amsterdam 2000.
L. Manderson, *Women, politics and change*, Oxford 1980.
A. McClintock, *Imperial leather. Race, gender and sexuality in the colonial contest*, New York 1995.
F. Mernissi, *Women and Islam. A historical and theological enquiry*, Oxford 1991.
P. Mille and A. Delmaison, *La femme et l'homme nu*, Paris 1924.
H. Ming, Barracks-concubinage in the Indies, 1887–1920, in *Indonesia* 35 (1983), 65–93.
H. Ridley, *Images of imperial rule*, New York 1983.
E. Sadka, *The protected Malay states, 1874–1895*, Kuala Lumpur 1968.
A. L. Stoler, Carnal knowledge and imperial power, in M. Leonardo (ed.), *Gender at the crossroads of knowledge*, Berkeley 1991, 82–5.
——, A sentimental education. Native servants and the cultivation of European children in the Netherlands Indies, in L. J. Sears (ed.), *Fantasizing the feminine in Indonesia*, Durham, N.C. 1996, 71–91.
——, *Carnal knowledge and imperial power. Race and the intimate in colonial rule*, Berkeley 2002.
A. Summers, *Damned whores and God's police*, Camberwell, Vic. 2002.
N. Yuval-Davis and F. Anthias (eds.), *Women, nation, state*, Houndmills, Basingstoke, Hampshire 1989.

Susanna G. Rizzo

Egypt

The onset of British occupation of Egypt in 1882 dealt a critical blow to independent Egyptian modernization and signaled the colonial restructuring of the society. Nowhere were the new relations of power between colonizer and colonized more apparent than in the area of gender relations and policies. British colonial government used the education of Egyptian women to prove its civilizing mission to its Oriental subjects. While some women writers ignored and/or were critical of that Orientalist discourse, which assumed the inferiority of the Orient and the superiority of the Occident, many men and women internalized it in their writings on gender roles and relations. More seriously, Egyptian nationalists found themselves in the paradoxical position of having to defend the status of women in Islamic societies while recognizing the need to overcome their backwardness. As a result, their gender discourses and policy agendas reflected a strong underlying belief in the necessity of following in the footsteps of the Occident as a developmental other.

ʿĀʾisha Taymūr's *Natāʾij al-ahwāl fi al-aqwāl wa al-afʿāl* (Consequences of changing conditions as they relate to speech and deeds) offered the first commentary on the crises of dynastic government and community that paved the way for British occupation and colonialism. Published in 1888 under strict British censorship, it stressed the need to struggle to overcome these crises through the transformation of Islamic traditions as a guide for the reorganization of the key political, economic, and social institutions of society. With that aim, Taymūr advocated the nationalization of dynastic government and the overcoming of class cleavages through the revival of fraternal relations of solidarity and the downsizing of polygamous marriages as means of infusing Islamic society with new sources of dynamism (Taymur 1888).

In contrast, Syrian Christian and Jewish women, who were graduates of missionary schools where the Orientalist discourse on knowledge and society was part of the curriculum, used a derivative of that discourse in the earliest women's journals calling on the Orient to copy the gender roles in the Occident. Toward that goal, the early journals, which included Hind Nawfal's *al-Fatā* (Girl, 1892), Louisa Habbalin's *al-Firdaws* (Paradise, 1896), Maryam Mazhar's *Mirʾat al-ḥasnāʾ* (Mirror of beauty, 1896), Alexandra Avierino's *Anīs al-jalīs* (The familiar companion, 1898), and Esther Azhuri's *al-ʿĀʾila* (Family, 1899), emphasized womens' education as part of the development of modern domesticity in the family (Baron 1994, Fawwaz n.d., 7–16, Hatem 2002).

When in the 1890s the British colonial government finally turned its attention to education in general and girls' education in particular, it declared itself to be committed to the expansion of girls' education as part of the civilizing mission. Paradoxically, its educational policy was restrictive (Tucker 1985, 125) and focused on the acquisition of basic literacy skills at the elementary school (*kuttab*) level and channeling very young girls into the study of domestic sciences (ibid. 126). It ended free public education for girls and relied on private schools to satisfy the needs of the middle classes.

This represented a break with the precolonial

educational policy where the approach was less gendered and less restrictive. It is best described by the three public schools that catered to the educational needs of young girls before 1882 and the changes that they had to endure under British control. The oldest of these schools was for midwives and was established in 1832. At the beginning, it had difficulty recruiting students, but eventually it attracted many working-class girls who upon graduation were employed by the state in the different provinces (Kuhnke 1990). In 1888, the school was transformed into a British-style nursing school in which students were trained to be helpers of male physicians who from then on monopolized the study and the practice of obstetrics to which the early graduates had access (Mahfouz 1935, 75–76). The other two public schools located in Cairo, al-Suyufiyya (1873) and Qurabiyya (1875), provided general education for girls. In the 1880s, the two schools were combined into one as al-Madrasa al-Saniyya in 1889 with a curriculum that reflected the new emphasis on domestic sciences. The first graduates of al-Saniyya, who included the feminist writer Malak Ḥifnī Nāsif and the distinguished educator Nabawiyya Mūsā, went on to train at the Teachers' College in 1901 and eventually worked as teachers at schools for girls (Kamal 2001, 179). Even though private primary education for girls continued to expand during the first two decades of the twentieth century, the establishment of preparatory and secondary school education for girls had to wait for Egyptian formal independence in 1923.

The rudimentary colonial view of girls' education was shared by Egyptian nationalists and modernists who claimed to be supporters of the liberation of women. Among them was judge Qāsim Amīn, who with other Egyptian nationalists such as Saʿd Zaghlūl, the Egyptian minister of education in 1906, worked closely with the British consul, Lord Cromer. Amīn apologetically defended Islamic gender practices in response to the Orientalist attack by Duc d'Harcourt's *L'Egypte and les Egyptiens* (1894) and then used his book *Taḥrīr al-marʾa* (The liberation of women), published in 1899, to reiterate the negative Orientalist representations of Islamic society and to blame Muslim women for its backwardness (Hatem 2002, 17–21). Unfortunately, the title of the book, its call for the abolition of the veil, and the attack launched against it by Muslim conservatives led most readers and analysts to assume that it had a progressive message. Recent analyses have moved beyond this superficial view to criticize Amīn's embrace of the colonial views of Lord Cromer (Ahmed 1992, 155–57) and the assumptions and categories of the Orientalist discourse (Hatem 2002, 17–21).

The colonial government had hoped that its abolition of corvée labor and the downsizing of the draft system would make it popular among the peasant classes. In fact, peasant men and women continued to view British soldiers in their midst with hostility (Tucker 1985, 145–6), culminating in the outbreak of violence in Dinshway (1907) where soldiers shooting pigeons accidentally shot a peasant woman and set fire to a barn, causing the peasants to attack them. In response, the colonial government whipped and executed the peasants involved.

The new colonial economy, which relied on the presence of a large landowning class and their support, did not improve the economic conditions of the peasant majority. Their plight was ignored by the modernist nationalist intellectuals of the early period who either maintained friendly relations with the Egyptian landed classes or were themselves members of that class. For example, Qāsim Amīn presented a simultaneously romantic and condescending view of peasant women and men in his writings. He argued that unlike the urban well-to-do women who were unproductive and did not share their husbands' education, peasant women were the economic partners of their husbands and shared their level of knowledge. In his view, peasant men and women led a "naive Beduin-like existence where the needs of the family were limited" (Amīn 1984, 32, 42).

The romanticization of the work of rural women overlooked their poverty and limited the satisfaction of their many needs. During the early part of the twentieth century, urban poor women faced equally difficult work conditions in the markets and in cigarette factories (Sālim 1984, 20). These conditions of work differed markedly from those facing middle-class women who developed an interest in public work in the first decade of the twentieth century. Their education provided them with better material, if not social, conditions as the memoirs of Nabawiyya Mūsā suggest. It was understood that working middle-class women had to leave their jobs once they were married. Malak Ḥifni Nāsif, one of the first graduates of al-Saniyya school, ended her teaching career when she married the notable ʿAbd al-Sattār al-Bāsil bek. More atypical was Nabawiyya Mūsā, the prominent educator, who chose not to marry and had a long career teaching first in public schools and then in her own private schools.

While Mūsā supported women's right to education and work in her writings, Nāsif developed the earliest and most powerful critique of the modernist-nationalist discourse espoused by the *al-Jarīda* group (which included Amīn and Zaghlūl), especially its blame of Egyptian women for the backwardness of the Muslim family and the society. As the only woman writer who had a column in the mainstream *al-Jarīda* newspaper, she suggested that men were using this new discourse and the goal of liberating women to impose their gender agenda on women, belittling the latter's perspective on such matters as the veil, polygamy, and public policy (El-Sadda 1994, 1998). In an effort to develop a distinct voice for women, Nāsif argued that the abolition of the veil was less important than changing the social and economic conditions that were responsible for the subordination of women. She also underlined the continuing role that men played in the reproduction of conditions that oppress women through polygamy, divorce, and resistance to an expanded public presence of women (Hatem 2001, 31–2).

The death of Nāsif in 1918, at the age of thirty-two, evoked numerous public testimonials by men and women that acknowledged her contributions to the development of an independent voice for women. The outbreak of a national revolution in 1919, calling for the end of British rule, contributed to a switch in perspective that strengthened the leading role played by the male nationalist elite and their modernist-nationalist discourse in shaping the public agendas of women. Upper- and middle-class women were mobilized by the women's committee of the Wafd party, which led the revolution. While the newspapers of the period pointed out that urban working-class women participated in industrial strikes, with rural women joining their men in the demolition of railway tracks and telegraph poles, the upper- and middle-class women's peaceful orderly demonstration monopolized national and international attention. The Wafd's women's committee also organized a successful boycott of British goods and wrote to local and international newspapers as well as to the British government voicing their views on the political issues of the day (al-Subkī 1986, 25).

The political mobilization of women in support of the 1919 revolution contributed to their co-optation by the nationalist discourse and its gender agenda. For example, Hūdā Shaʿrāwī, whose husband was an original member of the Wafd, concurred with the leaders of the revolution that Egyptian women were not yet ready for political rights. She utilized the new visibility and the skills she developed as one of the leaders of the Wafd's women's committee in the formation of the Egyptian Feminist Union in 1923, which undertook the task of preparing women for these rights through education and extensive social work among the poorer classes. As one of the wealthiest Egyptian women of her time, she quickly allied the union with the International Alliance for Women's suffrage, embracing its Western gender agenda and attending its different international conferences (Shaʿrāwī 1981, 248–60). Here, the desire for national independence from British colonialism did not coincide with the rejection of Western feminist agendas. These remained as the only social and political model for feminist organizing in Egypt. The union, its French journal, *L'Egyptienne* (1925–40), and the Arabic journal, *al-Miṣrīyāt* (1937–40) appealed to an audience that was primarily Westernized and well-to-do (Badran 1995).

Like the Western women of the alliance, the union used its dispensary and domestic school to present itself as the caretaker of women of poorer classes, seeking to socialize them into middle- and upper-class domesticity with classes that taught them family hygiene and genteel domestic skills such as sewing (Mariscotti 1994). The result was another variant of the hegemonic modernist-nationalist discourse first introduced by Amīn at the end of the nineteenth century that sanctioned domesticity as the primary role of women. Not only was this discourse oblivious of the fact that urban and rural working-class women have always had to juggle work inside and outside the home, but it also ignored the professional aspirations of middle-class women who were increasingly interested in public work. By the time Shaʿrāwī died in 1947, other middle-class women's organizations, such as Bint al-Nīl led by Durriyya Shafīq, began to eclipse the Egyptian Feminist Union with a platform that addressed the more complex political and professional needs of this new generation of women (Nelson 1996). The 1952 revolution, which put an end to colonial rule, embraced this new middle-class agenda and used it as a source of national and international support.

In conclusion, the gender claim of the civilizing mission of colonial rule proved empty. It did not improve the economic, social, or political conditions under which women lived or worked. Nor was it associated with the advancement of women and/or their rights. The prominent Orientalist assumptions and categories of the colonial discourse indirectly influenced the development of the modernist-nationalist discourse that constructed the identities of Egyptian men and women, their views of themselves and of each other. It privileged the views of middle- and upper-class men as the agents of modernity and treated women as the party responsible for the backwardness of the nation. This discourse continues to shape postcolonial society. The results of its modernizing project are modest at best. More seriously, it failed to give women an independent voice and has historically survived by enlisting the support of middle- and upper-class women for a narrow social agenda that neglects the needs of their rural and urban working-class counterparts.

BIBLIOGRAPHY

L. Ahmed, *Women and gender in Islam*, New Haven, Conn. 1992, 155–7.

Q. Amīn, *Taḥrīr al-marʾa*, Cairo 1984.

M. Badran, *Feminists, Islam and nation*, Princeton, N.J. 1995, chapter 5.

B. Baron, *The women's awakening in Egypt*, New Haven, Conn. 1994), chapters 1, 6, 7.

H. Elsadda, Malak Ḥifnī Nāsif. Ḥalqa mafqūda min tārīkh al-nahḍa, in *Ḥajar* 2 (1994), 109–19.

——, Notions of modernity. Representation of the "Western woman" by female authors in early twentieth century Egypt, in *The Arabs and Britain. Changes and exchanges*, Proceedings of a Conference organized by the British Council 23–5 March 1998, Cairo 1998, 352–66.

Z. Fawwaz, *al-Durr al-manthūr fī rabaṭ ṭabaqāt al-khudūr*, Kuwait n.d.

M. Hatem, Malak Ḥifnī Nāsif bayn ru'ya qadīma wa-jadīda, in H. al-Ṣadda (ed.), *Min rāʾidāt al-qarn al-ʿishrīn. Shakhṣīyāt wa qaḍāyā*, Cairo 2001.

——, *The nineteenth century discursive roots of the continuing debate on the social contract in today's Egypt*, San Domenico, Italy 2002.

H. Kamal, Muḥāḍarāt al-faraʿ al-nisāʾ fī al-jāmiʿa al-miṣriyya, in H. al-Ṣadda (ed.), *Min rāʾidāt al-qarn al-ʿishrīn. Shakhṣīyāt wa qaḍāyā*, Cairo 2001.

L. Kuhnke, *Lives at risk. Public health in nineteenth-century Egypt*, Cairo 1990, chapter 7.

N. Bey Mahfouz, *The history of medical education in Egypt*, Cairo 1935.

C. Mariscotti, Consent and resistance. The history of upper and middle class Egyptian women reflected through their published journals, 1925–1939, Ph.D. diss., Temple University 1994, chapters 2–3.

C. Nelson, *Doria Shafik. Egyptian Feminist*, Cairo 1996, chapter 8.

L. M. Sālim, *al-Marʾa al-Miṣriyya wa-al-taghyīr al-ijtimāʿī 1919–1945*, Cairo 1984.

H. Shaʿrāwī, *Mudhakkirāt Hudā Shaʿrāwī rāʾidat al-marʾa al-ʿArabiyya al-ḥadītha*, Cairo 1981.

A. K. B. al-Subkī, *al-Ḥaraka al-nisāʾiyya fī Miṣr mā bayna al-thawratayn 1919–1936*, Cairo 1986.

ʿĀʾisha Taymūr, *Natāʾij al-ahwāl fi al-aqwāl wa al-afʿāl*, Cairo 1888, chapters 1, 3.

J. E. Tucker, *Women in nineteenth-century Egypt*, Cambridge 1985.

MERVAT F. HATEM

French North Africa

The position of women in colonial society in North Africa was ambiguous; so too was the question of gender. European women were from the perceived "superior" civilization. As such they were above North African men and women in the colonial hierarchy but below European men. North African women were at the base of the gender pyramid. Colonial gender frameworks were more traditional than in metropolitan France, making their circumvention complex. Perceptions of women and women's agency in the colonial enterprise were also complicated by the fact that the military dominated the early years of colonial conquest and rule in Algeria (1830–70) and Morocco (1907–34). In addition, French occupation of Algeria, considered to be a part of France, preceded that of the two protectorates, Tunisia (1882) and Morocco (1912), by 52 and 82 years respectively. These factors shaped the experiences of women in the three regions of French North Africa in different ways.

During the military administration in Algeria little interest was shown in women, whatever their origin. The French/European civilian population was small and suffered from high mortality. Women who survived experienced the hardships of a pioneering society. Their agency in the colonial enterprise and their contact with local women were limited to the private sphere. As for North African women, a few officers chose wives from the two main ethnic groups, Arab and Berber, but on the whole their condition was deemed to be lamentable and was often cited as evidence of the inferiority of Islamic civilization. The French did make some distinction between Arab and Berber women, the latter being seen to be more independent than Arab women. French troops in Algeria were struck by the fact that Kabyle (a sub-group of the Berbers) women had joined in the fray of battle ululating and urging their warriors on to victory. This perceived Amazonian quality differentiated them from Arab women.

As colonization progressed, artists seeking exotic inspiration came to North Africa. Their influence contributed to the fabrication of the "Oriental" female as exotically erotic. Men (Delacroix, Fromentin, Chassériau) as well as women (Smith-Bodichon, Anderson) contributed to this development, which was extended, during the twentieth century, to the art forms of literature and photography. Sexuality was therefore a mediating framework between the cultures of France and North Africa.

The ambiguous nature of colonial practices and processes toward indigenous women arose out of their objectification and the contradictory images that emerged during the early decades of colonial rule in Algeria. As colonization progressed and spread to Tunisia and Morocco, the belief that women were a possible key to successful assimilation was added to perceptions of their backwardness or eroticism. If the French could access their private lives and erode their status as guardians of local tradition by instilling French values the women would pass them on to their children. To educate North African women, the French would have to break down the barriers of cultural resistance that had developed during the occupation. French women, the colonial authorities believed, were best suited to this task. In 1900 the French feminist Hubertine Auclert wrote a treatise on the condition of Algerian women. Derogatory in tone, it was not anticolonial but rather an appeal to the colonial authorities to improve the Algerian woman's lot. As they settled into the Maghrib some French women followed in Auclert's footsteps in an attempt to draw North African women into the French fold (Bugéja 1921, Célarie 1925).

North African women's response to these and other attempts at their colonization varied over time and space. During the early decades of colonization, North African women were encumbered with a double yoke of domination: colonial and gender. Algerian women undoubtedly felt the colonial burden most intensely due to the length and intensity of the French occupation. Land sequestration and the imposition of French legal structures caused material and moral deprivation that affected women with particular intensity. The commodification of land and the French principle that all land was alienable had an impact on family structure and size. Together with the imposition of heavy taxation and protracted warfare (in Algeria and Morocco) families had to sell their land to meet the costs of occupation. Furthermore, until the Second World War, with the exception of the elites and some urbanites, most North African women remained illiterate, making it difficult for them to respond to juridical and fiscal constraints. Women reacted to the changes in their situation by retrenching within the family, which became a bulwark against colonialism. Until the final stages of the nationalist struggle for independence, women's resistance was largely passive. It was effective, nonetheless, insofar as they created an oral tradition of anticolonialism that was passed from one generation to the next.

North African women did not, however, remain totally removed from colonial society. Large numbers of them entered domestic service in settler homes. Whereas the relationship between the two groups of women symbolized the colonial framework and represented the major contact point between the two, it nonetheless served as a site of acculturation for both.

Schools for girls were established in North Africa on a sporadic basis in the period following the Ferry laws (1880s). To begin with their focus was on skill acquisition, whether it was French-style home management or proficiency in certain arts and crafts. Missionary schools were among the first to appear, but due to parental reticence in the face of a Christian environment, enrolment was limited. From 1919 onwards there was a slow expansion of educational opportunities for women, but women only really started to enjoy the privileges of education after 1945. A French education introduced women to French republican concepts providing them with the intellectual arsenal with which to refute colonialism. At decolonization, therefore, educated North African women, such as the Tunisian Gisèle Halimi, entered the public arena taking their place alongside their male counterparts. It was not only an educated minority that took part in the struggles for independence, however. Literate and illiterate alike, North African women joined and aided the nationalist movements in the hope of ridding themselves of the double yoke of colonialism and gender inequality. Although they achieved the former, the latter proved to be a longer struggle.

Bibliography

M. Alloula, *The colonial harem*, trans. M. Godzich and W. Godzich, Minneapolis 1981, 1986[2].

H. Auclert, *Les femmes arabes en Algérie*, Paris 1900.

M. Bugéja, *Nos soeurs musulmanes*, Algiers 1921.

H. Célarie, *Nos soeurs musulmanes. Scènes de la vie du désert*, Paris 1925.

J. Clancy-Smith, La femme arabe. Women and sexuality in France's North African empire, in A. E. Sonbol (ed.), *Women, the family, and divorce laws in Islamic history*, New York 1996, 52–63.

——, Gender, work and handicraft production in colonial North Africa, in M. L. Meriwether and J. E. Tucker (eds.), *A social history of women and the family in the Middle East*, Boulder, Colo. 1999, 25–62.

——, L'école rue du Pacha à Tunis. L'éducation de la femme arabe et "la plus grande France" (1900–1914), in *Clio. Histoire, femmes et sociétés* 12 (2000), 33–55.

——, Educating the Muslim woman in colonial North Africa, in B. Baron and R. Matthee (eds.), *Iran and beyond. Essays in Middle Eastern history in honor of Nikki Keddie*, Costa Mesa 2000, 99–118.

M. Lazreg, *The eloquence of silence. Algerian women in question*, London 1994.

S. Monneret, *L'Orient des peintres*, Paris 1989.

Patricia M. E. Lorcin

Middle East, British

With its vast imperial holdings in the nineteenth and twentieth centuries, Great Britain ruled over millions of Muslim women. Often using women's social roles as benchmarks of civilization, British imperial agents used women to legitimate their imperial oppression of indigenous societies in vast areas of the Islamic world, including large territories in the Arab Middle East. However, although imperial agents claimed their agendas were meant to advance women's social positions, the experience of imperialism was often less than rewarding for women's personal and public lives.

At its height, the British Empire was deeply entrenched in the Arab world, directly administering and/or controlling the governments of Egypt, Sudan, Palestine, Transjordan (now Jordan), Aden (now in the Republic of Yemen), Kuwait, Iraq, Qatar, Bahrain, and Oman. Some nations, such as Egypt, were directly ruled, while others, such as Iraq and Transjordan, were established as mandatory nations with Arab monarchs at the head of government. In all of these territories, British imperialists assaulted local Islamic culture from several angles in the name of women's liberation. Male political leaders, feminists, and missionaries were all anxious to denigrate local leadership and culture in the name of freeing local women from oppression. However, an unavoidable consequence of such a tactic was tremendous resentment against the imperialists, whom their subjects viewed as hypocrites unwilling to admit their real goals for imperial control: the exploitation of local people and resources to create greater wealth and power for Britain.

One of the most decisive locations for gendered rhetoric in the British Empire was in Egypt. Formally occupied by Britain in 1882, British rulers often used what Leila Ahmed (1992) has called "colonial feminism" to claim the need for British rule in the name of liberating Egyptian women from native patriarchy. Casting Islam as a primary force oppressing Egyptian women, the British leader Lord Cromer used visible markers such as the *ḥijāb* and the practice of maintaining harems as evidence for his case in destroying local autonomy in Egypt. Cromer claimed that British rule would usher in a new era for Egyptian women, at the expense of Islamic leadership and culture, which he believed was morally and spiritually corrupt.

However, British policies focused on window-dressing, rather than actual change for the betterment of native women's lives. A highly sexualized discourse denigrating the practices of veiling and polygamy drove anti-Islamic theories in the imperial theater and the metropole, while imperial policies continued to decrease women's actual mobility through society. For instance, the British government in Egypt increased tuition costs for elementary education, making education for girls less accessible, at the same time that leaders such as Cromer were decrying education statistics among Muslims in the empire.

Such practices were often interpreted by British subjects as typical of an oppressive ruling elite out to destroy native leadership and values. At the same time, they were reinforced by other Britons working in non-official capacities to promote the empire's social, spiritual, and political leadership in Islamic nations. Feminists sought to export ideas about women's social and political participation to Arab women, while missionaries were eager to convert Muslim and Christian Arabs to Protestantism. Although these groups did not always agree in Great Britain, missionaries and feminists alike expended tremendous energy abroad to establish their ideals of domesticity, education, and spirituality. They also reached out to Muslim women living outside the purview of direct imperial rule, hoping to erode indigenous patriarchy in places such as the Ottoman Empire. In this way, they paved the way for more formal colonial rule in places such as Palestine before the Ottoman Empire was dismantled after the First World War.

Missionary bodies such as the Church Missionary Society, the Society for Promoting Female Education in the East, the Jerusalem and the East Mission, and the London Missionary Society established scores of churches, schools, and "houses of industry" aimed at drawing Muslim women away from Islam and toward Protestant Christianity. The predominant discourse directed toward would-be converts was a firm belief that Islam was an evil religion, and an indicator of its wickedness was the seclusion and veiling of women. Although missionaries often found themselves in conflict with British governmental authorities, their message of the superiority of British modes of religion, domesticity, and child-rearing usually assisted the larger imperial effort to expand British influence and domination.

British feminists, too, traveled throughout the empire, disseminating their beliefs in women's education and public participation among Muslim women. They often focused their attention on a desire to remove the veil from the bodies of Muslim women, attacking the cultural context of Islamic civilization and promoting Western dress as the first step toward Westernization in other aspects of life as well. British feminists put forward their nation's models of education, dress, and marriage practice among imperial subjects, even at a time when they themselves did not have equal property rights in their own country, or the right to vote or attend most institutions of higher learning. Although frequently fighting their own battles against patriarchy at home, they were actively engaged in supporting the expansion of British patriarchy abroad, in the name of women's liberation.

In the wake of social, political, and spiritual attacks on local culture, some Muslims living under British rule came to adopt values promoted by the imperial elite. However, many embraced ideals of Westernization in an effort to combat imperial authority. Qāsim Amīn, for example, became an advocate for women's education and the expansion of women's public participation in Egypt as a result of his experiences in Europe. Ardently convinced of the superiority of Western nations, he nonetheless advocated the adoption of Western models in an effort to regain independence (ʿAmara 1976). Amīn, and other subjects of the British, had something in common with the imperialists. Like them, he used local women's social positions, their physical presences, and their religious values as indicators of the worth of native attitudes. By embracing colonial ideologies of Muslim women, Amīn and others inadvertently reinforced them.

The result of British colonial practices on the lives of the millions of Muslim women ruled by the empire in the Middle East was mixed. As feminist and nationalist movements emerged in colonized lands, women struggled to shine a spotlight on the patriarchies that oppressed their full participation in society, both local and colonial. However, the association between imperialism and Western feminism, and the subsequent denigration of Islam by British politicians, missionaries, and feminists, laid the groundwork for deep distrust between colonized people and those espousing their ideas about women's roles in native societies. Some women embraced colonial notions, others cast them aside; but throughout the British Empire, Muslim women were used by colonizers and colonized as templates for or against their particular sociopolitical agendas.

Arab nationalists were eager to rally women to the cause of independence, and women in Egypt, Palestine, and other Middle Eastern nations organized conferences and demonstrations calling for more inclusive political and personal rights for women in the context of independent nations free from British rule. However, nationalist leaders, like the imperialists, did not extend substantial rights to women once the British relinquished control, despite their use of women's issues to bolster their struggles for independence. This resulted, in part, in the continued festering of the Woman Question, promoted by imperialists during their rule of the Middle East, deep into the postcolonial era. Such reification of women's existence continues to stand as a potent and contentious point between Muslims in former colonial nations and Westerners, long since the end of British rule in Muslim countries.

BIBLIOGRAPHY

L. Ahmed, *Women and gender in Islam. Historical roots of a modern debate*, New Haven, Conn. 1992.

M. ʿAmara (ed.), *al-Aʿmāl al-kāmila li Qāsim Amīn*, 2 vols., Beirut 1976.

M. Badran, *Feminists, Islam, and the nation. Gender and the making of modern Egypt*, Princeton, N.J. 1995.

N. Chaudhuri and M. Strobel (eds.), *Western women and imperialism. Complicity and resistance*, Bloomington, Ind. 1992.

E. Fleischmann, *The nation and its "new" women. The Palestinian women's movement, 1920–1948*, Berkeley 2003.

B. Melman, *Women's Orients. English women and the Middle East, 1718–1918. Sexuality, religion and work*, Ann Arbor 1992, 1995².

E. W. Said, *Orientalism*, New York 1978.

NANCY L. STOCKDALE

Russian Colonial Domains of the Caucasus and Central Asia

The social environment of Muslim women in the Islamic parts of Russia, which included Azerbaijan and today's Central Asia (that is, Kazakhstan, Kyrgyzstan, Turkmenistan, Tajikistan, and Uzbekistan) during the Tsarist period (1865–1917) is a topic not extensively studied. Despite this intellectual hindrance, there is some evidence that the Tsarist government reinforced the hierarchical, patriarchal social structure of the Islamic lands by choosing not to disturb ancient attitudes that had been held over millennia.

The history of Central Asia and its surrounding region has been shaped by Persian, Turkic, and to a lesser extent, Mongolian and Arab cultures, which at the beginning, or at least in time, respected the cultural and religious practices of the population. The emergence of Russia, a Christian, Slavic power, however, appeared to change that and created a major dilemma and concern for the Muslim population. Unlike previous conquerors, this new power was not going to integrate itself, culturally or religiously, with the Muslim population. The leaders of the Islamic areas made every effort to confront this new power, ranging from military battles to intellectual clashes, and to defend their cultural and religious independence. The final result was a social and legal concession by the Russians not to interfere in the Muslim population's social and, at times, legal practices.

This attitude developed partly as a result of the

Russians' own beliefs in gender inequality but more importantly because of their understanding of the role Islam would play in this part of the empire. Aware of the relationship between Islam and culture and the danger in directly challenging this arrangement, the Russians established an unwritten contract with the leaders of the Muslim republics to allow them to maintain certain practices that were based on cultural as well as religious traditions. The non-interference agreement encompassed several different elements, each reinforcing the patriarchal social structure of the Muslim population. One was the infusion of religious doctrine and law into the daily activities of the Muslim population.

Because the center of social as well as religious life of every city was the mosque, the religious leaders, the *ʿulamāʾ*, codified customs that they deemed best for the society through religious decrees and Islamic education, thereby religiously endorsing attitudes toward women. By interpreting Islam in a manner that supported their individual views on women and the society as a whole, the *ʿulamāʾ* prevented any direct challenge to their authority, because they invoked the Qurʾān and hence claimed divine sanction. At times, however, religious interpretations varied from republic to republic. In Uzbekistan, for example, because the type of Islam that was taught in schools reflected a more conservative attitude toward women and this attitude was transferred into the daily social practices of the society, any form of contact between men and women, outside of marriage, was virtually forbidden. In Kyrgyzstan, in contrast, Muslim women exercised greater social freedom than their Uzbek counterparts. Because of their society's nomadic nature and harsh climate, female participation was essential in daily life. As a result, there was a more liberal and less restrictive attitude toward women. Kyrgyz women, for example, did not have to fast during the month of Ramadan or pray five times a day. However, despite these differences, the Kyrgyz society was also one of patriarchy where men dictated the moral behavior of the family. In addition to Islamic education, the Russians permitted the Sharīʿa to remain the guardian of law in the region, even though the most serious crimes cases came under the jurisdiction of Russian courts (Akiner 1986, 262). For example, in addition to the civil office, the *ʿulamāʾ* recorded birth, marriages, and deaths of the population. The arrangement between the state and the *ʿulamāʾ* allowed the Muslim population not only to continue to preserve what they believed to be their heritage but also to guard against cultural practices that they may have viewed as a threat to the existing social structure.

The other factor that helped to strengthen traditional attitudes toward women was the decision of the Russians not to interfere in the patriarchal system of the Muslim societies, in other words to leave all the domains of the "home" untouched. Governed by a patriarch, who was expected to make all the decisions, the Muslim family was a closely knit institution, where membership was achieved by birth, adoption, or marriage, and the line was preserved through the son. Within this system, the patriarch defined the "moral" tone of the family, particularly when it came to women. A Muslim woman, regardless of her socioeconomic background, was required to behave in a manner that was synonymous with her cultural surroundings. She was, for example, to dress in a manner that represented her individual culture, religious beliefs, and social status. In Uzbekistan social rules demanded very little contact between men and women. They also compelled Uzbek women to dress in a manner that was not that different from the men. They wore long trousers and long shirts and covered themselves with a long gown and a heavy black veil. The reason for the veil was not so much religion as social protection. Because certain Muslim women had broken with traditional practices, either by divorcing or wearing Russian style clothing, they were perceived as "immoral." So, in order to protect herself from charges of immorality, an Uzbek woman covered her head with a veil.

But by the beginning of the twentieth century some of the Islamic communities, perhaps influenced by Russia's social habits, began to allow greater social rights for women. The upper and middle classes of Kazakhstan and Kyrgyzstan, for example, allowed girls to go to school and to obtain an education. In several parts of the region female poets began to publish their work and became well-known literary figures. In Azerbaijan, the first all girls' schools were opened in the early 1900s. Yet, despite these opportunities, the social environment of the majority of Muslim women remained largely the same because the changes were targeted toward the small urban upper elite.

During the Russian occupation the women of Central Asia and the Caucusus lived in an environment where ancient cultural attitudes combined with religious doctrine dictated their social behavior. Partly fueled by an attempt to maintain their heritage and partly because of personal beliefs, the various peoples who made up the Russian Islamic republics, supported at times by women, advocated values that not only represented their past but also marked their future. These values would continue to be in practice even during the Soviet era, where every attempt was made to Sovietize the Muslim population.

Bibliography

S. Akiner, *Islamic peoples of Soviet Union*, London 1986.

E. Allworth, *Central Asia. 120 years of Russian rule*, Durham, N.C. 1989.

S. Becker, *Russia's protectorates in Central Asia. Bukhara and Khiva, 1865–1924*, Cambridge, Mass. 1968.

E. Dunn, Post-revolutionary women in Soviet Central Asia, in *Canadian-American Slavic Studies* 9:1 (1975), 93–100.

R. Frye and W. W. De Jong, The heritage of Central Asia. From antiquity to the Turkish expansion, in *Indo-Iranian Journal* 41:2 (1998), 190.

R. Girshman, *Iran from the earliest times to the Islamic conquest*, Harmondsworth, Middlesex 1965.

K. Gronbech, *The Turkish system of kinship*, Copenhagen 1953.

J.-A. Gross (ed.), *Muslims in Central Asia. Expressions of identity and change*, Durham, N.C. 1992.

G. Hogg, Who were the Soviet people? A guide to materials on the non-Russian nationalities of the former USSR, in *Reference Services Review* 21:1 (1993), 25–36.

W. Jochelson, *Peoples of Asiatic Russia*, New York 1970.

L. Kader, *Peoples of Central Asia*, Bloomington, Ind. 1966.

B. Manz, *Central Asia in historical perspective*, Boulder, Colo. 1994.

H. Masse, *Persian beliefs and customs*, New Haven, Conn. 1954.

B. A. Nazarov and D. Sinor (eds.) with D. DeWeese, *Essays on Uzbek History, Culture, and Language*, Bloomington, Ind. 1993.

S. G. Wilson, *Persian life and customs. With scenes of incidents of residence and travel in the land of the lion and the sun*, New York 1895.

R. Wixman, Everyday Islam. Religion and tradition in rural Central Asia, in *Slavic Review* 54:3 (1995), 822.

Mitra Raheb

Sub-Saharan Africa

This entry traces women's contributions to Muslim African societies during the colonial period that generally lasted from the 1890s to 1960.

The history of Islam in colonial Sub-Saharan Africa is often depicted through men's participation in trade routes and Sufi orders. There has been little mention of women in culture or politics. While Islam expanded and changed during European colonial administration, local historical processes and colonial policies de-emphasized gender and women's roles. Yet Muslim African women continued to influence diverse social arenas. In the process, African women reshaped Muslim identity and local gender ideologies.

Islam had a long history in Africa by the time of European colonial expansion in the late nineteenth century. In British East Africa, Swahili-speaking Muslims populated coastal Kenya and Tanzania (formerly German Tanganyika). Indian Ocean contacts dating to the eighth century and a long history of adaptation of Islam resulted in a unique Swahili society. Marriage and local migration patterns may have been important to Islam's spread into the East African interior during the colonial period (Sperling 1999, 282). In the Horn of Africa, Britain, France, and Italy carved up largely Muslim territories. Prior to European intervention, Egyptian imperialism shaped women's and men's attitudes toward both Islam and external intervention in that region (Boddy 1988). In West Africa, the Sahelian region just south of the Sahara Desert had been the site of Islamic learning from at least the fourteenth century, though the earliest contacts date back to the eighth century. Women served as crucial links in these networks through economic activity, marriage, and religious scholarship (Boyd and Last 1985, Robinson 2000, 166). In West Africa, the British claimed Nigeria with its northern Hausa-Fulani speaking Muslims and an increasing number of southern Yoruba-speaking Muslims. Otherwise, France colonized most of West Africa. Finally, South Africa's Muslim population mainly resided in Cape Town, Durban, and later Transvaal. Many South African Muslims were Asian immigrants forced out of Southeast and South Asia by the seventeenth century. Enslaved African women and men who converted to Islam also made up part of the Muslim population by the nineteenth century (Shell 1999). These diverse contexts provided challenges and opportunities for women to contribute to local society and Islamic culture.

European colonial policies and attitudes acted as another variable in Muslim African communities. On one hand, European officials saw Islam as an improvement over indigenous African religious practices. On the other, European official and popular discourse also viewed Islam negatively, particularly in its treatment of women. In an uneven fashion, European policymakers portrayed Islam as local "tradition" or as an alien imposition. For example, Great Britain applied its famed practice of "indirect rule" in different ways. Based on a model developed in Muslim northern Nigeria, indirect rule ideally made use of existing power structures and recognized local leaders as intermediaries. In northern Nigeria, British policies maintained the emirate system while restricting access to Western education and other resources in the name of Muslim "tradition." Yet British officials ignored women's positions of power in precolonial Muslim Hausa-Fulani society (Cooper 1998). Using a different approach, despite the centuries-long influence of Islam in British Somaliland, British officials emphasized local traditions and clan differences (Kapteijns 1999b, 237–9). In British East Africa, new towns and centers emerged which brought Islam to non-Muslim areas via Muslim traders who acted as colonial agents. However, literate African Christian converts eventually displaced Muslim intermediaries (Sperling 1999). In each case, British administrators (initially) focused on (Muslim) male actors while often denying all female resources.

The difference between British "indirect rule" and French colonial policies is often overstated since colonial governments employed a variety of policies. Nevertheless under the model form of French "direct rule" (particularly prior to the First World War), French colonial administrators often displaced indigenous authorities, or replaced legitimate local leaders with favorites of the French. Sometimes Muslims were placed in control of largely non-Muslim populations. At the same time, French colonial administrators ultimately developed relationships with key Muslim leaders, particularly in the Senegal-Mauritania region. Because of its North African colonies and relationships with expanding Muslim populations, French officials represented France as a "Muslim power" (Triaud 1999, Robinson 2000). However, an underlying suspicion of pan-Islamic movements always simmered beneath any pretense of French favor toward Islam. To assuage these fears, French-scholar-administrators postulated a theory regarding *Islam noir* (Black Islam). The concept of *Islam noir* suggested that West African Islam was too unorthodox and localized to partner with Arab or pan-Islamic movements based in North Africa or the Middle East. The French colonial administration partly isolated Islamic practice and scholarship in West Africa. Islam's peculiar relationship with French colonialism also consolidated the power of Muslim leaders in particular ways (Triaud 1999, 181–2). French colonial documents focus on clerics and leaders from specific regions and provide little information on women's participation in Islamic culture through religious practice, kinship networks, and scholarship. Instead, Muslim women's participation in indigenous forms of worship takes precedence (Coulon 1988, 113–15). These perceptions of women's Islamic practice partly explain how European administrators ignored women's influence in Muslim African communities. The examples below explore the implications of Muslim religious expansion and Muslim women's religious expression during the colonial period.

Gender played an important role in the different paths of Islamic expansion in French-controlled southern Niger versus British-controlled northern Nigeria. The nineteenth-century reform movement (jihad) of Usman dan Fodio had different effects in the Hausa-speaking area that straddles the Niger-Nigeria border. Dan Fodio's movement, which gained control over what became northern Nigeria, encouraged women's education and right to inheritance. However, the practices of veiling and seclusion limited the physical and economic independence of women. The Maradi valley in southern Niger resisted dan Fodio's policies. In Maradi, women continued to farm, moved freely in public, and participated in Bori. Bori (known as Zar in Sudan and North Africa) is a spirit possession ritual that recognizes both Islam and indigenous religious practices. Bori also provided an avenue for political power and social influence for women that both French and British colonial administrative policies overlooked. Meanwhile, European colonial policies had various effects on both sides of the border. The opening of trade between northern Nigeria and southern Niger during the colonial period brought practices such as veiling and seclusion into fashion in southern Niger by the end of the colonial period. Yet, in southern Niger, women used their access to farming to gain real estate and Bori remained a social force. In northern Nigeria, women's groups have drawn upon the history of women's education and interpretation of Islamic texts. Women's participation in Muslim society in this border region reflects precolonial dynamics, colonial policies, and women's initiative (Cooper 1998).

In Senegal, the presence of a leading woman in a Sufi *ṭarīqa* (brotherhood) similarly resulted from internal local dynamics. In 1943, following her father's death, Sokhna Magat Diop succeeded her father as *khalīfa* or leader of a small Mouride *ṭarīqa*. Her ascent suggests that "popular" Islam in Sufi brotherhoods suits and supports women's involvement in Muslim religious practice. Diop also personally cultivated *baraka* or charisma through her ascetic and humble lifestyle (Coulon 1988). Diop's ability to manipulate colonial relationships like earlier Senegalese Muslim leaders is less clear. Her father reputedly instructed her in the ways of the French colonial administration. She also engaged in politically useful marriage alliances. The Diop case is not so much a singular biography as it is an example of local innovation and possible shifts in African Islam that occurred against the background of European colonial activities.

In other parts of the continent, colonial policies and Muslim religious expansion intersected in indirect ways. In Mombasa on the Kenyan coast, elite

Muslim women and descendants of slaves shifted the meaning of Muslim Swahili identity. Despite increased marginalization under the British colonial regime, Swahili women recast their Muslim identity through wedding dances and new economic practices (Strobel 1979). In the colonial city of Nairobi, Islam served as a social inroad into urban society for poor rural female migrants in the early part of the twentieth century. As some of these female migrants participated in the labor process, particularly through prostitution, their activities showed the limits of British colonial control over labor processes and social values. Before the 1930s, Muslim ideas of hierarchy and respect shaped certain neighborhoods and relationships more than colonial directives. Islam also provided a means for women to attain property and landlord status (White 1992, 58–65, 223). In Kenya, existing Muslim communities altered in self-definition and composition partly due to the economic and social initiative of women.

In northern Sudan, Zar or spirit possession serves as a site to explore women's experience of Islam and colonialism. Turco-Egyptian occupation in the early nineteenth century gave way to Anglo-Egyptian rule by the end of the nineteenth century. In this context of war and devastation during the nineteenth century, Zar reputedly emerged in northern Sudan. Zar potentially serves as a counterdiscourse of resistance to outside influence, including well-established Islamic practice. Through their participation in Zar, women act outside the boundaries of their femininity and village identity. Zar thereby challenges local order while providing therapeutic care and self-awareness. From a local to a broader Islamic cultural context, women in northern Sudan who participate in Zar ceremonies have the potential to alter, contest, and reconstruct the relationships between women and men within local Islamic culture. The emergence and expansion of Zar during the colonial period suggests the interaction between the colonial imposition, local constraints, and women's mobility within Muslim cultural boundaries (Boddy 1988).

In northern Somalia, songs, poems, and sayings similarly serve as a site for debate over women's roles and gender norms in a Muslim, largely pastoral, society. The tumult of colonial rule and a 20-year long anticolonial movement took a toll on the economic and social development of the region during the twentieth century. Much Somali orature from this period reaffirmed male views of social norms, particularly in relation to women's proper behavior. Somali women sang religious songs or *sitaat* that celebrated women's roles through an evocation of celebrated female Muslim figures. Women's oral performance in Somalia suggests how poetry, work songs, and religious songs made social commentary, reflected social norms, and claimed a gendered, Muslim identity (Kapteijns 1999b).

The invisibility of these histories and actors in Islamic and colonial African history illustrates various power dynamics. After the devastation of the First World War, European colonial officials in Africa refocused their attention on masculine domains of power. In the eyes of colonial administrators, the rapid introduction of "civilization" had threatened male control and social order (Conklin 1997). Colonial administrators sought to re-establish an imagined, idyllic African past through more intrusive control over women and women's bodies. Key policies included the codification of customary law, birthing clinics, and domestic training for women (Chanock 1985, Hunt 1999). These programs and policies emerged most forcefully among Christian women or women who engaged in indigenous worship. These non-Muslim cases, together with the Muslim examples above, illustrate the integral part gender played in European imperial efforts in Africa (Summers 1991).

This entry highlights the connection between European colonial policies, gender, and Islam in a variety of locations in Sub-Saharan Africa. Muslim African women influenced religious and non-religious domains throughout history in multiple ways (Dunbar 1999). Brief examples here illustrate how Muslim women reconfigured the meaning of Muslim identity in southern Niger and Mombasa. Women affected colonial economies through their participation in labor processes and markets in Nairobi and northern Nigeria. Women's religious scholarship and spirituality in Senegal, Sudan, and Somalia expanded the realm of Muslim religious expression. The lack of attention to Muslim African women reflects the colonial record and the general focus on Muslim men's trade and learning. This brief exploration of Muslim African women's religious observances, socioeconomic activities, and cultural strategies challenges the standard view of Islamic history on the continent. Attention to diverse (especially marginalized) groupings of women, youth, migrants, and others, expands both African and Islamic history.

Bibliography

J. Boddy, Spirits and selves in Northern Sudan. The cultural therapeutics of possession and trance, in *American Ethnologist* 15 (1988), 4–27.

J. Boyd and M. Last, The role of women as *agents religieux* in Sokoto, in *Canadian Journal of African Studies* 19 (1985), 283–300.

M. Chanock, *Law, custom, and social order. The colonial experience in Malawi and Zambia*, Cambridge 1985.
A. Conklin, *A mission to civilize. The republican idea of empire in France and West Africa, 1895–1930*, Stanford 1997.
B. Cooper, Gender and religion in Hausaland. Variations in Islamic practice in Niger and Nigeria, in H. Bodman and N. Tohidi (eds.), *Women in Muslim societies. Diversity within unity*, Boulder, Colo. 1998, 21–38.
C. Coulon, Women, Islam, and Baraka, in D. B. Cruise O'Brien and C. Coulon (eds.), *Charisma and brotherhood in African Islam*, Oxford 1988, 113–33.
R. A. Dunbar, Muslim women in African history, in N. Levtzion and R. L. Pouwels (eds.), *The history of Islam in Africa*, Athens, Ohio 1999, 397–417.
N. R. Hunt, *A colonial lexicon of birth ritual, medicalization, and mobility in the Congo*, Durham, N.C. 1999.
L. Kapteijns, Ethiopia and the Horn of Africa, in N. Levtzion and R. L. Pouwels (eds.), *The history of Islam in Africa*, Athens, Ohio 1999a, 227–50.
L. Kapteijns with M. O. Ali, *Women's voices in a man's world. Women and the pastoral tradition in Northern Somali orature, c. 1889–1980*, Portsmouth, N.H. 1999b.
D. Robinson, *Paths of accommodation. Muslim societies and French colonial authorities in Senegal and Mauritania, 1880–1920*, Athens, Ohio 2000.
R. C.-H. Shell, Islam in Southern Africa, 1562–1998, in N. Levtzion and R. L. Pouwels (eds.), *The history of Islam in Africa*, Athens, Ohio 2000, 327–48.
D. C. Sperling with additional material by J. H. Kagabo, The coastal hinterland and interior of East Africa, in N. Levtzion and R. L. Pouwels (eds.), *The history of Islam in Africa*, Athens, Ohio 1999, 272–302.
M. Strobel, *Muslim women in Mombasa (1890–1975)*, New Haven, Conn. 1979.
C. Summers, Intimate colonialism. The imperial production of reproduction in Uganda, 1907–1925, in *Signs* 16:4 (1991), 787–807.
L. White, *The comforts of home. Prostitution in colonial Nairobi*, Chicago 1990.

Lorelle Denise Semley

Constitutions

The Caucasus and Central Asian States

To review the interrelations between women, gender, and constitutions, and assess the role and significance of constitutions as a legal base to provide a regulatory framework for gender relations in Caucasian and Central Asian societies, it is important to look at the overall historic background. During the pre-Soviet era (before 1917), the countries known now as Azerbaijan, Armenia, Georgia, Kazakhstan, Kyrgyzstan, Tajikistan, Turkmenistan, and Uzbekistan, belonged to the Russian Empire, which maintained varying degrees of control over its colonial territories. Indigenous societies, however, were allowed to exercise customary laws to a certain extent, with women generally excluded from public life and subject to strong paternalistic attitudes. Since then, during the twentieth century, these societies have been through a radical transformation that affected all aspects of life, but the status of women especially. This changed image of "Eastern" women, who during the Soviet regime gained access to education, employment, generous social welfare, health services, and enjoyed far more freedom when compared to Muslim countries with similar income levels, was one of the principal trump cards of Soviet propaganda.

Soviet times (1917–1991)

After the Bolsheviks seized power in October 1917, all legal norms of ex-colonial territories of the Russian Empire were proscribed and the legal norms adopted in Bolshevik Russia were to be followed (Saidbaev, 1984). The Soviet doctrine based on the theoretical assumptions of Vladimir Lenin, Inessa Armand, Nadezhda Krupskaya, and other Bolshevik ideologues who attached particular importance to the liberation of women and equality between the sexes began to be implemented. The objective of these policies was to achieve universal literacy for women and actively involve them in public life and thus ensure their high participation in the workforce. In these policies, emancipation of "suppressed women of the East" was one of the strategic priorities and one of the most important political considerations of the central organs of the Communist Party in Moscow from its earliest days of rule.

The first decrees of the Bolshevik government in 1918, and then the first Soviet constitution adopted in 1922, contained provisions to equalize women and men. Equal rights at that time meant equal rights to vote, to marry, or instigate divorce. In 1918, early marriages were abolished and the official registration of marriage was made mandatory. Still, these important legal acts remained declarative, and the constitution alone was not able to change deeply traditional societies. Therefore, constitutional provisions for equality remained unclaimed, and had to be reinforced by other measures (legal acts, decrees, and decisions) of the Bolsheviks. In Central Asia, specific policy measures to liberate women and engage them in socioeconomic life were also required.

With adoptions of new constitutions in the Soviet Union, in 1936, and then in 1977, to reflect the changing situation and political agenda of the Communist Party of the Soviet Union, the articles declaring equality between sexes continued to form an important part of the supreme law. By the 1960s and 1970s, constitutional law provided women with rights and social entitlements such as legal guarantees for equality, property and inheritance rights, greater access to education, increasing opportunities in the public sphere, child allowances, state-sponsored childcare, lengthy maternity leaves, and guaranteed return to employment after maternity leave.

The status of women in the Caucasus and Central Asia changed significantly within one generation (from the 1920s to the 1960s). However, throughout Soviet history, constitutions primarily served as a tool for ideological purposes to demonstrate to the world how the Soviet government "cared" for the needs of women. There were no mechanisms created to implement the constitutional provisions other than political will and pressure coming from the ruling Communist Party. Equality between sexes was interpreted as "equality before the law," and remained limited, being largely perceived as sameness or similar identity. At the same time, the paternalistic approach toward women's specific needs arising from their biological roles led to the development of "protectionist" legislative measures that, in turn, further enhanced perceptions of women as mothers, bearing sole responsibilty for family and children. Therefore, in spite of impressive achievements in the area of employment, education, social welfare, especially visible in the context of Central Asian and Caucasian countries, equality of sexes remained illusionary as hidden discrimination continued to exist. It found its reflection in gender disparities and unequal gender roles when women had a disproportionate burden of responsibilities and men were alienated from the family sphere.

Post-Soviet times

Constitution in its modern role of a supreme national law, providing legitimacy and symbolizing sovereign statehood, has been considered as an important tool in the process of nation-building in Caucasian and Central Asian states. After the collapse of the Soviet Union in 1991, all these countries renewed their legal frameworks, and adopted new constitutions. This did not apply to the parts of the Caucasus that remained as constituencies of the Russian Federation (namely Abkhazia, Chechnya, Daghestan, and Osetia).

Constitutional law in the Caucasian and Central Asian states, as in the Soviet past, recognizes fundamental human and civil rights and freedoms, and guarantees equality regardless of sex, race, ethnicity, language, religion, social origin, political convictions, or individual and social status, according to the principles and standards of international law. All states have also signed and ratified the Convention on the Elimination of All Forms of Discrimination against Women (CEDAW) without reservation, and have made other international commitments in terms of the protection and promotion of gender equality.

As the Soviet regime suppressed freedom of conscience and other human rights related to spiritual faith, expectations arose at the beginning of the 1990s that the newly independent countries, in search of national identity, would turn to Islam as the principal religion in the region. Over the last decade the situation has remained complicated, but the legal and constitutional frameworks of these countries, especially with respect to gender equality, have remained secular.

While most Soviet social, economic, and political rights continue to be upheld, they have not been implemented, as throughout the region governments have failed to mobilize resources for adequate social spending. Another problem is that policies aimed at equality of sexes repeat mistakes once made under the Soviet governments: clear definition of discrimination based on gender is absent from the legal domain, as well as mechanisms to implement equal rights. The *de facto* situation reveals serious gaps in terms of implementation of the constitutional provisions. Moreover, such provisions do little to counteract common mindsets in terms of traditional gender roles that form the root of many gender-related inequalities and problems in the region.

Bibliography

D. Alimova, *Women's issues in Central Asia. A history of studies and current problems*, Tashkent 1991.

S. Akiner, Between tradition and modernity. The dilemma facing contemporary Central Asian women, in M. Buckley (ed.), *Post-Soviet women. From the Baltic to Central Asia*, Cambridge 1997, 261–304.

V. Asatryan and A. Harutyunian (eds.), *Women status report. Impact of transition* (available in English and Armenian), Erevan 1999.

Gender Development Association, Georgia, *Status of Women in Georgia* (available in English and Georgian), Tbilisi 1999.

Islam and women of the Orient. History and present day [in Russian], collection of articles, Academy of Science of Uzbekistan, Tashkent 1990.

M. B. Olcott, Women and society in Central Asia, in W. Fierman (ed.), *Soviet Central Asia. The failed transformation*, Boulder, Colo. 1991, 235–56.

S. Saidbaev, *Islam and society. Results of historic and sociological study* [in Russian], Moscow 1984^2.

S. Tadjbakhsh, Between Lenin and Allah. Women and ideology, in H. L. Bodman and N. Tohidi (eds.), *Women in Muslim societies. Diversity within* unity, Boulder, Colo. 1998, 163–87.

M. Tokhtakhodjaeva, *Between the slogans of communism and the laws of Islam*, Lahore 1995.

UNDP (R. Ibrahimbekova coordinator), *The report on the status of women of Azerbaijan Republic* (available in English and Azeri), Baku 1999.

Dono Abdurazakova

Indonesia

A constitution can be defined as "a set of fundamental laws, customs and conventions which provide the framework within which government is exercised in a state" (Ebert 1981, 4). Its basic contents are: the framework or structure of government; the power of government; and relations between the governors and the governed, especially rights of the latter.

Women and gender issues within the Indonesian constitutional system can be viewed from several aspects, such as women's participation in the constitution making process and the protection of women's rights in the constitution and in implementing legislations.

The constitution making process

The importance of women's involvement in a constitution making process can be explained by the argument that "the effectiveness of a constitution requires acceptance by the community and ownership of its provision," and to achieve this purpose, particular attention should be paid, among other things, to the process by which a constitution is made (Saunders 2002, 2). The process should undoubtedly involve all constituents within the community, including women. Sadly, looking at the experience of various countries, women are usually underrepresented in the process (ibid.). Yet women play important supporting roles in practice, as academics, researchers, or organizers.

Indonesia is no exception. Looking back to Indonesian constitutional history, there were only 2 women out of 69 members of the Badan Penyelidik Usaha-usaha Persiapan Kemerdekaan Indonesia (BPUPKI, Committee for examination of Indonesian independence), which was in charge of drafting the 1945 constitution. They were Mrs. R. Siti Soekaptinah Soenarjo Mangoenpuspito and Maria Ulfah Santoso, who later became the Indonesia's first woman minister (State Secretariat 1998).

The 1945 constitution was amended four times between 1999 and 2002 and women again played a minimal role in the formal drafting of amendments as they constitute only 9.2 percent of the total members of the Majelis Permusywaratan Rakyat (MPR, People's consultative assembly), which is in charge of amending the constitution (Ani Soetjipto 2002, 15). However, outside the assembly, women activists and women's organizations, for example, the Koalisi Perempuan Indonesia untuk Keadilan dan Demokrasi (KPI, Indonesian women's coalition for justice and democracy) and the Jaringan Perempuan dan Politik (JPP, Network of women and politics), have made significant contributions by conducting seminars, preparing the drafts of amendments that deal specifically with women and gender matters, and conducting lobbies. The movements resulted in, among other things, the adoption of new provisions relating to the protection of women's rights in the amended 1945 constitution.

Protection of women's rights in the 1945 constitution and its amendments

Article 27, paragraph (1) of the 1945 constitution states that "all citizens have equal status before the law and in government, and shall abide by the law and the government without any exception." Although the words "men" and "women" are not used it is commonly accepted that the constitution upholds the principle of equality for men and women. However, the KPI argues that the article only recognizes the principle of equality before the law, rather than equality of men and women (KPI 2000, 15). Therefore, the KPI suggests the inclusion of the principle of anti-discrimination on the grounds of race, ethnic origin, sex, age, religion, or political ideology (ibid., 15). Implementation of the equality principle should be accompanied by affirmative action (ibid., 16).

In 2000, in response to the public demand for extending the recognition of human rights provisions, the People's Assembly made the Second Amendment to the 1945 constitution. Some important provisions relevant to women's rights are stipulated in Articles 28H paragraph (2) and 28I paragraph (2). The former states that "each person has the right to assistance and special treatment in order to gain the same opportunities and benefits in the attainment of equality and justice" while the latter states that "each person has the right to be free from discriminatory treatment on any grounds and has the right to obtain protection from such discriminatory treatment." It can be concluded that the amended 1945 constitution provides the principles of equality and paves the way for using affirmative action policy in any field to enhance women's rights.

Legislation relevant to women's rights and gender

Prior to the Second Amendment of the 1945 constitution by the People's Assembly, the Dewan Perwakilan Rakyat (DPR, House of representatives) and the president enacted a new law on human rights, Law Number 39 of 1999, in Part 9 of which women's rights are explicitly provided for. Part 9 directs that the political and electoral system as well as the appointment mechanism in the executive and judiciary arms of government should guarantee women's representation. It also guarantees the right to determine citizenship, the right to obtain special protection in the workplace concerning any matter that might affect a woman's reproductive function, the right to legal action based on her own conduct, and so forth.

It is recognized that some obstacles to women's participation in parliament still exist in Indonesia. These include "political obstacles, socio-economic obstacles and ideological and psychological hindrances" (Shvedova 1998). One possible way out is to introduce a quota system. Unfortunately, the amended 1945 constitution does not contain any single article that deals with a quota for women in the national parliament. Rather, it is covered by Law Number 12 of 2003 on General Election. Article 65 of this law states that "each participating political party may nominate candidates for the DPR,

Provincial DPRD, and Regency/Municipal DPRD, for each electoral district, giving consideration to representation of women of at least 30 percent."

BIBLIOGRAPHY

M. Ebert, Women and constitutional renewal, in A. Doerr and M. Carrier (eds.), *Women and the constitution in Canada*, Ottawa 1981, 3–27.

Indonesia, 1945 Constitution, translation, <http://www.gtzsfdm.or.id/documents/laws_n_regs/con_decree/Const_Law_1945.pdf>.

Indonesia, State Secretariat, *Notes from the session of the Committee for Examination of Indonesian Independence and the Committee for Preparation of Indonesian Independence 28 May 1945–22 August 1945* [in Indonesian], Jakarta 1998.

KPI (Koalisi Perempuan Indonesia untuk Keadilan dan Demokrasi), *Women, human rights and the constitution* [in Indonesian], Jakarta 2000, 1–33.

C. Saunders, Women and constitution making, paper presented at the international conference on Women, Peace Building and Constitution Making, Colombo 2002, 1–23.

N. Shvedova, Obstacles to women's participation in parliament, in A. Karam (ed.), *Women in parliament. Beyond numbers*, Stockholm 1998, 19–41.

A. Soetjipto, Increasing women's political participation through constitutional and electoral reforms, in International IDEA, *Strengthening women's political participation in Indonesia*, Jakarta 2003, 7–18.

SUSĪ DWĪ HARĪJANTĪ

The Islamic Republic of Iran and Afghanistan

IRAN

The constitution of the Islamic Republic of Iran emerged from the Islamization of the revolution of 1979, in which Iranian women of various social strata took part, as did Iranian men. At that time there was already a constitution formally in force, which had come out of the revolution of 1906–7 (Raḥīmī 1978), and which was much less bound to Islamic provisions. The new constitution acquired its legitimacy in a referendum that took place in 1980, where the majority of women, like the majority of men, voted for it. It outlines an Islamic state, in which "all penal, financial, economic, administrative, cultural, military, political, and other laws and regulations must be based on Islamic criteria" (Art. 4). In actual legislations these criteria are determined by the Guardian Council, consisting of twelve jurists, of whom six are to be clergymen (*fuqahā*). The council has, among other powers, the right to ensure that no legislative proposal, approved by the parliament, runs counter to the principles of the Shīʿī Sharīʿa. Binding legislations to Sharīʿa is an obligation that, to begin with, discriminates against women in their private and social life.

The position of women as described in the constitution of the Islamic Republic may be summarized as follows:

1. The "decisive role of women," as part of the faithful, in the revolution is recognized by acknowledging that they were "actively and massively present in a most conspicuous manner at all [its] stages" (the Preamble).

2. It is declared as "natural" that women, because of the "greater oppression" they suffered under the old regime, "should benefit from a particularly large augmentation of their rights." The oppression this statement refers to lies in "women being regarded as an object or instrument in the service of promoting consumerism and exploitation" (the Preamble).

3. Art. 3, note 14, obliges the state to secure "the multifarious rights of all citizens, both women and men." But Art. 20 makes it clear that the relevant steps have to be taken "in conformity with Islamic criteria." This stipulation is repeated in Art. 21, where the state is bound to "ensure the right of women" in all "material and intellectual" respects and to "create an environment favorable for the growth of women's personality." The concrete measures that are to be implemented according to this article are for the purpose of "protecting mothers, particularly during pregnancy and child-rearing," "establishing competent courts to protect and preserve the family," "providing special insurance for widows, aged women, and women without support," and "awarding of guardianship of children to worthy women, in order to protect the interest of the children, in the absence of a legal guardian." The last clause means that a mother gets the right of guardianship of her children only when the father and his male ancestors are not alive.

The constitution of the Islamic Republic is not explicit about women's suffrage, which most prominent Islamic *fuqahā* opposed before the 1979 revolution. The reason why election laws have conceded women this right after the revolution should be seen in light of the increase in women's social and political power during and after the revolution, a fact that cannot be ignored any more.

AFGHANISTAN

The turbulent twentieth-century history of Afghanistan has resulted in at least five constitutions since 1923. However, all of them declare Islam as the state religion and stipulate in different formulations that in Afghanistan no law shall run counter to "the principles of Islamic faith." Only the constitutions of 1977, 1987, and 1990 state explicitly that "women in the Republic of Afghanistan have equal rights with men." The constitution of 1964 formulates this provision as "equal rights" for the people of Afghanistan "without discrimination." During the rule of the Taliban (1996–2001) the constitutional basis of the state was the Sharīʿa. The departure of the Taliban paved the way for a conference held in Petersberg (Germany) between 27 November and 5 December 2001 in which representatives of the most influential political groups of Afghanistan took part. The conference decided, among other things, that a committee would draft a constitution that would be considered for approval in a constitutional Assembly to be held in 2003. Until then the constitution of 1964, without its monarchic components, was to be the legal basis of the administration governing Afghanistan.

The constitution of 1964 stipulates, apart from binding legislation to the "provisions of the Ḥanafī doctrine of Islam" (Art. 2 and 64), that in the fields in which there are no laws the provisions of Ḥanafī jurisprudence of the Sharīʿa "shall be considered as law" (Art. 69). In addition to further stipulations reflecting its patriarchal foundation, this constitution implicitly favors a movement initiated by King ʿAbd al-Raḥmān in 1883, aiming at reforming the legal and social conditions of women. The movement, although frequently interrupted by the opposition of the Islamic clergy and by other traditionalist opponents of the reform, did achieve some of its goals. The extension of suffrage to women and the nomination of women as ministers are some of the measures that were taken before monarchy was replaced by a republican state in 1973. Urged on by the radical and/or communist administrators of the new republic, the situation of women improved more rapidly. Offering posts of minister to women, admitting them to universities, and protecting those who were willing to unveil were some of the steps taken by the government, along with the agitation that accompanied them. These reforms took place when the opposition to them was not much weaker than in earlier times. The increased influence of Islamicists caused by the Soviet invasion of Afghanistan in 1979 and by the leading role that they played in resisting this invasion impeded the development of the position of women inside the country. Reaching its culmination under the Taliban rule, the setback ended after the Taliban were defeated by international forces. The situation of women has been improving since 2001: about 200 women took part in the emergency assembly in June 2002 and women were given two ministerial posts in the new government. It remains to be seen whether the new constitution for Afghanistan will be more favorable to women than the constitution of 1964.

Bibliography

Afghanistan Online, <http://www.afghan-web.com/history/> (for the Afghanistan constitutions).

F. Azari, *Women of Iran. The conflict with fundamentalist Islam*, London 1983.

C. Benard and E. Schlaffer, *Veiled courage. Inside the Afghan women's resistance*, New York 2002.

ICL – Iran – Constitution, < htpp://www.oefre.unibe.ch/law/icl/ir00000_.html>.

Feminist Majority Foundation, <http://www.feminist.org/afghan/intro.asp>.

J.-H. Grevemyer, *Afghanistan. Sozialer Wandel und Staat im 20. Jahrhundert*, Berlin 1987.

C. Nölle-Karimi, C. Schetter, and R. Schlaginweit (eds.), *Afghanistan. A Country without a state*?, Frankfurt am Main 2002.

P. Paidar, *Women and the political process in twentieth-century Iran*, Cambridge 1995.

M. Raḥīmī, *Qānūn-i asāsī-i Īrān va ūsūl-i dimūkrāsī*, Tehran 1978.

A. Schirazi, *The constitution of Iran. Politics and the state in the Islamic Republic*, London 1997.

A. Tabari and N. Yeganeh (eds.), *In the shadow of Islam. The women's movement in Iran*, London 1982.

Asghar Schirazi

South Asia

The place of women and the working of gender in the constitutions of modern South Asian states, including India, Pakistan, and Bangladesh, to varying degrees reflect the cultures of their sizeable Islamic populations and have sparked considerable political contestation.

PAKISTAN

Although the successive constitutions of Pakistan have included some progressive policies for women, and Pakistani women have drawn on Islam to demand rights, a history of discriminatory, purportedly Islamic ordinances, reversions to authoritarian rule, and persistent judicial failures to protect fundamental rights have hurt the position of women. In the early years after the formation of Pakistan in 1947, women were able to invoke Islamic law to demand rights to inherit property. In the wake of additional pressure from women's organizations, including the Women's Voluntary Service (WVS), later the All Pakistan Women's Association (APWA), the 1956 constitution included equality of status, some economic rights, and reserved legislative seats for women. After a reversion to military rule, the 1961 Family Laws

Ordinance provided some safeguards for women in the area of divorce law, but the 1962 constitution removed rights to directly vote women into reserved seats. The 1973 constitution under elected leader Zulfiqar Ali Bhutto included equality before the law, non-discrimination on the basis of sex in government service, and reserved legislative seats for women at the local and national levels (Ali 2000).

After ousting Bhutto, military ruler Zia ul-Haq appealed to religious parties and patriarchal interpretations of Islam to consolidate his power. Women were central to General Zia's "Islamization" program, including the Hudood Ordinances passed in 1979, which made women pursuing rape cases vulnerable to charges of adultery. The opposition of women's organizations such as the Women's Action Forum (WAF) was able to restrict to the realm of finance another law reducing the value of women's testimony to half that of men's (Weiss 1994, 418).

Since his death in 1988, General Zia's "Islamic" amendments to the 1973 constitution have persisted, although various governments have appointed female judges, put in place women's quotas for government employment, and in 1996 agreed to become party to the UN Convention on the Elimination of All Forms of Discrimination against Women (CEDAW). Even the first female prime minister of a Muslim state, Benazir Bhutto, daughter of Zulfiqar Ali Bhutto and initially opposed to the Hudood Ordinances, found it politically untenable to repeal them once in office. The eighth amendment, passed under Zia, contributed to her difficulty by necessitating a two-thirds vote in the National Assembly to repeal the laws that had been passed by Zia's government. Returning Pakistan to military rule in 1999, Pervez Musharraf has criticized reactionary Islamists yet also further undermined judicial independence (Cotran and Yamani 2000, 162–3). The imperative to focus on legal rights has meant that the women's movement in Pakistan has had limited ability to focus on broader social and economic development issues (Ali 2000).

BANGLADESH

After the creation of Bangladesh (formerly East Pakistan) in 1971, a secular constitution was put in place in 1972. Interrupted by extended periods of military rule, democracy re-emerged with the 1991 elections. Despite efforts to achieve gender equality in the constitution and the dominance of two female leaders in contemporary Bangladesh, Begum Khaleda Zia, leader of the Bangladesh Nationalist Party (BNP) and Sheikh Hasina, leader of the Awami League (AL), the political influence of most women in Bangladesh remains low.

The constitution reserved 15 seats for women in the parliament, a number raised to 30 (nearly 10 percent of total seats) in 1979. After a lapse of three years starting in 1987, a 1990 constitutional amendment reinstated the 30 reserved seats. Women have successfully contested non-reserved seats as well. Politicians who have benefited from these reservations have mixed feelings about the ability of such policies to empower women (Commonwealth Secretariat 1999, 27–37).

The constitution guarantees women's equality in public life but not in the personal sphere, which is governed by the personal laws of religious communities. Muslim personal laws in Bangladesh, applicable in cases of marriage, divorce, inheritance, and child custody, discriminate against women, despite reforms in 1961. Men's rights to polygamy, easier divorce, larger inheritance of property, and authority over children after divorce are examples of inequities in personal laws (Khan 2001, Akhtar 2001).

Special ordinances against gender-based violence originated in 1983 and were expanded to include children in the 1990s. The government of Bangladesh is also a signatory of CEDAW, yet enforcement of these domestic, constitutional, and international initiatives remains limited by corruption and weak enforcement mechanisms. As in the rest of South Asia, many women, particularly poor women, are not aware of their rights (Asian Development Bank 2001, 6).

INDIA

Unlike Pakistan and Bangladesh, India is not a Muslim-majority state, but its 12 percent Muslim population makes it one of the largest Muslim countries in the world. India's constitution, in place from 1950 to the present, declares it a secular republic, committed to equality. Personal laws varying by religious community (applicable in cases involving marriage, divorce, maintenance, guardianship, adoption, inheritance, and succession) are one mechanism to achieve religious minority rights, yet they have raised questions about both secularism and equity, particularly with regard to women's rights (Larson 2001).

Debates over whether India should have a uniform civil code came to the forefront of Indian politics with the Supreme Court case of Shah Bano, a divorced Muslim woman demanding maintenance. The Supreme Court circumvented Muslim personal law to grant Shah Bano ongoing maintenance in

1985, causing controversy that continued with the subsequent Muslim Women's Bill, an effort to shore up personal law. Many women's organizations, such as the Joint Women's Programme, a national association with members of various religious backgrounds, opposed the Muslim Women's Bill. Muslim women were divided on the issue (Engineer 1987, 237–42). The increasing political power of Hindu nationalists and their support for a uniform civil code continues to alarm many Muslim politicians. Many analysts feel that political considerations rather than equity concerns have steered much policy regarding minority women (Hasan 1999, 123).

The actual impact of constitutional and legal provisions for women on their status was scrutinized most thoroughly by the Committee on the Status of Women in India in their 1975 report, which documented continuing gender imbalances in terms of sex ratios, work participation, literacy, and election to political office (India 1975). The women's movement in India continues to press for change in all of these areas, yet faces internal divisions along caste, class, regional, and religious lines.

Amendments to the constitution in 1992 reserved one third of seats for women in the *panchayat* system of local councils. Legislative attempts to amend the constitution and reserve one third of seats for women in the parliament have failed, in part because of controversial demands for subreservations for Muslim and lower caste women (Jenkins 2003). In addition to such challenges to women's unity, feminist legal scholars have drawn attention to the way legal discourses, despite formal legal equality, continue to reinforce ideologies of female duty and dependence (Niranjana 2000, 273).

In South Asian polities, group-based policies, particularly religious personal laws, have resulted in gender inequities even when constitutions purport to assure gender equality. Likewise, many initiatives to advance women in South Asian countries, such as reserved legislative seats, are group-based, "women's" rather than universal policies. Rights activists have often struggled with balancing their interests as women and as Muslims in political and constitutional contexts that rarely reflect the nuances of overlapping identities and interests.

Bibliography

S. S. Ali, Law, Islam and the women's movement in Pakistan, in S. M. Rai (ed.), *International perspectives on gender and democratization*, New York 2000, 41–63.

S. Akhtar, The status of widows in Bangladesh, in P. Grimshaw, K. Holmes, and M. Lake (eds.), *Women's rights and human rights. International historical perspectives*, Basingstoke, Hampshire 2001, 220–28.

Asian Development Bank, *Women in Bangladesh*, Manila 2001.

Commonwealth Secretariat, *Women in politics. Voices from the Commonwealth*, London 1999.

E. Cotran and M. Yamani, *The rule of law in the Middle East and the Islamic world*, London 2000.

A. A. Engineer (ed.), *The Shah Bano controversy*, Hyderabad 1987.

J. L. Esposito with N. J. DeLong-Bas, *Women in Muslim family law*, Syracuse, N.Y. 2001[2].

Z. Hasan, Muslim women and the debate on legal reforms, in B. Ray and A. Basu (eds.), *From independence towards freedom. Indian women since 1947*, Oxford 1999.

India. Committee on the Status of Women in India, *Towards equality. Report of the committee on the status of women in India*, New Delhi 1975.

L. D. Jenkins, Women's reservations and representation, in L. D. Jenkins, *Identity and identification in India. Defining the disadvantaged*, London 2003, 156–74.

R. Kapur and B. Cossman, *Subversive sites. Feminist engagements with law in India*, New Delhi 1996.

S. Khan, Good governance and judiciary. Equal rights of women, in H. A. Hye (ed.), *Governance. South Asian perspectives*, Karachi 2001, 137–44.

G. Larson (ed.), *Religion and personal law in contemporary India. A call to judgment*, Bloomington, Ind. 2001.

S. Niranjana, On the women's movement in India, in P. R. de Souza (ed.), *Contemporary India. Transitions*, New Delhi 2000, 264–81.

B. N. Ramusack and S. Sievers, *Women in Asia. Restoring women to history*, Bloomington, Ind. 1999.

A. M. Weiss, The consequences of state policies for women in Pakistan, in M. Weiner and A. Banuazizi (eds.), *The politics of social transformation in Afghanistan, Iran, and Pakistan*, Syracuse, N.Y. 1994, 412–44.

Laura Dudley Jenkins

Sub-Saharan Africa

The many countries that make up Sub-Saharan Africa lodge numerous ethnic groups within their borders. Most of these groups still hold to their customary laws, and are Muslims, Christians, or followers of African traditional religions. Gender refers to ways in which masculinity and femininity are constructed, lived, reconstructed, and negotiated by people living in the context of different communities (van Santen and Willemse forthcoming). There may be apparent conflicts between the constitutional guarantees of gender equality and the traditional status of women in many cultures in Africa, including the various Muslim communities, for example, over forced or child marriages (Ibhawoh 1999, 11). Cultural traditions may contain norms, institutions, and constitutional provisions that support gender equality – fairness of treatment by gender – as well as norms and institutions that are antithetical in relation to globally accepted relations of equality. Concerning gender, most Muslim societies use a mixture of Islamic contexts and interpretation of Islamic texts (Qur'ān and *ḥadīth*), pre-Islamic culture, tradition, custom, and the interests of those who hold the reigns of power (Shamina 1997, Creevey 1996).

Islamic communities in Sub-Saharan Africa have had to deal with non-Muslim members within their own cultural regions, which has sometimes caused them to draw boundaries and define interactions between "us" and "them." This may lead to confrontations, but can also bring about constructive cooperation and mutual interdependence between communities with national or state policies that are reflected in the political structures and constitutions. Even in regions where Muslims are a majority there are often groups, sometimes of a fundamentalist nature, who consider themselves to be good believers and consider other Muslims to have an inadequate understanding of Islamic faith and principles, and who therefore try to convert or reconvert their population. Such is the case, for example, in Sudan, where the regime has taken on increasingly Islamic course, although its constitution acknowledges the right to equality (art. 21) and freedom of religion (art. 24). As sources of the Sudanese constitution include Islamic law, referendums, the constitution itself, and custom, the personal status of women is subject to the relevant provisions of the Qur'ān (Bantekas and Abu-Sabeib 2000, 540). In North Cameroon Islamic purifying movements are also active, but they place strong emphasis on education for women and a larger role for them in the public and political space, which the national constitution provides for but which traditional pre-Islamic society often denies.

In some African countries national constitutions disfavor equal gender relations and need to be brought into accord with Islamic law and constitution to favor women's position; in other countries the contrary is the case. In Nigeria, famous for the Sharīʿa court death sentence by stoning prescribed for women accused of adultery, the 1999 constitution, Section 6/1 vests judicial power in the federation of diverse lower courts. However, final appeal can be made in the Nigerian states' Court of Appeal and the Supreme Court (Essien 2000).

Some governments deal with the differences between their Islamic and non-Islamic populations explicitly; for example, in Mauritania the constitution adopts Islam as a state religion but application of Islamic laws depends on the conditions given by state laws (Monteillet 2002). Other nation-states do not mention the discrepancies of Islamic law in relation to the state. In Uganda, for example, a new constitution was enacted in 1995 in which most of the critical provisions concerning both Muslim and non-Muslim women were accepted. These provisions were enacted after an enormous struggle on the part of women's groups to have a female representative from each of the 39 districts on the Constitutional Commission (Matembe 2002, 196–7). In South Africa an entire chapter of the new constitution of 1996 was dedicated to institutions supporting constitutional democracy, such as the Human Rights and Gender Equality Commission (Ebrahim 1998).

The constitutions of certain countries, such as Senegal and Mali, are based on former colonial constitutions, rendering them secular republics with a governmental structure adapted from the French colonizers and modified to suit national needs (Creevey 1996, Clark 1999). In other countries new constitutions were adopted after a process of democratization and the preceding national conferences. Chad, for example, a country with a large Islamic population which has long been divided by internal wars, adopted a new constitution in 1996 (Lanne 1996) that mentions equality of the sexes in article 6.

In Sub-Saharan Africa constitutional provisions against gender discrimination are reinforced by the obligation assumed by different states as signatories to the United Nations Convention on the Elimination of All Forms of Discrimination against Women (CEDAW) and the African Charter on Human and People's Rights. Article 18(3) of CEDAW explicitly states: "The state shall ensure the elimination of every discrimination against women and ensure the protection of the rights of women and the child as stipulated in the Universal Declarations conventions" (Mugwanya 2000, 761, Ibhawoh 1996, 46). However, as Mugwanya argues for Uganda, many states urgently need to reform their legal systems, as well as those practices and customs in both public and private spheres that are antithetical to the rights and dignity of women. Female genital mutilation (FGM) is an example. CEDAW and the United Nations' Beijing Declaration and Platform for Action on Women's Rights recognized FGM as a form of violence against women. Its practice is unambiguously forbidden in some state constitutions, such as Burkina Faso, where practitioners have been prosecuted in connection with the death of young girls (Ibhawoh 1999, 70). In other countries, however, such as Sudan, attempts to enforce legislation against FGM have caused popular outcries and have been abandoned. In 1990 the government of Kenya announced that it had officially banned FGM, but no law was passed in parliament to prohibit it. The Nigerian constitution is in conflict with the 1990 United Nations Convention on the Rights of the Child, article 24(3), but little has been done to prevent the practice.

Gender issues in the context of national constitutions arise in connection with questions of inheritance, marriage, and the dissolution of marriage. Most Muslim countries in Sub-Saharan Africa follow Muslim laws on these matters. In Nigeria, Niger, Mali, Cameroon, Senegal, and the Gambia women are married and allowed divorce according to Islamic laws, though those laws are interpreted differently in various Muslim communities. Female children may inherit the half share alloted them by Islamic law, and this does leave Muslim women with the possibility of inheriting land (Meager 2000), while women of most non-Muslim ethnic groups have just the usufruct, even though the constitutions of most African countries entitle them to rights to land and other property. In countries such as Mali and Senegal, where historically Islam served as a basis for social organization and a vehicle for mediation and negotiation between a weak state and a predominantly Muslim society, the leadership of brotherhoods such as the Tijāniyya and the Murides continue to wield enormous power (Clark 1999). In such circumstances, Islamic beliefs and the accompanying cultural baggage may negatively influence women when Muslim leaders are conservative and constitutional declarations do not work efficiently because of the interdependence of the government and the Muslim leaders who restrict the authority of each of them over society (Creevey 1996, 302).

Finally, a clause dealing with a legal construction of homosexual and sexual orientation was included in the 1993 interim constitution of South Africa (De Vos, 1996), but is either absent or negatively interpreted in the legal discourse of most African states.

Bibliography

A. N. Abdullahi, Article 39 of the Ethiopian constitution on secession and self determination. A panacea to the nationality question in Africa?, in *Verfassung und Recht in Übersee* 31:4 (1998), 440–55.

A. A. An-Naʿim, Towards an Islamic hermeneutics for human rights, in A. A. An-Naʿim et al. (eds.), *Human rights and religious values. An uneasy relationship?*, Amsterdam 1995, chapter 16.

I. Bantekas and H. Abu-Sabeib, Reconciliation of Islamic law with constitutionalism. The protection of human rights in Sudan's new constitution, in *African Journal of International and Comparative Law* 12 (2000), 530–53.

A. F. Clark, Imperialism, independence and Islam in Senegal and Mali, in *Africa Today* 46:3/4 (1999), 149–67.

L. Creevey, Islam, women and the role of the state in Senegal, in *Journal of Religion in Africa* 26:3 (1996), 268–307.

P. Devos, Pious wishes or directly enforceable human rights? Social and economic rights in South Africa's 1996 constitution, in *South African Journal on Human Rights* 13:1 (1997), 67–101.

H. Ebrahim, *The soul of a nation. Constitution making in South Africa*, Oxford 1998.

E. Essien, Conflicting *rationes decidendi*. The dilemma of the lower courts in Nigeria, in *African Journal of International and Comparative Law* 12 (2000), 23–30.

B. Ibhawoh, *Between culture and constitution. The cultural legitimacy of human rights in Nigeria*, Copenhagen 1999.

B. Lanne, Tchad. La constitution du 14 Avril 1996. Présentation, in *Afrique contemporaine* 182 (1997), 63–88.

M. Matemde and N. R. Dorsey, *Gender, politics and constitution making in Uganda*, Kampala 2002.

K. Meagher, Veiled conflicts. Peasant differentiation, gender and structural adjustment in Nigerian Hausaland, in D. Bryceson et al. (eds.), *Disappearing peasantries?*, London 2000, 81–99.

S. Monteillet, L'islam, le droit et l'état dans la constitution mauritienne, in *L'Afrique politique* (2002), 69–100.

G. W. Mugwanya, Augmenting the struggle for gender equality in Uganda. A case for the domestication of international human rights standards, in *African Journal of International and Comparative Law* 12 (2000), 754–98.

E. I. Nwogugu, *Family law in Nigeria*, Ibadan 1990.

H. Rushwan, Female circumcision, in *World Health* (September 1995), 16–17.

J. C. M. van Santen, "In between-sons." Mafa system of land, property and sustainable "land-use" in and outside the Mandara mountains, in M. Ali et al. (eds.), *Management of fragile ecosystems in the North of Cameroon*, Leiden 2001, 221–33.

——, "They will be pulled into hell with a rope around their balls." Femininity, masculinity and the Islamic fundamentalist wave, the case of North-Cameroon, in A. Breedveld and J. C. M. van Santen, *The dynamics of Islam and identity in Africa*, Brill (forthcoming).

J. C. M. van Santen and K. Willemse, Islam at the frontier. Dynamics of Muslim identities in relation to the changing role of the state in post-colonial Africa, NOW Research Proposal 2003.

——, The issue of "Islamic fundamentalisms." Masculinities and femininities, in A. Breedveld and J. C. M. van Santen, *The dynamics of Islam and identity in Africa*, Brill (forthcoming).

Shamima, paper presented at the MYM Islamic Tarbiyyah Programme 1997, 19–23 December, As-Salaam, KwaZulu-Natal 1997.

K. Willemse, The burden of boundaries. Islamist discourse and constructions of gender in Darfur, West-Sudan, in A. Breedveld and J. C. M. van Santen, *The dynamics of Islam and identity in Africa*, Brill (forthcoming), notes 4–5.

José C. M. van Santen

Democracy Ideologies

Arab States

Democracy is representation for the people by the people. A true democracy must include women who are representative of half of the population. Arab states that do not allow women to participate politically either implicitly or explicitly demonstrate, in this fact alone, their commitment and desire to democratize. As is evidenced from Table 1, regime type and economic and social status play little role in women's entrance into parliament. Indeed, societal obstacles which hinder women from entering such positions can in many cases be overcome by foreign influence and then, in most instances, by a quota system.

Political culture in the Arab world is shaped by informal groups and kinship relations, even within the formal political systems. Arab political structures include traditional and conservative monarchies, republics, and secular and Islamic regimes. Western democracy ideologies are often juxtaposed against these various structures of Arab political culture. Therefore, much of the political cultural analysis of the Arab world tends to dilute the possibilities of democratic advancement by labeling these states as "democratically challenged." The reasoning for such a consensus stems from religion, cultural beliefs, authoritarian Arab leaders, political economy, or a rejection of foreign influence. Yet, reform processes are taking place in Arab countries, albeit slowly, which aim to establish democratic methods of governing.

Certain religious interpretations adopted by religious groups contribute to the stagnation of the Arab reform process. Some scholars (such as Kedourie) believe that democracy is an alien concept to Islam while some Arab thinkers (Khālid Muḥammad Khālid) believe that the Islamic principle of *shūra* (consultation council) corresponds to the idea of democracy.

The evidence regarding obstacles to democracy are more clearly understood by examining the issue of women's status according to Sharīʿa law (Islamic law), which Islamic movements strive to uphold. Islamic law allows men to unilaterally divorce their wives, accepts polygamy, considers a woman's testimony to equal half that of a man, and allows a woman to inherit only half of what a man may inherit. Interpretation of women's inferior status in Islam is further reinforced by the patriarchic structure of the Arab family. An inferior view of women clearly represents a major obstacle to democracy, by not considering a woman a full participant in society.

Full participation is a right of every individual in society. Human rights organizations and women's organizations are at the forefront in creating a more pluralistic society in attempts to break up patterns of control and exclusionary tendencies in the Arab states. The ideologies of the women's movements and democracy share characteristics such as equality, dignity, autonomy, power-sharing, liberation, and human rights. While women's movements and democracy are ideologically united, women's presence in elected positions of formal government in the Middle East and North Africa region has been the lowest (regionally) in the world. Causes of this phenomenon are conventionally related to religious and cultural gender roles, tribal affiliations, or the existence of a patriarchal society.

Conventional wisdom suggests that if women's role in the social and economic sectors of the public sphere were to improve then women would more easily make the transition into politics. Table 1 shows that it is the external factor (whether conditionality of foreign aids or resisting foreign hegemony and influence) rather than socioeconomic factors that creates a conducive environment which allows women to enter the political realm. Foreign influence is the strongest variable affecting women's entry into the political realm.

Table 1

State	External Factor	Political Participation Rate	Female Labor Force
Jordan	Conditionality	5.4%	16.0%*
Morocco	Conditionality	10.0%	11.0%
Syria	Resistance	10.4%	25.0%
Lebanon	Minimal	2.0%	30.0%
Kuwait	Minimal	0.0%	33.8%

Source: World Bank GenderStats
* Department of Statistics, Government of Jordan, 2002

Table 1 examines five different states in terms of external factors, political participation rates of women, and percentage of female labor force. By viewing the external factors in relation to women's participation rates in politics a clear parallel is illustrated with foreign influence. The impact of increased foreign aid money granted on a conditional basis and resistance to foreign influence plays a major role in creating a kind of representative democracy. Surprisingly, the strongest female labor force rates (Lebanon and Kuwait) are associated with the lowest rates in political participation and the least involvement with outside forces either through conditional aid or resistance participation.

Women's political participation in the Arab world can be seen to run parallel to a strong foreign influence either in a direct (Jordan and Morocco) or indirect (Syria) way. Interestingly, the direct influence of the United States on both Jordan and Morocco has yielded positive outcomes as both countries have enacted a quota system to overcome the social obstacles that face women entering political positions and to further their democratic reform processes. United States suggestions to Jordan are closely linked with hundreds of millions of dollars in development and military aid. The Moroccan move toward democracy and women's involvement in political positions is similarly based on external forces, namely, foreign aid from the United States, which quadrupled from 1999 to 2000, the fall of the Berlin wall, the collapse of dictatorships, Western calls for democracy and human rights, and the aftershocks of 11 September 2001.

The Jordanian and Moroccan states, which are dependent on foreign aid, have had to implement certain measures to allow women's entry into parliament. Although women have campaigned in both countries success has been marginal due to the patriarchy and religiosity of society. The quota system provided a solution. By issuing royal decrees both Jordan and Morocco pleased the foreign providers of aid and broke through cultural barriers which inhibited women's entry into parliament. The quota system in Jordan ensures women 6 out of 110 seats in parliament to women, the quota in Morocco ensures 30 out of 300. The quota system provokes impassioned support and fervent opposition. A supportive argument maintains that over the years qualified women have been discriminated against solely on gender grounds. The quota system therefore is seen not as a favor to women but as an essential move toward creating a truly representative government. An oppositional argument declares that the quota system blatantly discriminates against men and, further, doubts that women have the capacity to fulfill the required duties in the formal political sphere.

Unlike the situation in Jordan and Morocco, Syrian women's involvement in politics can be traced back to the need to resist the process of Turkification which posed a genuine threat to the Arab sense of identity. This trend continued in 1919 when Syrian women were politically active in demonstrating against the French occupation and when in 1935 they participated in the Arab Women's Conference in Cairo in resistance to the Zionist infiltration. Syrian women received the right to vote in the same year as a result of demonstrating participatory approaches against threatening external forces. Lebanese and Kuwaiti women have had little experience in terms of political participation against external forces and therefore have low to non-existent rates of political participation. Furthermore, the Lebanese and Kuwaiti regimes are rarely candidates for Western pressure.

Arab politics, including women's movements, are shaped by and large as a response to external pressure. The success of democracy in the Arab world is contingent upon a kind of assertive linkage between foreign aid and demands for genuine democratic reform. Given the centrality of the external factor in Arab politics, internal variables such as kinship, tribal and religious groups, and socioeconomic factors should not be seen as a major stumbling block in the path of women's entry into politics.

Bibliography

Primary Sources

J. Caivano, Women's participation in the democratic process. The OAS Permanent Council in conjunction with the Unit for the Promotion of Democracy and the Executive Secretariat of the Inter-American Commission of Women, 25 November 2002, Washington, D.C. <http://www.upd.oas.org/lab/ information/democratic_forum/11_25_2002_washington_dc_joan_caivano.html>.

Jordan, Department of Statistics, *Jordan in Figures. June 2002*, issue 4, Amman, <http://www.dos.gov.jo/dos_home_e/main/index.htm>.

A. Karam, Strengthening the role of women parliamentarians in the Arab region. Challenges and options, 8 April 2002, United Nations Development Programme-Programme on Governance in the Arab Region, <http://www.pogar.org/publications/gender/karam2/section3.html>.

Inter-Parliamentary Union, *Plan of Action*, Paris, 26 March 1994.

Inter-Parliamentary Union, Women in national parliaments. Situation as of 31 May 2003, <http://www.ipu.org/wmn-e/arc/world310503.htm>.

Woodrow Wilson International Center for Scholars, More than victims, Washington, D.C., 12 September 2002, <http://wwics.si.edu/topics/pubs/womenpeacerpt.pdf>.

World Bank, Gender and development in the Middle East and North Africa. Women and the public sphere, November 2003, <http://lnweb18.worldbank.org/mna/mena.nsf/Attachments/GenderReport-overview/$File/GENDER-REPORToverview.pdf>.
World Bank, GenderStats, <http://devdata.worldbank.org/genderstats/home.asp>.

SECONDARY SOURCES
L. Anderson, Democracy in the Arab world, in R. Brynen et al. (eds.), *Political liberalization and democratization in the Arab world,* i, *Theoretical perspectives*, Boulder, Colo. 1995, 77–92.
N. Ayubi, Islam and democracy, in D. Potter et al. (eds.), *Democratization*, Cambridge. 1997, 345–66.
J. Bill and R. Springborg, *Politics in the Middle East*, New York 2000.
A. Ehteshami, Is the Middle East democratizing?, in *British Journal of Middle Eastern Studies* 26:2 (November 1999), 199–217.
F. Faqir, Engendering democracy and Islam in the Arab world, in *Third World Quarterly* 18:1 (1997), 165–74.
R. Husseini, Women's parliamentary quota proving to be a double-edged sword, in *Jordan Times*, 15 January 2003.
——, Female candidates in the capital explain platform, debate issues, in *Jordan Times*, 12 June 2003.
J. S. Makdisi, The mythology of modernity. Women and democracy in Lebanon, in M. Yamani (ed.), *Feminism and Islam*, New York 1996, 231–49.
A. Odibat and R. F. Bahou, *Gender and democratization in the Arab region*, Amman 2004.
A. Phillips, *Engendering democracy*, Cambridge 1991.
R. Voet, *Feminism and citizenship*, London 1998.

LINDSEY FAUSS

Asia-Pacific Region

INTRODUCTION

The recent interest in women and democracy is premised on women's increasing access to and control over representative institutions. Political participation is considered the key to the enhancement of the status of women and the institutionalization of democracy. Women activists are no longer happy to see women only vote in elections and sign petitions. For them gender inequality needs to be viewed from a broader context by focusing on women's disadvantaged position in terms of income and work. Political participation for women is only meaningful if women are in a position "to elect a government more responsive to women's poverty, one committed to a better programme of equal pay for equal work, combined with a set of welfare policies that would cater for women's needs" (Phillips 1993, 103). The quest for equality for women in politics has been a continuing concern for both feminists and the United Nations for the last three decades. The United Nations organized five major international conferences on women between 1975 and the present to increase women's participation in politics.

The significance of the role of women in politics in general and in democracy in particular is important for several reasons. Issues involved in the analysis of women in Third World politics are based on three assumptions that differ substantially from the case of men (Waylen 1996, 6). These assumptions are: politics does not have the same impact on women as it does on men; the political process often alters gender relations; and women often participate in political activity as political subjects. These assumptions show that men and women participate quite differently in formal politics in the First as well as the Third World, both in getting issues onto the political agenda and in policy-making and implementation (Ackelsberg 1992). One of the outcomes of this difference is that there is a distinct tendency for women to participate less than men in formal politics in higher echelons of power (Peterson and Runyan 1993).

This entry analyzes the situation of women vis-à-vis democracy in the Asia-Pacific region. In the process attempts are made to show differentiation and interrelationships between the key phrases "women and Islam" and "women and democracy."

WOMEN AND ISLAM

When Islam emerged in Arabia in the seventh century C.E. it was not only a new religion but also a movement of social reform with particular relevance to the status of women (Minces 1980, 15). Islam gave women a legal status, with rights and duties. Social responsibility in Islam is derived from the Qurʾān: "And [as for] the believers both men and women – they are friends and protectors of one another: they [all] enjoin the doing of what is right and forbid the doing of what is wrong" (9:71). This verse requires women and men to act for the betterment of society. Political involvement is a means to fulfill obligations to society. The history of Islam contains examples of women performing political roles, for example, voting in elections and holding positions of legislators and judges. But in many Muslim countries women have been denied some of their basic rights. This is contrary to Qurʾānic teaching. The Qurʾān proclaims that all believers who perform good deeds, whether male or female, "shall enter the garden and they shall not be dealt with unjustly" (19:60). From this and other verses it can be inferred that the Qurʾān intends to maintain equality between sexes (Engineer 1994, 51).

Women and democracy

There is now a consensus that for a political system to be called democratic it must have certain characteristics: open political competition, a multiparty system, civil and political rights guaranteed by law, and accountability operating through an electoral relationship between citizens and their representatives (Luckham and White 1996, 2). There has also been continuing tension within democratic theory between popular sovereignty and the power of the elite, between representatives and participatory principles, and between partial interests and common interests (Luckham and White 1996, 3). Criticisms leveled against democracy range from questioning its theoretical foundations to its adverse impact on women in democracies. Liberal democratic theory is considered essentially gendered and it perpetuates patterns of patriarchy and gender subordination both in polity and society (Rai 1996). For feminists, liberal democracy has failed to serve the interests of women (Mendus 1992, Phillips 1993). It has also been stated that women never have been and still are not admitted as full and equal members in any democratic country (Pateman 1989, 210). The feminist critique of democracy is premised on women's subordinate position in economy, polity, and society. Feminists point out that the underrepresentation of women in liberal democratic polities is due to emphasis on the individual as the legitimate actor in democratic politics and the division between public and private spheres (Rai 1996). In the context of the Third World it has been argued that this division inhibits mass participation of women in politics and consequently in the democratic process affecting them (Rai 1994, 209).

The basic objection of feminists is that the objective of democratization has not materialized in democratic systems. Democratization is expected to take place under conditions in which power resources have become so widely distributed that no group is any longer able to suppress its competitors or maintain its hegemony (Vanhanen 1997, 5). Feminists have challenged the relationship between democracy and democratization. They contend that a separation has been made between democracy (a political method) and institutional arrangement from democratization (a social and political process) (Pateman 1996, 7). The resultant dichotomy further weakens position of women vis-à-vis men because women may be enjoying certain rights in democracy while in the wider arena, namely democratization, they may be denied certain other rights that are products of sociopolitical interactions, belief systems, and capacities of individuals in particular societies (Khan 2001, 3).

Asia-Pacific region

The Asia-Pacific region consists of diverse countries with different populations and cultural heritages (Chung 1991, 103). The region's population reached 3.4 billion in the early 1990s (UN 1993, 2). The social landscape of this region has a wide spectrum of variations in the circumstances of women in such areas as workforce participation rates, earning opportunities, levels of education, health status, fertility, political representation, and participation in government. Such differences are in part accounted for by the extent, type, and quality of interventions of government on behalf of women in society (Sobhan 1992, 1).

The large number of countries in the region have various kinds of political systems. In South Asia, Bangladesh, India, Nepal, and Sri Lanka there are democracies while Pakistan remains under military rule. In East Asia, Japan has been a stable democracy for half a century and South Korea and Taiwan have carried out significant democratic transitions during the past decade. China, North Korea, and Vietnam are non-democracies. In Southeast Asia, Malaysia, Thailand, Indonesia, Singapore, and the Philippines have in place competitive elections, parliament with opposition representation, reasonably well-established norms of political competition, rule of law, and legalized opposition political parties. Burma remains firmly under the control of a military junta. In the Pacific region, Australia and New Zealand have remained vibrant democratic systems. Papua New Guinea has maintained a democratic system since gaining independence in 1975.

A survey of the region shows that women are far from achieving equal participation in decision-making and leadership positions. By 1995 only 24 women had ever been elected as heads of state or government (Corner 1997, 2). In 1994 women held 5.7 percent of posts of cabinet minister. There has been a wide level of variation in terms of women's parliamentary representation.

Though female leaders such as Indira Gandhi and Sonia Gandhi of India, Khaleda Zia and Sheikh Hasina of Bangladesh, Benazir Bhutto of Pakistan, and Srimavo Bandaranike and Chandrika Kumaratunga of Sri Lanka have dominated the political scene in recent decades, women in South Asia still have the lowest rates of participation in systems of governance. Women occupy only 7 percent of parliamentary seats; only 9 percent of cabinet ministers are women; and only 20 percent of members of local governments are women (HDC 2000, 136).

At the grassroots level women on the whole constitute a much smaller membership of political parties than men. Naturally, this means that the numbers elected to representative bodies are also low (see Table 1). While women generally remain underrepresented in formal politics, this does not imply that policies formulated and implemented within the political process do not have a critical impact on the lives of different groups of women. Therefore, while examining policy-making and its outcomes, the gendered nature of the state comes under significant scrutiny. Usually large numbers of women work in the public sector but only a few occupy top positions. This scenario is seen in all types of political systems.

Data indicate that in the year 2000 the highest proportion of female public sector administrative and managerial personnel is found in New Zealand (44 percent), followed by Fiji Islands (20.7 percent), and Australia (19.5 percent) (see Table 2).

In Southeast Asia, Corazon Aquino of the Philippines was elected to the presidency after the fall of the Marcos regime. Megawati Sukarnoputri of Indonesia is now the president of her country. Female representation in top elected political bodies in Southeast Asia still remains rather low. Women's representation in ministerial and sub-ministerial positions in some of the Southeast Asian countries in 1996 was: Thailand 3.8 and 4.5 percent, Singapore 0 and 7.1 percent, Malaysia 7.7 and 4.7 percent, the Philippines 8.3 and 26.3 percent, and Indonesia 3.6 and 1.4 percent (UNDP 1996).

The situation of women in terms of political representation is not much different in East Asian countries. In Japan the percentage of women in the lower and upper houses are 2.3 and 14.7 percent respectively (Yoko et al. 1994, 396). In South Korea 2 percent of legislators are women (Sohn 1994, 436). In China women hold 11.1 and 21.1 percent posts at ministerial and sub-ministerial levels (UNDP 1996).

These data point to a rather disappointing state of affairs. The "virtual exclusion and marginalization of women from formal politics" (Chowdhury and Nelson 1994, 15) cannot be explained by referring only to women's socially shaped choices and social norms. Rather, predominance of a male ethos of formal politics and culture and formal political institutions, including political parties, contributes to the situation. It has been argued that future enhancement of women's political engagement needs to be viewed from a much broader perspective taking into cognizance gender construction of the family, civil society, the economy, and official institutions (Chowdhury and Nelson 1994, 21).

For many years political participation of women has been used as an indicator of development of a country and of the status of women in that particular country. Women's participation has been measured against certain critical variables including their right to vote; their role in political associations; their participation in various elections; their success rate in elections; and their role in top policy-making bodies. Data on these variables are important, but to be useful they need to be evaluated in terms of social and historical context of each individual country (Manderson 1980, 10).

A comparatively high proportion of women active in the political arena may be due to the class structure of a particular society that allows women belonging to the upper strata to participate in much larger numbers compared to lower-class women and men.

The rise of all female prime ministers and presidents in politics in South Asia and Southeast Asia is due to primarily due to the kinship factor. They all inherited and benefited from political positions of their late fathers and husbands.

Female leaders, activists, and academics in Muslim majority countries such as Bangladesh, Indonesia, Malaysia, and Pakistan do not feel that Islam is antithetical to democracy ideologies or that it hinders women's active participation in formal politics. They believe that the spread of education and opening of economic opportunities for women will facilitate the challenge to those conservative religious interpretations that specifically discriminate against women's participation in public life. They believe that Islam upholds the principles of justice, dignity, and equality (Anwar 2000, 4). These principles are in clear conformity with democracy ideologies.

Conclusion

The present state of women's participation in democratic systems is unacceptable and needs to be changed. It is strange that the talent, experience, and wisdom of the vast majority of women in the Asia-Pacific region remain untapped. In order to institutionalize democracies and enhance women's participation in politics a number of things must happen. First, commitment, vision, and foresight of political leadership are important. Second, appropriate institutions need to be established and nurtured. Third, structural and legal impediments to the advancement of women need to be removed. Fourth, governments in Muslim majority countries should be able and willing to keep conservative political leaders under check. Finally, a strong and vibrant civil society should be able to operate without undue governmental restrictions.

Table 1: Gender empowerment measure (GEM)

Region/ Country	GEM Rank	Seats in parliament held by women (as % of total)**	Female legislators, senior officials and managers (as % of total)	Female professionals and technical workers (as of % of total)	Ratio of estimated female : male earned income
East Asia					
China	n.a.	21.8	n.a.	n.a.	n.a.
Japan	32	10.0	9*	45	0.44
Hong Kong, China	n.a.	n.a.	25	38	n.a.
Korea, Republic of	61	5.9	5	34	0.45
South Asia					
Afghanistan	n.a.	n.a.	n.a.	n.a.	n.a.
Bangladesh	66	2.0	5*	35 d	0.57
Bhutan	n.a.	9.3	n.a.	n.a.	n.a.
India	n.a.	8.9	n.a.	n.a.	n.a.
Nepal	n.a.	7.9	n.a.	n.a.	n.a.
Pakistan	n.a.	-j	9*	26*	n.a.
Sri Lanka	64	4.4	4	49	0.48
Southeast Asia					
Indonesia	n.a.	8.0	n.a.	n.a.	n.a.
Malaysia	43	14.5	20*	45*	0.46
Myanmar	n.a.	-I	n.a.	n.a.	n.a.
Philippines	35	17.2	35*	66*	0.59
Singapore	23	11.8	23	42	0.50
Pacific					
Australia	10	26.5	26	48	0.69
Fiji Islands	n.a.	n.a.	n.a.	n.a.	n.a.
Maldives	62	6.0	15	40	0.60
New Zealand	9	30.8	38	54	0.67
Papua New Guinea	n.a.	1.8	n.a.	n.a.	n.a.
Samoa	n.a.	6.1	n.a.	n.a.	n.a.
Solomon Islands	n.a.	0.0	n.a.	n.a.	n.a.
Vanuatu	n.a.	0.0	n.a.	n.a.	n.a.

* Data are based on the International Standard Classification of Occupations (ISCO-68) as defined in ILO 2001.
** Data are as of 8 March 2002. Where there are lower and upper houses, data refer to the weighted average of women's shares of seats in both houses.

Source: UNDP 2002, 226–9.

Table 2: Women in the public sector in the Asia-Pacific region

Region/Country	Women in government at ministerial level (as % of total) 2000
East Asia	
China	5.1
Japan	5.7
Hong Kong, China	n.a.
Korea, Rep of	6.5
South Asia	
Afghanistan	
Bangladesh	9.5
Bhutan	n.a.
India	10.1
Nepal	14.8
Pakistan	n.a.
Sri Lanka	n.a.

Table 2 (*cont.*)

Region/Country	Women in government at ministerial level (as % of total) 2000
Southeast Asia	
Indonesia	5.9
Malaysia	n.a.
Myanmar	n.a.
Philippines	n.a.
Singapore	5.7
Pacific	
Australia	19.5
Fiji Islands	20.7
Maldives	n.a.
New Zealand	44.0
Papua New Guinea	0.0
Samoa	7.7
Solomon Islands	n.a.
Vanuatu	n.a.

Source: UNDP 2002, 239–42.

Bibliography

M. Ackelsberg, Feminist analyses of public policy, in *Comparative Politics* 24:4 (1992), 477–93.

Z. Anwar, Perspective from Malaysia, in Asia Foundation, *Democratic transitions and the role of Islam in Asia*, 18 October 2000, 3–7.

N. Chowdhury and B. J. Nelson, Redefining politics. Patterns of women's political engagement from a global perspective, in N. Chowdhury and B. J. Nelson (eds.), *Women and politics worldwide*, New Haven, Conn. 1994, 3–24.

Y. Chung (ed.), *The Asia-Pacific community in the year 2000. Challenges and prospects*, Sejong Institute Monograph Series 91–01 (no. 6), Seoul 1991.

L. Corner, Women's participation in decision-making and leadership. A global perspective, 1997, <http://www.unifem-eseasia.org/resources/techpapers/wleaders.htm>.

A. A. Engineer, Muslim family law, in L. Sarkar and B. Sivaramyya (eds.), *Women and law. Contemporary problems*, Dhaka 1994, 50–62.

HDC (Human Development Centre), *Human development in South Asia 2000. The gender question*, Dhaka 2000.

ILO (International Labour Organization), *Yearbook of labour statistics*, Geneva 2001.

M. M. Khan, Problems of democracy. Administrative reform and corruption, in *BIISS Journal* 22:1 (2000), 1–24.

R. Luckham and G. White, Introduction. Democratizing the South, in R. Luckham and G. White (eds.), *Democratization in the South. The jagged wave*, New York 1996, 1–10.

L. Manderson, *Women, politics and change*, Kuala Lumpur 1980.

J. Minces, Introduction. A confessional universe, in J. Minces, *The house of obedience. Women in Arab society*, trans. M. Pallis, London 1980, 13–25.

S. Mendus, Losing the faith. Feminism and democracy, in J. Dunn (ed.), *Democracy. The unfinished journey 508 BC to AD 1993*, Oxford 1992, 207–19.

C. Pateman, *The disorder of women. Democracy, feminism and political theory*, Cambridge 1989.

——, Democracy and democratization, in *International Political Science Review* 17:1 (1996), 5–12.

V. S. Peterson and A. Runyan, *Global gender issues*, Boulder, Colo. 1993.

A. Phillips, Must feminists give up on liberal democracy?, in D. Held (ed.), *Prospects for democracy. North, South, East, West*, Cambridge 1993, 93–111.

S. Rai, Gender and democratization. Or what does democracy mean for women in the Third World?, in *Democratization* 1:2 (1994), 209–28.

——, Gender and democratization. Ambiguity and opportunity, in R. Luckham and G. White (eds.), *Democratization in the South. The jagged wave*, New York 1996, 220–42.

R. Sobhan, *Planning and public action for Asian women*, Dhaka 1992.

B.-C. Sohn, Women's political engagement and participation in the Republic of Korea, in N. Chowdhury and B. J. Nelson (eds.), *Women and politics worldwide*, New Haven, Conn. 1994, 436–47.

UN (United Nations), *The United Nations in the Asia-Pacific region*, Bangkok 1993.

UNDP (United Nations Development Programme), *Human development report 1996. Economic growth and human development*, New York 1996, <http://hdr.undp.org/reports/global/1996/en/>.

——, *Human development report 2002. Deepening democracy in a fragmented world*, New York 2002, <http://hdr.undp.org/reports/global/2002/en/>.

T. Vanhanen, Introduction, in T. Vanhanen, *Prospects of democracy. A study of 172 countries*, London 1997, 3–9.

S. Walby, Gender, globalization and democracy, in *Gender and Development* 8:1 (2000), 20–8.

G. Waylen, Analysing women in the politics of the Third World, in H. Afshor (ed.), *Women and politics in the Third World*, London 1996, 7–24.

E. Wormland, Rhetoric, reality, and a dilemma. Women and politics in Papua New Guinea, in N. Chowdhury and B. J. Nelson (eds.), *Women and politics worldwide*, New Haven, Conn. 1994, 560–74.

N. Yoko et al., The U.N. Convention on Eliminating Discrimination against Women and the status of women in Japan, in N. Chowdhury and B. J. Nelson (eds.), *Women and politics worldwide*, New Haven, Conn. 1994, 397–414.

Mohammad Mohabbat Khan

Iran and Afghanistan

Democracy ideologies are based on gendered concepts of citizenship. They define a citizen as a free and autonomous contract-making individual, a property owner, the male citizen. Democracy ideologies exclude women from the state. This exclusion is accentuated by the attempts to separate state and civil society, civil society and the private sphere, and the state and the private sphere. The works of Alexis de Tocqueville (1805–59), the French philosopher and historian, present an example of the gendered character of democracy ideologies. In his much acclaimed work *De la démocratie en Amérique* (1835–40), he makes an ideological distinction between state and civil society, considers women as custodians of religion and mores, advocates sex segregation and women's exclusion from the public sphere, argues that women's social and political inequality is a natural fact, and maintains that democracy is guaranteed through women's exclusion from the state, or what he calls women's political powerlessness.

By marginalizing women and excluding women from the state and the public sphere democracy ideologies deny women individuality, autonomy, and independence. Indeed, they do not perceive women as individuals but as family members whose rights and obligations are defined in relation to male relatives, leaders, and protectors of women.

In Iran and Afghanistan, modern centralizing states, although antidemocratic, more or less included women in their general program of modernization and national development, but did not challenge gendered distinction between public and private spheres. Women obtained the right to education and to work and were later granted political rights. But with their institutionalization of gendered relations, these states did not challenge gendered systems of social stratification or gendered relations within the family and did not remove from family and religion their social functions. These modernizing states submitted women to the control of the men of their community and privileged women mothers and wives over women citizens. The reformer Afghan King Amān Allāh (1921–9) promoted women's education and introduced a family code in 1921 outlawing child marriage as contrary to Islamic principles, followed by other measures in 1924, including the right of Afghan girls to choose their husbands. Although the introduction of a civil legal code went against traditionalist values of the tribal society and customs, it did not, however, intend to question patriarchy and male domination. In Iran under Reza Shah (1925–41), the number of girls' schools increased sharply in urban areas and the foundation of Tehran University in 1936 allowed women access to higher education and to work mainly in the administration. The veil was outlawed in 1936 but the new family code promulgated in 1933 was entirely founded on Islamic law.

Patriarchal system and gender inequality persisted in the 1960s and 1970s despite the grant of voting rights to women (1963 in Iran, 1964 in Afghanistan), statutory changes, and urban women's increasing presence in the public sphere. Women mothers and wives were still privileged over women citizens. The application of Islamic laws in the aftermath of the Iranian Revolution and following the downfall of the communist government in Afghanistan reinforced patriarchy and denied women their citizenship rights.

In Iran and Afghanistan the Western liberal notion of the citizen, which implies a masculinized construct, has been predominant in democratic discourses that also shared the Western construct of nation-state. As a consequence, attempts to ensure women's legal and citizenship rights, as major factors in the building of democracy, have been largely absent from democratic discourses. Anti-clerical, reformist, and Jacobin-minded Iranian intellectuals such as Aḥmad Kasravī (assassinated in 1945 by the Fidā'iyīn-i Islām, a fundamentalist group), Ḥasan Taqiʿzāda, and Muḥammad ʿAlī Jamālzāda shared the principle of patriarchy and male domination. Despite their different viewpoints on the question of women's emancipation, like de Tocqueville and John Stuart Mill (1806–73), they considered domestic work, and child-bearing and rearing as women's main social function and natural role. Kasravī even argued that women's political participation was in contradiction to their natural characteristics. Several religious reformist intellectuals in post-revolutionary Iran, including ʿAbd al-Karīm Surūsh (known as the standard-bearer of religious intellectualism in post-revolutionary Iran) and ʿAbbās ʿAbdī, who are against political Islam and advocate democracy, also largely share a gendered concept of citizenship. Surūsh's lack of interest in the Woman Question is paramount when we compare his writings on women to the vast corpus of his published work. He has so far devoted only two paragraphs to women. His discussion of gender issues is limited to some lectures and interviews where he criticizes both traditional understandings of women's status in Islam and equal rights advocates. In ʿAbdī's view, the question of women and their legal and citizenship rights is not intertwined with the building of democracy and therefore does not constitute an urgent issue for democracy ideologies.

Over two decades of civil war in Afghanistan, and the rule of the Taliban (1996–2001) have led to the disintegration of the state, social destructuring, and deprivation of women in terms of education, health facilities, work, and social and political participation. Although in the post-Taliban era women have obtained the right to education and to work, many years are needed to reconstruct the country and to empower women. The building of democracy is further hindered by poverty, lack of political stability, and fundamentalist opposition to women's social and political participation, as illustrated by the low representation of women at the Loya Jirga (traditional assembly), and to the presence of women as cabinet ministers or in other decision-making posts. President Hamid Karzai dismissed Sima Samar, the first minister in charge of women's affairs, following pressure by traditionalists, who had dubbed her the Afghan Salman Rushdie. Indicative of the lack of attention of the new Afghan government to women's problems is the fact that Habiba Sarabi, the new minister, was forced to dismiss 150 of her female staff due to financial shortfalls. Faced with structural, political, and cultural impediments to women's empowerment, educated Afghan women, who are conscious that democracy cannot be attained unless women' rights are established, have started to mobilize. Habiba Sarabi maintains: "The situation is very saddening but I'm determined to struggle." Women members of the editorial board of *Rooz*, the first post-Taliban women's magazine published in Kabul, as well as founders and members of women non-governmental organizations share this determination.

In Iran, despite the rule of Islamic law and important obstacles in the way of women attaining authority and power, building capacity for democracy is increasing due to higher literacy rates for women (80 percent of females aged six and over are literate), higher education for young women (50 percent of the 1,500,000 students are female), women's increasing social, cultural, and economic activities, and their increasing political involvement. Moreover, women's representation at local and municipal councils is growing (an 80 percent increase in the 2003 elections compared to 1999). Women's local civic activity combined with their involvement in national politics is likely to enhance grassroots bottom-up democracy.

Bibliography

ʿA. ʿAbdī, Rawshanfikrī-i dīn-i va masāʾil-i fawritar az masāʾil-i zanān, in *Zanān* 58 (2000), 38.

F. Collin, E. Pisier, and E. Varikas, *Les femmes de Platon à Derrida*, Paris 2000.

S. Joseph and S. Slyomovics, Introduction, in S. Joseph and S. Slyomovics (eds), *Women and power in the Middle East*, Philadelphia 2001, 1–19.

A. Kian-Thiébaut, Intellectuels religieux et clercs iraniens face à la modernité occidentale, in *Revue française de science politique* 47 (1997), 776–97.

A. Matin-Asgari, ʿAbdolkarim Sorush and the secularization of Islamic thought in Iran, in *Iranian Studies* 30 (1997), 95–116.

Z. Mir-Hosseini, Religious modernists and the "Woman Question," in E. Hooglund (ed.), *Twenty years of Islamic revolution. Political and social transition in Iran since 1979*, Syracuse, N.Y. 2002, 74–95.

A. Najmabadi, Hazards of modernity and morality. Women, state and ideology in contemporary Iran, in D. Kandiyoti (ed.), *Women, Islam and the state*, London 1991, 46–76.

P. Paidar, *Women and the political process in twentieth-century Iran*, Cambridge 1997.

H. Sarabi, interview with M. F. Colombani, La vie à Roz, in *Elle* 30 (2003), 158–60.

ʿA. Surūsh, Qabz va bast-i ḥuqūq-i zanān, in *Zanān* 59 (2000), 32–7.

A. de Tocqueville, *De la démocratie en Amérique*, 2 vols., Paris 1961.

Azadeh Kian-Thiébaut

Israel

Israel defines itself as both the Jewish state and a democracy. The Declaration of Establishment of the State of Israel, signed on 14 May 1948, explicitly calls for "the natural right of the Jewish people to be masters of their own fate, . . . in their own sovereign State"; it also stresses Israel's commitment to democratic principles including elections, social and political equality, and "freedom of religion, conscience, language, education and culture" (Israel 1948). Israel lacks a constitution, instead relying on a series of Basic Laws such as the 1992 Basic Law of Individual Freedom and Dignity, which guarantees the protection of all life, personal property, and individual liberties.

Many Israelis articulate identity by referencing dichotomies that highlight tensions within Israel over nationalism (Jewish/Palestinian), ethnicity (European/Oriental), and religion (secular/religious, Jewish/non-Jewish). For example, a feminist, left-leaning, secular woman of Moroccan parents might explain her civil identity in terms of politics that emphasize democracy, her national identity as Jewish, and her ethnic identity as Oriental or Moroccan while a Christian Palestinian woman might describe her national identity as Palestinian, her religious identity as Roman Orthodox, and her civil identity as Israeli. Such categorical distinctions deeply structure and affect a person's experience and participation within the state as one element within each pair carries more political, social, economic, and cultural power (Domínguez 1989). For marginalized groups within Israel, the state's embrace of democracy affords possible redress of civil discrimination; democracy and civil society are perceived as more flexible than Judaism or Zionism, which emphasize heritage.

Within academic and popular debates, scholars, politicians, and citizens regularly use the terms "Zionism," "Jewish," and "democracy," yet an overview of the terms illustrates that few shared meanings surface beyond the basic recognition that these terms belong to specific discourses related to Israel's existence. Moreover, individuals often obfuscate the ways in which normative ideas of the state drive descriptive analyses. Uneven and inconsistent democracy ideologies have real consequences for structurally marginalized groups – especially women and Palestinian citizens – when translated into policy. In the case of divorce and the absence of civil marriage in Israel, women receive different legal consideration in the civil and religious courts (Adelman 1997) or, with Palestinian femicides (honor killings), women find themselves subject to codes that further victimize the woman and stigmatize Palestinians (Faier 2004).

Israel is not a liberal democracy; its legislative, judicial, military, and religious bodies codify and institutionalize its Jewish character and Zionist underpinnings. State symbols reinforce the centrality of "Jewish" as a defining feature: the flag (Star of David) and national anthem (HaTikvah, The Hope) signify Jewish meanings and further distance non-Jews from the state. Falah (1996) argues that state land planning policies act in counter democratic ways by seeking to establish Jewish demographic dominance and, thus, Jewish ideological and physical boundaries in predominantly Palestinian areas.

Consequently, many Israelis and non-Israelis question whether Israel can be both Jewish and democratic. Some contend that as Zionism and democracy are fundamentally incommensurate, only a one-state solution ensures equality for all citizens. Post-Zionists share a similar stance by rejecting Zionism as a political organizing philosophy and calling for democratization. However, this literature stresses differing goals and processes because, as Silberstein (1999) illustrates, post-Zionism has metamorphosed from early assertions that the establishment of Israel fulfilled Zionist ideals to current wide-ranging critiques directed at state institutions, the distribution of power, and political processes.

Recent debates in the journal *Israel Studies* highlight ongoing concerns about how best to describe Israel's political ideologies and practices. According to Smooha (1990), Israel is an ethnic democracy that grants elevated status to Jews but does not prohibit the simultaneous realization of national and civil rights by Palestinian citizens. Ghanem, Rouhana, and Yiftachel (1998) reject Smooha's argument, stating instead that Israel's classification should be as an ethnocracy because of the inclusion of religion within the political structure of the state. Others maintain that while the absence of religion is not a precondition of democracy, the meaning of "democracy" or "the Jewish State" is disputed and riddled with inconsistency, misinterpretation, and uneven application (Gavison 1999).

What is striking about Israel's democracy debates is the diminished role gender plays as an issue theoretically linked to political ideologies, discourses, and practices (Kimmerling 2001). Although women (Jewish) serve in the military, run in parliamentary elections, and participate fully in daily life, the paucity of material that addresses gender and democracy as referential raises the question as to whether national conflict in Israel supersedes gendered issues (see Chatty and Rabo 1997 for other Middle Eastern contexts). Available literature and ethnographic data suggest that despite popularized discourses of gender equality in Israel, women face discrimination daily (Swirski and Safir 1991), find themselves challenged when they diverge from expected gendered life trajectories (Sa'ar 2001), and experience state and society through masculinist and nationalist contexts (Espanioly 1994).

In addressing gaps in democratic process, the women's movement focuses on the interrelationship between the political and the personal. Through its non-governmental organizations (NGOs), coexistence activities, peace groups, networks, and other groups, the women's movement offers opportunities for critiquing the status quo, organizing community action, and seeking alternative forms of social and/or political organization. For example, the organization Isha L'Isha (Woman to Woman) Haifa Feminist Center runs a media watch program that examines the impact of negative stereotypes on both the perception of women and their experiences. Women in Black and other women's peace groups have sought to locate their resistance within gendered discourses that draw from ideas of democracy and equality but do not replicate them (Shadmi 2000, Sharoni 1995). Magno (2002) examines the obstacles and possibilities for women's NGOs to produce social and political capital while Faier (2004) explores attempts by Palestinian female NGO activists to gender citizenship and nationalism in the face of risk and uncertainty.

Deep and established division among Israeli

women, usually along ethnic (Ashkenazi/Mizrahi, that is, European/Oriental) or national (Palestinian/Jewish) lines obscure how class, colonialism, and state categorization affect both women's lives and their experiences of the state (Shohat 1989). Kanaaneh (2001) illustrates how Palestinian women situate themselves and are situated as sites of power where demographic conflict, Palestinian nationalism, family planning, and the politics of gender within Israel play out. Similarly, Kahn (2000) explores reproductive technologies among unmarried Jewish women, drawing out the complicated ways fertility and reproductive debates invoke Jewish law as well as democratic access to state health services. According to Torstrick (2000), coexistence groups that desire social and cultural integration between Jews and Palestinians but not changes in Israel's political structure reinterpret the ideals of democracy along cultural idioms rather than risk exposing contradictions within the state's democratic fabric. Emmett (1996) shows that while female coexistence activists attempt to subsume politics within the personal, larger political conflicts seep into and infuse the interpersonal, challenging distinctions between public and private as well as self and nation.

Democracy in Israel is a hotly contested political ideology. Democracy ideologies interchange with larger conversations about civil society, nationalism, religion, and identity, opening up possibilities for revealing and perhaps benefiting from contradictions and inconsistencies within the state. Clearly, other concerns – namely the maintenance or contestation of the Jewish character of the state and the protracted Israeli-Palestinian conflict – temper the definition, articulation, and practice of democracy in Israel. Given these parameters, women face the doubly difficult task of interjecting their voices within state discourses and in turn, negotiating the form and substance of gendered ideologies of democracy and citizenship.

Bibliography

Primary Sources

Association for Civil Rights in Israel, <http://www.acri.org.il/english-acri/engine/index.asp>.

M. Freedman, *Exile in the promised land. A memoir*, Ithaca, N.Y. 1990.

D. Grossman, *Sleeping on a wire. Conversations with Palestinians in Israel*, New York 1993.

Haifa Women's Coalition Homepage, <http://www.haifawomenscoalition.org.il/>.

Israel, Ministry of Foreign Affairs, <http://www.mfa.gov.il/mfa>.

A. Shammas, *Arabesques. A novel*, trans. V. Eden, New York 1988.

Women's Voice, Women's Center, <http://kolhaisha.israel.net/engindex.html>.

Secondary Sources

M. Adelman, Gender, law, and nation. The politics of domestic violence in Israel, Ph.D. diss., Durham N.C. 1997.

D. Chatty and A. Rabo (eds.), *Organizing women. Formal and informal women's groups in the Middle East*, Oxford 1997.

V. Domínguez, *People as subject, people as object. Selfhood and peoplehood in contemporary Israel*, Madison, Wis. 1989.

A. Emmett, *Our sisters' promised land. Women, politics, and Israeli-Palestinian coexistence*, Ann Arbor 1996.

N. Espanioly, Palestinian women in Israel. Identity in light of the occupation, in T. Mayer (ed.), *Women and the Israeli occupation. The politics of change*, London 1994, 106–20.

E. Faier, *Organizations, gender, and the culture of Palestinian activism in Haifa, Israel*, New York 2004.

G. Falah, Living together apart. Residential segregation in mixed Arab-Jewish cities in Israel, in *Urban Studies* 33 (1996), 823–57.

R. Gavison, Jewish and Democratic? A rejoinder to the "ethnic democracy" debate, in *Israel Studies* 4 (1999), 44–72.

A. Ghanem, N. Rouhana, and O.Yiftachel, Questioning "ethnic democracy." A response to Sammy Smooha, in *Israel Studies* 3 (1998), 253–67.

Israel, Ministry of Foreign Affairs, 1948, <http://www.mfa.gov.il/MFA/Peace+Process/Guide+to+the+Peace+Process/Declaration+of+Establishment+of+State+of+Israel.htm.>

S. Kahn, *Reproducing Jews. A cultural account of assisted conception in Israel*, Durham, N.C. 2000.

R. Kanaaneh, *Birthing the nation. Strategies of Palestinian women in Israel*, Berkeley 2001.

B. Kimmerling, *The invention and decline of Israeliness. State, society, and the military*, Berkeley 2001.

C. Magno, *New pythian voices. Women building political capital in NGOs in the Middle East*, New York 2002.

A. Sa'ar, Lonely in your firm grip. Women in Israeli-Palestinian families, in *Journal of the Royal Anthropological Institute* 7 (2001), 723–40.

E. Shadmi, Between resistance and compliance, feminism and nationalism. Women in Black in Israel, in *Women's Studies International Forum* 23 (2000), 23–34.

S. Sharoni, *Gender and the Israeli-Palestinian conflict. The politics of women's resistance*, Syracuse, N.Y. 1995.

E. Shohat, *Israeli cinema. East/West and the politics of representation*, Austin, Tex. 1989.

L. J. Silberstein, *The post-Zionism debates. Knowledge and power in Israeli culture*, New York 1999.

S. Smooha, Minority status in an ethnic democracy. The status of the Arab minority in Israel, in *Ethnic and Racial Studies* 13 (1990), 389–413.

B. Swirski and M. Safir (eds.), *Calling the equality bluff. Women in Israel*, New York 1991

R. Torstrick, *The limits of coexistence. Identity politics in Israel*, Ann Arbor 2000.

Elizabeth Anne Faier

Divorce and Custody: Contemporary Practices

Arab States

The practices and social implications of divorce and custody are discussed here by looking at how women live with divorce before, during and after marriage. How do Arab women deal with the threat of divorce? What are their means to influence the divorce process? And what are its social and economic consequences? Historical studies of court archives have provided interesting insights into how women pursued or resisted divorce in court and added to its analysis from a legal perspective (Mir-Hosseini 2000, Ahmad 1972, Gibb and Kramers 1974, El-Alami and Hinchcliffe 1996, Sonbol 1996, Esposito and DeLong-Bas 2001), but information on women's actual experiences is scant and fragmented. Women's divorce experiences vary greatly, depending not only on the particular religious, customary, and national laws locally adhered to, but also on class, urban or rural locality, context of migration or dislocation, and individual circumstances.

Before marriage

Before marriage, girls and their parents try to reduce the risk of future divorce or its harmful consequences by choosing a marriage partner from comparable family background, preferably the father's brother's son or another kinsman. He is expected to show respect and responsibility for a wife who is related to him, and she will feel more comfortable living with relatives. No figures are available to confirm whether familial endogamy indeed reduces the divorce rate. Another strategy is to demand a sizable bridal gift (*mahr* or *ṣadāq*). This is thought to deter divorce because the man would lose this investment, which becomes her property if he divorces her. Estimations of the divorce risk are most expressed in the deferred *mahr*, the part due upon dissolution of the marriage, which is set higher for previously divorced or unrelated grooms. Cousins pay less, which may leave a woman divorced by her cousin with less property than if she had married a stranger. Bride-exchange between families exacerbates the precariousness of marriage for the women involved, because when one wife is repudiated the other must return to her parents too; and both women have less security in gold, because hardly any *mahr* is paid. Girls who are divorced before the marriage is consummated are expected to return the *mahr*, as Moors found for Palestine (Moors 1995, 145). A last means to empower women in divorce matters is through the stipulations Muslim women are allowed to write into their marriage contract. When any stipulated right, for example, to study, work, or remain the sole wife, is not granted, women can demand divorce (Chérif-Chammari 1995). Feminists advise the use of this strategy, but in practice it is difficult because girls depend on their male matrimonial guardian and male notaries, who are reluctant to negotiate and register uncommon clauses. Moreover, most girls prefer not to think of future marital problems, and some even fancy divorce as a way to become free.

During marriage

After the wedding, the conjugal tie is challenged by the young man's loyalty and obligations toward his mother and patrilineal kin. He needed their financial support for his marriage, which gives them the power to interfere in the couple's life. His family's demands for financial and emotional support are frequently a source of marital tensions (Mir-Hosseini 2001, 120). Accusations of magic in North Africa express this antagonism among in-laws (Jansen 1987, 115–20). Women know the marriage bond can be broken easily, and fear the fragility of their husband's love. Children are essential to secure the bond. Infertile women in the Maghrib sometimes say they are pregnant with a "sleeping fetus" to ward off the threat of divorce (Jansen 2000). Women also protect themselves by collecting gold, especially in the first years of marriage, or by saving their housekeeping money or salary. The tendency – and legal right – of employed women to spend their income on themselves rather than their family unit, is a source of conflict among better-educated urban couples.

Women's strategy to keep close social and financial ties with their family of birth, by a regular exchange of gifts or by leaving them their share of inheritance, is a source of security for women, but can equally be a source of marital conflicts, and can facilitate a separation. Maher explained the higher divorce rates she found in Moroccan villages compared to the nearby town by the fact that rural women could fall back on their families to whom they had left their land and with whom they had kept up intimate relations. Poor women in town who were cut off from the support of their families or without land rights in their villages of origin had no means to request a separation (Maher 1974a, 191–221, 1974b).

Marital discord is generally attributed to the wife's disobedience or disagreeable character. Among the Moroccan poor the discrepancy between the legal model of men as the sole providers and the social reality of the wife being in many cases the main breadwinner is an important underlying reason for marital breakdown. A common way for unemployed men to respond to the dishonor of being dependent on their wife's work or network, is to reclaim authority by violence or by deserting the family (Mir-Hosseini 2000, 120–1).

Divorce

In the divorce process, women have fewer rights than men. The dominant form of divorce in Islam is the *ṭalāq*, whereby a man simply declares: "I repudiate thee." When he does so three times the divorce becomes irrevocable. He need not give a reason, nor need his wife be present or informed. This superior male right dominates the general discourse on divorce. It is expressed by the use of the passive form ("he has repudiated her" rather than "they separated") in stories of men randomly divorcing their wives and in male threats during conflicts. This discourse fuels women's fear of divorce more than actual knowledge of divorce rates; accurate statistics on this issue are remarkably absent or unreliable in most Arab countries. Most Arab states have limited excessive use of this male prerogative. Many now require registration of the *ṭalāq* by a notary, and consider repudiations made under certain circumstances invalid, for example, when the husband is intoxicated or in a fit of anger or violence, or pronounces a triple repudiation in one formula, or when the wife is menstruating. In Egypt since 1979 the wife must be informed of the action and is entitled to remain in the rented marital home when she assumes custody of the children (Rugh 1984, 179). In Tunisia a divorce can only be obtained in court.

Despite such adaptations, women remain disadvantaged in terms of divorce. Simple registration does not suffice, and women must request divorce through a court. Nearly all divorce cases treated in court are therefore instigated by women, although men initiate divorce twice as often as women (Mir-Hosseini 2000, 84–5, Rugh 1984, 177). Unlike men, women need to have good reasons to petition for divorce, such as the husband's impotence or suffering from a dangerous contagious disease, repeated and extreme violent abuse, failure to provide maintenance, or desertion.

An alternative for women to effect separation is to convince the husband to divorce her. In this *khulʿ* divorce by mutual consent, the wife must pay the husband compensation for agreeing to release her: she "buys her head" as people say in the Maghrib. It should not be seen, however, as a "woman's divorce" in which women have equal rights. Men can abuse this option to avoid paying divorce dues. Rather than pronouncing a *ṭalāq* a man can make his wife's life so miserable that she leaves him and pays for a *khulʿ* divorce. Moreover, he can make her pay dearly for her freedom. She commonly has to return the *mahr* and to relinquish her right to the deferred *mahr*, but often she also gives up her maintenance during the waiting period (*ʿidda*), the maintenance of the children, or even the right to custody. A woman thus has to give up the very property that was meant to protect her against divorce and its financial consequences. Lower-class women without economic means or familial support will therefore seldom request a *khulʿ*. Instead, they fight to retain their *mahr* and maintenance. It is mainly women from upper and middle strata of society who request a *khulʿ* divorce in court. Since 2000, Egyptian women can do so without the husband's agreement. By exploiting the possibilities of *khulʿ* to the full, they can gain more gender equality in access to divorce. But they still bear the brunt of its consequences: the required arbitration process reinforces the extant familial control over divorce arrangements, women must return the *mahr* and other gifts, and stand up to public opinion, which condemns *khulʿ* as disrespectable (Tucker 2003).

Several women's organizations take a stand against gender discriminatory family laws and court practices or provide concrete support to divorcees (Collectif 95 1995). Divorce rates are likely to increase with the growing participation of women in the labor market and in politics. Christians in Islamic countries divorce less often than Muslims. The divorce rules of their churches vary from a total ban on divorce to allowing it under specific circumstances. Christian women have less fear of divorce and no protection in the form of a deferred *mahr*. Occasionally, a Christian who wants to divorce becomes Muslim or, more commonly, converts to another Christian denomination that accepts divorce.

After divorce

A divorced woman is expected to return to her family of birth and then remarry. A women's impetus to leave her husband is influenced by her chances of remarriage and the fear of losing her children. Only young women without children who can easily find a new partner willingly request divorce; post-menopausal women or women with several children seldom voluntarily do so (Maher 1974b, 191–221). The second marriage reveals a drop in social status: the *mahr* is lower and the second husband less attractive in terms of age, income, or civil status (Jansen 1987, 2–3). Moreover, a woman can seldom take her children into the new marriage. If her female relatives cannot take care of them, her ex-husband has the right to take the children away from her. Unlike men, women must observe a legal waiting period (*ʿidda*) before they can remarry. During this period of three menstrual cycles, or when they are pregnant until they have given birth, the man can take his wife back.

Not all families are able or willing to welcome back a divorcee with several children, despite the strong ideology of family support. They will pressure her to reconcile with and obey her husband, or when that fails, to sue the ex-spouse to pay maintenance. When he is too poor, the family often cannot but reproachfully accept that the divorcee earns her own living and that of her children. Divorcees are as a result over-represented among employed women.

The work of divorcees in public space and their movements outside male control contribute to the ambiguous reputation of divorcees as both morally degraded and joyfully free. Divorcees are often referred to in pejorative terms. Married women fear them for their seductive powers. In songs and gossip, divorcees and other "women without men" are associated with looseness, drunkenness, and prostitution. The choice of some divorcees to make a living in the entertainment business is seized upon to stigmatize the whole group, and forces others to go to extreme lengths to prove their decency (Jansen 1987, 196–8). On the positive side, divorcees are less constrained in their behavior than married women. They can experience economic independence and decision-making power, and taste the pleasures of mobility and exploration of the outside world. Despite the envious gossip and moral reprobation, some divorcees have come to enjoy life without a partner.

The mother is recognized as the most suitable caretaker of the children after divorce. If she cannot raise the child, or when she remarries, the right of care (*ḥaḍāna*) passes to her mother, or another woman in her family, before going to the child's paternal grandmother. This female prerogative does not prevent conflicts concerning the children. In some legal systems women's rights to the children are temporary. This gives fathers a hold over the mother and her children, whether they reclaim the children after a certain age or not. Another reason is that a father keeps his rights to guardianship (*wilāya*), provided he pays for the child's maintenance. It gives him the right to decide on its education, residence, travel or marriage, and the mother must obey him in anything that concerns the child. The major source of contention concerning the children, however, is the insufficiency or absence of maintenance. Among middle and upper classes, the fathers who do pay for their children still need regular prompting. Most broken marriages are found among the poor, and here men often forego their guardianship rights because they cannot afford to pay maintenance or prefer to spend their meager income on their new family. Women's privilege of custody means that they have to carry the full economic burden.

Bibliography

K. N. Ahmad, *The Muslim law of divorce*, Islamabad 1972.

A. Chérif-Chammari, *Le mariage. Guide des droits des femmes*, Tunis 1995.

Collectif 95 Maghreb Egalité, *One hundred measures and provisions for a Maghrebian egalitarian codification of the Personal Statute and Family Law*, Rabat 1995.

D. El-Alami and D. Hinchcliffe (eds.), *Islamic marriage and divorce laws of the Arab world*, The Hague 1996.

J. L. Esposito with N. J. DeLong-Bas, *Women in Muslim family law*, Syracuse, N.Y. 2001.

H. A. R. Gibb and J. H. Kramers, Ṭalāḳ, in *Shorter encyclopaedia of Islam*, Leiden 1974, 564–71.

W. Jansen, *Women without men. Gender and marginality in an Algerian town*, Leiden 1987.

——, Sleeping in the womb. Protracted pregnancies in the Maghreb, in *Muslim World* 90 (2000), 218–38.

Koran. With a parallel Arabic text, trans. N. J. Dawood, London 1990 (5th rev. ed.), 2:227–31, 33:49, 65:1–7.

V. Maher, *Women and property in Morocco*, London 1974a.

——, Divorce and property in the Middle Atlas of Morocco, in *Man* 9 (1974b), 103–22.

Z. Mir-Hosseini, *Marriage on trial. A study of Islamic family law in Iran and Morocco*, London 1993.

A. Moors, *Women, property and Islam. Palestinian experiences, 1920–1990*, Cambridge 1995.

A. B. Rugh, *Family in contemporary Egypt*, Syracuse, N.Y. 1984.

A. E. Sonbol, *Women, the family, and divorce laws in Islamic history*, Syracuse, N.Y. 1996.

J. E. Tucker, Tracking the woman's divorce. *Khulʿ* in historical context, paper presented at ISIM, Leiden, 14–16 March 2003.

Willy Jansen

Australia

The majority of Australian Muslim women involved in divorce and custody problems are required to negotiate their way through two sets of social and legal systems – the Islamic system, which governs their religious belief and culture, and the Western, secular Australian system, which operates under different principles and procedures. To date, there have been few, if any, formal studies of the way in which Australian Muslims deal with divorce and custody, and the information in this entry is based on a small number of informal surveys, responses from Islamic welfare organizations, and anecdotal evidence.

The Muslim community in Australia is small, recent, and very diverse. According to the 2001 census, 281,578 persons out of a total population of over 19 million identified themselves as Muslims. This number represents about 1.5 percent of the Australian population. Substantial migration of Muslims to Australia began only in the early 1970s, and so the majority of Muslims are recent migrants, the children of migrants, or their grandchildren. The Muslim population originates from more than 60 different countries, with different languages, and cultures and following different schools of Islamic law.

The majority of Muslim migrants to Australia come from countries where divorce, custody, and similar matters are regulated by Islamic law, and to most of them the Sharīʿa remains binding on the conduct of their family affairs. The Australian government does not recognize Islamic law. The Australian legal system is secular and is applied without distinction of ethnicity, race, or gender to all Australians. There is therefore some tension in the minds of Muslim Australians about how to accommodate both systems in case of family breakdown.

Under the Australian Family Law Act 1975, there is only one ground for divorce – irretrievable breakdown of marriage, evidenced by the fact that the parties have lived separately and apart for a period of at least twelve months. There are no fault grounds for divorce and no inquiry into the reasons for the marital breakdown. Either husband or wife may unilaterally decide to end the marriage and lodge an application for divorce with the family court. After proof of service of the application on the respondent spouse, the court can grant a divorce, provided that it is satisfied that proper arrangements have been made for any minor children of the marriage.

Ancillary matters such as child custody and access (residence and contact orders) are dealt with by separate applications. There is no presumption in favor of either parent and the welfare of the child is the paramount consideration. In recent years, the courts have placed much more emphasis on mediation as a way of resolving disputes concerning children. Although mainstream mediators undergo cross-cultural training, there are very few Muslim mediators and there is no culturally specific counseling service available to Muslims. In the first instance, women will normally seek the help of a sympathetic shaykh or imam, and in some communities there is strong social pressure not to involve institutions outside the Muslim community.

However, family members may not be present in Australia to help mediate family disputes, and women complain that male community leaders are too close to other men in the community and not prepared to support women even in cases of domestic violence. Women are frequently exhorted simply to exercise patience (*ṣabr*). There is only one refuge for Muslim women who have been forced to leave their homes. This was set up by the Muslim Women's Association in Sydney in 1988 to provide protection to Muslim women in an Islamic environment, since it was found that Muslim women were reluctant to enter culturally inappropriate mainstream refuges.

In some cases, women encounter community disapproval for seeking help about marital problems and are simply expected to endure bad marriages. There is still some social stigma attached to divorce in some communities, and divorced women may find it difficult to remarry.

Accessing the Australian court system is usually a last resort, although anecdotal evidence is that people from some communities, for example, the Turkish community, are more willing to do so. This may be because migrants from Turkey are used to having their family affairs regulated by a secular legal system. Where there is a dispute over child custody and it is feared that a child may be removed overseas, the Australian court system is more frequently used to obtain the necessary orders to prevent the child leaving Australia without the consent of the custodial parent.

Other than this, it is difficult to generalize about the way in which Muslim women deal with divorce and its consequences, because of differences in cultural background, level of education, and level of adherence to religious tradition. Some Muslims rely entirely on Islamic principles, entering into religious marriages and divorcing by *ṭalāq*, bypassing the Australian legal system completely. Other people with marital difficulties engage in forum shopping, accessing whichever system seems to suit their needs. Women who want a religious divorce, in circumstances where the husband refuses to pronounce *ṭalāq*, are unable to access an Islamic religious court, since none exists in Australia. A small number of shaykhs are willing to assist women, by persuading the husbands to pronounce *ṭalāq*, or by granting a divorce in other circumstances.

Rates of divorce among Muslims are relatively higher than among the mainstream population in younger age groups (Saeed 2003, 90). After the age of 30, the incidence of divorce drops to well below that of the non-Muslim majority. No studies have as yet been undertaken to explain this situation, but it may be that the encouragement to early marriage in some communities results in early divorce as couples mature and find they do not have as much in common as they had hoped.

Other marriages break up because of migration stresses, particularly among refugees and the newly arrived. Factors such as lack of family and community support networks, uncertainty about the future (particularly in the case of refugees on Temporary Protection visas), and non-recognition of overseas qualifications leading to reduced socioeconomic status (Kamalkhani 2002) all contribute to the likelihood of marital breakdown, affecting both men and women.

Bibliography

Islamic Welfare Centre, *The true position of women in Islam*, Sydney 2003 (pamphlet produced by local Muslim group).

Z. Kamalkhani, Recently arrived Muslim refugee women coping with settlement, in A. Saeed and S. Akbarzadeh (eds.), *Muslim communities in Australia*, Sydney 2001, 97–115.

A. Saeed, *Islam in Australia*, St. Leonards, N.S.W. 2003.

Jamila Hussain

Canada

Divorce has been of some consequence in the interaction of Muslims and the West throughout history, since the alleged ease with which Muslim men could divorce their wives was often used by European critics of Islam as proof of inequities and lack of modernity within the tradition. For example, the primary legalities of divorce are laid out in the Qurʾān, by which the male uttering of the *ṭalāq* formula ("I divorce you") three times in succession constitutes the legal end of the relationship. Since the Qurʾān had no equivalent procedure for the wife, the claim of inequity before the law was often made. Muslim social law was therefore assumed to be inferior to Western law by Western legists. Moreover, when the earliest Muslims (ca. 1880s) came to Canada, the legal system in place necessitated many modifications of Muslim expectations: 1. Muslim men could not have more than one wife and were expected to have divorced those not eligible to be the "first wife." 2. Muslim divorce practice was not legally recognized in Canada, so regardless of whether the formula had been pronounced, Canadian legal procedures in the courts had to be undertaken. 3. Children from severed Muslim unions under most schools of Islamic law were assigned to the mother until they were pubescent, when they were typically assigned to the care of the father; in Canadian jurisdiction, the courts had no precedence in affirming the Islamic code, so cases were decided on the basis of the court's judicious evaluation of the evidence. In the earliest times this meant the children were assigned to the mother. 4. Muslim law had various ways of providing for women after divorce, but none as clear-cut as the alimony/child support legislation in Canada, with the attendant responsibility falling on the husband. Muslim men, therefore, preferred to divorce under Muslim law.

The division of responsibilities between the federal and provincial governments in Canada has had an impact upon Muslims. Section 91 of the British North America Act of 1867 allowed the federal government control over the "capacity" of marriage, divorce, and custody, whereas solemnization jurisdiction rested with the provinces. Canada's case is further complicated by the fact that Quebec law differs significantly in its origins and formulations, with the Civil Code providing the basis for such social relationships as marriage. Some areas of dispute, such as matrimonial property, are provincial responsibilities. As a rule of thumb, the federal rules apply to all matters relating to setting up the legalities of these social relationships, but the provinces handle all practical matters of delivering the capacity to the people. In the early days, before imams were available, Muslims could not have marriages solemnized in a religious manner, and Muslims in remote areas had to rely upon the authorities validated by the province, making Muslim marriage, for example, an entirely secular matter. Furthermore, as in many aspects of federal-provincial relationships, Canadians discover that provincial custom defines the nuances much more readily than the federal law seems to imply. Thus, in matters of divorce, for example, local judges have great latitude regarding division of property, which allows for the enlightened judge to take Muslim law into consideration. A different judge, or one in an area not familiar with Muslim law, many not be so disposed. Moreover, since many Muslims came to Canada in the postwar period, they were subject to the changing perceptions of the legal fraternity. Statutes covering divorce in Canadian law changed in 1968 with the advent of the Divorce Act; its provisions made divorce easier and less humiliating. Under it, Muslims who agreed to divorce could make the claim that the pronouncing of the formula was evidence of the absolute break of the marriage bond, and the court could then accept that "irreconcilable differences" had ended the marriage. Revised, and eased further in 1985, the statutes allowed the court wide jurisdiction in interpreting the breakdown of a relationship, and one aspect that came to be respected by the courts was that a registered divorce in an Islamic context would have the same weight in Canada. Furthermore, unless there was good reason for challenging the Muslim legal case, courts could and did accept the legal school of the litigants as binding with regard to the children. If the mother contested that ruling, then Canadian law would apply. Under Canadian law to this date, the courts have acted as *parens patria*, that is, as having parental responsibility for the child's welfare, and that has been interpreted to mean that all aspects of foreign law could and might be considered in the application of custody. Normally, however, this means undertaking to determine what the children themselves wish, and only secondarily a consideration of Muslim law. Under amending legislation that is now under consideration, the word "custody" has been removed from the text. This has arisen from arguments that parents have no inherent custodial rights over their children in divorce, since the court holds that prerogative. Consequently, Muslim laws assigning children to the father at age twelve are even less likely to be given priority in Canadian courts.

Canadian courts have, however, shown some developments in accepting Muslim notions of female independence. If the wife had monies under her ownership prior to marriage (such as a dowry), the courts have shown some willingness to maintain those as her personal wealth after the breakdown of the marriage, as is the case under Muslim law. However, these kinds of rulings can also be overridden in provincial law, where the property brought to the marriage and used by both parties during the marriage is considered common property. Muslim women are at a disadvantage in such proceedings, since typically the males carry on the business of the family, and the men are more familiar with the disposing of assets. Finally, some women, married under Muslim law but divorced under Canadian law, sense a disjunction in their emotional life arising from the secular nature of the divorce; more than a few have complained of still feeling bound by Muslim religious marriage bonds even after several years of being divorced in Canada.

Beyond these areas of concern, Muslim women in Canada have demonstrated an inventive mind when it comes to Muslim law; they have, for example, developed a facility to explore various schools of Muslim law and to move from one legal school to another as it best fits their perception of their case. Canada thus allows them a freedom that they would not have in their "home" jurisdiction, where they are deemed to have been born under the jurisdiction of a certain legal school and are therefore subject to its codes.

BIBLIOGRAPHY

A Bissett-Johnson, Family law, in J. H. Marsh (ed.), *The Canadian encyclopedia*, i, Edmonton, Alta. 1985, 613–14.
M. Eichler, *Families in Canada*, Toronto 1983.
A. A. Engineer, *The rights of women in Islam*, New Delhi 1992.
Z. Husaini, *Muslims in the Canadian mosaic*, Edmonton, Alta. 1990.
D. Laberge and P. Lanreville, Law, in J. H. Marsh (ed.), *The Canadian encyclopedia*, ii, Edmonton, Alta. 1985, 984–6.
L. Larson, J. Walter Goltz, and B. Munro, *Families in Canada. Social context, continuities and changes*, Scarborough, Ont. 2000.
R. B. McGowan, *Muslims in the diaspora. The Somali communities of London and Toronto*, Toronto 1999.
E. Waugh, S. M. Abu-Laban, and R. Qureshi (eds.), *Muslim families in North America*, Edmonton, Alta. 1991.

EARLE WAUGH

The Caucasus and Central Asia

INITIATION OF DIVORCE

The ability to end a marriage is an important facet of women's rights. Women frequently could not dissolve their marriages on their own initiative because of the economic conditions that bound them. If they divorced, they had to give back the *kalym* (bride-money) as decided by the court of *biy* in Kyrgyz in the late nineteenth and early twentieth centuries. A woman had the right to divorce through the court in the following cases: the husband was incapable of performing his marital duties; the husband withheld from his wife food and clothes for six months and 13 days; the husband treated his wife cruelly; the husband had a mental disorder; and physical defects of the wife hindering her work. The judge had the right to decide on the dissolution of the marriage, on return of the *kalym*, and on a large fee for himself.

As a rule, husbands initiated divorce. A husband could divorce his wife at any time and on any pretext. He had only to repudiate her by unilateral declaration (*ṭalāq*); he could then take his word back and go on living a married life. A woman who was divorced on her husband's initiative had no right to her dowry or her children.

A woman who initiated a divorce had no right to an allowance, while a woman divorced on the initiative of her husband had an allowance until the *ʿidda* expired.

Childlessness would often constitute grounds for divorce. The birth of a girl could also justify polygyny. The divorced woman lost the right to bring up her children. In the case of divorce or the father's death, children (in particular boys) remained in the care of the father's relatives. In this connection, adoption of boys was widely practiced in the countries of Central Asia (in particular among the Uzbek and the Kyrgyz).

After Central Asian and Caucasian states became integrated into the Russian Empire, courts began to dissolve marriages on women's initiative. Under Soviet rule, the Muslim communities of Central Asia and the Caucasus gradually began to relinquish Muslim laws: however, they retained power and continued existence as sociocultural values.

While according to the family law divorce can be initiated by either spouse, in traditional Muslim societies divorce is an unseemly act, especially for women. A report presented by human rights activists states: "In Uzbekistan in many cases divorce is the result of domestic abuse. A woman attorney assures us that all her clients filed for divorce because their husbands had beaten them. Thus, the divorce process normally begins when a woman wants to free herself of domestic violence" (Minnesota Advocates 2000, 53).

A woman's right to divorce is restricted by public opinion, by the attitude of the community, relatives, and parents. Her parents close the door of the parental house to her. It is more difficult to marry off the daughters of divorced mothers; younger sisters of a divorced woman will not be able to marry because the stamp of the divorced sister is on them. Old Uzbek proverbs about marrying off a daughter say: "May your dead body return from there," and "Flesh for you and bones for us."

After divorce

The most frequent problem today upon divorce in the countries of Central Asia is that of where a divorced woman can live. In most cases, the wife has no right to her part of the house belonging to her husband's parents. After divorce, small children remain in the care of the wife (contrary to the traditions of the Caucasian peoples, where children can remain in the father's family). There is also a problem with work. A woman who has remained at home without working outside the home loses whatever qualifications she may have had before marriage; if she was not educated before the birth of children, in most cases a woman has no opportunity to acquire or continue education. For such women there is only work that is underpaid, dirty, intensive, and unskilled. Alimony does not cover all the expenses of maintaining children because of the low level of wages. Many women refuse alimony to prevent the subsequent claim on the part of the father for return of the alimony when the children attain majority. If a father pays alimony for the children's maintenance he is entitled to demand 25 percent of their wages for his own maintenance in his old age. If a divorced woman is engaged in commercial business, she is more likely to work a more flexible schedule, allowing her more time to be with her children; and she earns a better income.

Children

Under Islamic law in the pre-Soviet period, trusteeship (*wilāya*) could be established for minors and the mentally disabled. Trusteeship was carried out by the father, a trustee (*walī*), or a judge (*qāḍī*). It began before a minor achieved sexual maturity and stopped upon the death of a ward. The trustee had to be a Muslim; a woman could also be a trustee.

After divorce in the post-Soviet period, a young woman is always offered for marriage again. However, if she already has a child, her parents always try to take the child away from her. Childless families adopt children of close relatives. Sometimes a child is taken to a childless family from a large family against his or her mother's will. Such children learn who their true mother is only in adulthood. This frequently creates shock and stress. Adoptive parents prefer to hide the truth from the child unless extraordinary events force them to reveal it. The real mother has little role in the bringing up of her child. Frequently, adoptive parents take children from poor families for trusteeship. They often do not accord the same status to their adopted children as to their biological children. The girls are usually married off earlier than the biological daughters; they do not receive education equal to the biological children; they are loaded with housework more often; and they are often used as workers in the house. The attitude is the same toward boys. They become helpers in the house or on the farm; the adoptive parents are less concerned with their education and intellectual growth. The food and clothing of adopted children leave much to be desired.

The eldest daughters (less often sons) are sometimes left to be brought up by their lonely and aged grandmothers and grandfathers. Frequently, these are grandmothers and grandfathers living in the countryside, while the parents live in cities with the other children. An insuperable gap in education and language emerges between these children. A woman takes this step only in extreme and desperate and dire situations: a divorce, hard material conditions, or temporary economic difficulties. In the Soviet period, this often happened when parents have to pursue their education.

Frequently, close relatives assume custody of children born out of wedlock to their daughters or sons. Such children are adopted and brought up in families as younger brothers or sisters. Their real origin is hidden from relatives.

Among post-Soviet Caucasian peoples and ethnic groups with Muslim traditions the question of adoption in inter-ethnic marriages is more complex. There are cases of mothers being fully separated from their children on religious grounds, where the father has a local nationality (the Chechens and Daghestans). This is observed in societies under the strong influence of national and religious extremism. Mothers in such families are compelled to migrate to their historical homelands. Their children are violently taken away from them and remain in the families of their fathers. Close relatives are engaged in their education. These children are encouraged to have a hostile attitude toward their biological mothers of a different confession, who allegedly would not accept Islam even for the sake of children. Mothers of such children have no opportunity to meet their children for many years (no statistics available).

Bibliography

A. Chaikovsky, Issik Kul province in 1869–1871 [in Russian], in *Turkistanskiye vedomosti* 45 (1872).

Human Rights Watch 13:4(D) (June 2001), Uzbekistan.

N. A. Kislyakov, *Essays on the history of family and marriage among the peoples of Central Asia and Kazakhstan*, Leningrad 1969.

Minnesota Advocates for Human Rights, Domestic Violence in Uzbekistan, December 2000, <mnadvocates.org>.

O. Osaulenko, *Gender norms of religious and common law* [in Russian], Bishkek 2000.

A. S. Saidov (ed.), *Hidāya*, vol. II. Tashkent 1998.

Marfua Tokhtakhodjaeva and Almaz Kadirova

Iran and Afghanistan

Unequal divorce and custody rights in Iran and Afghanistan are the main reasons behind the social system that places men at the head of the household and fathers in control of children. In effect, many of the gains women secured as citizens have been nullified through family laws that make their freedom of movement, their desire to work or study, or to end their marriage subject to the approval of their husbands. Thus women are rendered subjects rather than partners of their husbands. While men have had, by religious convention and law, a unilateral right of divorce, women have had access to divorce on only very limited grounds and even then, to prove their case, often have to go to the unfamiliar and unwelcoming courts. Thus women must often look to alternative strategies to obtain a divorce, even assuming they can face the social stigma and economic hardships.

Although both Afghan and Iranian societies pay lip service to motherhood, mothers are given few rights in regard to custody of their children, who are viewed as belonging to their fathers. The custody rights of a mother in Iran exist up to the age of two for boys and seven for girls; while in Afghanistan among different cultures it can vary from five to seven years for boys and from five to puberty for girls. However, these rights are frequently ignored, and even when observed, should the mother remarry the custody reverts to the father. Visiting rights of mothers are the grayest part of Muslim jurisprudence and traditional practices in both societies. Even where mothers' visiting rights are legally recognized, there are no enforcement mechanisms. Frequently, belligerent husbands take away the children in order to punish their ex-wives. The threat of such eventualities constitutes a disincentive for any wife's disinclination to toe the line. Consequently, women may remain in an unhappy marriage so as not to lose their children. In both Iran and Afghanistan many widowed women feel obliged to accept marrying their brothers-in-law in order not to lose custody of their children. Years of war and high male mortality have brought the lack of custody rights for mothers to the forefront of Afghan women's concerns. Interestingly, widows of the Iran-Iraq War (1980–8) managed to successfully organize and pressure the Islamic Republic of Iran into changing the law to allow them to retain custody of their children even after remarrying. Women hoped the law would extend to all mothers in Iran although thus far resistance to such a development has been very strong.

Historically the male unilateral right of divorce has wreaked havoc in women's lives by rendering them economically and socially vulnerable. The practice of oral divorce continues to put women in an uncertain situation. As divorcees, women can not claim maintenance and yet on occasions women who remarried have been accused of bigamy (with severe legal and social consequences for them and their families) by the erstwhile husbands who have denied divorcing them. Thus an end to oral divorce has been a major demand by women in both societies. Under Iran's modern, centralized state there is compulsory registration of marriage and divorce and a resulting diminution of oral divorce. However, in Afghanistan, after two decades of war and the destruction of state institutions, the limited gains women had secured have almost totally evaporated. Thus oral divorce and, worse yet, lack of obligation on the part of the husband to ever communicate the divorce to the wife has seriously compromised women in Afghan society.

Although recent reforms in Iran have increased the possibility for women to obtain divorce if they can prove domestic abuse or severe addiction, the long and often costly procedure as well as the unwelcoming atmosphere discourages women from using these channels. They often, in effect, buy their divorce and occasionally the custody of their children by making their husband an offer. This kind of divorce is called *khulʿ* and traditionally women would give up their *mahr*, the gift that at marriage a husband pledges to give to his wife as a part of the marriage contract. As a counter strategy, increasingly husbands are demanding much more than the *mahr*, assuming they do not refuse the divorce outright. In some ethnic groups, such as the Pashtuns and Persians, a bride's family will tend to demand a more substantial although deferred *mahr* as a sort of marriage security for the bride. Among many other ethnic groups the *mahr* remains a small nominal sum and sometimes is paid to the father of the bride at the time of marriage. Nonetheless these culturally grounded strategies partially explain why women and their families in Afghanistan resisted attempts by the government in 1978 to limit the *mahr* to 300 Afghanis (US$5 today), particularly since there were few other mechanisms in place to protect women against abuses by the husband and his family. Indeed, Iranian women launched a successful public campaign to bring about a law that allowed for the *mahr* to be reassessed at the time of payment by taking inflation into account. An earlier campaign had made it compulsory for men to pay wages for the housework that women had performed during the years of marriage before husbands could legally divorce their wives. An obstacle to realizing these options has been that many Afghan women and some Iranian women have no marriage certificate, or the certificate does not stipulate the *mahr*, thus limiting women's leverage.

A final ploy for women has been to take advantage of the long-existing marriage contracts and to insert various useful clauses including an unconditional right of divorce. This strategy is rapidly becoming popular and is viewed by many women as the main vehicle to help them become more equal partners in their marriages. It could be argued that the above are cosmetic reforms that neither satisfy women's demands nor question the fundamentally unequal nature of divorce and custody laws. They nonetheless have increased many women's negotiating power in obtaining a divorce.

BIBLIOGRAPHY

M. Centlivres-Demont, Afghan women in peace, war, and exile, in M.Weiner and A. Banuazizi (eds.), *The politics of social transformation in Afghanistan, Iran, and Pakistan*, Syracuse, N.Y. 1994, 333–65.

N. H. Dupree, Revolutionary rhetoric and Afghan women, in M. Shahrani and R. L. Canfield (eds.), *Revolutions and rebellions in Afghanistan*, Berkeley 1984, 306–40.

H. Hoodfar (ed.), *Shifting boundaries in marriage and divorce in Muslim communities*, Women Living Under Muslim Laws, France 1996.

——, *The women's movement in Iran. Women at the crossroad of secularization and Islamization*, Women Living Under Muslim Laws, Montpellier 1999.

——, Families on the move. Impact of forced migration on the role of Afghan women and family structure, in *Hawwa. Journal of Women of the Middle East and the Islamic World* 2:2 (2004), 142–71.

M. H. Kamali, *Law in Afghanistan. A study of the constitutions, matrimonial law and the judiciary*, Leiden 1985.

M. Kār, *Sākhtār-i ḥuqūqī-i niẓām-i khānavādah dar Īrān*, Tehran 1999.

Z. Mir-Hosseini, Stretching the limits. A feminist reading of the Sharia in post-Khomeini Iran, in M. Yamani (ed.), *Feminism and Islam. Legal and literary perspectives*, Reading, U.K. 1996, 285–319.

V. Moghadam, *Modernizing women. Gender and social change in the Middle East*, Boulder, Colo. 1993.

HOMA HOODFAR

South Asia

Across South Asia there are many commonalities regarding marriage and divorce as they affect women. These arise out of a common cultural familial kinship pattern in many parts of the region and the common historical experiences regarding the development of Muslim personal law. There have been divergences in the development of family law during the last 50 years in India, Pakistan, and Bangladesh but on the whole the experiences of women regarding divorce are alike. This is because the expectations regarding gender roles in the society, the relation between wife-givers and wife-takers and the responsibilities incumbent on each with reference to marriage, especially the exchanges at marriage and even subsequently, remain similar in many parts of these countries. Variations exist due to class and region and the type of kinship system (matrilineal or patrilineal), which can make the experience of divorce and its aftermath different for different social groups.

Reliable information on the experiences of divorce is difficult to come by because of the few systematic empirical studies of the topic. Legal issues dominate the literature, and the work of social workers, non-governmental organizations, and others dealing with women's issues provides some information regarding women's experiences of the formal legal system. Studies reported in Ahmad (2003) show that there is considerable social stigma attached to divorce. Divorce is more frequent among families from the lower socioeconomic strata than among the middle and upper classes. The most commonly practiced procedure for divorce is the unilateral *ṭalāq*, where the husband pronounces the divorce formula three times on the same occasion, thus making the divorce irrevocable and final. Though from the religious point of view this is considered reprehensible, not only is it legal, but it is also generally believed to be the proper procedure. Commonly cited reasons for divorce are the inability of the wife to have children, a second marriage of the husband, non-maintenance of the wife by the husband, or insufficient dowry provided by the wife's family.

In a situation where few women are economically independent, where there is a high rate of female illiteracy, and where divorce carries a stigma, only a small proportion of women are able to take advantage of the rights given under the Dissolution of Muslim Marriages Act of 1939, which is the operative law dealing with divorce initiated by women in Bangladesh, India, and Pakistan. The problem of having to prove the grounds for divorce, which may be compounded by the time lag between separating from the husband and filing the case, ignorance of the procedure involved in establishing proof (such as prior police complaints in the case of violence), the expense of litigation, and the uncertainty of the outcome, all make the court option a distant one for most women. The fact that a large number of cases do not reach completion in the courts points to the possibility that out of court settlements are reached. Case studies suggest that recourse to the court can be initiated as a pressure tactic to get the husband to grant a divorce, which he may be refusing to do in order to avoid paying the dues of *mahr* and maintenance that the court would require.

The imbalance in the law is compounded by social norms and practices that put women in an inferior position economically and socially. Marriage is practically universal, and is considered to be the foremost source of security for a woman. Cultural ideals, such as that "a woman should leave her husband's home only in a coffin," deter women from opting out of a marriage even if it is highly abusive. The unrestricted right of divorce means that the threat of divorce can be used as a means of controlling the behavior of the wife. The cultural norm that the wife's side does not take any initiative that could jeopardize the marriage means that women do not press for divorce, living in hope that their situation will change for the better. Since most women are not in a position where they can be financially and emotionally independent, major considerations for a woman if she wants to separate from her husband are to minimize the stigma that arises from accusations of being responsible for the divorce and to arrange for her own financial security. Often women prefer to remain separated from the husband, accepting polygamous marriages, violent marriages, or even non-support, rather than to press for divorce and its attendant insecurity. On the other hand, since the oral divorce allows for considerable misuse, for instance, leaving women uncertain as to their marital status, women are often forced to initiate divorce proceedings in order to clarify their marital situation, especially if there is a possibility of their remarriage. The uncertainty of marital status can have dangerous repercussions if, for instance, the wife who believes she has been divorced remarries and is then charged with adultery by the former husband, as has happened in Pakistan. A trend that has been reported with reference to cases registered in the Sharīʿa courts or with the local kazi (judge) is that there is an increase in cases of *khulʿ* in recent years. This increase appears to indicate that women are being forced to purchase their freedom by agreeing to give up their right to *mahr* and maintenance, rather than that they are initiating divorce. The unequal relations between wife-givers and wife-takers is also illustrated in the dowry system, where gifts are expected to flow from the bride's family to the groom and his family. The *mahr*, which is a gift given by the husband to the wife in consideration of the marriage, and which could act as a security for the wife in case of divorce, thus does not fit into the cultural norm. More often than not the *mahr* is a token amount of Rs. 786, Rs. 555, or even as low as Rs. 50. In communities where the *mahr* is fixed at a high rate, often the assumption is that it is not actually to be paid. Though a high *mahr* is seen as a way of deterring divorce, in practice, a husband can succeed in making the wife agree to give up the *mahr* and sometimes even pay some amount in exchange for a divorce. Post divorce or even post separation, most women find themselves dependent on their natal families, along with their children.

The formal legal system, however, touches on the lives of only a fraction of the people in South Asia. Marriage and divorce are widely seen as belonging to the private sphere, over which the more appropriate authority is that of the family or community-based organizations (known in different regions by various names such as the *biraderi*, the *jamaat* council, *jirga, panchayat*). As pointed out by Shaheed (1998, 69) in Pakistan, where women's mobility is severely restricted, female illiteracy is rampant, and women's access to information about state laws or even practices elsewhere in the country is limited or absent, the operative practices of the community become the absolute standard. These community-based institutions are usually dominated by men who rarely have training in the legalities of divorce procedure or knowledge of the rights of women under the Sharīʿa. Here too the wife or her family can find themselves at a disadvantage. Customary norms discourage women from taking the initiative to establish their case and thereby jeopardize the marriage, while the husband, through his personal contacts, may be able to establish his version of the situation over a long period before the final break is sought. Moreover, he can simply disregard a decision that does not suit him, as these institutions depend on moral rather than legal authority and cannot enforce their decisions other than through community-based sanctions, which are rarely brought into play for matters such as divorce. Though studies on the working of these institutions are not available, it is possible to see that the procedure for divorce and settlement of dues can involve long negotiations as each side uses the informal and formal resources available to them to establish their case and to avoid losing their position in the community, and sometimes takes advantage of the plural adjudication systems in the country.

Anthropological accounts give some idea of the variations in practices of separation and divorce especially where the formal legal system does not hold sway. Among the Gujar Bakarwals of Jammu and Kashmir, and the Meos of Rajasthan, it has been reported that men rarely divorce their wives. However, if a woman wants to leave her husband she may elope with another man. Among the Meos if the woman wants to marry another man, he must pay compensation (*jhagra*) to the first husband. Unless this amount is amicably settled, elopement can lead to serious feuds, which sometimes last for generations (Ahmad 1976).

In the matrilineal society of Lakshwadeep there is a minimum dislocation for a woman and her children in the event of divorce (Dube 1999). Women do not move to their husband's home after marriage. The husband in fact visits the wife. The children are brought up in the mother's household. The divorce rate is very high and both women and men reported multiple marriages. The formalities of the Sharīʿa are followed in that the husband is pressurized to pronounce the *ṭalāq* formula. If a woman has to pay compensation to the husband to obtain the divorce, she can sometimes prevail upon her next prospective husband to pay the amount. There is little stigma attached to divorce.

A number of the problems described here have been controlled through marriage contracts that incorporate stipulations regarding women's right to divorce and other matters. This procedure was adopted as far back as a century ago (Caroll 1982), though today it is hardly used.

BIBLIOGRAPHY

I. Ahmad (ed.), *Family, kinship and marriage among Muslims in India*, Delhi 1976.

——, *Divorce and remarriage among Muslims in India*, Delhi 2003.

N. Alam et al., Determinants of divorce in a traditional Muslim community in Bangladesh, in *Demographic Research* 3 (2000), <www.demographic-research.org/volumes/vol3/4/3-4.pdf >.

L. Caroll, *Talaq-i-tafwid* and stipulations in a Muslim marriage contract. Important means of protecting the position of the South Asian Muslim wife, in *Modern Asian Studies* 16:2 (1982), 277–309.

L. Dube, The meaning and content of marriage in a matrilineal Muslim community, in *Journal of the Asiatic Society of Bombay*, n.s. 74 (1999), 78–95.

F. Shaheed et al. (eds.), *Shaping women's lives. Laws, practices and strategies in* Pakistan, Karachi 1998.

NASREEN FAZALBHOY

Western Europe

In Islam marriage is regarded as a civil contract between two adults, which entails an offer by one partner and acceptance by the other in the presence of two witnesses. The *qāḍī*, or official, usually solemnizes the marriage in a mosque, or court, or any other location. The marriage contract sets the defined rights and duties for each party. Because marriage is not a sacred union, divorce in Islam has always been permissible. Although the Qurʾānic legislation (at least in theory) on divorce aims at protecting women and allowing them to free themselves from the marital bond if it becomes necessary, there is today a huge gap between divine principles and reality. In most Muslim countries female divorce is a controversial issue and women are seldom allowed to exercise their right without establishing strong evidence of mistreatment or male sexual impotency. This is primarily because the treatment of divorce, whether in the schools of law or in various modern rules and regulations, reflects patriarchal understanding of the Qur'ān and the *sunna*. For example, in all schools of law the right to end the marital tie rests exclusively in the hands of the husband, who has the power to repudiate his wife any time he wishes. In doing so, he needs neither grounds nor the consent of his wife. This kind of divorce is known as *ṭalāq* and it is the unilateral prerogative of the husband – no one else has the right to pronounce it. The ease with which *ṭalāq* takes place has led to abuse and misuse, and despite the fact that on many occasions Muḥammad condemned the arbitrary practice of it, the jurists were and are still generally unwilling to alter the status quo.

A woman can obtain a divorce only if her husband agrees to it. In this context, she can secure her release via a *khulʿ* agreement in which she pays her husband a sum of money (especially if she is the one who initiates the process) in return for her freedom, or through a so-called mutual agreement between the two parties to dissolve the marital bond with no payment on either side. The woman can also obtain a divorce if she stipulates in her marriage contract the right to do so. This form of divorce is known as delegated divorce: the husband agrees to delegate the right to divorce to his wife, or to someone else who acts as an agent to release her on his behalf (notice that the delegated divorce neither affects the husband's right to *ṭalāq* nor relieves the wife from going to court to effect the divorce).

If the wife fails to secure her husband's agreement, her only recourse is to apply for court intervention; this is called judicial divorce, in which the judge (subject to approval) can either compel the husband to pronounce *ṭalāq* or pronounces it on his behalf. The grounds upon which a wife can demand separation vary from one country to another depending on the school of law to be followed. In this context, the most restrictive is the Ḥanafī school, while the most liberal is the Mālikī school. Nevertheless, female divorce is limited even with convincing evidence of mistreatment. The actual legislation in most Muslim countries is rigid and the cultural setting is patriarchal; these combine to ensure that female divorce is a difficult and protracted process. If the woman does not have a very strong reason, she can easily be refused divorce and sent back home to an unwanted husband. This is in contrast to the Qur'ānic verse 2:29 and the *ḥadīth*, especially the *ḥadīth* about the wife of Thābit b. Qays, both of which offer clear and adequate legal basis to allow women to obtain a divorce relatively easily, even without powerful justification.

Divorce has been grossly abused. Indeed, in most cases, it has been deliberately used to suppress, control, and humiliate women. The same attitude can be found among Muslims living in Western Europe; for example, in the United Kingdom, tensions can easily arise in the area of divorce for Muslim women. When marriages break down women are often abandoned and find it difficult to get divorced. This is primarily because of strong pressure from the community to force women to stay within the marital bond at all costs. Very often, when a wife has problems with her husband, the general attitude of the community is to blame her and try and talk her into better behavior; if she asks for divorce, the tendency is to persuade her to be patient and considerate even in matters where the husband is guilty of transgressing the terms of the contract. If her husband (as happens in most cases) refuses to cooperate, she is faced with the difficult choice of having to seek judicial divorce. There are at least two problems associated with this: first, as Islamic law is not recognized in Europe, there is no recognized body at the national level that could act as a court or as a judge, leaving the wife at the mercy of the individual representative. Here, the Islamists disagree on who should assume the role of a judge: some say an imam, shaykh, or learned person could do the job, while others insist on an Islamic-educated scholar. Second, the form of Sharīʿa applied in Europe among Muslims with regard to personal status law leaves little opportunity for women to obtain a divorce.

Muslims in the United Kingdom are predominantly South East Asians who are mainly followers of the Ḥanafī school of law, the most restrictive school in terms of women's issues in family law. This means that Muslim women here face an uphill struggle in their efforts to effect an "Islamic divorce." An Islamic Sharia Council was founded in London in the 1980s to deal with family issues, especially marital disputes, from the Islamic perspective. Its members, according to the council, are drawn from all over the United Kingdom and represent the five different schools of law; its main clients are women who are seeking divorce from reluctant husbands. Although the council claims to serve Muslims in the United Kingdom, with many branches in cities such as Birmingham, Manchester,

Bradford, and Glasgow, it is by no means a nationally recognized body, at least among Muslims. In fact, a large number of Muslim people are not aware of its existence. It is primarily a self-constituted body, has no legal status and deals solely with Islamic divorce; civil marriages dissolved by the British courts and issues related to maintenance and child custody fall outside its purview. The council can claim success in some of the cases presented to it, but the fact remains that these are a tiny minority. Also, despite the fact that its decisions are binding, it has no legal base to enforce them if the husband decides not to cooperate. Its ability to handle divorce cases efficiently is called into question; at the moment there is only one secretary who manages the daily work of the council. The result is lack of communication, misinformation, and long delay; it is estimated that a resolution dispute could take up to three years.

When women fail to secure divorce via a Muslim mediator, very often they go to British courts to obtain civil divorce; this can be done if they have marriage status according to United Kingdom law. A number of Muslim women in Britain do not have marriage status, primarily because they did not marry according to United Kingdom law. As such, they are left in limbo at the mercy of their husbands who refuse to grant them *ṭalāq*. Once a woman petitions for divorce in a United Kingdom court, apart from some obstacles related to cost, ignorance of the Islamic Sharīʿa, and lack of faith-sensitive support during the crisis and after it is resolved, she is able to obtain a decree absolute, maintenance, and control and custody of the children. This is because the majority society as well as the British authorities tend to be sympathetic toward women in disputes concerning divorce and child custody. However, even after obtaining civil divorce, a Muslim woman is still not completely free to start a new life. This is because civil divorce is not recognized in Islamic law and therefore she is still technically not free to remarry. Here, the woman could easily be blackmailed into submission by a brutal husband; the price could be financial, or, much more importantly, child custody. In Islam, child custody rules are based on scholarly opinions and vary considerably from one school to another. These rules, in general, favor the father, especially if the mother decides to remarry after separation. In this context, the husband can strike a good deal in return for Islamic divorce, undermining the benefit she gains from the civil divorce regarding finance and child custody.

Bibliography

L. Carroll, Muslim women and Islamic divorce in England, in *Journal of Muslim Minority Affairs* 17:1 (1997), 97–115.

H. Jawad, *The rights of women in Islam. An authentic approach*, Houndmills, Basingstoke, Hants. 1998, 71–82.

——, Historical and contemporary perspectives of Muslim women living in the West, in H. Jawad and T. Benn (eds.), *Muslim women in the United Kingdom and beyond. Experiences and images*, Leiden 2003, 1–17.

Z. Mir-Hosseini, *Marriage on trial. A study of Islamic family law. Iran and Morocco compared*, London 1993, *Marriage on trial. Islamic family law in Iran and Morocco*, London 2000 (rev. ed.).

A. S. Roald, *Women in Islam. The Western experience*, London 2001, 213–36.

S. N. Shah-Kazemi, *Untying the knot. Muslim women, divorce and the Sharia*, London 2001.

Haifaa Jawad

Domestic Violence

Arab States

Domestic violence – acts of violence between two individuals who have had an intimate or a family relationship – encompasses physical, sexual, psychological, economic, and verbal aggression between men and women, brothers and sisters, parents and their children. According to the United Nations Declaration on the Elimination of Violence against Women, domestic abuse includes: "battering, sexual abuse of female children in the household, dowry-related violence, marital rape, female genital mutilation and other traditional practices harmful to women, non-spousal violence and violence related to exploitation" (Office of the United Nations High Commissioner for Human Rights 1994). In Arab countries, occurrences of domestic violence may also comprise expelling wives from their marital homes, forced marriages, polygamy, and "honor killings" (also referred to as "femicide").

Domestic violence is deeply rooted in societal norms, including gender roles and expectations, and codified in legal systems that privilege male authority over women in the domestic and public spheres. The 1995 Egyptian Demographic and Health Survey demonstrates the extent to which violence against women is socially sanctioned: in that study one out of every three married women was beaten, usually by her husband. Eighty-six percent of Egyptian women surveyed condoned violence under the following circumstances: wife refuses to have sex (69.9 percent), wife answers back (62 percent), wife talks to other men (64.2 percent), and wife burns food (27.2 percent). While those findings point to the pervasiveness of violence across social class, religious, ethnic, and regional divides, other research indicates that two factors contribute to women's increased risk of domestic violence in the Arab world: early marriage and substantial difference in ages between spouses (LCRVAW 1998).

In a context of widespread social acceptance of domestic violence, women are often not aware of their rights being violated and reluctant to speak out against perpetrators because of the stigma attached and their fear of retribution. The absence of reliable data, the paucity of laws and policies that account for such violence and penalize its practices, and the poor training of medical providers and law enforcement agents to screen for violence all contribute to the hidden nature of domestic violence. In countries where laws do exist, there is often a lack of awareness of pertinent legislation and of where proper counsel can be found. Research furthermore underscores the influence of social pressure on women survivors of violence not to speak out against perpetrators. In addition, law enforcement agents may limit the ability of populations to exercise their rights under existing laws, especially abuse that results from sexual violence (Shalhoub-Kervorkian 2000).

The impact of domestic violence is widespread and includes negative effects on women, children, families, men, communities, and societies. The short-term health impacts for women include bruises and cuts, while long-term sequels can involve chronic disabilities, mental disorders, pervasive fear and depression, and unwanted pregnancies. The far-reaching repercussions of domestic violence, and the costs that it entails to individual women and to already over-extended health care systems, are demonstrated in a study in Alexandria, Egypt, that shows that domestic violence was the leading cause of injury to women, accounting for 28 percent of all visits to hospital trauma units (Graitcer and Youssef 1993).

Despite the prevalence, severity, and cost of domestic violence, the silence attributed to the social sanctioning of the practice has made it difficult for women's and rights groups to research the problem, develop effective interventions, and advocate for legal and societal change. Measures are increasingly being taken, however, to raise public awareness, protect women, prevent crimes, and change the social norms that ignore or condone such violence. Strategies to address violence against women in the Arab states tend to be three-fold: to document and analyze the types, magnitude, and consequences of domestic violence; to assist individual women who suffer from violence; and to challenge societal norms, institutions, and legal frameworks that condone such practices (New Women's Center for Research and Training 1994, Tunisian Association of Democratic Women 1995, Collectif 95 1999, LCRVAW 1998, Women's Center For Legal Aid and Counseling 2001, Ait-Hamou 2003).

Consequently, research in several Arab countries highlights the prevalence of domestic violence, the strategies developed by women, the necessity of changing laws that condone aggression, and the importance of situating violence in the broader sociocultural and political context of the respective countries. Studies also underscore the need to develop cultural understanding of violence, and context-specific models of intervention. An additional area of investigation addresses the challenges that service providers and therapists face in their efforts not to doubly victimize women who speak out against violence and seek counsel (Shalhoub-Kervorkian 1999).

The interventions developed by women's and rights groups include: opening shelters to ensure women's safety while assisting them with legal counsel; establishing hotlines to provide support for women and assistance in obtaining child custody; finding employment; and locating a home. Groups have also organized human rights education training for law enforcement agents, journalists, health workers, lawyers, women's organizations, and individuals (Ait-Hamou 2003).

In the area of legal reform, activists in several countries have focused their efforts on abolishing one of the most repressive laws, which stipulates that rapists be acquitted of all criminal charges if they marry the woman or girl who was raped. In Egypt, this law was overturned in 1999. Other changes are sought for equal rights in matters of divorce, inheritance, custody, nationality, political representation, and respect for state obligations under international legislation.

Several regional initiatives have been created to support country-level activities. Created in 1996, the Arab Women's Court to Resist Violence Against Women comprises organizations across 11 Arab countries interested in raising awareness of discriminatory factors in existing personal status codes, and creating alternative texts that honor states' obligations to respect women's safety and equality under international laws. This followed the first public hearing on women's experiences with violence, organized in 1995 in Lebanon, which included women's live testimonies from 14 different Arab countries. More recently, an Arab regional resource center on violence against women was established in Jordan to serve as a clearinghouse for related information and documentation across the Arab states and link women researchers and activists working in this area.

The awareness of the effects of violence against women across the Arab states has increased as demonstrated in the media coverage of this issue, and related research and interventions. Future activities could be strengthened if a wider range of civil society and government actors were to include violence against women as a focus of their work.

Bibliography

L. Ait-Hamou, Violence against women. The case of Algeria, paper presented at the Arab regional conference on Violence against Women, Cairo, 12–13 May 2003.

Collectif 95 Maghreb Egalité, *Les Maghrebines entre violences symboliques et violences physiques (Algérie, Maroc, Tunisie)*, Rabat, Morocco 1999.

F. El-Zanaty et al., *Egypt demographic and health survey*, Cairo 1993.

P. Graitcer and Z. Youssef, *Inquiry in Egypt. An analysis of injuries as a health problem*, Washington, D.C. 1993.

LCRVAW (Lebanese Council to Resist Violence Against Women), Violence against women. A report based on a sample of 92 victims, November 1998, http://www.lebanesewomen.org/cases.htm>.

New Women's Center for Research and Training, *Violence against women. A field study in preparation for the Fourth World Conference on Women in Beijing* [in Arabic and English], Cairo 1995.

Office of the United Nations High Commissioner for Human Rights, *Declaration on the elimination of violence against women*, Geneva, General Assembly Resolution 48/104 of 20 December 1993.

N. Shalhoub-Kevorkian, The politics of disclosing female sexual abuse. A case study of Palestinian society, in *Child Abuse and Neglect* 23:12 (1999), 1275–93.

——, Blocking her exclusion. A contextually sensitive model of intervention for handling female abuse, in *Social Service Review* 74:4 (2000), 620–34.

Tunisian Association of Democratic Women, *La violence à l'égard des femmes*, Tunis 1995.

Women's Center for Legal Aid and Counseling, *Report on the status of Palestinian women based on the CEDAW (Convention on the Elimination of Discrimination against Women) framework* [in Arabic], 2001, <http://www.wclac.org/ publications1.html>.

Leila Hessini

Canada

Domestic violence remains an issue of concern for Muslim women in Canada as it does for many women in societies worldwide. The specific character of domestic violence among Muslim communities in Canada is strongly shaped by the immigrant status of most members of the Muslim community and by the unique dynamics of the meeting of Islamic culture with Canadian society and culture. To understand the significance of these two features it is important first to review the key demographic characteristics of the Muslim minority community in Canada and to review the identity challenges that starkly face Canadian Muslim women.

Demographic traits

The 2001 census indicated that the Muslim population in Canada stood at 569,645, representing 2 percent of the Canadian population, rendering Islam the largest non-Christian religion in the country (Husaini 1999, 15–16). This represented a remarkable growth since 1970 when the Muslim population stood at only 33,370. By far the largest element in this growth is extensive immigration, which has been supplemented by relatively high rates of fertility and to some lesser degree by conversion.

The Canadian Muslim population is highly diverse and in many ways mirrors the Muslim world. Immigrants and refugees have come from virtually all parts of the Muslim world and from diaspora communities in the Caribbean, Africa, and Europe. The largest ethnoracial groups are South Asian (42.1 percent) and Arab (22.8 percent) in origin. In addition, large numbers of refugees have come in the last two decades from Iran, Afghanistan, and Somalia. Further adding to the mix is the presence of representatives from virtually all major doctrinal schools and offshoots of Islam including various strands of both the major Sunnī and Shīʿī groups. A variety of orientations to Islam are also notable in the Canadian Muslim population. Migrants positively disposed to traditional Islamic norms have come from many countries, alongside those who seem secular and indifferent, some of whom have fled political and cultural forms of Islamic expression.

Muslims in Canada are primarily resident in urban centers across the vast country. The largest concentration is to be found in the greater Toronto area where 254,110 Muslims lived in 2001. Toronto alone had 44 percent of the Canadian Muslim population. The significant concentration of Muslims in cities has resulted in many outward signs of Muslim religious and cultural life. In Montreal, and in particular in Toronto, mosques, Muslim religious schools and halal restaurants and food stores are now noticeable. Forms of traditional Muslim attire, especially the *ḥijāb* (headcover), are also now commonly observed.

The diversity of the Muslim community has contributed to a highly decentralized and uncoordinated structure of community involvement and representation. A number of national organizations exist, but most Muslims are undoubtedly more connected to their local mosques and community organizations. Among the more significant Muslim organizations for women is the Canadian Council of Muslim Women, a nationwide organization founded in 1982, which has been active in organizing conferences and seminars and fostering research and literature about Muslim women in Canada.

Issues of identity

Literature concentrating specifically on Muslim women in Canada is just emerging. Recent contributions in this area have focused attention on the experience of Muslim women adapting to life in Canada (Hoodfar 2003, Khan 2002, McDonough 2003, Meshal 2003, Zaman 1999). These contributions emphasize that Muslim women are subject to competing prescriptions emerging from mainstream society and from Muslim communities. They demonstrate how identity is negotiated for a number of Muslim women in Canada in response to factors of normative Islamic teachings, gender, race, ethnicity, migration, and minority status, amidst the apparent polarity of Islam and the West. Diversity and variety is a common theme emerging from each of these contributions, as it is clear that Muslim women in Canada self identify in a vast number of complex ways. This diversity in self-identification is mirrored in the diversity of ways in which Muslim women live in Canada. Many Muslim women live in traditional role structures within the home while large numbers are involved in a number of activities outside the home. While the majority of Muslim women in Canada do not wear *ḥijāb* an increasing number are doing so (Meshal 2003). Observance of the *ḥijāb* has been cited as a key factor in discrimination and harassment of Muslim women seeking employment (Persad 2002).

Issues of domestic violence

Mainstream Canadian media frequently focus attention on the presence in some Muslim societies of specific forms of domestic violence often associated with Muslim culture including, most significantly, forced marriage, honor crimes, and female genital mutilation. However, unlike well-publicized situations in Muslim communities in Europe and the United States, no concrete examples of these types of domestic violence occurring in Canada have arisen in scholarly or popular media reports.

Arranged or semi-arranged marriages remain the norm in most immigrant Muslim families, in both first and second generations, but no issues of compulsion have generally been raised (Hogben 1991, Qureshi 1991). Undoubtedly the social and sexual activity of most Muslim women remains significantly constrained relative to norms in mainstream Canadian society, but indications of honor-based violence directed at women for violating religious and cultural norms have been isolated (Hogben 1991). The Ontario Human Rights Commission produced a policy paper regarding female genital mutilation (OHRC 1996). This paper indicated that the policy was developed in response to suggestions from key community contacts that female genital mutilation was found among some immigrant communities in Canada. Again, no concrete incidents were cited to illustrate this. It is possible that these practices exist to some degree in pockets of the Muslim community coming from parts of Africa where the practice remains common, but to say anything more than this would be largely speculative.

Spousal abuse is a more clearly established form of domestic violence of concern for Muslim women in Canada. Research and literature about, and community response to, spousal abuse in the Muslim community has developed more than that on any other area of domestic violence. Major Canadian surveys of violence against women have found that some form of spousal abuse is common throughout Canadian society, but these surveys have not produced religious or ethnic community level specification (Johnson 2002). It is notable that research and literature on spousal abuse lumps Muslim women with national or ethnic groupings intersecting with the Muslim community (South Asian, Arab, Somali, and so forth) or with immigrant and refugee women in general (Bannerji 2002, Papp 1990, Moussa 2002, Schmidt 2000). Only Azmi's qualitative studies on wife abuse and the welfare response to it in the Muslim community in Toronto have focused attention on wife abuse specifically in the Muslim community (1996, 1999).

It is not clear from the literature to what degree Muslim women face spousal abuse in Canada. No quantitative data exist that compare the presence of spousal abuse found in countries of origin with its presence in Canada, nor do quantitative data exist to compare the presence of this form of domestic violence with its presence in other communities in Canada. At the very least it is clear that spousal abuse of various types and degrees exists in Muslim communities and that it is a recognized issue of concern within both the Muslim community and mainstream institutions.

Clearly the experience of spousal abuse among Muslim women is similar in many regards to that of spousal abuse in other mainly immigrant communities. Many immigrant Muslim women, like other immigrant women, are particularly isolated and vulnerable. Language barriers significantly impede their awareness of Canadian legal and social norms. They often lack extended family and community support networks, and are often economically dependent on their spouses. This situation is further complicated in situations where women have been sponsored for immigration by their spouses and for whom fear and threat of deportation is at least a perceived concern.

Also like other immigrant women, many Muslim women face serious issues of shame and denial. The role of wife and mother is a comparatively significant one in the cultural and religious understanding of many immigrant women and especially so for Muslim women. The threat of marital and family breakdown is particularly difficult to accept and as a result many Muslim women are often reluctant to report abuse unless it becomes particularly severe.

Along with immigration status issues, the experience of domestic violence for Muslim women in Canada has been heavily influenced by a pervasive and ongoing competition between normative Islamic and mainstream Canadian ideological and cultural outlooks. These competing ideological perspectives lead to varying visions of the nature of spousal abuse and appropriate welfare responses to them. Muslim religious community initiatives in responding to wife abuse tend to view spousal abuse as a product of religious and spiritual decline and put considerable emphasis on the provision of religious and spiritual counseling for both spouses, and on the preservation of the family as a major goal alongside issues of the safety of abused women. In contrast, mainstream providers of services for abused women tend to focus on unequal gender relationships as the primary cause of spousal abuse and emphasize the safety of abused women as the sole and overriding goal (Azmi 1996, Valiante 1992).

Mistrust of the mainstream society's initiatives responding to spousal abuse has led religious sectors of the Muslim community to develop alternative services that are perceived to better conform to religious norms. In Greater Toronto, where the Muslim community in Canada has experienced its most significant institutional development, a number of services parallel to mainstream ones have been developed by religious institutions and organizations. Most significant in this regard was the establishment in 1996 in Greater Toronto of the Muslim Welfare Home for Needy Women and Children. This 27-bed shelter was the first of its kind in Canada to provide shelter for women fleeing abusive relationships. The shelter is open to all women regardless of religious affiliation but reflects the need of the Muslim community to provide shelter inspired by religious values.

The immigrant experience and the meeting of Islamic religious perspectives with those of mainstream secular Canada are two significant factors that have shaped the experience of Muslim community life in Canada. These two factors have been, and will likely continue to be, major factors influencing issues of domestic violence in the Muslim community in Canada for decades to come.

BIBLIOGRAPHY

S. Azmi, Perceptions of the welfare response to wife abuse in the Muslim community of metropolitan Toronto, Ph.D. diss., University of Toronto 1996.

——, Wife abuse and ideological competition in the Muslim community of Toronto, in H. Troper and M. Weinfeld (eds.), *Ethnicity, politics, and public policy. Case studies in Canadian diversity*, Toronto 1999, 164–89.

H. Bannerji, A question of silence. Reflections on violence against women in communities of colour, in K. McKenna and J. Larkin (eds.), *Violence against women. New Canadian perspectives*, Toronto 2002, 353–70.

W. M. Hogben, Marriage and divorce among Muslims in Canada, in E. H. Waugh, S. M. Abu-Laban, and R. B. Qureshi, *Muslim families in North America*, Edmonton 1991, 154–84.

H. Hoodfar, More than clothing. Veiling as an adaptive strategy, in S. S. Alvi, H. Hoodfar, and S. McDonough (eds.), *The Muslim veil in North America. Issues and debates*, Toronto 2003, 3–40.

Z. Husaini, Historical background, in S. Zaman (ed.), *At my mother's feet. Stories of Muslim women*, Kingston, Ont. 1999, 13–19.

H. Johnson, Methods of measurement, in K. McKenna and J. Larkin (eds.), *Violence against women. New Canadian perspectives*, Toronto 2002, 21–54.

S. Khan, *Aversion and desire. Negotiating Muslim female identity in the diaspora*, Toronto 2002.

S. McDonough, Voice of Muslim women in S. S. Alvi, H. Hoodfar, and S. McDonough (eds.), *The Muslim veil in North America. Issues and debates*, Toronto 2003, 105–20.

R. Meshal, Banners of faith and identities in construct. The hijab in Canada, in S. S. Alvi, H. Hoodfar, and S. McDonough (eds.), *The Muslim veil in North America. Issues and debates*, Toronto 2003, 72–105.

H. Moussa, Violence against refugee women. Gender oppression, Canadian policy, and the international struggle for human rights, in K. McKenna and J. Larkin (eds.), *Violence against women. New Canadian perspectives*, Toronto 2002, 371–402.

Ontario Human Rights Commission, *Policy on female genital mutilation (FGM)*, Toronto 1996.

A. Papp, *Report on abused South Asian women in Scarborough*, Toronto 1990.

J. Persad, *No hijab is permitted here*, Toronto 2002.

R. B. Qureshi, Marriage strategies among Muslims from South Asia, in E. H. Waugh, S. M. Abu-Laban, and R. B. Qureshi, *Muslim families in North America*, Edmonton, Ont. 1991, 185–212.

S. Schmidt, Why does wife abuse occur in Somali refugee families settling in Canada when it rarely occurs in Somalia?, essay, New College, University of Toronto 2000.

W. Valiante, Domestic violence and the South Asian family. Treatment and research issues, unpublished manuscript, Toronto 1992.

S. Zaman (ed.), *At my mother's feet. Stories of Muslim women*, Kingston, Ont. 1999.

SHAHEEN HUSSAIN AZMI

The Caucasus

Domestic violence, a taboo subject in Caucasian culture, is deeply embedded in traditions of family privacy and autonomy. As it is a matter of private concern, the culture does not permit the society at large either to discuss or adjudicate violence within the family. It differs from other forms of violence in that it occurs in an enclosed space.

Historically, family autonomy evolved as an institution for survival and protection. In Caucasian culture the family consists of the immediate nuclear family and a wide circle of relatives. But acquaintances may also take part in resolving family problems. The expression, "My family is my business alone," expresses the exclusion of the state and legal institutions, and there is no legal definition of domestic violence.

The mechanisms of domestic violence rest on the fact that in the family the males control the resources and therefore women are subservient to them. In the extended family the greatest conflicts occur between pairs: wife and husband, daughter-in-law and mother-in-law, and son-in-law and mother-in-law. The role of violator and victim changes according to region and ethnicity, although the traditional perception is that it is mainly the wife and mother-in-law who instigate conflict. The exception is the mother who is the idealized icon.

Young people do not see domestic violence as an acute problem. Not particularly concerned with the internal family dynamics of domestic violence, they see only external causes and suggest only external solutions: adopt laws, improve economic and living conditions, and make violence a problem for open discussion in the public arena. Although domestic violence is influenced by education, inequality of family income, social environment, and attitudes, adults give priority to internal family relations: mutual understanding between spouses, children, and extended family. An absolute majority of the victims of violence suffer the consequences of economic power over them and the absence of protective institutions. According to research by Pkhakadze (2002), female victims of domestic violence do not report it for the following reasons: shame in the face of public exposure (32 percent); fear that it will give the family a bad reputation (10 percent); conviction that revelation will have no effect (29 percent); and fear of divorce and losing children (6 percent). Five percent of women think that domestic violence is normal and 20 percent fear being beaten for revealing domestic violence. As long as the attitude toward domestic violence confines it to the privacy of the family, there can be no meaningful social discussion.

BIBLIOGRAPHY
A. M. Alikhanov-Avarski *In the mountains of Daghestan. Travel impressions and stories of the Caucasus* [in Russian], St. Petersburg 1985, 1–339, 1986, 55–337.
A. G. Bulatova, Traditional winter games and entertainment in the mountains of Daghestan, in A. Alibov (ed.), *Problems of social life among the peoples of Daghestan in the nineteenth and twentieth centuries* [in Russian], Makhachkala 1987.
A. Dubrovnik, *Cherks* [in Russian], Nalchik 1991.
S. S. Gajiev, *Family and marriage among the peoples of Daghestan, from the nineteenth to the beginning of the twentieth centuries* [in Russian], Moscow 1985.
U. U. Karpov, *Notes on traditional social life. Materials of ethnographic field research* [in Russian], St. Petersburg 1996[3].
——, *The place of women among the peoples of the Caucasus* [in Russian], St. Petersburg 2001.
M. Kuchukhidze, *Family violence* [in Georgian], Tbilisi 2000.
M. C. Kudaev, *Wedding rites* [in Russian], Nalchik 1988.
G. Nizharadze, Woman and conflict, in G. Kutsishvili (ed.), *Alternatives to conflict* [in Georgian], Tbilisi 1999, 3–4.
P. Pkhakadze, *Family violence* [in Georgian], Tbilisi 2002.
L. Surmanizde, *Attitudes toward gender violence* [in Georgian], Tbilisi 2000.
G. Tevdoradze, *Five years in Pshavi and Khevsureti* [in Georgian], Tbilisi 1941.

FERIDE ZURIKASHVILI

Central Asia

By tradition in the Central Asian region boys are regarded as the bearers of the family line, while girls are temporary members of the family and the community. Thus boys and girls have a different social status and are educated in different ways. As research has demonstrated (Karasaeva 1996), the second-class status of women is fixed in the social consciousness, characterized by scorn for women that begins even before they are born. The result of research conducted by the OSCE (Organization for Security and Cooperation in Europe) in Uzbekistan (Tashkent and Tashkent Province) demonstrates that the majority of women are second-class members of the family and are inferior to every other family member (husband, mother-in-law, father, mother, brothers).

This is observed in every stratum of society. Custom and prejudice take precedence over law and the norms of human rights when it comes to the position of women in the family. According to tradition the woman is alienated from her basic rights of choice and freedom in her life. Research shows the following: 52 percent of women do not have the right to choose their husband; 82 percent of women have no voice in family decisions; 64 percent of women have no access to the family income; and 60 percent of women are deprived of the right to express their opinions on family problems. As a result, by custom 98 percent of women experience deprivation of their rights; 43 percent of women cannot independently decide on family planning issues; and childlessness serves as a reason for divorce of 54 percent of women.The patriarchal custom of bride theft, with few exceptions, is met with complete social acceptance and in reality hides the rape of young women, forcing them to reproduce. "The husband must be on a higher level than his wife," admonishes a well-known Muslim aphorism. These conditions form the basic rules for choosing mates in adult life (personal and business). This is the basis for the unjust distribution of rights and obligations in the family, and for the discrimination against women in the family. Frequently, this discrimination takes the form of domestic violence.

The most widespread form of violence in the culture is domestic violence, both the actual act and the threat of the act, which afflicts and damages women, physically, psychologically, economically, and morally. In six months in 1999 there were 2,497 incidents of domestic abuse in families; this is more than 33 percent of the total number of criminal acts. Acts of violence perpetrated on women composed 30 percent of the general number of murders (81 women were killed), 77 percent of suicides, 44 percent of cases of deliberate infliction of harm to health, 60 percent of beatings, and 21 percent of all threats of violence (CEDAW 2000, 27).

The statistical data on domestic violence from crisis centers – Shanse, Sezim, and the Umud shelter in the city of Bishkek (Kyrgyzstan) – corroborate the statistics of the ministry of internal affairs of the Kyrgyz Republic. In the course of three years of work with more than 9,000 women and girls in these establishments, 37 percent experienced physical force in the family, 23 percent psychological force, and 7 percent sexual abuse (Tugelbayeva 2001, 34)

The official attitude toward domestic violence differs from one republic to another in Central Asia. The governments of Kazakhstan, Tajikistan, and Kyrgyzstan publicly discuss the problems of domestic violence and struggle against its negative consequences. In Uzbekistan and Turkmenistan public discussion of these topics is forbidden. Indeed, in these republics domestic violence has a quasi-legal status. The facts of domestic violence are either hidden or discussed as isolated cases. The term "domestic violence" is not used in juridical practice. "Not a single case of family violence that we investigated ever reached the courts, therefore one cannot speak definitively about the relationship of the legal establishment to these matters. Attorneys, judges, and the militia consistently gave us to understand that the majority of cases of family violence, even in the presence of the police, never get to the courts" (Interview, Human Rights Watch, 8 June 2000). These are the words of one of the judges: "Even when a victim is criminally treated, such cases are normally hidden from the very beginning" (Interview, Human Rights Watch 22 May 2000, *Human Rights Watch* 2001).

Most important is that the great majority of women and girls who experience domestic violence consider this to be an integral element of family relations. For them it is a structural part of the overarching patriarchal legacy, supported by countless tenacious traditions and customs. It is precisely the patriarchal culture that preserves violence toward women as a system of exacting obedience and eliciting terror; it is like a virus that reproduces itself from generation to generation. Only a profound reformation of social and cultural norms will change this state of affairs, which is validated by the attitudes of centuries (Tugelbayeva 2001, 21).

Bibliography

CEDAW, National report, Republic of Kazakhstan, 2000, <http://www.un.org/womenwatch/daw/cedaw/reports.htm#k>.

Human Rights Watch 13:4(D) (June 2001), *Uzbekistan*.

A. Kadirova, *The discriminatory influence of certain customs and prejudices on the position of women in the family* [in Russian and Uzbek]. Proceedings of the conference on Overcoming of gender stereotypes, OSCE (Organization for Security and Cooperation in Europe), 18–19 September 2001, Tashkent.

A. K. Karasaev, *The Kyrgyz community. The tradition of violence against women* [in Russian], Bishkek 1996.

L. Sadikova (ed.), *The rights of women in Kyrgyzstan. Muslim tradition, Islamic values, and contemporary law* [in Russian and Kyrgyz], Bishkek 2001.

B. Tugelbayeva (ed.), *Violence against women. Prevention and struggle against the consequences* [in Russian and Kyrgyz], Bishkek 2001.

Marfua Tokhtakhodjaeva and Almaz Kadirova

Iran and Afghanistan

In this entry the phrase domestic violence is used to describe a variety of actions and omissions that occur in different family relationships. These include incidents of physical attack and/or psychological or mental violence (Davis 1994, Martin 1979, Viano 1992).

As far as Iran and Afghanistan are concerned, literature on the subject is scarce and field studies very recent in Iran and practically non-existent in Afghanistan. There exist no statistics or articles written solely about domestic violence against women in Afghanistan, possibly due to the sociopolitical upheavals of the past two decades. Only anecdotal evidence is found, from the mass media and non-governmental organizations (NGOs), that incidences of domestic violence have increased as a result of the war, displacement, and poverty.

Broadly speaking, two related gender issues affect the problem of domestic violence in both countries: one is attitudinal and based on norms and values; the other relates to legal doctrines and the Sharīʿa.

Patriarchal norms and values

Patriarchal values and a family system based on male supremacy, hierarchy, and obedience to the oldest male are prevalent (Nassehi-Behnam, 1985). Children socialized at home and in educational institutions that reflect a discriminatory image of women (Mohceni 1978, Taleghani 1994) learn to accept the practice and transfer of archaic gender roles and thus maintain patriarchal norms and attitudes. The consequences of this can be observed in different spheres of female life: a higher female child mortality due to discriminatory attitude of mothers toward food distribution (Nassehi 1996); the existence of a wide gap in the literacy rates of men and women (Aghajanian 2000); and the early marriage of girls when financial resources are limited.

Islamic law

Because of the existence of religious and legal doctrines inspired by Sharīʿa, the Iranian and Afghan civil codes concerning marriage, divorce, child custody, pension (*nafaqa*), family residence, right of citizenship, guardianship, and inheritance place women in a highly disadvantageous position in the social order (Behnam 1990).

In dominant interpretations of Islamic law, the right of punishment is reserved solely to men. But beating a woman is not recommended. Nevertheless in the mentality of certain men, religious as well as secular, an "untamed" woman must be trained. The response of clerics to a question on domestic violence is: "Islam does not recommend men to beat their wives, nevertheless, if a wife is not compliant (*nāshiza*), they are authorized to beat her. A woman is called 'untamed' if she refuses to satisfy the desires of her husband (*tamkin*). Husband's sexual satisfaction being part of *tamkin*, the rape of a wife cannot be considered as an assault! Thereafter, punishing her becomes a right for men" (Ardalan and Khaksar 1994). Even in the realm of crime the supremacy of men is blatant. According to Islamic criminal law (*qiṣāṣ*), a woman's life is equal to half that of a man, a situation that often results in the male escaping punishment after committing a crime.

Although the Iranian government joined the UN Convention on Children's Rights in 1993 and the parliament adopted a resolution proposed by activist women (September 2000) to raise the legal maturity age from 9 to 15 for girls and from 15 to 17 for boys, the problem remains unsolved. The Guardian Council rejected the resolution on grounds of incompatibility with Islamic law (Kian 2002). Nevertheless, bargains are being made, but the situation remains inconclusive. Young children can be married off as long as the father, grandfather, or guardian allow it (Kar 2000). The child must obey and respect his parents (article 1177) and parents have the right to punish and beat him if necessary (article 1179). *Qiṣāṣ* thus gives the father the right to treat the child the way he deems fitting, even as far as killing the child; if a father kills his child, the act is not punishable by law (article 220) (Ebadi 1999). Given the legal abuses, it becomes difficult to define violence and punishment in such cultures.

Women

According to the content analysis of a Persian daily newspaper (*Īrān*) during 1995 (Nassehi-Behnam 1999, 135), women were the usual victims of violence in the home and men the habitual perpetrators (85 percent men, 15 percent women). In most of the cases men acted violently toward women whereas women's aggressiveness was self-inflicted (attempted or successful suicide). Forty percent of reported domestic violence incidents resulted in the death of the victim, 2.5 percent in suicide, 3.5 in attempted homicide, and the rest in disputes and assaults that were taken to court.

Victims of male aggression are mostly wives, children, wife's parents, and siblings. Men often consider their parents-in-law responsible for their wife's behavior. Female violence is scarce and often involves threatening men (suicide attempt and self-burning) rather than injuring another person. But among women who attempted self-burning many have lost their lives (Moghissi 1994). Two cases of female homicides (a co-wife and the child of a co-wife) show, contrary to what some Muslims pretend, how intolerable a polygamous marriage may become to the first wife.

A documented study of violence (Kār 2001) concludes that violence against women is a partially hidden phenomenon because Iranian women have traditionally learned to tolerate and accept male violence and avoid reporting incidents of abuse. Legal organizations do not help the dissemination of data concerning domestic violence. That is the reason why statistics do not reflect the gravity of the situation of women's lives. Kār mentions the negative consequences of divorce in Persian culture, such as gender inequality in child custody and the lack of safeguards (economic and effective) for divorcees, as the main reasons for such subordination. A survey on divorcees in Tehran confirms the absence of any protection systems for these women, who are considered deviants in traditional societies (Nassehi 1980).

A survey of battered women in Tehran (E'zazi 2001) reveals that in 53 percent of the cases, violence against women is practiced at home and the rest in public places. A considerable number of the women interviewed did not know why they were beaten. Among respondents only 7 percent reacted to light physical attacks. Most women said they tolerated their husbands' violence to avoid being divorced, since they thought their husband's aggression was to make them ask for a divorce without the benefit of their bride-price (*mahr*). Others accept men's brutality as part of normal male behavior. Sixty-three percent were forced into marriage or went through arranged marriages. A considerable number of marriages were heterogamous. The reasons battered women gave for domestic violence are: jealousy, family disputes resulting from interference by in-laws or visits of wife's family members, financial problems, and alcohol or drug addiction.

Statistics from a report on people who consulted the Iranian Legal Medical Office during a period of 30 months (Kohani 2001), indicate that among approximately 2.5 million plaintiffs, more than half reported quarrels, and 24.5 percent of these were battered women. Of this number, 9 percent wanted to officially record their complaints for future decisions (*osr va haraj*), 31 percent to obtain a divorce, and 60 percent just to scare their aggressors and prevent future attacks.

An RDS report (2000) on the situation of Afghani women says: "the Human Rights situation for women was extremely poor . . . As lawless fighting continued in some areas, violence against women occurred frequently, including beatings, rapes, forced marriages, disappearances, kidnappings and killings. Such incidents generally went unreported, and most information was anecdotal . . . Prostitution and beggary are the only options especially for widows to survive and feed their children." The Human Rights Watch report of September 2002 on West Afghanistan confirms these allegations through testimonies.

Children

A study of violence toward children in three child dispensaries in Tehran shows that among 3,019 children (1,578 boys and 1,441 girls) who were brought to these dispensaries, 367 (12.2 percent) were abused. The percentage of boys who were physically assaulted was 14.5, and of girls 9.6. Child abuse was mostly due to plurality of children (large family), drug addiction, and stress. Among abusers, 34.1 percent had themselves been victims of violence during their childhood and 26.4 percent had prior abuse cases. According to the conclusion of this study, there is a positive correlation between physical assault and age, sex, place of residence, marital status, and history of violence in the family.

A Persian film called *Homework*, based on research on violence toward children, reflects the oppression that parents inflict upon their children at home.

A survey conducted by the UNHCR (United Nations High Commissioner for Refugees) in Afghanistan (1997) estimated the number of street children in Kabul at 28,000, of whom 20 percent were girls. Children as young as five years of age are forced to go out and earn a living for their disabled parents or young sisters.

Conclusion

What is presented here is but a vague estimation of what happens in Iran and Afghanistan. Scientific, long-term investigations must be carried out to obtain the true picture of domestic violence in these countries. Nevertheless, it is certain that, especially in Iran, both governmental organizations (such as police departments and the ministry of hygiene, healing and medical training) and NGOs (such as the Institute for Women's Studies and Research) have become conscious of the gravity of the situation and try not only to prevent domestic violence but also to protect the victims (Kār 1996). To improve the situation however, it is imperative that the judicial system be revised in these countries.

Bibliography

A. Aghajanian, The status of women and female children in Iran, in M. Afkhami (ed.), *In the eye of the storm*, Syracuse, N.Y. 1994, 44–61.
Ardalan and Khaksaz, Ta hāla shodah hamsaritān rā bazanid?, in *Zanān* (Tehran) 18 (June–July 1994), 6–19.
V. Behnam, Zan, khānuvāda va tajadud, in *Iran nameh* (Bethesda, Md.) 11:2 (1990), 241.
M. Davies, *Women and violence*, London 1994, 1.
S. Ebadi, Atfāl va khushūnat, in V. Nassehi-Behnam (ed.), *Violence and family*, *Nimeye Digar* 2:5, (1999), 72–81.
S. E'zazi, *Khushūnat-i khānuvādagi. Zanān-i kutak khurda*, Tehran 2001.
Homework, a Persian film by A. Kiarostami, based on research by Sholeh Dolatabadi, 1987.
M. Kār, Aya hanuz ham zarurāt-i ta'asis-e khanaḥy-i amn iḥsās nāmāshavad, in *Zanan* 29 (1996), 2–3.
——, Barisiy-i khushūnat 'layh-i zanān dar huquq-i inqilābiy-i Īrān, in V. Nassehi-Behnam (ed.), Violence and family, *Nimeye Digar* 2:5 (1999), 55–71.
——, *Pizhūhishī darbārah-'i khushūnat 'alayh-i zanān dar Īrān*, Tehran 2000, 145.
A. Kian, *Les familles iraniennes entre Islam, état et famille*, Paris 2002, 103.
M. D. Kohani, Paper presented to the Seminar on Violence and Family and reported in a special issue (*Vezeh nameh*) published by the University of Social Welfare and Rehabilitation Sciences, Tehran, November 2001, 19.
J. P. Martin, Some reflections on violence and the family, in J. P. Martin (ed.), *Violence and the family*, New York 1978, 346–59.
H. Moghissi, Ḥuqūq-i zan va bunbasthāy-i farhanki-i 'ijtimāy-i jumhurīy-i islām, in *Chashm Andāz* (Paris) 13 (Spring 1994), 42–53.
N. Mohceni, *Taṣvīr va naqsh-i zan va mard dar kitabhāy-i darsīy-i kudakān*, Tehran 1978.
G. Nassehi, *Situation analysis of women and children in the Islamic Republic of Iran*, UNICEF limited publication, March 1992, rev. 1996, 60.
V. Nassehi-Behnam, Change and the Iranian family, in *Current Anthropology* 26:5 (December 1985), 557–62.
——, Khushūnat dar khānavāda va bāztāb-i ān dar matbū'at-i Īrān, in V. Nassehi-Behnam (ed.), Violence and family, *Nimeye Digar* 2:5 (1999), 135.
V. Nassehi-Behnam et al., *The study of the situation of divorcees in Tehran* [in Persian], Tehran 1980.
RDS, Contemporary women's issues. Based on country reports (Afghanistan) on human rights practices for 2000, <http://rdsweb2.rdsinc.com>.
A. A. Sayyary et al., Barisīy-i kudakāzari jasmāni dar murāja'n-i sah darmānkāh-i takhasusīy-i darujān kūdakān dar shahristān-i Tihrān, in *Rehabilitation Science Quarterly* 6/7 (Fall 2001), 7–13.
M. Taleghani et al., *Portrayal of women in primary school textbooks before and after the Revolution*, UNESCO 1994.
E. C. Viano, Violence among intimates. Major issues and approaches, in E. C. Viano (ed.), *Intimate violence. Interdisciplinary perspectives*, Washington, D.C. 1992, 3–12.

Vida Nassehi-Behnam

Israel

Domestic violence, a subset of gender violence, refers to family-based sexual abuse, battering of women, and "honor killings." Researchers and activists point to intergenerational transmission of violence, political and economic hardship, gendered structural inequality, and/or patriarchal proprietary objectification of women as keys to domestic violence.

The location of Muslims within Israeli society helps to contextualize this complex phenomenon. Between 1948 and 1966, Palestinian Arab citizens (including Muslims, Christians, and Druze) were regulated under a military administration. Muslims constitute a majority of the non-Jewish Palestinian Arab national minority, with 1.7 million persons making up 16 percent of the Israeli population within the Green Line, but including East Jerusalem. Most Muslims live in Arab towns of fewer than 20,000 residents. Larger towns range in size from Taibeh (30,000), to Umm el-Fahm (38,000), and Nazareth (41,500), where confidentiality in social services and policing is often compromised. Muslims in Israel are amongst the youngest and least educated of the population, and also experience the highest levels of unemployment and poverty (especially Beduin living in the Negev). Socioeconomic marginalization, compounded by weak representation in local and national politics, intensifies battered women's entrapment. Palestinian feminists also argue that such second-class citizenship within a militarized society inspires critiques of political violence but creates silences about gender violence.

In this family-centered society, national tensions link marriage and motherhood to Palestinian identity. Marriage and motherhood enforce national and religious autonomy, evidenced, for example, in the exclusive jurisdiction of male *qāḍī*s in Sharīʿa courts (which are exempt from Israeli legislation on women's equality) over marriage and divorce, and the five-year struggle, won in 2001 by the Coalition for Equality in Personal Status Laws, to amend the Family Courts Law (1995), to open civil courts to Muslims to determine maintenance and child custody. Muslim men who batter rely on the state's lax enforcement of the 1959 anti-polygyny law and the legal prohibition against forced divorce, whereby a husband unilaterally pronounces his wife divorced, a tenet of Islamic divorce law. Threats of unilateral divorce enforce subordination and quell battered women's resistance, especially for Muslim women who, for economic reasons, fear of abandonment, family rejection, and the loss of social status or child custody, wish to stay married. Indeed, marriage rates are high and divorce rates lowest within the Muslim community, where living alone as a single or divorced woman is relatively rare. Muslim women marry on average at 21.5 years of age and have the highest number of children, when compared to Druze, Christian, and Jewish Israelis.

It was Jewish feminist activists who established the first battered women's shelter in 1977 in an Arab neighborhood in the city of Haifa. However, not until the 1990s did Arab and Jewish women, based in non-governmental organizations (NGOs) and public agencies, successfully transform violence against women from a personal harm into a social problem and firmly establish violence against women or family violence in the Israeli lexicon. As part of the global anti-gender violence movement, women organized centers for victims of sexual violence, opened hotlines and shelters, called for alternatives to violent and controlling forms of masculinity, and demanded legal changes and funding for victim services. Muslim women won limited recognition of their unique living conditions and related needs. In 1991, legislators gave victims access to restraining orders, although this option has limited utility for the majority of Muslim women who live adjacent to their husband's family. The first and only Israeli shelter staffed by and for Arabs was founded by Palestinian activists in 1993. Public monies partially support these and other shelters and regional prevention centers, but few are located in majority Muslim locales. Additionally, limited Arabic language materials on gender violence exist.

Israeli police estimate one out of every five married women is physically battered; the ministry of labor suggests one in four men chronically use physical violence against wives and children. Drawing on research among Palestinians that indicates similar prevalence rates, Aida Touma-Suliman, director of the Nazareth-based NGO Women Against Violence (WAV), estimates that one in four Palestinians in Israel beat their wives at least once a year. Approximately one in five engaged women report their partner's use of physical aggression against them. Taken together, the pervasive nature of domestic violence, the tendency to consider it a family issue, and men's justification of wife beating contributes to the normalization of physical violence and other behaviors intended to intimidate and control women. In concert with allied organizations, such as Kayan and Al Siwar, members of WAV work to end the familial ideology of privacy that upholds violence against married and unmarried women, and so-called "honor killings," where male relatives execute and thus punish a woman for breaking gender codes of comportment and mobility. Overall, about one third of victims of family-based threats and violence who seek support report the abuse to the police. In 2001, the police documented over 22,000 new cases of domestic violence in the population at large, yet representatives of law enforcement and the judiciary often dismiss violence against Muslim women as "cultural" and intervene in ways that at times ultimately endangers those seeking protection.

Palestinian women in Israel, working together and at times in coalition with Jewish Israeli feminists and/or members of the anti-occupation peace movement, continue to call for gender equality within a national framework, in order to make violence against women in all its forms unacceptable.

Bibliography

Primary Sources

M. Bassok, Census. One quarter of Israel's children are Muslims, 2 February 2004, <www.haaretzdaily.com>.

M. Freedman, *Exile in the promised land. A memoir*, Ithaca, N.Y. 1990.

Israel, Central Bureau of Statistics, *Statistical abstract of Israel, no.* 49 [in Hebrew], Tel Aviv 1998.

E. Konur, State funding for organizations that serve victims of violence against women 1990–2000, Adva Center, Tel Aviv March 2000, < http://www.adva.org/violence1999.html>.

Sikkuy, *The Sikkuy report 2001–2002. Monitoring civic equality between Arab and Jewish citizens of Israel*, Jerusalem 2002.

Working Group on the Status of Palestinian Women in Israel, *The status of Palestinian women citizens of Israel*, NGO parallel report submitted to CEDAW July 1997.

Secondary Sources

M. Adelman, No way out. Divorce-related domestic violence in Israel, in *Violence Against Women* 6:11 (2000), 1223–54.

——, The military, militarism, and the militarization of domestic violence, in *Violence Against Women* 9:9 (2003), 1118–52.

M. Adelman, E. Erez, and N. Shalhoub-Kevorkian, Policing violence against minority women in multicultural societies. "Community" and the politics of exclusion, in *Police and Society* 7 (2003), 103–31.

N. Berkovitch, Motherhood as a national mission. The construction of womanhood in the legal discourse in Israel, in *Women's Studies International Forum* 20 (1997), 605–19.

A. Ghanem, *The Palestinian Arab minority In Israel, 1948–2000. A political study*, Albany, N.Y. 2001.

M. Haj-Yahia, Patterns of violence against engaged Arab women from Israel and some psychological implications, in *Psychology of Women Quarterly* 24 (2000), 209–19.

——, Beliefs about wife beating among Arab men from Israel. The influence of their patriarchal ideology, in *Journal of Family Violence* 18 (2003), 193–206.

N. Shalhoub-Kevorkian, Law, politics, and violence against women. A case study of Palestinians in Israel, in *Law and Policy* 21 (1999), 189–211.

R. Torstrick, *The limits of coexistence. Identity politics in Israel*, Ann Arbor 2000.

Madelaine Adelman

The Ottoman Empire

Although several modern legal codes make reference to domestic violence, Islamic law (Sharīʿa) addresses it through the concept of *ḍarar* (harm) that encompasses several types of abuse against a spouse. For example, *ḍarar* can include the failure of a husband to provide obligatory support (*nafaqa*) for his wife, which includes food, shelter, and clothing. A husband's absence from the home, his inability to fulfill his wife's sexual needs, or mistreatment of his wife's family members can result in dissolution of the marriage. *Ḍarar* also includes physical abuse against a spouse. The laws concerning *ḍarar* maintain that if a woman is harmed in her marriage, she can have it annulled: "the most important proof needed was to show that the husband had broken the marriage contract or that the marriage caused the woman harm" (Sonbol 1996, 281). Physically assaulting a wife violates the marriage contract and is grounds for immediate divorce.

There are very few studies available on domestic violence in Islamic history. Colin Imber (1997) mentions it in the context of Ottoman fatwas. Ottoman law tends to treat cases of *ḍarar* in accordance with the Sharīʿa; this is reflected in a sixteenth-century fatwa from the Ottoman Şeyhülislām Ebu's-suʿud (Abū al-Saʿūd) that reads: "Question: Zeyd hurts his wife Hind in many ways. If the *qāḍī* knows about it, is he able to separate Hind from Zeyd? Answer: He is able to prevent his hurting her by whatever means possible" (Imber 1997, 216). Further evidence of Ottoman treatment of *ḍarar* can be found in studies currently being undertaken using Sharīʿa court records from the Ottoman period. For example Sharīʿa court cases from Aleppo, Syria reflect the ability of women to seek retribution when subjected to abuse. The courts of Aleppo ruled against abusive husbands in several cases of domestic violence. In one court case from May 1687 Fāṭima bt. Ḥajj ʿAlī filed a lawsuit against her husband testifying that he was abusing her; he had hit her with a stick on her body and on her mouth causing her to bleed. She claimed that he was constantly abusive. In her defense she brought along five witnesses. The court reprimanded the abusive husband, ordering that he be given *taʿzīr* (discretionary punishment) (SMH 36:78:214 16 Rajab 1098 A.H./May 1687).

In the Sharīʿa courts women had several strategies for defense. First, a woman could bring witnesses to testify on her behalf and strengthen her case. Second, she could include a clause against domestic abuse in her marriage contract that would offer her further protection if her husband ever abused her. Including these conditions in a marriage contract was an option in any Muslim marriage and offered the bride an opportunity to protect herself legally. For example, women could use their rightful conditions in the marriage contract to bar a man from his legal right to a second wife. When any condition was violated it led automatically to divorce. However, during the nineteenth-century reform period modern laws eliminated the ability of women to insert conditions in their marriage contracts.

It has been a commmon misinterpretation that Islam condones violence against women. In the Qur'ān there is a controversial verse stating: "As to those women on whose part ye fear disloyalty and ill-conduct, admonish them [first], [next], refuse to share their beds, [and last] beat them [lightly]; but if they return to obedience, seek not against them means [of annoyance]" (4:34). First, it is important to state that punishment is reserved for disobedient (nāshiza) wives. In Islamic law the husband's obligation in marriage is to provide for his wife; in return she owes him obedience (ṭāʿa). In Yūsuf ʿAlī's translation cited here, he interprets the the the original Arabic "iḍribuhuna" as "beat them [lightly]" when in fact the phrase literally means "beat them." This is because of dominant interpretations in juridical writings of tafsīr (Qurʾānic interpretation) that have settled the matter. In his interpretation of this verse, Ibn Kathīr cautions men to "refrain from severe reprimand . . . beat them non-violently and do not break their bones" (Ibn Kathīr i, 386). In another passage Ibn Kathīr states that jurists prohibited men from beating and disfiguring their wives. Some juridical writings prescribe more than divorce for abusive husbands. Condemnation of a husband who abuses his wife can be found in the writings of nineteenth-century Syrian jurist Ibn ʿĀbidīn in his Radd al-muḥtār ʿala durr al-mukhtār, where he addresses the issue of a man who beats his wife in a chapter entitled "Excessive Beating." He writes of a man who beats his wife excessively and "breaks bone," "burns skin," or "blackens" or bruises her skin: "if he does so without justification, taʿzīr is mandatory" (Ibn ʿĀbidīn iii, 190). Ibn ʿĀbidīn does not state what form the punishment should take. Interestingly, Ibn ʿĀbidīn's writings from the nineteenth century are consistent with the formulations of the Sharīʿa court case from Aleppo mentioned earlier in which taʿzīr was given as punishment to Fāṭima's abusive husband. Muslim jurists repeatedly admonished men who committed violence against their wives and the Sharīʿa court upheld their position.

Amira Sonbol's exploration of the nineteenth-century reform era in Egypt has noted the detrimental effects of legal reform on women's rights. Looking at the relationship between ṭāʿa and ḍarar she found that in the nineteenth century the burden of proof on women plaintiffs increased. Furthermore, disobedient wives had their rights gradually taken away by their husbands who wielded new state-endorsed authority over their wives. Included in a husband's new-found power was the institutionalization of the bayt al-ṭāʿa or "house of obedience" in which a husband could forcibly confine his wife if she was disobedient. Nineteenth-century personal status laws also allowed a wide range of discretion as to what disobedience entailed: some husbands interpreted it as taking a job, shopping, or visiting friends (Sonbol 1998, 287). Sonbol found that increasingly women had difficulty challenging these cases in court and often lost. Dalenda Larguèche's study of the incarceration of women in Tunisia shows a striking similarity: disobedient wives could be sent by a judge to Dār Juwayd, a system of domestic prisons, for correction. There was an increase in the number of these prisons in the nineteenth century. These institutions were used to modify the behavior of disobedient wives "so as to 'bring them around' to the prescribed norms of conduct and morality" (Larguèche 1996, 260). Both Sonbol and Larguèche problematize the connection between obedience and ḍarar in the modern period as the patriarchal state commingles with the Sharīʿa. These pioneering studies question the notion that modernization is a springboard for progress as several areas of the law drastically limit the legal options afforded women in earlier periods.

Although in the rubric of Western law, murdering a wife in a crime of passion has been placed in the same legal category as domestic violence, this is not the case in Islamic law. There is no mention in the juridical texts of condoned or permissible murder of a wife. However, some modern laws, such as Jordan's Penal Code (1960), contain clauses for "excuse for murder" or offer reduced sentences for men who murder a wife or a female relative suspected of sexual misconduct (Sonbol 2003, 193–4, Abu-Odeh 1996, 143). Authors such as Amira Sonbol and Lama Abu-Odeh have argued that there is a legal connection between "excuse for murder" and "crimes of passion" in the European tradition through the focus on circumstance and the criminal intent of the murderer. Modern legal reforms borrowed from French criminal codes freed the criminal of responsibility so long as the element of surprise was present (Sonbol 2003, 196). In contrast, crimes of passion, prejudicially called "honor crime" in the context of the Islamic world, have mistakenly been associated with Sharīʿa despite their stark connexion with tribal law. The areas with the highest instance of honor crime, namely

Yemen and Jordan, are regions that have large populations of recently sedentary Arab tribes and are best understood in that context.

Although this entry illuminates the way in which domestic violence was treated in the Ottoman and modern periods there is no comprehensive study dealing with the issue of domestic violence. With so few studies on *ḍarar* available it is not possible to perform a comparative study at the moment. By the same token, with a dearth of information available it leaves the path open to future researchers to pursue this area of much needed study.

Bibliography

Primary Sources

M. Ibn ʿĀbidīn, *Radd al-muḥtar ʿala durr al-mukhtār*, 7 vols., Cairo n.d.

I. Ibn Kathīr, *Mukhtaṣar tafsīr Ibn Kathīr*, 3 vols., Beruit, 1981.

al-Qurʾān, trans. Yusuf ʿAlī, Beruit n.d.

SMH (Sijillāt al-maḥkama Ḥalab), Aleppo court records, Syrian National Archives, Damascus, Syria.

Secondary Sources

L. Abu-Odeh, Crimes of honor and the construction of gender in Arab societies, in M. Yamani (ed.), *Feminism and Islam. Legal and literary perspectives*, New York 1996, 141–94.

C. Imber, *Ebu's-suʿud. The Islamic legal tradition*, Stanford, Calif. 1997.

D. Larguèche, Confined, battered, and repudiated women in Tunis since the eighteenth century, in A. E. Sonbol (ed.), *Women, the family, and divorce laws in Islamic history*, Syracuse, N.Y. 1996, 258–76.

A. E. Sonbol, Law and gender violence in Ottoman and modern Egypt, in A. E. Sonbol (ed.), *Women, the family, and divorce laws in Islamic history*, Syracuse, N.Y. 1996, 277–89.

——, Tāʿa and modern legal reform. A rereading, in *Islam and Christian-Muslim Relations* 9:3 (1998), 285–94.

——, *Women of Jordan. Islam, labor, and the law*, Syracuse, N.Y. 2003.

Elyse Semerdjian

South Asia

In South Asia, violence against women takes many forms, ranging from slapping, pushing, hitting, and kicking to dowry-killings, acid-throwing, nutritional deprivation, stove burning, polygamy, unilateral divorce, and sexual abuse. Information on violence against Muslim women in Nepal, Sri Lanka, Bhutan, and the Maldives is almost nonexistent. The print media has focused largely on Bangladesh and Pakistan – two Muslim majority countries in South Asia – and India, where about 125 million Muslims live. In these three countries, women's groups, non-governmental organizations, and feminist voices have been effective in disseminating information on gender violence and articulating women's responses. Most of this information has concentrated on public violence and trafficking in women and girl children; very little data have been collected on domestic violence, which is usually considered a private matter until murder, suicide, or attempted murder within a family takes place (Khondker 1994). Even so, many suicide cases go unreported and no government statistics or systematic police records exist for domestic violence.

Violence against women is part of the history of South Asia (Jayawardena and De Alwis 1996). Over time, Islam in South Asia has been experienced, interpreted, and practiced differently under colonization, imperialism, and nationalism and in the process has been transformed. In 1947, after 200 years of British rule, India was divided into two parts: India, a predominantly Hindu state, and Pakistan, a Muslim state. Since then, Islam as a religion has played a vociferous role in the subcontinent. Despite the separation of Muslim Pakistan from India, religion failed to hold Pakistan together. In the 1971 liberation war, Bangladesh, a province linguistically and culturally separated from the rest of the provinces of Pakistan, emerged as an independent country. During the liberation war, Pakistani military forces, all Muslims, conducted countless acts of violence on Bangladeshi women (more than 80 percent of the population were Muslim) through individual rape, gang rape, torture, and killings (Mascarenhas 1975, Imam 1986). This war in the Indian subcontinent culminated in a public outcry about male violence against women and ushered in what Kabeer (1988) describes as "a feminist consciousness," one that revealed the common thread of women's oppression across classes and religions.

Contrary to the pervasive perception of the family in South Asia as a tightly knit, well-integrated, primary-support kinship organization, gender-based domestic violence occurs throughout Muslim women's lives regardless of sect, class, education, geographical location, or rural/urban variation. In India, for example, female genital mutilation to control female sexuality is practiced among Bohra Muslims (an Ismāʿīlī Shīʿī sect); however, within South Asia this custom is never recognized as domestic violence (Ghadially 1991). In Bangladesh, it is accepted that a husband can inflict several sorts of violence: sexual, psychological (for example, a threat), or vicarious (smashing a plate, beating a child, or damaging something) (Shailo 1994). In Pakistan, a 1989 survey conducted by the Women's

Division suggested that domestic violence occurs in approximately 80 percent of the country's households (ADB 2000). An Asian Development Bank (ADB) report states: "During 1998, 282 burn cases of women were reported in Punjab. Of these, 65 percent died of their injuries. Data collected from two hospitals in Rawalpindi and Islamabad over a period of three years since 1994 reveal 739 cases of burn victims" (ADB 2000, xi). Such stove burning more often happens not as a result of a woman's negligence in the kitchen but because of attempted murder either by the husband or by the husband's family. (The Indian movie *Fire* graphically shows an example of stove burning inflicted on a woman by a husband.) In Bangladesh, India, Nepal, and Pakistan, demand for a huge dowry (ranging from money, gold ornaments, television, car, refrigerator, or furniture to land) by either the groom or the groom's family can cause enormous psychological pressure on the prospective bride and her family. In an effort to reduce the number of brides killed because of dowry, an anti-dowry law was enacted by the Jatiyo Sangsad (parliament) of Bangladesh in 1980. However, as Anam reports, "The Home Minister disclosed in Parliament on 22 November [1993] that there were 21,622 [women] reported suicides since January 1992. Most of these are cases of dowry deaths, domestic violence, etc., whereby women are murdered in a planned way and their husbands or relatives report that they have committed suicide. In other cases, their lives are made so unbearable that they are forced to commit suicide" (1993, 1). An ADB report on Nepal states that in the SAATHI and Asia Foundation survey (1997), "knowledge of violence related to dowry was reported by 38 percent of respondents in Banke, a western Terai district with a predominantly Muslim population" (ADB 1999, 20). To regulate, restrict, and eventually eliminate the custom of dowry, a number of laws have been passed in South Asia. These include the Dowry Prohibition Act of 1980 in Bangladesh (Akanda and Shamim 1985), and the Dowry and Bridal Gifts (Restriction) Rules of 1976 in Pakistan (Ali and Naz 1998). Although these laws have been in effect for over 20 years, customs and social norms and, most of all, the ineffectiveness of the governments in South Asia allow dowry killing to continue.

The patrilineal and patrilocal as well as the patriarchal nature of the social system gives males responsibility for protecting the welfare of women and children. In rural areas, where more than 70 percent of Bangladeshi women live, women's lives are restricted by the social institution called *shamaj*, which dictates the lives of rural people, especially women, in numerous ways. For example, in the case of domestic conflicts, a local rural community court called the *salish* (composed entirely of male members) plays a key role in arbitrating conflict. The woman must be represented by an adult male, who is considered the woman's guardian (World Bank 1990). Moreover, in rural and urban areas, a gender-based division of labor, as well as socially prescribed reproductive roles, ensures that women's labor is taken for granted and unremunerated in many households. As a result, many women are economically dependent and are especially vulnerable to abusive/violent relationship, desertion, divorce, or widowhood.

In Pakistan, the constitution of 1973 guarantees two fundamental rights in Article 25: all citizens are equal under law, and there shall be no discrimination based on sex (Mumtaz and Shaheed 1991). The existence of contradictions between these legal doctrines and women's actual status reveals the marginalized situation of women and children in Pakistani society, and ultimately perpetuates domestic violence. An ADB report states: "The official figure for the murder of women during 1998 was 1,974; the majority of them were victims of their own relatives – husbands, brothers, fathers, and in-laws" (2000, 19). A number of laws on marriage, divorce, maintenance, and child custody, which were enacted during the British colonial rule under the Shariat Application Act of 1937, meant that Muslims would be guided by their personal law or Sharīʿa (Mumtaz and Shaheed 1991). These laws have been amended and modified since then, but the fundamental constitutional principle of Pakistan as an Islamic state has solidified the role of patriarchy, namely, the existence of male supremacy in sociopolitical, legal, and economic institutions. This principle jeopardizes a woman's safety not only in the public domain, but also in her own home. For example, the Family Laws Ordinance of 1961 made the registration of marriage mandatory, but the right of irrevocable divorce remained with the husband. The husband had the authority to delegate his wife the right to divorce him in the *nikanama* (marriage registry), but this right is rarely awarded. A 1998 mini-survey conducted in three areas of Peshwar found that during the last 20 years, "in the Spin Jummat (University Town area), not a single *nikanama* contained a delegation of the right of divorce. Likewise, the Sunehri *Masjid Nikah* Registrar said that his registrar also did not have any case with a *talaq* (divorce) . . . It was only in the Nauthia area that the *Nikah* registrar reported two marriage contracts . . . [which contained] delegation of the right of divorce to the wife" (Ali and Naz 1998, 118). Lack of women's rights to divorce perpetuates an indentured relationship in a marital contract and, in too many cases, perpetuates male violence against women within a family. Moreover, the social norm emphasizing the value of virginity makes it almost impossible for women who are divorced to find another suitable marriage. To delegitimize and reduce the incidence of child marriage, the colonial Child Marriage Restraint Act (1929) and the Muslim Family Laws Ordinance (1961), were joined recently by a law requiring a woman's consent in marriage. Despite these laws, Shaheed reports what happens in practice: "A recent national survey (of 1609 women respondents) showed that 75 percent either had not been consulted or their opinion given no weight at all. Child marriages continue . . . and the Option of Puberty that allows minors to rescind unconsummated child marriages before reaching 18 years of age has never been heard of by an overwhelming number of those it is intended to provide relief to" (1998, 71). Child marriage or women's marriage without consent is condoned by society in the name of custom/tradition. However, these practices are rarely identified as domestic violence.

In India, there are nearly 60 million Muslim women, making up the second largest female Muslim population in the world (Hasan 1998, 72). In contrast with Bangladesh and Pakistan, Muslim women in India have not witnessed any changes in personal, or religion-based, family laws (Hasan 1998, Kumar 1995). In fact, Muslim personal laws in India institutionalize "easy divorce and polygamy" (Hasan 1998, 78). Customs (dowry), social traditions (patrilineality), and age-old discriminatory family and personal laws are entrenched in Muslim women's lives and facilitate the perpetuation of gender violence in the family.

All over South Asia – in Bangladesh, Pakistan, and India – women's groups have articulated the need to fight against domestic violence. Two actions these groups advocate are a Uniform Family Code and the implementation of the United Nations Convention on the Elimination of All Kinds of Discrimination against Women (CEDAW). Still, the question remains: how to implement a Uniform Family Code and other much needed reforms without jeopardizing religious minority rights? Until this question is resolved, the level of domestic violence against women will not change in South Asia.

Bibliography

ADB (Asian Development Bank), *Women in Nepal*, Programs Department (West), Manila 1999.

——, *Women in Pakistan*, Programs Department (West) and Office of Environment and Social Development, Manila 2000.

——, *Women in Bangladesh*, Programs Department (West), Manila 2001.

L. Akanda and I. Shamim, *Women and violence. A comparative study of rural and urban violence against women in Bangladesh*, Dhaka 1985[2].

S. S. Ali and R. Naz, Marriage, dower and divorce. Superior courts and case law in Pakistan, in F. Shaheed, S. A. Warraich, C. Balchin, and A. Gazdar (eds.), *Shaping women's lives. Laws, practices and strategies in Pakistan*, Lahore 1998, 107–42.

S. Anam, Stop, please stop this violence, *Daily Star* (Dhaka), 25 November 1993.

Bangladesh, Mahila Parishad, *Status of women in Bangladesh*, Dhaka 1992.

R. Ghadially, All for "izzat." The practice of female circumcision among Bohra Muslims, in *Manushi* 66 (September–October 1991), 17–20.

Z. Hasan, Gender politics, legal reform and the Muslim community in India, in P. Jeffery and A. Basu (eds.), *Appropriating gender. Women's activism and politicized religion in South Asia*, New York 1998, 71–88.

J. Imam, *Of blood and fire. The untold story of Bangladesh's war of independence*, trans. M. Rahman, Dhaka 1986.

R. Jahan, Women in Bangladesh, in *Women for women, Bangladesh 1975*, published for Women for Women Research and Study Group, Dhaka 1975, 1–30.

K. Jayawardena and M. De Alwis (eds.), *Embodied violence. Communalising women's sexuality in South Asia*, London 1996.

N. Kabeer, Subordination and struggle. Women in Bangladesh, in *New Left Review* 168 (1988), 114–15.

R. Khondker, Domestic violence is a more hush-hush affair, *Morning Sun* (Dhaka), 3 February 1994.

R. Kumar, From chipko to sati. The contemporary Indian women's movement, in A. Basu (ed.), *The challenge of local feminisms. Women's movements in global perspective*, Boulder, Colo. 1995, 58–86.

A. Mascarenhas, *The rape of Bangladesh*, New Delhi 1975.

K. Mumtaz and F. Shaheed, Historical roots of the women's movement. A period of awakening 1896–1947, in F. Zafar (ed.), *Finding our way. Readings on women in Pakistan*, Lahore 1991, 3–25.

F. Shaheed, Engagements of culture, customs and law. Women's lives and activisim, in F. Shaheed et al. (eds.), *Shaping women's lives. Laws, practices and strategies in Pakistan*, Lahore 1998, 61–80.

I. Shailo, The main targets of violence, *Morning Sun* (Dhaka), 24 February 1994.

World Bank, *Bangladesh. Strategy paper on women in development*, Washington, D.C. 1990.

S. Zia, The legal status of women in Pakistan, in F. Zafar (ed.), *Finding our way. Readings on women in Pakistan*, Lahore 1991, 26–42.

Habiba Zaman

Sub-Saharan Africa

The term domestic violence refers primarily to physical battery in the context of the household or the family. But battering lies on a continuum of gender violence in the private sphere that includes sexual assault, psychological torment, and deprivation of the capacity to meet basic human needs. Domestic violence is most common where the social structure favors male power and the dominant ideology legitimates women's subordination. In Africa, domestic violence emerges from many of the same patterns of economic, political, and legal discrimination found worldwide. Women's economic dependence on men makes leaving a violent household difficult or impossible. Domestic violence acts as a form of social control, enforcing women's low status and discouraging them from seeking political change. Legal systems tend to enforce patriarchal norms and provide only limited resources for preventing or punishing violence. The everyday experience of domestic violence in Africa also reflects local realities and cultural context.

Domestic violence in cultural context

Any inquiry into the place of violence in African life runs the risk of reproducing a stereotypical image of a homogeneous and "uncivilized" part of the world that has helped to justify Western racism, colonialism, and paternalism. An accurate assessment of gender violence in Africa therefore requires recognition of Africa's great cultural diversity, as well as the context of colonialism and international inequality that continues to shape contemporary African societies.

The incidence of domestic violence varies across Africa, with research indicating higher rates in Ghana, Senegal, South Africa, Tanzania, Uganda, Zimbabwe, and lower rates in countries where it is generally considered socially unacceptable, such as Côte d'Ivoire, Djibouti, Eritrea, Gabon, Madagascar, Malawi, Mauritania, Somalia, Swaziland, and Togo. However, these findings should be considered in the context of the problems of under-reporting, the "culture of silence" surrounding domestic violence in many African societies, and the incomplete and ongoing nature of domestic violence research in Africa.

Aspects of culture that shape domestic violence include relative acceptance of physical force in marriage, gender role expectations, and family structure. All of these undergo stress in response to deteriorating economic conditions and political repression, fostering violence and making redress more elusive.

In some predominantly Muslim countries, such as Senegal, Islam provides a rationale for male battering under the label of "correcting" wives who misbehave. In non-majority Muslim countries like Ghana, comparable legitimation derives from oral tradition and popular culture. In some contexts, such as Zimbabwe and Uganda, a majority of women report that battering is justifiable under certain circumstances. Many Africans throughout the continent see domestic violence as a private matter subject to local norms and family authority, not public scrutiny or state intervention. These beliefs present a challenge to activists working to change attitudes and laws. However, over-generalizations about the acceptance of gender violence in Africa belie the diversity of views both among and within African societies. In Senegal, for example, many men and women argue that battering is at odds with the precepts of Islam.

Patterns of family authority provide the structure within which acts of violence and responses to violence occur. Hierarchical male authority, common in Africa, makes women's resistance difficult. Some practices may exacerbate the incidence of violence in particular instances. Polygyny, a significant though minority practice in many African countries, may create conditions of unique vulnerability for battered women. In Uganda, some polygamous men use physical force to manage conflicts between co-wives. Ugandan women may also tolerate violence for fear of divorce and economic abandonment by a husband with additional wives. The payment of bridewealth may also exacerbate battering, as well as marital rape. Originally, this practice symbolized the bond between families and compensation for a daughter's labor. But in many African countries today, including Botswana, the Central African Republic, Mozambique, South Africa, and Uganda, bridewealth constitutes the "purchase" of a woman's body by her husband, helping to justify abuse.

The economics of gender violence have grown harsher in the aftermath of the economic crisis of the 1980s and severe structural adjustment policies. Women who are economically dependent on men and their families cannot afford to protest or to escape violent households. Men unable to fulfill traditional economic roles carry frustration and conflict into family life. Battered women, their health and energy drained, cannot contribute fully to the economic well-being of their families or the development of their societies.

Sexual violence

As with battering, sexual violence in much of Africa is met with silence or defined as part of a socially acceptable range of behavior. As in the rest of the world, most rape in Africa occurs between acquaintances, including intimates and family members. Alongside battery, rape creates a climate of terror and oppression in the domestic sphere that damages both physical and mental health. Rarely criminalized, marital rape commonly falls under the principle of "marital exemption" by which the private sphere is protected from state intervention. While laws prohibiting marital rape do exist in a handful of countries, including Ghana, Zimbabwe, and South Africa, they are rarely enforced.

Gender violence is also a common feature of large-scale conflict in Africa. In Burundi, the Democratic Republic of Congo, Liberia, Rwanda, Sierra Leone, and Somalia, rape is part of women's everyday experience of violence. In Burundi's civil conflict, for example, soldiers and members of armed political groups have used rape to humiliate and terrorize the population. The stigma attached to rape can also do long-term damage to a woman's position in her family and community. In Rwanda, children born to Tutsi women raped by Hutu men have become outcastes. Refugees from Africa's conflicts, living in desperate conditions and far from family and community mechanisms that may mitigate abuse, are especially vulnerable to both rape and battering.

The impact of domestic violence on health

Battering and rape directly threaten the health of women and girls. Rape also facilitates the spread of HIV/AIDS and other diseases, and results in unwanted and high-risk pregnancy. In Swaziland and Uganda, for example, high rates of HIV infection among girls and women correlate with the incidence of both marital rape and domestic violence.

Controversy surrounds the question of whether female genital cutting, in its mild and severe forms, constitutes violence against girls and women or a defensible cultural custom. In Kenya, for example, local activists protest against the practice while many Gikuyu women see it as an essential rite of passage. However, its widespread negative impact on women's health and sexuality shares much in common with battery and rape. Alongside the pain of the procedure and subsequent painful sexual activity, the risk of infection, HIV transmission, and complications during childbirth are all associated with the practice. The range of efforts to limit this procedure centers on challenging the misconception that it is a requirement of Islam, finding alternative employment for professional circumcisers, educating people about the health risks, medicalizing the procedure to make it safer, and criminalization.

Legal responses to domestic violence

Africa possesses a broad array of non-state dispute resolution mechanisms and formal legal processes that vary from country to country, most of which contain a blend of customary, religious, and European law. Traditional sanctions against gender violence remain an invaluable resource in much of Africa, but they have weakened in the face of urbanization, economic crisis, forced migration, and war. The common mediation approach to family disputes may backfire when battered women are compelled to respond in a conciliatory manner.

Throughout Africa, criminal rape prosecutions are rare, and with few exceptions marital rape and domestic violence are not crimes. Where such laws do exist, there are typically problems with both police and judicial enforcement. In South Africa, for example, police systematically treat domestic violence as less serious than other types of assault. In Senegal, judges discourage women from seeking divorce as a way out of a violent marriage. In countries such as Nigeria, where the Sharīʿa plays a major role in family law, prosecutions have been rare as some legal activists apply Islamic legal principles in domestic violence cases, while others appeal to international human rights law.

Gender violence entered international human rights discourse in force with the United Nations Decade for Women ending in 1985, and while absent from the original Convention on the Elimination of All Forms of Discrimination against Women (CEDAW) in 1979, new language was adopted in 1992 and 2003 declaring gender violence as a human rights violation. In 1998, the United Nations International Criminal Tribunal for Rwanda ruled that rape is a form of genocide, and in the same year the International Criminal Court listed sexual violence as a crime falling within its jurisdiction. The human rights approach to gender violence in Africa must contend with the charge of many Africans that international standards exhibit Western bias and disrespect for African cultures. Activists inside and outside Africa respond that the goal of ending gender violence should be in harmony with African cultural values, and that any disharmony indicates the need for change. Ultimately, the effectiveness of national and international struggles in ending domestic violence in Africa must draw on existing cultural resources while working to transform the economic, political, and legal context in which African women live.

Bibliography

Amnesty International, *Burundi. Rape – the hidden rights abuse*, New York 2004.

Carnegie Council on Ethics and International Affairs, Human Rights Dialogue, Violence against women, Series 2, 10 (Fall 2003), <http://www.cceia.org/viewMedia.php/ prmID/1061>.

Center for Women's Global Leadership (ed.), *Gender violence and women's human rights in Africa*, New Brunswick, N.J. 1994.

R. E. Dobash and R. Dobash, *Violence against wives*, New York 1979.

N. Green, *Gender violence in Africa. African women's responses*, New York 1999.

Human Rights Watch, *Shattered lives. Sexual violence during the Rwandan genocide and its aftermath*, New York 1996.

——, *Just die quietly. Domestic violence and women's vulnerability to HIV in Uganda*, New York 2003.

S. London, Conciliation and domestic violence in Senegal, West Africa, in *Political and Legal Anthropology Review* 20 (1997), 83–91.

S. E. Merry, Women, violence, and the human rights system, in M. Agosin (ed.), *Women, gender, and human rights*, New Brunswick, N.J. 2001, 83–97.

R. Ofei-Aboagye, Domestic violence in Ghana. Some initial questions, in M. A. Fineman and R. Mykitiuk (eds.), *The public nature of private violence. The discovery of domestic abuse*, New York 1994, 260–84.

M. J. Osirim, Crisis in the state and the family. Violence against women in Zimbabwe, in African Studies Quarterly. The Online Journal for Africa Studies 7 (2003), <http://web.africa.ufl.edu/asq/v7/v7i2a8.htm>.

F. Oyekanmi (ed.), *Men, women and violence*, Dakar 1997.

United Nations Population Fund, *State of world population 2003*, New York 2003.

C. Watts, S. Osam, and E. Win, *The private is public. A study of violence against women in Southern Africa*, Harare 1995.

World Health Organization, Understanding women's attitudes toward wife beating in Zimbabwe, in *Bulletin of the World Health Organization* (2003), 501–8.

SCOTT LONDON

Turkey

Almost all forms of violence against women in the family are widespread in Turkey. There is no female genital mutilation (FGM) or dowry killing but honor crimes do occur. According to the Turkish Civil Code marriage is only possible between opposite sexes; thus violence occurring in same-sex relationships is not covered here. Domestic violence includes physical, economic, sexual, and verbal violence, isolation, constant criticism, attacks against self-esteem, and so forth. In short, most forms of violence can be seen in the family. Violence is based on inequality of power between spouses and is seen as the best way of controlling women. A Turkish proverb demonstrates this attitude: "A woman's womb should not be left free from a fetus and her back should not be left without a stick."

There is no specific article or chapter regarding domestic violence in the Turkish Penal Code. General rules applied to physical violence are applied to domestic violence as well. Articles 414, 415, and 416 deal with rape, seduction of children, and assault on chastity and Article 417 covers aggravating circumstances connected with these crimes. The age of consent is 15. Articles 414 and 415 of the Turkish Penal Code deal with the rape of persons under the age of 15; Article 414 refers to "whoever rapes an infant under the age of 15" and Article 415 refers to "whoever attempts to assault the honor and chastity of an infant under the age of 15." Article 416 covers rape and assault that leads to sexual violence against a person who is over 15 by use of any means of coercion, deceit, fraud, and the like. Article 478 regulates the maltreatment of family members, including children, with imprisonment of offenders ranging from three months to three years. Article 417 deals with the punishment of rape, seduction of children, and assault on chastity. However, none of the articles in the Penal Code mention domestic violence directly. Rape in marriage is not considered a felony. Although articles related to rape do not make any differentiation between rapes occurring within or outside marriage, both decisions of the Criminal Court of Appeal and legal theory state that marriage is the place where people satisfy their sexual desires legitimately. By accepting marriage, each spouse implicitly gives consent to sexual intercourse and it is therefore not possible to talk about rape in marriage. In the Turkish Civil Code, violence against a wife may form a ground for moral compensation and divorce. The Turkish Penal Code is about to undergo a total change. In the new proposals pending at the Turkish Grand National Assembly, rape within the family is considered a crime (Article 105/2). Sexual crimes are covered under the heading "Crimes against Sexual Inviolability."

The official State Institute of Statistics does not collect data on violence against women, in either general or domestic matters. The only statistics on domestic violence have been collected either by private researchers or universities. Thus the extent of domestic violence or rape or any other form of violence against women in Turkey is unknown.

Separate from the provisions in the Civil Code and the Penal Code against maltreatment, there is also the Law on the Protection of Family, law number 4320, issued on 14 January 1998. This law was promulgated as a result of the women's movement in Turkey. According to Article 1, if a spouse or child or another member of the family living under the same roof is subject to abuse, and notification is made either by the victim or by the public prosecutor, a justice of the peace can pass a protection order including one or more of the following rulings or take any other measures that are deemed appropriate in addition to provisions of the Civil Code. The accused spouse can be ordered:

1. not to use violence or threatening behavior against the other spouse or children (or other members of the family living under the same roof);
2. to leave the abode shared with spouse or children, if there are any, and not to approach the abode occupied by spouse and children or their places of work;
3. not to damage the property of the spouse or children (or of others living under the same roof);
4. not to cause distress to the spouse or children (or others living under the same roof);
5. to surrender a weapon or other similar instruments to the police;
6. not to arrive at the shared abode while under the influence of alcohol or other intoxicating substances or to use such substances in the shared abode.

These measures can be applied for a period not exceeding six months and if the accused does not abide by the rulings he or she will be warned that he or she is liable to arrest and confinement. The judge will take into account the standard of living of the victim and rule on maintenance payments accordingly.

According to Article 2 of the law, the court entrusts a copy of the protection order to the public prosecutor. The public prosecutor monitors the application of the order through the police. In the event of an order being issued, the police will conduct an investigation without the need for the victim to submit a written application. The public prosecutor can file charges at the penal court against a spouse who does not abide by an order, the penalty for which is a prison sentence of between three and six months.

The inclusion in the law of family members living under the same roof is positive. Violence against family members is not always committed by the husband; brothers, sons, sometimes daughters, and in-laws from both sides can be perpetrators. The law is inadequate in that it excludes ex-spouses, spouses living out of wedlock, those who are dating but not living under the same roof, and homosexual couples. There is a proposal prepared by women's non-governmental organizations to improve the law.

Bibliography

V. Savaş and S. Mollamahmutoğlu, *Türk ceza kanunun yorumu*, iii, Ankara 1995.

Cânân Arin

Domesticity

The Caucasus

This entry deals mainly with Azerbaijan. This is because of the shortage of relevant scholarship on the rest of the Muslim Caucasus. In this region the pre-Soviet religious prescriptions on the seclusion of women reinforced the association between the domestic and the feminine. In the wealthy urban homes the gendered division of space confined women to *ichari ev* (inner home). What survived from this tradition in the Soviet era was the notion that it is the husband/father's duty to conduct the household's dealings with the outside world: shopping (especially trips to a baker or a butcher), taking things for repair, even taking the garbage out, were considered very much male tasks. It confirmed male prestige and a woman's dignity, though in practice women also participated in searching for scarce goods and joining long queues (Heyat 2002b, 117).

Following the Soviet revolution state ideology promoted the communalization of all housework and childcare in order to free women from such chores. But in later decades economic imperatives and other factors led to the abandonment of such utopian ideals. Instead, it was expected that women be equal citizens, loyal workers, and devoted mothers and wives who rather than rejecting family roles fulfilled them perfectly well, taking pride in their capacity to serve. Modernization and rationalization of domesticity was advocated by the state and Communist Party officials in the context of the communalization of family life. But this only took place in urban centers where canteens, wash houses, nurseries, and kindergartens were established. At the same time, the close association between women and domesticity persisted under the Soviet system, particularly in the rural regions. In Daghestan, girls were taught cooking skills from a very young age and by their teens were involved in heavy domestic labor as well as arduous farm work (Chenciner 1997).

In Azerbaijan, as elsewhere in the Soviet Union, despite the increasing public roles assumed by women, strong gender divisions of domestic labor persisted. Culturally this was reflected in the close association between the feminine and the domestic, and its converse: the masculine and avoidance of domestic chores. This is denoted by the way the label *aghabaji* (effeminate master) is given to men who involve themselves in housework, especially cooking and cleaning. Washing clothes and dishes are considered strictly female tasks. However, in households where there were no daughters present, because of difficulties of access to paid labor, sons and husbands also participated.

In the Azeri culture domesticity is a highly valued dimension of femininity (Heyat 2000a, 2002b). Women's domestic skills, *evdarlik*, are in fact crucial to maintaining a high standard of hospitality, *gonakhparvarlik*, in the form of generous offering of food and great respect toward guests, *gonakh*. This is reflected in the folklore and literature of Azerbaijan as far back as the medieval epics of *Dede Korkut*. It is also a source of ethnic pride through which Azeris distinguish themselves from the Russians and other Slavic and European peoples (Tohidi 1996, 1998). As in the rest of Caucasus and the Middle East, a tradition of hospitality still remains an integral element in the system of honor and prestige. In the later Soviet era, with a flourishing alternative economy (Heyat 2002c), investment in feasts became an important feature of maintaining personal networks that facilitated access to goods and services (Mars and Altman 1987). Given that the work was done entirely by women in the family, domestic skills of cooking and entertaining were a matter of pride and prestige as well as a necessity for women, including highly educated professional women.

In the post-Soviet era, however, for the small sector of the new rich, women's greater access to labor-saving devices, the abundance of processed and part-prepared food, and the development of the catering industry, particularly in the major cities, has reduced their domestic burden. Most women of this class have assumed the role of full-time housewives. For those of the younger generation the question of prestige is not based so much on their domestic skills but their looks, maintaining slim, fashionable figures, their knowledge of a Western language, and travel to Europe or the United States (Heyat 2002b, 185). Meanwhile, for the majority of the population the drastic decline in income and new poverty has entailed adopting survival strategies such as subsistence farming, hand-crafting of goods, petty trading, and provision of services that draw on their domestic skills. In the foreseeable future, therefore, the construction of women's identity through their domesticity will continue throughout the Muslim Caucasus, even across most of oil-rich Azerbaijan.

BIBLIOGRAPHY

R. Chenciner, *Daghestan. Tradition and survival*, London 1997.

F. Heyat, Azeri professional women's life strategies, in F. Acar and A. Güneş-Ayata (eds.), *Gender and identity construction. Women of Central Asia, the Caucasus and Turkey*, Leiden 2000a, 177–201.

——, *Azeri women in transition. Women in Soviet and post-Soviet Azerbaijan*, London 2002b.

——, Women and the culture of entrepreneurship in Soviet and post-Soviet Azerbaijan, in R. Mandel and C. Humphrey (eds.), *Markets and moralities. Ethnographies of postsocialism*, Oxford 2002c, 19–31.

G. Mars and Y. Altman, Alternative mechanism of distribution in a Soviet economy, in M. Douglas (ed.), *Constructive drinking. Perspectives on drink from anthropology*, Cambridge 1987, 270–9.

N. Tohidi, "Guardians of the nation." Women, Islam, and the Soviet legacy of modernization in Azerbaijan, in H. L. Bodman and N. Tohidi (eds.), *Women in Muslim societies. Diversity within unity*, Boulder, Colo. 1998, 137–161.

FARIDEH HEYAT

East Asia, Southeast Asia, and Australia

The grand gender narrative that has dominated East and Southeast Asia over the last five hundred years is the definition of woman as wife and mother ("bearer of sons" is the East Asian variation). This metanarrative remained uncontested until the late twentieth century when the rise of second wave feminism and women's activism raised alternative definitions of woman as worker and citizen. The corollary of this limited construction of the feminine as wife and mother (and this applies to women in both Muslim and non-Muslim societies in the region) is women's conflation with domesticity. Hence, both Muslim and non-Muslim women in East and Southeast Asia were similarly defined by cultures which delineated men as heads of households and women as mothers responsible for childrearing and for domestic duties – the caring of the home. Although some official discourses may pronounce women "queens of the households," in actual practice men still had authority over household decisions. There is a wide gap between official discourses of the ideal woman embedded in domestic bliss, or the ideal woman as housewife, and reality, since many peasant and lower-class women have been workers (and in Southeast Asia have dominated the marketplace) throughout the centuries. The other interesting irony is that although second wave feminism has officially raised alternative narratives for women, the rise of Islamic revivalism in the 1970s (coinciding with second wave feminism) reinforced the traditional gender narrative and raised women's domesticity as an ideal. In Malaysia for example, "'upwardly mobile' women were keen to demonstrate their 'Muslimness' and modernity by their identification with domesticity, motherhood and the consumption of religious and material paraphernalia which marked the Muslim home" (Healey 1994, 109). The "feminine" woman is "domestic" (Healey 1994, 109). This cultural deification of the woman as domestic is also endorsed by state ideologies of women, particularly in Malaysia, Indonesia (during the Suharto years), and Singapore.

The woman as housewife confined to the domestic sphere is also an elite or middle-class ideal since in reality many women have to work in order to make ends meet. Those who can afford it hire domestic helpers. These helpers are mostly women as well, thus reinforcing the view that women are best suited to domestic tasks. Consequently, the study of domesticity, Islam, and women in the Southeast Asian context is more about constructions of the feminine than it is about the realities of women's daily lives. Nevertheless domesticity is a very powerful ideology endorsed by culture, Islam, and the state even in the midst of the desire to become "modern" (Stivens 1998, 60).

State ideologies promoted women's domesticity. In the last 30 years of the twentieth century state ideologies and Islamic revivalism both emphasized women's domesticity. According to Evelyn Blackwood: "In Indonesia, in addition to state efforts to identify women with the domestic domain, mainstream Islamic discourse on womanhood portrays women as wives and mothers above all else" (1995, 126). In Indonesia during the New Order (1965–98) the state enshrined the notion that men are heads of households and families and women's roles are as housewives and mothers. Feminist scholars have labeled this ideology State Ibuism (*ibu* means mother), interpreting the state's definition of *ibu* as limited to its biological meaning: "State Ibuism defines women as appendages and companions to their husbands, as procreators of the nation, as mothers and educators of children, as housekeepers, and as members of Indonesian society – in that order" (Suryakusuma 1996, 101). These views were codified in programs that promoted the importance of motherhood and the belief that women were primarily responsible for their children and their family's health, care, and education (Blackwood 2000,

88). The state women's organization, the PKK (Family Welfare Organization), established in 1973, and the Dharma Wanita (the organization of wives of civil servants) propagated a middle-class ideology of womanhood in which women's domesticity in the nuclear household was paramount (Blackwood 2000, 89). The media (advertisements and television in particular) also reinforced state ideologies of domesticity. One popular television series, *Sinetron* (from a government owned television station), had as one of its underlying messages the proposition that the good woman is a domestic person (Blackwood 2000, 89, Aripurnami 1996, 252). One of the writers for the series, Novaris Arifidiatmo, told *Femina*, Indonesia's most prominent magazine, that "the theme is that of the good woman as a *domestic* person" (quoted in Aripurnami 1996, 252) and of course its opposite, a woman "not utterly domestic" was likely to be intrinsic to the "bad" woman (Aripurnami 1996, 252). The Sinetrons considered "the best films ever produced" endorsed the philosophy that a woman's place is in the home. Women characters in the paid workforce were positively presented if they conformed to traditional female occupations such as domestic helpers. After all, the housemaid's role was within the framework of domesticity that coincided with the government's encouragement of this type of paid labor (even if the women went overseas) (Sunindyo 1993, 138–9). This ideology extended to the big screen of New Order Indonesia, where women played subsidiary roles. In films categorized as "women's films" a common concern was the definition of the destiny of women and this was presented as "mother" within the space of the family (Sen 1993, 117). In Indonesian films, men were located in the paid public sphere while women were confined to the roles of reproductive agents in the unpaid domestic sphere (ibid., 119). In cinema there has yet to be a re-evaluation of the position of women because they are either depicted as mothers in the domestic sphere or prostitutes outside it (ibid., 130).

Islamic leaders in Indonesia have also interpreted the woman's primary role as wife and mother. Indonesian Muslim women in high government positions or who are leaders of women's organizations endorse these same statements supporting the state policy in which women are defined through domesticity (Blackwood 2000, 90). These state ideologies are so influential that even women who are not technically housewives claim to be housewives even if they are not the housewives of the state ideology, prompting Evelyn Blackwood to label them "contradictory housewives" (2000, 91).

In Malaysia too, both the state and religion endorsed the view of men as heads of households and families (Stivens 1998, 60). Maila Stivens argued that "the desired effect of the state pronatalism seems to be that women remain housebound, co-ordinating the mass consumption their fecundity is supposed to guarantee" (ibid., 60). Interestingly, Malaysia's preoccupation with modernity (post 1970s) isolated (if somewhat reinvented) women's domesticity as intrinsic to the new Malaysian modern woman.

Women are largely responsible for "the 'domestic' construction of the Malay middle classes" (Stivens 1998, 62), as women's magazines give instructions on household décor, child rearing, and cuisine as well as specific advice on how to prepare for Muslim holy days and festivals (ibid., 63). Since the family is highly politicized in Malaysia, the moral panic about working mothers producing delinquent children heightened fears about the family in crisis. The state responded in recent years with campaigns about "happy families" in which the father is head and protector of the family and the mother is his warm and supportive helpmeet (Stivens 2000, 26).

Singapore has remained since its independence an unabashedly patriarchal state. State policies applied to all women (whether Chinese, Malay Muslim, or Indian) and thus, Singapore's Muslim women have been defined alongside their non-Muslim sisters. The authoritarian nature of the regime meant that the policies were implemented quite forcefully across all classes of women. Men were defined as heads of households and women were to be wives and mothers morally bound to the home. State policies on education, health benefits, housing allocation, and citizenship all affirmed this view of women: "The government defines women's primary role in the family as that of child raising" (Chan 2000, 47). Educational policy for example, made home economics a compulsory subject for all girls whereas boys were enrolled in technical studies (1969) (Chan 2000, 47, Kong and Chan 2000, 522). Although the need for women to join the workforce meant that the policy was relaxed in 1977 (girls could study either home economics or technical studies, with boys studying technical studies), by 1987 home economics was again compulsory for girls and technical studies for boys, advocating the premise that "girls should be girls" and that boys' priority should not be home matters (Kong and Chan 2000, 522). What was more alarming about this educational policy was that it intended to fashion the new Singaporean woman of the future as a homemaker (Kong and Chan 2000,

523). In 1983 Prime Minister Lee Kwang Kyu unleashed the Great Marriage Debate in which he outlined the crisis discourse – Singapore's graduate women tended to have fewer children and therefore if nothing was done Singapore's competitiveness was at stake. The use of eugenics in his arguments further reiterated the view that the future of Singapore depended on women's roles as mothers. Intelligent women – graduate women – should be mothers producing "smart" children to keep the nation competitive in the global marketplace.

There is still a vacuum in the scholarly literature on women, Islam, and domesticity in East Asia. Japan's Muslims are mostly immigrants – male contract laborers rather than women. Likewise, the history of women in the Chinese Islamic diaspora "is largely unacknowledged and even now only barely documented" (Jaschok and Shui 2000, 45; see also state of the field essay Gladney 1995, 371–4). In the People's Republic of China since 1950, the experiences of Muslim women have been similar to those of non-Muslim Chinese women (Jaschok and Shui 2000, 138). Research in the central China region (Zhongyuan) disclosed the cultural axiom that "a woman's primary reason for living is her husband and family" (ibid., 139). Before the 1950s women were confined to their houses, particularly in North Henan where men's roles were to perform outside work and women's roles were to look after the children at home. This binary division was essentialized in the maxim: "man working outside, woman doing housework at home" (ibid., 140, 143). Since the 1950s, although both husbands and wives earn salaries, many husbands and some women still isolate housework as a "woman's task" (ibid., 145). Jaschok and Shui's fieldwork with Muslim women married to Muslim teachers, scholars, or religious leaders led to the conclusion that "their duties are limited to housework; they look after the husband's needs and raise their children in the strict observance of Islam" (ibid., 146). Clearly, domesticity is still a powerful ideology defining Muslim women of contemporary China.

Muslim women in Australia come from the Muslim migrant population who have immigrated as part of a family unit (Yasmeen 2001, 74). A study on Muslim women's settlement needs in Perth underscored the women's prioritization of education, training, and employment as essential to their sense of self-esteem and independence (Yasmeen 2001, 82). But these same women preferred to postpone their ambitions and focus instead on their roles as homemakers as they assumed primary responsibility for child-rearing, care of the aged, and housework. While the roles these women performed may not differ much from those in their countries of origin, in Australia the high unemployment rate of Muslim men (25.3 percent compared to the national average of 8.8 percent) has had the impact of restricting women's space in the home. Men's larger role in the domestic arena has resulted in the shrinking of space available to women (Yasmeen 2001, 84). Whether Muslim women attend Islamic schools or not they are still subject to the Australian syllabus. Hence, Australia's female Muslims are in much the same position as mainstream women with respect to domestic duties. Most women do their own housework; some husbands help and some do not; some women who can afford it can outsource household tasks (ironing, cleaning) while some may be full time mothers (Hussain 2003).

Domesticity is therefore a very powerful ideology shaping cultural constructions of women in this region of enormous diversity. Despite the appearance of alternative narratives that launched debates about the "modern" Asian woman (Roces and Edwards 2000) contemporary state ideologies and the rise of Islamic revivalism have reinforced rather than contested this enduring gender narrative.

Bibliography

S. Aripurnami, A feminist comment on the Sinetron presentation of Indonesian women, in L. J. Sears (ed.), *Fantasizing the feminine in Indonesia*, Durham, N.C. 1996, 249–58.

E. Blackwood, Senior women, model mothers, and dutiful wives. Managing gender contradictions in a Minangkabau village, in A. Ong and M. G. Peletz (eds.), *Bewitching women, pious men gender and body politics in Southeast Asia*, Berkeley 1995, 124–58.

——, *Webs of power. Women, kin and community in a Sumatran village*, Lanham, Md. 2000.

J. Chan, The status of women in a patriarchal state. The case of Singapore, in L. Edwards and M. Roces (eds.), *Women in Asia. Tradition, modernity and globalisation*, Sydney 2000, 39–58.

D. C. Gladney, Islam in Chinese religions. The state of the field, in *Journal of Asian Studies* 54:2 (1995), 371–7.

L. Healey, Modernity, identity and constructions of Malay womanhood, in A. Gomes (ed.), *Modernity and identity. Asian illustrations*, Melbourne 1994, 96–121.

J. Hussain, personal communication, 2003.

M. Jaschok and Shui J. J., *The history of women's mosques in Chinese Islam. A mosque of their own*, Richmond, Surrey, U.K. 2000.

L. L. L. Kong and J. Chan, Patriarchy and pragmatism. Ideological contradictions in state policies, in *Asian Studies Review* 24:4 (2000), 501–31.

M. Roces and L. Edwards, Introduction. Contesting gender narratives, in L. Edwards and M. Roces (eds.), *Women in Asia. Tradition, modernity and globalisation*, Sydney 2000, 1–15.

K. Sen, Repression and resistance. Interpretations of the feminine in New Order cinema, in V. M. Hooker (ed.), *Culture and society in New Order Indonesia*, Kuala Lumpur 1993, 116–33.

M. Stivens, Modernizing the Malay mother, in K. Ram and M. Jolly (eds.), *Maternities and modernities. Colonial and postcolonial experiences in Asia and the Pacific*, Cambridge 1998, 50–80.

——, Becoming modern in Malaysia. Women at the end of the twentieth century, in L. Edwards and M. Roces (eds.), *Women in Asia. Tradition, modernity and globalisation*, Sydney 2000, 16–34.

S. Sunindyo, Gender discourse on television, in V. M. Hooker (ed.), *Culture and society in New Order Indonesia*, Kuala Lumpur 1993, 134–48.

J. I. Suryakusuma, The state and sexuality in New Order Indonesia, in L. J. Sears (ed.), *Fantasizing the feminine in Indonesia*, Durham, N.C. 1996, 92–119.

S. Yasmeen, Settlement needs of Muslim women in Perth. A case study, in A. Saeed and S. Akbarzadeh (eds.), *Muslim communities in Australia*, Sydney 2001, 61–79.

Mina Roces

Iran and Afghanistan

Domesticity is a social, cultural, and historical construction with multiple layers of meaning, including a type of space, a kind of work (paid or unpaid), and a relationship of power or organization (Hansen 1992). Constructions of domesticity in Iran and Afghanistan in the mid-nineteenth century to the present were shaped by broad economic developments and social and cultural practices, such as urbanization, the emergence of a middle class, state-building, and nationalist and missionary ideologies.

Differences among women based on ethnic and tribal group, region, social class, mode of subsistence, and family make it difficult to generalize about domesticity in relation to gender roles, identities, and ideologies. For example, in Afghanistan among the nomadic pastoralist Durrani Pashtuns, women are responsible for milking the animals and weaving the tent awnings, whereas among the Ghilzai Pashtuns men handle such tasks. Many women in Iran and Afghanistan work in agricultural production and make goods and crafts at home for sale in markets and private households. In many rural and poor urban families, children do the household work and caring for younger siblings and the flock. However, even though women perform important economic roles in both the household and larger society, throughout history they were defined primarily as wives, mothers, and the carers of children. In addition, a division of labor existed whereby women were confined to domestic activities, while the economic and political decisions outside the domestic sphere belonged to men.

Domesticity has served as an index of class. In the nineteenth and early twentieth centuries in Iran and Afghanistan, a steady supply of domestic servants and relatives among people of means made up for the lack of modern household technology and amenities. This is still the case in Afghanistan today. Thus, some wealthy Iranian and Afghan women had an identity beyond what was defined by domesticity in that they enjoyed more leisure and recreational time and could entertain family and friends and partake in charitable, philanthropic, and political events. This strengthened their identity as actors in the public arena. Similar factors also allowed other poorer and middle-class women to utilize their domestic skills in commercial enterprises, such as embroidery or carpet-making.

Features of the patriarchal social structure were more entrenched in Afghanistan due to the predominance of pastoral nomadism as a mode of subsistence and the weaker role of the state in instituting "modernizing" reforms. For example, women's reproductive roles were more fetishized in the context of Afghanistan's ethnic, tribal kinship-based patriarchy in which women, labor, and land were owned by males (Moghadam 1999, 175). In contrast, even though the nomadic tribal population in Iran was also sizeable, a larger urban, middle class emerged in the early to mid-twentieth century.

In both Iran and Afghanistan, early twentieth-century reforms sought to modernize the role and status of women. Reza Shah Pahlavī of Iran (1925–41) and King Amān Allāh of Afghanistan (1919–29) instituted reforms in education, marriage, and dress. State-building projects that shaped domestic ideologies were influenced by the development of modern scientific thought that sought to rationalize the home and create a new hierarchy of power within it. Domesticity as a state project was a symbol of modernization and social transformation of the nation and its women. For projects of modern state building, women frequently become markers of political goals and cultural identity. Scientific domesticity as a state project and ideology involved disciplining and civilizing women. During the modernization periods of the early twentieth century in Iran and Afghanistan, the unveiled woman who was a household manager trained in the science of domesticity and proper hygiene signified modernity and progress. On the other hand, the veiled woman lacking an education in scientific domesticity symbolized backwardness and superstition. Women's range of experiences and appearance was defined by the cultural and political goals of the state.

Studies of domesticity in the Middle East are in part about encounters between European and North American colonial and missionary projects and local communities in the settings of schools, women's organizations, and the periodical press. Unlike Afghanistan, Iran experienced considerable British, French, and especially American missionary influence in education. However, cultural encounters between missionaries and Iranians often inspired struggle over the content and meaning of domesticity.

American missionary notions of domesticity were based on belief in the "dignity of labor" of wife and mother as an ingredient of the modern, hygienic, scientifically ordered household, nation, and society. For example, the American Presbyterian girls' school Iran Bethel, established in 1895, introduced a course called "Household Arts." The curriculum included domestic science subjects such as designing and decorating a home, plumbing and water-gathering, heating, lighting, washing clothes, cooking, and sewing. Missionaries considered this type of education vital for modern Iranian womanhood and believed that it also secured the missionary influence on the Iranian household. However, the earliest students at Iran Bethel were from Iran's most wealthy and prominent families and were not accustomed to performing housework, which they viewed as best left to their servants.

Even though Iranian students initially resisted missionary models of domestic science education, reformers and certain segments of elite Iranian society embraced important notions of scientific domesticity. Feminists of the early twentieth century in particular used it to stake their claim in the educational and public arenas. As adherents of nationalist ideology, they argued that if Iran were to become a modern nation, the Iranian family, and particularly women who raised children, needed access to proper education and training. The Iranian women's journals *Dānish* (Knowledge, 1910–11) and *Shukūfah* (Blossom, 1914–18), founded by female editors Dr. Kahhal and Muzayyan al-Saltanah respectively, *ʿĀlam-i Nisvān* (Women's universe, 1921–34), edited by graduates of Iran Bethel, and the Afghan women's journal *Irshād-i Nisvān* (Women's guidance, 1921–5), established by Queen Ṣurayyā, published articles on childcare, household affairs, and increased rights for women.

Domestic science education and elite women's writings had a concrete impact on Iranian and Afghan households. In the twentieth century, the rise of the urban middle classes, especially in Iran, led to the transformation of scientific domesticity into actual domestic practices.

BIBLIOGRAPHY

M. Centlivres-Demont, Afghan women in peace, war, and exile, in M. Weiner and A. Banuazizi (eds.), *The politics of social transformation in Afghanistan, Iran, and Pakistan*, Syracuse, N.Y. 1994, 333–65.

V. Gregorian, *The emergence of modern Afghanistan*, Stanford, Calif. 1969.

V. Moghadam, Reform, revolution and reaction. The trajectory of the "woman question" in Afghanistan, in V. Moghadam (ed.) *Gender and national identity. Women and politics in Muslim societies*, London 1994, 81–109.

——, Revolution, religion, and gender politics. Iran and Afghanistan compared, in *Journal of Women's History* 10:4 (1999), 172–95.

A. Najmabadi, Crafting an educated housewife in Iran, in L. Abu-Lughod (ed.), *Remaking women. Feminism and modernity in the Middle East*, Princeton, N.J. 1998, 91–125.

J. Rostam-Kolayi, Foreign education, the women's press, and the discourse of scientific domesticity in early-twentieth-century Iran, in N. Keddie and R. Matthee (eds.), *Iran and the surrounding world. Interactions in culture and cultural politics*, Seattle 2002, 182–204.

N. Tapper, *Bartered brides. Politics, gender and marriage in an Afghan tribal society*, Cambridge, 1991.

K. Transberg Hansen (ed.), *African encounters with domesticity*, New Brunswick, N.J. 1992.

JASAMIN ROSTAM-KOLAYI

Sub-Saharan Africa: Hausa Societies

Occupation of domestic roles, engagement with domestic labor, and association with domestic spaces of the home are central to the identities of Muslim Hausa women in Northern Nigeria. The identities of millions of ordinary rural and urban Muslim Hausa women are formed largely through their lived experiences of daily domesticity. The lives of women, especially adult married women, are strongly rooted in the domestic sphere, primarily via their occupation of the domestic space of the *gida* (courtyard home) within which they perform the daily tasks of domestic labor. Time use studies show that for both rural and urban Muslim Hausa women much of their time is occupied with domestic tasks. Dominant ideologies and prevailing socioreligious discourses also express, reflect, and ensure that women's place is in the home bearing and rearing children, preparing food, washing clothes, and engaging in the myriad of tasks essential to the daily and generational reproduction of the family, community, and society. With respect to the construction of Hausa women's identities via domesticity, the widespread practice of wife seclusion is one of its most fundamental aspects.

For many married women seclusion in the domestic sphere is part of the Hausa cultural environment today and dates back to the early nineteenth century and the Sokoto Jihad – a powerful campaign of Islamic religious reform that had major impacts on gender relations in the region that still resonate today. It is the ideologies and practices of seclusion that keep married Hausa Muslim women largely within their domestic courtyards screened from the public male gaze by high compound walls. The image of "leisured" domesticity associated with seclusion indicates high social status. Thus, with increased prosperity, or aspirations in that direction, wives find themselves increasingly tied to the domestic sphere by seclusion. Conversely, it is also argued that Hausa women opt for seclusion in order to boost their own social status and to reject the hard work of agriculture (associated with slave status of former times).

Geographically and historically Muslim Hausa women's identities, as constructed through notions and practices of the domestic, reflect past and present ideological constructions and practices. Ideologies around domesticity are not monolithic, but intersect with other ideological terrains around gender, seclusion, marriage, ethnicity, and so on. Individuals and groups of people negotiate within and across these ideological fields. Ideologies and practices of domesticity shift with political and economic changes, but always involve conflict, power relations, and reconstruction of ideological fields in arenas of contestation and negotiation.

Seclusion is claimed to tie women to the domestic sphere, reduce their spatial mobility, limit their opportunities for income earning and increase their dependence on men and children. However, within their domesticity many Muslim Hausa women operate as secluded traders with economic roles that are diverse and in many circumstances fundamental to their household's economic survival. There are, however, class variations, such that a few urban women work in the professions and the formal sector, thereby transcending the domestic sphere to work in public space(s) and in non-domestic occupations. Thus, not all Hausa women's identities are defined by domesticity.

Up to the 1980s at least, in cities such as Katsina, another minority of Hausa women pursued alternatives to domesticity (that is, marriage, seclusion, and domestic labor) by supporting themselves as courtesans. This was also known in the past in rural areas with the existence of *gidan mata* (houses of women). Similarly and alongside courtesans, Hausa women Bori (spirit possession) adepts are dissociated from domesticity in that they do not observe seclusion, may go on *ḥajj* without their husbands, and suchlike. However, even Hausa women Bori adepts, while portrayed as powerful independent agents, are also recognized as being affected by the strong gendered social norms of Hausa femininity and its equation with domesticity and seclusion, in that relative to male Bori adepts their mobility is nonetheless restricted. With growing Islamism, options for women to pursue lifestyles as courtesans and Bori adepts were becoming less tenable by the 1990s.

Early insights into the domesticity that so overwhelmingly permeates the lives of many Hausa women are to be found in the account of Baba of Karo – an ordinary rural Muslim Hausa woman who recounted her life story to the anthropologist Mary Smith in the mid-twentieth century. Rural women today are much more widely secluded than in Baba's time.

In the literature there are two contrasting and contradictory representations of Hausa women as formed through domesticity and their engagement with domestic labor: Hausa women as victims (domestic drudges) and in contrast Hausa women as agents (powerful matriarchs). Although this is a somewhat crude and caricaturing binary division, it nonetheless draws out the extent of diverse portrayals of Hausa women. In many ways both sets of representations are (regulatory?) fictional identities, in addition to being rather narrow and unidimensional. Alternative discourses and subject positions might be provided by Hausa women themselves, but we have very little information on how Hausa women would account for themselves. Clearly, who does the reporting partially determines how Hausa women are viewed and represented. Even such accounts as there are derived from Hausa women themselves contain contradictions. Baba of Karo provides evidence both of Hausa women actively resisting seclusion (Smith 1954, 80) and initiating divorce (ibid. 107–8), but also as victims of violent domestic abuse from their husbands (ibid. 169, 204, 232–5).

Discourses of Hausa women as victims of domesticity see them as subjugated by patriarchal oppression, subordinate, dependent on men/children, dispirited drudges, constrained, restricted to the home, immobile, to be pitied, imprisoned by seclusion, and controlled by husbands, men, and patriarchy; they are illiterate, poor, ignorant, powerless, and isolated.

At the other end of the spectrum, discourses of Hausa women as domestic agents portray them as intelligent, creative, strong, independent, self-reliant, and even subversive individuals actively resisting patriarchy and domestication. Albeit operating within and from the domestic realm, they are seen as powerful individuals, initiators of divorce, able to hold husbands in debt, control children's labor, and advise and influence male leaders. Images of Hausa women as agents illustrate how they are socially, economically, politically, and culturally active within and despite the domesticity that dominates their lives. These Muslim women are in control of their own lives, their children, and the economic and other affairs of their households. Such women are seen to have strong networks within and beyond the domestic realm and to be powerful, active traders, courtesans, Bori adepts, and so on. Some argue that because Hausa women subvert the restrictions of domesticity they are not victims. For example, while women may not be able to choose to reject seclusion, they can and do manipulate its conditions, constantly devising ways to exploit and work around restrictions of occupying and being occupied by the domestic.

Despite their limited spatial mobility and physical restriction to the domestic space of the courtyard and home (*gida*), secluded Muslim Hausa wives have an impact (albeit indirect) on external political affairs through influencing their husbands and the upbringing of their children. This is especially true for the elite, most domesticated, and tightly secluded of all Hausa women – the royal wives in the Kano Palace. A tiny minority of highly educated Hausa women scholars and poets (mostly from the past, but some today) are similarly portrayed as influential in political and social matters, albeit from within their domestic roles as model wives and mothers.

The discourse that emphasizes women's agency sees Hausa women occupying domestic women's worlds that are portrayed as sites of strength and separateness, reflecting feminine value systems. This is a valorization of the domestic, private sphere in which men are not welcomed and from which they remain largely absent. It is a domesticity within which women are viewed as culturally autonomous, active agents (rather than passive victims) who wield the potential for subverting established male power. Thus, although appearing thoroughly domesticated, Muslim women in Northern Nigeria resist domestication through covert or indirect bargaining (albeit not in overt organized ways), in face-to-face relations with husbands, children, co-wives, other kin, friends, and neighbors with such strategies as diversion of food, income, or labor resources.

BIBLIOGRAPHY

J. Boyd and B. B. Mack, Women's Islamic literature in Northern Nigeria. 150 years of tradition, 1820–1970, in K. W. Harrow (ed.), *The marabout and the muse. New approaches to Islam in Islamic literature*, London 1996, 142–58.

B. Callaway, *Muslim Hausa women in Nigeria. Tradition and change*, New York 1987.

C. Coles and B. B. Mack (eds.), *Hausa women in the twentieth century*, Madison, Wis. 1991.

A. M. Imam, Politics, Islam, and women in Kano, Northern Nigeria, in V. M. Moghadam (ed.), *Identity politics and women. Cultural reassertions and feminisms in international perspective*, Boulder, Colo. 1994, 123–44.

A. Koko and J. Boyd, Nana Asma'u, in B. Awe (ed.), *Nigerian women in historical perspective*, Lagos 1992, 37–54.

R. Longhurst, Resource allocation and the sexual division of labor. A case study of a Moslem Hausa village in northern Nigeria, in L. Beneria (ed.), *Women in development*, New York 1982, 95–117.

B. B. Mack, Authority and influence in the Kano harem, in F. Kaplan (ed.), *Queens, queen mothers, priestesses and power. Case studies in African gender*, New York 1997, 159–72.

S. O'Brien, Pilgrimage, power, and identity. The role of the Hajj in the lives of Nigerian Hausa Bori adepts, in *Africa Today* 46 (1999), 10–40.

R. Pittin, Houses of women. A focus on alternative lifestyles in Katsina City, in C. Oppong (ed.), *Female and male in West Africa*, London 1983, 291–302.

——, Social status and economic opportunity in urban Hausa society, in F. A. Ogunsheye et al. (eds.), *Nigerian women and development*, Ibadan 1988, 264–79.

E. Robson, Wife seclusion and the spatial praxis of gender ideology in Nigerian Hausaland, in *Gender, Place and Culture. Journal of Feminist Geography* 7 (2000), 179–99.

E. Schildkrout, Hajiya Husaina. Notes on the life history of a Hausa woman, in P. W. Romero (ed.), *Life histories of African women*, London 1988, 78–98.

E. B. Simmons, A case-study in food production, sale and distribution, in R. Chambers, R. Longhurst, and A. Pacey (eds.), *Seasonal dimensions to rural poverty*, London 1981, 73–80.

M. F. Smith, *Baba of Karo. A woman of the Muslim Hausa*, London 1954, repr. 1981.

——, *Baba of Karo* [in Hausa], Kano 1991.

ELSBETH ROBSON

Turkey

After the foundation of the republic in 1923, Turkey went through an immense and profound process of modernization, which in the Turkish case meant the adoption of Western social, cultural, and economic structures and the abolition of traditional institutions. As part of this grand project, the Kemalist reforms were initiated, which radically affected the status of women. Such reforms included the introduction of a secular Civil Code that banned polygamy and granted women enhanced property rights. Although women had property rights in the Ottoman Empire, the scope and the use of such rights remained very limited and covered only upper-class and educated women. With the reforms, however, the scope of property rights expanded to a universal scale. In addition, all free religious schools were banned; primary education was made compulsory for both boys and girls; and Western codes of dressing were supported. These reforms were significant in their ascription of a new role for women, who were to take part in the public sphere as a sign of Westernization. The republican elites were of the opinion that women were not only to act as a medium of modernization but were also to take on an instrumental role. Women as homemakers and as mothers who would raise the future generations of citizens according to the ideals of the state were to distribute the values of the republic and to construct a modern family. This was not a means of confining women to the domestic sphere; in addition to their roles in the household, women were to take part in the public sphere by way of education and work.

Although the Kemalist reforms resulted in the increasing visibility of women in the public sphere, this reflected more the case of elite families in urban areas who were committed to the republican ideals (Abadan-Unat 1991, 183). The peripheral masses, mostly in rural areas, were dominated by Islamic values that asserted the segregation of the sexes and confined women to domesticity. This section of society was reluctant to send its daughters to schools beyond primary level. In order to convince traditional families to allow their daughters to be educated without disrupting the patriarchal ideology and prescribed gender roles, in the 1930s the Turkish state started to establish girls' institutes in accordance with the Kemalist reforms. This development illustrates the consensus between the Kemalist modernizers and the traditional families on the gender roles of women centered on domesticity.

The girls' institutes were single-sex educational institutes at high school level where daily contact with the opposite sex was curtailed. In these schools students were trained to be good housewives and mothers. The establishment of the girls' institutes emerged out of a policy of compromise between the state and the society: female children were to be educated, but along the lines of their gender roles and not in a coeducational environment. With the girls' institutes, the state would ensure women's education and women would spread a modern and Westernized lifestyle to society.

The education program of the girls' institutes served to rationalize and modernize domesticity. Subjects offered at the institutes included needlework, handicrafts, knitting, courtesy, painting, child development, family economics, nutrition, and so forth. With the aim of becoming good housewives, the students were taught how to sew and iron Western attire, how to welcome guests with Western etiquette, how to use dinner services and serve food at a table. At a time when food was eaten with wooden spoons on the floor, these courses served to implement the modern lifestyle. In order to become good mothers, the students were taught how to bring up the future generation with scientific and medical knowledge. For instance, they learned that feeding bottles and diapers needed to be sterile and that when children became ill, they were not to be cured by old wives' techniques but by medical doctors and nurses. After centuries of women doing the same work of mothering and housekeeping, transferring their know-how from generation to generation, students were now being taught in public institutions with schoolteachers under a scientific curriculum.

The institutes' objective of modernizing traditional femininity in the service of the republic's orientation toward the West resulted in two paradoxes (Ş. Toktaş 2002, 427). First, although these schools trained students how to be good housewives, some of the graduates did not become housewives exclusively. With the high school diplomas they had earned they worked in the public sphere as civil servants in state offices such as post offices or banks. Second, among the graduates who chose to work, some did not marry and become mothers as anticipated (motherhood in Turkey is strictly confined to marriage). These outcomes became possible with the specific track of Turkish modernity and the opportunities it offered to women. The Kemalist reforms, imposed from above, enabled women to take part in the public sphere and women in return adopted these reforms willingly and elaborated them. Women who perceived themselves empowered by education and work were able to stand on their own feet. Women were able to redefine their gender roles and take a greater part in public life.

In 1974, the girls' institutes were changed into girls' vocational high schools and the educational program was reformed. The restructured schools prioritized vocational education and employment. Due to the industrialization of Turkey and the incompatibility of the former education program with the labor markets, the curricula of the vocational schools were more oriented toward the needs of industry. Today, the courses given at girls' vocational high schools are industrial design, textile painting and weaving, pastry cooking, interior decoration, food analysis, electronics, jewelry making, hairdressing, and the like. The change from the girls' institutes to vocational high schools marks the difference in the approach to women: the former aimed to produce housewives and mothers, the latter members of the workforce.

BIBLIOGRAPHY

N. Abadan-Unat, The impact of legal and educational reforms on Turkish women, in N. R. Keddie and B. Baron (eds.), *Women in Middle Eastern history. Boundaries in sex and gender*, London 1991, 177–94.

Ş. Toktaş, Engendered emotions. Gender awareness of Turkish women mirrored through regrets in the course of life, in *Women's Studies International Forum* 25 (2002), 423–31.

ŞULE TOKTAŞ

Family Relations

The Caucasus

This entry deals mainly with Azerbaijan. This is because of the shortage of relevant scholarship on the rest of the Muslim Caucasus. Family relations in the Muslim Caucasus are based on gender and generational hierarchies whereby the elders command great respect and authority over the young. In the pre-Soviet era men had absolute authority over their wives and children, as reflected in the phrase *ar Allahin kolgasidir* (a husband is the shadow of God). The Soviet revolution attempted to alter many of the patriarchal aspects of family and gender relations by banning the practices of polygamy, and underage and forced marriages, and through setting up women's committees, "zhensoviets," which campaigned for women's emancipation and intervened in cases of violence against women. Gender equality was established in legislation concerning marriage, custody of children, inheritance, and employment (Heyat 2002, 80).

During the Soviet era extended family and kinship relations continued to form the most fundamental basis of support for the individual and the focus of their loyalties (Chenciner 1997, Tohidi 1996, 1998). However, there were subtle and profound changes in family and gender relations, especially in the industrialized urban centers in Azerbaijan. The liberalization in intergenerational relations was most marked in mother/daughter-in-law relations. It was transformed from a highly authoritarian relationship where a young bride was expected to act as a maid in the service of the husband's household, to one of mutual support and loyalty. Similarly, husband/wife relationships, particularly among the intelligentsia, were significantly transformed, as noted in the change of term for a spouse, *hayat yoldash* (life comrade/friend). Nevertheless, the husband, *ar*, remained the nominal head of the family and the main breadwinner (Heyat 2002, 145).

In the later Soviet era as women entered employment *en masse* (in the rural areas as members of collective farms, *kolkhoz*) they became breadwinners as well as largely assuming charge of household affairs and the education of children. The Soviet media and the state regularly promoted the position of mothers, awarding medals and rewards to women with many children. The system of strong reciprocal support within the close-knit extended family also reinforced the mother's position, since it was often the maternal grandmother and aunts who helped with the care of children (Heyat 2000). Mothers and grandmothers generally wield overwhelming influence over their offspring in matters of education, marriage, and residence. However, fathers also retain close relations with their children, especially with their sons. Among the siblings, brothers often assume authority over sisters regarding issues of sexual propriety and female conduct. This is less so among the educated professional strata of society where male-female relations are more liberal.

Given the strength of the institution of family, relations with cousins, whether on the paternal or maternal side, are often very close. It is not uncommon for people to refer to their first cousin as their brother or sister. The mutual support and loyalty expected from the kin group, particularly the first degree family members, makes it incumbent on the adult children to care for elderly parents. Traditionally, the youngest son is expected to remain with his parents after marriage and eventually to inherit the family home. Widows normally live with their youngest son and his family. Under the Soviet system shortage of housing reinforced the practice of multiple generations living in a single household (Chenciner 1997). However, this also led to increased tension in the household and friction between generations, in particular with in-laws. In cases of family disputes, the customary arbiter is a well-respected elder member, the *ak sakkal* (gray beard). The *ak birchek* (gray hair), female elder, often mediates disputes between women members. It is rare for Azeri families to resort to the legal system to resolve a conflict with a relative.

In Azerbaijan, and generally among the Muslims in the Caucasus, the family as a network of support and control, particularly of women, led to few incidents of runaway children. In Soviet times, in cases of serious conflict within the family a child could move on to live with a close relative, or failing that, to a state boarding house caring for orphaned or abandoned children. In many of these state homes, especially in the larger cities, the degree of care and concern for the children's welfare was reasonably high. However, since independence, there is a growing population of displaced and homeless young people in the major cities. The vulnerability of runaway girls, in the absence of family protection and state provisions, is further escalated with the increase in prostitution and the post-Soviet lawlessness.

BIBLIOGRAPHY
R. Chenciner, *Daghestan. Tradition and survival*, London 1997.
F. Heyat, Azeri professional women's life strategies, in F. Acar and A. Güneş-Ayata (eds.), *Gender and Identity Construction: Women of Central Asia, the Caucasus and Turkey*, Leiden 2000, 177–201.
——, *Azeri women in transition. Women in Soviet and post-Soviet Azerbaijan*, London 2002.
N. Tohidi, Soviet in public, Azeri in private, in *Women's Studies International Forum* 19:1/2 (1996), 111–23.
——, "Guardians of the nation." Women, Islam, and the Soviet legacy of modernization in Azerbaijan, in H. L. Bodman and N. Tohidi (eds.), *Women in Muslim societies. Diversity within unity*, Boulder, Colo. 1998, 137–61.

FARIDEH HEYAT

Central Asia

The traditional Central Asian family is extended, patrilineal, and patrilocal. There are many variations over this vast area, especially between the historically sedentary and the nomadic peoples. These were intensified by differential exposure to Sovietization, Tajikistan being the least influenced and Kazakhstan the most, with urban populations more affected than rural.

There are also significant similarities, particularly in basic gender characteristics. Inculcated in children from birth, in order to induce appropriate behavior patterns, and in Central Asia both sex and age dependent, these are crucial to family relationships. Since this region is a gerontocracy, young men and women are expected to be submissive to parents but gain power as they age. However, gender stereotypes depict the mature controlling man and the young sexually pure, submissive women, thus naturalizing older male dominance. In much of the region, young people have little, if any, choice over marriage arrangements and mothers have been known to force even their sons into unwanted unions. Nevertheless, in many more educated and/or urban circles young people may choose their own spouses, with parental approval. At least among Tajiks and Uzbeks, marriage between first cousins is frequent, while Kazakhs marry exogamously. Traditional family organization is often maintained even by the most highly educated, and the worst thing that could happen to a Central Asian family is to lose its honor (*nāmūs*) through improper gender-related behavior from either sex.

Traditional family relations are strongly formalized. Relational rather than proper names are used when addressing, and talking about, members, and teknonymy is prevalent in all but the most Russianized environments. The strictest customs regulate the conduct of the daughter-in-law (*kelin*), particularly as a new bride. *Kelin* literally means incomer and at least until they have consolidated their relationship within their marital family by bearing sons, brides remain on sufferance and must strive hard to please. They should remain silent and work hard. A man's first allegiance is to his natal family, so a *kelin* will rarely have anyone on her side if she has problems with one of her in-laws.

It is important for a *kelin* to bear a child as soon as possible, with patrilocal residence intensifying son preference. In Soviet times large families were prevalent, especially in Tajikistan and Turkmenistan, with 15 or more children not uncommon in rural areas. While desired numbers of children have dropped since independence, the tendency remains on the high side. One son, often the youngest, will be expected to remain with his parents for life and he and his wife will have the primary responsibility for their care. It is considered shaming to abandon old people, and large families mean that childless individuals can usually find someone to look after them. Barrenness is highly stigmatized, usually blamed on women, and considered an acceptable reason for polygyny or divorce.

Especially among newly-weds, divorce is greatly on the increase in most of Central Asia, owing to economic pressures, social instability, and, in Tajikistan at least, a dearth of young men. In that republic divorce is almost as often initiated by mothers-in-law as by husbands. However, women who make a good living, whose husbands, unemployed, and thus a drain on resources, refuse to carry out traditionally female domestic and childcare tasks, are starting to instigate divorce. Despite legal equality, women often suffer hardship upon divorce, including social opprobrium as well as material difficulties. In pre-Soviet times children were held to belong to the patrilineage. However, since Soviet courts almost always awarded children to divorced mothers, even after a religious divorce, mothers today very often take the children. As there is little or no shared custody, the parent who does not take the children may rarely, if ever, see them again.

Legally, divorcees and widows have a right to remain in the family home. However, if this belongs to their in-laws they are more likely to move back in with their parents. Remarriage is not stigmatized, although for those with large numbers of children this may be difficult. Levirate marriage, common before the revolution, is less prevalent today. Much to women's dismay, polygyny is on the increase, especially among labor migrants, who may have a wife in more than one place.

Major decisions are usually discussed in family councils in which traditionally men are the main locutors. In some circles women may voice their opinions directly, in others only through husbands or other males. Conflicts are similarly settled in these councils, or with the help or support of religious leaders or *maḥalla* tribal elders. However, young people can rarely appeal against the edicts of their parents, especially over choice of spouse. While boys have considerable mobility and so can distance themselves from family disputes, girls' movements are more restricted to the home, where many feel alienated and isolated.

In Kyrgyzstan and Karakalpakstan the practice of bride stealing, either with the girl's compliance or against her will, is common. Suicide is one response to forced marriages, particularly in Tajikistan and Uzbekistan, usually by self-immolation, drowning, or imbibing industrial-strength vinegar. Another option for girls under severe pressure is to run away from home, if possible to a relative. Otherwise, they may end up among the increasing numbers of street children, who hang around market places trying to earn enough to eat, and sleep under bridges or in other sheltered places. Rates of sexually transmitted diseases are on the rise among this cohort, many of whom resort to prostitution to survive.

The post-Soviet period has seen an increase in family violence, mainly committed by husbands, but also by parents and in-laws. This is worsened by drug addiction, and compounded by rhetoric, legitimized by appeals to religion that situates men as the masters in the home, and the discourse of honor that limits women's rights to protest or reveal family problems. Most republics now have non-governmental organizations that provide some protection and support for victims of domestic violence but despite laws against this, it is rare for officials to take action. Instead they remain complicit with tradition, which, notwithstanding the decades of Soviet rule, remains the most important influence on Central Asian families.

Bibliography

C. Blackwell, *Tradition and society in Turkmenistan. Gender, oral culture and song*, Richmond, Surrey 2001.

C. Harris, Muslim views on population. The case of Tajikistan, in J. Meuleman (ed.), *Islam in the era of globalization. Muslim attitudes towards modernity and identity*, London 2002, 211–22.

——, *Control and subversion. Gender relations in Tajikistan*, London 2004.

E. Hvoslov, The social use of personal names among the Kyrgyz, in *Central Asian Survey* 20:1 (2001), 85–95.

S. Kadyrov, Some questions on the study of the Turkmen family, in *Central Asian Survey* 12:3 (1993), 393–400.

K. Kuehnast, Let the stone lie where it has fallen. Dilemmas of gender and generation in post-Soviet Kyrgyzstan, Ph.D. diss., University of Minnesota 1997.

M. Tokhtakhodjaeva, *Between the slogans of communism and the laws of Islam*, Lahore 1995.

M. Tokhtakhodjaeva and E. Turgumbekova, *The daughters of Amazons. Voices from Central Asia*, Lahore 1996.

C. Werner, The dynamics of feasting and gift exchange in rural Kazakstan, in I. Svanberg (ed.), *Contemporary Kazaks. Cultural and social perspectives*, New York 1999, 47–72.

T. A. Zhdanko and G. P. Vasil'eva, *The new and the traditional in the daily life of rural families in Central Asia and Kazakhstan* [in Russian], Moscow 1980, 47–72.

Colette Harris

South Asia

While Muslims in South Asia are divided between India (14 percent of the population), Pakistan (97 percent), Bangladesh (85 percent), and Sri Lanka (9 percent), their history is common before 1947, and different after that largely according to the politics of each state.

In all South Asian families, the birth of a female infant is celebrated less joyously than that of a male. In spite of government family planning efforts, as in India from the 1960s, most Muslim families are unconvinced about birth control methods. The preference for sons leads to large families. The prospect of dowry payments and of losing the daughter to the spouse's family makes daughters less respected and cherished in perceptible ways, although parental love may be the same for girls as for boys.

The infant begins to be constructed as a gendered being almost immediately after birth. As the child grows up, the allotment of family resources in all areas of life is in favor of men over women. The majority of Muslims in India are either farmers in rural areas, or artisans in urban areas. Girls as daughters and women as wives are almost never given apprenticeship in a craft, but they do play an indispensable role in the family's occupation. This role goes unacknowledged, and all women are regarded as primarily cooks, servers, and nurturers, not workers. Women who are acknowledged as wage earners are usually in weaker economic and political positions than men with similar skills. Middle-class women are progressively better educated and pursue work outside the home. However, their image also remains predominantly that of home-maker.

While the acquisition of knowledge is enjoined on all, the knowledge is limited for most children, and specially for girls, to the learning by rote of some portions of the Qur'ān. In the colonial period, because Muslims were accused of being "backward" partly because of the condition of Muslim women, reform of this backwardness, such as the attempts of Sir Sayyid Aḥmad Khān, stressed the importance of education. While schools and educational programs for girls came to be seen as indicative of progress, it was considered essential to retain signs of the community, such as the practices of purdah and seclusion, alongside education.

Important family sacraments include the *nikāḥ*, marriage contract, which is a *sunna* of the Prophet. The bars to marriage are blood relationship or consanguinity between the woman and her male ascendants and descendants, and relationship by marriage or affinity. Dowry is a practical bar to celebrating the birth of girls on an equal footing with boys. Although theoretically undesirable in Islam, it is prevalent, like purdah, across class divisions, but markedly in upwardly mobile families. Divorce (*ṭalāq*) is permissible, and though not frequent, is discriminatory against women. *Mahr*, or the bride-price settled specifically upon women, could theoretically be a counter to easy divorce, except that most *mahr* amounts are relatively low, and most women are prevailed upon to forego *mahr* payments. Women are guaranteed rights to inheritance but, as with *mahr*, may be dissuaded from claiming them, and only a few cases of non-observance are taken to court.

The nationalist state in India, with its constitution of 1950, guarantees equal rights to all its citizens and makes special provisions for women. But the Indian state has been "communal" in that it has relied on an identity that was Sanskritic and on institutions such as personal law to cover the areas of marriage, divorce, adoption, and inheritance. Personal law, defended by the community as essential for its self-definition, and condemned by both progressivists and fundamentalists as regressive in its denial of rights to the individual, is itself a hybrid. It was concocted over two hundred and more years by the colonial state with its fears and prejudices, from selected oral testimonies, Indian interpreters' reports, colonial constructions, and internal debates within classes of people in India. Muslim personal law may be criticized for its adherence to polygamy, easy divorce by men, and unequal rights of inheritance. The state, in its continued acceptance of this law, as well as through all other legal and political measures, supports the community in its gendered exercise of power.

While modesty and chastity in both men and women are highly prized, and the Qur'ān asks both men and women to lower their eyes, it is women who are veiled. Everyday life, to be properly Islamic, is supposed to be defined by *sharm* (modesty and self-effacement on the part of women). Purdah as the worn garment or veil indicates varying exercise of control and agency. Its wearing is largely in inverse relationship to modern education, occupation, and self-consciousness. But its wearing also permits a degree of autonomy and freedom, and is liberating for women in giving them the ability to move about almost freely and engage in almost any occupation. In contemporary times, the covering of the self can also be a political statement of women's control over their own choices and lives.

Purdah, literally curtain, or the physical seclusion of women, is practiced also through the separation of public/outside space and private/inside space, and then through the segregation of domestic space as men's and women's. Whether it be one room or a self-sufficient section of a capacious house, there is a "separate world" for women, enforced by the design of spaces and buildings. This confinement, while a hindrance to equality, is also a source of agency and power for women.

In Pakistan and Bangladesh there is a patriarchal unity of purpose between the state and the community, and change in inegalitarian gender relations within the family occurs gradually through reform. In India, there is, ironically, a similar unity between a secular/Hindu state and the Muslim community, but reform becomes more elusive because, as in colonial times, the community can claim its autonomy from "external" interference and resist legal and educational change.

BIBLIOGRAPHY

I. Ahmad (ed.), *Family, kinship and marriage among the Muslims*, Delhi 1976.

——, *Divorce and remarriage among Muslims in India*, Delhi 2003.

V. R. Bevan Jones and L. Bevan Jones, *Women in Islam. A manual with special reference to conditions in India*, Lucknow 1941, repr. Westport, Conn. 1987.

N. Haksar, Campaign for a uniform code, in A. R. Desai (ed.), *Women's liberation and politics of religious personal laws in India*, Bombay 1986, 47–51.

Z. Hasan (ed.), *Forging identities. Gender, communities and the state*, Delhi 1994.

P. Jeffery, *Frogs in a well. Indian women in purdah*, London 1979, repr. 2000.
D. Kandiyoti (ed.), *Women, Islam and the state*, Philadelphia 1991.
G. Minault (ed.), *The extended family. Women and political participation in India and Pakistan*, Columbia, Mo. 1981.
H. Papanek and G. Minault (eds.), *Separate worlds. Studies of purdah in South Asia*, Delhi 1982.
Z. Pathak and R. S. Rajan, Shah Bano, in *Signs* 14:3 (1989), 558–82.
T. Saliba, C. Allen, and J. A. Howard (eds.), *Gender, politics, and Islam*, Chicago 2002.
C. Vreede-de-Stuers, *Parda. A study of Muslim women's life in northern India*, Assen, Netherlands 1968.

NITA KUMAR

Sub-Saharan Africa: Fulbe Societies

Terminology alone does not offer a sensible guide to intimate family relationships between husband and wife, siblings, children and parents, and extended kin. Rather, in order to discuss the complex interaction of gender, Islam, and family in sub-Saharan Africa, one has to examine the relationships between individuals and within domestic groups that are characterized by continually shifting relationships of authority, influence, emotional solidarity, and conflict. Family and gender are better explored as negotiated processes than terms to be defined. Several aspects of these relationships are addressed in this entry, such as power, access to resources, political economy, marriage patterns, mobility, inter-generational relationships, fostering, social status, and kinship. Attention must be paid to the embedded nature of gender as a material, social institution and as a set of ideologies located in a particular politico-economic and historic context. Abu-Lughod argues for "ethnographies of the particular" by which she locates the effects of extra-local and long-term processes as manifested locally and specifically, produced in the actions of individuals living their particular lives, inscribed in their bodies and their words (Abu-Lughod 1999, 150). Following Abu-Lughod's model, this entry raises these broader theoretical and practical issues related to the study of family, gender, and Islam and then situates these ideas within a particular social, geographic, and historic context – that of the Muslim Fulbe of West Africa.

Fulbe is the term used in the Futa region of Guinea to describe the people who speak the language Pular, known elsewhere as Fula, Fulani, Peul, or Haalpulaaren. The Fulbe are one of West Africa's most populous ethnic groups and are widely scattered across the sub-region in a more or less continuous belt, stretching from The Gambia and Senegal in the west to Cameroon and beyond in the east (Oppong 2002, 28). While they are considered one of the major cattle-keeping peoples of the world (Riesman 1984, 171), they are also known as farmers, traders, and learned Islamic teachers. The Fulbe brought Islam to the Guinea/ Senegal region in the mid 1700s, when the pastoralist nomads settled down in villages with their conquered slaves. The jihad provided the initial justification for the enslavement of the infidels, a practice perpetuated through the Fulbe social hierarchy of nobles, ex-captives, and artisan groups. Most Fulbe practice a syncretic form of (Tijāniyya) Sufism, in which cultural beliefs and norms are combined with Islamic principles.

In the traditional view of a rural Fulbe household in Guinea, the child is born into the *suudu* (hut), given to her *neene* (mother) by her *baaba* (father). He or she generally shares the *suudu* with full siblings or *neene-gotoobe* (children of the same mother) who are raised according to their sex and birth order. Since many marriages are polygynous, the household may be composed of several buildings that house co-wives and their children and correspond to discrete household economies. Each wife has her separate set of tools, utensils, and foodstuffs for daily activities and is usually responsible for producing items for sauce such as tomatoes, beans, onions, and okra from her *suntuure* (household garden) and for purchasing clothing, shoes, and medicine for her children. Money gained from the sale of items from the *suntuure*, from income-generating activities outside the household, or from grain harvested in a field given to her exclusively for cultivation by her husband are considered hers to keep. The *beyngure*, or entire domestic unit into which an individual is born, might be extremely large and widespread. Usually the oldest male is considered the head of the household and is the one in charge of all the different domestic units situated in the fenced area, of which there may be many. Included may be aging parents, semi-permanent visitors, children who are being fostered, a tenant who is farming for the season or practicing a trade, or a son who has married and is living with the family.

Family relationships tend to be more normative in rural than urban areas because there is strong community power to sanction behavior and relationships. For the patrilineal Fulbe, parallel cousin marriage is preferred in order to maintain wealth and land within the family. The Fulbe refer to this as the best and worst type of marriage, as there is simultaneously great familial support and intense social pressure for the marriage to succeed and to avoid divorce. Levirate marriages are common, where a widow is remarried to her late spouse's brother, and women past childbearing age tend to be married for respectability and stature in the community.

Discussions about the family are often based on the males' point of view rather than looking at the rights and responsibilities transferred through marriage to women, such as domestic labor, sexuality, and children. There is often a significant age difference between a man and his wife because of the demands on men to accumulate sufficient bridewealth and to attain the appropriate status in the family to have the support of the father, uncles, and other influential family members. For women, access to resources is made possible through marriage, though it can be especially problematic in polygynous unions. The move to her husband's house/village upon marriage marks the transition from girl to woman. Marriages are most often arranged by the parents of the young woman. Unlike many other West African societies, Fulbe consider neither premarital sex nor dating as precursors to marriage, as the resulting union would be impure before Allah (Furth 2004, 94). In fact, Fulbe prohibit girlfriends and boyfriends from marrying, especially in cases where sexual relationships are confirmed in pregnancy. Virginity is highly prized for brides, although recent estimates of sexual activity among teenagers in Guinea (Görgen et al. 1998) suggests that virginity may be more symbolic than real, reflected by the decrease in the practice of displaying bloodstained sheets after the marriage is consummated or the willingness to fabricate proof in order to protect the families' honor (Furth 2004, 104).

Power differences within families based on parity and gender differently affect members' ability to access resources such as land, housing, money, and education. For those who move with their husbands, migration is a source of new ideas and skills, but for those who are denied resources within the marriage, migration may become a means to financial independence. Women in rural areas generally face greater family-related social and economic constraints than their male counterparts and may view mobility, as well as extra-marital sexual networking, as alternatives. The process of leave-taking is a catalyst for change and negotiation of social roles for women that clearly merits further exploration and research.

The pilgrimage to Mecca is another transformative experience for women, as the Hadja title is a religious, social, and economic status symbol. For a woman to have her child finance the pilgrimage to Mecca is a sign of success: she has raised her children to be contributors to the family economy, according to Islamic principles. Status in the community and family has traditionally been based on hereditary positions and religious learning, perpetuated through marital alliances. However, the ability of young men to make their fortune through labor migration has led to an increase in interethnic marriages and marriages between high and low status families. Movement from rural areas to urban centers also allows for temporary, informal living arrangements between men and women where the consent of the families is not sought, for example relationships that are called *tap to me* (Krio for "cohabit with me") by Fulbe in Sierra Leone (Andrews 2004). While these extra-familial relationships are not commonly discussed or condoned, they are an important example of how migration to urban African cities and beyond provides an expansion of cultural norms and gender roles.

Kinship is a strategic resource in this context where migration is a durable feature of everyday life and seizing opportunities in other regions may depend on the presence of kin, whether real or practical, to ease the initial pressures of the move. Particularly in Guinea, Sierra Leone, Liberia, and Côte d'Ivoire, many Fulbe, who may have originally arrived as economic migrants, have now become forcibly displaced because of war. For Fulbe, practical kin are created through sharing household resources, care of children, and having a common place of origin. While the existence and importance of a biological caregiver is assumed, children may spend a substantial amount of time away from blood relatives. Fostering is a common practice; children may go to live with a childless aunt, an older relative who needs assistance, or family in an urban area who can provide support while the child is at school. Children provide a link between scattered family members, particularly for a group like the Fulbe who continue to be migrants for economic and political reasons. The maintenance of family ties through marriage, remittances, fostering, and visits for funerals and other important ceremonies remains vital in maintaining a sense of Fulbe identity.

Bibliography

L. Abu-Lughod, *Veiled sentiments. Honor and poetry in a Bedouin society*, Berkeley 1986, 1999 (updated ed.).

L. Andrews, Sembakounya camp life, in K. Jacobsen (ed.), *Refugee camps. A problem of our time*, Palgrave MacMillan Publishers (forthcoming).

M. Di Leonardo (ed.), *Gender at the crossroads of knowledge. Feminist anthropology in the postmodern era*, Berkeley 1991.

R. Furth, Marrying the forbidden other. Marriage status and social change in the Futa Jallon Highlands of Guinea, Ph.D. diss., University of Wisconsin, Madison 2004.
R. Görgen et al. (eds.), Sexual behavior and attitudes among unmarried urban youths in Guinea, in *International Family Planning Perspectives* 24 (1998), 65–71.
Y. Oppong, *Moving through and passing on. Fulani mobility, survival and identity in Ghana*, New Brunswick, N.J. 2002.
P. Riesman, The Fulani in a development context. The relevance of cultural traditions for coping with change and crisis, in E. P. Scott (ed.), *Life before the drought*, London 1984, 171–91.
——, *First find your child a good mother*, New Brunswick, N.J. 1992.

B. Lacey Andrews

Turkey

Gender and family relations in Turkey are influenced by traditions stemming from the Ottoman-Islamic heritage, pre-Islamic Turkic origins, and Mediterranean culture, all interacting with the processes of a revolutionary modernization. Turkey is an extremely heterogeneous country and women's positions and gender relations in the family vary significantly according to place of residence, level of education, and professional status.

The position of women in the family and society changed considerably after the Kemalist reforms, which had the aim of establishing a secular nation-state. However, the first initiatives for the emancipation of women and democratization of family relations were taken during the Tanzimat period, in the latter half of the nineteenth century. The leading ideologue of Turkism, Ziya Gökalp, asserted that a family morality based on ancient Turkish cultural values included norms such as democracy in the family, the equality of men and women, and monogamous marriage (Kandiyoti 1995). Gökalp's ideas had a great influence on Mustafa Kemal Atatürk in the processes of Westernization, secularization, and nation-building.

In 1926, the Turkish Civil Code, modeled after the Swiss Code, was adopted. This law abolished polygamy, and endorsed compulsory civil marriage, the right of divorce for both partners, and egalitarian inheritance laws. However, the civil law failed to establish full legal equality between the sexes since it contained several clauses that endorsed a traditional male-headed family model and institutionalized women's dependence on men (Arat 1994). In 2001, the Civil Code was amended. The "head of the household" clause was eliminated, each spouse acquired the right to represent the conjugal union, and a new regime ensuring sharing of property after divorce was adopted.

While legal reforms were important in securing women's rights, a basic ambiguity influencing women and family relations was also institutionalized. Even though women's education and participation in the public sphere were encouraged, their main and most sacred duty was specified as motherhood. The persistence of traditional role patterns within families, the double burden of working women, and strict control of female sexuality has led to a labeling of Turkish women as "emancipated but unliberated" (Kandiyoti 1987).

The success of legal reforms in changing women's conditions was limited to the extent that Islamic traditions concerning sex roles have remained socially valid, especially in rural areas (Toprak 1981). There have not been radical changes in the status of peasant women who work full time as unpaid family workers. Arranged marriage, demand for bride price, marriage of underage girls, and boy preference are common practices in rural areas.

In urban areas, arranged marriage is rapidly declining and young people are afforded a relative autonomy in their marriage decisions (Sunar 2002). Marriage in order to start a family is almost universal: the marriage rate is above 90 percent. The divorce rate is still low, with only around 6 per cent of all marriages ending in divorce. Cohabitation without formal marriage is rare and is often morally stigmatized. Fertility rates vary significantly with women's level of education. While women with lower levels of education give birth to an average of 2.5 children, this number declines to 0.8 children for women with higher education (SIS 1998).

The bilateral kinship system in Turkey, in which descent is traced equally through both males and females, shows more similarity to Mediterranean countries than to the patrilineal descent system of most Middle Eastern Islamic countries (Baştuğ 2002). Kinship loyalties are strong and ties between parents and children are very close. Children of both sexes remain with their parents until marriage and frequent interaction is maintained after marriage. Families try to live near other kin and routinely exchange goods and informal services. The social security system is not well developed in Turkey and close family ties extending into kinship relations serve an important function of security in times of crisis and conflict. Wider kinship relations are extremely important in both rural and urban areas in Turkey among all social classes, despite the high percentage of nuclear family residence (Duben 1982). The modern Turkish family does not exhibit the pattern of separateness and autonomy of members from one another and their wider kin but one of continued emotional interdependence (Kağıtçıbaşı 1985).

In Turkish families, women have the main responsibility for housework, childcare, and care of the elderly. When they receive help, it is mainly other women – their daughters, mothers, or paid female helpers, not their husbands – who share their workload. This traditional division of labor remains valid even for a majority of dual-earner, professional couples (Sümer 2002). Family members are highly dependent on each other for the care of small children and the elderly. A familistic gender regime prevails in Turkey (Drew, Emerek, and Mahon 1998). The assumption that childcare and care of the elderly should be met within the family (that is, by women) leads to low public provisions and supports the male-breadwinner/female-housewife family model.

Bibiliography

Z. F. Arat, Turkish women and the republican reconstruction of tradition, in F. M. Göcek and S. Balaghi (eds.), *Reconstructing gender in the Middle East. Traditions, identity, and power*, New York 1994, 57–78.

S. Baştuğ, The household and family in Turkey. An historical perspective, in R. Liljeström and E. Özdalga (eds.), *Autonomy and dependence in the family. Turkey and Sweden in critical perspective*, Istanbul 2002, 99–115.

E. Drew, R. Emerek, and E. Mahon (eds.), *Women, work and the family in Europe*, London 1998.

A. Duben, The significance of family and kinship in urban Turkey, in Ç. Kağıtçıbaşı (ed.), *Sex roles, family, and community in Turkey*, Bloomington, Ind. 1982, 73–100.

Ç. Kağıtçıbaşı, Intra-family interaction and a model of family change, in T. Erder (ed.), *Family in Turkish society*, Ankara 1985, 149–65.

D. Kandiyoti, Emancipated but unliberated? Reflections on the Turkish case, in *Feminist Studies* 13:2 (1987), 317–38.

——, Patterns of patriarchy. Notes for an analysis of male dominance in Turkish society, in S. Tekeli (ed.), *Women in modern Turkish society*, London 1995, 306–18.

SIS (State Institute of Statistics), Republic of Turkey, <www.die.gov.tr>.

S. Sümer, Global issues/local troubles. A comparative study of Turkish and Norwegian urban dual-earner couples, doctoral diss., Department of Sociology, University of Bergen 2002.

D. Sunar, Change and continuity in the Turkish middle class family, in R. Liljeström and E. Özdalga (eds.), *Autonomy and dependence in the family. Turkey and Sweden in critical perspective*, Istanbul 2002, 217–37.

B. Toprak, Religion and Turkish women, in N. Abadan-Unat (ed.), *Women in Turkish society*, Leiden 1981, 28–92.

Sevil Sümer

The United States

The family is the major social institution in the Muslim world, as well as among Muslim Americans. Other institutions, political, religious, and social, may compete for importance, but seldom succeed. Women play an extremely important role in the family, but males have privilege through a kinship system of patrilineality, also found in most of Asia. Islam, originating in Saudi Arabia, reflects patrilineal privilege and often enforces the kinship system in family laws, especially in countries experiencing an increase of religious ideology. This entry examines the effect of the traditional Muslim family system on women of Middle Eastern and Asian origin in the United States.

Muslim families in the United States differ along lines of socioeconomic background and individual histories and experiences. Factors such as residence in a close ethnic community or scattered in the suburbs, the number of relatives or people sharing the same country of origin who assist or restrict activities, economic class, education, generation, and pre-migration patterns are all variables that may affect behavior even more than religious identity. However, the ideology of family rules includes being large and extended, is based on intimate social reciprocal obligations, and for most is patrilineally organized. Visiting among the members is expected and frequent. Women play a big part in this sociability, by planning, negotiating, influencing children's marriages, spreading information, hosting, and preparing food.

Chain migration, where one member in a family migrates to the United States, then brings other members of the family, contributes to this pattern. Families are important for economic survival in a new country. Upper-class immigrants sometimes migrate without families and form fictive kin groups. Social gatherings tend to be large, and the hostess is never exactly sure how many guests will attend. Umm Hassan comments, "Every weekend, I feed all these people. My daughter and I are tired from bringing them coffee and tea and fruit all day. My husband's niece and her husband leave, then his nephew comes" (Walbridge 1996, 310).

Kinship rules and the effect on family and women

Understanding the rules of patrilineal kinship is essential for contextualizing women. Sometimes confused with patriarchy, which means male power, patrilineality is a comprehensive kinship system in which a person, son or daughter, becomes a member of the father's descent group at birth, and shares many special rights and obligations with that group. A person's behavior reflects favorably or unfavorably on that name and group, not merely upon self or parents. Through rules of patrilineality, Muslim men are permitted to marry out with more ease than women, since the children are seen to follow the man's religion and culture. It is expected that the children of women who marry out will follow their father's line. The honor or reputation of the family acts as a strong mechanism of social control. The mother's family is not unimportant. However, since it is often an emotional support group, migration may increase its importance if the father's family is dispersed.

Being socialized as a member of a group rather than of a nuclear family is a basic difference between Muslim and many other American families where the emphasis is on individualism and individual space. This is at variance with the idea of shared obligations, which may come at the price of individual pursuits. When a young Muslim was asked why she went to the movies with her cousins rather than her friends, she replied, "But they are my friends." Other Asian, Mediterranean, South American and Third-World ethnic groups such as Chinese, Indians, Italians, and Mexicans with large families also share this experience.

Male privileges in Islamic patrilineal systems include the possibility of multiple wives in the Middle East, more inheritance, fewer restrictions on sexuality, and more power given to males, especially elders, in the patriline. The latter power is termed "patriarchy." Parents are called the father and mother of the eldest son, Abu and Umm Ahmed for example, and a son's birth receives much attention. Fathers are treated with respect in public and often receive preferential treatment at home. Wives should not contradict husbands in public. There are generational differences as well. When asked how it was growing up as an Arab Muslim girl, one elderly immigrant woman whose father used a belt on her says, "It is different today. A girl of five might as well have been a woman then . . . My Dad was definitely the boss. My mother would say, 'Don't you know, God is first and your husband second.'" (Aswad 1997, 233).

The males of the patriline are seen both as the protectors of women and as the enforcers of behavior. Outsiders see the resulting modesty and disproportionate public restrictions placed on females, especially young unmarried girls, yet do not observe the support system. The control of female sexuality and the insistence on female virginity before marriage relates to the need for sure knowledge that a child belongs to the father. That this is more a cultural than a religious norm is clear from the fact that the same sanctions and pressures are placed on, for example, Christian Asian women.

The custom of patrilocality, by which men in the patriline try to live near each other, has traditionally accompanied patrilineality and serves to reinforce male power. In Muslim cultures, women may be separated from their lineage and sources of protection and social support when they move to their husband's locale after marriage. The custom of cousin marriage within the patriline (marriage of a girl to her father's brother's son) eases this separation since the father and his brother will try to live near each other. While patrilocality does not always pertain to the United States, women often experience similar feelings of separation in a new and alien environment. In the United States, first cousin marriage is prohibited, but cousins can marry in the Middle East and then transfer to the United States. An early survey of a Muslim Arab immigrant community found that 50 percent were married to relatives (Aswad 1974, 67). Marriages are strongly influenced and sometimes planned by parents, who feel it is their duty to secure a good marriage for their children by examining the credentials of a mate and the economic situation of his or her parents.

Economic factors and women

The Middle Eastern and Asian patriline is involved in economic ventures such as land control and store ownership, and often affects the political realm. It is difficult for women to struggle against male power because it is embedded in a vast range of lineage obligations, not just patriarchy. In contrast, women may gain power if they are members of a strong or rich patriline. Instances where they have even occasionally replaced their fathers in government, such as former Prime Minister Benazir Bhutto of Pakistan who inherited much of her father's power, are often confusing to Westerners.

During the immigration process, the power of lineages may break down and allow new opportunities for lower-class people as well as for women. Migration may also disrupt the structure and composition of families, making life difficult emotionally and economically. Sometimes children are left in the home country. Situations of warfare in the Middle East or South Asia also bring great strains on families who are separated because of immigration to the West (Aswad 1992).

Economic class affects family interaction. In the United States, many upper-class immigrants live in suburban areas, and had fewer family members when they first migrated. The 1965 immigration laws gave preference to relatives and professionals with skills needed by the United States. Immigrants made links with persons from their regions of origin, religion, and/or class and occupation, such as doctors and successful business people. Among these upper-class immigrants, there are many educated professional women. Pharmacy is a popular occupational choice among immigrants and later generation Muslim women.

Muslim women have successfully used their social networking in numerous businesses. Among Iranian Muslims in Los Angeles, Dallafar found women actively participating in their ethnic economy using their class, ethnic, and gender resources to open small businesses. Many of these are run from the home, or are family-run enterprises (1996, 123). For many women employment is full-time and they often have multiple roles such as seamstress, cashier, and public relations. In many cases, rather than being secondary to the husband, they are "central to the survival of the small ethnic entrepreneurial business" (ibid.). Dallafar points out the importance of women's social and family networks, which they use in the home and transfer to a business environment. This networking is evident in small stores across the United States, and also among those who have been successful in the real estate business and major companies where they serve clients from the Middle East. Among working-class families in industrial areas, immigrant Muslim women historically have worked in clothing and to a lesser degree on assembly lines. Most families try to influence their daughters to follow professions that restrict interaction with non-related males.

Muslim men are still considered the providers and protectors of the family. Those without educational or language skills in the United States suffer feelings of diminished status. They may feel guilty or embarrassed if a wife works or receives welfare. Most, however, support their daughters' education, although it may be less valued than a son's.

Muslim women of the lower classes have received welfare in the United States, and, as in other cultures, welfare has affected gender relations since it usually goes to women. Some lower-class men welcome governmental assistance, and before it was mandated that welfare recipients must seek employment, saw it as a means of assistance while their wives stayed at home with the children. Others worry that welfare unduly strengthens the women's role: "Welfare will fulfill her needs rather than her husband. She will think she is financially independent without me. It will weaken or destroy my role" (Aswad 1996, 186). Generally Muslim Lebanese immigrant women feel it threatens the male role more than those from Yemen (ibid.). Having many children is a status symbol among Muslim lower classes, and requires women to be at home. Poor women have come to view welfare as a method of contributing to income and achieving more economic leverage in the family while trying to carry out their duties of raising a family.

Youth behavior, dating, and socializing

Muslim customs are at variance with a culture where marriage involves dating, love, and a great measure of freedom of choice in choosing a mate, even though the ideology of that freedom may be exaggerated. There is both a generational and a cultural gap for Muslims. Today most parents fear their children will marry non-Muslims, though attitudes change according to historical periods. Until the late 1960s the emphasis was on assimilation into the United States. Anglo names were common and many Muslims married non-Muslims. Educated Muslim male professionals of the 1960s often married non-Muslim women whom they met in college. As the number of Muslims in the United States has increased, the emphasis has moved for many from assimilation to self-identity as both Muslim and American. With this has come an incrased emphasis on Muslim children, especially girls, marrying within the faith.

The behavior of Muslim American children reflects not only on the honor of the father's family, but also on the mother who is expected to raise her children in the correct fashion. Sometimes the strongest strains may be seen in the family between girls and their mothers, when daughters enter the more permissive American culture. Sons are given more leniency in dating than daughters due to the expectation of female but not male virginity at marriage. A son's ability to marry outside the faith more easily than a daughter's is also a factor.

Muslim children are expected to obey and respect parents, but girls are more restricted. Opinions about this vary. Farida says, "From the time you are born until the day you die you always respect your parents. No matter what. If you take a beating from them, you take a beating." Hanaa disagrees, "If I feel I'm right, I stick up for myself. If they yell, I yell right back." The asymmetry of sexual control over women is particularly felt in the area of dating. Farida says, "If I could change one thing, I'd change how the Muslim guys get more freedom than the girls" (Eisenlohr 1996, 254). Hanaa agrees. "I tell my mother that I would let my daughter have more freedom." Lubna adds, "A lot of Arab girls aren't allowed out at night" (ibid. 255).

Some feel that rules are stricter now than they used to be. "In the 1950s and 1960s," says one woman, "Arab boys and girls here could date, and not just in groups. The boys may have started dating American girls, but then the girls followed suit, dating Arabs and sometimes non-Arabs . . . None wore scarves, and many girls wore shorts; my sister still does at 65 years of age. Now with the immigrants from the Middle East, there is much less going out by the girls." (Aswad 1997, 233). Her own marriage had been arranged by an imam to a man 20 years older than she, but she did not arrange her sons' marriages, both of whom married non-Arabs and non-Muslims. Socializing across sexes today often tends to be among kin or friendship groups, especially among recent immigrants. Brothers have the responsibility to guard their sisters, but often assist them in keeping secrets.

Mothers, daughters, and brothers

Mothers have power usually not seen outside the community. Their success in raising children is important, and through their traditional role in planning marriages they acquire power over sons as well as daughters. They are usually the mediators between father and children. Shryock comments, "Most Arab immigrants accept as a fact of life that a man should be head of the house, even if 'the mother is the neck that moves the head'" (2000, 586). Widows are to be cared for by their eldest son. Women find power through women's groups and visiting patterns that engage in gossip and knowledge of relationships, of which men are often ignorant. Occasionally they dominate husbands, but most try to embrace a balance of influence, hard domestic work and increasingly outside employment, negotiating, and manipulation, characteristics shared by many women in the world.

Daughters bear the greatest responsibilty for good behavior. They bond with sisters and female cousins, and seek their brother's assistance with their parents on issues of dating or marriage. Brothers have privileges over sisters. Usually they protect them and may side with them against parents. Others exploit this power and mistreat their sisters, sometimes without parental rebuff. Zobeida says, "My brother helps me. When my parents say no, he says, "Why are you doing this? Let her do this" (Eisenlohr 1996, 260). Nehmeh adds, " I have three brothers who don't live at home, but I see them just as much as if they did. One might say 'If I find out what you're doing and I don't like it, then you're in trouble'" (ibid., 259).

Mistreatment and divorce

Some girls have threatened suicide and others have run away. If an issue of misbehavior becomes public, and is not worked out by other members of the family, clergy, or community social agencies, male members of the patriline, usually a father or brother, may abuse a girl. In the extreme, they may murder her. This seldom occurs in the United States but remains as a threat. Rarely does a woman harm or murder a man. Family relations are considered private, and domestic violence is usually hidden, as in much of the world. The greater emphasis on Islamic values has generated arguments over Qurʾānic verses used to condone the beating of wives. A predictor of domestic violence is the restriction of women's ability to leave the family setting (Hajjar forthcoming).

Divorce rates, while low, are rising and have reached 10 percent among Arab Muslims. This reflects the pressures on employed women, as well as the ability to leave an abusive husband and retain custody in the United States. Some men restrict their wife's employment for this reason. Pressures against divorce include a strong stigma, family influence, lack of job skills or other economic resources, alternative domestic arrangements, and the still present possibility of losing custody of children (Hajjar forthcoming). A recent study in Dearborn found that Muslim immigrant women felt, rightly or wrongly, that their husbands would be deported if they called the police (Kulwicki 2000).

Non-Muslim counselors should be cognizant of the moral role of males and extended families to intervene and protect females as well as their potential to harm them. When domestic violence occurs, each situation needs to be treated with special sensitivity. Muslim women seeking to gain their rights, achieve independence, and yet maintain emotional and physical support from the family face a strong system of social and emotional obligations and customs. It is not an easy balance, but one that many American Muslim women are working hard to achieve.

Bibliography

N. Ahmed, G. Kaufman, and S. Naim, Southern Asian families in the United States. Pakistani, Bangladeshi, and Indian Muslims, in B. C. Aswad and B. Bilgé (eds.), *Family and gender among American Muslims*, Philadelphia 1996, 155–72.

B. C. Aswad, The Lebanese Muslim community in Dearborn, Michigan, in A. H. Hourani and N. Shehadi (eds.), *The Lebanese in the world*, London 1992, 167–88.

——, Attitudes of Arab immigrants toward welfare, in M. W. Suleiman (ed.), *Arabs in America*, Philadelphia 1999, 177–91.

—— (ed.), *Arabic speaking communities in American cities*, Staten Island, N.Y. 1974.
B. C. Aswad and B. Bilgé (eds.), *Family and gender among American Muslims*, Philadelphia 1996.
B. Bilgé, Turkish-American patterns of intermarriage, in B. C. Aswad and B. Bilgé (eds.), *Family and gender among American Muslims*, Philadelphia 1996, 59–106.
L. Cainkar, Palestinian women in American society, in E. McCarus (ed.), *The development of Arab American identity*, Ann Arbor 1997, 85–105.
A. Dallafar, The Iranian ethnic economy in Los Angeles. Gender and entrepreneurship, in B. C. Aswad and B. Bilgé (eds.), *Family and gender among American Muslims*, Philadelphia 1996, 107–28.
C. Eisenlohr, Adolescent Arab girls in an American high school, in B. C. Aswad and B. Bilgé (eds.), *Family and gender among American Muslims*, Philadelphia 1996, 250–70.
L. Hajjar, Domestic violence and Sharīʿa, in L. Welchman (ed.), *Islamic family law*, Zed Press (forthcoming).
S. Howell, Finding the straight path, in N. Abraham and A. Shryock (eds.), *Arab Detroit*, Detroit 2000, 241–8.
J. Kadi (ed.), *Food for our grandmothers*, Boston 1994.
A. Kulcicki and J. Miller, Domestic violence in the Arab-American population, in *Mental Health Nursing* 20:3 (1999), 199–216.
A. Shryock, Family resemblances. Kinship and community in Arab Detroit, in N. Abraham and A. Shryock (eds.), *Arab Detroit*, Detroit 2000, 573–610.
L. S. Walbridge, Five immigrants, in B. C. Aswad and B. Bilgé (eds.), *Family and gender among American Muslims*, Philadelphia 1996, 301–17.

Barbara C. Aswad

Western Europe

Recent changes in family relationships and gender hierarchy among European Muslims are due to women's pragmatic use of their migration experience, and to the fact that younger generations, especially women, born and socialized in Europe, have marked the difference between cultural traditions and Islamic faith.

Women did not come to Europe simply following their husbands: far from being passive participants, women have their own migratory project inside the context of family migration. Since the 1990s, in Italy and Spain women have also arrived on their own. Emigration imposes confrontation and adaptation; it prolongs and perfects the changes that have already begun in the societies of origin. Insertion into Europe does not result in estrangement from the culture of origin: it generates an attempt at critical synthesis, typical of the diaspora condition, in which women play a role both conservative and innovative. This process is of course neither obvious nor painless.

As critical and pragmatic participants, women experience emigration as an opportunity to make changes in their private life (freer marital choices, access to work, shifting in the dynamics of the couple), but also as a chance to strengthen certain values that in their eyes are non-negotiable, such as the priority given to motherhood, and faithfulness to the ethical principles of Islam as a framework for behavior.

Fewer and fewer marriages are arranged by parents, and they do not necessarily take place between members of the clan, or of the same ethnic and/or national group. Women still accept arranged marriage, but only as long as the free choice of the individual is respected.

Family constraints were, for the first European cohorts, the main reason behind the departure of runaway girls, whose rebellion against parental dictates led to exclusion from the family and separation from the community. Nowadays, in the name of respect for the Islamic rule prohibiting coercion, which renders any action invalid in the eyes of God, women utilize religious tradition to break free from cultural pressure.

However, the real turning point is in marital relationships. All the empirical research on the European diaspora shows female demands that traverse all national communities (be they Turkish, Moroccan, or Pakistani). Women demand, in the following order: more equity, reciprocal esteem and respect, and real communication between partners. They express explicit refusal of polygamy. They demand acknowledgment of equal shared responsibility by the couple, especially regarding the education of children, an implicit criticism of the traditional masculine model of authority. This general wish for change is faced with the following paradox: on the one hand the still ingrained custom of choosing endogamic unions, on the other hand the shortage of potential husbands in a marital market where a partner meeting this description is rare merchandise in the breeding ground of "mummy's pets" educated like son-kings. Among North African women in France, aged between 25 and 29, only 38 percent are married, alongside an already not particularly high national average of 48 percent. In the eyes of the fathers, yielding to a career appears preferable to the dreaded choice of exogamy. The increase of celibacy and the postponement of marriage show the new feminine demands synthesized in the irony of the joke: "a good husband must not be like a mother-in-law" (Schmidt di Friedberg and Saint-Blancat 1998).

Traditional patriarchal relationships are nevertheless unconsciously very strong. An individual is still not completely autonomous from his/her family and kindred. Fathers, brothers, cousins have rights over him/her, and he/she duties to them.

These contradictions nowadays create conflict between generations and genders.

Breaking free from their role is also a difficult task for men. In Muslim families, males are still socialized to practice their superiority over women and their right to control them as a given fact. Protected and always defended by their mothers, they have more freedom than their sisters or cousins, particularly regarding sex. In case of a mixed marriage, the family, though displeased, does not banish the male, as they would his sister. Male authority derives also from the duty to sustain wife and family. Losing jobs, for the fathers who are first generation immigrants, or having difficulty in finding jobs, for their sons (in France the unemployment rate of North Africans aged between 20 and 29 is 40 percent, twice the national average), contribute to the weakening of gender hierarchy. The instability of male identity, faced with both contradictory family expectations and indirect social discrimination in many European societies, gives rise to humiliation and frustration, which result in rising alcoholism, forms of deviance, and the kind of control, sometimes violent, enforced on daughters, mothers, and sisters.

Women do not question one of the fundamental conceptions of their culture: the pre-eminence of the mother role above all others, which often delays in time, or relegates to a secondary position, the choice of profession for many. For most women, motherhood remains an unavoidable and non-negotiable step on their way to identification and affirmation on a personal level, and to contribution on a community level. The priority of motherhood does not at all exclude a general tendency toward fewer births. For women, the ideal number of children (2 or 3 at most) is a sign of the decrease in fertility rates, both in Muslim societies and in diaspora communities.

Regarding work, the traditional family model considers salary as a male prerogative. Female work is seen as an additional income. Only widows and divorcees need to work, if they do not have a brother, an adult son, or a generous brother-in-law on whom they can count. Work is appreciated as an economic contribution to the needs of the family, as an agent of external socialization and personal growth, but it is still not considered as rewarding and gratifying as dedication to raising and educating the children. However, the paths chosen by socialized women in the diaspora or by the increasing number of women who come to Europe on their own, progressively show an autonomous choice to attempt to conciliate working life with the primary value of motherhood. Women prefer independent jobs, which gratify them and give them the possibility to freely organize their working time.

Women's demands do not appear to be caused from the outside, by the sole comparison with European family models; they are born of the interiorization of religious norms that coincide with the identity of women and their gender role; in brief, from the heart of Islam itself, where the principles of justice and equality lead all conduct.

Not all women are able to find their way between what is written in the Qur'ān and what has been enforced by social tradition, under the control of men. Many, however, make a clear distinction between religious law and traditional customs. It is therefore to be expected that the means by which women will be able to shake the foundations of both patriarchal and theological hegemony, hence modifying their social status, will be renewal of religious interpretation (*ijtihād*) itself. Only through critical work on Islamic law and a growing capability of mastering Qur'ānic tradition, combined with secular knowledge acquired in European universities, will women be able to breach the normative orthodoxy of learned Islam, which has always been reserved for and governed by men. There is a long way to go, but that breach can hardly be closed. In the words of Nouria, a young Turkish girl of 17, "When I discovered my religious sources and was finally able to study them, I realized that Islam gave me rights my father was denying me: the possibility to study, my assent to the choice of my husband, who does not necessarily have to be a Turk . . . This brought revolution to our home; I finally had arguments not to let them run my life . . . I managed to enforce my values without having to suffer for them in an institution, as my elder sister had been forced to do" (Bouzar 2003, 46).

Young women are progressively retrieving gender identity through the prism of religion. They no longer want to marry a "Muslim in tradition," but a "Muslim in heart." Polysemous usage of the *ḥijāb* is another example of this autonomy of conduct: by choosing or refusing to wear it, women express a demand for individual and plural interpretation of religious practice. Women have begun to challenge the principle of their submission, which they do not find in the spirit of the Qur'ān. They are aware of the role they may play in the future if they manage to act on the content of religious transmission, and thus on the transformation of family roles.

Bibliography

L. Ahmed, *Women and gender in Islam. Historical roots of a modern debate*, New Haven, Conn. 1992.

L. Babès and T. Oubrou, *Loi d'Allah, loi des hommes*, Paris 2002.

D. Bouzar and S. Kada, *L'une voilée, l'autre pas*, Paris 2003.
D. Bouzar, Réappropriation de la référence musulmane, parenté et citoyenneté, in *EMPAN* 50 (2003), 45–50.
N. Göle, *The forbidden modern. Civilization and veiling*, Ann Arbor 1991.
N. Guénif Souilamas, *Des "beurettes" aux descendantes d'immigrants nord-africains*, Paris 2000.
G. Jonker, Islamic knowledge through a woman's lens. Education, power and belief, in *Social Compass* 50:1 (2003), 35–46.
C. Lacoste-Dujardin, *Des mères contre les femmes. Maternité et patriarcat au Maghreb*, Paris 1996.
A. Ramirez, La inmigración marroquí. Los procesos de cambio en las relaciones de género y el papel del Islam, in V. Maquiera and M. J. Vara (eds.), *Género, clase y etnía en los nuevos procesos de globalización*, Madrid 1997, 183–91.
A. S. Roald, *Women in Islam. The Western experience*, London 2001.
C. Saint-Blancat, *L'islam de la diaspora*, Paris 1997.
O. Schmidt di Friedberg and C. Saint-Blancat, L'immigration au féminin. Les femmes marocaines en Italie du nord. Une recherche en Vénétie, in *Studi Emigrazione/ Migration Studies* 131 (1998), 483–98.
N. Tietze, *Jeunes musulmans de France et d'Allemagne. Les constructions subjectives de l'identité*, Paris 2002.
M. Tribalat, *Faire France*, Paris 1995.
S. Vertovec and A. Rogers (eds.), *Muslim European youth. Reproducing ethnicity, religion, culture*, Aldershot, England 1998.
N. Weibel, *Par-delà le voile. Femmes d'islam en Europe*, Paris 2000.

Chantal Saint-Blancat

Families: Metaphors of Nation

Overview

Introduction

Benedict Anderson observes that nationalism is akin to kinship in that it rests on assumptions of putative "blood" connections between those regarded as fellow nationals/fellow citizens (1991, 5). Nationalist rhetoric is replete with images of blood and earth evoking birth and autochthony. The status of citizen, the sense of belonging to the nation, arises on the basis of birth, of blood connections, like membership of a family. (Indeed the word nation derives from the Latin *nasci*, to be born.) In some instances, the nation and the family are explicitly connected through metaphorical equations that naturalize the exercise of state power, rendering it inevitable and even God-given. More commonly, the equation is more imminent, with woman's role within the family serving as a homology for her role as a citizen, or her performance of citizenship linked to domestic/maternal roles. The "Western construct of the nation-state, which became the compulsory form for the rest of the world, is based on citizens as detached from communities, as individuals. In fact – in the Arab world, the Third World, and much of the West – persons are deeply embedded in communities, in families, in ethnic and social groupings" (Joseph 1997, 64). Just as men and women are not necessarily equal within families, the connection to the nation is not equally available to men and women. They are differentiated in terms of civil and political rights, these differences commonly deriving from their family roles.

In his path-breaking work on nationalism, Anderson does not pursue the connection of the nation with kinship, except insofar as his argument posits the imagining of the nation as a community, a fraternity. Scholars of nationalism have not tended to see the nation as a social entity that exhibits a deep gender asymmetry, even though the language of nationalism is replete with gender imagery. The national subject is represented as male, in both nationalist rhetoric and in scholarship. The theoretical insights required to analyze the gendered basis of the nation have been developed within feminist political theory, and these tools are now being applied by (mainly female) scholars in analyses of specific nations/nationalist movements. Gender relations, both in the private world of the family and in the public order, are foundational to analysis of the nation.

Women's citizenship and nationalist struggles

In an oft-cited formulation, based on a wide-ranging historical review, Yuval-Davis and Anthias (1989) have outlined the terms on which women have been offered citizenship – terms that are, on the whole, different for men: as biological reproducers of the members of the national collective; as reproducers of the boundaries of national groups (through restrictions on sexual or marital relations); as active transmitters and producers of the national culture; as symbolic signifiers of national difference; and as active participants in national struggles. These idealized roles in the political life of the nation are linked to their duties within the private world of the family. Eickelman and Piscatori (1996, ch. 4) discuss the centrality of the link between women's role in the moral order and the upholding of the civic virtue of the nation in modern Islamic political thought.

Jayawardena has documented the important ways in which women, and women's issues, were integral to the articulation of the ideal of the nation in many struggles for national independence. Claims for women's civil and political rights – most commonly in marriage and family law, education, and suffrage – have often originated independently of the influence of the first wave of feminism in the West. Indeed, the "first arena in which women as a group began to be involved in political action was that of nationalist struggles" (Jayawardena 1987, 258). There are few published materials on the imaginings of nation by these women, but it is clear that they were articulating a modern notion of women's rights as part of their vision.

Reviewing nationalist movements in twelve nations (including five with majority Muslim populations), Jayawardena concludes that the reform of the family and women's roles were important symbolic elements of the strategies of bourgeois nationalist reformers in their quest for a national consciousness and for modern secular political structures. For these reformers, family structures that oppressed women were associated with old orders and the bourgeois family was central to the modern nation. Practices such as polygamy, concubinage, and divorce were regarded as "social evils" that threatened the stability of bourgeois family life. There was an "in-built conservative bias" in many nationalist movements at the same time ensuring that "women should retain a position of traditional subordination within the family" (Jayawardena 1987, 15). But others opted for more radical change as part of the social reconstitution associated with national independence. Moves to transform the family and the roles of women were opposed not just by colonial rulers, but also by traditional political and religious elites, who countered with responses such as isolationism or fundamentalism (Jayawardena 1987, 6).

Moghadam contrasts two styles of leadership in contemporary Islamic nations (using Iran and Afghanistan as case studies): modernizing (secular nationalist) elites, "particularly, but not exclusively, those with a socialist orientation" (1993, 125), who see the emancipation of women as integral to their agenda for development; and emerging "fundamentalist" movements, which seek a return to the past, including the (re) instatement of traditional sex roles. In the latter case, the family encodes the social role of women, their citizenship duties, their relation to the nation. That is, different national visions imply different bases of citizenship for women.

Articulation of the nation as family

Fanon linked the metaphor of the nation as family to the psychodynamics of colonial domination: "Militarization and the centralization of authority in a country automatically entail a resurgence of the authority of the father" (1967, 141–2) – the state borrows and enlarges the domestication of gender power within the family. "Fanon understands brilliantly how colonialism inflicts itself as a *domestication* of the colony, a reordering of the labor and sexual economy of the people, so as to divert female power into colonial hands and disrupt the patriarchal power of colonized men" (McClintock 1995, 364). He understands the different ways in which men and women are implicated in nationalist movements, and "recognises the power of nationalism as a *scopic* politics most visibly embodied in the power of sumptuary customs to fabricate a sense of national unity" (ibid., 365). For men, women become the visible signs of the emerging nation, and hence "subject to especially vigilant and violent discipline," such as the "emotive politics of dress" (ibid.).

McClintock has most clearly identified the manner in which the family trope has been fundamental to articulating the nation in authoritarian political thought. The family "offers a 'natural' figure for sanctioning national hierarchy within a putative organic unity of interests" (1993, 63). Echoing this view, Joseph has commented, "Hierarchy tends to genderize: those in superordinate position are masculinized, and subordinates are feminized" (Joseph 1997, 66).

The family trope was explicitly employed by the Egyptian nationalist leader Muṣṭafā Kāmil (1874–1908). He worked to develop a new sense of national belonging beyond local community or tribe by promoting the idea of the nation as one family. According to Baron, he did this to de-emphasize religious difference. This idea was adopted by his successor Saʿd Zaghlūl – his home became *Bayt al-Umma* (the house of the nation) and his wife *Umm al-Maṣriyyin* (The mother of all Egyptians). In turn, this name evoked *umm al-muʾminīn* (mother of all believers) that was given to ʿĀʾisha, Muḥammad's favorite wife (Baron 1993, 248–50).

Depicting the nation as a family, with a common symbolic home and mother, was an attempt to heal communal rifts and bridge class divides. These images were also meant to inspire male hearts with love and instill in them the sense that they had a duty to protect the honor of the family/nation (Baron 1993, 252).

The nation-as-family trope is fundamental to the assertion of a style of politics manifesting "Asian Values" in Indonesia, Malaysia, and Singapore, where ruling elites have aspired to a form of national politics deemed to be unique, and based on core values rooted in putative history. Central to this is the embracing of the patriarchal family as a cornerstone of a unique Asian world-view that brings social stability. In the island state of Singapore, with a minority Muslim population, the ruling elite claims a congruence between the place of the individual in a "natural institution like the family" (Heng and Devan 1992, 356) and the citizen's loyalty to a state that intervenes in all areas of their lives. Women are represented as loyal daughters of the paternal state, as well as patriotic mothers bearing the nation's children; "the transfer of the paternal signifier *from* the family *to* the state" renders natural an "omnipresent government" (ibid.). The model of paternal authority is an important underpinning of authoritarian rule.

In the case of Indonesia, the fictive patriarchal family has been elevated to the status of a core element of state ideology, particularly under the long authoritarian rule of President Suharto (1966–98). Indonesian political leaders have argued for an autochthonous political tradition that gives central place to "the notion of the state as a family, organically united in love, and governed by a father-head who best understands the needs of its members" (Reid 1998, 25). Not only was Suharto – who presided over a corrupt and crony-ridden regime – known as the "Father of Development" and his wife universally referred to as Ibu Tien (Mother Tien), but the state ideology enshrined a notion of familial harmony as a quintessential "Indonesian" characteristic in order to counter demands for the political contestation associated with democracy. For Indonesia's women, this ideology was reflected in discriminatory legal instruments as well as in a systematic campaign to mobilize them in state-sponsored organizations intended to nourish their roles in the private sphere of the family as the expression of "good citizenship" (Robinson 1999).

Women, the Family, and Boundaries

In the invocation of the nation as family, women and their fecundity are seen as important "boundary markers" of both ethnic group and nation. The symbol of the family represents a homogenizing version of the nation that suppresses plurality – and indeed this has been a strong effect where this trope has been deployed.

The former, long-standing president of Singapore, Lee Kwang Kyu, proposed that the state intervene in the marriages and reproductive choices of educated Singaporean women for eugenicist purposes, through a combination of incentives for childbearing and experiments in state-brokered marriages. He linked this appropriation by the state to traditions where families arranged marriages, often without their daughters' knowledge or consent, and also speculated on the possibility of reintroducing polygamy (in fact, polygyny). The proposal was directed at the majority Chinese residents, manifesting anxiety that their social precedence may be challenged by Indian and (Muslim) Malay minorities. A similar invocation to "breed" was made by Prime Minister Mahathir, to Muslim Malay citizens of Malaysia, manifesting anxiety that the Muslim Malay majority of Malaysia would be overrun by Chinese citizens. Mahathir stressed the unique qualities of the Malays, strongly rooted in their Islamic religion: in this vision, the Malay family, and women in their role as mothers, are fundamental to a (Malaysian) Islamic modernity.

Women act as identity markers by preserving dress codes and other manifestations of public behavior that define national boundaries, and boundaries between nation/ethnic groups. In Egypt, the strong promotion of public veiling by Muṣṭafā Kāmil's wife Ṣafiyya was linked to the fact that Ṣafiyya's honor (as mother of the nation) had become the nation's honor. "The vocabulary and signs employed to disseminate nationalism thus reinforced certain deeply embedded beliefs about gender, reaffirming ideals of sexual purity, morality and motherhood" (Baron 1993, 252).

Women are seen as the repositories of tradition and are often enjoined to marry endogamously. In situations of political conflict, within and between nations, the connection between nation-women-family-honor provides a language of violation. Within the "microcosm" of the family, should a woman be compromised or violated, there must be redress lest the honor of the family be spoiled, and so in conflict situations, rape becomes a direct attack on the nation (which, like the family, is conceptualized in terms of blood and relatedness). This idea was developed in Egyptian nationalist struggles against the British: "the notion of the collective was expanded, and with this a new sense of collective honour developed" (Baron 1993, 246). Dishonor was increasingly associated with the inability of Egyptian men to protect their women, an expression of the homology between the family and the wider collective, the nation.

Motherland/Fatherland

A common invocation of the familial trope is the conceptualization of the nation as mother or father. Nasta suggests the idea of "motherland" is a common colonial trope, inherited by patriarchal postcolonial male leaders: "In the iconographies of nationalism, images of mothers have conventionally invited symbols suggestive of primal origins – birth, hearth, home, roots, the umbilical cord of being – as encapsulated by terms such as 'mother-tongue,' 'mothercountry'" (1991, xxi).

Toward the end of the nineteenth century, many modernist Islamic thinkers embraced French political thought. This was especially the case in Egypt, which was at the forefront in the reform of Islam (Jayawardena 1987, ch. 3), and ideas flowing from Egypt were influential in other Middle East countries. Donohue and Esposito argue that Rifāʿa Rāfiʿ al-Ṭahṭāwī (1801–73) was the first writer to introduce these new concepts into Arabic (1982, 11), expressing the French notion of fatherland (*patrie*) by the Arabic *waṭan* (home area), and patriotism by *waṭaniyya*. He wrote:

> there are some indications that God disposed men to work together for the improvement of their fatherland and willed that they relate to one another as members of one family. God willed that the fatherland would . . .

> take the place of father and mother and tutor and would be the locus of happiness shared by men. Thus, it is not fitting that one nation be divided into numerous parties on the basis of different opinions, because partisanship begets contradictory pressures, envy and rancour with consequent lack of security in the fatherland (1982, 11).

Here the exposition of the fatherland expresses organicist political thought: the family brings harmony. But al-Ṭahṭāwī also envisages a modern democracy in which men are free and equal and membership of the "family" incurs obligations.

The ideas flowing from the French Revolution influenced Namık Kemal (1840–88), one of the most important intellectual leaders of the Young Ottomans in the later nineteenth century. He popularized the use of *waṭan* and these new meanings "took hold in all the main Middle East languages" (Keddie 1995, 243).

In his modernizing project for the Turkish nation, Mustafa Kemal (1881–1938) – Atatürk or Father of the Turks – employed images of the Father State (Devlet Baba) and the Motherland (Anavatan). While the idea of the "father state" had been employed under the Ottoman Empire, he embraced the concept in a new way, in particular by pairing it with the feminized "motherland." This was intended to provide a more overarching sense of identity than the *millet*s (nations) acknowledged under Ottoman rule: these were usually confessional groups, into which one was born, distinguished by a particular language and ethnic group (Delaney 1995, 179).

Delaney argues strongly for the translation of *vatan* (*waṭan*) in Turkish as "motherland," rather than the "fatherland" implied by the French translations of the activists mentioned above. Tohidi recounts a similar notion of homeland (*ana vatan*) as meaning "motherland" in Azerbaijan (1998, 118). (In Indonesian, *waṭan* is given a non-gendered gloss, but invokes the ideal of kinship – the *tanah tumpah darah*, or "land where the blood was spilled.") Palestinian nationalists have invoked gendered images of "the fertile mother-nation" and "Palestine as the Father's land" (Abdo 1994). In Azerbaijan, and in Palestine, the image of the mother nation or motherland conflates family and national morality: as mother, her honor must be defended and protected at all costs.

There is need for further scholarship on the articulation of national ideals and the use of the family trope, or derivative metaphors such as "motherland" and "fatherland." What are the implications for the everyday performance of gender, and of articulation of civic rights, of the invocation of such metaphors? How does the idea of defending the honor of the motherland flow into the vigilant and violent discipline of women that is especially associated with fundamentalist national regimes? How does the family metaphor condition the moral imperatives surrounding women's performance of femininity?

The origin of familial thinking

The idea of the family as a model for harmony tends to be historicized, the connection with ideas of "blood relations" asserting it as an autochthonous political theory. In discussing this move in Indonesian political thinking, Reid comments, the familial metaphor can be historically linked to "the current of organicism in European political thought, now discredited in the West because of its association with fascism" (Reid 1998, 25). In Indonesia, the historical trajectory can be traced, through the Leiden Law school and its influence on constitutional arrangements in the colonial period, and on the thinking of Indonesian nationalist lawyers who authored the 1945 constitution (which allows for centralization of executive power). Reid also links these ideas to the Japanese occupation during the Second World War and their idea of the family state (*kazoku kokka*).

Discussing the organicist familial model, Reid writes:

> The political features held to grow out of these principles are the organic unity of state and society, harmony and consensus rather than open debate and majority decision . . . the primacy of group needs over individual needs . . . and rejection of the standard elements of liberal constitutionalism, such as separation of powers and individual rights (1998, 25).

This ideology became a tool of political control for the Suharto regime, which ruled through domination of a state party. Each social "interest" was represented and bound together in a political process that disallowed open competition under the rubric of (familial) harmony, while in practice enshrining the rule of the father through a regime of state terror.

Fundamentalism represents itself as delving into the autochthonous roots of the nation, envisaged through Islamic texts. It is interesting that the "post-Confucian" Singapore, the theistic but not Islamic Indonesian New Order, and both secular and fundamentalist Islamic movements can utilize family metaphors as the basis of "nation." There is room for further explorations of the connections between the construction of women, the family, and the nation in fundamentalist and secular nationalist thought, seeking out links to other philosophical traditions and the force of those influences.

Family relations as "anti-history"

The familial/organic trope is not autochthonous, but it provides modes of political organization with the imprimatur of "history" or "tradition." Invocations of the cultural category "family" utilize the naturalizing power of ideology (drawing on notions of blood ties/nature). McClintock links the metaphorical equation of nation and family to the evolutionary modes of historical thought that emerged in the nineteenth century. After 1859 and the advent of Social Darwinism, the idea of the evolution of races/nations was conceptualized as a family tree in which "the family offered an indispensable metaphoric figure by which national difference could be shaped into a single historical genesis narrative which naturalized the idea of evolutionary progress, with the European family as the apogee. Within this narrative of progress, women were seen as 'inherently atavistic,' as the 'conservative repository of the national archaic'" (1995, 359).

The idea of the family as the national archaic was picked up by (male) secular nationalist reformers, in ideals about reforms in gender/family relations as part of the revolutionary social transformation that was to accompany moves to postcolonial independence. However, in many instances, colonial authorities as well as middle-class reform and nationalist groups left existing gender relations largely intact. Whereas colonial authorities did not tolerate the operation of Islamic law in areas such as criminal law, it was seen to be appropriate in family law/family relations. Eickelman and Piscatori comment that in Islamic nations there has been more resistance to changes in the arena of family law than in other spheres (1996, 94). (It is also an area where there is most difficulty in obtaining cooperation in international law.)

This has contributed to a scenario in which domestic life is regulated by Islam/custom; for example Tohidi comments on Azerbaijan in relation to Soviet rule: "The family thus becomes the *dār al-Islām* (domain of Islam) to be protected from the penetration of the dominant 'other'" (1998, 155). That is, the family (and particularly the mother) functions as the site of resistance against assimilation to the dominant culture. So the hierarchical structures and male control are reproduced, in a language of resistance and cultural preservation. Paradoxically, this has been possible because the Soviet Union left the Muslim male's domination of his private territory – women and the family – intact (1998, 118). Both secular nationalist and fundamentalist discourses have invoked ideals of Islamic morality in social control. Whether or not the state has a civil family code or whether Sharīʿa is allowed to operate without state intervention become important issues. "In many Third-World countries, Arab ones included, kinship and community are crucial organizers of social life. I don't see state institutions or civil society operating independently of kin-based relations . . . The people themselves don't separate public and private" (Joseph 1997, 68).

Sources

The printed word is inextricably linked to the genesis of the idea of nation and the achievement of nationhood (Anderson 1991). Nationalist movements leave volumes of written material but the development of national consciousness is also tied to new forms of narration, including ways of narrating the self – rich sources in the form of biographies and autobiographies as well as novels.

> The postcolonial female writer is not only involved in making herself heard, in changing the architecture of male-centered ideologies and language, or in discovering new forms and language to express her experience, she has also to subvert and demythologize indigenous male writings and traditions which seek to label her . . . In countries with a history of colonialism, women's quest for emancipation, self-identity and fulfilment can be seen to represent a traitorous act, a betrayal not simply of traditional codes of practice and belief but of the wider struggle for liberation and nationalism (Nasta 1991, xv).

Women's writing can "subvert and question the 'father tongue' and make way for a multiplicity of perspectives" (ibid., xvii). Boehmer suggests it is a source of counter-symbolic images of gender. Mary Poovey asks, "Did historically specific nationalisms . . . contribute to the normalization of an interiority constituted as trans-individual? Was this interiority gendered? How does it exist alongside that constituted by the family?" (cited in Hall 1993, 102). The question is how these iconic images are brought into play, and how they are challenged. Fictional writing can be a way to explore this. Does the icon of the mother have the same meaning for women as men? "Do nationalist vocabularies not implicate women in certain paradoxes of identity and affiliation?" (Boehmer 1991, 4). Boehmer suggests that "where male nationalists have claimed, won and ruled the 'motherland,' this same motherland may not signify 'home' and 'source' to women" (ibid., 5).

The historical records of nationalism and nationalist thinking (like many historical records) are gendered – men are more likely to operate in the public domain and to leave written records, while in most countries women's literacy has lagged behind that of men. Women writers, in particular, have drawn attention to the ways in which the illiterate participate in and reproduce nationalist thought. Other cultural materials are important; hence the analysis of rituals, sermons, symbols, and forms of oral expression, including poetry and song, and visual media including film and art/craft works.

Conclusions and further questions

An important task is the revisiting of nationalist discourse in regard to the translation of terms employed in familist and gendered metaphors. Have colonial stances in regard to families, gender regimes, and law impacted on familist and gendered tropes in nationalist thought? What are the continuities of political thought from European traditions, including the French and American revolutions, and in what ways do they involve familial metaphors? What have been the impacts of these transformations in bourgeois thinking for other social spheres? McClintock reminds us that "nations are not simply phantasmagoria of the mind, but are historical and institutional practices through which social difference is invented and performed" (1993, 61). The *Feminist Review* (1993) raises the question of the ways in which narratives of national identity become forms of individual subjectivity. How is affect mobilized on behalf of the nation? This question is especially important when investigating the emotive issues of motherhood, family, and honor and their relationship to issues of national identity and citizenship. What is required to achieve ideals of citizenship that are not gendered, notions of difference that do not imply/invoke inequality?

Islamic nationalism (in the sense of anticolonial and liberation struggles) can become caught up in a broader conceptualization of the struggle across national borders for the achievement of a united Islamic *umma* that transcends national boundaries. The limiting intimacy of the family trope is at odds with this. Is there an inherent tension between non-fundamentalist modes of Islamic political thought and the power of the (inherently authoritarian) family metaphor?

Bibliography

N. Abdo, Nationalism and feminism. Palestinian women and the intifada – No going back?, in V. M. Moghadam (ed.), *Gender and national identity. Women and politics in Muslim societies*, London 1994, 148–70.

M. Afkhami, Introduction, in M. Afkhami (ed.), *Faith and freedom. Women's human rights in the Muslim world*, Syracuse, N.Y. 1995, 1–16.

B. Anderson, *Imagined communities. Reflections on the origin and spread of nationalism*, London and New York 1991 (rev. ed.).

B. Baron, The construction of national honour in Egypt, in *Gender and History* 5:2 (Summer 1993), 244–55.

E. Boehmer, Stories of women and mothers. Gender and nationalism in the early fiction of Flora Nwapa, in S. Nasta (ed.), *Motherlands. Black women's writing from Africa, the Caribbean and South Africa*, London 1991, 3–23.

C. Delaney, Father State, Motherland, and the birth of modern Turkey, in S. Yanagisako and C. Delaney (eds.), *Naturalizing power. Essays in feminist cultural analysis*, New York 1995, 177–200.

J. J. Donohue, and J. L. Esposito (eds.), *Islam in transition. Muslim perspectives*, New York 1982.

D. F. Eickelman and J. Piscatori, *Muslim politics*, Princeton, N.J. 1996.

F. Fanon, *Black skin, white masks*, New York 1967.

Feminist Review, Special issue on nationalisms and national identities, 44 (Summer 1993).

Gender and History, Special issue on gender, nationalisms and national identities, 5:2 (1993).

C. Hall, Gender, nationalisms and national identities. Bellagio Symposium, July 1992, in *Feminist Review* 44 (Summer 1993), 97–103.

G. Heng and J. Devan, State fatherhood. The politics of nationalism, sexuality and race in Singapore, in A. Parker et al. (eds.), *Nationalisms and sexualities*, New York 1992, 343–64.

K. Jayawardena, *Feminism and nationalism in the Third World*, London 1987.

S. Joseph, Gender and civil society (interview with J. Stork), in J. Beinin and J. Stork (eds.), *Political Islam*, London 1997, 64–70.

D. Kandiyoti (ed.), *Women, Islam, and the state*, Basingstoke, Hampshire 1991.

N. R. Keddie, *Iran and the Muslim world*, New York 1995.

A. McClintock, Family feuds. Gender, nationalism and the family, in *Feminist Review* 44 (1993), 61–80.

——, *Imperial leather. Race, gender and sexuality in the colonial contest*, New York 1995.

V. Moghadam, Revolution, Islam and women. Sexual politics in Iran and Afghanistan, in A. Parker et al. (eds.), *Nationalisms and sexualities*, New York 1992, 424–46.

——, Patriarchy and the politics of gender in modernizing societies. Iran, Pakistan and Afghanistan, in *South Asia Bulletin* 13:1–2 (1993), 122–33.

——, *Gender and national identity. Women and politics in Muslim societies*, London 1994.

S. Nasta, Introduction, in S. Nasta (ed.), *Motherlands. Black women's writing from Africa, the Caribbean and South Asia*, London 1991, xiii–xxx.

A. Reid, Political "tradition" in Indonesia. The one and the many, in *Asian Studies Review* 22:1 (1998), 23–38.

K. Robinson, Women. Difference versus diversity, in D. K. Emmerson (ed.), *Indonesia beyond Suharto*, New York 1999, 237–61.

R. B. al-Tahtawi, Fatherland and patriotism, in J. J. Donohue and J. L. Esposito (eds.), *Islam in transition. Muslim perspectives*, New York and Oxford 1982, 11–15.

C. Timmerman, Muslim women and nationalism. The power of the image, in *Current Sociology* 48:4 (2000), 15–27.

N. Tohidi, "Guardians of the nations." Women, Islam and the Soviet legacy of modernization in Azerbaijan, in H. L. Bodman and N. Tohidi (eds.), *Women in Muslim societies. Diversity within unity*, Boulder, Colo. 1998, 137–61.

N. Yuval-Davis, *Gender and nation*, London 1997.

N. Yuval-Davis and F. Anthias (eds.), *Woman, nation, state,* Basingstoke, Hampshire 1989.
Women's Studies International Forum, special issue, Links across differences. Gender, ethnicity and nationalism, 19:1/2 (1996).

Kathryn Robinson

Family: Modern Islamic Discourses

Canada

This entry examines the debate over Islamic law in Canada and also introduces Irshad Manji, a controversial Islamic feminist.

The debate over the use of Sharīʿa (Islamic law) tribunals to settle disputes between Muslims in Canada has divided the Muslim community. Proponents of the Sharīʿa courts stress the importance of Islamic arbitration in cases concerning family law, although the courts can be used to solve any civil disputes. In Ontario, some Muslims have been using Islamic arbitration since 1991, when the Ontario Arbitration Act opened civil law cases to alternative arbitration. More recently a movement to standardize and generalize the use of Sharīʿa courts has gained momentum, with the goals of widening the scope of these courts beyond Ontario to all Canada, encouraging courts to uphold decisions made under Sharīʿa law, and rendering the Sharīʿa court's decisions binding for the parties involved. Canadian and international women's rights associations have responded by establishing a vigorous counter-movement against Sharīʿa law in Canada.

Retired lawyer Mumtaz Ali, the chief proponent and spiritual leader for the advancement of Sharīʿa law in Canada, founded the Islamic Institute for Civil Justice (Dār al-Qaḍāʾ) to forward the movement's aims in October 2003. Ali contends that since living under Sharīʿa law is a religious obligation for Muslims, Canada's recognition of the tribunal's legitimacy is an issue of human rights and religious freedom. Furthermore, he argues that the right to Sharīʿa tribunals is fully in accordance with the ideals of the Canadian Charter of Rights and Freedoms, since the use of these courts will be voluntary for all parties involved. However, as Ali's feminist critics are quick to point out, it is questionable whether the Sharīʿa option can be considered truly voluntary, given the internal pressures that will be placed upon members of the community to seek its services. This point is evinced by Ali's rhetorical polarization of the issue, in which he equates the desire to live under Sharīʿa law with the status of being a good Muslim. In a 1995 interview/address to his community, he tells Canadian Muslims that whoever prefers governance by secular Canadian family law over Sharīʿa law cannot claim to believe in Islam as a religion and a complete code of life actualized by the Prophet. He also claims that participation in the movement to establish Sharīʿa law constitutes a necessary moral duty for Canadian Muslims.

Although Ali stresses that Muslims are obliged to seek governance under Islamic law, he has limited the extent of his Sharīʿa campaign to issues concerning family law, content to leave penal and other law codes under the scope of secular law. Ali explains this apparent contradiction pragmatically, claiming that since family law is an area in which the Canadian judicial system could feasibly accommodate Muslim minority concerns, his decision to confine his movement to family issues is far more realistic and practical than trying to establish recourse to other aspects of Sharīʿa for Canadian Muslims.

In his online essay, "Complementarity Equanimity," Ali addresses the singular importance of family law for Muslims as a comprehensive system of rules for married life that governs the "delicate and diverse aspects of gender temperaments." He explains that for Muslims, the ideal of personal, psychological, rational, and physical harmony between spouses can be reached exclusively through reference to Sharīʿa law. Since marital harmony serves as a cornerstone for moral conduct and proper social behavior in general, the Sharīʿa-governed family must serve as the foundation for any Muslim society. A strict version of gender complementarity lies at the heart of Ali's ideology. Although the woman is afforded employment and property rights, Ali asserts that liberty of the woman does not run contrary to a general policy of Islam, which prescribes that the male take on the role of the head of the household and manage the affairs of the family.

Muslim Canadian women's associations have mobilized against the advancement of Sharīʿa law in Canada and this issue has garnered the attention of the international Muslim women's community as well. Most importantly, in crafting their statements of opposition, these groups offer alternative perspectives from which to see the debate to those provided by Mumtaz Ali. For example, the standpoint of the Canadian Council of Muslim Women (CCMW), Canada's most prominent Muslim women's organization, is developed from within an

Islamic framework, and thus successfully resists Ali's polarizing statements that categorize any opposition to his vision as un-Islamic. In its online position statement, the CCMW identifies itself as a pro-faith national organization that is not opposed to Sharīʿa in general, but that rather opposes the current plans to apply Sharīʿa in Canada. Against Ali's claims, the position statement points out that while Muslims have five beliefs and five pillars of practice, there is no sixth pillar or belief which states that Muslims have to practice *fiqh*, or Islamic arbitration.

The CCMW, with chief spokesperson Alia Hogben, have leveled their chief argument against the Sharīʿa campaign by challenging the notion that those who will use the Sharīʿa courts will do so voluntarily. Rather, because of sociocultural factors, many Canadian women will be coerced into choosing the Sharīʿa courts over the Canadian ones. They specify the written statements made by Mumtaz Ali, which stress that not following the Sharīʿa option is "tantamount to heresy-apostasy" as a particular focus of concern, identifying his rhetoric as coercive and as evidence against the voluntary nature of the Sharīʿa option. The CCMW position statement significantly explores the cultural and historical specificity of Muslim women in diaspora, and pinpoints their particular vulnerabilities to pressures from both their culture of origin and their host countries. Hogben points out that as newer immigrants, Canadian Muslims are searching for markers to identify themselves as a faith group, and the use of Sharīʿa serves as one such marker. Hogben expresses her concern that some Canadian Muslim women may be persuaded to use Sharīʿa, rather than seeking protection under the law of the land, as part of a struggle for identity rather than a search for justice. She calls attention to the role that the fears and anxieties of being new immigrants and a minority has in driving Canadian Muslims to construct an identity that incorporates diverse elements, including living under Muslim law, and cautions Muslim women that not all of these diverse elements are essential to living in Canada as practicing Muslims.

The position statement further challenges Mumtaz Ali's assumptions by proposing that a non-Muslim law, which is judged to be in harmony with the spirit of Islamic law, could serve as suitable basis for Islamic society in diaspora. The CCMW strongly states that it does not recognize any compelling reason to live under any form of law in Canada other than Canadian law, and demands the right to live under the same laws as other Canadian women. The association praises the Canadian Charter of Rights and Freedoms as a document that safeguards and protects women's equal rights, and claims that the values of Canadian law are also the cornerstones of Islam. In inverse relation to the goals of the Sharīʿa movement, the CCMW identifies its objective as assisting Canadian Muslim women to live under Canadian laws, which are congruent with Islamic ideals of social justice and equality.

The International Campaign for the Defense of Women's Rights in Iran is another organization leading a vigorous campaign against the Sharīʿa courts in Canada, although it adopts a secular framework from which to make its claims. Led by coordinator Homa Arjomand, this organization has engaged in awareness-raising through appearances on radio and television; Internet publications and newsletters; a sophisticated website; appeals to key government and judicial figures; panels for discussion and debate; and an online petition, which had been signed by 1,981 people by April 2004. Arjomand argues that adoption of the Sharīʿa tribunals constitutes a move against secularism, modernism, egalitarianism, and women's rights, and would send a message to women that they are undeserving of human rights protection. She points out that since the government is responsible for ensuring the safety and protection of all individuals and the civil rights and liberties of all citizens living in Canada, it is ultimately responsible for curtailing the influence of the Sharīʿa movement.

Besides being the locus of a heated debate over Sharīʿa law, Canada is also the home and base of a highly provocative Muslim woman speaker and writer, Irshad Manji. A television journalist and author of the bestselling book, *The Trouble with Islam: A Wake-Up Call for Honesty and Change*, Manji has garnered international attention, including death threats. In the first weeks after its publication, her book made front-page news across Canada and received immediate attention in Europe and the United States.

A native of Uganda, Manji emigrated to Vancouver, British Columbia with her family at the age of four, and joined the growing Islamic immigrant community there. Throughout her life and career, Manji has continued to question what she considers to be the inflexibilities of dominant Islam. Her message centers on the revivification of *ijtihād* (interpretation of religious texts), and she urges all Muslims to engage in critical reflection about their religion. Among her most controversial views are her questioning of the infallibility of the Qurʾān, her sympathy with both Arabs and Jews in Palestine, and her privileging of the West as the most suitable site from which to initiate Islamic reform.

Despite her radical views, Manji refuses to give up her Muslim identity, and instead levels her critique of dominant Islam from the vantage point of an insider. As a lesbian and a feminist, she diverges a long way from the usual standards of those who speak for Islam.

Bibliography

M. Ali, Complementary equanimity, 1992, <http:muslimcanada.org/equanimity.html>.

Canadian Council of Muslim Women, Position statement on the proposed implementation of sections of Muslim law in Canada, 2004, <http://www.ccmw.com/Position%20Papers/Position_Sharia_Law.htm>.

International Campaign Against *Sharīʿa* Court in Canada, 2004, <http://freehost14.websamba.com/noshariacourt/>.

Islamic Institute of Civil Justice, <http://muslim-canada.org/DARULQADAform.html>.

I. Manji, *The trouble with Islam. A wake-up call for honesty and change*, New York 2003.

R. Mills, Interview with Syed Mumtaz Ali. A review of the Muslim personal/family law campaign, 1995, <http://www.muslim-canada.org/pfl.pdf>.

Alisa Perkins

Central Asia

"We Central Asians are Muslims, so we must all marry and have children. Our parents are supposed to choose our husbands, unlike Russian girls. *They* have to manage by themselves and they cannot always find one," explained a Tajik girl from Dushanbe.

The family is at the center of Muslim society, and the relationship between spouses is prescribed in the Islamic family code, which is generally supposed to give men domination over their wives. In pre-revolutionary sedentary Central Asian families, each sex had distinct duties, women's centering round childbearing and housework, while men's were to protect and regulate the family, and provide material resources. The Sharīʿa allowed girls to be married as young as 9 and boys from 15 years of age, but parents might betroth their children at birth. Women were generally secluded. In theory, men might have up to four wives, whom they could easily divorce, but in practice most had difficulty in saving bride price and wedding costs for even one, and could ill afford to divorce her. On sufficient grounds women could petition the *qāḍī* courts for divorce, but this was rare, especially as it could be hard to support themselves afterwards. Even secluded women could earn money, which they were not obliged to contribute toward family finances, except in the poorest households.

In the nomadic societies, women were not secluded and could mix with men. Their responsibilities included putting up the *yurt* that was their portable dwelling place, and taking charge of the household for long periods, while the men took their livestock to pasture. Nevertheless, in these families men also dominated and women were little freer than their secluded sisters.

After the revolution, the Soviet government tried to transform the Central Asian family. Attention was particularly focused on a small set of traditional practices considered to result from the pernicious effects of religion. Starting in the 1920s polygyny, child marriage, forced marriage, and bride price (*kalym*) were all banned. The state tried to substitute civil marriage and divorce ceremonies for religious ones, and discouraged religious funerals and circumcision. Women were encouraged to abandon seclusion, educated, and taken into the workforce, thus upsetting the customary division of labor within the family, although men rarely took on domestic tasks in compensation.

Central Asians resisted these strategies by attempting to preserve traditional family values, legitimizing this by appeals more to religious norms than to the defense of their cultural heritage. Even those Central Asians who modernized their attitudes toward education and the workforce tended to retain traditional attitudes toward family relationships. Weddings of underage girls and polygynous unions were celebrated by *nikāḥ* without civil registration. Most marriages were still arranged, especially in rural Tajikistan and Uzbekistan. Brides had to submit to their husbands and obey their mothers-in-law, who often treated them as servants. Even women with high public status were expected to subordinate themselves at home. Frequently, all monies were placed in a common pot, so that women's earnings did not serve to gain them increased decision-making powers. Such changes as did occur were more often due to official pressures rather than individual commitment to modernity. For instance, parents who married underage daughters were liable to imprisonment, as were mullahs who officiated at marriage ceremonies.

Since independence, the governments of Central Asia have derived the construction of new national identities from religiously based traditional values that identify women with domesticity. This has been accompanied by Islamist discourses that strongly suggest that women's roles should be limited to those of housewife and mother, and also by a popular resurgence in customs formerly proscribed by the Soviet government but never completely abandoned, including polygyny. Proposals to legalize this last were unsuccessfully debated in the parliaments of several countries, including

Kyrgyzstan and Tajikistan. Nevertheless, men openly practice it, justifying this by religious doctrine.

Islamist discourse, especially in Uzbekistan, represents men as social, political, economic, and spiritual leaders for both nation and family, while women are portrayed as subordinate to their husbands, physically and emotionally dependent on them, owing to their supposed bodily frailty and weakness. Women are strongly encouraged to withdraw from the workforce into dependence. Some accept with relief the chance to terminate their labor burden but the more educated are appalled and resist.

While Islamists preach male dominance, many women seek greater equality in the home, and battle to educate their daughters, backed by women's non-governmental organizations that campaign for greater social equality. Even women who generally favor traditional gender identities have expressed dislike of current trends, especially polygyny.

Thus, the post-Soviet family is becoming a locus for struggle not just between men and women but also among different schools of thought – the traditional, the religious, the Sovietized, and the Westernized. The first two are based on differing interpretations of Islam, but even those favoring the last two still accept the importance of religious principles.

BIBLIOGRAPHY

F. Acar and A. Ayata (eds.), *Gender and identity construction. Women of Central Asia, the Caucasus and Turkey*, Leiden 2000.

T. Dahl, *The Muslim family. A study of women's rights in Islam*, Oslo 1997.

C. Harris, *Control and subversion. Gender relations in Tajikistan*, London 2004.

A. Ilkhamov, Impoverishment of the masses in the transition period. Signs of an emerging "new poor" identity in Uzbekistan, in *Central Asian Survey* 20:1 (2001), 33–54.

M. Kamp, *Unveiling Uzbek women. Liberation, representation and discourse, 1906–1929*, Chicago 1998.

K. R. Kuehnast, Let the stone lie where it has fallen. Dilemmas of gender and generation in post-Soviet Kyrgyzstan, Ph.D. diss., University of Minnesota 1997.

G. Tett, Ambiguous alliances. Marriage and identity in a Muslim village in Soviet Tajikistan, Ph.D. thesis, University of Cambridge 1995.

M. Tokhtakhodjaeva, *Between the slogans of communism and the laws of Islam*, trans. S. Aslam, ed. C. Balchin, Lahore 1995.

M. Tolmacheva, The Muslim woman in Soviet Central Asia, in *Central Asian Survey* 12:4 (1993), 531–48.

Women Living Under Muslim Laws, *For ourselves. Women reading the Quran*, Lahore 1997.

COLETTE HARRIS

Iran and Afghanistan

Iran and Afghanistan are neighboring Muslim countries with long historical ties that evolved somewhat differently in the course of the twentieth century. They have had divergent encounters with modernity, and varied levels of socioeconomic development (urbanization, industrialization, class formation) and state capacity. Yet in the late twentieth century, both countries experienced revolutions and religio-political conflicts in which discourses about women, gender, and the family figured prominently.

IRAN

The Iranian Revolution against the Shah, which unfolded between spring 1977 and February 1979, was joined by countless women. The large street demonstrations included huge contingents of women wearing the veil as a symbol of opposition to Pahlavī bourgeois or Westernized decadence. The idea that women had "lost honor" during the Pahlavī era was a widespread one. The Islamists in Iran felt that "genuine Iranian cultural identity" had been distorted by Westernization. Islamists projected the image of the noble, militant, and selfless Fāṭima – daughter of the Prophet Muḥammad, earlier popularized by the late Islamist scholar ʿAlī Sharīʿatī – as the most appropriate model for the new Iranian womanhood (Tohidi 1994, Najmabadi 1994).

Such views shaped the new Islamic regime's policies and laws on women, gender, family, and religion. The 1979 constitution spelled out the place of women in the ideal Islamic society that the new leadership was trying to establish: within the family, through the "precious foundation of motherhood," rearing committed Muslims. The Islamic Republic emphasized the distinctiveness of male and female roles, a preference for the privatization of female roles (although public activity by women was never barred, and women retained the vote), and the socially valuable nature of motherhood and domesticity. *Ḥijāb* and sex-segregation in public spaces were made compulsory, and certain fields of study, professions, and occupations were decreed to be off-limits to women. With the abrogation of the Pahlavī state's family law, the Islamic state lowered the age of marriage for girls to puberty, made access to contraception difficult, reinstated polygyny, permitted men the right to easy divorce (but all but denied women the right to divorce), and granted men total headship over families, including sole custody over children after divorce, and the right to "discipline" wives and children. Wives were required to obtain the permission of husbands for purposes of travel or employment. The new policies and laws were enacted under the banner of the promotion of Islam, the struggle against colonialist and imperialist plots, and the protection of culture, morality, and family.

AFGHANISTAN

In April 1978 the People's Democratic Party of Afghanistan (PDPA) seized power in what came to be called the Saur (April) Revolution and established the Democratic Republic of Afghanistan (DRA). The DRA introduced a radical reform program to modernize Afghan society. These included the government promulgated Decree No. 7, which would enhance the status of women and girls within the family while also reducing the high costs of marriage and the prevalence of indebtedness among rural households.

The first two articles in Decree No. 7 forbade the exchange of a woman in marriage for cash or kind, customarily due from a bridegroom on festive occasions; the third article set an upper limit of 300 afghanis, the equivalent of $10 at that time, on the *mahr.*

Articles 4 to 6 of the decree set the ages of first engagement and marriage at 16 for women and 18 for men. The decree further stipulated that no one could be compelled to marry against his or her will, including widows. Aware that abolishing polygamy would engender considerable hostility, the PDPA prohibited its members from practicing it.

The PDPA attempts to change marriage practices, expand literacy, and educate rural girls met with strong opposition. Unlike Iran, the Afghan state was not a strong one, able to impose its will through an extensive administrative and military apparatus.

Discourses of women, gender, family, and Islam have figured prominently in political developments in Iran and Afghanistan since at least the late 1970s. In Iran, compulsory veiling signaled the (re)definition of gender rules, and the veiled woman came to symbolize the moral and cultural transformation of society. In Afghanistan, uncovering women, raising their status within the family, and promoting their schooling and social participation were the chief markers of the socialist modernizing project of the DRA. Further divergences, however, took place in the late 1990s and into the twenty-first century. Iranian women's rights activists, both Islamic and secular, succeeded in effecting some changes to discriminatory gender policies and the family law. Moreover, as their educational attainment rates rose, women began to marry later and have fewer children. Meanwhile, Afghan women experienced a draconian gender regime under the Taliban, who claimed that Islam and Afghan tradition mandated the confinement of women to their homes and the *burqaʿ*. The post-Taliban transition brought about some relief, but schooling was still inaccessible to most rural girls, for whom marriage and childbearing remain the main life option. The new constitution of the Islamic Republic of Afghanistan (approved January 2004) stipulates the equality of all Afghan citizens, women and men, and calls on the state to "devise and implement effective programs for balancing and promoting of education for women" (Article 44). It also states that the "family is a fundamental unit of society and is supported by the state. The state adopts necessary measures to ensure physical and psychological well being of family, especially of child and mother, upbringing of children and the elimination of traditions contrary to the principles of sacred religion of Islam" (Article 54).

BIBLIOGRAPHY

H. Emadi, *Repression, resistance, and women in Afghanistan*, Westport, Conn. 2002.

V. Gregorian, *The emergence of modern Afghanistan. Politics of reform and modernization, 1880–1946*, Stanford, Calif. 1969.

V. M. Moghadam, Patriarchy and the politics of public space in Afghanistan, in *Women's Studies International Forum* 25:1 (Spring 2002), 1–13.

——, *Modernizing women. Gender and social change in the Middle East*, Boulder, Colo. 1993, 2003[2].

A. Najmabadi, Power, morality, and the new Muslim womanhood, in M. Weiner and A. Banuazizi (eds.), *The politics of social transformation in Afghanistan, Iran, and Pakistan*, Syracuse, N.Y. 1994, 336–89.

G. Nashat (ed.), *Women and revolution in Iran*, Boulder, Colo. 1983.

S. K. Nawid, *Religious response to social change in Afghanistan 1919–1929. King Aman-Allah and the Afghan ulama*, Costa Mesa 1999.

A. Tabari and N. Yeganeh (eds.), *In the shadow of Islam. The women's movement in Iran*, London 1982.

N. Tapper, Causes and consequences of the abolition of brideprice in Afghanistan, in N. Shahrani and R. Canfield (eds.), *Revolutions and rebellions in Afghanistan*, Berkeley 1984, 291–305.

N. Tohidi, Modernity, Islamization, and women in Iran, in V. M. Moghadam (ed.), *Gender and national identity. Women and politics in Muslim societies*, London 1994, 114–47.

VALENTINE M. MOGHADAM

Turkey and the Caucasus

Throughout history, the family has been considered the backbone of Turkish and Caucasian societies, and its importance was reinforced by religion. Among the Turkish societies of the region, the family is seen as sacred and protected by God, and women are regarded as such an integral part of the family that the Turkish word for family, *aile*, is sometimes used to refer to a wife. However, the position of women in the family and society varies greatly and may seem both emancipatory and restrictive, as it has historically been the target of both progressive and traditional orientations. In this entry, women's intra-family status is considered within a sociohistorical context by examining similarities and differences between Turkey and the Caucasus.

One common element is that the states of both the Turkish Republic and the former Soviet Union, the two major sovereign sociopolitical powers in the area, were involved in initiating changes in women's status, which was seen as pivotal to efforts at modernization. In these secular polities women were encouraged and given the opportunity to live public lives, involving educational and occupational attainments.

Beyond this apparent similarity, however, the role envisaged for women in the policies of these two states has been radically different. In the Caucasus, the reforms were seen as being imposed by the ruling Soviet state, in order to benefit from the economic potential of women's labor. Educated, career-oriented women who in the public realm symbolized Soviet emancipation were, in the private realm of the family, expected to be the custodians and perpetuators of religious and familial traditions. At home the Islamic component of their identity was an important marker of differentiation from the Russians (Shami 2000). Caucasian women had to reconcile the varied, and at times conflicting, expectations of the Soviet state and their Muslim communities. The assertive professional women of the public realm resorted to docility and submission at home to protect their men's sense of masculinity in the quasi-colonial context of the Soviet period (Tohidi 2000), and played a significant role in providing religious education, and in resisting the process of Russification (Heyat 2000, Shami 2000). Thus, the emphasis put on the persistence of the traditional family (and the related patriarchal values and religio-ethnic norms) entailed paradoxical gender implications: the family served as a buffer against external pressures by offering support and solidarity but it also functioned as a repressor of women's independence and personal growth. Though some women expressed resentment, most regarded the family as a "mixed blessing," "the *dar al-Islam* to be protected from the penetration of the dominant 'other'" (Tohidi 2000, 281).

In contrast, in Turkey, rather than being imposed by an external ruling power, as in the Caucasus, the well-educated, professional women prototype was regarded as the building block of the new modern outlook of the Turkish national republican identity. This outlook was rooted in the nationalist ideologies going back to the modernization efforts of the Ottoman Empire in the nineteenth century (Jayawardena 1986). The demands for women's rights had legitimacy according to the authentic nationalist and religious traditions, that is, the original Turkic roots, and "the tenets of pure Islam cleansed of misinterpretations" (Minai 1981, 48); and many laws and regulations were accepted to secure gender equality in different domains of life.

Beliefs and traditions often tend to lag behind legal changes, particularly in rural areas. Urban settings respond more quickly. Today, in spite of certain difficulties, particularly concerning the slow change in the role of the male, as well as problems in maintaining relationships with the extended families, Turkish urban families, on the whole, seem to be moving in the direction of achieving a state of cooperative interdependence based on relative egalitarianism, with increases in socioeconomic development (Imamoğlu 2000). Age at marriage and education play an important role in the emergence of a modern outlook toward marriage and family, especially for women. Better educated urban women are more likely to marry husbands of their own choice and at older ages, to contribute more as breadwinners, and to participate more in family decisions. Women's power in the family tends to increase with increases in their socioeconomic status and modernism, whereas the more modern husbands of higher socioeconomic status tend to wield less power than the more traditional husbands of lower socioeconomic status. Although the nuclear family type is widely prevalent, ties with the extended family are often very close (Imamoğlu 2000).

The process of transformation of Turkish women's traditional roles has been interlocked with the process of constructing a new progressive nation-state and national identity in this Muslim society with a secular state. Because the Islamic cultural heritage has been regarded as an inseparable aspect of Turkish nationalism, the modernization efforts of the secular state toward becoming a part of the international system have been, for the most part, embraced by the great majority of the Turkish people (Olson 1985), although religiosity still tends to be generally associated with a more authoritarian outlook and traditional attitudes toward gender (Imamoğlu 1999).

In the Caucasus, although egalitarian gender relations constituted an important aspect of the nationalist writings of the Turkic ethnic groups of the area when they were colonized by Russia (Rorlich 2000), in the new states, in contrast, nationalist efforts often involve a rejection of anything associated with Soviet colonialism, and hence pose problems for women. As compared to the early Turkic nationalists, contemporary nationalists of the post-Soviet Caucasus have adopted more conservative interpretations of Islam, which has come to represent an opposition to the Soviet-imposed communism and Westernization. Patriarchal relations and traditional gender division of labor are increasing as part of such nation-building efforts; for example, the tendency to marry at a younger age and bear many children is held up as the sacred duty of women to their nations; many women do not object to this because of their feeling of having been worn down by the "double burden" of the Soviet era (Tohidi 2000). Thus Caucasian women face the major burden of the current difficulties of the economic transformation of the socialist states; these indirectly influence women's family status by reinforcing gender-based traditional division of labor and hampering their public participation (Shami 2000).

Thus, in spite of some progressive changes, issues involving gender and family are so closely identified with the Islamic cultural traditions that they continue to elicit conservative political reactions, even today. The strong family traditions and religion of the people of this region, who have recently been exposed to the widespread tensions of rapid change in different areas of life, have been important sources of support and meaning as well as a means of restriction. Still, the more liberal and democratic trends among the progressive segments of the area may pave the way toward promoting more egalitarian, gender-sensitive relationships in these societies, as suggested by the Turkish urban trends.

Bibliography

F. Heyat, Azeri professional women's life strategies in the Soviet context, in F. Acar and A. Güneş-Ayata (eds.), *Gender and identity construction. Women of Central Asia, the Caucasus and Turkey*, Leiden 2000, 177–201.

E. O. Imamoğlu, Some correlates of religiosity among Turkish adults and elderly within a cross-cultural perspective, in L. E. Thomas and S. S. Eisenhandler (eds.), *Religion, belief, and spirituality in late life*, New York 1999, 93–110.

——, Changing gender roles and marital satisfaction in Turkey, in F. Acar and A. Güneş-Ayata (eds.), *Gender and identity construction. Women of Central Asia, the Caucasus and Turkey*, Leiden 2000, 101–16.

K. Jayawardena, "Civilization" through women's emancipation in Turkey, in K. Jayawardena, *Feminism and nationalism in the Third World*, London 1986, 1989[3], 25–42.

N. Minai, *Women in Islam. Tradition and transition in the Middle East*, New York 1981.

E. A. Olson, Muslim identity and secularism in contemporary Turkey. "The headscarf dispute," in *Anthropological Quarterly* 58:4 (1985), 161–71.

A. Rorlich, Intersecting discourses in the press of Muslims of Crimea, Middle Volga and the Caucasus. The woman question and the nation, in F. Acar and A. Güneş-Ayata (eds.), *Gender and identity construction. Women of Central Asia, the Caucasus and Turkey*, Leiden 2000, 143–61.

S. Shami, Engendering social memory. Domestic rituals, resistance and identity in the North Caucasus, in F. Acar and A. Güneş-Ayata (eds.), *Gender and identity construction. Women of Central Asia, the Caucasus and Turkey*, Leiden 2000, 306–31.

N. Tohidi, Gender and national identity in post-Soviet Azerbaijan. A regional perspective, in F. Acar and A. Güneş-Ayata (eds.), *Gender and identity construction. Women of Central Asia, the Caucasus and Turkey*, Leiden 2000, 249–92.

E. Olcay Imamoğlu

The United States

It is helpful to characterize Islamic discourses on family in the United States by distinguishing four social constellations: early migration followed by adaptation; the rise of African-American Islam; the developments attending the feminist agenda; and the reactions to the rise of Islamism (fundamentalism). While each has its own trajectory, none operates without interaction with the others. Despite attending complexities, the constellations do provide structures through which the Islamic experience can be understood.

Early migration followed by adaptation

The stage was set for Islam in the Unites States to be gendered in a specific way by migration patterns. The earliest Muslim migrants were males who came to work. They came without spouses. It is important to note this fact because one of the ideological bases of traditional Islam has been the critical role of family in defining Muslim life. Family is essential to *umma* (community) formation, which itself is a kind of family writ large, but it is also significant because of the theologically-sanctioned relationship of the sexes, which is gendered while being cohesive. This theological ideology began with the Qurʾān, and it has remained a central feature of Islamic societies ever since.

In effect, then, the beginnings of Islam in the United States arose without Muslim women being present, a situation unnatural from a religious point of view. Furthermore, restricted by laws that curtailed the immigration of certain nationalities (such as the Arabs), Muslims discovered that establishing families often required extraordinary effort (importing a spouse from a distant country). Not until 1965 were these laws to relax and allow a much more free-flowing creation of family life to occur. American Muslim women faced the additional problem that they could not marry unless the husband-to-be professed Islam. Spousal conversion is a significant theme encountered from the inception of Islam in North America. When it failed, parents had to send daughters back to the country of original to procure suitable mates, usually through the good offices of a relative. Poor families could not afford this luxury and even wealthier Muslims found it problematic. Moreover, while arranged marriages are the norm in Islam, such marriages usually only apply to the first, with the result that divorced immigrant women, or women whose husbands are deceased, must rely on their own initiative or well-placed community resources to find a further spouse.

Another area of conflict was the Muslim acceptance of polygamy, a practice at odds with law in the United States; those who had more than one wife had to adopt divergent means, such as maintaining a second household, but without the legal benefits accorded the first wife under the law of the country. Clearly the roadblocks to appropriate marriage spurred adaptation, and marriages were often brokered with a Muslim from a different ethnic group, or even of a different, but related religious group, such as Christian Arabs, providing continuity at least in cultural if not in religious affairs.

Early on, Muslim gendered differentiation also had an impact on attitudes toward premarital sex. Values derived from Muslim countries affirmed the central role of the female in maintaining family legitimacy and/or Islamic veracity, and for the immigrant community, great emphasis was placed on a segregated and honor-bound space for Muslim girls. By contrast, while sexual experimentation with non-Muslim women was officially denounced by religious authorities, it was often tolerated for young males. By the twenty-first century these concerns had shifted. Faced with the threat to family integrity posed by HIV and other sexually-transmitted diseases, families became equally concerned that both males and females adhere to a Muslim standard, whether they be male or female. Where parents of daughters were almost universally concerned about the perils of sexual involvement with young men, now many American Muslim parents fret just as much over the potential waywardness of sons. Hence resistance to the perceived rampant sexual freedom in American society is now enjoined upon all youth. Since arranged marriages continue to be the vehicle of choice for Muslim youth of immigrant families, the concept of marriage as a contract between families, rather than individuals committing themselves to each other, continues to be an important feature of Islamic life.

The rise of African-American Islam

With the advent of the Moorish Science Temple in 1913, Timothy Drew began the articulation of a discrete and crucial element in contemporary American culture: the African-American Muslim movement. Its most vigorous and empowered son was to be Elijah Muhammad (1897–1975), whose Nation of Islam succeeded in reaching the poor and largely neglected inner city ghettos. The movement was partly successful because Elijah Muhammad insisted on the validity of the Nation's family life. For him, broken homes with many children, all without the required Islamic male supervision, were wreaking havoc in African-American society. He set out to re-establish the traditional Islamic family structure through several innovative ways: he built upon the strength of women to construct his educational institutions and women's organizations; he insisted on the training of girls as much as boys; he reinforced the role of women in the home and family by highlighting their achievements; and he assigned his paramilitary organization, the Fruit of Islam, a role in disciplining recalcitrant males. He aggressively insisted on the Fruit's role in re-directing male responsibilities toward spouses and children. He affirmed the Islamic norm of marriage contracts and commitments. All these actions, and others of similar intent, were to have a powerful impact on the burgeoning growth of the movement.

The success of Elijah Muhammad may be the most spectacular, but it is not the only African-American story. Charged by a religious sense of *hijra*, or migration, African-Americans clustered into little communities, attempting to withdraw from the larger society into a space bordered by an Islamic consciousness. Such social experiments as Jabul Arabiyya in West Valley, New York, or the Universal Islamic Brotherhood in Cleveland established a sense of distinctiveness and promoted a connectedness to Muslim culture in the Middle East and Africa. Key to the founding of these communities was the Islamization of gender, marriage, and family. Thus, Imam Da'ud, founder of the Universal Islamic Brotherhood, insisted on the segregation of boys from girls in his schools, instituted the use of veils for all women and girls, and promoted a sense of equal but distinctive space within the community, in effect, a gendered space similar to that found in the Middle East. Moreover, marriage was not only planned by parents, and approved by the imam, but the youthful adolescents who were married lived under the supervision of adults until such time as they were deemed sufficiently mature to manage on their own. All this was in keeping with the belief that Islamic society required strong disciplinary leadership to protect the community against the sexual evils of society at large, and to foster a true women's role. These utopian communities looked to the Prophet Muḥammad's political position in Medina, and to his relationships with his wives as models for constructing a valid American Muslim identity.

The developments attending the feminist agenda

Feminist ideology has also had a marked impact on Muslims in the United States. Concerns over the role and position of women in a patriarchal society developed into a full-blown critique of the inequities between men and women in Western culture. However, it is important to note that the roots of the feminist critique begin not with feminist contentions of the twentieth century, but with Western critiques of Islam from the medieval period, when Christian adversaries singled out Muḥammad's relationships with women as demonstrative of Islam's inferiority. The result was that females and their roles in Islam became a lightning rod for anti-Islamic fervor in the West. The intensity of this critique guaranteed that gender issues would dominate the symbolic world of cultural knowledge, making it virtually impossible today to comprehend the nuances of Muslim women's actual lives. Reactions to the virulence of this campaign began to be felt in the Muslim world, with the result that such elements as Muslim dress codes became ways of expressing identity, difference, and ultimately rejection of the West. In sum, many contemporary aspects of Muslim women's lives, and the meaning of their gendered existences, arise out of an agenda imposed by or in reaction to the Western interpretation of the feminine.

It is not surprising, then, that Islamic sensitivities to the feminist critique should take several contentious forms. There are advocates of Islamic feminism, Islamicist (fundamentalist) feminism, and Islamic womanism in various permutations throughout the United States. The first accepts that the Western critique of Islamic society and the way it treats women is somewhat justified; Muslim scholars such as Mernissi, Ahmad, and Hassan portray Muslim society as patriarchal, while carefully disengaging the Qurʾān from their critique. They insist that Islam must return to the equality present in the Qurʾān's teachings and in the life of the Prophet in order to free itself from the distortion that centuries of patriarchal exegesis have introduced. Moreover, some American Muslim women see both the conceptualization of woman's body and the submissive discourse within traditional Qurʾānic understandings as problematic for the true achievement of an equal gender ideology. Fundamentalist or Islamicist feminism eschews this discourse, holding that such analyses are merely the application of secularist doctrine to a religious culture that rejects the secular outright. These feminists argue for an Islam disengaged from its cultural moorings, and point to an Islam of religious power and authority affirming the original vision of God's Holy Book. Writers such as Dunya Maumoon insist on the veracity of the Qurʾān's depiction of women and their rights; furthermore, Mahmood and others see ample evidence of a distinctive affirming of women's body and a contextualized meaning of submissiveness within Islamicist doctrine. Still others react to long-standing Muslim antagonism to the very term feminism, and try to shape a new perspective that will embrace the best within Islamic culture without challenging the basis of the Qurʾān's own wording. Dubbed Islamic womanism, this trend regards the distinctive emphasis placed on the "feminine" to be quite foreign to Islam, insisting that the true Islamic understanding of gender is one of complementarity. Theoretically akin to Dove's argument for postcolonial Africa, womanist discourse sees "traditional" Muslim society as importantly, but differently, matriarchal, with roles and responsibilities that allow gender to function synergistically in the wider Islamic culture. Womanists see this as anything but a passive discussion; rather they insist upon the gender equality in the Qurʾān as the foundation for discourses within Muslim homes and communities, a kind of participatory process of determining true Islamic identity. Barazangi terms this "participatory feminism," but it is feminist only to the extent that it begins its analysis from what women contribute to the corporate Muslim whole. Within the American context, then, feminism has been a catalyst that has sparked a heated debate both within and without the *umma*, and has cognate significance for Muslim women, gender issues, and family life.

Reactions to the rise of Islamism (fundamentalism)

While feminist discourses have been carried on largely at the formal and academic levels, it is important to note that they have also had a significant impact on the street. Islamicist and revivalist trends have heightened conflicting positions. The use of the *ḥijāb* among women is a rising feature within Muslim enclaves in major cities, signaling an awareness of the distinctiveness of American Muslim culture; arguments for specifically Muslim social services, based on "Muslim values" or "multiculturalism" can regularly be heard, and just as regularly contested; voices against a distinctive Muslim dress code have been raised within American institutions, based on the visibility prejudices attending the attacks of 11 September 2001; separate schools for Muslim boys and girls are now found throughout the United States, along with the implied rejection of American public educational culture; males are insisting on their position as the public representative of the family, even while mosque organizations struggle to articulate an "official" role for women; the hegemony of males over religious and social institutions is being challenged within the local communities by effective women leaders; veiled women have once again been singled out as in need of liberation, even as Islamic feminists carry new Qurʾānic interpretations into the nation's television and media outlets.

The very violence of the Islamist agenda has upset other Muslim women, who urge that their image of nurturing and shaping the next generation is being hijacked by an Islam over which they have little control, and to which there is only limited commitment within the community at large. Many Muslim women have pointed out that the United States has sustained their families, promoted their well-being and allowed them to grow, all values consistent with the Islam they embrace. Those women who self-identify with radical Islam have little in common with the ordinary Muslim woman in the United States, who finds the foregrounding of killing in the name of Islam antithetical to her treasured role as mother and community builder.

All four constellations interact with varying intensities among Muslims in the United States today.

Bibliography

L. Ahmad, *Women and gender in Islam. Historical roots of a modern debate*, New Haven, Conn. 1992.

N. H. Barazangi, Muslim women's Islamic higher learning as a human right. Theory and practice, in G. Webb (ed.), *Windows of faith. Muslim women scholar-activists in North America*, Syracuse, N.Y. 2000, 22–47.

——, Participatory feminism, at <www.einaudi.cornell.edu/parfem/working paper.htm>, 2003.

R. M. Dannin, The greatest migration, in Y. Y. Haddad and J. I. Smith (eds.), *Muslim minorities in the West. Visible and invisible*, Walnut Creek, Calif. 2002, 59–76.

N. Dove, African womanism, in *Journal of Black Studies* 28:5 (1998), 515–40.

R. Hassan, Muslim women and post-patriarchal Islam, in P. Cooey, W. Eakin, and J. McDaniel (eds.), *After patriarchy. Feminist transformations of the world religions*, Maryknoll, N.Y. 1991, 39–63.

S. Mahmood, Feminist theory, embodiment, and the docile agent. Some reflections on the Islamic revival, in *Cultural Anthropology* 6:2 (2001), 202–36.

D. Maumoon, Islamism and gender activism. Muslim women's quest for autonomy, in *Journal of Muslim Minority Affairs* 19:2 (October 1999), 269–83.

F. Mernissi, *The veil and the male elite. A feminist interpretation of women's rights in Islam*, trans. M. J. Lakeland, Reading, Mass. 1991.

——, *Women and Islam. A historical and theological enquiry*, trans. M. J. Lakeland, Oxford 1991.

K. M. Moore, *Law and the transformation of Muslim life in the United States*, Albany, N.Y. 1994.

A. Sachedina, Woman, half-the-man. The crisis of male epistemology in Islamic jurisprudence, in F. Daftary (ed.), *Intellectual traditions in Islam*, London 2000, 160–78.

S. Yousef, *Islamic work. Muslim women misunderstood*, Chicago 1993.

Earle Waugh

Fatwa

Overview

In Islamic legal parlance, fatwa (*fatwā*, pl. *fatāwā*) refers to a clarification of an ambiguous judicial point or an opinion by a *mufti*, a jurist trained in Islamic law, in response to a query posed by a judge (*qāḍī*) or a private inquirer (*mustaftī*). It is not a binding judgment or verdict – that is for a judge to deliver. Although the practice of issuing fatwas dates back to the earliest days of Islam, the term gained worldwide notoriety in 1989 following Ayatollah Khomeini's fatwa against the British author Salman Rushdie; Khomeini charged Rushdie with blasphemy in his novel *The Satanic Verses* and pronounced a death sentence on the author. Soon there were reports of similar fatwas against the Egyptian novelist Naguib Mahfouz and the Bangladeshi novelist Taslima Nasreen. The greater awareness of and attention to the term fatwa since the late 1980s is reflected in both the increased international media coverage of current fatwas as well as the greater number of scholarly works on historical and contemporary fatwas that has been produced in both Muslim and non-Muslim contexts. It would be inaccurate, however, to attribute the increasing number of fatwas pertaining to women (the primary concern in this entry) in Islamic societies entirely to the renewed prominence of the term itself. Throughout Islamic history, fatwas have been sought in greater than usual numbers during times of change and transition, and this is also true of the late twentieth century; as a result of state policies, the efforts of non-governmental organizations (NGOs), as well as the growth of Islamist politics, women in Muslim societies are increasingly confronted with new public roles and opportunities. Thus, while in the nineteenth century Muslims in Iran, Algeria, and India sought fatwas on how to interact with the new non-Muslim colonial powers, laws, and customs in their midst, today Muslims pose such questions as: what is appropriate dress for women? Can women shake hands with men? Are beauty pageants contrary to Islam? Can women vote? Can women participate in Christian-funded development activities?

The high profile fatwas mentioned earlier raise important questions that are relevant to a broader discussion of the role of fatwas today and how they affect the lives and behavior of ordinary women in Islamic societies. By issuing a fatwa on behalf of the Muslim *umma* (community of believers), Khomeini granted himself the authority to speak on behalf of Muslims everywhere. The question then arises, who has the authority to issue a fatwa? The varied responses to Khomeini's fatwa among Muslims themselves lead to a second related question: upon whom is a fatwa binding and under what circumstances? Finally, on what topics can fatwas be issued? This entry explores these questions in the context of recent decades, with particular attention to fatwas pertaining to women in two populous Muslim-majority countries, Egypt and Bangladesh.

Muslim countries today vary in the importance they attach to official muftis. Egypt, for instance, has had an official Dār al-Iftā' (office that issues fatwas) since 1895, headed by the country's grand mufti. In addition to the Dār al-Iftā', Egypt is home, of course, to that venerable seat of Islamic learning, al-Azhar University, headed by the grand shaykh. For some observers, both institutions' close ties to the Egyptian state have given their decrees legitimacy; according to critics, they have become mere pawns of an undemocratic government. Interestingly, recent years have seen open disagreement between the two institutions on many controversial issues, including international politics. Bangladesh, which came into existence only in 1971, was established as a secular state and has no comparable national institution for fatwas. There, the term fatwa exploded onto the national scene in the early 1990s with a fatwa against Taslima Nasreen, issued by an obscure group that accused her of blasphemy and offered a reward for her execution; the international media quickly dubbed her the "female Rushdie." This was accompanied by reports of rural fatwas – decrees by village-based religious leaders – against village women accused of having behaved in an un-Islamic manner. The norms of Islamic jurisprudence would deem these men unqualified to issue fatwas, yet local villagers took their pronouncements as binding decrees and went on to commit acts of often brutal violence against the women in question.

While there is some confusion then in Muslim societies about who exactly is authorized to give a fatwa, most Muslims do assume that only men can issue fatwas; indeed, there have been no official female muftis anywhere in the Muslim world.

Although women learned in Islamic law have been giving unofficial religious advice, essentially fatwas, through the ages, there is still no official sanction for a woman mufti. In 1999, Dr. Suʿād Ṣalāḥ, head of the department of *fiqh* (jurisprudence) in the faculty of Islamic and Arabic studies for girls at al-Azhar University, approached Grand Mufti Naṣr Farīd Wāṣil offering to serve as his assistant, without salary, and be responsible for fatwas solely on women's affairs. She pointed out that there was nothing in the Qurʾān or *ḥadīth* to suggest that this would be contrary to Islam, yet she never received a response from him.

A relatively new development that may open up possibilities for women to offer fatwas is the world of cyber-fatwas. While, traditionally, a private individual in need of religious advice would travel as far as necessary to pose his question in person to an appropriately qualified and respected mufti, today Muslims throughout the world can send their queries across cyberspace with the click of a mouse. There are advantages and disadvantages to the phenomenon. The greatest advantages perhaps are that, first, individuals who would be hesitant or for any reason unable to travel to a "live" mufti can seek information as long as he or she has access to the Internet (a fairly small group of course); second, individuals can pose questions about intimate matters that they would be loathe to broach in person. The disadvantages are that it is not possible to verify the qualifications of the mufti or the authenticity of the information he or she provides; moreover, given the global nature of the web, it is unlikely that the mufti has solid knowledge of the local context within which the *mustaftī*, the person posing the question, operates. One solution seen in Egypt today are the Egyptian tele-evangelists, websites, and "dial-a-fatwa" hotlines; these represent modern alternatives to the traditional muftis yet are sufficiently locally situated that they can draw on both their knowledge of local practices and religious texts when preparing a fatwa.

EGYPT

Significant early twentieth-century Egyptian fatwas regarding women included: permission for family planning as early as the 1930s; a 1942 sanction for women to pray in mosques; a 1952 prohibition on women's suffrage on the grounds that voting and running for election are rights restricted to men (though Egyptian women did receive both rights in 1956). In 1979, Grand Mufti Jād al-Ḥaqq ʿAlī Jād al-Ḥaqq openly expressed his support for the so-called Jihān law; in response to outrage at the new law on the part of many members of the Islamic establishment, Jād al-Ḥaqq issued a long fatwa arguing that laws making polygamy more difficult for men and permitting women to leave their homes without their husbands' permission were very much in accordance with Islam. Islamists responded by declaring him a puppet of the government. Like most countries of the world at the time, in the midst of the United Nations Decade for Women, Egypt was under international pressure to take visible steps to empower the country's women. In the mid-1980s, Acting Grand Mufti Mujāhid and his successor Grand Mufti Shaykh Muḥammad Ṭanṭāwī were both called upon to decide whether the *ḥijāb* (women's dress covering head and entire body) or the *niqāb* (*ḥijāb* plus a veil covering the face and gloves for the hands) was the more appropriate dress for Muslim women. Both men issued similar statements: based on their examination of the Qurʾān and *ḥadīth*, they declared that the *ḥijāb* was the correct dress for Muslim women and the *niqāb* was unnecessary; neither man, however, discussed any possible disadvantages to wearing the *ḥijāb*. As Jakob Skovgaard-Petersen points out, the study of fatwas can be very useful in establishing a chronology of changing social norms. Given that the first questions posed about the *niqāb* date only to the mid- to late-1980s, it seems reasonable to conclude that the face veil and gloves were fairly recent phenomena then and far from being in common use.

In June 1988, Ṭanṭāwī issued a long fatwa in response to recent controversy over the sex-change from man to woman of Sayyid ʿAbd Allāh, a medical student at al-Azhar University. The fatwa concluded that it was permissible to perform the operation in order to reveal hidden male or female organs and that indeed it was obligatory to do so when advised by a doctor; but it was not permissible if the person simply wished to change sex.

The 1994 United Nations Population Conference was a controversial event for religious groups of all persuasions. Within the Islamic world, the governments of Saudi Arabia, Sudan, and Lebanon refused to attend following critical fatwas by their countries' religious authorities. Like the Vatican, they saw the conference as focused on encouraging promiscuity and limiting the number of people on earth despite God's wishes. The most contentious issue to arise from the conference, however, was that of female genital surgery. A CNN broadcast of an actual female genital surgery at the time of the conference thrust the issue into Egyptian public discourse for the first time. An embarrassed Egyptian government quickly promised to curb the practice; although a ban had been in effect since 1959, the practice had persisted unhindered. Shortly after the conference, Jād al-Ḥaqq, then grand shaykh of al-Azhar, issued a fatwa declaring that uncircumcised girls tend to "a sharp temperament and bad habits" and are like to fall prey to "immorality and corruption." He described genital cutting as "a laudable practice that does honor to women" and as a religious practice as important as praying to God. The government's response to this fatwa was to lift the ban and require that the service be available at government hospitals one day a week. The rationale was that at least then the surgery would be conducted under safe hygienic conditions; however, given that the government hospitals charged five times more than the going street rate, this initiative was unlikely to attract poorer families and was doomed from the start. Interestingly enough, Ṭanṭāwī's statement on the subject was in clear contradiction to Jād al-Ḥaqq's position. He argued that the modesty of young girls depended not on circumcision but on a proper religious and moral education and upbringing; furthermore, he had found no evidence that the Prophet had had his own daughters circumcised. The Egyptian Organization of Human Rights filed a lawsuit against Jād al-Ḥaqq for his support of female circumcision. A court later dismissed the suit; in any case, by then, Jād al-Ḥaqq had passed away and Ṭanṭāwī was the new grand shaykh of al-Azhar. In June 1996, the government finally banned female circumcisions in all hospitals, public and private, and prohibited any licensed medical professional from performing the surgery. The following year, however, the new grand mufti, Shaykh Naṣr Farīd Wāṣil, issued a fatwa decreeing that female circumcision should be permitted even though it is not obligatory under Islam. Soon after, a court overturned the government's directive prohibiting licensed health workers from conducting the surgery on the grounds that the government could not interfere in professional practice through a ministerial decree.

In 1998, Wāṣil issued a fatwa that a woman who had been raped was entitled to surgery that would "restore" her virginity; because state and society had failed to protect her, he argued, it was up to them to provide this service so that she might go on to lead a normal life. This controversial fatwa provided an excuse for media and public discussions on the issue of rape; some critics expressed concern that such surgery would serve to deceive the woman's future husband, while others, such as women's groups, did not see the mufti's proposal as the most appropriate way to meet the needs of a raped woman.

BANGLADESH

In Bangladesh, where there is no official fatwa-issuing authority comparable to the Dār al-Iftāʾ or al-Azhar University of Egypt, the fatwas that have made national and international headlines are of a very different nature. In addition to the death sentence against the writer Taslima Nasreen, throughout the 1990s there were reports of incidents in which ordinary landless village women were publicly humiliated, beaten, and in one case, burned to death following local *salish* (village tribunal) indictments, usually under charges of adultery. While a *salish* comprising the old wise men of the village was a traditional part of the rural informal justice system, the use of the term fatwa to describe its decision on a case was a distinctly new phenomenon. In addition, women who had become involved in NGO projects in order to earn money, receive medical care, or attend literacy classes, became the subject of fatwas by local religious leaders: some fatwas called for these women to be ostracized from the community, others declared them apostates and automatically divorced from their husbands. Finally, in a number of areas, local religious leaders issued fatwas stating that it was "un-Islamic" for women to vote in local and national elections. In many of the cases investigated, it was found that the women were proxies in larger fights between families and that the "fatwas" were endorsed by the wealthier party in these disputes. This helps to explain why the poorer and less powerful members of the community felt they had no alternative but to go along with the fatwas issued, even when they considered them unjust or even un-Islamic. Non-Muslim women were not spared the brunt of this new form of gendered oppression: a Hindu teenager was punished by a *salish* in 1994 simply for talking to a Muslim man.

The public response to such fatwas in Bangladesh has been divided between secularists and Islamists. For the former, these incidents simply confirm their worst fears regarding the public use of religion: if state and society are not restored to the secularist principles on which the country was founded, the country is doomed to medieval barbarism. According to the Islamists, half-educated village religious leaders have been able to get away with their unlawful fatwas precisely because there is no national and official fatwa board in the country that can issue genuine Islamic fatwas. They insist that fatwas are an integral part of Islamic jurisprudence and are horrified that the secularists have coined the derogatory term *fatwabaz* to refer to anyone who issues a fatwa.

Many of the NGOs working in rural areas made a deliberate effort to educate villagers about the dangers of these unlawful fatwas. The Dhaka-based legal aid organization Ain o Salish Kendra (ASK, Law and mediation center) took the lead in documenting cases of such fatwas and of filing charges against the perpetrators whenever possible; the center estimated that there were about 180 reported incidents of fatwa-related violence between 1993 and 2001. Recognizing that the *salish* provides poor villagers an invaluable, inexpensive, and locally-rooted alternative forum for dispute resolution to expensive formal courts, ASK, Banchte Shekha (Learning to survive), and other NGOs undertook projects to develop this institution while minimizing its worst aspects. Thus they educated poor village women as well as local elected officials on the intricacies of state law so that they could challenge inappropriate decrees made by religious leaders in a salish. Activists achieved a major victory in 2001 when the Bangladesh high court ruled that all fatwas issued by individuals without legal authority are illegal and non-binding and called on parliament to enact laws to stop this dangerous practice. While human rights activists celebrated, Islamist leaders responded by declaring the two judges responsible for this ruling *murtad*s (infidels) and called on all true believers to take action against them.

IRAN

In Iran, where Shīʿī Islam bestows upon clerics a degree of authority and official power not found in Sunnī Islam, the personality of an individual religious leader can make all the difference. Grand Ayatollah Yusef Saanei, for instance, is among the twelve most revered clerics in Shiʿism. He believes that the Qurʾān calls for the equality of all people, men and women, Muslim and non-Muslim. He has issued fatwas banning discrimination on the basis of race, gender, or ethnicity; he has declared that women can hold any job, including his; and he has stated that abortion is permitted in the first trimester for reasons other than the mother's health or fetal abnormalities. He has even written letters of consent for women who are seeking abortions to take to their doctors. He rationalizes such fatwas on the grounds that Islamic laws should be interpreted in accordance with changes in science and social realities. A second cleric, Ayatollah Mustafa Mohaqeqdamad, has argued that men should not be permitted to divorce their wives simply by uttering "I divorce you" three times. His rationale is that an Islamic marriage requires the consent of both parties and therefore, surely, divorce should require the same.

As this entry shows, although the practice of giving fatwas has been part of the Islamic tradition from its earliest days, it has come to be understood very differently in different contexts at the turn of the twenty-first century. In countries with official fatwa-issuing institutions, fatwas are seen generally as authoritative statements on issues of concern to contemporary state and society; in some instances, as in Egypt, state muftis have lost some credibility because they are regarded as being in too close an alliance with the state. In Iran, on the other hand, independent and powerful ayatollahs have been able to issue controversial fatwas challenging traditional ideas of gender roles. In Bangladesh, finally, which does not have an official fatwa-board, the term has been appropriated by village religious leaders to target and punish women they feel are behaving inappropriately.

BIBLIOGRAPHY

S. M. S. Alam, Women in the era of modernity and Islamic fundamentalism. The case of Taslima Nasrin of Bangladesh, in *Signs. Journal of women in culture and society* 23:2 (1998), 429–62.

A. S. Dallal, Fatwa (modern usage), in *The Oxford encyclopedia of the modern Islamic world*, ii, New York 1995, 13–17.

T. I. Hashmi, *Women and Islam in Bangladesh. Beyond subjection and tyranny*, New York 2000.

M.-A. Hélie-Lucas and H. Kapoor (comps.), *Fatwas against women in Bangladesh*, Grabels, France 1996.

M. K. Masud, B. Messick, and D. S. Powers (eds.), *Islamic legal interpretation. Muftis and their fatwas*, Cambridge, Mass. 1996.

M. R. Khan, *Fatwabaz* [in Bengali], Dhaka 1996.

E. Shehabuddin, Contesting the illicit. Gender and the politics of fatwas in Bangladesh, in *Signs. Journal of women in culture and society* 24:4 (1999), 1012–44.

J. Skovgaard-Petersen, *Defining Islam for the Egyptian state*, Leiden 1997.

M. Zeghal, La guerre des fatwâ-s. Gad al-Haqq et Tantawi. Les cheikh-s à l'épreuve du pouvoir, in *Cahiers de l'Orient* 45 (1997), 81–95.

ELORA SHEHABUDDIN

Freedom of Expression

Australia

This entry is concerned with the ways in which Muslim women in Australia experience religious racism as a restriction on their freedom of religious expression. Recently a number of initiatives have tried to gather information on levels of religious racism and have tried to address related issues (New South Wales Anti Discrimination Board 2003, DIMIA 2003, HREOC 2004, Dunn 2003). Schools are places where young Muslim women experience particularly high levels of racism; however, many Muslim women have strategies of resistance to allow them to subvert the racism and continue to express their religious identities publicly and proudly.

In recent years there has been increasing recognition that Australia has a number of issues to deal with in relation to its minority Muslim population. Of particular concern have been increasing levels of religious racism Muslims experience, particularly those Muslim women who wear *ḥijāb*, as they are the most easily visible members of Australia's Muslim communities. In 2003, the New South Wales Anti-Discrimination Board, in an attempt to understand the nexus between media coverage and representation of events involving or affecting Muslims, published a report entitled *Race for the Headlines*. This report recognized that Australia has a "long history of institutionalised racism" (New South Wales Anti-Discrimination Board 2003, 3) against a range of peoples including, most recently, people of Middle Eastern background and Muslims. It also recognized that "it is virtually impossible to isolate the ways in which media coverage of current events, political commentary and rhetoric, and community attitudes interact" (New South Wales Anti Discrimination Board 2003, 4) and therefore that religious racism against Muslims was not to be "blamed" solely on either the media or individuals in the community.

Shortly after this report was published, Australia's Human Rights and Equal Opportunity Commission (HREOC) began a series of consultations with Arab and Muslim Australians in order to gather qualitative data relating to experiences of racism, based on both religion and ethnicity. HREOC called this consultative process "Isma-Listen" because their primary goal was to listen to the stories and experiences of racism and to ask Arab and Muslim communities what they felt would be appropriate government responses or solutions to their concerns. During the consultations the HREOC facilitators made it clear to participants that HREOC was aware that Arab and Muslim Australians, particularly women who wear *ḥijāb*, experienced extremely high levels of racism but that HREOC and its state-based counterparts rarely received official complaints. The Isma-Listen process was an opportunity for individuals to speak out under the freedom of anonymity and without the obligation of pursuing the case through official avenues. What these consultations established was that Muslim (and Arab) Australians were not confident that their complaints would be taken seriously, or that they feared further negative repercussions if they pursued an official complaint (HREOC 2004).

Even prior to the HREOC consultations, the Australian government had recognized that Muslims are one of Australia's minorities most likely to experience racism (Dunn 2003). In response to this the "Living in Harmony" initiative was instituted with the aim of encouraging "tolerance" and "anti-discrimination" (DIMIA 2003). Through the distribution of small grants to community groups who were involved in projects or events that aimed at reducing barriers between religious and ethnic communities and who facilitated opportunities for "cultural exchange," the Australian government believed that racism would be reduced. However, as the Isma consultations demonstrated, measures such as "Living in Harmony" are largely ineffective in reducing the racism experienced by ordinary Muslims, particularly veiled Muslim women.

One of the areas that the HREOC Isma consultations reported was the experience by Muslims of high levels of racism in schools. Unlike countries such as France, Singapore, and Germany, Australia's view of itself as a secular country does not require that its citizens refrain from outward expressions of religiosity such as the wearing of *ḥijāb*. However the current global context (particularly since 11 September 2001) is one of hostility toward Muslim women who wear *ḥijāb* as an open and public display of their commitment to Islam. Consequently, the experience of many young Muslim women who wear *ḥijāb* in Australian schools is one of overwhelming hostility and negativity. The Isma-Listen consultations reported that schools were often places of fear and distress for Muslim women as, in many cases, schools were ill-equipped, or unprepared, to deal with either racism or the special needs of Muslim students. Students did not feel safe in practicing their religion as they would become the target of abuse, bullying, physical attacks, and hostility from both staff and other students. One of the major effects of these experiences is to make young people, particularly women, feel alienated from the Australian education system, and society more broadly, and to increase their feelings of persecution, fear, and vulnerability. Despite being assured that they are free to practice their religion, many of the students spoken to felt that the current climate prevented them from freely expressing their religiosity. Often these young people, even when permitted to practice particular aspects of their religion such as dress codes, dietary habits, and certain forms of social interaction (such as a lack of physical contact between the sexes), felt as if this "permission" was tenuous and that approval could be withdrawn at any moment.

In research conducted with young women in Australian schools, this researcher has heard many narratives of religious racism. One of the most powerful came during an interview with a 17–year-old woman named Shakira. Having recently begun wearing *ḥijāb*, she was well aware that doing so would increase her visibility and that she might well become a target of racism, but she was determined not to let this deter her. Her first obstacle was whether her school would treat her new clothing choice with respect. In discussions with the head of the school Shakira was assured that provided she wore a cream colored *ḥijāb* so that it blended in with the school uniform she was more than welcome to wear it. After a few months in which Shakira felt that her new, active religiosity was gradually becoming accepted by staff and students an incident occurred which showed her that hostility toward her *ḥijāb*, and thus her identity as a Muslim woman, had been simmering under the surface waiting for an opportunity to erupt.

The school commissioned a large color photograph of all staff and students and Shakira took part in this. When she received her copy of the photo, she initially found it difficult to locate herself in the image because, in order to erase her Muslim identity as embodied in her *ḥijāb*, the school had air-brushed her *ḥijāb* in such a way that it appeared to look like brown hair. Shakira's fury and hurt at this action meant that she felt unable to continue at the school she had attended for many years. The injustice she had suffered was compounded as she then had to settle into a new school, find new friends, and accommodate to a different set of teachers and expectations while her original school continued unaffected by the incident.

Other young women interviewed as part of the same study spoke about their school's refusal to provide them with a space in which to perform their midday prayers despite the women's flexibility about the size and location of the room. They felt that this decision was unfair as the (public) school had made generous provisions to Christian youth groups operating during lunchtimes at the school. They felt that if the school, which publicly promoted itself as a multifaith, multicultural environment, wished to live up to this claim then it should support students of all faiths in their practices, or, alternatively, not support the practice of any faith by its students.

The young women also spoke about the willingness of their schools to provide a range of food options at their school canteens as against their continued refusal to provide halal (or kosher) food, even where Muslim students made up a significant portion of the schools' populations. During the research it also became clear that schools were largely unwilling to re-evaluate pedagogical practices that affected their female Muslim students' ability to comfortably participate in lessons. For example, many of the young women felt uncomfortable in having to work closely with male classmates, particularly on lengthy projects that would involve working together on weekends and after school. Similarly they were reluctant to participate in certain school activities such as swimming carnivals because these were inappropriate according to their sense of religiosity. All the young women said that their schools often told them that it would be willing to accommodate any special religious needs but that although schools occasionally made special provisions, this was rare and the constant pressure of having to request special treatment meant that the young women felt constrained and resentful toward the education system that so clearly did not support their choice to be actively Muslim. In many instances when they did make special requests these were not catered for appropriately or, in some cases, at all.

While Australia might profess to be a society in which there is total religious freedom, the experiences of young women in schools, as well as other Muslims, tell a different story. A nation does not need to legislate in order to make it difficult for individuals to practice their religion as is the case in France recently (Willms 2004); it only needs a majority population willing to perpetuate negative representations and hostility toward them. Even if racism does not result in a change in religious practice, either internal or external, the racism itself is a curtailment of religious freedom of expression. Many of the young women involved in a variety of research projects have stated that it is racism and hostility to their Muslim identity that makes them feel oppressed. This stands in direct contradiction to ideas of Muslim women as always being oppressed by their menfolk. As one woman put it in HREOC's consultations, "Muslim women are portrayed as being oppressed by their husbands but in fact we are being oppressed by the society where we can't feel comfortable wearing our *ḥijāb* and practicing our religion" (HREOC 2004, 77).

However, when dealing with racism, Muslim women in Australia refuse to become victims and enact strategies of resistance. For example, in a number of Australian cities Muslim women have come to agreements with fitness centers and swimming pools to ensure that men are excluded from certain sessions each week in order that Muslim women (and other women) have a comfortable environment in which to work out or swim. While these arrangements have often come under pressure from some sectors of the community, the women have not allowed racism to deter them from expressing their religious identities as well as participating in the broader society (New South Wales Anti Discrimination Board 2003). Other examples of resistance to racism are more subtle, however.

In research with female Muslim school students they repeatedly spoke of the importance of networking with other young Muslim women so that if an incident of racism occurred each woman had an immediate support network who understood her situation and who could assist in the healing and reparation process. These networks were not substitutes for friendships but provided key support to the young women and enabled them to continue to publicly identify as Muslims in instances where, without these support networks, the racism may otherwise have led them to hide their religiosity in fear of their safety.

For many Muslim women who wear *ḥijāb* in Australia, religious racism is something they must confront on a daily basis. Partly as a result of being members of a minority Muslim community within a majority non-Muslim country and partly because of their visibility, a visibility that evokes popular ideas of Muslim women being oppressed and therefore victims, Muslim women bear the brunt of hostility and negativity (Deen 2003, Kampmark 2003, Mubarak 1996, Sukkarieh and Zahra 2002). However, they do not passively accept such racism. Rather, they actively resist and subvert both the racism they experience directly and the negative stereotyping and representation in the media and popular culture. Although it may be difficult for these women to freely express their commitment to Islam in a variety of ways, most commonly and most visibly through wearing the *ḥijāb*, they continue to find ways to do so while simultaneously being mindful of their safety.

Bibliography

H. Deen, *Caravanserai. Journey among Australian Muslims*, St. Leonards, N.S.W. 1995, Fremantle, W.A. 2003 (new ed.).

DIMIA (Department of Immigration and Multicultural and Indigenous Affairs), "Living in Harmony" Initiative, 2003, <http://www.immi.gov.au/multicultural/harmony/ index.htm>.

K. Dunn, Racism in Australia. Findings on racist attitudes and experiences of racism, paper presented at the conference on "The Challenges of Immigration and Integration in the European Union and Australia," University of Sydney, 18–20 February 2003.

HREOC (Human Rights and Equal Opportunity Commission), Isma-Listen national consultation on eliminating prejudice against Arab and Muslim Australians, 2004, <http://www.hreoc.gov.au/racial_discrimination/isma>.

B. Kampmark, Islam, women and Australia's cultural discourse of terror, in *Hecate* 29:1 (2003), 86–105.

F. Mubarak, Muslim women and religious identification. Women and the veil, in G. Bouma (ed.), *Many religions, all Australians*, Kew, Australia 1996, 123–46.

New South Wales Anti-Discrimination Board, *Race for the headlines*, Sydney 2003.

O. Sukkarieh and M. Zahra, Silence that speaks and dreams that cry, in Borderlands e-journal 1:1 (2002), <http://www.borderlandsejournal.adelaide.edu.au/vol1no1_2002/sukkarieh_silence.html>.

J. Willms, France unveiled: making Muslims into citizens, in OpenDemocracy, 2004, <http://www.opendemocracy.net/email/ed3500/willms_1753.jsp>.

Alia Imtoual

Iran

The Constitutional Revolution of 1905–11 was a turning point in the lives of Iranian women. Women participated in huge numbers and gained important sites for expressing their views, including journals, schools, and associations that flourished in the following period (1911–24) (Afary 1996).

The defeat of the Constitutionalists (1921–5) and the consolidation of power by the highly dictatorial Reza Shah (1925–41) had two contradictory impacts. Independent women's journals and groups were destroyed, while the state implemented social reforms such as mass education and paid employment for women. Reza Shah also banned wearing the Islamic *ḥijāb*. Under Reza Shah's rule, women, like other sectors of the society, lost the right to express themselves and dissent was repressed. Reza Shah brutally repressed non-Persian ethnic minorities (Azerbaijanis, Kurds, Arabs), nomadic tribal groups (Bakhtiaris, Qashqais), dissident Shīʿī clerics, and Sunnīs. Compliant Shīʿī clerics were granted funds to develop seminaries in the city of Qom.

From the 1850s, non-Muslims constituted between 1 and 4 percent of the population, Sunnīs between 8 and 10 percent, and Shīʿīs between 89 and 94 percent (Abrahamian 1982, 12, Limbert 1987, 30). Under Reza Shah Armenians were viewed with suspicion following their massive participation in the Constitutional Revolution and their general sympathy with progressive forces. Other non-Muslim religious minorities (Zoroastrian, Jewish, and to a lesser extent Assyrian) were allowed social freedom as long as they did not engage in politics. However, during the period 1934–41, religious minorities (Bahai, Armenian, and Assyrian) were targeted for discrimination, and their schools were closed (Abrahamian 1982, 163).

The period after Reza Shah's abdication in 1941 until the 1953 coup was the freest period in Iran's contemporary history. Various political groups mobilized workers, women, and ethnic groups. The August 1953 coup brought to an end a period marked by extensive civil liberties where all groups – including women's, religious, and ethnically-based groups – were free to publish their political and ideological perspectives and organize to demand their rights.

The period 1953 to late 1978 witnessed the return of Pahlavī authoritarianism, which combined repressive measures with reforms financed by oil revenues. The massive oil income in the 1960s and 1970s allowed mass education, including higher education for women at unprecedented levels, with a huge increase in women entering into salaried professions and blue-collar employment.

Despite participation of women in higher education and employment in substantial numbers, they (along with the rest of the society) were not allowed freedom of expression, or the right to establish independent journals or groups. Many young university women were attracted to left-wing groups, but in the early 1970s women's rights were not prominent as such; they were subsumed under other guises, either the anti-imperialist struggle or class demands (Kazemzadeh 2002). The Islamist groups, by and large, opposed the Shah's programs as wholesale importation of Westernized norms alien to Islamic values and identity. Secular liberal democratic groups emphasized the repression of individual and political rights by the Shah's regime.

The anti-Shah movement from early 1977 to February 1979 included diverse groups. After coming to power, however, Khomeini and his fundamentalist allies instituted gender policies that were resisted by large numbers of women. These struggles revolved around the compulsory *ḥijāb*, dismissal of female judges, dismissal of employed women, limiting women's access to higher education, and reinstitution of Sharīʿa laws. Feminist, liberal democratic, and leftist forces publically criticized and resisted the fundamentalist policies until June 1981, when a violent reign of terror succeeded in silencing all voices. Mass executions, in the tens of thousands, crushed all non-fundamentalist forces.

Religious minorities (Sunnī, Bahāʾī, Armenian, Assyrian, Jewish) lack many civil and political rights in Iran today. Many religious minorities, particularly the non-Muslims, left the country after the 1979 revolution in order to escape persecution and discrimination.

The deteriorating economic conditions, suffocating cultural environment, and harsh discrimination against women gave rise to a widespread passive resistance throughout the 1980s, which eventually forced the regime to renege on many of its earlier policies in the 1990s.

In May 1997, a large number of women participated in the elections and overwhelmingly voted for Hojatolislam Mohammad Khatami, a reformist cleric who had promised reduction of repression and toleration of civil society institutions. His election opened a period when dissidents could voice their ideas, with many becoming increasingly bolder in their demands and in their criticisms.

At the beginning of the twenty-first century, the fundamentalist regime has lost its ideological hegemony and political legitimacy but not its ability to coerce and subdue. The proliferation of satellite television, foreign-based radio broadcasts, and the Internet have progressively undermined the regime's ability to restrict political ideas. The Internet has enabled the exchange of information via undetectable email: opponents of the regime can easily publish articles and photos on the Internet under pseudonyms. Iranian youth, particularly young women, have found it safe to write their views on personal weblogs in Persian. Use of these new media has allowed increased and undetected communication and contact between the opponents of the regime residing abroad with people living in Iran, but also, more significantly, it has enabled activists in Iran to meet fellow activists.

Numerous feminist Internet sites based abroad as well as inside Iran provide a plethora of information, feminist literature, and solidarity. The awarding of the Nobel Peace Prize to Shirin Ebadi, an Iranian human rights and feminist activist, further emboldened Iranian feminists inside Iran and cemented their relationships with Iranian feminist activists abroad.

Bibliography

E. Abrahamian, *Iran between two revolutions*, Princeton, N.J. 1982.

J. Afary, *The Iranian constitutional revolution, 1906–1911. Grassroots democracy, social democracy, and the origins of feminism*, New York 1996.

F. Azari (ed.), *Women of Iran. The conflict with fundamentalist Islam*, London 1983.

M. Kazemzadeh, *Islamic fundamentalism, feminism, and gender inequality in Iran under Khomeini*, Lanham, Md. 2002.

J. W. Limbert, *Iran. At war with history*, Boulder, Colo. 1987.

A. Najmabadi, Hazards of modernity and morality. Women, state, and ideology in contemporary Iran, in D. Kandiyoti (ed.), *Women, Islam and the state*, Philadelphia 1991, 48–76.

G. Nashat (ed.), *Women and revolution in Iran*, Boulder, Colo 1983.

P. Paidar, *Women and the political process in twentieth-century Iran*, Cambridge 1995.

E. Sanasarian, *The women's rights movement in Iran. Mutiny, appeasement, and repression from 1900 to Khomeini*, New York 1981.

A. Tabari and N. Yeganeh (eds.), *In the shadow of Islam. The women's movement in Iran*, London 1982.

Masoud Kazemzadeh

South Asia

The issue of freedom of religious expression has acquired increasing significance in the context of South Asia in light of the rise of right-wing movements and their attack on religious minorities. Hateful writings and speeches played a role in political events such as the destruction of the Babri Masjid in Ayodhya in December 1992; the vituperative and vitriolic speeches and writings of the Hindu Right against the Muslim community in 1992 and 1993 framed the context within which the Bombay riots took place in September 1992 and January 1993; and the fatwa issued against Taslima Nasreen in May 1994 represented a contest over who has the right to speak for whom.

The right to freedom of speech is guaranteed as a fundamental right under article 19 of the Indian constitution, article 39 of the Bangladesh constitution, article 14 of the Sri Lankan constitution, and article 19 of the Pakistan constitution. In each country, reasonable restrictions on the right to free speech are permitted, for example, in the interests of public order and decency. The penal codes in each country also have provisions that prohibit words or representations that promote disharmony or enmity between different religious, caste, or racial communities, between language or regional groups, or that deliberately outrage the religious feelings of any class by insulting its religion or religious beliefs. The codes also have provisions against obscenity and affront of a woman's modesty. Many court decisions indicate that the legal provisions against hateful speech have been primarily used to protect minority religious groups from various attacks on their religion and religious beliefs. Most prosecutions have involved quite vicious and outrageous attacks on the religious beliefs or practices of the concerned community. However, the increasingly overt religious climate and rise of right-wing politics have led to the erosion of the rights to free speech and expression of women and religious minorities.

India

In India, the Hindu Right is increasingly successful in promoting the perception of the persecution of the majority by the minority and asserting itself as the spokesperson for what constitutes Hindu culture, religion, and history. It has promoted its agenda partly through the right to free expression, while simultaneously attacking the right of anyone who dissents from or challenges its agenda.

In the context of Muslim women, the Hindu Right avails every opportunity to denounce the Muslim community because of the way it treats women. They invoke their free speech rights to report any atrocity or indignity committed against Muslim women, whether within the Muslim community in India or within the surrounding Muslim countries. For example, the Hindu Right took up the cause of Taslima Nasreen, in the fatwa controversy that emerged around this Bangladeshi writer. The fatwa was issued in September 1993, after the publication of her novel, *Lajja*, a story of the plight of a Hindu family in Bangladesh persecuted in the aftermath of the destruction of the Babri Masjid in December 1992. In a newspaper interview in May 1994, Nasreen called for a reform of religious texts that oppress women and the fatwa was reasserted. Facing protests and calls for Nasreen's death, the Bangladeshi government charged Nasreen with blasphemy. Nasreen fled the country to live in exile.

In this controversy, the Hindu Right positioned itself as the defender of free speech from the threat of fundamentalist censors. Women's rights groups also defended Nasreen's rights to free speech. In the hands of the Hindu Right, the rhetoric of freedom of expression was deployed to construct the Muslim "other" as the violator of democratic rights and to deflect attention from the similar absence of a respect for free expression within its own ranks. The Hindu Right became the self-appointed champion of the rights of Nasreen, a Muslim, and deployed the violation of these rights as a way of attacking the Muslim community as a whole. Women's groups championed Nasreen's right to free speech as an assertion of her civil and human rights. However, they also found themselves in the awkward position of being aligned with the Hindu Right, who opposed the fundamentalist attack on Nasreen to further constitute itself as secularist.

BANGLADESH

The right to women's sexual expression and sexual autonomy in Bangladesh is also enjoined by cultural practices and the rise of right-wing fundamentalism that views women's conduct through a moral lens. For example, in rural areas a *salish* or tribunal is frequently used to settle local disputes. Women are excluded from participating in the *salish*. Village religious leaders have developed the practice of making declarations, which they call fatwas, on individual cases dealing with marriage or divorce, or meting out punishments for perceived moral transgressions. These proceedings have been manipulated by local religious leaders to find women guilty of extramarital sexual affairs and other acts. Punishments are dispensed in accordance with religious laws as interpreted locally, and these are often in contravention of the existing penal code. Some women have been flogged publicly and a few have also committed suicide.

In January 2001 the high court ruled illegal all fatwas, or expert opinions on Islamic law. Generally, only muftis (religious scholars) who had expertise in Islamic law were authorized to declare a fatwa. While the court's intention was to end the extrajudicial enforcement of penalties by religious leaders, primarily in the villages, the ruling declared all fatwas illegal and resulted in violent public protests. The appellate court stayed the high court's ruling and the case is pending further hearing.

The moral framework in which sexual expression is addressed finds its most explicit manifestation in the Anti-Terrorism Ordinance of 1992. The ordinance provides punishment for all kinds of terrorism including harassing women. Sexual harassment provisions should promote women's rights to equality, sexual autonomy, and sexual expression. However, the equation of sexual harassment with terrorism associates women's sexual purity, honor, and dignity with the honor, dignity, and security of the nation-state. The ordinance does not enhance women's rights to sexual autonomy or expression, but rather recasts her sexual integrity as an expression of nationhood. Securing her sexuality is equated with securing the nation. Women's conduct and sexual behavior are strictly monitored and they are harshly dealt with if implicated in any moral transgressions.

Women's rights to free speech and expression must be understood against the increasingly conservative nature of the government and its moral clean-up campaign. In 1999 police forcibly removed 267 sex workers from a large brothel district in Tanbazar and Nimtoli, Narayanganj as part of its clean-up and cultural purity efforts. Authorities claimed that the women wanted to be rehabilitated. The women asserted that they had the right to live in their homes, and practice their trade. The women were confined in a center for vagrants, where some alleged that they were abused. Eventually all of the women were released, and most returned to work in other locations. The case triggered a major campaign against the eviction, though women's claims to sexual expression were not simultaneously endorsed. The speech issue in this instance was overshadowed by the right to freedom of association and the challenge to the arbitrary actions of the government. The conservative moral authority of the state to restrict women's rights to sexual speech and expression was not in any way challenged or altered.

PAKISTAN

In Pakistan, the right to free speech of women is being threatened with the rise of the religious fundamentalist parties in the North-West Frontier Province. These groups have successfully lobbied for the adoption of Sharīʿa law in the province. The government is seeking to establish a Vice and Virtue Department "to restrict the faithful from wrongdoing." Girls over the age of twelve must wear the *burqaʿ*. Young men are tearing down billboards with images of women whose faces are unveiled. The dominance of hardline Islamic parties and the support they have previously expressed for the Taliban has added to fears that the province is a new breeding ground for Taliban-style ideology. These parties are intent on imposing their values, by force if necessary, and are against all forms of modernity, especially women's rights.

Another complex area is the right to free speech of women in minority communities in Pakistan.

Those at particular risk of abuse are the members of the Aḥmadiyya community. Aḥmadīs, members of a religious group founded in the nineteenth century, consider themselves to be Muslim, but orthodox Muslims regard them as heretical. In 1974, a constitutional amendment introduced by then Prime Minister Zulfikar Ali Bhutto declared Aḥmadīs a non-Muslim minority. Subsequent legislation passed in 1984 made it a criminal offence for Aḥmadīs to call themselves Muslim, and profess, practice, and propagate their faith as Muslims.

The blasphemy laws are a major tool used to harass, intimidate, and detain members of the minority community or members of the majority religion who in some way interpret, teach, or debate their religion in a non-orthodox manner. The blasphemy laws continue to be used by the present government to arbitrarily detain members of the minorities. Charges are also filed under those sections of the penal code specifically directed against Aḥmadīs and entail trial by the special anti-terrorism courts. Women are unable to acknowledge their religion or speak out against the discrimination they experience for practicing their faith. They are also prevented from criticizing practices within their own community that harm women, for fear of betraying the community, which already faces external threat and persecution.

BIBLIOGRAPHY

A. Basu, Feminism inverted, The real women and gendered imagery of Hindu nationalism, in T. Sarkar and U. Butalia (eds.), *Women and the Hindu right*, London 1995, 158–180.

K. Crenshaw, Beyond racism and misogyny. Black feminism and "2 Live Crew," in M. J. Matsuda, C. R. Lawrence III, R. Delgado, and K. W. Crenshaw (eds.), *Words that wound. Critical race theory, assaultive speech and the first amendment*, Boulder, Colo. 1993, 54–61.

D. Kandiyoti (ed.), *Women, Islam and the state*, Philadelphia 1990.

R. Kapur, Who draws the line? Feminist reflections on speech and censorship, in *Economic and Political Weekly*, 20–27 April 1996, WS15–WS22.

RATNA KAPUR

Sub-Saharan Africa

The record of freedom of expression of women in Sub-Saharan Islamic cultures has been mixed and historically conditioned – that is, if we take freedom of expression broadly to include the space of free articulation of ideas, feelings, opinions, and identities in verbal, non-verbal, and symbolic forms.

Freedom of expression presumes unfettered access to the tools and means for the exercise of that freedom. Foremost among these are intellectual, linguistic, and literary skills imparted in specific educational settings. In the majority of Muslim societies in Sub-Saharan Africa, classical Arabic and higher realms of Islamic learning were almost the exclusive preserve of men. As a result, the space to articulate a particularly woman centered reading of Islam and women's place within it has been undermined by patriarchal control of Islamic learning and knowledge.

Since the beginning of the democratization process in the early 1990s, however, many of these societies have experienced the emergence of political Islam with movements such as Izala in Nigeria and Niger. This development has created new conditions in which Muslim women have begun to develop their own initiatives to study classical Arabic and to understand and use Islam from their own perspectives – ranging from orthodox to liberal and secular positions (Gamatié-Bayard 1992, Alidou 2000).

In instances where Muslims constitute the preponderant majority in the nation, as in Niger, Mali, and Senegal, this Muslim women's activism rooted in new readings and uses of Islam has inspired minority Christian women to engage in similar efforts to interrogate afresh the place of women in Christianity itself and in the wider Muslim polity (Marut 2002, Ganda and Galadima 1992, 3).

Where Muslim women's readings of Islam in predominantly Muslim nations have departed from received patriarchal interpretations, the women have often been victims of violence and aggression and subject to accusations of selling out to Western interests. In nations where Muslims are not in the majority, in contrast, as in Kenya, Uganda, Malawi, and South Africa, similar developments among Muslim women have led to their being associated not only with Western interests, but also with the interests of the non-Muslim "other," namely Christians, in the nation-state. For example in Kenya, the (gender) Equality Bill was opposed by most Muslim men, and some conservative Muslim women's associations supported this particular protest on the ground that the proposed bill was a Western-Christian inspired legal document (Mazrui 1999).

Gender disparity within education, however, is evident not only within the world of Islam, but also in the more recent domain of secular education. Religious, colonial, and postcolonial conditions, including forces of globalization, have combined to the disadvantage of women in modern schools, especially at the higher levels. As a result, Muslim women's acquisition of ex-colonial languages and educational qualifications that have become requisite in critical areas of public expression such as the government, parliament, and electronic and print media has been disproportionately lower than that of their male counterparts (Callaway and Creevy 1994, Djibo 2001, Hamani 2000, 127–69).

If the development of pluralist politics has had implications for women's education, however, it has also affected the expression of their identities. Nowhere is this development more evident than in dress discourses, especially in urban landscapes. The rise of political Islam in this new context has led to the emergence of a dress code, such as *ḥijāb* (veiling), to which Muslim women are expected to adhere. Women who choose not to express their Muslim identity through the *ḥijāb* code have sometimes been victims of verbal and physical assault by extremist Islamist males. In Kenya, Muslim women of the coastal areas who did not wear *buibui* – a wide, black floor-length cloak with attached veil (Hirsch 1998, 48–56) – suffered physical assault from young male members of the Islamic Party of Kenya.

In contrast, especially in societies where Muslims are in the minority, Muslim women in *ḥijāb* have experienced discrimination and hostility in educational institutions and places of work. For example, in inland Kenya, Muslim women students took their schools to court to challenge their suspension on the ground of wearing the *ḥijāb* (*Coastweek* 17–23 April 1999).

The 11 September 2001 tragedy in the United States has also had implications for the dress expression of identity in Sub-Saharan Africa. Several African countries, including Kenya, Tanzania, Uganda, Ethiopia, and Djibouti, have been under pressure by the United States government to enact "anti-terrorist" legislation that bears a strong resemblance to the United States Patriot Act (Kelley 2003). This has certainly included Muslim profiling through bodily appearance. The *ḥijāb* among Muslim women and the *jallābiyya* (long white robe) among bearded Muslim men as expressions of Islamic identity have now become a political liability in the post-September 11 dispensation. Spring and summer 2003 saw a massive student demonstration in the capital city of Gambia, Banjul, against a high school superintendent who dismissed female students wearing *ḥijāb* to school (*Independent* [Banjul] 3 June 2003).

If the expression of Islamic identity has suffered under certain conditions, Muslims themselves have sometimes violated the freedom of expression of others. It is widely accepted, for example, that spirit possession and exorcism, both predominant among women in Sub-Saharan Africa, are sacred spaces for the expression of women's feelings, ideas, and desires that are taboo for women to express in other domains within Islamic patriarchy. In many Islamic cultures there was, for a long time, a co-existence and even a symbiosis between Islam and indigenous African spirituality such as Bori in Hausaland (McIntyre 1996, 257–74, Cooper 1998, 28–31). But some Islamist movements in Niger, Nigeria, Mali, and Senegal have in many cases led to a new antagonism against these important rituals, condemning them as expressions of *bidʿa* (innovation) that are antithetical to authentic *sunna* (tradition) of the Prophet Muḥammad. In the same spirit of Islam, Niger even went to the extent of passing a law in the 1980s that criminalized rituals of spirit possession, especially in the holy month of Ramadan. It was only under the pressure of pluralist politics of the 1990s onwards that the law became dormant and the rituals, which had become clandestine in urban areas especially, regained their free space of expression.

In spite of instances of hostility generated by religious fundamentalism of all types and the shortcomings of the new democratic experiments in Sub-Saharan Africa, the new politics of pluralism has, without doubt, granted Muslim women the space to inscribe their agency in an overt expressive manner, sometimes at the risk of being victimized. A case in point is the national tension arising from the women's campaign for the constitutional adoption of an egalitarian family law in Niger (Dunbar 1991, Niger Republic 1995, Reynolds 1997). It has also offered, in a number of countries, new possibilities for Muslim women to join other women in coalitions across boundaries of religion to advocate for the rights and freedoms of women, as in the case of the horrifying so-called Sharīʿa trial of Amina Lawal in Katsina, North Nigeria, on charges of adultery. This is clearly illustrated by the commendable work of women activists and scholars such as Ayesha Imam of Baobab (a human rights non-governmental organization) and others working in the African Center for Democracy and Human Rights Studies in Mali to educate Muslim and Christian as well as non-Muslim and non-Christian women about religious and secular laws and policies that violate women's rights and freedoms.

Bibliography

O. Alidou, Islamisms, the media and women's public discursive practices in Niger, paper presented at the Conference on Islam in Africa sponsored by the Institute of Global Cultural Studies at the State University of New York, Binghamton 13–15 April 2000.

B. Callaway and L. Creevey, *The heritage of Islam. Women, religion and politics in West Africa*, Boulder, Colo. 1994, 55–186.

B. Cooper, Gender and religion in Hausaland. Variations

in Islamic practices in Niger and Nigeria, in H. L. Bodman and N. Tohidi (eds.), *Women in Muslim societies. Diversities within unity*, London 1998, 21–37.

H. Djibo, *La participation des femmes africaines à la vie politique. Les exemples du Niger et Sénégal*, Paris 2001.

R. A. Dunbar, Islamic values, the state and the development of women. The case of Niger, in C. Cole and B. B. Mack (eds.), *Hausa women in the twentieth century*, Madison, Wis. 1991, 69–89.

M. Gamatié-Bayard, Le harem, in *Le Démocrate* (Niger), 10 August 1992, 3.

S. Ganda and A. Galadima, Debate on secularism in Niger. The reaction of the church, in *Le Démocrate* (Niger), 28 September 1992, 5.

S. F. Hirsch, *Pronouncing and preserving. Gender and the discourses of dispute in an African court*, Chicago 1998.

K. J. Keley, US launches terror initiatives in East Africa, in *East African* (Nairobi), 1 September 2003.

J.-C. Marut, Les particularismes au risque de l'islam dans le conflit casamançais, in *Politique africaine*, Paris 2002, <http://www.cean.u-bordeaux.fr/pubcean/particularismes.pdf>.

A. Mazrui, The equality bill. An alternative Islamic perspective, a Kenyan human rights position paper, Nairobi 1999.

J. McIntyre, A cultural given and a hidden influence. Koranic teachers in Kano, in D. Parkin, L. Caplan, and H. Fisher (eds.), *The politics of cultural performance*, London 1996, 257–74.

Niger Republic, Ministry of Social Development and Population and the Promotion of Women, *Rapport national. Conférence mondiale sur les femmes et développement*, Niamey 1990.

E. M. Reynolds, The democratic transition in Niger (1991–1996). Women leaders' theories and organizational strategies for the empowerment of women, masters thesis, Clark University 1997.

Ousseina Alidou

Turkey

Turkish women enjoy a broad array of constitutionally guaranteed rights that remain largely unparalleled in the rest of the Muslim world. Turkey's drive to become a full member of the European Union (EU) has added great impetus to democratization in general and to the expansion of free expression in particular. Yet, Turkey's rigidly prosecular policies, while enabling women to compete with men professionally and socially, have also restricted free religious expression of openly pious women.

Bans on the Islamic-style headscarf in government institutions and in both state and privately run educational institutions are viewed by overtly pious Turks as one of the chief restrictions on religious freedoms. Merve Kavakçi, a Western-trained engineer, who covers her head, was stripped of her parliamentary seat and of her Turkish nationality after appearing at the parliament's inaugural session in 1999 wearing her headscarf. Her candidacy on the ticket of the Islam-oriented Virtue Party in the 1999 parliamentary elections was also cited as one of the main reasons for the party's closure by the constitutional court in 2001 on the grounds that it was seeking to overturn secular rule.

The French parliament's decision in February 2004 to ban religious "symbols" including the headscarf in state-run primary schools and lycées was perceived as a blow by Turkish women campaigning to lift such bans in Turkey as it provided ammunition for those who argue that the headscarf is a political symbol used to advocate Islamic militancy. Fearing retribution from the military, the conservative Justice and Development Party (AKP), led by a group of former Islamists, which came to power alone in the November 2002 elections, did not field any female candidates who wore the Islamic-style headscarf either then or during municipal elections held in March 2004. The wives of AKP cabinet members, including the wife of Prime Minister Recep Tayyip Erdogan, continue to be barred from attending state functions because they cover their heads. Some pious women have resorted to wearing wigs over their headscarves so as to circumvent the ban, especially in high schools and universities. Religiously observant Turks are especially irked by the fact that the headscarf is not allowed even at coeducational state run religious schools where imams and preachers are trained and students, in addition to learning all subjects taught in secular schools, are taught about the life of the Prophet Muḥammad and how to read the Qurʾān.

Turkey's powerful armed forces continue to label Islamic fundamentalism as the main threat to the country's security and have played a major role behind the scenes in clamping down on any overt expression of Islam in public life. Turkey's own peculiar brand of secularism is exercised through the strict control of all aspects of religious life through the state-run Religious Affairs Directorate, which appoints all the country's imams. Members of Turkey's minority Alevi sect, who practice a liberal form of Shīʿī Islam, have long accused the state of discriminating against them by not including information about their faith in mandatory religion classes taught in government run schools. They also accuse the Religious Affairs Directorate of bias because it regards them as a cultural rather than a religious group. Tensions between the Alevis and Turkey's Sunnī Muslim majority have occasionally escalated into outright violence. In one of the worst such incidents, in 1993, some 37 Alevi intellectuals, writers, and poets were burned to death in a hotel in the eastern province of Sivas by a crowd of people emerging from Friday prayers at a local Sunnī mosque. The failure of Islamist activists to condemn the Sivas massacre, as it came to be known, has left a deep scar in the Alevi psyche.

Indeed, the debate over secularism and the role of Islam in society and politics continues to be one of the major issues dividing modern Turkey as it strives to cement over three decades of largely uninterrupted democratic rule.

Turkey's current constitution was drawn up in 1982 by the rigidly pro-secular military after it had seized power directly for the third and last time in 1980. The constitution imposed stiff curbs on free expression, with the result that thousands of Turkish nationals have since been jailed for so called non-violent "thought crimes."

A separatist insurgency launched in the country's predominantly Kurdish southeastern provinces by the outlawed Kurdistan Workers' Party (PKK) led to a sharp rise in human rights violations throughout the 1990s as government forces resorted to brutal methods, including arbitrary detentions, torture, and the forcible evacuation of thousands of Kurdish villages, to stamp out the rebellion. In 1994 a special state security court sentenced four ethnic Kurdish members of parliament to 15 years in jail on thinly supported charges that they were linked to the PKK; among them was Leyla Zana, a female Kurdish parliamentarian from the southeastern province of Diyarbakır, whose chief offense was to have addressed the parliament in the Kurdish language during an inaugural session in 1991. All four were released pending an appeal on 9 June 2004 in a move aimed in part to persuade the EU to begin membership talks with Turkey by the end of 2004. The same day Turkish state-run television aired its first ever program in the most widely spoken Kurdish dialect, Kurmanji.

In 2003 the parliament passed legislation lifting bans on teaching Kurdish as a language in privately run language courses, but teaching in the Kurdish language is forbidden still. Turkey's human rights record has been repeatedly cited by EU governments as one of the main reasons why Turkey has been denied entry to their organization so far.

Bibliography

N. Pope and H. Pope, *Turkey unveiled*, London 1997, 324–5.

United Nations, Convention on the Elimination of All Forms of Discrimination against Women, Committee on the Elimination of Discrimination against Women, Combined fourth and fifth periodic reports of States parties, Turkey, August 2003.

United States Department of State, Turkey, Country Reports on Human Rights Practices – 2002, Washington, D.C., <http://www.state.gov/g/drl/rls/hrrpt/2002/18396.htm>.

United States Department of State, Turkey, International Religious Freedom Report 2003, Washington, D.C., <http://www.state.gov/g/drl/rls/irf/2003/24438.htm>.

Amberin Zaman

The United States

Muslim women struggle against demeaning stereotypical images depicting them as incapable of being productive elements in society. They often find themselves confronting cultural trends within the Muslim community that hold them to a high standard of moral discipline yet deny them any significant role in shaping the future of their own community. But Muslim women are diverse along lines of ethnicity, religious attitude, and occupation. Their experiences and views on gender and freedom of expression issues are even more complex.

Muslim women wearing *ḥijāb*, the attire that varies in style but usually covers the hair, neck, and body except for the face and hands, have been the most vocal in recent years in pressing for their right to practice their faith. Feeling empowered by the constitutional protection of freedom of religion, many Muslim women share the view that being American does not mean shedding their religious convictions. After all, the United States is a pluralistic society that has produced and marketed many modes of dress around the world. So, while the ethnic South Asian shalwar kameez and the Arab *thawb* have given way to contemporary North American clothing styles, the *ḥijāb* has survived because it stems from deeply held religious beliefs.

While the *ḥijāb* has caused controversy, for example, in uniformed occupations, the issue is increasingly regarded as a matter of freedom of religion in the workplace and at school. The Equal Employment Opportunity Commission, a federal government agency set up to implement the employment clauses of the Civil Rights Act of 1964, has advocated the right of women to wear *ḥijāb* at work. The law requires employers to offer reasonable accommodation to the religious practices of employees.

Often the discriminatory treatment experienced by women wearing *ḥijāb* is overt and could conceivably be challenged in court. However, most potential plaintiffs are not willing to make waves, cannot afford the usually high cost of legal counsel, or simply are unaware of their legal rights. In many cases, Muslim women denied their First Amendment right to wear *ḥijāb* look for other jobs or relax their fulfillment of religious requirements to fit the demands of employers, just as some Muslim men shave their beards or take off the *kūfī* they wear for religious reasons in order to keep their jobs.

A few corporations have taken steps to recognize the need to accommodate religiously inspired modes of dress. For example, on 18 May 2001, United Airlines, whose uniform policy was challenged by Muslim women in a number of incidents, announced that its customer service employees across the United States would be "allowed to wear a company-sanctioned hijab, turban or yarmulke as part of their uniform." Explaining the decision, the company stated, "We want our workforce to reflect the diversity of our global customer base."

For the public, *ḥijāb* has become a Muslim identifier. Outside the workplace, women with *ḥijāb* are frequently the targets of anti-Muslim attacks. In schools, girls with scarves are taunted; in shopping malls women with *ḥijāb* are harassed or denied service. Traveling Muslim women also reported humiliating experiences at airports, especially after the 11 September 2001 attacks on the World Trade Center and the Pentagon. On the other hand, Americans demonstrating sympathy and tolerance to Muslims wore *ḥijāb* to express solidarity with Muslim women when anti-Muslim hate crimes peaked after 11 September 2001. In one case of passenger profiling involving a Muslim woman, a coalition of groups led by the American Civil Liberties Union filed a law suit against private security personnel at O'Hare International Airport in Chicago for the degrading treatment of a Muslim passenger wearing *ḥijāb*, charging that the woman's freedom of religion and constitutional protections against unreasonable search and seizure had been violated.

Women who convert to Islam have indicated additional pressures. Some have faced rejection by family members who do not approve of their decision to embrace another religion; some families have become so intolerant of the change that they have severed relations and disinherited their convert daughters. In a few such cases, parents of converts have even attempted to gain custody of their grandchildren. In other cases family members and friends may express tolerance toward their relatives converting to Islam but treat them as if they have become disloyal citizens.

Muslim women with an ethnicity-based identity may face a different set of pressures related to racial and national origin prejudice. The immigrants in this subset of Muslim women struggle while attempting to strike a balance between assimilation and acceptance, being American without losing pride in their roots and core values. Some find the problematics of freedom relate more to the discriminatory treatment they face from family members who, for example, consider it unacceptable for their female relatives to date but are not bothered by the same behavior from their male counterparts.

Many women view their identity in terms that are much larger or even different from ones confined to religion and ethnicity. Regardless of orientation, most Muslim women are concerned about balancing the demands of work, family, and society. Experiences differ. Immigrant women coming from patriarchal cultures face a more difficult task in meeting the demands of career while fulfilling the demands of husbands who expect them also to cook, clean, and care for children. In some instances women have been forced to make a choice between marriage and work outside the house. In the United States, Muslim women generally place high value on education; many refuse to consider marriage or job before finishing college. Parents generally support such a tendency.

Many Muslim men are adjusting to the requirements of family life where both husband and wife are employed to sustain a household. Among many Muslim women a sense of sisterhood has been established around the need to support one another in pursuing a multi-faceted life inside and outside the house. Some have developed childcare services based on reciprocity; others have established day care businesses to support the desire of their Muslim sisters to earn a living or participate in public functions.

Because of the lingering male bias that often claims legitimacy on the basis of tradition, some intellectual Muslim women are joining forces to reexamine religious scholarly works. A number of contemporary female authors argue that religious texts have been misinterpreted for centuries by male jurists who did not have women's interests – or, for that matter, particularly Islamic interests – in mind. These women are only beginning to offer religious interpretations they believe to be free of male bias. This movement, however, is still in its infancy and has yet to make any significant impact on the discourse on the status of Muslim women.

Muslim women's roles outside the home include organizing on the basis of gender to promote the involvement of Muslim women in civic life. Such involvement is constrained by a gender gap between Muslim men and women regarding the social and political roles of women. More women than men are enthusiastic about the involvement of women outside the house. Still, the reality is that Muslim women participate in community life in a variety of ways, although women struggle for representation in leadership positions. A number of

Muslim community organizations in the United States are responding to women's call for inclusion. The Islamic Society of North America had its first female vice president in 2001. The American Muslim Alliance elected a woman to serve on its board in 2004. Nearly half the staff and a board member of the Council on American-Islamic Relations are women. Among young Muslims, the inclusion of women is being institutionalized. For example, some Muslim Student Association (MSA) chapters, such as MSA-Northwestern University in Chicago, now have by-laws requiring co-presidency by males and females. On 25 June 2004, MSA National elected its first female president. As women gain access to higher education and job related skills, they enhance their contribution to community and society and increase their chances to improve their status and assume leading roles.

BIBLIOGRAPHY

M. Afkhami, *Faith and freedom. Women's human rights in the Muslim world*, Syracuse, N.Y. 1995.

C. Anway, *Daughters of another path. Experiences of American women choosing Islam*, Lee's Summit, Mo. 1996.

Y. Y. Haddad and J. L. Esposito (eds.), *Islam, gender, and social change*, New York 1998.

J. I. Smith (ed. and intro.), *Women in contemporary Muslim societies*, Lewisburg, Pa. 1980.

A. Wadud, *Qur'an and woman. Rereading the sacred text from a woman's perspective*, New York 1999.

G. Webb (ed.), *Windows of faith. Muslim women scholar-activists in North America*, Syracuse, N.Y. 2000.

MOHAMED NIMER

Western Europe

Fundamental rights are protected legally at different levels in Western Europe. Do Muslim women living in the member states of the European Union fully experience these rights? Do they benefit from more freedom of expression and religious expression than in Muslim countries?

Freedom of expression and freedom of religious expression are part of the fundamental rights that are guaranteed and protected by law at the national and European Union level. These fundamental rights have individual and collective dimensions that may in some case interfere with and even contradict each other. Moreover, in Western European countries, the complex history of the relationship between state and religion is central to understanding the specific political culture of every national context. Western Europe may in fact appear from the outside as a relatively uniform religious landscape (Christian). The difficulty of the task of analyzing freedom of expression and freedom of religious expression of Muslim women living in Europe lies in the extreme diversity of the national settings when attempting to interpret the meaning of these fundamental rights and putting them into practice. This may be the main reason for the problem Western European societies have in recognizing and guaranteeing these fundamental rights to Muslim populations.

In the European Union, a set of legal provisions has been implemented aimed at protecting the fundamental rights of individuals. Recently, the European directive on the creation of a general system for equal treatment in employment and work (2000/78/EC of 27 November 2000) makes religion an individual criterion for discrimination, which for the first time appears explicitly in a juridical text. However, there is no unitary "religious" European public policy. Religion remains potentially a highly controversial issue as demonstrated in the discussion of the text of the Preamble to the future European Constitution and the quotation of an explicit reference to a set of "common religious values." In this picture, Muslims in many respects appear as latecomers and even as troublemakers. For instance, now that the economic, juridical, and political standards for admission into the European Union are closer than ever, the perspective of the accession of Turkey, a secular republic but still a Muslim society, is more openly questioned in terms of religious identity.

The situation of Muslim women in this context is the same as for other women, at least from a purely juridical perspective. Indeed, if Muslim women do have European citizenship through access to that citizenship in their country of residence, they fall within the scope of European jurisdiction as far as personal status is concerned. This, however, is not the case for those who are still citizens of Muslim countries and still subject to the rule of law of these countries. This is of peculiar importance for marriage and divorce, and also for decisions concerning children in such cases. Freedom of expression and fundamental rights remain under foreign legal influence and may contradict the fundamental principles of the European Union. A particularly vivid illustration is the reality of a child kidnapped (mainly) by his or her father after a divorce in a Western European country and brought back to his country of origin.

If we try to map the situation of Muslim women in Western European societies, a distinction has to be made between women who have access to education and professional skills, allowing them employment and financial autonomy, and those who remain under the very strong influence of the family structure. Time changes the situation for many. For the most part, the first category is composed of women who arrived when very young or who were born in the European countries where their parents decided to move. The situation is quite different for those women arriving in their twenties as the first of their family to migrate. This is particularly true of the young Muslim women who continue to be brought from the country of origin to be married to young Muslim men already living in Europe. At first glance, this may appear from a sociological perspective to be a matrimonial strategy implemented to obtain access to new positions through physical and social mobility. Recent qualitative studies conducted among young Muslim girls from Turkey, however, have demonstrated that in terms of personal autonomy and in particular of contact with European societies, the circumstances of these women are highly dependent on their educational skills, as well as their ability to construct their own autonomy vis-à-vis the family.

Another issue is that of the collective visibility of Muslim women in the public space in Europe. Here the discussion relates to many issues. The first level is a political one: no Western European country forbids women to participate in political life, either as a political candidate or as a voter. Once they acquire citizenship in the European country in which they live, Muslim women benefit from this right. The situation is again different for Muslim women who are not European citizens. The second level is that of religious organizations. In most European countries, Muslims are organized in associations that provide a range of different activities, either related to religious practices and education (mosques, praying rooms, Qur'ān courses), or oriented toward social and even economic activities (sports, halal business, library, women's groups, schools, and so on). As in many other associations, women are underrepresented, with the exception of women's groups oriented to specific activities, mostly related to the education of children. This is also the case with the internal membership on boards of directors or steering committees of national Muslim federations in many countries. At a third level, if we remain in the realm of religious authorities and observe the composition of the various structures that function as the national partner of a state, very few women can be found. It seems nevertheless that a general movement toward empowerment of Muslim women in these religious circles is emerging. This empowerment is often based on new skills in Islamic knowledge (Jonker 2003) and on a growing familiarity with European ideals and principles of gender equality (Roald 2001).

Finally, we must note the opportunities that residence in Western Europe may have given to women that would not have have been available to them in most Muslim societies. Western European countries present an ambiguous face. On the one hand, for women coming from Muslim societies where certain religious signs such as headscarves are perceived as highly political and therefore strongly controlled or forbidden (as in Turkey and Tunisia), European countries represent places of freedom where praying or walking with a veil in the street is not a problem. This idea of Europe as a space of religious freedom is mostly true for countries where religion and politics have found an institutional way of coping with each other. The United Kingdom, Italy, and Germany are perhaps the most obvious cases. In contrast, some limits to this religious freedom may appear and open up highly controversial discussions when it comes to recognizing the individual's right to wear a headscarf at school, at work, or on an ID card. Here again, national political cultures and the way the "neutrality" of the state is articulated with regard to religious pluralism have to be considered in a historical perspective to understand why this topic is so difficult to manage in some contexts, while in others it is rather smoothly discussed. The wish to wear the veil in daily life emerged at the same moment in many European contexts (Belgium, France, Germany, the Netherlands, the United Kingdom). While in most (but not all) cases it has been quite easily managed when the veil is worn at school, matters are different when women make the same claims for religious freedom in the workplace and in particular in the public sector. The tension between two principles – individual rights to practice freely a religion versus state neutrality (as expressed, for instance, by civil servants) – appears obvious. It remains a national debate, not yet a European one. This may eventually change once the European Court for Human Rights produces a case law helping Muslim women to have this specific claim recognized as an individual right to freedom of expression and of religious expression. This is, however, not yet the case (see the recent decision of the European Court for Human Rights, 44774/98 on 29 June 2004.

Bibliography

J.-Y. Carlier and M. Verwilghen (eds.), *Le statut personnel des musulmans. Droit comparé et droit international privé*, Brussels 1992.

G. Jonker, Islamic knowledge through a woman's lens. Education, power and belief, in *Social Compass* 50:1 (2003), 35–46.

A.-S. Roald, *Women in Islam. The Western experience*, London 2001,
W. A. R. Shadid and P. S. van Koningsveld (eds.), *Religious freedom and the neutrality of the state. The position of Islam in the European Union*, Leuven 2002.

Valérie Amiraux

Friendship

Arab States

Recent studies of women, gender, and friendship in Arab states can be roughly divided into two often overlapping categories: studies that focus on the use of the discourse of kinship, broadly defined, in creating and describing women's most central friendships; and studies that draw out the relationship between women's friendships and the geographies and practicalities of women's daily social lives. Recognizing how women create meaningful social relationships through the use of a kinship idiom takes us past a biogenetic, familial-based determinism focusing on the role of the Arab family to a nuanced understanding of how women create a range of meaningful relationships. Traditionally, scholars have emphasized the form and functions of the genealogically-defined extended family, while often excluding other meaningful sources of relationships for women. At issue here is the fact that many women in communities throughout Arab states use the idiom of kinship to describe meaningful relationships of all sorts. Scholars who take this discourse as a simple reflection of biological fact miss the use of the kinship discourse as commentary on the social construction of meaningful social relationships.

Further, by recognizing the roles of neighbors and the socially constructed geographical boundaries of the social lives of Arab women, we may learn how key cultural and political economic forces affect women's intimate lives. Cultural limitations imposed on women's movements and, thus, on women's opportunities for forming close relationships, may not necessarily be seen as oppressive by the women themselves; on the other hand, when international and nationalist politics create artificial borders and boundaries between and among communities, the repercussions for friendships and families alike are often severe and keenly felt as inherently oppressive. Yet because they have often been understood to be both limited to and entrapped by the domestic (rather than public) sphere, women's social circles have often been simplistically assumed to be limited to their family members. Debunking these commonly held misconceptions about women's isolation within the family and carefully delineating the layers of meanings found within the use of the kinship idiom have been central goals of recent scholars.

Finally, studying friendships of women in Arab states may serve to help us consider what exactly constitutes "friendship" in specific cultural settings and lead us to a greater recognition of its culturally and historically constructed qualities, rather than presuming that friendship is an ahistorical, timeless, or "natural" relational category.

Friendship and family

Recent scholarship emphasizes how, in both practice and ideology, notions of family and friend are both closely related to each other and/or distinguished from each other, depending upon context. Thus, although often distinguished linguistically, in practice friend and kinship relationships may be difficult to tell apart. For example, as Geertz points out, although in Morocco speech distinctions are made between kin and non-kin, "the operative, everyday, acted-upon premises do not rely on sharp and simple distinctions among family, friend, and patron" (1979, 315).

Reflecting the closely related character of good friends and one's family is the fact that women's most meaningful friendships are often described as being similar to good kin relations. For example, Lila Abu-Lughod, in a study of Beduin women in Egypt, describes how Beduin who live together and develop close relationships may stress the "link of paternal kinship" in discourse, whether or not it exists, as a means of describing the nature of their friendships; long-time neighbors may thus be considered "quasi-kin" (Abu-Lughod 1986, 63). Soraya Altorki similarly notes for elite women in Saudi Arabia, "old friends are treated as if they were close kin" (1986, 103). Formality is significantly lessened among friends (as it is among family members), and visits are not based on a strict basis of reciprocity. Friendship ties may play a key, supportive role in women's lives, a role that is at times as important as the roles played by kin. Anne Meneley, in her study of Yemeni women in the town of Zabid, notes that the word for "neighbor" has an "emotionally evocative quality," calling up a sense of comfortableness, familiarity, and feeling "like kin" (1996, 54).

These examples demonstrate that, for many

women in the Arab world, the family is a central model for creating meaningful relationships with others. They do not suggest, however, that women are unaware of, or indifferent to, the difference between those who are biologically-related family members and those who are not. Nor does it suggest that friends who are spoken of and/or treated as kin are equated with biological kin. Further, it is important to note that just as relationships among genealogically-related women may be shaped by personal preference, antagonistic histories, or the hope for closer future ties, so too are the relations among friends. Thus, women use the discourse of family to imbue their friendships with culturally appropriate meanings. Ideally, one's extended family members should be one's friends; one's friends, if not from the extended family, should be treated as if they are so related.

Friendship and the geography of social life

Women's friendships in Arab states are shaped not only by expectations of kin-like relations, but also by geographical location, a factor that is intrinsically affected by international and national politics and economics, as well as local practices of gender segregation and, in some instances, seclusion. Geographical constraints and opportunities, always socially and politically constructed, are consequently imbued with cultural, political, symbolic, and emotional meanings.

The importance of closely located neighbors as sources for women's closest friendships is undeniable in places where women's movements are located primarily in, or restricted to, the neighborhood. Wikan, for example, argues that in the case of Sohar, Oman, where women's lives are strictly defined by patterns of sex segregation and by remaining far from the public eye, women maintain circles of diverse companions usually chosen from among their neighbors; women do not use the word "friend" to describe their relationships with one another; rather, men use the word "friend" to describe their relationships with peers. Wikan argues that "the very diversity [in terms of ethnicity, age and wealth] of these circles indicates that physical closeness and convenience are major considerations in their formation" (1982, 116).

Spaces that are primarily female are also important for the formation and maintenance of women's friendships. Suad Joseph argues that, for women in an urban lower-class neighborhood in Lebanon, the requirements of men's work away from their neighborhood left the street a female domain; for women, "co-residence in a street became a basis for intimacy" (1978, 545). Similarly, Rothenberg (2004) has argued that for Muslim villagers in the West Bank, the "kind of family that matters" for many women is shaped by a sense of friendship created, in large part, through the circumstance of being physically close to one another. The role of international as well as local politics is also central here: in the West Bank, the ready existence of a history of ties that can be found to link almost any two neighbors, coupled with the pressure for emigration from the village and the fact that many families are forcibly divided because of Israeli restrictions on who was allowed to return to the West Bank after the occupation that began in 1967, make enduring physical presence as well as individual preference key factors in creating important social ties. Indeed, if almost anyone can be considered kin (albeit to varying degrees) and, simultaneously, the threat of departure from the village is seen as always imminent, the people who matter are those upon whom one can rely and those about whom one cares.

New developments

The ethnographic examples discussed here reflect the linkage between notions of friends and family, as well as close relationships of all kinds and geographical location. A number of relatively recent developments in the Arab world have impacted on and will continue to affect women's experiences of friendship in the decades to come. A process already in motion is women's increasing access to higher education and the workforce, experiences that change the shape and nature of women's friendship networks. It has been demonstrated, for example, that women may become involved in political organizations with their peers on university campuses (for example, El Guindi 1981) and have experiences which are certain to affect their choices of friends. The growth of the nuclear family structure also affects women's opportunities and preferences for large networks of friends; while nuclear family arrangements may allow women some increase in the freedom to make their own choices about with whom to spend their time, it also often increases their workload, as there are fewer adult women to share the work of the household. Finally, the increasingly widespread use of the Internet and "chat rooms" have made both international and cross gender "virtual" friendships possible in ways that were unthinkable a generation ago. These and other changes as yet unforeseen will shape and be shaped by the experience of friendship for women in Arab states and will pose interesting possibilities for future research.

BIBLIOGRAPHY
L. Abu-Lughod, *Veiled sentiments*, Los Angeles 1986.
S. Altorki, *Women in Saudi Arabia*, New York 1986.
F. El Guindi, Veiling infitah with Muslim ethic, in *Social Problems* 28:4 (1981), 465–83.
H. Geertz, The meaning of family ties, in C. Geertz, H. Geertz, and L. Rosen (eds.), *Meaning and order in Moroccan society*, New York 1979, 315–91.
S. Joseph, Women and the neighborhood street in Borj Hammoud, Lebanon, in L. Beck and N. Keddie (eds.), *Women in the Muslim world*, Cambridge, Mass. 1978, 541–58.
A. Meneley, *Tournaments of value*, Toronto 1996.
C. Rothenberg, *Spirits of Palestine*, New York 2004.
U. Wikan, *Behind the veil in Arabia*, Chicago 1982.

CELIA E. ROTHENBERG

The Caucasus and Central Asia

Among the values preserved by the various ethnic groups living in the Caucasus and Central Asia are the maintenance of gendered space and the concept of family honor. Women maintain family reputation and honor by demurely staying in the background and exercising restraint. This often means that women's friendships are primarily forged within the extended family structure, as women of conservative Muslim and Orthodox Christian families traditionally were/are enjoined not to socialize with those unrelated to them. While conservatism is not solely found in rural areas, village life is somewhat more prone to keep within traditional norms due to the intimate living conditions of small settlements. Urban life allows more flexibility and openness because of the anonymity cities provide. This makes it easier for women to create bonds of friendship outside the family circle and widen their webs of social relationships.

How significant friendships between women are when viewed from a socioeconomic and political perspective is difficult to ascertain and represent in numbers and statistics. Currently, there is little if any research material available that specifically addresses the role of friendships in Central Asia or the Caucasus. This may reflect a disinterest of scholars to investigate the importance of informal relationships in general, or women's private lives in particular. It may also indicate a lack of available funding for research that does not translate into economic or political applications. Then again, it may simply be a matter of the difficulty encountered when scholars try to enter into personal discourse with informants who wish to remain anonymous, or mistrust foreigners who apparently represent institutional entities, or – even worse – governments.

Friendships are an integral part of the social network that facilitates local micro-economies and makes survival possible in severely distressed economies of the slowly developing civil societies. Hence, women's friendships are of immense importance as they not only represent an emotional and social outlet for them, but also because they provide access to networks that help pool and redistribute scant resources in areas devastated by Soviet economic policies that created an ecological disaster zone across the vast expanse of Central Asia.

As can be gleaned from numerous scholars of the region whose work originates in different disciplines, women's friendships are essential for the survival of all social groups. Attempts at creating civil societies in the independent states have made the role of friendship among women in given neighborhoods and with women from foreign non-governmental agencies more visible in recent years. Within grassroots organizations run by and for women, friendship between women of different ethnical, religious, and socioeconomic backgrounds are opening channels of communication as well as venues for political agency.

Still, popular religion is often the only acceptable social outlet for many women. Rituals and ceremonies are fertile grounds for renewal, maintenance, and creation of friendships. Unlike most men, women venture past class and professional boundaries in search of social connections. They cast their nets wider in forming friendships and use religious and religiously sanctioned gatherings, especially when sponsored by the *maḥalla* – the traditional community based on patrilineal clan organization – to build networks.

The social life of the community centers on the *maḥalla*, a bastion of traditionalism that situates women in a "safe" and (usually) unassailable discursive space. Within that framework, women's friendships are articulated according to traditionalist sensibilities. In this context, religious instruction by an *otin*, a woman who teaches Islam to girls and women, festivals, rituals, and prayer meetings are welcome diversions and present additional opportunities to connect with the world outside family boundaries.

Most women depend on their friends for emotional support, especially as many of the younger women often find themselves utterly powerless and isolated as junior wives at the mercy of their mother-in-law. A "good wife" is silent, does not leave her house without her husband, and subordinates herself completely to her mother-in-law. This translates into high suicide rates for young brides who are isolated from family and childhood friends, as marriage generally means living with the new husband's family. Especially in rural areas, where not even the illusion of privacy exists, friendships with equally powerless young neighborhood women are crucial in maintaining sanity. Urban life by comparison is somewhat more liberal and anonymous. Town women have more opportunities to meet in the context of the workplace and social outings that cross class and age barriers. Hence, their opportunities to build friendships are enhanced when compared to those of rural women.

Women in post-Soviet space still experience the double burden of being part of the paid labor force as well as being responsible for all domestic chores. Although it appears that there is a revival of pre-Soviet social norms that limit women's role in public positions, the political leadership at least still appears to further women's political engagement. Whether this is mere window dressing to attract Western investment, or represents any deep felt conviction that women ought to have a voice in public and international discourse is open to debate. The fact remains that women in government positions occupy positions of relative powerlessness when compared to their male counterparts. Here again, the role of friendship ought to be investigated. Could women with strong bonds with others in similar situations create a climate of egalitarianism on an official level that could eventually trickle down to the private sphere and domestic discourses? Relevant research remains to be done in this regard.

BIBLIOGRAPHY

F. du P. Gray, *Soviet women. Walking the tightrope*, New York 1989.

P. A. Michaels, Kazak women. Living heritage of a unique past, in H. L. Bodman and N. Tohidi (eds.), *Women in Muslim societies. Diversity within unity*, Boulder, Colo. 1998, 187–202.

J. Nazpary, *Post-Soviet chaos. Violence and dispossession in Kazakhstan*, London 2002.

S. P. Poliakov, *Everyday Islam. Religion and tradition in rural Central Asia*, trans. A. Olcott, ed. and intro. M. B. Olcott, Armonk, N.Y. 1991.

M. H. Ruffin and D. Waugh (eds.), *Civil society in Central Asia*, Seattle 1999.

S. Tadjbaksh, Between Lenin and Allah. Women and ideology in Tajikistan, in H. L. Bodman and N. Tohidi (eds.), *Women in Muslim societies. Diversity within unity*, Boulder, Colo. 1998, 163–86.

N. Tohidi, "Guardians of the nation." Women, Islam, and the Soviet legacy of modernization in Azerbajian, in H. L. Bodman and N. Tohidi (eds.), *Women in Muslim societies. Diversity within unity*, Boulder, Colo. 1998, 137–62.

ANDREA GIACOMUZZI

Iran and Afghanistan

Friendship plays a significant part in the lives of Iranians and Afghans, who do not generally value solitude or privacy, but enjoy forming and maintaining acquaintance and companionship. Women show warmth and affection to their female relatives and friends. Because Iranian and Afghan families often maintain tight ties and most females are generally restricted from movement outside kin circles, the closest friendships are often with mother, sisters, cousins, or aunts.

For females, friends offered support and reprieve from sometimes oppressive husbands or in-laws. Poorer or rural women might be able to confide their stories of mistreatment to neighbors, weep, and receive sympathy. In less well-off and traditional families, males could go out and find friends and activities outside their family and relatives. Especially before large-scale schooling of girls, females faced more severe limitations on developing friendships outside family, female relatives, and neighbors. Class, finances, and level of seclusion affected a female's ability to spend time interacting with others. Women in the socially conservative Pukhtun ethnic group, who form the majority of Afghanistan's population, usually were not able to leave their courtyards or small kin groups and faced barriers to forming friendships outside these circles. Urban and better off rural women in Iran, with its higher standard of living and much larger population, enjoyed a social life of interacting with other women. Rural women looked forward to weddings, visits to the cemetery on Thursday afternoons, and even mourning rituals, as opportunities for talking with other women. Better off women often engaged in rounds of visits and gatherings during which they could converse and keep up friendships. Iranian and urban Afghan women could participate in religious rituals at home, attend segregated life cycle rituals, or perform pilgrimage at shrines together.

Because of the informal and personalistic nature of society, when women mobilized to attain aims, they generally worked with their friends. Some urban Iranian women cooperated with their female friends in supporting the Constitutional Revolution and developing newspapers, journals, and schooling for females in the earlier part of the twentieth century.

Early marriage and moving away to the home of a husband generally disrupted young female friendships. Obligations to husband, children, household, and in-laws, as well as expectations of modesty left little time or opportunity for a young wife to keep up friendships. In her later years, freedom from responsibilities to husband and children, and the greater latitude allowed a post-menopausal woman, enabled her to spend time with friends.

In the 1960s and 1970s, with more girls going to school, and even a minority to university, and then taking jobs, in Iran more so than in Afghanistan, females found opportunities to make friends with their classmates and work associates. Well-off families often participated in one or more circles of people who met on a regular basis, weekly or monthly, for food and conversation. Wealthier women who were not working might take turns hosting elaborate lunches. High school girls might follow suit, their parents driving them to the home of a classmate on a weekend for a good meal cooked by the mother, and then a movie in the afternoon. Even less educated and less economically advantaged women could participate in regular women's religious gatherings to listen to recitations of the passion of Shīʿī Muslim saints. Educated and modernized females in Iran and in the tinier middle- and upper middle-class urban Afghanistan could develop extensive networks outside religious and kin circles. Based more on specific common interests and world-view rather than on proximity, such friendships might last a long time, even after marriage. In urban Iran, groups of couples could enjoy weekend outings and eat out at restaurants together.

In Afghanistan, the war with the Soviet Union, the conflict between factions after the expulsion of the Soviets, and then finally the Taliban rule forced many Afghans to become refugees. Friendships and ties with family and relatives were disrupted. Often Afghan women living as refugees away from their own neighborhoods and villages in Afghanistan faced severe seclusion. Under the Taliban, women were not permitted to leave the house without a male family member escort, and thus were cut off from friends and relatives. Under the insecure conditions of post-Taliban Afghanistan, families fear for the safety of their females, and often do not allow girls to go to school, or visit in other homes without a male family escort, thus reducing opportunities to interact with friends.

In Iran, women met with friends to discuss personal and public issues. Women mobilized their friends for various organizations and participation in political marches for supporters of the revolution against the Pahlavī regime. After the revolution and the subsequent formation of the Islamic Republic of Iran, the religious/political leaders mandated increased gender segregation and women's modesty. In the early years of the republic, women were restricted in their movements and activities and were thus less able to maintain interaction with friends outside religious and kin gatherings. However, after these early policies were modified, even those from rural, lower-class and more conservative families began to attend high school and university in greater numbers, thereby gaining opportunities to develop friendships outside the family. Women's segregated religious gatherings to study the Qur'ān and other religious sources have increased in popularity. Some women are working through their friendship networks to try to bring about positive change in women's rights and opportunities.

In Afghanistan, women cooperated with friends to try to form home-based, secret schools for girls during the Taliban period and to oppose the severe Taliban restrictions on females.

Those Iranian women, and the much smaller percentage of Afghan women, who work outside the home have little time for intensive rounds of visiting and attending religious ritual, neighborhood, kin, and friendship group gatherings. However, they continue to place great importance on socializing, intimate or intellectual exchange, and developing close relationships with other women.

BIBLIOGRAPHY

V. Doubleday, *Three women of Herat*, Austin, Tex. 1988.

H. Emadi, *Repression, resistance, and women in Afghanistan*, London 2002.

S. Farman-Farmaian, *Daughter of Persia. A woman's journey from her father's harem through the Islamic Revolution*, New York 1992.

E. Friedl, *Women of Deh Koh. Lives in an Iranian village*, New York 1991.

M. Hegland, Women and the Iranian Revolution. A village case study, in M. J. Diamond (ed.), *Women and revolution. Global expressions*, Dordrecht, The Netherlands 1998, 211–25.

Z. Kamalkhani, *Women's Islam. Religious practice among women in today's Iran*, London 1997.

M. Kousha, *Voices from Iran*, Syracuse, N.Y. 2002.

H. Moghissi, *Populism and feminism in Iran*, New York 1996.

A. Nafisi, *Reading Lolita in Tehran*, New York 2003.

P. Omidian, *Aging and family in an Afghan refugee community. Transitions and transformation*, New York 1996.

E. Sanasarian, *The Women's rights movement in Iran. Mutiny, appeasement and repression from 1900 to Khomeini*, New York 1982.

N. Tapper (Lindisfarne), The women's subsociety among the Shahsevan nomads of Iran, in L. Beck and N. R. Keddie (eds.), *Women in the Muslim world*, Cambridge, Mass. 1978, 374–98.

——, *Bartered brides. Politics, gender and marriage in an Afghan tribal society*, Cambridge 1991.

A. Torab, The politicization of women's religious circles in post-revolutionary Iran, in S. Ansari and V. Martin, (eds.), *Women, religion, and culture in Iran*, London 2002, 143–68.

MARY ELAINE HEGLAND

South Asia

Like ripples of water hit by a pebble, the social life of Muslim women in South Asia emanated outwards from the center at a speed dictated by the Islamic ideology of purdah and its attendant concepts of *ʿizzat* (honor) and *sharm* (dishonor) on one hand, and embracing Western education and its concomitants on the other. Little is known about the social life of women in the early twentieth century. Literary and survey sources focus on the family and kin as sources for social relations. Women, especially sisters, functioned both as siblings and friends. Zeenat Futehally dedicated her novel *Zohra* (1951) to her three sisters. Elite women had the privilege of social access to Parsee, Hindu, and English women. This is portrayed in Attia Hossain's short story, "The First Party" (1991). Unlike the world of family and kin, this constituted a formal social world and less of an intimate emotional one. Unlike elite Muslims who lived in multiethnic locations, their less privileged sisters were clustered in *moholla*s (ethnic enclaves). Besides family and kin their social network spilled into the neighborhood. Ismat Chughtai's short story, "The Wedding Suit" (2001), set in North India, describes the role of neighborhood women in assisting each other in preparing the bride's trousseau as girls in various households reached marriageable age. In Gujarat when men were away at work, women sat on the *otlo* (porch) of their residential building and gossiped with neighbors, a practice that continues to this day. The purpose of the network was instrumental in scope – religious and life cycle rituals – rather than for leisure. With few exceptions the site for friendship was limited to the domestic space and contacts centered on same sex, sect, and class but across generations as well. There is no scholarship on lesbian relationships within the *zenana* (women's quarters). Ismat Chughtai's short story, "The Quilt" (2001), written in the 1940s, depicts a lesbian relationship between a woman and her maidservant, as seen through the eyes of a child.

Cross-gender contact, not to mention friendships, were strictly taboo. However, unlike the Hindus, Muslims practiced purdah primarily toward non-related males. As a result, across class and sect, relations between kinsmen and women were relaxed and as cousin marriages were favored there was teasing leading to romantic overtures. This is depicted in several literary works such as Qurratulain Hyder's short story, "Memories of an Indian Childhood" (1991). Contact with unrelated males was not completely absent. In her autobiographical work, *The Brocaded Saree* (1946), Ishvani mentions how as a young doctor her grandfather trained the women of the community to assist him in taking the pulse of women and delivering their children into the world.

The publication of Muslim women's journals and the formation of Muslim women's associations extended the social boundaries of women to a greater geographical sphere. The publication of *Tahzib un-Niswan*, *Khatun*, and *ʿIsmat* in the twentieth century initiated the spread of ideas of women's education and social change. Muhammadi Begum, the co-editor of *Tahzib un-Niswan* wrote in *Adab i-Mulaqat*, an etiquette book dealing with social gatherings, on how to offer hospitality at such "modern" functions as tea parties and what to do when visiting. Minault (1998) writes, "This was especially useful information for *purdah*-observing women who were just beginning to socialize beyond the immediate family circle and were unsure how to behave." The All India Muslim Ladies' Conference (Anjuman-i-Khawatin-i-Islam) was formed in Aligarh in 1914. It established regional branches and advocated female education and a purdah observance based on Islamic injunction rather than the stricter variety dictated by custom. Minault highlights some of the friendships among its office bearers and hosts from different parts of the country and the increased sense of community it fostered among Muslim women. In a limited way, it also expanded exposure to non-kin men.

By the 1930s the acceptance of higher education for girls, relaxation of purdah rules, and Gandhi's political activism opened possibilities for the integration of women into a network that transcended regional, religious, and sectarian lines. Schools and colleges functioned as new sites from where friends could be drawn. The postcolonial disintegration of joint family and business, alteration in residential patterns, and improved public transport brought additional possibilities in women's friendship patterns. Anees Jung (1993) on Muslim women describes Rashida, 20 and unmarried, who sits amidst a group of women who gather every week at a welfare center. The women talk about their homes, problems of raising children, husbands who dominate, and elders who squabble.

Despite dramatic changes, women's friendships remained firmly rooted in their ethno-sectarian communities. International migration resulted in dispersal, but identity politics and Hindu-Muslim riots have pushed many back to their ethnic enclave and undone the social achievements of the past century. This is best illustrated by the women of the Daudi Bohra Ismāʿīlī sect of Shīʿī Muslims who continue with their practice of friendship, prevalent since the early twentieth century, variously known as *menij* (turn), *sayoo* (friends), or *goth* (an arrangement). This is a circle of ten to twelve women similar in age and class who meet on a rotation basis every month in a member's home. Entry is established by puberty and is formalized by a few basic rules such as collection of annual dues, charge of a fee for failure to adhere to one's turn, and so forth. The cash collected is spent going to movies, restaurants, and picnics. From time to time extra dues are collected for travel. The main purpose is to pass time, have good food, pray together, and exchange information pertaining to women's concerns. Women enjoy the company of other women as it addresses their special interests, reduces their dependency on men, and gives them privacy. As a concession to modernity, the community has added a new dimension to friendship known as "couple-company" consisting of married men and women who follow a similar pattern. Social contact between the sexes is still dictated by the Islamic ideology of purdah and the nature of political economy. Jeffery (1979), describing the lives of women of *pirzade* men (custodians of a shrine in Delhi), writes that accommodating male guests posed a serious challenge as women had to be made invisible to them. These extremes reflect the diversity of women's experience in South Asia.

Bibliography

M. Asaduddin (ed.), *Lifting the veil. Selected writings of Ismat Chughtai*, Delhi 2001.
Z. Fatehully, *Zohra*, Bombay 1951.
A. Hosain, The first party, in L. Holmstrom (ed.), *The inner courtyard. Stories by Indian women*, Delhi 1991, 106–11.
Q. Hyder, Memories of an Indian childhood, in L. Holmstrom (ed.), *The inner courtyard. Stories by Indian women*, Delhi 1991, 39–55.
Ishvani, *The brocaded saree*, London 1946.
P. Jeffery, *Frogs in a Well. Indian women in purdah*, London 1979.
A. Jung, *Night of the new moon. Encounters with Muslim women in India*, Delhi 1993.
G. Minault, *Secluded scholars*, Delhi 1998.

Rehana Ghadially

Sub-Saharan Africa: West Africa

Your presence in my life is by no means fortuitous. Our grandmothers in their compounds were separated by a fence and would exchange messages daily. Our mothers used to argue over who would look after our uncles and aunts. As for us we wore out wrappers and sandals on the same stony road to the koranic school . . . We walked the same paths from adolescence to maturity, where the past begets the present. My friend, my friend, my friend. I call upon you three times (Mariama Bâ, *So Long a Letter*).

Types of women's intimate relationships

Friendship is a voluntary relationship based upon trust that one chooses to engage in and that provides mutual rewards, including personal and social support. Unlike the formally structured interactions of kinship and other socially institutionalized roles, which are ultimately about meeting the needs of groups in society, friendships are primarily about meeting the needs of individuals, including expressions of intimacy and the privileging of and by another. Such relationships are more easily entered into over the course of an individual's lifetime but are also more easily abandoned, a brittleness that may at times prove useful.

Female friendships throughout Sub-Saharan Africa, including Muslim regions, tend to be distinguished by age groups and gender. From among one's contemporaries are chosen the majority of one's friends – those acquaintances whom one is always happy to see and who are greeted warmly at the market-place or at school; those "useful to know" people with whom one may exchange gifts and even the formalized mutual obligations of a patron/client relationship; and those who are the "most-trusted friends," with whom people share the joys and sorrows of their lives. This type of relationship is the focus here. It may last longer than many marriages and may transcend time and space. Such longstanding intimacy is illustrated sensitively in the novella *So Long a Letter* (1981) by Senegalese author Mariama Bâ, who uses the device of an exchange of letters between two educated Wolof women, friends since childhood. At times, a woman's intimate associations with other women may take precedence over her bonds of kinship and marriage; they certainly help her cope successfully with the demands of such ties.

In general, women friends form mutual aid societies, complementing the ranks of female kinswomen. They watch each other's homes, children, and at times, husbands, and often send food back and forth to each other. Indeed, this exchange of food can be an important way of establishing or reinforcing a friendship. When spouses quarrel it is often a female friend who intervenes to heal the breach and who seeks to keep the dispute from escalating out of bounds. She counsels patience and restraint to both parties. Since marriage in Sub-Saharan Africa is rarely just between two people, this function of the friend as mediator can play an important role before representatives of the families have to become involved. Female friends will also come to the aid of a woman who gives birth far from her female relatives. They take over all household duties for the first week and check in on her as she gradually resumes her household tasks.

This sharing of the minutiae of daily life is highly characteristic of women's friendships as is the frequent intersection of female kin (relatives) and non-kin (friends). One of the few to study friendship in Africa was Paul Riesman who examined personality formation among the Muslim Fulbe of Burkina Faso. He comments on these matters when he elucidates the Fulbe proverb, "*giDo yaaye womnata BiDDo*" (It's the mother's friend who will make the baby dance). He explains that playing with a baby by bouncing it on one's lap and tossing it up slightly is known as "making the baby dance"; thus, a true friend is a person who will help not only the individual but also one's relatives, represented by the image of playing with the child (Riesman 1992, 118).

Islam and the conventions of friendship: the example of the Muslim Hausa

Muslim Hausa women in Sub-Saharan Africa are bound by social convention – believed to derive from the prescriptions of the Qurʾān – to entertain friends only in their households. Married women should be attractive only in their homes since their husbands will blame them if any other man finds them attractive. To decrease the odds that this will happen, formal visits between friends take place after nightfall, which also coincides with the end of the workday and the completion of daily chores.

Married men generally are not close to their wives nor women to their husbands. Men tend to stay out of women's quarters in other homes and only rarely enter these quarters in their own homes. They feel freer in visiting older sisters and other female relatives than they do in visiting younger sisters. In these female quarters, then, women have a great degree of freedom from male scrutiny and censure. Visits are one way that Hausa women develop and maintain their own networks as well as their ongoing involvements in their extended families. Religious ceremonies such as marriages and naming ceremonies are constant events in Hausa communities and provide other opportunities for women to meet, develop connections, and exchange information without any male presence. Through these networks they influence developments in their wider communities.

Women's visiting networks have become especially important in the contemporary urban centers, places such as the barracks of Kano, Nigeria studied by Katja Werthmann. The barracks area of Kano is part of the new section of town and the layout of houses is quite different from that in the Old City of Kano. In the Old City there is a clear division of public and private space and women's spaces are safely away from the public gaze. The barracks houses, however, do not afford this privacy. The old entrance hall is gone and there is no public space to replace it. Moreover, the outer area is not shaded as in traditional houses so men spend their days near mosques or in other areas where they can more comfortably meet. Women are almost the sole occupants of the neighborhood for much of the day and have used this opportunity to more fully develop their friendships. Because the women living in this neighborhood of Kano come from all over Nigeria there is a virtual absence of women's kinship networks. Instead, women have replaced these local kin networks with ones of non-kin friends throughout the city and reinforce these key support relationships with systematic visiting practices.

The ties of kinship and of friendship may intersect in other contexts as well. Hausa life cycle celebrations illustrate this point. Men and women remain separated for most of the events. For example, the bride is never present at a Hausa wedding, while the groom is typically present if the wedding is his bride's first marriage. The woman receives her guests and gifts at her father's home. Her female relatives and friends take care of the preparations for the celebration. The bride recites verses from the Qurʾān in a display of her piety and knowledge in front of her relatives. As she does so, her female friends are there to support her, but traditionally hidden from view until the women join together in their party afterwards. The women then announce the marriage to the larger community by taking cakes and other treats home with them, thus spreading the news of the marriage through distributing a female-associated domestic product, processed food.

Gender segregation and celebration with friends also characterizes Hausa naming celebrations. The naming ceremony for a newborn child has two parts. In the early morning, the ceremony occurs at the mosque. It is for men only and here the baby receives its name. Then there is a later celebration that begins late in the morning. This ceremony is for women only. It generally gets loud and festive and takes up most of the remainder of the day. There is ceremonial drumming, performed by Hausa males who are allowed in despite the restrictions of purdah. They begin with Hausa style drumming but move to a more generic Muslim style as the day continues. Then music fills the air and women dance with one another. They have the time to relax, eat, catch up on each other's news, exchange information, and enjoy one another's company.

BIBLIOGRAPHY

M. Bâ, *So long a letter*, trans. ModupéBodé-Thomas, Oxford 1981.

L. Creevey and B. Callaway, *The heritage of Islam. Women, religion, and politics in West Africa*, Boulder, Colo. 1994.

D. A. Donahoe, Measuring women's work in developing countries, in *Population and Development Review* 253 (1999), 543.

B. House-Midamba and F. K. Ekechi (eds.), *African market women and economic power. The role of women in African economic development*, Westport, Conn. 1995.

P. Riesman, *First find your child a good mother. The construction of self in two African communities*, New Brunswick, N.J. 1992.

F. A. Salamone, *The Hausa people. A bibliography*, New Haven, Conn. 1983.

——, *God and goods in Africa*, Salem, Wis. 1985.

——, The problem of magic and religion. Further explorations into the relationship of missionaries and anthropologists, in *Proceedings of the New York State Sociological Association*, Oakdale, N.Y. 1994.

——, The Bori and I. Reflections of a mature anthropologist, in *Anthropology and Humanism* 19 (June 1995) 15–19.

——, Law and ritual. A Nigerian case, in *Papers of the commission's Xth international congress*, Faculty of Law, University of Ghana, Legon, Ghana, 21–4 August 1995, 14–38.

——, Review of William Miles, *Hausaland divided*, in *American Ethnologist* 23 (1996), 161–2.

——, Ethnicity and Nigeria since the end of the civil war, in *Journal of Dialectical Anthroplogy* 22 (1997), 303–33

——, The illusion of ethnic identity. An introduction to ethnicity and its uses, in L. L. Naylor, *Multiculturalism and diversity in the United States*, Westport, Conn. 1997, 117–26.

——, The Waziri and the thief. Hausa Islamic law in a Yoruba city. A case study from Ibadan, Nigeria, in *Journal of Legal Pluralism* 42 (1998), 139–55.

——, Children's games as mechanisms for easing ethnic interaction in ethnicially heterogeneous communities. A Nigerian case, in S. M. Channa (ed.), *International encyclopedia of anthropology*, iv, New Delhi 1998, 751–65.

——, Religion and repression. Enforcing feminine inequality in an "egalitarian society," in S. M. Channa (ed.), *International encyclopedia of anthropology*, xi, New Delhi 1998, 2551–62.

——, Hausa, in J. F. Rodriguez (ed.), *The historical encyclopedia of world slavery*, 2 vols., San Francisco 1998, 333–44.

——, Bornu-Kanem Sultanatein, in *Magill's guide to military history*, Pasadena 2000, 222–4.

—— with V. Salamone, Kirki. A core value of Hausa culture, in *Africa* (Italy) 48 (1993), 359–81.

——, Erikson in Nigeria. Exploring the universality of the theory of psychosocial development, in *Anthropos* 88 (1993), 87–98.

K. Werthmann, Matan bariki, "women of the barracks." Muslim Hausa women in an urban neighbourhood in northern Nigeria, in *Africa* 72:1 (2002), 112–30

FRANK A. SALAMONE

Gender Socialization

Central Asia

Although the development of gender socialization throughout Central Asia shares a common history, the Soviet period created fundamental changes. Currently this process is expressed through socio-economic, cultural, and political differences among Central Asian republics.

Throughout Central Asia the concept that women belong to men is ubiquitous: their social status is acquired through father, brother, husband, and son (Tokhtakhodjaeva 2001). Socialization is geared to gender roles: for the woman, the role of wife, mother, and housewife; for the man, provider and head of household.

The family is the main agent of socialization, especially for Muslim women; even in the Soviet period, women, essentially excluded from the public sphere, lived mainly within the home and family (Pal'vanova 1982). In the traditional Central Asian family children, male and female, understand their gender identity at a very early age. The birth of a boy is joyfully celebrated by everyone (Andreev 1953). Girls are rarely accorded such attention. The parents, especially fathers, openly express emotional attachment to their young sons, even through play emphasizing the boy's gender significance (Kisliakov 1969). Fathers are significantly less attentive to female children. Mothers prepare girls to take care of themselves and to take on their allocated obligations. At the age of five and six years girls take care of younger siblings. From earliest childhood girls are taught to tolerate deprivation and limitations in food, sleep, and comforts. A capricious girl is not tolerated, while the family accepts capricious and demanding boys. Mothers and grandmothers promote these attitudes. Using her own experience a mother prepares her daughter for her subsequent difficult life as a wife in the husband's home, where she will be subservient to the husband and his relatives (Sharipova 2002). The strictly hierarchical relationship between bride and mother-in-law is a frequent source of family conflict, especially in recent times, when young wives (even in rural areas) are better informed about their rights and have a better developed sense of their own worth than women of the older generation.

Observing the father's power in the family's daily life, boys recognize their superiority over girls; they know that they have the right to punish them if they deviate from the norms of their gender status. Boys are encouraged to activity, to self-defense, to aggressiveness. They spend a great deal of time outside the home in the company of men.

Both family and community exercise strict control over girls' behavior. Girls know that they must serve other family members, especially the males. They must be modest, obedient, and fear all men: male kin may punish them for disobedience and strange men may cast aspersions on their honor and good name. A girl's good name is the capital that defines her worth in the family and the community. That good name includes not only preserving her virginity until marriage, but modesty in clothing and speech, and not showing herself in social spaces with unrelated men. Control over girls' and women's sexual behavior is a fundamental element in Central Asian gender socialization. Traditional norms encourage asexuality in women of all ages. Expressing sexuality in any form is considered deviant behavior (Sharipova 2002). However, in the post-Soviet period preserving virginity until marriage is more or less a formality. Both premarital and extramarital sex are practiced, especially in the big cities and regions influenced by polyethnic culture (Tabyshalieva 1998).

Gender segregation is especially rigid in the plains of Tajikistan, Uzbekistan, Turkmen villages, and the southern areas of Kazakhstan and Kyrgyzstan. In the mountainous areas of Tajikistan gender segregation is less rigid than in the plains and women are more independent, since the household is in women's hands (Andreev 1953). In the cities of Kazakhstan and Kyrgyzstan where polyethnic groups predominate, traditional norms and the Sharīʿa are more of a formality (Tabyshalieva 1998).

The role of education in the socialization of Central Asian Muslim women was important in the Soviet period. Formal education for all and obligatory work for women outside the home led to the formation of a female social group within class: worker, peasant, intelligentsia. The intelligentsia encouraged education for girls that was geared to professions differentiated by gender. Thus, teaching and medical work were considered appropriate for women, commensurate with their roles of mother, wife, housekeeper. Soviet modernization gave rise to a special form of male and female conformism, a double standard between Russified norms of behavior at work and in social spaces, but the observation of traditional norms of behavior within the family and in personal relationships between men and women.

Mass communication has had an enormous influence on gender socialization. In the post-Soviet period Muslim ideology and the formation of a model Muslim woman are furthered through the mass media, literature, and art. Secular publications portray a synthesis of the stereotype of the new Central Asian woman, a blend of wife and mother with worker. There is also an element entirely new to the Central Asian mentality, namely public sexuality. Advertisements for cosmetics and clothing and the arrival of beauty contests create a feminine ideal through the female body.

The socioeconomic crisis and the influence of globalization in the post-Soviet period have weakened the role of male as provider. More women must become full- or part-time providers for their families. This, of course, changes traditional concepts of masculinity and femininity (Kasymova 2002). The working woman who feeds her family will spend the greater part of her day at work and she will go on business trips, while the husband remains at home and takes care of the children and the household. These changes create external and internal conflicts evidenced by discrimination toward women. Domestic violence, sexual abuse at work and in social places increase the vulnerability of Muslim women. These factors contribute to deviant behavior by women, such as prostitution, illegal business undertakings, and suicide. Female self-immolation is observed mainly in Tajikistan and Uzbekistan. These tendencies are present not only in the cities but in rural areas through Central Asia (Tabyshalieva 1998).

BIBLIOGRAPHY

Andreev, *Tajik valleys of Khuf* [in Russian], Stalinabad 1953.

A. Bauer, N. Boshman, and D. Grin, *Women and gender relations in Kazakhstan. Social consequences* [in Russian], Manila 1998.

A. Dzhalilov, *On the history of women in Central Asia before and after the introduction of Islam* [in Russian], Dushanbe 1974.

C. Harris, *Control and subversion. Gender and socialism in Tajikistan*, Manchester, U.K. 2000.

Islam and Eastern Women [in Russian], Tashkent 1990.

S. Kasymova, Gender relations in traditional Tajik society [in Finnish], in *Idantutkimus* (Helsinki) 2 (2002), 45–55.

N. Kisliakov, *Studies in the history of the family and marriage among the peoples of Central Asia and Kazakhstan* [in Russian], Leningrad 1969.

B. Pal'vanova, *Emancipating the Islamic woman* [in Russian], Moscow 1982.

A. Tabyshalieva, *Reflections of time. Notes on the history of Central Asian women* [in Russian] Bishkek 1998.

M. Tokhtakhodjaeva, *Exhausting the past. The position of women in Uzbekistan, a society in the process of reclaiming Islam* [in Russian], Tashkent 2001.

Women in Kyrgyzstan. Tradition and new realities [in Russian], Bishkek 1995.

Sofia Kasymova

Iran and Afghanistan

Girl children are socialized into sex segregation, dependency, lack of authority, and severely limited access to resources through example, admonition, contradictory gender messages, stories, heavy demands, and violence (especially in Afghanistan). In popular gender ideology girls differ from boys and have contradictory characteristics: infant girls need more food (are weaned later) but older girls need less food; girls are smaller and weaker yet more resilient; better tempered yet fickle; more emotional yet secretive; sweeter yet valued less although fathers can sell them for a bride price, especially in Afghanistan; and frail yet hard working. Their reason (*ʿaql*) is firmer (they assume responsibilities earlier than boys), yet women's reason is weaker than men's. As part of their father's kin group, their loyalty is challenged after marriage. These purported differences within the gender hierarchy, authoritarian relationships (responsibility from men downwards, obedience upwards to men), and patrilineality with preference for male children account for differences in socialization. They also lead to benign and explicit neglect of girls, including differential access to food, health care and schooling, and to traffic in children (in Afghanistan). Population statistics suggest a gender imbalance favoring males in Iran, but figures are unreliable.

A girl's beauty is praised yet girls hear that their attractiveness threatens men. Even female toddlers are told to be modest (be well covered, sit with folded legs, not laugh or speak in front of men). Girls are told to trust male relatives yet also to perceive men as threats (like wolves) and to be suspicious of them. The avoidance of unwanted male attention and aggression is a major concern, and girls admonish and chaperone each other and avoid public spaces, especially in Afghanistan. Until the age of about six, they can appear in public bareheaded; later, modesty dictates attire ranging from colorful head-scarf and short, tight coat over jeans in cities in Iran today to the all-encompassing veil almost everywhere in Afghanistan. In Iran, some young urban women date men (especially on the telephone) and appear in public unmolested with make-up and minimal compliance with the dress code, setting examples for others. In Afghanistan girls still learn that only the veil, strict segregation, and home mean safety and propriety, and are punished for transgressions by women and men.

Males older than nine may claim authority over females. In all social strata this creates power struggles between sisters and younger brothers who demand compliance but whom sisters still see as the wards they had been as toddlers. Girls come to expect brothers to be more restrictive than fathers and more likely to be violent. Public improprieties will bring punishment because they suggest a girl's poor management by father or brothers and thus diminish the men's honor. In Afghanistan women may use men's fear of losing control over their women to subvert male authority, but girls learn through their stories that this is dangerous.

Obedience requires the instillment of respectful fear (*tars*) in children. Girls, taken to be more compliant than boys, develop respect mostly through admonition, scolding, and intimidation while for boys additional harsh threats and beatings are deemed necessary in most traditional families. Girls witness aggression among male relatives, toward women and themselves, and come to see it as a lamentable fact of life. Staying close to home, girls have unparalleled intelligence abilities and functions and thus are suspected especially by their brothers of possessing secret knowledge. Lacking authority, they learn to exert power by manipulating people and knowledge and through dissimulation, at the price of being called untrustworthy. Most learn to see that they are the property and wards of men (especially in Afghanistan) and that their position is one of servitude, that their restricted access to important things from money and inheritance to religious rituals is immutable, and to regard their marital future as fate beyond their control. Depression among women and girls is high in both countries and discussed widely in Iran.

Formal education reaches most children in Iran, while in Afghanistan it is unavailable to most, especially to girls. The Iranian government pushes girls' education to meet women's needs in the Islamic society; this led to a surge of women into education. In the sex segregated schools female students do not defer to males but compete among themselves, which benefits their self esteem. Middle-class girls are encouraged to emulate professional women. Even young rural and low-class women now see education as an alternative to early marriage and large families, however unrealistic it is for most. In Afghanistan religion was used to rationalize banning girls from all schooling and is still used to justify the transmission to girls of traditional, premodern patterns of life for women in all classes and regions, including the notion that marriage, motherhood, and dependency form the only God-ordained, reasonable female existence. Child betrothal and early marriage of girls are still practiced widely in Afghanistan while even in rural Iran most girls now expect a say in marriage arrangements. Polygyny, divorce, and the sorry fate of "fallen" women are popular themes in the media and among women everywhere. Although relatively rare (especially in Iran), polygyny and divorce are a source of power for men and of anxiety for women, and this is communicated to children and produces fear of loss of mother.

Girls learn skills, outlook on life, and patterns of behavior, thinking, and feeling by observing men and imitating women. They rehearse infant care and chores along with the expression of affect and pain, elicitation of support and pity, supplication of saints, and resistance (for example, dodging demands). Teasing and lying as tools of control lead to general distrust, but experience also teaches girls to feel safe with their mother and female relatives (especially in Iran). They also learn that competence leads to confidence and that support of males, even to the detriment of women, gains approval. Yet, everywhere girls also come to realize that "good" (self effacing, compliant) women are less successful as persons, mothers, and wives than those who earn money and are vocal, manipulative, and pushy.

Bibliography

A. Aghajanian, The status of women and female children in Iran. An update from the 1986 census, in M. Afkhami and E. Friedl (eds.), *In the eye of the storm. Women in post-revolutionary Iran*, Syracuse, N.Y. 1994, 44–60.

E. Friedl, *Children of Deh Koh. Young lives in an Iranian village*, Syracuse, N.Y. 1997.

S. Guppy, *The blindfold horse. Memories of a Persian childhood*, Boston 1988.

M. Kousha, *Voices from Iran. The changing lives of Iranian women*, Syracuse, N.Y. 2002.

G. Mehran, Socialization of schoolchildren in the Islamic Republic of Iran, in *Iranian Studies* 22 (1989), 35–50.

A. Najmabadi, Crafting an educated housewife in Iran, in L. Abu-Lughod (ed.), *Remaking women. Feminism and modernity in the Middle East*, Princeton, N.J. 1998, 92–125.

N. Rachlin, Would I have become a writer without my sister? in E.W. Fernea (comp. and ed.), *Remembering childhood in the Middle East. Memoirs from a century of change*, Austin, Tex. 2002, 320–8.

Save the Children, *Afghanistan's children in crisis*, Westport, Conn. 2002.

A. C. Shalinski, Learning sexual identity. Parents and children in northern Afghanistan, in *Anthropology and Education Quarterly* 11 (1980), 254–65.

N. Tapper, *Bartered brides. Politics, gender, and marriage in a tribal society*, Cambridge 1991.
B. S. Yasgur, *Behind the burqa. Our life in Afghanistan and how we escaped to freedom / by "Sulima" and "Hala" as told to Batya Swift Yasgur*, Hoboken, N.J. 2002.

ERIKA LOEFFLER FRIEDL

The Ottoman Empire

Muslim women's place in Ottoman society was constructed on a complex foundation of ideals and actualities. As in other Islamic communities, the internal configuration of the family and the socioeconomic location of the household were shaping conditions. In combination with these, the patriarchally inclined customs and expectations of the larger society, particularly as projected in Islamic law, served to define women's roles. However, the ambiguities and contradictions of law and custom, and women's own efforts to operate within that interpretive space, moderated patriarchal rigidities, enabling women to achieve a larger share of familial and communal power.

Although women were generally excluded from Ottoman narratives of empire, their experience in real-life terms emerges from less hierarchical documentation. Court records, which are uniquely voluminous for the Ottoman period, have overturned the received wisdom of strictly enforced female seclusion and subordination. The degree of women's autonomous action cannot be compared to that of the present era, but Ottoman women, despite misogynistic popular discourse and restrictive government policies, were able to affect decisions about their own lives and to exercise control over others.

As in the premodern world generally, Ottoman women's social existence and personal identity centered on the family. Marriage, childbearing, and participation in the family economy were paramount. Family members were the principal – usually the only – source of female instruction in religion, social conduct, and work. Most young women married into domestic households like those of their mothers and grandmothers. Virgin brides, prized for their youth, sexual innocence, and tractability, fetched the highest bride-price (Arabic, *mahr*; Turkish, *mehr*), but previously married women were not at all shunned. Divorcees, widows, and the deserted, prompted by the absence of independent economic opportunities for women, sought and found new husbands.

Despite the idealization of female submission, factors internal and external to the family often compelled more egalitarian practice. The size of the Ottoman Empire, its heterogeneous demographics, and the difficulties of communication before the nineteenth century, promoted regional distinctions. Different understandings of appropriate female behavior also arose from changes in provincial governors, shifts in women's productive roles, and other structural and historical factors.

Probably no one geographical area or socioeconomic arrangement was consistently more liberal than others with respect to women's status and roles. Women in Cairo seem to have enjoyed greater public visibility and voice than women in Istanbul, but the evidence is not systematic for the entirety of Ottoman rule. In any case, as the imperial capital, Istanbul was the main arena for the exemplary projection of government power. Thus Istanbul's women were subject to more frequent and forceful policing than women elsewhere. Even in kindred Turkish-speaking cities such as Bursa and Edirne, women had to contend with fewer official limitations on their movements and dress. Veiling, including concealment of the face, was the norm for all classes on urban streets, but styles of head and face covering differed from place to place and across ethnic groups as well as between classes. In Istanbul, the fashion center of the empire, the prescribed dress for Muslim women in the seventeenth through the mid-nineteenth centuries was the *ferace* dust-coat with separate pieces of fabric for the head wrap and veil. Poorer women, tribal women, and provincial visitors obeyed the spirit of the law with respect to facial and bodily anonymity, but adoption of Istanbul's female uniform was not always necessary if women kept to their own residential neighborhoods or enclaves.

In general, women were denied access to institutions and collectivities that bespoke sociopolitical equality with male members of the community. Thus women were discouraged, if not forcibly prevented, from attending congregational mosques at prayer time, and with few exceptions over the centuries women were kept from active membership in the craft guilds. Again, though, restrictions varied, especially with regard to mosque attendance. Istanbul's massive cathedral mosques, physically and psychologically located at the center of power, tended to be off-limits to female worshippers. Some other mosques, in the capital and elsewhere, were more genuinely communal. Women's long-recognized patronage of popular forms of worship, notably local pilgrimage and saint reverence, helped compensate for their exclusion from male-gendered rituals. The most revered of the shrines frequented by women in the Ottoman Turkish-speaking world was the burial place of Abū Ayyūb

(Eyüp) al-Anṣārī, a Companion of the Prophet who died in a seventh-century Muslim siege of Byzantine Constantinople.

Women's involvement with the empire's justice system, particularly the Islamic courts, reflects the relative openness of this mainstay of imperial legitimacy. For reasons that have still to be explained, women's use of the court system varied from place to place. For example, seventeenth-century court cases from the Anatolian towns of Kayseri, Amasya, Karaman, and Trabzon reveal that women's participation in legal actions ranged from 17 percent to a surprising 42 percent (Jennings 1975, 59). The variety of female commercial and financial litigation further refutes the stereotypes of female passivity and isolation. On the other hand, most women who came to the court did so as plaintiffs, and most plaintiffs were in conflict with husbands and ex-husbands.

The high incidence of divorce, child custody, support, and property cases in the court records of the seventeenth to the nineteenth centuries illuminates the paradox of family – especially conjugal – instability in the Ottoman Islamic patriarchal setting. Recourse to formal adjudication points to women's social vulnerability and their difficulty in gaining entitlements without legal arm-twisting. Women showed their willingness to pursue claims in a public forum, sometimes speaking in their own voices, at other times through designees. The fact that there were courts in which they could make their case was a particular mark of Ottoman rule, which took care to establish and staff hundreds of courts throughout its territories.

The natural and man-made disasters afflicting the Ottoman Empire in the seventeenth through the nineteenth centuries also challenged prescribed gender roles. The proportion of women who headed their own households waxed and waned with warfare, plague, banditry, and male migration. As in today's Middle East, Ottoman men were highly, though episodically, mobile. Islamic law's provisions for women to inherit from husbands and fathers, and to receive compensation from divorcing husbands for *mahr* balances and other debts, lessened women's economic dependency overall. Independent means as bargaining leverage was most evident in the case of mature widows or divorcees contemplating remarriage. In fact, there is some evidence that wealthier women sought to avoid remarriage.

In the eighteenth century, the empire's military and economic incapacities and its growing susceptibility to European intervention were manifested in domestic politics in a heightening of gender tensions. Sumptuary laws, particularly restrictions on clothing, were issued with increasing frequency and severity to force women and other targeted groups to adhere to the colors, fabrics, and styles that had traditionally been prescribed for them. The moralist critique of the legislation resembled that of other Islamic – and non-Islamic – regimes with respect to the causal link between women's comportment and social order. Women's behavior was often a convenient foil for larger state worries. Prior to the eighteenth century, however, women were usually singled out in connection with specific historical occurrences. The barrage of decrees affecting women in the eighteenth and early nineteenth centuries served similar purposes in Ottoman politics. Nonetheless, the constant focus on women through both conservative and reformist sultanates in the late Ottoman centuries suggests newly enduring social and political anxieties with which women were consistently and inextricably linked.

Bibliography

R. C. Jennings, Women in early 17th-century Ottoman judicial records. The sharia court of Anatolian Kayseri, in *Journal of the Economic and Social History of the Orient* 18 (1975), 53–114.

A. E. Sonbol (ed.), *Women, the family, and divorce laws in Islamic history*, Syracuse, N.Y. 1996.

M. C. Zilfi (ed.), *Women in the Ottoman Empire. Middle Eastern women in the early modern era*, Leiden 1997.

Madeline C. Zilfi

South Asia

Muslims came to the Indian subcontinent in the eighth century and established trading relations between India and Arabia. Nearly a century later Muslim warriors from across its northern borders, including Afghans, Persians, and Turks invaded India and established political hegemony. The Muslim population in India grew both through conversion of Hindus to Islam and intermarriage with local women, as the invading armies did not bring their wives along with them. The Muslim population of India is the largest in South Asia. According to the census of 1941 (the last census before the 1947 partition into India and Pakistan and the 1971 division of Bangladesh from Pakistan), Muslims were nearly a quarter of the total population of India. Post-partition the Muslim population was larger in India than in Pakistan or Bangladesh, and it continues to be so.

South Asian Muslims are not a monolithic community and cannot be represented by a uniform Islamic image. Muslims in South Asian countries have been greatly influenced by the local socioeconomic and cultural conditions. The countries of the subcontinent share a common cultural heritage, predominantly Hindu, highly patriarchal, and characterized by a high level of gender discrimination and suppression of women that finds expression in the socializing practices of girls. The social position of Muslim women has been influenced by the corresponding position of Hindu women. In the compounding of Hindu and Muslim cultures the conservative and restrictive elements of Hindu tradition neutralized the liberal elements of Islam, so that Muslim women lost out on the Islamic right of widow remarriage and women's rights to inheritance, which were denied to Hindu women. In turn, Hindu women adopted the Muslim restrictive tradition of purdah (seclusion).

Socialization of girls in South Asia starts from early childhood. Little girls are fed on the model of submissive, passive, obedient, sacrificing, serving, and pious non-persons, who are to live and die as daughters, wives, and mothers, and who should never as much as even aspire to have an identity of their own. Female role behavior is instilled into girls through socialization and the socializing agents are, ironically, women themselves. The socializing process takes place at different levels, in the family, at educational institutions, and through the mass media.

Girl children are socialized into being different from boys; from the time of birth they are clothed differently: newborn infant girls are dressed in a pink embroidered or smocked frock while infant boys are dressed in a simple loose upper garment. From the very start girl babies are given different toys to play with, mostly dolls and kitchen utensils, while boys are given balls, toy motor cars, airplanes, and even small guns. The girls are brought up to be defenseless, non-aggressive, and dependent. They are taught to look upon their fathers and brothers, even younger brothers, and after marriage their husbands, as their protectors and providers. Girls are not socialized into being economically independent; they are generally denied professional skills that could enable them to take up jobs. Socialization of girls aims at stifling and curbing natural instincts of curiosity and adventure, and at molding them into domesticated, non-aggressive, submissive beings. Girls are discouraged from playing outdoor games. Running, jumping, climbing, swimming, and even kite-flying is disapproved for girls.

The concept of *ʿizzat* (honor) in the subcontinent plays an important part in the process of socializing girls. *ʿIzzat* is closely associated with women's sexuality, around which gender relations are structured. A woman is central to the concept of *ʿizzat*, as she can lose or enhance her family's *ʿizzat* through her sexual conduct. So she is guarded and her sexuality controlled. There is duality in this respect: while girls' sexuality is enhanced for the consumption of men, and girls are taught to take care of their physical appearance and be shy and coquettish, they are socialized into suppressing their own sexuality. They are kept ignorant of sexual knowledge, and segregated from boys and adult men. Any deviant behavior is most severely punished as it brings shame and disgrace to the family, and a socially deviant girl may not find a good husband. It is the responsibility of parents to marry off a daughter with her virginity intact.

Nothing can sully a family's *ʿizzat* as much as the loss of virginity of an unmarried girl. A girl is, therefore, instructed to cover her body; at the slightest sign of puberty she must cover the upper part of her body with a long scarf, even inside the house. Girls' interactions with adult men are closely watched and restricted. Girls are mostly confined inside the house, but if they are obliged to go out they must cover themselves with the *burqaʿ*, a garment that covers the body from head to toe with netting over the eyes to enable vision. The *burqaʿ* is common in India and Pakistan and a girl is usually required to use it from the age of nine or ten. Purdah is mostly observed by upper- and middle-class women. In lower classes women are required to work outside their homes and cannot afford to live in seclusion. However in urban areas and with the rise of fundamentalism, and a desire to emulate the Islamic countries of West Asia, the *burqaʿ* is gradually being replaced with the *ḥijāb*, a square scarf tied round the head to cover hair. Those girls and women who resist using the *burqaʿ* are considered shameless.

The concept of shame permeates every aspect of a girl's life. Girls are watched closely and admonished severely if their behavior deviates even slightly from the prescribed female norms. Girls are taught to avoid unbecoming behavior: they should not raise their voice, walk fast, or eat too much. Girls should not become fat. Among North Indian Muslims a baby girl is breast-fed for one year and nine months while a baby boy is breast-fed for two years and three months; it is believed that baby boys need to grow physically stronger than baby girls. The gender discrimination in feeding practices starts from infancy and continues throughout life. Girls are socialized into serving the best of food to men of the household, and prepare the menu according to their tastes.

Obedience to men forms an important aspect of female socialization, and is expressed through women being respectful and obedient to men. This requires total submission to the will of men and elders, especially male elders. The message given to every girl is that she should not answer back or argue with her father or husband and should accept her situation ungrudgingly. Avoiding the use of a person's first name is regarded as a sign of respect and girls are taught not to address their husbands by their first name, and to use the pronoun "aap," rather than "tum," which signifies familiarity and disrespect. Girls learn about the higher value of men compared to women by observing and participating in rituals and superstitions signifying male superiority. Two goats are sacrificed at the *ʿaqīqa* (naming ceremony) of a baby boy but only one at the naming of a baby girl. Married women try to conceive during moonlit nights and sleep on their right side to give birth to baby boys in order to enhance their position in the family. Girls are forbidden from eating a twin growth of any fruit or vegetable to avoid having a co-wife. Because polygamy is permitted on the subcontinent, Muslim women live in constant fear of their husband taking another wife.

Formal education was traditionally not considered necessary for girls. However, with the introduction of British rule in the subcontinent, liberal-minded men felt that girls could be given some elementary education in order to bring up their sons to better adjust to the changing society. In the early twentieth century, separate girls' schools were started where girls wore *burqaʿ* and traveled in covered vehicles. The curriculum for girls' schools was designed to enhance only their role as mothers and housewives. Textbooks were written exclusively for girl students emphasizing female virtues of chastity, sacrifice, submission, and obedience. In recent years in urban areas co-educational schools and colleges are becoming more common, although separate girls' schools and colleges also continue and Muslims prefer to send their daughters to them. Those girls who go to co-educational institutions follow the common curriculum, which includes sciences and computer training.

The mass media also reflect the social conditioning of males and females. Songs, dramas, and films depict women's helplessness, their dependence on men, and their preoccupation with domestic chores and the enhancement of their physical assets to keep their husband's attention. Television programs, advertising bites, and exclusive women's magazines are full of fairness creams, slimming devices, and beauty tips, in addition to recipes and home-making suggestions. These indirectly socialize girls and boys into being different along conventional lines.

Bibliography

Z. Bhatty, Socialisation of Muslim female child in India, in K. Karuna (ed.), *Socialisation, education and women. Explorations in gender identity*, New Delhi 1988, 231–9.

——, Fundamentalism, symbolism, and women, in S. M. Naseem and K. Nadvi (eds.), *The post-colonial state and social transformation in India and Pakistan*, Karachi 2002.

A. A. Engineer, *Islam, women and gender justice*, New Delhi 2001.

Government of India, *Hindu women's marriage act*, 1955.

——, *Hindu inheritance and adoption act*, rev. version 1956.

R. Hasan, Feminism in Islam, in A. Sharma and K. Young (eds.), *Feminism and world religions*, Albany, N.Y. 1999, 248–78.

Z. Hasan (ed.), *Forging identities. Gender, communities and the state*, New Delhi 1994.

Zarina Bhatty

Sub-Saharan Africa: Swahili Societies

Unyago is an initiation ritual performed as part of the socialization process in Swahili societies. These societies along the coast of East Africa and on the nearby islands have absorbed many different cultural traits through close ties within Africa and across the Indian Ocean. Girls' initiation rituals were introduced in Swahili societies by female slaves from Tanganyika, Zaire, Mozambique, Malawi, and Zambia who continued to perform their rituals after they arrived on the coast. The rituals continued after slavery was abolished and women who were previously freeborn joined the various ritual groups, bringing their daughters for initiation (Strobel 1979). Over the years, the rituals have been modified according to social and religious customs as well as to notions that were prevalent in the various Swahili societies (Caplan 1976, Larsen 1990, Middleton 1992), together with the widespread Muslim faith that constitutes a basis for a shared moral code and cultural practices. Although several virtues such as assiduity in religious devotion, formal and religious education, generosity to the poor, and hospitality are endorsed as important for both genders, girls and boys from an early age are assigned different activities and positions. While girls are expected to be involved in domestic tasks and the care of younger children, boys are sent outside to play with friends of their own age. In contrast to boys, girls are continuously reminded about the significance of virginity and chastity (Caplan 1976, Larsen 1990, Topan 1995). When puberty approaches sex segregation becomes crucial with regard to the much lauded ideal of purity and notions of respectability and shame. Many girls, for instance, at this time in life will leave their educational program in order not to be too exposed in gender-mixed milieus. The physical segregation between women and men is managed through the organization of social space and the material environment, division of labor by sex, and clothing, such as the women's veil called *bui-bui* (Larsen 1990). Ideally, knowledge about sexuality and sexual relations should remain taboo, especially for girls, until their initiation ritual and their first marriage. A girl's mother will chose a *somo* for her daughter. The responsibility of a *somo* is to teach the girl, *mwari* (which refers generally to girls from their first menstruation until marriage), first about how to behave in relation to menstruation and later about matters relating to sex and sexuality. These themes are never explicitly dealt with between mothers and daughters. A girl will only gradually come to know her *somo*, and the first time a girl goes to stay with her *somo* is during her first menstruation. From then on the relationship becomes formalized; it is the *somo*, not the mother, who brings the girl to her initiation (*unyago*). *Unyago* is seen to produce social, not physical, maturation. Young women should be initiated before their first marriage. Not all women become members of a ritual group; nor do all women go through the initiation rituals. Although *unyago* has never been universally performed, its existence has played an important role in the formation of female gender identity (Caplan 1976, Larsen 1990, Eile 1990). Initiation rituals are basically understood to have a socialization function (Richards 1956) and concern what is called "social puberty," while puberty rituals mark "physical growth" (Van Gennep 1960). In some places along the coast the term *unyago* refers to both girls' and boys' initiation rituals, while in other areas boys' rituals are called *jando*. Only male initiation rituals include circumcision.

Unyago rituals

Unyago is surrounded by secrecy. It is usually performed on the outskirts of the town or in the forest and the initiates remain secluded until the teachings are finished. At the onset of the ritual *mwari* has to be purified and prepared in order to receive and accommodate new knowledge. During the ritual, *mwari* has to learn secret riddles by heart as well as secret names of objects and actions associated with women's everyday tasks and activities. It is said that during her initiation *mwari* has to learn everything by rote, and that only later when she is exposed to married life will she understand the meaning of the teaching she receives. The various trials to which *mwari* is exposed focus on fertility and reproduction, and the dance movement and the dance performed by all women present, called *kata kiuno*, focuses on sensuality, desire, and sexual pleasure. Dancing women sing a number of songs that only initiated women (*warombo*, sing. *mrombo*) are expected to know. During the dancing *mwari* is ordered to move in certain prescribed ways by the ritual leader, called *nyakanga*, and the other initiated women present punish her when she fails. The ritual ends with a common meal and a coming-out ceremony in which the initiates receive particular ritual names. This also marks the girl's initiation into the ritual group. From this point on, she has access to knowledge about adult life and thus about sexual relations. Nothing regarding the teaching received during her initiation is explained to her by the ritual leader (*nyakanga*), her *somo*, and the other initiated women (*warombo*), if she is not herself able to formulate relevant questions. The idea is that only on the basis of experience will a girl be able to ask the right questions and reflect upon, and thus grasp, the "meaning behind the meaning" (*mana ndani kwa ndani*) in the various songs, riddles, and trials. To reach this level of understanding implies that a girl has learned to cope as a woman in relation to a man and in society.

There is a hierarchy of knowledge among initiated women, with the ritual leader or *nyakanga* in first rank, and a line of distinction between those who are initiated and those who are not. If a woman is not initiated she will, equally with men, not have access to women's *unyago* knowledge, which is considered to represent the actual meaning of gender difference. At present, various reasons are given by those who do not participate or who do not want their daughters to be initiated in *unyago* (Larsen 1990, 2000). Some claim that *unyago* is against Islam, and that what women learn and do during the ritual is incompatible with being a good Muslim. Others say that the rituals are old-fashioned (*-ya zamani*) and that girls today can learn all they need to know from school, and from television, videos, and magazines. Some girls claim that they will not go through *unyago* because it implies suffering and harassment by the ritual leader and the other women present. To participate in *unyago* is taken by some as a sign of not being "modern" (*-endelea*, *-kwenda na wakati*). Still, for those who participate in *unyago* the ritual practice and the knowledge involved do not contradict Islamic values or what they consider a modern lifestyle. In general in Swahili societies there is an idea that both girls and boys have to be transformed into women and men, rather than simply becoming adults as a result of physical growth. Within this context, the female initiation ritual deals with a woman's understanding and representation of her position in the world and of the relations involved according to experience rather than to abstract moral ideals.

BIBLIOGRAPHY

P. Caplan, Boys circumcision and girls' puberty rituals among the Swahili of Mafia Island, in *Africa* 46:1 (1976), 21–33.

L. Eile, *Jando. The rite of circumcision and initiation in East African Islam*, Lund 1990.

A. van Gennep, *The rites of passage*, London 1960.

K. Larsen, *Unyago – from girl to woman. The construction of female gender identity in the light of initiation rituals, religiosity and modernisation in Zanzibar*, Oslo 1990.

——, The other side of "nature." Expanding tourism, changing landscapes and problems of privacy in urban Zanzibar, in V. Broch-Due et al. (eds.), *Producing poverty in Africa*, Lund 2000, 198–219.

J. Middleton, *The world of the Swahili. An African mercantile civilization*, London 1992.

M. Ntukula, The initiation rite, in Z. Tunbo-Masabo et al. (eds.), *Chelewa, chelewa. The dilemma of teenage girls*, Uppsala 1994, 96–119.

A. Richards, *Chisungu*, London 1956.

M. Strobel, *Muslim women in Mombasa 1890–1975*, New Haven, Conn. 1979.

M. J. Swartz, *The way the world is. Cultural processes and social relations among the Mombasa Swahili*, Berkeley 1991.

F. Topan, Vugo. A virginity celebration ceremony among the Swahili of Mombasa, in *Journal of African Language and Cultures* 8:1 (1995), 87–107.

KJERSTI LARSEN

Turkey and the Caucasus

The gender socialization of women in Turkey and the Caucasus has been subject to the particular cultural norms and societal values determining the role and position of women according to region, class/social status, and the state ideologies governing these societies. These norms and values underwent fundamental changes in the twentieth century, with Kemalist modernization programs in Turkey and the Soviet revolution in the Caucasus.

Broadly speaking, the institution of the family has been the most crucial support system in the lives of women. Much of the early socialization of girls is through the role models provided by mothers and grandmothers. The latter are particularly significant in the case of urban centers in the Caucasus where under the Soviet system large numbers of women who were employed outside the home shared childcare with their own mothers. Given the rather distant father-daughter relationships, and the more authoritarian attitude of brothers, mothers are very often the mediators in settling disputes and negotiating differences. The different socialization patterns for girls and boys are based on the assumed male and female roles within the household and outside in society. For girls, housekeeping and childcare, almost solely female responsibilities, are arenas of activity in preparation for their future role as wife and mother, in addition to any formal education. The internalization of women's double burden begins early on from the end of primary school age. The boys, in contrast, are left free to engage far more in play, socializing with friends and family, and performing outdoor chores. The sense of authority, confidence, and self-esteem gained by the male children as they develop social skills is further reinforced through their privileged status as the future head of the family. This is especially the case for boys who are only sons.

TURKEY

The issue of *nāmūs* (male honor related to female sexual propriety) is a primary determinant in regulating girls' mobility, autonomy, and interaction with unrelated males. There is strict expectation of chastity (virginity) before marriage for girls, made the more crucial as marriage is considered their primary goal in life regardless of level of education and family status. The exceptions here are the secularized middle and upper classes in western Turkey for whom the question of a girl's educational attainment and career may be of greater concern than her marriage prospects. Attitudes to premarital sexual relations have also altered significantly among the young in this stratum of Turkish society (Kandiyoti 1981). Nevertheless, gender asymmetry is still reflected in the expectations of a greater level of education for a husband than for his wife. In Turkey's rural areas and small towns a high level of education in a girl is actually considered detrimental to her marriage prospects. This accords with the subservient position a wife is expected to assume in relation to her husband, particularly when living communally with his family. In later years, however, when the wife's children have grown up, there is a shift in power relations with regard to both the husband and the in-laws. Sociability in these regions is also very much along the traditional gender segregated pattern: males gathering outside the home (tea and coffee houses, civic centers, and so forth) and women paying house visits to friends and family (Kıray 1981).

More generally, women's position in Turkish society and their experience of socialization have undergone significant changes over the last few decades with the acceleration of capitalist development in the country and the high rates of internal and external migrations. This is especially noted for women dwellers of shanty towns (*gecekondu*) and those running households of male migrant workers. These women's aspirations for their children and expectations of gender power balance are more akin to the modern attitudes prevailing in the large urban centers than those in their rural points of origin. Among such communities a change in the male authority relations is observed in the greater autonomy women are able to assume, whether it is in the choice of marriage partners, consumption patterns, or the management of family finances (Abadan-Unat 1981). Similarly, in the case of working-class households with women breadwinners, the girlhood dream of being a perfect wife and mother (commended for domestic skills such as cooking, sewing, and maintaining hygiene) conflicts with the modern ideal of role-sharing demanded in consequence of outside employment (Cihan Bolak 1981).

The stereotype of the perfect housewife/mother is one that still dominates the ideal of womanhood even among the professional middle classes. This is despite the large numbers of Turkish women entering white-collar work and a range of professions. The media promote domesticity for women through the popular press and television programs that constantly deal with love and emotions, valorizing housework and home life (as, for example, with the Latin American soap operas). They further project the image of gentility, understanding, and devotion to the family as the undisputable core of femininity, whilst adapting to requirements of modernity (Saktanber 1991). The education system, however, reinforces gender discrimination through the sexist content of primary level textbooks and the range of subjects (particularly at the vocational school level) deemed suitable for male and female students (Gök 1991). The growing spread of religious functionary schools since the 1970s is a further reinforcement of conservatism in the educational agenda for women, and a platform for the Islamist forces that have entered Turkish politics in a major way. The Islamic model of womanhood presented by these establishments and the media controlled by them contrasts the pious Muslim woman, who is an obedient wife and devoted mother, with the overworked, exploited, and oppressed Westernized woman (Acar 1991).

THE CAUCASUS

In the Caucasus, where there is as yet little intrusion by the outside Islamist groups, women's education, outside employment, and power relations vary greatly according to the specific region and rural/urban divisions. In the rural areas a strongly patriarchal system dominates women's gender and intergenerational relations, and women have little control over their fertility. In mountainous Daghestan it has been noted that women constitute a highly exploited labor force, engaged in very heavy physical work (Chenciner 1997), a situation similar to the Black Sea region of Turkey a few decades ago.

In Azerbaijan, where early capitalist development of the oil industry in the tsarist period led to a degree of modernization, including the education and unveiling of women of elite families, large-scale industrialization and modernization took place in the seven decades following the Soviet revolution. By the 1980s Azeri women had already entered the workforce en masse, forming a majority in some fields, such as education and medicine (see Heyat 2002 for a study of women in Azerbaijan). This has entailed profound changes in women's status in society, and their gender and inter-generational relations, particularly in urban areas. The authoritarian mother/daughter-in-law relations prevalent in many Muslim societies, for instance, have been mostly transformed to mutual support and bonds of affection and loyalty. More generally, the institution of family has been central to enabling women to cope with the multiple tasks expected of them: housewife, career woman, and educator of the children. For the professional Azeri women dealing with the double burden of career and heavy domestic duties a crucial factor was the vertical support across generations, particularly that of grandmothers. The system of kin-based loyalty and support also enabled these women to call on the labor of others for the management of household chores. This was particularly crucial under the Soviet system, given the difficulties of obtaining hired domestic labor, unlike in Turkey and other Muslim Middle Eastern countries where professional women may easily rely on this sector.

In Azeri culture there is a strong association between domesticity and ideals of femininity, whilst masculinity is associated with tasks that require dealings outside the home. The codes of hospitality are very demanding, in part due to investment in personal networks that were crucial to gaining access to scarce goods and services under the Soviet system. All this required a great deal of time and attention from women. It also placed them in a central position in regulating social relations, which subsequently empowered women in subtle ways. Moreover, expectations of womanhood in Azerbaijan were subject to the conflicting demands of the socialist state's egalitarianism, including gender equality, and the patriarchal and authoritarian features of the ethnic Azeri culture. This led to an ambiguous and complex gender system that varied in its degree of male bias and adherence to traditions according to urban/rural divide, as in the example of Baku, the cosmopolitan and Europeanized capital city, and the surrounding villages.

A particularly crucial gain for women was the state's promotion of female education, which is at a level above all other Muslim countries. Consequently, higher education for daughters is valorized, increasing their chances of marriage, even among the lower strata of society. In the area of school curriculum, some gender differentiation is maintained in the way boys are offered practical skills in building, carpentry, and electrical work and encouraged to take up outdoor sports, whilst girls are offered domestic skills and almost never taught swimming, though in science and mathematics girls are equally encouraged. At the same time there is a strong emphasis on the gender division of domestic labor, highlighting women's servicing role in the home. Whilst femininity is closely associated with domesticity, masculinity is associated with avoidance of domestic chores (washing and cleaning in particular). However, these cultural norms are mostly adhered to depending on practical imperatives. For example, in the urban households with only sons, given that most women were employed outside, the males had to participate in housework.

The strong stereotyping of gender roles in the home begins early with children in the immediate family. In the case of families with both sons and daughters the brother-sister relationship contributes to socializing children into appropriate gender roles. Otherwise a similar process may take place within the extended family between male and female cousins. The extended family is still a very important institution in conducting social relations in Azeri society, and the primary locus of socialization for the children. For girls this is further reinforced by the notion that women are the custodians of Azeri custom and tradition, to be passed on through the female line (Heyat 2002, Tohidi 1998).

In the past, gender segregation, in tandem with sexual division of labor and maintenance of codes of sexual propriety, was manifested outside the home through restriction of public places such as tea houses and cafes to males (even at restaurants women only attended in the company of family members). In the post-Soviet era much of this has changed in Baku, the center of the oil industry and the largest city in the Muslim Caucasus, though not much in small towns and other regions. The media, heavily influenced by the West, via Turkish and Russian television broadcasts, have projected images of femininity that orient women toward consumerism, following of Western fashions, and generally the cult of the "beautiful." At the same time, for a small sector of women of the new rich and those with knowledge of Western languages new opportunities in employment and travel abroad have opened the way to greater autonomy and eventually alterations in gender roles and relations. Thus for the middle-class professional families today, the daughters' attainment of higher education and career development are of major consideration in their upbringing.

Generally, for the vast majority of the girls in the region socialization still takes place within the kin group, with mothers and grandmothers as the primary agents. In Azerbaijan, as in other former Soviet republics where primary and secondary education are compulsory, schools are also important sites of socialization for children and young teens. In the Soviet era, the pioneer and Komsomol groups were further sites of socialization as they regularly organized extra-curricular activities. For the girls, values, beliefs, and attitudes that govern their process of socialization concern notions of domesticity, motherhood, and sexual propriety, with "good" marriage as the primary goal. Nonetheless, in the post-Soviet era in the Caucasus, as in Turkey, perceptions of women's role and function in the home and in society, and cultural norms governing their code of conduct are undergoing significant changes according to region, class, status, and economic position.

Bibliography

N. Abadan-Unat, Turkish women and social change, in N. Abadan-Unat (ed.), *Women in Turkish society*, Leiden 1981, 5–31.

F. Acar, Women and Islam in Turkey, in Ş. Tekeli (ed.), *Women in modern Turkish society. A reader*, London 1991, 46–65.

R. Chenciner, *Daghestan. Tradition and survival*, London 1997.

H. Cihan Bolak, Towards a conceptualization of marital power dynamics. Women breadwinners and working-class households in Turkey, in Ş. Tekeli (ed.), *Women in modern Turkish society*, London 1991, 173–98.

F. Gök, Women and education in Turkey, in Ş. Tekeli (ed.), *Women in modern Turkish Society*, London 1991, 131–40.

F. Heyat, *Azeri women in transition. Women in Soviet and post-Soviet Azerbaijan*, London 2002.

D. Kandiyoti, Intergenerational change among Turkish women, in N. Abadan-Unat (ed.), *Women in Turkish society*, Leiden 1981, 233–58.

M. B. Kıray, The women of small town, in N. Abadan-Unat (ed.), *Women in Turkish society*, Leiden 1981, 259–74.

A. Saktanber, Women in the media in Turkey. The free, available woman or the good wife and selfless mother, in Ş. Tekeli (ed.), *Women in modern Turkish society*, London 1991, 153–69.

N. Tohidi, "Guardians of the nation." Women, Islam, and the Soviet legacy of modernization in Azerbaijan, in H. Bodman and N. Tohidi (eds.), *Women in Muslim societies. Diversity within unity*, Boulder, Colo. 1998, 137–63.

Farideh Heyat

Gossip

Arab States

The expression *kalām al-nās* (talk of the people) is a common term for gossip throughout much of the Arab Middle East and how information in the form of gossip circulates in communities can be quite important.

Gossip, positive or negative, can be used to reinforce group norms or to negotiate and further differing interests. Comments can be embellished to highlight basic points or outright falsified, perhaps backfiring upon the speaker. Men may depend upon wives or female relatives for certain types of information and vice versa. Secrets may be kept or revealed, including by eavesdropping children. People may recall events inaccurately. Public opinion may be of one mind or many minds. In such ways, the spoken word is very much the lived word.

Positions of honor and status of an individual or a family can be achieved, lost, or stay the same through gossip. The hospitality shown to guests at a home by one person, for instance, can reflect upon the honorable reputation of their entire family. In the United Arab Emirates, where people reportedly dreaded being the subject of bad gossip, violating the rites of hospitality would expose the host family to severe social disapproval. If the hostess failed to meet the guest's expectations, gossip ensued: "God forgive us, not even coffee was offered." Whereas, when the guest was satisfied, the praise to others could be: "They honored me, they fulfilled their duty toward me" (Kanafani 1993, 133–4). This continues to be true in many places.

Gossip and social control

When there is a family dispute, the gossip of visitors and neighbors can be the channel by which a family member makes the problem public, whether by accident or deliberately. In Egypt, a young Beduin woman who had left her husband to have her marital problems formally mediated by her father had this to say about her mother-in-law's attempt to generate negative gossip against her, just before she left:

> Nowadays people get each other into disputes through talk. I took my good clothes along to my father's because I was upset, for my husband and I had had an argument. And some clothes which I didn't want and had no need for – if I had tried to give them to a poor, old woman, even she would not have accepted them – I had taken them and I had burned them. My husband's mother came and said, "She has burned her house, and now she wants to burn ours and go." I *always* burn the garbage there, but she just wants to talk empty talk so that people will say that I am wrong and she is good and such. She says meaningless things. People know I would not burn good things.

The mother-in-law had rushed over from her house next door screaming those remarks. An elderly neighbor visiting the mother-in-law heard the loud marital argument and the mother-in-law's reaction, as did others nearby. This incident took place in a tribal village in South Sinai where gossip was being used by both genders as a method of social control to keep women and older girls at, or near, home. It was considered immodest for them to be outside, in increasingly crowded conditions (Gardner 2000). Yet public support, garnered by sympathetic gossip, could also have a bearing on the resolution of a marital dispute. The young wife was confident that people would not be swayed by her mother-in-law, who was known for having a flash temper and exaggerating. She was right.

In more serious situations, South Sinai Beduins can be held responsible for slander. When another woman was repeatedly slandered by her unhappy husband and his family to others, the offenders were found liable in a tribal court. Both of these cases took place in 1990 but being a topic of gossip could have long-term, dangerous effects. Some of the most stubborn evil-eye illnesses in women are considered by believers to be the result of attention caused or compounded by gossip, as the young wife who had left her husband thought was the case when she became chronically ill.

Women, judgment, and honor

An activist group of Palestinian women in Israel, al-Fanār (The lighthouse), stressed how controlling and damning gossip can be:

> Damage to the reputation of a girl by means of the rumor and gossip system means damage to the reputation and honor of the family. This leads to the mobilization of all the "family forces" to uphold this honor, usually by inflicting heavy punishments on the young woman, the victim. It should be noted that the degree of truth of this gossip and its relation to reality is usually unimportant (*al-Fanār* newsletter 1991, 7).

Such gossip can contribute directly to femicide, when a male murders a female family member for being deemed as having had improper relations outside of wedlock. These murders have especially been reported in some Arab communities in Israel and also in Jordan, with researchers examining the role that gossip plays and how men are held to a different standard of behavior (Glazer and Abu Ras 1994, Faqir 2001). Yet protecting the family honor can sometimes mean just trying to keep the information out of the public eye. In the Negev Desert, for example, Beduin "informants claimed that when marriage is conducted between parallel cousins and the girl turns out not to be a virgin it is highly unlikely that the matter be disclosed to the community" (Jakubowska 1990, 889).

While both women and men gossip, it is the women who are often in a position to observe other women and girls. In the Muslim Moroccan community of the Spanish border enclave Ceuta, it is even considered heretical for women to openly gossip about men's behavior in critical terms, but not about women's behavior (Evers Rosander 1991, 226). In some other areas, it is deemed improper to gossip about either gender. Social anthropologist Unni Wikan found that in the town of Sohar, Oman, "they did not gossip and thereby tell me about neighbors, acquaintances, and local events. They did not judge others and thereby reveal their own values. They did not chatter idly – indeed, they often hardly even talked" (1991, 10–11). Humor could still be an acceptable way to gossip and judge though, for more than half of the women's neighborhood group conversations that took place in her presence were devoted to talk and jokes about sexual matters such as infidelity and non-virginity (136–7). They did not, however, talk about specific people.

The Qurʾān states, "O ye who believe! Shun much suspicion; for lo! some suspicion is a crime. And spy not, neither backbite one another. Would one of you love to eat the flesh of his dead brother? Ye abhor that (so abhor the other)! And keep your duty (to Allah). Lo! Allah is Relenting, Merciful" (49:12). This is commonly read as a directive for both men and women not to gossip.

From Morocco, in a book with examples of gossip, comes this admonishment related to a group of women, including the author, by a gossip who was having concerns about her own conduct:

> There was a man who prayed and fasted and was charitable and went to Mecca. There was little to prevent him from going to paradise. But he used to talk. And that gossip sent him to hell. One arm records the good, the other records the bad. His bad accounts added up and he got the fire on the spot (Kapchan 1996, 221).

Bibliography

al-Fanār, al-Ishāʿāt wa-al-aqāwīl wa-dawrahā fī qamʿ al-marʾa, in al-Fanār newsletter, June 1991, 6–7.

F. Faqir, Intrafamily femicide in defence of honour. The case of Jordan, *in Third World Quarterly* 22:1 (2001), 65–82.

A. Gardner, At home in South Sinai, in *Nomadic peoples* 4:2 (2000), 48–67.

I. M. Glazer and W. Abu Ras, On aggression, human rights, and hegemonic discourse. The case of murder for family honor in Israel, in *Sex Roles. A Journal of Research* 30:3/4 (1994), 269–89.

L. Jakubowska, Terra e onore. La sessualitá femminile fra i Beduini sedentari, in *Quarderni Storici* 75:3 (1990), 879–94.

A. Kanafani, *Aesthetics and ritual in the United Arab Emirates*, Beirut 1983, adapted as Rites of hospitality and aesthetics, in D. L. Bowen and E. A. Early (eds.), *Everyday life in the Muslim Middle East*, Bloomington, Ind. 1993, 128–35.

D. Kapchan, *Gender on the market. Moroccan women and the revoicing of tradition*, Philadelphia 1996.

M. Pickthall (trans.), *The Koran*, New York 1930, repr. 1992.

E. Evers Rosander, *Women in a borderland. Managing Muslim identity where Morocco meets Spain*, Stockholm 1991.

U. Wikan, *Behind the veil in Arabia. Women in Oman*, Chicago 1982, repr. 1991.

Ann Gardner

Iran, Afghanistan, and South Asia

The notion of *ghaybat* or talking in a negative way about a woman behind her back plays a significant role in the lives of Iranian, Afghan, and South Asian women. Fear of gossip puts pressure on them to uphold traditional and restrictive gender expectations. Given the emphasis on female chastity and modesty, reports about a female's improper behavior, even if unfounded, can ruin a reputation and chances for a good marriage, and even result in physical chastisement or, in extreme cases, death. Women are more at risk than men of harm from gossip. Most women maintain consciousness about how any dress, behavior, interaction, or location can result in people talking and lead to serious harm to their social position and well-being.

In addition to severely restricting women's behavior and mobility, the notion of gossip plays a part in the formation of gender identity. People view gossip negatively. Women are the ones who gossip, people generally believe. The association of gossip with femaleness conveys a characterization of women as lacking character, dignity, and restraint. Women, with their assumed tendency to gossip, are seen as idle, weak-willed, unreliable, and frivolous. Often women themselves view speaking negatively about others behind their backs as a sin, and think women are the ones who participate in this social evil. Women even fear that other women will not keep disclosed information to themselves.

Women may try to avoid revealing transgressions, weaknesses, or distress, worrying that others may take a perverse satisfaction from their misery or be unable to avoid the temptation of passing on some juicy, scandalous, privileged information. Such caution may have negative effects. Frequently women suffer in silence rather than risk confiding in others. The reputation of a female influences the status and social standing of her family, the marriage opportunities for its young people, and even its economic and political interests. As people highly value social ties and interaction, they are extremely sensitive about leaking incriminating information and becoming the object of gossip. Much of people's sense of well-being, for females more so than males, depends on enjoyable interaction and relationship with others. Females fear the potential of gossip to provoke disrespect, rupture relationships, or cause ostracism or perhaps the need to leave a setting. People often put on a good front and keep unpleasant realities out of sight to avoid blame, critical commentary, and public discussion. Fearing that they themselves will be seen as the cause, women may keep domestic abuse, philandering of husbands, or children's problems to themselves. Sometimes a woman may find a friend who is outside her circle of neighbors and relatives with whom she may be more spontaneous and less censored.

People frequently hold that women waste much time in idle and even sinful talk about other people. Males often have a tendency to look down on females, believing them to engage in frivolous, useless, undignified, destructive gossip, unable to restrain their verbal activity. Unfortunately, the negative connotation placed on the word "gossip" in the languages of these areas and the association of women's talk with this negative word results in the obliteration of the important work that women achieve through their verbal exchanges.

Although fearful that sensitive information might fall into the wrong hands, women may find other women with whom they can share confidences and problematic situations. A women might unburden her heart, perhaps weeping as she tells her story, to a neighbor, relative, or friend, and feel catharsis through doing so. Through practice and observation, women generally are adept in a listening, comforting, and counseling role. Women's intimate exchanges with each other, particularly in situations where marriages are arranged, provide close social ties and crucial emotional support. Women frequently work with one another, assuming a role much like that of a therapist. Women learn which women provide good support and advice and which women might gossip to others about disclosures. Some women gain the reputation of extending wise assistance to other women and maintaining confidentially, and thereby the respect and admiration of the community.

Particularly in times of more rigid gender segregation and where women were not occupied with schooling and work outside the home, they spent much time in telling each other stories of their own or other women's difficulties. Generally not disclosed to men, these stories and the telling of them developed as underground networks of communication and reservoirs of tales of women's troubles, frequently involving males. Women may use these stories for various purposes – to provide guidance, elicit compassion and assistance, build a sense of community of women as mistreated by males, show a young relative in an unhappy marriage how well off she is comparatively, or to arouse awareness of violence against women and a desire to bring about change.

Males often left the home, courtyard, and neighborhood to go to school or work. Females stayed in the home and neighborhood and interacted with other females more frequently than with males, sometimes even communicating little with their own husbands. Such verbal exchange constituted a main source of a woman's enjoyment. In groups and networks, through the use of their fine conversational abilities, women developed gratifying social lives for themselves, positions of respect within the world of women, and reservoirs of knowledge and relationships that could be useful personally, socially, politically, and economically. Through such communication networks, a woman could present her family in a positive light, attempt to persuade people to her own or a family member's viewpoint on a situation, disseminate information about a conflict, or collect data for the benefit of herself, her family, or her faction.

Women wield their verbal abilities for their group and goals in local factional, political, and sectarian competition and conflict. They cooperate to help other women and to force males into different behavior. They teach and discuss religion. They organize gender-segregated religious rituals. They work to develop and maintain social networks through their organizing and verbal work in the area of religion, as well as other areas such as poetry, literature, sports, women's rights, philanthropy, political parties, kinship, education, and so on. During the Iranian Revolution of 1978–9, female activists discussed the issues at stake, spread information about developments, and attempted to persuade others toward their own viewpoints. Although most Afghan women are more secluded than their more economically advantaged, modernized Iranian counterparts, some Afghan women worked to promote female education, resisted the Taliban's rigidly discriminatory treatment of women, and tried to provide support for each other in loss and suffering, both inside Afghanistan and as refugees outside the county. Pakistani Muslim women host gender-segregated religious rituals, participate in party politics, especially in attracting the female vote, and organize and mobilize for sectarian competition, as do Muslim women in India.

In the smaller, more localized communities of years past, women greatly enjoyed opportunities to talk with other women and appreciated the sense of support and community built through frequent and relatively spontaneous interaction with women. They developed much of their sense of well-being, identity, and self-worth through their verbal exchanges. Women did most of the work of spreading news. The fact that everyone seemed to know everyone else's business carried many advantages. Learning that someone was ill or had suffered the death of a loved one, or was looking for a spouse for a child, other women could go to visit and extend sympathy and advice. However, some women mention the freedom from being the object of close observation and extensive discussion as one of the advantages of moving from village to a somewhat more impersonal urban setting. With women's education, migration, and modernization, women are no longer as available for regular intensive verbal exchange. As women gain many other interests and spheres of activity, their thoughts and discussions are no longer limited to other people in their immediate circles and their behavior. With modernization and globalization, over the last few decades communities, family groups, and social networks have been growing looser, particularly in oil-rich Iran. As economic and political relations become more regularized and institutionalized, women's "gossip" becomes less crucial for these spheres. In Afghanistan, particularly among the majority ethic group, the Pushtun or Pukhtun, women were secluded in their own courtyard or kin group. They focused their verbal activity on their own or their children's interests within the family. Because of the war with the Soviet Union and subsequent fighting among Afghan factions, many Afghans became refugees. Often living in Pakistan and concerned about their women surrounded by strangers, Afghani men secluded their womenfolk and thereby restricted their verbal exchanges all the more severely. In Pakistan and India, some Muslim females have been able to gain an education and then work outside the home, but the majority become stay-at-home wives and mothers upon marriage. Many Pakistani and Indian Muslims are socially conservative. These women may be limited in their access to verbal interactions beyond their own family, kin, neighborhood, and religious groups and networks and thus look positively on opportunities for verbal exchanges as entertainment and emotional support. Given the sectarian conflict and violence, in Pakistan between Sunnī and Shīʿī Muslims and in India between Hindus and Muslims, women's verbal work of persuading, building networks, creating unity, mobilizing, and disseminating information continues to promote the interests of their religious groups. In all of these countries, even if in a tiny minority, some women have been using their verbal skills to work with other women and speak out to try to improve conditions for women and in society in general.

Bibliography

S. Ali, *Madras on rainy days*, New York 2004.

F. Barth, *Political leadership among Swat Pathans*, London 1986.

M. Behnam, *Zelzelah. A woman before her time*, London 1994.

A. Betteridge, The controversial vows of urban Muslim women in Iran, in N. A. Falk and R. M. Gross (eds.), *Unspoken worlds. Women's religious lives*, Belmont, Calif. 1989, 102–11.

V. Doubleday, *Three women of Herat*, Austin, Tex. 1988.

T. Durrani with W. and M. Hoffer, *My feudal lord*, London 1994.

Z. Eglar, *A Punjabi village in Pakistan*, New York 1960.

H. Emadi, *Repression, resistance, and women in Afghanistan*, London 2002.

S. Farman-Farmaian, *Daughter of Persia. A woman's journey from her father's harem through the Islamic Revolution*, New York 1992.

E. Friedl, *Women of Deh Koh. Lives in an Iranian village*, New York 1991.

——, Sources of female power in Iran, in M. Afkhami and E. Friedl (eds.), *In the eye of the storm. Women in post-revolutionary Iran*, Syracuse, N.Y. 1994, 151–67.

B. Grima, *The performance of emotion among Paxtun women*, Austin, Tex. 1992.

S. Guppy, *The blindfold horse. Memories of a Persian childhood*, Boston 1988.

S. Haeri, *No shame for the sun. Lives of professional Pakistani women*, Syracuse, N.Y. 2002.

M. E. Hegland, Political roles of Aliabad women. The public-private dichotomy transcended, in N. R. Keddie and B. Baron (eds.), *Women in Middle Eastern history. Shifting boundaries in sex and gender*, New Haven, Conn. 1991, 215–30.

——, Flagellation and fundamentalism. (Trans)forming meaning, identity, and gender through Pakistani women's rituals of mourning, in *American Ethnologist* 25 (1998), 240–66.

——, Gender and religion in the Middle East and South Asia. Women's voices rising, in J. E. Tucker and M. L. Meriwether (eds.), *Social history of women and gender in the modern Middle East*, Boulder, Colo. 1999, 177–212.

——, Talking politics. A village widow in Iran, in L. S. Walbridge and A. K. Sievert (eds.), *Personal encounters. A reader in cultural anthropology*, New York 2003, 53–9.

J. Howard, *Inside Iran. Women's lives*, Washington, D.C. 2002.

P. Jeffery, *Frogs in a well. Indian women in purdah*, London 1989.

Z. Kamalkhani, *Women's Islam. Religious practice among women in today's Iran*, London 1997.

M. Kousha, *Voices from Iran*, Syracuse, N.Y. 2002.

S. Lateef, *Muslim women in India. Political and private realities*, New Delhi 1990.

C. Lindholm, *Generosity and jealousy. The Swat Pukhtun of Northern Pakistan*, New York 1982.

F. Milani, *Veils and words. The emerging voices of Iranian women writers*, Syracuse, N.Y. 1992.

K. Mumtaz and F. Shaheed, *Women of Pakistan. Two steps forward one step back?*, London 1987.

A. Nafisi, *Reading Lolita in Tehran*, New York 2003.

P. Omidian, *Aging and family in an Afghan refugee community. Transitions and transformation*, New York 1996.

P. Paidar, *Women and the political process in twentieth-century Iran*, Cambridge 1995.

N. Rahat, The role of women in reciprocal relationships in a Punjab village, in T. S. Epstein and R. A. Watts (eds.), *The endless day. Some case material on Asian rural women*, Oxford 1981, 47–81.

A. Rauf, Rural women and the family. A study of a Punjabi village in Pakistan, in *Journal of Comparative Family Studies* 18 (1987), 403–15.

V. J. Schubel, *Religious performance in contemporary Islam. Shīʿi devotional rituals in South Asia*, Columbia, S.C. 1993.

F. Shaheed, Controlled or autonomous. Identity and the experience of the network, Women Living Under Muslim Laws, in *Signs. Journal of Women in Culture and Society* 19 (1994), 997–1019.

N. Tapper (Lindisfarne), The women's subsociety among the Shahsevan nomads of Iran, in L. Beck and N. R. Keddie (eds.), *Women in the Muslim world*, Cambridge, Mass. 1978, 374–98.

——, *Bartered brides. Politics, gender and marriage in an Afghan tribal society*, Cambridge 1991.

A. Torab, Piety as gendered agency. A study of *jalaseh* ritual discourse in an urban neighbourhood in Iran, in *Journal of the Royal Anthropological Institute* 2 (1996), 235–51.

A. M. Weiss, *Walls within walls. Life histories of working women in the old city of Lahore*, Boulder, Colo. 1992.

S. Wright, Prattle and politics. The position of women in Dushman-Ziari, in *Anthropological Society of Oxford Journal* 9 (1978), 98–112.

MARY ELAINE HEGLAND

Honor

Iran and Afghanistan

"Honor," a translation of *nāmūs, sharaf*, and a number of related concepts, is a central term in the languages and cultures of Afghanistan and Iran. In spite of the amazing diversity of the two countries – in culture, ethnicity, religion, language, class, and social formations – honor bridges the historical and geographic divides, and regulates the exercise of gender power with remarkable consistency.

Nāmūs, in Persian, Dari, Tajik, and other languages of the region, is at the core of a semantic field, which includes synonyms such as *ābirū*, reputation, *sharaf*, honor, dignity, *ʿiffat*, chastity, *ʿirḍ*, reputation, honor, *ʿiṣmat*, chastity, *hayāʾ*, timidity, *ḥujb*, shyness, modesty, *najābat*, decency, *pākdāmanī*, chastity, and *sharm*, shame. Although polysemic, these concepts point to the hierarchical organization of female and male sexualities, as well as class and status. Some are defined primarily as female qualities (*pākdāmanī, ʿiṣmat, ʿiffat*, or *ḥujb*) and are used as female personal names (ʿIṣmat and ʿIffat) or names of women's institutions (for example, Nāmūs Girls' School). Each noun or its derivatives has antonyms (*bīābirūʾī, bīḥayāʾī*, and so forth), which, in spite of their pejorative meanings, depict the ability of women to deviate from the strictly regulated regime of gender relations. Men also violate rules of honor by engaging in *hatk-i ʿiṣmat* or *hatk-i nāmūs* (*hatk*, tearing, rending, rape), *zinā*, adultery, and incest.

A female, her body, sexuality, name, and fame, is the bearer or, rather, the repository of *nāmūs*, and is always liable to lose it through extra- or premarital relations, real or imagined, with or without her consent, for example, in rape or incest. A woman's *nāmūs* belongs to the male members of the family, kin, community, tribe, and nation. One of the meanings of *nāmūs*, in a number of languages including Persian, is "wife, and all the women belonging to a man, such as mother and sister and daughter and the like; female (members) of a family" (Dihkhudā 1994).

The violation of a female's honor generally leads to the loss of her life. The family, kin, and community, including females, participate, directly or indirectly, in the killing by expecting it to happen. While pre-Islamic in origins and non-Qurʾānic, honor killing is sanctioned in Sharīʿa texts, which in turn inform modern penal codes that do not criminalize it or are lenient in punishing the killers. In the Islamic Republic of Iran and Afghanistan, married adulterers are killed judicially through public ceremonies of stoning to death (*sangsār kardan* or *rajm kardan*).

Honor-centered norms of propriety, although rooted in the male control of women's bodies and female sexuality, are not limited to the regulation of sexual relations. Honor is a complex social institution, which is crucial for the (re)production of patriarchal social relations.

Honor is closely inscribed in the values of bravery, courage, pugnacity, fearlessness, and generosity, all of which are meanings for the word *mard*, man and *mardānagī*, manliness, in Persian (Dihkhudā 1994) and other languages of the region. The defense of the family, kin, tribe, village, city, and country is an honor conferred on the members of the male gender. In Persian oral and written traditions, the word *zan*, woman, is the antonym of *mard*. It implies, among other pejorative connotations, timidity, cowardice, and weakness (intellectual and physical). While this gender regime does not leave much room for females to lead an "honorable" life, individual women can achieve honor, fame, and respect on accounts of bravery, hospitality, piety, generosity, knowledge, and wisdom. In princely or aristocratic families, for instance, individual women have occasionally ruled over tribes, regions, and territories, although always in the absence of a male member of the ruling family, and anticipating the transfer of power to a male child on adulthood. Since the early 1970s, women have participated in armed struggles against the state.

The practice of honor varies according to context, for example, class, socioeconomic formation, religion, education, and ethnicity. For instance, among the Bilbas tribal confederacy in Kurdistan, it has been an honor for a woman to elope at least once in her life, whereas such a practice would bring shame to urban upper-class families (Mengurī 1999). While shyness and delicacy define the ideal urban upper-class woman, female strength and stubbornness are highly valued in pastoral-nomadic and agrarian formations, where women are a major force in the labor-intensive production system.

While individual women have always resisted the honor-based hierarchy of gender power, conscious efforts to change the status quo began, in Iran, with the emergence of women's rights ideas in late nineteenth-century poetry and journalism, and especially during and after the Constitutional Revolution of 1905–11. In Afghanistan, too, urban intellectuals took the first steps toward challenging the status quo in the early twentieth century. Legal reforms granting women limited rights from the 1920s and 1930s could not displace the ancient hierarchies of honor. In the mid-1950s, Furūgh Farrukhzād (1935–67) revolted, in her poetry and personal relations, against the male-centered regime of propriety and morality (Hillmann 1987). Although by the mid-1960s women were granted suffrage rights, an important step toward legal equality, honor values continued to regulate gender relations in and outside the body politic.

By the end of the twentieth century, the theocratic regimes in both countries tried to reverse what they considered to be Westernization of gender roles. They constructed detailed codes of propriety based on the Sharīʿa, in order to restore the dignity and honor that Muslim women had lost to modernity. In Iran, Fāṭima (the Prophet's daughter and the wife of Imām ʿAlī) and Zaynab (Fāṭima's daughter) were promoted as role models to be emulated by the new Muslim woman. The Islamic Republic created a network of patrols, including the Sisters of Zaynab, which toured the streets in special cars and warned, arrested, or punished women who deviated from the new propriety. The Islamic Emirate of Afghanistan (1996–2001) created a regime of gender apartheid closely monitored by the al-Amr bi-al-marʿūf wa-al-nahy ʿan al-munkar (Ministry of enjoining good and forbidding evil). Men, too, had to observe codes of propriety by emulating the Prophet Muḥammad (Haj Bābāyī 2002). The fall of the emirate did not visibly change the status quo, while in Iran women's resistance has led to relaxation in implementing propriety codes. In 2004, honor killing and women's suicide continued unabated in both countries.

Bibliography

M. Haj Bābāyī, *Qavānīn-i Mullā ʿUmar. Majmūʿi-yi qavānīn-i Talibān dar Afghānistān*, Tehran 1381/2002.

ʿA.-A. Dihkhudā, *Lughatnāmi*, Tehran 1373/1994.

M. Hillmann, *A lonely woman. Forugh Farrokhzad and her poetry*, Washington, D.C. 1987.

M. M. A. Mengurī, *Beserhatî siyasî Kurd. Le 1914ewe heta 1958*, Sweden 1999.

Shahrzad Mojab

South Asia

Honor (*ijjat, ezzat, paxto*) refers to good character, doing what is appropriate and moral for one's gender, age, kin relations, caste, and religion. Honor often centers on the family, male authority, and community linkages. Both men and women construct notions of female honor. However, they are not always in agreement. A woman's honor may be subsumed into family obligations of reciprocity and hospitality or it may be particular to her gender.

Moore (1998a) describes a Muslim community in northeastern Rajasthan where the exercise of honor is fairly typical of rural South Asian customs. In the male council, honor is defined by the men in terms of control: elders over juniors, men over women, and the groom's family over the bride's family. Parents are responsible to see that a child is married near the age of puberty. Rahman notes that in rural Bangladesh "the marriage of a daughter at an 'appropriate age' brings honor – social and symbolic capital – for the household" (1999, 94). Jewelry that women receive at the time of their marriages should be passed to a daughter's dowry. Reciprocal money donations are recorded in red ledgers as the village community marries its sons and daughters. Girls are married to men outside their villages. The wedding is performed in the bride's village but the groom's female kin should not attend. Following notions of hypergamy, after a daughter is married, it is honorable for a bride's family to give lavishly to the groom's family but not to visit or take from them. The young daughter-in-law in an extended family is expected to work hard for her mother-in-law. In a custom that was not expected in her natal village, she now draws her head shawl over her face in the presence of any male her husband's age or older. The council of male elders says, "a wife must live with her husband, however he keeps her 'wet or dry'" (Moore 1998a, 117, 1998b).

Divorce and the patrilineal community's inability to control their women are threats to honor. In this area, affairs are somewhat common. Male elders threaten beatings and even murder but most cases are settled by outcasting. Women, too, define women's moral obligations in terms of staying with and serving her husband, caring for her children, respecting her in-laws, and caring for the elderly. However, the obligation that outweighs all others is the duty to a woman's children (Moore 1998a, 148). A female villager commented, "If you want to have an affair do it here; why run away!" (ibid., 147). Running away and abandoning land would ruin a woman's house, life, and children. Although many villagers spoke of a family's right to kill a daughter who conceives outside marriage, today family honor is more often preserved through an abortion. Men and women explained that today women love their daughters too much to bring themselves to kill them. Many villagers still argued that a family with honor would kill their daughter unless she already had children that needed her. "In the past the lover would be hung from the tree and his limbs would be broken," a villager remembered (Moore 1998a, 152–3). In recent years the state has outlawed these local remedies. Still, crimes of honor are not totally obliterated. Communities swear their members to secrecy and perjure themselves in court to protect their right to administer their own justice (ibid., 150).

Among Paxtun women in Pakistan's Northwest Frontier Province *paxto*, *gherat*, and *sharm* define honor. Grima notes that men and women demonstrate honor in distinct ways. Adult women exchange gifts, songs, visits, and personal narratives at times of great sadness or joy. Women show shame, modesty, and subservience by remaining silent in the presence of designated others, obedience, and eating after the men (1992, 37). Veiling of adult women in public is expected as part of the honor complex, but throwing off the veil or "forgetting" to wear it in public is used by women as an expression of severe pain and trauma (ibid., 39–40). This is important because enduring great suffering and the sharing of hardships is at the core of women's identity and honor. Grima concludes that women hold the key to men's honor: "She can help or hinder honor, but she cannot control it" (ibid., 164). A woman's honor should be under the control of a man; if alone or with a weak man, the community sees her as without honor. "*Paxto* makes no allowances for a woman alone" (ibid.).

Rahman writes about women and microcredit in rural Bangladesh. He notes that hierarchical control in patrilineal, patrilocal villages, notions of honor and shame, and a village council that is responsible for maintaining moral conduct are all manipulated to help ensure there are high repayment rates at the bank. According to Rahman, the microcredit industry uses women's "positional vulnerability" to ensure repayment of loans. Loans are most often used by men but given to women who are seen as "more disciplined (passive/submissive)" than men. These loans must be repaid in weekly installments or the group of peer borrowers will not be granted future loans. The recalcitrant borrower will be humiliated in public, bringing *durnam* (bad reputation) to the household, lineage, and village. For a man the same humiliation would mean almost nothing (Rahman 1999, 75). Thus women and household members try to arrange women's loan installments on time to safeguard the family honor.

Traditionally, a woman's working outside the home for pay was considered dishonorable. Women were expected to remain modestly within the domestic sphere or work in the family fields. Men were expected to protect and provide for women. Today, the relationship between women, purdah, and social status is changing in both rural and urban areas. In Bangladesh, poverty combined with microcredit loans leads families to allow Muslim women to travel abroad or migrate to urban areas for work (Rahman 1999, White 1992, Zaman 1996). Kabeer spoke with female garment workers in Dhaka, Bangladesh where she found that women were pragmatic about their financial needs, the breakdown of traditional family ties, and community safety nets. Women argued for individual responsibility, a "purdah of the mind," instead of lineage control (2000, 91). Family honor was reinterpreted in terms of factory honor where co-workers were seen as fictive kin and workers were instructed on moral factory behavior (not talking to others, not retaliating insults, and concentrating on work). Kabeer found that levels of tolerance to change were different for women and men. Women welcomed the added income for their families while men felt that women's work challenged men's masculinity and their material privileges.

Shaheed found that challenges to control-based notions of honor in Pakistan come most from women who are educated, unmarried, or heads of households. Honor codes were most strictly enforced with young reproductive wives. A persistent complaint was that strictly controlled mobility affected women's leisure, socializing, studies, work, and coping with crises (1998, 151).

Rahman noted that notions of honor are focused on the status of women in society irrespective of religious beliefs, Hindu or Muslim (1999, 74). Jeffery and Jeffery agree. They comment, "Casting slurs on another man's womenfolk or subjecting them to sexual harassment are means through which men compete for dominance. All women, then, regularly experience controls over their mobility and demeanor that structure their experience of the world beyond their homes" (1998, 123–4).

Bibliography

B. Grima, *The performance of emotion among Paxton women*, Austin, Tex. 1992.

P. Jeffery and R. Jeffery, Gender, community and the local state in Bijnor, India, in P. Jeffery and A. Basu (eds.), *Appropriating gender. Women's activism and politicized religion in South Asia*, New York 1998, 123–41.

N. Kabeer, *The power to choose. Bangladeshi women and labour market decisions in London and Dhaka*, Dhaka 2000.
D. Mandelbaum, *Women's seclusion and men's honor. Sex roles in North India, Bangladesh, and Pakistan*, Tucson 1988.
E. P. Moore, *Gender, law and resistance in India*, Tucson 1998a.
——, *Keep her under control. Law's patriarchy in India*, ethnographic film, contact author, 1998b.
A. Rahman, *Women and microcredit in rural Bangladesh*, Denver, Colo. 1999.
F. Shaheed, The other side of the discourse. Women's experience of identity, religion, and activism in Pakistan, in P. Jeffery and A. Basu (eds.), *Appropriating gender. Women's activism and politicized religion in South Asia*, New York 1998, 143–64.
F. White, *Arguing with the crocodile. Gender and class in Bangladesh*, Dhaka 1992.
H. Zaman, *Women and work in a Bangladesh village*, Dhaka 1996.

Erin Patrice Moore

Turkey and the Caucasus

The initial formulations of the "honor and shame code," which dominated the literature on social and sexual relations in the Mediterranean and the Middle East into the 1980s, held men's honor to be proportionally linked to women's chastity (Peristiany 1966). While the significance of honor as an index of personal and group prestige is still acknowledged, scholars have challenged the ways in which the honor/ shame model obscured other relevant factors in the construction of honor beyond sexual propriety (Herzfeld 1987, Wikan 1984), as well as the model's assignment of honor exclusively to the realm of men, when, in fact, women strive for honor as well (Abu-Lughod 1986).

Before focusing on sexual honor, therefore, it is important to recognize that honor also extends to cultural practices of hospitality, reputation, social status, and family in Turkey and the Caucasus. Honor in the sense of esteem (*itibar*) is as important for women as it is for men, and is related most conspicuously to women's role as mothers and nurturers. Sirman's (1990) ethnographic research among rural women in western Turkey demonstrates, however, that women do not achieve social status merely by becoming mothers or by being appropriated into their husbands' households. Rather, they need to develop strategies toward forming networks of solidarity with other women in the community. Being sought as a host and for advice, along with the public avowal of particular skills – from picking cotton quickly to story telling to cooking – are integral to women's reputation. Similarly, fieldwork by Yalçin-Heckman (1990) among seminomadic Kurds in southeast Turkey reveals that women's reputations are earned through working fast and fastidiously, especially in jobs of high prestige such as baking bread, carpet weaving, and milk production, and assuming a nonchalant posture even under a heavy workload.

Seniority and the competition among women in the same household also pertain to women's honor. Although the bride takes on most of the housework and services, the respect and honor from their noteworthy execution often accrue to the mother-in-law, who gains further esteem by having a hard-working, agreeable daughter-in-law (Sirman 1990). Likewise, in Circassian households in Adygeia, grandmothers vie for authority over their daughters-in-law through laying claims to their grandchildren's upbringing and to religious knowledge, as well as through the invocation of memories of hardship and exile during Soviet rule (Shami 2000). Women across the Caucasus are also constructed by honor as bearers of authenticity, measured through their difference from the perceived image of the "Russian other" (Heyat 2002).

Nonetheless, sexual honor (*namus*) remains primary throughout the region. In a recent survey in Azerbaijan, *namus* was ranked as the most important theme in early socialization, with women's chastity being the primary connotation (Tohidi 2000). In Turkey, beginning with puberty, girls are strictly socialized into codes of modest demeanor – from dress to speech to body gestures – that will protect and affirm their chastity. A woman's sexual misconduct or even rumors thereof tarnish not only her own reputation, but also bring shame and dishonor to her family/lineage. The importance of women's purity as an icon of family honor manifests itself linguistically in the myriad of injunctions against "staining the family honor." What is designated as sexual misconduct, however, varies greatly. In parts of Turkey, the very possibility of unsupervised interactions with boys may provide sufficient grounds for an "honor killing," the murder of the dishonored girl by male kin. By contrast, it is taken for granted in Circassian communities that adolescent girls will attend parties and mingle with several potential suitors (*kashen*) (see box). The freer attitudes among Circassians may be attributed to the Soviet influence as well as to the absence of institutionalized forms of Islam, though the latter have been gaining increasing prominence in the post-Soviet era (Shami 2000).

Indeed, a major question has been over the influence of Islam on the persistent link between women's purity and family honor. Pointing to the fact that ideas of honor and shame are embedded in the monotheistic religions, Delaney (1991) has argued for the determining role of Islam in the Turkish context. According to the theory of procreation in Islam, men are creators; they *produce* by providing the "seed" in the making of the child. Women, however, are mere receptors; they *reproduce* because they only provide the "soil" on which the seed is fertilized. Women, therefore, need to be closely monitored, for the legitimacy of paternity – and thereby the honor of men – can only be assured through the monogamy of women.

Other scholars have found the attribution of such a definitive role to Islam ahistorical, noting that the notion of honor is contingent on the nationalist histories and social policies of each nation-state (Kandiyoti 1987). Attention to the role of the state is also crucial to avoid confining the concern with honor to the traditional rural community. The Turkish modernizing elite, for example, who took it upon themselves to emancipate Turkish women, granted women legal rights and fashioned the image of the public, modern woman, while simultaneously reaffirming the importance of women's virtue and chastity. Women who entered the public sphere thus had either to downplay their female sexuality to the point of invisibility or contain it within the boundaries dictated by men (Arat 1997, Durakbaşa 1988). Furthermore, now that women were unveiled and no longer confined to the private sphere, their honor, previously monitored through kinship networks, came under the surveillance of the modern state, as evidenced by the existence until 1999 of state enforced virginity examinations, which were routinely performed on political detainees, women suspected of prostitution, and on girls in state orphanages, dormitories, and high schools (Parla 2001).

Soviet modernization, on the other hand, did not concern itself with women's chastity, and was far more successful in promoting gender equality and ensuring education and careers for women. However, its effects with regard to gender and honor among its Muslim minority echo the Turkish case. Women in the Caucasus, too, faced a double burden: on the one hand, they had to fulfill the communist requirement to participate equally in the workforce and in public life and on the other hand, they were expected to sustain the call of their ethnic communities for modesty (Heyat 2002).

WWHR – New Ways

Espousing the view that honor crimes are only the tip of the iceberg beneath which lies a system of patriarchal traditional norms limiting women's control over their own bodies and sexualities, Women for Women's Human Rights (WWHR) – New Ways, an autonomous women's organization based in Turkey, has been working toward the realization of women's sexual rights since its foundation in 1993. The publication of a reader entitled *Women and Sexuality in Muslim Societies* (Ilkkaracan 2000) aimed at rendering visible the voices and efforts of women activists, academicians, poets, and cartoonists living in Muslim countries against practices such as honor crimes that are wrongfully justified in the name of Islam. Most recently, WWHR – New Ways has assembled a working group, composed of feminist activists, lawyers, academicians, and representatives of nongovernmental organizations, to draft a reform of the Turkish Penal Code from a gender perspective, a pressing task as the code continues to sanction the concept of honor that links the honor of the family and community directly to women's sexual behavior.

BIBLIOGRAPHY

L. Abu-Lughod, *Veiled sentiments. Honor and poetry in a Bedouin society*, Berkeley 1986.

Y. Arat, The project of modernity and women in Turkey, in S. Bozdoğan and R. Kasaba (eds.), *Rethinking modernity and national identity in Turkey*, Seattle 1997, 95–112.

C. Delaney, *The seed and the soil. Gender and cosmology in Turkish village society*, Berkeley 1991.

A. Durakbaşa, Cumhuriyet döneminde kadın kimliğinin oluşumu, in *Tarih Toplum* 51 (1988), 43.

M. Herzfeld, "As in your own home." Hospitality, ethnography, and the stereotype of Mediterranean society, in D. Gilmore (ed.), *Honor and shame and the unity of the Mediterranean*, Washington, D.C. 1987, 75–89.

F. Heyat, *Azeri women in transition. Women in Soviet and post-Soviet Azerbaijan*, London 2002.

P. Ilkkaracan (ed.), *Women and sexuality in Muslim societies*, Istanbul 2000.

D. Kandiyoti, Emancipated but unliberated? Reflections on the Turkish case, in *Feminist Studies* 13 (Summer 1987), 317–38.

A. Parla, The "honor" of the state. Virginity examinations in Turkey, in *Feminist Studies* 27 (Spring 2001), 65–89.

J. G. Peristiany (ed.), *Honour and shame. The values of Mediterranean society*, Chicago 1966.

S. Shami, Engendering social memory. Domestic rituals, resistance and identity in the North Caucasus in F. Acar and A. Guneş-Ayata (eds.), *Gender and identity construction. Women of Central Asia, the Caucasus and Turkey*, Leiden 2000, 306–31.

N. Sirman, State, village and gender in Western Turkey, in N. Sirman and A. Finkel (eds.), *Turkish state, Turkish society*, London 1990, 21–51.

N. Tohidi, Gender and national identity in post-Soviet Azerbaijan. A regional perspective, in F. Acar and A. Guneş-Ayata (eds.), *Gender and identity construction. Women of Central Asia, the Caucasus and Turkey*, Leiden 2000, 249–92.

U. Wikan, Shame and honour. A contestable pair, in *Man* 19 (1984), 635–52.

L. Yalçın-Heckmann, Aşiretli kadın. Göçer ve yarı-göçer toplumlarda cinsiyet rolleri ve kadın stratejileri, in Ş. Tekeli (ed.), *1980'ler Türkiye'sinde kadın bakış açısından kadınlar*, Istanbul 1990, 1995[5], 277–90.

Ayşe Parla

Honor: Crimes of

Overview

Definition

While it was anthropologists and sociologists who studied the cultural construct "honor" (and its corollary "shame") in Muslim countries, it was mostly human rights activists and lawyers who took on the phenomenon of crimes of honor. "Crimes of honor" refers to the legal regulation of a cultural practice known as "honor killings." In some Muslim cultural contexts, an honor killing takes place when a woman is killed by a male member of her family for engaging in, or for being suspected of engaging in, a prohibited sexual practice before or outside marriage. The spilling of the blood of the victim is seen as necessary to erase the shame she has brought upon her family by her sexual misconduct. Sometimes an honor crime is merely an attempt to mask a more serious crime that has taken place within the family, such as rape or incest, or is carried out with the intent to disenfranchise the woman of her property or inheritance. The most common relation the male perpetrator has to his female victim is that of either father or brother. Husbands and lovers commit "honor killings" too, although in this instance, their action tends to be understood as driven by a different cultural idea, namely, "passion," or rage of sexual jealousy. Which countries to include in the list of those where honor killings occur depends on the understanding of the relationship between honor and passion: is an honor killing the same as a passion killing, continuous with it, or sharply distinct from it? Should Brazil, where passion crimes occur, be treated as not dissimilar from Jordan, where honor crimes occur, or should they be treated as distinct because a culture of passion is distinct from that of honor?

Honor killings often occur within immigrant communities living in the West where the country of residence is usually more at home legally with the notion of a crime of passion than that of honor. Such killings raise the issue of "cultural defense" for the particular Western legal system: should the immigrant killer be allowed to appeal to the culture of origin to justify his killing and to get sympathetic understanding from the court/jury?

Islamic law

Most schools of Islamic jurisprudence treat as legitimate the killing by private individuals of a married person caught committing adultery red-handed. They argue that since death is the *ḥadd* punishment assigned under Islamic law for adultery committed by married persons, an adulterer has made his blood *ḥalāl*. The same is true for killing an unmarried person caught fornicating, even though the punishment assigned under Islamic law for fornication is a mere one hundred lashes. Some jurists justify legal tolerance for the killing in this case on the basis of "provocation" and they limit it to women the killer is related to. Most jurists, however, justify killing on the basis of "the duty to fend off sin," which they treat as a religious duty. In this case, the killing is tolerated whether it includes women the killer is related to or not. It is important to note that if a later court judgment determines that adultery/fornication did not in fact take place, the killer is punished for murder. It is also a rule of Islamic jurisprudence that retaliation is not inflicted against a parent who kills his/her child in the course of correction. Killing for honor is seen as such an instance. There is evidence to suggest that the Ottomans, rulers and jurists alike, tolerated the practice of honor killings and left it to the domain of self-help. In contrast, sixteenth- and seventeenth-century muftis of Syria condemned the practice as un-Islamic. Contemporary Saudi Arabia, which characterizes its own legal system as Islamic, allows the killing of females if they disgrace their family on the basis of custom (*ʿurf*). *ʿUrf* is treated as one of the sources of the law.

The contemporary liberal Muslim response to this cultural practice insists that honor killings are un-Islamic. It argues that there is no such sanction, whether in the Qurʾān or *ḥadīth*, that allows a person to take the life of another. When a woman or a man is accused of *zinā* (illicit sexual behavior), the Qurʾān requires that four men must actually have witnessed the act of sexual intercourse taking place. If guilt is proven, the same punishment is inflicted on men and women. Moreover, if a person accuses another of such a crime and the accusation transpires to be baseless, then the accuser is punished.

Modern law

The legal regulation of honor killings in various Arab and Islamic countries varies from complete prohibition of the crime, to partial tolerance, to indifference through either lack of regulation or lack of prosecutorial enforcement. Judges often interpret the gaps, conflicts, and ambiguities in the rules with an eye of sympathy for the male perpetrator of the crime. Arab criminal codes (originally legal transplants from Europe) vary in their attitudes toward honor killings, each offering a different kind of excuse (total exemption from penalty or partial reduction in penalty) to different kinds of male perpetrators (father, brother, husband), depending on the particular code. Which kind of excuse offered to which kind of male relative determines the extent to which the particular code is tolerant of the idea of an "honor" defense, or alternatively, that of "passion." Most criminal codes represent a compromise between the two ideas. Arab judicial practice in Jordan, Syria, and Egypt has the tendency to reinterpret the criminal codes of their respective countries to increase the legal tolerance of these crimes.

Bibliography

L. Abu-Lughod, *Veiled sentiments*, Berkeley 1986.

L. Abu-Odeh, Crimes of honour and the construction of gender in Arab societies, in M. Yamani (ed.), *Feminism and Islam. Legal and literary perspectives*, Reading, Berks, U.K. 1996, 141–94.

——, Comparatively speaking. The "honor" of the "East" and the "passion" of the "West," in *Utah Law Review* 2 (1997), 287–307.

S. Al-Khayyat, *Honor and shame. Women in modern Iraq*, London 1993.

R. T. Antoun, *Arab villages. A social structural study of a Trans-Jordanian peasant community*, Bloomington, Ind. 1977.

ʿA. al-Q. ʿAwda, *al-Tashrīʿ al-jināʾī al-Islāmī muqāranan bi-al-qānūn al-waḍʿī*, Cairo [1985?].

A. Basarudin, Are Islam and human rights compatible? Revisiting Muslim women's rights, <http://www.iifhr.com/Global%20Fellowship/Azza%27sFellowPape.html>.

D. D. Gilmore (ed.), *Honor and shame and the unity of the Mediterranean*, Washington, D.C. 1987.

S. Haeri, The politics of dishonor. Rape and power in Pakistan, in M. Afkhami (ed.), *Faith and freedom. Women's human rights in the Muslim world*, Syracuse, N.Y. 1995, 161–74.

C. Imber, *Ebu's-Suʿud. The Islamic legal tradition*, Edinburgh 1997.

M. Lippman, S. McConville, and M. Yerushalmi, *Islamic criminal law and procedure. An introduction*, New York 1988.

S. Mackey, *The Saudis. Inside the desert kingdom*, Boston 1987.

H. Maguigan, Cultural evidence and male violence. Are feminist and multiculturalist reformers on a collision course in criminal courts?, in *New York University Law Review* 70 (1995), 36–99.

F. Mughayzil and M. ʿAbd al-Sātir, *Jarāʾim al-sharaf. Dirāsa qānūniyya*, Beirut 1999.

B. Sarwar, . . . On suspicion of illicit relations, in M. Davis (ed.), *Women and violence*, London 1994, 220–22.

Strategies to address "honour crimes," roundtable held at School of Oriental and African Studies, University of London, 15–17 February 2002, transcript of proceedings.

J. E. Tucker, *In the house of the law. Gender and Islamic law in Ottoman Syria and Palestine*, Berkeley 1998.

Lama Abu-Odeh

Sub-Saharan Africa: Northern Nigeria

Discussion of gender and violence in Muslim societies in Sub-Saharan Africa quickly brings to mind the issue of stoning to death for adultery in the northern states of Nigeria. Because this is such an important region, and because it has been the scene of such well publicized issues, this entry focuses on northern Nigeria, and on the relationship between legal practice and violence, with comments where relevant on other centers of Muslim population south of the Sahara.

Observers might conclude from the public support for restoring Islamic penal law in the northern states of Nigeria that this region offers a graphic example of Islamic values underwriting patriarchal violence against women. However, a close examination can lead to different conclusions. While at least one sentence of lashing has been carried out, the sentence of stoning to death in the widely discussed case of Amina Lawal was rejected by a Muslim court in September 2003. Moreover, "honor killing" is not a common phenomenon in northern Nigeria. Indeed, as a conservative Muslim region where honor killing seldom takes place, the northern states of Nigeria offer an important comparative case to help in assessing the roots of "honor killing" in other predominantly Muslim societies.

The northernmost tier of Nigerian states, which includes much of the former Sokoto Caliphate and the Sultanate of Bornu, comprises one of the most heavily Muslim areas of Sub-Saharan Africa, with the proportion of Muslims in many localities being 90 percent or more. Islamic penal law, with the exceptions of stoning for adultery, amputation for theft, and death for apostasy, was applied in the region under British rule up until the implementation of the Northern Region criminal and penal codes in 1959. This is a pattern found in no other area of Sub-Saharan Africa, and in few other areas of the Muslim world. While civil and commercial law were handled by Muslim judges (*alkali*, pl. *alkalai*), criminal law was in the hands of the emir's judicial councils, and so its application was closely bound up with the image and practice of traditional rulership.

"Honor killing" is a term used to refer to the killing by male patrilineal kin of women whose perceived behavior is thought to have brought shame to the family. While it is well documented in a number of modern Muslim societies, notably in the Middle East and Southwest Asia, it is difficult to gauge its frequency over the longer historical term.

Islamic law is relevant to this phenomenon in two ways. First, Islamic law calls for the punishment of adultery (*zinā*), with lashing for those never married, and stoning to death for those married or formerly married. Both the man and woman involved are liable for punishment. But in most schools of Islamic law, it is difficult to prove adultery since four witnesses are required. Thus the law condemns adultery in the most severe of terms, yet makes it difficult to punish by formal legal process.

This reality may suggest that because the courts are constrained by legal technicalities it is legitimate for male kin to take matters into their own hands. Islamic homicide law is also relevant, for it treats homicide as a tort rather than a crime, except when it occurs in the context of highway robbery or rebellion – in other words when it challenges state authority. The built in assumption is that killing usually involves conflict between lineages. When the court finds that homicide has taken place it authorizes the aggrieved male patrilineal next of kin to take proportional revenge, or to claim compensation. The court can also exact "Allah's right" (*ḥaqq Allāh*) and apply its own punishment to the guilty individual. In northern Nigeria this was typically one hundred lashes and a year in prison. When a killing takes place within the patrilineal group, as it does in the honor killing of an adulteress, only this second punishment is relevant. This legal pattern may help explain modern situations such as that in Jordan, where the courts apply a lesser punishment in cases of honor killing.

The legal setting in northern Nigeria adds a further wrinkle. Here it is the Mālikī school of Islamic law that is applied, and in this school pregnancy out of wedlock is accepted as circumstantial proof of adultery. Of course, short of DNA testing, this proof is only relevant to the woman. In the past, Mālikī jurists in North Africa and Spain came up with a number of ingenious devices to curtail the impact of this. For instance, they agreed that it was possible for a child to sleep within its mother's womb for up to five years. European colonial legal scholars scoffed at the unscientific character of this doctrine, but clearly it had a humane intent. The use of force, deception, or magic might also constitute a valid argument against the charge of adultery. In a curious way, the Mālikī system may have worked to lure cases into the courts where they would die a slow death through legal technicalities, saving the life of a woman who, in areas under the ostensibly more liberal schools such as the Ḥanafī or Shafiʿī, might have been quickly put to death in an honor killing carried out under the informal authority of "tribal law." One conclusion, also suggested by women's roles in Muslim courts in East Africa, is that courts grounded in a formal tradition of written law can provide a counterweight to social norms unfavorable to women's rights.

In searching for insights as to why northern Nigeria lacks honor killing, one also needs to investigate social and cultural patterns. In Muslim societies where honor killing is common, and apparently sanctioned by public opinion, lineages often have key roles in social and political life. Marriage articulates the lineage internally, and it cements external alliances. But among the Hausa, the predominant ethnic group in northern Nigeria, lineage does not have a prevalent role. Hausa society is best characterized as territorial and hierarchical. Individuals are identified by village, or urban quarter of residence, rather than by lineage. Social interactions in lineage based societies are often egalitarian and competitive. In Hausa society they are characterized instead by an emphasis on deference and decorum.

In lineage based Muslim societies, violence often erupts between competing lineages who share a larger cultural identity. In northern Nigeria, the most frequent examples of violence are those that involve attacks on individual outsiders, or conflicts between culturally different communities. Legal records show the frequent killing of thieves. At least in the early twentieth century these were frequently slaves or ex-slaves – outsiders with no kin to support their rights or claim compensation. Since the 1950s, there have been periodic eruptions of intercommunal violence involving southerners or, in the case of the 1980 Mai Tatsine disturbances, a dissident Islamic sect.

There have been occasional notorious acts of violence against women in northern Nigeria that have come before the courts and received widespread publicity. One dramatic case was recorded in the register of the Emir of Kano's Judicial Council in 1913. In this case, a prominent man, Sarki Maiduwa, killed his wife, Hafsa, by striking her on her neck and head. The motive for this, revealed in testimony of her mother, was that Hafsa had refused to countenance her husband's taking her bed and giving it to his concubine. He claimed that an attack of *jinn*, malevolent spirits, had been the cause of her death. The written account suggests that there was an expectation that Sarki Maiduwa would be held guilty, but in the end, because there was only circumstantial and hearsay evidence, he was let off. In 1980 in Kano there was a highly publicized case involving Nafiu Rabiu, son of a prominent Kano businessman. He killed his wife, whom he had kept confined in an urban Kano apartment by locking her in. The trial was held in a court presided over by Kano's last British judge, who found him not guilty. Public rumor had it that the judge departed Kano airport with his bags stuffed with cash given him by Nafiu Rabiu. There was such a public outcry that a new trial was held, under a Nigerian judge, and Rabiu was convicted of manslaughter and sent to prison.

These two cases suggest that the dominant motive in violence against women is not family honor but rather the dynamics of jealousy and resentment that are commonplace in the polygynous household. Public opinion certainly does not ascribe an honorable rationale to such violence, in contrast to the case for honor killing. There are no allegations of sexual misbehavior on the part of the woman in these cases, but rather suggestions that she was assertive enough to arouse her husband's ire. The reference to illness caused by *jinn* may suggest a recognition that a woman's depression is closely connected to the dynamics of violence. Both cases can probably be understood as excesses of domestic violence that occurred normally but did not result in death.

In examining the support for stoning to death for adultery that has surfaced since 1999, one needs to ask whether this is a reversion to tradition or instead needs to be seen as a new phenomenon, the product of new forces in the society. In records from the pre-colonial and early colonial periods there are no references to this penalty. It was outlawed by the British, but if it had been common there would certainly have been cases arising from the informal application of this punishment. Yet there are none. This supports the argument that deteriorating economic conditions since the 1980s must be suspected as having a role in the present situation, creating situations where adultery occurs, and perhaps lending to growing hostility to independent women. The sharp deterioration in economic conditions may explain a greater frequency of situations in which women are divorced and left on their own, but can find no man who can afford to marry them. They are thus left vulnerable to sexual victimization. This factor can be seen in the most widely publicized case, that of Amina Lawal. Apprehension over rising rates of HIV/AIDS may also contribute to the focus on adultery.

There is wide recognition in Nigeria that women such as Amina Lawal are victims, not criminals. There are women's rights groups such as Baobab that speak out strongly in their defense. Northern Muslim men in positions of responsibility tend rather to follow the traditional jurist's tack of quietly pursuing legal arguments to prevent a finding of adultery. When such a case is brought to court, as opposed to being settled informally as with the honor killing pattern, the court can provide a forum for public discussion of all the issues involved, a discussion that can put the incident into reasoned and compassionate perspective.

Bibliography

Baobab for Women's Human Rights, <http://www/baobabwomen.org>.

J. Boyd and B. B. Mack, *One woman's jihad. Nana Asma'u, scholar and scribe*, Bloomington, Ind. 2000.

Centre for Democratic Development and Research Training, <http://www.ceddert.com>.

A. Christelow, *Thus ruled Emir Abbas. Selected cases from the Emir of Kano's Judicial Council*, East Lansing, Mich. 1994.

C. Coles and B. B. Mack, *Hausa women in the twentieth century*, Madison, Wis. 1991.

B. Cooper, *Marriage in Maradi. Gender and culture in a Hausa society in Niger (1900–1989)*, Portsmouth, N.H. 1997.

R. A. Dunbar, Muslim women in African history, in N. Levtzion and R. Pouwels (eds.), *The history of Islam in Africa*, Oxford 2000, 397–418.

S. Hirsch, *Pronouncing and persevering. Gender and the discourses of disputing in an African Islamic court*, Chicago 1998.

C. Fluehr-Lobban, *Islamic law and society in the Sudan*, London 1987.

M. Smith, *Baba of Karo. A woman of the Muslim Hausa*, New Haven, Conn. 1981.

Allan Christelow

Honor: Feminist Approaches to

Overview

Recently, human rights activists and feminist scholars have turned their attention to crimes of honor and have mobilized their efforts to combat this social practice, especially in the context of some Arab and Islamic countries. Surveying the literature on crimes of honor that Western as well as non-Western feminist legal scholars and human rights activists have produced, it is clear that the kind of feminism the particular activist or scholar adopts influences the way she frames crimes of honor conceptually. The framing determines the way the feminist understands the wrongs of the crime, the way it relates to other cultural phenomena, and the particular remedies she proposes to abolish the crime. It is important to note, however, that since the fight against crimes of honor consists of an alliance between local activists and activists involved in international human rights organizations, the feminist discourse deployed to fight those crimes has been trafficking back and forth from the international to the local and back again. This trajectory affects the discourse's internal coherence, as users mix and match ideas between different theories of feminism. It also loses memory of its place of origin, so that what is "Muslim" and what is "Western" about these feminist discourses becomes lost along the way.

Liberal feminists

Liberal feminists, for whom "equality" is the main analytical category, argue that the trouble with the legal regulation of honor killings is that it discriminates between men and women. According to these feminists, not only are the social norms more tolerant of men's extramarital sexual conduct where men are rarely killed for honor, but the legal norms themselves rarely punish men for such conduct. This is evident from the criminal codes of Turkey, the Arab states, Bangladesh, and Pakistan. Moreover, criminal codes fail to award the same kind of procedural protection to women as they do to men. When a woman is tried and executed privately by her family for dishonoring them and the legal system tolerates such private acts, what this in effect means is that extrajudicial trials are allowed when they involve female victims. This would never happen if the victims of the homicides were men. Such discrimination, liberal feminists argue, is a violation of a woman's right to life.

Liberal feminists typically evoke the language of international human rights to support their claims of discrimination against women. They argue that domestic laws are in violation of international laws such as the Convention on the Elimination of All Forms of Discrimination against Women (CEDAW) and need to be reformed to bring honor crimes in line with other homicides. Killers of women should be given as harsh a treatment as killers of men.

For some liberal feminists, passion as a motivation for crime is seen as different from that of honor. Killing for passion, as when a man kills his wife and her lover when he catches them having sex, is different from killing for honor, as when a father kills his daughter for sexual misconduct to erase the shame she has brought upon him. For these feminists, an honor killing is instrumental in nature; it is calculated murder to avoid shame. Passion, in contrast, is driven by jealousy and rage, and is inherently involuntary. A possible liberal feminist response therefore is to maintain that when it comes to passion killings women should be awarded the excuse as well, because women have feelings too.

Regarding matters of sexuality and sexual practice, liberal feminism is generally libertarian in its attitude. A given sexual practice is legitimate as long as it is based on the consent of the parties involved. Generally though, liberal feminist activists tend to say little about the disciplinary function of crimes of honor on women's sexuality. Instead of protesting at the crime as a violation, say, of a woman's right to consent to sex, they resort to the liberal arguments outlined here: right to life, right to equal access to due process, and so forth. There are two reasons for this kind of avoidance: right to life arguments work better than right to sex in more traditional societies such as the Arab and Islamic ones. Moreover, "right to sex" evokes fears of "Western cultural imperialism" in many. Indeed if matters of sex have to be referred to, the "right to privacy" and the "right to bodily integrity" are usually evoked, as in the case of state virginity controls in Turkey.

Against the grain of this practice, some Muslim feminist scholars called for the equalization of sexual mores in Arab societies: either virginity is eliminated as a social expectation or it is expected equally of both men and women. Also, a minority of Western human rights activists have argued for the formulation of a new human right, namely, "sexual autonomy," to combat practices associated with honor.

Radical feminists

Radical feminists, for whom "patriarchy" and "violence against women" are the main analytical categories, treat honor killings as a symptom of a larger regime of patriarchy or male dominance over women. These killings are not an instance, singular and unique, of particular cultures, but are on a par with and similar to other forms of violence inflicted on women by men, universally and in all cultures. Coercing minors to marry, domestic abuse, rape, polygamy, are all acts of male violence against women and are on a continuum with the crime of honor. In a sense, they are all crimes of honor. Each culture has its own peculiar variation of male acts of violence.

Most of these practices of violence, in the view of radical feminism, go unremedied. What is required therefore is a more severe response from the legal system: acts of violence against women, including crimes of honor, should all be grouped together and treated more seriously. Indeed, the sexual dimension of the crime of honor cries out for special treatment (harsher punishment) not equal treatment (to other types of homicides) as liberal feminism contends.

According to radical feminism, passion is the same as honor. Both honor crimes and crimes driven by passion are symptoms of a regime of male dominance. Whether a man is overcome with the passion of jealousy or the shame of dishonor when he kills a woman makes no difference. Both types of killings function to subordinate women to men; they are the acting out of the societal script of male dominance.

Some feminist activists in the Islamic world find this brand of feminism appealing because of its insistence on the universality of male violence. It frees them from the sense of shame they might feel toward their own culture's practice of honor killings and its peculiar form of control of women's sexuality. Since passion crimes do occur in less sexually repressive cultures in the West, and since according to radical feminism passion is the same as honor, then one culture cannot hold itself morally superior to the other. We are all victims of male violence.

Radical feminism in general is skeptical of the liberal categories of consent and choice, especially when deployed in the arena of sexuality. Freeing women to have sex with men may only result in making women available to male violence and control. Both the idea that male violence is everywhere and the general skepticism concerning questions of sexual liberation allow radical feminists to avoid talking about sex in other cultures.

Some radical feminists influenced by cultural feminism argue that sexuality in honor cultures should be transformed to become more feminine: caring, sensitive, and communicative.

It is worth noting that many activists and scholars on the question of honor tend to mix, in their analytics and advocacy rhetoric, the two strands of feminism, liberal and radical. They believe in the universality of patriarchy and they are advocates of women's equality to men. Male violence is everywhere but women must reclaim their autonomy and agency.

Poststructuralist feminism

While poststructuralist feminists agree generally with the radical feminist idea of male dominance, they assert that violence against women does not work in the interests of all men against all women, but in the interests of some men against those of many women and men. Moreover, male dominance as a regime of power is not total because it is shot through with various forms of resistance everywhere by both men and women. Law works as a set of background rules, along with social norms, to influence the particular dynamic of power and resistance within the system. A la Foucault, poststructuralist feminism also believes that law plays a role in "subjection," that is, participating in the creation of forms of being a gendered subject.

Poststructuralist feminists note that in the societies where honor killings take place, women's virginity is a highly prized social practice, the loss of which is penalized in extreme cases through these killings. At the end of the day, this produces a hymenized space between men and women, where the preservation of men's virginity is no less the effect of the system than that of women's. This regime of virginity by command (for women) and virginity by default (for men) is no less taxing on women than it is on men. It coerces both genders to bargain their way around this particular form of prohibition to interact sexually. Such forms of being (virgin/virgin by default) and bargaining (different kinds of sexual deviance designed to preserve virginity while still having sex) are unique to the cultures that produce honor killings. According to this view, the interaction between the legal rules on honor killings a particular legal regime opts for, judicial practice of that regime through interpretation of those rules, and prosecutorial practice, leave a residue of social violence that influences those forms of being (a virgin) and bargaining (for sex) described here. In the modern Arab world, partial liberalization of the normative command of virginity was introduced by the nationalist elites that took power after Arab states gained independence. Desegregation of gendered public space through education and work wrapped the command of virginity with a particular form of ambiguity that allowed for sexual maneuvering that did not exist before. The criminal codes put in place by these elites reinforced this partial liberalization by combining rules taken from a "passion" legal regime with those taken from an "honor" legal regime.

Poststructuralist feminism deconstructs the liberal distinction between honor (seen as instrumental and rational) and passion (seen as driven by the irrational rage of jealousy). Honor killers can be driven by rage, seen culturally as a natural reaction, and passion crimes can be executed to maintain the honor of the killer. But poststructural feminism does not see passion and honor as the same, either, in the way radical feminism does. Rather, it asserts that passion and honor have a differential impact on the culture of sex. Which kind of rules a particular regime picks to award which kind of excuses to which kind of men will distribute power and sexual subjectivities differently between men and women. The difference makes a difference.

Poststructuralist feminists do not avoid talk about sex. Since honor killings are disciplinary of sexual practice, the goal is to open up resistance through reformed law and social norms that allow for more pleasure and new forms of pleasure.

BIBLIOGRAPHY

E. Accad, Sexuality and sexual politics. Conflicts and contradictions for contemporary women in the Middle East, in C. T. Mohanty, A. Russo, and L. Torres (eds.), *Third World women and the politics of feminism*, Bloomington, Ind. 1991, 215–36, repr. in P. Ilkkaracan (ed.), *Women and sexuality in Muslim societies*, Istanbul 2000, 37–50.

Amnesty International, Pakistan. No progress on women's rights, 1 September 1998, AI Index ASA 33/013/98, <http://web.amnesty.org/library/Index/ENGASA330131998?open&of=ENG-2S4>.

——, Pakistan. Violence against women in the name of honour, 22 September 1999, AI Index ASA 33/017/99, <http://web.amnesty.org/library/index/ENGASA330171999>.

——, Pakistan. Honour killings of girls and women, 1 September 1999, AI Index ASA 33/018/99, <http://web.amnesty.org/library/Index/ENGASA330181999?open&of=ENG-PAK>.

CEDAW (Convention on the Elimination of All Forms of Discrimination against Women), <http://www.un.org/womenwatch/daw/cedaw/econvention.htm>. See Article 2 (f) and (g).

Declaration on the Elimination of Violence against Women, G.A. res. 48/104, 48 U.N. GAOR Supp. (No. 49) at 217, U.N. Doc. A/48/49 (1993), <http://www.un.org/documents/ga/res/48/a48r104.htm>. See Preamble and Article 4(d).

F. Faqir, Intrafamily femicide in defense of honor. The case of Jordan, in *Third World Quarterly* 22:1 (2001), 65–82.

Human Rights Watch, Women's Rights Project, A matter of power. State control of women's virginity in Turkey, June 1994 <http://www.hrw.org/reports/1994/ turkey/>.

S. Y. Lai and R. E. Ralphy, Female sexual autonomy and human rights, in *Harvard Human Rights Journal* 8 (1995), 201–27.

F. Mernissi, Virginity and patriarchy, in *Women's Studies International Forum* 5:2 (1982), 183–94, repr. in P. Ilkkaracan (ed.), *Women and sexuality in Muslim societies*, Istanbul 2000, 203–14.

R. P. Petchesky, Sexual rights. Inventing a concept, mapping an international practice, in R. Parker, R. Maria, and P. Aggleton (eds.), *Framing the sexual subject*, Berkeley 2000, 81–103.

N. Shalhoub-Kevorkian, Femicide and the Palestinian criminal justice system. Seeds of change in the context of state building?, in *Law and Society Review* 36 (2002), 577–99.

M. Spatz, A "lesser" crime. A comparative study of legal defences for men who kill their wives, in *Columbia Journal of Law and Social Problems* 24 (1991), 597–638.

LAMA ABU-ODEH

Hospitality

Central Asia

The legendary hospitality of Central Asians was the consequence of several influences. Foremost was the role played by the Great Silk Road, which depended on hospitality to support caravans of goods. Village and neighborhood communal hospitality houses, as well as Beduin and Islamic norms, also bolstered Central Asian hospitality, as did the influence of Russian culture in the nineteenth and twentieth centuries.

Ethnographers have acknowledged the importance of hospitality in Central Asian culture exclusively from the male perspective. Among sedentary Central Asians, the role of women has remained secreted in the *ichkari* (interior of the house). The literature describes traditional communal hospitality houses (*alovkhona* and *mehmonkhona*) (Rahimov 1990). The *alovkhona* (house of fire) derives from the Zoroastrian temple of eternal flame and is usually attributed to the mountain Tajiks. It was a space for ritual practice and men's feasts as well as for guests.

Like the *alovkhona*, the communal *mehmonkhona* (guesthouse) was kept by the sedentary population in the Central Asian plains. However, they played an essential role for the nomadic population as well. Nomads always had extra *yurt*s for guests. In their winter settlements semi-nomadic tribes built stationary guesthouses, mosques, and enclosures for livestock before they built personal dwellings. The hospitality houses were maintained communally and provided hospitality without charge. There were also *mehmonkhona*s in private residences, usually a room remote from the women's part of the dwelling. Established originally in houses of rich Soghdians, they are now a focal point in every Central Asian dwelling.

Many sayings and expressions reflect an exalted idea of hospitality: the guest is a messenger of God (Tajik); God's guest (Kyrgyz); dearer than a father (Uzbek). The gates are always open to symbolize hospitality and the readiness to receive guests. The host is expected to share everything he possesses down to his last loaf of bread.

Male and female roles and responsibilities were sharply divided. Females of all ages and boys served. Women maintained a clean and orderly household in case guests arrived. Men were responsible for supplying refreshments (sweets and dried fruits) because women had limited access to public bazaars. When the Soviets lifted restrictions on women's socializing, women added the masculine obligations of hospitality (as well as working outside the home) to their traditional women's obligations.

It is customary for women and girls to prepare food. In public places such as the *mehmonkhona* or *choykhona* (teahouse) men cook and have feasts with various names depending on the region: Gap, Jura, Jumagap, Tukma, Gashtak, Gurung, Ziyofat (Rahimov 1990, Snesarev 1963), Joro bolo (Simakov 1984). Women also have gatherings. In these gatherings, as well as at weddings, funerals, and other women's occasions, an important woman specialist in rituals – the *dasturkhanchi* – plays a key role as master of ceremonies or hospitality leader. She is elected to this honorary position by women of the residential community. The *dasturkhanchi* initiates all ritual events; she monitors the correct sequence of observance, helps hostesses to receive and seat guests, and decides on the division of labor for preparation of meals or gifts. She is well versed in the details of ceremonies and the norms of behavior and etiquette during their observance (Alimova and Azimova 2000, Kandiyoti and Azimova forthcoming). Similar masters act for men but they are not elected.

Gifts are given on almost all occasions, such as guest receptions (esteemed male guests are garbed in ethnic robes, while women receive choice outfits and scarves), weddings, or other family life-cycle or community events, Islamic and secular holidays, and meetings of gender and age groups (in the latter case it is a host who receives a gift or cash from each member). Sometimes women pack food or sweets for guests to take home. Women also exchange special holiday recipes.

Etiquette determines the physical allocation of family members and guests. For instance, in traditional families women and children do not sit at the table with guests. While many families influenced by Russian culture no longer do this, they still practice ranking around the table. Guests occupy the best places at the head of table, which is always opposite to an entrance. Father and son sit next to guests, while mother and girls take peripheral positions. Men sit comfortably cross-legged on the floor, while women sit with one leg under them and the other with bent knee. This is convenient, for they always serve at the table and need to get up easily, and is also considered a sign of female modesty. Dishes are first served to guests and men.

The host and hostess meet the first guests together. Later guests are welcomed by one of them while the other entertains the guests who came earlier. When guests leave, hosts usher them to the gate. If there are grown sons in the household, they escort guests to a bus or home to ensure that they arrive safely.

Bibliography

Primary Sources

A. S. Agaronyan, *The culture of everyday life* [in Russian], Tashkent 1982.

D. Alimova and N. Azimova, Women's position in Uzbekistan before and after independence, in F. Acar and A. Güneş-Ayata (eds.), *Gender and identity construction. Women of Central Asia, the Caucasus and Turkey*, Leiden 2000.

M. A. Hamidjanova, Party for girls or Choygashtak in Stalinabad, in *Izvestiy AN Tadji SSR* 10–11, Stalinabad 1956.

D. Kandiyoti and N. Azimova, *The communal and the sacred. Women's worlds of ritual in Uzbekistan* (forthcoming).

K. Mahmudov, *Hospitality* [in Russian], Tashkent 1967.

V. Nalivkin and M. Nalivkina, *The everyday life of women in the settled native population of Fergana* [in Russian], Kazan 1886.

R. R. Rahimov, Men's houses [in Russian], in *Traditsionii Kulture Tadjikov*, Leningrad 1990.

Secondary Sources

S. M. Abramzon, K. I. Antipina, and G. P. Vasilyeva i dr., Everyday life of collective farms in Kirgiz Seleny Darhan and Chichkan [in Russian], in *Trudy Instituta Etnografii* AN SSSR, NS 37, Moscow 1958.

G. N. Simakov, The social role of popular Kirgyz entertainment [in Russian], in *Obshestvennye Funktsii Kirgizskih Narodnyh Razvlecheniy v Kontse 19 – Nachalo 20 Vekov*, Leningrad 1984.

G. P. Snesarev, Material on the origins of the vestiges of rituals and customs among the Uzbeks of Khorezm [in Russian], in *Materialy Khorezmskoy Ekspeditsii*, Vyp. 4, Moscow 1957.

——, Traditions of male associations and their contemporary variations among the peoples of Central Asia [in Russian], in *Material y Khorezmskoy Ekspeditsii* Vyp. 7, Moscow 1963.

K. L. Zadykhina, Vestiges of developing classes among the peoples of Central Asia [in Russian], in *Rodovoe Obshestvo*, Moscow 1951.

Nodira Khaitbaevna Azimova

The Gulf and Yemen

The hospitality of the Arabs is so famed as to seem sometimes stereotypical, yet the centrality of hospitality to women's lives is evident in ethnographic accounts of the Arabian Peninsula. While there are important regional variations, a common thread is that hospitality is often understood in a religious frame. Extending food and drink to a guest who arrives at one's home is held to be a religious obligation incumbent upon a pious Muslim. A miserly woman (*bakhīla*) is not only a bad person in an everyday sense, but one whose lack of generosity (*karāma*) will be punished in the afterlife. The offering and receiving of generous hospitality is fundamental to one's recognition in the social world; people who refuse to engage sociably with others are viewed with suspicion.

Engaging with others through the exchange of generous hospitality is a central way in which a woman maintains ties with kin, neighbors, and friends, ties that are vital to her quotidian social support. Visiting is also part of the important political work that women do for their families; through their practices of sociability, they maintain and keep viable ties between families. While visiting is, for many women on the Arabian Peninsula, a daily practice, extending and accepting hospitality is particularly important at key life cycle events, particularly birth, marriage, and death and key dates in the religious calendar. Yet while the everyday exchange of hospitality and generosity is vitally important to the production of a sense of community, it is often competitive, and indexes hierarchical relationships.

Greetings and words

Hospitality begins with vibrant greetings. A less than effusive greeting may be read as a snub. Verbal greetings in Zabid are accompanied by the exchange of kisses on hands, shoulders, or cheeks, varying according to the age and status of the women (Meneley 1996, 99–107). In contrast, women in the Omani village of Hamra greet with handshakes rather than kisses (Eickelman 1984, 124–5). In the Omani oasis town of Bahla, an initial greeting provides a phatic entrance to initiate the social visit. Not to exchange words in everyday conversation during social visits in Bahla would be as rude as not offering or accepting hospitality (Limbert 2002). Women's visits appear in the ethnographic literature as times of the exchange of gregarious conversation: in the Omani village of Hamra (Eickelman 1984); in the Iraqi village of al-Nahla (Fernea 1969); among the elite women of Jeddah (Altorki 1986) and the people of ʿUnayzah (Altorki and Cole 1989); and in the Yemeni cities of Sanaʿa (vom Bruck 2002), ʿAmran (Dorsky 1986) and Zabid (Meneley 1996). A notable exception is Wikan's account of Sohari women's silence during visits (1982).

Icons of hospitality

After greetings, guests in the Gulf and Yemen are offered refreshment, although what substance stands for appropriate hospitality varies. In Oman and the United Arab Emirates, coffee is central to hospitality; a United Arab Emirates proverb says offering coffee is considered "the aesthetic greeting of the Arabs: (*taḥiyat il ʿarab il fannānah*)" (Kanafani 1983, 39). In the United Arab Emirates, morning or afternoon visitors are given a *fuālah*, a hospitality ritual that involves first offering guests fruit, sweets, and nuts, followed by coffee served in tiny cups; when the visitor has had enough, she shakes the cup sideways (Kanafani 1983, 20–3). In the Omani town of Bahla, groups of neighbors drink coffee in the morning, each woman bringing and sharing her thermos of coffee and container of dates. Together with the exchange of words, coffee and dates are digested; balancing the exchange of these items serves as a metaphor for sociality itself (Limbert 2002). In Zabid, sweetened tea or *qishr*, a spiced drink made from coffee husks, is brought to a guest upon her arrival. In the Yemeni cities of Sanaʿa and Zabid, everyday sociability centers around chewing *qāt*, a leaf which contains a mild amphetamine. Hosts provide the cool, incensed water and waterpipes full of tobacco that are thought to enhance the pleasure of *qāt*, but guests bring their own *qāt*, which they often exchange with their hosts and the other guests present. In the Gulf, and parts of Yemen where women do not chew *qāt*, snack food, dates, and fruit tend to play a greater role in hospitality (for Oman, Eickelman 1985; for ʿAmran, Dorsky 1986). Deaths are occasions where the normal rules of hospitality are reversed. For instance, in Zabid, a staple of hospitality, sugar, is left out of the *qishr* during mourning visits. In the United Arab Emirates, the usual food snacks are not served in mourning visits, lest the enjoyment of the food take people's minds from the loss (Kanafani 1983, 79).

Aesthetics of hospitality: aromas, cleanliness, and adornment

Scents, perfumes, incenses, and flowers play a central role in hospitality all over the Gulf. In the United Arab Emirates, women take pride in making their own special blends of perfumes and incenses from scented oils and gums. The special blend of perfume that a hostess offers her guest lingers and is evaluated by those in the next house a guest visits (Kanafani 1983, 101). Omani hostesses in the village of Hamra offer their guests the fragrant herbs saffron and mahaleb with which to paint their faces (Eickelman 1984, 156), while in Bahla guests are offered an incense brazier and perfumes at the close of the visit (Limbert 2002). Zabidi hosts welcome a new bride or special guest with a string of aromatic jasmine flowers.

In the United Arab Emirates, houses should also be sweet smelling and clean (Kanafani 1983); Altorki notes that among the Jiddah elite a hostess should keep a "glittering, spotless, generous house valued by the community" (1986, 102). Just as it is a duty (*wājib*) for the hostess to honor the guest by being clean and well dressed, in a spotless house, it is also the duty of the guests to honor the hostess by appearing clean and nicely attired. As in so many aspects of social life in the Gulf and Yemen, the etiquette of hospitality is not separate from religious morality. Indeed, in the United Arab Emirates, the social obligation for people to be clean is understood in reference to a *ḥadīth* of the Prophet Muḥammad, who notes that the clean person is a considerate person (Kanafani 1983, 93).

A woman should be dressed and bejeweled according to her status; the inevitable differences in adornment index not only indicate the relative wealth of families, but gold jewelry also communicates a woman's moral worth and her husband's or father's love (*ḥubb*). In Yemen's capital, Sanaʿa, women's adult identities are constituted through adornment in the public sphere of *tafriṭa*, women's daily afternoon visits. Despite its association with marriage, adornment is appreciated beyond its significance for sexual attraction between men and women (vom Bruck 2002). Weddings are often the apotheosis of hospitality events; hosts and guests wear their nicest finery; in Zabid, this is the time when the host family's widest network of connections will recognize their generosity by partaking in the wedding lunch (Meneley 1996, 124–5).

There is a reciprocal effect to generosity: the host offers hospitality, but the guest must accept it properly. Not to accept what the host offers, or to appear inappropriately adorned at a formal social event is to dishonor the host. In this moral economy, prestige is garnered in the social world for generous hospitality. However, the wealthy are those who are most able to offer generous hospitality and therefore to reap the moral value perceived to redound from it, in this world and the next.

Bibliography

S. Altorki, *Women in Saudi Arabia. Ideology and behavior among the elite*, New York 1986.

S. Altorki and D. P. Cole, *Arabian oasis city. The transformation of ʿUnayzah*, Austin, Tex. 1989.

G. vom Bruck, Elusive bodies. The politics of aesthetics among Yemeni elite women, in T. Saliba, C. Allen, and

J. Howard (eds.), *Gender, politics, and Islam*, Chicago 2002, 161–200.
S. Dorsky, *Women of ʿAmran. A Middle Eastern ethnographic survey*, Salt Lake City 1986.
C. Eickelman, *Women and community in Oman*, New York 1984.
E. Fernea, *The guests of the sheik. An ethnography of an Iraqi village*, New York 1969.
A. Kanafani, *Aesthetics and ritual in the United Arab Emirates*, Beirut 1983.
W. Lancaster, *The Rwala Bedouin today*, Cambridge 1981.
M. Limbert, Of ties and time. Sociality, gender and modernity in an Omani town, Ph.D. diss., University of Michigan, 2002.
C. Makhlouf, *Changing veils. Women and modernization in North Yemen*, Austin, Tex. 1979.
A. Meneley, *Tournaments of value. Sociability and hierarchy in a Yemeni town*, Toronto 1996.
U. Wikan, *Behind the veil in Arabia. Women in Oman*, Chicago 1982.

Anne Meneley

Iran, Afghanistan, and South Asia

Hospitality is an extremely significant part of Muslim culture. The obligation to give hospitality confers status and honor on the host. Religious gatherings, and life cycle rituals for engagements, weddings, births, and mourning all entail hospitality. Until recent decades, such occasions and even political and economic meetings took place in homes, as did visiting and socializing. People rarely ate in restaurants. Restaurant food served only the needs of travelers and working people. Some men frequent tea and coffee houses or *kabābī*s and simple roadside food providers. By tradition females do not go to public places. They socialize in the home, sometimes at picnics in walled orchards or relatively secluded outdoor areas, in the company of family members.

Women, responsible for maintaining homes, shoulder great responsibilities for hospitality. In light of the relatively informal structure of social institutions, personal relations have been crucial to conducting business. Building trust and personal relations requires refreshments and conviviality in a comfortable setting. The work of women in providing hospitality and thereby gaining respect, emotional attachment, and a sense of obligation thus contributes not only to the conversation and social interaction valued in itself, but also to the social connections through which economics, politics, and religion operate.

Gendered division of labor resembles gender structure elsewhere. Females in the home clean and decorate interiors and process, prepare, and serve refreshments and food. In Iran and Afghanistan, females among herding nomads and in agricultural areas milk animals and produce buttermilk, yogurt, butter, and dried yogurt. They also use wool and hair of animals to make items necessary for entertaining guests. They weave, knot, and sew rugs, kilims, tents, and cushions. Nomadic and peasant women also gather wild herbs, fruits, nuts and vegetables to set before guests. Women care for chickens. They spend hours baking thin sheets of bread, the diet staple, with rice as an important dish in better off families. Iranian and Afghan women must always be prepared to boil water in a charcoal samovar and brew tea. They cut up sugar lumps from large cones to serve with the tea. Pakistani and Indian women stew tea with milk, sugar, and spices. Iranian cuisine includes a great variety of regional dishes with subtle spicing and unique combinations. Pakistani and Indian women carefully prepare, grind, and learn how to use spices.

Excelling in cooking delicious food brings a woman respect and admiration. The pleasures of eating well prepared food according to familiar recipes is accorded great value. Women with more resources and access to wider networks of information will subtly compete to provide different preparations and many dishes to guests. Girls learn to help their mothers at an early age. Cleaning rice, legumes, and greens for cooking are time consuming activities. Nomadic and peasant women cook over wood and charcoal fires, first gathering the wood and carrying water for cooking. The womenfolk of important men are especially busy cooking, and serving guests.

An important part of a wife's duty lies in serving her husband's guests to reflect well on him and his family. Given the segregated gender organization, males often visit without their wives, and the women who prepare the food are out of sight. In an earlier period and still today in more conservative homes, boys might actually bring the tea and food to seated males. Among the Pukhtun (also known as Pathan or Pushtun), better off men or families or neighborhoods arranged men's houses or separate areas within a home for receiving male visitors. In less rigidly segregated areas, women might serve tea and food to a visiting group of men discussing political or economic issues, or perhaps asking for the hand of a daughter. Being present to distribute refreshments or listening out of sight, women might learn about the proceedings of the meeting, then talk among themselves and later with the household men.

When men visit, hospitality usually assumes a higher level of formality and generosity. They are hosted in the best available room, provided with the most comfortable pillows and seating and served more refreshments. Because of women's lower status and traditional modesty, they can more easily than men drop in at a neighbor's or relative's home for a short, informal visit. Especially in better off families or when women do not work outside the home, they spend a great deal of time visiting each other's homes, giving and receiving hospitality. Failure to return visits or to attend a gathering can be interpreted as an insult. Gender segregation and the high value placed on relationships and social interaction create significant bonds between women.

In addition to informal visits, women, especially in higher class families, have many opportunities to entertain groups of women for specific purposes. Religious and kin-related gatherings provide a framework for women's segregated gatherings. Traditionally, celebrations of weddings or pilgrims returning from Mecca and mourning rituals are held separately for males and females, sometimes in different homes or at least in different rooms of a home. In mosques too women's and men's gatherings take place either at different times or in different sections. For Shīʿī women these gatherings often commemorate the martyrdom of Imam Ḥusayn and his male relatives and the female hostages taken on the plains of Karbala in present day Iraq in 680 C.E. Sunnī women might host Qurʾān readings and celebrations of the birthday of the Prophet Muḥammad and other religious figures. Menfolk generally permit women to attend such events, and women can participate in religious gatherings without harming their reputations. Women who arrange such gatherings achieve a sense of accomplishment and status. The gatherings are also a source of enjoyment, food, verbal interaction, social intimacy, emotional support, and entertainment. They are opportunities to spread and gather news, as well to participate in spiritual and religious rituals.

By the early decades of the twentieth century, modernization began to have a effect on hospitality, more so in oil-rich Iran than in poorer Afghanistan and South Asia. By the 1960s and 1970s many Iranian females were attending school and working as teachers and in other employment. The nuclear family became more important than the extended family. Girls and women busy with education and work were not as available to provide hospitality. It became increasingly expensive to maintain maids, who had often been poor little girls or perhaps women from rural areas. Even in poorer Afghanistan, Pakistan, and India, middle- and upper-class females were increasingly occupied with education and work and less available for home and hospitality work, despite the fact that families expected them to put the honor and interests of the family ahead of their own pursuits. Especially in Iran, with more people working in the modern sector and fast moving modernization, social gatherings in the upper-middle and higher classes became integrated. People began to entertain outside the home. Increasingly, rituals and life cycle commemorations were held in public spaces, with purchased catering and service. Although the strong pressure to drop everything to serve a guest remains, a few women find ways to evade the heavy responsibilities of hospitality. For example, a young woman might inform her visiting mother-in-law that she has a commitment to go elsewhere. Many women have become active in mosque gatherings. Places of employment may have halls available to employees for reasonable cost.

After the Iranian Revolution of 1979 and the establishment of the Islamic Republic of Iran, which emphasizes female modesty and segregation, the government attempted to reimpose gender segregation. Women's segregated religious gatherings in homes and religious buildings became more frequent. Among women in Afghanistan and South Asia, modernization has been much slower than in Iran, and women participate in schooling and work in professions in smaller numbers. But hosting women's religious gatherings and segregated life cycle rituals continue to be significant in women's social lives. Afghan females – refugees or victims of the war with the Soviet Union, internal fighting, and finally Taliban control – often found movement beyond the segregated home area severely restricted. Visiting and providing hospitality became more difficult. Some brave Afghan women attempted to secretly create schools for girls in their homes during the Taliban period. Some Iranian women meet at each other's homes to hold reading and study groups and strategize to improve women's lives under the gender restrictions of the republic.

Hospitality in Iran, Afghanistan, and South Asia continues to be significant for women and men alike in spite of restrictive government, warfare, work and study responsibilities, and economic constraints. The desire to provide hospitality, to treat the guest as God's beloved remains a main definition of a woman's reputation. Women who seek education, jobs and careers, and a larger circle of friends and associates and activities may find it difficult to balance hospitality demands and their own aims and interests. Whether they provide hospitality for their menfolk's guests or their female guests, the great majority of women still feel gratification and acquire status through their skill in tending to the comfort of guests.

BIBLIOGRAPHY
S. Ali, *Madras on rainy days*, New York 2004.
F. Barth, *Political leadership among Swat Pathans*, London 1986.
M. Behnam, *Zelzelah. A woman before her time*, London 1994.
A. Betteridge, The controversial vows of urban Muslim women in Iran, in N. A. Falk and R. M. Gross (eds.), *Unspoken worlds. Women's religious lives*, Belmont, Calif. 1989, 102–11.
V. Doubleday, *Three women of Herat*, Austin, Tex. 1988.
T. Durrani with W. and M. Hoffer, *My feudal lord*, London 1994.
Z. Eglar, *A Punjabi village in Pakistan*, New York 1960.
H. Emadi, *Repression, resistance, and women in Afghanistan*, London 2002.
S. Farman-Farmaian, *Daughter of Persia. A woman's journey from her father's harem through the Islamic Revolution*, New York 1992.
E. Friedl, *Women of Deh Koh. Lives in an Iranian village*, New York 1991.
——, The dynamics of women's spheres of action in rural Iran, in. N. R. Keddie and B. Baron (eds.), *Women in Middle Eastern history. Shifting boundaries in sex and gender*, New Haven, Conn 1991, 195–214.
——, Sources of female power in Iran, in M. Afkhami and E. Friedl (eds.), *In the eye of the storm. Women in post-revolutionary Iran*, Syracuse, N.Y. 1994, 151–67.
——, *Children of Deh Koh. Lives in an Iranian village*, Syracuse, N.Y. 1997.
B. Grima, *The performance of emotion among Paxtun women*, Austin, Tex. 1992.
S. Guppy, *The blindfold horse. Memories of a Persian childhood*, Boston 1988.
S. Haeri, *No shame for the sun. Lives of professional Pakistani women*, Syracuse, N.Y. 2002.
M. E. Hegland, Political roles of Aliabad women. The public-private dichotomy transcended, in N. R. Keddie and B. Baron (eds.), *Women in Middle Eastern history. Shifting boundaries in sex and gender*, New Haven, Conn. 1991, 215–30.
——, The power paradox in Muslim women's *majales*. North-West Pakistani mourning rituals as sites of contestation over religious politics, ethnicity, and gender, in *Signs. Journal of Women in Culture and Society* 23 (1998), 391–428.
J. Howard, *Inside Iran. Women's lives*, Washington, D.C. 2002.
P. Jeffery, *Frogs in a well. Indian women in purdah*, London 1989.
Z. Kamalkhani, *Women's Islam. Religious practice among women in today's Iran*, London 1997.
M. Kousha, *Voices from Iran*, Syracuse, N.Y. 2002.
S. Lateef, *Muslim women in India. Political and private realities*, New Delhi 1990.
C. Lindholm, *Generosity and jealousy. The Swat Pukhtun of Northern Pakistan*, New York 1982.
A. Nafisi, *Reading Lolita in Tehran*, New York 2003.
P. Omidian, *Aging and family in an Afghan refugee community. Transitions and transformation*, New York 1996.
P. Paidar, *Women and the political process in twentieth-century Iran*, Cambridge 1995.
N. Rahat, The role of women in reciprocal relationships in a Punjab village, in T. S. Epstein and R. A. Watts (eds.), *The endless day. Some case material on Asian rural women*, Oxford 1981, 47–81.
A. Rauf, Rural women and the family. A study of a Punjabi village in Pakistan, in *Journal of Comparative Family Studies* 18 (1987), 403–15.
V. J. Schubel, *Religious performance in contemporary Islam. Shīʿi devotional rituals in South Asia*, Columbia, S.C. 1993.
F. Shaheed, Controlled or autonomous. Identity and the experience of the network, Women Living Under Muslim Laws, in *Signs. Journal of Women in Culture and Society* 19 (1994), 997–1019.
Y. Suzuki, Negotiations, concessions, and adaptation during fieldwork in a tribal society, in E. Friedl and M. E. Hegland (eds.), *Iranian Studies. Special issue on ethnographic fieldwork* 37:4 (forthcoming).
N. Tapper (Lindisfarne), The women's subsociety among the Shahsevan nomads of Iran, in L. Beck and N. R. Keddie (eds.), *Women in the Muslim world*, Cambridge, Mass. 1978, 374–98.
——, *Bartered brides. Politics, gender and marriage in an Afghan tribal society*, Cambridge 1991.
A. Torab, The politicization of women's religious circles in post-revolutionary Iran, in S. Ansari and V. Martin (eds.), *Women, religion, and culture in Iran*, London 2002, 143–68.
A. M. Weiss, *Walls within walls. Life histories of working women in the old city of Lahore*, Boulder, Colo. 1992.
S. Wright, Prattle and politics. The position of women in Dushman-Ziari, in *Anthropological Society of Oxford Journal* 9 (1978), 98–112.

MARY ELAINE HEGLAND

North Africa

Although the Arab and Muslim cultural tradition of generous hospitality has long been recognized in literature on the Middle East and North Africa, the gendered nature of serving and attending to guests and the central role that North African women play in maintaining the family's status through their hospitality rituals has only recently received significant scholarly attention. Arab and Beduin traditions of generously providing food, drink, and accommodation to parched and lost visitors are documented in travelers' reports to the region as long ago as the Roman era, and even earlier. Such hospitality was not merely customary generosity, however, but a critical component of survival in nomadic society. Should members of the tribe become lost or injured in the harsh desert, they could count upon the hospitality of a nearby group to nurse them back to health. With the arrival of Islam, Arab values of generosity and hospitality became incorporated into religious tradition. Numerous verses in the Qurʾān, such as Sura 107 (*al-Māʿūn*, Neighborly Assistance), as well as various *ḥadīth* emphasize the importance of generously sharing one's wealth, food, and possessions with guests, the needy, and the community.

As Arab culture and Islam spread – first to the cities of the Arabian Peninsula and then throughout the Middle East and North Africa – lavish hospitality became not merely a form of aid to travelers but a symbol of the status, wealth, and honor of the host as well as his guest. At the height of the Islamic empire, travelers' accounts of the sumptuous tables, beautiful serving girls, and lavish entertainment provided in the palaces of various sultans and caliphs were legendary, continuing to this day in folklore, fables, and fairy tales such as the *Thousand and One Nights*.

In North Africa today, the tradition of offering guests the finest and most choice dishes, while patiently catering to all their needs for hours, or even days, continues to be a central matter of family pride and honor. Indeed, after an important visit or a special celebration such as a wedding or circumcision, the central topic of discussion in the community is invariably the expense and quality of the food, drink, and entertainment provided to the guests. Given that the most highly prized dishes typically require the most expensive ingredients (such as meat, nuts, or honey) and demand many hours of preparation, a special event, such as a wedding, can pose an intense economic and practical burden, particularly upon the poorer households of the community. Few things are a more humiliating slur to a family's honor and prestige than rumors that the hosts were rude, the food and drink poorly prepared and, worst offense of all, the guests were sent away early, hungry, tired, or mistreated. Hence it is not unknown for a household to almost bankrupt itself for an important guest or event, preferring to offer the family's only piece of meat or to prepare an expensive array of dishes to an honored guest rather than be perceived as stingy or inhospitable.

Although men will outwardly play the role of host to male guests, the preparation and serving of food and drink is primarily a woman's responsibility. Thus much of the burden of hospitality and demonstration of the family's honor falls directly on the women of the household. This largely unrecognized form of female labor for the household is defined by Papanek (1979) as "family status production": those activities that define and maintain the status and position of the family within the community.

Given that hospitality is primarily "women's work," households without women, or lacking adequate female labor, typically rely on an extended network of female relatives, friends, and neighbors to assist in social obligations. Thus single and widowed men commonly live with or near female relatives who can step in to serve guests when necessary. Likewise women without daughters or other females in the home will frequently call upon nearby female kin and neighbors to assist in providing missing ingredients, and preparing and serving food should an unexpected or important guest arrive. Major life cycle events such as weddings and circumcisions typically involve numerous generations of female kin working together to create a successful celebration.

Interestingly, despite the increasing entry of women into the workforce in North Africa, the time demands and expense of hospitality appear to have increased rather than waned. Working women often lead frantic lives in which their weekends are devoted to visiting, not only relatives, but now also work colleagues and former schoolmates. Frequently, women's added income is used to increase their ability to be a good hostess: paying for luxury goods (such as refrigerators, microwaves, and expensive foods) and services (such as maids and catering).

This conspicuous social consumption appears to result, in part, from the North African expectation that hospitality is a reciprocal relationship. While the quality and expense of food served does reflect upon the status of the host's household, it also indicates the status of the guest. To pay a visit to someone is to confer an honor: the higher the status of the guest, the higher the honor bestowed upon the host. With the exception of clearly unequal households (such as patron-client relationships), the honor of visiting is expected to be returned within a reasonable period of time, along with the understanding that an equivalent or more lavish spread will be offered. As a result, visits are generally made between households of similar status and wealth. Thus an upwardly mobile family will frequently seek to expand their visiting network by demonstrating their wealth through more extravagant hospitality.

Perhaps the most obvious indicator of the prestige of the guest, and correspondingly, the social importance of the visit is reflected in the North African tea ceremony. Regardless of the occasion, a sweet infusion of tea is expected to be offered at all visits: the status and importance of the visitor and host are reflected in the kinds of nuts and ingredients added to the tea, along with the quality of the tea leaves. Typically the serving of tea with very expensive nuts such as pine nuts indicates a very wealthy family and important visitor. Cheaper ingredients such as peanuts or mint indicate a less formal event or a poorer family.

Yet regardless of the status and wealth of the family, throughout North Africa hospitality continues to represent an important cultural value, the implementation of which is women's work.

BIBLIOGRAPHY
L. Abu-Lughod, *Writing women's worlds. Bedouin stories*, Berkeley 1993.
R. Bourquia, M. Charrad, and N. Gallagher (eds.), *Femmes, culture et société au Maghreb*, Casablanca 1996.
S. S. Davis, *Patience and power. Women's lives in a Moroccan village*, Bloomington, Ind. 1983.
P. Holmes-Eber, *Daughters of Tunis. Women, family and networks in a Muslim city*, Boulder, Colo. 2002.
A. S. Kanafani, Rites of hospitality and aesthetics, in D. L. Bowen and E. A. Early (eds.), *Everyday life in the Muslim world*, Bloomington, Ind. 1993, 128–35.
H. Papanek, Family status production. The "work" and "non-work" of women, in *Signs. Journal of Women in Culture and Society* 4:4 (1979), 775–81.

PAULA HOLMES-EBER

Turkey and the Caucasus

Three factors have played important roles in the social institution of hospitality in Turkey and the Caucasus. These factors are gender, age, and social status within the context of the Islamic culture and the non-Islamic layer of tradition (*ʿāda*, common practice).

Traditional culture is conventionally represented in familial and social everyday life by four basic tenets: reverence to older people, respect for women, mutual assistance, and hospitality.

The tradition of hospitality emerged long ago and it still exists, though in a somewhat altered state. There are certain rules of hospitality. The attitude toward guests has varied and still does, but the reasons for treating guests differently have changed. For example, the Adygs who lived in the Northwest Caucasus used certain criteria to define the level of "honorability" of the guest, such as how far the guest had to travel to get there, the social status of the guest in comparison with the social status of the host, the goals of the visit, special personal traits (talents or achievements) of the guest, his age, and the kind of kinship or camaraderie between the guest and the host. The way hospitality was conducted depended upon all these factors.

When the guest came, the partition of the house into male (*selamlık*) and female (harem) parts became of special importance. The guests were met in the *kunatskaya* (guesthouse, from *kunak*, comrade) or in the male half of the house. The *kunatskaya* is a part of the social (male) space in Turkey and the Caucasus. That is why the chief role in meeting the guests is played by the man, the head of the family.

Feasts in Turkey and the Caucasus have always been conducted according to principles of seniority and gender differentiation. When the guest came into the house, women had to go to their rooms. Women played attendant roles in hospitality: they cooked and helped with arranging of the hand-washing and sleeping arrangements. In the Caucasus since the second half of the nineteenth century young women have been allowed to enter the *kunatskaya* and attend to the guests during the meal. Sometimes the oldest woman in the family helped to wash the hands of the most honorable guests, but usually she only came into the *kunatskaya* to greet and welcome the guests. Women had the right to participate only in meeting the most honorable guests. The latter could even be invited to the female half of the house, as a sign of special honor. In former times, the guests were usually men. If the guest were a woman, she might be met in the female half of the house.

Under certain circumstances a woman also could be seen as a distinguished guest. In hierarchical Caucasian societies reception depended on the social status of the guest, his wife, and the host; for instance, a prince and his wife were always given a grand welcome. The wife of the clan leader or family head, or a woman with extraordinary talents (for instance, a medicine woman, a witch, or a woman who read or spoke Arabic) were also considered distinguished guests. At a party such a guest would have the prime seat and be accorded all the honors.

Hospitality in Turkey and the Caucasus has lost much of its peculiarities and functions, in particular the function of communication. In a sense the institution is preserved as a symbol and attribute of ethnic identity and has acquired a hue of purposeful display. Recently the number of female guests has grown sharply and receptions for men and women have become similar. Still, women's status and role have not seen much change: male guests are entertained by the host and the hostess does not take part in male receptions. When a mixed group comes, the hostess can join them for a meal if the host or one of the guests requests it; under very rare circumstances girls are allowed to attend.

BIBLIOGRAPHY
(all works cited are in Russian)
I. L. Babich, *Folk traditions in the social life of Kabardians*, Moscow 1995.
B. H. Bgazhnokov, *The etiquette of Adygs*, Nalchik 1978.
J. V. Chesnov, Women and the ethics of the Chehen's life, in *Ethnographic Review* (Moscow) 5 (1994).
D. E. Eremeev, The women of Turkey and traditions, in *Peoples of Asia and Africa* (Moscow) 3:4 (1978).
——, *Between Asia and Europe. Essay on Turkey and the Turkish woman and man*, Moscow 1980.
U. U. Karpov, *Female space in the culture of the Caucasian peoples*, St. Petersburg 2001.

A. I. Musucaev, *The traditional hospitality of Kabardians and Balkarians*, Nalchik 1990.
M. N. Serebrjakova, A few aspects of ethnoetiquette among modern Turkish women and men, in *Etiquette among the peoples of Middle East Asia*, Moscow 1988.
G. A. Sergeeva, The status of women in Daghestan, in *Caucasian Ethnographic Collection* (Moscow) 4 (1969).
J. S. Smirnova, The status of the elder women of the Caucasian peoples and their historical interpretation, in *Caucasian Ethnographic Collection* (Moscow) 8 (1984).

Irina Babich

Household Division of Labor

Central Asia

The status of family in Central Asia has always been very high. A family with many children is a symbol of wealth and prosperity; it is also a role model to respect and follow. In the Central Asian context, marriage is more than a union of two loving individuals – it is an important alliance, linking wider kinship networks. Family, being a reproductive unit, also serves as a survival mechanism, helping to cope with socioeconomic and political problems, at times of both crisis and peace, by providing relatives with mutual support and help.

The traditional extended family is predominant in Central Asia and usually represents a household with three generations (parents, married sons, and their children) living together. Big households are particularly common in rural areas where the majority of population lives (more than 60 percent in Uzbekistan and Tajikistan). The region is marked by high birth rates, especially in Uzbekistan and Tajikistan where, despite some decline in the early 1990s, population growth still remains the highest compared to other parts of the former Soviet Union.

Usually associated with a high level of consolidation, integrity, and solidarity of family members, at the same time big families are marked by strict regulations and strong gender-age hierarchy. Such traditional families are rarely open to change, and are an ideal instrument for passing traditional and religious values from older to younger generations. In turn, it is traditions and customs that give strength to these families. Sovietization of Central Asian society in the twentieth century aimed to uproot the pillars of the patriarchal family based on Islamic and traditional values, but its basic principles survived despite the revolutionary changes that occurred in other spheres of society. The relentless methods used by the Soviet regime to transform Central Asian societies in the 1920s and 1930s forced local culture and traditions inside family life, creating two parallel systems of values. Thus, newly imposed ideology could not succeed in eradicating traditional views and attitudes that continue to endure.

Gender roles and responsibilities in traditional families are predetermined and leave little space for informed choice or decision. Men are considered breadwinners and women mothers or "hearth guardians," with deviations from socially prescribed roles not easily accepted by public perceptions. Marriage is patrilocal, and a couple moves to the house of the husband's father, where the young dutiful bride is expected to do all domestic work, taking care of her husband, his parents, and unmarried brothers and sisters. According to custom, the newly married young woman occupies the lowest rank in a family hierarchy under the supervision of her mother-in-law and is exploited for her domestic labor – until she establishes herself by giving birth to sons. In the meantime, her numerous responsibilities include cleaning, washing, cooking, and other services, all performed with demonstration of respect and obedience to her parents-in-law. In rural areas, domestic chores also include work in plots of land adjoining the house, for food for family consumption, and often milking a cow. But even in smaller nuclear families more typical of the urban environment, women have a multitude of responsibilities ranging between paid and unpaid, productive and reproductive activities.

The realities of the Soviet period and the current transition from centrally planned to free market economy could not leave gender roles completely unchanged. It is now not only culturally accepted that women participate in the labor force and contribute to the family budget, but given the current downturn in the region's economy, families would not survive otherwise. However, it is men who continue to be considered and treated as head of the family.

In big households with extended families, the survival strategies dictate that women share their responsibilities, as in addition to numerous tasks they already have in both paid and unpaid work, women contribute to community level activities. This presumes more service-oriented work that includes (but is not limited to) preparation of special food for numerous weddings, funerals, and other traditional rituals involving large numbers of people. These tasks take the entire time and income of women, leaving no opportunity for them for self-improvement, personal development, or recreation. The biggest burden falls, however, on rural women, where lack of facilities (gasification, safe water, services such as health care, and the like) as well as bigger families, stronger traditional perceptions, and growing poverty, make life particularly hard.

The transition from centrally planned to free market economy has left many men in Central Asia out of work, with accompanying depression, alcoholism, and drug addiction that aggravate the problem. A disproportionate burden of domestic and community-based unpaid work placed on women and the high pressures placed on men as breadwinners turn families into sources of stress and tension, posing a serious threat to women. Studies conducted with the support of international agencies over the last decade show that domestic violence is common in the region, as the subservient role of women in the traditional environment makes them particularly vulnerable. Women's suicide may take a form of self-immolation. This act of desperation is typical of sedentary rural areas. In Uzbekistan, the first ever officially announced figure of female self-immolation was as high as 270 in 1986/7 (Alimova 1991). Due to lack of information, it is not possible to provide current figures, but according to some estimates the dynamics show an increase over the last decade.

Bibliography

D. Alimova, Women's issues in Central Asia. A history of studies and current problems [in Russian], Tashkent 1991.

M. Bikjanova, *Family in kolkhozes of Uzbekistan* [in Russian], Tashkent 1959.

D. Kandiyoti, Women and social policy, in K. Griffin (ed.), *Social policy and economic transformation in Uzbekistan*, Tashkent 1995, 129–47.

S. Poliakov, *Everyday Islam. Religion and tradition in rural Central Asia*, New York 1992.

M. Tokhtakhodjaeva, *Between the slogans of communism and the laws of Islam*, Tashkent 2000.

UNICEF, *Societies in transition. A situation analysis of the status of children and women in the Central Asian republics and Kazakhstan 2000*, Almaty 2000.

——, *Women in transition*, Florence 1999.

Dono Abdurazakova

Iran and Afghanistan

Important variables are the local gender philosophy and ideology; class, linked to modernization; and different labor demands in urban and rural life.

Popular gender ideology, supported (but not created) by Islam, endows men with bodily and moral strength and leadership qualities and women with frailty, empathy, and a natural inclination toward nurturing, care of husband, children, and house. In traditional families girls acquire appropriate skills as apprentice helpers to women in their father's or in-laws' house. Domestic labor is organized less by skills than social position: senior women (head women in Afghanistan) delegate work to junior women and girls. The more cooperative young, healthy women there are in a household, the better for all. A daughterless mother is pitied for her lack of help. Girls learn to work early; boys have no obligations in the house save to obey and serve elder men. Although belittled, women's work creates self worth and a small power base for women.

The more traditional a household is, the more will men and women be interdependent labor-wise, but unequally so: men demand services from women and children rather than render them. The male household head has to provide all means, including the house, by which the women can fulfill their duties; he has to keep the house repaired, supervise the household generally and represent it to the outside, and discipline/educate children, especially sons. Men are not responsible for housework and avoid it as demeaning, although most can cook simple dishes and prestige food such as kebab and can take care of children temporarily. Modern young men occasionally wash, even iron, their own clothes. A widow heading a household will likely take on male responsibilities (management, breadwinning, male chores) in addition to her female duties while a widower will remarry soon to get housework done. Shopping is a male responsibility, especially if it involves travel, but with great variations by location and class: in Afghanistan today women are less likely to be seen in the street for any purpose than in Iran; a middle-class woman is more likely to insist on choosing her clothes herself than a poor and uneducated one; rural and lower-class women have some cash for small purchases from itinerant vendors; among nomads women work in the open.

Household chores reflect the socioeconomic standing of the household. In wealthy, large houses, social obligations make time-consuming preparations of a variety of foods and the upkeep of clothes and furnishings a full-time chore for many hands while in poor households, baking or buying bread and some vegetables, hauling water, sweeping floors, brewing tea, cooking a simple dish, and washing pots and clothes constitute housekeeping. Most Iranian middle-class households now have indoor plumbing, a gas range, refrigerator, vacuum cleaner, meat grinder, rice cooker, and television set. Men buy appliances (often in fulfillment of marriage contracts) and keep them repaired; women use them. Men buy, drive, and maintain cars, but in Iran an increasing number of women drive as well. In Afghanistan household amenities are rare, especially in rural areas, and more women thus have to fetch water, wash, and cook unaided. Everywhere, women manage kinship networks. In middle-class families they elaborately care for and supervise children, especially in Iran. In well-appointed households with few children or where servants or several women share the work, women are underemployed and spend their time with embroidery (clothes, pillows, draperies), knitting, socializing (in Iran), and preparing hope chests for unmarried girls in the house (especially in Afghanistan.) In Iran women everywhere now aim for diversion and income-creating skills by taking courses where offered (literacy, cooking, languages, computers, make-up, sewing, even exercise.)

Among working women the double shift of job and housework is the norm, with few exceptions. For men home is the place to relax. Wherever women work at home on income-creating projects (spinning, weaving, embroidery, sewing, beadwork, stitching of cotton-yarn shoes), men market these goods, and the male household head usually controls this income like any other. There are exceptions, though: a traditional, pious father (husband) may refuse to touch his daughters' (wife's) money and will not allow it to be spent on anything he ought to provide (such as clothes); and working middle-class women increasingly demand and retain control over their income, especially in Iran.

In rural areas and nomadic camps women have many more chores of vital importance to the family's economy; again, their labor is less gender-restricted than is men's. Men are responsible for animals, fields, the upkeep of the family, and representation, but women provide help ranging from entertaining guests to collecting wild vegetables and berries, getting grass for cows, herding young animals, fetching and holding sheep and goats (by young girls) at milking, to hoeing, weeding, planting rice seedlings, harvesting legumes, sapping poppies, binding sheaves, picking fruit, and carrying things. Men herd, water, shear, market, and butcher animals. Women care for and control poultry. In pre-Islamic Nuristan (Afghanistan) goats were linked to the realm of fairies, too pure to be touched by women. Everywhere else women milk animals and process milk and wool. In Afghanistan felt rugs are made by women, in Iran mostly by male itinerant felt makers. The heaviest tasks for rural/ nomadic women are hauling water (traditionally in goatskin bags carried on the hip), handling heavy household goods including heavy tent planes and beams while pitching and razing tents, and carrying children and wooden cradles on the back. (In Iran, households increasingly are transported by trucks.) Collecting and lugging firewood and the transport of grain sheaves to threshing areas in some parts of rural Iran and Afghanistan are women's back-breaking tasks, as they were in the past. Women complain about these chores. In the absence of radical changes in rural women's work and in the gender division of labor generally, the relative leisure of urban lifestyles is becoming increasingly attractive to women. At present, women in rapidly modernizing, relatively wealthy Iran have better chances of attaining urban labor patterns than women in deprived Afghanistan.

BIBLIOGRAPHY

L. Beck, Women among Qashqa'i nomadic pastoralists in Iran, in L. Beck and N. Keddie (eds.), *Women in the Muslim world*, Cambridge, Mass. 1978, 351–73.

D. Bradburd, *Ambiguous relations. Kin, class, and conflict among Komachi pastoralists*, Washington, D.C. 1990.

V. Doubleday, *Three women of Herat*, Austin 1988.

S. Farman-Farmaian, *Daughter of Persia*, New York 1992.

E. Friedl, Women and the division of labor in an Iranian village, in *Middle East Report* 95 (1981), 12–18.

——, *Women of Deh Koh. Lives in an Iranian village*, Washington, D.C. 1989.

B. Glatzer, *Nomaden von Gharjistan*, Wiesbaden 1977.

B. Grima, *The performance of emotion among Paxtun women*, Austin, Tex. 1992.

H. Hansen, *The Kurdish woman's life*, Copenhagen 1961.

M. E. Hegland, Political roles of Aliabad women. The public-private dichotomy transcended, in N. Keddie and B. Baron (eds.), *Women in Middle Eastern history*, New Haven, Conn. 1991, 215–30.

W. Maggi, *Our women are free. Gender and ethnicity in the Hindukush*, Ann Arbor 2001.

G. S. Robertson, *The kafirs of the Hindu-Kush*, London 1896.

N. Tapper, *Bartered brides. Politics, gender and marriage in an Afghan tribal society*, Cambridge 1991.

B. Tavakolian, Sheikhanzai women. Sisters, mothers and wives, in *Ethnos* 52 (1987), 180–99.

ERIKA LOEFFLER FRIEDL

South Asia

South Asia represents considerable cultural, religious, ethnic, and linguistic diversity that is reflected in domestic and cultural life. The lives of Muslim women are as diverse across South Asia as the lives of Hindu and Christian women. These differences influence women's participation in paid work but their implications for gendering of work within the home is less evident. Regional diversity can be characterized by a general northwest/south split and in some indicators the east has distinctive features as well (Dyson and Moore 1983). Women in the south fare better in education and survival than women in the north, although even in the south women have relatively low autonomy and mobility compared to the rest of the world.

According to the Demographic and Health Surveys (Table 1), women's education and workforce participation, as measured by mean years of education and percentage of all women who report working for a salary, vary regionally for Hindu and Muslim women alike. In general, within most states Muslim women have lower education and considerably less work participation than Hindu women. However, in two of the largest states of the south, Tamil Nadu and Andhra Pradesh, Muslim women have higher education than Hindu women and Muslim women's education and workforce participation in the southern states are higher than those of Hindu women in the north or the east.

In Bangladesh, Hindu women have higher education and workforce participation than Muslim women. These levels and religious differentials are similar to the states of India that surround Bangladesh, specifically those of West Bengal. Overall levels of educational attainment are low everywhere in Pakistan but there is a range in the levels of workforce participation among Muslim women. The proportion of Hindus in Pakistan is negligible and it is not possible to estimate rates from national surveys. As with Bangladesh and areas of India surrounding it, perhaps more striking than the variation within Pakistan is the similarity with contiguous regions across the border – Muslim women in both Punjabs (India and Pakistan) have exactly the same workforce participation rate of 13 percent. Sindh and Balochistan have somewhat higher rates than Punjab and levels are similar to the neighboring region of Rajasthan.

Table 1: Mean years of education and percentage of women working for salary by religion and state, ever-married women, Bangladesh (1996–7), India (1998–9), Pakistan (1990–1)

	Average Years of Education		% Working for Salary	
	Hindu	Muslim	Hindu	Muslim
Bangladesh	5	3	44	19
India, East				
Assam	4.0	2.4	22	10
Bihar	2.0	1.0	19	15
Manipur	5.9	2.5	54	13
Meghalaya	2.9	1.2	30	–
Mizoram	3.2	5.3	22	33
Nagaland	2.7	0.9	34	27
Orissa	2.9	2.5	26	17
Sikkim	3.7	4.2	19	13
West Bengal	4.1	2.2	27	17
Arunachalpradesh	3.9	1.7	16	11
Tripura	5.0	2.6	19	15
India, North				
Gujarat	4.3	4.3	33	20
Haryana	4.0	0.8	10	3
Himachal Pradesh	5.2	2.5	9	9
Jammu	3.9	1.8	10	15
Madhya Pradesh	2.5	3.2	33	20
Punjab	6.1	2.2	11	13
Rajasthan	2.0	1.2	15	19
Uttar Pradesh	2.7	1.8	11	10
New Delhi	7.5	3.6	20	11
India, South				
Andhra Pradesh	2.8	3.8	46	19
Goa	6.1	4.4	33	22
Karnataka	4.0	3.2	38	35
Kerala	8.3	6.4	31	8
Maharashtra	4.6	4.8	38	19
Tamil Nadu	4.4	5.3	46	23
Pakistan				
Punjab	–	2	–	13
Sindh	–	2	–	17
NWFP	–	1	–	3
Balochistan	–	0	–	19

Source: author's calculations from Demographic and Health Surveys, Bangladesh, 1996–7, India 1998–9, Pakistan 1990–1.

Much less is known about division of labor within the household and variations regionally. A study of time use data collected in six states in India (Table 2) shows that, regardless of region, women in India bear all of the responsibility for domestic work – men account for less than 5 percent of all domestic or care-giving activities (Narasimhan and Panday 2000). Women's time in productive work also does not vary systematically by regions represented by the six states. The only indicator of variation across states is that women in the northern states of Haryana and Gujarat are far less likely to be paid for work while women in the southern state of Tamil Nadu are more likely to be paid for productive work and also have the lowest number of hours spent in such work.

Table 2: Average number of hours per week by type of activity, rural areas in six states, 1998–9

State	Women's Domestic Work	Women's Productive Work	% of Women's Productive Work Unpaid
Haryana, North	23.5	30.7	86
Madhya Pradesh, North	23.0	35.5	52
Gujarat, North	24.0	37.5	45
Orissa, East	19.0	35.3	69
Tamil Nadu, South	23.5	29.5	33
Meghalaya, East	29.0	34.5	76

Source: Narasimhan and Panday 2000.

Time use data are seldom found disaggregated by religion. A survey of married adolescents in Bangladesh showed that Hindu and Muslim women do not differ much in the average hours of time spent in domestic work versus productive work (6.35 hours for Muslim women compared to 6.73 hours for Hindu women) (data from Amin, adolescent survey, 2001).

Table 3 shows detailed daily time accounts from rural women living in agricultural households in Bangladesh, West Bengal, and Rajasthan. The table shows that there is more similarity in time use pattern by region than by religion. Surveys conducted among Bengali women in Hindu and Muslim villages in India and Bangladesh showed they had similar patterns of work. The main contrast shown in the table is that women in Rajasthan spend an average of three hours a day in crop production related activities and thus have longer hours of work overall. By contrast women in Bengal spend less than half an hour in crop production.

Table 3: Average hours worked per day in various tasks by rural women in four studies in India and Bangladesh

Activities	Mohanpur, Bangladesh 1991	West Bengal, India 1976	Char Gopalpur, Bangladesh 1976	Rajasthan, North India 1976
Dominant Religion	Muslim	Hindu	Muslim	Hindu
Crop Production	0.22	0.56	0.28	3.03
Wage Work	0.15	0.13	0.49	0.03
Animal Care and Other Non-Domestic	0.86	0.52	0.56	0.61
Rice Processing	0.30	0.26	1.29	0.21
Childcare	0.32	0.32	0.80	0.91
Handicrafts	0.27	0.36	0.28	0.03
Fuel Collection	0.81	0.36	0.36	0.55
Food Prep/Housework	4.35	5.12	4.24	3.64
Total Hours Worked	7.32	7.82	7.81	9.01
Persons Observed	215	381	174	189

Source: Amin 1997.

Muslim influence is frequently invoked to explain the relatively low status of women in the north but there is little evidence to support a causal influence. While it is true that Mughal influence is more evident in the north relative to the south or the east in terms of music, art, architecture, and cuisine, it appears not to extend to the treatment of women (Morgan et al. 2002, Jejeebhoy and Sathar 2001). Indeed, there is strong numerical dominance of Muslims in Sri Lanka, Kerala, and Karnataka, three states where women's status indicators are most favorable.

Dyson and Moore (1983) suggest that regional variation in women's autonomy is related to kinship systems of patrilineality and exogamous marriage that differ systematically between the north and south and influence all religious groups. These differences result in women in the south being more active outside the home while the pattern in the north is one of confinement to the home with women having very limited mobility. These underlying differences are importantly associated with gendered notions of public space.

Bibliography

S. Amin, The poverty-purdah trap in rural Bangladesh. Implications for women's roles in the family, in *Development and Change* 28:2 (1997), 213–33.

Demographic and Health Surveys, <http://www.measuredhs.com/>.

T. Dyson and M. Moore, On kinship structure, female autonomy, and demographic behavior in India, in *Population and Development Review* 9:1 (1983), 35–60.

S. Jejeebhoy and Z. Sathar, Women's autonomy in India and Pakistan. The influence of religion and region, in *Population and Development Review* 27:4 (2001), 687–712.

S. P. Morgan et al., On Muslim and non-Muslim differences in female autonomy and fertility, in *Population and Development Review* 28:3 (2002), 515–38.

R. L. Narasimhan and R. N. Pandey, Some main results of the pilot time use survey in India and their main policy implications, 2000, <www.unescap.org/stat/meet/timeuse/Programme.htm>.

Sajeda Amin

Southeast Asia

Islamic teachings on gender roles

The conjugal relationship is marked by rights and duties since Muslim marriage is a contract. By Islamic law, a man is contractually obliged to provide lodging, clothing, food, and general care for his wife according to his means: "Lodge them where you are lodging, according to your means, and do not press them, so as to straiten their circumstances . . . Let the man of plenty expend out of his plenty. As for him whose provision is stinted for him, let him expend of what God has given him. God charges no one beyond his means. After difficulty, God will soon grant relief" (Qur'ān 65: 5–6, as cited in Ali 1977, 150). The rationale for a man's role as provider stems from the notion that he is head of the family: "Men are the protectors and maintainers of women, because God has made some of them to excell others, and because they support them from their means (Qur'ān 4: 34, as cited in Khan 1995, 82).

Should a man fail in his obligation (*nafaqa*), his wife has the right to initiate a divorce. In the same vein, the wife is bound by law to contribute to the success and blissfulness of the marriage. Her role includes managing the affairs of the household by meeting her husband's needs, nurturing the children, and protecting the family property and name (Ali 1977, 168–9), as shown by this Qur'ānic verse: "The woman is the guardian of her husband's home and she is accountable for it" (Bukhari, *Ṣaḥīḥ*, as cited in Khan 1995, 89).

Although tutoring the children in religious matters is regarded as a joint responsibility, the wife may adopt a leading role (Roberts 1982, 116), assuming she spends more time at home. A Muslim woman also understands that her husband has been granted authority over her and that she is obliged to obey him, failing which the division of labor in the family is said to be meaningless (Khan 1995, 86). Hence, it is the duty of men to support women, implying that women need not work but rather focus on the affairs of the household.

Although the wife is expected to manage the hearth, she is not obliged to take on the role of food provider; instead this task is regarded the marital obligation of the husband who either carries out the role himself or employs a cook. In the event a man cannot afford to employ a cook, and his wife decides to take on this task out of willingness (*ṣadaqa*), she stands to gain religious merit (*pahala*) for this gracious act.

Cultural notions of men's and women's roles

In spite of Islamic teachings on gender roles in the family, indigenous cultural ideologies persist across Southeast Asia. Among Malays, tradition (*adat*) dictates that women oversee the private domain and its activities, while men dominate public activities. In rural Malaysia, a striking gender division of labor is evident in families where women manage the household, in contrast to men who were said to have had "other things to do" (Firth 1966, 24–5, Laderman 1984). Carsten (1987, 154) found a similar separation of gender roles in Langkawi with Malay women fostering kinship bonds within and beyond the family. Men who were absent from the house for a substantial part of the day were found engaged in fishing, and activities in the local *surau* (mosque) and village politics, and were frequently seen in the village coffee-shops (Carsten 1995, 111).

But Southeast Asian women are not entirely indifferent to engagement in the economic sphere to supplement the household budget. Many are active in income-generating activities, as were their sisters in precolonial Southeast Asia (Reid 1988, 634–5). Wealthier women of Lampung engage in petty trade, although this is always home-based rather than market-based (Elmhirst 2000). Among the coastal fishing households of Sabah, women operate small shops or engage in cottage industries to supplement the family income (Schulze and Suratman 1999, 73–87). In the Muslim fishing communities of Thailand, women are actively involved in the sale of seafood produce in the markets, which they buy from fishermen (Dorairajoo 2002). In the village of Kelantan, the bulk of the cutting of the rice grain is the women's task, while threshing is done by men (Yoshihiro 2001, 24).

Although women may partner men in the role of breadwinner, the home and family are clearly female domains. Some scholars have argued that this division of labor persists because of widespread acceptance of the nature of the sexes, which governs men's and women's self expectations and social behavior (Brenner 1995). Brenner's ethnographic explorations in Solo, central Java amongst the merchant community, revealed that women believe "they have a naturally stronger bond with their offspring than their husbands do, which leads them to take the burden of securing their descendants' futures more heavily on their own shoulders" (ibid., 36). Exceptions may be unmarried daughters who return home from a hard day's work in wage employment. In a *barangay* in Darangen city in central Mindanao, young working daughters are exempted from household chores, which are carried out by the other women residing in the same household (Hilsdon 2003). Here, the practice of veiling meant that married women were most likely to remain in the home executing the household labor, while men sought after wage employment to maintain the household, thus spending more time outside the home.

Given that women manage the hearth, they also act as managers of the household finances. Whether the husband (father) or children work, cash is always handed over to the wife (mother) for the expenses of the household in Lampung (Elmhirst 2000). Although women retain the money, decisions as to how it is spent may be jointly made by a couple, as was found in central Java (Hull 1975, as cited in Wolf 2000). The Islamic teaching that men are ascribed the role of providers is clearly seen in how finances are budgeted among Malays in Singapore. The husband pays for daily essentials, including rent, utilities, the children's education, basic foods such as rice, oil and milk, and other major objects such as the refrigerator, furniture, and television set (Li 1989, 18–19). Although it is not obligatory, the wife usually pays for supplementary items such as her own and her children's clothing, other smaller consumer goods, and major items such as a washing machine or kitchenware. Should the food budget run out, the wife usually pays and is later reimbursed by her husband. When the wife goes out of her way to supplement the household budget or to provide extras for her family, this is viewed by the couple as her voluntary contribution or a gift to the family.

Although men are obliged to take on the role of provider in the family, male responsibility for provision of food is not explicitly defined in the Qurʾān (Devasahayam 2003). Thus, it is common practice for Malay men to purchase food, leaving the women to cook it. In urban Malaysia, a Malay man may either shop for food independently or accompany his wife on food shopping trips, although he pays for the purchases. This gender division of labor was observed in earlier generations, as well as among rural folk (Devasahayam 2001, 207–8). By no means does this suggest that men do not engage in cooking. Instances when men are enlisted to cook are in the public domain as part of ritual or social service, such as in mosques or at a village feast (*kenduri*) for a marriage. While men's engagement in public cooking may have emerged because they dominate activities outside the house (Carsten 1989, 138), celebratory events reverse traditional forms of normal household practices (Carsten 1987, 164). In public cooking, however, women are never entirely disengaged from the scene; instead they play a significant role in a supportive capacity by cutting and chopping up the foodstuff before it is cooked (Carsten 1987, 164, Devasahayam 2001, 186–9). Thus, while cooking is identified with women in the domestic context, when food is prepared in public, the activity does not conform to the dominant gender ideology connecting women to food.

Symbolically linked to food, women are also associated with the kitchen. This link is reinforced by the fact that when Kelantanese women of the east coast of Malaysia trade in the marketplace, they liken this work to "searching for side dishes" (*cari lauk*) (Rudie 1995, 239). Cultural values positing cooking as the prerogative of women are inculcated at a very young age when girls (*anak dara*) are taught by their mothers skills related to household management (Carsten 1989, 120, 121, Laderman 1982, 82). When girls in the past received a formal education, they were usually enrolled in vernacular girls' schools where they learned to cook, weave, and sew (Manderson 1979, 239–40).

The intent for a girl to learn these skills was to refine her female deportment (Omar 1994, 28–9) and create feminine qualities that would enable her to secure a spouse and maintain a household later on in life. That traditional gender role patterns are demanded by the older women of younger girls in Kelantan has been argued to "have an almost all-embracing grip on role formation" (Rudie 1983, 137–8). Yet this "grip" has been seen to be positive in that it creates a cooperative network among women who even help each other by selling produce in the marketplace for those who cannot make the trip themselves.

State constructions of gender roles

State discourses have also reinforced women's caretaker role in the family. Malaysia's modernity project as captured in Vision 2020 calls for the active contribution of women from the middle and upper income echelons to wage employment, while stressing that they continue to retain their role of mother in the family. The dichotomy of gender roles was echoed in earlier policies such as the 70 million target National Population Policy and the National Policy on Women or Dasar Wanita Negara. In the Family Development section of the Sixth Malaysia Plan (1991, 424, as cited in Puthucheary 1991, 11–12), which principally emphasized women's role in providing a "conducive and harmonious family environment," while being simultaneously actively engaged in the country's wage economy, work was defined as an added dimension to a woman's familial responsibilities, thus reinforcing the rhetoric of the "ideal" woman as one who is able to successfully balance the roles of worker and mother/wife (Puthucheary 1991, 12). For many urban women who want a career and family, the employment of a foreign domestic worker has been the solution (Chin 1998).

In Indonesia, official discourses assign women to take the lead role in the performance of reproductive duties. In contrast, the husband is recognized as the head of the household whose primary role is that of breadwinner. Although colonial and post-independence regimes subscribed to this dominant discourse, it only became vigorously institutionalized during Suharto's reign through two key state institutions – the Family Welfare Movement (PKK) and Dharma Wanita (Parawansa 2002, Brenner 1995, Wolf 1992). Through these institutions, the ideals of state "Ibuism" (maternalism) were propagated, emphasizing the primary functions of women as producers of the nation's future generations, loyal companions to their husbands, mothers and educators of children, managers of households, and useful members of society (Sen 1998, Wolf 1992). However, PKK and Dharma Wanita failed to recognize women's worker identity – whether as paid employees or executors of unpaid family labor. A shift occurred when the Ministry for the Role of Women began to portray women in their dual roles in both the domestic and public spheres (Parawansa 2002, Sen 1998, 43). From then onwards, the term *peran ganda* (dual role) was frequently echoed in the official discourses of the New Order regime. However, Indonesian feminists picked up on the implications of *peran ganda*, highlighting the actual workload of women in raising a family. This led to the formulation of the Broad Outlines of State Policy (GBHN) (1993–8), emphasizing shared responsibility of men and women in the domestic sphere, especially in the education of children and the "cultural and philosophical guidance of children" (Sen 1998, 45). In redefining gender equity, however, the economic well-being of a household was left out of the equation, thereby disregarding the experiences of working-class urban and rural women who were unable to afford hired help. Since the Suharto era, efforts at promoting gender equity in the family, society, and nation continue; yet official discourses of gender roles and identities have remained unchanged (Parawansa 2002).

Bibliography

H. ʿAbd al-ʿĀṭī, *The family structure in Islam*, Indianapolis 1982.

S. Brenner, Why women rule the roost. Rethinking Javanese ideologies of gender and self-control, in A. Ong and M. Peletz (eds.), *Bewitching women, pious men. Gender and body politics in Southeast Asia*, Berkeley 1995, 19–50.

J. Carsten, Analogues or opposites. Household and community in Pulau Langkawi, Malaysia, in C. MacDonald (ed.), *De la hutte au palais. Sociétés "à maison" en Asie du Sud-Est insulaire*, Paris 1987, 153–68.

——, Cooking money. Gender and the symbolic transformation of means of exchange in a Malay fishing community, in J. Parry and M. Bloch (eds.), *Money and the morality of exchange*, Cambridge 1989, 117–41.

——, Houses in Langkawi. Stable structures or mobile homes?, in J. Carsten and S. Hugh-Jones (eds.), *About the house. Levi-Strauss and beyond*, Cambridge 1995, 105–28.

C. B. N. Chin, *In service and servitude. Foreign female domestic workers and the Malaysian "modernity" project*, New York 1998.

T. W. Devasahayam, Consumed with modernity and "tradition." Food, women, and ethnicity in changing urban Malaysia, Ph.D. diss., Department of Anthropology, Syracuse University 2001.

——, Empowering or enslaving? What *adat* and *agama* mean for gender relations and domestic food production in Malay households, paper presented at Urban Malaysia. Eat Drink, *Halal Haram*: Food, Islam and Society in Asia Workshop, 3–5 December 2003, Asia Research Institute, National University of Singapore.

S. Dorairajoo, "No fish in the sea." Thai-Malay tactics of negotiation in a time of scarcity, Ph.D. diss., Department of Anthropology, Harvard University 2002.
B. Elmhirst, Negotiating gender, kinship and livelihood practices in an Indonesian transmigration area, in J. Koning, M. Nolten, J. Rodenburg, and R. Saptari (eds.), *Women and households in Indonesia. Cultural notions and social practices*, Richmond, Surrey 2000, 208–34.
R. Firth, *Housekeeping among Malay peasants*, London 1943, 1966².
A.-M. Hilsdon, Violence among Maranao Muslim women in the Philippines, in L. Manderson and L. R. Bennett (eds.), *Violence against women in Asian societies*, London 2003, 20–40.
M. W. Khan, *Woman in Islamic shari'ah*, trans. F. Khanam, New Delhi 1995.
C. Laderman, Putting Malay women in their place, in P. Van Esterik (ed.), *Women of Southeast Asia*, Detroit, Mich. 1982, 79–99.
——, *Wives and midwives. Childbirth and nutrition in rural Malaysia*, Berkeley 1984.
T. Li, *Malays in Singapore. Culture, economy, and ideology*, Oxford 1989.
L. Manderson, A woman's place. Malay women and development in Peninsular Malaysia, in J. C. Jackson and M. Rudner (eds.), *Issues in Malaysian development*, Singapore 1979, 233–72.
R. Omar, *The Malay woman in the body. Between biology and culture*, Kuala Lumpur 1994.
K. I. Parawansa, Institution building. An effort to improve Indonesian women's role and status, in K. Robinson and S. Bessel (eds.), *Women in Indonesia. Gender, equity and development*, Singapore 2002, 68–77.
M. Puthucheary, *Government policies and perceptions of policy makers and women leaders on the status and role of women in society. Status and role of Malaysian women in development and family welfare*, Research report no. 2, Faculty of Economics and Administration, University of Malaya, Kuala Lumpur 1991.
A. Reid, Female roles in pre-colonial Southeast Asia, in *Modern Asian Studies* 22:3 (1998), 629–45.
D. S. Roberts, *Islam. A Westerner's guide*, London 1982.
I. Rudie, The significance of "eating." Cooperation, support, and reputation in Kelantan Malay households, in W. J. Karim (ed.), *"Male" and "Female" in developing Southeast Asia*, Oxford 1995, 227–45.
——, Women in Malaysia. Economic autonomy, ritual segregation and some future possibilities, in B. Utas (ed.), *Women in Islamic societies. Social attitudes and historical perspectives*, London 1983, 128–43.
H. Schulze and S. Suratman, *Villagers in transition. Case studies from Sabah*, Sabah, Malaysia 1999.
K. Sen, Indonesian women at work. Reframing the subject, in K. Sen and M. Stivens (eds.), *Gender and power in affluent Asia*, London 1998, 35–62.
D. Wolf, *Factory daughters. Gender, household dynamics and rural industralization in Java*, Berkeley 2000.
T. Yoshihiro, *One Malay village. A thirty-year community study*, trans. P. Hawkes, Kyoto 2001.

Theresa W. Devasahayam

Sub-Saharan Africa

The gendered division of labor within the family in societies in Sub-Saharan Africa is a consequence of the particular historical conditions under which family structures emerge and the ways in which family relations are constantly renegotiated.

Islam

Islam is practiced today by the majority of men and women in Mauritania, Senegal, Mali, Niger, Nigeria, Gambia, Guinea, Chad, Sudan, Somalia, Djibouti, and the Comoro Islands. Additionally, Islam is an important minority religion in the East African countries such as Kenya and in the Gulf of Benin countries (Coulon 1983, 6). The mass appeal of Muslim reform movements throughout Sub-Saharan Africa at the turn of the twentieth century can be understood in part by transformations taking place in the domestic sphere. These changes took place in the context of a social crisis that was engendered by the French conquest and the disintegration of the political structures in the region, particularly West Africa, which destabilized the material basis of social production. Though early converts to Islam were, as Robinson (1991) suggests, "weary of war," most likely they also sought land and bridewealth. Former slaves as well as young men converted to Islam to acquire land through the patronage of Muslim shaykhs. Klein (1998) suggests that many people in the region of the Senegambia turned to Islam to escape slavery and focuses on the ways in which former slaves were incorporated into social and familial structures under Islam. Though Muslim missionaries, traders, and scholars spread Islam throughout much of Sub-Saharan Africa, Launay and Soares argue that the Islamization of many communities was the "unintended consequence" of French colonial rule. Islamic reform movements can be understood in terms of "the emergence of a qualitatively new 'Islamic' sphere; conceptually separate from 'particular' affiliations such as ethnicity, kin group membership or slave origins, as well as from the colonial state" (1999, 497).

Slave trade and labor migration

Colonial rule and the Atlantic slave trade fundamentally altered the social basis of rural and urban artisanal economies in West African societies (Sow 1985, 567). In other parts of Africa during the colonial period men from many communities, particularly in Eastern and Southern Africa, left their rural homes in search of employment in colonial projects such as road building, portage, and mining, in addition to work on agricultural plantations. On the heels of this largely male migration to the urban centers of production, many adult women followed to provide services and in search of a livelihood through restaurants or prostitution. During the two world wars many men in French and British colonies were conscripted to fight for the Allies with the encouragement of Muslim shaykhs; many were not paid by the European powers for their services. The slave trade and labor migration were thus major factors affecting the relations of production within the household economy, with wide ranging consequences for the economy proper.

Postcolonial period

The French anthropologist Claude Meillassoux (1975) analyzed West African agricultural communities and their articulation with capitalism through the process of colonization to illuminate the connections between the kinship structures that control reproduction and the exploitation of workers. Meillassoux thus considered the historical and material conditions that contributed to the development of this particular form of social organization to avoid thinking of the family as an extra social given.

In the postcolonial period, many agriculturally based communities have suffered environmental degradation as a result of poor farming practices related to monocropping during the colonial period. They have come to rely increasingly on trade in local, national, and overseas markets and overseas remittances as the prices for raw goods have fallen in the global market and their currencies have been devalued through structural adjustment programs of the International Monetary Fund and the World Bank. As a result, men have become increasingly involved in overseas migration and women have become increasingly involved in domestic markets. Women are thus often the consumers and distributors of good imported by their male counterparts. In some societies, such as northern Nigeria, women practice seclusion and must rely on exchanges between households to earn money rather than working outside the home.

Thus the household division of labor within the family is not comprised of a fixed set of duties and responsibilities, but rather by a set of obligations that are the product of a process of constant renegotiation in the context of changing social, political, and economic conditions. The division of labor within the family is influenced in part by Qurʾānic law and by the *ḥadīth*, the sayings of the Prophet Muḥammad (Sow 1985, 563). For example, in Senegal, men and women place a premium on generosity. For men this means giving charity and alms as well as gifts to religious leaders and aid to friends, associates, and business partners. Ideas about generosity form the basis of relations of patronage that reach up toward the state. For women, the emphasis on generosity means giving liberally at family ceremonies and staging elaborate feasts. Thus men and women often come into conflict concerning the allocation of household resources.

In many families across the continent, women participate in rotating credit unions and Islamic forms of banking that avoid payment of interest, which is prohibited in Islam. These economic organizations may be composed of family members, neighbors, religious devotees, or participants in local development projects sponsored by nongovernmental organizations. One such organization that has been very successful is ENDA T.M. in Senegal. Exchange relations, and their affective qualities, go beyond family to encompass rotating credit unions, and ritual, neighborhood, and political associations. Relations among women neighbors have become a significant resource pooling unit, much like the kinship unit.

Qurʾānic law is applied differently to varying forms of family structures and relations of obligation across the continent. What is universal is the emergence of a discourse about how Qurʾānic law ought to be interpreted with respect to the generation and distribution of resources along the lines of age and gender. Arguments concerning the division of labor and household economy play out over the manipulation of rules of filiation, paternity, engagement, marriage, and inheritance. But as Sow argues, "the advent of Islam in black Africa did not lead to acute conflict of family structures and law" (1985, 563). She gives two reasons, the first of which is a historical argument based on the pluralistic basis of many of these societies and the second is that "Koranic thought lends itself to interpretation (*ijtihad*), in the sense of adaptation" (1985, 563).

Conventionally, the head of the family is a senior male. This person is in a position to control the production, exchange, and distribution of resources; this includes material resources such as land and cash and symbolic payments such as bridewealth within the extended family. This person also distributes work along the lines of age and gender, provides for the needs of the family members, and endeavors to establish good relations beyond the household (Sow 1985, 564). Women aim to sustain good relations within the household and extended family. Authority follows the lines of age and generation in the first order and gender in the second, in most cases. With regard to relations of alliance, mothers-in-law have control over the productive and reproductive possibilities of their daughters-in-law. Thus younger women often take on the burden of domestic labor, freeing their in-laws for ritual work outside the household, which often involves elaborate forms of reciprocal gift exchange, an important source of wealth and authority within the lineage and neighborhood. Thus while it may appear that men dominate and control economic life, women divert those resources toward the production of their power and authority through family ceremonies that require enormous outlays of cash.

Increasing male migration in relation to economic liberalization in many regions of the continent has meant that women have become *de facto* heads of households. They have used remittances from male kin to shore up the household economy and to engage in their own productive endeavors, such as trading, and have diverted these earnings into their ritual economies. In many communities there is discourse concerning a crisis of social production that is related to neoliberal reform. Men in particular discuss their failure to constitute relations of kinship and alliance due to their prolonged sojourns abroad and the absence of the kinds of resources necessary to sustain these alliances.

BIBLIOGRAPHY
M. Klein, The impact of the Atlantic slave trade on the societies of the western Sudan, in J. Inikori and S. Engerman (eds.), *The Atlantic slave trade. Effects of economies, societies and peoples in Africa, the Americas, and Europe*, Durham, N.C. 1992, 25–47.
C. Meillassoux, *Maidens, meal and money. Capitalism and the domestic community*, Cambridge 1975.
D. Robinson, Beyond resistance and collaboration. Amadu Bamba and the Murids of Senegal, in *Journal of Religion in Africa* 21:2 (1991), 149–69.
F. Sow, Muslim families in Black Africa, in *Current Anthropology* 26:5 (1985). 563–70.

BETH ANNE BUGGENHAGEN

Turkey and the Caucasus

In general, the domestic division of labor varies with contextual factors such as the labor market and industrial structure, and with household characteristics such as family structure, social class, income source, ethnicity, and relative factor endowments of male versus female family members. To identify patterns across the region, it is useful to focus on the interplay between social norms and everyday practices producing gendered definitions of work. Social norms either differentially assign obligations to men and women, or differentially prohibit them from certain tasks.

Throughout Turkey and the heavily Turkic areas of the Caucasus, cultural expectations dictate that adult men earn a living and protect the domestic unit (and the nation) against external threats. Women are responsible for childcare, food preparation, and quotidian household maintenance. Failure to fulfill these obligations results in loss of self-respect and social respectability, for both men and women. Men are generally prohibited from performing female duties, whereas the converse rarely holds. For example, a man who is forced by circumstance to regularly cook or to take care of children is considered much more gender-deviant than a woman who is forced to provide for her family or take up arms in defense of home and country. In other words, the norms that impose prohibitions on women's work are considerably more flexible than those for men, and are more easily overridden when in conflict with the family's needs. Thus, most of the regional variability in domestic arrangements is accounted for by the wide range of tasks that women perform in response to varying outcomes of the constant negotiation between broad cultural expectations and the practical requirements of daily survival. For the same reason, women's work has undergone more dramatic changes than men's in response to socioeconomic transformations.

Agricultural production in the region is dominated by small-scale family holdings where both men and women engage in crop cultivation and animal husbandry. Clearing and plowing of fields are generally men's work, while weeding (hoeing), transplanting, and hand-irrigation are mostly performed by women aided by children. The whole household works in the fields during the harvest. The maintenance of poultry and milking of livestock are also women's work. Women, aided by children, process raw agricultural products into fuel, cooking ingredients (such as cracked wheat, yogurt-wheat-soup mix [*tarhana*], noodles, tomato paste, dried vegetables, smoked meats, cheese, and butter), and crafting materials (such as straw for basket-weaving, thread, and yarn). Along the Black Sea coast where farms are relatively small and the major crops (tea, tobacco, hazelnuts) do not require annual plowing, women are frequently the major cultivators while adult men engage in seasonal cash-earning activities.

In rural households, the physical strength requirement of a task is rarely a determining factor in its gendering. For example, women frequently haul heavy loads of straw, kindling, and water across long distances, even when adult males are available. It is not unusual for rural women to carry the stones or bricks for a building while men do the masonry (Erdentuğ 1959). Additionally, rural women are almost solely responsible for childcare, cooking, cleaning, knitting, weaving, and sewing.

Even in cases where the resulting products are marketed, constituting significant contributions to household income, these activities are generally regarded by both men and women as either leisure or simply part of womanhood (Berik 1987, Kağıtçıbaşı 1982, 13–14).

In urban households where the husband's income can support a comfortable standard of living, a woman who chooses full-time homemaking is not regarded as deviant as long as she fulfills domestic and childcare obligations. These duties are performed by (usually female) domestic servants if household income can support their wages without threatening the secure survival of the family. Since supervision of domestic servants is easily combined with full-time employment, it is common for (especially younger) women from affluent households to pursue professional and managerial careers without breaking serious gender norms (Öncü 1981, Erkut 1982). However, an able-bodied woman who does not contribute to a household income that is insufficient for a culturally expected level of security and comfort invites social disapproval. Thus, in urban households where adult men are un(der)-employed, women commonly engage in income-earning activities ranging from taking in piecework (White 1994), to waged work in both the informal and formal sectors (Ecevit 1998, İlkkaracan 1998). However, men's contribution to housework and childcare is considered inappropriate by the majority except in times of family crisis, and there appears to be a consensus that under those circumstances, the most suitable domestic chore for adult men is shopping (Başaran 1985).

These asymmetries in definitions of gender-appropriate work impose serious strains on women, especially in low-to-middle-income households. Additionally, and somewhat paradoxically, they create and maintain two highly gender-segregated domestic role clusters and relative autonomy for (especially older) women carrying out female-appropriate daily tasks. Consequently, most scholars of the Turkish family agree that it follows a duofocal pattern rather than a classical patriarchal one (Olson-Prather 1976, Olson 1982)

Though by no means unique to the region in its broad outlines, the particulars of this division of labor nonetheless bear the marks of a highly specific set of historical and sociocultural factors. Male and female duties clearly derive from Islamic family norms, as does the dependence of masculinity on the ability to distance itself from feminine tasks, and the resulting autonomy of women within the domestic sphere (Ahmed 1982). Norms governing women's roles outside the home, however, underwent drastic revisions under the Kemalist reforms in Turkey and the Bolshevik Revolution in the Caucasus.

Both movements incorporated women's emancipation as an integral part of their program, and as a litmus test of success. Observing gender asymmetries in domestic labor, Bolshevik reformers concluded that women, and not the working class, were the truly exploited and hence were their potential allies in the predominantly Muslim areas around the Caucasus (Massell 1974). In Turkey, the modernization of women was a key component of Atatürk's reformist agenda. Through speeches and legislative reforms, he actively coaxed Turkish women into the public sphere of work, career, and politics. The female comrade in Soviet revolutionary culture (Wood 1997) and the (especially rural) woman within the Turkish discourse of national liberation and rebirth (Atatürk 1923) are both represented as strong workers and brave fighters. Both discourses, however, were silent about domestic labor except to reassert women's importance as mothers. Consequently, neither reform movement significantly altered masculine duties and prohibitions as defined by Islamic law and practice, while they drastically widened the scope of female duties and aggressively challenged prohibitions against women's public roles. In other words, women's emancipation came with high labor costs.

Bibliography

L. Ahmed, Western ethnocentrism and perceptions of the harem, in *Feminist Studies* 8 (1982), 521–34.

M. K. Atatürk, *Atatürk'ün söylev ve demeçleri*, ii, Istanbul 1952, 84–7, 148–54.

F. Başaran, Attitude changes related to sex roles in the family, in T. Erder (ed.), *Family in Turkish society. Sociological and legal studies*, Ankara 1985, 167–82.

G. Berik, *Women carpet weavers in rural Turkey. Patterns of employment, earnings and status*, Geneva 1987.

Y. Ecevit, Türkiye'de kadın emeğinin toplumsal cinsiyet temelinde analizi, in A. Hacımirzaoğlu (ed.), *75 yılda kadınlar ve erkekler*, Istanbul 1998, 267–84.

N. Erdentuğ, *A study on the social structure of a Turkish village*, Ankara 1959.

S. Erkut, Dualism in values toward education of Turkish women, in Ç. Kağıtçıbaşı (ed.), *Sex roles, family, and community in Turkey*, Bloomington, Ind. 1982, 121–32.

İ. İlkkaracan, Kentli kadınlar ve çalışma yaşamı, in A. Hacımirzaoğlu (ed.), *75 yılda kadınlar ve erkekler*, Istanbul 1998, 285–302.

Ç. Kağıtçıbaşı, Introduction, in Ç. Kağıtçıbaşı (ed.), *Sex roles, family, and community in Turkey*, Bloomington, Ind. 1982, 1–32.

G. J. Massell, *The surrogate proletariat. Moslem women and revolutionary strategies in Soviet Central Asia, 1919–1929*, Princeton, N.J. 1974.

E. Olson, Duofocal family structure and an alternative model of husband-wife relationships, in Ç. Kağıtçıbaşı (ed.), *Sex roles, family, and community in Turkey*, Bloomington, Ind. 1982, 33–72.

E. Olson-Prather, Family planning and husband-wife relationships in contemporary Turkey, Ph.D. diss., University of California, Los Angeles 1976.
A. Öncü, Turkish women in professional occupations. Why so many? in N. Abadan-Unat, D. Kandiyoti, and M. B. Kıray (eds.), *Women in Turkish society*, Leiden 1981, 181–93.
J. B. White, *Money makes us relatives. Women's labor in urban Turkey*, Austin, Tex. 1994.
E. Wood, *The baba and the comrade. Gender and politics in revolutionary Russia*, Bloomington, Ind. 1997.

Nilüfer A. İsvan

Household Forms and Composition

The Caucasus

This entry deals mainly with Azerbaijan. This is because of the shortage of relevant scholarship on the rest of the Muslim Caucasus. At the turn of the twentieth century in the Caucasus, where the great majority of the population lived in rural areas, *aila ijmasi* (family communes) were the common form of household composition. These were based on common ownership and use of land and livestock by large extended families. The complex organization of such social groups was marked by a rigid system of etiquette governing intergenerational and affinal relations, with the male elders, *ak saqqal*, predominating in authority. But on matters concerning women, the *ak birchek*, female elder, would also be the authority referred to (Heyat 2002, 60). Generally, the status of an elder was achieved as much through their personal qualities of leadership as their age.

Later, through the early part of the twentieth century with developments in trade and industry (especially the oil industry), family communes began to break up and nuclear families started to evolve. This process was greatly accelerated by the Soviet system; under collectivization the rural family unit lost much of its economic function and power. From the 1970s the nuclearization of families further accelerated with urbanization and the increase in apartment building and the housing stock generally. However, in the rural areas households of three or more generations living as one unit were very common. In Baku composite households of different generations with the addition of young relatives from the regions was not uncommon. For young people from rural areas who came to study at the capital city one of the means of being accommodated was to move in with a relative. This was often done in exchange for child minding or other domestic chores. Hiring domestic labor often had to be disguised as an interfamily arrangement of labor and financial exchange.

Today in the Muslim Caucasus, the tradition of closely-knit extended families seeking residence in close geographical proximity to each other and maintaining frequent contact continues (Chenciner 1997, Hortaçsu and Baştuğ 2000). The economy of shortages and the all-pervasive Soviet system of nepotism had reinforced reliance on family members as the core of personal networks essential for access to scarce resources and employment opportunities (Tohidi 1998, Heyat 2000). In the present post-Soviet era, despite the emergence of money as a source of power and influence, the need for pooling of family resources as a means of survival in the face of severe economic difficulties has led to the continuity in the strength of the extended family.

In Azerbaijan, the demographic, social, and cultural changes following the economic breakdown, transition to free market, and the war with Armenia in the early 1990s have led to the departure from the country of large numbers of men in search of work in Russia, other former Soviet republics, and further afield (Heyat 2002, 175). Consequently, there are today far greater numbers of female-headed households than there have ever been in the region's history. The economic empowerment of young people with knowledge of Western languages and expertise working for multinational organizations, Western non-governmental organizations, and foreign companies in Baku has also led to the formation of single occupancy households there. In the past, given the shortage of housing, living alone was highly unusual and not socially condoned, especially for women.

In the present free market era, there is a growing gap in wealth and social distinctions (Heyat 2002). As the new rich are able to build and acquire much larger accommodation space, some in the form of mansions, their household size is reduced since newly married couples and even some of the single young professionals are able to afford their own separate apartments. At the same time, economic difficulties and the influx of foreigners have led to some families in Baku renting out their homes and moving in with parents, in-laws, or even siblings in order to gain an additional income. This has meant a contra-nuclearization process in which three or more generations, or adult siblings and their respective families, cram into apartments previously assigned to a nuclear family household. In the rural areas, however, there is increasing gender and generational imbalance as young people in search of work, particularly the males, depart for urban centers or abroad. In Azerbaijan, female-headed households and households where the adult males are mostly absent, or often in transit, have increasingly become the norm.

Bibliography
R. Chenciner, *Daghestan. Tradition and survival*, London 1997.
F. Heyat, Azeri professional women's life strategies, in F. Acar and A. Güneş-Ayata (eds.), *Gender and identity construction. Women of Central Asia, the Caucasus and Turkey*, Leiden 2000, 177–201.
F. Heyat, *Azeri women in transition. Women in Soviet and post-Soviet Azerbaijan*, London 2002.
N. Hortaçsu and S. Baştuğ, Women in marriage in Ashkabad, Baku and Ankara, in F. Acar and A. Güneş-Ayata (eds.), *Gender and identity construction. Women of Central Asia, the Caucasus and Turkey*, Leiden 2000, 75–100.
N. Tohidi, "Guardians of the Nation." Women, Islam, and the Soviet legacy of modernization in Azerbaijan, in H. L. Bodman and N. Tohidi (eds.), *Women in Muslim societies. Diversity within unity*, Boulder, Colo. 1998, 147–67.

Farideh Heyat

Central Asia

A significant characteristic of the Central Asian family is its flexibility in make-up and also, in many aspects, in location. This was even more marked before the 1917 Russian Revolution when there were several distinct lifestyles in Central Asia: the nomadic Kazakhs and Kyrgyz, and the sedentary Uzbeks and Tajiks, with the Turkmens, Karakalpaks, and other related groups drawing on elements from both.

The nomadic peoples typically lived in tents, or *yurts*, easy to dismantle structures divided into men's and women's quarters, with separate sleeping sections for the parents and a central kitchen. Their household can be conceptualized as a group of family units residing in a cluster of *yurts*, forming a camp or *aul*, and jointly owning the family herds. These *auls* usually moved location from winter to summer and did not always consist of an identical group of people.

The sedentary household was situated within a courtyard (*havli*), containing anything from one room to a large group of houses/rooms, each accommodating a family unit. The 1897 Central Asian census data indicated an average of 5.5 people per household but this figure obscures large differences in size, from one-person households to those containing 50 or more (Krader 1971, 147–9).

Both nomadic and sedentary peoples lived in extended patrilineal families, usually consisting of a patriarch, his wife or wives, and their unmarried offspring, married sons and their wives and children, and in larger households the patriarch's younger brothers, their wives and progeny, and perhaps also distant cousins. Thus, most male members would be related by blood, with wives marrying in. Richer men might live between several households, each run by a different wife, sometimes in a different town.

When they became too big or at the patriarch's death, households would split, each son forming his own. In smaller households a son would separate soon after marriage or at the marriage of the following son, except for the youngest, who would remain with his parents for life and inherit the *yurt* or *havli* after their death. However, wives who did not get along with their in-laws might try to persuade their husbands to split from the extended family sooner. Families without sons might prevail upon a son-in-law to move in with them permanently to carry on the line.

Those too poor to afford their own homes could serve the rich. Poor women might work as indoor servants. They might even accompany a daughter married to a wealthy man as her servant. In nomadic areas men with insufficient herds to support themselves could act as servants to those with large herds until they could afford independence. Similarly, among the sedentary, poor men would hire out their services to wealthier ones in whose households they would live. An impoverished man might arrange to give bride labor instead of the usual bride-price, living as a servant in his future wife's household meanwhile. In general, class distinctions were not strong, servants frequently intermarried with their employers' families, and there was little differentiation between kin and non-kin within the household.

After the revolution, the Soviet regime encouraged the development of nuclear households throughout the region. Nevertheless, in rural areas today the extended family remains the norm, despite changes in economic relations as a consequence of collectivization and the forcible settling of the nomadic tribes. In urban areas the government tried to enforce its policies by building apartments too small for extended families. However, even when fathers and sons live in physically separate residences, they and their families may spend most of their free time together, functioning virtually as an extended family, so that it is often difficult to decide where to draw the line round the household unit. Moreover, offspring often give their eldest child to their parents to rear, which also skews the division of households into nuclear units.

The Soviet government provided dormitories for factory employees from rural areas. Today these may house whole families, each living in a single room and sharing bathrooms. Some workers have a home elsewhere. However, for the poorest, and especially single mothers, their dormitory room may be their sole accommodation, and thus might be considered to contain a household.

Family size changed during Soviet times as improved health conditions allowed increasing numbers of children to survive to maturity. As of 1996, for instance, the average family size in Tajikistan was 7.1 (Tajikistan 1996, 82). Recently, economic pressures have reduced birth rates. Simultaneously, however, they also make it harder for families to afford to live separately. For the first time, divorce rates have risen so high that for want of other living quarters adult women have started to return to their parents' home in significant numbers, usually accompanied by their children. As a result, overall household size has increased.

Especially in postwar Tajikistan, numbers of female-headed households have grown considerably, both nuclear households, where a woman lives alone with her children, and extended ones where her married sons reside with her.

New forms of polygynous residence have also arisen. That least encountered consists of two wives living in the same home. More commonly, one wife is chosen by, and resides with, her husband's parents, while he additionally marries a woman of his own choice, either establishing her in an urban apartment or moving in with her if she already has her own place. This happens frequently when men from rural areas migrate to work in a town, whether in Central Asia or the Russian Federation. In Tajikistan at least, the imbalance between the sexes has led to women consenting to become third and even fourth wives rather than never marrying. Such women may continue to reside with their natal families and be visited only occasionally by their husbands, who take little or no responsibility for them or their offspring.

While multiple wives can be married by *nikāḥ*, civil law permits only one wife. If parents do not register the first marriage then the husband can register his second. Since civil registration is entered into one's passport some men "lose" these and obtain a second one so as to register a second time, thus effectively committing bigamy. Registration of marriage is especially important for marriages in Russia for the purpose of obtaining residence permits.

Same-sex households remain rare. Divorced or widowed men usually remarry, invite a female relative to keep house, or move in with another family member. They tend to live together only as a last resort, such as during labor migration to the Russian Federation. Most homosexual men marry or live with their parents.

Slightly more common are households consisting of one or more women, with or without children and/or siblings. These are unlikely to be lesbians but rather sisters, mothers and daughters, or even friends. I have also come across rare cases of apparently intersexed persons living together in what resemble women-only households in that those concerned may present themselves as females, irrespective of genetic make-up.

BIBLIOGRAPHY

E. E. Bacon, *Central Asians under Russian rule. A study in cultural change*, Ithaca, N.Y. 1966.

L. Krader, *The peoples of Central Asia*, Bloomington, Ind. 1971.

A. Meakin, *In Russian Turkestan*, London 1903.

L. F. Monogarova, Contemporary urban family structure in Tajikistan (on materials from Ura-Tyube and Isfary) [in Russian], in *Sovetskaya Etnografia* 3 (1982).

V. Nalivkin and M. Nalivkina, *A study of women's lifestyles among the settled indigenous population of Fergana* [in Russian], Kazan 1886.

E. Schuyler, *Turkistan*, New York 1876.

Tajikistan/UNDP, *Tajikistan. Human development report*, Dushanbe 1996, <http://www.undp.org/rbec/nhdr/1996/tajikistan/>.

T. A. Zhdankova, Study of changes in the traditional structure of family among the peoples of Central Asia under the conditions of socialism [in Russian], in *Slovensky Narodopis* 31:3 (1983), 414–25.

COLETTE HARRIS

Iran and Afghanistan

Households vary with class and location. Traditional agricultural/pastoral households contain an extended patrilineal/patrilocal family spanning several generations, forming a production and consumption unit with complementary sexual division of labor. In urban and non-agricultural households women do not produce much (except children); they prepare food and provide care with materials provided by the men. These households change to nuclear family patterns earlier than agricultural ones under the influence of changing work patterns, limited urban spaces, and modernist ideas. Traditional wealthy urban households usually are the largest, including multiple wives of the household head, an extended family, other relatives, and servants.

Structurally, the developmental logic of the extended family informs household composition and relationships: a man will try to exert control over wife (wives) and sons as early and as long as possible, staying in his father's house, compound, or camp and identifying with his father's and brothers' interests as long as necessary or advantageous for him. Eventually, he will establish an independent nuclear household, which leads to the next extended family as his sons bring their wives into the household. The sons, in turn, will start the circle anew. Households of extended families are structurally unstable.

Practically, this household form ranges from a production and consumption unit under one roof (including several wives) to a loosely cooperating production unit with different contributions (cash from a teacher son, labor from a farmer son) and separate consumption, as different nuclear families (or mother and children units in polygynous families) live in separate rooms in a compound, apartments in a house, or tents in a camp. Built into these structures are the demand for cooperation, resentment of authoritarian relations, and competition for resources especially among married brothers. It is said that nothing breaks up a household faster than brothers' wives fighting with each other and with their mother-in-law. Co-wives are proverbially adversary. This is mostly due to the household structure: co-wives are pitched against each other as are sons' wives, and all against their mother-in-law over resources and workloads; mothers-in-law back their sons, especially in polygynous marriages, because sons are their source of power and of support in old age. The often bad relationship between mother-in-law and daughter-in-law leads to many old women's reliance on their own visiting daughters for care.

Rich men are more likely to be polygynous than are poor men (although any man may be saddled with his dead brother's widow in addition to his own wife), but they can also maintain separate homes for their wives, minimizing contact and potential strife among them. Such households in effect are headed by a woman, with a visiting husband. There are reports of older wives selecting a young wife for their husband for various reasons. The first wife will usually stay in charge of the household, including management of co-wives and supervising work. In the wealthy households of the past, male and female servants did most of the menial chores; with the trend toward nuclear families such large households have become rare. Modernity is expected to lower the rate of polygyny, but especially in Iran today many wealthy professional men are said to maintain several wives. Women in Iran today are admonished to stipulate a separate home if they contract a marriage with a married man.

While sons may stay in their father's household with their wives, daughters leave upon marriage and are replaced by their brother's wives. As strangers to the husband's people and to each other, ignorant of the new household's customs, the young wives must expect to be everybody's servants. Unless the mother-in-law is amiable and the young woman is hard-working and cooperative, tensions and emotional and physical abuse are frequent. Expected to keep wives and children under control and to side with father, brothers, mother (in this order), a man will not likely support his wives against his own people. Contrary to Islamic law, daughters especially in lower classes and rural areas do not inherit, making them the more vulnerable economically. In instances of hostile relations, only through separation from the extended household can a woman gain peace and control over resources in the house, including, eventually, over her own daughters-in-law. An old or widowed woman expects to live in the nuclear-to-extended household of a son (the youngest, where ultimogeniture is practiced). Only if earlier she had established warm relationships with the daughter-in-law who now is responsible for her care can she hope realistically to be treated well. Recently, there is a notable increase in the number of old women (but not old men) living alone by choice, especially in Iran, with financial assistance of their sons. An old widower will stay with a son if he does not take another wife and establish a new nuclear household. Since about 1990, as marriage age and divorce rates are increasing (in Iran), single-person households have increased in cities as have households of several unmarried young women (or men) renting an apartment to share costs, and even women-headed households with children. Any household, especially in cities, at times will include temporary residents such as a wife's parents, a relative who is indigent, in need of education or medical care, or who can provide childcare.

Men have few household duties and skills and rely on service from women. In the traditional households with many children and complementary gender roles, the division of labor made sense to people. In the new, nuclear middle-class households with fewer children (in Iran), women accuse men of being lazy and indolent, especially if the women work outside the home. New patterns for household forms and relationships are developing especially in socially dynamic Iran, where people aspire to middle-class lifestyles, while war and the social ideology of the Taliban in Afghanistan have encouraged large, traditionally structured households including many children, the extended family and/or multiple wives and other relatives.

BIBLIOGRAPHY

M. Afkhami, Death of the patriarch, in E. W. Fernea (ed.), *Remembering childhood in the Middle East*, Austin, Tex. 2002, 157–62.

V. Doubleday, *Three women of Herat*, Austin, Tex. 1988.
S. Farman-Farmaian, *Daughter of Persia*, New York 1992.
E. Friedl, *Women of Deh Koh. Lives in an Iranian village*, Washington, D.C. 1989.
S. Guppy, *The blindfold horse. Memories of a Persian childhood*, Boston 1988.
H. Hansen, *The Kurdish woman's life*, Copenhagen 1961.
M. Kousha, *Voices from Iran. The changing lives of Iranian women*, Syracuse, N.Y. 2002.
N. Tapper, *Bartered brides. Politics, gender, and marriage in an Afghan tribal society*, Cambridge 1991.

ERIKA LOEFFLER FRIEDL

The Ottoman Empire

Etymology and Methodology

The household, usually termed *hane*, was the base layer of society in the Ottoman Empire. Administratively, the term meant a fiscal unit until the nineteenth century, but after the first census was carried out in 1828–9, the term came to mean a census unit. Substantial research has been done since Ömer Lutfi Barkan discovered that the *hane*s recorded in *taḥrīr* (survey) registers in the fifteenth and sixteenth centuries could be important sources for the study of historical demography (Barkan 1953). Research on households in the Ottoman Empire before the nineteenth century is rare, however, with only a few instances (for example, Laslett and Clarke 1972). Even after the nineteenth century, because of limited accessibility to census records, analysis is primarily in urban areas such as Istanbul, Cairo, and Damascus (Duben and Behar 1990, Fargues 1999–2000, Okawara 2003). Households in rural areas are not well understood except for some Balkan and Egyptian examples (Hammel 1972, Cuno 1995). Only Maria Nikolaeva Todorova's study (1993) of Bulgarian households covers both urban and rural areas.

A variety of approaches and definitions have been applied to household forms and composition. The definition adopted by the Cambridge Group for the History of Population and Social Structure, the most widely used criterion at present, defines a household as a domestic group, members of which slept habitually under the same roof (a locational criterion), shared a number of activities (a functional criterion), and were related to each other by blood or by marriage (a kinship criterion). Resident servants or maids are also members of the household (Laslett 1972, 23–7).

Household Formation

The most typical Ottoman household formation system is the joint family household, a kind of multiple family household characterized by early marriage for men and rather earlier marriage for women, young married couples frequently starting life together in a household in which an older couple is in charge, and formation by the fission or fusion of one or more existent households. The death of a household head is more important than marriage in this type of household formation. The system contrasts with the northwest European system, which is characterized by later marriage for both sexes, all couples in charge of their own households after marriage (neolocalism), and young people frequently circulating between households as servants before marriage (Hajnal 1983, 68–72).

The joint family household system became the ideal in the Ottoman Empire for three reasons: property holding, living space, and family strategies. For example, Islamic law (Sharīʿa) requires an equalized inheritance system (a female's share, however, is half that of a male), and therefore a household's property can easily be subdivided further between heirs. Households in rural areas that include agricultural land, and urban households that include large estates, seemingly prefer to maintain a joint household for economic reasons. The system is also confirmed by the large courtyard-style houses that afforded ample living space for such a household, and by the domestic servants and maids who took care of domestic affairs before, and in some cases even after, the abolition of slavery. Finally, in terms of family survival strategies a simple family household was not preferable because high mortality and short life expectancy would increase the risk of extinguishing the family.

Household Composition and Size

Even in societies where the joint family household was ideal, such as Ottoman societies, households did not always tend toward a large and complex structure. In reality, any joint family household was difficult to continue through generations; a father had no guarantee that his son(s) would arrive at maturity and marry.

The domestic cycle was also a problem. The rule for Ottoman-Turkish domestic cycle households is as follows: a simple family household is transformed into a multiple family household, composed of married offspring and their children in patrivirilocal residence. Daughters leave their natal households as they marry. The fission of the household into extended or simple family households is precipitated by the death of the father (Duben 1985, 84). In contrast, the rule for the Ottoman-Syrian domestic cycle is that even after the death of the patriarch, and even after the death of the mother, *frérèches* (households of married brothers) live together, and thus fission of the household did not take place easily (Okawara 2003, 63–4). This is also the rule in Egyptian rural households (Cuno 1995, 490).

These findings indicate that any household could experience the stages of simple family, extended family, and multiple family, depending on its domestic cycle. An average for the duration of a joint family household could affect the proportion of households in any given period and place. For example, simple family households were dominant in Istanbul in 1907 (40.0 percent), while multiple family households were dominant in Damascus in the same year (40.1 percent). Their mean household sizes also differ, 4.2 in the former and 6.6 in the latter (Okawara 2003, 60–3).

Women, gender, and household

How did the Ottoman household system affect the status, life course, and fate of Ottoman women? First, in matters of marriage the system was often harsh to women. For example, female early marriage, particularly child marriage, was sometimes a source of trouble. In general, marriage was likely to be arranged by the patriarch for the purpose of reproduction of the patriarchal system (Pierce 2003, 129–31, Meriwether 1999, 103). Also, a female's position was shakier than that of a male, as indicated by the domestic cycle. Daughters might have to leave their natal households as they marry, return if they divorce, or leave again if they remarry, and new brides, as yet lacking their own identity, had to establish full membership in the husband's household by childbearing and child-rearing rather than by marriage itself (Pierce 2003, 150).

Various fiscal registers and census records before 1877–8 serve as evidence of this because they exclude women from their listings. Even census records after that date prefer male to female as a rule. In census records, therefore, female household heads appear in solitaries or no family households, which may consist of a divorcee, aged woman, female slave, or the like. Some simple, extended or multiple family households are also composed of female members only. Such a household rarely lasts long, and is likely to be fused with another household of relatives. In Istanbul, some independent households in the second half of the nineteenth century were composed of manumitted female slaves (Behar 2003, 144).

Nuclearization

The nuclear or simple family household exists in any society to some extent. As for Ottoman societies, even in the Istanbul of 1907, which set trends for the rest of the empire, the simple family household was not overwhelmingly dominant. At the same time, late marriage and a decline in fertility, which are important factors of nuclearization, were increasing in Istanbul due to modernization and the more comprehensive integration of the empire into the world economy. The empire itself, however, had disintegrated before the nuclearization trend prevailed throughout its realm.

Bibliography

Ö. L. Barkan, "Tarihi demografi" araştırmaları ve Osmanlı tarihi, in *Türkiyat Mecmuası* 10 (1953), 1–26.

C. Behar, *A neighborhood in Ottoman Istanbul. Fruit vendors and civil servants in the Kasap İlyas mahalle*, Albany, N.Y. 2003.

K. M. Cuno, Joint family households and rural notables in 19th-century Egypt, in *International Journal of Middle East Studies* 27 (1995), 485–502.

A. Duben, Turkish families and households in historical perspective, in *Journal of Family History* 10 (1985), 75–97.

A. Duben and C. Behar, *Istanbul households. Marriage, family and fertility, 1880–1940*, Cambridge 1991.

P. Fargues, The stage of the family life cycle in Cairo at the end of the reign of Muḥammad ʿAlī, according to the 1848 census, in *Harvard Middle Eastern and Islamic Review* 5 (1999–2000), 1–39.

J. Hajnal, Two kinds of pre-industrial household formation system, in R. Wall, J. Robin, and P. Laslett (eds.), *Family forms in historic Europe*, Cambridge 1983, 65–104.

E. A. Hammel, The Zadruga as process, in P. Laslett and R. Wall (eds.), *Household and family in past time*, Cambridge 1972, 335–73.

P. Laslett, Introduction. The history of the family, in P. Laslett and R. Wall (eds.), *Household and family in past time*, Cambridge 1972, 1–89.

P. Laslett and M. Clarke, Houseful and household in an eighteenth-century Balkan city. A tabular analysis of the listing of the Serbian sector of Belgrade in 1733–4, in P. Laslett and R. Wall (eds.), *Household and family in past time*, Cambridge 1972, 375–400.

M. L. Meriwether, *The kin who count. Family and society in Ottoman Aleppo 1770–1840*, Austin, Tex. 1999.

T. Okawara, Size and structure of Damascus households in the late Ottoman period as compared with Istanbul households, in B. Doumani (ed.), *Family history in the Middle East. Household, property, and gender*, Albany, N.Y. 2003, 51–75.

L. Peirce, *Morality tales. Law and gender in the Ottoman court of Aintab*, Berkeley 2003.

M. N. Todorova, *Balkan family structure and the European pattern. Demographic developments in Ottoman Bulgaria*, Washington, D.C. 1993.

Tomoki Okawara

South Asia

Modern scholars have defined the South Asian household as a co-residential and commensal unit. This scholarship has been fashioned by two different trends. Social historians, frustrated by finding that the records came from ruling households rather than from peasants or commoners, felt free to ignore them as unrepresentative. Only historians interested in state formation studied the ruling households of the region. Thus Blake (1979) studying the Mughal Empire (1526–1858) found it necessary to focus on the imperial household as a microcosm of the "patrimonial-bureaucratic empire." Social anthropologists, on the other hand, have written much on the household but have paid little attention to religion (Vatuk 1989, 109). Since neither the historians nor the anthropologists have seen Islam as significant for the household, it is at present only possible to outline a history of Muslim households in the subcontinent.

Islam arrived in South Asia in the seventh century. By the middle of the twentieth century, Sunnī Islam had become the dominant school though other variants of Islam maintained a strong presence within the Muslim community. This long history was marked by enormous diversity in the ethnic-cultural practices that shaped Islamic institutions. The first Arab Muslim migrants were joined by large numbers of Muslims from Central and West Asia, and East Africa. The group and individual conversion of South Asians to Islam increased the diversity of belief and practice within the community. Thus Muslims were linguistically, ethnically, and socially diverse. Through the centuries, connections developed between soldiers, courtiers, scribes, and rural societies organized around Islamic holy men, and class-rank distinctions and hierarchies were elaborated within the South Asian Muslim community.

Of these four main social groups, only women from the courtly groups have left any significant literary traces. A comparative study of such records allows us to simultaneously locate significant continuities in Muslim elite conceptions of "family," "ancestry," and "kinship" as well as to glimpse the tectonic shifts that had occurred by the twentieth century. Structurally speaking, the multi-layered household described by a sixteenth-century Mughal princess in her *History of Humāyūn* resembles those depicted in twentieth-century memoirs of women from the landed gentry of Northern India. But while the sixteenth-century household may have contained the multiple wives of a Mughal grandee, later elite households in the region were rarely polygynous. In both periods, however, these households contained multiple generations of consanguineous kin, as well as large numbers of unrelated people. The wealthier households encompassed large numbers of dependents who were either distant kindred or elderly kinswomen, or non-kin recipients of charity. Since believing Muslims are enjoined to give a portion of their income to charity, the presence of unrelated or very minimally related people within these households was itself a public display of piety. But charitable intent notwithstanding, such households were also organized to extract, and differentially reward, labor services of various kinds. It is always, therefore, difficult to distinguish the dependent but free kinsman or kinswoman from the dependent non-free servitor.

All accounts record an elaborate hierarchy of female and male servants. Elderly supervisors and wet-nurses were the most powerful and new young slaves the least powerful. But the same accounts also record change: thus wet-nurses often acquired the status of foster-parents to children they had suckled; and the children of wet-nurses were to be regarded as foster-siblings by their charges. This elevation would be registered during ceremonial moments in the life cycle of the child and of the household. The longer the record of service, the greater the moral claim of such a servant upon the attention and resources of the household.

With the spread of British colonialism in the nineteenth century, attention shifted to the gender-segregated and secluded nature of women's lives within such households. While some accounts may be exaggerated, it is important to understand that seclusion practices were being adopted by growing numbers of Muslims as part of intensified social stratification. While some ruling groups lost their wealth and fell in status, families of scholars, artisans, and substantial peasants began to claim higher rank. Since seclusion had been an important symbol of social position, upwardly mobile groups in the nineteenth century also adopted this aristocratic practice. Purdah, or the seclusion of women, accompanied claims to genealogical depth, and/or "foreign" origins and served to consolidate social prestige among Muslims.

Another social practice associated with a particular moment in the ascent of such a lineage was increasing marital exclusivity. Anthropologists refer to this as the adoption of endogamous marriage for junior members. Endogamous marriages were justified by the learned as required by *kafā'a* (Arabic) or *barabari* (Urdu) (similarity of status of bride and groom). The criteria for status, however, differed between groups. Among the southern Indian Muslim followers of the Shāfiʿī law, the principal criteria in the nineteenth century were descent, freedom, religion, and occupation. Some even required a formal assent to a certain austerity in marriage rites and celebrations. Simultaneously, the northern Muslims following Ḥanafī law applied the criteria of pedigree, generations elapsed since conversion to Islam, religiosity, wealth, occupational status, and intellect.

This attention to legal detail in social life coincided with the increasing "purification" of Islam within South Asia during the nineteenth century. In this social and legal context, memories of accepting brides from socially distinct or even non-Muslim communities became an embarrassment in the contemporary Islamic scale of values. While the historical record for many such households in the subcontinent reveals a range of relationships from slave-concubinage to ritualized unions with daughters and sisters of local non-Muslim hegemons, the indigenous language histories produced by these Muslim households either tended to erase these women from the relevant family histories or spoke of them as *mankūḥa*. This last usage inverted the formal meaning of *nikāḥ* (Islamic nuptials) by recording it as a ceremony inferior to the elaborately performed *shādī* in South Asia. So custom continued to operate alongside a growing reference to Sharīʿa among many Muslim households.

The role of the colonial administration in both reshaping and maintaining customs among Muslims in South Asia is a deeply contentious one. In some annexed provinces like Punjab (annexed in 1849), colonial administrators maintained customary practices such as unilineal descent, patrilineal inheritance, and primogeniture. This legitimized deviation from the system of proportionate shares allotted to women in Islamic law, and appears to have seriously affected the property rights of daughters, sisters, and widowed and divorced Muslim women.

Imperial British law directly reshaped household customs at another level too. While diverse sexual relationships could co-exist within the same household from the sixteenth to the eighteenth century, colonial legal measures and interpretations of Islamic laws diminished the viability of such patterns by classifying children born of non-ritual unions as illegitimate. This process also led to the degradation of earlier fosterage and adoption practices that had prevailed in these households, and now began to be identified by Muslim legists too as un-Islamic.

These changes significantly altered relations within substantial households. Hortatory Islamic literature in the nineteenth century addressed women in print for the first time. Texts began to urge women of upwardly mobile Muslim groups to become knowledgeable and skilled laborers. This signals both the entry of new groups without established claims upon, and the older elites' loss of command over, servile and dependent labor. The autobiographies of educated Muslim men in the nineteenth century suggest that skilled labors by women, particularly as seamstresses and spinners, in turn sustained households through the stress of economic and social transition.

Muslim households everywhere were affected by the Partition of 1947. Large numbers of Muslims migrated from India to the newly established nation of Pakistan. Joint-family households were split up. Property-owning Muslim households in both nations appear to have responded to financial and political stresses by becoming ever more vigilant about marriage and family constitution. In some areas, the survival strategies of Muslim households headed by widows and unmarried women reinforced kinship claims upon the younger males, who would reside in multiple households by rotation. Such membership of multiple households may be located in a continuum that includes the dual residence (rural-urban) households of incipient professional groups of the nineteenth century and the households from which males migrated as precolonial soldiers and postcolonial blue-collar workers in the Middle East. In sum, the shape and function of Muslim households in South Asia should be seen as historically responsive to the challenges faced by diverse Islamic groups, rather than as fixed and permanent through all time.

Bibliography

I. Ahmed (ed.), *Caste and social stratification among the Muslims*, New Delhi 1973.

S. P. Blake, The patrimonial-bureaucratic empire of the Mughals, in *Journal of Asian Studies* 39:1 (1979), 77–94.

R. Brara, Kinship and the political order. The Afghan Sherwani chiefs of Malerkotla (1454–1957), in T. N. Madan (ed.), *Muslim communities of South Asia. Culture, society and power*, New Delhi 2001.

L. Carroll, The Muslim family in India. Law, custom and empirical research, in *Contributions to Indian Sociology* 18 (1983), 293–300.

I. Chatterjee, *Gender, slavery and the law in colonial India*, New Delhi 1999.

—— (ed.), *Unfamiliar relations. Family and history in South Asia*, New Brunswick, N.J. 2004.

S. Dale, *Islamic society on the South Asian frontier. The Mappilas of Malabar 1498–1922*, Oxford 1980.

R. M. Eaton, *Essays on Islam and Indian history*, New Delhi 2001.

—— (ed.), *India's Islamic traditions 711–1750*, New Delhi 2003.

Gulbadan Begam, *History of Humāyūn (Humāyūn nāma) by Gulbadan Begam (Princess Rose-Body)*, trans. A. S. Beveridge, London 1902, repr. Delhi 2001.

J. Habibullah, *Remembrance of days past. Glimpses of a princely state during the Raj*, Karachi 2001.

G. R. G. Hambly (ed.), *Women in the medieval Islamic world. Power, patronage and piety*, New York 1998.

S. S. Ikramulla, *Behind the veil*, Karachi 1953, repr. 1998.

S. M. Khan, *The Begums of Bhopal*, London 2000.

Lutfallah, *Autobiography of Lutfullah, a Mohamedan gentleman; and his transactions with his fellow-creatures*, ed. E. B. Eastwick, London 1857.
B. D. Metcalf, *Perfecting women. Maulana Ashraf ʿAli Thanawi's* Bihishti Zewar, Berkeley 1990.
Mrs. B. Mir Hasan ʿAli, *Observations on the Mussulmauns of India*, ed. and intro. W. Crooke, Karachi 1974[2].
S. Vatuk, Household form and formation. Variability and social change among South Indian Muslims, in J. N. Gray and D. J. Mearns (eds.), *Society from the inside out. Anthropological perspectives on the South Asian household*, New Delhi 1989.
——, The cultural construction of shared identity. A south Indian family history, in P. Werbner (ed.), *Person, myth and society in South Asian Islam*, special issue of *Social Analysis* 28 (1990), 114–31.
——, Identity and difference or equality and inequality in South Asian Muslim society, in C. J. Fuller (ed.), *Caste today*, Delhi 1996, 227–62.
A. M. Weiss, *Walls within walls. Life histories of working women in the old city of Lahore*, Boulder, Colo. 1992.

INDRANI CHATTERJEE

Sub-Saharan Africa

Centering on women in Muslim communities of Sub-Saharan Africa, this entry begins with an overview of household forms and composition; it then emphasizes the complexity of women's experiences by considering households in the context of broader social processes, including intra- and inter-household dynamics.

All statistical data in the entry, unless otherwise noted, comes from Demographic and Health Surveys (2003), which includes all countries in the region with significant or majority Muslim populations.

OVERVIEW

The household is the residential unit. It is generally patrilocal; that is, upon marriage women move to men's households. Most houses are owned by men, but in some towns along the Swahili coast 85 percent are owned by women (Askew 1999). Six primary household forms include: three elementary types (single parent, nuclear, and polygynous); two extended types (three-generational and lateral); and same sex. In addition, "hearth-holds" (Ekejiuba 1995) are nested within most households. Over their lifetimes, most women reside at least briefly in each of these forms. By most definitions, each household includes a head. Twenty-five percent are female-headed. Nuclear households are the norm; that is, slightly more households are nuclear than any other form. There is no evidence that nuclear households are becoming more common or smaller (Bongaarts 2001). Three-generational and lateral households, about equal in number, are the next most common; these are followed closely by polygynous and same sex, also roughly equal in number. Single-parent households are by far the least common.

The mean household size is about six, including 2.8 adults and 3.2 children. Twenty percent of households have only one or two members, whereas 15 percent have nine or more members. Extended households are generally larger than elementary ones, but no systematic evidence exists linking household form and size. Twenty-five percent include at least one foster child. Although no statistical data is available, many households include residential domestic workers.

Single-parent households consist only of a head and his or her children. The majority are female headed.

Nuclear households consist only of a head, one spouse, and their children. A tiny minority are female-headed.

Polygynous households consist only of a male head, two to four spouses, and their children.

Three-generational households include grandparents, their adult male offspring often together with their wives, and their grandchildren. Very few are female-headed. Typically they are headed by either a grandfather or the eldest male of the middle generation.

Laterally extended households often include siblings and sometimes their spouses, cousins and other relatives of the head, and sometimes friends of the siblings, usually of the head. The vast majority are male headed.

Same sex households consist primarily of either adult males or females, who may or may not be relatives. Females head all female same sex households.

Hearth-holds are mother-children units within households, symbolically defined by the hearths owned by virtually all adult women.

LIVED EXPERIENCES OF WOMEN IN HOUSEHOLDS

This overview of general patterns provides only a snapshot view of household forms and composition. "The household" is not a static institution. Household forms have evolved through centuries of complex interaction between Islam and African models, and through a century in adaptation to colonialism, urbanization, capitalism, nationalism, and global media. Households are not discrete entities; they are embedded within wider structures and broader systems of production, consumption, and distribution (Guyer and Peters 1987). Household forms are "in continual flux as the domestic cycle unfolds and as families respond to changing opportunities and constraints" (Gage et al. 1997, 299).

Households are the dynamic center of female social life. Girls are born and mature in households. Women do most of their work and socializing, and experience marriage, sex, and motherhood, and die in households.

Power and interpersonal relations

While some researchers insist that women are categorically subordinate in the household, recent studies reveal a far more complex reality. In practice, even in cases where a woman is the main provider for the household, a man is often designated as its head. Even so, as noted earlier, 25 percent of households in the region are female-headed according to survey data. Five percent of female heads live with husbands, and "high proportions of married women are living separately from their husbands" (Guyer 1981, 104).

Merely identifying a head reveals little about hierarchical power relationships within households, obscuring the agency of women. Power is complex in the household, all "participate in the decision-making process. A patriarch rarely makes decisions alone" (Sow 1985, 564). Households are sites "of separable, often competing, interests, rights, and responsibilities" (Guyer and Peters 1987, 210). Innovative terms such as "hearth-holds" reveal that virtually all women enjoy some measure of independence within broader households. Senior women command respect and deference from junior women.

Women's money-making jobs are a source of significant power in households. The vast majority are self-employed; "they manage their own business affairs, with little or no input from males other than from those the women specifically ask for advice or whom they employ" (Sudarkasa 1985, 56). Women control their own incomes, which often exceed men's (Cooper 2001, Quimby 1979, Sudarkasa 1985). Despite Muslim family law, which stipulates that husbands must provide food, shelter, clothing, and medical care for all their wives and children, women "increasingly take on the burden of feeding themselves and their children" (Cooper 2001, 268).

Pervasive gender segregation of space and activities can be a source of great power and autonomy for women, including wives in seclusion. Many women value the household as a refuge from a hostile world where they are fighting a difficult struggle for the "right to be seen publicly without being stigmatized morally" (Cooper 2001, 268). Only female visitors are permitted to enter. Complex women's networks and voluntary associations are created by systematic visiting patterns and meetings in households.

Women's interpersonal relationships in households are highly variable. Many enjoy loving, kind, and hardworking husbands, and close relationships with other women, including co-wives (Sudarkasa 1982). In contrast, many women suffer from domestic violence and other abuse at the hands of men. Furthermore, tension between co-wives is a widespread problem. In the Hausa language, the term for co-wife is *kishiya*, "jealous one." Women's music and dance often expresses anger regarding all of these problems (Askew 1999, Quimby 1979).

Membership

Defining household membership is difficult. Individuals regularly enter through marriage, birth, adoption, and immigration, and regularly leave through divorce, death, and emigration. Muslim Sub-Saharan Africans experience some of the highest rates of nuptiality, fertility, adoption, and migration in the world, and divorce is fairly common. The hardships of living with in-laws endured by married women with migrant husbands, including being treated disrespectfully and facing increased workloads, is one of the most common themes in women's oral literature and emerging voice in published novels, poetry, and short stories (Buggs-Boyd and Scott 2003).

Boundaries between household forms and particular households are often highly permeable. For example, polygynous households are often embedded in three-generational households. In some places, polygyny is practiced non-coresidentially (Tipple et al. 1994). Many women maintain overlapping memberships by spending roughly equal amounts of time in their rural nuclear households, their natal three-generational households, and in urban same-sex households as migrant workers.

Activities

Households are also defined by their activities. This includes sleeping under the same roof or within the same self-contained compound dwelling. Most women, including all women in polygynous households, have their own spatially separate living and sleeping space. This can be a separate room within one structure, or more typically a stand-alone single-room dwelling within the compound. Household members share costs and contribute labor toward its maintenance. Most of the actual labor in women's income generating jobs – typically as food processors, traders, crafts producers, and purveyors of cooked foods – is performed in households. Mothers play an essential role in the socialization process: "before the child is seven, the father has no direct role in childrearing" (Sow 1985, 565). Women are responsible for all household cleaning and cooking, except in same sex male households. Most meals are taken at the same time within the household in gender and age segregated groups.

Material living conditions

Compounds include one or more households. Compounds are enclosed spaces, usually square in shape, bounded by two-meter high walls. There is only one entrance. Houses are built against the outer walls, with their doors and windows facing an interior courtyard. Households consist of a mean of three rooms each about twelve square meters, including a living room and two sleeping rooms with a mean of three persons per sleeping room. Houses are constructed of either local, handmade mud bricks or thatch, in roughly equal prevalence. A tiny minority are built with industrially manufactured bricks.

Most households lack industrially manufactured amenities. Only 25 percent have electricity, and only 33 percent enjoy piped water. Only 7 percent include flush toilets, while 49 percent have pit toilets, and 44 percent have no toilet. Fifty-five percent have dirt floors. Fifty percent of households own radios, while only 10 percent have televisions, and 2 percent have telephones.

Bibliography

K. Askew, Female circles and male lines. Gender dynamics along the Swahili coast, in *Africa Today* 46 (1999), 67–102.

J. Bongaarts, Household size and composition in the developing world in the 1990s, in *Population Studies* 55 (2001), 263–79.

D. Boyd-Buggs and J. H. Scott (eds.), *Camel tracks. Critical perspectives on Sahelian literature*, Trenton, N.J. 2003.

B. Callaway, Ambiguous consequences of the socialisation and seclusion of Hausa women, in *Journal of Modern African Studies* 22 (1984), 429–50.

B. Cooper, The politics of difference and women's associations in Niger. Of "prostitutes," the public, and politics, in D. Hodgson and S. McDurdy (eds.), *"Wicked" women and the reconfiguration of gender in Africa*, Portsmouth, N.H. 2001, 255–73.

Demographic and Health Surveys, <http://www.measuredhs.com>.

F. Ekejiuba, Down to fundamentals. Women-centered hearth-holds in rural West Africa, in D. Bryceson (ed.), *Women wielding the hoe. Lessons from rural Africa for feminist theory and development practice*, Oxford 1995, 47–62.

A. Gage et al., Household structure and childhood immunization in Niger and Nigeria, in *Demography* 35 (1997), 295–309.

J. I. Guyer, Household and community in African studies, in *African Studies Review* 24 (1981), 87–137.

J. I. Guyer and P. E. Peters, Conceptualizing the household. Issues of theory and policy in Africa, in *Development and Change* 18 (1987), 197–213.

K. Hansen, Introduction. Domesticity in Africa, in K. Hansen (ed.), *African encounters with domesticity*, New Brunswick, N.J. 1992, 1–33.

L. Quimby, Islam, sex roles, and modernization in Bobo-Dioulasso, in B. Jules-Rosette (ed.), *The new religions of Africa*, Norwood, N.J. 1979, 203–18.

F. Sow, Muslim families in contemporary Black Africa, in *Current Anthropology* 26 (1985), 563–70.

N. Sudarkasa, African and Afro-American family structure, in J. Cole (ed.), *Anthropology for the eighties*, New York 1982, 132–60.

——, Female employment and family organization in West Africa, in F. Steady (ed.), *The black woman cross-culturally*, Rochester, Vt. 1985, 49–63.

G. Tipple et al., House and dwelling, family and household. Towards defining housing units in West African cities, in *Third World Planning Review* 16 (1994), 429–50.

Scott M. Youngstedt

Turkey

European travelers often described Ottoman Muslim households as patriarchal extended families having large numbers of slaves and servants. They focused their descriptions on harem life, polygynous marriages, and concubines. They degraded Muslim women, seeing them as sexual objects who were kept strictly inside the harem. This Orientalist perspective was adopted by the modernizing elites in Turkey, who criticized family life in their writings. Only during the last two decades have serious studies on Ottoman families and harem life emerged and the Orientalist myths about Muslim families and women been refuted (Duben 1985, Geber 1989, Duben and Behar 1991, Peirce 1993).

Using the 1885 and 1907 Ottoman census records (*Taḥrīr Defterleri*), Duben and Behar (1991) showed that the dominant household type in Istanbul was the simple family. Polygyny was practiced in not more than 2 percent of households. Late marriage and low fertility levels, comparable to the large European cities, were prevalent in Istanbul at the turn of the century. Even in rural Anatolia the majority lived in simple family households from the nineteenth century (Duben 1985). High mortality and poor economic conditions meant few could live in extended family households with large numbers of kin and non-kin members. In addition, late age at marriage (particularly of men) was responsible for the dominance of simple families in Istanbul.

Domestic slave use was widespread among the Muslim elites. Ubicini (1998) claimed that some households had hundreds of slaves and that slaves constituted one third of the Muslim population of Istanbul in the early nineteenth century. Restriction of slave trade, economic crises, and the spread of Western ideas gradually reduced the total number of slaves. In 1907, about one fifth of the households had slaves; most of these had one or two slaves (Özbay 1999).

In the period from the Ottoman-Russian War in 1877 to the establishment of the republic (1923), war casualties, internal conflicts, and mass migration from the Balkans and Caucasia to Anatolia led to a radical increase of single-parent families, non-family, and single person households. In 1885 the proportion of non-family and single person households reached 30 percent in Istanbul and declined to 20 percent in 1907 (Duben and Behar 1991). Even in 1907, 14 percent of all households heads were female. This proportion often did not include single-parent households. Women tended to declare their sons, no matter how young they were, as heads. During these years, for the first time Muslim women were allowed to work in urban areas (Özbay 1998a). Thousands of girl orphans and daughters of poor villagers had to work as residential servants in middle-class urban households (Özbay 1999).

Patriarchal extended family living, though not a dominant type, was idealized by the masses. The nationalist state advocated monogamous, simple families with no servants as the ideal national family (*milli aile*). It required that religious marriage be contracted only after fulfillment of the civil marriage contract, which was part of the Civil Code, in which polygamous marriage was restricted and inheritance and divorce rights for women were given, yet male headship was acknowledged. Accordingly, the law allowed men to decide upon the location of the marital house, and a woman had to obtain the permission of her husband to work outside the house. The family was considered to be the basis of society and this statement was included in the constitution. The state encouraged marriages and high fertility. This exaggerated concern with the family shaped the place of women in the family as well as in society. When the male deficiency in population recovered women retired from the labor force and many of them devoted their life to their family members and to good housekeeping activities in order to be "modern" and good citizens.

The findings of the first nationwide survey on family indicated that the dominant type was a nuclear family household in both urban and rural areas in 1968 (Timur 1972). Patriarchal extended households were found among well-to-do families. Thirty years later, in 1998, the proportion of simple family households increased to 72 percent. Multiple family households declined considerably to 10 percent. Research conducted in an Anatolian town, Ereğli, revealed that while former multiple family households of the elite rapidly turned to the nuclear form, a relatively small proportion of such household type was adopted by lower-middle classes solely as a survival strategy between 1962 and 1982 (Özbay 1998).

The average household size was 5.6 persons in 1968 and declined to 4.2 in 1998. This was partially related to declining fertility. In 1965 the state adopted a policy to reduce family size and advocated family planning methods for couples who wanted to control their family size. Total fertility rate declined from 7 to 2 children per family between 1950 and 2000 (Yavuz 2003).

Consanguineous marriages constituted 25 percent of the total marriages in 1998 (Hancıoğlu et al. 2001). This high proportion helps maintain the prevailing family-oriented lifestyles. Children usually stay with their parents until they marry (Koç 2002). Turkish families are protective of their elderly members, who, however, prefer to live in separate households close by. The incidence of co-residence with the elderly was low (20 percent), and that of living nearby was quite high (50 percent) in 1988 (Aytaç 1998). Increased life expectancy did not lead to a higher proportion of extended living, but instead to an increasing proportion of solitary, simple, and other non-family living patterns. Single person households (5 percent) were mostly females, widows and particularly elderly women, although those with young and unmarried single people consisted mostly of men. The proportion of non-family households was low (2 percent), though it slightly increased between 1978 and 1998; they mostly consisted of kin members. Gay and lesbian living is not significant.

The proportion of female-headed households is low (10 percent in 1998) but shows an increasing trend. These households consist of single-parent as well as solitary and non-family households. They are poorer than the average (Yavuz 2003).

Long years of feminist pressures coming from inside and outside Turkey resulted in a new Civil Code in which gender inequality was eliminated in 2002. Wives are no longer assistants of their husbands, but are equals with them in the eyes of the law. In practice, gender inequality in the family continues. Division of labor within the household between husband and wife reflects this inequality. Even in households where both marital partners are working outside, husbands do not share any housework responsibilities; women often care for children and the sick, cook, wash, clean the house, and iron alone. In only about 20 percent of households do women have domestic help (Koç and Ergöçmen 2001).

Studies show that domestic violence is considerably high across the classes (AAK 1995). The prevalence of honor killing is especially a problem for women in less developed eastern Turkey. The state issued the Law for the Protection of the Family in 1998. The primary aim of this law is to protect the family in cases of domestic violence by recommending the "faulty party" – often men – to behave themselves.

Bibliography

A.A.K. (Aile Araştırma Kurumu), *Aile içi şiddetin sebep ve sonuçları*, Ankara 1995.

I. Aytaç, Intergenerational living arrangements in Turkey, in *Journal of Cross-Cultural Gerontology* 13 (1995), 241–64.

A. Duben, Turkish families and households in historical perspective, in *Journal of Family History* 10:1 (1985), 75–97.

A. Duben and C. Behar, *Istanbul households. Marriage, family, and fertility, 1880–1940*, Cambridge 1991.

H. Geber, Anthropology and family history. The Ottoman and Turkish families, in *Journal of Family History* 14:4 (1989), 409–21.

A. Hancıoğlu et al., Türkiye'de akraba evlilikleri. 1998 Türkiye nüfus ve sağlık araştırması, in *Nüfusbilim Yazıları* 3 (2001), 1–14.

İ. Koç, Female headed households in Turkey and socio-demographic and economic characteristics of female household heads, in *Turkish Journal of Population Studies* 19 (1997), 73–99.

——, Timing of leaving home in Turkey and its relationship with other life course events, in *Turkish Journal of Population Studies* 23 (2001), 16–24.

İ. Koç and B. Ergöçmen, Analysis of the relationship between women's modernity level and women's attitudes, beliefs and values about intra-household relation, in *Women's Studies Review* 7 (2001), 31–44.

F. Özbay, Türkiye'de kadın emeği ve istihdamına ilişkin çalışmaların gelişimi, in F. Özbay (ed.), *Küresel pazar açısından kadın emeği ve istihdamındaki değişimler. Türkiye örneği*, Ankara 1998a, 147–81.

——, Türkiye'de aile ve hane yapısı. Dün, bugün, yarın, in A. B. Hacımirzaoğlu (ed.), *75 yılda kadınlar ve erkekler*, Istanbul 1998b, 155–72.

——, *Turkish female child domestic workers*, Istanbul 1999.

L. Peirce, *The imperial harem. Women and sovereignty in the Ottoman Empire*, New York 1993.

S. Timur, *Türkiye'de aile yapısı*, Ankara 1972.

M. A. Ubicini, *Osmanlı'da modernleşme sancısı*, Istanbul 1998.

S. Yavuz, Household composition and complexity in Turkey. Findings from the Turkish Demographic and Health Survey, 1998, M.A thesis, Hacettepe University, Ankara 2002.

Ferhunde Özbay

The United States

Household form and membership among Muslims living in the United States differ greatly according to country of origin, education, class, generation since emigration, and many other factors. Some young Muslims who came to the United States for education live on their own or with roommates. Sometimes siblings or other relatives may share a home. The mother who can afford it may accompany one or more children who have come to attend high school or college. Often a young person coming for education may live for a while with relatives. Even when people finish school, start working, and become settled in the United States, households may fluctuate as parents and other relatives come to visit for extended periods of time.

In general, household boundaries among people of Muslim background are relatively permeable and flexible. Visits to family, relatives, and friends are frequent and may involve staying for several nights. Even when people are living separately, they may frequently gather together, maintain daily telephone contact, and cooperate closely with such tasks as cooking or childcare. A nephew or niece, grandparent or other relative may live with a family for a time. Some families of means own two homes, one in the United States and one in the country of origin to accommodate their transnational households.

Parents of Muslim background generally want their children to attend a university close by so that they can continue to live at home. Even if children go to another city for educational purposes, they may frequently live with their parents again upon graduation. Muslim parents generally expect their children, and especially females, to live at home until they marry, despite social or educational class. Especially among first and second generation emigrants, ideas of female modesty and the emphasis on female virginity and chastity influence residential choice for young, unmarried females and even for divorced and widowed adult women. Often parents expect children, especially females, to stay at home and engage in any outside activities with the family rather than with peers. Among conservative families, sometimes a young girl will be sent back to the country of origin for schooling, in order to keep her away from the more liberal interaction between sexes in the United States. Conversely, males may go back to the country of origin to find a bride who has not lived in the freer American environment. Generally only young adults from educated, modernized, secularized, middle- or upper-class backgrounds will consider cohabiting before marriage. As homosexuality is generally not tolerated among Muslims, gay cohabitation is relatively rare and will usually be kept a secret. Only unusually open minded parents from Muslim backgrounds will tolerate a son or daughter's gay sexual orientation and welcome a partner to their family gatherings.

Among first and second generation working-class emigrants from socially conservative Muslim countries, parents may play a strong role in marriage choice, and often continue to marry their daughters at a relatively young age to somewhat older men. Often in such families there is little emphasis on birth control. The marital relationship and family hierarchy may continue to follow home country cultural expectations, with women relatively isolated within the home. For more modern, well-off, educated, and Westernized Muslims, age of marriage, marriage choice, marital and family dynamics, and postponement and spacing of children will generally become more similar to those of other United States couples.

Generally people from Muslim backgrounds place great importance on obtaining a separate residence for a bridal couple, even if a young couple traditionally lived with the groom's parents for a period in their country of origin. Sometimes, young couples are able to find homes near parents or other relatives, especially in more localized Muslim communities. Depending on class and level of education, modern couples may live at a distance to take advantage of career possibilities. Although relatives may be scattered among the home country and other countries abroad, generally they attempt to maintain close relations through frequent telephoning and visiting.

Polygyny, allowed in Islam although illegal in the United States, does exist in rare instances, particularly among people from less modern, more conservative Muslim backgrounds. Some African American sectarian movements allow for multiple wives. A second wife and her children may live in a separate residence, although financial pressures often result in common residency. People may be cautious about revealing a polygynous marriage, and a second wife may be presented as a sister or other relative, rather than a spouse.

Although in past decades even middle-class families in Muslim countries of origin often had live-in servants, this practice is rarely followed in the United States. American Muslim households are relatively self-sufficient, and members generally attend to home and childcare work themselves. Professional families may hire yard workers, house cleaners, or other help, as is common among American upper classes and increasingly among the middle class as well. People of Muslim background are generally hesitant to hire baby-sitters or send pre-schoolers to childcare facilities although professional or wealthy families and women who must work and have no other alternatives may do so.

In general, depending on different circumstances, families from Islamic cultures are becoming increasingly nuclear. As young people attend university in different parts of the country and find jobs in cities away from their parents, they may find a spouse who is either from their own country of origin or another Muslim country, or even a non-Muslim American. Parents usually want their children to marry a Muslim from the same country, but outmarriage, especially among more educated modern groups is not unusual. Rarely will a young couple live with parents in an extended family situation beyond a period of time that some less advantaged couples need to establish themselves economically. When parents still live in the country of origin or when the spouse is not from the same background, interaction and amount of time spent together will generally be minimized. In the American environment, as young wives are more often educated, have been enculturated into higher expectation of personal autonomy, and work outside the home, the influence and interference of parents-in-law in their lives and decision-making is declining.

Especially among the better off and educated Muslim emigrant populations, divorce rates are rising. Thus the proportion of households with a single parent, especially a mother, is increasing. Although among more conservative American Muslims pressures still exist to prevent a female living by herself, among modernized groups divorced and single women often live alone.

Until recently elderly parents commonly lived with their children, or one or more children and their families continued to live in the parental home. Such extended family households are becoming less common in the United States. Among more conservative, less advantaged groups whose parents are with them and do not know English, parents often live with the children. Among better off groups, when parents come to the United States to be closer to their children, they often live separately. Even widowed mothers may live in their own homes. Some families look for homes with a semi-separate section or adjacent structure for older parents. If they do not know English, older parents may feel lonely and isolated, even if living with their children, when the middle generation are all out working and the children are in school. Sometimes better off older parents living in the

United States make regular trips back to home countries to visit relatives and friends. Conversely, more financially comfortable older parents living in home countries may come and stay with their children in the United States for extended periods of time. Not unusually, older parents, more often mothers, will care for grandchildren on a regular basis, either living in the same home or not far away, so that the mother can work or attend university.

A small minority of elderly Muslims live in senior facilities and nursing homes, especially those without families, or those who need constant care and whose children are working. Muslims place high value on caring for parents within the home and, when circumstances force them to seek care facilities for their parents, they feel emotionally distressed. Slowly Muslim communities are beginning to establish clubs, centers, and day care or activity centers for seniors. Because Muslim men tend to marry younger women, and also because of women's greater longevity, women are widowed more commonly than men. Further, widowed or divorced men more often tend to remarry, or to live with one of their children or another relative, or at least receive care from a daughter who may come regularly to cook and clean.

Bibliography

M. Afghami (ed.), *Women in exile*, Charlottesville 1994.
S. Ali, *Madras on rainy days*, New York 2004.
B. C. Aswad and B. Bilgé (eds.), *Family and gender among American Muslims. Issues facing Middle Eastern immigrants and their descendants*, Philadelphia 1996.
T. Bahrampour, *To see and see again. A life in Iran and America*, Berkeley 1999.
F. Dumas, *Funny in Farsi. A memoir of growing up Iranian in America*, New York 2003.
Y. Y. Haddad, *The Muslims of America*, New York 1991.
Y. Y. Haddad and J. I. Smith (eds.), *Muslim communities in North America*, Albany, N.Y. 1994.
M. E. Hegland, Iranian women immigrants facing modernity in California's Bay Area. The courage, creativity, and trepidation of transformation, in G. Amin (ed.), *The Iranian woman and modernity. Proceedings of the ninth international conference of the Iranian Women's Studies Foundation*, Cambridge, Mass. 1999, 35–62.
K. Hosseini, *The kite runner*, New York 2003.
R. Kelly and J. Friedlander (eds.), *Irangeles. Iranians in Los Angeles*, Berkeley 1993.
P. Omidian, *Aging and family in an Afghan refugee community. Transitions and transformation*, New York 1996.
S. Pari, *The fortune catcher. A novel*, New York 1997.

Mary Elaine Hegland

Human Rights

Overview

The area of human rights is a "limited exception" to the general absence and impact of women from and on the substance and process of international law (Charlesworth and Chinkin 2000,16). The term human rights refers herein to the human rights norms established in the international system in and following from the Universal Declaration of Human Rights 1948 (UDHR). The discourse of "women's rights are human rights" is one of several ongoing discourses and debates provoked by a consideration of women, gender, and human rights, and indicates the relatively recent concentration on the specific subject of women's rights by "traditional" human rights institutions and organizations. Another is the debate on universality of rights versus cultural relativity, and closely related to this is the discourse of "Islamic human rights," the compatibility or otherwise of the "status of woman in Islam" with the requirements of international human rights standards. This in turn involves both state practice, in terms of the determinations made by Muslim majority states as to the requirements and applications of Islamic law on matters to do with the status and position of women, and the debates in Muslim communities (domestically, regionally, and internationally) as to these requirements. Issues of "voice," of "authority," and of representation figure prominently in these debates, linking to the discourses of postcolonialism and feminism.

Commentators credit the efforts of women's nongovernmental organizations (NGOs) in securing provisions in the United Nations Charter (1945) prohibiting discrimination on the grounds of sex and providing for equal rights of men and women, in advance of the UDHR. Similar efforts secured the establishment of the United Nations Commission on the Status of Women (CSW) in 1946. The CSW has always had a majority of women delegates, and maintains close links with the women's NGO movement. Despite the CSW's considerable achievements, Connors observes that on the specific subject of human rights, "its existence has, ironically, contributed to the neglect by both the traditional United Nations human rights framework and human rights NGOs of issues of concern to women" (1996, 152). For the first decades, most women's NGOs focused on the CSW rather than the mainstream human rights mechanisms. Women's organizations did participate in the 1960s in the drafting processes for the two International Covenants, on Civil and Political Rights (ICCPR) and on Economic, Social and Cultural Rights, which include the requirements of non-discrimination and equal rights. Nevertheless, writing in 1997, Gallagher noted "a near-unanimity amongst women human rights activists that 'specialization' has become 'marginalization' – that women and their concerns remain on the sidelines of United Nations activity for the protection and promotion of human rights" (1997, 285). One reason advanced by commentators for this marginalization is the "public/private divide" (contested in postcolonial and feminist discourses) that tended to leave abuses in the "private" sphere of the home and family outside the purview of state-focused international human rights law.

A formal call for the "mainstreaming" of women's rights in the United Nations system was made at the Second World Conference on Human Rights in Vienna in 1993. In the final document of the conference, states agreed that the human rights of women were "an inalienable, integral and indivisible part of human rights." For Sullivan, the most striking result at Vienna was that "the conference crystallized a political consensus that various forms of violence against women should be examined within the context of human rights standards and in conjunction with gender discrimination" (1994, 152). The intense preparatory and lobbying efforts of women's rights and NGO activists worldwide are generally credited with the achievements at Vienna. Links between women's rights and human rights organizations were strengthened, and the 1990s also saw increasing attention paid to abuses of women's human rights by the "traditional" international human rights NGOs. This period also saw a preference for the term "gender" over the use of "women." In 1994, the United Nations Commission on Human Rights appointed the first Special Rapporteur on Violence against Women, in this action mandating the first gender-specific brief for a Special Rapporteur. In 2000, the Human Rights Committee issued in its General Comment 28 an analysis of the gender-specific implications of the ICCPR, article by article. This particular effort at mainstreaming gender perspectives came nearly two decades after a specialized convention on women's rights came into force, its origins lying in the CSW. Most recently, some observers and activists have questioned the effectiveness of the "mainstreaming" approach.

In 1965, a resolution was sponsored at the United Nations General Assembly by a group of Eastern European and developing countries calling for a declaration on the elimination of discrimination against women. The declaration was voted on in the General Assembly in 1967 and the CSW tasked with overseeing its implementation. In advance of the International Women's Year declared by the United Nations General Assembly for 1975, the CSW set up a working group to prepare for a convention specifically addressing discrimination against women. The International Women's Year Conference in Mexico City decided on an International Decade for Women (1976–85) and formally called for the drafting of a convention. The Convention on the Elimination of All Forms of Discrimination against Women (CEDAW, also referred to as the Women's Convention) was adopted by the General Assembly in 1979 and opened for signature; it entered into force in 1981. According to Charlesworth and Chinkin, the approach of the Women's Convention "acknowledges that, for women, protection of civil and political rights is meaningless without attention to the economic, social and cultural context in which they operate" (2000, 217). This meant, *inter alia*, tackling the "private sphere" and the conduct of non-state actors. Among its provisions, the Women's Convention requires states parties to take appropriate measures to modify laws, customs, and practices that constitute discrimination against women, and to ensure equality of rights for women and men in a range of matters relating to marriage and the family. These areas are central to the debates on cultural relativity and on women's rights in Islam.

Although Muslim majority states were involved from the inception of work on the Women's Convention at the CSW, the General Assembly debates were long and intense, and several involved issues presented as in conflict with the requirements of Islamic law or, more precisely, the Sharīʿa. A number of Muslim majority states abstained on specific articles and five abstained on the final vote for the convention. Today most Muslim majority states are parties. As at 3 June 2003, the convention had 174 states parties; of the 57 members of the Organization of Islamic Conference (OIC), 49 are parties to CEDAW, with 6 of the exceptions also being members of the League of Arab States.

The Women's Convention has drawn an unusual number of reservations from states parties across the world, prompting commentators to question the actual commitment of the world community of states to the implementation of women's rights (Cook 1990, 644). According to Connors, however, "the most notorious reservations to the Women's Convention have been made by countries who apply, to a greater or lesser extent, the Islamic *sharīʿa*" (1996, 352). The controversial nature of reservations entered by certain Muslim majority states arises from their generality, purporting to subject commitments under the entire convention to the principles or norms of Sharīʿa law or applying a reservation to the general undertaking (in article 2) to take legislative action to eliminate discrimination. Substantive articles of the convention frequently reserved by Muslim majority states parties are article 15, which provides for equality of women with men before the law, including in legal capacity and at all stages of court procedure, and in "the law relating to the movement of persons and the freedom to choose their residence and domicile"; and article 16 requiring states to "take all appropriate measures to eliminate discrimination against women in all matters relating to marriage and family relations." A number of states have also made reservations to article 9 regarding equal rights to nationality and to the nationality of children.

In the 1980s, following the entering into force of the Women's Convention, objections were filed by co-parties to the convention to certain reservations including the broad texts submitted by Egypt and Bangladesh, and the Committee on the Elimination of All Forms of Discrimination against Women (responsible for monitoring implementation of the Women's Convention) proposed in its General Recommendation 4, in the context of its general concern at the number and type of reservations entered to the convention, that the United Nations should "promote or undertake studies on the status of women under Islamic laws and customs and in particular on the status and equality of women in the family . . . taking into consideration the principle of El Ijtihad in Islam." Debates on these issues at the United Nations were heated; Connors reports allegations of "cultural imperialism and religious intolerance" and warnings against "using the Convention as a pretext for doctrinaire attacks on Islam," and the General Assembly subsequently agreed that no further action be taken on the CEDAW suggestion (1996, 362). Objections continue to be filed to similar reservations entered by certain Muslim majority parties who have become parties to the convention in more recent years, such as Saudi

Arabia, the Maldives, and Mauritania, and the committee continues to seek information from states on progress toward the withdrawal of reservations.

Such debates raise the substantive question of compatibility of such reservations with the Women's Convention, on the one hand, and the compatibility of the convention with Islamic law on the other. Also arising is the substance and interpretation of "Islamic law," or "the Islamic Sharīʿa," as presented by state representatives at the United Nations and in their domestic legal systems. In terms of process, they also illustrate the politicized nature of debates when "Islamic law" and "international women's rights" are posed as conflicting norms of competing authority. The risk that certain interventions may be perceived or presented as "attacks on Islam" poses particular challenges to advocates of women's human rights, both domestically and internationally. More recently, the General Assembly has seen similarly heated interventions and a lack of consensus in debates on draft resolutions on the subject of eliminating crimes against women committed in the name of honor; in 2000, the majority of the 25 abstentions to the resolution on this subject were from Muslim majority states, with delegates objecting to the apparent singling out of a particular "culture" and the perceived association of "honor killings" with Islam.

Muslim majority states articulate concern at the exploitation of the human rights discourse for political ends. The 1997 OIC summit, while recalling the objectives of the UDHR, called on members "to continue to actively coordinate and cooperate among themselves in the field of human rights in order to strengthen Islamic solidarity to confront any initiative leading to the exploitation of human rights as a means of exerting political pressure against any Member State." While Muslim majority states under criticism for their human rights record in international forums have political interests in seeking to divert and undermine such criticism, it is the case that in the Muslim world more generally there is a perception of selectivity in the application of human rights discourse and principles by powerful "Western" states. According to Mayer, "to Muslims, this suggests that the West is biased against Islam and more inclined to charge Muslims than others with rights violations, while at the same time the West minimizes or disregards the sufferings of Muslims deprived of their rights" (1994, 313). The question of Palestine is among grievances contributing to this perception. More broadly, Moosa sets "the abuse of human rights discourse" in the context of the "hegemony of market capitalism and the globalization of Western political culture," observing that "it has become a political weapon in the hands of powerful nations in order to subdue emerging nations and those communities contesting the monopoly of global political power." He combines this with a criticism of the response of some "Islamic nations" to describe "a monumental, unrelentingly bleak account of the status of human rights in the international discourse" (2000–1, 205). These issues have been heightened in the aftermath of the attacks in the United States of 11 September 2001.

As well as being implicated in these dynamics in Muslim communities, the international women's human rights discourse is a central feature in the debate on cultural relativity versus universality of rights. Charlesworth and Chinkin observe that "it is striking that 'culture' is much more frequently invoked in the context of women's rights than in any other area" (2000, 222). Central to the debate is the equality paradigm, which underpins the women's human rights norms and discourse, and which is held by critics to illustrate the "Eurocentrism" of human rights norms. The universality/cultural relativity debate was a contentious issue at the 1993 Vienna World Conference on Human Rights, and likewise at the Fourth World Conference on Women in Beijing in 1995. At the latter, the term "gender" also became an issue, with certain Muslim majority states joining the Holy See and others to oppose any inference of sexual orientation in its usage.

In response to the equality norm, Muslim majority states have argued for "equitable" or "equivalent" rights for men and women. Illustrative of this is the approach of the Cairo Declaration of Human Rights in Islam, adopted in 1990 by OIC member states to serve "as a general guidance for Member States in the field of human rights." The declaration states that "woman is equal to man in dignity, and has her own rights to enjoy as well as duties to perform" while making the husband "responsible for the maintenance and welfare of the family." This approach points to the gendered text and practice of laws and norms presented by governments, and by the dominant and traditional discourses in Islamic jurisprudence, as an integral part of Islamic culture and indeed religion, particularly although not only in the "private sphere" of marriage and the family. Many Muslim critics, while stressing that numerous areas of traditional Islamic law are entirely consistent with international human rights norms, including certain rights of women, argue against the particularity of "Islamic human rights schemes," and against laws and practices justified by reference to Islam that constitute discrimination under international human rights standards.

The debate on "human rights in Islam" includes what Moosa has described as a "vibrant debate taking place in almost all Muslim societies about the status of women" (2000–1, 204). An important focus is the presentation in state or societal practice of what Islam requires or mandates regarding women's rights, and different understandings of these requirements formulated by a broad spectrum of critics. These understandings range from "Islamist" positions eschewing international human rights norms as a framework in holding that the Sharīʿa gives women all their rights if implemented in full under a Muslim authority, to "secularist" positions that states should leave matters of religion to individuals in their private faith practices. Among the different approaches, some scholars and activists call for a new approach to the text and principles of the sources of Islamic law, a reformulation or reconstruction of Islamic jurisprudence expanding the existing common ground with human rights norms. Among the more recent discourses is "feminist *ijtihād*"; al-Hibri, for example, criticizes the culturally inspired "social and political assumptions" in traditional, historically-conditioned Islamic jurisprudence as giving rise to "a then common model of state and family relationships which are best described today as authoritarian/patriarchal" (1997, 5).

A number of the Muslim scholars applying themselves to the source texts in this way are based in the West. Challenging the dominant discourses in this regard, whether through textual approaches or through advocacy and activism aimed at state policy, remains a controversial undertaking in different Muslim societies and states. Challenges to advocates of women's human rights include the conflation of "cultural" or "national" with a particular "authoritative" articulation of Islamic norms in the rise of identity politics. States' political interests may be served by the invocation of Islam over contested areas of law and policy, while "Islamist" groups may attack the discourse of women's rights to undermine the credentials of existing regimes. Advocates of international women's human rights may be accused of alienation, a lack of cultural authenticity, and of seeking to undermine the unity and stability of the Muslim family, and by extension Muslim society, through the importation of Western ideas associated with moral laxity. Opponents of the discourse of gender equality situate it, along with the discourses of "Western feminism," within the larger context of colonial and neocolonial agendas, cultural imperialism, and hostility to Islam.

Within the rights movements, there is criticism of a Western influence over the agenda of the human rights movement in general and the women's human rights movement in particular, seeking, for example, greater prioritization of socioeconomic rights and the disproportionate effect on women in the South of structural adjustment policies and the economics of the global market. Generally, there is a consensus on the need to increase internal resonance with human rights norms and discourse, as well as to focus on national and international state law and policy, in order to increase the prospects for implementation of the range of women's human rights in Islamic cultures.

Bibliography

A. A. An-Naʿim, Human rights in the Muslim world. Socio-political conditions and scriptural imperatives, in *Harvard Human Rights Journal* 3 (1990), 13–52.

M. Baderin, Establishing areas of common ground between Islamic law and international human rights, in *International Journal of Human Rights* 5:2 (2001), 72–113.

H. Charlesworth and H. Chinkin, *The boundaries of international law. A feminist analysis*, Manchester, U.K. 2000.

J. Connors, Non-governmental organizations and the human rights of women at the United Nations, in P. Willetts (ed.), *"The conscience of the world." The influence of non-governmental organizations in the United Nations system*, London 1996, 147–80.

——, The Women's Convention in the Muslim world, in M. Yamani (ed.), *Feminism and Islam. Legal and literary perspectives*, Reading, U.K. 1996, 351–71.

R. Cook, Reservations to the Convention on the Elimination of All Forms of Discrimination against Women, in *Virginia Journal of International Law* 30 (1990), 643–716.

A. Fraser, Becoming human. The origins and development of women's human rights, in *Human Rights Quarterly* 21 (1999), 853–906.

A. Gallagher, Ending the marginalization. Strategies for incorporating women into the United Nations human rights system, in *Human Rights Quarterly* 19 (1997) 283–333.

A. al-Hibri, Islam, law and custom. Redefining Muslim women's rights, *American University Journal of International Law and Policy* 12:1 (1997), 1–44.

A. E. Mayer, Universal versus Islamic human rights. A clash of cultures or a clash with a construct?, in *Michigan Journal of International Law* 15 (1994). 307–404.

E. Moosa, The dilemma of Islamic rights schemes, in *Journal of Law and Religion* 15:1/2 (2000–1), 185–215.

D. Otto, Holding up half the sky, but for whose benefit? A critical analysis of the Fourth World Conference on Women, in *Australian Feminist Law Journal* 7 (1996), 7–28.

D. Sullivan, Women's human rights and the 1993 World Conference on Human Rights, in *American Journal of International Law* 88:1 (1994), 152–67.

Lynn Welchman

Arab Gulf and Yemen

The current general status of women's human rights conditions in Yemen and the Arab Gulf states is broadly characterized by international and local human rights non-governmental organizations (NGOs) as being abysmal. Progressive changes toward achieving equality for women, particularly in states that maintain religiously based personal status laws that discriminate against women, have been slow. Despite the existence of regional commonalities, reasons for this gloomy status are numerous and vary from country to country. One principal reason, however, relates to the weak status of civil movement for women's human rights.

Civil activism pertaining to women's human rights is widely conditioned by the political framework within which civil society operates in the region. Historically undemocratic state regimes and ostensibly self-declared Islamic ruling elites have consistently inhibited the emergence of effective civil activism for promoting gender equality. Using a plethora of techniques that range from official refusal, to registering local human rights NGOs, to openly imposing life-threatening experiences, harassment, and imprisonment on activists, autocratic regimes in the region have continuously repressed the maturity of not just women's civil activism but credible human rights movements in general (An-Na'im 2001). Existing NGOs representing women's issues are either influenced or controlled by the ruling regimes, a factor that renders them suspect of being government showcases to foreign human rights monitors. Consequently basic human rights enjoyed by women in the region, such as the right to work and to education, are attained not through a history of civil activism but by government sanctions. This reality of inhibited civil activism subjects gender related human rights to the ideological dispositions as well as the political positions of the ruling regimes vis-à-vis internal conservative and religious pressure elements the state may face. Historically, and in the face of thriving political Islamist groups, the autocratic states of the region often appear, paradoxically, as the protectors of women' rights, albeit in limited ways, against the excessive demands of internal politico-religious movements in connection with women's rights.

Commonly in the societies of the region, gender related human rights are intrinsically conditioned by larger normative legal rights granted or suspended by the Sharīʿa, a divinely ordained system of law that covers the totality of the Muslim way of living, including gender relations and rights. Consequently, actual rights and triumphant dialogues on women's status within society tend to be those rights and dialogues consistent with interpretations of the Sharīʿa. External systems of women's human rights norms, such as the universal rights proposed by the United Nations and international conventions, are incorporated when and if they can be rationalized within the internal Sharīʿa norms.

In the moderate countries of the region, such as Yemen and Bahrain, international human rights standards pertaining to gender equality are incorporated as constitutional rights of all female citizens. Such incorporation, however, cannot override the power of the Sharīʿa law, which the constitution assigns as the supreme basis of all civil rights, including those regulating marriage contracts and inheritance. Consequently the rights stipulated under the Sharīʿa override the constitutionally proclaimed rights. Those universal human rights proposed by international organizations are generally faced with difficulties when they contradict or undermine the gender related rights prescribed by the Sharīʿa.

Despite the Sharīʿa's evident supremacy, there are other sources that prescribe gender relations, status, and rights. Centuries-old patriarchal customary laws and contemporary socioeconomic factors often coalesce and provide the rationale under which gender inequalities and the violations of women's human rights are perpetuated in this region. In Yemen, for example, legalized insurance policies provide only half the financial indemnities and compensations due to female victims in cases of automobile accidents. The genesis of these policies is a tribal customary law that assigns women half the blood retribution in cases pertaining to homicide or accidental death. Another case is a state decree in the Kingdom of Saudi Arabia that denies Saudi women as well as foreign women living in the kingdom the right to drive vehicles. It would be inconceivable to rationalize this law under the Sharīʿa since women in the early Islamic period had the right to ride camels and horses, the era's means of transportation. Reasons cited for officially suspending such rights relate to social insecurities allegedly associated with the presence of a high percentage of single foreign male migrant workers in the kingdom. Following the Iran-Iraq War (1980–8), a group of 20 Saudi women activists challenged this law by taking to the streets of Riyadh driving cars. Their actions were seen as illegally mutinous and prompted brutal governmental responses. Severe humiliation accompanied by imprisonment and loss of employment opportunities befell those involved.

In spite of the overarching similarities pertaining to suppressed or weak civil activism, autocratic state regimes, and the supremacy of the Sharīʿa, gender related human rights conditions in the region are hardly monolithic. In some countries, for example, Bahrain, Qatar, and Yemen, there exist recently adopted democratic reforms (freedom of press, elections, and legalized political parties) that have benefited women. These reforms depart from the undemocratic conservativeness of the remaining countries, especially Saudi Arabia, Oman, and Kuwait, where civil activism and human rights monitoring are entirely prohibited or severely restricted and gender equality still looms rudimentary (An-Na'im 2001). Under these favorably democratic environments, women tend to enjoy a relatively high degree of political freedom. In Yemen and Bahrain, women have equal voting rights. In the former, women's political rights are further advanced than any other country in the region and women can be elected to parliament. Yet these plausible rights do not alter the fact that the largest women's NGO in the country is currently run as a governmental branch.

Gender related human rights civil activism and conditions are not only varied but also have been subject to historical and political transformations. For example, in the case of southern Yemen under two decades of socialist regime in the 1970s and 1980s, radical laws pertaining to gender equality were executed by the state, thereby undermining pre-existing tribalist customary laws and conservative applications of the Sharīʿa. Yet these reforms did not come as a result of gender related civil movements but as the ambitions of the socialist state that sought to build a welfare society in which citizens were all productively accountable vis-à-vis the power of the state (Molyneux 1981, Seif 1995, 1997, 2002). The abruptness with which these advantageous human rights conditions were removed in the 1990s following south Yemen's unification with conservative north Yemen attests to the absence of a strong women's movement that could protect gender related rights. Women in Kuwait and Bahrain, on the other hand, are currently benefiting from recently flourishing waves of democratic processes and debates that may allow them full political participation in elections in the general assemblies (*majlis al-shūrā*).

Similarly, and in spite of inhibited civil activism, several countries in the region including Bahrain, Kuwait, and Yemen have recently appointed or are in the process of appointing ministerial level posts, offices, and committees for the protection of human rights, all of which will have positive effects on the status of gender related human rights in the future. In the case of Yemen, a woman heads the new ministry for human rights.

Notwithstanding these general positive changes, there exist specific groups of women in the region whose basic human rights are systematically violated due to reasons that go beyond societal discriminatory approaches to generalized sexual difference. In Yemen, for example, long histories of cultural persecution and prejudices against minority social groups often subject women perceived to be of African origin to different sets of discrimination and human rights abuses. Equally true is the existence in the region of thousands of foreign female workers from Asia who suffer severe human rights abuses through their status as non-citizen domestic workers. Currently, with no credible human rights civil movements, neither the states themselves nor human rights groups within them seem to be effectively engaged with the protection of the human rights of these groups of women. The gender related basic human rights of women from marginalized minority groups and those of migrant domestic workers, like the rights of all female citizens in the region, still remain unprotected.

BIBLIOGRAPHY

Amnesty International, *Report on Saudi Arabia*, New York 2000.

A. A. An-Na'im, Islamic foundations of religious human rights, in J. Witte Jr. and J. D. van Vyver (eds.), *Religious human rights in global perspective. Religious perspectives*, The Hague 1996, 337–59.

——, Human rights in the Arab world. A regional perspective, in *Human Rights Quarterly* 23:3 (2001), 701–32.

A. E. Mayer, *Islam and human rights. Tradition and politics*, Boulder, Colo. 1991, 1995².

M. Molyneux, *State policies and the position of women workers in the People's Democratic Republic of Yemen, 1967–77*, Geneva 1982.

H. A. Seif, Contextualizing labor and gender. Class, ethnicity, and global politics in the Yemeni socio-economy, in J. Peters and A. Wolber (eds.), *Women's rights, human rights. International feminist perspectives*, London 1995, 289–300.

——, Social impediments to girls' access to education in Yemen, Unicef report, Sanʿa 1997.

——, Moralities and outcasts. Domination and allegories of resentment in Southern Yemen, Ph.D. diss., Columbia University, 2003.

United States Department of State, Bureau of Democracy, Human Rights, and Labor, *Country report on human rights in Saudi Arabia*, Washington, D.C. 2002.

HUDA A. SEIF

Canada

Human rights movements and non-governmental organizations (NGOs) in Canada serve to assist

Muslim Canadians attain and retain their rights and civil liberties within Canada as well as to highlight their concerns. Women play significant roles as active members of these organizations

The Muslim community in Canada maintains a vibrant and visible role as its largest minority group, with a population of over 650,000 Muslims. In order to assist Canadian Muslims in understanding their role, and to address and disclose injustices they may confront, several organizations have been formed to educate the average citizen about his/her civil rights and freedoms within Canadian society. In 2004, the major organizations include the Muslim Lawyer's Association (MLA); the Canadian-Muslim Civil Liberties Association (CMCLA); the Canadian Council of Muslim Women (CCMW); the Federation of Muslim Women (FMW); the Council of American Islamic Relations-Canada (CAIR-CAN); and the Canadian Islamic Congress (CIC).

The human rights movements in Canada reflect parallel objectives, such as advocating for equal participation of Canadian Muslims in social, educational, legal, and political spheres in accordance with the Canadian Charter of Rights and Freedoms; highlighting educational and legal avenues to guarantee the affiliation of health, social, and public services in order to ensure that they are culturally sensitive and fully accessible to Canadian Muslims; undertaking relevant aspects of public education; disseminating and publicizing material in relation to Islam and Muslims; making resources available in reference to Islam and Muslims; developing, publishing, and distributing resource materials concerning discrimination and cross-cultural education; and presenting the Islamic perspective on issues of importance and relevance to the Canadian public and academia.

The MLA unofficially began in 1992 and was officially inaugurated in 1998. The group consists of individuals of diverse backgrounds in the legal profession. The goals of the MLA are networking, peer support, educational outreach to the Muslim community, and professional advocacy. The organization exists to interact with and assist Muslim lawyers, law students, the Muslim community, the legal profession and the public at large. Women within the organization comprise less than half of the membership and work primarily with the government, NGOs, and commercial companies or organizations. The disproportion of male and female membership of the MLA is due neither to the scarcity of Muslim women lawyers nor their qualification. Following graduation from law school female lawyers face realities such as difficulty in finding an appropriate practice, reduced or changed interest, or their personal preference to tend to domestic responsibilities. Few women have occupied leadership positions. Yusra Siddiquee, an immigration lawyer, was the first and only female interim governor of the MLA, 1994–97. Siddiquee occupied the position of vice-chair and assisted in helping to formalize the organization in light of the constitution. Haniya Sheikh, a woman lawyer in the area of commercial, regulatory, health, malicious prosecutions, and negligence who works for the Government of Canada in the Department of Justice, is a current governor of the MLA. After 11 September 2001, the MLA became a nationwide network. Various internal concerns were phased out as the organization considered its services in relation to the demands of the community. The MLA is an important resource for the Canadian Muslim community in educating its members of their rights and identifying and connecting them with lawyers and other resources best capable of advising and/or representing them in issues, challenges, and injustices they may confront.

The CMCLA was founded in 1994 to address matters that reflect the intricacies of Muslim life in Canada. Members of the CMCLA consist of concerned individuals, scholars, students, and community activists who are versed in the Canadian legal system, including those who have worked in the area of social policy-making as well as activists in the field of education and the mass media. The CMCLA maintains long-term goals on the national front in order to assert change at both institutional and political levels. It also works at the grassroots level by providing assistance to individuals and communities when resources are available. The organization has maintained a predominately male board, but it has depended upon the involvement of women at all levels of various CMCLA campaigns. The organization also relies on the volunteer experience and assistance of women and has had women supervise many projects. Sajidah Kutty has been the only female board member of CMCLA, 1994–2001, and has assisted in the public relations sector. She has also directed a fund-raising and awareness campaign and assisted in daily communication endeavors. CMCLA strives to empower the Muslim community in Canada through legal, political, and social avenues.

Canadian-based Muslim women's organizations such as the CCMW, founded in 1982, and the FMW, founded in 1997, serve as catalysts for Muslim women to attain a voice within the larger Islamic movement and the Canadian community at large. Both organizations were established with the mandate to attain and maintain equality, equity, and empowerment for Canadian Muslim women in the North American setting, and to develop a vibrant human rights sector within their organizations. The CCMW collaborates with the Canadian government at the municipal, provincial, and federal levels in order to achieve its objectives. It also seeks to develop strategies to counteract racism and violence against women, publishes reports and newsletters, hosts conferences and workshops, and initiates local and national projects to disseminate information that further their objectives. The FMW engages in initiatives similar to those of the CCMW, and in addition deals with such issues as violence against children, rights of physically and mentally disabled citizens, alleviation of poverty, and discrimination against *ḥijāb*-wearing Muslim women.

The CAIR was inaugurated in the United States in 1994. Subsequently, the CAIR-CAN chapter was launched in 2000. The CAIR-CAN undertakes tasks such as monitoring local and national media in order to challenge stereotyping, hosting information seminars and workshops, formulating and distributing action alerts, and assisting with intercommunity relations. Physicist Sheema Khan is its founder and current chairperson and is responsible for overseeing most of its projects. CAIR executive members and members-at-large include men and women who may play parallel roles within the media-related organization.

The CIC was founded in 1998 with numerous objectives including education of Canadians about Islam and Muslims, networking with all levels of government and with NGOs, and undertaking national research initiatives. Wahida Chishti Valiante, a family counselor, is a founding member and the current vice president of the CIC. While overseeing the various CIC initiatives, she lectures regularly at both national and international conferences, and is an author of major research papers related to media and social work. Similar to the CAIR, CIC executive members and members-at-large include men and women who may play parallel roles within their organization.

Muslim women are increasingly evident in human rights movements and NGOs in Canada, representing the wide diversity of cultures, races, languages, and ethnicities within the Muslim Canadian community.

Bibliography

CAIR-CAN (Council of American Islamic Relations-Canada), <http://www.caircan.ca/>.

CCMW (Canadian Council of Muslim Women), <http://www.ccmw.com/>.

CIC (Canadian Islamic Congress), <http://www.cicnow.com/>.

CMCLA (Canadian-Muslim Civil Liberties Association), <http://www.cmcla.org/>.

FMW (Federation of Muslim Women), <http://www.fmw.org/>.

MLA (Muslim Lawyer's Association), <http://www.muslimlaw.org/>.

Nadira Mustapha

Iran

This entry examines Iranian women's use of the human rights discourse to contest legal limitations under an Islamic regime. Based on field research in the year 2000, findings indicate human rights ideals serve as instruments of reform for women seeking to revise their legal, social, and political rights in Iran. This struggle takes place in the context of a reform movement that began in 1997.

Discovered in 1878 at the Babylon excavation cite, Cyrus the Great's cuneiform cylinder was declared the first ever human rights charter by the United Nations in 1971. Most Iranians take pride in this historical tie with the human rights movement. However, the development of this movement in Iran has differed from its progress in the West.

With roots in the ideals of enlightenment, human rights ideology generally places great importance on individualism. Islam, however, values the roles that individuals play in society. Hence, the rights movement in Iran has often relied on this paradigm, focusing on the rights of women as mothers, children, and students, that is, within a social location.

The Iranian women's rights movement gained particular visibility in the early twentieth century after the Constitutional Revolution. Secret women's organizations were formed dealing with wide-ranging issues including the right to participate in government, vote, publish women's magazines, and mandated education for girls (Price 2000).

After the Second World War, the United Nations was created to protect individuals from oppression at the hands of their governments. Concurrently, the Pahlavī regime was in the process of Westernizing and secularizing Iran (Mackey 1996). This historical backdrop provided an ideal impetus for the advancement of women's efforts for equality. By 1962 women gained the right to vote, and in 1968 the Family Protection Law expanded women's rights in marriage, divorce, and custody (Mir-Hosseini 1993). Many of these rights were lost after the Revolution of 1979. In 1998 the Supreme Council decided Iran would not become party to the Convention on the Elimination of All Forms of

Discrimination against Women (CEDAW) because many of its provisions contradict Islamic law.

Some argue that for the human rights ideology to succeed in non-Western nations, it must allow for multiculturalism. Others argue that allowing special privileges for cultural and religious practices of diverse ethnic groups potentially threatens gains made by feminists (Okin 1999). The refusal to sign CEDAW can be viewed as an example of the negative aspects of multiculturalism.

The tension between multiculturalism and universal human rights has created a dual system of laws that govern women's status in Iran. A conflict is caused by the adoption of modern legal systems in a country that also codifies Islamic law, the Sharīʿa, giving rise to "two parallel but distinct notions of legitimacy: Shari'a and legal" (Mir-Hosseini 1993, vii). Laws derived from dominant readings of the Sharīʿa, such as marriage, divorce, and custody laws, usually contradict secular norms derived from human rights principles concerning, for example, legal equality between the sexes. Often, one of these notions of legitimacy is challenged in court, blurring the boundaries between the secular and the religious. Women renegotiate their legal status through manipulation of these obscure boundaries (Mir-Hosseini 1993).

Today, Iranian women play a vital role in various human rights non-governmental organizations. One such group is the Society for Protecting the Rights of the Child (SPRC), headed by activist female lawyer, Shirin Ebadi. Shirin Ebadi was the first female judge in Iran in 1975. After the 1979 Revolution, women judges were dismissed, forcing Ms. Ebadi to step down from the bench. She continued her work as an attorney and a human rights activist. In 2003 Ms. Ebadi was awarded the Nobel Peace Prize making her the first Iranian, the first Muslim woman, and the third woman ever to receive the award.

The work of SPRC and other such groups often falls in the obscure gap between modern legal standards (international human rights) and religious laws (governing marriage, custody, and the family). SPRC relies on human rights law to improve children's rights. However, the use of these principles in conjunction with the group's focus on family and custody laws exemplifies reliance on prescribed gender roles to promote women's rights.

In 1997 SPRC and Ebadi succeeded in codifying a proposed amendment to the custody law, prohibiting automatic custody of children to unfit fathers. Such victories demonstrate women's use of human rights standards to improve child welfare, reinvent their own rights as mothers, and legitimize their roles as activists in the reform movement.

Through activism in human rights organizations and adherence to prescribed gender roles, Iranian women are engaged in everyday forms of resistance. Relying on human rights ideology and focusing on traditionally female roles has legitimized women's struggle for equality.

Bibliography

S. Mackey, *The Iranians. Persia, Islam and the soul of a nation*, New York 1996.

Z. Mir-Hosseini, *Marriage on trial. A study of Islamic family law. Iran and Morocco compared*, London 1993.

S. M. Okin, Is multiculturalism bad for women?, in S. M. Okin with respondents; J. Cohen, M. Howard, and M. C. Nussbaum (eds.), *Is muticulturalism bad for women?*, Princeton, N.J. 1999, 7–26.

M. Price, A brief history of women's movements in Iran (1850–2000), <www.iranonline.com/History/women-history/4html>, 2000).

Niaz Kasravi

Mashriq Arab States

Women's rights activists in the central Arab States point to discrimination and violence against women as major violations of women's rights. The systematic nature of the subordination of women as embedded in law and social practice permeates nearly every aspect of women's lives. The inferior legal status of women in the region is rooted in personal status codes (PSC) that are religiously derived. These laws discriminate against women and privilege men in both the public and private spheres. Modern legislation on nationality, penal, and other laws has generally reinforced the discriminatory clauses of the PSC. This discrimination is translated and put into practice in civil, political, and economic life with the rights, statuses, and roles of men and women organized hierarchically.

Women's subordinate status in society limits their access to education, employment, and political representation, in addition to making them more vulnerable to violence. Laws on violence against women in the region do not sufficiently address the size and scope of the problem, and the few laws that exist lack enforcement mechanisms to guarantee their implementation. The notion of marital rape does not exist in the law, and unmarried women with children and rape victims are particularly vulnerable and not always protected under the law. In addition, lack of official quantitative and qualitative statistics on the extent, forms, and manifestations of violence against women, enables states in the region to shun their responsibilities, notably to take the necessary legal measures to set up shelters and to train doctors, police, and magistrates in how to deal with cases of violence against women.

Female illiteracy rates in the region are still very high, an average of 42 percent in comparison to 21 percent for males. The average female participation in the workforce peaks at 29 percent though it is 39 percent for countries with comparable revenues. Discrimination against women in paid employment is widespread, and is reinforced by the absence of laws and enforcement mechanisms that protect women from wage discrimination and sexual harassment in the workplace. Furthermore, women have traditionally worked in agriculture, which, as well as their household work, is not accounted for in the national economy of their countries. This has led to to further marginalization of women's contribution to their respective societies.

The constitutions of countries in the region guarantee in principal equal political rights for men and women. Yet, in practice the participation of women in political decision-making processes is among the weakest in the world. Some countries, like Jordan, have adopted affirmative action by introducing a quota for female parliamentary members. However, with the regimes in the region suppressing and controlling the right of any citizen to freely participate in political life, the mere presence of women in powerless institutions will not necessarily improve women's status. In some cases, affirmative action even has the reverse effect, providing the state with the opportunity to demonstrate its commitment to women's rights, and thus making it all the more difficult to argue in favor of genuine empowerment of women in political decision-making.

Governments in the region have signed and ratified international pacts and conventions relating to women's rights, particularly the Convention on the Elimination of All Forms of Discrimination against Women (CEDAW), but have added reservations that go against the spirit and letter of those conventions. They have been particularly hesitant over articles 2, 9 (paragraph 2), 15 (paragraph 4), and 16 of CEDAW. Article 2 demands parties to condemn all forms of discrimination against women and thereby establish legal protection for women; article 9(2) demands equality between men and women with respect to the nationality of their children; article 15(4) demands equality for women in regard to their freedom of movement and freedom to choose their residence and domicile; and article 16 demands the elimination of discrimination in all matters relating to marriage and family relations. States often resort to cultural and religious explanations for not implementing the provisions of these international conventions. Furthermore, international human rights norms are usually not integrated in the national legislation of these countries.

However, despite or even because of the exclusion of women from the official political sphere, women have been active in associational life in many countries in the region. The history and evolution of women's rights organizations in the region varies enormously across political, social, and economic contexts. Traditionally, the women's rights movement has been linked to national liberation movements and today there is a strong link between the women's rights movement and the movement for human rights and democracy.

Particularly during the United Nations Decade for Women 1976–85, women's rights activists from the region began to attend regional and international meetings on women's rights. By the 1990s they began building regional networks such as Aisha, Court of Arab Women, Sisterhood is Global Institute (SIGI), Maghreb/Mashrek Network for Information and Training on Gender, along with many other unofficial networks. Women's rights organizations and networks are involved in different activities, such as campaigning on specific issues pertaining to violence against women, or more generally informing women about their rights and providing legal aid and counseling. Yet, despite these activities in promoting women's rights, there is still a lack of information about the status of women in the region and a tendency to stereotype women in the media as suppressed and thereby to overlook their capacities and the role they play in implementing change in their respective societies.

The relationship of the women's rights movement in the region with the ruling regimes and Islamist factions poses a serious challenge to the movement. The ruling powers attempt to limit, curb, and exercise total control over civic initiatives through legislation on public and associative freedoms. Thus, in the name of fighting the Islamist groups, the ruling powers try to co-opt or control the women's rights movement and use it for their own ends. In Syria and in Egypt, for example, organizations require government authorization in order to be registered and receive funding. Another means of control is for the regime, as is the case in Jordan, to create para-official structures in the guise of independent NGOs – the so-called GONGOs (government organized non-governmental organizations) – which often receive funding from international donors, while presenting themselves as national networks uniting the whole of the women's rights movement.

The Islamists, whose model for society and women's role within it often corresponds with society's cultural references, accuse women from the women's rights movement of being in the pay of the West. They try to cast doubt on the women's religious beliefs and morals by arguing that they misappropriate funds from donors for personal gain or that they promote homosexuality and want to ruin family values. They claim that international human rights instruments are the tools of a vast Western conspiracy against Islam and the Arab countries.

In addition, women's rights organizations face internal challenges regarding organizational structuring, leadership, transparency, funding, and reaching out to a wider constituency. These challenges to the women's rights movement, both external and internal, have translated into different strategies among women's rights activists regarding the promotion of women's rights in the region. One strategy focuses on disseminating knowledge of international women's rights instruments and lobbying for states to lift their reservations to CEDAW and adopt the Beijing Platform for Action. They also call on states to raise public awareness of discrimination and violence against women, tackle the social bias against women, and provide protection for women from discrimination and violence. The other strategy is to encourage a more progressive interpretation and historical reading of the religious texts in regard to women's rights and law reform.

BIBLIOGRAPHY

M. Afkhami, Introduction, in M. Afkhami (ed.), *Faith and freedom. Women's human rights in the Muslim world*, New York 1995, 1–16.

M. Badran, Toward Islamic feminisms. A look at the Middle East, in A. Afsaruddin (ed.), *Hermeneutics and honor. Negotiating female "public" space in Islamic/ate societies*, Cambridge, Mass. 1999, 159–88.

A. Basu, Introduction, in A. Basu (ed.), *The challenge of local feminisms. Women's movements in global perspectives*, Boulder, Colo. 1995, 1–21.

C. Bunch, Women's human rights. The challenges of global feminism and diversity, in M. Dekoven (ed.), *Feminist locations. Global and local, theory and practice*, New Brunswick, N.J. 2001, 129–46.

R. Cook, Women's international human rights law. The way forward, in R. Cook (ed.), *Human rights of women. National and international perspectives*, Philadelphia 1994, 3–36.

S. Graham-Brown, Women's activism in the Middle East. A historical perspective, in S. Joseph and S. Slyomovics (eds.), *Women and power in the Middle East*, Philadelphia 2001, 23–33.

S. Joseph, Gendering citizenship in the Middle East, in S. Joseph (ed.), *Gender and citizenship in the Middle East*, New York 2000, 3–30.

D. Kandiyoti, Contemporary feminist scholarship and Middle East studies, in D. Kandiyoti (ed.), *Gendering the Middle East. Emerging perspective*, New York 1996, 1–28.

——, Beyond Beijing. Obstacles and prospects for the Middle East, in M. Afkhami and E. Friedl (eds.), *Muslim women and the politics of participation. Implementing the Beijing Platform*, New York, 1997, 3–10.

——, The Politics of gender and conundrums of citizenship, in S. Joseph and S. Slyomovics (eds.), *Women and power in the Middle* East, Philadelphia 2001, 52–8.

S. Kazi, Muslim law and women living under Muslim law, in M. Afkhami and E. Friedl (eds.), *Muslim women and the politics of participation. Implementing the Beijing Platform*, New York 1997, 141–6.

Lawyers Committee for Human Rights, *Islam and justice*, New York 1997.

——, *Islam and equality*, New York 1999.

A. Mayer, Rhetorical strategies and official policies on women's rights. The merits and drawbacks of the new world hypocrisy, in M. Afkhami (ed.), *Faith and freedom. Women's human rights in the Muslim world*, New York 1995, 104–32.

R. Naciri, Engaging the state. The women's movement and political discourse in Morocco, in C. Miller and S. Razavi (eds.), *Missionaries and mandarins. Feminist engagement with development institutions*, London 1998, 87–111.

R. Naciri and I. Nusair, *The integration of the human rights of women from the Middle East and North Africa in the Euro-Mediterranean partnership*, Denmark 2003.

al-Raida Magazine, *Arab women's movements*, 100 (2003).

M. Tallawy, International organizations, national machinery, Islam and foreign policy, in M. Afkhami and E. Friedl (eds.), *Muslim women and the politics of participation. Implementing the Beijing Platform*, New York 1997, 128–40.

M. Yamani, Introduction, in M. Yamani (ed.), *Feminisms and Islam. Legal and literary perspectives*, New York 1996, 1–27.

ISIS NUSAIR

North Africa

Human rights discourse emerged throughout the Maghrib as part of the anti-colonial struggle (arguing against inequality between colonizer and colonized with regard to work, education, health, and so forth). Against this general background, the way in which women contributed to the discourse and to the development of a focus on women's rights varied from country to country. The steps to promote women's rights that were taken during the first decades after independence were the product of state action, supported by state-dominated women's organizations; later, a second generation of reforms, starting in the 1980s, was a consequence of the struggle undertaken by the new feminine elites working within women's non-governmental organizations in civil society. Among these were l'Association marocaine des droits des femmes, la Ligue démocratique pour les droits des femmes (Morocco), the Collectif 95 Maghreb Égalité, l'Association pour l'égalité devant la loi entre les hommes et les femmes (AELHF, Algeria), l'Association pour la défense et la promotion des droits des femmes (ADPDF, Algeria), l'Association tunisienne des femmes démocrates (ATFD), l'Association des femmes tunisiennes pour la recherche et le développement (AFTURD). These associations were composed of women who were born around the time of independence, raised within the new state's education system, and who were primarily middle-class. The associations grew in force in a context of civil society democratization, mass education, economic crisis, and structural adjustment, and what might be termed external factors (such as new notions of development), and where women were finding themselves marginalized in structures of political opposition. It was also a context in which they saw movements based on religion as threatening (following the Iranian Revolution in 1979) and in which they struggled to find space for expression in the sphere of civil society (Marzouki 1999). Organizations that arose during this period and their successors continue to contribute today to the debate on human rights and women's rights (Dwyer 1991), democracy, and the establishment of the rule of law (Belarbi 2002, 141–57).

The legal context of the struggle for women's rights differed from country to country and measures to establish and reinforce women's rights were adopted at different times. The civil codes governing these issues – the Mudawwana in Morocco, the Family Code in Algeria, and the Personal Status Code in Tunisia – while differing significantly, have some points in common. An underlying tension in all these codes – on the one hand the recognition of equality between the sexes and in citizenship rights, in conformity with international law and, on the other, the inequality in personal civil rights related to the application of Sharīʿa and to laws that have their source in religious decrees – has been a motor of women's activity throughout the struggle of feminists for an equal civil status. *Ijtihād* and the secularization of family law – the Tunisian model being the one that has adopted the most liberal reading – are dimensions that distinguish these societies from one another.

MOROCCO

Among the positive aspects of the Mudawwana in Morocco, which was introduced in 1957 and in 1959, are that the eligible marriage age for girls was raised to 15 and for boys to 18; a woman's freedom to exploit and dispose of her own wealth and inheritance was reaffirmed; and she gained the right to divorce in certain circumstances. Her obligation to obey her husband was legally abolished in 1993, except in cases where immoral conduct was feared. Significant legal changes were introduced to the Mudawwana in 2004, including the principle of equality, whereby the spouses run the family jointly; the *mahr* is merely symbolic; the eligible marriage age is the same for men and women; obedience to the monogamy clause in the marriage contract (if this is accepted at marriage) is obligatory; polygamy is limited to two wives; and divorce requires a judicial proceeding (discontinuing recognition of non-judicial repudiation). Also, civil marriages performed abroad (between 40 and 50 percent of emigrants are women) are now recognized as legal. One change that weakens the rights of women is that in cases of separation the father gains the right to designate a guardian for his children, whereas in 1993 the mother had been awarded guardianship. For Moroccans living abroad, the procedures related to polygamy and an unmarried woman's right to adopt a child under the regime of *kafāla* (a customary form where the child keeps his/her birth name) have not been specified. In the workplace the rule of non-discrimination between the sexes has not been legally affirmed.

ALGERIA

Upon independence in 1962, Algeria extended the colonial statute of 1959, which did not allow repudiation, and this law continued in effect until 1975. The Algerian Family Code is, among the three countries of the Maghrib, the most prejudicial to women's rights and when proposed to the national assembly in 1981, it led to protests, but without effect. Although not having a religious foundation the code, finally adopted in 1984, treats women as minors. It recognizes polygamy, guardianship over the woman, and the woman's obedience to her husband. Following this, the mobilization of Algerian women took on an unprecedented dynamic.

In addition to early and continuing protest against the Family Code in Algeria, women also were active, starting in 1990, in opposing measures taken in municipalities dominated by the Islamic Salvation Front (Front islamique du salut, FIS) by which the veil was imposed upon women working in the administration, women's sports facilities were closed, girls were forbidden to study music and dance in public conservatories, and the separation of sexes on beaches was applied. Women also mobilized in favor of democracy and in solidarity with the families of "disappeared" persons. In 1997, a number of women's civil society associations launched an appeal to collect a million signatures to promote significant amendments to the Family Code and, in 2004, the group "20 years, enough!" bears witness to continuing mobilization for women's rights. In October 2003, the government established a commission to examine raising the eligible marriage age for women to 19; the woman's right to marry without her family's consent; increased financial support from the husband in cases where he decides unilaterally on separation; housing support for the children and the mother; and stricter rules on polygamy. Unlike in Morocco, in Algeria laws mandate equality of the sexes in the workplace but, in the Maghrib, Algeria has the lowest proportion of working women. As in Tunisia, legal statute mandates that wages be equal for both sexes, but inequality appears in the differential access each has to employment, to credit, and to education. Finally, whereas in Morocco the presence of women in religious institutions and in business is the most visible of the three countries, Algeria saw the participation of a woman candidate in the presidential elections of April 2004.

TUNISIA

In Tunisia, the Personal Status Code introduced in 1956 adopted the principle of equality between men and women, and guaranteed it by constitutional and legislative texts. Polygamy was outlawed, the eligible marriage age for girls was raised to 17 and her consent was required, and guardianship was given to the mother in case of the father's death. Adoption was made legal. In 1968, the same penalties were instituted for the adulterous man as for the adulterous woman. In 1981, the right to live in the family residence was given to the woman in case of divorce as was custody of the children. Starting in 1993, amendments introduced imposed upon both spouses the obligation of treating one another with kindness and mutual aid in running the household and caring for the children. The woman's duty to obey the husband was abolished. The mother shares in managing the affairs of her children and the married girl who is still a legal minor has the right to control her own life and wealth. A fund to guarantee the payment of food support for the divorced woman and her children was established and a woman married to a non-Tunisian may transmit her nationality to the children, with the consent of the father. In cases of conjugal violence, the situation of matrimony is considered to be an aggravating circumstance, leading to more severe penalties; and violence against a spouse for acts such as adultery are now treated simply as crimes, with so-called attenuating circumstances no longer considered. Since 1996, maintenance payments are awarded to the mother who has custody of the children, orphan's payments continue up to the age of 25 if the youth remains in education, and the possibility of both spouses to contract an individual loan to buy a residence is introduced. In the workplace, nondiscrimination between the sexes is mandated.

Now that women have gained new rights and protective mechanisms, varying greatly from country to country, several general problems remain throughout the region. The first involves maintaining the effort to gain further advances. Second, the awareness women have of their rights needs to be extended and implementation of these rights improved – a problem that is particularly acute among rural women and other underprivileged sectors. Third, in the absence of a democratic political culture (both on the level of formal politics as well as within women's movements themselves), women's movements are at risk of being weakened without having accomplished the deconstruction of dominant representations: on the one hand, dependence on foreign funds and discourse raises a number of problems; on the other, they are in danger of being instrumentalized by their states that may be looking for legitimacy from hegemonic forces abroad as a way to shore up their own internal authority.

BIBLIOGRAPHY

A. Belarbi, Femmes et société civile. Réflexions sur le cas du Maroc, in A. Belarbi et al., *Droits de citoyenneté des femmes au Maghreb. La condition socio-économique et juridique des femmes. Le mouvement des femmes*, Casablanca 1997, 249–72.

K. Dwyer, *Arab voices. The human rights debate in the Middle East*, London 1991.

I. Marzouki, *Femmes d'ordre ou désordre de femmes?*, Tunis 1999.

M. K. Remaoun, Le mouvement des droits des femmes entre visions spécifiques et visions sociétales, in O. Derras (comp.), *Mouvements associatifs au Maghreb*, Oran 2002, 141–57.

LILIA LABIDI

Sudan

Sudan's history regarding women's rights and human rights is a mixed one. Important advances were made by indigenous activists in the post-independence period after 1956; international pressure on the issue of female genital mutilation (FGM) has yielded some positive results; however, since 1989 Sudan has been cited by human rights groups as a "human rights disaster" for its longstanding civil war affecting its southern citizens, and also for its treatment of women in the north.

The Sudanese constitution of 1973 provides for equal rights of all citizens irrespective of gender, and women have held responsible positions as government ministers and judges at various times. However, since 1989, under an Islamist regime led by the National Islamic Front (NIF), questions of citizenship and human rights of women have been raised in the following areas: 1. mandatory wearing of *ḥijāb* in public and empowering morals protection police and courts to enforce public morality. Cases of lashing for immoral public behavior have been brought to international attention by human rights groups; 2. the purging of non-NIF women from government employment and the judiciary. The few public female figures are closely associated with the NIF, such as Wisal al-Mahdī, the wife of Islamist leader Ḥasan al-Turābī; and 3. application of the *ḥadd* punishment of stoning for adultery or fornication to women.

Sudan was once a leader in legal reform of Sharīʿa marriage and divorce laws (Fluehr-Lobban 1987). Judicial divorce for women on the grounds of harm or abuse (*ḍarar*) was allowed in Sudan in 1915, years before such reform was undertaken in Egypt and elsewhere in the Muslim world. In the 1970s Sudan continued its path of legal innovation under the leadership of the last *qāḍī al-quḍāt* (supreme judge), Shaykh Muḥammad al-Jizūlī, who took the bold move to appoint women judges to the Sharīʿa courts and who expanded legal divorce for women using the concept of ransom (*fidya*) whereby a woman could use her bride-price (*mahr*) to obtain her release from a harmful marriage.

After 1983, Sharīʿa was made state law, and since 1989 conservative legal opinion has been influenced by the NIF. Non-Muslim men and women as well as Muslims in northern Sudan have been sentenced to the *ḥadd* penalty of stoning for adultery. Southern non-Muslim women have been sentenced to this penalty in remote parts of the country (Darfur), but as of this writing no sentence of stoning has been carried out. However, numerous amputations for theft have been carried out upon men since 1983.

Historically, the struggle for Sudanese women's rights was part of the larger nationalist movement. The first organized group of women, the Sudanese Women's Union, was formed in 1946 as part of the Sudanese Communist Party. After independence, through the 1950s and 1960s, the Women's Union published its *Ṣawt al-marʾa* (Woman's voice) in which numerous issues relating to the political and social status of women were raised, such as polygamy, divorce reform, and female circumcision. Suffrage was extended to women, not at the time of independence, but after the 1964 popular revolution against the Abboud military government, when women openly and enthusiastically demonstrated for popular democracy. Fāṭima Aḥmad Ibrāhīm, a founder of the Women's Union, was the first woman elected to parliament in 1965. The Women's Union was also influential in agitating for the reforms in the Sharīʿa law of marriage and divorce that took place in the 1960s and early 1970s. In 1993 Fāṭima Ibrāhīm accepted the United Nations Human Rights Prize on behalf of the Sudanese Women's Union. Since 1989 the Islamist regime of ʿUmar al-Bashīr has officially suppressed all democratic organizations, including the Sudanese Women's Union, banning their publications and ability to speak freely in public.

Also since 1989, female supporters of the NIF have had greater opportunities defending the regime's policies toward women internally and in external media outlets. Sudanese Islamist feminists were especially active at the 1995 Fourth International Congress on Women held in Beijing, raising challenges to human rights activist criticism of Islamist regimes. They argued that Islam and the Sharīʿa provide comprehensive legal, political, and religious rights for women. Their critics, especially the Republican Brothers and Muslim liberal secularists, counter-argue that the ban some Muslim countries impose on women as heads of state and their lack of equal legal rights in divorce and inheritance amount to a violation of women's rights as human rights.

Since independence in 1956 the movement for women's rights has been dominated by northern Muslim women and their supporters while the rights of southern women were left out of the process, or merely offered lip service. Rural women have also all but been forgotten.

The special issue of FGM has attracted the greatest attention by international human rights groups. The topic of "female circumcision" has been a subject of fascination, horror, and feminist agitation in the West. The current NIF government has reinstituted a ban on female circumcision; however, it remains to be seen how this latest ban will be enforced.

Allegations of the revival of slavery in the context of the civil war since 1983 have focused on the abduction of southern women and children by "Arab" militias in the border areas between north and south, especially Bahr al-Ghazal. American and European Christian groups have intervened to slow or stop such abductions as they perceive the civil war in Sudan to be a conflict between the Muslim north and Christian south.

While equal rights for women are protected in the Permanent Constitution of 1973, a great deal remains to be addressed in practice, including a national approach to family law reform, increased political participation of women at all levels, and a concerted effort to include women in development planning and economic development. The historically secular women's movement and Sudanese feminists have been critical of the recent drives toward greater Islamization. With a peace agreement close to being signed in 2004 a national approach to the Sharīʿa and the status of women becomes a priority in a country in which a third of its population is non-Muslim.

BIBLIOGRAPHY

C. Fluehr-Lobban, *Islamic law and society in the Sudan*, London 1987.

R. Lobban, R. Kramer, and C. Fluehr-Lobban, *Historical dictionary of the Sudan*, Lanham, Md. 2002³, see Sudanese women's movement, 282–3.

N. Toubia, *Female genital mutiliation. A call for global action*, New York 1995.

CAROLYN FLUEHR-LOBBAN

Sub-Saharan Africa

Women engaged in law in Africa, and Muslim women in particular, have a long history of participation in the over 19 currently existing general professional organizations for lawyers and judges. Some of these same professional women have also organized themselves around their Muslim identity.

Women's rights as human rights came into their own in preparations for the Vienna World Human Rights conference sponsored by the United Nations Commission for Human Rights (now the Office of the High Commissioner for Human Rights) in 1993. The move reflected the spectacular progress made in global consciousness of women's rights since the last world meeting on human rights in Tehran in 1968, when the women's rights movement was still in an embryonic stage. The 1993 conference resulted in the creation of a new office, that of the Special Rapporteur on Violence against Women.

The Regional Report from Africa prepared in Tunis in 1992 for the 1993 Vienna Conference made an appeal to African governments and the international community to rapidly eliminate "all forms of discrimination against women" in Africa by allocating resources for the provision of legal aid services with a view to the promotion and protection of human rights. The African states were also called upon to encourage non-governmental organizations (NGOs) to participate in the advancement of women. The effects of religion on women were specifically highlighted. African states were to take "all appropriate measures in order to promote the rights of women, to put an end to discrimination based on sex and to protect women from all forms of violence and traditional practices of intolerance and extremism, particularly religious extremism, affecting their rights and freedoms" (UNCHR 1992).

In 1990 the Ford Foundation provided funding for the Women in Law and Development in Africa (WILDAF) network. With a boost from the Vienna resolutions in 1993, the Ford Foundation pushed women's rights to center stage, leading to an expansion of WILDAF into regional centers in eastern, southern, and most recently western Africa. These NGOs combine research and advocacy for women's rights as human rights. Individual Muslim women experts have joined. Various WILDAFs have also paired up with local national professional organizations, for example, with the Tanzania Media Women's Association in East Africa, which has key Muslim members, in order to assure a broad dissemination of research findings. WILDAF's strategy is to get women's rights legislation passed and to initiate litigation challenging gender adverse laws. Women's issues are not divided according to religion or ethnicity. Test litigation in African courts has been supported by the International Women's Rights Action Watch (IWRAW, based in Minnesota, USA), founded in 1985 at the Women's World Conference in Nairobi with the aim of making the United Nations Convention on the Elimination of All Forms of Discrimination against Women (CEDAW) a global reality. The IWRAW newsletter established strong links with women in Africa who sent information on all discriminatory customs and laws, whether secular or religious. The WILDAF legal support has been supplemented in South Africa since 1999 by a religiously neutral organization called the Women's Legal Center, which has litigated cases in order to advance equality for women under customary and Muslim laws. It is funded in part by the Ford Foundation and the International Commission of Jurists.

Alongside women's human rights NGOs in Africa, in which Muslim women participate, are organizations that are founded by Muslim women, but that do not have a Muslim identity as such. One example is Amanitare, a well-known organization focusing on health, sexuality, and reproduction as women's human rights issues, and the elimination of violence against women. Amanitare, which is coordinated by the Research, Action and Information Network for the Bodily Integrity of Women (Rainbo), was founded by a Muslim Sudanese medical doctor in 1994. The Amanitare/Rainbo project, started in 1999, bases its mandate on the Vienna Conference, the Cairo International Conference on Population and Development (1994), and the Beijing World Conference on Women (1995). One of its key research projects involves the progressive reduction of female genital mutilation (FGM) in Africa, including African Muslim societies. The organization has published a guide to laws on FGM (2000). Another example is the Gender Desk (founded 1993) of the Muslim Youth Movement (MYM 1970) in South Africa. Shamima Shaykh, a Muslim woman activist, worked with MYM to involve Muslim youth in the politics of the anti-apartheid movement. With the coming of political freedom, she founded the Gender Desk in order to promote the interests of Muslim women in the gender policy of the new political order. More specifically, she sought equal access for women to Muslim religious institutions and positions.

Other women's organizations have an explicit Muslim identity and focus. The 1993 Vienna Conference spurred the Ford Foundation to support organizations that had consolidated their activities earlier as a result of the 1985 Nairobi International Women's conference. The major Muslim women's organization from that era founded by Muslim women in 1984–5 was Women Living Under Muslim Laws (WLUML), with its headquarters in France. It mobilized initially around the imprisonment of Algerian feminists and extended its concerns to all women affected by Muslim laws globally. Its object is to network and encourage women "to reflect, analyze and reformulate the identity imposed on them through the application of Muslim laws and by doing so, to assume greater control over their lives." In the 1990s, Ford Foundation grants greatly boosted the organization's networking and global communications capabilities. With headquarters now located in London, the WLUML works throughout the Muslim world primarily through local sister NGOs that have a rights centered approach. One of its major coordinating organizations for Africa and the Middle East is BAOBAB for Women's Human Rights, in Nigeria (founded 1996). BAOBAB's mandate includes improving development of rights under religious and customary laws. Like WILDAF, BAOBAB involves itself in court litigation among other activities. It has supported Muslim women brought to trial under recent Islamic criminal laws in northern Nigeria.

Umbrella organizations with a Muslim focus such as WLUML and BAOBAB have long operated alongside non-rights oriented older Muslim women's organizations in Sub-Saharan African countries. This is fast changing, however. The Ghanaian Federation of Muslim Women's Association, funded by the Women's Global Fund, promotes human rights over against traditional practices such as female circumcision. The Muslim Sisters Network in Kenya has joined the national constitutional debate to give voice to both traditional and liberal perspectives on Islamic law. The corresponding role of the Ugandan Muslim Women Vision (UMWV) in the debate on the draft domestic relations bill, which would prohibit polygamy and has been contested publicly by the mufti of the Uganda Muslim Supreme Council (March 2004), is not widely known. Also with headquarters in Nigeria is the Federation of Muslim Women's Associations of Nigeria (FOMWAN), which participated in the 1985 International Women's Conference in Nairobi. It was created in 1985 as a result of dissatisfaction with the liberal academic feminist philosophy of the Nigerian National Council of Women's Societies. FOMWAN is faith oriented and participates in forming opinions on social and political issues for women from the less educated strata of society. It has organized, for example, forums on HIV/AIDS and expanding women's education. Some of its branches have become members of Nigeria's democracy and governance project funded by grants from Johns Hopkins University. The Nigerian Federation has sister federations in Gambia, Ghana, Liberia, and Sierra Leone. In 2003, at a meeting in Accra sponsored by the Ghana Center for Democratic Development, the Africa Democracy Forum expressed interest in encouraging a new activity for Muslim women's organizations. They hope to bring Christian and Muslim activists and communities together, along the lines of the work of Women in Black in former Yugoslavia and the joint peace efforts of Muslim and Christian women in an organization called The Women's Movement that Cares for Maluku (GPP, founded in 2003) in Maluku Province in Indonesia.

The latest continent-wide legal development for women's human rights has been the signing in Maputo of the Protocol to the African Charter of Human and Peoples' Rights on the Rights of Women in Africa, known in short as the Charter for Rights of Women in Africa (July 2003). The protocol addresses and proscribes controversial African religious and customary practices involving, *inter alia*, inheritance, gives women the right to protection against HIV/AIDS, and guarantees women the right to participate in the determination of cultural policies and equal representation at all levels of decision-making (which presumably includes the judiciary). The protocol is a triumph for the efforts of the African regional office in Nairobi of the Lawyers Alliance for Women, an initiative of Equality Now (based in New York). Several states have already made reservations to the protocol on grounds of conservative jurists' interpretations of Islamic law. The role of African Muslim women's organizations in the drafting and, now more urgently, the implementation of the protocol has yet to be fully researched.

It is clear that all the major women's NGOs need international finance and high profile participation in United Nations women's international conferences in order to survive. The extent of financial underwriting from wealthier Muslim governments has not been comprehensively researched. There is a further need to study the organizational culture of African Muslim women's NGOs as well as the role of Muslim women in non-Muslim women's human rights organizations. Such studies would include mapping whether and how African Muslim women should organize themselves to create a Muslim human rights identity, and how they decide whether to coordinate with other religiously neutral organizations on human rights affecting all women.

BIBLIOGRAPHY

BAOBAB for Women's Human Rights, <www.baobabwomen.org>.

Equality Now, The Law Project, <www.equalitynow.org/English/ law_project/law_project_en.html>.

FOMWAN (Federation of Muslim Women's Associations of Nigeria), <www.ifh.org.uk/ fomwan.html>.

International Women's Rights Action Watch, <http://iwraw.igc.org>.

Jakarta Post, Christian, Muslim women promote peace in Maluku, 1 January 2003, <www.infomaluku.net/arc/03/030101jp.html>.

Jenda. A Journal of Culture and African Women Studies, <www.jendajournal.com>.

A. Kiondo, Policy advocacy. The case of Tanzania Media Women Association (TAMWA), <www.eldis.org>.

Legalbrief, Kenyan leader to block rights bills, 16 November 2003, <www.legalbrief.co.za>.

MYM (Muslim Youth Movement) of South Africa, <http://shams.za.org/gender.htm>.

New Vision (Kampala), Muslims warn on marriage bill, 8 March 2004, <http://allafrica.com/stories/printable/200403080969.html>.

Protocol to the African Charter on Human and Peoples' Rights on the Rights of Women in Africa, 11 July 2003, <www.africa-union.org>.

A. Rahman and N. Toubia, *Female genital mutilation A guide to laws and policies worldwide*, London 2000.

Research, Action and Information Network for Bodily Integrity of Women (RAINBO), <www.rainbo.org>.

A. Samiuddin and R. Khanam (eds.), *Muslim feminism and feminist movement in Africa*, 2 vols., Delhi 2002.

TAMWA (Tanzania Media Women Association), <www.tamwa.or.tz>.

UMWV (Uganda Muslim Women Vision) <www.wougnet.org>.

UNCHR (United Nations High Commission on Human Rights), Report of the regional meeting for Africa, Tunis, 2–6 November 1992, <http://www.unhchr.ch/html/menu5/wctunis.htm>.

Virginia Gildersleeve International Fund, Project Grants Library, No. 1512, Muslim Women's Action Against Traditional Practices, Tamale, Northern Region, Ghana, <www.thegildersleeve.org>.

WILDAF (Women in Law and Development in Africa), <www.wildaf.org.zw>.

WLUML (Women Living Under Muslim Laws), <www.wluml.org>.

CHRISTINA JONES-PAULY

Turkey

Turkish women, who have had the vote since 1934, still experience human rights violation and discrimination in modern Turkey. There is no clear form of Kurdish dress but Kurdish nationalists, both male and female, are exposed to discrimination regardless of whether they dress according to secular or Islamic norms. However, recent international pressure, especially from the European Union (EU), has promoted greater human rights for women and encouraged them to more freely express their demands. The new Civil Code of 2001 consolidated the equal status of women within the family by annulling men's position as head of family, supporting women's right to take decisions in marital matters, and granting them an equal share of the assets accumulated during marriage.

Nonetheless, numerous Turkish laws on sensitive matters such as the Kurds, military interference in politics, and political Islam still curtail freedom of expression and association. Violation of these laws is punished by fines, imprisonment of journalists and politicians, and closure of Kurdish and Islamic political parties. The leaders of these parties lose their political rights, as well as their right to publish their newspapers and broadcast on television. These restrictions are based on the assumption that the use of the Kurdish language and Islamic discourse threatens national security. In other words, the rationale for these restrictions is that to acknowledge the ethnic and religious heterogeneity of Turkish society could undermine the republic's unitary and secular structure. These fears have been exacerbated by two decades of armed clashes between the separatist Kurdish guerillas and the Turkish security forces and by the rise of Islamic fundamentalism.

Dissidents are frequently "disappeared," tortured, and ill-treated, particularly in southeastern Turkey, inhabited mainly by Kurds. Detainees, routinely blindfolded during interrogations, are held incommunicado. They are harshly beaten, stripped naked, and deprived of sleep, food, drink, and toilet facilities. Their torturers administer electric shocks, hang them by their arms, spray them with cold pressurized water, and sexually abuse them. The perpetrators are rarely tried in court, while victims are often charged with insulting members of the security forces. This discourages victims from seeking justice. In particular, victims rarely report sexual assaults because of the grave limitations on impartial and comprehensive independent investigation.

In the case of women, the violation of human rights is exacerbated by gender discrimination. Female detainees are strip-searched and raped by male officers when they are in police custody or in prison, often in the sight of their husbands or family members, to force them to confess (*Human Rights Watch World Report 2002*). In addition to the physical and psychological effects of such sexual assaults, the female survivors risk death, further violence, forced marriage, and ostracism by their families as a result of the state's cynical utilization of "honor" to demean them before the community. Revealing that they have been exposed to sexual violence encourages a discriminatory culture that threatens all women. Moreover, the forced virginity test in custody is a form of abusing women's sexuality and physical integrity; to refuse to submit to this test is assumed to be a sign of stained honor. The woman who survives sexual abuse and humiliation suffers further serious consequences, because the intact hymen of an unmarried woman is regarded as material proof of virginity. It is not only a matter of individual choice, but also a sociocultural construct within the protection of the family (Cindoğlu 2000, 215–16). Such sexual violence has led women detainees to commit suicide, especially in southeastern Turkey, or to flee their homes, with or without their families. There is, however, nowhere to go; the number of shelters for such women is limited in Turkey. Further, male relatives are known to practice the "honor murders" of sexually "impure" women to cleanse family honor: this is justified by the Turkish Penal Code, which pronounces the victim's behavior as grave provocation.

Since the 1980s the number of female students with *başörtüsü* (headscarf) has mushroomed in the universities, "the castles of modernity" (Göle 1996). Their demands for higher education pervade the Turkish daily agenda. There were debates in the early 1980s in the Council of Higher Education (YÖK) to prohibit the headscarf but allow the *türban*, a kind of scarf that covers the head but not shoulders. In 1982 a law abrogated the wearing of the *türban*, but was resolved in 1988 by the Constitutional Courts by leaving the issue to the individual decision of universities in 1989 (Özdalga 1998, 41–6).

On 28 February 1997 the military generals in the National Security Council promulgated an extrajudicial decree that prohibited the headscarf in order to buttress secularism. This demonstrated the vulnerability of Turkish democracy to interference by the military, which decided that the headscarf is the "ideological uniform" of fundamentalism. But the decision led to the greatest massive civil disobedience for freedom of education in Turkish history when three million people formed a human chain throughout Turkey on 11 October 1998 demanding women's right to wear the headscarf. At the time of writing, the government of the Islamic Justice and Development Party (AKP), with its overwhelming parliamentary majority and zeal to develop human rights, backed by the EU for its possible membership, has frozen the headscarf problem, the frontline between Islamists and the military.

The terrifying experiences of Kurdish women and the protests of headscarved women as a form of political activity deepened women's awareness of human rights. They question state oppression and also their traditional gender status. It is to be hoped that such violations of human rights will cease as Turkey adopts the EU's *acquis communautaire*.

BIBLIOGRAPHY

Y. Arat, Women's rights as human rights. The Turkish case, in *Human Rights Review* 3/1 (2001), 27–34.

Z. Arat (ed.), *Deconstructing the images of Turkish women*, New York 1998.

S. Bozdogan and R. Kasaba (eds.), *Rethinking modernity and Turkish identity in Turkey*, Seattle 1997.

D. Cindoğlu, Virginity tests and artificial virginity in modern Turkish medicine, in Women for Women's Human Rights (ed.), *Women and sexuality in Muslim societies*, Istanbul 2000, 215–228.

N. Göle, *The forbidden modern. Civilization and veiling*, Ann Arbor 1996.

Human Rights Watch World Report 2002, <www.hrw.org/wr2k2/europe19.html>.

A. Kadioğlu, Women's subordination in Turkey. Is Islam really the villain?, in *Middle East Journal*, 48 (1994), 654–60.

D. Kandiyoti, *Women, Islam and the state*, Philadelphia 1989.

E. Özdalga, *The veiling issue, official secularism, and popular Islam in modern Turkey*, Richmond, Surrey 1998.

S. Tekeli, *Women in modern Turkish society. A reader*, London 1991.

MURAT ÇEMREK

Identity Politics

Central Asia

Identity politics in Central Asia exists on different levels – international, regional, and local. In the first, East (tradition) confronts West (modernity). In the second, attempts are made to distinguish among the various national groupings of the region, while the third focuses on internal differences, at national, local, or clan level. In all three, much of the discourse takes place around gender identities, and images of women are used as counters in male political games.

During the 1920s the Bolsheviks attempted to re-engineer Central Asian gender identities, especially femininity, characterized by submission to male control and sexual purity. The region's women found themselves contested terrain between the Soviet state and their own cultures. Throughout the Soviet period, images of veiled Muslim women and Sovietized female workers were used in struggles over identity politics, with different meanings by each side, so that Asian women retained their central place in the continuing battle between opposing, albeit shifting, visions of identities. Notwithstanding the ideological variations among the successive Soviet leaders, which shaped the relationship of different generations of Central Asian women with socialism and nationalism (Kuehnast 1997), the basic dichotomy between Sovietized modernity and Central Asian traditions continued to be expressed through much the same female images.

Since 1991, in their endeavors to legitimize their existence as distinct nations, the governments of all Central Asia's five republics have acknowledged Islam as an integral part of their heritage. Here, pride in nation (as well as, in Kazakhstan, Kyrgyzstan, and Turkmenistan, clan or tribe) is underpinned by images of heroic masculinity, in which is embedded control over women. The imagined new nationhood is to be supported by women's return to a notional pre-Soviet submission and domesticity, with a combination of Islam and nationalism employed to legitimize both the new states and male claims to power, situating women who refuse to comply as potential traitors both to the nation-building project and their religion. This resurgence of traditional gender identities coexists with national constitutions that in general legalize formal equality between the sexes, in keeping with both Soviet and international law.

Opposition forces, especially in Tajikistan and Uzbekistan, also make use of gender identities in their political strategizing. The most important are the Islamic parties, who challenge state-run religious establishments with images of bearded men and women in *ḥijāb*, important issues both in the Tajik civil war and in recent political clashes in Uzbekistan. To the governments of Central Asia, the specter of Afghanistan is sufficient to legitimize serious repression of Islamic movements. Beards have been banned from the Tajik army and those wearing them have been beaten by police in Uzbekistan, where veiled students also encounter problems.

Women's endeavors to negotiate their identities through these political minefields are very varied. Older educated women may prefer a Sovietized image, while many younger ones are fascinated by representations of fashionable Western women portrayed in advertisements and soap operas. While neither of these conforms to current political trends, neither do the *ḥijāb* wearers, who, in Uzbekistan at least, are practically considered enemies of the state.

Governments promote traditional identities, partway between these extremes, using local media to encourage a concept of Asian women as primarily housewives and mothers, supported by breadwinner husbands. Thus, implicitly they concur with religious extremists' calls for women to renounce paid labor and secular higher education.

In the current depressed economy, such feminine identities permit to go unchallenged the significant decrease of women's participation in politics and public life in general. They were the first to be laid off from state enterprises and the last to be rehired; they have noticeably been discriminated against in such matters as the redistribution of land from the former collective and state farms. Ironically, high male unemployment and low wages have forced large numbers of women to enter the informal labor market. They thereby retain notional domesticated identities while simultaneously making a living, thus partially satisfying the demands of the conservatives while reducing the obligations of governments to provide jobs.

In all five states, personal identities are strongly

connected to sub-national groupings, tribes or clans in Kazakhstan, Kyrgyzstan, and Turkmenistan, locality (*maḥalla*) in Tajikistan and Uzbekistan. Just how important these are became apparent during the Tajik civil war, when political factions divided sharply along *maḥalla* lines, with gender identities serving as important distinguishing characteristics. After the war, the political positioning of the *maḥalla*s became increasingly unequal, with the president's locality hogging the best posts, while people from *maḥalla*s that had supported the wartime opposition, as well as non-titular nationalities, were disadvantaged. In Central Asia generally, pressures toward group and/or national endogamy are growing, with access to political posts, patronage, and other resources often dependent on membership in internal groupings. In all of this gender identities serve as cultural markers, and have thus come to play a role at all levels of identity politics.

Bibliography

S. Akiner, *Tajikistan. Disintegration or reconciliation?* London 2001.

L. Handrahan, Gender and ethnicity in the transitional democracy of Kyrgyzstan, in *Central Asian Survey* 20:4 (2001), 467–96.

M. Kamp, Unveiling Uzbek women. Liberation, representation and discourse, 1906–1929, Ph.D. diss., University of Chicago 1998.

K. Kuehnast, Let the stone lie where it has fallen. Dilemmas of gender and generation in Post-Soviet Kyrgyzstan, Ph.D. diss., University of Minnesota 1997.

A. Kuru, Between the state and cultural zones. Nation building in Turkmenistan, in *Central Asian Survey* 21:1 (2002), 71–90.

N. Lubin, *Central Asians take stock. Reform, corruption, and identity*, Washington, D.C. 1995.

W. Mee, Country briefing paper. Women in the Republic of Uzbekistan, Asian Development Bank 2001, <www.adb.org/Documents/Books/Country_Briefing_Papers>.

N. Megoran, Theorizing gender, ethnicity and the nation-state in Central Asia, in *Central Asian Survey* 18:1 (1999), 99–110.

M. Tokhtakhodjaeva, *Between the slogans of communism and the laws of Islam*, trans. S. Aslam, ed. C. Balchin, Lahore 1995.

M. Tolmacheva, The Muslim woman in Soviet Central Asia, in *Central Asian Survey* 12:4 (1993), 531–48.

Colette Harris

Iran and Afghanistan

A century of political and social upheavals in Iran and Afghanistan, beginning in the late nineteenth century, situated women at the heart of diverse class, ethnic, national, and religious "imagined communities." In both countries, the link between gender and modernity played a significant role in shaping and representing the nation, women in the nation, and various subnational identities. Neither Iran nor Afghanistan was formally colonized, and both countries underwent periods of indigenous reform and revolution in the twentieth century.

During the Iranian Constitutional Revolution (1905–11), nationalists used female images – the daughters of Iran, wives/women of the *millat* (nation), and homeland (*vatan*) as mother – not only to define the concept of *tajaddud* (modernity), but also to link national, sexual, and religious boundaries. Contemporary press reports about the trafficking of peasant Shīʿī girls by Sunnī Turkmen tribes and Armenians of Ashkhabad, for example, produced a tragic context for collective ethnic and religious grievances and led to the emergence of new legal codes for the construction of "Iranianness." Notwithstanding women's political participation, secular nationalists (from Muslim as well as Armenian, Assyrian Christian, Jewish, Bahāʾī, and Zoroastrian communities) and Islamic conservatives used the concept of educated mothers and wives to debate various visions of the constitution.

Before Afghanistan's independence in 1919, Pushtun political dominance over Tajiks, Uzbeks, and Turkmens, with its emblematic tattoo on women's bodies and animals as private properties, strengthened the pre-Islamic feudal and *qabīla* (tribe) patriarchal concepts of women as signifier for sexuality, *fitna* (temptation), and *nāmūs* (honor) to enforce a Sunnī Sharīʿa identity for nation. Rebelling against King Amān Allāh's modern nationalist reforms, tribal chiefs demanded he divorce the queen for her unveiled presence at Loya Jirga assemblies and ceremonies. Women were caught between two opposing visions of Afghan's nationhood: the 1926 reformist Family Law with its symbolic urban-based modern representation of femininity and the conservative 1928 Loya Jirga's Nizām-nāmeh with its legitimization of purdah (seclusion).

The Pahlavī legal sanction on tribal clothing and women's veiling was instrumental in the consolidation of a unified state against Iran's diverse tribal and ethnic authorities (Azeris, Bakhtiaris, Gilanis, Kurds). The newly emerged nation-state and its icon, public women, conflicted with Iran's "national honor" – the familial position of women within Sharīʿa – and created a heterogeneous concept of nationhood, combining modern and traditional, Iranian culture and Islam. While the modernization of gender relations caught urban elite women between these two visions, the modernization policies of the "Great Civilization" dislocated the tribal productive center, the family, and turned village women from the owners of their produce into factory laborers and consumers. The acceleration of migration to the cities generated ideological and material tensions for the young generation of the popular classes, exposing them to new, public Westernized roles of women in mass media, higher education, and the professions. In the 1970s, intellectual, Islamic, and leftist responses to the monarchy's constructed metaphor of the modern nationhood addressed the regime's dominant "lipsticked" image of the modern emancipated (and sexualized) women as a threat to the moral fabric of society. Jalāl Āl Aḥmad's socially committed female characters in his literary works, ʿAlī Sharīʿatī's formulation of the linkages between women's oppression and "cultural imperialism," his elevation of an Islamic role model for women within family and nation, and Fidāʾiyīn-i Khalq's "masculinization" of women offered alternative identities. Āl Aḥmad's notion of *gharbzadigī* (Westoxification) pitted a nation of good and authentic Iranian men and women against a corrupt autocracy and its alien consumer-capitalist and neocolonialist agenda.

An "innovative" language of Shiʿism, elevating the militant sister and wife of *shāhid* (martyr) Imām Ḥusayn (grandson of the Prophet) in the "Tragedy of Karbala" (680 C.E.), and various female-specific symbols idealizing the cultural spectacle of the Islamization of gender – scarves, segregation of sexes in university classrooms, and female-led religious gathering – emerged as an indigenous, yet modern and progressive politics of the Islamic Revolution's identity, to mobilize women in the name of national unity. Despite a constitutional ban on the commercial use of the images of women, ideal images of veiled mothers, who raise "pious children for the Prophet's Kingdom," were used on posters, billboards, and stamps during the Iran-Iraq War, not only to elevate the concept of Iran's national identity but also to distinguish Shīʿī Iran from Sunnī Iraq. In the midst of crushing the country's workers' movement during the 1980s, valorizing "good *ḥijāb*" versus "bad *ḥijāb*," family over profession, the government used an invented tradition to create a sharp identity division between secular middle-class urban women and the Islamist provincial women of the popular class, asserting the future direction of Iran as well as controlling and making women conform to an idealized construct of womanhood. Since the emergence of a moderate state in the 1990s, and pressured by the Islamist and secular feminists who have found common ground to claim a counterculture to the politicization of gender identities, the government has adopted a policy of Islamic/Shīʿī modernization that attempts to reconcile the images of women as mothers and housewives with Iranian women's aspirations and achievements in public and professional life.

Kabul's Nixon Market shopping center symbolized modernist Westernization in the 1960s and early 1970s. However, mini-skirts, beauty pageants, co-education, and women's presence at nightclubs and rock concerts bore little relation to the experience of rural women. The 1978 Saur Revolution, the 1979 invasion by the Soviet Union, the 1992 seizure of power by the Mujāhidīn, and the 1996 takeover by the Taliban linked the major dichotomy between modernity and tradition with a politicized, gendered demarcation of Afghan's national identity. The PDPA's (People's Democratic Party of Afghanistan) support for Soviet occupation produced a split between secular, pro-Soviet women's organizations and feminist, anti-Soviet women's movements (for example, RAWA, the Revolutionary Association of the Women of Afghanistan). The subjugated women under the culturally and politically loaded symbol of the *burqaʿ* replaced the socialist image of women, ranging from urban educators in the countryside to singers and stage performers, and marked the nation's identification with a political yet conflictive tribal Islam, clearly expressed in Sebghatullah Mojaddadi's election speech, which, while claiming the equality of men and women under Islam, called the election of a woman president as a sign of a "nation in decline."

In Iran and Afghanistan, the search for a postcolonial modernity – Western, socialist, and Islamic – with its metaphorical association of new womanhood with new nationhood, has failed to subsume traditional and subnational identities within a hegemonic national culture. In both countries, the struggles over the nation and its "fragments" (women, ethnic and religious communities, popular classes) have always been strongly gendered. Women, though included like men as citizens, were given a limited space – as mothers and symbols of national and cultural identity – in the project of the national process. At the crossroads of modernization and the globalizing discourse of consumerism, human rights, and identity politics, women in Iran and Afghanistan will continue to contribute to the shaping of the meanings of "woman" and "nation."

Bibliography

J. Afary, Shiʾi narratives of Karbala and Christian rites of penance. Michel Foucault and the culture of the Iranian Revolution, 1978–1979, in *Radical History* 86 (2003), 7–35.

B. Anderson, *Imagined communities*, New York 1991.

C. M. Amin, *The making of the modern Iranian woman.*

Gender, state policy, and popular culture, 1865–1946, Gainesville, Fla. 2002.
A. Brodsky, *With all our strength. The Revolutionary Association of the Women of Afghanistan*, New York 2003.
P. Chatterjee, *The nation and its fragments. Colonial and postcolonial histories*, Princeton, N.J. 1993.
N. Dupree, Revolutionary rhetoric and Afghan women, in M. N. Shahrani and R. L. Canfield (eds.), *Revolutions and rebellions in Afghanistan*, Berkeley 1984, 306–40.
D. Ellis, *Women of the Afghan war*, Westport, Conn. 2000.
H. Emadi, *Repression, resistance, and women in Afghanistan*, Westport, Conn. 2002.
H. Esfandiari, *Reconstructed lives. Women and Iran's Islamic Revolution*, Washington, D.C. 1997.
J. de Groot, Coexisting and conflicting identities. Women and nationalisms in twentieth-century Iran, in R. R. Pierson, N. Chaudhuri, and B. McAuley (eds.), *Nation, empire, colony. Historicizing gender and race*, Bloomington, Ind. 1998, 139–65.
V. Moghadam (ed.), *Gender and national identity. Women and politics in Muslim societies*, Oxford 1994.
——, *Identity politics and women. Cultural reassertions and feminisms in international perspective*, Boulder, Colo. 1995.
A. Najmabadi, Hazards of modernity and morality. Women, state, and ideology in contemporary Iran, in D. Kandiyoti (ed.), *Women, Islam, and the state*, Philadelphia 1991, 663–87.
——, *The story of the daughters of Quchan. Gender and national memory in Iranian history*, Syracuse, N.Y. 1998.
G. Nashat, *Women and revolution in Iran*, Boulder, Colo. 1983.
P. Paidar, *Women and the political process in twentieth-century Iran*, Cambridge 1995.
E. Sanasarian, *The women's rights movement in Iran. Mutiny, appeasement, and repression from 1900 to Khomeini*, New York 1982.
F. Shirazi, *The veil unveiled. The hijab in modern culture*, Gainesville, Fla. 2001.
N. Yuval-Davis, *Woman, nation, state*, New York 1989.

FAKHRI HAGHANI

South Asia

Although South Asia is segmented along various axes of difference – ethnic, caste, class, gender, religion, language – the mobilization of these identities is the result of particular configurations of local and global political, social, and economic forces and of the emergence of specific constituencies and identity politics based on new forms of politicized religion. Located in a broader crisis of modernity and state legitimacy, identity politics based on politicized religion are modernist with a clear political project for control over the state and imposition of their agenda on others. This was seen in the Islamization campaign during Zia ul-Haq's regime in Pakistan, under General Ershad's rule in Bangladesh, and in the propagation of the Hindutva ideology espoused by the ruling Bharatiya Janata Party in India.

Since the 1980s a new configuration and redefinition of the contours and boundaries of the state, community, and the family in the region has emerged. Multiple identities are being particularized into singular religion-based identities imposed through force as well as embraced through affinity. Women in particular have been subject to contradictory political, economic, and social pressures and they have defined themselves, and have been defined and redefined, in their identities as women and as members of a nation, community, caste, and class group. That these identities are often at the cost of equal citizenship rights is epitomized by the following statement by Nur Jahan, a working class Muslim feminist from India: "If by making separate laws for Muslim women, you are trying to say that we are not citizens of this country, then why don't you tell us clearly and unequivocally that we should establish another country – not Hindustan or Pakistan but Auratstan [women's land]" (Chhachhi 1994, 74).

The characterization of the emergence of politicized religion in the region is contested. Analysts continue to debate whether contemporary states and particular religio-political identity groups should be labeled fundamentalist, communalist, nationalist, Islamist, majoritarian, fascist, or right-wing – each characterization reflecting particular political positionings. Although there are variations in the strength of politicized religion in each country there are common features in the ways in which the boundaries of the nation/community/family are constructed, (re)defined and protected with women/gender relations figuring as a crucial marker and signifier of identity.

A key determinant of identity politics in the South Asian region today is the role of the state in mobilizing and reproducing politicized religious identities. The process of the formation of India, Pakistan, and Bangladesh was itself based on an ideological mobilization that equated the nation with a particular community identity, despite avowals of secularism. The often forced recovery of women abducted by both sides during Indian partition was cast within a discourse of protection/ contamination/control over women's bodies in which citizenship was defined in religious community terms. In India and Pakistan each side emphasizes its difference through external discourses and internal processes of "othering" through the media, history textbooks, and popular discourses, often using the masculine/feminine dualism to bolster a militarized masculinity.

In India, nationalist identity was derived from a Sanskritized upper caste version of Hinduism, excluding other communities, tribals, and *dalits* (untouchables) at the same time as it incorporated a particular notion of gender relations and womanhood. Indian nationalism contained in itself the seeds of divisions that proliferated in the post-independence period. The continued existence of separate religion-based laws (called personal laws) to regulate marriage, inheritance, divorce, and adoption constructed a sharp disjunction between the professed secularism of the Indian state and the legal structure that governed the private domain. In the post-independence period the controversies over personal law led to a questioning of the state ideology of secularism itself. Social citizenship remains based on membership of a community and in all personal laws women are denied equal rights in varying degrees. These laws and the appropriation by Hindutva forces of the feminist demand for a uniform civil code have become a battleground for the defense of "authentic" minority Muslim and majority Hindu community identities. This defense is ironic since the process of codification of these laws for Hindus, Muslims, and Christians incorporated colonial Victorian assumptions and selective interpretation of texts by priests and mullahs, thereby constructing "imaginary" boundaries of each community and the family. Given the minority status of Muslims in India a progressive-regressive movement has determined the construction of Muslim identity and equal citizenship rights for Muslim women have been subordinated to the defense of the community. The upsurge in majoritarian Hindu fundamentalism, the destruction of the Babri Masjid in 1992, and the pogrom against Muslims in Gujarat in 2003 have once again led to a defensive reassertion of personal law as a symbol of Muslim identity.

Pakistan resolved the dilemma posed at its birth of whether it was a country "of Muslims" or "for Muslims" by constructing a national identity through a twin process of homogenizing Islam and enhancing the differences between men and women and Muslim and others. This was constructed through gender segregation, dress codes (shalwar kameez versus sari and chador and *chardiwari*) and legislating secondary status to women, minorities, and all Muslim sects other than Sunnī. From 1977 onwards issues of sexual, geographical, cultural, and moral boundary protection became central in public discourse and the private realm of the family came under increasing state supervision and control. The Hudood Ordinances, which combined misogynist views with public morality to control women's sexuality, were accompanied by an increase in public violence against women – those who transgressed social norms as well as those who were victims (for instance, rape was redefined as adultery in the Zina Ordinance).

The creation of Bangladesh on the basis of ethnic/linguistic/cultural nationalism (which required the dismantling of a Muslim identity uniting both wings of Pakistan) also contained contradictions. Contestations over secularism were subsequently framed within religious discourse as later military regimes moved away from the nationalist/socialist project of the Mujib period and slowly incorporated Islam as a state religion in the constitution and built alliances with fundamentalist groups. The government hence failed to prevent or control the increased issuance of fatwas by rural religious leaders backed by village elites ordering the burning or stoning to death of women, the harassment of intellectuals, the banning of the work of "blasphemous" writers, and attacks on non-governmental organizations

Global alliances have also played a significant role in bolstering fundamentalisms in the region – Saudi oil connections and patronage in Bangladesh, United States support to Pakistan as a frontline state against the Soviet supported Afghanistan, which fostered the Taliban, and the financial support from the Hindu diaspora for Hindutva in India. Integration into a global economy, capitalist markets, urban consumerism and political alliances have led to the emergence of particular constituencies – primarily middle-class – who support the political agenda of Islamization in Pakistan and Bangladesh and Hindutva in India.

In all three countries the state is neither monolithic nor are its policies uniform. Concurrent with the carving of national/communal identities with specific gender constructs, modernization policies have drawn women into the labor force, granted degrees of political representation at the national and local level, and provided for education. Similarly regime types do not necessarily indicate internal processes. In Pakistan the Family Laws Ordinance 1961, which gave women some rights in relation to marriage, divorce, and child custody was passed by a military government; while the Hudood Ordinances were not repealed by the democratic government, the Jamaat-e-Islami, a fundamentalist group, expanded under a democratic government in Bangladesh; and the worst forms of violence have been unleashed against Muslims and Christians in democratic secular India.

Central to the projects of religio-political groups is the control over women's bodies, mobility, sexuality, and reproductive capacity, and a reinscription of gender relations. The increase in public violence against women and the gendered and sexualized discourse of fundamentalist groups is in part a response to the increasing public visibility of women, the undermining of hegemonic masculinity in traditional patriarchal structures, and the growing consciousness and assertion of women's rights in the region.

Increasing numbers of women in all three countries are entering the more visible sectors of employment – export industries, banks, and offices – and in some cases taking on hitherto male jobs. Simultaneously there are reports of numerous cases where women have started asserting their rights to choice in marriage, property, maintenance, and divorce. It is in this changing context of modernity that the state and community has responded with measures to reassert control and redefine the contours of identity. State discourses and legal measures have wider implications since they sanction the right of control over women from the family/community to any man on the street. For instance, in Pakistan the institutionalization of laws such as Hudood, Evidence, and Qisas and Diyat – which reduce women to second-class citizens – have been primarily used against poor working-class and destitute women, but they also expose upper- and middle-class women to the constant threat of surveillance by the police, mullahs, and the evidence of any man. In Bangladesh community control was asserted through fatwas against women who transgressed social norms. In India the controversy over Muslim personal laws (the Shah Bano case) reasserted community control over Muslim women who sought to assert independent citizenship rights. There has been escalation in direct forms of violence against women ranging from tarring the midriffs of women wearing saris in Bangladesh, acid throwing, honor killings, to the glorification of *sati* (widow immolation) as a symbol of true Indian/Hindu womanhood. The centrality of sexual violence in the Hindutva political project was manifest in the pogrom in Gujarat in 2003. Violation of Muslim women's bodies/community boundaries, by acts of public rape and targeted attacks on their reproductive organs functioned to eliminate/humiliate/violate the minority community and simultaneously forge a new form of Hindu hegemonic masculinity that was virile and omnipotent.

Women have been agents as well as objects in the discourse and practice of religious fundamentalist movements in South Asia. The extensive mobilization and activism of women in fundamentalist movements in the region have raised problematic questions about agency, activism, and empowerment. Women in fundamentalist movements have incited, participated and justified violence against the "other" community. Despite supporting an agenda that curtails their rights and constructs images of the dependent, self-sacrificing, dutiful wife/mother, women in these movements have also experienced freedom from traditional restrictions on early marriage and mobility and have gained access to physical training and participation in the public political sphere. This feature of Hindu fundamentalism has been characterized as "controlled emancipation." The paradoxical nature of women's complicity and collusion in communalized identity politics is an area for further research and political engagement for women's movements that stress the significance of feminist agency.

The complexity of identity politics in the region is reflected in the diversity of political positions within the women's movements of the region. There are broadly three kinds of group: those who continue to speak on the basis of an undifferentiated notion of women, see religion as inherently irrational and patriarchal, and argue for a secular nonsexist law that guarantees equal citizenship and justice; those who articulate a dual identity as Muslim and Christian feminists and focus on reforming religious laws drawing on progressive reinterpretations of the Qur'ān and the Bible; and those who propose a combined strategy of reform plus a secular code of equal rights for women. New identity groups continue to emerge, such as the *dalit* feminist group in India who argue from an epistemological standpoint of the most oppressed and are critical of the mainstream women's movement. Women's groups in the region have also linked with transnational networks such as Women Living Under Muslim Laws as well as established regional and cross-border alliances, such as South Asian feminist networks and peace and democracy coalitions, thereby linking the issue of women/gender and identity politics with militarism and democratization in the region.

Bibliography

F. Agnes, Women, marriage and the subordination of rights, in P. Chatterjee and P. Jeganathan (eds.), *Community, gender and violence*, New Delhi 2000, 106–37.

P. Baccheta, Hindu nationalist women as ideologues. The Sangh, the Samiti and differential concepts of the Hindu nation, in K. Jayawardena and M. de Alwis (eds.), *Embodied violence. Communalising women's sexuality in South Asia*, London 1996, 126–67.

A. Basu, Hindu women's activism in India and the questions it raises, in P. Jeffery and A. Basu (eds.), *Appropriating gender. Women's activism and politicized religion in South Asia*, New York 1998, 167–84.

C. Bayly, *The origins of nationalism in South Asia. Patriotism and ethical government in the making of India*, Oxford 1998.

U. Butalia, Muslims and Hindus, men and women. Communal stereotypes and the partition of India, in T. Sarkar and U. Butalia (eds.), *Women and the Hindu right. A collection of essays*, New Delhi 1995, 58–81.

A. Chhachhi, The state, religious fundamentalism and women. Trends in South Asia, in *Economic and Political Weekly* 24:11 (1989), 567–78.

——, Forced identities. The state, communalism, fundamentalism and women in India, in D. Kandiyoti (ed.) *Women, Islam and the state*, London 1991, 144–75.

——, Identity politics, secularism and women. A South Asian perspective, in Z. Hasan (ed.), *Forging identities. Gender, communities and the state*, New Delhi 1994, 74–95.

S. Feldman, Manipulating gender, shifting state practices, and class frustrations in Bangladesh, in P. Jeffery and A. Basu (eds.), *Appropriating gender. Women's activism and politicized religion in South Asia*, New York 1998, 33–52.

F. Gardezi, Nationalism and state formation. Women's struggles and Islamization in Pakistan, in N. Hussain, S. Mumtaz, and R. Saigol (eds.), *Engendering the nation-state*, i, Lahore 1997, 79–110.

M. Guhathakurta, Religion, politics and women. The Bangladesh scenario, in Women Living Under Muslim Laws, Dossier 25 (2003), 71–6, <http://www.wluml.org/english/publistype.shtml?cmd%5B72%5D=c-1-Dossiers>.

T. Hansen, Controlled emancipation. Women and Hindu nationalism, in F. Wilson and B. D. Frederiksen (eds.), *Ethnicity, gender and the subversion of nationalism*, London 1994, 82–94.

N. Hussain, S. Mumtaz, and R. Saigol (eds.), *Engendering the nation-state*, i, Lahore 1997.

International Initiative for Justice, Threatened existence. A feminist analysis of the genocide in Gujarat, Bombay/ Delhi 2003, <http://www.onlinevolunteers.org/gujarat/ reports/ iijg/2003/>.

A. Jalal, The convenience of subservience. Women and the state in Pakistan, in D. Kandiyoti (ed.) *Women, Islam and the state*, London 1991, 77–114.

K. Jayawardena and M. de Alwis (eds.), *Embodied violence. Communalising women's sexuality in South Asia*, London 1996.

P. Jeffrey, Agency, activism, and agendas, in P. Jeffery and A. Basu (eds.), *Appropriating gender. Women's activism and politicized religion in South Asia*, New York 1998, 221–44.

P. Jeffery and A. Basu (eds.), *Appropriating gender. Women's activism and politicized religion in South Asia*, New York 1998.

P. Jeffery and R. Jeffery, Gender, community, and the local state in Bijnor, India, in P. Jeffery and A. Basu (eds.), *Appropriating gender. Women's activism and politicized religion in South Asia*, New York 1998, 123–42.

N. Kabeer, The quest for national identity. Women, Islam and the state in Bangladesh, in D. Kandiyoti (ed.), *Women, Islam and the state*, London 1991, 115–43.

N. Keddie, The new religious politics and women worldwide. A comparative study, in *Journal of Women's History* 10:4 (1999), 11–34.

N. Menon, Women and citizenship, in P. Chatterjee (ed.), *Wages of freedom. Fifty years of the Indian nation-state*, New Delhi 1998, 241–66.

J. Mirza, *Between chaddor and the market. Female office workers in Lahore*, Oxford 2002.

S. Rege, A *dalit* feminist standpoint, in A. Rao (ed.), *Gender and caste*, New Delhi 2003, 90–101.

S. Rouse, The outsider(s) within. Sovereignty and citizenship in Pakistan, in P. Jeffery and A. Basu (eds.), *Appropriating gender. Women's activism and politicized religion in South Asia*, New York 1998, 53–70.

T. Sarkar, Woman, community, and nation. A historical trajectory for Hindu identity politics, in P. Jeffery and A. Basu (eds.), *Appropriating gender. Women's activism and politicized religion in South Asia*, New York 1998, 89–106.

F. Shaheed, The other side of the discourse. Women's experiences of identity, religion and activism in Pakistan, in P. Jeffery and A. Basu (eds.), *Appropriating gender. Women's activism and politicized religion in South Asia*, New York 1998, 143–66.

——, Constructing identities. Culture, women's agency and the Muslim world, in Women Living Under Muslim Laws, Dossier 23/24 (2001), 1–11, <http://www.wluml.org/english/publistregional.shtml?cmd%5B24%5D=c-1-International>.

S. Shobhan, National identity, fundamentalism and the women's movement in Bangladesh, in V. M. Moghadam (ed.), *Gender and national identity. Women and politics in Muslim societies*, London 1994, 63–80.

P. van der Veer, *Religious nationalism. Hindus and Muslims in India*, Berkeley 1994.

AMRITA CHHACHHI

Turkey

Images of women have played a central role in Turkey's national project since the creation of a secularist republic in 1923. "Turkish" identity emerged from the process of nation-building that was associated with the transition from the Ottoman Empire, with its ties to Arabic and Persian Islamic culture, to the Republic of Turkey, which looked to Turkic roots and modern secularism as sources of identity. "Turkishness" was retrieved from folk culture (Mardin 2002) to become the vehicle of "modern" culture. In the process of shaping Turkish secular, national identities, policymakers sought to suppress ethnic diversity. In a continuation of reforms based on European models that had begun in the nineteenth century, Atatürk's government aimed to create a nationalist Turkish identity by transforming not only state institutions but also everyday life and customs, dress, bodily practices, and gender relations. The government abolished the fez (a distinctively Ottoman hat worn by men and often associated with the Islamic Sufi orders) in 1926, banned the headscarf in government buildings including schools, and generated an ideological promotion of gender equality. In this "state feminism," women were expected embody national ideals by appearing in public spaces, getting an education, entering the political realm, and pursuing unorthodox careers, a role epitomized by Atatürk's adopted daughter Sabiha Gökçen, who became a fighter pilot (Altınay 2004). But Altınay and other feminists have argued that women have also faced growing pressures to be loyal wives and sacrificing mothers, that the public image of the modern Turkish woman had little impact on everyday gender relations (Sirman 1989), and that women's liberated bodies have been the source of a "schizophrenic identity," which has left little room for women's personal fulfillment (Tekeli 1990) or even a sexualized or gendered identity.

The goals of the early Turkish Republic equated secularization and Westernization, which were contrasted with traditional Islamic practices. The traditionally dressed woman wearing a headscarf was the embodiment of backwardness and the Ottoman past. In the secularist imagination, such women continue to inhabit the margins of modern society, epitomized in Turkey's villages which have not yet been fully modernized and in the shanty towns on the outskirts of major cities where migrants from rural areas congregate and form the lowest class.

With the rise of Islamism, women's dress and the organization of gender became the focal point of yet another controversy over identity and national policy. In 1984, political protests erupted over the government's policy of banning headscarves on university campuses (Olsen 1985). Before this, women adopted modern dress when they entered schools and universities, giving up the headscarf as a sign of the traditional uneducated woman. Young Islamist women in the early 1980s were at the vanguard of a movement that had developed a new perspective on the relationship between national identity and the West. Influenced by the writings of thinkers such as Maudūdī in Pakistan and al-Quṭb in Egypt, Islamism was a growing transnational movement; it disrupted Orientalist dichotomies which equated modernity, technological development, and the West and contrasted them with the backwardness of the Muslim world. For many Islamists, the position of women and the headscarf became key symbols for asserting the relevance of Islam for the modern world. Women's identity in the Islamist movement is sharply distinguished from what both Islamists and secularists label the "traditional" Muslim woman, whom both see as a passive bearer of habits and local practices. The Islamist woman's headscarf is worn in a style distinctively different from that of the traditional village woman but similar to that of Islamist women across the globe, marking a Muslim identity that transcends national differences and identities.

The woman who adopts the Islamist headscarf is asserting a Muslim identity based on a conscious, personal decision rather than on submission to her community or to the authority of men (Göle 1996, Ewing 2000). Becoming knowledgeable about Islam through study groups and maintaining public visibility are important elements of women's Islamist practice which contrast with the traditional organization of gendered spaces. Some women have asserted an Islamic feminist position. When the Islamist Welfare Party first came to power for a short time in the late 1990s, some women who had played an active political role in the party were disappointed when their male colleagues failed to give them significant positions in the new government, and openly spoke out against efforts to relegate them back into the home. The Islamist headscarf also has a class dimension (White 2002): many of these women have gained access to higher education, seek professional careers, and lead urban middle-class lives. They assert an identity, not against modernity, but against specific forms of secularism and the dominance of Western European cultural ideals.

Bibliography

A. Altınay, *The myth of the military nation. Militarism, gender and education in Turkey*, New York 2004.

F. Acar, Women and Islam in Turkey, in Ş. Tekeli (ed.), *Women in modern Turkish society. A reader*, London 1995, 46–65.

Y. Arat, Feminists, Islamists, and political change in Turkey, in *Political Psychology* 19:1 (1998) 117–31.

F. M. Coşar, Women in Turkish Society, in L. Beck and N. Keddie (eds.), *Women in the Muslim world*, Cambridge, Mass. 1978, 124–40.

C. Delaney, *The seed and the soil. Gender and cosmology in Turkish village society*, Berkeley 1991.

K. P. Ewing, The violence of non-recognition. Becoming a "conscious" Muslim woman in Turkey, in A. Robben and M. Suárez-Orozco (eds.), *Cultures under siege. Collective violence and trauma in anthropological and psychoanalytic perspective*, Cambridge 2000, 248–71.

N. Göle, *The forbidden modern. Civilization and veiling*, Ann Arbor, 1996.

A. Kadıoğlu, Women's subordination in Turkey. Is Islam really the villain?, in *Middle East Journal* 48 (1994), 645–60.

D. A. Kandiyoti, Women and the Turkish state. Political actors or symbolic pawns?, in N. Yuval-Davis and F. Anthias (eds), *Woman, nation, state*, London 1989, 126–49.

——, End of empire. Islam, nationalism, and women in Turkey, in D. A. Kandiyoti (ed.), *Women, Islam, and the state*, London 1991, 22–47.

D. A. Kandiyoti and A. Saktanber (eds.), *Fragments of culture. The everyday of modern Turkey*, New Brunswick, N.J. 2002, 191–217.

Ş. Mardin, *Religion and social change in modern Turkey*, Albany, N.Y. 1989.

Y. Navaro-Yashin, *Faces of the state. Secularism and public life in Turkey*, Princeton, N.J. 2002.

E. Olsen, Muslim identity and secularism in contemporary Turkey. "The headscarf dispute," in *Anthropological Quarterly* 58:4 (1985), 161–9.

A. Saktanber, Becoming the "other" as a Muslim in Turkey. Turkish women vs. Islamist women, in *New Perspectives on Turkey* 11 (Fall 1994), 99–134.

N. Sirman, Feminism in Turkey. A short history, in *New Perspectives on Turkey* 3:1 (Fall 1989), 1–34.
Ş. Tekeli, The meaning and limits of feminist ideology in Turkey, in F. Özbay (ed.), *Women, family and social change in Turkey*, Bangkok 1990, 1–12.
J. B. White, *Islamist mobilization in Turkey. A study in vernacular politics*, Seattle 2002.

KATHERINE PRATT EWING

The United States

In the United States Muslims face a constant challenge to assert their identities as Muslim, but also have a legitimate stake in being "American." This is due to the widespread racism, prejudice and negative stereotypes of Islam as a backward and violent religion, oppressive of women. Mainstream society suspects an American cannot also be a Muslim.

Research into Muslim women's identity in the United States is still in its infancy, with many studies focusing only on the issue of *ḥijāb*, rather than on broader questions of identity (Read and Bartkowski 1999, Alvi, Hoodfar, and McDonough 2003). Shahnaz Khan's *Muslim Women: Crafting a North American Identity* is an exception. Though her study focuses on women in Toronto, it can be easily argued that her findings are equally applicable to the United States (due to the similarity in political, economical, and social/cultural mores and contexts). Khan identified a "third space" for Muslim women's identity – an ambiguous, even hybrid identity, where Muslim women carve out a space between the mainstream racism and discrimination they face as Muslims, and any patriarchal religious dogmas that seek to control them (Khan 2000).

An identity not deeply explored by Khan in her book, but highlighted by Aminah Beverly McCloud in her work on African American Muslims (1995), is one not of hybridity, but more of synthesis. McCloud looks at the ways African Americans, who already have an American identity, take on or adapt Islamic practices, beliefs, and customs when becoming Muslim, or establishing Muslim communities. Her observations on the fusion of these two identities (American and Muslim) are also applicable to immigrants, and especially the children of immigrants. Racism, discrimination, and a sense of being cut off from one's home culture often galvanize Muslim women into feeling pride in their heritage, so that they seek to become observant and pious Muslims while retaining a strong sense of the right to be modern American women. This is one of the most interesting aspects of Muslim women's identity in the United States in the twenty-first century.

Observant Muslims in the United States are usually associated in some way with one of the major Muslim associations, whether as formal members, as recipients of a magazine, or as regular attendees at national or regional conferences. Major associations such as the Islamic Society of North America (ISNA), the Islamic Circle of North America (ICNA), the Council on American-Islamic Relations (CAIR), the Muslim American Society (MAS) broadly agree on issues related to Muslims as United States citizens, namely that the United States Constitution offers Muslims rights and guarantees to practice their faith and to be full citizens in the United States polity. These mainstream associations promote a vision of Islam that stresses peaceful co-existence, interfaith dialogue, and integration into mainstream United States society, while at the same time maintaining Islamic heritage. (See numerous articles in *Islamic Horizons*, the ISNA's magazine, and news releases by CAIR.) At the 2003 Annual ISNA Convention, held in Chicago, the American Muslim Political Coordinating Council (made up of the American Muslim Alliance, the American Muslim Council, CAIR, and the Muslim Political Action Committee) distributed an open letter to the ISNA attendees urging Muslims to vote in the next federal election. Voting is presented as Muslims' fulfilling their "duty to [their] religion in part by fulfilling [their] duty to [their] nation" (CAIR 2003).

Muslim women are not well represented in the executive bodies of these associations, though they are involved as activists at all other levels (as well as behind the scenes, as wives of executives, see Ali 2003, 16–24). Nevertheless, the associations themselves promote the concept that men and women are equal in Islam. A new generation of Muslim women, especially the youth born in the United States to immigrant parents, along with those converting to Islam from United States society, has been influenced by this discourse. Hence, right across the United States there are self-assured, dynamic young women who also embrace their Islamic faith with confidence (see the profile of Asma Gul Hasan in Rhodes 2002). Some creative synthesis of traditional Muslim practices and traditional United States customs are taking place.

For instance, many of the young women in this category embrace the traditional Islamic dress of *ḥijāb*. But their rationale for doing so is tied to an inverted Western feminist discourse. Mainstream Western feminists view the *ḥijāb* as a symbol of Muslim women's oppression (Govier 1995). These young women claim the *ḥijāb* as an empowerment for women. Their argument is based on the Western feminist critique of the male gaze and the "beauty myth" (Wolf 1992). *Ḥijāb* is seen as liberation from mainstream American culture's obsession with and promotion of the beautiful, thin female body. In newspaper articles, these young women emphasize that their body is their own, that in *ḥijāb* they are not sex objects, and that they have been liberated from the "thin is beautiful" pressures that lead many of their non-Muslim friends into anorexia or bulimia (Farooqi 2002, Bullock 2002).

The *ḥijāb* itself is usually an adaptation of mainstream American fashion. Rather than a traditional wide piece of cloth wrapped around the body, many will wear Western dress – a skirt from Gap, a shirt from Chateau, and shoes from Payless – with a headscarf pinned under the chin. This outfit allows for greater freedom of movement than the traditional wrap. Many will play sport, attend a gym, or ride a bicycle dressed in this way.

Another creative adaptation of a traditional American institution is the emergence of an "all-girls Muslim prom." Since the pious Muslim cannot date or attend dances with men, the high school ritual of the prom is an existential dilemma for many Muslims. Not wanting to succumb to the pressure of being "too nerdy" not to have a date for the prom, many girls want to attend, even without a date. The prom occasions power struggles between parents adamant the teen should not go, and the teen adamant she should. A creative solution has emerged in San Jose and other towns across the United States. For the 2003 graduates in San Jose, a banquet hall was hired. The girls arrived at the hall in their *ḥijāb*, but removed it once inside, being dressed in a typical prom outfit, with make-up, jewelry, and their hair done. They sat down to eat a three-course meal, and then danced to Britney Spears. And at sunset, they turned the music off, donned their *ḥijāb*, and prayed the *maghrib* (sunset) prayer (Brown 2003).

Muslim women in this category of those attempting to synthesize being American and being Muslim have a strong sense of their equality with men in Islam. Many will argue that equality need not mean identicality as liberal feminists promote; rather they align more with the "different but equal" school, more akin to French feminism (Badawi 1995). They believe, like Aminah Assilmi, a popular Muslim woman speaker at religious conferences, that they adhere to true Islam, rejecting the cultural "baggage" of practices from their countries of origin that may be oppressive of Muslim women (Assilmi and Disuqi). Indeed, as Cayer found for young women in Toronto, though it can be replicated across the United States also, many young women embrace Islam and the headscarf as a way of resisting parental pressures that they find limiting and restrictive, especially parental pressure to marry someone from their own ethnic background ("I have the right in Islam to say 'no' to your suggested candidate") or as a way to promote their desire for education and a career ("Islam gives me the right to be educated, and if I am covered and a practicing Muslim woman, no one can deny me the right to a career") (Cayer 1996). So while embracing an observant Muslim lifestyle (praying, fasting, wearing *ḥijāb*), these young Muslim women are not jettisoning a modern or American lifestyle. Many expect to have careers, and if they marry, to have husbands who will do housework and share childcare (Bullock 2002).

Another example of creative synthesis is the growing Muslim music industry in the United States: this conforms to traditional Islamic law's eschewing of all instruments but the drum, but addresses the needs and concerns of the youth. Songs in English, such as "Do you think you can fool him?" by Mustaqim Sahir, or "Allah is enough for me," by Zain Bhikha, praise the Prophet Muḥammad, extol the beauties of Paradise, stress the necessity of prayer, and warn of the dangers of a United States "sex and drug" culture.

All this has also had an impact on immigrant parents, and it is not uncommon, as I have seen, to find mothers adopting the headscarf after their daughters have done so, or to find themselves praying and observing Ramadan, while in their twenties in their countries of origin they may not have (Bullock 2003). In addition, many Americans, from all walks of life (Native, African, Latino, Caucasian), are attracted by the vision of Islam this youth movement adheres to, and are converting in large numbers to Islam, adopting an observant practice of the religion. Thus many Muslims negotiate their identity in the United States as an effort at synthesizing a modern American lifestyle with an observant Islamic lifestyle.

Bibliography

Primary Sources

S. Ali, Building a movement. A woman's work, in *Islamic Horizons* (May/June 1424/2003), 16–24.

A. Assilmi and R. al-Disuqi, *Rights of Muslim women and their potential for impact in society*, video lecture produced by MeccaCentric Da'wah Group.

P. Brown, At Muslim prom, it's a girls-only night out, in *New York Times*, 9 June 2003, 9.

CAIR (Council on American-Islamic Relations), America Muslim News Briefs, 2 September 2003, email distribution list.

M. Farooqi, Wearing hijab changed my life, *Las Postias College Express*, 29 October 2002, 10.

K. Govier, Shrouded in black, *Toronto Star*, 25 September 1995, A19.
A. J. Rhodes, Riding tall. A Muslim cowgirl, in *Azizah Magazine* (Winter 2002), 68–70.

SECONDARY SOURCES
S. S. Alvi, H. Hoodfar, and S. McDonough (eds.), *The Muslim veil in North America. Issues and debates*, Toronto 2003.
J. Badawi, *Gender equity in Islam. Basic principles*, Plainfield, Ind. 1995.
K. Bullock, *Rethinking Muslim women and the veil. Challenging historical and modern stereotypes*, Herndon, Va. 2002.
C. Cayer, *Hijab*, narrative, and the production of gender among second generation, Indo-Pakistani, Muslim women in greater Toronto, M.A. thesis, York University, Toronto 1996.
S. Khan, *Muslim women. Crafting a North American identity*, Gainsville, Fla. 2000.
A. B. McCloud, *African American Islam*, New York 1995.
J. Read and J. P. Bartkowski, Identity negotiation in contemporary Islam. Muslim women's view of the veil, Association Paper, American Sociological Association (ASA) 1999.
A. S. Roald, *Women in Islam. The Western experience*, London 2001.
N. Wolf, *The beauty myth. How images of beauty are used against women*, New York 1992[2].
J. Zine, Redefining resistance. Towards an Islamic subculture in schools, in *Race Ethnicity and Education* 3 (2000), 293–316.

KATHERINE BULLOCK

Western Europe

THE POLITICAL MOBILIZATION OF MUSLIM MINORITIES IN THE WEST: A GENDER (UN)FRIENDLY PROJECT?

Mass migration movements are very symptomatic of this age we call global. Massive flows of people move from north to south, from east to west to seek a better future for themselves and their children (Appadurai 2000). During the 1950s and the 1960s a sizeable number of Muslims participated in an exodus from south to north within the scope of larger labor agreements that brought them to Western Europe (see, for example, the case of Belgium in Martens 1976). Having left with the hope of returning home after a few years of hard work, they found that the few years became an indefinite period once the second generation was born. Today this diaspora of Muslims, which is ethnically very heterogeneous in its composition, forms with its 12 million citizens one of the largest religious minorities in Western Europe (Dassetto et al. 2001). However, the considerable unemployment rate and low level of education make this group also one of the weakest groups on the sociopolitical level. In most Western European countries the Muslim populations are locally perceived as a problem category, which can only be dealt with through adjusted policy measures focused on the key concept of integration. Events like those of 11 September 2001 have added to this problematic perspective through inscribing this group into a wider, global discourse in which terrorism and security are the key words (Zemni 2002, Shahid and van Koningsveld 2002). The actual development of European Islam is monitored on the premise that certain tendencies may develop that could threaten the national security.

In a context in which Islam is perceived as a threat and Muslims are seen as a problem, several counter-movements have been developing to contest these a priori racist positions. At first these protest movements mainly organized themselves as a reaction against the electoral successes of extreme right movements in several European countries and also against the persistent exclusion of Muslims. The driving ideology of universal humanism of this first anti-racist movement, however, has underrated the importance that minorities accord to the recognition of their cultural and religious identities (Modood 1997). This importance in the last decades has become clear through the mobilization of different groups around cultural and religious claims, for example the Islamic headscarf issue in most Western European countries. More than just seeking socioeconomical and political equality, these groups redefine the notion of citizenship, including a recognition of their religious and cultural identity (one of the clearest illustrations of this development can be found in the spectacular rise of the Arab European League in Belgium and in Holland). The so-called neutrality of the universalistic premises of citizenship is defied and unmasked as a particular white middle-class self definition (Werbner 2003).

The notion of identity politics – to which this last political mobilization refers – is, however, not an undisputed concept, either in politics or in theoretical writing. In a large sense identity politics refers to any political mobilization centered around a particular identity, be it ethnic, sexual (women's issues, gay movement), or functional (labor movement centered around the workers as a defined category) (Calhoun 1994). In this entry this concept is used primarily to refer to the mobilization of ethnic and religious groups. The entry tries to offer a summary elaboration of this issue through a focus on the relationship between identity politics and women's rights. When the political mobilization of Muslim minorities in Western Europe is discussed, the issue of gender quickly pops up into the foreground.

Women's rights or group rights?

When identity claims are articulated by Muslim groups, feminist critiques arise immediately. Political mobilization of Muslims is often criticized because of its lack of attention to gender issues. One of the most famous essays offering this argument is that of Okin (1999). She states that the widely heard call for recognition of cultural rights sustains the patriarchal structure of these groups. To illustrate this statement, she refers to the Islamic societies where practices such as female genital mutilation are present.

Following the same line of argument, though from a different theoretical perspective, are authors such as Yuval-Davis (1993, 1997) who analyze the genesis of nationalism and other ethnic movements. While Okin can be situated within the liberal school of thought, Yuval-Davis rather belongs to classical "gender studies," combining poststructuralist, politologist, and anthropological perspectives. She takes over Benedict Anderson's argument for the definition of nations or ethnic groups – which she equates analytically in her argument – as "imagined communities." To maintain this collective imaginary, boundaries have to be constructed and kept. To achieve this, women take key positions: they are designated as the transmitters of cultural traditions and customs, and often symbolize the collective honor. When the ethnical or national group is threatened, the control of women and their sexual activity will be the first target of the group (Yuval-Davis 1993). Consequently, Yuval-Davis argues, in a context in which the ethnic group is in constant defense, such as is the case with migration, women will be subjected to a much greater control from the community. Every identity claim will go in the direction of more "cultural purity" and more control of the women. Again, the example of Muslim women in Great Britain is offered to illustrate this position (Yuval-Davis 1997, 201).

What is needed, then, is a transversal policy in which women of different identities ally themselves for the struggle, without losing the ethnical rootedness that would generate a constant dialogue and negotiation among the women (Yuval-Davis, 1997, 202). Other alternatives are found in the creation of a "third space" – a term developed by Homi Bhabha – in which neither the culture of origin nor the dominant culture would rule, a space of hybridity in which ethnicity would not be reduced to a particular vision over culture, and in which women could recompose their cultural identity and contest the patriarchal order of their community (Thiara 2003, Khan 1998).

Empowerment through identity politics

In the first line of arguments outlined here, a skeptical position was taken as to the possible compatibility of political mobilization through an ethnic line and the effects it would have for female members of that community. This argument assumes the a priori position of an oppressive patriarchal ethnic community. Any political measure that would empower the community as a whole would be negative for women. Though it is a fact that issues related to women are regularly marginalized in the political struggle for cultural recognition – just as they are marginalized an *any* struggle for political rights that is not explicitly feminist – we argue that this opposition, which is presented between ethnic mobilization and women's rights, is based on an essentialization of both the community and the women.

A first reason to argue against this opposition is the homogeneous and oppressive description that is given of minority cultures, and more specifically of Muslim cultures. It is quite striking to see how an opposition is made between the majority culture in which oppressive structures would not be as active, and an Islamic minority culture in which they are dominant. This vision underestimates the complexity and diversity present among Muslim minorities; it also reproduces the Orientalist view in which a liberated Western majority is contrasted with an oppressive Muslim minority (Ahmed 1994, Khan 1998). Furthermore, by stating in advance that an identity politics approach that is organized across ethnic lines can only reproduce the patriarchal structures, the same equation of ethnicity with culture, criticized by authors such as Yuval-Davis (1997, 200), is made. The ethnic group is equated with a particular vision of their culture, which undercuts any dynamism. The diverse and hybrid characteristic of culture is, however, not an objective to strive for, but is rather the *reality* from which analysis ought to depart (Friedman 1997). To fully understand the dynamism of identity politics, a dissociation has to be made between ethnicity – which refers to a "we-belonging" related to common origin (Roosens, 1998) – and culture. This means understanding these political claims as claims for *recognition*, in which religion plays a fundamental structuring role of identification for the group here concerned (Calhoun 1994, Modood 1997, 1998, Werbner 2003). It also means analyzing how this political struggle for recognition always goes together with a constant internal renegotiation of the different dynamics that are present among the community. Political struggle does not change the complexity of the social reality, it merely reduces its representation in order to attain goals. Arguing the contrary would serve to reduce the social reality to the political representation of it (see also Modood 1998 382).

A second fundamental reason why we argue against this opposition is because of the construction and definition of emancipation in relation to the women here concerned. Firstly, the only relationship this vision acknowledges between a woman and her community is one of victimhood. Women – and certainly Muslim women – can only be oppressed. Secondly, the only true emancipation for these women will be attained through an individual, secular process of emancipation. This affirmation not only reproduces a very particular definition of emancipation – a Western liberal definition in which the individual is artificially cut off from the group – it also and foremost ignores the empowering processes that are active within the community precisely through the use of group-logics. Only a few women will accept a vision of feminism that puts them in conflict with their origin and ethnic background. They will rather seek for a way of emancipation that respects all aspects of their identity (Khan 1998, Thiara 2003). Several empirical studies on Muslim women in a migration context and in the homeland show how one can speak of an "Islamic feminism" that does not oppose the essential structuring role that religion takes in the self-identity of the group (Amiraux 2003, Göle 2003, Torab 1996). Several authors have, however, debated the feminist calibre of these movements (see, for example, Moghadam 2002). The empowering of women is legitimized through the construction of alternative interpretations of the religious sources that are women-friendly and contest patriarchal dominance. To ignore the fact that these women are racialized and ethnicized next to being women, and thus that a struggle for ethnical and/or religious recognition is as important to them as it is for their fathers and brothers, is to ignore a fundamental dimension of their identity and emancipation.

Bibliography

L. Ahmed, *Women and gender in Islam. Historical roots of a modern debate*, New Haven, Conn. 1992.

V. Amiraux, Discours voilés sur les musulmanes en Europe. Comment les musulmans sont-ils devenus des musulmanes?, in *Social Compass* 50:1 (2003), 85–96.

A. Appadurai, *Modernity at large. Cultural dimensions of globalization*, Minneapolis 2000.

C. Calhoun, Social theory and the politics of identity, in C. Calhoun (ed.), *Social theory and the politics of identity*, Oxford 1994, 9–36.

F. Dassetto, B. Maréchal, and J. Nielsen (eds.), *Convergences musulmanes. Aspects contemporains de l'islam dans l'Europe élargie*, Louvain-la-Neuve 2001.

J. Friedman, Global crises, the struggle for cultural identity and intellectual porkbarrelling. Cosmopolitans versus locals, ethnics and nationals in an era of de-hegemonization, in P. Werbner and T. Modood (eds.), *Debating cultural hybridity. Multi-cultural identities and the politics of anti-racism*, London 1997, 70–89.

N. Göle, Musulmanes et modernes. Voile et civilisation en Turquie, Paris 2003.

S. Khan, Muslim women. Negotiations in the third space, in *Signs. Journal of Women in Culture and Society* 23:2 (1998), 463–94.

A. Martens, *Les immigrés. Flux et reflux d'une main-d'œuvre appoint*, Louvain 1976.

T. Modood, "Difference," cultural racism and anti-racism, in P. Werbner and T. Modood, (eds.), *Debating cultural hybridity. Multi-cultural identities and the politics of anti-racism*, London 1997, 238–54.

——, Anti-essentialism, multiculturalism and the "recognition" of religious groups, in *Journal of Political Philosophy* 6:4 (1998), 378–99.

V. M. Moghadam, Islamic feminism and its discontents. Towards a resolution of the debate, in *Signs. Journal of Women in Culture and Society* 27:4 (2002), 1135–71.

S. M. Okin, *Is multiculturalism bad for women?*, Princeton, N.J. 1999.

E. Roosens, *Eigen grond eerst? Primordiale autochtonie. Dilemma van de multiculturele samenleving*, Leuven 1998.

W. A. R. Shahid and P. S. van Koningsveld, The negative image of Islam and Muslims in the West. Causes and solutions, in W. A. R. Shahid and P. S. van Koningsveld (eds.), *Religious freedom and the neutrality of the state. The position of Islam in the European Union*, Leuven 2001, 74–94.

R. K. Thiara, South Asian woman and collective action in Britain, in J. Andall (ed.), *Gender and ethnicity in contemporary Europe*, Oxford 2003, 79–96.

A. Torab, Piety as gendered agency. A study of Jalaseh ritual discourse in an urban neighbourhood in Iran, in *Journal of the Royal Anthropological Institute* 2:2 (1996), 235–52.

P. Werbner, The politics of multiculturalism in the New Europe, in B. Saunders and D. Haljan (eds.), *Whither multiculturalism. A politics of dissensus*, Leuven 2003, 47–58.

N. Yuval-Davis, Gender and nation, in *Ethnic and Racial Studies* 16:4 (1993), 621–32.

——, Ethnicity, gender relations and multiculturalism, in P. Werbner and T. Modood (eds.), *Debating cultural hybridity. Multicultural identities and the politics of anti-racism*, London 1997, 175–80.

S. Zemni, Islam, European identity and the limits of multiculturalism, in W. A. R. Shadid and P. S. van Koningsveld (eds.), *Religious freedom and the neutrality of the state. The position of Islam in the European Union*, Leuven 2001.

Nadia Fadil

Infanticide and Abandonment of Female Children

Overview

Female infanticide has been practiced from earliest times to the present in a wide variety of cultures. The practice usually results from a combination of poverty, lack or scarcity of resources, patriarchal social order, preservation of family honor, and the low status of women. If inheritance goes through the male line, if sons and not daughters support their parents in old age, if daughters join their husbands' families and thereafter contribute their labor to them, if families must furnish daughters with dowries upon marriage, if adequate food and care is available only in quantities sufficient for existing children, then a newborn daughter may be considered a burden and the preference for a male child may be a rational if regrettable economic choice.

In Muslim societies, the practice of female infanticide is the subject of an extensive and well-known religious discourse. The Qurʾān addresses the practice in a famous and much-quoted verse: "When the sun shall be darkened, when the stars shall be thrown down, when the mountains shall be set moving, when the pregnant camels shall be neglected, when the savage beasts shall be mustered, when the seas shall be set boiling, when the souls shall be coupled, when the buried infant shall be asked for what sin she was slain, when the scrolls shall be unrolled, when heaven shall be stripped off, when Hell shall be set blazing, when Paradise shall be brought nigh, then shall a soul know what it has produced" (81:1–14). This passage refers to the events that will precede the Day of Judgment. Taken together, events such as polluting the earth with blood from an infant buried alive or of her accusing her murderers who must face the harshest of judgments for their crime are unimaginably horrific calamities. Virtually all jurists have taken this passage to confirm that female infanticide is in Islamic law equivalent to the crime of murder. Criticizing the attitudes of such parents who reject their female children, the Qurʾān further states: "And when any of them is given the good tidings of a girl, his face is darkened and he chokes inwardly, as he hides him from the people because of the evil of the good tidings that have been given unto him, whether he shall preserve it in humiliation, or trample it into the dust. Ah, evil is that they judge!" (16:58–9).

Other passages reinforce the illegality of infanticide and place a high value on family relations: "Say: 'Come, I will recite what your Lord has forbidden you: that you associate not anything with Him, and to be good to your parents, and not to slay your children because of poverty; We will provide you and them" (6:151). Similarly, we read, "And slay not your children for fear of poverty; We will provide for you and them; surely the slaying of them is a grievous sin" (17:31); "What, has your Lord favored you with sons and taken to Himself from the angels females? Surely it is a monstrous thing you are saying!" (17:42).

According to the Qurʾān, providence determines the sex of the fetus: "To God belongs the Kingdom of the heavens and the earth; He creates what He will; He gives to whom He will females, and He gives to whom He will males or He couples them, both males and females; and He makes whom He will barren. Surely He is all knowing, All-powerful" (42:49).

The *ḥadīth* literature also contains many sayings of the Prophet Muḥammad that express his high regard for daughters and for their proper upbringing. According to both Bukhārī and Muslim, the Prophet said, "Whoever maintains two girls till they attain maturity, he and I will come on the Resurrection Day like this; and he joined his fingers." Similarly, Ibn Ḥanbal reported, "Whosoever has a daughter and he does not bury her alive, does not insult her, and does not favor his son over her; God will enter him into Paradise," and "Whosoever supports two sisters till they mature, he and I will come in the Day of Judgment as this (and he pointed with his two fingers held together)." Islamic modernists have cited these and other *ḥadīth*s to demonstrate that Islam calls for kind and respectful treatment of daughters.

In recent years, women's rights advocates have built on the work of the Islamic modernists to show that Islam does not favor males over females. Indeed, they insist, the Qurʾān from the outset called for women's equality and inherent rights. Verse 16:59 quoted earlier is among the passages taken to demonstrate that Islam condemns all forms of violence against women. The usual approach is to emphasize the low status of women before Islam, which is proven by the practice of female infanticide, and the improved status of women after Islam was revealed, which is proven by the many verses guaranteeing women's rights. Islam's most fundamental guarantee of women's rights is simply the right to live. Islam then calls on parents to treat both male and female children with kindness, thereby making gender equality central to its message. Islam, they argue, clearly protects the rights of women but also the disadvantaged such as orphans, the infirm, and the aged, indicating that its goal is to secure social justice for all. Nevertheless, the Qur'ān and *ḥadīth* do not determine behavior as much as interact with local custom, family honor, and economic need to produce guidelines, which vary enormously from region to region. In some regions mothers may decide to commit infanticide or abandon a newborn child when an older child is still nursing. The mother knows that the older child will die without adequate nutrition and if the older child is healthy and male and if the newborn is female or perhaps handicapped or sickly, the latter may be killed or abandoned. This is considered regrettable but not a crime. The real crime, of course, is the global and regional economic inequality that forces families to make such unhappy choices.

In recent years, new reproductive technologies such as ultrasound and amniocentesis procedures have enabled prospective parents to determine the sex of the unborn and this has led to the intentional abortion of female fetuses and to the prevalence of male infants in certain regions and social strata in India, China, and many other societies. Worldwide, at least 80 million girls who would otherwise be expected to be alive are "missing," as a result of sex-selective abortions, infanticide, or neglect.

Islamic authorities have viewed the new reproductive technologies with favor only if the purpose is to enable an infertile couple to have children. The use of egg or sperm donors is generally frowned upon because it tampers with family lineage. While opinions vary on the legality of abortion for the purpose of family planning, abortions for the purpose of sex selection are not approved.

Despite the views of the religious authorities, many women are caught in a dilemma. They must produce sons or risk social censure and abandonment. The woman who successfully produces sons for her husband's family can expect to gain marital stability, higher social status, greater authority within the family, and material rewards. Often a young woman will accept a low status within her marriage in the expectation of a higher status at a more senior age. It is a means of self-preservation in families and societies constrained by patriarchal customs. The woman has been socialized to understand that rebelling may mean the end of her marriage, loss of status, and economic loss not only for herself but also for her kinship network. While the stable nuclear or extended family remains the basis of Muslim society in theory, the reality for many women is very different. Divorce, the former husband's failure to pay alimony and child support, and outright abandonment confront many women. Such fears may make sex-selected abortion the best course of action for individual and family survival. Some women also state that they do not wish to bring daughters into a social context in which they are not wanted. Such women, and indeed their families, should not be condemned, for they are trying to advance their mutual or divergent interests in a discriminatory and difficult environment.

In Pakistan, women activists have been exceptionally visible in campaigning against sex-selective reproductive practices. In utero diagnosis has enabled physicians to identify hundreds of diseases at an early stage of pregnancy, but the valuable medical procedure can easily be misused. Ultrasound is more often than not used to determine the sex of the fetus and female fetuses are aborted not only by impoverished women but also by women in the middle and upper classes who find it in their interests to bear male children. Such women and their marital families covet the prestige associated with producing male children and social pressure can be considerable. Pakistani medical personnel increasingly refuse to disclose the sex of the fetus because of the prevalence of sex selection, but prospective parents may then seek another more cooperative medical care provider. The result is a disproportionate number of male infants and perhaps 3.1 million missing females in Pakistan.

Neglect of female infants may be more common than infanticide or sex-selected abortion in some areas. In Egypt, more than 600,000 females are missing from the Egyptian population, thereby skewing the expected male:female sex ratio. Impoverished parents give inferior food and medical care to the less valued female infants and children who may then succumb to respiratory infections, diarrhea, and malnutrition. Researchers in Egypt conducted a national survey, which showed that while infant mortality was lower for females for the first month after birth, it rose rapidly after the neonatal period, indicating parental or care-giver neglect. To date there are few statistical surveys on the neglect of female infants elsewhere, though indications are that the practice is far from rare in impoverished regions.

In Sudan, female or male infanticide is illegal and rare but is considered less shameful than is pregnancy in unmarried women. Often a family may abandon the infant to avoid damaging family honor. Such infants may end up in orphanages where care is limited. Sudanese families wanting household servants sometimes informally adopt female children from the orphanages, but males usually remain without a respectable social role. Reliable statistics on the abandonment of female children in Sudan and elsewhere are virtually non-existent, although anecdotal evidence suggests a need for a viable childcare system in many urban areas.

In recent years, human rights activists have made female infanticide, neglect, and abandonment the first of many human rights violations that threaten women's lives. Critics have argued that the human rights framework ignores political, social, cultural, and economic constraints on women's behavior and derives in part from assumptions that non-European peoples and cultures are encased in passive and unchanging traditions that are fundamentally oppressive to women. The universalizing human rights discourse has indeed confronted local ethnic, religious, and cultural norms that may command the loyalty of women and men. The solution is to emphasize the wide range and variation in cultural practices within any given tradition, the many ways to interpret religious texts, and the fact that all cultures are formed from multiple influences and evolve with the times.

It is not clear whether the international women's human rights campaigns against violence against women will help advance Muslim women's rights. Certainly the new medical technologies have enabled governments and extended families to extend their control over women's sexuality and reproductive practices. Sex-selective feticide is considered more humane and certainly far easier than infanticide, neglect, or abandonment and is far more common than the earlier means of sex selection. The resulting imbalance between males and females may cause social disturbances in the future including trafficking in women, forced prostitution, and other social ills. The human rights campaigns may draw attention to the problem and the heightened awareness may lead governments and non-governmental organizations to press for reforms.

Change may come in part through criminalizing feticide, abandonment, and neglect, but more importantly through family law reform that gives women equal rights in marriage and divorce, inheritance, child custody, alimony, and a choice of domestic arrangements. Women of all social classes and in urban and rural areas need improved access to education and work opportunities. Governmental incentives such as extra educational and work provisions, social security programs, tax credits, and improved medical facilities for women and girls along with limitations on dowries and prohibition of sex-selective medical procedures will help to correct the male: female ratio. These reforms, however, will not suffice or even be possible unless the enormous inequalities produced by the global economic system, the structural adjustment programs, and the spiraling debts held by developing nations are addressed.

BIBLIOGRAPHY

A. J. Arberry, *The Koran interpreted*, New York 1955.

J. Bargach, *Orphans of Islam. Family, abandonment, and secret adoption in Morocco*, Lanham, Md. 2002.

F. M. Denny, *An introduction to Islam*, New York 1994.

E. Gruenbaum, *The female circumcision controversy*, Philadelphia 2001.

M. Inhorn, *Infertility and patriarchy. The cultural politics of gender and family life in Egypt*, Philadelphia 1996.

——, *Quest for conception. Gender, infertility, and Egyptian medical traditions*, Philadelphia 1994.

R. A. Kanaaneh, *Birthing the nation. Strategies of Palestinian women in Israel*, Berkeley, Calif. 2002.

D. Kandiyoti, Bargaining with patriarchy, in *Gender and society* 2 (1988), 274–90.

F. Rahman, *Health and medicine in the Islamic tradition*, New York 1987.

NANCY GALLAGHER

Inheritance: Contemporary Practice

Arab States

The last decades have seen major shifts in academic studies about women and inheritance. If earlier work often considered legal texts either as having a determining impact on social practice or as irrelevant for social practice, more recent work questions such dichotomies and investigates the multiple, complex relations between legal texts and social action. This has also been encouraged by the use of a wider variety of sources and methods, such as court records, ethnography, and oral history.

This entry starts with a discussion of the various laws of succession in the Arab world, and then moves on to social practice. If women are legally entitled to inherit, this raises the question whether they indeed receive their inheritance share, or rather, which women are able to claim their inheritance and what inheriting actually means.

Laws of succession in the Arab world

In those areas once part of the Ottoman Empire, succession is legally regulated through two different law systems. Property held in full ownership (*mulk*), such as urban real estate, buildings, vineyards, orchards, and movables, is inherited in accordance with the Islamic law of succession. Most agricultural land (but not the plantations) is not *mulk* but *mīrī*, land to which individuals could acquire rights of usufruct and possession, but with ultimate ownership remaining vested in the state. This right of possession is also inheritable, but in this case a secular law of succession is applied.

Within these two systems gender, marital status, kin relation, and the presence of contending heirs impact upon inheritance rights. The Sunnī Islamic law of inheritance is prescriptive and strongly partible; it restricts the right of testation and stipulates allotments to a large number of heirs, divided into two categories. First in line are the Qurʾānic heirs (*ahl al-farāʾiḍ*), who are entitled to a fixed percentage of the estate, varying from one-half to one-sixth. This category mainly consists of close kin, such as the father, mother, daughter, and sister of the deceased, and the widow or widower. The remainder is divided amongst the male agnatic heirs (the *ʿasaba*), with the nearer agnate excluding the farther. Certain categories of women, such as the daughter and the sister, turn from *farāʾiḍ* into *ʿasaba* heirs if there are male heirs of the same category; in that case they receive one-half of the share of their male counterparts. A widow is entitled to a fixed share of one-eighth of her late husband's estate if he had children (not necessarily by her) and one-quarter if not. A widower in a similar situation would take twice as much: one-quarter and one-half of his wife's estate respectively. Daughters receive a fixed share if the deceased has no sons: one daughter is entitled to half the estate, two or more sharing two-thirds of it. Thus, if a man dies without leaving sons, a considerable part of the estate goes to his male agnates, usually his brothers. If, on the other hand, there are sons, these are the first heirs and daughters turn into agnatic heirs, entrusted with one-half the share of a son. Shīʿī law, in contrast, does not give such preference to agnates, as parents and lineal descendants exclude all other heirs. This allows for limited partition of the estate; an only daughter may inherit the whole estate, even excluding the grandfather.

While *mulk* property is inherited according to Islamic law, a very different law of succession is applied to *mīrī* land: the Ottoman *intiqāl* (succession) system. Its main principles are gender equality and distribution of the estate on the basis of generations. The major heirs are the children of the deceased, and if there are none, then the parents, with the surviving spouse receiving one-quarter of the estate if the deceased had children and one-half if there were none.

In contrast to what may seem apparent in the foregoing, the Islamic inheritance system was, and to some extent still is, flexible as it allowed for donations *inter vivos* and for family endowments that make it possible to designate particular family members and descendants as beneficiaries. Whereas, as Powers (1990, 27–8) has argued, these forms of property transmission were widely practiced, the system became more rigid under the impact of colonialism when the system of family endowment came under widespread attack. Contemporary debates about reforming inheritance law have remained limited. Most legal systems have remedied the problem of the exclusion of orphaned grandchildren. One interesting case is the Iraqi family law reform of 1959, which extended the gender-neutral rules for state (*mīrī*) land to all forms of property. As early as 1963, however, the law was amended to basically apply the order of succession in Shīʿī inheritance law to the Sunnī population as well (Coulson and Hinchcliffe 1978, 47). In Jordan reform has gone in a different direction: from 1990 on, the rules of Islamic law were extended to *mīrī* land (Brand 1998, 105, 134).

The nature of the property

One major divide in the literature about inheritance is that between urban and rural women. Historians working on Ottoman cities using court documents have emphasized that women indeed received their share in the estate (Gerber 1980, 232, 240, Jennings 1975, 98, 111, Marcus 1985, 120, Reilly 1990). Anthropologists doing fieldwork in rural areas have underlined that in practice women often did not receive their inheritance share (Granqvist 1935, 256, Rosenfeld 1960, 66, Antoun 1972, 140). Looking more closely at the nature of the property involved, other differences come to the fore. The Ottoman historians have pointed out that urban women had more access to residential than to commercial or agricultural property (Jennings 1975, 101, Gerber 1980, 233, Marcus 1983, 144), while anthropologists have also provided examples of settings in which women as a rule took their share (Peters 1978 for South Lebanon and Mundy 1979 for Highland Yemen, even if in the latter case usually when they were in mid-life and had adult sons to transfer the land to). Whether women inherit or not seems to tie in with the structures of production, in particular with the nature of the property-holding unit; women stand a better chance to inherit land if it is individually owned rather than held by a collectivity (Peters 1978, Mundy 1988). Yet, in the latter case they may receive compensation in the form of movable property (Pastner 1980, 152), while they may also keep a claim to land held collectively. Doumani (1998, 36ff) highlights the importance of particular political economies in a comparison of family endowments in Tripoli and Nablus in the early nineteenth century. In the former, where the major economic activity was horticulture with land held in private ownership, women did inherit or were beneficiaries in family endowments; in the latter, where land was collectively owned and the key source of wealth was control of the rural surplus that demanded personal mobility and political participation in non-kin patron-client relationships, women had only limited rights in family endowments.

The women involved: twentieth-century Nablus

The remainder of this entry investigates inheritance practices of daughters in twentieth-century Nablus, underlining the importance of taking factors such as the absence or presence of competing heirs, class positions, and marital status into account. If for the sake of brevity structural elements are highlighted in a rather generalizing manner, this does not mean that these can be taken as a blueprint. Rather, they point to the field of possibilities that frames women's ability to act.

Case studies, such as Moors (1995, 1996) about Jabal Nablus, point out that it is not so much the nature of the property that counts (*mulk* or *mīrī*, urban or rural), but rather the presence of contending heirs. A daughter in a small property-owning household often prefers to give up her share in the estate in order to reaffirm and strengthen her ties with her brothers (see also Granqvist 1935). Also, after marriage women tend to identify with their own kin and feel a special closeness to their natal household, while at the same time they may well be dependent on their male kin for their economic security, especially if they have no access to education and employment. By not claiming her share, a woman enhances the status of her brothers (and by implication her own) and accentuates their obligations toward her, as they are in the position of owing their sister. If, in contrast, a woman demands her share in the estate, she may receive this, but then is often no longer able to invoke her brother's help and support, which in turn undermines her position vis-à-vis her husband. The situation is different if a daughter does not have brothers. Then it is socially accepted if she claims her share (that otherwise would go to her father's brothers). Still, the attempts to claim of daughters without brothers are not easily successful and such daughters often receive considerably less than what they are legally entitled to.

Women tend to stand a better chance to inherit if their families are wealthy or if they are single. It is true that also in better off families productive property and real estate are often transmitted patrilineally and remain under (male) family control. If, however, enough cash is available, giving daughters a share in their father's estate is seen as enhancing the status of the family as a whole. In the case of large estate owners whose major resource was agricultural land, a common solution was to allow a daughter to marry only her paternal cousin, so the land would remain in the same lineage; if it was not possible to arrange such a marriage, such a daughter would have to remain single (also Peters 1978, 337).

The inheritance question of elderly single women is structurally different from that of married women. In the case of a single woman without means of her own, her brothers are legally obliged to provide for her. In a sense, a brother's contributions to his sister are hard to distinguish from a gradual pay-off of her inheritance share. If tensions arise, these tend to be expressed in terms of maintenance rather than in terms of inheritance. Elderly single women usually hold strong usufruct rights to their father's house. Especially when it became increasingly common for married sons to move soon after marriage into a house of their own, the most convenient solution often was for an elderly unmarried daughter to remain in her father's house.

One particularly interesting case is women inheriting gold, as it often argued that rural women tend to inherit gold rather than land. However, it may not be so much the nature of the property that is at stake, but the relation between testator and heir. Gold is, after all, mostly inherited from mothers. Because of the often strong bonds between a mother and her daughter it is rather common for a woman to support her daughter through (premortem) donating some of her gold to her. And even if she does not do so in her lifetime, this close mother-daughter tie gives women a particular claim on their mother's estate, which often consists of gold. In that sense it seems more difficult to disinherit women from gold than from any other type of property.

The multiple meanings and power effects of inheriting property

Much of the literature on women and inheritance in the Arab world assumes that claiming inheritance rights is an indication of gendered power. Yet inheriting property has multiple meanings and divergent power effects. If women from this area often refrained from claiming their inheritance rights, this was not necessarily an expression of their subordination, nor was claiming their rights in the estate an indication of power. Some women received (part of) their share automatically because they were from an urban wealthy family background, where men would raise their own status by "giving" to their sisters. Their inheriting was first and foremost an expression of their class position, rather than of gendered power. Others inherited because their husbands put great pressure on them to claim their share. Rather than an indication of power, under such circumstances inheriting property may well undermine a woman's position. These women were not only likely to lose kin support, but, as a result, would also often find themselves in a weaker position in regard to their husband and his kin. Then there were women, in particular daughters without brothers, who claimed their share because they were in a highly vulnerable situation. On the other hand, when daughters renounced their rights to the estate, they often did so as in order to underline their close kin's obligations toward them, expecting to gain more from giving up their rights to the estate than from claiming them. This implies that legal texts, even if not implemented, are still important. For it is the widespread awareness of women's rights to inherit that produces these effects.

Bibliography

R. Antoun, *Arab village. A social structural study of a trans-Jordan peasant community*, Bloomington, Ind. 1972.

L. Brand, *Women, the state, and political liberalization. Middle Eastern and North African experiences*, New York 1998.

N. Coulson and D. Hinchcliffe, Women and law reform in contemporary Islam, in L. Beck and N. Keddie, *Women in the Muslim world*, Cambridge, Mass. 1978, 37–52.

B. Doumani, Endowing family. Waqf, property devolution, and gender in Greater Syria, 1800 to 1860, in *Comparative Study of Society and History* 40 (1998), 3–41.

H. Gerber, Social and economic position of women in an Ottoman city, Bursa, in *International Journal of Middle East Studies* 12 (1980), 231–44.

H. Granqvist, *Marriage conditions in a Palestinian village II*, Helsinki 1935.

R. Jennings, Women in early 17th-century Ottoman judicial records. The Sharia court of Anatolian Kayseri, in *Journal of the Economic and Social History of the Orient* 18 (1975), 53–114.

A. Marcus, Men, women and property. Dealers in real estate in eighteenth-century Aleppo, in *Journal of the Economic and Social History of the Orient* 26 (1983), 137–63.

A. Moors, *Women, property and Islam. Palestinian experiences, 1920–1990*, Cambridge 1995.

——, Gender relations and inheritance. Person, power and property, in D. Kandiyoti (ed.), *Gendering the Middle East. Emerging perspectives*, London 1996, 69–84.

M. Mundy, Women's inheritance of land in Highland Yemen, in *Arabian Studies* 5 (1979), 161–87.

——, The family, inheritance, and Islam. A re-examination of the sociology of fara'id law, in A. al-Azmeh (ed.), *Islamic law. Social and historical contexts*, London 1988, 1–123.

C. Pastner, Access to property and the status of women in Islam, in J. Smith (ed.), *Women in contemporary Muslim societies*, Lewisburg, Pa. 1980, 146–86.

E. Peters, The status of women in four Middle Eastern communities, in L. Beck and N. Keddie (eds.), *Women in the Muslim world*, Cambridge, Mass. 1978, 311–51.

D. Powers, The Islamic inheritance system. A socio-economic approach, in C. Mallat and J. Connors (eds.), *Islamic family law*, London 1990, 11–31.
J. Reilly, Properties around Damascus in the nineteenth century, in *Arabica* 37:1 (1990), 91–115.
H. Rosenfeld, On the determinants of the status of Arab village women, in *Man* 40 (1960), 66–74.

Annelies Moors

Iran and Afghanistan

Inheritance laws in both countries are based on the Sharīʿa. They assign females regardless of age precisely defined shares of an estate according to detailed genealogical considerations. These shares are always less than a male's of equal genealogical position. This "Golden Rule" is praised as a great improvement for women over pre-Islamic customs regarding property. Its inherent gender inequality is defended within an ideology of practicality: men need resources for their obligations to care for and protect their dependents, including women, while women have no such obligations and can spend their resources frivolously; the *mahr* (bride-price) women receive from their husband at the time of marriage together with their father's inheritance (half of a brother's share) is enough for their discretionary spending; in cases of special hardship (for example, a sick daughter), a man may bequeath extra funds through a testament.

In both countries local inheritance customs supersede these laws, to the effect that women – with exceptions – are not considered heirs. The traditional gender philosophy justifies this exclusion: women are considered part of a man's estate rather than heirs (as shown, for example, in the custom of the levirate and in the term "buy," colloquially used for the acquisition of a wife); a woman's God-ordained main function is to bear and raise children for her husband's group and to work for the benefit of her family (first natal, later conjugal-extended), while men's obligations are manifold – in order to fulfill them men need to inherit, women do not; in the logic of patrilineal descent and management of property, women as heirs alienate property from the agnatic group by passing it to the husband and his children; a woman should not be trusted with agnatic property because she will have to obey a husband's and son's potential order to surrender her inheritance; women are said to be weak stewards of property because of their purported lack of managerial inclinations and skills and their weakness of resolve, which again will compel them to give in to the inevitable pressure by men for control of the inheritance anyway. For these reasons a compassionate, wise woman will pardon her inheritance for the benefit of her male relatives, most likely her brothers (as a sister) and her sons (as a widow).

The commonsensical inequality informing traditions and Qurʾānic laws is also evident in legal reforms. The 1931 Civil Code and the Family Protection Act of 1967 in Iran retained unequal inheritance despite modernist goals. In addition, men rarely apply these laws voluntarily, and women either are ignorant of their rights or choose not to press for them. Likewise, legal changes in Afghanistan under Soviet rule made little difference to most common people – the laws were ignored, just as the Taliban-ordained Qurʾānic laws were later. Then as now, in both countries women who claim their legal share of an inheritance likely belong to the small, educated, West-oriented elite, to local traditional, wealthy families in leadership positions, or to those who have access to consciousness-raising religious instruction. Rarely is a woman able to press a claim on her own, especially not a rural or uneducated woman, for reasons of logistics and of compromising family honor by going to court. Frequently, women who claim inheritance do so at the instigation and under the guidance of a husband or son who risks his cordial relationships with the woman's relatives trying to enrich himself through her.

In practice, therefore, inheritance considerations are embedded in family politics: a daughter who claims her share of her father's inheritance strains relationships with her brothers; a widow who insists on her share of her husband's estate may start a fight with her sons or husband's brothers; a successful claim by one sister may lead to discontent among the others. But even accepting an inheritance when offered may undermine a woman's position: her brothers will chalk it up as their generosity; her husband or son may withhold support by referring to her own property. In contrast, a woman who pardons her share may strengthen her political position: the beneficiary will be obliged to her. A father who passes on property to a daughter's children as a gift in lieu of the inheritance to his daughter will raise his moral standing with his daughter's husband. Even a husband can benefit by turning his wife's pardon of her share into the morally superior position of generosity toward his wife's male relatives.

As long as patrilineal structures and women's dependency on men continue in either country, inheritance practices will not change much. Where these structures become weaker, as today in the modern middle class in Iran with its scores of well-educated, knowledgeable women, inheritance claims are increasing and will increase further, but Sharīʿa law will not allow for gender equality.

Bibliography

H. Emadi, *Repression, resistance, and women in Afghanistan*, London 2002.

H. A. Jawad, *The rights of women in Islam*, New York 1998.

M. Kazemzadeh, *Islamic fundamentalism, feminism, and gender inequality in Iran under Khomeini*, New York 2002.

A. Moors, Debating Islamic family law. Legal texts and social practices, in M. L. Meriwether and J. E. Tucker (eds.), *Social history of women and gender in the modern Middle East*, Boulder, Colo. 1999, 141–60.

N. Tapper, *Bartered brides. Politics, gender, and marriage in a tribal society*, Cambridge 1991.

Erika Loeffler Friedl

South Asia

Inheritance laws in South Asia fall within the jurisdiction of personal laws. These are not universal, but are differentiated by religious denomination. However, in precolonial times, the civil law of the land, now defined as customary law, tended to be homogeneous. Thus Muslim daughters frequently did not claim their full share of inheritance, permissible under Qurʾānic laws. They gave their share to their brothers to protect their right to return to the family home in case of conflict, divorce, or widowhood. Significantly, Hindu daughters rarely inherited from fathers under the laws of the Dharmashastras (law books), but were permitted a limited share under custom (Agarwal 1998). Both were compensated through gifts mainly of immovable property at the time of marriage, a practice that continues today. The underlying principles were to keep landed holdings intact so as to maintain the power and prestige of families in the male line.

The principle of property ownership and management by Muslim women was accepted, however. It was only under colonial rule, through the introduction of the category of *pardanishin,* or veiled lady, in an 1867 court case in Calcutta, that officials sought to curtail their unlimited right of property alienation: they were required to prove that independent advice had been obtained before making any transactions (Murshid 2002). Numerous cases under this category reached the Privy Council, the highest court of appeal. These demonstrate the wealth of the litigants, and the fact that women inherited landed property both as daughters and as widows.

From the nineteenth century, inheritance rights of Indians were regulated through customary practice, legislation, and court proceedings. The contrary claims of religion and custom under British colonial rule determined the regional variation in the nature and implementation of inheritance laws. Religion was paramount in formulating the inheritance laws of Bengal, whereas, in the Punjab, custom defined those rights (Mahmood 1977).

Contrary to popular perceptions, personal laws were not always based on perceived religious injunctions. For example, through an 1847 landmark decision, the Bombay Supreme Court exempted the Khojas and Memons from the application of Anglo-Muhammadan Law, which would have permitted daughters a share of the inheritance. Justice C. J. Perry argued that the Company Charter had made no absolute enactment for the adoption of the Qurʾān in matters of inheritance, and that the practice of excluding females from inheritance had become a Muslim custom (Perry 1988 reprint).

Appealing to religion to bring about legal changes was common. Based on the Qurʾānic principle that charity begins at home, Muslims created family endowments and charitable trusts (*wakf*s) to protect future generations from hardship and poverty. Only the remaining properties were available for disposal under inheritance laws. Classical theory acknowledged that although Islamic inheritance laws were egalitarian, they led to the fragmentation of properties, and eventually made them economically unviable. British Orientalists, like their French counterparts in Algeria, argued that these endowments were un-Islamic (Powers 1989). Indian courts held that endowments had to be primarily charitable to be legal under Islamic law. Muslims were accused of wanting to escape the rules of their religion. The effect of this ruling was to break down large holdings, cripple the old aristocracy, and free up land for the land market. It was only through popular pressure backed by political mobilization that the Privy Council decision was overturned through legislative enactments. Indian Muslims led by Muhammad Ali Jinnah and supported by the Congress Party secured the Muslim Wakf Validating Act 1913. However, it was given retroactive effect only after the passage of the Muslim Wakf Validating Act 1930. The long-term impact was to diminish the practice of establishing family endowments in South Asia.

The courts often deprived women of the ownership of property: daughters frequently were not permitted to inherit, even if it could be proved through the record of customs called the Riwaj-i-am that the practice would be welcomed by the community. In 1934, the Lahore Full Bench argued that a valid custom had to date back to time immemorial, rather than be the expressed wish of a community (*Indian Law Reporter* 1935). Thus, in practice, the inheritance rights of Muslim daughters were similar to those of Hindu daughters.

Widows were favored over daughters to an extent in being permitted the use of inherited property, but without any powers of alienation. There was evidence to prove that widows became *maliks* or absolute proprietors in Dewa (Oudh). However, in a 1929 landmark case, the Privy Council decided that in the absence of sons, widows succeeded to a life estate only, rather than one with survivorship. The ruling brought the property inheritance rights of Muslim widows to the same level as those of Hindu widows (Murshid 2002). But, there was an anomaly in the conceptualization of these rights. A Hindu widow was permitted a limited inheritance as a member of the husband's joint family, whereas a married daughter was not as she technically belonged to another family. However, the joint family as a legal concept was not applied to Muslims in matters of property ownership, although the notion was invoked in mediating the inheritance claims of Muslim widows.

These cases highlight three features. The limited rights of inheritance by women demonstrate that the administrative objective of preserving landed estates was pursued at the cost of female ownership. The colonial state reserved the right to determine customary law by selecting authentic custom. Finally, it formulated Anglo-Muhammadan Law through creating binding rules of decision, which could only be overturned by acts of legislature.

Colonial officials admitted to interference in one area only: that of inheritance and succession in the case of apostasy. Through the 1850 Caste Disabilities Removal Act (XXI), the legislature provided that renunciation of religion or loss of caste would not impair the right of inheritance in the Company Courts (Grady 1869).

The workings of Anglo-Muhammadan Law were unsatisfactory in that it placed too much emphasis on custom in regions such as the Punjab, or on religion in provinces such as Bengal. Muslims resented their inability to exercise absolute control over land through powers of alienation, wills, or bequests of more than one-third of their property. To a lesser extent, they were concerned about the limited rights of inheritance available to women (Murshid 2003).

It was in this context that the demand for a Shariat act arose in western India. The Muslim Personal Law (Shariat) Application Act 1937 overrode all custom and usage in favor of personal law in matters of adoption, inheritance, gifts, marriage, divorce, trusts, wakfs, and so forth, and was made binding on all Muslims.

After independence, the states of South Asia modified their family laws, but left the minorities untouched. There were few changes in Muslim inheritance laws. The Hindu Code of 1956 recognized formal equality between the sexes, but in practice continued the status quo. The Succession Act of 1956 favored the *mitakshara* system whereby only males were coparceners, and had the right to will away their shares in joint property. The right of a daughter to a share in the self-acquired property of her father was restricted. Husbands' relatives were given rights to inherit women's property or *stridhan*, not their parents. Moreover, fathers and brothers often made women sign away their inheritance rights before they married. Thus the law and the practice facilitated the disinheritance of women, in the interest of preventing fragmentation. In reality, it permitted individual males to dispose of their properties without hindrance, which suited big businesses (Kishwar 1994, 2156).

Opponents of the Succession Act cited Muslim law to seek protection for Hindu women. In theory at least, Muslims could will away one-third of their property, or gift away all of it during their lifetime. At wedlock, Muslim wives often received gifts in property, which could not be affected by debt.

The only changes to the inheritance laws in Pakistan and Bangladesh stem from the 1961 Muslim Family Laws Ordinance. It accepted the principle of inheritance by grandchildren, where the father had already died. While this principle continues to be observed in Bangladesh, it was annulled in Pakistan during President Zia ul-Huq's Islamization drive.

Bibliography

B. Agarwal, Widows versus daughters or widows as daughters? Property, land and economic security in India, in *Modern Asian Studies* 32:1 (1998), 1–48.

S. G. Grady, *A manual of Mahomedan law of inheritance and contract. Comprising the doctrines of Soonee and Sheea schools and based upon the text of Sir W. H. Macnaghten's Principles and Precedents together with the decisions of the Privy Council, and high courts of the presidencies in India*, London 1869.

M. Kishwar, Codified Hindu law. Myth or reality, in *Economic and Political Weekly*, 13 August 1994, 2145–61.

G. C. Kozlowski, *Muslim endowments and society in British India*, Cambridge 1985.

T. Mahmood, *Muslim personal law. Role of the state in the sub-continent*, New Delhi 1977.

T. Murshid, Law and female autonomy in colonial India, in *Journal of the Asiatic Society of Bangladesh. Humanities* 47:1 (2002), 25–42.

——, Social construction of Shariah. Validating difference, paper given at the Centre d'Etudes de l'Inde et de l'Asie du Sud, Paris, 20 May 2003.

E. Perry, *Cases illustrative of Oriental life decided in H. M. Supreme Court at Bombay (1847). The application of English law to India*, London 1853, repr. New Delhi 1988.

D. S. Powers, Orientalism, colonialism and legal history. The attack on Muslim family endowments in Algeria and India, in *Comparative Studies in Society and History* 31:1 (1989), 535–71.

CASES

Mst Sardar Bibi v. Haq Nawaz Khan, *Indian Law Reporter*, Lahore 1935, 425–59.

Roshan Ali Khan v. Chaudhuri Asghar Ali, *Indian Law Reporter*, Lucknow 1930, 70–80.

TAZEEN MAHNAZ MURSHID

International Conventions

Overview

Introduction

International law is a significant symbolic tool, but may be a very weak device in reality to assist in improving the actual lives of women around the world, including Muslim women. This entry examines one major aspect of international law – the role of conventions or treaties, which are "international agreements concluded between States in written form and governed by international law" (art. 2(1)(a), Vienna Convention on the Law of Treaties). They cover a wide array of topics, including human rights, arms control, trade, international humanitarian law, and terrorism. Since conventions constitute agreements that bind governments, these documents are usually negotiated and drafted by representatives of those states, whether the individuals work in a foreign ministry or other executive branch agency or in an international institution like the United Nations. Multilateral treaties with a large number of countries involved may be drafted at special diplomatic conferences where each state has a delegation that includes legal advisers.

As women were rarely represented in the professional upper echelons of these entities during the twentieth century when most conventions were drafted, female input and the concerns of women have been minimal in the development and application of most international treaties. Many conventions lack any references to gender or sex, such as environmental agreements like the Convention for the Protection of the Ozone Layer, or trade agreements like the Uruguay Round Final Act, creating the World Trade Organization. Even human rights agreements like the Convention on the Elimination of Racial Discrimination (CERD) may not mention gender. As such conventions are "genderless," one view is to regard them as applying to "people" or "human beings," so that they should not be applied in any gendered manner, that is, only to one sex. Thus, protecting the ozone, for example, would be seen as equally applicable to both genders. Another view is that since these types of conventions cover "people," they include either or both genders. It would thus be permissible to apply them to one gender. For example, CERD could be applied to assist minority group women, including Muslim women of color in non-Muslim predominantly white countries like the United States, who face special kinds of multiple or intersectional discrimination (Wing 2003).

Some conventions may specifically mention the masculine "he." For example, the Convention against Torture, and Other Cruel, Inhuman, and Degrading Treatment or Punishment (CAT) defines torture as "intentionally inflicted on a person for such purposes of obtaining from him . . . a confession" (art. 1, CAT). One interpretation is to regard "he" in the "traditional" fashion as the generic term for he or she. Both men and women are tortured around the world, including in a number of Muslim countries. Another view is to read such phrases literally, as only applying to men, leaving women outside the scope of protection.

Other agreements clearly state that the convention applies equally to men and women. The International Covenant on Civil and Political Rights (ICCPR) says, for instance, "The States Parties to the present Covenant undertake to ensure the equal right of men and women to the enjoyment of all civil and political rights" (art. 3, ICCPR). Its companion agreement, the International Covenant on Economic, Social and Cultural Rights (ICESCR) requires that states protect the equal rights of males and females to enjoy economic, social, and cultural rights (art. 3, ICESCR).

Some conventions contain language clearly meant to refer in part to women, such as the Genocide Convention's definition of genocide including, "imposing measures intended to prevent births within the group" (art. 2(d), Convention on the Prevention and Punishment of the Crime of Genocide). This statement could include abortion against the will of the mother or the killing of pregnant women and their fetuses. During the 1990s, there were also examples of Bosnian Serbian Christian fighters impregnating Bosnian Muslim women and holding them as captives to ensure the birth of non-Muslim babies, the religion of the child being determined by the father's (Wing and Merchan 1993). These kinds of clauses could also be applied to men as well. Using the same example, rounding up, imprisoning, and exterminating Bosnian Muslim men and boys clearly affected births in the group.

There are some conventions that may disproportionately affect women, such as the Hague Convention on the Civil Aspects of International Child

Abduction. With respect to the Muslim world, there are numerous examples where Western court child custody decrees grant custody to the mother, and fathers from Muslim countries abduct the children and take them to their home country, where the law recognizes that the child in a divorce belongs to the father after a certain age (Andrews 2000). This convention is designed to prevent such abductions and make sure the children are returned to the custodial parent.

Finally, a few international agreements were designed specifically to apply to women, the most comprehensive being the Convention on the Elimination of All Forms of Discrimination against Women (CEDAW), written in part to remedy the gaps in the previously mentioned approaches. CEDAW had 174 States Parties as of June 2003. Other treaties range from the post-Second World War Convention on the Political Rights of Women (1953), the Convention on the Nationality of Married Women (1957), to the twenty-first century International Labor Organization Maternity Protection Convention (2000).

Even when a treaty is designed specifically to apply to women, there can be glaring omissions. For example, CEDAW does not explicitly mention violence against women, although various provisions could be interpreted as covering that topic. The 1994 Declaration on the Elimination of Violence against Women tries to fill in the gaps, but like all declarations, is not binding in international law. With respect to violence, CEDAW does not specifically mention customary practices of some countries of the Islamic world such as honor killings. Valuing female chastity and modesty, male members of a family feel justified in killing any female relative, including their own mothers, sisters, or wives. Practices like dating, wearing clothes regarded as revealing, leaving the house without permission, or being seen in the presence of male non-relatives, may invoke lethal force to avenge the insult to the family "honor." Scholars have analyzed these killings as violation of CEDAW obligations in countries such as Jordan, where the domestic law still treats honor killers lightly (Arnold 2001).

A superficial analysis of the text of a convention for applicability to women is only the first step in determining whether an agreement might be helpful for female concerns, including those of Muslim women. Once a multilateral convention or treaty is finalized, it must "enter into force," to have any significance. This occurs once a certain number of states designated in the treaty have accepted the agreement (art. 24(1), Vienna Convention). In many instances, a country signifies that it is willing to be bound by "signing," "ratifying," "accepting," "approving," or "acceding" to it (art. 11). There are some agreements that are not yet in force for lack of signatories or ratifications. For example, the Protocol to the Banjul Charter for the Establishment of the African Human Rights Court was adopted in 1998, but had not yet entered into force as of April 2003, since it only had 6 of the 15 ratifications it needed. Such a court might have jurisdiction over situations where African countries prioritize customary or religious practices that discriminate against women over their obligations under the Banjul Charter on Human and Peoples' Rights.

The most accepted treaty in the world is the Convention on the Rights of the Child (CRC), which has been ratified by every country, except the United States and Somalia. This convention applies irrespective of the child or parent's gender and specifically uses male and female pronouns throughout the agreement (CRC, art. 2).

States do not have to completely accept all aspects of an agreement, which is one reason why the wide variety of states have been able to join so many conventions. They have the opportunity to make exceptions to their ratification of a treaty by issuing a "reservation," "declaration," "understanding," or "clarification." A reservation, for example, "excludes or modifies the legal effect of certain provisions of the treaty in their application to that State" (art. 2 (d), Vienna Convention). Reservations are generally allowed unless the treaty prohibits them, or only permits certain types, or they are "incompatible with the object and purpose" of the treaty, the latter being very difficult to determine in many instances (art. 19). Unfortunately, the treaty with the most reservations is CEDAW, most of which exempt the states from complying with any provision that undercuts their existing customs or religion (Clark 1991). Since most gender discrimination is based upon patriarchal customs and religious practices, these kinds of reservations gut the treaty. States gain approbation from the international community for joining the treaty, yet in reality have committed themselves to nothing more than they were already doing.

Many of the Muslim states that have ratified CEDAW have made such reservations. For example, Egypt's reservation states that it complies with Article 2, condemning discrimination against women, but only to the extent that it does not conflict with Islamic Sharīʿa law (Brandt and Kaplan 1995–6, Multilateral Treaties 1995). Kuwait ratified CEDAW, but made a reservation justifying the continued failure to permit women to vote.

Scholars have vigorously criticized these sorts of reservations as incompatible with the object and purpose of the treaty (Mayer 1995b).

Understandings or declarations occur when a nation states what a certain provision means, usually for domestic political or legal reasons. Courts in that country may invoke the understanding to interpret the treaty. If the government does not intend the understanding to have effect between it and other states, it will not be considered a reservation (Buergenthal and Maier 1990). The end result is that the understanding or declaration may have almost the same text as a reservation. In other words, a Muslim state may make an understanding that ICCPR article 2 does not require men and women to have the same opportunities in violation of Islamic principles, whereas another country would have called the same statement a reservation.

Since it is well understood that reservations can undermine the application of a treaty, there are several choices one state can make if it does not like the reservation of another state party. It can do nothing and just ignore the issue. It can accept that the reserving state is a party to the convention, but ignore their reservation. It can object to the reservation as well, which a number of Western states have done with respect to Islamic countries reservations to CEDAW. For example, Sweden objected to Egypt's reservations concerning CEDAW (Mayer 1995b). Alternatively, it can decide that it will not even acknowledge that the reserving state is a party to the treaty (art. 20, Vienna Convention). An objecting state can even take the matter to an international court like the International Court of Justice (ICJ) for a ruling. Unfortunately, since the ICJ and other international tribunals have no effective police power to implement their decisions, the opinions can be ignored or flouted much as the United States flouted the ICJ's Nicaragua decision holding the mining of the Nicaraguan harbors to be a violation of international law. Thus, the embarrassment of the large number of reservations to CEDAW is unlikely ever to be rectified.

While the international level is the place to begin regarding the implementation of conventions, it is the national level where real change must then take place to affect the lives of women. A major problem that can arise with international agreements is that even if a state properly ratifies an in-force treaty with no reservations, it may never follow national law procedures to implement the treaty, such as revising existing or passing new legislation. Since most treaties are not "self-executing," a lack of implementing legislation means the treaty is meaningless. For example, article 15(4) of CEDAW says that "States Parties shall accord to men and women the same rights with regard to the movement of persons and freedom to choose their residence and domicile." Some Muslim countries have customs and laws that give a husband legal control over his wife's or wives' movements, ranging from the most restrictive in which a wife needs permission of the husband even to leave the house to slightly less restrictive policies on holding a job or traveling outside the country. Assuming for the moment that the country made no reservation on this matter, if the national law is not amended to bring it into compliance with CEDAW, then article 15 remains irrelevant.

Even if the proper legislation is passed, the treaty may still have no penetrative ability; the branches of government may make no effort or have limited capacity to change practices required to implement the treaty. Using the last example, suppose the national law is changed and a husband still refuses to let his wife leave the house. Making the large assumption that the wife hears about the new law and manages to leave the house, her efforts to appeal to the local police or a court are likely to be rebuffed, as deeply rooted customs and laws are hard to change in the minds of the enforcers. Of course, the likelihood that the wife would dare even attempt to bring a claim under the new law is mooted by the fact that she, even if illiterate, could properly weigh the consequences. The sequelae range from being beaten (which may be legal), to being thrown out of the house permanently, divorced against her will with no recourse, left without any financial resources by the major or sole breadwinner, rejected by her birth family who might refuse to then support her, and losing any access to her children (who remain the legal property of their father).

Since a country can not be put into a literal prison, few remedies exist for noncompliance. The weak remedies available usually include bringing the matter to the attention of whatever body is created to oversee implementation of the treaty. For example, there is a 23-member CEDAW committee of experts that meets for only a few weeks a year to review reports of state parties, make recommendations, and develop links with other organizations (arts. 18, 21, 22, CEDAW). The committee is several years behind in reviewing reports, and many nations are years behind in submitting their documents, which may be superficial in nature. The committee has little ability other than shame to make recalcitrant governments live up to their obligations.

Universalism versus cultural relativism

A major issue intertwined with the foregoing discussion that arises with respect to implementation of international conventions is the debate between universalism and cultural relativism, namely, whether the convention is to be universal in its application or relative depending on the culture. In other words, even if a country signs and ratifies a convention without reservations and passes implementing legislation and is prepared to enforce the convention, a provision will not mean the same thing in different countries. For example, the ICCPR provision on treating men and women equally may not mean that women will have the same opportunities for access to jobs, education, property, and health care as men in two different countries.

The issue of universalism versus cultural relativism in implementation of international conventions is a major one with respect to the Muslim world and gender issues. Various human rights organizations originating in the West as well as Western governments point to practices in many Islamic countries as violations of human rights conventions. Most of the practices implicate women's rights. With respect to clothing, the veiling of Muslim women is often the most prominent symbol of Islam portrayed as a human rights violation in the West. The practices range from wearing an Afghani *burqaʿ* to an Iranian chador to a mere headscarf covering the hair. The Islamic practice of polygamy, which permits a Muslim man to have up to four wives who are either Muslim, Christian or Jewish, but a Muslim woman to only have one husband, who must be a Muslim, is often mentioned as well. There have been internationally publicized incidents of Muslim Nigerian women being faced with the Islamic punishment for adultery of being stoned to death for bearing a child out of wedlock, while their partners go free for lack of four male witnesses (Dowden 2002). Under Islamic inheritance laws women only inherit a half share as compared to men of the same degree of relationship. Customary practices that predate Islam ranging from female genital surgeries to dowries, arranged marriages, and honor killings, may be mentioned as well.

The notion is that human rights documents such as the International Bill of Rights consisting of the Universal Declaration of Human Rights (1948), the ICCPR (1967), and the ICESCR (1967), were conceptualized and drafted by Western countries. Some Muslim nations and scholars claim that adhering to these documents without violating Islamic law is impossible, and thus making reservations is justified (Entelis 1997). Some scholars such as An-Naim (1987) claim that it is possible to reconcile Islam and international human rights. Al-Hibri (2000) focuses on the need to omit patriarchal interpretations. Mayer (1995b) has pointed out that Western nations are often hypocritical, criticizing Islamic nations, while their own laws remain sexist. For example, the United States signed CEDAW during the Jimmy Carter administration, but has yet to ratify it. United States feminist efforts to pass a gender equality amendment to the United States Constitution failed decades ago, and have not been revived.

The Islamic world has begun to develop its own human rights instruments. There is a Universal Islamic Declaration of Human Rights (UIDHR), which was developed in 1981 by the International Islamic Council. While declarations are not binding treaties, the UIDHR is clearly an attempt to present an Islamic perspective as opposed to a Western view on human rights issues. Western scholars have found that it constrains Islamic women (Mayer 1995a). For example, article 19 states, "Within the family, men and women are to share in their obligations and responsibilities according to their sex, their natural endowments." Such a statement can be interpreted as confirming the customary limitations on Muslim women.

Bibliography

A. Al-Hibri, Deconstructing patriarchal jurisprudence in Islamic law, in A. K. Wing (ed.), *Global critical race feminism. An international reader*, New York 2003, 221–33.

D. M. Andrews, Non-Muslim mothers v. Egyptian Muslim fathers. The conflict between religion and law in international child custody disputes and abductions, in *Suffolk Transnational Law Review* 23 (2000), 595–630.

A. An-Naim, The rights of women and international law in the Muslim context, in *Whittier Law Review* 9 (1987), 491–516.

K. Arnold, Are the perpetrators of honor killings getting away with murder? Article 340 of the Jordanian Penal Code analyzed under the Convention of the Elimination of All Forms of Discrimination against Women, in *American University International Law Review* 16 (2001), 1343–1409.

B. Clark, The Vienna Convention reservations regime and the convention on discrimination against women, in *American Journal of International Law* 85 (1991), 281–321.

M. Brandt and J. A Kaplan, The tension between women's rights and religious rights. Reservations to CEDAW by Egypt, Bangladesh and Tunisia, in *Journal of Law and Religion* 12 (1995–6), 105–42.

T. Buergenthal and H. G. Maier, *Public international law*, St. Paul, Minn. 1990.

R. Dowden, Death by stoning, in *New York Times Magazine*, 27 January 2002, 28.

J. Entelis, International human rights. Islam's friend or foe? Algeria as an example of compatibility of international human rights regarding women's equality and Islamic law, in *Fordham International Law Journal* 20 (1997), 1251–1305.
A. E. Mayer, *Islam and human rights. Tradition and politics*, Boulder, Colo. 1991, 1995a², 102–9.
——, Rhetorical strategies and official policies on women's rights. The merits and drawbacks of the New World hypocrisy, in M. Afkhami (ed.), *Faith and freedom. Women's rights in the Muslim world*, Syracuse, N.Y. 1995b, 104–32.
Military and Paramilitary Activities in and against Nicaragua (Nicaragua v. US), Merits, I.C.J. Reports 1986, 14, <http://www.studiperlapace.it/documentazione/nicaragua86.html>.
A. K. Wing (ed.), *Critical race feminism. A reader*, New York 2003.
A. K. Wing and S. Merchan, Rape, ethnicity and culture. Spirit injury from Bosnia to Black America, in *Columbia Human Rights Law Review* 25 (1993), 1–48.

International Treaties

African Charter on Human and Peoples' Rights (Banjul Charter), 21 I.L.M. 59 (1981).
Convention against Torture and Other Cruel, Inhuman, or Degrading Treatment or Punishment, 23 I.L.M. 1027 (1984).
Convention on Rights of the Child, 28 I.L.M. 1448 (1989).
Convention on the Elimination of All Forms of Discrimination against Women, 19 I.L.M. 33 (1980).
Convention on the Nationality of Married Women, 309 U.N.T.S. 65 (1957).
Convention on the Political Rights of Women, 193 U.N.T.S. 135 (1953).
Convention on the Prevention and Punishment of the Crime of Genocide, 78 U.N.T.S. 277 (1948).
Declaration on the Elimination of Violence against Women, 33 I.L.M. 1049 (1994).
Hague Convention on the Civil Aspects of International Child Abduction, 33 I.L.M. 225 (1993).
International Covenant on Civil and Political Rights, 999 U.N.T.S. 171 (1966).
International Covenant on Economic, Social and Cultural Rights, 993 U.N.T.S. 3 (1966).
International Convention on the Elimination of All Forms of Race Discrimination, 5 I.L.M. 352 (1966).
International Labor Organization Maternity Protection Convention, No. 183 (2000).
Universal Declaration of Human Rights, U.N. G.A. Res. 217 (1948).
Universal Islamic Declaration of Human Rights (1981), <http://www.alhewar.com/ islamdecl.html>.
Uruguay Round Final Act, 33 I..L.M. 1143 (1994).
Vienna Convention on Protection of the Ozone Layer, 26 I.L.M. 1516 (1987).
Vienna Convention on the Law of Treaties, 1155 U.N.T.S. 331 (1969).

Adrien Katherine Wing

International Organizations

Overview

The end of the Second World War and the emergence of the United Nations system and the official international intergovernmental organizations (IGOs) ushered in a new era in the women's movement and women's rights along with the expansion of human rights ideology. Added impetus to the concept of development came later, mainly through the United Nations Decade for Women (1976–85), which brought women, particularly those of the developing countries, into the limelight of development discourse. Meanwhile, in the 1970s, the work of Esther Boserup brought about a paradigm shift in demonstrating the skewed relationship of women to men. She showed that the underrepresentation of women in agricultural statistics led to a male-biased development. She maintained that twentieth-century modernization produced a dichotomy in which men work in a sector of enhanced productivity, either in farming for the market or in migrant urban and industrial labor, while women remain in an untransformed sector in which they use traditional and low-productivity technology to farm for subsistence (Boserup 1970). The historical dominance of men over women was attributed to two prime factors. Women lag behind men because of the reproductive behaviors of women followed by the formation of rational behavior emanating from the protection of their offspring (Rubin 1975). Such understanding of the skewed relationship between men and women influenced gender planning to correct the situation for women through the interrelationship between gender and development, the formulation of gender policy, and the implementation of gender planning practice (Moser 1993), with particular emphasis on the identification of women's strategic gender needs and practical gender needs (Moser 1989). The understanding of gender planning opened a floodgate for the promotion of particular gender norms as manifested in Women in Development (WID), Woman and Development (WAD), Gender, Environment and Development (GED), Gender and Development (GAD), and the like.

Gender, international organizations, and Muslim societies

The question that needs to be addressed is: what happens when gender programs and projects are implemented at the level of organizations and societies in Islamic developing countries? In the first place there is a need to develop an understanding of the nature of Muslim societies. Muslim societies, in general, include a hierarchy of social structures and relations that start with the ideology of the Muslim *umma*, institutionalized Islam, and family laws. The Muslim *umma* lays emphasis on a community within which all – women and men – are equal in their relationship to Allah. The notion of *umma* has, at least theoretically, curtailed the power of men over women and allows women to enjoy their rights. The Quʾrān provides many rights for women and women's rights over men (Doi 1993). While the notion of *umma* emphasizes the balanced nature of gender relations, the historical process of the formation of Islamic societies has systematically excluded women from the power structures of institutionalized Islam. The problem of representation of women in power structures is that when different Islamic schools of thought interpreted the Qurʾān, the interpretation appeared to be gender blind. The male theologians have historically misinterpreted the equal Qurʾānic rights of women in order to produce a male biased system of Islamic laws and interpretations (Hassan 1991a, 1991b, 1994). Islamic laws are concerned with inheritance, marriage, and simliar issues, and these constitute a social system that encourages the reproduction of extended family groupings (Rippin 1993, 115–16). The ideology of reproduction of family places pressure particularly on women to undertake all types of household tasks and duties, and to bear and raise children. A contradiction in present Muslim society is that while the ideology of Islamic *umma* emphasizes gender equality in all spheres of life, Muslim men create obstacles to equitable participation of women in the traditional institutions. The organizations of Islamist women, which are rapidly growing, are relentlessly working to rectify the incorrect view of women so long promoted by male Islamic scholars.

Thus, unlike in the West, the women's movement did not evolve from within Muslim society to establish gender norms. On the contrary, gender issues are gaining prominence in Muslim societies because of the proactive measures taken by international organizations. The effort of international organizations to spread particular gender norms is in contest with the notion of women embedded in the laws of Islam as stated in the Qur'ān. In Islam, women have non-negotiable rights to be paid as wives and mothers and to be respected as women (Afshar 2002, 134). Globalization has made the two world-views on women even more complex and confusing. Globalization has led to the emergence of a category of Westernized elite women who are willing to embrace Western values including those relating to gender ideologies. At the same time, Western education has transformed large numbers of women who readily accept Western economy and technology but reject the ideology of the West. These are the Islamist women who use their modern education to actively support Islamification that may mean that women are returning to their roots, rediscovering Islam and demanding their non-negotiable rights given to them by the Qur'ān. The Islamist women invoke a backlash, which is an outcome of disillusionment born out of the failure of industrialization and modernization to liberate women, against the West and its values (Afshar 2002, 133).

Although the international organizations and their partners in Islamic developing countries enjoy organizational and financial support from the West, they are prone to show weakness when it comes to the question of implementing gender programs and projects. The weakness lies in the way they create spaces for women and recruit modern elite women staff from the privileged and affluent classes for whom Islam has a weak appeal. These elite women uncritically accept Western gender norms without understanding the historical context in the West through which the concept of gender has evolved. Thereby, they also give a new meaning to gender in the context of development and Islam. They often interpret gender not as a mere development of balanced relationship between men and women, but as a condition for binary opposition to set women against men under the notion of positive discrimination. Now women replace men and different facilities and opportunities are provided to women, but these severely delimit any organizational approach for developing gender policies to deconstruct the male dominated environment. Moreover, the proponents of gender are unable to see and comprehend how the broader environment reproduces and nurtures the male-dominated culture and adopts policies that are not conducive to the needs of women.

These elite women staff are conversant with Western models of gender relations, but have hardly any understanding of how Islamic values and society shape the everyday reality of the rural poor women – their ultimate customer. They provide a universal analysis of women ignoring differences of class, cultural, and religious backgrounds of women in different societies. Many gender practitioners suggest that the sheer presence and practices of elite women reproduce capitalist patriarchy within the international organizations and their partner non-governmental organizations (NGOs). Capitalist patriarchy is operational as Western males often place local modern elite women at the head of the international organizations and their partner organizations as their counterparts and colleagues. The capitalist patriarchs take it for granted that purdah (seclusion) prevails across Muslim society. They fail to see that it is not the practice of purdah but rather hierarchical social structures and relationships that are largely responsible for the backwardness of women.

The failure to deconstruct and comprehend the broader environment by international organizations creates obstacles in the way of their operations. Paradoxically, international organizations and their partners, while trying to promote gender parity and world-view, continuously reproduce within their rank and file the broader Islamic cultures and values. When these organizations implement projects and programs by ensuring women's participation in the project planning cycle, they confront an Islamic patriarchy. Islamic patriarchs are the rural elite, village elders and religious leaders who practice orthodox Islam sustained by the hierarchy of Islamic culture. Despite organizational contradictions, the promotion of gender programs by international organizations has brought a favorable change among male and female staff in development organizations and NGOs. The growing awareness has now led government and international organizations to grant aid for setting up sections or focal points to be responsible for integrating women's issues into administrative projects (Østergaard 1992, 7). All organizations ensure the reflection of gender issues in project planning cycles. Despite the complex problem of separating the impact of projects on men and women, the usual approach to understanding the impact of gender on a project is to assess the outcome or product of an organization and explore how this effects men and women differently (Roche 1999, 236).

While international organizations and their partners have initiated a process of increased gender sensitivity, the same cannot be said to be true for the rural societies where organizations carry out projects. Transformative politics begins when development organizations mobilize women through implementing different projects, which also brings out women from their private sphere in households. The participation of women in development activities then gives them visibility in the male dominated public sphere. The mobilization of women from the private to the public sphere also gives women a discursive identity and new image of their womanhood. The discursive identity poses problems to both international organizations and Islamists, as they are unsure as to how to deal with the new image of women. The new image of women is also a source of rift and tension over the construction of women's identities between the international organizations and Islamists. International organizations and NGOs see the new identities as an element of modernization and secularism. The development organizations, particularly the World Bank, consider the visibility of women as engendering development (King et al. 2001), which they understand as the transformation of traditional women into modern and secular women. On the contrary, Islamists see the new identities as undermining of traditional norms and nuances, values and visions. Islamists consider women's visibility as an effort on the part of modern organizations for "de-Islamization." De-Islamization is a process in which Islamic faith and beliefs of women are systematically deconstructed and distorted to induce a belief that Islam cannot free the poor from abject poverty. De-Islamization may in some cases be a first step in the process of converting women into Christianity (Mannan 2000).

Concluding thought

The net outcome of the tensions between the gender programs and the de-Islaminization of women produces at least three fractional images of women in Muslim societies. First, there is the image of modern and secular women promoted by the work of development NGOs. These women are measured against a poverty scale upon which the international organizations map the modernity and progress of poor women. The paradigm of modernity is designed to "developmentalize" women. Second, there is the image of a Muslim woman upheld and promoted by Islamic patriarchy. The women adopt *ḥijāb* as a symbol of Islamic modernity. Moreover, Islamic actors believe that the North, as in colonial days, is either employing NGOs to create more poverty or to pollute their Islamic belief and faith. Finally, there is the image of a woman based on the prevailing reality construed by local customs, beliefs, culture, and ecology (Shiva 1988). In reality, women continue to exist beyond the Western and Islamic paradigms as a part of a historical stream to form subaltern subjects. These three contending interpretations compete with each other to control the lives of women.

In the last analysis, the historically evolved gender norms in developed countries have split into concepts of gender in developing Islamic countries. As both capitalist patriarchy and Islamic patriarchy try to construct women's identities with their respective paradigms, they create problems for their partner organizations. All partner NGOs and international organizations locate themselves in the tension between capitalist patriarchy and Islamic patriarchy. As a logical outcome, many NGOs in the name of gender try to maintain the status quo; others adopt a reformist approach, but women's movements and gender ideologies still have a long way to go to bring about positive changes in the life of women in Islamic cultures.

Bibliography

H. Afshar, Gendering the millennium. Globalising women, in D. Eade (ed.), *Development and culture*, Oxford 2002, 336–47.

N. Berkovitch, The emergence and transformation of the international women's movement, in J. Boli and G. M. Thomas (eds.), *Constructing world culture. International nongovernmental organizations since 1875*, Stanford 1999, 100–26.

E. Boserup, *Women's role in economic development*, London 1970.

A. R. Doi, *Women in the Qur'an and the Sunnah*, London 1993.

R. Hassan, The issue of woman-man equality in the Islamic tradition, in L. Grob, R. Hassan, and G. Gordon (eds.), *Women's and men's liberation. Testimonies of spirit*, New York 1991a, 65–82.

——, Muslim women and post-patriarchal Islam, in P. M. Cooey et al. (eds.), *After patriarchy. Feminist transformations of the world religions*, Maryknoll, N.Y. 1991b, 39–64.

——, Women's interpretation of Islam, in H. Thijssen (ed.), *Women and Islam in Muslim societies*, The Hague 1994, 113–21.

E. M. King et al., *Engendering development. Through gender equality in rights, resources, and voice*, Washington, D.C. 2001.

M. Mannan, Islam, gender and conflict models. NGOs and the discursive process, paper presented to the European Network for Bangladesh Studies Conference, Oslo 2000, <http://www.bath.ac.uk/cds/enbs-paperspdfs/mannan.pdf>.

C. O. M. Moser, Gender planning in the Third World. Meeting practical and strategic gender needs, in *World Development* 17:11 (1989), 1799–1825.

——, *Gender planning and development. Theory, practice and training*, London 1993.

L. Østergaard, *Gender and development. A practical guide*, London 1992.

A. Penrose, Partnership, in D. H. Robinson and J. Harriss (eds.), *Managing development. Understanding inter-organizational relations*, London 2000, 243–60.

A. Rippin, *Muslims. Their religious beliefs and practices*, ii, *The contemporary period*, London 1993.

C. Roche, *Impact assessment for development agencies. Learning to value change*, Oxford 1999.

G. Rubin, The traffic in women. Notes on the "political economy" of sex, in R. Reiter (ed.), *Toward an anthropology of women*, New York 1975, 157–210.

V. Shiva, *Staying alive. Women, ecology and survival in India*, New Delhi 1988.

MANZURUL MANNAN

Jewish Women

Overview

The status and condition of Jewish women living in Muslim societies are based on Jewish law and traditions and influenced by Muslim law and practice, conditions specific to individual regions and developments over time. Thus, while there are those basics common to Jewish women in general, specifics change due to neighboring cultural and societal influences and historical and economic developments.

The status of women as subordinate to men is stated at the very beginning of the Bible, in the story of the creation of the human race. According to one version, the first man, Adam, was created by God in his own image "male and female He created them" (Genesis 1:27), thus giving women the same divine origin as men. Nonetheless, another story of creation is more popular and better known. It states that Adam was created by God from the dust of the earth and the first woman, Eve, was formed by God from the rib of Adam, aimed to serve the man and be his companion and helper (Genesis 2:7, 21–3). Accordingly, women were to be subordinate to men, mainly under their husbands' rule and their chief function in life was childbearing. Thus, the primary reason for the creation of two sexes was not companionship and service but reproduction, and much of the difference in Judaism between the status of men and women derives from this.

In Biblical times marriage was usually arranged between parents, but the woman's approval was requested. In later periods, this latter option often remained only a formality and the daughter did not have much say in the selection of the bridegroom. In some regions, there were occasions in which young Jews could see each other and choose a mate, although parental approval was required. In Tripoli, Libya, on the last day of Passover, Jewish maidens stood at the gate of their home, beautified and nicely dressed, and young Jewish men walked by to look at them. Afterwards, the men went to the woman's parents to ask for her in marriage. In villages, young people could often see each other at the well, and then try to arrange an engagement. At times, in Tripolitania, Jewish men got the help of Muslim tribal chiefs for that purpose. Usually, however, marriage was arranged by parents, and was the beginning of an alliance. Even when it grew into companionship, it was rarely one between equals, as the husband remained the master and the wife took care of his needs.

Until the twentieth century, Jewish brides in Muslim countries were often very young, between the ages of 8 and 14. In some regions, even babies were promised in marriage. In Yemen, this practice was justified as a prevention measure, so that the Muslim state could not claim "protection" over Jewish orphans and Islamize them. This practice, however, was often used to enable old men to marry young girls. Among the crypto-Jews of Mashhad, Iran, the practice was used after the 1839 forced Islamization to prevent intermarriage with Muslims. When foreign schools were established in Muslim countries, they tried to postpone the marriage age of Jewish girls.

Virginity was considered of paramount importance. When it was found that a woman was not a virgin when married for the first time, she was brought to the door of her father's house and stoned to death by the town's people (Deuteronomy 22:20). In many Jewish communities under Islam, it was common for the mother of the bride to wait until the marriage was consummated and then show the bloody dress or sheet as a proof of her daughter's virginity.

Although Biblical law allowed polygamy, the more common practice was monogamy. Since childbearing was considered the woman's chief function, barreness could be a reason for bigamous relations and divorce, in order to enable men to have children: it was the woman who was considered the guilty party when a couple did not have children. In later periods, if the couple did not have children for ten years, the husband had to take another wife or divorce his first wife if she refused to accept his marrying a second wife. In the case of a man with no heir special arrangements were developed in Biblical times and elaborated later. His widow had to marry his brother, or in the absence of a brother another close relative. This practice (*yibum*, levirate marriage) could cause polygamous marriages. When the widow refused to marry the relative, she had to receive his approval and undergo an elaborate and humiliating ceremony, *ḥalitsah*, removal (of the shoe of the man and spitting at his face). These rules are still in force, and men might demand a hefty sum for releasing the widow from an enforced marriage. Since medieval times the common view was that *ḥalitsah* has priority over *yibum*, though not all rabbis (for example, Maimonides, who lived in Egypt in the twelfth century) and communities (for example, Algeria) accepted this view.

Biblical law permits divorce, but only the husband can initiate it. While numerous regulations were added to the process over time the principle remained the same, and the wife cannot initiate divorce, except in a very limited number of cases (for example, when the Jewish court of law agrees that the husband is incompetent physically or mentally). Thus, husbands can prevent wives from being absolved of a failed marriage and starting a new life, and men might require a large payment and put forward difficult conditions for divorcing their wives. One of the most painful problems in this regard is when a husband disappears without leaving trace (for example, missing in action, gone on business trip). The deserted wife (*ʿagunah*, "anchored" to her husband) cannot then be divorced, nor is the Jewish court of law able to force her husband to divorce her. Though attempts were made over time to solve this problem, it is still an acute one.

In the medieval period, Rabbi Gershom, the "Light of the Diaspora" (ca. 960–1028), of Germany prohibited polygamy and divorcing a wife against her will. This became known as the "Ban of Rabbi Gershom," the violation of which carried severe judicial sanctions by the Jewish court of law. These prohibitions are still followed by the Ashkenazi communities (that is, by most European Jews) and were influenced by the prevalent Christian laws requiring monogamy. This is one of the major differences between the condition of Jewish women under Christianity and under Islam. In the latter, the Ban of Rabbi Gershom was not observed, influenced by the Muslim acceptance in principle of polygamy. Sephardi and Mizrahi communities (Jews originating from Spain and their offspring as well as those originating from Muslim countries) did not accept Rabbi Gershom's Ban, while Ashkenazi communities generally did, even after Ashkenazim settled in Muslim countries. This does not mean, though, that polygamy was prevalent among Jews under Islam, but it was allowed and occasionally did take place even in the twentieth century.

Both genders were subject to strict laws of purity, and women were regarded as impure during their menstrual period followed by another 7 "clean" days (Leviticus, 15). Women were also considered impure for 7 days following the birth of a son and were forbidden to touch consecrated objects or visit a sanctuary for the following 33 days; both figures were doubled when women gave birth to a girl (Leviticus 12:2–5). While impure men and women are forbidden to each other, only women are under a mandatory period of impurity. Over time, the regulations regarding purification and immersion in the ritual bath (mikva) became very elaborate, and they are still in force. Conjugal relations were stipulated as a duty in the marriage contract, and it became customary to have them at least on those Friday nights in which the woman was "clean."

Women's various tasks within the family included service to their husbands, maintaining the home, and taking care of her children, for which they were praised as a good wife and mother. Influenced apparently by the sociocultural attitudes of twelfth-century Egypt, Maimonides ruled that if a wife refuses to carry out her duties toward her husband, such as washing his hands and feet, or serving him at the table, she is to be chastised with a rod. This was not, however, the common view among contemporary rabbis who objected, stating that they never heard that it was permitted to raise a rod to a woman. This was also contrary to the practice in Ashkenazi communities at the time, where husbands were not allowed to beat their wives. This is not to say, however, that Jewish battered wives did not exist.

The division between the public and private realm was strongly observed among Jews in Muslim countries. Since women were basically restricted to the private realm, and contacts with non-kin men were frowned upon, men did the shopping in the market. Women usually went out in groups or chaperoned by a male relative, and their visits were mostly to other female friends and relatives, to the mikva, the synagogue, the cemetery, or to saints' shrines. Although women's work was mostly at home or in its vicinity (for example, in the vegetable garden), it was usually the women's job in rural areas to draw water and to fetch wood – activities that were usually conducted by a group of women. Most Jewish women did not work outside their homes until the late nineteenth century. Some women, though, worked in exclusively female jobs, such as midwives, cosmeticians (mainly for brides), and mikva supervisors. Others became maids when economics forced them, but usually only until they married. A few were peddlers, merchants, or in finance. Some women worked at home and sold their extra produce (embroidery, sewing, spinning, or foodstuffs). With the advent of female formal education, women trained in professions, but the society was slow to accept their participation in the job market, where most women were both young and unmarried or older widows.

Not only was women's role in life and in the family viewed as different from that of men, but the Bible also regards their basic character as different. While Adam is shown as God-fearing and obedient, disobedience is attributed to women: it was Eve who ate from the forbidden tree in the Garden of Eden, and convinced Adam to follow suit, whereupon their eyes were opened and they gained wisdom. While this is usually presented as an act of sacrilege and disobedience, it can also be interpreted as independent thinking and desire for knowledge. This dichotomy was further developed in later periods, attributing to women earthly, sensual, lascivious behavior in contrast to men's spiritual character. It is the man who is described as innocent, and he is warned to beware of the evil temptress who seeks to beguile him.

Over time, additional negative qualities were attributed to women: they were said to be greedy, eavesdroppers, lazy, and jealous, as well as querulous, garrulous, and "light-minded," namely, frivolous, inconsistent, and unstable. It was also claimed that "ten measures of speech descended to the earth; women took nine." Moreover, women were feared as a source of temptation, and it was specifically stated that their voice, hair, and legs are a sexual incitement. Consequently, various restrictions were placed on women, though none on men, and nowhere was it explained why men are so easily tempted, while women are not. Thus, women were forbidden to sing and dance in public in front of non-kin men. Besides, the hair of married women had to be covered as well as most of their body. In many regions under Muslim rule, Jewish women used the veil, similar to Muslim women, but at times there were differences in color and shape. During the Safavid period in Iran (1501–1731), Jewish women had to sew bells on the bottom of their veil to warn Muslims of their arrival. During the nineteenth century, they had to cover their faces with a black piece of fabric, contrary to the white used by Muslim women. In Kurdistan, they were not allowed to cover their faces, when this was a sign of looseness and immorality, and their veils were of two colors. These practices ended in Iran in 1936 with the official unveiling of women.

The general attitude toward women in later periods is reflected in the wording of the benediction recited daily by men, praising God for not having made them women. From the context one might conclude that the thanks are for the greater opportunities men have because they have to carry out more precepts (mitzvot) than women: while men have to carry out all precepts, women are exempt from precepts that depend upon a specific time. Still, this acknowledges that Judaism provides women with fewer opportunities to fully carry out religious obligations. Moreover, the prevalent interpretation of the benediction is indeed that men regard themselves fortunate for being born male and not female, and that they view men as superior to women.

In Biblical times, the three annual pilgrimages to the Temple of Jerusalem were mandatory only for men although women could accompany their husbands. In post-Biblical times, when the synagogue gradually replaced the Jerusalem Temple as the center of religious worship, the status of women regarding worship did not change and they could not actively participate in the service. Moreover, according to Maimonides, women should not be appointed to any communal office. This had physical and spiritual-educational implications for women. As time passed and procedural regulations became more elaborate, a special section was set up in the synagogue for women who wanted to be present at the service and observe it. This section (*ʿezrat nashim*) was often in a balcony or at the rear of the auditorium, constructed in such a way that allowed women to watch and hear the service without letting the men see them lest they be distracted during their prayers. Synagogues in Muslim countries, especially in rural areas, were slower to add a women's section. Women, though, used to clean the synagogue and its vicinity and viewed it as a great privilege. Women also composed special songs in the vernacular in honor of the synagogue and the Torah scroll and regarded it as a special omen to kiss the latter or other sacred objects. Women also used sacred objects as talismans guaranteeing health and longevity for themselves and for family members.

Since women were not obliged to participate in the service in the synagogue and had no role in the temporal and religious administration of the community, the latter did not regard it as mandatory to provide formal education for women. There were, however, girls who received formal education, usually when their brothers were tutored at home or when they had no brothers and their fathers were learned men who often taught them themselves. Some communities had religious primary schools that allowed young girls to study together with little boys before they reached puberty, and in any case only for two or three years. But the general practice was not to provide formal education for girls. One of the most radical statements in this regard was "whosoever teaches his daughter the Torah it is as though he teaches her lasciviousness." Consequently, girls were educated at home by their female relatives, who taught them how to maintain a Jewish home. This included not only manual work but also prayers and related Jewish laws (for example, kosher food, times of work and rest, especially as regards the Shabat, and purity laws). Thus, boys and girls received different education, leading toward different goals based on the perceived place in the world destined for each gender.

It would be wrong to conclude that girls were less educated than boys, but it is true that they received what the Jewish community perceived as the less prestigious education. Since the main goal of boys' education was to enable them to participate in the service in the synagogue, they learned to read the Hebrew holy scriptures, mainly the Pentateuch. Nonetheless, they usually could only recite the text without properly understanding it, because the spoken language of Jews in most communities of the Jewish diaspora was a Jewish dialect of the local language (for example, Yiddish, Ladino, Judeo-Arabic, Judeo-Persian). Only relatively few men became religious scholars who understood the holy scriptures and other religious writings, and even fewer could write in Hebrew or in the vernacular. Adult education for men in the synagogue was usually limited to recitation of religious texts in Hebrew and Aramaic, which most of the audience did not understand. Girls' education was experience-based and was much more creative and individualistic than that of boys. Moreover, women developed oral poetry in the vernacular, which was understood by all and was constantly changed by individuals based on current events and personal feelings. Women were also involved in other branches of art such as embroidery, singing, and dancing (the latter two only in front of women or close family members). Every woman could contribute to these constantly evolving art forms based on her inclinations and talents, regardless of her level of formal education or socioeconomic status. Women were often the ones passing on tradition to children. This was an important issue among the crypto-Jews of Mashhad who after the forced Islamization of 1839 tried to keep their Jewish faith alive in secret. Since women were secluded, it was easier for them to clandestinely pass on tradition to their children.

Modern schools, especially those for girls, were established in Muslim countries later than in the West. At first, schools were established by Western institutions, most of which were Christian religious ones. Later on, Jewish European organizations opened schools so that local Jews could receive a combination of modern and Jewish education. The next step was the establishment of modernized Jewish communal education for boys and state schools for both genders. As a result of these developments, Jewish girls could receive formal education, and contrary to Jewish boys, all female formal education was modern. However, Jewish girls often received an education that was not in tune with their cultural and social environment.

Bibliography

S. D. Goitein, *A Mediterranean society. The Jewish communities of the Arab world as portrayed in the documents of the Cairo Geniza*, Berkeley 1967–93.

R. Lamdan, *A separate people. Jewish women in Palestine, Syria, and Egypt in the sixteenth century*, Boston 2000.

B. Lewis, *The Jews of Islam*, Princeton, N.J. 1984.

A. Rodrigue, *Images of Sephardi and Eastern Jewries in transition. The teachers of the Alliance israélite universelle, 1860–1939*, Seattle 1993.

H. Sarshar (ed.), *Esther's children. A portrait of Iranian Jews*, Beverly Hills 2002.

R. Simon, *Change within tradition among Jewish women in Libya*, Seattle 1992.

——, Between the family and the outside world. Jewish girls in the modern Middle East and North Africa, in *Jewish Social Studies* 7 (2000), 81–108.

N. A. Stillman, *The Jews of Arab lands. A history and source book*, Philadelphia 1979.

Rachel Simon

Jihad

Arab States

There is, especially in the West, a popular misconception that jihad means "holy war," referring only to military struggle against non-Muslims with the purpose of spreading Islam. Both scholars of Islam and Muslim activists alike, however, stress the wider meaning of jihad, which refers more generally to praiseworthy and pious efforts, "the struggle against one's bad inclinations," and "the struggle for the good of Muslim society and against corruption and decadence" (Peters 1996, 116). Muslim authorities have taken different positions on the appropriateness of women's participation in various forms of jihad. Jihad has been deemed an obligation for all Muslims, but its purposes, forms, and participants have been explained, justified, and mobilized differently over time, depending on the sociopolitical circumstances. The variable conceptions and practices of jihad have both challenged and reinforced dominant gender relations in different contexts. There is a notable dearth of research into the topic of women and jihad, and even fewer scholarly treatments focus on the non-military aspects of the concept.

Islamic history

A *ḥadīth* (one of the sayings of the Prophet) reports that Muḥammad, on returning from a battle, exclaimed "we have come back from the lesser jihad to the greater jihad." When asked what he meant by the "greater jihad," he answered "the jihad against oneself." Throughout Islamic history, Muslim women have publicly participated in jihad, including both the "great jihad" of internal struggle for self-improvement, and the "little jihad" of martial struggle against the enemies of Islam. Four famous women from the time of the Prophet Muḥammad joined the jihad to defend Islam against its foes, all having been involved in battle: Khadīja, Muḥammad's first wife, ʿĀʾisha, his youngest wife, Zaynab bt. ʿAlī, his granddaughter, and Nusayba bt. Kaʿb. The latter, also referred to as al-Najariyya and al-Mazayniyya, is one of the most famous jihad warriors. She fought at the battle of Uhud in 625 C.E. and is reported to have personally defended the Prophet Muḥammad there (Cooke 2002). These historical figures became models for future Muslim activists, who cited them as precedents when justifying their participation in jihad and their calls for Muslims, including women, to struggle likewise in the path of God (Cooke 2000, 55).

Layla bt. Ṭarīf is also mentioned as a fighter among the seventh-century Khārijīs (Cooke forthcoming). Based on the fact that women fought with the Prophet Muḥammad and accompanied him in battle, the Khārijīs argued that fighting jihad was not only legitimate, but a religious requirement for women. Other women, such as the famous poet al-Khansāʾ, were present at battles, encouraging Muslim warriors with their verse (Ahmed 1992, 71–2).

The dominant orthodox Muslims fighting the Khārijīs opposed women's participation in jihad and "killed and exposed naked the women captured in their battles with the Kharijis" (Ahmed 1992, 71). In the period following the death of the Prophet Muḥammad, it was claimed that women should not be visible in public, nor should they fight. Jihad was portrayed as a male domain, especially after the fight against the Crusades (Cooke 2002, 230).

Egypt

Sayyid Quṭb (1906–66), a modern Egyptian Islamist ideologue and a leader of the Ikhwān al-Muslimīn (Muslim Brotherhood) was influential in shaping the thought and agenda of much contemporary Islamic revivalism. Jihad was a concept central to his interpretation of Islam, and he considered military jihad, as part of Islam's "pragmatic activistic system of life," to be a precondition for the *daʿwa* (call to Islam) to proceed, such that a just Islamic society could be established. He wrote that while peace is the essential character of Islam, so too is jihad a necessity against forces that would impede the dominance of Islam (Haddad 1983).

Quṭb argued that preaching, persuasion, as well as the use of force "to set human beings free from the yoke of human enslavement and make them serve the One and Only God" are principles of equal importance. Quṭb's exegesis of the history, meanings, and purpose of jihad in one of his most well-known tracts, *Milestones*, does not articulate a position on women's role in jihad. Saudi preacher Fāṭima Nasīf, however, cites Quṭb as affirming that women may participate in jihad if absolutely necessary (Cooke forthcoming).

The Egyptian Zaynab al-Ghazālī, prior to becoming a leader in the Muslim Brotherhood, formed the Muslim Women's Society in 1936. While she emphasized the domestic role as women's proper form of participation in jihad, her own politico-religious endeavors went far beyond this. During Nasser's crackdown against Islamists, al-Ghazālī helped organize the Brotherhood to resume its activities, and made "a vow to God to struggle even to the point of death in the path of His call." She also refused to let her husband get in the way of her "struggle in the path of God," asking him to sign an agreement promising his non-interference. In her prison memoirs, *Days From My Life* (1986), she expressly refers to famous warriors from the time of the Prophet as being role models (Hoffman 1984).

In the current Islamist "piety movement" in Egypt, of which the women's mosque movement is a part, participants focus on learning Islamic scriptures and proper practice of Islam as part of their ethical self-fashioning. In their efforts to cultivate virtuous selves, careful enactment of moral behavior and thought, including modesty, honesty, and self-willed obedience to religious strictures are paramount concerns (Mahmood 2003).

PALESTINE

Unlike Egyptian Islamists whose jihad has been geared toward the establishment of an Islamic state, Palestinian efforts are aimed at ending the Israeli occupation, and are motivated by a mix of nationalist and, only for some, religious, concerns. In this political context, jihad has taken on a meaning that encompasses several notions of struggle: for land, for country, for freedom, and for religion.

Palestinian women have been involved in political and military efforts to block Zionist colonial settlement since the 1936–9 Arab Revolt led by Shaykh ʿIzz al-Dīn al-Qassām, and throughout the "revolution" in the 1960s when the Palestine Liberation Organization (PLO) began its armed guerilla movement. Several women became famous for their military operations, including Layla Khālid, a member of the Popular Front for the Liberation of Palestine (PFLP), and Fatah operative Dalāl al-Mughrabī, but their involvement in these largely secular political organizations was not necessarily framed in terms of jihad. ʿĀṭif ʿAlyān, a member of Islamic Jihad, was arrested before carrying out a suicide attack using a car bomb in Jerusalem in 1987.

On 27 January 2002, Wafāʾ Idrīs became the first of several Palestinian woman to execute what most Palestinians refer to as a "martyrdom operation," exploding herself, killing one Israeli and injuring 100 others in Jerusalem. The discourse surrounding her act, and that of the other women who carried out similar attacks, included an explicitly gendered challenge, directed both at Palestinian society and the international community. The communiqué issued by the Al-Aqsa Martyrs' Brigades, the Fatah-linked militia that facilitated Idrīs's bombing, described her as being "a woman, but worth a thousand men." The defiant challenges of their messages and actions did not, however, disrupt traditional gender roles. In the video-taped final testimony of female suicide bomber, Ayāt al-Akhras, she declared that her action was in revenge for women who had lost their children, and those who were orphaned. She criticized the Arab leaders for neglecting Palestine to such an extent that even Palestinian girls are fighting. Women combatants such as these are popularly considered martyrs and heroes, but not always referred to as *mujāhidāt*. Another woman suicide bomber, however, Darīn Abū ʿĀʾisha, was labeled a *mujāhida*, and her death was recognized as being for the sake of God. In her final note she specifically framed her act as being part of struggle "in the way of God," and claimed for women the right to jihad against oppression, since women's role is no less than that of the (male) *mujāhidīn*. While some scholars interpret women's use of jihad rhetoric as being an excuse and justification for what is actually feminist behavior (Cooke 2002, 229), this development in women's militancy has not translated into overall shifts in gender roles, or into women's greater political participation.

Women's militant anti-occupation activities have sparked another level of debate in the ongoing discussion of the religious legitimacy of suicide bombings. Shaykh Yūsuf al-Qaraḍāwī, a leading Egyptian Muslim scholar, and president of the European Council for Fatwa and Research, declared that martyrdom operations are the highest form of jihad. While other Islamic scholars echoed his opinion, it was not a universally held ruling among muftis. As for women's participation, Shaykh al-Qaraḍāwī also declared that this is permitted, because when the enemy attacks part of the Muslim territories, jihad becomes an individual duty of all. Woman can participate in this form of jihad "according to her own means and condition." Qaraḍāwī's fatwa included strategic reasoning when he maintained that women could carry out attacks and reach places that men could not. This recalls the emergence of *mujāhidāt*, women militants of the Algerian Revolution who became heroines in the 1960s for transporting bombs in their dresses, thus evading French capture (Moghadam 2003).

Leaders of the Palestinian Islamic Resistance Movement, Hamas, a branch of the Muslim Brotherhood established in 1988 in Palestine, concurred with Qaraḍāwī's reasoning. But the Hamas spiritual leader, Shaykh Aḥmad Yāsīn, said that women need not be deployed so long as there are men volunteering for such attacks. Sayyid Quṭb's thoughts on the subject of jihad are echoed in the charter of Hamas. Article 12 of its charter declares that jihad against the enemy is an individual obligation of every Muslim man and woman when the enemy invades the land of the Muslims. In this situation, a woman can fight even without her husband's permission. Jihad, which the charter discusses in nationalist terms as being necessary to the solution of the Palestinian problem, is expansively defined in Article 30: "*Jihad* is not confined to carrying arms and clashing with the enemy. The good word, the excellent article, the useful book, support, and aid – all that, too, is *Jihad* for the sake of Allah, as long as the intentions are sincere to make Allah's banner paramount." A woman's role in the war of liberation is described as being no less than that of men, but is focused on her reproductive and domestic capabilities as a "manufacturer of men." Women are seen to play a major role in guiding future generations by educating children so they will be prepared for jihad (Mishal and Sela 2000, 182–95).

After women started carrying out suicide attacks, the general response in Palestine was to say that it was no surprise, as women have always been part of the resistance against occupation, and continue to be gravely oppressed, just as men are. This directly contradicts those Western sources that claim that these women have been exploited, and their female fragility taken advantage of. It also belies the Orientalist explanation of suicide bombers which, disregarding political motivation and sociohistorical context, holds that Middle Eastern men are seduced to commit such acts, lured by the promise of 70 doe-eyed virgins in heaven.

LEBANON

Women have been active participants in other resistance movements, including Amal and Hizballah (established in 1982), both Shīʿī groups fighting in the Lebanese civil war (1975–91) and against the Israeli occupation of Lebanon. In 1985, a young woman drove a car full of explosives into an Israeli checkpoint in Lebanon, killing two soldiers. Attitudes toward women's participation similar to those found in Palestine and Egypt were voiced by Mūsā al-Ṣadr, founder of Amal, who said that women complemented men's role in the struggle, and equaled them in heroism, nobility, and glory. Women's primary responsibility was in the domestic sphere, nurturing children, supporting men, and preparing them for jihad, but they could be called to fight if the political situation required it (Shehadeh 1999). Contemporary women's jihad among Shīʿī Muslims has been parsed into three major forms: resistance jihad of those participating in the Islamic Resistance, the personal jihad of self-improvement and building self-confidence, and gender jihad, which involves struggling for equity between women and men (Deeb 2003).

BIBLIOGRAPHY

L. Ahmed, *Women and gender in Islam. Historical roots of a modern debate*, New Haven, Conn. 1992.
M. Cooke, *Women claim Islam. Creating Islamic feminism through literature*, New York 2000.
——, Islamic feminism before and after September 11th, in *Duke Journal of Gender Law and Policy* 9 (2002), 227–36.
——, Women's *jihad* before and after September 11, in S. Zuhur (ed.), *Women and gender in the Middle East and Islam today*, University of California Press (forthcoming).
L. Deeb, An enchanted modern. Gender and public piety among Islamist Shiʿi Muslims in Beirut, Ph.D. diss., Department of Anthropology, Emory University 2003.
V. Hoffman, An Islamic activist. Zaynab al-Ghazali, in E. Fernea (ed.), *Women and the family in the Middle East. New voices of change*, Austin, Tex. 1984, 233–54.
S. Mahmood, Ethical formation and politics of individual autonomy in contemporary Egypt, in *Social Research* 70:3 (Fall 2003), 837–66.
S. Mishal and A. Sela, *The Palestinian Hamas. Vision, violence, and coexistence*, New York 2000.
V. Moghadam, *Modernizing women. Gender and social change in the Middle East*, Boulder, Colo. 2003.
R. Peters, *Jihad in classical and modern Islam. A reader*, Princeton, N.J. 1996.
L. Shehadeh, Women in the Lebanese militias, in L. Shehadeh (ed.), *Women and war in Lebanon*, Gainesville, Fla. 1999, 145–66.

LORI A. ALLEN

East Asia, Southeast Asia, and Australia

This entry deals with modern interpretations and expressions of jihad (literally meaning "struggle") and the role of Muslim women in jihad in East Asia, Southeast Asia, and Australia. Muslim women have been passionate defenders of religion in multiple ways, but most of them have placed less emphasis on armed struggle against the infidels than on the intellectual and moral struggle against backwardness, poverty, and social injustice. Although Muslim women agree on the universal applicability of jihad and on the high position of women in Islam, they interpret and apply jihad according to social, cultural, political, and economic circumstances.

EAST ASIA

In modern China, jihad has become part of civil society in the form of the women's movement. A number of women's organizations, including the Women's Association for Muslim Widows and Orphans, have been involved in the efforts to better the life of the marginalized, especially poor and uneducated women and children. Women teachers at the Shanghai Women's Mosque, for example, have also been progressive in their ideas and activities in seeking greater equality and justice. In Hui Muslim villages and townships, there has been a culture of resistance against the stagnation of faith (*weiganji*), youth disenchantment, criminality, economic backwardness, and the neglect of religious education. An example of the latter is the attempt to educate Chinese children and women for the defense of faith by publishing Chinese literature. Yet, for many Chinese women, jihad primarily means self-purification in the context of the three prevailing, often competing traditions: traditional Chinese law, modern law, and Islamic law.

In Japan, Muslim women have to reconcile diverse competing traditions. Most Muslim women in Japan converted to Islam through marrying Muslim immigrants from South Asia, Iran, and Central Europe. For many, the primary concern is the shift from a Japanese tradition to an Islamic identity. Japanese women converts often face ostracism from their family and alienation from friends. Struggle against the predominant Japanese culture takes different forms. If they work, they face the problem of performing daily prayers in a workplace where there is no prayer room and no break time for prayer. They also have to change their diet. Women encounter difficulties in educating their children about Islam and often face problems in dealing with authorities regarding school regulations.

For those who grow up in a nation focused on material development while religion is often kept in the background, jihad means primarily the search for meaning. The veil (*ḥijāb*) continues to be stressed not as a symbol of oppression but as a sign of identity. By wearing the veil many Japanese Muslim women become self-confident, serene, and dignified. For these women, *ḥijāb* and jihad have become closely intertwined: *ḥijāb* has become not only a sign of modesty and religious faith but also a symbol of the defense of Islam (jihad), the preservation of family, and therefore the identity of Muslim society. Associations like the Islamic Center of Japan, the Islamic Cultural Association, and the Japan Muslim Association aim to ensure self-purification and to preserve a sense of Islamic community. Providing men and women with a wide variety of Islamic information and services, they have become religious, social, and cultural spaces for Muslim families and their children to promote mutual Islamic fraternity.

In Korea, women's jihad has both internal and external dimensions. Because Christianity and Buddhism dominate the religious scene in modern Korea, Islam has developed as an outsider. While struggling for self-empowerment, Korean Muslim women have to counter stereotypes and misunderstandings about Islam. Recently, the Muslim Association has engaged in an increasing number of activities intended to improve public understanding of Islam. Some efforts are bearing fruit. For example, Islam is now accorded a status almost equivalent to that of Christianity and Buddhism in revised textbooks for middle and high school students. As in Japan, Muslim women in Korea interpret jihad in terms of proper observance of Islam.

SOUTHEAST ASIA

In the country with the largest Muslim population, Indonesia, contemporary Muslim women have become increasingly diverse in their understanding and implementation of jihad. In Aceh, with its history of seventeenth-century queens and nationalist female leaders, jihad symbolizes armed struggle against the infidel (*kāfir*), first in the form of Dutch colonialism and then the Indonesian nation-state. However, in most of the other regions, the term jihad connotes fighting against poverty, ignorance, and social injustice. In the colonial era, Aisyiyah, the women's wing of the Muhammadiyah (founded in 1912) established the Laskar Sabilillah (Defenders of God's path) and Laskar Hizbulwatan (Defenders of the nation), but in the postcolonial period such paramilitary organizations were deemed irrelevant. The meaning of jihad has therefore shifted from armed struggle to enjoining good and forbidding evil (*amar maruf nahi munkar*) in a wide variety of areas previously dominated by men, including politics, education, and religious propagation. Aisyiyah now runs orphanages, maternity clinics, hospitals, day-care and family planning centers, and girls' dormitories. Women are taught how to set up cooperatives and how to market their products in order to increase the family income. Similar organizations were established, including Muslimat, the women's wing of the Nahdlatul Ulama (founded in 1926).

Muslimat has focused on educating and empowering women mostly in rural areas, aiming to eradicate illiteracy and encouraging women to be more independent. Together with Aisyiyah and other smaller organizations, Muslimat has stressed economic progress, efficiency, and productivity. More recent feminist organizations, such as Rahima (Center for Training and Information on Islam and Women's Rights Issues), based in Jakarta, are particularly concerned to apply an Islamic perspective to women's empowerment and liberation. These women activists have avoided associating jihad with holy war. Resistance against state oppression, male supremacy, gender inequality, and injustice are for them much more relevant and urgent.

In modern Malaysia, Islamization has become the concern of both the state and civil society. For many women, jihad has meant a struggle for a greater conformity toward Islamic orthodoxy, but for liberal women activists, such as Sisters in Islam (SIS), jihad should signify women's liberation in all aspects of public and private life. These women, mostly middle-class, have taken the lead in opposing the Islamic establishment in the country as well as Islamic literalism. For example, they criticized the 1993 Sharīʿa Criminal Code (II) of the State of Kelantan and the 1994 Domestic Violence Act. SIS has also been vocal in advocating women's rights. The SIS leader Zainah Anwar argues that cultural traditions affirm women's public contribution and participation in often positive, non-hierarchical ways. Another kind of jihad has been promoted by missionary (*daʿwa*) movements, which flourish in schools, campuses, and businesses. The latter have been seeking economic autonomy and ritual segregation and have been promoting their own concept of gender equity, based on their interpretation of the Qur'ān and the *ḥadīth*, rather than on Western feminism. There are also moderate Muslim women who insist that there is no discrimination by God between men and women in any of their work. These moderate women believe that Muslim women should be able to reconcile authenticity and modernity. For these women, jihad should open up a wide variety of opportunities for female advancement, but pursuit of these should be peaceful.

In the Philippines, the meaning of jihad similarly varies according to different individuals and groups. Bangsamoro Muslim women, for example, are not monolithic in their beliefs. To them, jihad has meant armed resistance to the aggressive actions of martial law, personified by Ferdinand Marcos (president 1965–86) as well as actions by subsequent governments. Jihad has implied the continuous effort to defend their cultural tradition, property, land, livelihood, and life. Their rebel songs provide a unique indication of how they interpret jihad in relation to the defense of the indigenous community of the believers and their homeland. As the result, homeland (*inged*) and jihad have become closely interwoven in Bangsamoro thinking. However, in contemporary times, even for the Moro Islamic Liberation Front (MILF), jihad has come to convey more complex meanings. While it retains the old connotations (namely, fighting against colonialism and the enemy from within), it has also come to signify a moral struggle that aims to bring about a positive transformation of the inner self and the socioeconomic and political order.

Although many women are actively involved in the armed struggle and are trained in military camps, many others engage in medical services and educational or economic activities. Among the educated women are activists who have established foundations, such as the Salama Women Foundation and the Bangsamoro Women's Foundation for Peace and Development. Among Bangsamoro women who have excelled in the educational field are Bai Matabay Plang, Bai Tanto Sinsuat, and Bai Yasmin Sinsuat. The first Bangsamoro Women's Assembly was held in April 2003, where some 100,000 women tackled various concerns of Bangsamoro women in the context of the raging war in Mindanao, where the victims were mostly women and children. Unlike the MILF and other Moro fronts, important initiatives in Bangsamoro civil society have been promoting peaceful alternatives to solve the conflict – to bridge the gap of misunderstanding between the Manila government and the Bangsamoro people.

AUSTRALIA

The notion of jihad as armed struggle has never entered the minds of Muslim women in Australia. However, since the Australian constitution recognizes freedom of religion in the sense that the Commonwealth cannot make any law imposing religious observances or prohibiting the free exercise of any religion, Muslim women are increasingly realizing that Muslims continue to encounter problems in obtaining and practicing their rights, whether personal, human, or religious. Jihad for Muslim women in such contexts is thus not physical but intellectual and spiritual. They feel the need to demonstrate their overlapping Australian and Islamic identities, and have attempted to be the defenders of Islamic heritage in Australia's multicultural environment. They have to demonstrate their loyalty to Islam while avoiding placing themselves on the periphery of the wider Australian community. Amatullah Armstrong, a follower of

Sufism, for example, emphasizes that jihad is essentially the conquering of selfhood. She insists that the struggle along the spiritual path in Australia is great, for not only must a Muslim woman struggle against the enemies within herself but she must wage determined war against the irreligious tide in an era of decadence. For her, jihad is the battle to bring peace to the earth – not the physical earth out there – but the earth of the self.

Muslim women in Australia have been active in advocating Muslim rights. The Islamic Women's Welfare Council of Victoria (IWWCV) is the most famous in providing Islamic information and services. Their struggles have included an effort to correct misconceptions about Islam, including the meaning of jihad as holy war. According to IWWCV, the concept of jihad is generally misconstrued and limited to holy war. More broadly, jihad means to struggle and make an effort in any activity carried out for the sake of God. The greatest jihad is the struggle of the inner self. Since Islam is stereotypically associated with Arabs, especially after the 11 September 2001 terrorist attacks in the United States, Muslim women in Australia often suffer discrimination, harassment, and assault. Under these circumstances, they attempt to challenge the often biased media and politicians in order to improve the representation and public understanding of Islamic symbols. Jihad in Australia is therefore largely interpreted and implemented in the context of a multicultural society through mass media and education.

Referring to both an internal and external struggle, the passion attached to the Islamic concept of jihad has never been lost. Jihad provides the language of struggle in contexts where religious ideas and symbols are central. Women's jihad has accommodated a broad, diverse, and complex meaning according to different agencies and environments. However, although Muslim groups in certain parts of Southeast Asia still emphasize the military aspect of jihad, the vast majority of Muslim women in East Asia, Southeast Asia, and Australia have stressed its non-military aspects, especially in the context of the struggle against illiteracy, poverty, and social injustice.

Bibliography

T. Alawiyah, International seminar on women in Islam, conference report, Jakarta 2000.

A. Armstrong, *And the sky is not the limit. An Australian woman's spiritual journey within the traditions*, Karachi 2001.

B. Baried, Islam and the modernization of Indonesian women, in T. Abdullah and S. Siddique (eds.), *Islam and society in Southeast Asia*, Pasir Pajang, Singapore 1986, 139–54.

S. R. Dzuhayatin, Gender and pluralism in Indonesia, in R. W. Hefner (ed.), *The politics of multiculturalism. Pluralism and citizenship in Malaysia, Singapore, and Indonesia*, Honolulu 2001, 253–67.

A. Feillard, Indonesia's emerging Muslim feminism. Women leaders on equality, inheritance, and other gender issues, in *Studia Islamika* 4:1 (1997), 83–111.

P. G. Gowing, *Muslim Filipinos. Heritage and horizon*, Quezon City 1979.

Hsiung P.-C., M. Jaschok, and C. Milwertz (eds.), *Chinese women organizing. Cadres, feminists, Muslims, queers*, Oxford 2001.

R. Israeli, *Islam in China. Religion, ethnicity, culture, and politics*, Lanham, Md. 2002.

Istiadah, *Muslim women in contemporary Indonesia. Investigating paths to resist the patriarchal system*, Clayton, Vic. 1995.

M. Jaschok and Shui J. J., *The history of women's mosques in Chinese Islam. A mosque of their own*, Richmond, Surrey 2000.

W. J. Karim, *Women and culture. Between Malay adat and Islam*, Boulder, Colo. 1992.

L. Marcoes-Natsir et al. (eds.), *Conference on Indonesian Islamic women. Textual and contextual studies* [in Indonesian], Jakarta 1993.

S. Marden, Heirs of oppression or progeny of optimism? Muslim women in modern China in the light of traditional Chinese and Islamic perspectives, M.A. thesis, University of Hawaii at Manoa 1997.

T. M. McKenna, *Muslim rulers and rebels. Everyday politics and armed separatism in the Southern Philippines*, Berkeley 1998.

R. L. P. Moore, Women and warriors defending Islam in the Southern Philippines, Ph.D. diss., University of California, San Diego 1981.

L. Z. Munir, *Positioning woman's character. Women and change from women's perspective* [in Indonesian], Bandung 1999.

L. Y. Nakano, Muslim women in Japan, in *Japan Times*, 19 November 1992.

Pimpinan Pusat Aisyiyah, *A history of the rise and development of Aisyiyah* [in Indonesian], Yogyakarta 1995.

S. Rozaria, On being Australian and Muslim. Muslim women as defenders of Islamic heritage, in *Women's Studies International Forum* 21:6 (November–December 1998), 649–61.

I. Rudie, Women in Malaysia. Economic autonomy, ritual segregation, and some future possibilities, in B. Utas (ed.), *Women in Islamic societies. Social attitudes and historical perspectives*, London 1983, 12–143.

S. M. Samarai, History and development of Islam in Japan, paper presented at the symposium on Islam in East Asia: History and Culture, in Seoul, Korea, 22–4 August 1997.

L. R. Shehadeh, *The idea of women in fundamentalist Islam*, Gainesville, Fla. 2003.

J. A. Siapno, *Gender, Islam, nationalism and the state in Aceh. The paradox of power, co-optation and resistance*, London 2002.

J. Sleboda, Islam and women's rights advocacy in Malaysia, in *Asian Journal of Asian Studies* 7:2 (2001), 94–136.

Muhamad Ali

Iran and Afghanistan

In Western vocabulary the term "jihad" has been especially used to denote the "sacred war" of Muslims against their enemies. The 11 September 2001 tragedy has led to the identification of jihad, which was largely unknown to the Western public, with terrorism. But jihad also means "effort" made in social and political domains in order to enhance the territorial expansion of Islam. Religious authorities are unanimous in maintaining that neither this "offensive jihad" nor the "sacred war" is compulsory for Muslim women. Martyrdom (*shahāda*) associated with participation in these two forms of jihad is therefore peculiar to male warriors. In 1979, when the Islamic Republic of Iran was engaged in a war in Iranian Kurdistan, Ayatollah Khomeini, the leader, declared: "Some women asked me for authorization to fight in Kurdistan. They said they wanted to be martyrs. I did not agree, arguing that it was not convenient for women, that the army would do the job." For a number of religious authorities, including Ayatollah Khomeini, if a Muslim country is invaded by non-Muslims, "defensive jihad" becomes mandatory for all Muslims regardless of their gender, age, or status. Women and men alike should mobilize to defend the honor of Islam. For this reason Khomeini endorsed women's military training and their enrolment in the army and the *pasdaran* (revolutionary guards).

During the Iran-Iraq War (1980–8) women volunteers demanded authorization to go to the front. The Ayatollah argued that at the time of the Prophet women went to the front but their main role was to treat the wounded. Committed Iranian women participated in "defensive jihad" mainly through a multitude of activities ranging from taking care of the wounded or the families of martyrs, to baking bread or sewing uniforms for the soldiers of Islam. Although Marziyeh Haddidchi-Dabbagh, a confidante of Khomeini, one of his bodyguards, and a member of the second, third, and fifth Islamic parliaments was appointed commander of the *pasdaran* in western Iran, women were not asked to sacrifice their lives to the community. They were expected to show their commitment to Islam and to the Islamic Republic by accepting gendered roles. As presumed main guardians of traditions they were required to reinforce Islamic family ties, thereby maintaining social cohesion.

In Afghanistan, following the Soviet army's invasion in 1979, the religious authorities did not ask women to take arms and to fight against the army of infidels but they and the *mujāhidīn* (combatants of jihad) required women to contribute to the cause of jihad. The punishment for those who did not was severe. Mina Keshvar Kamal, a health worker and founding member of RAWA (Revolutionary Association of the Women of Afghanistan, a leftist group campaigning for women's rights and providing education and health facilities for women and children), was accused by the Hezb-i Islami (a fundamentalist group founded by Golboddin Hekmatyar within the *mujāhidīn*) of anti-jihad activities. She was assassinated in 1987 in Quetta.

In Iran as in Afghanistan women are especially required to participate in a different form of jihad called *jihād-i nafs*, or the effort made by all Muslim believers to raise themselves to the level of human perfection through piety and worldly asceticism. Although *jihād-i nafs* concerns both men and women, its symbols are gendered: the blood of the martyr and the Islamic veil, with equal symbolic values. Committed women's participation in *jihād-i nafs*, however, is not limited to their individual spiritual or inner struggle against the vices. Through engaging in the public sphere, they conduct an openly political and ideological jihad against poverty, illiteracy, and the like, in order to construct an Islamic society. The aim is to empower women to better serve the society and to be better mothers and wives. The Fatemeh Zahra Religious Seminary for women in Tehran trains women *mujtahid*s (legists engaged in theological interpretation); it also financially and morally assists deprived women in order to boost their activities in the public sphere. The seminary established a credit system, which collects money from the pious rich and grants interest-free loans to the poor. It helps poor families in Tehran and Qom, paying for the education of their children, and provides several female university students with financial assistance. Fatemeh Amini, its founder, who established the first religious seminary for women in 1972 declared: "Our goal is to contribute to women's development by giving impetus to their creativity, thereby also increasing their self-esteem." Women are also active in the Nehẓat-i Savād Āmūzī (Literacy movement organization) established in December 1979. It provides literacy education for adults, especially women, who comprise the majority of adult learners. The objectives are to teach reading and writing, and the promotion and dissemination of Islamic culture. It is believed that an Islamic society cannot be built unless women are educated. The female role models presented in literacy books are Fāṭima and Zaynab, respectively the daughter and granddaughter of the Prophet, symbols of courage and devotion, of women's pivotal role in the home and their active presence in the society. Although taking good care of the husband is presented as the holy task of women, equivalent to jihad in the path of Allah, booklets promote equal worth of male and female offspring and the need to treat children justly. When, contrary to pro-birth traditions of Islam, the Islamic Republic re-established the family planning program in 1989 to lower the birth rate, committed women took active part in educating rural and lower class women, promoting the idea that they can be better mothers with fewer children. This political and ideological jihad however, has had unintended social, cultural, and political consequences for the power elite. Iranian women, who are now better educated than before (51 percent of women aged 15 and over are now literate against 30 percent in 1976), have a much lower number of children (2.1 in 2001 against 7 in 1976), and play a more active role in the society, challenging patriarchal order and male domination. In Iran as in Afghanistan women also increasingly reject divine justifications for segregation policies.

Bibliography

Fatemeh Amini, personal interview, Tehran 1994.

H. Hoodfar, Reforming from within. Islamist women activists in Iran, in Women Living Under Muslim Laws, *Reconstructing fundamentalism and feminism. The dynamics of change in Iran*, Grabels, France 1995, 12–38.

G. Kepel, Jihad, in *Pouvoirs* 104 (2003), 135–42.

R. Khumaynī (Ayatollah Khomeini), *Ṣaḥīfa-yi nūr*, Tehran 1989, ix, 242.

A. Kian-Thiébaut, Women's religious seminaries in Iran, in *ISIM Newletter* 6 (2000), 23.

——, *Les femmes iraniennes entre islam, état et famille*, Paris 2002.

G. Mehran, Lifelong learning. New opportunities for women in a Muslim country (Iran), in *Comparative Education* 2 (1999), 201–15.

V. Moghadam, Revolution, the state, Islam, and women. Gender politics in Iran and Afghanistan, Women Living Under Muslim Laws, Dossier 7:8 (1991), 32–41.

Women living Under Muslim Laws, *Women's situation in Afghanistan*, Grabels, France 1998.

Azadeh Kian-Thiébaut

South Asia

In South Asia, the dominant feature of women's way of life is known as purdah (Papanek and Minault 1982). This tradition is respected by both Muslim and Hindu women. Strictly observed, purdah can lead to the complete seclusion of women. Despite this, Muslim women, like their male counterparts, recognize two different kinds of jihad: the physical *jihād-e asghar* and the spiritual *jihād-e akbar*. As early as the eleventh century, Muslim mystics distinguished the two jihads.

Jihād-e asghar

The *jihād-e asghar* or "lesser" jihad is the battle enjoined as a religious duty when Islam and the Muslims are threatened by infidels. In the history of Muslim South Asia, there are a few instances of women taking up arms, or even ruling the country, for example Raziyya Sultāna (d. 1240), who ruled the Delhi sultanate for three-and-a-half years. In the modern Indian subcontinent, Shāh Walī Allāh and his son and successor Shāh ʿAbd al-ʿAzīz issued fatwas in which they officially declared as *dār al-harb* the part of India that was under British rule. During the colonial period, it seems that the different jihads upheld by Indian Muslims did not involve women.

Recently, the situation has changed. After the attacks on the United States on 11 September 2001, the feminist wings of the Islamist parties were asked to attend protest rallies in the larger cities of Pakistan. Women were seen in the streets with banners demanding jihad against the American coalition during the war against the Taliban in Afghanistan. Some women were members of the Jamaat-e-Islami, but the most active were linked to the so-called *jihādī* groups, such as the Lashkar-i Tayba and Jaysh-i Muḥammad, which published newspapers for women in which they were asked to give their jewelry for the sake of jihad. Another example of ways in which women participated in the jihad effort is the letters in which mothers, sisters, and wives eulogized the sacrifice of their dear ones, the *shahīds*. In November 2001, the *jihādī* newspaper *Dharb-i-Muʾmin*, reported that 5,000 armed and veiled women had expressed their desire to take part in a jihad to help the Taliban in Afghanistan. These cases remain marginal because it is paradoxical to require women to live in seclusion and take an active role in a physical fight. Despite this attitude, when Dr. Farhat Hashmi, who ran Qurʾānic classes in Al-Huda Institution for Islamic Education, stated that women had many important things to achieve before thinking of jihad, she was called a *kāfir* by an *ʿālim*.

Jihād-e akbar

Here the situation is quite different. *Jihād-e akbar*, "greater" jihad, is the Sufi fight against the self (*nafs*). In the patriarchal society of South Asia, nothing forbids women from devoting their lives to religion, though there are very few Sufi-related organizations for women. An individual woman can nevertheless, in certain circumstances, turn to the mystic way, although this is not common because of the role women play in the family sphere. The *jihād-e akbar* is understood as the control of the *nafs* and it is not necessarily conducted in a Sufi group. But given the difficulty of this inner fight, the conditions of the Sufi life are more convenient for attaining the goal. Some women who are on the way of the *jihād-e akbar* can even choose the *qalandarī* way (that is, free of any Sufi order). If the *qalandars* do not form a real congregation or even a group, the *jihād-e akbar* can be realized through their participation in different kinds of Sufi rituals, such as *piyālo* (initiation), *dhikr* (meditation), *dhammāl* (ecstatic dance), and so forth. It is noteworthy that in the Sufi context no gender discrimination is generally observed. The *sajjadā nashīn* can be the spiritual guide of a woman, and she can be his murid, although it is nevertheless difficult to find women saints. Moreover, the traditional guise of the *qalandar* is the dress of a woman, with bangles, earrings, long hair, and ostentatious jewels and it is hard to distinguish a man from a woman.

Literature gives another view of the *jihād-e akbar* as it relates to women. In folk poetry of Sindh, for example, the figure of the bride is a polysemical symbol. The heroine always plays the most important role in the narrative proper, and she is also the symbol of the divinity such that the union of her bridegroom with her is understood as his union with God. The seeker must therefore attain immersion in God through the mediation of the female. The ultimate goal of the *jihād-e akbar* is the *fanāʾ fī Allāh*. There are many allusions to the *virahinī*, the woman who longs for her beloved, namely God or the Prophet. In his *Shāh-jo Risālo*, the great poet Shāh ʿAbd al-Lātif (d. 1757) gives a detailed description of the *jihād-e akbar* performed by the heroine Sūhnī: "Do not encumber yourself with self-consciousness or ego in your journey to the beloved" (1985, iii, 1675). Many references to marriage can also be found in other Muslim devotional literature in South Asia. In the hymns (*ginān*s) sung by the Khojās, who are Aghākhānī Ismāʿīlīs, Pīr Ḥasan Kabīr al-Dīn uttered: "O Master, how long can I remain alone, while my days pass in lack of love? Banish this lack of love, Master, and turn it into a married bliss" (cited in Shackle and Moir 1992, 99). In another *ginān*, Pīr Mīra Sayyid Khān addresses God with the following verse: "Listen, my Consort, and do as I say. Do not remain so aloof from me, your wife" (ibid., 95).

BIBLIOGRAPHY

S. Ali, Les romancières pakistanaises de 1947 à nos jours, doctoral thesis, University of Paris III 1985.

M. Boivin, Jihâd and national reassertion in post-9/11 Pakistan, in S. Shafqat and B. Spooner (eds.), *New perspectives on Pakistan. Contexts, realities, and visions for the future*, Columbia University Press (forthcoming).

C. Dedebant, *Le voile et la bannière. Mouvements féministes du Pakistan*, Paris 2001.

B. Metcalf (ed. and trans.), *Perfecting women. Maulana Ashrafʿ Ali Thanawi's* Bihishti Zewar, Berkeley 1990.

H. Papanek and G. Minault (eds.), *Separate worlds. Studies of purdah in South Asia*, Columbia, Mo. 1982.

C. Shackle and Z. Moir, *Ismaili hymns of South Asia. An introduction to the ginans*, London 1992.

Shāh ʿAbd al-Lātif, *Shāh-jo risālo*, Hyderabad 1985.

A. Weiss, *Walls within walls. Life history of working women in the old city of Lahore*, Boulder, Colo. 1992, Oxford 2002².

MICHEL BOIVIN

Sub-Saharan Africa: West Africa

Jihad in West Africa is a complex phenomenon, initially expressed in a series of reform movements in the seventeeth and eighteenth centuries and culminating in the creation of a number of Islamic states in the eighteenth and nineteenth centuries. These progressive revolutions impacted a region stretching from present-day Senegal and Gambia in the east to Cameroon in the west. Although there had been African Muslims in the region since the eleventh century, their connections and allegiances to the faith were through North Africa and across the Mediterranean. The leaders of the jihads created Islamic authorities where none had existed before and brought West Africa fully into the Dār al-Islām. They accomplished this by combining the religious goal of returning to a purer form of Islam with military action, territorial expansion, and state building.

There were a number of key "links" in the jihadic chain, starting with late seventeenth-century scholarly reformist traditions. Important eighteenth-century developments were the Futa Jallon jihad and the Futa Toro jihad, providing the ideological blueprint for the Sokoto jihad of Usman dan Fodio, which became the model – and at times legitimization – for subsequent nineteenth-century jihads. The imposition of European colonial rule in the late nineteenth and early twentieth centuries brought to an end this period of West African jihads. Yet, as elsewhere in Sub-Saharan African, Western colonialism itself provided the impetus for later calls to jihad, albeit with limited military success, as have post-independence reformist movements that evoke their great predecessors.

There were many shared features among the eighteenth- and nineteenth-century jihads. These include dominance by the Fulbe, an ethnic group who were primarily rural pastoralists; a leadership outside the established political system; the conquest of urban states; and a belief in Sufi ideas and practices (the Qādiriyya and Tijāniyya orders were important theological influences). These religious teachings encouraged the development of new doctrines and pious literatures and the use of vernacular languages, which in turn led to new roles for women.

One legacy of these jihads was the spread of Muslim beliefs from urban centers to the countryside where people from a variety of ethnic groups were encountered, some nominally Muslim, others following traditional religions. Conversion became a goal, especially in combating local spiritual practices. This particular struggle was often a gendered project and the battle one of words. For example, the Fulbe scholars of the Labe region of Futa Jallon wrote religious verse in their own language instead of Arabic in order to proselytize women and slaves (that is, non-Muslims) and free Fulbe Muslim women were enlisted to be teachers and pedagogues.

The leadership role of women was especially important in the establishment of the Sokoto Caliphate, founded by Usman dan Fodio (1754–1817). The explicit purpose of his military jihad was to establish a society where men and women could be Muslims under Muslim organizations and where un-Islamic behavior, epitomized by adherence to Bori spirit possession practices, would not be allowed. Dan Fodio came from an intellectual Fulbe elite (his family is believed by some to descend from Futa Toro reformists), which for generations had chosen to live in village settings, remote from the distractions of urban commerce and rule, that is, a form of *hijra* (migrating away from disbelievers). In his family it was normal for women to be educated, some becoming highly trained scholars. He said it was a positive duty to instruct women, and criticized men who kept their wives in ignorance: "Men treat these beings like household implements which become broken after long use, and which are thrown out on the dung-heap" (from Usman dan Fodio, *Nūr al-Albāb*, Hodgkin 1960).

Children were taught that the heart had to be purified from the whisperings of Satan, pride, false hope, anger, envy, and showing off. They were told they had to turn away from anything superfluous to a simple life. This training in the inner struggle was directed by women teachers, notably dan Fodio's wives Aisha and Hawwa, who both outlived him by 20 years and promoted post-jihad standards throughout the caliphate.

Dan Fodio started preaching in the 1790s and after inspiring large numbers of people to join his community, became a threat to the Hausa status quo and the jihad ensued. From February 1804 to October 1808 the Shehu was on the move, sometimes in retreat, sometimes on the attack. Losses were considerable and the privations suffered affected the women and children who traveled with the army, there being no safe haven for them. These women had to do things they had never dreamed of doing. In one crucial battle it was recorded,

> Then, they [the enemy] turned away and most of them were struck down by arrows,
> And there were slain among them about fifty impious men,
> And our women added to it by stoning and leaving them exposed in the sun (A. Danfodio 1963).

By 1808 the period of intensive warfare was over although military actions continued for decades. When Usman dan Fodio's son and eventual successor, Muhammad Bello, began building a defensive *ribāṭ* at Sokoto, he had as his objectives the safeguarding of the frontier, the resettlement of a huge number of captives, and the reconciliation of all factions of the population.

The young female slaves who became concubines posed a threat to the integrity of the new caliphate because they were ignorant of Islam, while at the same time being knowledgeable about the spirit world of Bori. The Bori spirit cult originated and is most associated with the Hausa of Nigeria and Niger. Dan Fodio's establishment of the Sokoto Caliphate in Northern Nigeria involved the consolidation of a number of Hausa emirates that had included both Muslim and "pagan" Hausas, Muslim and "pagan" Fulbes, and members of other ethnic groups. This possession cult included such un-Islamic practices as the use of hallucinatory herbs, hypnotic drumming, confidence in magic, belief in the efficacy of animal sacrifice, and female religious leaders such as the Inna of Gobir. The invasion of the Sokoto wives' domains by foreign women who, in due course, bore their masters' children presented a threefold challenge. First, the wives had to accommodate the newcomers emotionally, exercising tact and patience. Second, they had to strive to keep the homogeneity of the caliphate heartland intact by educating the concubines and requiring from them religious conformity. Third, they had to ensure that the children of the concubines received proper training and grew up as Muslims.

In the postwar period, educated women were

highly useful to the new caliphate. Of the 29 female scholars known by name, several of dan Fodio's daughters were outstanding leaders, including Maryam, Fatima, and Asma'u. Nana Asma'u (1793–1864) is the most famous. Her brother Caliph Muhammad Bello recognized and used her creative and organizational talents in furthering his aim of promoting Islam to women.

An important development in the consolidation of the post-jihadic state occurred in the 1830s when Asma'u directed her educational message to rural women. She identified senior village women and authorized them to bring groups of girls and grandmothers to her. Their task was to memorize the verses she composed for them and then to return home and teach others. These associates, the famed Yan Taru, flourished for decades and continue to make their journeys to Sokoto in the twenty-first century. The room she used as a classroom is still in use today, 140 years after her death.

Asma'u's deep concern for the women at the fringes of society ensured that her memory lived on, but it was her scholarly writings that guaranteed her fame. In more than 60 works, written over a period of 40 years in three languages, she expressed herself on a variety of subjects. Her translation of her father's poem *Tabbat Hakika* (Be sure of this) on rights and responsibilities in an Islamic state is now part of the Sokoto tradition together with her history of the jihad, *Wakar Gewaye* (The journey). Nothing so convincingly shows how her influence spread from the world of women to that of men as the elegant verses she exchanged with scholars such as a visiting Mauritanian shaykh or the admonishment she sent to a misbehaving provincial governor. Interviewed in 2003 on the eve of the 200th anniversary of the caliphate, Alhaji Mohammadu Maccido, the Sultan of Sokoto, said that Asma'u primarily helped women because as a woman she was limited to teaching them rather than men, but her knowledge was of benefit to everyone, men and women alike.

Hajiya Saʿadiya Omar, Director of the Centre for Hausa Studies at Usmanu Danfodiyo University, is the leader of the Sokoto branch of the Federation of Muslim Women's Associations of Nigeria (FOMWAN). Interviewed on Nigerian television in 2003, she spoke of the meaning Asma'u's life had for her and for her four female colleagues who appeared on the same program – a physician, a lecturer in modern European languages, a librarian, and an engineer:

> The aim of FOMWAN is to upgrade the status of Muslim women through increasing their religious awareness and education – exactly what Nana Asma'u did. She mobilized women and brought them together, she taught and reformed them making them better members of society. Our inspiration came from her and we look on her as a model. Whatever we achieve is indigenous. Our ideas do not come from the United States, nor the United Kingdom, nor from Saudi Arabia. We have our model here. We may learn from others but our upbringing, our development is through Nana Asma'u.

Bibliography

N. Asma'u, *The collected works of Nana Asma'u*, ed. J. Boyd and B. B. Mack, Lansing, Mich. 1997.

R. Botte, Pouvoir du livre, pouvoir des hommes. La religion comme critère de distinction, in *Journal des Africanistes* 60:2 (1990), 37–51.

A. Danfodio, Tazyīn al-waraqāt, ed. and trans. M. Hiskett, Ibadan, Nigeria 1963.

M. Hiskett, *The development of Islam in West Africa*, London 1984.

T. L. Hodgkin, ʿUthman dan Fodio, *Nur al-albab*. Extract, in T. L. Hodgkin (comp.), *Nigerian perspectives. An historical anthology*, Oxford 1960, 194–5.

M. Last, Reform in West Africa. The jihad movements in the nineteenth century, in J. F. A. Ajayi and M. Crowder (eds.), *History of West Africa*, ii, London 1974, 1–29.

N. Levtzion, Islam in the Bilad al-Sudan to 1800, in N. Levtzion and R. L. Pouwels (eds.), *The history of Islam in Africa*, Athens, Ohio 2000, 62–91.

B. B. Mack and J. Boyd, *One woman's jihad. Nana Asma'u, scholar and scribe*, Bloomington, Ind. 2000.

D. Robinson, Revolutions in the western Sudan, in N. Levtzion and R. L. Pouwels (eds.), *The history of Islam in Africa*, Athens, Ohio 2000, 131–52.

Jean Boyd

Kinship, Descent Systems

Sahelian West Africa and North Central Africa (Chad/Sudan)

With the gradual conversion to Islam, Sahelian societies have been influenced by Islamic organization systems, reinforcing the patrilineality that already existed in these societies. However, within this organization matrilineal elements guarantee women room for negotiation and flexibility in gender relations.

In the West and Central Sahel, Islamization is a continuing process. The first contacts with Islam stem from more than a thousand years ago, when trade routes and traveling Muslims were the avenues for Islam and were closely related to early state-building (for example, the empires of Ghana, Mali, Gao [Songhai], Bornu, and Darfur). Islam has long been the religion of the elites. This changed during the nineteenth century when the Fulani empires in the Western Sahel were firmly established. Their rulers made an effort to spread Islam among the common people and tried to impose Muslim rule. It could not, however, be imposed on everyone. First, many did not want to become Muslim, and second, those who imposed Islam did not want their entire slave reservoir depleted through conversion since it was forbidden to enslave fellow Muslims.

Today Islam touches all ethnic groups in the area. The interpretation of Muslim rule at the popular level takes many different forms in a continuous dialogue between custom and religion (Launay 1992, Holy 1991). It is very difficult to disentangle the influence of Islam and the so-called pre-Islamic elements in the social and cultural organization of these diverse ethnic groups. It is therefore not easy to attribute the dominant patrilineal organization, which is neither exclusive nor fixed, to Islamic culture. Differences between ethnic groups and social categories, and between urban and rural areas, must also be considered.

Political hierarchies of the widely spread nineteenth-century empires made a clear distinction between noble and non-noble people, one that generally still pertains. The distinction, linked to adherence to Islam, influences social organization and gender relations. The noble warriors and political elites were and still are strict Muslims (especially Hausa, Fulani, Tuareg, Moors, Kenembou, and Arabs). They live in large villages and towns and claim to be descended from the nineteenth-century kings. They are patrilineally organized and follow the inheritance rules of Islam. Women are sometimes secluded in a rigorous way and are not allowed to live alone. Widows are immediately remarried, or go to their brother's home until marriage takes place. Social organization is explained in Muslim terms (VerEecke 1989, de Bruijn and Van Dijk 1995, Fortier 2001, Coles and Mack 1991).

The social organization of the noble semi-nomadic pastoralists is more flexible so as to respond to the vagaries of the climate and allow them to best raise their livestock (Baroin 1984, Bernus 1993, de Bruijn and van Dijk 1995). In general, political and economic relations are defined in patrilineal terms, while relationships of care are defined along matrilineal lines. The basic unit of production is the patrilineal household, and the basis for reproduction and care of family members is the union between mother and children, defined as the "hearthhold" (de Bruijn 1997). As most of these groups have a pre-inheritance system, the children of the hearthhold are the proprietors of the livestock. The Tuareg have a special inheritance system that they call "the living milk." A portion of the cattle is inherited through the matrilineal line. During the past few decades this inheritance system has led to many disputes, with the result that the Islamic form of inheritance has been gaining influence (Oxby 1990). An important matrifocal element in these societies is the preference for cross-cousin and parallel cousin marriages sometimes including the matri-parallel cousin, a partner forbidden by Muslim law. These alliances are not exclusive, however, since distance marriages are frequent. Furthermore, divorce rates are very high.

Slaves are people without history and in principle without a clear kinship system. After the abolition of slavery and in the gradual formation of their own society, former slaves have copied the model of the noble strata and developed a patrilineal system. Today most of them are sedentary and work in agriculture. Among the Tuareg, Moors, and Tubu they are also herders and nomads. They do not restrict their women as much as the nobles do because women play an important role in the economy of daily life (on Riimaybe, former slaves of Fulani, de

Bruijn and van Dijk 1995, Gibbal 1994; on Tuareg, Bouman 2003; on Tubu, Baroin 1984).

The agricultural and sedentary groups are considered by the nobles to have a status equal to that of non-nobles. Among these are the Berti, the Zaghawa, and the Wolof who are today Islamized, but in whose culture other religious forms are recognizable, comparable to the situation of pastoral semi-nomads. Others, like the Dogon, Kapsiki, Hadjerai, and Nuba were in contact with Islam, but in a negative way especially in the eighteenth and nineteenth centuries when they were subject to slave raids. Conversion of these groups to Islam began in the twentieth century, most intensively after the Second World War. Islamization often goes together with migration to towns (van Santen 1993), or with repression during war (Davidson 1996, de Bruijn, van Dijk, and Djindil 2004, Manger 1994). In one village and even within one family a mixture of religious forms can be found. For example, the Dogon in Mali have a marabout mask in their ritual dances (Joly 1994) and the Hadjerai in Chad both conserve their altars in the mountains and go to the mosque. These groups are all more or less patrilineally organized, which fits their livelihoods well. In what way the conversion to Islam influenced the kinship system is not very clear. For the Kapsiki in Cameroon, for instance, the turn to Islam goes together with a decreasing importance of the maximal clan. For the Hadjerai the introduction of Islam not so much influences the descent system as affects the position of women as their role as animistic priestess diminishes, a process also described for the Jola in Senegal (Linares 1992).

BIBLIOGRAPHY

C. Baroin, *Anarchie et cohésion sociale chez les Toubou. Les Daza Kĕšerda (Niger)*, Cambridge 1984.

E. Bernus, *Touaregs nigériens. Unité culturelle et diversité regionale d'un peuple pasteur*, Paris 1993.

A. Bouman, *Benefits of belonging. Bella in Burkina Faso*, Amsterdam 2003.

M. de Bruijn, The hearthhold in pastoral Fulbe society, central Mali. Social relations, milk and drought, in *Africa* 67:4 (1997), 625–51.

M. de Bruijn and H. van Dijk, *Arid ways, cultural understandings of insecurity in Fulbe society, central Mali*, Amsterdam 1995.

M. de Bruijn, H. van Dijk, and N. Djindil, Chad revisited. Long-term effects of war and drought in central Chad, manuscript, Leiden 2004.

C. Coles and B. B. Mack (eds.), *Hausa women in the twentieth century*, Madison, Wis. 1991.

A. P. Davidson, *In the shadow of history. The passing of lineage society*, New Brunswick, N.J. 1996.

M. Dupire, *Peuls nomads. Étude descriptive des Wodaabe du Sahel nigérien*, Paris 1962.

C. Fortier, Le lait, le sperme, le dos, et le sang? Représentations physiologiques de la filiation et de la parente de lait en islam malekite et dans la société maure, in *Cahiers d'études africaines* 41:161 (2001), 97–138.

J. M. Gibbal, *Genii of the river Niger*, Chicago 1994.

L. Holy, *Religion and custom in a Muslim society. The Berti of Sudan*, Cambridge 1991.

O. F. Linares, *Power, prayer and production. The Jola of Casamance, Senegal*, Cambridge 1992.

L. Manger, *From the mountains to the plains. The integration of the Lafofa Nuba into Sudanese society*, Uppsala 1994.

C. Oxby, The "living milk" runs dry. The decline of a form of joint ownership and matrilineal inheritance among the Twareg (Niger), in P. T. W. Baxter and R. Hogg (eds.), *Property, poverty and people. Changing rights in property and problems in pastoral development*, Manchester, England 1990, 222–7.

J. C. M. van Santen, *They leave their jars behind. The conversion of Mafa women to Islam*, Leiden 1993.

C. VerEecke, *Cultural construction of women's economic marginality. The Fulbe of Northeastern Nigeria*, Working Paper 195, Michigan State University 1989.

MIRJAM DE BRUIJN

East Asia, Southeast Asia, Australia, and the Pacific

INTRODUCTION

This entry discusses kinship, descent, and inheritance systems in Southeast Asia, East Asia, and the Australia-Pacific regions. Due to the multiplicity of ethnic groups with varieties of local customs in these regions, the entry focuses on certain ethnic groups that exemplify how Islamic rule is in conflict with, or has adapted to or co-opted local pre-Islamic laws. The argument is that the acculturation of Islamic law and local customary laws has had different effects on the women living in these regions.

SOUTHEAST ASIA

Although as early as the seventh and eighth centuries Arab Muslim traders traveled throughout the islands of Southeast Asia, Islam started to affect the region after the first settlement of a Muslim town, established around the late thirteenth century, in the Pasai region of North Sumatra (Reid 1993, 133). It is said that Islam's popularity and its acceptance by local people was due to the Islamic propagators' ability to syncretize Islamic ideas with existing local beliefs and display tolerance toward local pre-Islamic practice (Osman 1985, 44). The dissemination of Islam into Southeast Asia has significantly affected the structures of its social organization, especially in relation to its gender relations and inheritance systems. The fact that Islamic principles of descent and inheritance favor men has led to conflict with more gender-equal customs in many places in Southeast Asia. The entry here focuses on the Minangkabau social organization that favors women in order to explore ramifications of the integration of Islamic rules into a pre-existing matrilineal society.

The acculturation of *adat* (a collective term for Minangkabau laws and customs) and Islam in the Minangkabau culture of West Sumatra is expressed in the ideological aphorism: *Adat basandi syarak, syarak basandi Kitabullah. Syarak, mangato, adat mamakai. Alam takambang jadi guru*, which roughly translates as "Minangkabau customary laws are based on religious laws; the religious laws are based on the Holy Book, the Qur'ān. For religious law, orders, *adat* applies. Nature is the teacher of humankind."

The integral impact of Islam on the practice of Minangkabau *adat* in daily life can be seen from the fact that there is a modification of the standard norm for a family pattern in Minangkabau society. Matrilineal Minangkabau kinship system considers a husband/father as an outsider (*orang lua*) to his wife's family. His children will automatically become part of their mother's family, and will bear the mother's clan name rather than their father's. Furthermore, it is a *mamak*'s (maternal uncle) responsibility to take care of his sisters' children. The relationship between a *mamak* and his *kamanakan*, niece/nephew, is close and is perhaps even stronger than that between a father and his own son with *mamak* representing the "sociological father" of his sisters' children. A *mamak* also bequeaths his wealth to his *kamanakan*. His *sako*, inheritance of position, will pass to his nephews, while his *pusako*, inheritance of wealth, will pass to his nieces. According to *adat*, traditionally the smallest family unit is a mother and her children, known as *samande* (one mother) and is headed or owned by a woman as a mother. However, based on research undertaken in West Sumatra by the Indonesian Supreme Court in 1976, *samande* has now been modified to refer to a nuclear family, consisting of mother, children, and the father who is regarded as the family's head. This modification may partly be influenced by Islamic rule that positions the man as the head of the family (Qur'ān 4:34). However, in practice a woman (as a wife or mother) is still the *de facto* leader of the family, notwithstanding the fact that *de jure* a man (as a husband or father) is the head of the family. This situation is also found in Acehnese society.

While the Acehnese kinship system, like the Malay, is bilateral, tracing descent through both male and female sides, the residence system is matrilocal. The implementation of the matrilocal residence system requires that a married couple lives in the household or place of the bride's kin. This marginalizes men's role and authority within households (Siegel 1969). Despite the influence of Islamic law, the concept of household is still the domain of women (Siapno 2002, 63).

Another impact of the imposition of Islamic values on *adat* can be seen from the change of the inheritance system in Minangkabau society. In order to integrate *adat* with Islamic laws, the Minangkabau assembly, which consists of the representatives of Minangkabau clan heads, village leaders, religious scholars and intellectuals, and an Indonesian government representative who functions as a witness, was held in Bukit Tinggi on 2–4 May 1953. The assembly members, most of whom were men, launched a regulation that while *pusaka tinggi* (ancestral property) is still inherited based on matrilineal principle, *pusaka rendah* (self-acquired property) is inherited based on *syariah* (Islamic law) (Hamka 1963, 7). According to *syariah*, sons inherit twice as much as daughters. This consensus was made in order to avoid dispute between the rights of a person's own children and that person's sisters' children. But in practice, the matrilineal system is still very influential. Maila Stivens's research on the Rembau of Negeri Sembilan, Malaysia, whose ancestors are from Minangkabau, suggests that there has been a reconstitution of the inheritance system there. She terms this shift a feminization of property relations. It means that female-centered inheritance practices are not confined to ancestral land but also operate in a new way in relation to acquired property land, which is frequently registered under women's names, sometimes passing on occasion from parents to daughters, or from brothers to sisters (Stivens 1996, 6).

It is misleading to assume that the practice of Islamic values has categorically disadvantaged women. On the contrary, these practices have given benefits to women such as in the modification of the customary law among the Batak Karo of North Sumatra who mark their ethnicity by clan identities. The five-clan social system distinguishes the Batak Karo from the Malays, their closest neighbors, who do not have a clan system. Clan membership is assigned unequivocally and automatically through patrilineal descent into one of its five clans. In order to be able to trace clan membership unambiguously through father only, the Batak Karo practice exogamic marriage and prefer matrilineal cross-cousin marriages (Kipp 1996, 33). At some points Islamic law conflicts with Batak Karo *adat* law, for example, in marital and inheritance law. According to the practices of patrilineal descent system and patrilocal residence, inheritance, specifically land, also goes through a father to a son. Traditionally, a daughter will not inherit from her parents as after marriage she belongs to her husband's family. Although receiving unequal shares under Islamic law, a daughter has a right to inherit her parents' property.

The Batak Karo concept of marriage is also in conflict with Islamic marital law. The Batak Karo consider marriage within the same clan as incest and punish it severely by exclusion from the Batak Karo world. Islamic law, on the other hand, allows marriage within one clan as long as the persons are not closely related by blood. Islamic rule only prohibits a man from marrying his own mother, daughter, sister, parent's aunt, or niece. This prohibition is extended to include to step, foster, and in-law relations (Qur'ān 4:23). Among the Batak Karo, the Malay system is partly identified with Islam and the practice of "incest." Because of that Batak Karo refer to a person who has committed incest as having becoming Malay (*menjadi Melayu*), therefore ceasing to be Batak Karo. Like Christian Batak Karo, Muslim Batak Karo, who are a minority, try to reconcile their religion and *adat* law by obeying religious rules as well as whatever norms are appropriate for their society (Kipp 1996, 234).

EAST ASIA

China, Korea, and Japan are considered to be most typically patriarchal and patrilineal among East Asian societies. Chinese, Korean, and Japanese cultures are rooted in Confucian principles, founded in China by Kung-futze, "Master Kung" or Confucius (551–479 B.C.) (Hwang 1979, 11). These principles, incorporated into Chinese law in 210 BC and adopted as the state ideology by the Japanese Tokugawa Bakufu dynasty (1603–1868) and the Choson dynasty in Korea (1392–1910), form a code of conduct by which to live (ibid.). Confucianism had a tremendous impact on the social systems in these communities. It is fundamentally patriarchal: the sole authority in the family rests with the father and only those on the paternal line are considered relatives. Social class and rights are transmitted only from fathers to sons who have higher status than daughters, and first-born males hold the right to lineal succession. Its residence pattern is patrilocal. After marriage, a woman forfeits her natal family membership and becomes a member of her husband's family, joining them in their family ancestral ceremonies. A woman does not have rights to inherit family property. However, as a housewife, she can control the family property and manage the family household, although this may not be seen outwardly (Lee 1997, 52).

Islam is a relatively new religion in Japan and Korea, whereas China has known Islam since as early as the seventh century. There are some Islamic rules that differ from local customs in these countries. For example, Islamic law decrees that a married woman can hold two agnatic group memberships. She can retain her natal family membership while she is also part of her husband's. Moreover, women as daughters and wives have a right to inherit property from their parents and husbands. Islam has not yet greatly affected these communities, especially in relation to women's rights. In order to survive over the centuries Chinese Muslims, known as Hui, while maintaining their identity as devotees of Islam, have had to become increasingly integrated into Han Chinese society (Voll 1987, 141).

There have been some changes that benefit women. For example, the Korean government launched the Family Law Act of 19 December 1989, which states that all property is divided equally between all children regardless of sex in the absence of a will (Hampson 2000, 175). Although in modern times in most East Asian societies women's status has been made to equal that of men by regulating non-gender-bias law and constitutions, to some degree women still face inequality in both the public and private spheres as it is difficult to change a culture that favors men.

AUSTRALIA-PACIFIC REGION

As in the East Asian region, Muslims are also a minority in the Australia and Pacific region. According to the census taken in 2001 the number of Australian Muslims was approximately 1.5 per cent of the total population. The majority of the Australian Muslim population were born overseas in countries such as Lebanon, Pakistan, Bosnia, and Indonesia (Saeed 2003, 1–2). The fact that these people come from different social and ethnic backgrounds is reflected in the way they apply Islamic values, which are varied and rooted in their own cultural traditions.

There are some social and legal problems surrounding the practice of Islamic laws that are in conflict with Australian law or mainstream culture, for example, child custody and property settlement in divorce cases. Australian law tends to favor an equal division of assets, irrespective of whether both parties have earned income, while under Islamic law division depends on the amount of contribution of each party during the duration of the marriage. Moreover, Australian mainstream norms favor the mother's role in child rearing. In contrast, in Islamic law the father generally gains custody of children once they reach a particular age (Humphrey 1984, 43).

Traditionally, mainstream Australia is a bilateral society and the concept of the family is that of a nuclear family consisting of a husband and his wife who live with their children apart from the relatives of either spouse. One-parent families, *de facto* couples, heterosexual or homosexual, with or without children, and childless couples are becoming much more common as family units. This concept is at variance with Islamic family law, which strictly prohibits both *de facto* and homosexual relationships and prevents illegitimate children from inheriting wealth from the father. In Australia, most Muslim migrants try to maintain their traditional values, although some of them are being affected by Australian values. This has led to conflict between spouses, parents and children, as well as relatives in Australia and abroad (Hussain 2001, 163).

Conclusion

As a result of the adaptation of Islamic law alongside local customary law, women often act or are treated differently from their traditional roles. It seems that the implementation of Islamic law in patriarchal societies tends to give more benefit and advantages to women than they have previously experienced. However, the dissemination of Islamic law in matrilineal societies such as the Minangkabau of West Sumatra has adversely affected women in relation to materialist concerns such as inheritance and social position.

Bibliography

Byung, T. H., Confucianism in modernization. Comparative study of China, Japan and Korea, Ph.D. diss., University of California, Berkeley 1979.

Hamka, *Minangkabau customary laws facing revolution* [in Indonesian], Djakarta 1963.

S. Hampson, Rhetoric or reality? Contesting definitions of women in Korea, in L. Edwards and M. Roces (eds.), *Women in Asia. Tradition, modernity, and globalisation*, St. Leonards, N.S.W. 2000, 170–87.

R. W. Hefner and P. Horvatich (eds.), *Politics and religious renewal in Muslim Southeast Asia*, Honolulu 1997.

M. Humphrey, Islamic law in Australia, in M. Humphrey and A. Mograby (eds.), *Islam in Australia*, Sydney 1985, 36–47.

J. Hussain, Family law and Muslim communities, in A. Saeed and S. Akbarzadeh (eds.), *Muslim communities in Australia*, Sydney 2001, 161–87.

R. S. Kipp, *Dissociated identities. Ethnicity, religion, and class in an Indonesian society*, Ann Arbor 1996.

Kwang Kyu Lee, *Korean family and kinship*, Seoul 1997.

Mahkamah Agung (Indonesian Supreme Court), Research on customary laws related to inheritance matters within the area of the Appellate Court of Padang [in Indonesian], Jakarta 1980.

M. T. Osman, Islamization of the Malays. A transformation of culture, in A. Ibrahim, S. Shiddique, and Y. Hussain (eds.), *Readings on Southeast Asia*, Singapore 1985.

A. Reid, *The making of an Islamic Political discourse in Southeast Asia*, Clayton, Vic. 1993.

A. Saeed, *Islam in Australia*, Sydney 2003.

J. A. Siapno, *Gender, Islam, nationalism and the state in Aceh. The paradox of power, co-optation and resistance*, London 2002.

J. Siegel, *The rope of God*, Berkeley 1969.

M. Stivens, *Matriliny and modernity. Sexual politics and social change in rural Malaysia*, Sydney 1996.

J. O. Voll, Soviet Central Asia and China. Integration or isolation of Muslim societies, in J. L. Esposito (ed.), *Islam in Asia. Religion, politics, and society*, New York 1987, 125–51.

Mina Elfira

Kinship, Descent Systems and State

Afghanistan

Afghanistan is a multiethnic, tribal society with a predominantly rural population. Islam as the foundation of the value system is the common denominator that binds together diverse ethnic groups. About 85 percent of Afghans are Sunnī Muslims and adhere to Ḥanafī law; the rest are Shīʿīs. Small populations of Hindus and Sikhs live in urban centers.

The Pashtun, Tajik, Hazara, Uzbek, Turkmen, Baluchi, and Nuristani ethnic groups (*qawm*) vary in patrilineal kinship, language, and regional customs. Kinship networks constitute the foundation of wealth and security. Loyalty to kin and tribe (*qabīla*) has historically posed a challenge to the authority of the state. Patriarchal values dominate the kinship-based society. In the eastern and southeastern regions, inhabited principally by Pashtun tribes, the tribal code of behavior (Pashtunwali) governs all aspect of tribal life, including kinship and gender relations. Concepts of honor and shame prescribe appropriate behavior for men and women. Women symbolize family honor (*nāmūs*) for all Afghans. They are protected within the extended family system and compelled to comply to accepted norms of behavior.

The practice of female seclusion varies with age, regional customs, and lifestyle. Before the process of modernization began in Afghanistan, urban women were required by a strict interpretation of Ḥanafī law to cover their faces and wear the all-enveloping *chadari*, or *burqaʿ*, outside the home. Covering the face was not required in the countryside, where peasant and nomadic women were often needed to work on farms and in pastures.

Most marriages take place between members of the same lineage. Since tribal membership is determined by patrilineal lines, a woman who marries outside a tribe has to leave her tribe. Therefore, marriage between cousins and second cousins is encouraged to secure kinship bonds and lineage solidarity. Marriage among close relatives, as Dupree has pointed out, keeps female family members together in groups: "Intimate aunt-niece relationships, as well as daughter-in-law mother-in-law closeness strengthens the already strong matri-core in the society" (1973, 181).

Although Islam permits men to marry up to four wives, the vast majority of Afghan men have only one wife. The practice of polygamy is a sign of wealth and power and a means of forging alliances with other powerful families or tribes (see, for example, Anderson 1975). At the end of the nineteenth and the beginning of the twentieth centuries concubinage was common among the elite. The concubines came from Tajik, Kafari (Nuristani), and mostly Shīʿī Hazara ethnic groups; they were captured and sold in slave markets in Afghanistan and Central Asia (Kakar 1979, 173–6). As in most other parts of the Muslim world, the children born of a slave mother had exactly the same rights as those born of a legal wife and were integrated in their father's pedigree.

Local customs in some instances contradict the Sharīʿa on gender issues. For example, although the Sharīʿa grants women the right of inheritance, Pashtunwali denies it. In rural areas marriages are arranged by exchanging one girl for another or by paying the customary bridal price, *shirbaha*, also known as *walwar* and *qailin*. Unlike *mahr*, which is sanctioned by the Sharīʿa and is paid to women in the instance of divorce, *shirbaha* must be paid to the bride's family at the time of marriage. In northern Afghanistan, where a woman's skills as a carpet weaver contribute significantly to a family's income, the bridal price is based on carpet weaving and other skills. In the areas inhabited by the Pashtuns, tribal and subtribal disputes are usually settled by giving one or several women in marriage to the family of the victim without having to pay the bridal price (Tapper 1991). These practices vary significantly between urban and rural areas.

State policies on gender and kinship

The first systematic attempt by the state to change the social structure of the country was undertaken in the 1920s during the reign of King Amān Allāh. Amān Allāh's social reforms were intended to weaken kinship and undermine the exclusive claims of family by legislating against arranged marriages and by emancipating women. The abolition of slavery in 1920 freed hundreds of women from the bondage of concubinage. The family law, issued shortly afterwards, discouraged marriage between close relatives and the payment of bridal money to the bride's family. A new code, issued in the following year, imposed restrictions on polygamy and outlawed the Pashtun practices of bartering women as retribution for crime and forcing a widow to marry the closest male relative of her deceased husband. Both of these practices were declared to be contrary to Sharīʿa law.

The state's efforts to regulate and monitor family matters provoked widespread hostility and resistance. Opposition to these and other social reforms resulted in general revolts in 1928, the abdication of King Amān Allāh, and the repeal of his social reforms. Kinship and tribal loyalties remained prevalent despite modernization attempts and economic development during the 1950s, 1960s, and 1970s. Although urban women, a small segment of the total population, benefited from development projects in the areas of education, employment, and political representation, the situation of women in rural areas remained essentially unchanged. Uneven development actually widened the gap between urban and rural populations.

In 1978, the pro-Soviet People's Democratic Party of Afghanistan (PDPA) gained power in a military coup referred to as the Saur (April) Revolution. The new regime targeted first the structure of "tribal-feudalism" and pushed for radical changes. In 1979, the Revolutionary Council of the Marxist regime issued several decrees to transform the traditional bases of economic and social exchange that held extended families together and "knitted them into a *qawm* or tribe" (Rubin 1995, 116). Women's emancipation was integral to this policy. Decree No. 7 issued in October declared the equal rights of women and men and the regime's goal "to free the toiling women of Afghanistan from humiliating feudalistic relations and provide opportunities for their advancement at all levels." The land reform act (Decree No. 8), issued a month later, awarded each family about 15 acres of first quality land and defined family to include a husband, wife, and unmarried children under 18 years of age. In conformity with other reforms, land reform was intended to replace the extended family system and larger kinship units with nuclear families dependent on the state. As Rubin points out, the reforms undertaken by the Marxist government would have changed the social fabric of Afghanistan, had they been implemented (Rubin 116–17). As it turned out, the government's revolutionary approach stirred up resentment in the countryside that impeded the implementation of social reforms, even those of previous regimes, particularly those relating to the rights of women.

Effects of war

Islam became the rallying point in uniting various ethnic groups in a jihad (holy war) against the regime and its Soviet backer. The war of resistance (1978–92) and the ensuing civil war that lasted until United States military operations in 2001, had disastrous social consequences. About two million Afghans were killed or wounded and about six million more, mostly women and children, were dislocated internally or fled into Pakistan and Iran as refugees. A systematic study of the impact of displacement on kinship and extended family in Afghanistan has not been yet undertaken. Reports prepared by various international relief societies, however, confirm that thousands of women lost their homes and their husbands, fathers, and sons and were left with no means of support. The majority of these women were forced to assume new responsibilities as the head and breadwinner of their household.

Bibliography

J. W. Anderson, Tribe and community among the Ghilzai Pashtuns. Preliminary notes on ethnographic distribution and variation in eastern Afghanistan, in *Anthropos* 70 (1975), 575–601.

A. Banuazizi and M. Weiner (eds.), *The state, religion, and ethnic politics. Afghanistan, Iran, and Pakistan*, Syracuse, N.Y. 1986.

H. Bradsher, *Afghan communism and Soviet intervention*, Karachi 1999.

L. Dupree, *Afghanistan*, Princeton, N.J. 1973.

N. H. Dupree, Revolutionary rhetoric and Afghan women, in M. N. Shahrani and R. L. Canfield (eds.), *Revolutions and rebellions in Afghanistan*, Berkeley 1984.

H. Kakar, *Government and Society in Afghanistan. The reign of Amir Abd al-Rahman Khan*, Austin, Tex. 1979.

N. Lindisfarne (Tapper), *Bartered brides. Politics, gender, and marriage in an Afghan tribal society*, Cambridge 1991.

S. Nawid, *Religious response to social change in Afghanistan. King Aman-Allah and the Afghan ulama, 1919–1929*, Costa Mesa 1999.

O. Roy, Le double code afghan. Marxisme et tribalisme, in *Revue française de science politique* 36 (December 1986), 846–61.

B. Rubin, *The fragmentation of Afghanistan. State formation and collapse in the international system*, New Haven, Conn. 1995.

B. Sultan and G. Wardel, *Capitalizing on capacities of Afghan women. Women's role in Afghanistan's reconstruction and development*, International Labor Organization, Working Paper 4, Geneva 31 December 2001.

Senzil Nawid

The Caucasus

Kinship in the Caucasus is discussed in this entry in light of the general debate in anthropology on patrilineal descent societies, with specific reference to works in anthropology on kinship in the Middle East and Central Asia and to the author's own research results in Azerbaijan.

Recently published works on the Caucasus and Central Asia point to the existence of genealogically defined patrilineal and patrilocal descent groups, regarding them as still important today despite the economic and social changes during the Soviet regime. Patrilineal descent reckoning and the transmission of economic resources along the male line are considered as structural characteristics of these agnatic groups and held responsible for the social devaluation of women.

Such descriptions of unilineal descent groups are strictly based on the British functionalist lineage theory, in which an opposition between agnation and matrilaterality was created. Women as daughters, sisters, and wives were defined exclusively with reference to fathers, brothers, and spouses and were condemned to jural irrelevance. Even criticism of this functionalist design continued to define women in an agnatic perspective and independent kinship classifications were not enlarged upon.

An analysis of patrilineal descent groups according to the functionalist theory relieves these groups from their embeddedness in the political, social, economic, and religious contexts of their states and is, therefore, inadequate. The author's research in rural Azerbaijan has shown that kinship systems do develop in these contexts and that they are in fact dependent upon them. Patrilineal descent categories exist in the consciousness of people. However, they neither form a permanent social structure nor do they include every individual. Patrilineal descent categories are not a structure but an option which is chosen in specific situations, for instance, when particular economically successful members gain material advantage through the enmeshment of primarily agnatic kin in the state bureaucracy. Only then are solidarity groups formed, whose members support one another in all social, political, and economic matters. Yet, since these groups are extremely dependent upon the economic success and the social networks of their prominent members, the durability of their solidarity is fragile and could collapse at any time. Indeed, these solidarity groups follow the well-known pattern of genealogically recruiting members, but these are modern adaptions from the ideological reservoir of patrilineal descent.

Patrilineal descent systems are held responsible for the disadvantaged position of women. In the perspective of patrilineal descent groups, daughters or sisters who are given in marriage to other groups are lost members. The solidarity groups in Azerbaijan do not comply with this. Because of their economic strength married daughters remain incorporated in the group. For the women in question the consequence is that even after marriage their status as daughter/sister prevails over their status as daughter-in-law; like their brothers they continue to participate in the decision-making of the group. Social marginality rests upon their husbands, provided that they have no solidarity group of their own.

Kinship terminology in Azerbaijan differentiates between agnatic and uterine kin: agnatic kin is conceived as *sümük qohumluq* (kinship of the bone) and uterine kin as *süd qohumluq* (milk kinship). Just as *sümük qohumluq* refers to the patrilineal descent category, *süd qohumluq* describes the uterine kin, who are firstly the descendants of both sexes of a remembered great-grandmother. Seen genealogically *süd qohumluq* describes the transmission of milk. However, it is not uterine descent that is marked, but the equality of uterine positions (mother, mother's mother, mother's sister, and so forth), and this equality is based on the central concept of motherhood. In its very essence *süd qohumluq* evolves after the birth of the first child of the daughter. It is ritually marked but does not emphasize the continuity of groups, but rather the life process in general.

Süd qohumluq between women dissects the socially dominant borderlines of agnatic solidarity groups and dispels them. This is manifested in the context of feuds between two groups who have an affinal relationship with one another. While the men of the two groups are obliged to their agnatic bonds and interrupt the existing affinal relationship between the two parties, the women continue their relations of *süd qohumluq* with the women of the other group.

In principle, the two sexes always belong to both, *sümük* and *süd qohumluq*. However, men as a category are associated with *sümük* (bone) and women with *süd* (milk). Just as men cannot pass milk to the next generation, women are excluded from the transmission of agnatic descent. In sum, various aspects are concealed behind the terms *sümük* and *süd*, depending one's perspective. *Sümük qohumluq* refers primarily to men, is realized through agnation, objectivates "milk" during the marriage process and regards the wife as alien. *Süd qohumluq* refers primarily to women, emphasizes uterinity and stresses with the concepts of motherhood and birth the life process itself. But *sümük* and *süd* equally denote the unity of the sibling group, of "brother" and "sister"; the value of consanguinity is placed hierarchically before the value of affinity.

The topic of the general life process is encountered again in the field of religion and cosmology. Here, the meaning of the life process is constituted in conflict with the concepts of the newly arising so-called orthodox Islam. It is the relationship of the female body to Islamic purity rules which is formulated differently. In the life cycle rituals of the *qırx* (literally "forty"), female impurity after marriage and birth is no longer negatively defined, as part of the social exclusion of women. Quite the contrary, female impurity and fertility stipulate each other and are dependent on one another.

BIBLIOGRAPHY

S. Baştuğ and N. Hortaçsu, The price of value. Kinship, marriage and meta-narratives of gender in Turkmenistan, in F. Acar and A. Güneş-Ayata (eds.), *Gender and identity construction. Women of Central Asia, the Caucasus and Turkey*, Leiden 2000, 117–40.

P. Bourdieu, *Outline of a theory of practice*, trans. R. Nice, Cambridge 1976.

R. Callois and G. E. von Grunebaum (eds.), *Le rêve et les sociétés humaines*, Paris 1967.

J. Collier and S. Yanagisako, *Gender and kinship*, Stanford 1987.

T. Dragadze, Islam in Azerbaijan. The position of women, in C. F. El-Sohl and J. Mabro (eds.), *Muslim women's choices. Religious belief and social reality*, Oxford 1994, 152–63.

M. Fortes, The structure of unilineal descent groups, in *American Anthropologist* 55 (1951), 17–41.

H. A. Habilov, *Ethnography of Azerbaijan* [in Azeri], Baku 1991.

L. Holy, *Kinship, honour and solidarity. Cousin marriage in the Middle East*, Manchester, England 1989.

A. Kuper, Lineage theory. A critical retrospect, in *Annual Review of Anthropology* 11 (1982), 71–92.

J. Marcus, *A world of difference. Islam and gender hierarchy in Turkey*, London 1992.

I. Pfluger-Schindlbeck, *Verwandtschaft, Religion und Geschlecht in Aserbaidschan*, Reichert Verlag (forthcoming).

N. Tohidi, Gender and national identity in post-Soviet Azerbaijan. A regional perspective, in F. Acar and A. Güneş-Ayata (eds.), *Gender and identity construction. Women of Central Asia, the Caucasus and Turkey*, Leiden 2000, 249–92.

INGRID PFLUGER-SCHINDLBECK

South Asia

INTRODUCTION

Officially, Islam entered South Asia in 712 C.E., with the conquest of Sindh by an Arab general, but the rise of Islam in Arabia impacted South Asia much earlier, since trade in the Indian Ocean area had existed since prehistoric times. Much of this impact was mediated by women – a fact largely ignored by history books that tell only of conquering "Muslim armies," forcible conversions, and gentle Sufi persuasion. These early female mediators were South Asian non-Muslims who attended to and lived, possibly in *mutʿa* marriages (Bouchon 1986), with merchants, sailors, and fishermen from the Gulf and the Hadramawt, who had converted to the new faith. Later South Asian non-Muslim women even lived with East African slave converts traded by Arabs and Persians till the late nineteenth century. Living over generations as wives, mothers, and daughters with Muslim men, these women combined the new faith with much of their pre-Islamic (notably Hindu or Buddhist) cultures. From the thirteenth century onwards Muslim women from Iran and Central Asia came in as wives, companions, and slaves of the elite, and transmitted to their descendants their blend of pre-Islamic and Islamic practice – often construed in the South Asian setting as "ideally Muslim." Between the ninth and the twentieth centuries Muslim women in South Asia toiled as peasants, pastoralists, professional craftswomen, and artistes; they ruled over territories and lived as bonded labor; they were among the fabulously wealthy and the abject destitute; they acquiesced with invading powers and resisted them, as for example in the struggle against British colonialism. Today, South Asian Muslim women play complex roles in the broader framework of relations between Muslims and non-Muslims at the levels of both community and state. This entry touches upon some of the numerous issues concerning Muslim women, kinship, and Islam in different South Asian states with large Muslim populations – Bangladesh (ca. 130 million), India (ca. 150 million), Maldives (ca. 0.30 million), Nepal (ca. 0.96 million), Pakistan (ca. 145 million), and Sri Lanka (ca. 1.35 million). At the outset it must be stressed that there has always been great variation within every region and micro-region, according to specific community, locality, particular religious denomination, and, above all, class.

DESCENT, RANKING, AND COMMUNITY

Transmission of nationality in South Asia is a male prerogative in Bangladesh and Pakistan and was so in India till 1992. Most South Asian communities were and are patrilineal and patrifocal, and the advent of Islam brought little change, if any. The primacy of agnatic kin is marked even when kinship terminology is bilateral, as among the Pakistani Baluch (Pastner 1978). More bilinear in practice, but not in ideology are the Sidi of Gujarat, India (Basu 1995). The few matrilineal communities – notably the Māppilla of Kerala, the people of Lakshadweep (both in India), and of the Maldives – continued to remain so even after adopting Islam. Here, men have rights of usufruct over property held in common by the matrilineal group, while the transmission of individually owned property is governed by the principles of the Shāfiʿī school of Sunnī Islam (Dube 1969, 1994, Kutty 1972). Traditional residence patterns were matrilocal, with the system of visiting husbands. In recent decades, with increasing interaction with dominant non-Muslim communities in India and Muslims in the Gulf, matrilocality here is giving way to patrilocality among both Muslims and non-Muslims. Simultaneously, elsewhere in South Asia, long-term male labor migration within and beyond the subcontinent is forcing many patrilineal communities to become "matri-weighted" (Naveed-i-Rahat 1990) in practice, though not in ideology.

While matri-centered socioeconomic units have long existed in many Muslim and non-Muslim agricultural and herding communities – for example in Rajasthan (India) and Sindh (Pakistan) – where men entrust the cash earned for safe-keeping to mothers and wives, among most traditional Muslims, Hindus, and Sikhs direct female participation in production processes outside the precincts of the household economy depends on and is an indicator of family wealth and social status and the concept of (male) honor. The less the visibility of such participation, the higher the status, especially in urban areas (Jeffery 1979, Mandelbaum 1988, Vreede-de Stuers 1968), but also in many rural settings (Kotalová 1993, Lindholm 1982, Naveed-i-Rahat 1990).

Status among South Asian Muslims is also closely related to concepts of "origin," pedigree and blood (*nasab*), caste (*jāt*/*jātī*) and lineage (*birāderi, khāndān, kaum*/*qoum, kul, nukh* are among terms used, depending on locality). This is despite the fact that for several centuries, community boundaries remained fairly flexible, because of individual and group conversions and immigration from surrounding regions. Only in the early sixteenth century did the Māppilla, for instance, evolve into an endogamous community. Almost identical, language-specific kinship terminology and (especially female) first names among Muslims and non-Muslims, as well as the numerous communities who blended Islam and non-Brahmanical Hinduism – Bishnois, Guptis, Hussaini Brahmins, Pranamis, and so forth – may indicate a degree of intermarriagc. This continued between Muslims and Hindus into the late Mughal and early colonial period among the ruling elite (for example, the Rajputs) and certain lower status professional groups (for example, classical musicians). In remoter regions (for example, Ladakh) Muslims and Buddhists intermarried till even the late twentieth century, when general religious fanaticism encouraged by state policies intervened. In Bangladesh no laws bar inter-faith marriages, but social pressure to convert to Islam is strong. Pakistani law prohibits a Muslim woman from marrying a non-Muslim and a Muslim man from marrying a Hindu, while in Nepal a Hindu loses his/her legal (and social) identity on marrying a Muslim (Gaborieau 1995). In India, under the Special Marriage Act 1954, Muslims and non-Muslims may marry and retain their respective religions; to remain valid such a marriage must be monogamous. In reality, however, when Hindu girls marry Muslim boys, increasingly the couples, their respective families, and their possessions are targeted by gangs affiliated to various Hindutva organizations; the couples are forcibly separated, the boys charged with abduction and the girls put away – all this usually with the connivance of the local police.

Ritual sororal and sibling bonds across religious boundaries played major roles in subcontinental history and still unite individuals and groups in village India. The cognitive flexibility regarding community boundaries did not clash in practice with the primacy accorded to traits transmitted through paternal blood and maternal milk (Rao 2000). Female mediated "fictive kinship" across religious and community boundaries was most clearly embodied in the precolonial elite institution of the wet nurse, which existed well into the early decades of the twentieth century. Based on the principle that through the milk, the child would imbibe the traits of the community/caste of the wet nurse, it united families, while also following the Islamic rule governing *riḍāʿa*.[1]

Well ensconced in the overarching hierarchy of the local version of the caste (*varna-jātī*) system – with the partial exception of the (Indian administered) Kashmir Valley, some Pakistani "tribal areas" (but see Barth 1971), and parts of Bangladesh (Bertocci 1995) – Muslims also observe the norms of caste stratification (albeit often with less extreme adherence to notions of purity and pollution) that prevail in socioeconomic interaction within any given micro-region (Ansari 1960, Eglar 1960). Islamization of local communities and immigrant Muslim groups may have introduced a certain spirit of egalitarianism, but they also brought along other principles of ranking, which had been well worked out, for example by jurists of the Ḥanafī school that predominates in South Asia. As Ahmad observes, "caste among Muslims . . . owes . . . directly to Hindu influences, but . . . has been reinforced by the justification offered for the idea of birth and descent as criteria of status in Islamic law" (1978, 15). Status is intimately connected to norms governing marriage, which vary regionally and according to specific community, rather than creed only.

Forging alliances: marriage, economics, and politics

While in December 2003 a constitutional Pakistani court ruled that an adult woman may marry without her guardian's permission, in July 2004, the Muttahida Majlis-i Amal, the ruling party in Pakistan's North West Frontier Province drafted the Hisbah Bill, a law according to which marriage without parental consent will be construed as an act of disobedience, and hence forbidden (Rahman 2004). Indeed, among all South Asians marriage continues to be overwhelmingly arranged by parents or other elders, often against the explicit wishes of the adult woman, or minor girl. Though often interpreted as expressions of mystic love, the famous legends of *Hīr-Rānjhā, Ḍholā-Maru, Mahendra-Mūmal*, and others, eulogizing romantic love, are often sung at engagement ceremonies, which, however, only males may attend. Female sexuality is recognized exclusively within the bounds of heterosexual marriage, which is considered essential. Significantly, no legal provisions exist regarding the maintenance of unmarried major Muslim women during their father's life time. Even prostitutes in Bangladesh are "married" to "banana trees . . . the sun or the moon" (Kotalová 1993, 194) as part of their professional initiation rites. The only category of unmarried Muslim women who were provided for were perhaps courtesans who, drawing on economic resources intended for the legitimate domestic unit, provided cultured noblemen of past centuries with intelligent companionship, taught them refined manners and the fine arts, and sometimes also initiated their sons into the pleasures of sexuality.

Birth rituals draw heavily on local pre-Islamic customs, and though in India active female infanticide is minimal among Muslims as compared to Hindus, daughters tend to be neglected throughout South Asia. Wedding rituals also largely resemble local non-Muslim practice, the signing of the *nikāḥ* (marriage contract) being an additional, obligatory act. In India if such *nikāḥ* marriages are additionally registered under the Special Marriage Act of 1954, the husband may bequeath a greater share of inheritance to his wife and children than would be permissible under the existing traditional *fiqh* laws. The Pakistan Muslim Family Ordinance of 1962 makes *nikāḥ* registration compulsory. In Bangladesh the registration of marriages is rare in rural areas; so is polygamy, though the Bangladesh Muslim Family Ordinance of 1961 allows it. In Indian-administered Kashmir, though the Dukhtarān-e Millat, a militant women's organization closely linked to the local Jamāʿat-i Islāmī advocates polygamy, its practice is extremely rare. In Pakistan polygamy is restricted by law to cases where the court certifies that the first wife is barren or suffering from terminal illness and requires her consent. Practice, however, does not always adhere to these legal restrictions. Even after marriage, Muslim women retain membership of their patri-group and act as major socioeconomic balancing links between their natal and conjugal families, for example through the continued exchange of gifts incorporated in the institutions of *vartan-bhānji* and *salāmi* in Pakistani Punjab (Alavi 1995, Eglar 1960, Naveed-i-Rahat 1981). Preferential lineage and/or caste endogamy is the norm, and giving a daughter/sister in marriage outside such a unit is tantamount to lowering social status and publicly acknowledging this decrease. While many groups prefer cousin marriage, some who were closely linked to non-Muslim elites avoid marrying close kin (Ahmad 1976, Donnan 1988, Rao 2000). In parts of pre-partition urban India, marriages with close kin appear to have been less frequent, partly because the pool of potential partners was larger and partly because the sense of social insecurity as a minority community was absent. Exchange marriages of siblings or other close kin, sometimes over generations, are not rare. These consolidate existing networks and are usually less expensive, with low marriage prestations. They also inhibit excessive conflict between a man's wife and mother (and other senior female kin) and further enable some relaxation of the otherwise strict avoidance behavior vis-à-vis his senior male kin. The disadvantages of preferential exchange are the lack of individual freedom and the dangers of one unhappy marriage in such a set easily affecting the other, especially given the strong emotional bonds between siblings. Short stories by noted Muslim women authors portray further problems inherent in such preferential systems in rapidly changing socioeconomic environments, where women from poor, traditional families wait in desperation for the wealthier and less traditional cousin's family to propose.

The choice of a spouse for one's child and the

practice of marriage reflect the inextricable intermeshing of kinship rules and social organization with dominant economic and political structures. Dowry has no legal sanction in Bangladesh, India, or Pakistan, but the ban is not enforced. Irrespective of religion, such transactions are the norm among most groups, except the tribally organized, such as the Baluch, among whom the bride gets some jewelry, clothes, cash, and household goods from her father, which he in turn received as *māl* from the groom's family. Even communities with bridewealth or equivalent transaction systems are increasingly adopting dowry – in India as a sign of upward socioeconomic mobility, in Bangladesh because of rising male unemployment (Rahman 2001). With spiraling demands, women are increasingly victimized and even killed by their husbands or other conjugal kin for not having provided "enough" dowry, and legal action against the culprits is rare. When dowry is absent (for example, among the Ithnā ʿAshariyya Shīʿīs of Indian Uttar Pradesh, Roy 1984), a married woman receives clothes and jewelry for herself and her children from her natal family throughout her life, as compensation for her unclaimed share of parental property. At least in India, most Muslim women appear unaware of the size of their share (Lateef 1990, 143). In pre-partition South Asia, this did not include agricultural land, which was governed by customary laws rather than by the Shariat Act. This still applies to northern India, but almost everywhere, sisters relinquish their rights to all paternal inheritance in favor of their brothers. Though rarely recorded formally, such relinquishing is universally appreciated and construed as done in exchange for the right to fraternal asylum, were her conjugal household to fall apart due to divorce or widowhood. Often, however, brothers cannot or do not fulfill their part of such informal agreements, and especially widows are at the mercy of one and all (Chen 1986, Haram 2002). Widow remarriage is not socially approved except in some communities in the form of levirate. In urban Kashmir widows and even fiancées whose grooms die are considered inauspicious (Manchanda forthcoming). Till recently, however, divorce carried little stigma in rural Kashmir if the woman's agnates or new husband returned the bridewealth. But elsewhere, divorce can be highly stigmatizing, and while it must be registered in court in Pakistan and Bangladesh, in the latter alimony is not always paid. Indeed, with growing globalization and male mobility, women are being increasingly divorced, or simply abandoned. Thus in July 2003, a Kerala court ordered a husband to pay maintenance to his abandoned wife, saying that although she was a minor at marriage, both partners were post-pubertal and the marriage was performed following customary law. Increasingly women also find themselves in legal limbo, due to modern technologies used in contracting both marriage and divorce. Notably migrants to the Gulf are divorcing their first wives back home via SMS, email, or telephone. In these so-called "triple *ṭalāq*" cases (*ṭalāq-ul bidaʿ/ṭalāq-e badai/ṭalāq-e bain*) divorce pronounced by the husband in one sitting is considered binding by most Ḥanafī Sunnīs (but not by Ahl-i Ḥadīth and not by Ithnā ʿAshariyya or Mustaʿlian Ismāʿīlī Shīʿīs), provided it was originally pronounced in the presence of Muslim witnesses and later confirmed by a Sharīʿa court. Such practice tends to leave the divorcees without a minimum of financial security, and the gravity of the situation is apparent from the current debate surrounding the issue among Muslim Indians. At the time of writing, *ʿulamāʾ* of various persuasions (Barelvi, Deobandi, Ahl-i Ḥadīth and Shīʿa) who are members of the Muslim Personal Law Board in India are at odds concerning the theological validity of this manner of divorce and its associated practice of *ḥalāla*, following which a divorced woman may not remarry her divorced husband unless she first marries another man. As long as she does not remarry, a divorced mother usually retains the rights and duties of *hiḍānat* (physical custody and daily care) toward a male toddler and a pre-pubertal female. Thereafter, the father alone is entitled to guardianship over the child's person and property (the right of *wilāyat-e nafs* and *wilāyat-e nikāḥ* respectively). Fatherless children are considered "orphans," and few wish to marry such girls.

South Asian states encourage the intermeshing of kinship, politics, and economics, implicitly by recognizing and tolerating specific customs and "traditions," and explicitly through legislation. The following examples illustrate this issue:

1. In addition to millions of deaths and rapes, the partition of colonial India led to the abduction of at least 50,000 Muslim and 33,000 non-Muslim women in India and Pakistan respectively. They did not accompany the roughly 8 millions crossing the newly formed borders. Between 1948 and 1956 the Central Recovery Operation of the newly formed Indian government sought to "recover" abducted and forcibly converted women on either side of the border. Following what it considered the moral bonds of kinship, the state forcibly "returned" some 30,000 women, the great majority of whom were Muslim, to their original families, often against their own wishes (Böck and Rao 2000,

29ff), thus underscoring the principle of the appropriation of women through the community and the state. Ever since, marriages across the borders are fraught with danger and the looming threat of especially rural women being imprisoned as illegal immigrants.

2. On 8 October 2003, Shazia Khaskheli, a bank officer's daughter and her husband, Mohammad Hassan Solangi, originally from the lowly fisherman (*machi*) caste, were tortured and murdered in the presence of thousands. It was one more case of "honor killings"[2] (*karo kari*) in Sind, Pakistan, where the first three months of 1999 and the first nine months of 2003 saw 132 and 176 women respectively (and dozens of men) thus murdered. According to figures obtained from the Human Rights Commission and the Pakistan and Sindh Graduates Association 286 women were similarly killed in 1999 in Punjab. Official statistics presented before the Pakistani Senate in July 2004 put the total number of lives lost through such killings between 1998 and 2004 at 4,000 (Dawn 2004). The murdered (and the hundreds of other forcibly divorced) women had soiled the honor of their families and communities, by flouting social norms (Shazia had married beyond her tribe and a lower caste man as well). Among many communities in Pakistan and Azad Kashmir marriage entails transfer of all rights over the woman from her natal to her conjugal family, including that of killing her, often on the slightest suspicion of marital infidelity. Such infidelity constitutes an attack on the husband's honor and he must retaliate by killing the woman and her presumed lover (Ahmed and Ahmed 1981). Her natal family has the right of revenge, by killing a kinsman of the murderer, or demanding a young girl of his family as marital compensation. If the infidelity is genuine, the murdered woman's family gains in status by forgiving the murderer. The Pakistani law of Qisas and Diyat (concerning physical injury, manslaughter, and murder) permits the victim's heirs to decide the fate of the murderer, thus accepting that women may be murdered and/or used as objects of compensation. The December 2003 court ruling in Multan (Pakistan) ordering a man's public blinding and imprisonment for having blinded his fiancé with acid – an increasingly frequent occurrence in both Pakistan and Bangladesh – also indicates such tacit approval of gender-related "custom."

3. Some 20,000 women languish in Pakistani prisons, charged with adultery under the Hudood Ordinances 1979 (Burney 1999, Jahangir and Jilani 1990) promulgated as part of the government's declared "Islamization program." Many are rape victims, charged with adultery for failing to provide four male witnesses on their behalf. Others were charged in revenge, by their parents for marrying against their will, or by their divorced husbands because they wished to remarry; yet others are charged by brothers or neighbors to deprive them of their property. Ongoing efforts to repeal these laws, which include death by stoning, are meeting with great opposition.

4. A current controversy in Indian administered Jammu and Kashmir concerns the rights of women who marry outside this region. At stake is their status, guaranteed by the Kashmiri constitution, as "permanent residents" (or "state subjects") of the territory, that enables them to inherit immovable property and obtain state employment within the territory. While the non-state subject wife of a male state subject can acquire such rights as long as she resides in the territory, the position of female state subjects who marry non-state subjects appears uncertain. Most Kashmiris perceive this issue as essential to their specific political identity, as is evident from its current manipulation by various Kashmiri and Indian political parties.

5. In precolonial and colonial South Asia community-specific customary laws prevailed over creed-specific personal laws. Thus, in Baluchistan, *lub*, promised to a wife on divorce (unless she was barren, unfaithful, or remarried) was managed by her agnates and inherited by her children. In Indian-administered rural Kashmir customary laws still regulate most lives, despite recent transforming attempts by groups adhering to more scriptural readings of Islam. In practice, customary and personal laws in India vary depending on region and community, but formally, the Muslim Personal Law (MPL), based on the Shariat Act 1937 and on what was known as the Anglo-Mohammedan Law, regulates the civil concerns of Muslim Indians. The ongoing debate in India about a uniform civil code (UCC) received much publicity with the so-called Shah Bano case (Rao 1992) and reflects the discursive importance of Islam in the formation of the postcolonial Indian state. Article 44 of the Indian constitution advocates as a directive principle that the state endeavor in future to secure a UCC, primarily through social evolution (Dhagamwar 1989, Faruqi 1985, Mahmood 1977, 1995, Parashar 1992, Wahiduddin Khan 2001). Today, some favor the enactment of an UCC to promote "gender equality," and/or "national integration." Others see it as an onslaught by fanatical Hindutva hegemonists on Muslim religious identity, especially in a state whose rulers and educated elite increasingly flout the constitutional principles of secularism and

democracy. But even among those who reject a UCC, there have been many diverging voices, going back more than 30 years (Fyzee 1971), who plead strongly for reforms within the MPL, and for a conceptual distinction between what they consider the path ordained by God and the man-made corpus of jurisprudence.

Conclusion: Muslim women as symbols and targets

Authored by men, reformist literature of the mid-late nineteenth century (for example, *Mirʾāt al-ʿarūs* [The bride's mirror] by Nazīr Aḥmad in 1869 and *Bihisht-i Zewar* [Heavenly oranaments] by the Deobandi scholar Ashraf ʿAlī Thānawī) served upper-class Muslim women as practical guides to family and religious life. Simultaneously, with the Muslim conception of Islamic law being confined by British rule "to the parameters laid down for it by colonial imperatives," "reformist fervor focused on women's rights in marriage, divorce and inheritance" (Jalal 2001, 72), and MPL became the core of South Asian Muslim identity. The All-India Anjuman-i-Khawatin-i Islam (Muslim Women's Conference) attempted several reforms (Minault 1998), passing a resolution against polygamy in 1918 and lobbying to enable women to initiate divorce through delegation (*ṭalāq-i tafwīḍ*). In postcolonial India, Muslims as an increasingly embattled minority must necessarily perceive any change in personal laws as a threat to community identity and survival. Here, women are projected as the cornerstone of this identity, both by those who attack it and those who defend it. Though in practice polygamy is at least as frequent among non-Muslims as among Muslims, and because of greater poverty live births among Muslims are lower than among Hindus, fascist Hindutva rhetoric in India has cobbled up an image of the "Muslim woman" as a breeding ground for millions of fanatic, violent, and "backward," "anti-national" Muslims. Simultaneously, the shades of opinion among Muslims regarding wide ranging reforms within the MPL are largely ignored, in attempts to portray the community as a homogeneous, threatening whole.

Since women are used as symbols of their respective communities, they are also targeted as such. A much publicized case was the persecution of the Bangladeshi novelist Taslima Nasreen for, among other things, writing about the repression of women and its effects on their health. Less known perhaps, is how individual and gang rape are used as instruments of repression: during partition in 1947, thereafter in every "communal riot" in India, by the Pakistani army in Bangladesh, and by Indian security personnel in Kashmir. The Gujarat genocide of 2002 (IIJG 2003) highlights how central sexual violence is to the state sponsored Hindutva project and its newly constructed notions of honor and virility. But women are also perpetrators. Mothers and mothers-in-law instigate, encourage, and participate in "honor killings," just as much as men do. Upper-class Pakistani women lauded their raping soldiers for attempts to "improve the race" of Bangladeshis, and in September 2003 women activists of the Pakistani Jamaat-e-Islami demonstrated against the proposed repeal of the Hudood Ordinances. Women members of Hindutva associations and even women members of parliament from extreme right-wing parties in India have abetted young Hindu men to attack Muslims and their places of worship, spurring them on in the name of "male honor" and "national pride."

Social, economic, and political conflict at various levels of South Asian society exacerbate the situation of all women, including Muslim women, and deep-seated fear of social boycott and physical reprisal coupled with the state's implicit if not explicit complicity in crimes against women tend to force the victims into silence. While the frequency of abductions and rapes of village girls by state sponsored gunmen in Indian-administered Kashmir exemplifies their defencelessness in the context of a war economy that has long ruptured a variety of social institutions, the widespread sexual abuse of children in Pakistan (nearly half of all children there, according to Human Rights reports, see Terzieff 2004) by village landlords and other men in positions of authority and power testifies to the weakness in practice of normative values. All South Asian states have ratified the United Nations Women's Convention, and there are increasingly active women's movements in all these countries. It remains to be seen how far their efforts will impinge on the multiple ways in which the ideologies and practice of kinship affect Muslim women and their relations with the state.

Notes

1. In Islam the kinship of milk (*riḍāʿa*), like that of blood, restricts marriage between those considered to be milk-siblings; by the same token it also functions to broaden bonds between individuals and groups (for an anthropological overview see Rao 2000, 107–12).

2. Similar "honor killings" (also known in certain regions as *vani*) are equally prevalent in parts of northern India among non-Muslims, especially middle- and upper-caste Hindus and Sikhs, but no figures appear to be available. Such killings are also practiced among the South Asian diaspora, for example in Britain and in Sweden.

Bibliography

I. Ahmad (ed.), *Family, kinship and marriage among Muslims in India*, Delhi 1976.

——, Introduction, in I. Ahmad (ed.), *Caste and social stratification among Muslims in India*, Delhi 1978, 1–17.

A. S. Ahmed and Z. Ahmed, "Mor" and "Tor." Binary and opposing meanings of Pakhtun womanhood, in T. S. Epstein and R. A. Watts (eds.), *The endless day. Some case material on Asian rural women*, New York 1981, 31–46.

H. Alavi, The two biraderies. Kinship in rural west Punjab, in T. N. Madan (ed.), *Muslim communities of South Asia. Culture, society, and power*, Delhi 1995, 1–62.

G. Ansari, *Muslim caste in Uttar Pradesh*, Lucknow 1960.

F. Barth, The system of social stratification in Swat, North Pakistan, in E. R. Leach (ed.), *Aspects of caste in South India, Ceylon and North-West Pakistan*, Cambridge 1971, 113–46.

H. Basu, *Habshi Sklaven, Sidi-Fakire. Muslimische Heiligenverehrung in westlichen Indien*, Berlin 1995.

P. J. Bertocci, Community structure and social rank in two villages in Bangladesh, in T. N. Madan (ed.), *Muslim communities of South Asia. Culture, society, and power*, Delhi 1995, 177–209.

M. Böck and A. Rao, Indigenous models and kinship theories. An introduction to a South Asian perspective, in M. Böck and A. Rao (eds.), *Culture, creation, and procreation. Concepts of kinship in South Asian practice*, Oxford 2000, 1–49.

G. Bouchon, Quelques aspects de l'islamisation des régions maritimes de l'Inde à l'époque médiévale (xiie–xvie s.), in M. Gaborieau (ed.), *Islam et société en Asie du sud. Puruṣārtha* 9 (1986), 29–36.

S. Burney, *Crime or custom? Violence against women in Pakistan*, Washington D.C. 1999.

U. Butalia, Community, state and gender. On women's agency during partition, in *Economic and Political Weekly* 28:17 (1993), 12–24.

M. Chen, Poverty, gender, and work in Bangladesh, in *Economic and Political Weekly* 21:5 (1986), 217–22.

Dawn (newspaper, Pakistan), Editorial, Law on honour killing, 11 July 2004.

V. Dhagamwar, *Towards the uniform civil code*, Delhi 1989.

H. Donnan, *Marriage among Muslims. Preference and choice in northern Pakistan*, Delhi 1988.

L. Dube, *Matriliny and Islam. Religion and society in the Laccadives*. Delhi 1969.

——, Conflict and compromise. Devolution and disposal of property in a matrilineal Muslim society, in *Economic and Political Weekly*, May 1994, 1273–84.

Z. Eglar, *A Punjabi village in Pakistan*, New York 1960.

Z. al-H. Faruqi, Orthodoxy and heterodoxy in India, in M. Hasan (ed.), *Communal and pan-Islamic trends in colonial India*, Delhi 1985, 382–99.

A. A. A. Fyzee, *The reform of Muslim personal law in India*, Bombay 1971.

M. Gaborieau, Muslims in the Hindu kingdom of Nepal, in T. N. Madan (ed.), *Muslim communities of South Asia. Culture, society, and power*, Delhi 1995, 211–39.

N. Haram, *Muslim widow*, Delhi 2002.

IIJG (International Initiative for Justice in Gujarat), *Threatened existence. A feminist analysis of the genocide in Gujarat. Redressing violence against women committed by state and non-state agencies*, Bombay 2003.

A. Jahangir and H. Jilani, *The Hudood Ordinances. A divine sanction?* Lahore 1990.

A. Jalal, *Self and sovereignty. Individual and community in South Asian Islam since 1850*, Delhi 2001.

P. Jeffery, *Frogs in a well. Indian women in purdah*, Delhi 1979.

J. Kotalová, *Belonging to others. Cultural construction of womanhood among Muslims in a village in Bangladesh*, Uppsala 1993.

A. R. Kutty, *Marriage and kinship in an island society*, Delhi 1972.

S. Lateef, *Muslim women in India. Political and private realities 1890–1980s*, Delhi 1990.

C. Lindholm, *Generosity and jealousy. The Swat Pakhtun of northern Pakistan*, New York 1982.

T. Mahmood, *Muslim personal law. Role of the state in the Subcontinent*, Delhi 1977.

——, *Uniform civil code. Fictions and facts*, Delhi 1995.

R. Manchanda, Kashmiri women and the armed conflict. From icon to agency, in T. N. Madan and A. Rao (eds.), *The valley of Kashmir. The making and unmaking of a composite culture?*, Berghahn Books and Manohar (forthcoming).

D. G. Mandelbaum, *Women's seclusion and men's honor. Sex roles in North India, Bangladesh, and Pakistan*, Tucson 1988.

G. Minault, Women, legal reform and Muslim identity, in M. Hasan (ed.), *Islam, communities and the nation. Muslim identities in South Asia and beyond*, Delhi 1998, 138–58.

Naveed-i-Rahat, The role of women in reciprocal relationships in a Punjab village, in T. S. Epstein and R. A. Watts (eds.), *The endless day. Some case material on Asian rural women*, New York 1981, 47–81.

——, *Male outmigration and matri-weighted households. A case study of a Punjabi village in Pakistan*, Delhi 1990.

A. Parashar, *Women and family law reform in India*, Delhi 1992.

C. M. Pastner, The status of women and property on a Baluchistan oasis in Pakistan, in L. Beck and N. Keddie (eds.), *Women in the Muslim world*, Cambridge, Mass. 1978, 434–50.

M. J. Rahman, Shariah in Nowshera, in *News International*, 10 July 2004.

S. Rahman, Women in Bangladesh. Reflections on women and violence in 2000, 2001, <http://www.ahrchk.net/hrsolid/mainfile.php/2001vol11no5/67/>.

A. Rao, Die Stellung der Frau und die Ehre der Gruppe. Einige Bemerkungen zur Situation islamischer Frauen in Nordindien, in *Sociologus* 42:2 (1992), 157–79.

——, *Autonomy. Life cycle, gender, and status among Himalayan pastoralists*, Oxford 1998.

——, Blood, milk and mountains. Marriage practice and concepts of predictability among the Bakkarwal of Jammu and Kashmir, in M. Böck and A. Rao (eds.), *Culture, creation, and procreation. Concepts of kinship in South Asian practice*, Oxford 2000, 101–34.

S. Roy, Concept of zar, zan and zamin. A cultural analysis of Indian Islamic tradition of inheritance and kinship, in *Man in India* 64:4 (1984), 388–96.

J. Terzieff, Child rape victims struggle for justice in Pakistan, in *San Francisco Chronicle*, 28 June 2004.

C. Vreede-de Stuers, *Pardā. A study of Muslim women's life in northern India*, Assen 1968.

M. Wahiduddin Khan, *Uniform civil code. A critical study*, Delhi 2001.

Aparna Rao

Kinship, Idiomatic

Iran

Kin terms vary considerably by language and local dialect, all within a bilateral structure with patrilineal emphasis. Terms for the father's relatives carry more authority, respect, and distance than for the mother's, which more likely carry familiarity. Women are said to be more attuned to correct use and subtle meanings of kin terms than are men. These meanings can be manipulated by the speaker: endearing *maman* may change to formal *mādar* (mother), conveying insistence or urging attention. The suffix *jān* (life, soul) emphasizes endearment; the prefix *khān* in connection with "mother's brother" (*dāī*), conveys respect. Increasing genealogical distance increases formality. Recently, names started to replace kin terms: adults use personal names within the speaker's generation and for younger relatives, last names for older and more distant ones, often with polite titles such as "madam/sir."

The most versatile kin terms one may extend to unrelated people to create so-called fictive kinship are those for members of the nuclear family and for parents' siblings. Children may use their parents' kin terms for a person regardless of their own actual kinship relationship. Thus, a child may call any man "mother's brother" whom the child's father calls "mother's brother," although the man actually is a "father's brother" (*amū*) to the child. Older children adopt appropriate kin terms for their relatives or avoid addressing them directly, and in reference or when in doubt use a descriptive term – "mother's brother's wife" (*zān-i dāī*).

For children, the default term for friendly, unrelated females (mother's friends, for example,) is "mother's sister" (*khāla*), connotating kindness and generosity: "All *khāla*s are good except *khāla* Bear" says a proverb. It may also cover female caretakers, nannies, and old female servants. Familiar but unrelated men such as elder sisters' husbands likely are called "father's brother," emphasizing respect over familiarity. Adults often admonish young children to call other young children "sister" (*khuwāhar*) or "brother" (*barādar*), encouraging friendly interaction. Children do not extend terms for parents.

Spouses may use each other's kin-terms for in-laws: a wife may call some of the husband's relatives, especially close, female ones, by his terms for them. This practice is less common for husbands for distant-formal relatives, in rural areas, and in traditional-formal families. A few people generally become known as "uncle (*amū*, *dāī*)/aunt (*ʿamma*, *khāla*) plus personal name" in their kin group, even neighborhood, regardless of actual kinship. The spouses of some relatives may be called by the gender-appropriate equivalent of the term used for the connecting relative: thus the husband of a "father's sister" becomes a "father's brother." Terms for mother's siblings are more readily extended than those for father's siblings.

When a man and an unrelated woman must interact, they may use kin terms as a buffer, to stress a non-sexual, supportive, or submissive intent. If they presume age and status equality, they use "sister" or "brother." (The old terms *dādā, kākā*, still used by Luri speakers today, also covered slaves or servants in the past.) Great age difference requires the use of "son, daughter" (*pisar, dukhtar*) and "mother, father," even "grandmother" (*nānā*) or, rarely, "grandfather" (*bābā*). Only the most formal term for mother and father (*pidar, mādar)* is extended; colloquial-intimate forms (such as *maman*, "mom," *baba*, "dad"*)* are limited to one's own parents and, rarely, grandparents. All these terms suggest the religiously lawful (*maḥram)* relationships within the nuclear family.

Two unrelated women may use "sister" or "mother's sister" for each other if they are of about equal age and status; or else father's sister, often teknonymously. This is tricky, though, as a woman may take offense at being reduced to a "mother's sister" by a younger or lower-ranking woman, while one addressed as "father's sister" may resent being made older than the speaker is: *ʿamma* carries respect and deference due paternal relatives; *khāla* carries familiarity and intimacy, suggesting the easy-going relationship with mother's relatives. Kin terms express status as well as age differences between speaker and the addressed.

When two unrelated men of about equal age and status wish to address each other informally – asking for help, for example – they will probably use one of several terms for "brother," in this order of increasing familiarity: *barādar, dādash, kākā* (Luri also *gyegu*). Unequal age and status require terms that cross a generation ("my father/my son").

An adult, especially female, speaker is likely to add the possessive suffix *man* or *am* to extended kin terms to emphasize positive qualities connected with closeness (*madare-man,* "my mother"); without the possessive, *pisar* and *dukhtar* are condescending and belittling, stressing authority over closeness.

In the political language of the Islamic Republic, "brother" and "sister" appear in speeches, when officials want to persuade, reprimand, or demand something of people, and in titles for religious organizations (for example, Sisters of Zaynab). This use emphasizes equality and the obligations Muslims have toward each other in the family of believers.

Bibliography

F. Barth, *Nomads of South Persia*, New York 1961.
L. Beck, *The Qashqa'i of Iran*, New Haven, Conn. 1986.
D. Bradburd, *Ambiguous relations*, Washington, D.C. 1990.
E. Friedl, *Children of Deh Koh*, Syracuse, N.Y. 1997.
S. Guppy, *The blindfold horse. Memories of a Persian childhood*, Boston 1986.
I. Pezeshkzad, *My Uncle Napoleon*, Washington, D.C. 1996.
B. Spooner, Kinship and marriage in Eastern Persia, in *Sociologus* 15 (1965), 22–31.

Erika Loeffler Friedl

Kinship and State

Arab States

Although the Arab world is geographically vast and features considerable sociocultural diversity, its peoples have in common patrilineal kinship, a way of organizing kin relations that places emphasis on agnatic descent groups. Patrilineages have long formed the basis for other modes of social organization, including the tribe and the state (Khoury and Kostiner 1990). They may have been preceded by matrilineages in pre-Islamic Arabia (Keddie 1991), although this is disputed. Matrilineal relations remain important during an individual's lifetime and provide an alternative to the idealized patrilineal family (Joseph 2000, 125). However, they do not persist structurally through time as do patrilineages.

Impingement by kinship modalities on systems of governance, and the reverse phenomenon, have occupied analysts of Arab societies at least since the advent of Islam. For Ibn Khaldun, writing in the fourteenth century, a successful society is best organized along kinship lines, which naturally produce *ʿasabiyya* (group feeling) (1969, 98). He even argued that a successful caliph needed this in addition to the requisite divine mandate to rule (ibid., 160). But he then noted that the Qurʾān discourages it, citing Qurʾān 49:13 and its admonishment to leave behind "pride in ancestry," allowing that, "still, we find that Mohammed censured group feeling and urged us to reject it and leave it alone" (ibid.). Anthropologist E. R. Wolf also regards the advent of Islam as introducing a new concept of territoriality – one based on religion rather than kin relationships, breaking with "the traditional notion of a territory's belonging to a certain kin group and representing its inviolable property" (2001, 109).

Despite these early mitigations, however, observers have argued that the Arab family "constitutes the dominant social institution through which persons and groups inherit their religious, class, and cultural affiliations. It also provides security and support in times of individual and societal stress" (Barakat 1993, 98). A significant number of theorists have argued that Arab states both encompass and are constituted by this dominant social institution in what is both a fraught and inextricable relationship whether in "weak" states, such as Lebanon, or "strong" states, such as Baʿthist Iraq, and that Arab family structures have proven remarkably adaptive to political change.

Cultural logics of kinship and state

Many people in Arab and Mediterranean societies adhere to a cultural logic in which the male/female binary is strongly linked to thinking about territoriality, autochthony, governance, and succession and in which woman is to soil as man is to seed (Delaney 1992), sovereignty over land is akin to sexual consummation (Layoun 2001), and marriage (for a man) is like the purchase of a plot of land (Bourdieu 1977, 46). The metaphorical and lived similarities between political and kinship systems are multiple. Peteet (1992, 176) argues that the Arab family is fundamentally male-centered, even when circumstances work against this as in the case of Palestinian families in which men are absent from the household due to migration for political or economic reasons. Others have theorized that Arab states are likewise male-centered, bestowing their fullest citizenship rights only on men (for example, Joseph 2000), that Arab kin groups famously seek to acquire and maintain honor while avoiding shame (for example, Peristiany 1966), and that the bodies of the women and girls who are members of the lineage, and by extension the clan or tribe and state, are their most powerful repository. Kin groups restrict/protect these living repositories from non-kin, usually by limiting mobility and autonomy, through social pressure within affectively close communities linked by "patriarchal connectivity" (Joseph 1993). Correspondingly, Arab states limit women through jural codes, such as in Saudi Arabia, where they are not allowed to drive or to be seen in public unaccompanied by a male kinsman. As with kin groups, the goal is protection from exogenous threats, including "the age-old antagonism between Islam and Christendom . . . [which] created an area of cultural resistance around women and the family" (Kandiyoti 1991, 7).

In all Arab states, then, it appears that patrilineal kinship, or what Joseph (1997, 80) calls "patriarchal kinship" forms the model for the state. This model has endured through the centuries and, during the past hundred years, since the demise of the

Ottoman state, through the intensification and decline of European colonialism, and the advent of the modern Arab state.

Women living enmeshed in the kin relations and networks found in these states face a host of consequences that compromise or deny their rights as citizens. If suspected of sexual relations outside marriage a girl or woman may face severe reprimand ranging from banishment to honor killing, in which a male family member kills her in order to restore the family's honor. In many states this is sanctioned by the law in that the perpetrator is subjected to a lighter sentence than for a different type of murder. Women are likewise often barred from the workplace and from public life. In some cases the state has even reversed gains made in recent decades, such as in Iraq during the 1990s, when the government, pressured by economic sanctions imposed by the West, introduced policies aimed at removing some women from the workplace (Human Rights Watch 2003).

Modern Arab states and family as metaphor

Among modern Arab states there exists considerable diversity in governance, including republics, single-party military dictatorships, and monarchies. But across these diverse Arab states the metaphor of state leader as father is frequently invoked and images of the Arab state as a family writ large are seemingly ubiquitous. Eickelman and Piscatori (1996, 83) note instances in which Palestinian leader Yasser Arafat and King Hussein of Jordan referred to their political constituents as their "family." Wedeen describes Hafiz al-Asad's role as head of the Syrian "national family" which manifested itself in "a chain of filial piety and paternal authority that culminates, and stops, in Asad" (1999, 49–65). The various versions of this chain are portrayed as both a bottom-up movement, in which "the political leader has been seen as a family member, an honorary family patriarch" (Joseph 1997, 87), and a top-down movement of the kind suggested by Iraqi leader Saddam Hussein, who made a point of being photographed playing with a child during the start of his 1991 invasion of Kuwait – a reminder to his followers of "the extreme need of the vulnerable for protection exercised by an all-powerful father" (Saghieh 2000).

Changes in kinship and gender often accompany, or are at least expected to accompany, the modernization process. But as Sharabi and others after him argue, the contemporary Arab state simply reshapes and preserves patriarchy, creating a modernized form of it called "neopatriarchy" that is "in many ways no more than a modernized version of the traditional patriarchal sultanate" (1992, 7). Sharabi identifies this state's "central psychological feature" as "the dominance of the Father (patriarch), the center around which the national and natural family are organized. Thus between ruler and ruled, between father and child, there exist vertical relations: in both settings, paternal will is the absolute will mediated by a forced consensus based on ritual and coercion" (1992, 7).

The central role of kin loyalties in the nascent modern Arab states was evident from the beginning. Early Arab nationalist Khalil al-Sakakini wrote in his diary of families in post-First World War Jerusalem, "The family interest comes before any other interest . . . If you assign someone to vote . . . he will vote for the elder of his family, whether or not that person is fit for the job" (al-Sakakini 1990, 115, cited in Segev 2001, 103).

As the new Arab states searched for their footing, they both were offered and looked for new father figures. Thompson describes a 1918 speech by occupying French general Henri Gourand in which he welcomed his Lebanese hearers "to France's colonial family" (2000, 39) and stated that "colonial children who were loyal would be rewarded" and resistors punished. Thompson notes that Gourand was, in his subtext, competing with another father figure, King Faysal (ibid., 40). What had brought about this "crisis of paternity" in the first place? The demise of the Ottoman Empire, in which "each sultan had ruled as a father" (ibid., 41).

In her 2002 presidential address to the Middle East Studies Association of North America, Lisa Anderson described the region as featuring "decades of despotism, once fed by Cold War imperatives [that] continued as if by inertia." The "inertia" she describes might well be the mutual constitution of state and kinship in the Arab world. Libyan president Muʿamar Qaddafi, one of the major figures of the "decades of despotism" (presumably her remarks apply to Arab North Africa as well as to the Middle East), lays out his political philosophies in his *Green Book*, a tract analogous to Mao's *Little Red Book*. "The nation," he writes, "is a large family which has passed through the stage of the tribe . . . The family, likewise, grows into a nation only after passing through the stages of the tribe and its ramifications . . . Inevitably this is achieved over long periods of time" (Qaddafi 1980, 19–20). Several pages later (22) he states that he regards a state as rightly being comprised of a nation. Qaddafi's remarks portray a seemingly attractive sense of nested collective identities and a *telos*, but unfortunately whitewash the despotism, marginalization of women, and other realities inherent in the conflation of patriarchy and state.

BIBLIOGRAPHY

L. Anderson, Scholarship, policy, debate and conflict. Why we study the Middle East and why it matters, 2003 MESA presidential address, *Middle East Studies Association Bulletin* 38:1 (2004), <http://fp.arizona.edu/mesassoc/Bulletin/Pres%20Addresses/Anderson.htm>.

H. Barakat, *The Arab world. Society, culture, and state*, Berkeley 1993.

P. Bourdieu, *Outline of a theory of practice*, Cambridge 1977.

C. Delaney, *The seed and the soil. Gender and cosmology in Turkish village society*, Berkeley 1992.

D. F. Eickelman and J. P. Piscatori, *Muslim politics*, Princeton, N.J. 1996.

Human Rights Watch, Human rights watch briefing paper, Background on women's status in Iraq prior to the fall of the Saddam Hussein government, New York 2003, <http://www.hrw.org/backgrounder/wrd/iraq-women.pdf>.

Ibn Khaldun, *The muqaddimah. An introduction to history*, trans. F. Rosenthal, ed. and abridged N. J. Dawood, Princeton, N.J. 1969.

S. Joseph, Connectivity and patriarchy among urban working-class Arab families in Lebanon, in *Ethos* 21 (1993), 452–84.

——, The public/private. The imagined boundary in the imagined nation/state/community. The Lebanese case, in *Feminist Review* 57 (1997), 73–92.

—— (ed.), *Gender and citizenship in the Middle East*, Syracuse 2000.

D. Kandiyoti, Introduction, in D. Kandiyoti (ed.), *Women, Islam and the state*, London 1991, 1–21.

N. Keddie, Introduction, in N. Keddie and B. Baron (eds.), *Women in Middle Eastern history. Shifting boundaries in sex and gender*, New Haven, Conn. 1991, 1–22.

P. S. Khoury and J. Kostiner, *Tribes and state formation in the Middle East*, Berkeley 1990.

M. N. Layoun, *Wedded to the land? Gender, boundaries, and nationalism in crisis*, Durham, N.C. 2001.

J. G. Peristiany (ed.), *Honour and shame. The values of Mediterranean societies*, Chicago 1966.

J. Peteet, *Gender in crisis. Women and the Palestinian resistance movement*, New York 1992.

M. al-Qaddafi, *The green book, Part III. The social basis of the third universal theory*, Tripoli 1980.

H. Saghieh, Saddam, manhood and the image, in M. Ghoussoub and E. Sinclair-Webb, *Imagined masculinities. Male identity and culture in the modern Middle East*, London 2000, 236–248.

K. al-Sakakini, *Such am I, o world* [in Hebrew], Jerusalem 1990.

T. Segev, *One Palestine, complete. Jews and Arabs under the British Mandate*, New York 2001.

H. Sharabi, *Neopatriarchy. A theory of distorted change in Arab society*, Oxford 1988, repr. 1992.

E. Thompson, *Colonial citizens. Republican rights, paternal privilege, and gender in French Syria and Lebanon*, New York 2000.

L. Wedeen, *Ambiguities of domination. Politics, rhetoric, and symbols in contemporary Syria*, Chicago 1999.

E. R. Wolf, *Pathways of power. Building an anthropology of the modern world*, Berkeley 2001.

DIANE E. KING

The Ottoman Empire

The Ottoman Empire included diverse ethnic and religious groups that adhered to a variety of kinship practices. To establish legitimacy and power over these groups, the Ottomans regularly co-opted kinship units of the different populations into the organization of the Ottoman state. For example, rival Turkish and Arab tribal groups and leaders were often given regional powers within the Ottoman state apparatus. This tactic allowed the Ottoman Empire to expand its boundaries and its sovereignty over people and resources, even as each of the various ethnic groups was able to maintain a fair amount of autonomy within their respective territories. While the relationship between kinship and state in the Ottoman era is a complex topic, this entry focuses specifically on how the Ottoman dynasty of the classical era (1300–1600) used kinship discourse to help consolidate its power and legitimate itself as the dynasty whose right to rule was mandated by Turkish tradition and by association with the Prophet Muḥammad. This resort to kinship to justify positions of power differentially implicated women in the Ottoman dynasty, depending on the context of the legitimating discourse.

Early in its history the Ottoman dynasty's right to rule over the numerous territories and peoples of Anatolia was repeatedly contested by various rivals. After the Seljuk Turkish sultanate of Anatolia crumbled during the thirteenth century, Mongol invaders and various Turkmen tribes competed for control of the Anatolian lands; the Ottoman tribe emerged as dominant by the end of the fourteenth century. In 1395 the Ottoman ruler Bayezid I sought to reinforce political supremacy in Anatolia by petitioning the ʿAbbāsid emperor for the official title of Ṣultān al-Rūm (ruler of the Byzantine territories), which was a designation that had traditionally belonged to the Seljuk rulers. But the Mongol leader Tamerlane and his successor Şahruh countered the Ottoman drive for dominance by laying claim to all former Mongol territories in Anatolia gained during the Mongol invasion of the thirteenth century. To frustrate this challenge, the Ottomans produced a long, largely fabricated, genealogy connecting the Ottoman lineage to the ancient and glorious Turkish khans of Central Asia, who were extolled as *gazi* leaders – that is, warriors in the service of jihad. Early Turkish historians claimed that Osman I (ca. 1299–1324), the founder of the Ottoman Empire, was descended directly from the legendary Oğuz Khān, and that an assembly of Turkish beys of the frontier had formally recognized Osman as the rightful heir to Oğuz's rule. At the same time, the Ottomans purposely revived ancient Turkish traditions to reinforce their connection to the Turkish khans and to justify their claim to the Islamic sultanate of Anatolia and Rum (Byzantine lands).

The practice of fabricating a lineage that connects a current ruler with mythic or ancient rulers is a legitimating practice in many dynastic contexts – both Muslim and non-Muslim – and the Ottomans were no exception. Two points bear emphasizing here. First, the practice of polygyny guaranteed the continuity of the Ottoman lineage. Unlike some monarchies, the Ottoman Empire was entirely identified with the Ottoman dynasty, so that the production of an heir to the throne was of paramount importance not only for the continuity of the dynasty but also for political stability. This problem was easily solved through polygyny, a practice probably derived from Islamic law that gave the Ottoman lineage the necessary flexibility and strength to guarantee many sons and a continuous dynasty.

Second, the lineages drawn up by Turkish historians reflect the fact that the Ottomans were decidedly patrilineal, meaning a child inherited all titles and power from the father while the mother's culture and background were largely inconsequential to a child's identity. By the fifteenth century, the practice of capturing non-Muslim slave women to serve as concubines – and not wives – to the sultan and become mothers of the princes became established, based on the logic that a converted slave woman would not introduce fanatical or heretical religious ideas into the inner sanctum of the palace. Indeed, after Orhan I (ca. 1324–62), only Süleyman the Magnificent (1520–66) chose to marry one of his concubines, his beloved Hürrem Sultan. Whether the sultan's consort served as a wife or a slave-concubine had no effect on the legitimacy of his offspring. What established a child's royal pedigree was not the mother's blood but the father's.

Once the Ottomans were established as the heirs of the Byzantine Empire (after the capture of Constantinople in 1453) and as the seat of the caliphate (after 1517), asserting the Ottoman dynasty's right to rule over far-flung and multiethnic populations remained an important political issue. By the sixteenth century the Ottomans adopted a legitimizing kinship discourse that sought to link the Ottoman house to the house of the Prophet. Certainly the Ottomans could never claim any direct genealogical link to the Prophet and his family, as was common among Muslim rulers throughout the history of Islam. Early Ottomans did assert that their renowned ancestor Oğuz Khān and his descendents were all Muslims, had close contact with early Muslim leaders, and were involved in the spread of Islam from the beginning. Yet the importance of linking the Ottoman dynasty to the Prophet's family was clearly recognized. Rather than connect males (members of the Ottoman bloodline) to the Prophet's lineage, legitimizing discourse adopted the practice of linking the women of the Ottoman house – particularly the concubines and mothers of the sultans – to the women of the Prophet's family, who were also not blood members of the Prophet Muḥammad's lineage. For example, royal Ottoman women were given honorific titles, such as the "Khadīja of the age" or were likened to ʿĀʾisha, the youngest wife of the Prophet. As Leslie Peirce (1993) has suggested, linking the dynasty to the Prophet's family through women demonstrates a discursive function that royal women, but not royal men, could serve. That is, the royal women could be likened to the Prophet's family precisely because they were not blood members of the Ottoman lineage or house, just as Muḥammad's wives were not members of his lineage. The notion of conversion also played into this. Just as the Ottoman slave concubines were foreign elements who converted to Islam, so were the wives of Muḥammad some of the first converts from paganism to Islam.

In sum, kinship discourse was an important, if not exclusive, means of legitimizing Ottoman power first over the inhabitants of Anatolia and then over the widely dispersed peoples of the Ottoman Empire. In the case of the Ottomans, legitimacy of birth and legitimacy of power were one and the same.

Bibliography

Primary Sources

İ. T. Ahmedî, *Dastan ve tevarih-i müluk-i al-i Osman*, in N. Atsız (ed.), *Osmanlı tarihleri*, Istanbul 1947, 1–35.

O. Bon, *The sultan's seraglio. An intimate portrait of life at the Ottoman court*, trans. R. Withers, London 1996 (first published ca. 1650).

M. N. Mevlana, *Kitâb-ı Cihan-nümâ. Neşri tarihî*, 2 vols., ed. F. R. Unat and M. A. Köymen, Ankara 1949–57.

R. al-D. Ṭabīb, *Jāmiʿ al-tavārikh*, trans. Z. V. Togan, *Oğuz destanı*, Istanbul 1982.

Turhan Hadice Sultan, Süleymaniye Library 150.

Tursun Beg, *The history of Mehmet the Conqueror*, ed. and trans. H. İnalcık and R. Murphey, Minneapolis 1978.

Secondary Sources

D. Goffman, *The Ottoman Empire and early modern Europe*, Cambridge 2002.

G. Goodwin, *The private world of Ottoman women*, London 1997.

C. Imber, The Ottoman dynastic myth, in *Turcica* 19 (1987), 7–27.
H. İnalcık, *The Ottoman Empire. The classical age 1300–1600*, trans. C. Imber and N. Itzkiowitz, London 1973.
C. Kafadar, *Between two worlds. The construction of the Ottoman state*, Berkeley 1995.
L. Peirce, *The imperial harem. Women and sovereignty in the Ottoman Empire*, New York 1993.
S. J. Shaw, *History of the Ottoman Empire and modern Turkey*, i, *Empire of the Gazis*, Cambridge 1976.

KIM SHIVELY

Southeast Asia, East Asia, Australia, and the Pacific

Recent transformations in many countries of the Asia-Pacific region, home to the world's largest Muslim population, have dramatically reconfigured gender relations. In both Muslim majority and Muslim minority nations, the complex interplays between development (often state-led), consumer capitalist culture, economy, polity, and religious practice have had profound implications for women's and men's everyday lived experiences, and for wider processes of identity formation. Expanding education, the entry of large numbers of women into modern labor sectors, rapidly rising ages at marriage, the decline of arranged marriages, changing divorce rates, and birth rates declining well below replacement level in a number of countries, notably Japan, Singapore, and Thailand, have all meant widening opportunities for some women, and deepening exploitation for others. Women have been important political actors, especially in their engagements with states over issues of family law and violence against women; but they have also frequently found themselves placed ideologically by state nation-building projects and media as keepers of family and bearers of cultural and national identity and honor (Ong and Peletz 1995, Sen and Stivens 1998, Edwards and Roces 2000).

Although the so-called Malay World contains the world's largest Muslim population, it is often treated as peripheral within discussions of Islam. Muslims, however, account for over 88 percent of Indonesia's 220 million inhabitants, 65 percent of Malaysia's 23.27 million population, the majority of Brunei's 300,000 plus population, 14 percent of Singapore's 4 million population, and are a significant presence in the Southern Philippines and Southern Thailand. Indeed, Malay identity in Malaysia and Singapore is synonymous with being a Muslim. Outside the Malay World, in other parts of Southeast Asia, in East Asia and in Australasia, Muslims form important minorities (although Gladney has counseled against understanding the concept of "minority" to imply any simple idea of marginality, 1991).

The intensifying Islamization of the last few decades has had particular implications for Muslim women, especially in the area of personal laws. From the colonial period, issues concerning Muslim women's situation and Islamic family law have formed a site of extensive social and cultural contests in both the majority and minority societies of the region, with divisions within communities of believers between conservative and modernist, liberal forces. Debates around polygamy and divorce have been especial concerns. In Indonesia, Malaysia, and the Philippines, for example, colonial legal apparatuses set up separate spheres for Islamic family law, alongside the remnants of customary law (*adat*) and the new civil laws. This often produced confusing, contradictory, and disparate legal systems, with an overall lack of uniformity of laws and their application (ADB 2002). It is notable, however, that the everyday kinship practices of most Muslim social groups within the Malay World are in fact often strongly female-centered, in contrast to dominant images of Muslim family life in global discourses. Although the complexities of modernity have greatly modified the underlying bilateral and female-centered kinship patterns, these continue to have significance.

Recent Islamization has also brought new sources of identity and identity politics: in embracing a "revived" Islam, many women have become important new religious agents in their own right, and shapers of contemporary local, regional, and globalizing Islam. But women's long-term significance as religious agents, both acting as such, and in instructing the young from generation to generation, has not been adequately recognized either in political spheres or in scholarship.

MUSLIM MAJORITIES

It is often argued that women in the Malay World possess a degree of relative autonomy that contrasts with women's experiences in East and Southeast Asia: it is suggested that East Asian kinship and family relations have tended to be more male centered and patriarchal, whereas Southeast Asian kinship has mostly been bilateral (kinship links traced through both males and females), according greater gender equality in inheritance. These advantages are ascribed to women's economic importance in the precolonial economies of the region. Such categorizations, however, can oversimplify the complex histories of interrelationships between gender, indigenous kinship relations, state, and religious ideologies and practices from the colonial period onwards: the long and cosmopolitan history of the region, especially the Malay World's position at the crossroads of East and West, has produced enormous social diversity and complexity. Moreover, the model of the autonomous woman has given way in recent decades to more critical versions, in which women's previous autonomy is often assumed to be undermined by intensifying social change.

Kinship patterns in the Malay World fall into several categories historically: a majority bilateral principle, which has often favored the female side, especially in residence patterns; systems of marriage exchange like those of eastern Indonesia; and a unilineal kinship pattern, which includes the more male emphasis of Balinese kinship practices, and the famous matrilineal practices of the Minangkabau of West Sumatra in Indonesia (population of nearly 4 million in 1990) and their small daughter society Negeri Sembilan in Malaysia, who trace descent through women. In rural areas the elementary or extended family has normally been the basic unit of production and consumption, even when several such families co-reside (Bowen 1992).

Anthropologists emphasize the ways in which this bilateral kinship grid has underlain diverse kinship beliefs and practices, supporting relatively egalitarian ideas of gender across the region (Bowen 1992). They also underline the importance of sibling relationships within these systems. Thus everyday inheritance practices have frequently emphasized both the male and female sides, although they have also reworked into local patterns the formal requirements of both Muslim law and local kinship (Stivens 1996). In Minangkabau, for example, scholars have seen a long-term accommodation between the female-focused *adat* (customary law) and Islamic rules (Blackwood 2000). Naming, however, mostly follows the Muslim practice of tracing descent from the father. There is disagreement about the extent of male authority in households historically, although many researchers view colonial and modern states as frequently supporting the rights of males in households over those of females.

Muslim patterns of marriage and fertility in Southeast Asia are distinctive. They share the regional pattern of rising ages at marriage and falling birth rates, but divorce trends have deviated from the assumed "modern" patterns characterizing the West: the very high rates of the 1950s, especially in the first years of marriage, have declined to rates that are in some cases only a third of those in the West (Jones 1994). The possible causes are highly complex and variable, but include growth in incomes, rising ages at marriage, and the decline of arranged marriages (ibid.). Muslim populations mostly have fertility rates above the prevailing averages, although their birth rates have also been falling. Contemporary Muslim women clearly experience in common with other women in the region the relentless pressures between rising demands both at home and at work caused by modern economic developments and globalization. Negotiations within households around these demanding domestic labor divisions, especially among "modern" middle-class dual income families, are growing. Latterly, governments under pressure to acknowledge some of the realities of modern gender divisions, have incorporated more images of the working woman into representations of women, as in Indonesia (Sen and Stivens 1998). But negotiations within households can also be forestalled, as among the middle classes in Malaysia and Singapore, where the employment of domestic workers has reshaped the domestic arena. Often recruited from neighboring countries such as Indonesia and the Philippines, these workers have joined other waves of transnational migration in facing sizeable risks of abuse and exploitation.

There has been a long history of women's organizations working for women's interests in pre-and post-independent Indonesia and Malay(si)a. Muslim women have been particularly active in past and contemporary campaigns to reform Islamic family law, especially divorce and polygyny provisions. Campaigns against domestic violence have been a feature of the last decade. In Indonesia, the government established the National Commission on Anti-Violence against Women in October 1998, with a draft bill working its way toward enactment. In Malaysia the Domestic Violence Act of 1994 came into effect in 1996. Groups engaged in campaigns for sexuality rights have also arisen, including Pink Triangle in Malaysia and Gaya Nusantara in Indonesia. The activities of reformist groups like the Sisters in Islam in Malaysia promoting a social justice agenda within Islam have been especially important in forging new public spaces for Muslim women intellectuals and activists.

Muslim minorities

Muslims form important sectors of the population in the other countries under discussion, where their integration has long been contentious politically: there have been active separatist movements in the Philippines, Thailand, and Burma, for example. In the Philippines, Muslims comprise an estimated 5–7 percent of the total population of 82 million, concentrated on the southern islands. In Thailand, Muslims constitute an estimated 5–10 percent of the 62 million population: a significant population of Malay-speaking Muslims in Southern Thailand share cultural and historical ties with Malays, which have been promoted within a recent ethnic resurgence; in Indochina as well, the Cham, many of whom are Muslim, have formed an important minority (Nakamura 1999). Nakamura also describes Indian Muslims in Indochina, who form small groups there, as in many other parts of Southeast and East Asia.

Philippine, Thai, and Singapore Malay Muslim family and kinship practices follow versions of the basic insular Southeast Asian bilateral, extended, female-focused kinship patterns, but as in Indonesia and Malaysia, there are separate family law provisions for Muslims in each of these countries. In the areas affected by separatist movements, however, there has been extensive disruption of family and kinship patterns. There is little focused information on the kinship practices of Muslims in Indochina, although Nakamura has reported female-centered kinship and family patterns among the Cham (1999; see also EWIC I, 228–31).

The 1990 census in China lists 17.6 million Muslims in China, mainly in the northwest and central provinces. Jaschok and Shui (2000) note how Islamic law defines the relationship between husband and wife in a way that overlaps with Chinese "traditional" (sic) practices, granting men a range of rights over women in households. Jaschok and Shui see women's engagement in the post-revolutionary, modern labor force as bringing a greater degree of equality, and divorces, once infrequent, are on the rise. They argue that Muslim women's instrumentality in China, especially within female mosques, preserves and invigorates the faith. Gladney also sees Hui Muslim Chinese marriage networks across large geographical distances as an important way of preserving cultural identity (1991, 255). In the other East Asian countries, Muslim numbers are small, and information sparse, although transnational migrants, such as Indonesian domestic workers, are a growing presence in places such as Hong Kong.

Among the 280,000 Muslims in Australia (from 70 countries), women have higher than average post-school qualifications and involvement in nonstandard occupations, marry at a younger age than average, and divorce more frequently, with Islamic beliefs around marriage and divorce subjected to Australian family law (Saeed 2003). Muslim women have been active in organizations, including the influential Muslim women's National Network of Australia. Saeed notes that there is extensive disagreement among Australian Muslims about women's roles, especially segregation and dress codes (2003).

In the Pacific, the main Muslim presence is the 16 percent of Indo-Fijians who are Muslim. (Descendants of indentured plantation labor, Indo-Fijians comprise 44 percent of Fiji's 830,000 population.) There is little focused material on Indo-Fijian gender, family, and kinship relations, but Lateef (1993) reports the re-establishment in the diaspora of some patterns from India, extensive change in family and kinship patterns recently with modernization, a persistence of arranged marriage (albeit via marriage bureaus), and growing numbers of love marriages which parents still try to contain. Women's groups have highlighted issues of domestic and ethnically-based violence toward Indo-Fijian women.

Bibliography

ADB (Asian Development Bank), Sociolegal status of women in Indonesia, Malaysia, Philippines, and Thailand, Poverty Reduction and Social Development Division, Poverty and Social Development Paper No. 1, January 2002, <http://www.adb.org/Documents/Studies/Sociolegal_Status_Women/sociolegal.pdf Publication>.

D. J. Banks, *Malay kinship*, Philadelphia 1983.

E. Blackwood, *Webs of power. Women, kin, and community in a Sumatran village*, Lanham, Md. 2000.

J. R. Bowen, Family and kinship in Indonesia, in M. L. Cohen (ed.), *Asia. Case studies in the social sciences. A guide for teaching*, Armonk, N.Y. 1992.

L. Edwards and M. Roces (eds.), *Women in Asia. Tradition, modernity and globalisation*, St. Leonards, N.S.W. 2000.

D. Gladney, *Muslim Chinese. Ethnic nationalism in the People's Republic*, Cambridge, Mass. 1991.

M. Jaschok and Shui J.J., *The history of women's mosques in Chinese Islam. A mosque of their own*, Richmond, Surrey 2000.

G. W. Jones, *Marriage and divorce in Islamic South-east Asia*, Kuala Lumpur 1994.

S. Lateef, Indo-Fijian marriage in Suva. A little love, a little romance, and a visa, in R. A. Marksbury (ed.), *The business of marriage. Transformations in Oceanic matrimony*, Pittsburgh 1993, 205–23.

R. Nakamura, Cham in Vietnam. Dynamics of ethnicity, Ph.D. diss., Department of Anthropology, University of Washington 1999.

A. Ong and M. G. Peletz, *Bewitching women, pious men. Gender and body politics in Southeast Asia*, Berkeley 1995.

A. Saeed, *Islam in Australia*, St. Leonards, N.S.W. 2003.

P. Saihoo, Social organization of an inland Malay village community in Southern Thailand (with emphasis on the pattern of leadership), D.Phil. thesis, University of Oxford 1974.

K. Sen and M. Stivens (eds.), *Gender and power in affluent Asia*, London 1998.
M. Stivens, *Matriliny and modernity. Sexual politics and social change in rural Malaysia*, St. Leonards, N.S.W 1996.

MAILA STIVENS

Kinship: Milk

Overview

This entry examines the legal-ethical rules and practices, prevalent in Muslim societies, past and present, which stem from the idea that transmission of milk from a nursing woman to a strange (that is, another woman's) nursling creates impediments to marriage.

The idea that the relations created through lactation between a nurse and her (strange) nursling are similar, from the viewpoint of prohibitions of marriage, to blood relations, is based on a pre-Islamic Arabic concept. In Arabic medical writings of the classical period of Islam this idea was supported by the notion, found in ancient Greek learned medicine, that the breast milk is formed of the blood of the mother's womb undergoing, after birth, a slight change in the breasts. It was, moreover, believed that the milk influenced not only the physical as well as psychological traits of the nurse's own offspring but also those of her strange nurslings. Documenting milk kinship is, therefore, essential in drawing the social map of relationships in Islamic societies.

Like their counterparts in the first centuries of Islam, Muslim doctors and jurists today encourage mothers to breastfeed their own babies. Maternal lactation for relatively long periods of time was and still is very popular (as emerges from recent child and family health surveys), particularly in village societies, in the Muslim world. It plays, however, a less important role nowadays among mothers of the urban elites.

Early Islamic religious and medical writings supported voluntary non-maternal lactation by relatives, friends, neighbors, and the like, and allowed for mercenary wet nursing, viewing both as the most acceptable alternative when the mother herself proved incapable of breastfeeding her own infant. As shown by recent ethnographic and anthropological studies, no less than in the past Muslims today are well aware of the legal-moral implications of non-maternal lactation. Similarly, contemporary religious scholars, particularly in the fatwas they issue on the subject, but also Muslim physicians, reveal a great concern for impediments to marriage through milk kinship. For instance, unlike in the West, milk banks in Muslim countries remain largely a theoretical issue because pooling the milk of several donors for potential, as yet unknown, consumers precludes the possibility of establishing legal marriage ties. Still, the issue is widely discussed because it serves as a useful foil when it comes to outlining the legal ramifications of milk kinship.

By adding milk mothers and milk sisters to the list of those with whom a man may not have sexual relations, the Qurʾān, in a single verse, laid down the foundation for the Islamic rules of milk kinship: "Forbidden to you are your mothers, your daughters, your sisters, your parental aunts, brothers' daughters, sisters' daughters, those who are your mothers by having suckled you, those who are your sisters by suckling" (4:23, English translation by Richard Bell). Thus, following pre-Islamic Arabic custom, the Qurʾān extended the range of incest beyond its definition in Judaism and Christianity.

Qurʾān exegeses in the first centuries of Islam regard this verse, which mentions only a milk mother and milk sisters, as intended to duplicate for milk relationships the list of those blood relatives with whom a Muslim man is forbidden to contract marriage. According to this widely accepted concept which was, in fact, adopted by Islamic law, a man is forbidden to marry his milk niece (maternal and paternal), milk aunt, milk daughter, and the milk mother of his wife. He is also forbidden to have simultaneous intimate re-lationships with women who are milk sisters.

Ḥadīth reports attributed to the Prophet Muḥammad and his companions add another dimension to this idea by postulating a connection between the nurse's milk and her husband's semen: it is the man's semen that causes the breast milk to flow in the woman it made pregnant. The man, therefore, is the actual "owner" of the milk as the term "sire's milk" (*laban al-faḥl*) indicates. This means, among other things, that suckling creates ties similar to blood ties not only between the nursling and his or her (strange) nurse but also between the nursling, on the one hand, and the nurse's husband and his relatives, on the other. Thus, for instance, a woman and a man who, in their infancy, separately suckled from two women unrelated to one another but married to the same husband are not allowed to get married since, as Mālik b. Anas (the eponym of the Mālikī school of law, d. 795 C.E.) puts it, "the semen which impregnated both [wet nurses] and which was the source of the milk of both was one and . . . the two sucklings had thus become as though they were the children of the two women's husband" (1977, 414).

By enabling it to form the basis for a complex and ramified network of impediments to marriage, Islamic law made non-maternal breastfeeding play an important role in much wider circles of social life. Firstly, it influenced the way in which relations between different families were established. Like adoption in other societies, Islam emphasized the importance of milk relationships as a means to create legal pseudo-familial relations with people or groups outside the original framework of kinship. Breastfeeding was practiced in the early Islamic community so as to broaden the network of relatives on whom one could rely for assistance and cooperation. Assuming that the Prophet Muḥammad's biographies reflect patterns of social behavior in the first centuries of Islam, one may conclude that wet nursing functioned as a means of creating relations, for instance, between sedentary communities and the tribes of the desert. The Prophet's biography by Ibn Isḥāq and Ibn Hishām (eighth-ninth centuries C.E.) gives detailed information about the ancestry of Muḥammad's Beduin milk parents – Ḥalīma and her husband of the Banū Saʿd b. Bakr – as if they were his blood parents. There are indications to the effect that breastfeeding was continually used for the purpose of establishing relations between strange families. Ibn Bābawayh, the Shīʿī scholar of the tenth century, no doubt had this in mind when he distinguished between wet nurses who offer their services to make a living and those who seek nurslings to gain nobility and glory.

Second, by creating milk kinship with neighbors, who often would be members of the same extended family, non-maternal breastfeeding probably led to a reduction in endogamous marriages, in any case limited by the Qurʾān to patenal cousins only. *Ḥadīth* reports tell us how Muslims, including the Prophet Muḥammad himself, had to cancel marriage plans, or even break off existing marriage ties, because a milk relationship was found to exist between the two people involved. A survey of the *fatwas* section of *Majallat al-Azhar,* the monthly periodical issued by al-Azhar University in Cairo, shows that such situations are also familiar to Muslim societies today. It seems that in early Islam believers were encouraged to seek their marriage partners beyond the boundaries of their own patrilineal-patrilocal extended families so as to consolidate a larger community based not only on blood ties but also on common values and aims.

Third, establishing milk relationships with neighboring families creates semi-private spaces which allow women greater freedom of conduct, for instance, to appear unveiled and do work like cooking and washing clothes outside their houses.

It was the effect non-maternal nursing had in obstructing the common practice of paternal cousin marriages which probably aroused reservations even among the early representatives of the "great tradition" of Islam. Being loyal to local patrilineal-patriarchal traditions, quite a few of them began to look for ways to reduce the effect of the rules on prohibitions of marriage. Thus, there are *ḥadīth* reports which exclude "suckling a grown-up" (*riḍāʿat al-kabīr*), claiming that as far as impediments to marriage are concerned only the suckling of infants not older than two years, that is, suckling intended to "stave off hunger" is effective. Two years, the formal minimal period of nursing, according to Qurʾān 2:233, is regarded as crucial for the physical development of the infant. Establishing the minimum number of suckling sessions that, within the first two years of a nursling's life, would guarantee milk kinship was another source of discord. There was, on the one hand, the notion, based on a literal interpretation of Qurʾān 4:23, that a single suck, of even one drop of milk, was enough to create impediment of marriage between the nursling and its nurse and her relatives. On the other hand, a group of *ḥadīth* reports claimed that no less than five, or even ten successive sucklings are required to create milk bonds.

The tension between these two tendencies, namely, to reduce the occurrence of the rules concerning prohibitions of marriage by making boundary conditions, on the one hand, and to stick to the more comprehensive attitude of the *ḥadīth* in this regard, on the other, is well reflected in legal (*sharʿī*) writings. Muslim jurists in their collections of positive law (*furūʿ*), fatwas, and *nawāzil* (real-life cases and the way they resolve them) from the eighth-ninth centuries onwards devoted long and detailed discussions to milk kinship. This is in an environment of a fully developed Muslim urban civilization outside the Arab peninsula, where mercenary professional wet nursing, for instance, was probably common within the circles of the elite. Among the legal questions they dealt with in this context were: is there symmetry between blood relationships and milk relationships as far as prohibitions of marriage are concerned or not? Are milk relationships created between strange nurslings and the nurse's husband, the actual owner of the milk, and his relatives? Which ways of transmitting milk from a nurse to a nursling create an impediment to marriage? Is it direct suckling from the nurse's breast to the nursling's mouth only or also other, indirect ways, such as pouring milk from the breasts of a woman into a strange infant's mouth with no act of sucking, giving an infant the milk of a strange woman from a vessel, feeding an infant with bread or with other kinds of food mixed with a strange woman's milk, or pouring strange woman's milk into an infant's nose, eye, ear, and so forth? What is the minimal number of sucklings that create an impediment to marriage? What is the maximal age at which breastfeeding creates an impediment to marriage? Does the absorption of the milk of a dead woman create an impediment to marriage? Legal discussions on these themes reveal there was much disagreement among those Muslim jurists who tried to define exactly under which circumstances breastfeeding created impediments to marriage. Fatwas, in many cases reflecting aspects of daily life, are an indication of the relevance of these questions in Muslim societies throughout premodern times.

In Shīʿī Islam, the rules of milk kinship were developed along more or less the same lines as in the Sunnī law. However, the discussion of milk kinship in the writings of contemporary religious scholars in Iran reveals some differences. For instance, according to Ayatollah Khomeini, a minimum of fifteen suckling sessions in succession are needed to create a milk relationship between a nursling and a non-maternal nurse, and the milk must be suckled at the breast. Moreover, it is recommended that the wet nurse be a practicing Twelver Imāmī Shīʿī Muslim. In practice, non-maternal nurses have been employed in contemporary Iran only when it was absolutely essential and attention has been paid to avoid the choice of a wet nurse that could affect future marriage arrangements.

Bibliography

S. Altorki, Milk-kinship in Arab society. An unexplored problem in the ethnography of marriage, in *Ethnology* 19 (1980), 233–44.

Bahrain, Ministry of Health, *Bahrain child health survey 1989*, managing editor S. Farid, Manama 1992.

G. J. Ebrahim, Cross-cultural aspects of breast-feeding, in Ciba Foundation, *Breast-feeding and the mother*, Amsterdam 1976, 195–204.

A. Giladi, Breastfeeding in medieval Islamic thought. A preliminary study of legal and medical writings, in *Journal of Family History* 23 (1998), 107–23.

——, *Infants, parents and wet nurses. Medieval Islamic views on breastfeeding and their social implications*, Leiden 1999.

F. Héritier, *Les deux soeurs et leur mère. Anthropologie de l'inceste*, Paris 1994.

A. al-Kaḥlāwī, *Bunūk al-laban. Shubuhāt ḥawla bunūk al-laban. Dirāsa fiqhiyya muqārana*, Cairo 1998.

J. Khatib-Chahidi, Milk kinship in Shiʿite Islamic Iran, in V. Maher (ed.), *The anthropology of breast-feeding. Natural law or social construct*, Oxford 1992, 109-32.

——, Sexual prohibitions, shared space and fictive marriages in Shiʿite Iran in S. Ardener (ed.), *Women and space. Ground rules and social maps*, London 1981, 112–35.

V. Maher, Breast-feeding in cross-cultural perspective. Paradoxes and proposals, in V. Maher (ed.), *The anthropology of breast-feeding. Natural law or social construct*, Oxford 1992, 1–35.

Mālik b. Anas, *al-Muwaṭṭaʾ*, n.p. 1977.

ʿA. M. al-Najjār, Mawqif al-islām min bank laban al-ummahāt, in *Majallat al-Azhar* 59 (1986), 447–55.

Oman, Ministry of Health, *Oman child health survey*, ed. M. J. Suleiman, A. al-Ghassany, and S. Farid, Muscat 1992.

Oman, Ministry of Health, and Council of Health Ministers of GCC States, *Oman family health survey 1995. Principal Report*, ed. A. J. M. Suleiman, A. al-Riyami, and S. Farid, Muscat 1996.

Qatar, Ministry of Health, *Qatar child health survey*, ed. A. Salman, K. al-Jaber, and S. Farid, Doha 1991.

Saudi Arabia, Ministry of Health, *Saudi Arabia child health survey*, ed. Y. al-Mazrou and S. Farid, Riyadh 1991.

J. Schacht, J. Burton, and J. Chelhod, Raḍāʿ or Riḍāʿa, *Encyclopaedia of Islam*, new ed., viii, 361–2.

United Arab Emirates, *United Arab Emirates child health survey*, ed. A. al-Muhaideb et al., Abu Dhabi 1991.

Avner Giladi

Kurdish Women

Overview

"Kurdish women" are members of a non-state nation, the Kurds, who have lived since ancient times in their homeland, Kurdistan, a contiguous territory divided, since 1918, among the neighboring countries of Turkey (southeast), Iran (northwest), Iraq (north), and Syria (northeast). They also live in small and large communities scattered outside Kurdistan in each of the four countries, in Caucasus and Central Asia, and as refugee and immigrant communities in Lebanon, Europe, North America, Australia, New Zealand, Japan, and other countries.

In the absence of census figures, estimates of the size of the Kurdish population vary between 25 and 35 million, making them the fourth largest ethnic people of the Middle East, outnumbered by Arabs, Turks, and Persians. While the population is densely Kurdish, other peoples such as Armenians, Assyrians, and Jews have lived in Kurdistan.

The Kurds are often depicted in both the Middle East and the West as a "nomadic and tribal Muslim people." However, Kurdish society, throughout its recorded history, has been complex, including tribal-nomadic, rural-feudal, and urban non-agrarian social and economic formations. It is now highly differentiated in terms of social class, profession, religion, politics, and culture. The majority religion is Sunnī Islam, with minorities such as Shīʿīs, ʿAlawīs, Yazīdīs, and Ahl-e Haqq.

The two powerful empires of the region, Ottoman Turkey and Iran, engaged in unceasing wars for the control of Kurdistan, and divided it into two parts in 1639, but failed, until the mid-1850s, to overthrow Kurdish mini-states and semi-independent principalities. Kurdish political life has so far been characterized by, often concurrently, statehood and statelessness (for a general history, see McDowall 2000; for a pictorial history, see Meiselas 1997).

Kurdish women: a historical sketch

Our knowledge about the early history of Kurdish women is limited by both the dearth of records and the near absence of research. *Sharaf-Nāmi*, the first history of the Kurds, written in 1597 by the Kurdish prince Sharaf al-Dīn Bidlīsī, is a chronicle of Kurdish dynasties, mini-states, and principalities. More or less silent on women and non-princely classes, it makes references to the women of the ruling landowning class, and their exclusion from public life and the exercise of state power. According to this source, the Kurds, following the Islamic tradition, took four wives and, if they could afford it, four maids or slave girls (*jāriyya*). This regime of polygyny was, however, practiced by a minority, which included primarily the members of the ruling landowning class, the nobility, and the religious establishment. Daughters and sisters were given or exchanged in marriage as a means of settling wars and blood feuds. When one side was defeated, the victor took over the women of the enemy as booty and as proof of the humiliating defeat of the adversary. Although state power was exercised only by males, Bidlīsī mentions three women who, after losing their husbands, assumed the reins of power in order to transfer it to their sons upon their adulthood. While generally referring to women using degrading words such as "weakling," Bidlīsī extols the ability of the three women to rule in the manner of males, and calls one of them a "lioness" (Bidlīsī 1964, 33, 176, 184, 226, 228, 497, 508).

In the mid-seventeenth century, the Turkish traveler Evliya Çelebi confirmed the picture depicted by *Sharaf-Nāmi*. He was associated with the Ottoman court, and stayed in a number of Kurdish cities as the guest of Kurdish rulers. In the court of the powerful Bidlis principality, he found the female members of the prince's family, together with maids or slave girls, confined to the harem. Apparently exaggerating, he noted that women were not allowed into the marketplace, and would be killed if they went there. At the same time, Çelebi noted that in Kurdish principalities where rule was hereditary, women did occasionally assume power, to the extent that the Ottoman state accepted the succession of a male ruler by a female in Kurdistan (Çelebi 1990, Bruinessen 1991).

By the mid-nineteenth century, Mela Maḥmūd Bayazīdī, a learned mullah, provided the first Kurdish account of the life of women in tribal, nomadic, and rural communities. In his *Customs and Manners of the Kurds* (1858–9), he noted that the majority of marriages were monogamous. Women did not veil, and together with men participated in production work as well as singing, dancing, and other entertainment. Nomadic women did all the work related to animal husbandry, which was the main source of livelihood. When the tribe was attacked, women took part in war alongside men. They were "unique" in so far as they were, simultaneously, men's "wives, slaves, and guards" as well as fighters. By contrast, settled rural women were not as courageous, and were much less involved in agricultural production. Nomadic and rural women were, according to Bāyazīdī, as free as the women of Europe in socializing with men. However, the family would kill them with impunity if they engaged in or were suspected of extra- or pre-marital sexual relations. The goal was to instill fear in women so that they refrained from such "bad deeds." Elopement was also punished by death, although compromise was usually reached if the couple could take sanctuary with a tribal chief, a respected or religious figure, and seek mediation. Documenting male domination in Kurdistan, Bāyazīdī believed: "Kurdish women are much wiser, accomplished, perceptive and humane than men. They are very affectionate and very compassionate with those from other lands and strangers" (Bāyazīdī 1963, 138–9, also 75, 98, 115, 174, 180–1).

Kurdish oral tradition, collected since the latter part of the nineteenth century, depicts a complex regime of gender relations. In oral literature, one finds both the patriarchal regime presented in the written sources cited earlier, and a tribal quasi-matriarchal order in, for instance, *Beytî Las û Xezal* (Ballad of Las and Khazal). In this ballad, two women, each the ruler of a tribe, openly compete over a lover, a man who chooses one and freely socializes with the other. In patriarchal contexts, peasant women are subjected to the violence of male feudal lords, for example, in *Beytî Kake Mîr û Kake Şêx* (Ballad of Kaka Mir and Kak Sheikh, both texts in Mann 1906). At the same time, women resist being sold as property or exchanged in marriage in the interests of the male members of the family. This resistance takes the form of eloping with their lovers, an act which may risk their lives, for example, *Beytî Xec û Syamend* (Ballad of Khaj and Syamand), or leaving their family and tribe in search of their lovers, for example, *Beytî Şoř Mehmûd û Merzîngan* (Ballad of Shor Mahmud and Marzingan, text in Fattāhī Qāḍī 1970). Proverbs, too, treat women in conflicting, though patriarchal, ways, ranging from "source of life" to "pain" (Rohat 1994). The Kurdish language, like other languages studied so far, is lexically and semantically androcentric, sexist, and misogynist (Hassanpour 2001).

Western travelers and scholars have found Kurdish women notably different from other "Muslim" or "Oriental" women. Although travel literature points to the existence of harems and gender segregation in upper-class families, it finds Kurdish rural women enjoying more freedom than their Arab, Persian, and Turkish sisters. The evidence cited in support of this relative freedom includes, among other things, the absence of veiling, free association with males including strangers and guests, and a list of female rulers (Galletti 2001).

The majority of women lived, until the late twentieth century, in rural areas. Unlike rural women, urban women, especially in well-to-do families, were largely confined to the domestic realm. Until the late twentieth century, the majority of women were illiterate. Literacy was limited to the all-male clergy, scribes, and certain members of the feudal and mercantile classes; however, women in these social milieus acquired literacy through private tutoring. Thus, a few female names appear in the list of poets who lived before the First World War. The only well-known intellectual, Māh Sharaf Khānum, known as Mastura Kurdistani (1805–47), was a member of the court of Ardalan principality. She was a poet, writer of a brief work on Islamic doctrine, and is known as the first female historian of the Middle East. A considerable part of her poetry laments the untimely death of her husband, the young ruler of the principality (Māh Sharaf Khānum 1948). In her work, there is no evidence of consciousness about gender inequality or women's rights (Mojab 2001e).

Women, nationalism, and the nation-state

The fall of Kurdish principalities eliminated the last trace of Kurdish self-rule, and extended Ottoman and Iranian power over all parts of Kurdistan; however, rural areas and their population remained largely under the control of tribal and feudal chiefs. This centralization of state power was part of the administrative, financial, and military reforms in the latter half of the nineteenth century. The reforms occurred, in part, due to the pressure from emerging liberal-minded elites and nascent democratic movements, and, to some extent, under the pressure of Western powers interested in a safe environment for their economic pursuits.

The constitutionalization of monarchical regimes in Ottoman Turkey (1876 and 1908–9) and Iran (1906) did not immediately turn the subjects (*raʿāyā*) into citizens. Inspired by European constitutions, the Iranian and Ottoman documents denied women full citizenship. The emerging nation-state was, like its Western counterparts, a male entity, which denied women the right to participate in the exercise of state power. Women were expected to contribute to nation-building primarily by producing and nurturing good sons and daughters. While state power remained male gendered, it was also ethnicized on the basis of Turkish ethnic identity. In the same vein, the Iranian state emerged as a patriarchal unitary regime centered on Persian ethnicity.

In the wake of the defeat of the Ottoman state in 1918, Ottoman Kurdistan was re-divided, and incorporated into the newly formed states of Iraq (under British rule, 1918–32) and Syria (under French rule, 1920–46), and Turkey. The small Kurdish population of Russia came under Soviet rule by 1921. The five states – Turkey, Iran, Iraq, Syria, and the Soviet Union – pursued different policies in integrating women into their nation-building projects, and thus shaped the lives of Kurdish women in diverse ways.

Modern state- and nation-building has often entailed the use of violence. In this region, identified as a "zone of genocide" (Levene 1998), the Ottoman regime and the Republic of Turkey eliminated the Armenian and Assyrian peoples in the course of genocidal campaigns from the late nineteenth century to 1923. Beginning in 1917, the government forcibly moved hundreds of thousands of Kurds to the western parts of the country; many perished during these operations. State violence in the form of genocide, ethnocide, linguicide, or ethnic cleansing continued throughout the twentieth century in republican Turkey, in Iraq under the Baʿth regime, and, to varying degrees, in other countries (Fernandes 1999). The gender dimension of this violence has not received adequate research attention.

Women in the Kurdish nationalist project

Nationalist and feminist consciousness emerged, more or less simultaneously, in the Ottoman Empire in the latter part of the nineteenth century. The Kurdísh aristocrats and intellectuals exiled in Istanbul formed literary, political, and journalistic circles, which promoted the idea of a distinct Kurdish nation with claims to self-rule within the Ottoman state. The circle, led by the uprooted Badir Khan rulers of Botan principality, launched the first Kurdish newspaper in Cairo in 1898. One of the members of this group, Haji Qadir Koyi (1817?–97), a mullah and poet, emerged later as the ideologue of Kurdish nationalism. He encouraged the Kurds to embrace modern science and education, and learn from the national liberation movements of the time. Part of his modernist politics was advocacy of women's education. Referring to the Prophet Muḥammad's saying that Muslims should search for knowledge by going as far as China, Koyi addressed the Kurds: "There is no difference between males and females in this saying, if the mullah forbids it [women's education], he is a non-believer" (Koyi 1986, 186–7). The emerging modernist Kurdish intelligentsia, mostly males, developed this nascent idea of gender equality into a full-fledged nationalist discourse on the Woman Question between the 1908 constitutional revolution and the formation of the Turkish Republic in 1923.

For the intelligentsia, the Kurds constituted a nation because they possessed a homeland, a distinct language, a literary tradition, and their own culture and history. They conferred on women a prominent role in these early efforts to map the conditions of a modern Kurdish nation. Women constituted half the nation, and had to be equal to men in rights and privileges. Moreover, women, especially those in rural areas, were the bearers of genuine Kurdish language and culture, which distinguished the Kurds from the Turks, and conferred on them national rights including self-determination. Rural women were the embodiment of a distinct nation in so far as they enjoyed more freedom than Muslim Turkish women, and at the same time were bearers of a pure language and culture not tainted by the Turkification rampant in the cities. However, women whose illiteracy and domestic life had protected them from assimilation into the dominant nation had to be educated so that they could contribute to Kurdish nation-building (Klein 2001). Religion was not a constituent of nationhood and womanhood since the Kurds were, like their adversary, the Ottoman state, predominantly Muslims. Nationalists founded the first Kurdish women's organization (*Kürd Kadınları: Teali Cemiyeti*, Society for the advancement of Kurdish women) in 1919 in Istanbul where the size of the Kurdish population had been growing due to forced migrations and war (Alakom 1995).

The Republic of Turkey (since 1923)

Turkish nationalists led by an army officer, Mustafa Kemal Pasha, later celebrated as Atatürk, "Father of the Turks," defeated the invading foreign armies, and declared the formation of the Republic of Turkey in 1923. Formally abolishing the Ottoman regime, Atatürk replaced it by a secular, Western-type, and nationalist order based on Turkish ethnic identity. Women were assigned a special role in this project, which included reforms such as the separation of state and religion, and

Westernization of dress and calendar. Unveiled women, studying in coeducational institutions and participating in public life, and universal suffrage (as of 1934) were the hallmark of the modernizing state.

The Kemalist project of building a unitary, secular, and ethnically Turkish nation-state met with considerable resistance from Kurdish religious and nationalist leaders. A series of revolts from 1925 to 1938 were brutally suppressed. The suppression of the Dersim revolt of 1937–8 has been identified as genocide. The army targeted males and females, and many women committed suicide in order to escape rape and abuse (McDowall 2000, 207–10, van Bruinessen 2000). Ethnic cleansing projects included forced resettlements of Kurds in western provinces, the banning of all expressions of Kurdish identity including the names "Kurd" and "Kurdistan," and the criminalization of the use of the Kurdish language. All Kurdish organizations, including the women's society of 1919, and publishing disappeared after the 1925 revolt.

Official propaganda and the media identified Kurdish resistance to Turkification as tribalism, feudalism, religious fanaticism, reactionary politics, backwardness, and banditry, all directed against a civilizing state. The emancipated women of the republic were recruited to highlight the civilizing role of the Turkish nation. Sabiha Gökçen, an adopted daughter of Atatürk, was promoted as the world's first woman combat pilot, who dropped the bomb that killed the leader of the Dersim revolt, and brought it to a successful end (Mojab 2001c). The only alternative open to Kurds, women or men, was to discard their national or ethnic identity, and become Turks.

In assessing eight decades of nationalist intervention in gender relations, Turkey's feminists of a critical persuasion argue that male dominance and patriarchal structures remain intact in spite of the progress made in legal equality and the remarkable advances in women's access to the public domains of life (Arat 1994, Müftüler-Bac 1999). If state feminism failed to displace patriarchy in Turkey, it also failed to assimilate Kurdish women into its ethnicist project. By the mid-twentieth century, the number of educated women in Kurdish provinces was increasing, and in the 1980s, a stratum of professionals and intellectuals had already changed the fabric of Kurdish society. The new wave of Kurdish opposition movements of the 1960s and 1970s was different from the revolts of the 1920s and 1930s in so far as they were urban, secular, cultural, political, and led by communists, leftists, and nationalists. The movements, involving mostly students and youth, continued to be male dominated, but the left was interested in women's emancipation without authorizing independent feminist organizing. Still, by the time the leaders of the 1980 military coup d'état suppressed leftist movements and crushed any trace of civil society, the Kurdish Marxist director Yilmaz Güney raised the question of women's oppression, and strongly condemned, in his movie *Yol* (Road, 1982), the patriarchal violence prevalent in rural Kurdish society (Benge 1985).

After the 1980 coup, women undertook independent feminist initiatives, and feminism gained more currency. This trend was still Kemalist, and denied the existence of Kurdish women. The political environment changed, however, when in 1984 the Kurdistan Workers Party (known as PKK in its Kurdish acronym) began armed struggle aimed at Kurdish self-determination. By the mid-1990s, thousands of women had joined the ranks of the PKK and its guerrilla army. The organization was identified as "terrorist" by Turkey and its Western allies, and the government and the mainstream media launched a misogynist propaganda campaign against women guerrillas, vilifying them as "prostitutes" (Kurdistan Information Centre Publications 1992, 1995). Under conditions of harsh state violence against the Kurds, gender consciousness was overshadowed by nationalism.

Another development was the resurgence of Islamist political movements in Turkey and throughout the Middle East in the wake of the establishment of the Islamic Republic of Iran in 1979. Turkish Islamist movements, in spite of their own cleavages, do not deviate from the Kemalist line of denying the Kurds national rights. While they share with Kurdish Islamists a politics of Islamization of gender relations, their devotion to Turkish ethnicity distances them from the Kurds. At the same time, the secular Turkish state, faced with the challenge of Kurdish nationalism, has used Islam and religious divisions among the Kurds including the ʿAlawī/Sunnī divide against this nationalism. For its part, the secular PKK responded by endorsing religion as a legitimate component of Kurdish life, and thus recruiting Islamists and ʿAlawīs. Under these conditions, ethnic, national, and religious cleavages created a regime of ever shifting alliances (Houston 2002), which undermined the potential for non-sectarian feminist organizing.

The military operations against the PKK included the destruction or evacuation of more than 3,500 villages, the uprooting of the population, forced urbanization, and countless disappearances and extrajudicial killings. Women in custody of armed and security forces were subjected to various forms of "sexual torture," including rape. The mothers of the disappeared organized into a vocal group called Saturday Mothers, and demonstrated every Saturday in Istanbul, which has emerged as the city with the largest Kurdish population (Kurdish Human Rights Project 2002).

In 2002, Turkey took new steps in extending legal gender equality. However, in the Kurdish provinces (officially called the "southeast"), violations of women's rights were prevalent in, for instance, domestic violence including honor killing, polygyny, wife exchange, and early, forced, arranged, and child marriages. Women were not aware of their rights under the existing legal system (Ilkkaracan 1999). However, non-official and non-party feminist initiatives emerged in Istanbul and major cities, which ranged from "Islamic feminisms" to radical secular projects. While the phrase "Kurdish woman" was officially considered "separatist propaganda" and a crime against the "indivisibility of the Turkish nation," Kurdish women had formed their own feminist groups, and launched feminist journals (for example, *Roza* and *Jujîn*, both launched in 1996), rights advocacy groups (for example, K. Ka. DaV, The foundation for solidarity with Kurdish women and research on the Woman Question, Istanbul), shelters, and literacy and skills training programs (for example, Ka-Mer, the women's center in Diyarbakir). They also engaged in debate or dialogue with Turkish feminists.

IRAN

Demands for the reform of gender relations in Iran date back to the late nineteenth century, when nationalist and liberal intellectuals questioned the oppression of women, especially veiling, segregation, polygyny, seclusion, and illiteracy. During the Constitutional Revolution of 1905–11, social democrats and radical members of the new parliament demanded women's suffrage rights, and there was considerable women's grassroots organizing in the Caspian region. The violent suppression of the revolution in 1911 silenced radical voices, although outside the sphere of the state, women continued their organizing activities, journalism, advocacy of equal rights, and opening girls' schools (Afary 1996). Most of these activities were confined to Tehran and major cities, leaving Kurdish provinces and much of the country marginally affected. Opposition to women's demands came especially from conservatives among the clergy and in the government.

Kurdish women were a target of the armies of Russia and Ottoman Turkey when they invaded the northern parts of Kurdistan during the First World War. In 1915, the Russian army massacred the male population of Sauj Bulaq (Mahabad) and took away about two hundred women for abuse (Fossum 1918).

State intervention in gender relations in Kurdistan was more visible after the 1921 coup d'état, when the central government further expanded its military and civil administration to all the cities and towns. Reza Shah, army officer and founder of the Pahlavī dynasty (1925–79), established a highly centralized dictatorial regime largely through the use of military power. By the early 1930s, he had suppressed all independent women's activism and crushed the religious centers of power. Much like republican Turkey, and inspired by it, the Pahlavī monarchy was a nationalist, secular, modernizing, and Westernizing unitary state, which assigned women a major role in its nation-building project. In this multiethnic and multicultural country, women had to be modern, Westernized, and Persian(ized).

The most visible intervention in gender relations, Reza Shah's 1936 decree on the unveiling of women, was enforced largely through coercion. According to confidential government correspondence of the period, there was no need for unveiling in the rural and tribal areas of the country, especially in Kurdistan, where women were always unveiled. However, the colorful and distinctly Kurdish clothing of women was treated as "ugly and dirty," and had to be replaced by the "attire of civilized women," that is, Western-type dress (Iran National Archives 1992, 171, 250, 249, 273). In Kurdistan, this state-imposed "unified dress" was known as Pahlavī or Persian (*ʿecemî*) rather than European clothing. Another official initiative was the opening of the first public schools for girls in Kurdish cities in the 1930s, of which there were few.

The Soviet Union and Britain occupied Iran during the Second World War, and replaced Reza Shah with his son Mohammad Reza in 1941. Soon after the war ended, Kurdish and Azerbaijani nationalists established their short-lived autonomous governments in northwestern Iran in 1946. The National Government of Azerbaijan granted women suffrage rights, while the Kurdish Republic encouraged women's participation in public life outside the sphere of the family. The Kurdistan Democratic Party (KDP), founder of this mini-state, launched a women's party (Hizbî Jinan), which promoted women's education and rallied them in support of the republic. Women teachers and students from girls' schools appeared unveiled in official ceremonies and other public spaces wearing their uniforms, and wore the Kurdish national dress.

The short-lived experience of the two governments, overthrown within a year through Tehran's military offensive, demonstrated the failure of the Pahlavī monarchy to integrate non-Persian women into the unitary ethnicist state. In fact, Kurdish nationalists created their own alternative, a Kurdish state based on Kurdish ethnicity, with its language, culture, history, homeland (*niştman*), in other words Kurdistan, with its own ideal "Kurdish woman." This Kurdish woman shared more with the women envisioned by the Kurdish nationalists of the late Ottoman period than the modern "Iranian women" fostered by the Pahlavī state (Mojab 2001b).

Participants in the 1978–9 Revolution against the monarchy were extremely diverse socially and politically, and pursued different goals. In Kurdistan, the struggle was predominantly nationalist and secular, and the demand was autonomy within a democratic and federal state structure. Even the two Kurdish Islamic leaders who came to prominence in 1978–80 called for self-rule. The Islamic theocracy is, like the monarchical regime, a unitary state rooted in Persian ethnicity (its language, religion, and culture), and rejects the idea of autonomy for non-Persian nationalities. "Muslim women" were given a special role in the Islamization of the ancient monarchical state; they were expected to play a leading role in reversing the social and cultural changes that had occurred in Iran since the constitutional revolution. In Kurdistan, resistance against the Islamization of gender relations assumed a nationalist dimension, although religious cleavages were present (most Kurds are Sunnīs while the Iranian theocracy is Shīʿī). Resistance included, among others, using Kurdish, non-Islamic, female names, and violating Islamic dress codes by wearing Kurdish clothing, and participating in weddings, which are centered on mixed dances and music.

Kurdish opposition parties engaged in armed resistance when the army launched a major offensive, in August 1979, to wipe out the autonomy movement. One of the political organizations, Komele, the Kurdistan organization of the Communist Party of Iran, and other leftist groups recruited hundreds of women into their military and political ranks. Komele's military camps formed a sharp contrast to the gender apartheid regime imposed throughout Iran. The organization abolished gender segregation, and women participated in traditionally male domains such as combat and military/political training, while men undertook traditionally female work such as cooking, washing, and cleaning.

By 2000, the Islamization of gender relations had failed in Kurdistan, where the active presence of "Kurdish woman" was in sharp contrast with the contested, state-sponsored, "Muslim woman." While a considerable number of Kurdish women had entered the non-domestic labor force, both skilled and unskilled, an increasing number of poets (for example, Miryam Hula and Zhila Huseini), writers (for example, Nasrin Jaʿfari and N. J. Ashna), musicians (for example, Qashang Kamkar), teachers, and artists pointed to the formation of an intelligentsia. At the same time, the unprecedented increase in women's suicide, especially through self-immolation, revealed the pressures of both theocratic patriarchy and domestic violence (Yūsifī and Yūsifī 1997), all exacerbated by the wars of the 1980s, poverty, and a ruined economy.

IRAQ

Formed under British occupation (1917–20) and mandate (1920–32) supervised by the League of Nations, the Iraqi state accepted the existence of the Kurds as a people with limited rights to use their language in primary schools, publishing, and broadcasting. However, Britain rejected Kurdish demands for autonomous status within a federal Iraqi state, fearing that it would spread Kurdish nationalism to the neighboring countries, and inhibit the integration of the Kurds. Unlike the nationalist regimes of Turkey and Iran, Britain did not adopt "state feminism" in the course of building Iraq as a monarchical Arab state. In fact, British authorities complained to the League of Nations about incessant Kurdish educational demands (Great Britain 1930, 139–40), including more girls' schools. The monarchical regime (1932–58) continued the policy of ignoring gender equality. The Communist Party of Iraq, like its counterparts in Iran, Syria, and Turkey, was vocal in advocating women's rights.

Resisting assimilation into the Arab state, Kurdish nationalists emphasized their ethnic, linguistic, cultural, territorial, racial, and historical distinctness, which included the claim to the relative freedom of Kurdish women. However, the autonomous government of Sheikh Mahmoud formed in the early 1920s was a patriarchal, feudal regime with no interest in women's rights. Still, intellectuals, ranging from religious to nationalist to Communist, denounced the oppression of women. The most prominent modern poet, Abdullah Goran (1904–62), condemned, in his poetry, gender and class violence, especially honor killing. The KDP of Iraq published, clandestinely, the first issue of *Dengî Afret* (Woman's voice) in 1953.

In the more or less open environment following the overthrow of monarchy in 1958, the Communist

Party's powerful women's organization cooperated with the Union of Kurdish Women, and lobbied for legal reform, which brought marriage under civil control, and abolished the tribal custom of honor killing. The Baʿth regime, which came to power in 1968, used military might to crush the Kurdish autonomist movement, and in 1988 perpetrated a genocide officially named *Anfāl*, "spoils of war" (Ismael and Ismael 2000). The coercive organs of the state institutionalized rape as a method of punishment, which violated the honor of both women and the (Kurdish) nation. The entire adult male population of the Barzani tribe was eliminated and women were kept in concentration camps and subjected to rape and terror (Makiya 1993, 135–50, 289–98).

After the defeat of Iraq in the Gulf War of 1991, much of Kurdistan came under the rule of two Kurdish organizations, the KDP and Patriotic Union of Kurdistan (PUK), which created the Kurdistan Regional Government (KRG). Six of the 105 members of the parliament were women (5.7 percent). However, in the course of parliamentary elections, male and female voters were segregated at the voting centers. Although virtually independent from Baghdad, the KRG, especially its KDP faction, refused to repeal the Baʿth regime's personal status codes and other laws that were lenient on honor killing. In 1994, women marched from Sulaymaniyya to Arbil in protest at the civil war between the KDP and the PUK, which lasted, intermittently, until 1996, and led to the formation of two Kurdish governments. The genocide and the 1991 Gulf War disrupted the fabric of Kurdish society, and unleashed extensive male violence including honor killing; suicide through self-immolation, previously a rare phenomenon, occurred regularly. In the wake of continuing protest, the PUK-led government issued resolutions aimed at criminalizing honor killing, although they remained on paper. The KDP, however, justified patriarchal violence as part of Islamic and Kurdish traditions (Çingiyanî 1993).

The Baʿth regime's policy of creating a "new Iraqi woman," one who is totally devoted to the ideology and politics of the party, failed largely due to Kurdish nationalist resistance. However, the experience of self-rule from 1991 revealed that Kurdish nationalism in power, as in other cases, Western and non-Western, ensures women's loyalty to the state. By the late 1990s, feminist knowledge and critique was gaining ground, and women were already resisting indigenous national patriarchy. Several women's groups and magazines ranging from secular to Islamic, and communist to nationalist, engaged in debates on issues such as legal reform, violence against women, and especially honor killing.

SYRIA

Built largely under French rule (1920–46), the Syrian state was, like Iraq under British rule, without a "state feminist" project. The majority of the Kurds lived in rural areas of the northeast, although there were sizeable Kurdish settlements in Damascus, Aleppo, and other cities. A nationalist movement emerged in the 1920s among the urban notables and intelligentsia, but there was no Kurdish women's movement. However, individual women of the aristocratic families were active in education and culture in the 1930s and 1940s. The ruling Baʿth party has eliminated all opposition movements since it came to power in the mid-1960s, and revoked the citizenship of thousands of Kurds.

THE SOVIET UNION (1921–91)

Women were granted suffrage rights once Soviet power was established, in 1921, over the Caucasian regions of Armenia and Azerbaijan, where most Kurds lived in rural areas. Tribal-feudal socioeconomic relations, considered the engine of patriarchy, were promptly dismantled; women were expected to be active in the building of socialist society and economy (Abdal 1960). In sharp contrast to other parts of Kurdistan, where female illiteracy rates in the villages are still as high as 50 percent, illiteracy was eliminated in the Soviet Union by the early 1930s. The reform of gender relations entailed extensive educational and ideological work in the newly established Kurdish print media, film, and schools. By the mid-1950s, a generation of professional women were active in areas such as teaching, journalism, broadcasting, medicine, agriculture, and music. Also sharply different from the case in Turkey and Iran, Kurds enjoyed the freedom to use their language and maintain their culture. None of the states in the region allowed any contact with the Kurdish women of the Soviet Union. After the fall of the Soviet regime, the size of the Kurdish population was reduced and displaced due to the war between Armenia and Azerbaijan, and Kurdish linguistic, cultural, and human rights were restricted (McDowall 2000, 490–4, Russo 2000).

THE DIASPORAS

The Kurdish diasporas that emerged since the 1960s, in the West and elsewhere, consist of around one million "guest workers" (mostly in Germany), refugees, and immigrants. Gender relations among the Kurds enter into complex relationships with the prevalent regime in each country. Patriarchal relations ranging from arranged marriages to honor killing persist in the first generation, while resistance, including feminist organizing, has also emerged.

Conclusions

The modernizing projects of the nation-states to transform "Kurdish woman" into "Iranian woman," "new Turkish woman," "new Iraqi woman," or "Muslim woman" have failed. Eight decades of forcible assimilation have, in fact, contributed to the formation of the polity of "Kurdish woman." While there is no single definition of Kurdish womanhood, the ideal "Kurdish woman" is predominantly nationalist, secular, and modern. At the same time, the persistence of tribal-feudal forms of Kurdish patriarchy and the failure of Kurdish nationalism to democratize gender relations has encouraged feminist awareness and organizing. Leyla Zana, the first and only Kurdish woman member of Turkey's parliament, defended Kurdish rights, and was sentenced in 1994 to 15 years in prison. She has stated, "I view my imprisonment as synonymous with the freedom of my people" (Zana 1999, 111). Fadime Şahindal, a young Kurdish-Swedish woman killed by her father for reasons of "honor" in Sweden in 2002, revolted against indigenous patriarchal violence. Leyla and Fadime both spoke of significant developments in the lives of women in the transnational, non-state, Kurdish nation (Mojab 2001a, Savelsberg 2000).

Bibliography

Primary Sources

M. Bayezidi, *Customs and manners of the Kurds* [in Kurdish and Russian translation], ed. and trans. M. B. Rudenko, Moscow 1963.

Sh. Bidlīsī, *Sharaf-nāmi*, Tehran 1964.

E. Çelebi, *Evliya Çelebi in Bītlīs*, trans. and ed. R. Dankoff, Leiden 1990.

Secondary Sources

A. Abdal, La structure sociale des Kurdes de la Transcaucasie, trans. M. B. Nikitine, in *L'Afrique et l'Asie* 49 (1960), 61–6.

J. Afary, *The Iranian constitutional revolution, 1906–1911. Grassroots democracy, social democracy, and the origins of feminism*, New York 1996.

R. Alakom, *Kurdish women. A new force in Kurdistan* [in Kurdish], Spånga, Sweden 1995.

——, Kurdish women in Constantinople at the beginning of the twentieth century, in Sh. Mojab (ed.), *Women of a non-state nation. The Kurds*, Costa Mesa 2001, 53–70.

Z. F. Arat, Kemalism and Turkish women, in *Women and politics* 14:4 (1994), 57–80.

A. Benge, Güney, Turkey and the West. An interview, in *Race and class* 26:3 (1985), 31–46.

M. van Bruinessen, *Kurdish ethno-nationalism versus nation-building states*, Istanbul 2000, 10–11, 70–5.

——, From Adela Khanum to Leyla Zana. Women as political leaders in Kurdish history, in S. Mojab (ed.), *Women of a non-state nation. The Kurds*, Costa Mesa 2001, 95–112.

C. Çingiyanî, An interview with four women belonging to the Union of the Women of Kurdistan, in *Xermane* 9–10 (1993), 122, 124.

A. Dzhindi (ed.), *Kurdish epic song-stories* [in Kurdish and Russian], Moscow 1962.

Q. Fattāhī Qāḍi (ed. and trans.), *Mandūmi-yi kurdīyi shur mahmūd va marzīngān*, Tabriz 1970.

D. Fernandes, The Kurdish genocide in Turkey, 1924–1998, in *Armenian Forum* 1:4 (1999), 57–107.

L. O. Fossum, The war-stricken Kurds, in *The Kurdistan Missionary* 10:7 (1918), 5–6.

M. Galletti, Western images of the woman's role in Kurdish society, in Sh. Mojab (ed.), *Women of a non-state nation. The Kurds*, Costa Mesa 2001, 209–25.

Great Britain. Colonial Office, *Report by His Majesty's Government in the United Kingdom of Great Britain and Northern Ireland to the Council of the League of Nations on the administration of ʿIraq for the year 1929*, London 1930.

H. H. Hansen, *Daughters of Allah. Among Muslim women in Kurdistan*, trans. R. Spink, London 1960.

——, *The Kurdish women's life. Field research in a Muslim society, Iraq*, Copenhagen 1961.

A. Hassanpour, The (re)production of patriarchy in the Kurdish language, in Sh. Mojab (ed.), *Women of a non-state nation. The Kurds*, Costa Mesa 2001, 227–63.

C. Houston, *Islam, Kurds and the Turkish nation state*, Oxford 2001.

P. Ilkkaracan, Exploring the context of women's sexuality in Eastern Turkey, in *Women living under Muslim laws*, Dossier 22 (1999), 100–13.

Iran National Archives, *Violence and culture. Confidential records about the abolition of hijab, 1313–1322 H. Sh* [in Persian], Tehran 1992.

J. S. Ismael and Sh. T. Ismael, Gender and state in Iraq, in S. Joseph (ed.), *Gender and citizenship in the Middle East*, Syracuse, N.Y. 2000, 185–211.

Kurdistan Information Centre/Kurdistan Solidarity Committee Publications, *Resistance. Women in Kurdistan*, London 1992.

——, *Kurdish women. The struggle for national liberation and women's rights*, London 1995.

J. Klein, En-gendering nationalism. The "woman question" in Kurdish nationalist discourse of the late Ottoman period, in Sh. Mojab (ed.), *Women of a non-state nation. The Kurds*, Costa Mesa 2001, 25–51.

H. Q. Koyi, *Dîwan [collected poems] of Hacî Qadirî Koyî* [in Kurdish], Baghdad 1986.

Kurdish Human Rights Project, *State violence against women in Turkey and attacks on human rights defenders of victims of sexual violence in custody. Trial observation report*, London 2001.

M. Levene, Creating a modern "zone of genocide." The impact of nation- and state-formation on Eastern Anatolia, 1878–1923, in *Holocaust and genocide studies* 12:3 (1998), 393–433.

Māh Sharaf Khānum (Mastūri Kurdistānī), *Divan of Mastūr-i-yi Kurdistānī*, ed. S. Safīzādi, Tehran 1998.

K. Makiya, *Cruelty and silence. War, tyranny, uprising and the Arab world*, New York 1993.

O. Mann, *Die Mundart der Mukri-Kurden*, Berlin 1906.

D. McDowall, *A modern history of the Kurds*, London 2000.

S. Meiselas, *Kurdistan. In the shadow of history*, New York 1997.
S. Mojab (ed.), *Women of a non-state nation, The Kurds*, Costa Mesa, 2001a.
——, Women and nationalism in the Kurdish Republic of 1946, in Sh. Mojab (ed.), *Women of a non-state nation. The Kurds*, Costa Mesa 2001b, 71–91.
——, Introduction. The solitude of the stateless. Kurdish women at the margins of feminist knowledge, in Sh. Mojab (ed.), *Women of a non-state nation, The Kurds*, Costa Mesa 2001c, 1–21.
——, The politics of "cyberfeminism" in the Middle East. The case of Kurdish women, in *Race, gender and class* 8:4 (2001d), 42–61.
——, Theorizing the politics of 'Islamic feminism', in *Feminist review*, 69 (1 November 2001e), 124–46.
——, No "safe haven" for women. Violence against women in Iraqi Kurdistan, in W. Giles and J. Hyndman (eds.), *Sites of violence. Gender and conflict zones*, Berkeley 2004.
S. Mojab and A. Hassanpour, *The women of Kurdistan. A subject bibliography*, Greenwood (forthcoming).
M. Müftüler-Bac, Turkish women's predicament, in *Women's studies international forum* 22:3 (6 May 1999), 303–15.
Rohat, *The sovereignty of women in Kurdish folklore* [in Kurdish], Sweden 1994.
D. Russo, *Azerbaijan and Armenia. An update on ethnic minorities and human rights*, London 2000.
E. Savelsberg et al. (eds.), *Kurdische Frauen und das Bild der kurdischen Frau*, Münster 2000.
M. H. Yūsifī and F. Yūsifī, A survey of the causes of self-immolation in the city of Sanandaj in 1995–96 [in Farsi], *Abidar* 8 (1997), 5.
L. Zana, *Writings from prison*, Watertown, Mass. 1999.

Shahrzad Mojab

Law: Access to the Legal System

Afghanistan

With a well-defined judiciary in the constitution and jurisprudence composed of the Sharīʿa, Civil Code, and traditions of its ethnic groups, Afghanistan does not lack laws. Women's access to and ability to use the judicial system are mainly affected by lack of legal literacy, cultural pressure, and inadequate judicial infrastructure. The concept of claiming and taking rights does not exist in the society. Men and especially women believe rights are given to them. They seldom understand the relationship of rights and laws to the official bureaucracy and processes of a court system. Ninety-nine percent of Afghans being Muslims, Islamic literacy is widespread in the areas of marriage, divorce, and inheritance. With illiteracy at around 90 percent for women and 80 percent for men, this has implications on how fast Afghanistan can – and perhaps should – implement more civil codes. Knowledge of Islamic rights, transmitted mostly through oral interpretations, is mixed with ethnic traditions and currently imbued with extremist political ideologies that utilize negation of rights of women as their axis of control. Very few Afghans have ever read either the Afghan constitution to understand their rights and the judiciary, or the Qur'ān translated into their own languages. Fewer still know Arabic. This is why the Afghan Women Roqia Center for Rights, Studies and Education in Kabul has published, and distributes gratis, a translation in Dari of the Qur'ānic verses pertaining to women.

In addition, the obstacles to women using law are the cultural mores and traditions of the ethnic groups and the pervasive social patriarchy. This is more pronounced among the tribal Pashtuns whose oral code of conduct, the Pashtunwali, counts *zan, zar, zameen* (women, gold, land) the most important things in life. All Afghans consider women to represent the family honor and/or an economic opportunity. Losing face and being shamed is the highest disgrace. The code of silence to show family/clan/tribal solidarity is very strong. Thus, marriages occur in front of a mullah, not a judge, divorces happen in front of family, or men sell their wives to other men for as little as two rifles; rarely is any of this reported to the court and so justice for women is affected. Suffering and injustice occur not because the Sharīʿa gives daughters half of the inheritance received by sons. Rather, due to sociocultural pressures daughters can rarely claim and/or get that half from brothers or uncles (often sons also suffer this difficulty). Daughters claiming this right are often subjected to being disowned for life by the family (*qat'-e kleegary* in Pashtunwali).

Another factor affecting women's access to law is the state of the judiciary in contemporary Afghanistan. After long decades of war, much of the infrastructure has been destroyed. Courthouses do not exist everywhere; roads to reach a courthouse are impassable; judges are no longer trained in Afghan jurisprudence (most have Sharīʿa training); the legal reference books were reassembled and reprinted in 2002 (17 tons of them) but have not yet been distributed to each courthouse. Lawyers are in short supply as are law enforcement officers and other paralegal professionals around a courthouse. In such a situation, in faraway villages or less accessible provincial towns the population in general and women in particular have difficulty reaching a court.

Bibliography

N. Gross, *Steps of peace and our responsibility as Afghans* [in Dari], Falls Church, Va. 2000.

Nasrine Gross

Arab States

Until the 1970s, scholarship neglected the question of how women might have fared in premodern legal systems. This was due to lack of archival sources, but also to scholars' basic assumption that the discriminatory provisions of Islamic law as found in legal text books (*muṭūn*) would predetermine how women fared in legal systems. When Ottoman archival sources became more widely accessible in the 1970s and 1980s, scholars discovered that women of all walks of life fared better than expected in Ottoman courts. In contrast, the selective codification of Islamic law, the bureaucratization of procedures, and the patriarchal nature of modern state institutions appear to have limited women's access to colonial and postcolonial courts.

Contemporary legal systems in the Arab states are diverse, ranging from systems based on selective combinations of Islamic legal concepts with French law (North Africa, Egypt), Ottoman law (Jordan, Syria, Palestine), and English law (Kuwait, Yemen, Gulf states). All Arab court systems recognize a hierarchy of courts and some have specialized jurisdictions. Only Iran, and more recently Egypt, have specialized courts for family matters. Otherwise, personal status matters are handled by Sharīʿa courts (Jordan, Lebanon, Palestine, Syria, United Arab Emirates) or by courts with general jurisdiction (Algeria, Tunisia, Yemen, Kuwait, Morocco, Saudi Arabia), sometimes also called Sharīʿa courts.

While Arab constitutions generally provide for citizens' right to bring legal action, actual access to the legal system is hampered by several factors, some affecting women and men differently. Those who work in Arab legal systems often cite corruption, slowness, and lack of enforcement of legal rulings as the main issues affecting access to and respect for the legal system. Widespread illiteracy in rural areas and among the urban poor make these groups dependent on the advice of legal specialists, thus creating yet another obstacle and increasing the costs. While court fees are often regulated, constituting a percentage of the value of the civil case, lawyers' fees tend to be high; in addition there are many hidden fees.

Court proceedings tend to be drawn out. In the last decades, Egyptian women suing for divorce spent between three and seven years on the different aspects of their cases (Brown 1997, 200, Fahmi 1987, 15, 61–70, 73, Hill 1979, 43). Reliable statistics on length of proceedings are, however, hard to come by. The same holds true for a gender-relevant analysis of cases brought to and decided by courts; court registers are difficult to access, often requiring extended fieldwork. However, the Jordanian office of the *qāḍī al-quḍāt* (supreme judge) has published its 2000 breakdown of personal status law cases (www.sjd.gov.jo/html/fahresn.htm); the Moroccan ministry of justice runs a website advising citizens about personal status law and legal procedure (www.justice.gov.ma/justfamille/mariage.htm); and a Tunisian site has a comprehensive FAQ section on family, criminal, and civil law to facilitate access to the legal system (www.jurisitetunisie.com). But judicial statistics, even where published, appear not to be very accurate (for Egyptian crime statistics, Bernard-Maugiron and Dupret 2002, li).

Access to courts, courts' efficiency, and implementation of rulings are among the most under-researched topics in respect to contemporary legal systems. Attempts to reform Arab legal systems, particularly with an eye to improving women's access to the courts, often therefore suffer from lack of information, as recent studies funded by the United Nations Development Programme on judicial reform in the Arab states have pointed out (see www.pogar.org).

Legal literacy and the legal profession

Whereas most citizens in the Arab states hold notions of what is right in moral terms, knowledge about national legal codes is as rudimentary among lay people as elsewhere in the world. In some countries, local leaders, such as village headmen or tribal leaders, have some legal knowledge, but they often attempt to persuade parties to avoid legal proceedings; in addition their services are targeted solely at men.

Numerous donor-funded projects support legal literacy campaigns in the Arab states. The impact of these programs is hard to evaluate; when focusing on the production of written material, impact would be highest among urban, educated middle-class women.

All Arab legal systems allow, some even mandate, legal representation by professionals at all stages. Where it is not mandatory, the bureaucratic nature of court proceedings is often only manageable with a lawyer, even at the primary stage (Mir-Hosseini 1993, 112 for Morocco; compare Würth 2000, 117 for Yemen and Brown 1997, 190 ff. for Egypt). Legal services differ in quality; top lawyers are as expensive as elsewhere, hampering access to high-quality legal representation for everybody but the well-off middle and upper classes.

In all Arab states, legal professionals are educated in universities. Judges usually receive between one and three years' postgraduate judicial training. Curricula differ widely in respect to the amount and depth of Islamic law teaching and specialization.

While women make up a large proportion of law students, they are usually not well represented in the legal profession; there are, however, no reliable statistics. Countries such as Saudi Arabia, Kuwait, and the United Arab Emirates do not permit women in the judiciary. Even in countries where women enter the judiciary, they are a tiny minority. The police is likewise an overwhelmingly male domain; only very few Arab states employ women officers and most of them work as warders in women's prisons.

Cultural contexts and constraints

While factors like corruption and inefficiency affect men and women alike, women's access to the legal system is in addition hindered by other factors. Whereas many women do make it to court – in a number of countries women appear to be the majority of litigants in family law at the primary stage (Rosen 1997, 93, Würth 2000, 144) – they only do so after overcoming cultural and social negative images of court proceedings, especially against a blood relative or spouse. This holds particularly true in family law, where the better off favor out-of-court resolutions and only resort to the courts if all else fails (Hill 1979, 15, Moors 1995, 140). For women, taking a family member to court thus tends to signify cultural and social failure at settling the dispute, and ultimately speaks to the lack of family standing. The repercussions depend largely on the case at hand; taking a brother or father to court for assault will obviously have different effects in a woman's family environment than divorcing an abusive husband.

Women's access to the criminal justice system is likewise disadvantaged by political, cultural, and legal factors. Many citizens are reluctant to report crimes to the police to begin with, the lack of rights awareness being one factor. In addition, Arab police forces have a well established record for mistreatment and extortion. Reporting violence and particularly domestic violence is risky, due to widely-held cultural assumptions that women are to blame if they become the victim of a violent crime. Initiatives like the Arab Women Court (http://www.arabwomencourt.org/womenscourt/aboutus/aboutus.htm) publicize testimonies of victims of domestic violence to change these stereotypes. While women can, in theory, invoke penal provisions of assault against perpetrators of domestic violence, marital rape is not defined as a criminal offense in any Arab state. In theory, rape by unrelated men is punished severely (Mohsen 1990 for Egypt). In contrast, a rapist could marry his victim and avert punishment in Egypt – only in 2000 were the respective provisions repealed. This type of provision has contributed to severe under-reporting of rape and impunity for those who physically and sexually assault women.

Scholarship

The *locus classicus* for the assumption on the part of Islamic scholars that women fared badly in premodern legal systems is J. N. D. Anderson's work, claiming that nineteenth- and twentieth-century legal reforms came as a blessing to Muslim women, who, due to the provisions of the Ḥanafī school, were unable to obtain a divorce should their husband have left them for prolonged periods (Anderson 1968, 224, 225 ff.). As Nahal (1979, 47) and Tucker (1998, 78–87) have shown, the Ottoman legal system was flexible enough to accommodate women in this situation, and permitted divorce rulings issued by Shāfiʿī judges.

If "immutable rigidity" was the catchword for scholars' perception of Islamic legal systems until the 1970s, access to Ottoman archives (*sijillāt*) led scholars to the contrary conclusion. Whatever the legal text books said, the *sijillāt* demonstrated a high degree of flexibility and plurivocality, accommodating changing needs of the population, minorities included, and particularly women's needs. Studies in Ottoman archives demonstrated that women did indeed use urban and rural courts, to secure property and financial rights, divorce their husbands, and gain custody of their children (Doumani 1985, Jennings 1999, Tucker 1985 and 1998). These studies also demonstrated, rather surprisingly, that minority women resorted to Muslim courts frequently, requesting a divorce not available to them under their denomination (al-Qattan 1999).

Studies based on a systematic reading of twentieth-century family law archives and jurisprudence have shown judges' different interpretations of relevant legal provisions (Shaham 1997), the selective reconstruction of Islamic legal concepts by courts (Dennerlein 1998), the relevance of class in the use of the courts (Hill 1979, Moors 1995, Würth 2000), and the political nature of family law reform (Welchman 2000).

But many intriguing social and legal questions remain: were and are women using the legal system representative of the larger female population or rather an exception? What do women win if courts rule in their favor and how can women secure the implementation of rulings, particularly if financial rights are involved? How do women fare in the different layers in the legal process? How do governments use legal and judicial reform and the reference to differing legal norms to enhance their own legitimacy? How have social change and economic crisis affected the use of courts and women's access to them?

These issues remain largely unresolved, but overall recent scholarship, often by women historians and anthropologists, has shown that women's access to contemporary Arab legal systems is determined by patriarchal and class-based understandings of proper behavior, by numerous factors common to Third-World judiciaries and judicial policies, and finally by women's strategies, often, but not always, mediated by their lawyers.

Bibliography

J. N. D. Anderson, The eclipse of the patriarchal family in contemporary Islamic law, in J. N. D. Anderson (ed.), *Family law in Asia and Africa*, London 1968, 221–34.

N. Bernard-Maugiron and B. Dupret, Introduction. A general presentation of law and judicial bodies, in N. Bernard-Maugiron and B. Dupret (eds.), *Egypt and its laws*, The Hague 2002, xiv–lii.
N. Brown, *The rule of law in the Arab world. Courts in Egypt and the Gulf*, Cambridge 1997.
——, *Arab judicial structures. A study presented to the United National Development Program*, August 2001, <www.pogar.org/publications/judiciary/nbrown>.
B. Dennerlein, *Islamisches Recht und sozialer Wandel in Algerien. Zur Entwicklung des Personalstatuts seit 1962*, Berlin 1998.
B. Doumani, The Islamic court records of Palestine, in *Birzeit Research Review* 2 (1985), 3–30.
G. H. El-Nahal, *The judicial administration of Ottoman Egypt in the seventeenth century*, Chicago 1979.
H. Fahmi, *Divorcer en Egypte. Etude de l'application des lois du statut personnel*, Cairo 1987.
E. Hill, *Mahkama! Studies in the Egyptian legal system*, London 1979.
R. Jennings, *Studies on Ottoman social history in the sixteenth and seventeenth centuries. Women, zimmis and Sharia courts in Kayseri, Cyprus and Trabzon*, Istanbul 1999.
Z. Mir-Hosseini, *Marriage on trial. A study of Islamic family law*, London 1993.
S. Mohsen, Women and criminal justice in Egypt, in D. Dwyer (ed.), *Law and Islam in the Middle East*, New York 1990, 15–34.
A. Moors, *Women, property and Islam. Palestinian experiences 1920–1990*, Cambridge 1995.
N. al-Qattan, Dhimmis in the Muslim court. Legal autonomy and religious discrimination, in *International Journal of Middle East Studies* 31:3 (1999), 429–44.
L. Rosen, A la barre. Regard sur les archives d'un tribunal marocain (1965–1995), in G. Boëtsch, B. Dupret, and J.-N. Ferrié (eds.), *Droits et sociétés dans le monde arabe. Perspectives socio-anthropologiques*, Aix-en-Provence 1997, 85–99.
R. Shaham, *Family and the courts in modern Egypt. A study based on decisions by the Sharīʿa courts, 1900–1955*, Leiden 1997.
A. E. Sonbol (ed.), *Women, the family, and divorce laws in Islamic history*, Syracuse, N.Y. 1996.
——, *Women, labor and the law in Jordan*, Syracuse, N.Y. 2003.
J. E. Tucker, *Women in nineteenth-century Egypt*, Cambridge 1985.
——, *In the house of the law. Gender and Islamic law in Syria and Palestine, 17th–18th centuries*, Berkeley 1998.
J. E. Tucker and M. L. Meriwether (eds.), *Social history of women and gender in the modern Middle East*, Boulder, Colo. 1999.
L. Welchman, *Beyond the code. Muslim family law and the Sharʿi judiciary in the Palestinian West Bank*, The Hague 2000.
A. Würth, *Ash-Sharīʿa fī bāb al-Yaman. Recht, Richter und Rechtspraxis an der familienrechtlichen Kammer des Gerichtes Süd-Sanaa (Republik Jemen) 1983–1995*, Berlin 2000.
M. C. Zilfi (ed.), *Women in the Ottoman Empire. Middle Eastern women in the early modern era*, Leiden 1997.

Anna Würth

The Balkans

This entry focuses on the successor countries of the former Yugoslavia with an emphasis on the Bosniaks. Bosnia and Herzegovina formed part of the Ottoman Empire from 1463, when Sharīʿa courts were introduced to the southern Slav lands, till the 1878 Berlin Congress, which accorded the administration of Bosnia and Herzegovina to the Austro-Hungarian monarchy. Austria-Hungary passed legislation applying Sharīʿa law to Muslim women in Bosnia and Herzegovina in family and inheritance matters, as a result of which the Sharīʿa courts were incorporated into the Dual Monarchy's state judiciary. Based on the provisions of the Treaty of St. Germain on the protection of minorities, the Kingdom of Yugoslavia retained state Sharīʿa courts for matters of family and inheritance law affecting Muslims. Access to the legal system was not uniform throughout the region – there were six legal systems, the result of the different histories and legal systems in the various parts of the country. In addition, the social role and legal status of women and men was determined by the dominant patriarchal cultural matrix, the impact of which still survives to this day.

1918–40: Kingdom of Yugoslavia

In this period, Sharīʿa courts were administratively a division of the civil courts, but in reality they constituted a separate entity within the state authorities, independently applying separate laws to a specific group of Yugoslav citizens. In their organization, character, staffing, and judicial practice, they were of the type of modernized judicial institutions to be found at that time in Muslim countries, and were the best system in the Balkans: this was because the Muslims were so numerous and because they had their own specialist law schools. Sarajevo had a Sharīʿa judges' school (1887–1937), founded by the Austro-Hungarian authorities, and an Islamic Sharīʿa and theological college (1935–45) for higher education in these subjects. From 1931, a specialist course in Sharīʿa law was offered by Belgrade's Faculty of Law. The operation of the Sharīʿa courts was influenced by the half-century's experience of encountering European administration.

Muslim women's status in marriage was similar to that of women from other religious communities, to whom the Austrian Civil Code applied. Freedom of movement and public activity were contingent on their husbands' approval. Muslim women had the right to manage, enjoy, and freely dispose of their own property, but pursuant to Sharīʿa law there were inequalities in their inheritance rights. In addition, Muslim women were too poorly educated and too isolated to be able to fully enjoy the right to work. For the majority of rural women, economic independence was impossible to achieve.

As regards access to the Sharīʿa courts, Muslim women also had difficulties in being represented; it was not considered fitting for women to appear in court. This was exacerbated by the fact that it was unknown in the history of the Sharīʿa judiciary for lawyers to represent their clients; as a result, the lawyers who did so in the Sharīʿa courts were not necessarily familiar with Sharīʿa law. Advocates' unfamiliarity with Sharīʿa law as much as the ignorance of the women themselves undermined the effectiveness of judicial protection.

1945–91: Socialist Federal Republic of Yugoslavia

In common with other communist states and countries in the region, women and men were declared to be equal constitutionally and before the law. This led to the abolition of the Sharīʿa courts by a law enacted on 5 March 1946. Their jurisdiction was transferred to the ordinary civil courts, and civil law was applied to Muslims in matters of personal and family status and inheritance. The common feature was the separation of the state, and its legal system, from religion and religious institutions. For example, only marriages conducted by the relevant state authorities were legally valid.

Religion and the culture associated with it still had considerable influence on the private lives of Muslims, though this differed in rural and urban areas. In the case of Muslim women from rural areas, it was reflected in their education levels. In conservative rural areas there were even cases of girls being kept out of school.

Although discrimination on the grounds of sex was prohibited in principle, in practice women failed to achieve full equality. The courts failed to provide effective protection against discrimination at work, sexual harrassment, or violence in the family. Access to justice and effective legal protection were also made more difficult by the length of time court proceedings took, lack of money to pay for legal representation, ignorance of the law, and women's lack of education.

After 1991: the successor countries

The common features of the region for this period are the experience of war, and economic and political transition. Gender analyses have shed light on the still present equality gap between men and women; studies have been written on the position and problems of women in the transition period; women's groups have been formed to promote women's rights; and the process of adopting legislation and other measures aimed at achieving gender equality and equality of opportunity for men and women is under way. As regards Bosnian women, within the Muslim community there are some small groups rethinking the position and rights of women and applying the standards and practice of other Islamic countries in the way they dress, in relations between men and women, and in married life and life in the community. The human rights context is the expression of specific religious features and cultural traditions. The current situation is characterized by constitutional and legal equality and efforts to introduce mechanisms to ensure equality of standing in practice. The grave economic situation, the absence of legal and civic education, and lack of self-confidence prevent women from using existing legal mechanisms to protect their rights on the one hand and ensure their personal advancement on the other.

Bibliography

Primary Sources

A. Božić, Position of women in private law [in Serbian], Ph.D. diss., Faculty of Law, Belgrade University 1939.

Z. Grebo, Social policy of employment of women and their social rights at work and in the family [in Bosnian], Ph.D. diss., Faculty of Political Sciences, University of Sarajevo 1971.

F. Karčić, Sharīʿa courts in Yugoslavia, 1918–1941 [in Bosnian], Sarajevo 1986.

F. Kožul, Self-management and legal status of women in Bosnia-Herzegovina [in Croatian], Ph.D. diss., Faculty of Political Sciences, University of Sarajevo 1972.

National report on implementation of the Convention on the Elimination of All Forms of Discrimination against Women [in Serbo Croatian], Edvard Kardelj Yugoslav Centre for the Theory and Practice of Self-Management, Ljubljana 1985.

United Nations Development Programme, *Human development report 1988. Bosnia and Herzegovina*, New York 1988.

——, *Human development report 2002. Bosnia and Herzegovina*, New York 2002, <http://www.undp.ba/nhdr/NHDR2002ENG.pdf.>

Women's human rights in Bosnia and Herzegovina, national NGO report published by a group of local non-governmental organizations in cooperation with the International Human Rights Law Group BiH Project, Sarajevo 15 May 1999.

Secondary Sources

B. Baranović, *Images of women in textbooks* [in Croatian], Zagreb 2000.

T. Bringa, *Being Muslim the Bosnian way*, Princeton, N.J. 1995.

O. N. Hadžić, *Islam and culture* [in Croatian], Zagreb 1894.
A. Hangi, *Life and customs of the Muslims* [in Bosnian], Sarajevo 1906, 1990³.
S. Pletikosić, *Arguments over the emancipation of women. Response to Hamdija Karamehmedović, et al.* [in Croatian], Opatija 1911.

JASNA BAKŠIĆ MUFTIĆ

The Caucasus

Caucasian legal history can be divided into two periods: the seventeenth century to 1917 and 1920 to 1990. Until the 1920s, the legal system of the Caucasus was a fusion of standards of ʿāda, Sharīʿa, and state law established by the Russian Empire during the nineteenth century.

PRE-SOVIET PERIOD

Some communities were dominated by ʿāda (Northwest and Central Caucasus) with Sharīʿa family norms disseminated throughout, others by Sharīʿa (East and Northeastern Caucasus: Chechnya, Daghestan, Azerbaijan). Imam Shamil's role in the dissemination of Sharīʿa in North Caucasus during the period of his imamate (1834–59) was important.

Criminal cases were heard according to the ʿāda and, later, Russian law; civil cases were subject to Russian legal standards. The family law norms that regulated divorce and division of property and inheritance filled a separate niche. This area of law was strongly influenced by Islamic law. Elements of Islamic land and finance law (bond norms, stale debt, fine imposition and payment) were found only in Daghestan and Azerbaijan.

Until the 1920s, the access of women to ʿāda, Sharīʿa, and the Russian legal system was significantly limited. The obstacles they faced were: inequality of rights and duties to the communal authority and court in ʿāda law; subjection of women in society and family; influence of Islamic restrictions on women's participation in social life; and ʿāda interpretation of crimes against women as a harm done to the group to which the victim belongs. These groups could be kindred unions (families of near relations, clans) or territorial unions (communities, community unions).

In customary law, the legal actors were: man, family, clan, community, community union. Men, relatives and communities could stand as a legal person in various circumstances.

With the introduction of Russian courts into the Caucasus in the nineteenth century (Highlander Verbal or Gorskiy Courts), women acquired the right to go to Russian courts independently. However, they still faced obstacles: the narrow range of cases tried by Russian courts and the pressure of Caucasian and Islamic standards regarding the social status of women. The Highlander Courts tried virtually no cases concerned with women. Caucasian women rarely used courts as a way to fight for their rights.

SOVIET PERIOD

Soviet law introduced the concepts of domestic crime (1920s–1940s) and useful and harmful customs (1950s–1980s). The useful aspects of customary law included such traditions as homage to elders, mediation at negotiations, peacekeeping, and property protection, while the harmful ones were blood revenge and subjection of Caucasian women.

Under Soviet law equal rights and duties for men and women of the Soviet Union were established. Women's rights were promulgated among hill-women. Propaganda campaigns were conducted to promote Soviet law. Women gained the right to receive higher legal education and the right to work in Soviet judicial bodies.

The criminal code of the Soviet Union and Caucasus of 1960 included a special category of crimes that represented the relics of local customs (chapter 11). There were three groups of crimes: crimes that affront the equality of women and men, namely payment and acceptance of the bride-price (*kalym*), compulsion of a woman to marry, compulsion of a woman to continue marital cohabitation, obstruction of a woman's marrying, abduction of a woman for marriage, bigamy, and polygamy; second, crimes that affect the physical or moral development of non-adults of either sex, namely marriage to an unmarriageable person or cohabitation with an unmarriageable person; and third, reconciliation evasion, blood feud murder, and femicide "on the basis of the relics of former attitudes towards women." In 1998 a new criminal code of the Russian Federation was passed in which this chapter was eliminated but the blood feud clause kept.

THE PRESENT

Women in the Caucasus have the opportunity to use the state legal system for defending their rights. Formally, Caucasian women can be both plaintiff and defendant, although in fact fathers, husbands, or brothers still appear for women in the courts. Women use the state court for fighting for their rights as rarely as before. Statistics on petitions show that the majority of cases are concerned with rape.

Major obstacles to the active use of the modern courts by Caucasian women are the preservation of the traditional sense of justice among Caucasian men and women and the preservation of the traditional social status of men and women, which partly relies on Islamic ideology.

BIBLIOGRAPHY
(all works cited are in Russian)

PRIMARY SOURCES
L. A. Chibirova (comp.), *The Caucasian periodical press on Osetia and the Osetians*, 5 vols., Ckhinvali 1981–91.
V. K. Gardanov (comp.), *Adygs, Balkarians, and Karachians in the materials of the European authors of the thirteenth–nineteenth centuries*, Nalchik 1974.
Gidatlinsky ʿāda, Makhachkala 1957.
B. A. Kaloev (comp.), *Osetians from the point of view of foreign travelers (thirteenth–fourteenth centuries)*, Vladikavkaz 1967.
H. O. Khashaev (comp.), *The monuments of Daghestan customary law of the seventeenth–nineteenth centuries*, Moscow 1965.

SECONDARY SOURCES
I. L. Babich. *The evolution of legal culture of Adygs*, Moscow 1999.
V. O. Bobrovnikov, *The Muslims of North Caucasus*, Moscow 2002.
Customary law in Russia, Rostov-in-Don 1999.
H. M. Hashaev, *Sharīʿa and ʿāda in Daghestan*, Moscow 1949.
L. G. Svechnikova, *The family law of Caucasian peoples in the nineteenth and twentieth centuries*, Moscow 1994.

IRINA BABICH

Central Asia

Securing equal access to legal assistance is a precondition for achieving equal justice in a society. In the Central Asian republics, equal access to justice is a right declared by constitutions and therefore the states have a legal obligation to provide the arrangements necessary to exercise this right. However, there are few reliable data sources, statistics, or specialized studies that could help to assess usage patterns, especially when it comes to indicators disaggregated by sex, age, ethnicity, and territorial division that may provide more precise information by highlighting underprivileged groups.

Overall analysis of the situation reveals that the use of court services and other judicial mechanisms for dispute resolution at family or community levels is not common among the Muslim population. With the collapse of the Soviet Union and the formation of independent republics, traditional approaches and mindsets become stronger, being associated with "national identification." The situation characterizing access to qualified legal services that was never ideal during Soviet times was further complicated by new economic, legal, cultural, historic, and other obstacles that emerged in the process of transition from centrally planned to free market economies.

The economic barriers to access to the legal system are significant in the Central Asian states. During the Soviet past, legal services as a rule were not free but could be afforded by the majority of population, as the principal costs were largely borne by the state. With the transition from centrally planned to free market economy and the commercialization of life, including legal and judicial systems, and growing poverty of the population in the region, many people without the necessary financial means are unable to obtain legal aid, and thus become discouraged from defending their interests in the courts that are often slow and expensive. Therefore, the affordability of legal action has become an important issue in the region.

Geographical distribution is a serious barrier, in the Central Asian context, in determining access to justice, given that the majority of the population live in rural areas where legal services, for both criminal and civil cases, are scarce. The situation is even worse in remote mountainous regions. In contrast, in urban areas, the quality of civil legal aid, lack of standards, and corruption lead to a high level of distrust of the judiciary.

Another important factor in influencing the ability to use the legal system is strong cultural and informational barriers. Central Asian women, especially in rural areas, are brought up in the spirit of obedience and subordination to the will of the elders and to the power of men. Traditions nurture and cultivate young women as patient and submissive wives. At the same time, women bear a disproportionate burden of household responsibilities and unpaid domestic work, with limited access to and control over resources, including any time they could use for self-improvement and learning. The claiming of rights by women, whether in the family or workplace, is not approved and is usually viewed as washing dirty linen in public. This is further exacerbated by the fact that the population (both women and men), although highly educated, has very low levels of legal awareness. As a result, women are vulnerable when it comes to protecting their own interests and rights through legal means, and this may partly explain why cases concerning polygamy or sexual harassment in the workplace, which have been legally prohibited in both the Soviet and post-Soviet periods, have almost never been instigated in the courts.

The survival of traditional approaches in regulating gender relations could be explained by the Sovietization of Central Asia (1917–91), which modified but did not change traditional societies by bringing a new social polarization unknown before: the Soviet-oriented ruling elite as against the rest of the indigenous population. The latter continued to preserve and even particularly value traditions at family and local neighborhood levels, in many ways as a means of silent and unconscious protest against the forceful Russification of social norms and education that penetrated Muslim societies but were never internalized by the masses, especially in rural areas. Therefore, relations between sexes and disputes at the family and community levels often continued to be regulated by customs that might not necessarily have been of Islamic origin (for example, bride kidnapping in the areas where nomadic culture had been dominant) but were "traditional."

Post-Soviet Central Asian countries have separated religion from the state, and the Sharīʿa (Islamic law) does not formally have any legal power. However, the services of mullahs are easily accessible for the wider population, especially in Uzbekistan and Tajikistan. This is facilitated by the fact that some provisions in secular laws and norms refer to traditional means in settling civil cases. For instance, in Kyrgyzstan, so-called *aksakal* (elderly people) courts in local communities have a right to represent public approval/disapproval when judging a situation through the lens of their life experience. In Uzbekistan, the *maḥalla* (neighborhood community) is given powers by the local authorities to act as a "clearance house" for couples before they apply to a court to file for divorce. Given traditional approaches, predominant among *maḥalla* dwellers, the goal is to reconcile families and prevent divorce at any cost, but most often at the high costs paid by women. A family code adopted in independent Uzbekistan contains a provision allowing referral to "customs and traditions" if the legislation does not provide a solution otherwise.

Meanwhile, the current environment provides little alternative. Qualified and free legal aid provided by public psychological-consultative and crisis centers is not a norm, but such centers are being established in Kazakhstan and Kyrgyzstan and, to a lesser extent, in Uzbekistan and Tajikistan, mostly by the efforts of non-governmental organizations (NGOs) and with support from international donor organizations. Over the past decade, the Central Asian NGOs have been active, through seminars and training programs, in educating legal professionals in issues such as domestic violence and human trafficking. They also have been active in conducting legal literacy programs that train rural residents, at community levels, in the principles of gender equality, setting up hot lines, and providing free legal aid to the neediest. However, such work has been neither systematic nor coordinated. It has been largely limited in scope and outreach. Equal access to the justice and legal system, particularly with respect to disadvantaged groups, remains a deeply underestimated issue, at the margins of the mainstream of policy-making in the Central Asian countries.

Bibliography

Academy of Science of Uzbekistan, *Islam and women of the Orient. History and present day* [in Russian], Tashkent 1990.

D. Alimova, *The Woman Question in Central Asia. Historical study and current problems* [in Russian], Tashkent 1991.

International Helsinki Federation for Human Rights (IHF), *Women 2000*, New York 2000.

M. B. Olcott, Women and society in Central Asia, in W. Fierman (ed.), *Soviet Central Asia. The failed transformation*, Boulder, Colo. 1991, 235–56.

S. Saidbaev, *Islam and society. Results of historical and sociologial study* [in Russian], Moscow 1984².

S. Tadjbakhsh, Between Lenin and Allah. Women and ideology in Tajikistan, in H. L. Bodman and N. Tohidi (eds.), *Women in Muslim societies. Diversity within unity*, Boulder, Colo. 1998.

M. Tokhtakhodjaeva, *Between the slogans of communism and the laws of Islam. The women of Uzbekistan*, trans. S. Aslam, ed. C. Balchin, Lahore 1995.

Dono Abdurazakova

Iran

Although Iranian women have made important strides regarding entry into public schools and institutions of higher learning, they continue to lack sufficient access to their limited legal rights. In pursuing their rights they either do not seek relief from the judiciary or, if they do, end up abandoning their demands as they discover that even with perseverance the judiciary remains unresponsive. The obstacles they face in their attempts to access the legal system include laws that explicitly discourage women from seeing themselves as individuals endowed with rights equal to those of men, a consequently low level of legal literacy required for the pursuit of the limited rights they do have, a legal structure that is not friendly to women, a paucity of legal advisors with sufficient knowledge of women's issues, and a cultural context that discourages women from litigating for their rights, particularly within the confines of family law.

Contemporary Iranian laws are explicit in their unequal treatment of men and women in the arenas of criminal, civil, and family law. This explicit inequality, for instance in giving men the absolute right to divorce and only a limited right to women, is itself an important obstacle to access. Women, particularly in the rural areas and smaller cities, often assume that they do not possess any rights even in situations in which the law does give them limited rights, such as the right to divorce in case of evident spousal abuse, spousal addiction to illicit drugs, or delinquency in financial support. Operating under a patriarchal mindset, they deem their husbands' actions to be immune to any legal recourse. Unmarried women also often assume the absolute authority of their fathers or paternal grandfathers in making decisions about their marriage even though the law allows a women to marry with the permission of the court if the father or paternal grandfather's opposition to the marriage is deemed unreasonable.

The paucity of lawyers specializing in women's rights adds to the problem of lack of knowledge about legal recourse. In many villages, smaller cities, or even larger cities outside the capital city of Tehran, lawyers are simply not available to women. This is an important drawback, because many of the rights with which women are endowed, particularly in the arena of family law, are ensconced in a very complicated legal framework that requires adequate legal representation for their attainment in a court of law.

In cases where women do pursue their limited rights, the embedded inequalities and the intransigence of the legal system force them to compromise and give up parts of their rights. For instance, the legal imbalance that exists usually leads women to forfeit all or parts of the financial claims they have in their years of marriage in exchange for the right to divorce.

Women are also inhibited in their legal access by the composition of the judiciary, which does not employ female judges. The new system of justice that came into effect after the Islamic Revolution of 1979 dismissed all female judges, gradually allowing women only to act as advisors in courts and not pass sentences. While women's groups continue to put pressure on the judiciary to change, the current essentially all male make-up of the judiciary is undoubtedly unfriendly to women and an important obstacle to access. In addition, the existence of widespread corruption in the judiciary makes its members open to bribes by husbands who are generally better off economically. Many lawyers report that their clients or even they themselves have been threatened by influential persons within the judiciary or other revolutionary institutions who were inspired to do so on the basis of bribes paid by husbands.

Finally, perhaps the most important set of obstacles to access to the legal system is generated by cultural and social impediments, particularly in the domain of family law. Even among families that are seemingly modern, litigation against fathers, paternal grandparents, or husbands is considered unseemly and a source of family shame. Women who are seeking the right to marriage without their father's permission, or divorce, often feel isolated, and married women cannot rely on other family members to act as witnesses in cases of abuse, and are prevented from making their cases public by social pressures.

BIBLIOGRAPHY

H. Afshar, *Islam and feminisms. An Iranian case study*, New York 1998.

M. Kār, *Rafʿ-i tabʿīz az zanān. Muqāyisah-ʾi Kunvānsiyūn Rafʿ-i tabʿīz az zanān bā qavānīn-i dākhilī-i Īrān*, Tehran 1999.

——, *Kudām ḥaqq? Kudām taklīf?*, Tehran 2001.

Z. Mir-Hosseini, Women, marriage and the law in post-revolutionary Iran, in H. Afshar (ed.), *Women in the Middle East*, London 1993, 59–84.

P. Paidar, *Women and the political process in twentieth-century Iran*, Cambridge 1995.

MEHRANGIZ KAR

The Ottoman Empire

The Ottoman legal system was a complex one that included administrative and public law (*kanun*), Islamic law (Sharīʿa), and customary law (*ʿurf*). The Sharīʿa had the most direct impact on women's lives, and this examination of women's access to the Ottoman legal system largely focuses on the Sharīʿa court (*muḥākama sharʿiyya*). Women in rural areas were also directly affected by customary law, but we do not have sources that would let us study how it affected women. Women had significant access to the Ottoman legal system; that they did so was closely linked to the role of the *qāḍī* (judge) and the Sharīʿa courts in imperial administration. To bolster their authority and legitimacy to a greater degree than in any previous Islamic state, the Ottomans formalized the role of legal scholars in the state by organizing *qāḍī*s into an official hierarchy and making them part of the state bureaucracy. They also developed a more institutionalized Islamic legal system throughout the empire with the establishment of a more uniform and extensive network of Islamic courts. Ḥanafī judges, trained in the *madrasas* of Istanbul and appointed by the central government, presided over the courts in the major provincial cities, assisted by local *ʿulamāʾ* who served as deputy judges, clerks, and intermediaries between the judge and the local population.

By the end of the sixteenth century Sharīʿa courts were found in all the major cities and towns throughout the empire. The larger cities of the empire had several courts to better serve the needs of the local population; for example seventeenth-century Cairo, the second largest city in the empire, had 15 (Hanna 1998, 11). The physical proximity of the Sharīʿa courts to the urban population facilitated their use. Women as well as men took advantage of the services the courts provided. The surviving records of these courts provide the single most direct evidence of women's access to the legal system. In the first study of women's use of the courts, Ronald Jennings noted that the women of seventeenth-century Kayseri, "came to court regularly, freely, and openly. Manifestly the court was accessible to them and relevant to their lives" (1975, 65). Much of the social and economic history of the Ottoman Empire written in the last 30 years is based on Sharīʿa court archives from all parts of the empire. This scholarship confirms the striking visibility of women in these sources; this visibility is itself evidence of women's participation in the social and economic life of the empire. Some evidence suggests that the number of women using the courts increased in the later centuries of Ottoman rule, a reflection that this participation of women was growing (Zarinebaf-Shahr 1998, 308).

The circumstances under which women utilized the courts were linked to the functions of the Sharīʿa courts, and women went to court for the same reasons that men did. First, the courts were similar to the notary offices of Europe – a place to register transactions that fell under the jurisdiction of the Sharīʿa, such as a property sale, a marriage contract, or the establishment of a religious endowment (*waqf*). The vast majority of the entries in the registers of the Sharīʿa court archives fall into this category. There is no requirement in Islamic law that these transactions be registered with the *qāḍī*, but registration provided a written record that might be useful evidence in the future. In other words the courts served as "communal witnesses" (Peirce 1998, 296). Women as well as men used the courts for this purpose. Having a written record might have been particularly important for women since their rights to property were more likely to be challenged.

The second function of the court was to resolve conflicts. If a dispute went to court, it usually meant that other means of mediation and resolution had failed. Most people did not want to take disputes to court, especially family conflicts, and women were under particular pressure not to do so. Nevertheless, some women sued their husbands, brothers, or fathers when they thought their rights had been violated and often these rights were upheld. The courts served as intermediary institutions that mediated family disputes and provided recourse where there were grievances

Women's access to the courts appears to have been facilitated by several factors, in addition to the physical proximity of the courts. One, the *qāḍī*'s court was seen as a "legitimate destination," a public space in which it was acceptable for women to appear (Seng 1998, 247). While some women were represented by *wakīl*s (agents) and did not appear, many others did attend court. Second, cases were handled expeditiously and court procedures, based primarily on oral testimony, were simple. Third, women expected that their legal rights would be upheld. Historians are generally in agreement that women were aware of their rights and used the norms, laws, and institutions available to them to defend those rights. "That so many women were capable of understanding and managing their own legal problems bespeaks a degree of sophistication on their part" (Jennings 1975, 65). The knowledge of their rights and how to use the system came from formal education, from access to courts and judges who were relatively close by, and/or from the exchange of information in female networks within extended families and urban neighborhoods. They went to court with the expectation that the *qāḍī*s would protect these rights when they were violated.

Despite the accessibility of the system to women, obstacles restricted access to the legal system for many women. Both class and place of residence played a large role in whether they had access to the courts. For all practical purposes the jurisdiction of the Sharīʿa courts did not extend into the rural areas, where customary law (*ʿurf*) remained in effect. Women in rural areas therefore rarely had access to the formal legal system and to whatever protection this system could provide. Class also played a role. Poor urban women, like their rural counterparts, did not usually have the opportunity or the means to seek protection from the courts. Most of the women who used the courts were women of the propertied classes, women of the social and political elites, though the records do include women of modest means. Women primarily used the courts to protect property rights. The registration of a property sale, a loan, or the establishment of a *waqf* provided a written record if challenged. When women were involved in litigation, it usually was a lawsuit over the denial of property rights. Finally, for all women the difficulties of going to court to protect their rights in the face of family opposition would have been daunting. Only women who had strong personalities or support networks would have been able to do so.

Urban middle- and upper-class women had access to the Ottoman legal system, and the legal system usually upheld the rights granted to women in the Sharīʿa. At the same time many women faced obstacles in using this system. Ultimately, the system upheld basic patriarchal structures of society.

BIBLIOGRAPHY

H. Gerber, *State, society, and law in Islam. Ottoman law in comparative perspective*, Syracuse, N.Y. 1995.

F. M. Göçek and M. D. Baer, Women's experience in Ottoman society through the eighteenth-century Galata Court records, in M. C. Zilfi (ed.), *Women in the Ottoman Empire. Middle Eastern women in the early modern era*, Leiden 1997, 48–65.

N. Hanna, *Making big money in 1600. The life and times of Isma'il Abu Taqiyya, Egyptian merchant*, Syracuse, N.Y. 1998.

R. Jennings, Women in early seventeenth-century Ottoman judicial records. The sharia court of Anatolian Kayseri, in *Journal of the Economic and Social History of the Orient* 18 (1975), 53–114.

L. Peirce, She is trouble, and I will divorce her, in G. R. G. Hambly (ed.), *Women in the medieval Islamic world. Power, patronage, and piety*, New York 1998, 267–300.

Y. J. Seng, Invisible women. Residents of early sixteenth-century Istanbul, in G. R.G. Hambly (ed.), *Women in the medieval Islamic world. Power, patronage, and piety*, New York 1998, 241–68.

A. E. Sonbol (ed.), *Women, the family, and divorce laws in Islamic history*, Syracuse, N.Y. 1996.

F. Zarinebaf-Shahr, Ottoman women and the tradition of seeking justice in the eighteenth century, in M. C. Zilfi (ed.), *Women in the Ottoman Empire. Middle Eastern women in the early modern era*, Leiden 1997, 253–63.

——, Women and the public eye in eighteenth-century Istanbul, in G. R.G. Hambly (ed.), *Women in the medieval Islamic world. Power, patronage, and piety*, New York 1998, 301–24.

MARGARET L. MERIWETHER

South Asia

South Asia's relatively well-established legal system allows Muslim women to exercise their rights in marriage, divorce, maintenance, custody, and inheritance under Sharīʿa and secular laws. Their ability to do so depends on their level of education, and their economic, political, and sociocultural situation. The continuation of feudal patriarchal social structures, poverty, widespread illiteracy, and cumbersome court procedures tend to work against women. The struggles over legislative changes in India and Pakistan demonstrate the difficulties faced by women in realizing their rights. Despite the ostensible success of the Indian women's movement in India (which before 1947 included Pakistan and Bangladesh), every legislative initiative that improved women's rights relating to inheritance, divorce, and polygamy was strongly resisted by conservatives of both Muslim and Hindu communities. Following partition, despite constitutional and legislated rights, the same forces actively oppose the realization of rights, often citing the same political and social reasons that devolve around family and community loyalty, adversely affecting poor, rural, and semi-literate women.

After 1947, with the creation of Pakistan and later of Bangladesh, the safeguards under Sharīʿa laws, such as a waiting and arbitration period after declaration of divorce, were legislatively and administratively tightened, as were laws on polygamy and inheritance. Indian Muslim law remained without such safeguards, but Sharīʿa laws interpreted by secular civil courts have benefited women.

INDIA

In India a number of cases have highlighted the inadequacies of the Dissolution of Muslim Marriages Act (DMMA) in the absence of safeguards particularly with regard to maintenance, divorce, and polygamy. The Indian courts had used the *mahr* or bridal gift as the compensation due to women at divorce in place of maintenance. In the Bai Tahira case the court, citing section 125 of the Criminal Procedure Code 1973, ruled that it was the obligation of a divorced husband to provide maintenance if the wife were indigent. This set a precedent for other maintenance cases, in particular Muhammad Ahmed v. Shah Bano Begum, which created a political furor and led to the passage of the Muslim Women (Protection of Rights on Divorce) Act 1986. This act provides some latitude to courts in Section 2, stating that a Muslim husband's obligation extends to reasonable and fair provision as well as the amount of *mahr* due or other properties promised at the time of marriage. This was demonstrated by Ali v. Sufaira in 1988 when it was noted "that the unmistakable intent of the 1986 Act was to protect the interests of divorced Muslim women" (Pearl and W. Menski 1998, 216–17). Indian Muslim law has effectively established the Qurʾānic basis for the husband's responsibility on divorce and the 1986 act has through its distinction between *mahr*, maintenance, and fair provision supported that (Pearl and W. Menski 1998, 222).

PAKISTAN

Pakistan enacted the Muslim Family Law Ordinance (MFLO) in 1961, which established codes for marriage, divorce, and inheritance. Arbitration councils and *nikāḥ* registrars would regulate unilateral divorce and polygamy by enforcing the waiting and arbitration period and the terms of the marriage contract. The Pakistan Women Lawyers Association has tried to compensate for the poverty and illiteracy of women by working to represent women and to advocate simplification of judicial procedures. Some changes are apparent. In 1952 the Supreme Court ruled in Syeeda Khanum v. Muhammad Sami that "if the wives were allowed to dissolve their marriage without consent of their husbands by merely giving up their dowers, paid or promised to be paid, the institution of marriage would be meaningless as there would be no stability attached to it." In 1959 the Lahore High Court ruled in Balquis Fatima v. Najm-ul-Ikram Qureshi that the court could grant the wife a divorce if the couple were incompatible, departing from accepted Ḥanafī law by quoting a Qur'ānic verse: "Unless they both fear they cannot comply with God's bounds . . . Then it is no offence if the woman ransoms herself" (2:28). This in effect utilized Mālikī law, which recognized marital discord as grounds for divorce. In rendering judgment the court referred directly to the Qur'ān's support of women (Esposito and DeLong 2001, 79–80). Pakistani women's groups have been extremely critical of the Hudood Ordinances passed in 1988, and of the Enforcement of Shariah Ordinance (which declared the Sharīʿa as the main source of law in Pakistan) as it failed to distinguish between rape and adultery and endorsed the unequal weight of testimony under the law of evidence, which favored men.

BANGLADESH

In Bangladesh the Shariat Act, the DMMA, and the MFLO laws were included in the legal system. In addition to the arbitration council, rural courts called *salish* were sought to be regulated by the Village Courts Ordinance 1976 and the Council of Dispute (Municipal Areas) 1979 (Hashmi 2000, 103–4). Village courts rulings, a mixture of rural tradition and conservatism, work against women. Non-governmental organizations that work on women's issues have been subjected to fatwas that denounce their activities (Hashmi 2000, 103–13). Federal courts have referred directly to the Qur'ān to support women's right to maintenance as in the case of Md. Hefzur Rahman v. Shamsun Nahar Begum in 1995 (Pearl and Menski 1998, 205) and that of Jesmin Sultana v. Mohammad Elias in 1977, upholding the right to *mahr* and maintenance unless the wife remits the *mahr* amount voluntarily (Pearl and Menski 1998, 374).

SRI LANKA

In Sri Lanka Shāfiʿī law is followed in the Sharīʿa courts, and under pressure from conservatives, women judges cannot be appointed despite the fact that in secular courts Muslim women were both lawyers and judges.

BIBLIOGRAPHY

J. L. Esposito and N. J. DeLong, *Women in Muslim family law*, New York 2001.

T. I. Hashmi, *Women and Islam in Bangladesh*, London 2000.

M. A. Nuhuman, Religious identity, religious fundamentalism and Muslim women in Sri Lanka, in Women Living under Muslim Laws, Dossier 21 (September 1998), 89–111.

D. Pearl and W. Menski, *Muslim family law*, London 1998.

SHAHIDA LATEEF

Southeast Asia

This entry describes and evaluates issues within the legal systems of the Southeast Asian nations (mainly Malaysia, Singapore, Indonesia, Brunei, the Philippines, and Thailand) and how they affect Muslim women's access to justice.

OVERVIEW OF THE LEGAL SYSTEMS IN SOUTHEAST ASIA

The legal systems of the Southeast Asian nations are typically characterized by pluralism. In a particular country there will be a generally applicable system of law enforced for matters common to the general population. This generally applicable law regulates the lives of citizens with regard to crime, commerce, and a broad spectrum of civil matters covering tort, contract, trust, and modern business and social transactions. In many of the countries, the commonly prescribed system of law is based on the legal system of a country's pre-independent colonial power. The prevailing legal systems of Malaysia, Singapore, and Brunei, for example, are broadly based on the common law originating in England. The Philippine system of law reflects Spanish and American influences. Colonial Dutch law, on the other hand, heavily influences Indonesia's legal system.

In the majority of the countries, however, matters pertaining to the major faiths and cultures of citizens are formally regulated by separate, co-existing systems of personal laws. These matters mainly consist of the observation of religious rituals and adherence to religious precepts. Most importantly they include rules on marriage and divorce and matters ancillary to these issues, such as maintenance, inheritance, guardianship of children, adoption, and the constitution and administration of personal court systems.

Muslims form significant percentages of the population in many of the Southeast Asian countries. Muslims constitute the majority population in Malaysia, Indonesia, and Brunei. In countries where Muslims are minorities, they have long histories of practicing Islamic law and way of life. Historically, governments of the day in these countries have allowed Muslims to continue applying Islamic rules and principles in many aspects of their private transactions. Thus, Islamic law develops into an important personal legal structure within many of the Southeast Asian legal systems featuring it as a distinct subset of legal pluralism in these countries.

In Malaysia, the mandatory prescription of Islamic law to Muslims for specific personal and family matters is constitutionally provided. The provision delineates the specific powers and jurisdictions of institutions to be charged with the legislation and administration of Islamic law. It includes a prohibition from interference by the ordinary courts and the federal legislature. In Indonesia, the Marriage Act (No. 1/1974) stipulates that a marriage is legitimate when it is conducted within the law of each of the parties' religion and belief. For a Muslim, the Compilation of Islamic Law provides that such a marriage must be conducted in accordance with Islamic law. Malaysia, Singapore, Brunei, and the Philippines have formal Sharīʿa court structures with jurisdictions and administrations separate from the ordinary courts. In Thailand, the enforceability of Islamic law is less clear. However, historical evidence shows that past governments have positively included Islamic law as a legitimate source of personal law for Muslims in the southern areas of the country where Muslims form the majority. The substance and structure of Islamic law as historically developed in these areas continue to prevail.

In many of the Southeast Asian countries, Islamic law is interpreted to suit local situations. It is enacted and codified through formal and contemporary processes of legislation. In Malaysia, each of the 13 states and federal territories has its own body of Islamic legislation that includes the Islamic Family Law Enactment and the Syariah Criminal Code. In Singapore personal law matters for Muslims are codified in the Administration of Muslim Law Act 1966, while in Brunei they are included in the Islamic Council and Kadi's Court Act (Term 77). Indonesia collates Islamic rules and principles to be applied to Muslims in its Compilation of Islamic Law. Muslim-governed provinces in Mindanao, in the Philippines, enforce the Muslim Code on Personal Law. Thailand regulates the prescription of Islamic law in a Royal Decree of 1945, which gives discretion to the Ministry of Internal Affairs to establish Islamic Committees, now known as the Islamic Councils, in provinces with significant percentages of Muslims. These councils advise the provinces' Administrative Committees on matters pertaining to Muslims.

Muslim women and Islamic law

Muslim women within these regions are significantly affected by the legal systems through their encounters with the substantive and procedural aspects of Islamic law as administered in the various countries. Since the use of Islamic law is prescribed mostly for matrimonial issues, women, disproportionately, become plaintiffs in cases involving divorce, maintenance, and guardianship of children.

Within this region, it is accepted that Islamic matrimonial law gives a husband a unilateral right to pronounce a divorce. Such a pronouncement, in effect, may be made at the husband's behest. Although a modern interpretation of Islamic law enables the legislature to deem a pronouncement outside of the Sharīʿa court a matrimonial offence, such a pronouncement is rarely considered to invalidate the divorce. A woman, in contrast, is not given similar freedom to dissolve her marriage. This means that a woman who intends to separate from her husband without his consent has to use the court to apply for an order of a dissolution of marriage. Similarly, if she disagrees with her husband's pronouncement of divorce, she must take steps to contest it in court.

A husband is also the person vested with the paramount responsibility for providing for the financial and material maintenance of his wife and children. When he fails to do this, and the wife has no other means of support, it often falls on her to seek redress in the court for herself and her children. Women also, more often than men, have to instigate court proceedings to settle issues relating to the custody of their children in cases of separation and divorce. Since Islamic law in many of the Southeast Asian countries stipulates that a father shall have the legal guardianship of his children, even when their physical custody is vested in someone else, a mother who has custody may find it difficult to deal with issues that require the consent of a legal guardian. Consequently, she has to go to court to seek redress. In these ways, women become primary plaintiffs in Islamic matrimonial proceedings and face many issues with regard to the substance and procedure of the law.

Substance and structure of Islamic legal systems affecting women's access to justice

Substantial aspects of Islamic law refer to the body of legal principles to be applied in resolving disputes. With respect to the Southeast Asian region, the substantial part of the law is legislated based on a particular community's interpretation of the Sharīʿa's primary sources, namely the Qurʾān and *ḥadīth*, or Prophetic traditions. Furthermore, a community's adherence to particular Islamic schools of thought (*madhāhib*) is also influential in determining the kind of legal principles developed. The resulting effect of such practice is that while Qurʾānic principles and provisions of the *ḥadīth* that are clearly stated are commonly accepted, those with more general statements are interpreted in varied ways within the region. The basic concept of a man's right to unilateral divorce, for example, is commonly adopted, but the ways in which a woman may seek a dissolution of marriage by an order of court differs quite significantly among the countries. In Malaysia and Singapore, the laws allow for three methods in which women may apply for such orders. These are the divorce for breach of a marriage stipulation (*taʿlīq*), divorce by way of *khulʿ* (returning of the *mahr*), and *faskh* (dissolution on specified grounds). Detailed provisions of these methods, however, vary substantially between the two countries. The Philippines regulates *khulʿ* and *faskh* divorces but not *taʿlīq*. In addition, it allows for divorce by *ṭafwīd* (delegation). In Brunei, a Muslim woman may seek a dissolution of marriage by way of *faskh* on a very general ground of "accordance with *hukum syarak* [principles of Islamic law]." A Muslim woman in Indonesia may bring a divorce suit in court on the grounds that include adultery, desertion, violence, physical incapacity, violation of *taʿlīq*, and apostasy.

Muslim women in the region are further affected by the procedural aspects of Islamic law. These refer to the rules governing access to courts and proceedings in them. The problem of the Islamic law structure in the Southeast Asian region emanates from its distinct position as a sub-system within the general legal framework. Since it constitutes a separate system, it operates with different modes of access and processes from the general court system. This can prove to be problematic to many Muslim women in the region. In Malaysia where each of the 13 states and federal territories have separate and independent legislative and judicial jurisdictions over Islamic law, a woman faces difficulties in proving she falls under a particular court's jurisdiction for a divorce case where her marriage has been contracted within a different boundary. Even where a court accepts jurisdiction, the enforcement of its judgment against the defendant husband may be problematic if he relocates to another jurisdiction.

Effective procedures are lacking in many of the countries with regard to controlling a husband's arbitrary pronouncement of divorce. Even where rules exist that render pronouncement outside of the court a matrimonial offence, such as in Malaysia and Singapore, the limited sentencing jurisdictions of the Sharīʿa courts means that they are unable to mete out effective sanctions against the action. In Malaysia, husbands willingly pay fines for making such pronouncements without their wives' knowledge. Upon payment, the courts declare the pronouncements valid.

Procedural issues in the region also occur where one party to a marriage converts or denounces Islam. They include questions such as whether the Muslim courts have jurisdiction to declare that a marriage subsists or is dissolved after a conversion or denouncement and whether the courts can make matrimonial orders against the non-Muslim spouses. Since Islamic law has limited jurisdiction over the population, when a woman converts to Islam, she may not be able to apply for a divorce in the ordinary courts if, as the case for Malaysia, the legal system specifies that Muslim marriages may only be ruled by Islamic law. On the other hand, she may not use the Sharīʿa court since the court will not have jurisdiction over her non-converting spouse.

A fundamental factor within the Sharīʿa legal sub-systems in the Southeast Asian nations that may affect Muslim women's access to justice is the elements of patriarchy that persist in the administration of Islamic justice. Judges of Muslim courts are mainly men and consequently decisions made are gendered, especially in issues such as domestic violence and guardianship of children. In many of the countries, women who flee their homes to seek shelter from wife abuse face problems when claiming maintenance in court in divorce cases. They are often considered *nusyuz* (disobedient) for leaving the matrimonial homes without their husbands' permission and are thus not entitled to maintenance. Many judges do not think domestic violence a legitimate ground to abrogate from the rules on *nusyuz* behavior.

In the case of guardianship of children, decision-making about the person and the property of minors are consistently deemed to be vested in the father or, in his absence, his relatives. Physical care, on the other hand, is usually considered the primary responsibility of the mother. In cases of divorce, women find this problematic since while caring for their children they are not able to decide on issues such as their children's birth registration and schooling.

Efforts to eradicate problems Muslim women face in obtaining access to the legal systems in the Southeast Asian region are substantially pervasive. They are carried out at local levels and regionally. In general, female advocacy activities are not instigated by religious-based but by cross-cultural organizations. However, where the Muslim population is the majority, programs that focus on the well-being of Muslim women often feature as major undertakings. Legal reform of the Islamic law structure is central to these pursuits.

BIBLIOGRAPHY

A. A. An-Na'im (ed.), *Islamic family law in a changing world. A global resource book*, London 2002.

A. H. Buang (ed.), *Islamic law in Syariah courts in Malaysia* [in Malay], Kuala Lumpur 1998.

Z. Kamaruddin (ed.), *Islamic family law issues 2000*, Kuala Lumpur 2001.

Sisters in Islam Regional Workshop, Islamic family law and justice for Muslim women. Divorce. Singapore, Indonesia, Philippines, Malaysia, unpublished, Kuala Lumpur 2001.

——, Islamic family law and justice for Muslim women. Financial provisions. Singapore, Indonesia, Philippines, Malaysia, unpublished, Kuala Lumpur 2001.

A. M. Yaacob (ed.), *Islamic family law and women in ASEAN countries* [in Malay], Kuala Lumpur 1999.

NORAIDA ENDUT

Sub-Saharan Africa

INTRODUCTION

The access of women to legal systems is integral to the consolidation of democracy and pursuit of good governance through the rule of law. The rule of law presupposes parity of rights, privileges, and opportunities for women to participate in and affect public deliberations, and gain greater control over their lives. Consistent with evolving international objectives, most national constitutions espouse anti-discrimination principles. However, the significance of inclusive paradigms and guarantees is circumscribed by gender stratification and asymmetry. The issues and challenges of women's access to the legal system in Sub-Saharan Africa are not peculiar. They share striking parallels with similar concerns in other parts of the world. In the African context, the concerns are exacerbated by cutbacks in social spending and the exigencies of oppositional movements fueled by legitimacy crises concerning the inherent inequities of the global political economy.

Legal pluralism characterizes many Sub-Saharan African states where contemporary legal institutions hammered out during the early post-independence years show various degrees of accommodation to customary, Islamic, and European-derived systems of law. There is considerable variation throughout the region regarding how central a role Sharīʿa (Islamic religious law) is accorded, from limited, mixed jurisdiction in minority Muslim states such as Ghana, Kenya, and Tanzania, to the regional authority of northern Nigeria, to the use of Sharīʿa as civil code in Sudan. However, there are some underlying similarities and these have resonance for women's experiences of the law. The Sharīʿa has long derived power in African societies because it is written law, unlike the oral-memory nature of customary law and in counterpoint to the written law of Europeans. It guarantees women basic rights in marriage, divorce, adoption, inheritance, and property. Most Sub-Saharan countries have a national Sharīʿa court of appeals to adjudicate disputes pertaining to family matters even where other kinds of law, such as criminal or commercial, have superseded Islamic law. Sharīʿa can therefore be applied to various aspects of life, varying by country in Muslim Africa, but it will always include the domestic concerns of women. For many, Islamic law is embodied in the person of the local *qāḍī* (Muslim scholar/judge) who hears disputes. The *qāḍī*s have knowledge of the extensive written commentary on the Sharīʿa and grasp the processes of selectivity, procedural precedent, and reinterpretation that can allow for a flexible and vital system. In recent decades, thinly-veiled protests against eroding material bases of patriarchal privileges and shifting thresholds of traditional authority are increasingly proffered to justify the systematic imposition of the Sharīʿa to govern gender relations, as in the high-profile case of the twelve northernmost Nigerian states. Religious injunctions and prohibitions are not the only determinants of women's access; nor are they invariably adverse. In interrogating and contemplating strategies to enhance the access of women to the legal system, the premium placed on resource distribution under the Sharīʿa is noteworthy. In fact, there are grounds to assert socioeconomic justice as a reciprocal and valid prerequisite for the enactment of the Sharīʿa penal and justice system in those areas that have adopted its criminal code, such as northern Nigeria. In some respects, the upsurge in the adoption of the Sharīʿa advanced the goals of decentralization and fostered the accessibility of grassroots communities to the legal system. Nevertheless, this dividend is offset by the gender backlash reinforced by the trend. Similarly, the value of expediting and settling disputes without strict adherence to written rules of procedure in Sharīʿa courts is discounted by disparate rules for testimonial competence that spell civil death for women and impinge on due process norms. The extent to which patriarchal prejudice informs the realities and options of women varies. Women are not a monolithic category; they are differentiated by socioeconomic status, ethnicity, and other variables that mediate their individual experiences. Furthermore, women are not passive objects of patriarchal institutions and discourses, but autonomous agents who actively negotiate their subjectivities. For example, Hirsch (1998), dealing with Swahili marital disputes, shows how Muslim women successfully navigate and at times manipulate the *qāḍī* court system in Kenya.

Impediments and remedies

Gender disparities characterize the access of women to the legal system. This phenomenon is attributable to a confluence of factors that are compounded by women's poverty and illiteracy. The burden that women bear magnifies the geographic distance of legal forums and ordinary challenges of the legal sector such as prohibitive costs, cumbersome procedures and technicalities, protracted proceedings, and language difficulties. The handicap posed by inadequate services and outreaches, the shortage of skilled or competent personnel, and the non-implementation of judgments and policy or legislative decisions, among other factors, attains harsher proportions in the face of persistent inconsistencies and conflicts of laws, lack of knowledge and understanding, social reprobation, and fear of reprisals. These constraints are further complicated in settings characterized by civil war and conflict.

Strategies to improve the access of African women to the legal system address considerations of demand, supply, and context to promote just outcomes, fair and equitable treatment, responsive and affordable procedures, comprehensibility, and predictability. Frameworks articulated to enhance the effectiveness, efficiency, credibility, and accessibility of the legal system often outline an inventory of interventions to inspire confidence and build capacity, stimulate enabling environment, and redress systematic gender bias in the content of law, the nature of legal processes, and the delivery of legal services. Some interventions give centrality to progressive reinterpretations of Sharīʿa, cultivating dynamic civil society, nurturing transparency and accountability, influencing favorable policy levers and legislative instruments, supporting participation and training of stakeholder and auxiliaries, and promoting gender-friendly legal education.

Other remedial measures give differing degrees of emphasis to contesting gender-specific derivative rights, regularizing rules of evidence and proof, streamlining exacting procedures, rethinking concessions to legal pluralism, dispelling fears and countering disincentives to access, establishing specialized tribunals and summary proceedings for gender-sensitive matters, instituting mobile clinics and courts, and safeguarding due process.

Conclusion

Effective access denotes the recognition of rights and entitlements, capabilities to assert rights and seek protection, and infrastructure to enforce remedies and catalyze autonomous agency. As antidiscrimination norms travel across radically different histories, cultures, and structures, substantive access to the legal system is fundamental to vindicate Muslim women's needs, constraints, and vulnerabilities. Gender-responsive legal reform initiatives typically privilege advocacy, policy dialogue or negotiation, and legislative review or reform. Once enacted, laws do not grow limbs with which to run after and apprehend transgressors. It takes the initiative of relevant beneficiaries to harness the transformative potentials of law.

Bibliography

M. Afkhami (ed.), *Faith and freedom*, Syracuse N.Y. 1995.

J. N. D. Anderson, *Islamic law in Africa*, London 1954.

A. Christelow, Islamic law in Africa, in N. Levtzion and R. L. Pouwels, *The history of Islam in Africa*, Athens, Ohio 2000, 373–96.

J. Ezeilo, L. M. Tawfiq, and A. Afolabi-Akiyode (eds.), *Sharia implementation in Nigeria. Issues and challenges on women's rights and access to justice*, Enugu, Nigeria 2003.

S. Golub, Beyond the rule of law orthodoxy. The legal empowerment alternative, in Carnegie Endowment for International Peace, Working Papers, Rule of Law Series, Democracy and Rule of Law Project 41 (October 2003), Washington, D.C., <http://www.ceip.org/files/Publications/wp41.asp?p=1&from=pubauthor.>

M. Greico, Women, legal reform and development in Sub-Saharan Africa, in World Bank, Findings, Africa Region 20 (1994), Washington, D.C., <http://www.worldbank.org/ afr/findings/english/find20.htm.>

S. F. Hirsch, *Pronouncing and preserving. Gender and discourses in an African Islamic court*, Chicago 1998.
M. H. Kamali, Appellate review and judicial independence in Islamic law, in C. Mallat (ed.), *Islam and public law*, London 1993, 49–83.
D. Manning, The role of legal services organizations in attacking poverty, 2001, <http://www.worldbank.org/legal/ljr_01/doc/Manning.pdf>, 24–6.
L. A. Obiora, Supri, supri, supri, Oyibo? An interrogation of gender mainstreaming deficits, in *Signs. Journal of Women in Culture and Society* 29:2 (2004), <www.journals.uchicago.edu/Signs/journal/issues/v29n2/290224/290224.html>.
L. Welchman (ed.), *Women's rights and Islamic family law. Perspectives on reform*, London 2004.
Women in Law and Development (WiLDAF), Access of women to legal and judicial services in Sub-Saharan Africa, Ghana 2000. See also Asian Development Bank, Legal empowerment. Advancing good governance and poverty reduction, in Law and Policy Reform Series, 2001, <http://www.adb.org/Documents/Others/Law>.

LESLYE AMEDE OBIORA

Turkey

The founding of the Turkish Republic in 1923 brought an end to the Ottoman Empire's system of parallel laws, which were applied depending on a citizen's religion, gender, community, and occupational status or sect, and established a single, secular, and standardized judicial system based the European system of law. The Turkish Civil Code of 1926, adapted from the Swiss Civil Code, abolished polygyny and granted women equal rights in matters of divorce, child custody, and inheritance. The Turkish Penal Code, also adopted in 1926, is based on the Italian Criminal Code.

An extensive reform of the Turkish Civil Code was accomplished in November 2001. The new Civil Code, which came into effect on 1 January 2002, abolished the supremacy of men in marriage and thus established the full equality of men and women in the family. It also set the equal division of property acquired during marriage as the default property regime, raised the legal minimum age of marriage to 18 for both men and women (previously 17 for men and 15 for women), gave children born out of wedlock the same inheritance rights as those born inside a marriage, and allowed single parents to adopt children. Another recent (October 2001) step toward gender equality in the Turkish legal system is the amendment of Article 41 of the constitution, redefining the family as an entity "based on equality between spouses" (WWHR – New Ways 2002).

However, it is evident that legal reforms alone are not sufficient to prevent gender discrimination and women's rights violations. The majority of women in Turkey are unaware of their legal rights and have very little access to pertinent information. Many women have little or no income and, until very recently, free or inexpensive legal counseling services for women were non-existent in Turkey. In the last decade, women lawyers have established some legal counseling services under the auspices of bar associations in the larger cities, but their number and capacity are very limited. A human rights education program, implemented by Women for Women's Human Rights (WWHR) – New Ways since 1998 in 30 community centers throughout the country in cooperation with the directorate for social services, aims to provide ongoing training sessions where women not only learn what their rights are, but are also given the skills and support that allow them to actively achieve those rights. An evaluation of the program shows that only 11 percent of those who participated had some knowledge of their legal rights prior to the training. The majority indicated that the knowledge and competencies acquired through the training have helped them achieve greater gender equality in both the home and the community (Kardam 2003).

In addition to lack of knowledge, education, economic means, and state resources for legal counseling, other factors limiting women's access to the legal system include the prevalence of customary and religious practices, language barriers for women belonging to non-Turkish ethnic groups living in Turkey, and oppression within the family preventing women from seeking their legal rights.

The lives of the majority of women living in Turkey continue to be shaped by a multiplicity of traditional practices that violate existing laws, including early and forced marriage, polygamous marriage, "honor" crimes, virginity testing, and restrictions on women's mobility. Research conducted with 599 women living in the eastern and southeastern regions of Turkey shows that 16.3 percent of women in the region were married earlier than the minimum legal age of 15 (raised to 18 in 2002). More than half of the women (51 percent) were married without their consent although consent of both parties is a precondition for marriage under Turkish law. One in ten women live in polygynous marriages, although polygamy was banned under the Civil Code in 1926 (Ilkkaracan and WWHR 1998).

Research findings also show that it is not uncommon for uncodified customary or religious laws to be applied in matters related to marriage, despite their lack of validity under the Turkish legal system. For example, only 54 percent of women in civil marriages indicated that, in the event of divorce, the Civil Code would dictate the terms; 23 percent said customary laws would govern divorce and 14 percent said religious laws would prevail (Ilkkaracan 1998).

Women who were married in a religious ceremony but who had no civil marriage constitute a distinct group without access to the legal system. According to the Turkish constitution and the Civil Code, only a civil marriage enacted by legally authorized officials is considered a valid marriage before the law. Religious marriage alone confers no legally binding rights. In fact, according to law, couples must have an officially documented civil marriage before a religious marriage ceremony can take place. Violation of this is a crime under Article 237 of the Penal Code, both for the person who conducts the religious ceremony as well as for the couple (WWHR – New Ways 2002). Despite these legal provisions, 8.3 percent of married women living in Turkey have only a religious marriage, and thus have no recourse to the legal system on matters relating to their marriage (SIS 1994).

Many women belonging to non-Turkish ethnic groups, including Kurds, Zaza, and Arabs, have little or no command of the Turkish language. They are thus severely disadvantaged in terms of accessing the legal system, as the official language of all governmental institutions, including judicial ones, is Turkish.

While the reform of the Turkish Civil Code constitutes a major step toward establishing gender equality in Turkey, lack of substantive reforms in legal, social, and political domains – such as a variety of coordinated state programs and services for women, including legal counseling services, and state programs to eradicate violence against women, prevent gender discrimination in the educational and economic spheres, and increase women's participation in political life – makes its real effect in eradication of gender discrimination less of a success story.

Bibliography

P. Ilkkaracan and WWHR (Women for Women's Human Rights), Exploring the context of sexuality in eastern Turkey, in *Reproductive Health Matters*, 6 (1998), 66–75, < http:// www.wwhr.org/?id=743>.

P. Ilkkaracan, Doğu Anadolu'da kadın ve aile, in A. B. Hacimirzaoğlu (ed.), *75 yılda kadınlar ve erkekler*, Istanbul 1998, 173–92.

N. Kardam, *WWHR – New Ways women's human rights training program (1995–2003). Evaluation report*, Istanbul 2003.

SIS (State Institute of Statistics), *Main indicators. Women in Turkey, 1978–1993*, Ankara 1994.

WWHR (Women for Women's Human Rights) – New Ways, *The new legal status of women in Turkey*, Istanbul 2002.

Pinar Ilkkaracan

Western Europe

The fifteen million-strong Muslim population of Europe is now a well established part of the Muslim diaspora, giving rise to a new form of "European Islam." The willingness and capacity of European societies to accommodate the presence of Muslims on the basis of religious difference has become a particularly challenging political issue in many states. The primary mechanism by which states have accommodated Islamic difference is through the establishment of particular legal provisions addressing specific needs. Such accommodation is problematic, however, as most European legal systems are avowedly secular in nature and aim to maintain a centralist and uniform legal system within national boundaries. The philosophy of secular liberalism that underpins most European conceptions of law has prevented such states from taking the more radical step of officially recognizing Sharīʿa as a legitimate counterpart to official state law. Thus, although there are fundamental differences of approach between European states in the extent to which official laws have recognized Muslim practices, states are united in their rejection of formal recognition of Islamic law having status and application equal to official laws. Consequently, the question of official recognition of Sharīʿa is one that affects Muslim men and women equally. Crucial differences arise, however, in the way legal rights are gendered to the detriment of women in Sharīʿa, and the extent to which these are sanctioned by European states.

Some of the main legal issues pertinent to Muslim women are marriage, divorce, rights of inheritance, child custody, the laws of evidence, and the wearing of the *ḥijāb* in public spaces such as the workplace and schools. The relationship between European laws and Sharīʿa can be categorized in terms of three models, all of which can be located on a spectrum which posits assimilation/absorption at one end and pluralism/multi-culturalism at the other. The first model consists of cases where the accommodation of Muslim difference is incorporated into the fabric of official law. For example, it is acknowledged that a woman must be afforded legal protection against possible discrimination in the workplace on the basis of wearing the *ḥijāb*. Individual states have been forced to comply with recent developments in European law such as the Equal Treatment at Work Directive (2000/78/EC), itself promulgated under Article 13 of the European Community Treaty, which outlaws discrimination in the workplace on a number of grounds, including religion. Muslim women who wear *ḥijāb* are among the main beneficiaries of state implementations of this significant directive.

The second approach is one whereby Muslims have developed means by which official laws can be legitimately avoided. Muslims are following those aspects of state law they consider appropriate or not in direct conflict with Islamic precepts. Bracketing together Islamic obligations with provisions in state law, a synthesized form of Sharīʿa is developed that avoids breaching official law. This hybrid form of law remains unrecognized by official law but is a potent and dominant force for many Muslim communities in European states. The area of marriage laws may be seen as an example of this approach whereby the *nikāḥ* ceremony, although not formally recognized by state law, functions as an integral part of the marriage ceremony and is incorporated within civil procedures. This has elements of both the pluralist and assimilationist models. There is no official recognition of Muslim difference and so assimilation takes place in the need to comply with the civil marriage procedure. However, the *nikāḥ* is tolerated at the margins of state law, giving rise to a nebulous form of legal pluralism.

The third model is found in the conflict between state laws and Sharīʿa injunctions. Here, liberal secular ideals come into play. There is a clear rejection of Muslim religious difference by the state on the basis that Muslim demands do not comply with so-called secular ideals such as gender equality. The assimilationist rationale underpins state rejections of such Muslim claims as men's unilateral right to divorce and polygyny, mothers' lesser rights of child custody, women's reduced rights of inheritance, the diminished weight accorded a woman's evidence against a man and, most recently, state restrictions on the wearing of the *ḥijāb*. It is important to note here the burgeoning feminist literature exploring women's legal rights in Islam and the new exegetical work on scripture that is challenging the restricted notion of such gendered rights. Muslims concerned with state rejection of Islamic family and personal laws also have the choice of bringing legal claims outside the official legal system and in Muslim organizations that apply Islamic law. The European-wide Fatwa Council and the British Shariah Council are examples of community institutions that will adjudicate and mediate within an Islamic legal framework.

Both the second and third models are leading to the development of legal measures for Muslim women that are less discriminatory than conservative interpretations of such rights under Sharīʿa. To take the model of hybridity, the fact that Muslim men have to comply with state procedures to register a marriage has resulted in the granting of important rights to Muslim wives and the prohibition of unfair practices, under the aegis of secular state laws. Thus women do not have to challenge their husbands' "right" to take on additional wives – it is simply banned by state law. Because the state registers marriages, women have greater custody rights of children upon divorce. The model of assimilation has also provided for greater rights for women in areas of inheritance, the rules of evidence, men's unilateral right to divorce and, of course, polygyny. The European picture is not one of homogeneity, however. Individual state systems vary in their approach, as do Islamic schools of jurisprudence and Islamic interpretations of women's rights in such discourses.

Legal protection of the right to wear the *ḥijāb* is a particularly pertinent issue in the light of European law. The wearing of the *ḥijāb* in schools is a good example of the inconsistency of rights in European states. The stances taken by Britain (tolerance) and France (proscription) illustrate the diversity of state laws in this area. The issue is further complicated by the fact that the European Convention on Human Rights 1950 gives European citizens the right to practice their religion (Article 9) and also the right not to be discriminated against on the ground, *inter alia*, of religion (Article 14). Thus, French Muslim women may challenge the ban as a human rights legal issue as they are being forced to choose between religiously mandated attire and access to public education. Additionally, a claim could be made under the French constitutional right to freedom of conscience, education, and expressions of religious belief. This example illustrates the situation in other European states where laws may be contradictory and inconsistent.

Powerful cultural norms and the stigma attached to such issues as divorce have resulted in women failing to access their legal rights – either in state or community courts. Many are unaware of their rights, under either Sharīʿa or state legal systems. State courts can also view Muslim women in a stereotypical manner, often as passive victims in cases such as forced marriage. State systems often require litigants to possess substantial financial and other resources, to which poorer Muslim women often do not have ready access. Migrant Muslim women may also encounter substantial language problems in instigating legal claims in state courts. The reliance on alternative dispute resolution in the form of local community courts may result in traditional interpretations of Sharīʿa and discriminate against women in the key areas outlined above. A continued problem is that many interpreters and enforcers of Sharīʿa are male community "experts" who interpret women's legal rights in a conservative manner, often reinforcing entrenched patriarchal interpretations of scripture. State legal systems also often rely on such "experts" to give definitive interpretations of Islamic law. Consequently, women's access to European state and community legal systems has been limited.

Bibiliography

M. D. Evans, *Religious liberty and international law in Europe*, Cambridge 1997.

S. Ferrari and A. Bradney (eds.), *Islam in European legal systems*, Aldershot, U.K. 2000.

S. Hunter (ed.), *Islam, Europe's second religion. The new social, cultural and political landscape*, Westport, Conn., 2002.

Q. Mirza, Islam, hybridity and the laws of marriage, in *Australian Feminist Law Journal* 14 (2000), 1–22.

J. Nielsen, *Muslims in Western Europe*, Edinburgh 1995.

——, *Towards a European Islam*, Basingstoke, Hampshire 1999.

D. Pearl and W. Menski, *Muslim family law*, London 1998.

S. Roald, *Women in Islam. The Western experience*, London 2001.

W. A. R. Shadid and P. S. Koningsveld, *Religious freedom and the position of Islam in Western Europe*, Kampen, The Netherlands 1995.

—— (eds.), *Political participation and identities of Muslims in non-Muslim states*, Kampen, The Netherlands 1996.

——, *Religious freedom and the neutrality of the state. The position of Islam in the European Union*, Leuven 2002.

S. Vertoc (ed.), *Islam in Europe. The politics of religion and community*, Houndmills, Basingstoke, Hampshire 1997.

Qudsia Mirza

Law: Articulation of Islamic and non-Islamic Systems

Arab States

Patricia Crone's *Roman, Provincial, and Islamic Law: The Origins of the Islamic Patronate* (1987) set the cue for focusing on the synthesizing nature of Islam and the syncretic pragmatic approach taken by Arab conquerors when confronted with ancient sophisticated societies in Persia and Egypt. The new conquerors built on the pre-existing bureaucratic and legal systems.

In regard to women, however, Islamic jurists presented Islam as a vast improvement over the pre-Islamic treatment of women. While Islam did indeed improve some practices detrimental to women, for example, the killing of girl babies, it restricted pre-Islamic rights of women in terms of their status as heads of households.

In the course of time the Qur'ān did not stand alone as the source of Islamic law. Much legal weight was given to the Prophetic tradition (*ḥadīth*, pl. *aḥādīth*) as a vital supplement to the Qur'ān. This process can be seen as an attempt by jurists to legitimate customs – Arab and non-Arab, Muslim and non-Muslim – as a valid source for developing Islamic law. The founder of the Mālikī school of law and author of one of the earliest Islamic legal books, the *Muwaṭṭa'*, a collection of *aḥādīth* rulings, stressed the use of local customs to formulate Islamic legal rules. Medinese rulings reflected consensus and custom in Medina. It was expected that Kufans and Basrans far away on the frontier would not imitate them but form whatever rules were needed for their situation. The rule of stoning adulterers, for example, exemplifies how local non-Arab and non-Qur'ānic customs influenced the development of Islamic penal law. The rule is based on a *ḥadīth* in which the Prophet applied the Mosaic law of stoning to a Jewish couple who came to him to settle a dispute. In inheritance law, the introduction of certain female heirs who are not mentioned in the Qur'ān reflects the influence of blood money customs. The *aḥādīth* uphold a grandmother's claim to inherit, but also convert female heirs into residuary heirs so as to reduce their Qur'ānic shares vis-à-vis male heirs and thus reconcile custom and revelation. Customs not so favorable to women were also incorporated into law as exemplified by the story of how 'Umar tried to convince the Prophet to adopt the Persian custom of veiling women.

Al-Ṭabarī's official history of Islam relates how the Arab Muslim leaders in the first century of conquest guaranteed in treaties with non-Arabs and non-Muslims the continuance of their local customs and faiths in exchange for their pledge not to ally with the military enemies of Arabs and Muslims. The Qur'ān acknowledges Christian and Jewish core beliefs (Mary's virginity, the law as the valid expression of faith, and so forth) and confers preferential status on monotheists. This legal autonomy coincided with the introduction of Arab Muslim women to military frontier posts, which constrained the right of Muslim Arab men to intermarry with local non-Muslim women. This evidences a restrictive interpretation of the Qur'ānic verse on intermarriage that was later expanded to allow only Muslim men to marry non-Muslim women.

As the Arab-Islamic empire grew in riches and the number of female slaves expanded, rules were devised to extend men's right to polygamy. The Qur'ān limited a man to four wives. The question arose as to whether the rule applied to sexual relations with enslaved women, be they non-Muslims or converts. This led to a debate not on whether polygamy should be restricted to marriage with widows with children, but on whether the Prophet, who left nine widows, intended that the Qur'ān be interpreted to allow nine wives for every man.

The differences between the Islamic schools of law over the right of an adult woman to marry with or without the consent of a guardian (*walī*), or the ease with which she could divorce her husband are probably due to different customs, although more research is needed on this point. The right of a husband to divorce (*ṭalāq*) without the consent of his wife and to condense the repudiation into one sitting, contrary to explicit Qur'ānic prescriptions of a process extending over three menstrual cycles, reflects the custom as revealed in the *ḥadīth* of men in pre-Islamic Arabia divorcing whenever and however they wished.

With the increased stability of the Islamic empire in its second century, the consensus was adopted that local custom was in principle a source of law. Muslims could decide whether they wanted to go to a judge who followed a particular *madhhab* (school of law) which honored certain rules and customs over others. A woman could choose the judge who gave her the most freedom. The present-day Tunisian Code of Personal Status, for example, explicitly allows courts to apply customary law in disputes over division of expensive gifts brought into the marriage by the wife and her family, such as shirts for the husband, household goods, and linens (Art. 28).

The guarantees in treaties initially concluded with the conquered non-Muslim populations were sustained throughout the centuries. Christians and Jews continued to choose to go to their own faith-based courts, including appealing to the Jewish high court in Jerusalem. This pattern prevails to this day in most Arab jurisdictions, for example, among the Copts in Egypt and the Orthodox Christians in Lebanon. The major change under Islamic imperial rule occurred in criminal matters. Islamic penal law became the law of the land, applicable to Muslims as well as non-Muslims, but with some modifications in terms of penalties. Market practices and professions also became subject to Islamic law. For example, midwives, whether Muslim or not, were under the control of the Islamic market administrator.

Contact during the Ottoman era with Europeans harboring imperial and colonial ambitions began to spur new approaches as to how Islamic law was going to synthesize the notion of a non-faith based legal concept, that is, a law applicable to all. The first step was to codify all the laws of the Ottoman Empire into one book known as the *Mecelle* or *Majalla*. This process raised issues about what options a Muslim ruler had: to codify the religious law of each and every community; to combine all non-Muslim laws with Islamic law into one code; or to formulate entirely new laws independent of faith. Before these questions could be resolved, the European conquest of the Arab regions of the Ottoman Empire was sealed. The Europeans found a collection of semi-autonomous faith based legal systems alongside overarching codes regulating criminal, commercial, and property matters, all the result of centuries of the Islamic process of synthesizing and syncretizing. The Europeans did not sweep the system away. They added a new dimension. The court system became divided along lines of discrimination. The European rulers, though Christians, did not go to the indigenous Christian courts created by their Muslim predecessors. They set up separate courts for themselves as Europeans, though not exclusively. The Mixed Court system of Egypt and the French courts in North Africa were established as "universal" courts, available to non-Muslims and Muslims alike. While Muslims were thus offered a choice, the local system was deprecated as beneath the dignity of a European, who was not given the choice of going to pre-European courts.

Colonial influence and rule resulted in the next 50 to 70 years in a more formalized and hierarchical syncretic court system which regulated the relation between Sharīʿa and other faith based courts and the new state courts. The European rulers continued codifying laws. The law of the land was, however, no longer Islamic, but rather state law which fused European and Islamic law. The law of procedure and evidence was codified along European lines. Islamic law was confined mainly to personal status. The nascent appellate system of the Ottomans evolved into a model based on the European notion of a strict hierarchy of courts.

Since the 1930s women have not hesitated to use and manipulate the system. For example, in Tunisia, when Muslim women with a Sharīʿa court order of child support could not get an enforcement order, they relied on the European-style courts. In Egypt, abused wives sued in government courts rather than in the Sharīʿa courts because of expedited enforcement of penalties against the husbands. Today in Egypt, non-Muslim women likewise cross lines (in 1998 and 2003) to find the justice most favorable to them, for example, seeking divorce relief from the Sharīʿa chamber of the national courts because under Coptic law adultery is the only ground for divorce for a woman.

On the periphery of the evolution of legal systems under the Ottomans and Europeans were the Arabian Peninsula and the Gulf states. Tribal custom allowed alternative approaches to mainstream Islamic rules, for example punishing adulterers with social ostracism and a symbolic pile of stones in front of their houses, or agreeing to very high rates of compensation for physical abuse or death of a woman, presumably because of her high labor value for the family and to discourage men from taking advantage of her exposure while tending family herds without a male protector.

Decolonialization in the 1950s and 1960s ushered in an era of consolidation of centuries of syncretic evolution. Official legislation and/or presidential, or kingly, decrees, even in the Saudi and Gulf regions continue the codification of the law. The classically trained jurists (*ʿulamāʾ*) lost their monopoly over the formulation and interpretation of Islamic legal sources. The state became the source of *ijtihād*, the process of reinterpreting Islamic law in light of new social circumstances and values. Constitutions were written according to international standards and included guarantees for gender equality as well as a Muslim identity. Arab countries began reconciling the demands of international law, classical mainstream Islamic legal opinions, and local customs. The process goes on today despite attempts of extremist Islamic political movements to come to power. Egypt's legislature, for example, enacted with the approval of the Shaykh al-Islām a divorce law that reaffirms the wife's right to divorce by returning her marriage dowry, without having to give elaborate reasons. The divorce, *khulʿ*, is an old practice, although the word does not appear in the Qurʾān. It can be found in the customary law of the Thonga in southern Africa. The Egyptian law aims to eradicate the customary practices of men that undermine the simplicity of the classical *khulʿ* divorce. Husbands had habitually negotiated not only the return of the *mahr*, but also release from child support and retention of all marriage gifts contributed by the wife and her family.

Of all the Arab countries, Tunisia took the boldest leap in reinterpreting personal status law. The law is fully rooted in the Qurʾān and *aḥādīth*, which were cited in the first version of the Personal Status Code of 1956. The dichotomy in courts and laws according to the faith of the litigants was abolished. All laws, including personal status laws, became applicable to all Tunisians irrespective of their faith affiliation. One law for all was based on the notion that all three monotheistic faiths could find something in common to agree upon. As a result, polygamy was abolished; divorce grounds were made equal for men and women; and the *mahr* was reduced to a symbolic value. Classical Islamic inheritance rules remained the same, but the law has allowed all citizens, Muslims or non-Muslims, to use gifts to equalize shares between female and male heirs.

In one sense, the Tunisian law has brought Islamic law back full circle. The Tunisian Islamic law reflects the original spirit of the Qurʾān; that is, Islam should be the means by which the other monotheistic faiths are harmonized and debates about women's rights are resolved in favor of equalization.

The process of legal consolidation since independence has cemented the state's centralization and homogenization of the interpretations of the Sharīʿa. This has to some extent reduced forum shopping on the part of women. Under the traditionally fragmented legal system, a woman could seek out a judge specializing in women's affairs or a *madhhab* known to favor women if, for example, she were seeking liberation from a marriage guardian. Centralization has narrowed the space for competition. Women now have to find new strategies to compete with the male voice. Centralization demands that women strive to access the literary sources of Islamic law (the Qurʾān, *ḥadīth*, jurists' compilations of interpretations) that governments consult. Beyond this, centralization also requires women to vie in the public political space, that is, the institutional world of legislating, administering, and adjudicating, where Islamic law and policy are now formed and *madhāhib* combined. How women decide to deal with the transition from fragmentation to homogenization will determine their future in Islamic law.

Bibliography

L. Ahmed, *Women and gender in Islam*, New Haven, Conn. 1992.

A. Bayindir, The functioning of the judiciary in the Ottoman Empire, in K. Çiçek (ed.), *The great Ottoman-Turkish civilisation*, iii, *Philosophy, science and institutions*, Ankara 2000, 639–56.

R. Brunschvig, Considérations sociologiques sur le droit musulman ancien, in *Studia Islamica* 3 (1955), 61–73.

N. J. Coulson, *A history of Islamic law*, Edinburgh 1964.

P. Crone, *Roman, provincial, and Islamic law. The origins of the Islamic patronate*, Cambridge 1987.

Egypt, Law 1 of 2000, Al-jarīda al-rasmiyya, No. 3, 29 January 2000, p. 10.

Egypt, Regulation of the personal status matters of the Orthodox Coptics, in A. Bergmann and M. Ferid, *Internationales Ehe- und Kindschaftsrecht*, Frankfurt/Main 1993, ongoing updates, 81–98.

S. D. Goitein, *A Mediterranean society. The Jewish communities of the Arab world as portrayed in the documents of the Cairo Geniza*, iii, Berkeley 1978.

E. Hill, *Mahkama! Studies in the Egyptian legal system*, London 1979.

K. A. al-Hilw and S. M. Darwish, *Customary law in northern Sinai*, ed. A. al-M. Haridi, trans. R. I. Dougherty, Cairo 1989.

M. Y. ʿIzz al-Dīn, *The theory and the practice of market law in medieval Islam. A study of* Kitāb niṣāb al-iḥtisāb *of ʿUmar b. Muḥammad al-Sunāmī (fl. 7th–8th century/13th–14th century) by M. Izzi Dien*, [Cambridge, England?] 1997.

C. Jones, Reforms in the Islamic legal judicial system and the Sharia inheritance and family law in Tunisia, in *Yearbook of African Law* 7 (1993), 3–23.

F. Kholeif, *A study on Fakhr al-Din al-Razi and his controversies in Transoxiana*, Beirut 1966.

F. I. Khuri, *State, religion and sects in Islam*, London 1990.

H. Pensa, *L'avenir de la Tunisie*, Paris 1903.

Fakhr al-Dīn Muḥammad ibn ʿUmar Rāzī, *Al-tafsīr al-kabīr*, ix, Beirut 1967³, 173ff.

R. Shaham, *Family and the courts in modern Egypt. A study based on decisions by the sharīʿa courts, 1900–1955*, Leiden 1997.

A. E. Sonbol (ed.), *Women, the family, and divorce laws in Islamic history*, Syracuse, N.Y. 1996.

J. Starr, *Law as metaphor. From Islamic courts to the Palace of Justice*, Albany, N.Y. 1992.

F. H. Stewart, The contract of surety in Bedouin customary law, in *UCLA Journal of Islamic and Near Eastern Law* 12:2 (2003), 163–280, citing F. H. Stewart, The woman, her guardian, and her husband in the law of the Sinai Bedouin, in *Arabica* 38 (1991), 102–29.

ʿA. Thaʿālibī, *Rūḥ al-taḥarrur fī al-Qurʾān/L'esprit libéral du Coran*, Paris 1905.

Al-Ṭabarī, *Taʾrīkh al-rusūl wa-al-mulūk*, Cairo 1960–77, Year 22.
J. E. Tucker, *In the house of the law. Gender and Islamic law in Ottoman Syria and Palestine*, Berkeley 1998.
Tunisia, *Majallat al-aḥwāl al-shakhsiyya*, Tunis 1956, 1970, 1998.
F. E. Vogel, *Islamic law and legal system. Studies of Saudi Arabia*, Leiden 2000.
D. Webster, *Abafazi bathonga bafihlakala*. Ethnicity and gender in a KwaZulu border community, in P. A. McAllister et al. (eds.), *Tradition and transition in Southern Africa*, Johannesburg 1991, 243–71.

Christina Jones-Pauly

The Caucasus and Turkey

A pluralistic legal system had developed in the Caucasus based on customary law (ʿ*āda*), Sharīʿa, and state laws (Russian). This system was applied until the 1920s when Soviet power and law were established and all other legal codes were declared unlawful.

THE CAUCASUS

Pre-Soviet period

Until the 1920s, criminal cases were judged according to ʿ*āda*, domestic cases according to the Sharīʿa, and other civil cases were subject to Russian law. The predominance of customary law in the Caucasus made it possible for women to feel relatively free in society, though upholding their rights was impossible for them.

Access to all the legal systems was limited for women due to their special social status originating in Caucasian national traditions and Islamic traditions that spread from the Ottoman Empire and Iran to the Caucasus from the tenth to the nineteenth centuries. If a man enjoyed a high social status, his wife was able to maintain her rights in the society. Married women with children also enjoyed a certain amount of legal freedom and protection. Islam introduced some legal protection into the family circle of Caucasian women. The following Sharīʿa regulations appeared: husband's correct deportment toward his wife; observance of divorce rules; and the introduction (in addition to the ʿ*āda* bride-price) of the *mahr*, and of the share of inheritance that was due to a woman, which equaled half a man's share (according to ʿ*āda*, women received nothing).

ʿ*Āda* and Sharīʿa legal procedures were conducted by between five and ten men who had knowledge of the ʿ*āda* and Sharīʿa norms. Caucasian social traditions emphasized veneration of the elders and arbitrators were selected from among the older men. In the Sharīʿa court, the *qāḍī* (judge) settled all the cases alone, using Arabic works on Sharīʿa, which had penetrated the Caucasus between the tenth and nineteenth centuries. Few women had knowledge of Arabic.

The ʿ*āda* and Sharīʿa courts initiated proceedings only if there were applications filed by the participants in the case in dispute or their relatives (near or distant). ʿ*Āda* and Sharīʿa legal proceedings comprised four stages: the plaintiff's case was heard; the defendant's plea was heard; the witnesses' testimony was taken; and the judgment was passed.

Women as plaintiffs

In general, women were able to take any legal action but they had to do it indirectly, through their male relations (father, brother, husband) or proxies. A relation between the type of case and the person who defended the woman's rights can be observed: the girl's father drew up the marriage settlement (*nikāḥ*); full brothers or first cousins took vengeance for an offence against the woman; and an uncle took part in negotiations to settle questions connected with the abduction of the bride (a traditional part of the arrangement of marriage). If a widow of a murdered man had no relations able to plead her cause, then proxies were appointed.

Women as defendants

A woman could not be a defendant in the ʿ*āda* or Sharīʿa courts. Her father or husband stood as defendant if she were being tried.

Women and testimonies

The following were considered as evidence in ʿ*āda* or Sharīʿa courts: the confession of the accused; physical evidence; and witnesses' statements under oath. A Qurʾānic oath was typical of the traditional legal procedure. The defendant was able to purge himself by means of the co-oath of his relatives or fellow villagers. Testimony of one man was equal to that of two women. Women's testimonies were used very rarely. Only men could evaluate testimony (Russian *atauly*, Kabardian *th'eryiueshchyh'et*).

In murder cases, after the court's decision was made, there was a rite in the Caucasus called a conciliatory feast (Ossetian *fynga* or *tuji fyng*, Russian *stol krovi*, blood table). The conciliatory ritual included visiting the mother of the murdered person: a delegation of authoritative mediators together with the criminal's relations went to the house of the mother, or sister if the mother was dead, and begged forgiveness.

Caucasian women were prohibited from taking part in ʿ*āda* or Sharīʿa legal proceedings, though there were other forms of action open to them. Women were able indirectly to participate in taking vengeance: they could ask their sons or husbands to act on their behalf. In cases involving disputing parties Caucasian women could remove their kerchief and break into a brawl or fight between men, and the latter were obliged to stop their conflict. A hillman who had committed any crime could hide from his pursuers in the female half of the house.

Introduction of Russian courts to the Caucasus (Highlander Verbal Courts, Gorskiy Courts) in the second half of the nineteenth century and the beginning of the twentieth century brought no significant changes to Caucasian women's life. Members of the Highlander Courts were male Russian officials. Cases related to the defence of women's rights were rarely brought before these courts and more usually passed to the ʿ*āda* or Sharīʿa courts.

The Soviet period

Soviet law was applied in the Caucasus from the 1920s to the 1980s. The Soviet judicial system engaged women in both legal proceedings and in defending their rights in the state court. The role in juridical life of women in Transcaucasia expanded noticeably. Women of the North Caucasus rarely exercised their right to be a judge in the state courts, which were still male.

The Soviet family code and court system did little to change the marriage and family traditions in the North Caucasus, which remained the domain of religious laws. Traditionally marriage was performed through abduction of the bride followed by *nikāḥ*, religious marriage registration. The bride-price was paid to the bride's family, and the bride received a *mahr*, which was hers to keep after divorce. Official Soviet laws failed to have a profound influence on North Caucasian woman's life, her rights or social standing. Soviet laws were more widely used in Transcaucasian republics (in particular in Armenia and Georgia, to some extent in Azerbaijan) where women saw significant emancipation, real freedom, and a chance to defend their rights in court.

Post-Soviet period

From the 1990s to the present there has been a slight development of the state law in the North Caucasus. A number of juridical traditions have been kept, such as marriage as a way to settle rape cases; traditional reconciliation when a girl is abducted for marriage; the drawing up of a marriage agreement (*nikāḥ*); and the institution of women encouraging their men to take vengeance. The process of revival of use of the Sharīʿa in matters concerning divorce and and division of property/inheritance is underway.

TURKEY

The history of the Turkish judicial system can be divided into two periods. From the fourteenth to the early twentieth century, Sharīʿa law was applied in the Ottoman Empire. After the Kemalist revolution (1926) a secular state was declared and Islam was made independent of the state, together with its legal system. A secular civil statute was established following the Swiss Civil Code and Islamic law was declared illegal. Formal equalization of men's and women's rights, equal access to legal procedures, and equal marriage, divorce, and property succession rights followed. Changes in gender status were slow. Informally, the Sharīʿa still applied, especially in rural areas, in matters of polygyny, Islamic weddings (*nikāḥ*), *mahr*, and divorce. The division of inheritance whereby a woman received half the share of a man also continued.

BIBLIOGRAPHY

PRIMARY SOURCES

(all works cited are in Russian)

N. M. Agishev, V. D. Bushen, and N. M. Reinke, *Materials concerning the Gorskiy court in the Caucasus*, St. Peterburg 1912.

H. M. Dumanov and F. H. Dumanova (comps.), *The legal norms of Adygs and Balkaro-Karachains*, Maikop 1997.

N. F. Grabovskiy, *Courts and criminal cases in Kabarda. A collection of information about the Caucasian peoples*, vol. 9, *Tbilisi* 1876.

H. O. Khashaev (comp.), *The monuments of the Daghestan customary law of the 17th–19th centuries*, Moscow 1965.

M. M. Kovalevskiy, ʿ*Āda of the Daghestan region and Zakatalsky Krai*, Tbilisi 1899.

——, *Law and tradition in the Caucasus*, 2 vols., Moscow 1890.

F. I. Leontovich, *Caucasian* ʿ*āda*, 2 vols., Odessa 1882.

SECONDARY SOURCES

T. Ansay and D. Wallace (eds.), *Introduction to Turkish law*, The Hague 1996⁴.

I. L. Babich, *The evolution of legal culture of Adygs* [in Russian], Moscow 1999.

V. O. Bobrovnikov, *The Muslims of North Caucasus* [in Russian], Moscow 2002.

Customary law in Russia [in Russian], Rostov-in-Don 1999.

D. E. Eremeev, *Islam in Turkey* [in Russian], Moscow 1990.

V. H. Kazharov, *The traditional social institutions of Kabardians and their crisis at the end of the 19th and*

the beginning of the 19th century [in Russian], Halchik 1992.
H. M. Khashaev, *Sharīʿa and ʿāda in Daghestan* [in Russian], Moscow 1949.
E. Örücü, Turkey. Reconciling traditional society and secular demands, in *Journal of Family Law* 10 (1986), 221–36.
E. Ural, *Handbook of Turkish law for foreigners*, Ankara 1991.

IRINA BABICH

Iran

From the Safavid period (1501–1722) Iran has been a Shīʿī country and its law is based on the rules of the Twelver Shīʿa. Shīʿī family law differs only in some minor points from Sunnī law, for example, in the pronunciation of the phrase of repudiation by the husband, the right of male and female lines to inheritance after the distribution of the property as prescribed by the Qurʾān, and the validity of the so-called temporary marriage (*mutʿa*, Persian *ṣīgha, izdivāj-i muvaqqat*).

In the nineteenth century legislation and jurisdiction were mainly influenced by the rules of the Sharīʿa, which were applied in *sharʿī* courts presided over by religious scholars, and by customary law (*ʿurf*). In his wish to create a modern nation state with a secular judicial system based on modern legal codes, Reza Shah Pahlavī (r. 1926–41) abolished the religious courts and reduced the influence of the Sharīʿa. Family law was codified between 1928 and 1935 as part of the Iranian Civil Code. In 1967 Mohammad Reza Shah (r. 1941–79) enacted the Family Protection Law, which was regarded at that time as one of the most modern family laws in the Islamic world. It was amended in 1975. However, as family law and the law of inheritance have always been regarded as central to the Sharīʿa, even in this Family Protection Law equality between the sexes was not achieved; rather, certain discriminatory rules such as men's right to arbitrary divorce, polygamy, and child custody were restricted. The woman was given permission to initiate divorce if her husband took another wife without her consent. Secularization of marriage and divorce was introduced through submission to the control of a family protection court. Divorce was possible only after reconciliation had failed. The responsibility for reaching agreement on maintenance and custody of children was placed on the couple. The court only intervened when agreement was not reached. The age of marriage was raised to 20 for men and 18 for women.

Despite its Sharīʿa origin, this law provoked a strong protest amongst the clergy. The Shīʿī clergy and especially the late leader of the Islamic Revolution, Khomeini, sharply criticized this law as contrary to Islamic law. In the Islamic Republic (1979) most of the stipulations of the Family Protection Law were revoked. Among others, the marriage age of girls was reduced to nine years. The Islamic state encouraged a proliferation of the practice of *ṣīgha* (second temporary marriage to the same man). However, this return to unrestricted Sharīʿa rules proved to be socially and politically unacceptable.

A legal discourse, especially among women, the clergy, and responsible state officials emerged in the following period. In 1992 a law was enacted that (as in 1967) outlawed divorces without a court certificate and required the registering of marriages. Female legal advisors were admitted at the family courts and the rights given to women in 1967 were reintroduced, this time legitimated on the basis of Islamic law. At the beginning of the twenty-first century the family law of the Islamic Republic did not differ substantially from the Shah's 1967 Family Protection Law.

Since the late 1990s the discourse on women's rights in Iran has been increasingly dominated by female voices. This discourse is shaped by the influence of different systems of law, especially the influence of modern Western law and the human rights discussion, but also by the obvious flexibility of the Sharīʿa rules. Interpretation of Sharīʿa rules, especially in matters of family law, is currently the subject of an ongoing public legal discourse.

Legal pluralism, the coexistence of different legal codes or legal cultural practices, for example, customary law and – more importantly – European law beside Islamic law, has further influenced legal reasoning of women. Nomadic customary law affected the position of women in nomadic societies before their gradual decline since the early twentieth century. Religious groups such as Christians (mostly Armenians) and Jews have their own legal systems concerning personal statute, which sometimes provides women with better legal or social conditions, allowing more political participation and a reduction of segregation.

The Islamic Republic of Iran propagated a concept of gender in accordance with Islamic law, favoring complementarity as opposed to equality of sexes. The Islamic Republic thus tried to create its own blueprint of the position of women in a modern society. However, in the face of the existing legal inequality of sexes in family law, women of different social, religious, and political backgrounds in Iran formed a movement to demand improvement in their legal position. These demands are formulated by women in women's journals such as *Zanān*. Women trained in Islamic jurisprudence have challenged some traditional interpretations of the sources of law (the Qur'ān and the sayings of the Prophet and the imams). They demand admittance of women as candidates in presidential elections and their appointment as judges. Several amendments to improve family law have been submitted to parliament. Islamic legislation can surely be said to have gained a new feminist dimension at the turn of the twenty-first century.

BIBLIOGRAPHY

H. Afshar, *Islam and feminisms*, London 1998.

K. Amirpur, Islamischer Feminismus in der Islamischen Republik Iran, in *Orient* 40 (1999), 439–52.

L. Beck, Women among Qashqa'i nomadic pastorlists in Iran, in N. Keddie (ed.), *Women in the Muslim world*, London 1978, 351–73.

N. J. Coulson, *A history of Islamic law*, Edinburgh 1964, repr. Delhi 1997.

S. Haeri, *Law of desire*, London 1989.

Z. Mir-Hosseini, *Marriage on trial*, London 2000.

——, Islam, women and civil rights. The religious debate in the Iran of the 1990s, in S. Ansari and V. Martin (eds.), *Women, religion and culture in Iran*, Richmond, Surrey 2002, 169–88.

P. Paidar, *Women and the political process in twentieth-century Iran*, Cambridge 1997.

S. Ṣadr, Ṭarḥ-i ʿaffāf va sāyir-i qaḍāyā, in *Zanān* 11 (2002), 16–17.

Sh. Sardar Ali, *Gender and human rights in Islam and international law*, The Hague 2000.

N. Tapper, The women's subsociety among the Shahsevan nomads of Iran, in N. Keddie, *Women in the Middle East*, London 1978, 374–98.

IRENE SCHNEIDER

Southeast Asia

Measured by conventional status indicators, the social and legal standing of Southeast Asian women in the pre-Islamic era was relatively strong (Tiwon 2003). Most importantly for present purposes, the predominant family structure in the region is based on bilateral descent and inheritance, though Southeast Asia also includes the world's largest matrilineal group. Women have also always been active in the region's mainly agricultural economy. Because Southeast Asian women have enjoyed relatively high social status as compared to other predominantly Muslim regions, a persistent theme in the history of Islamic law in Southeast Asia has been the tension between the distinctly patrilineal and patriarchal Sunnī legal doctrines and Southeast Asian social patterns and cultural norms. Opponents of recent Islamization efforts have pointed to the enduring social and cultural differences between the Arab society in which standard Sunnī legal doctrine developed and Southeast Asia as an argument against contemporary campaigns for broader enforcement of conventional understandings of Islamic law.

In addition to Indonesia and Malaysia, the Philippines, Singapore, and Brunei Darussalam also enforce Islamic legal doctrines, but the discussion here focuses on selected aspects of the two countries with the largest Muslim populations.

INDONESIA

Belief in one God is a foundational principle of Indonesia's state ideology, but there is no official state religion, and Indonesian law guarantees a limited freedom of religion. Efforts to implement a constitutional obligation to enforce Islamic law have been repeatedly abandoned for lack of support. A national system of Islamic courts exercises jurisdiction over Muslim marriage, inheritance, and charitable foundations.

In 1974 Indonesia enacted a National Marriage Law. The act and other important family and gender initiatives in the last decades of the twentieth century reflect the conservative gender policies of the New Order government of President Suharto, which ruled the country from the mid 1960s to the late 1990s. The Suharto government's family policy idealized female domesticity and small, stable families as the foundation of a stable and ordered nation. This policy was promoted through, among other means, a variety of governmental and quasi governmental organizations that emphasized the role of women as wives and homemakers whose function is to promote the careers of their husbands.

Although the National Marriage Act prescribes a single set of rules applicable to Indonesians of all religions, Islamic marriage doctrine is made applicable to marriages of Muslims through a provision stating that a marriage is "valid when carried out according to the religious law of the parties." The Marriage Act requires that marriage be based on the consent of the parties, and establishes minimum marriage ages of 19 years for males and 16 years for females. The minimum age rules were designed to reduce the practice, common among many communities, of parentally arranged marriages of very young couples. Although failure to comply with statutory age requirements does not necessarily invalidate the marriage, the frequency of arranged and underage marriage is declining.

The Marriage Act states that marriage is "in principle monogamous," but authorizes Muslim men to marry as many as four wives. The act establishes a number of conditions that must be satisfied by a husband desiring polygamy, including the permission of his existing wife or wives, and requires approval from the Islamic court.

A principal purpose of the Marriage Act was to reduce the frequency of divorce. The statute prescribes different divorce procedures for Muslim men and Muslim women. The procedure applicable to men involves a repudiation (*ṭalāq*) pronounced in the presence of the Islamic court. Women are required to present witnesses and prove statutory grounds for divorce. As interpreted by the courts, however, men are now also required to prove the same grounds for divorce as the wife before they will be permitted to utter the repudiation. These rules have not eliminated the practice of unilateral arbitrary repudiation, which remains common. Moreover, divorces initiated by wives often take longer to process than *ṭalāq* divorces.

The Marriage Act incorporates customary property doctrines as the marital property regime for Indonesian Muslims. Upon dissolution of the marriage each spouse retains ownership of separate property acquired prior to the marriage or obtained by gift or inheritance. Property accumulated during the marriage through the combined effort of the spouses is owned by the spouses jointly. Although not treated in the Marriage Act, the subsequent Kompilasi Hukum Islam (Compilation of Islamic Law) implemented in 1991 by presidential edict declares an equal division of marital property upon dissolution of the marriage by death or divorce.

As of 2003 Indonesian inheritance law had not been codified, but is treated in the Compilation. A government-backed proposal to equalize the shares of male and female children was dropped during the drafting process because of objections from the Muslim establishment, and the final version of the Compilation preserves the traditional rule granting sons a share equal to two daughters. One potentially significant innovation provides that children of predeceased heirs succeed to the share of the inheritance that would have passed to the predeceased heir had she or he survived.

Women have full political rights, and there are no formal barriers to women owning property or participating in the economy. The law requires that 30 percent of candidates nominated by political parties for the national legislature be women, though there is no mechanism for enforcing this requirement. While Indonesian women occupy important positions in both the private sector and public life, representation of women in the highest levels of business and government is low. In 2001 Megawati Sukarnoputri, a Muslim woman, became the country's fifth president despite pronouncements by several political parties and prominent political leaders that Islam does not permit a woman to serve as head of state. A substantial minority of Islamic court judges are women.

MALAYSIA

Indonesia and Malaysia share much in common, but while Indonesia is nearly 90 percent Muslim, Malaysia includes large non-Muslim Chinese and South Asian minorities resulting in a significantly more religiously plural society. Malay ethnicity is regarded as virtually synonymous with being Muslim, and Islamic law has been one of the means by which Malays have expressed their identity and asserted their claim to political dominance.

Malaysia also has a very different political structure from that in Indonesia. While Indonesia has until recently been highly centralized, Malaysia is a federally structured constitutional monarchy comprised of 13 states and 3 federal territories. The constitution declares Islam to be the state religion, but further states that all religions may be practiced in peace and harmony, and provides that discrimination on the basis of religion is forbidden. The ninth schedule to the constitution contains a list of matters reserved to the states, which includes the power to make laws on matters of Islam.

In the early 1980s the federal government enacted an Islamic Family Law Act for the country's three federal territories. The act was also intended to serve as a model to promote uniformity among the states. However, the family law of some states deviates from the federal model in several important respects.

The Federal Act and most states require the consent of the bride to marry and do not permit marriage by compulsion. However, the Family Law Enactment for Kelantan follows conventional Shāfiʿī doctrine in permitting the forced marriage of a virgin if the person who acts as her ritual marriage guardian (*walī*) is either her father or paternal grandfather (*walī mujbīr*).

In contrast to Malaysian civil marriage, Muslim marriages are regarded as polygamous in principle, even if the man has only one wife. The Federal Territories Act seeks to regulate the practice of polygamy to avoid injustice to women by imposing conditions to take a second wife. These conditions are not required in all states, and are not always strictly enforced. Some men have been able to evade compliance with legal restrictions on polygamy in their home states by contracting the marriage in another state where the rules are more lenient.

The Islamic Family Law Act seeks to limit arbitrary unilateral repudiations (*ṭalāq*) by requiring husbands to apply to the court for permission to pronounce the *ṭalāq* in court. Although extra-judicial repudiation is subject to punishment by fine and/or imprisonment not exceeding six months, imprisonment is rare. The law provides a number of avenues for wives to obtain a divorce, but legal proceedings for divorces initiated by women tend to be lengthier and more complex than requests by husbands for permission to pronounce the *ṭalāq*.

The law distinguishes between separate property and marital property (*harta sepencarian*). Upon dissolution of the marriage *harta sepencarian* is usually divided according to a ratio of two parts for the husband and one part for the wife. While the wife's contribution in maintaining the household is supposed to be considered in determining the division of the property, direct financial contributions are often given greater weight.

Upon divorce the mother takes custody of children who have not yet reached the age of discernment (*mumaiyyiz*). Children who have reached the age of discernment, considered to be between seven and nine years for boys and between nine and eleven years for girls, are allowed to choose which parent to follow. Based upon a disputed interpretation of a Prophetic dictum (*ḥadīth*), mothers can be deprived of custody upon remarriage, though the remarriage of the father does not affect his custody rights. The law requires the father to provide for the children financially.

Malaysian Islamic courts apply conventional Sunnī inheritance doctrines, including the rules that grant sons and male heirs a share equal to two females. In recent years the application of Islamic inheritance rules has been broadened, often to the detriment of women, by including, for example, lump sum provident fund pension benefits and insurance in the estate that is subject to inheritance, rather than assigning those assets to contractual beneficiaries. The practice found among some groups in southwestern areas of peninsular Malaysia of assigning control over inalienable clan properties according to female blood lines has been condemned as un-Islamic by some advocates for broad enforcement of Sunnī *fiqh* rules.

The constitution as implemented by federal statute grants states the power to enforce offenses against Islam subject to maximum penalties of fine not to exceed RM 5,000, three years imprisonment, or six strokes with a cane. The offenses falling within this jurisdiction include gambling, drinking intoxicating drinks, seclusion for an immoral purpose likely to lead to adultery or fornication, and disrespect of the fasting month. An effort to include domestic violence among the offenses punishable by the Syariah Courts was defeated. The possibility of state enforcement of dress regulations for women has been discussed, but as of 2003 no dress rules had been enacted.

In 1993 the state of Kelantan enacted a *ḥudūd* bill prescribing Islamic punishments (*ḥudūd*) for six offenses, including theft, highway robbery, unlawful sexual intercourse, slanderous accusation of unlawful intercourse that cannot be proven with four witnesses, wine drinking, and apostasy. The legislature for Trengganu passed a similar statute in 2002. The enactments have been criticized on a number of grounds, but two issues of particular concern to women are the rules disqualifying women from acting as witnesses in *ḥudūd* offenses, and the provision regarding unlawful intercourse (*zinā*). The enactments provide that an unmarried pregnant woman is presumed to be guilty of *zinā* unless she can prove to the contrary. This provision would have the implication of imposing on a pregnant rape victim the burden of proving rape, or facing punishment for committing *zinā* as well as for making an unlawful accusation of *zinā* (*qadhf*). Because the constitutional jurisdiction of the Syariah courts does not include general criminal matters, implementation of the *ḥudūd* law requires a constitutional amendment, which has not occurred.

Women have full political rights. While there are no legal impediments to women holding public office, representation of women in high public office is low, and leaders of the Pan-Malaysian Islamic Party (PAS) have voiced public opposition to women standing for public office. The head of state (Yang di-Pertuan Agong) is chosen from among the hereditary sultans from the states, who by tradition must be male. Although not prohibited by law, there are no women in the Islamic judiciary.

Bibliography

Primary Sources

Indonesia, *Law No. 1* [in Indonesian], 1974.

Indonesia, *Compilation of Islamic law* [in Indonesian], 1991.

Secondary Sources

M. Cammack, Inching toward equality. Recent developments in Indonesian inheritance law, in *Indonesian Law and Administration Review* 5 (1999), 19.

M. B. Hooker, *Islamic law in Southeast Asia*, Singapore 1984.

M. Hashim Kamali, *Punishment in Islamic law. An enquiry into the Hudud Bill of Kelantan*, Kuala Lumpur 1995.

——, *Islamic law in Malaysia. Issues and developments*, Kuala Lumpur 2000.

A. Ibrahim, *Family law in Malaysia*, Kuala Lumpur 1997[3].

J. Katz and R. Katz, The new Indonesian marriage law. A

mirror of Indonesia's political, cultural, and legal systems, in *American Journal of Comparative Law* 23 (1975), 653.
D. S. Lev, *Islamic courts in Indonesia. A study in the political bases of legal institutions*, Berkeley 1972.
M. Nakamura, *Divorce in Java. A study of the dissolution of marriage among Javanese Muslims*, Yogyakarta 1983.
N. Noriani Nik Badlishah (ed.) *Islamic family law and justice for Muslim women*, Kuala Lumpur 2003.
N. Othman, Grounding human rights arguments in non-Western culture. *Sharia* and the citizen rights of women in a modern Islamic state, in J. R. Bauer and D. A. Bell (eds.), *The East Asian challenge for human rights*, Cambridge 1999, 169–92.
S. Pompe, Mixed marriages in Indonesia. Some comments on the law and literature, in *Bijdragen tot de Taal-, Land-, en Volkenkunde* 144 (1988), 259.
S. Pompe and J. Otto, Some comments on recent developments in the Indonesian marriage law with particular respect to the rights of women, in *Verfassung und Recht in Ubersee* 4 (1990), 415–33.
J. Prins, Adatlaw and Muslim religious law in modern Indonesia, in *Welt des Islams* 1 (1951), 283.
N. Soewondo, Law and the status of women in Indonesia, in *Columbia Human Rights Law Review* 8 (1976), 123.
——, The Indonesian marriage law and its implementing regulations, in *Archipel* 13 (1977), 283.
S. Thalib, *Indonesian family law* [in Indonesian], Jakarta 1974.
S. Tiwon, Indonesia. Early 20th century to present, in EWIC I, Leiden 2003, 235–8.
C. Vreede-de Stuers, *The Indonesian woman. Struggles and achievements*, The Hague 1960.

MARK CAMMACK

Sub-Saharan Africa

Islamic law is an important part of legal thought and dispute resolution processes in much of Sub-Saharan Africa. The application and jurisdiction of Islamic law vis-à-vis other systems of law and social norms varies tremendously, however. In some African states, Islamic law constitutes a part of the official legal system. Elsewhere, Islamic law is not part of state law but informs local-level dispute resolution and influences community moral guidelines and ethical norms. Most African states that incorporate Islamic law into the state legal system do so only for matters of family law; Islamic legal institutions can therefore be arenas of great importance to women. In some areas, people refer to Islamic courts as "women's courts."

The spread of Islam into Sub-Saharan Africa brought important changes regarding law, dispute resolution, and women's social, legal, and political status. In Nigeria, the Islamic court system became widespread after Usman dan Fodio's jihad movement of 1804, which overthrew the rule of the Hausa Emirs and strove to establish a leadership derived directly from the Sharīʿa. Dan Fodio's daughter, the poet Nana Asma'u, supported his aims and sought to increase women's knowledge of Islamic law to improve their social position (Callaway and Creevey 1994).

With the spread of Islam, women sometimes gained rights and sometimes lost them. Women often won rights within the family, such as the right to the custody of children and to marital maintenance. Islamic law brought an increased focus on the rights of the individual over kin groups, which affected women's status through land usage and inheritance rights. In parts of Nigeria, women specifically benefited from Islamic inheritance rights that they had not previously enjoyed (Callaway and Creevey 1994). Elsewhere, as in eighteenth-century Sudan, women lost economic advantages when the adoption of Islamic legal norms influenced family economies by drawing women away from their conventional roles in household-level production (Spaulding 1984).

The relationship between Islamic and customary law played out differently from place to place. The distinction between what is appropriately "Islamic" and what is "customary" is often unclear, and even members of the same community may differ on this point. In some parts of Africa, custom was woven into the fabric of Islam. Elsewhere, distinctly recognized customary legal norms held sway. Among the Yao of Malawi, for example, Islamic norms regulated marriage, but customary norms of matrilineality controlled inheritance – only occasionally was wealth distributed to children and spouses according to Islamic norms (Anderson 1970).

In writing of the relationship between custom and Islam, some scholars have linked women with "custom" and men with "Islam." Eastman suggested that in East Africa, Islamic law was the domain of men while custom (in Kiswahili *mila*) was that of women (1984, 1988; see also Caplan 1982). Other scholars have criticized the assumption of two religio-legal spheres by arguing that men and women exert considerable influence in both arenas (Middleton 1992, Caplan 1995). Hirsch found that Kenyan Swahili women are less likely than men to move to an Islamic legal discourse in framing their disputes for a kadhi's (*qāḍī*) court, although both men and women will make use of Islamic discourse (1998).

In the colonial period, European rule brought changes that affected women's status through law. In many areas, Islamic legal institutions were already established, and colonial governments sometimes kept them in place; Britain, for example, kept such institutions intact in Nigeria and Zanzibar. Often, the jurisdiction of Islamic courts was restricted to family law, which was sometimes modified to improve women's rights. In 1930s Sudan, where the British supported the pre-existing centralized Islamic legal system, Islamic authorities encouraged legal reform that benefited women; for example, divorce through unilateral repudiation, *ṭalāq*, was made illegal (Fluehr-Lobban 1994). In some areas, despite popular conceptions that European law was more progressive in terms of women's rights, women often received greater benefit from Islamic courts. In colonial Zanzibar, a woman could obtain a divorce from an Islamic court on the grounds of a husband's cruelty but could not from a British judge. Rather, a judicial separation might be ordered to influence her husband to divorce her himself or to cease paying maintenance, which could lead to a divorce (Anderson 1970).

The dawn of independence sparked debates about women and Islamic law vis-à-vis other legal spheres in many African states, several of which had to address issues of religious pluralism, the coexistence of multiple legal systems, and women's status. Some states, such as Senegal and Mali, abolished Islamic courts. Issues of gender equality vis-à-vis Sharīʿa came to the forefront in others. Could a state committed to equality of all persons permit, for example, Islamic legal rules of witnessing and inheritance in which women and men are treated differently?

In Nigeria, the issue of Islamic law has been controversial since independence. Much of the debate centered on the Sharīʿa court of appeals, which became a symbol of the public role of Islam on the national level. Nigerian Muslims proposed that Islamic courts were a necessary component of religious freedom in a secular state, and argued that Muslims could not freely practice religion without them (Laitin 1986). The controversy peaked with the 1999 decision of twelve northern states to instate Islamic criminal law. The media frenzy surrounding the 2003 case of Amina Lawal, who was accused of adultery and sentenced to stoning by a primary Islamic court, fanned the flames. An Islamic appeals court eventually rescinded the lower court's decision by citing a violation of procedural law and the Mālikī legal principle of a "sleeping fetus," which asserts that a fetus can "sleep" in the womb for several years.

Controversy over Islamic law also raged in religiously plural Sudan. In the 1970s, al-Numayrī issued presidential decrees to improve the status of women by easing judicial divorce in abusive marriages and improving women's maintenance rights. In the 1980s, he declared Islamic law state law. Unlike elsewhere in Africa, Islamic law was to be applied to all matters – not just family law. This was very controversial, largely because of Sudan's substantial non-Muslim population, and led to civil war. Despite the controversy, in 1990 the Islamist government codified Islamic family law. The codification aimed to improve women's status by, for example, easing marriage restrictions and increasing benefits of marital maintenance (Fluehr-Lobban 1994).

Tanzania has a substantial Muslim minority, and with independence, Nyerere hoped to prevent religious strife by instituting different laws for different religions with the Marriage Act introduced in the early 1970s. Islamic courts were established in the Muslim-majority island state of Zanzibar, but not on the mainland. Though Islamic family law is not codified in Zanzibar, the Kadhi's Act of 1985 addressed gender issues in procedural law by requiring that judges give equal weight to the testimony of all witnesses, regardless of gender, ethnicity, or religion. The extent to which judges adhere to this is a different matter. On the mainland, experts in religious law advise the secular courts on Muslim family law. This is similar to the approach taken in Mali and South Africa.

Today, there is much regional specificity in the way in which Islamic law is incorporated and articulated vis-à-vis other legal orders. In religiously plural states like Nigeria, Kenya, and Niger, religious courts are important arenas for addressing gender and cultural pluralism. Islamic legal institutions can be an important way for Muslim women to assert rights, and in most Islamic courts, women open the majority of cases in court. They successfully present claims and win cases in courts that outsiders have often viewed as more favorable to men. Kenyan women, for example, use the courts to resist and challenge patriarchal relationships in the home (Hirsch 1997). In legally plural environments, it is common for women to make shrewd choices of judge or venue in hopes of a favorable settlement. In Niger, for example, women strategically use Islamic or customary law as a resource to secure land (Walker 1992).

Activists and scholars of gender policy assert the importance of reforming religious and/or customary personal status law to improve women's social and economic positions. Some propose that stricter adherence to Islamic law will improve women's status. In Zanzibar, for example, activists and Islamic scholars alike argue that following Islamic marriage laws would improve women's position. An example often cited concerns the *mahari* (*mahr*), the marriage gift paid by the groom to the bride, which the bride's elders often appropriate. If families followed Islamic legal norms, the argument goes, brides would have full control of the *mahari* and be in a better financial position in marriage (Stiles 2002).

Assessing the relationship between Islamic law, secular law, and social norms in Africa provides an important opportunity for gauging changes in women's status. Muslim women's movements have influenced the status of personal status law throughout Sub-Saharan Africa. The Federation of Muslim Women's Associations of Nigeria (FOMWAN), established in 1985, has attempted to engage Muslim women in political activity, and in the 1990s called for the establishment of Islamic courts and argued that women need to be more active in interpreting Islamic law (Callaway and Creevey 1994). In Niger, the Association of Nigerien Women has supported similar legal reforms (Dunbar 2000).

Bibliography

J. N. D. Anderson, *Islamic law in Africa*, London 1970.

B. Brown, Islamic law, qadhi's courts, and women's legal status. The case of Kenya, in *Journal of the Institute of Muslim Minority Affairs* 14 (1993), 94–101.

B. Callaway and L. Creevey, *The heritage of Islam. Women, religion and politics in West Africa*, London 1994.

P. Caplan, "Law" and "Custom." Marital disputes on Northern Mafia Island, Tanzania, in P. Caplan (ed.), *Understanding disputes. The politics of argument*, Providence, R.I. 1995, 203–21.

A. Christelow, Islamic law in Africa, in N. Levtzion and R. Pouwells (eds.), *The history of Islam in Africa*, Athens, Ohio 2000, 373–96.

—— (ed.), *Thus ruled Emir Abbas. Selected cases from the records of the Emir of Kano's judicial council*, East Lansing, Mich. 1994.

R. A. Dunbar, Muslim women in African history, in N. Levtzion and R. Pouwells (eds.), *The history of Islam in Africa*, Athens, Ohio 2000, 397–418.

C. Fluehr-Lobban, *Islamic law and society in the Sudan*, London 1987.

——, *Islamic society in practice*, Gainseville, Fla. 1994.

S. Hirsch, *Pronouncing and persevering. Gender and the discourse of disputing in an African Islamic court*, Chicago 1998.

D. Laitin, *Hegemony and culture. Politics and religious change among the Yoruba*, Chicago 1986.

J. Middleton, *The world of the Swahili. An African mercantile civilization*, New Haven, Conn. 1992.

R. S. O'Fahey, The past in the present? The issue of Sharia in the Sudan, in M. Twaddle and H. B. Hansen (eds.), *Religion and politics in East Africa*, London 1995, 32–44.

J. Spaulding, The misfortunes of some – the advantages of others. Land sales by women in Sinnar, in M. J. Hay and M. Wright (eds.), *African women and the law. Historical perspectives*, Boston 1982, 2–18.

E. E. Stiles, A kadhi in his court. Marriage, divorce and the Islamic legal tradition in Zanzibar, Ph.D. diss., Washington University 2002.

M. J. Swartz, Religious courts, community and ethnicity among the Swahili of Mombasa. An historical study of social boundaries, in *Africa* 49:1 (1979), 29–40.

A. H. Yadudu, The prospects for Shari'ah in Nigeria, in Islam in Africa Conference (Nigeria 1989), *Islam in Africa*, ed. N. Alkali et al., Ibadan 1993, 37–58.

Erin E. Stiles

Law: Criminal

Overview

Women in Islamic cultures, in common with women in other cultures, are likely to be subject to distinctly gendered criminal law and process. The majority of official actors in the criminal legal system – whether secular or Islamic – are male; this includes police officers, lawyers, prosecutors, and judges, as well as legislators. Another cross-cultural phenomenon is the under-reporting of crimes of violence – particularly sexual violence – against women and girls, including incest, rape, domestic violence, and sexual harrassment, both because of the nature of the complaint and prosecution process that may ensue, and because of shame that may attach to the victim/survivor in the eyes of society, community, or family. In the area of criminal law and women in Islamic cultures, particular attention is focused on the treatment of crimes related in one way or another to the sexual conduct (actual, alleged, or potential) of females and its control by formal or informal law. In recent years, a particular focus has developed among activist women's groups and among academics on "crimes of honor" against women, which involve not only an unwritten law considered by the perpetrator(s) to sanction a murder, but also the state criminal legal system (again, secular or Islamic) in viewing the perpetrator's claimed motivation with indulgence and hence in reducing the protections afforded by state law to the lives of women citizens. A further focus, in light of the "Islamization" of the legal systems of a number of states since the 1970s, has been the discriminatory impact upon women of the implementation of the *ḥadd* penalties for extramarital sexual relations. In addition, since the 11 September 2001 attacks in the United States, women in Muslim communities in the United States and Europe have been disproportionately affected by state actions – mostly against husbands and male family members – taken under anti-terrorism criminal and internal security legislation and criticized by civil society groups as not meeting due process and other human rights standards.

Since the 1970s, a number of Muslim majority states have announced programs of the Islamization of laws in which the codification of Islamic criminal law is a prominent and, according to observers, highly symbolic feature. These include Libya, Pakistan, Sudan, Yemen, and states in northern Nigeria. Typically such legislative programs include the *ḥadd* penalties stipulated for specific offences in traditional jurisprudence (*fiqh*) on the basis of the source texts of the Qur'ān and the *ḥadīth*, notably, for the purposes of this examination, the offence of *zinā*, unlawful sexual intercourse, that is, sex between any two persons who are not (and know that they are not) married to each other. The offence of *zinā* is punishable, according to the traditional interpretations of the source texts, by the *ḥadd* penalties of stoning to death for the married offender and by whipping for the unmarried offender; these penalties are criticized by many on human rights grounds. Although the penalties apply both to males and females, the implementation of such statutes has also been criticized *inter alia* on grounds of their discriminatory impact on women. Particular concerns raised in this regard are evidentiary rules or judicial practice establishing pregnancy of an unmarried woman as proof of *zinā*; the inclusion of the crime of rape in the *zinā* statutes; and the disqualification of women's testimony in *zinā* cases (Sidahmed 2001, Quraishi 1997).

It is commonly observed that the evidentiary standards for proving the occurrence of *zinā* liable to the *ḥadd* penalty are so high as to be practically impossible to meet, except in the case of voluntary confession to the offence; otherwise, the requirement of four adult male Muslim witnesses to the act of penetration brings the offence of *zinā*, as Quraishi (1997, 296) points out, very much into the public sphere rather than treating it as a matter of private conduct. However, reliance on a minority juristic opinion allowing pregnancy of an unmarried women to stand as evidence for *zinā* introduces a way of establishing the offence that applies only to the woman involved, and cannot be used against her partner. Sidahmed (2001, 203) observes that "the presumption of *zina* on grounds of pregnancy, whether corroborated by a confession or not, puts a woman defendant in a disadvantageous position compared to a man accused of the same offence" and ponders the implications of a modern-day legislature (in this case Sudan) explicitly introducing this minority opinion as part of statute law. A presumption of *zinā* is also of relevance to the treatment of rape as "forcible *zinā*" or "*zinā* under duress" (*zinā bi-al-jabr*) under the new statutes. While the use of force will exonerate the rape victim from the charge of and penalty for *zinā*, the same evidentiary standards are applied to the offence, making it extremely difficult for a woman to establish. Particular concern arises where women alleging rape risk being charged with *zinā* when they fail to establish the use of force against them (Sidahmed 1999, 198, Quraishi 1997, 302). In Nigeria, where starting in 1999 a number of northern states have implemented Sharīʿa penal codes, Amnesty International (2004) holds that "*zinā* as a criminal offence for Muslims only negates the principle of equality before the law." Against the background of considerable international attention to a number of *zinā* prosecutions against Nigerian women, Amnesty (2004) found that "the application of the death penalty for *zina* offences combined with the gender-discriminating evidence rules within the *Sharia* penal codes have meant that women have disproportionately been sentenced to death for *zina* in northern Nigeria since the introduction of new *Sharia* Penal Codes." In regard to Pakistan, Quraishi observes that the particular issue of rape and the misapplication of the Zina Ordinance is a "primary topic in women's human rights discussions globally, and stirs up an expected share of frustration, anger, defensiveness, and arrogance from all sides" (1997, 292).

In Muslim majority states that do not apply such codifications of Islamic criminal law and do not implement the *ḥadd* penalties, extramarital sexual relations may be criminalized under secular penal codes that historically differentiated the establishment of the offence and the length of the prison sentence on grounds of gender. Thus, for example, a husband might have to be openly involved with a woman other than his wife or to have had extramarital relations in the marital home in order for an offence of adultery to be proven against him, while no such developments on a single act of adultery would be specified for the wife. The crime of rape generally excludes marital rape but attracts very heavy penalties in case of prosecution and conviction. In some states, scholars criticize the categorization, in penal codes, of rape and sexual assault under sections dealing with, for example, crimes against public decency and morals (Jordan) or family order (Turkey) rather than in the sections on crimes against individuals. Abortion – which tends to be allowed only on therapeutic grounds (Bowen 1997) – may also be included as an offence under such sections. Mohsen finds infanticide to be "closely related to the crime of abortion" and reports that in Egypt, infanticide is "almost always a female crime," is strongly under-reported, and even where reported "is rarely prosecuted" – this last because "many law enforcement officers view such a crime as more the result of the woman's ignorance than of malicious intent" (1990, 17–18).

In many states, criminal law shows direct influence from previous colonial powers in the way it treats offences of particular relevance to women. Thus, various Middle Eastern and North African states have penal codes developed not only from the Ottoman but also the French penal codes of the nineteenth century; certain provisions of particular significance to women, notably the suspension of criminal proceedings against or punishment of the abductor of a woman in the event that she marries him, have parallels in the penal codes of some Latin American states. The French as well as Ottoman antecedents in criminal law are also illustrated in the penal codes of certain Arab states regarding "crimes of honor" (Abu Odeh 1996), to the effect that there remains a partial defence in law in the event that a man surprises his wife or one of his close female relatives in an act of *zinā* and kills her and/or her partner in the act; in Jordan, attempts to amend an article in the penal code providing an absolute defence in such circumstances have preoccupied sections of civil society and the legislature in recent years.

Increased attention to and research on crimes of honor against women, and particularly "honor killings," has shown that the above-mentioned articles are rarely if ever invoked as a legal defence by alleged perpetrators of honor killings; advocacy campaigns aimed at their amendment or repeal, and in some cases the opposition to such campaigns, indicate that they remain nevertheless highly symbolic. In the courts of various countries, different legal provisions combine to provide substantial reductions in penalties for the perpetrators of honor killings in circumstances that do not involve allegedly catching anyone in the act of illicit sexual liaison. Thus in some Arab states a partial defence to murder may be based on arguments akin to provocation – that is, that the perpetrator acted in a "fit of fury" and in defence of his honor (Abu Odeh 1996, Shalhoub-Kevorkian 2002a), while further reductions follow a waiving of personal rights in the prosecution by the victim's family. In Pakistan, although the statutes codifying Islamic criminal law do not recognize the partial defence of "grave and sudden provocation" previously available in criminal law, observers criticize implementation of the Qisas and Diyat Ordinance for reduced protection of women against murder (Amnesty International 1999). In Turkey, a partial defence of severe provocation may reduce the sentence to a third with further substantial reductions if, as is reported to be frequently the case, an honor killing is executed by a minor male (WWHR 2002). Turkish cases where the minor is chosen for the deed by a family council of male family members illustrate vividly the place such violence may occupy in parallel normative systems inadequately challenged by the state's criminal legal system (Sev'er and Yurdakul 1999). Research shows an apparent lack of attention and determination on the part of officials of the criminal justice system in investigating the murder or "suspicious deaths" of women in different states (Shalhoub-Kevorkian 2002a, Sev'er and Yurdakul 1999, Amnesty International 1999).

Increased domestic attention to crimes of honor in various Muslim majority states has been matched in recent years by increasing international attention, for example at the United Nations, where certain Muslim states have objected to a perceived association of honor killings with Islam. Domestically, the debate can be complicated by perceptions or assertions of Western pressure being behind attempts to amend the relevant legislation. From a different perspective, many activists and scholars situate manifestations of honor killings in the wider framework of violence against women; thus for example Shalhoub-Kevorkian (2002b, 590) observes that "naming femicide as 'crimes of passion' in the West and 'crimes of honour' in the East is one reflection of the discriminatory constructions of frames of analyses, which build a simplistic system that hides the intersectionality among political, economic, cultural and gender factors." The perceived association with Islam is also addressed explicitly. In her 2000 report, Asma Jahangir, United Nations Special Rapporteur on extrajudicial, summary, or arbitrary executions, noted that "the practice of 'honour killings' is more prevalent although not limited to countries where the majority of the population is Muslim. In this regard it should be noted that a number of renowned Islamic leaders and scholars have publicly condemned this practice and clarified that it has no religious basis." In a number of countries, those investigating and challenging crimes of honor in their domestic contexts have invested effort in demonstrating the fallacy of the idea that there is support for such practices in the bodies of principles and rulings that make up Islamic law. In responses to allegations of a relationship between Islamic law and crimes of honor (whether in practice or as countenanced in certain legal provisions) it is the "classical" law – or the dominant interpretations of Islamic criminal law – that are set out to establish that honor killings as commonly understood are not sanctioned. Among the points stressed are the stringent procedural requirements for the establishment of the *ḥadd* offence of *zinā*, the non-approval of extra-judicial action by private parties in punishing *zinā*, and the sin – as well as the crime – involved in the murder of innocents under the terms of Islamic criminal law.

The fact that existing legal provisions – and judicial interpretation of the same – may combine to provide seriously reduced penalties against those who kill women on alleged grounds of "honor" is exacerbated by a lack of attention on the part of state policy and agencies to the broader (indeed global) phenomenon of violence against women in the private sphere of the home and the family. Related areas of criminal law that appear to be under-enforced in various Muslim majority states and that have particular impact on women include the prohibitions on underage and forced marriage. Rendering criminal law more effective as deterrent and/or remedy is only one focus of the many individuals and women's groups campaigning around such issues in Islamic cultures, as indeed elsewhere. The particular manifestations of abuse intersect *inter alia* the enduring "maleness" of the legal process, perhaps particularly in criminal law; paradigmatic attitudes to women, sexuality, and property; and deliberate or negligent choices made by state authorities not to prioritize and systematize their responses to violence against women.

Bibliography

L. Abu Odeh, Crimes of honour and the construct of gender in Arab societies, in M. Yamani (ed.), *Feminism and Islam. Legal and literary perspectives*, Reading, U.K. 1996, 141–94.

Amnesty International, Pakistan. Violence against women in the name of honour, AI Index ASA 33/17/99, London 1999, <http://web.amnesty.org/ library/index/ ENGASA330171999>.

——, Nigeria. The death penalty and women under the Nigerian penal system, AI Index AFR 44/001/2004, London 2004, <http://web.amnesty.org/library/Index/ ENGAFR440072004?open&of=ENG-NGA>.

D. L. Bowen, Abortion, Islam and the 1994 Cairo Population Conference, in *International Journal of Middle East Studies* 29 (1997), 161–84.

CIMEL and INTERIGHTS, Annotated bibliography on "crimes of honour," <www.soas.ac.uk/honourcrimes>.

S. K. Mohsen, Women and criminal justice in Egypt, in D. H. Dwyer (ed.), *Law and Islam in the Middle East*, New York 1990, 15–34.

A. Quraishi, Her honor. An Islamic critique of the rape laws of Pakistan from a woman-sensitive perspective, in *Michigan Journal of International Law* 18 (1997), 287–320.

A. Sev'er and G. Yurdakul, Culture of honor, culture of change. A feminist analysis of honor killings in rural Turkey, in *Violence against Women* 7:9 (1999), 964–99.

N. Shalhoub-Kevorkian, Femicide and the Palestinian criminal justice system. Seeds of change in the context of state building, in *Law and Society Review* 36:3 (2002a), 577–605 .
——, Re-examining femicide. Breaking the silence and crossing scientific borders, in *Signs. Journal of Women in Culture and Society* 28:2 (2002b), 581–608.
A. S. Sidahmed, Problems in contemporary applications of Islamic criminal sanctions. The penalty for adultery in relation to women, in *British Journal of Middle Eastern Studies* 28:2 (2001), 187–204.
WWHR (Women for Women's Human Rights), *The new legal status of women in Turkey*, Istanbul 2002.

LYNN WELCHMAN

Afghanistan

Afghanistan's legal system includes the Sharīʿa and the Penal Code; in most cases penalties are not gender-based although the code does refer to certain parts of the Sharīʿa, such as *ḥudūd, qiṣāṣ*, and *diya*. Afghanistan has capital punishment. Women's crime rate is very low and mostly family related. In Kabul, with a population of nearly three million, the women's jail has only 28 inmates who live there with their children. From 1992 to 2001 in the free northern provinces of Kapissa and Parwan, there was only one female execution and one *qiṣāṣ* (requested by a widowed mother whose daughter was killed by a man she had refused to marry her daughter to). From 1996 to 2001, the Taliban militias stoned or executed many women publicly, imprisoned many more for violating their orders, and put into their correctional facility hundreds of young women and girls for as small an infraction as laughing in the street. While since December 2001 the reinstated 1964 constitution recognizes the rights of all citizens, has well-defined separation of powers, and does not admit fatwa as binding law, the Taliban operated only by fatwas from their leader, Mullah Omar.

An overall problem that will have to be dealt with in the criminal law domain is the fact that the judiciary is based on Ḥanafī law while a sizeable population follows Shīʿī Jaʿfarī law.

The largest number of crimes committed by women and against women are related to family violence. Often women who have suffered in these situations face criminal charges as well. Examples abound: an already married woman whose husband was working in another city ran away because her father wanted to marry her to another man (in return for money). The police found and jailed her, both to protect her from her father and to punish her for running away without permission from a male member of her family. Sometimes the fate of women in situations of family violence does not come to light until after their death. Authorities are reluctant to indict family members in such cases.

It remains to be seen if in the new constitution (adopted January 2004) and the legal institutions now taking shape in Afghanistan these issues are dealt with in a manner consistent with equality of men and women.

BIBLIOGRAPHY

M. H. Kamali, *Law in Afghanistan. A study of the constitutions, matrimonial law and the judiciary*, Leiden 1985.
J. E. Sihombing and H. A. Finlay (eds.), *Law Asia family law series*, editor-in-chief R. Watson, Singapore 1979.
H. G. Vafai, *Afghanistan. A country law study*, Washington, D.C. 1988.

NASRINE GROSS

Arab States

Criminal law in the Arab world derives, by and large, from Western European principles as well as from the Sharīʿa and *ʿurf* (tribal or customary law), although in Saudi Arabia law is not codified and the *ʿulamāʾ* (religious scholars) preside over matters of criminal law. It would not be correct to single out the Arab states as the only locus of legal disadvantage for women or discrimination against them. Until quite recently, many Western legal codes defined women as wives and dependents. Islamic legal principles treat women as reproductive and sexual beings to be constrained by the *umma* (the Muslim community), family, or tribe. Theoretically, as Islamic law developed, the adjudication of crimes shifted to the *umma*. Yet families and tribal councils continued to serve as guardians and to apply customary law.

Women's legal status affects their role in the judicial system. For example, women are excluded from giving testimony in the most serious category of crimes in Islamic law, the *ḥadd* (pl. *ḥudūd*), which are crimes against God. Women judges have presided in Syria, Yemen, Tunisia, and Lebanon but historical precedent and Islamist sentiments have prevented them from serving elsewhere. The key principles of most criminal categories are gendered and have serious implications for women.

MURDER

ʿUrf accorded a lesser monetary value to women's lives, and assigned a high value to virginity. Islamic law adopted these monetary distinctions, although it did outlaw cruel practices such as death by exposure of female infants. In tribal tradition, a life or limb was worth its equivalent but a woman's life was worth half that of a man's. Her reproductive value was taken into consideration, so in some areas, in a conflict between two tribes, a dead man's tribe could abduct a woman from the other tribe until she bore a son. Modern states restricted such practices, as in Section 7 of the Tribal Courts Law (1936) for Palestine.

Severe penalties such as amputations, or lashings, were imposed rather than imprisonment in the premodern era. In addition, retaliation often served to settle inter-clan disputes. *ʿUrf* and Sharīʿa law did not attempt to reform criminals; rather, public punishments were conceptualized as deterrent measures.

The worst crimes are those committed against God, the *ḥadd*, which have a fixed punishment, followed by *qiṣāṣ*, which may involve retaliation. Least serious are *taʿzīr*, crimes for which a judge formulates punishment. In the Sharīʿa, murder, manslaughter, and bodily injury or maiming are *qiṣāṣ* crimes. The victim's family can demand retaliation or *diya* (blood money). The penalty must represent equivalent harm, and be executed with the least pain possible. Female victims are entitled to *diya* at half the value of a man's; since men's inheritance was twice that of women's, the valuation was logical.

In modern law codes, prison terms have replaced acts of retaliation. Murder sentences should be equivalent, but in crimes of honor or passion, the guidance for sentencing varies.

Honor crimes

Honor crimes occur when male family members kill a woman for a perceived violation of the code of sexual behavior. Most penal codes exempt or reduce the sentence if the victim is seen as having "provoked" the crime. In Jordan, the average sentence for an honor crime is seven and a half months. Often, families will assign the task of killing sisters to minor males to mitigate penal sentences.

Modern Penal Codes which blur the distinction between murder and crimes of honor reinforce the notion that men have a right to punish women. Lebanon was the first Arab state to reform the article in its Penal Code of 1999, which provided exemptions or sentence reductions for honor crimes. A similar reform campaign in Jordan has yet to succeed. Articles permitting extenuating circumstances, or exemption from penalty, are discriminatory because most countries do not provide reduction of sentences for women who commit murder in such situations.

Adultery

Under Sharīʿa law, sex is permitted solely within licit marriage. The crime of *zinā* (adultery, fornication) merits lashing for unmarried persons, and lapidation for married persons. Such sentences are uncommon, even in Saudi Arabia, Sudan, and Libya. Under Western-influenced law codes such as that of Tunisia, women, but not men, could be punished for adultery prior to 1968. Tunisian law was subsequently reformed to apply equally to men and women. The Egyptian Penal Code previously specified a sentence of not more than two years for an adulterous woman. A man's sentence could not exceed six months, and male adultery was only so defined if it occurred in the marital home.

Rape

In Morocco, in 1993, Hajj Muhammad Mustafa Thabit testified to rapes of around 500 women over a period of 13 years and was swiftly executed. The incident revealed that such crimes occur in Arab society, contrary to popular discourse. All Arab states penalize rape, although not marital rape. Since rape victims may be killed by their families, the crime is underreported. *ʿUrf* treats rape as an act of physical damage and theft of sexual property, diminishing a virgin's financial worth. In countries following the Sharīʿa, penalties are now severe. In the past, financial compensation might suffice if jurists found an element of doubt (*shubha*). Civil penal codes differentiate between forced rape and consensual sex, and minor and adult victims, as was common in Western law as well. Reformers have protested at the fact that most Arab penal codes do not charge a rapist with a criminal act if he marries his victim. This clause was repealed in Egypt in 1999. In Lebanon, torture and gender-based abuse and rape of imprisoned women was reported despite penal code articles prohibiting torture.

Incest and sexual abuse

Incest is illegal under Sharīʿa law. Today, penalties range from execution to those less serious than for rape. Incest and sexual abuse victims are constrained by the honor code. Incest carries a sentence of only three years in Jordan, and a male relative must register the complaint, not the victim, or a shelter where she has taken refuge. A Palestinian women's center estimated that 75 percent of sexual assault cases involve close male relatives, with girls aged between 4 and 13 being most at risk.

Sexual abuse and harassment

As legal categories, sexual abuse and harassment are new concepts. Thus it was news when a Tunisian hospital worker filed a sexual harassment complaint in 2002, and a hospital disciplinary board swiftly convened against her. Political police surrounded the hospital and threatened the complainant and her attorneys with rape (OMCT 2002).

Arab women experience and complain of harassment in the streets and public areas. Penal or civil codes prohibit lewd behavior but are infrequently enforced.

Illegitimacy

The fear of violence from a female's family often prevents the birth of illegitmate children. In cases of such births, subterfuge or infanticide are usual, or informal adoption. In Morocco, a woman may be imprisoned for six months for bearing a child out of wedlock. Child abandonment is illegal although it does occur and is the reason for the existence of most state and private orphanages. If women kill their own children, sentences vary; in Jordan, a woman can receive a sentence of 5 to 10 years, but, as in Sudan and elsewhere, judges might reduce the sentence in such a case.

Abortion and new reproductive technologies (NRTs)

Tunisia liberalized its abortion law by greatly broadening the substantiating groups for obtaining the procedure. Egypt, Syria, Lebanon, Yemen, and Libya have criminalized abortion except to save the mother's life. In Morocco, Algeria, and Saudi Arabia, abortion is allowed to save the mother's life or preserve her physical or mental health. Sudan and Iraq allowed abortion in cases of rape and incest and Qatar permits it in cases of rape and fetal impairment.

NRTs are criminalized if they involve gamete donation; the rationale derives from religious principle. However, in Lebanon, Shīʿī jurists have agreed that couples may use donated eggs.

Prostitution, sexual trafficking, homosexuality

Poverty and tourism fuel the sex industry in Arab states. Prostitution may be fictionalized as marriage when Arab tourists "marry" young girls in Egypt and then abandon them. War conditions caused an increase in prostitution, kidnapping, and sexual trafficking of women in Iraq. In Saudi Arabia, Mauritania, Sudan, and Libya the penalties for *zinā* apply to prostitution. Elsewhere, prostitution is punishable by a fine or a prison sentence. It is legal in Lebanon and Djibouti, although pimping and coercion are not. Sexual trafficking has not yet been seriously tackled in the penal codes.

Homosexuality is illicit according to the Sharīʿa, contrary to nature and punishable, yet is often tolerated. Outside the Gulf states, Sudan, and Libya penalties include fines and/or prison sentences, and it is conceived as an offense against public morality.

Female genital mutilation (FGM)

Although the 1946 Sudanese Penal Code prohibited infibulation, while permitting the less radical *sunna* circumcision, infibulation has continued. In 1957 and again in 1991, this law was re-ratified, but FGM is not mentioned in the 1993 Penal Code.

In Egypt, FGM was permitted one day a week and performed by licensed health professionals with the rationale that "medicalization" of the process might save lives. Following a CNN live exposé of a circumcision, the Egyptian minister of health banned the practice in state facilities and private clinics in 1996. His decision was overturned, then revalidated in a higher court. The decree is frequently ignored, and some deaths have resulted. Activists from Arab and African nations called for specific legislation to address FGM.

Battering and domestic violence

Many Muslims believe that both Islamic law and custom mandate that women owe men obedience (*ṭāʿa*), proper care of the household, and sexual favors on demand. A wayward woman was classified as being *nāshiza* according to the Sharīʿa and a *ḥadīth* recommended remonstration, leaving the bed of a wife, and then lightly beating her. Liberal Muslims reject this interpretation.

Most countries penalize battery and assault, but lack articles that specifically apply to domestic violence. Moreover, the reduced penalties for honor crimes apply to batterers. Magistrates appear to discriminate in sentencing in favor of male batterers (Zulficar 1994, 86–7).

Conclusion

Penal codes that discriminate against women violate the Convention on the Elimination of All Forms of Discrimination against Women (CEDAW). Codes that include whipping, lapidation, and capital punishment also violate the international prohibitions against torture. The level and efficacy of legal reform in response to the CEDAW directive should be a priority for the Arab states, in spite of opposition.

Equality on the basis of gender is granted constitutionally to most Arab citizens. The disjuncture between statutory discrimination in the penal codes and women's constitutional rights provides a legal basis for reform.

BIBLIOGRAPHY

L. Abu Odeh, Feminism, nationalism, and the law. The case of Arab women, SJD thesis, Harvard Law School 1993.

Amnesty International, Lebanon. Torture and ill-treatment of women in pre-trial detention. A culture of acquiescence, AI Index MDE 18/009/2001, 22 August 2001, <http://web.amnesty.org/library/Index/ENGMDE180092001?open&of= ENG-LBN>.

J. N. D. Anderson, *Islamic law in Africa*, London 1954.

Association tunisienne des femmes démocrates, *Rapport aux décideurs. Les violences à l'encontre des femmes*, Tunis 2001.

M. C. Bassiouni (ed.), *The Islamic criminal justice system*, London 1982.

L. Brand, *Women, the state, and political liberalization. Middle Eastern and North African experiences*, New York 1998.

B'Tselem, Morality, family honour and collaboration, in Y. Be'er and S. 'Abdel-Jawad, *Collaborators in the Occupied Territories. Human rights abuses and violations*, Israeli Information Center for Human Rights in the Occupied Territories, January 1994, 89–99.

A. C. Chamari, *La femme et la loi en Tunisie*, Casablanca 1991.

Al-Fanar, Developments in the struggle against the murder of women against the background of so-called family honour, in *Women against Fundamentalism Journal* 6 (1995), 37–41.

C. Fluehr-Lobban, *Islamic law and society in the Sudan*, London 1987.

J. Ginat, *Blood revenge. Family honor, mediation, and outcasting*, Brighton, U.K. 1997.

S. Hammad, Violence against women. Honor crimes in Jordan, in *Civil Society. Democratization in the Arab World* 7:44 (December 1998), 17–20.

M. J. L. Hardy, *Blood feuds and the payment of blood money in the Middle East*, Leiden 1963.

F. A. al-Hayani, Legal modernism in Iraq. A study of the amendments to family law, Ph.D. diss., University of Michigan 1993.

R. Husseini, Honor killings, <http://www.pbs.org/speaktruthtopower/rana.html>.

P. Illkaracan (ed.), *Women and sexuality in Muslim societies*, Istanbul 2000.

T. Mahmood et al., *Criminal law in Islam and the Muslim world. A comparative perspective*, Delhi 1996.

C. Mallat and J. Connors (eds.), *Islamic family law*, London 1993.

A. E. Mayer, *Islam and human rights. Tradition and politics*, Boulder, Colo. 1991.

——, Libyan legislation in defense of Arabo-Islamic sexual mores, in *American Journal of Comparative Law* 28 (1980), 287–313.

N. M'jid, Sexual exploitation of children in the MENA region. An overview, paper presented at the Arab-African forum against sexual exploitation of children, Rabat, Morocco, 24–6 October 2001.

S. E. Nanes, Fighting honor crimes. Evidence of civil society in Jordan, in *Middle East Journal* 57:1 (Winter 2003), 112–30.

OMCT (Organisation mondiale contre la torture), also known as World Organization against Torture, The impact of economic, social and cultural rights of women on violence against women in Egypt, report prepared for the Committee on Economic, Social and Cultural Rights, Geneva April 2000.

——, International Secretariat. Case TUN 141102 VAW, <http://www.omct.org/>.

S. Ruggi, Commodifying honor in female sexuality. Honor killings in Palestine, in *Middle East Report* 28:1 (Spring 1998), 12–15, reprinted in P. Illkaracan (ed.), *Women and sexuality in Muslim societies*, Istanbul 2000, 393–98.

N. Shalhoub-Kevorkian, The politics of disclosing female sexual abuse. A case study of Palestinian society, in *Child Abuse and Neglect* 23:12 (1999), 1–19.

A. N. Wood, A cultural rite of passage or a form of torture. Female genital mutilation from an international law perspective, in *Hastings Women's Law Journal* 347 (Summer 2001), 347–86.

M. Yamani (ed.), *Feminism and Islam. Legal and literary perspectives*, Reading, Berks., U.K. 1996.

S. Zuhur, Criminal law. Women and issues of gender, sex, and sexuality in the Middle East, North Africa, and the Islamic world, in *KKHP/WWHR* (forthcoming).

M. Zulficar, *Women in development. A legal study*, Cairo 1995.

SHERIFA ZUHUR

Bangladesh

Bangladesh became independent as a result of the Indo-Pakistan war in 1971. Before and after 1971 the Penal Code of 1860, the Criminal Procedure Code 1989, and the Evidence Act of 1872 formed the statutory basis of the criminal law of Bangladesh. The government of Sheikh Mujibur Rahman enacted a constitution in 1972 that proclaimed secularism as one of the founding principles of state policy. Yet in subsequent years of military rule from 1975 to 1990 constitutional amendments revived religious-based parties and eliminated secularism as a state principle. This was feared by women's groups because of the risk of exposing women to discriminatory laws. The Suppression of Violence against Women and Children Act 2000 covers the offences of grievous hurt to women and children, trafficking of women, kidnapping and abduction of women and children, confinement of women and children for ransom, rape, murder accompanied by rape, or sexual assault, and committing murder or hurt in order to obtain a dowry. In spite of this law, these offences have not abated in any significant measure. Women's organizations in Bangladesh demand that real issues related to the management of crimes be addressed, namely indifferent police, corruption, criminalization of politics, poor participation of women in the policy-making sphere, and so forth.

RAPE

The common crime of rape in Bangladesh is controlled by section 376 of the Penal Code, the

Suppression of Violence Against Women and Children Act of 2000, and also punishable under the Special Powers Act of 1974 (As Amended) by the setting up of a special tribunal. But in practice criminal law does not provide enough protection to women against rape. In cases of rape the rule that prevents further action is that an independent witness is required to confirm a victim's statement. Other factors contributing to the fact that the crime is rarely reported are poor medical examination of the victim, bribery by the offender, and threats to life. Rape is also committed on women held in police custody where it is difficult to hold the offender accountable because the investigation is supposed to be carried out by his own colleagues. The social and emotional consequences of rape are endless. Marriage for victims of rape is virtually impossible. People still believe that rape is the victim's own fault and many victims of rape commit suicide.

Violence

Women are not sufficiently protected from domestic violence, including dowry deaths. Incidents of murder or attempted murder for dowry-related reasons are regular items in the country's daily papers. Acid burnings have also become a common form of violence; the main reasons for this crime are jealousy, refusal of sexual advance, revenge after an argument, or a husband seeking more dowries or permission for polygamous marriage. In 1984, a new provision, section 326A, was inserted in the Penal Code providing penalties up to capital punishment for those found guilty of this crime. The Suppression of Violence against Women and Children Act 2000 recognizes offences of sexual assault and sexual harassment. Under the Bangladesh Penal Code women cannot even be charged with adultery, but occasionally decisions are controlled by the local elders, led in particular by religious leaders. There have been cases where women were accused of *zinā* and sentenced to be caned. Sentences passed on women (sometimes called fatwas) issued by mosque imams and *madrasa maulanas* have included stoning, flogging, or social boycott.

Trafficking

Trafficking in women and children is a significant problem in the Bangladesh. The government has taken measures to curb the practice by introducing strict punishment to offenders in the Suppression of Violence Against Women and Children Act 2000, and strengthening border check posts. But due to socioeconomic factors there is a serious lack of implementation of laws and border police may become partners with the traffickers in order to supplement their income.

Bibliography

Ain o Salish Kendra, Threats of violence and violations of human rights by imams of mosques and the religious right in Bangladesh, unpublished collection of cases compiled for the period 1992–94, Dhaka 1994.

R. Bhuiyan, *Aspects of violence against women*, Dhaka 1991.

M. Guhathakurta, Gender violence in Bangladesh. The role of the state, in *Journal of Social Studies* 30 (1985), 77–93.

M.-A. Hélie-Lucas and H. Kapoor (comps.), *Fatwas against women in Bangladesh*, London 1996.

R. Jahan, Hidden wounds, visible scars. Violence against women in Bangladesh, in B. Agarwal (ed.), *Structures of patriarchy. State, community and household in modernizing Asia*, New Delhi 1988, 216–26.

S.-R. Khan, *The socio-legal status of Bangali women in Bangladesh. Implications for development*, Dhaka 2001.

R. Khondker, *Violence and sexual abuse. Legal cases studies from Bangladesh*, Dhaka 1990.

K. R. Redden, Bangladesh, in K. R. Redden (ed.), *Modern legal systems cyclopedia*, ix, Buffalo, N.Y. 1990.

A. Shaheena, *How far Muslim laws are protecting the rights of women in Bangladesh*, Dhaka 1992.

Rubya Mehdi

Iran

The source for understanding the standing of women in Iranian criminal law is the Islamic Penal Code. The origin of this Penal Code can be found in *Qanūn-i ḥudūd wa qiṣāṣ wa muqarrarāt-i an* (The law of retribution and boundaries and its ordinances) that was passed immediately after the revolution of 1979. This law was later amended and ratified as *Qanūn-i mujazat-i Islāmī: Ḥudūd, qiṣāṣ, diyat, taʿzīrāt* (The Islamic Penal Code: boundaries, retribution, compensation, corporal punishments) by a clergy-dominated Iranian parliament in 1982 and again amended in 1992.

The Islamic Penal Code, relying on often-ambiguous Islamic commands, allows for severe and violent physical punishments. In addition, public or state authorities are given permission to violate the citizens' private spheres on the pretext of combating moral crimes and violations. As such, the Islamic Penal Code not only conflicts with international human rights treaties, many of which the government of Iran had signed before the revolution, but is also at odds with the social transformation Iran has experienced in the past century. On the basis of this code, violence against women is encouraged, women's right to life is denigrated, a woman's testimony in court is either not valued or deemed as only half as credible as that of a man, and some of her most basic human rights, such as the right to wear what she wishes, are denied.

There are many instances of gender-based inequality that can be cited in the Islamic Penal Code but at the most fundamental level inequitable treatment is manifested in the minimum age of criminal culpability. The Islamic Penal Code itself does not specify the minimum age of criminal culpability and instead in Article 49 identifies a child as someone who has not reached the age of religious maturity. It is in Article 1210 of the Civil Code that the age of religious maturity of 9 for women and 15 for men is specified. As such, girls enter the arena of criminal liability six years earlier than boys and can be punished as adults. This contradicts the Convention on the Rights of the Child, which has been ratified and signed by the Islamic Republic of Iran. The Iranian judicial system has tried to lessen the impact of the existing laws and in some ways to offer a veneer of legitimacy to its practices by creating special corrective courts for children but the realities of Article 49 of the Islamic Penal Code and the unequal treatment it promotes on the basis of gender cannot be overlooked.

Iranian criminal laws also treat men and women differently in terms of the right to wear the kind of attire they wish. Immediately after the 1979 Revolution, not wearing a veil or not wearing it properly in public was considered a crime, punishable by as many as 74 lashes until 1996 when imprisonment or monetary fines replaced lashes. The situation is complicated by the fact while Article 638 of the Islamic Penal Code passed in 1996 identifies the new penalties, it continues to keep the category of "improper" veil undefined, leaving it open to interpretation by judges or implementers of the law who have found the legal vagueness a useful tool for harassing women.

There are many other areas in which men and women face varied and unequal criminal culpability, for instance in allowing for passion killing for men but not women (Article 630 of the Islamic Penal Code). The law also treats a woman's life as less worthy than a man's by making her blood money worth half that of a man's. If a man intentionally kills or maims a woman and in turn, based on the law of retribution, is sentenced to death or maiming, the woman's family must give half of the man's blood money to his family. The law does not require blood money for a woman who has been sentenced to death or murder. Such disparity in blood money compensation, and the fact that the family of the female victim ends up owing money to the family of the male criminal in its pursuit of justice, has the potential of promoting violence against women for the sake of financial gain.

There are also areas in the Iranian criminal law, such as sexual relations between unmarried adults (*zinā*) or adultery (*zinā-yi muḥṣina*), both criminalized in the Islamic Republic, in which the Islamic Penal Code seemingly treats men and women equally. But in practice women end up receiving harsher punishments. For instance, in the case of adultery, both the married man and the married women caught in extra-marital relationships are subject to the punishment of stoning on the basis of Article 83 of the Islamic Penal Code. However, more women have been stoned because, given the fact that men in Iran have the right to marry up to four wives, adulterous men have the option of identifying the woman with whom they have relations as their new wife, an option obviously not open to adulterous women. International pressures to end this practice have only led to the suspension of stoning by the judiciary and not its outright ban through parliamentary laws.

BIBLIOGRAPHY

M. Kār, *Rafʿ-i tabʿīz az zanān. Muqāyisah-ʾi kunvānsiyūn rafʿ-i tabʿīz az zanān bā qavānīn-i dākhilī-i Īrān*, Tehran 1999.

——, *Sākhtār-i ḥuqūqī-i niẓām-i khāvādah dar Īrān*, Tehran 1999.

——, *Pizhūhishī darbārah-ʾi khushūnat ʿalayh-i zanān dar Īrān*, Tehran 2000.

H. R. Kusha, *The sacred law of Islam. A case study of women's treatment in the Islamic Republic of Iran's criminal justice system*, Burlington, Vt. 2002.

F. Ṣāliḥī, *Diya yā mujāzāt-i mālī*, Tehran 1992.

MEHRANGIZ KAR

Pakistan

Since 1947, the Pakistan Penal Code 1860, the Criminal Procedure Code 1989, and the Evidence Act of 1872 have formed the statutory basis of the criminal law of Pakistan. In 1979 Islamic criminal law was partly implemented. Islamic criminal law is not compatible with the status that women already had in Pakistan. Woman's organizations mobilized and claimed that Islamic law had to face the challenges of the modern world. The women's movement in Pakistan holds that traditional Islamic law needs reinterpretation and that religion should not be confused with a patriarchal social structure. Islamization of the criminal law has shown clearly that there are differences of opinion concerning the interpretation of the Sharīʿa. The Islamization has affected women mainly through the aspects of criminal law described in this entry.

Law of rape

With the Islamization of the law changes were introduced in the law of rape making it part of the ordinance called The Offence of Zina (Enforcement of Hudood) Ordinance, VII of 1979 (the term *zinā* encompasses adultery, fornication, rape, and prostitution), and requiring Islamic standards of proof and punishments. The ordinance makes fornication and adultery, which were not regarded as crimes in Pakistan before 1979, crimes similar to that of rape. The ordinance has the following consequences: first, it is impossible to inflict the severe *ḥadd* punishment on the rapist because of the high standard of proof required. Second, for *ḥadd* punishment a woman's evidence has no value, in other words, the testimony of rape victims has less weight than the testimony of Muslim males. Third, for punishment of rape under *taʿzīr* a woman runs the risk of being accused of fornication/adultery if she fails to convince the court that rape has taken place. Fourth, the offence of fornication/adultery lies so close to the offence of rape that the severity of the rape offence as a serious crime is reduced.

Law of murder

The Criminal Law Amendment Ordinance VII of 1990, popularly known as the Qisas and Diyat Ordinance, subsequently became the Criminal Law Amendment Act 1997, which was passed without significant parliamentary or public debate. As part of the process of Islamization, it replaced the sections of the Pakistan Penal Code relating to murder and manslaughter and covers all offences against the human body. One profound change it effected is that direct control over cases involving murder does not lie with the state. Under Islamic law, the punishment for murder can either be in the form of *qiṣāṣ* (equal punishment for the crime committed) or *diya* (compensation payable to the victim's legal heirs). The act discriminates against women as victims and as heirs of victims.

The new law sets *diya* or blood money as punishment for unintentional murder (*qatl bi-sabab*) and in certain categories of murder (for example grave and sudden provocation) the court only has discretion to award *diya* and imprisonment of up to 14 years as *taʿzīr*. This is detrimental to the rights of women and the poor. Moreover, if a husband murders a wife by whom he has a child the case is treated differently from instances where strangers are involved; he cannot be sentenced to a normal penalty of death under section 302 of the Pakistan Penal Code. Instead a lesser punishment of *diya* is enforced, approximately US$ 4,500, and the court may additionally sentence him up to a maximum of 14 years imprisonment.

Women as the heirs of victims are also discriminated against under this law. In the matter of the disbursement of *diya* women have been treated unequally or altogether excluded:

(1) The law has made offences relating to the human body compoundable. Legal heirs have the right to negotiate with the offender under sections 309 and 310. Under section 309, legal heirs can forgive the murderer in the name of God without receiving any monetary compensation in the form of *diya*, while under section 310 the legal heirs can compromise after receiving *diya* in their respective shares. The minimum value of the blood-money is provided for under Section 323 PPC and is fixed by the federal government for each fiscal year. This varies according to the price of silver. The criteria for the distribution of blood-money are to be decided in accordance with the inheritance shares of men and women in Islam, which are not equal.

(2) In the matter of the compounding of *qiṣāṣ* (*ṣulḥ*) in *qatl-i-amd*, a mother of minor children having the right to waive *qiṣāṣ* may be excluded from speaking or deciding on behalf of her children. Under section 310, the right to compound *qiṣāṣ* in *qatl-i-amd* rests with the *walī* (heir). Under section 310(2) read with section 313, if a *walī* is a minor or insane, the right to compound vests in their father or in his absence in the paternal grandfather. If the minor or insane person has no living father or grandfather, the right to compound *qiṣāṣ* devolves upon the government, thus excluding altogether the mother and grandmothers.

Witnesses

The 1984 Evidence Act, known as the Qanun-e-Shahadat Order brought in substantial amendments to the 1872 Evidence Act. Section 17 of the 1984 act provides that in "matter pertaining to financial or future obligations," the testimony of "two men, or one man and two women" is required; and in all other matters, the testimony of one man or one woman, according to what the court may accept. In *ḥudūd* cases women are not considered capable of appearing as witnesses at all for the crimes mentioned in the four ordinances, namely, the Offences Against Property (Enforcement of Hudood) Ordinance, VI, 1979; the Offence of Zina (Enforcement of Hudood) Ordinance, 1979; the Offence of Qazf (Enforcement of Hadd) Ordinance, VIII, 1979; and the Prohibition (Enforcement of Hadd) Ordinance.

BIBLIOGRAPHY

A. R. Changez, The law of qisas and diyat, in *Pakistan Times*, 23 August 1984.

A. Jahangir, Stoning to death in Pakistan, in *Lawyers*, February–March 1988, 28–33.

A. Jahangir and H. Jilani, *The Hudood Ordinance. A divine sanction?*, Lahore 1990.

R. Mehdi, The offence of rape in the Islamic law of Pakistan, in *International Journal of the Sociology of Law* 18 (1990), 19–29.

——, *The Islamization of the law in Pakistan*, Richmond, U.K. 1994.

R. Patel, *Women and law in Pakistan*, Karachi 1979.

——, *Islamization of laws in Pakistan?*, Karachi 1986.

R. Shehab, Diyat of women in Islamic law, in *All Pakistan Legal Decisions* 36 (1984), 84–6.

Simorgh Collective and S. Hussain, *Rape in Pakistan*, Lahore 1990.

Women protest against qisas-diyat law, in *Viewpoint*, 16 August 1984.

RUBYA MEHDI

Turkey

Article 10/1 of the constitution of the Republic of Turkey provides for equality before the law: "All individuals are equal before the law, irrespective of language, race, color, sex, political opinion, philosophical belief, religion and sect, or similar considerations." However, some clauses in the Turkish Penal Code violate the principle of equality and some *de facto* situations discriminate against women as well.

Felonious acts that violate sexual freedom are described in "Felonies against Public Decency and Family Order," and are considered violations of public decency and family order. But there is no word for rape in the Turkish language. Instead, the act is described as behavior that "dishonor(s) or ravish(es) someone's honor or attack(s) someone's chastity." In other words, rape dishonors public decency and family honor. Males can be raped, but it is normally assumed that a rape victim is a female whose body is the property of her family, her husband, or the public. Thus, there is an article in the Penal Code (article 423) concerning the taking of a girl's virginity: "Whoever deprives a girl of 15 of her virginity by promising marriage shall be imprisoned for six months to two years." If victim and perpetrator marry, prosecution and punishment is suspended. However, if the wife sues for divorce within five years, public prosecution is revived or the punishment previously adjudged is executed.

The age of consent is 15 in Turkey. "Whoever ravishes a child under the age of 15 (the age of consent) shall be punished by imprisonment for not less than five years." Further, "when the offence is committed with force, violence, or threats or is committed against an child who cannot resist because of mental or physical defects . . . imprisonment shall not be less than ten years." Thus, all sexual intercourse with a person under 15 years of age is considered rape, regardless of the victim's sex.

A new Penal Code is now being debated between women's groups and the Commission of Justice. Article 429 of the Turkish Penal Code defines the penalty for abduction: "Whoever abducts a woman who has reached majority legally or by judicial decree and uses force, violence, threats or fraud, influenced by lascivious feelings or with the intent of marriage, shall be punished by imprisonment for three to ten years . . . If the abducted person is a married woman, imprisonment may not be less than seven years." Legislation accords more importance and respect to married women than unmarried women. The Penal Code (Article 434) states that "if the abducted girl or woman marries the accused, prosecution and/or punishment shall be suspended." If the couple divorces, the prosecution can be renewed and a previously rendered punishment can be executed. Thus the victim is forced to marry her abductor to protect her family honor.

Adultery was a crime according to Articles 440 and 441 of the Penal Code but as a result of a campaign by women's non-governmental organizations, the Turkish Constitutions Court decriminalized male adultery as in 1996 and female adultery in 1998. Adultery is no longer a crime and can only be a ground for divorce (Civil Code, Article 161).

Homicide is a serious crime. In the case of a "malicious murder of a newborn child to protect the dignity and reputation of the offender or of his wife, mother, daughter, grandchild, adopted daughter or sister, the offender shall be punished by imprisonment for five to ten years" (Penal Code, Article 453.e). Formerly, the murder of a family member was punished by death. In accord with European Union laws, capital punishment has been abolished, and the murder of a family member is now punished by life imprisonment.

In principle abortion is no longer a felony, but under certain circumstances it is punishable. The last of three articles in a chapter on "Felonies Regulating Lineage" in the Penal Code states: "Whoever commits one of the offences in the foregoing articles to protect the reputation of himself, his wife, mother, sister, descendant or adopted daughter, shall be imprisoned for one month to three years."

Another exception to the decriminalization of abortion based on protecting family honor is in "Felonies against the Integrity and Health of the Race." The punishment for felonies lessens if the crime is committed to "preserve the pride and reputation of oneself or a relative" (Article 472).

Worst of all was Article 462 which regulated the reduction of punishment in "passion crimes," but in reality applied to all "crimes of honor." This article was annulled by the Turkish National Assembly in June 2003 to satisfy the European Union.

Bibliography

Türk ceza kanunu 765, approved 1 March 1926, published in *Resmi Gazete* 320, 13 March 1926.

Türk medeni kanunu 4721, approved 22 November 2001, published in *Resmi Gazete* 24607, 8 December 2001, enacted 1 January 2002.

Cânân Arin

Law: Cultural Defense

Overview

Definition

The cultural defense is a legal strategy used sometimes in criminal cases in United States courts to excuse, justify, or mitigate criminal conduct. It is the admission of cultural evidence to explain the behavior of the defendant. Most often the accused is an immigrant, and in such cases the defense lawyer argues that judges and juries must consider such factors as "culture" when assessing the evidence against the accused. This form of defense is grounded in the argument that newcomers to the United States may be insufficiently assimilated to United States standards of conduct, and that foreign behavioral norms compel then to act outside United States law. Thus the accused may have acted under the influence of a particular custom or culture that is adverse to the standards of the host society, and should be considered less culpable under the law. The cultural defense seldom leads to an acquittal of the accused. Instead, it is used to argue for a mitigation of the penalty, seeking reduced criminal charges and/or a reduced sentence. The main point of the cultural defense is that people who are foreign, when acting in accord with the norms of their native culture, should not be held fully accountable under United States law for conduct that conforms to the prescriptions and proscriptions of the culture of their countries of origin.

While seemingly at odds with United States standards of individualized justice, the cultural defense fits within the existing framework in criminal law that assesses various degrees of culpability in considerations of intention, knowledge, recklessness, and negligence. United States courts recognize various defenses involving state of mind or diminished mental capacity, such as the insanity defense or the post-traumatic stress disorder defense. The cultural defense is similar to these types of defenses in that it recognizes how environment affects and defines an individual's rationality. The cultural defense asserts a causal connection between environment and law, and elaborates that connection in the context of an individual defendant on trial. The essence of the cultural defense in legal analysis rests on the contextualization of the offense(s) with which the defendant is charged, saying that the social system must bear part of the responsibility for the crime.

One type of cultural defense case involves a defendant carrying out customs that are accepted in his or her native land but outlawed in the United States. The defendant's argument is that "I may have committed a crime, but back home it is not a crime, and I should be judged by the laws of my country of origin." An example of this is the case of Mohammed Kargar, an Afghani refugee, who was convicted in 1996 by a state court in Maine on two counts of sexual assault after he was reported to have "kissed" his 18-month-old son's genitals. It was argued through expert testimony at a court hearing that the act would have been considered a customary show of a father's affection for his child in Afghanistan, with no sexual feelings involved.

Ultimately Kargar's cultural defense strategy was vindicated on appeal, as the Maine Supreme Court vacated his conviction on the grounds that his conduct had not been envisaged by the Maine legislature when it had enacted the penal statute on sexual assault. Kargar's conduct, motivated by paternal feelings and not by sexual gratification, was deemed to be something outside the parameters set by the law that criminalized sexually deviant and harmful behavior. The highest court in Maine held that "although it may be difficult for us as a society to separate Kargar's conduct from our notions of sexual abuse, that difficulty should not result in a felony conviction in this case" (*State v Kargar*, 679 A2d 81 [1996 Me. LEXIS 162] @ 85). However, the court also stipulated that the defendant must now know that the practice of genital kissing is prohibited by law in the United States, regardless of the motive. The Maine Supreme Court wrote, "Kargar does not argue that he should now be permitted to practice that which is accepted in his culture" (*State v Kargar*, 679 A2d 81 [1996 Me. LEXIS 162] @ 85, n. 5). The cultural defense was successful here because it did not raise the specter of permanence. Instead it conveyed the idea that assimilation is an integrative process, and newcomers must abandon questionable or offensive practices accepted in their countries of origin and learn to conform to United States legal and cultural standards. Kargar is not criminally liable for his past conduct given his present repudiation of the practice, even though the conduct itself remains criminal. While the courts may show mercy to defendants such as Kargar in an early stage of their assimilation, it is argued, maintenance of separate normative orders is not envisaged under the law.

The second type of cultural defense strategy argues that the defendant's state of mind was heavily influenced by cultural factors at the time of the commission of the offense(s). Here the judge is expected to take into consideration the defendant's state of mind and decide whether cultural factors played an aggravating role, in which case the charges might be reduced (for example, from second-degree murder to voluntary manslaughter). For example, in the case of a Sikh woman from Punjab, India, who attempted to kill her two children and then take her own life after she discovered her husband's infidelity, the argument was not that such parent-child murder-suicide attempts are accepted in India, but that conflicting cultural norms pressured the defendant and resulted in her feelings of disorientation and abandonment when it became clear her husband wanted a divorce. Illiterate and confined in an arranged marriage, the defendant, Narinder Virk, could not speak English, had no friends or employment and allegedly was abused by her husband. According to her attorney, Virk was trapped in the roles of a subservient wife and mother, and was driven to madness by a culture that measured her value by her domestic abilities and the success of her marriage, and threatened to disown her and her children if she failed. Expert testimony at the trial was used to argue that Virk's despair at her situation was exacerbated by the cultural standards in which she had been reared. Culture in this circumstance is viewed as contributing to the defendant's impaired mental state. Sometimes extreme emotional disturbance may only be understandable in a particular cultural context (see Piccalo 2000).

Examples of cultural defense cases

In the United States, "culture" has become an increasingly common defense in recent years, as defendants assert that a person's cultural background is relevant under the law. Historically the idea that culture matters has been encountered in cases as early as the 1920s, where judges in a number of cases accepted a defense based on cultural differences. For instance, Italian immigrants referred to "culture" to defend themselves against statutory rape charges when they seduced and married young Italian-American women without their parents' consent (Cleghorn). Most often the defense strategy that seeks the admission of cultural evidence to benefit the defendant has been associated with patriarchal practices that are harmful to women's interests (Coleman 1996, Maguigan 1995, Volpp 1994, 2000, 2003).

At the end of the twentieth century many reported cultural defense cases involved family relations. For example, in 1987 in New York a Chinese-born man, upon learning of his wife's infidelity, used a claw hammer to strike his wife in the head eight times until she was dead. At trial an anthropology professor from Hunter College testified on the defendant's behalf, explaining that in Chinese culture a woman's adultery is severely punished because it is proof of her husband's weak character and is "an enormous stain" on the reputation of himself, his offspring, and his ancestors (cited in Renteln 2003, 34). In China, the expert continued, a husband often becomes enraged and threatens to kill his unfaithful wife. However, the close-knit community usually intervenes and prevents the husband from carrying out his threat. The defendant's case was premised on the absence of a local Chinese community that would have presumably restrained the enraged husband and protected the intended victim. The court found the defendant guilty of the lesser crime of second degree manslaughter and sentenced him to five years probation.

In another case, in a Los Angeles suburb in 1994 the attorney for a man who had beaten his wife to death argued that the murder victim had violated the norms of their Iranian Jewish community by serving her husband – the defendant – a bologna sandwich on the eve of the Persian New Year, an occasion usually celebrated with a feast. Further evidence brought to light by the defense at trial demonstrated that the victim had continually ridiculed her husband in front of relatives and friends, calling him "stupid" and making him sleep on the floor, again violating the norms of Persian culture by undermining his dominance in the marital relationship. In his opening statement, the defense attorney promised the jury that they would hear evidence "about a culture that is vastly different from yours and mine," one that is male-dominated and pious (Moore 2002, 196). In this case the judge lowered the charges from first degree murder to voluntary manslaughter. The jury convicted the defendant on the lesser charge and he was sentenced to serve an eleven-year prison term.

Trials of persons accused of child molestation have also involved the cultural defense. An Albanian Muslim man named Sadri Krasniqi was arrested for allegedly molesting his four-year-old daughter during a martial arts exhibition in suburban Dallas, Texas, in 1989. Although Krasniqi was acquitted of criminal charges in 1994, due in part to the expert testimony of an anthropologist who argued that the touching of a child's genitalia is not considered sexual in Albania, he and his wife permanently lost the custody of their children in family court. Many Muslims in Dallas and nationwide were angered by the outcome of this case because of the court's severance of parental rights before the accused came to trial in a criminal court and the adoption of the Krasniqi children by a family who had the children convert to Christianity. In response to public protest, the judge involved in the civil case publicly refused to apologize and wrote that Krasniqi's defense in criminal court had been based on the offensive assertion that "molesting young girls is acceptable in Muslim culture" (Moore 2002, 198).

The judge in the Krasniqi case puts his finger on the problem with the cultural defense strategy. The argument that culture determines an individual's behavior imagines culture to be fixed and bounded as a static set of rules, beliefs, values, and institutions, instead of being a heterogeneous set of discourses and practices that are constantly being transformed through particular historical events and exchanges and through the activities of individuals. Particular constructions of "culture'" embedded in legal defenses associate offensive or questionable cultural factors with people who are then seen as primitive, unchanging, and inferior to United States standards of conduct. Thus, the assertion that touching a young child is acceptable in certain countries and cultures generalizes from the instance of the actions of one man to condemn the world's substantial Muslim population. The generalizations the cultural defense allows validate the core images of Islam and Muslims already structured in the dominant discourses.

Attempts have been made in the United States Congress to ban the use of the cultural defense in United States courtrooms in certain circumstances. In the case of female genital mutilation (FGM) – also known as female genital surgery or female circumcision – United States federal law adopted in the wake of the heavily publicized asylum case of Fauziya Kasinga in 1996 criminalized the practice of FGM in the United States and forbade any consideration of cultural imperatives in the defense against criminal charges arising from this practice. The law prohibits the court to consider the effect of any belief that the practice of FGM is required as a matter of custom or ritual. However, this has been construed as an inappropriate prohibition since the question of cultural belief is directly relevant to the state of mind of the defendant: at the time of the commission of the act for which he is criminally charged, did he have the requisite criminal intent? (see Maguigan 1999). For those who continue practices that have a cultural basis, cultural evidence continues to be admitted in court because it relates to the state of mind of the defendant.

Bibliography

K. H. Cleghorn, *The immigrant's day in court*, New York 1923, repr. 1969.

D. L. Coleman, Individualizing justice through multiculturalism. The liberal's dilemma, in *Columbia Law Review* 96 (1996), 1093–1167.

H. Maguigan, Cultural evidence and male violence. Are feminists and multiculturalist reformers on a collision course in criminal courts?, in *New York University Law Review* 36 (1995), 36–99.

——, Will prosecutions for "female genital mutilation" stop the practice in the U.S.?, in *Temple Political and Civil Rights Law Review* 8 (1999), 391–423.

K. Moore, Representations of Islam in the language of law. Some recent U.S. cases, in Y. Y. Haddad (ed.), *Muslims in the West. From sojourners to citizens*, New York 2002, 187–204.

G. Piccalo, Attorneys to cite similar incident in drowning case defense. Courts saying cultural values caused woman to kill her children. Lawyers will recall 1985 episode, in *Los Angeles Times*, 17 February 2000, Metro, Part B, 11.

A. D. Renteln, *The cultural defense*, New York 2003.

State v Kargar, 679 A2d 81 (Me 1996).

L. Volpp, (Mis)identifying culture. Asian women and the "cultural defense," in *Harvard Women's Law Journal* 17 (1994), 57–101.

——, Blaming culture for bad behavior, in *Yale Journal of Law and the Humanities* 12 (2000), 89–116.

——, On culture, difference and domestic violence, in *American University Journal of Gender, Social Policy and the Law* 11 (2003), 393ff.

Kathleen M. Moore

Law: Customary

Afghanistan

Customary law in Afghanistan needs to be understood in the context of the semi-autonomous segregated societies that have made up the Afghan landscape. These are self-defined by ethnicity or geographical location/boundaries. As the practice of customary law can be an identifying marker of a geographical group or ethnicity, legislation in the case of Afghan customary law needs to be understood outside the more common state-bound usage. Legislation occurs where adjudication takes place by the person who judges or arbitrates. Since there are no written codified laws in Afghan customary legal contexts and there is only a vague sense of precedence, legislation is the enactment of laws that are neither codified nor part of a corpus of state or regional laws. Rather, village councils (*jirga* or *shūra*) and leaders draw upon a variety of legal systems including local customs, tribal laws, Islamic law (Sharīʿa), and state laws. Village leaders are interested in reaching a decision which is most acceptable to the mood of the community at the time the matter under arbitration occurred, and which will be in the best interests of the community as a whole. The village community is, therefore, able to maintain a specific social order and religious-ethnic identity through village members enacting the norms of their customary law codes. In some cases, ethnic/geographical identity is intertwined with religious identity, hardly distinct from it, so that practicing customary law is the same as practicing Islamic law. Women are legislators of Afghan customary law in that they arbitrate like Afghan men both at the village level (though infrequently) and at the extended family level. There are only rare exceptional cases where women village leaders are members of the men's village councils.

As documented before the Soviet invasion, Afghan women, especially in sedentary and semi-sedentary societies, have their own sphere of legislative jurisdiction. Despite separate spheres, men have control over decisions affecting greater numbers of people and over allocations of larger resources, maintaining disparity of power distribution. Men and women in this kind of society inhabit separate worlds, yet together they contribute to the sustenance of the whole community. Anthropologists such as Audrey Shalinsky or Nancy Lindisfarne (formerly Tapper) search for women's authority or lack thereof by focusing on the boundaries in Afghan society that demarcated the public and private spheres. Through this lens men have control of the public sphere, where the "real" power is located, and women have control/authority over limited parts of the private sphere, with at best, the "soft" power of persuasion to influence men's decisions. In searching for women's power in men's public spheres, a few exceptional cases of female leaders can be found, for example, Nazo Anna (d. ca. 1715), the legendary "Mother of Afghan Nationalism," or Zarghona Anna (d. ca. 1772), who maintained governance in the capital of the early Afghan confederacy, while her son Aḥmad Shāh was away on military expeditions. However, by fine-tuning the perspective of where women's spaces are located, a very different picture of everyday women's authority and power in customary law practices can be revealed.

By looking at both gendered boundaries and private/public space boundaries through their homosocial organization, a new light can be shed on the power and authority women possess, especially in the sedentary and semi-sedentary societies of Afghanistan. "Homosocial" implies that men and women work and socialize almost exclusively with the same gender. However, the boundaries are porous and overlap where youth and elderly cross, and in certain circumstances such as celebrations or work environments.

In Afghan women's spaces, women gain authority through social networks, honorable reputation, seniority, and control of familial resources. Women who achieve authority and become village and family leaders arbitrate conflicts ranging from theft to stopping a revenge cycle (*badal*). In the case of the customary law code of the Pashtuns, Pashtunwali, under the rule of *nanawati* (literally, to enter into the security of a house) women leaders go to the houses of the feuding families and arbitrate a way for the conflict to stop, which the host must accept, especially if the leader who enters the house is from the enemy's family. These female leaders are at the top of their social hierarchies in the village or family and do not legislate through formal councils as men at the village level do. While it may seem that decisions are made unilaterally by the female leader, they are preceded by levels of informal consultation among the women since an unpopular decision would reduce the authority of the leader. The leader's control gives those whose conflicts she arbitrates incentives to follow her legislation, as she may withhold resources or contracts from those who do not.

Men are able to overturn women's decisions, especially those related to marriage and sexual misconduct of women. According to customary law codes, women have been given in marriage as blood compensation in the resolution of conflicts, or to alleviate a family's economic distress caused by high bride-price. If a woman's sexual conduct comes into question, customary law allows and sometimes encourages honor killings. Men legislate decisions that affect both the men's and the women's spheres of the family, such as reputation or economic situation. In other words, women have legislative control as long as the conflicts are within their jurisdiction only.

This view of women's authority is based in documented examples as well as in tropes in Afghan folk stories and poetry. However, over 25 years of war and displacement have left women's spheres and networks in tatters. Customary law is a continually evolving process and much of women's power of decision and control of resources has been lost due to the continual unrest and fear the war situation created. More displaced women are forced into types of seclusion they were unused to in their villages: they have to wear a *bughra* (*burqaʿ*) in the streets around their homes and they are cut off from their social networks. With the breakdown of women's social networks and spheres men gain more control over women's legislative power.

Bibliography

A. Ahmed, *Millennium and charisma among Pathans. A critical essay in social anthropology*, London 1976.

F. Barth, *Political leadership among Swat Pathans*, London 1965.

H. Christensen, *The reconstructions of Afghanistan. A chance for rural Afghan women*, Geneva 1990.

M. M. Ismati, *The position and role of Afghan women in Afghanistan*, Kabul 1987.

P. Kakar, Tribal law of Pashtunwali and women's legislative authority, in P. Bearman and F. Vogel (ed.), *Afghan legal history project*, Harvard University Press (forthcoming).

E. Knabe, Afghan women. Does their role change?, in L. Dupree and L. Albert (eds.), *Afghanistan in the 1970s*, New York 1974, 144–66.

N. Lindisfarne (Tapper), *Bartered brides. Politics, gender and marriage in an Afghan tribal society*, Cambridge 1991.

A. Pont, *Blind chickens and social animals*, Portland, Or. 2001.

F. Rahimi, *Women in Afghanistan*, Leistal 1986.

A. Shalinsky, *Long years of exile*, New York 1994.

Palwasha L. Kakar

The Caucasus

From the tenth to the nineteenth centuries, a dual system of customary law (*ʿāda*) and Sharīʿa developed in the Caucasus. The absence of a state system and state law favored the lasting preservation of *ʿāda* in North Caucasus. Three kinds of customary law can be distinguished: pre-reformation customary law (fifteenth to mid-nineteenth century), reformed customary law (second half of nineteenth to early twentieth century), and customary law of the Soviet and post-Soviet period (1920 to the 1990s).

The pre-reformation North Caucasian customary law can be described as an unwritten law combined with a community control system. The exception is Daghestan where systematization of *ʿāda* was carried out in the fifteenth to eighteenth centuries and customary law was written down in Arabic.

The reformed customary law developed after the Russian-Caucasian war, under the influence of the active policy of the Russian Empire in the Caucasus, legal reforms in the Russian Empire between 1860 and the 1910s, and the incorporation of the North Caucasian peoples into Russian state power and law system. *ʿĀda* was codified and made an element of Russian state law applicable in North Caucasus. Governmental verification of compliance with *ʿāda* court decisions (Kabardian *mendetyr*, Turkic *tere*, Ossetian *tarhon lagi* or *tarhoni lagtae*, Russian *mediatorskiy, posrednicheskiy*, or *treteiskiy* [arbitral]) and a system of fines for noncompliance were introduced. Legal procedure was still verbal, while the *ʿāda* court decisions began to be written down throughout North Caucasus.

The *ʿāda* decision included the following: composition of the court, names, ages, and social status of the judges; a brief description of the case; the amount of compensation; conditions and terms of payment; and arrangement of the conciliatory feast. The document was signed by every judge.

Rights and duties to the communal authorities and the court under *ʿāda* law were unequal. Factors that influenced the application of the *ʿāda* norms were: class hierarchy (Kabardian *uork habze*, code of honor of princes and uzdens), age and sex of the participants in the conflict, and the extent of the influence of Islam and Sharīʿa on *ʿāda* within the specific society.

Expansion of *ʿāda* within the ethnic communities of the Caucasus was conditioned by the degree of Islamization and establishment of legal standards of Islam (Sharīʿa) in all areas of the civil and criminal legislation. The Sharīʿa was implemented most strongly in Northeastern Caucasus (Daghestan, Azerbaijan). Criminal cases were usually tried according to the ʿ*āda* standards, and civil cases (mainly family) according to the norms of the Sharīʿa.

Underlying customary law is a collective sense of justice: any crime is harm done to the collective. The basic principles of Caucasian ʿ*āda* are vengeance for damage (blood feud) and reparation of damages (payment of compensation, blood money). Woman are part of a collective – the family or clan – and are defended by the (male) collective. According to the ʿ*āda*, a woman is not a legal person. The main types of harm done to Caucasian women are insult, rape, physical damage (wound or murder), abduction of the bride without her consent, non-payment of *kalym*, and neglect of her share of the property or inheritance being partitioned. Caucasian forms of insult include an alien man taking off the kerchief from the head of a married woman or violating the taboo on entering the female half of the house, and the smearing of the girl's house door with tar. The main types of harm perpetrated by Caucasian women include insults, quarrels, fights, and adultery.

ʿ*Āda* was used to try most crimes concerned with the life of Caucasian women. Some wrongs were not considered by either ʿ*āda* or Sharīʿa. Rapes were in most cases settled by marriage of the victim and the rapist. Punishment for rape depended on the class status of both victim and rapist as well as the woman's marital status: the rape of a married woman was considered a more important crime and could not be settled by means of marriage and, as in a case of murder, vengeance followed.

The perpetrator of vengeance (*krovnik*, one who was to take revenge, "bearer of blood") was the husband or a brother. A woman could not be an object of vengeance, even if she had incited a fight or brawl. Killing a boy was considered less offensive than killing a woman.

Harm done to a Caucasian woman (insult, wound, murder) necessitated the payment of compensation. The blood money for a woman was half as much as for a man. Another ʿ*āda* norm was also practiced: compulsory ejection of the collective (the criminal and his family) from the village (temporarily or permanently). Women were ejected along with men. In such cases, a woman indirectly shared legal responsibility for the crime committed by her husband. If the criminal was a woman, then a man (husband, brother, father) was legally responsible for it.

From 1920, when state law was established within the territory of the Soviet Union, ʿ*āda* standards have been applied fragmentarily and illegally. Women's rights and duties related to vengeance for damage (women have become an object of vengeance) and reparation of damages (in case of rape, the settlement of the conflict by means of marriage is used everywhere) have partly changed.

BIBLIOGRAPHY
(all works cited are in Russian)

PRIMARY SOURCES
V. K. Gardanov (comp.), *Material on Kabardian customary law*, Nalchik 1956.
Gidatlinsky ʿāda, Makhachkala 1957.
H. O. Khashaev (comp.), *Monuments of the Daghestan customary law of the seventeenth to nineteenth centuries*, Moscow 1965.
M. M. Kovalevskiy, *Law and tradition in the Caucasus*, 2 vols., Moscow 1890.
——, *ʿĀda of the Daghestan region and Zakatalsky Krai*, Tbilisi 1899.
F. I. Leontovich, *Caucasian ʿāda*, 2 vols., Odessa 1882.

SECONDARY SOURCES
I. L. Babich, *The evolution of legal culture of Adygs*, Moscow 1999.
V. O. Bobrovnikov, *The Muslims of North Caucasus*, Moscow 2002.
Customary law in Russia, Rostov-in-Don 1999.
H. M. Dumanov, *The customary law of property in Kabardian society*, Halchik 1976.
A. A. Pliev, *The blood revenge of Chechens*, Moscow 1969.

IRINA BABICH

Central Asia

The legal heritage of Central Asia comprises a multi-layered heritage of ancient Turkic and Persian traditions, Islam (since the seventh century C.E.), and Soviet law and practice (Kamp 1998). This is especially true for the "stans" (Kazakhstan, Kyrgyzstan, Tajikistan, Turkmenistan, and Uzbekistan), but Mongolia and Afghanistan were also heavily influenced by Soviet conceptions. Post-Soviet law has continued to reproduce Soviet norms, as well as drawing from legal reforms in the Russian Federation, and the United Nations human rights conventions now ratified by all these states.

Nomadic cultures were established in Central Asia by around 1700 B.C.E. The area was periodically overrun by Persians, Huns, Chinese, Mongols, and, with the advent of Islam, Arabs. Islam reached Central Asia only 20 years after the death of the Prophet Muḥammad, and during the Middle Ages Islamic art, philosophy, and law flourished in the kingdoms of Korasan, Bukhara, Herat, and

Samarkand (IFL 2000). The majority of Muslims in Central Asia belonged to the Sunnī Ḥanafī sect, the most liberal of the four Sunnī schools, so that Christians, Hindus, Sikhs, and Jews have also had significant influence.

Conditions of life for women varied greatly before Soviet control. The pre-Soviet Kazakhs had no tradition of veiling or seclusion, while in Islamic Bukhara women were routinely secluded or completely veiled in public. Tajik women also were almost totally secluded.

However from the seventh century, women in most of Central Asia had, according to Islamic law, the right to inherit, own, and sell both movable and immovable property. Women acquired wealth and property through marriage arrangements and through inheritance. A man was obliged by law to give his bride *mahr*, a negotiated amount of money, jewels or other property, which became her own possessions, subject to her own disposal, and which served as two-thirds of her settlement if her husband divorced her (Kamp 1998). Islamic inheritance law provided that a man's property was divided among his children first, with sons receiving a share twice as large as that of a daughter. Nevertheless, daughters received an inheritance too.

Once the Soviet Union gained complete control of the region, it abolished Sharīʿa law, and made polygamy and bride price illegal. Most of the region's 24,000 mosques were closed, pilgrimage to Mecca was prohibited, and printing and distribution of the Qurʾān was banned.

There are however a number of respects in which customary law has persisted through the Islamic and Soviet periods into the present day.

Research has shown that for Kyrgyz and other nomad peoples of Central Asia, shame and respect are the factors that sustain customary law, which is used more often than written law in relation to family and community relations (Giovarelli and Akmatova 2002). For example, Kyrgyz women interviewed in 2000 said that the custom they would most like to change is that of slaughtering as many animals at funerals as any other participant, which, despite official attempts at reform, remains strong, because of the effect of shame on the family.

Customary law has a number of other features. First is the strongly patrilineal and patrilocal family structure prevalent in most of the region, together with the influence of clan allegiances.

A second is the strong ethnic tradition predating Islam: the "cult of fertility," consequent high birthrate, and accompanying child mortality (Tabyshalieva 1998).

Third is the increasing prevalence in Uzbekistan and Turkmenistan of polygamous marriages. Although contrary to criminal law and religious law – they cannot formally be performed by a mullah – such marriages are in Uzbekistan often conducted in the mosque. In Turkmenistan polygamy is not only traditional, but is officially permitted.

Fourth, bride kidnappings (mostly consensual – often in fact elopement) are especially common among former nomadic peoples such as the Turkmen, Kyrgyz, and Kazakh. The real scale of kidnapping without the consent of the bride, especially in remote rural areas, is unclear. There are no programs to eliminate this practice, and discussion of it remains a taboo (Tabyshalieva 1998). Recent research shows that the shame of being unmarried after age 30 appears to be more intolerable than to be stolen because traditional society is so cruel to unmarried women and men (Giovarelli and Akmatova 2002).

Where conflicts exist between customary law and written law, customary law often takes precedence in rural areas, because written law fails to reflect the reality of the villagers' lives. For example, written law does not have the notion of family property or household property (where the land is held by whoever is in the family at that time). Judges are known to use provisions of the procedural code to sanction customary law over written law in such cases.

Bibliography

G. Capdevila, Central Asian women increasingly targeted by traffickers, IPS World News 17 August 2003, <http://www.oneworld.org/ips2/aug01 /23_56_072.html>.

R. Giovarelli and C. Akmatova, Local institutions that enforce customary law in the Kyrgyz Republic and their impact on women's rights, World Bank, Washington, D.C. March 2002, <http://lnweb18.worldbank.org/ESSD/ ardext.nsf/22ByDocName/Publications>.

IFL (Islamic Family Law), *Legal datasheet for Central Asia and Caucasus*, 2000, <http://www.law.emory.edu/IFL/region/centralasia.html>.

N. Ismagilova, Women in mind. Educational needs of women in Central Asia – general recommendations and strategies for development (2001), <http://www.mtuforum.org/resources/library/ismano2a.htm>.

M. Kamp, Land for women, too. Islam, communism, and land reform in Uzbekistan, 1925–1928, in *Columbia Caspian project. Women in Central Asia. The politics of change*, 15 August 1998, <http://www.sipa.columbia/ resources/caspian/wom_p12.html>.

F. Najibullah, Central Asia. Women's rights activists push for higher marriage age, *Radio Free Europe/Radio Liberty*, 10 February 2003, <http://www.rferl.org/nca/features/2003/02/10022003154421.asp>.

A. Tabyshalieva, Revival of traditions in post-Soviet Central Asia, 1998, <http://www.ifrs.elcat.kg/Publication/Anara>.

——, Central Asia. Increasing gender inequality, 2000, <http://www.ifrs.elcat.kg/Publication/Anara>.

M. Tokhtakhodjaeva, Women in Central Asian society, in *Women Against Fundamentalisms* 4 (1992/3), 29–31, <http://waf.gn.apc.org/j4p29.htm>.
Women Living Under Muslim Laws (WLUML), Uzbekistan. Polygamy in Central Asia, 31 October 2003, <http://www.wluml.org/english/>.

Bill Bowring

The Gulf and Yemen

Customary law is the term used for written and unwritten codes of conduct in rural tribal communities, both settled and nomadic, in the Gulf and Yemen. Urban communities in the region maintain that their legal systems are based on Sharīʿa, or Qurʾānic law, in contrast to rural systems based on custom. In reality, there has been considerable mutual borrowing between rural custom and urban law, especially in neighboring communities. Details of customary law vary with time and place, but rules always valorize the components of tribal honor: collective responsibility, autonomy, generosity, hospitality, the protection of the weak, equality within the tribal population, the sanctity of contract, and the importance of mediation. Known simply as "custom" in Arabic (*ʿurf, silf*) customary law not only specifies formal mechanisms for settling disputes within and between communities but also reciprocal obligations between and within kin groups. These are considered obligatory. For example, a woman in rural Yemen who attended a large wedding planning to dance among the guests was called upon by the hostess, "Oh wife of my cousin, come help knead dough [for the guests]." The guest ruefully acknowledged, "True, I am your cousin's wife," and joined the cooks in the kitchen. In this case, the hostess presented an obligation recognized as binding within this system (Adra 1982). By the same token, a guest can deride a stingy hostess or host in public because hospitality is not considered a personal issue but a social obligation (Adra 1982).

There are no accepted mechanisms of coercion in traditional tribal society in the Arabian Peninsula. A shaykh or mediator's influence is persuasive rather than coercive. In formal dispute mediation, an animal is sacrificed and/or money is handed over to signal that a settlement has been reached. Disputing parties generally share a meal to make the settlement binding. The basic format for mediation includes lengthy discussions in which each side presents its case until consensus is reached about the degree of blame and appropriate amends or reparations. The same format is followed informally in disputes within a household, or, with more serious intercommunity criminal acts or warfare, it may involve mediators from outside the community who are paid for their efforts.

Within a community, if women or men quarrel, others close to them (women or men) will try to mediate the dispute. The offender will be called upon to present a gift or money to make amends. If no acceptable apology or reparations are made at this point, a woman's male kin will institute formal mediation processes in which they represent her interests. Men may represent themselves.

Technically, only the testimony of mature, male tribal Muslims is accepted during formal mediation. Yet, in practice, women's input in community conflict resolution is important. During men's debates, women meet to discuss the same issues. In the evenings, women discuss the case further with husbands and brothers who then bring their opinions back to the mediation process the next day. When discussions are held in the tent dwellings of pastoralists, women participate actively, although in some areas they may do so from behind a curtain.

Disputes among women most often involve husbands or relatives through marriage. A woman who is insulted by her husband or his relatives may go to her father or brother's house in protest (*ḥanaq* in Yemen's northern highlands). Her husband is honor-bound to follow her, present her with a gift and ask her to return. In the case of repeat offenses, outside mediators may be brought in, and irreconcilable conflict may result in her family's demand for a divorce. If a man takes a second wife, his first wife almost always asks for divorce. There is no stigma attached to divorce in rural communities in this region, with serial marriage being common.

Customary law reflects the tribe's male orientation. All formal interactions between groups are negotiated through men. Rituals of tribal display, for example, *razfat al-ʿiyāla* in the Gulf, *barāʿa* performance and *zāmil* poetry in Yemen, as well as the blood feud, are male activities. Men usually represent women during legal transactions. Marriage is formally negotiated through male kin. In principle, women are kept away from the scrutiny of strangers and are not referred to by name in public. At formal functions, segregation by gender is the rule. Women, along with guests, clients, religious minorities, and children, constitute the unarmed population to whom tribesmen owe protection.

A system that is so ideologically male is, in practice, less detrimental to women than one would expect. Tribal custom's high valuation of the family and of alliances made through marriage lead to a respect for motherhood and an acknowledgment of the important roles women play in the tribal system. The birth of girls is celebrated rather than mourned as is reported elsewhere. Women's important, though informal, participation in conflict mediation reflects and inspires a corollary respect for women's intellect.

Among the most serious breaches of the principles of customary law is for a man to harm a woman, no matter what she has done to instigate his anger. Rural women's safety is thus ensured, and they enjoy considerable mobility, in contrast to urban women in the region who are secluded. Historically, during feuds and raids, women would take food and messages to their warring relatives without incurring any danger to themselves. In some places, women would bare their heads and accompany men in battle while beating drums to support their efforts. In contrast, situations have been recorded in which women, tired of war, would walk into the midst of fighting, take off their head covering or bare their breasts, thus putting their own honor on the line as an effective way of stopping the fighting.

While the laws of custom cover those aspects of tribal life that involve collective responsibility, they do not cover inheritance, marriage, economic transactions, or religious ritual, issues that fall under the rubric of personal status law. Formally, these are relegated to the domain of Islamic law. Thus, depending on the degree of her family's support, a woman may inherit land, choose her husband, or leave an unhappy marriage. On the other hand, she may not enjoy these rights if she does not have the backing of her immediate kin.

Bibliography

N. Adra, Qabyala. The tribal concept in the Central Highlands of the Yemen Arab Republic, Ph.D. diss., Temple University, Ann Arbor 1982, 104–211.

H. al-ʿAwdī, *Al-turāth al-shaʿbī wa ʿalāqatuhu bi-al-tanmiyya fī al-bilād al-nāmiyya. Dirāsa taṭbīqiyya ʿan al-mujtamaʿ al-Yamanī*, Sanʿa 1980.

D. Chatty, *Mobile pastoralists. Development, planning and social change in Oman*, New York 1996.

S. al-Muṭayrī, *Al-dīwān al-atharī. ʿĀdāt wa-turāth al-bādiya. Al-aʿrāf wa-al-muṭālaʿāt al-qabaliyya*, Kuwait 1984.

H. Qāyid, *Bādiya li-al-amārāt. Taqālīd wa ʿādāt*. U.A.E., n.d.

Najwa Adra

Indonesia

The main features of *adat* inheritance law

In Indonesian customary law (commonly called *adat*), the law of inheritance is comprised of rules governing the process of transfer and retention of family property, both material (such as land property, money, house) and immaterial (involving any legal rights and responsibilities of the deceased when alive, such as debts, mortgage, the right of land control, and similar matters), from one generation to the next (ter Haar 1950, 197). This is one aspect of *adat* substantive law that is inseparable from the law of marriage, in which the principles of life arising from a communal way of thinking are reflected very strongly in the teaching of preserving equilibrium and harmony within the family, the core component of the community structure. What makes the *adat* law of inheritance so distinct is that the process of transferring property does not focus on the death of the parents or of a particular person in one generation but is believed to have commenced with the family's original formation (Hadikusuma 1980, 18–19). Thus, although the death of a parent can be an important event for the future of the family bond, this does not mean that the transfer of property hinges on this fact, since the transfer is seen as a continuing process and can take place without any such event.

The importance of equilibrium in the community seems to be a legal foundation for dealing with transfer of property within the family, and this principle extends not only toward that which exists between man and nature but also between man and woman in the family sphere. As the welfare of the family means also in turn the welfare of the community at large, the estate transfer mechanisms should ideally be undertaken in such a way as to avoid disturbing the harmony of the family bond. Differently put, the property, whether material or immaterial, is transferred through whatever method of succession can best ensure the wellbeing of the next generation in the family, so that in turn the wellbeing of the community can be preserved. As a consequence, the mechanism of the inheritance law does not involve any complicated mathematical calculation of estate division. In principle, all the heirs can receive equal portions of the estate without consideration of gender, age, or religious belief. As long as the heirs belong to one genealogical network, the vertical transfer of property can theoretically be assumed.

On a practical level, more often than not preference is given to those heirs most in need of the estate. In this case, the economic function of the estate thus operates as a kind of primary reason for the transfer. If so, the first consideration is given not to the owner of the property in question but to the role of the estate as capital for assuring the welfare of the living members of the family. Therefore, in *adat* law, distribution of the estate can commence even while the parents are still alive. Whenever the children are in need of resources, the transfer of the property can be pursued. Nor is this regarded as a gift, because, when the parent dies, the child who had received the wealth before will not receive any further share of the estate. The main point of concern therefore lies in the variable of social justice among family members, since the main consideration is not how soon the wealth can be divided but how the estate can be used to the maximal benefit of all family members (especially children and any surviving parent) on an equal basis.

The position of women

In practical terms, the *adat* law of inheritance is inseparably linked to the clan system embraced in the community. For this reason, women can play a key role in division of the estate. Here, the procedure of transferring the estate in *adat* law theoretically follows a particular pattern depending on how the community organizes its clanship, whether along patrilineal, matrilineal, or parental lines (Hadikusuma 1991, 63–146).

In the patriarchal system, where a man is regarded as the head of the family, it is only the sons who are, theoretically, allowed to inherit the estate from the deceased. This means that women are marginalized, since the daughters or female members of the family will only receive shares if they happen to be the widow of the deceased or daughters who are entitled to be considered as sons by virtue of marriage. This pattern is found in some places that preserve the patriarchal system of clanship, such as that in Batak (North Sumatra), Lampung (Sumatra), Bali, and Rote Island in Eastern Nusa Tenggara. In many instances, the patriarchal pattern of the inheritance is characterized by a preference for designating the agnatic son – in many places the first-born son in the family – as the one responsible for the future of the whole of the family, especially when the father may be very old or incapable of taking care of the family, or even deceased. Here, the sense of the wealth as capital for the economic well-being of the family is very strong, and it is the son who seems to be the one expected to take on the economic burden. The preference shown to the son by entrusting him with the property is usually understood as giving him the means to discharge his responsibility. Thus in practice the estate is not to be divided among the heirs in advance but placed under the authority of the first-born son and kept undivided until all the heirs marry and establish their own families, at which time they usually need their share of the estate in order to get started in life. This is but one of two types of collective inheritance in *adat* law. The other is what is called the *mayorat* system, in which the estate is not divided but instead placed under the collective authority of all agnatic sons and not just the first-born, to be used as a resource for the family's well-being.

By contrast, in a matrilineal system of inheritance, women take precedence in division of the estate, in keeping with the tradition in matrilineal society where the female is the locus of authority within the family. In some matrilineal *adat* circles, such as in Minangkabau (West Sumatra) and some regions of South Sumatra, the mother and her family exercise leadership so that only relatives on the mother's side manage and share the estate of the deceased (Rajo Penghulu 1994, 113–18). Thus what we find in matrilineal collective inheritance is that the entire network of relatives on the mother's side retains authority over the estate and enjoys the right to benefit from it at the direction of a single female heir. In some places, this kind of management of the estate is common practice as regards the ownership of land originally owned by the predecessors of the mother's family. As in the patriarchal method, the *mayorat* system applies here too, although in the matrilineal model the first-born daughter takes responsibility along with the first-born son of the family, so that the two relatives work together to preserve the estate for the sake of the family's welfare.

In contrast to the gender-based underpinnings of these two models, the parental system prescribes that both sons and daughters have equal rights to the estate. Thus whereas in patrilineal or matrilineal communities either only men or only women control the inheritance (with the consequence that gender alienation may then result from such a framework), the parental system sees no point in differentiating between the two sexes, and assigns them equal rights in the succession. In consequence, the estate in the parental inheritance model devolves not only on the heirs on the mother's or father's side, but on all descendants of either sex. The children or heirs of the estate are therefore not viewed as belonging to one side of the family or the other, but are equally entitled to inherit from either parent. This is the system that is most commonly found in the *adat* law of inheritance in the Indonesian archipelago. In the *adat*-based communities of Aceh and North Sumatra, most regions in South Sumatra, Java, Madura, Kalimantan and Sulawesi, as well as in most of the eastern archipelago, the parental system of inheritance is favored (Hadikusuma 1991, 109). In contrast to the patrilineal and matrilineal systems, which are dominated by the collectivist approach to estate allotment, the parental system is, in practice, more individualist in nature since the division takes into account each of the heirs, irrespective of gender. As each individual heir has the right to an allotment from the estate, it is usually divided as soon as all the heirs come to an agreement as to its division. In the parental system, therefore, there is no concept of authorizing a particular successor or group of successors in a single family line to administer the estate as found in the matrilineal and patrilineal systems.

Gender equality in the rights of property

Regardless of the differences in the division of the estate inherent in the various clan systems described here, all *adat* law circles in the archipelago have this much in common: the assets owned by the father's or the mother's side before marriage are distinguished from those obtained subsequent to their marriage (Soepomo 2000, 85–90). The marriage thus becomes the dividing line: property accruing to the couple as a result of their engagement is treated in a distinct fashion from property acquired through earnings or other sources, an important consideration when calculating the estate on the death of one of the spouses. As a consequence, property of the first category obtained by each party before their marriage is counted as property that should be returned to or retained by the late spouse's original family line, while the second category, namely property obtained after the marriage, will automatically go to the heirs: the surviving spouse and their children. On a practical level, this legal norm varies greatly, depending upon how people value gender status in the society. In patriarchal societies, the authority over the couple's property is so decidedly in the hands of the father or his family line as to give him considerable power over the distribution of the family's wealth. This logic is largely repeated in matrilineal societies, where the mother and her family line dominate the wealth and keep much of her own family's wealth separate from the couple's.

The concept of common property, owned jointly by a couple, is more characteristic of the parental society, which sees the husband and wife as equal partners in the marriage bond. In this way claims to the property are based on the view of the wife and husband as having equal rights before the law (Prins 1950, 290–1). Since property acquired during the marriage is held jointly by both partners, they retain equal rights to it. Such property is viewed as indivisible, unless the marriage is dissolved, or until one of the couple dies. Even here the common feature prevails that they do not divide the estate directly but use it for preserving the lifestyle of the family. It is usually the surviving parent (widow or widower) who takes on the role of directing the estate, and if there is a decision to divide it, that parent will automatically receive a half share of the common property, while the other half will be distributed evenly to all the children of the marriage. Such a method is believed essential to maintaining peace within the family and, by extension, the equilibrium of the community at large.

This now appears to be the trend in modern Indonesia and it seems to reflect the Western concern for gender equality, which has in fact gained considerable ground in the country since its independence in 1945. Thus any legal values, whether from *adat* or Islamic law, that are viewed as raw material for the construction of a national law, are made to conform to this concept of gender equity (Bowen 2003). That the parental system of inheritance in *adat* is now meant to be the current model of inheritance law in the country is furthermore completely in line with the movement to interpret Islamic law in accordance with gender equality (Hazairin 1964).

Bibliography

J. R. Bowen, *Islam, law and equality in Indonesia. An anthropology of public reasoning*, Cambridge 2003.

B. ter Haar, *Beginselen en stelsel van het adatrecht*, Groningen 1939, 1950⁴.

H. Hadikusuma, *Adat inheritance law* [in Indonesian], Bandung 1980.

——, *Indonesian inheritance law* [in Indonesian], Bandung 1991.

Hazairin, *National family law* [in Indonesian], Jakarta 1962.

——, *Bilateral inheritance law according to the Qur'ān* [in Indonesian], Jakarta 1964.

J. F. Holleman, *Van Vollenhoven on Indonesian adat law*, The Hague 1981.

M. B. Hooker, *Adat law in modern Indonesia*, Kuala Lumpur 1978.

D. S. Lev, The supreme court and adat inheritance law in Indonesia, in *American Journal of Comparative Law* 11 (1972), 205–24.

I. H. Dt. Rajo Penghulu, *Basic knowledge of the adat of Minangkabau* [in Indonesian], 6th ed., Bandung 1994.

J. Prins, *Adat en Islametische Plichtenleer in Indonesië*, The Hague 1948, 1950².

——, Adat law and Muslim religious law in modern Indonesia, in *Die Welt des Islams*, 1 (1951), 283–300.

R. Soepomo, *Chapters on adat law* [in Indonesian], Jakarta 1967, 2000¹⁵.

Ranto Lukito

Mashriq Beduins

People of the rural Mashriq, who identify themselves as *badū* (nomadic) or *ḥaḍarī* (settled), by tribal or family descent or locality, understand customary law (*ʿurf*, from the root *ʿ r f*, to know, to recognize) as the knowledge of jurally based rules and customs known to all, predating Islam and embedded in existing social, economic, and political practices. *ʿUrf* resolves disputes so both parties reconcile their differences, and the community as a whole moves forward. *ʿUrf* maintains peace through the restitution of honor to the complainant by reconciliation and compromise, or by compensation for wrongs and injury from the defendant through the efforts of mediators or, if these fail, of arbitrators.

There are said to be private collections of *ʿurf* judgments and opinions in Arab countries. Juhayna (1983, 283) writes that in the small towns of pre-Wahhābī Najd, judgments concerning property transactions, endowments, wills, inheritances, criminal cases, and and other similar issues were recorded, unlike cases settled by reconciliation and compromise. This appears similar to mountain areas of the northern Gulf where people used *ʿurf* and Sharīʿa law, depending on context. In the 1970s, cases mediated by Rwala shaykhs of Syria were unrecorded. During the nineteenth and twentieth centuries, Western scholars recorded customary law: for example, Burckhardt (1831), Jaussen (1907, 1914, 1927), Musil (1928), Dickson (1949), and Hardy (1963). *ʿUrf* has common themes and processes yet varies among tribes, families, and villages. Women and their role in *ʿurf* have received little attention. Three aspects concerning women stand out. First, women remain jural members of their natal family throughout their lives. Second, a woman owns property outright; within marriage, she can invest her property, engage in enterprises, and the proceeds are hers. She may contribute to the household, but it is her husband's duty to support her. Third, women, through their behavior, are the guardians of family honor. Women participate in all aspects of customary law, except feud, raids, and war. Their participation is largely invisible, since male relations represent them in any public forum and where women are disputants, the process takes place at home.

Customary law underpins traditional economic activity. Since women are active economic agents (de Boucheman 1939, 91–2, Metral 1993, 208, Abu Rabia 1994, Lancaster 1981, Lancaster and Lancaster 1999, Lienhardt 2001, 62–3) they become involved in disputes over ownership, boundaries, access, distribution of shares of profits and losses, fulfillment of share contracts, payment of rents or wages, delivery of goods, and the like. Women's investments and enterprises, small and large, place them in the networks of customary contractual transactions underlying regional economic activities. Family economic disputes, usually between husband and wife or mother-in-law and daughter-in-law, are about management of the joint household purse, temporary use of property belonging to one or the other, clarification of exact ownership of shares in property, gifts to kinsmen and affines, and allocations of labor inputs between co-owners or co-users. Economic disputes between the two families are concerned with transfers of outstanding bride price, and the use of property inherited by women.

Women do not fight, except by default: *badū* women fighting in defense of their own property (Musil 1928); a woman whose camels were raided while her husband was absent raided them back (Lancaster 1981); or a woman may be killed by raiders (Lienhardt 2001, 104). In some tribes, the end of a long-standing feud is marked by a woman of the aggressor's family being given in marriage to the victim's (Jaussen 1907, Lienhardt 2001).

Customary law, in conjunction with Islamic law, regulated marriage and family relationships. Within a working descent group, many marriages are between relatively close paternal cousins; some involve more distant paternal cousins; and a few involve individuals of genealogically distant groups linked by marriage over generations. With such preferred marriages, most individuals have networks of close or distant relations from both parents that spread within and across tribe and family. The internal dynamics of male descent groups are achieved through women drawing families closer and distancing others. Marriage becomes legal through the transfer of bride price and its various components. Groups vary in details, but the general principles compensate a woman's family for the cost of her upbringing, establish the new family unit, and provide for the woman should there be a divorce.

Only husbands can pronounce divorce, but a woman has customary procedures to persuade her husband to divorce her. Initially, she appeals to his generosity and honor. If this fails, she can return to her home for the support of her father and brothers. If her father insists she returns, and her husband makes her an attractive present, the marriage continues. If the marriage worsens, she may try behaving so badly her husband divorces her. She may return home repeatedly, but if she gets no support from her father and brothers, she may decide to flee and take protection from a leading man of good public reputation, a shaykh. He cannot refuse her appeal, and makes her whereabouts known to the husband and her family so that a settlement can be reached. She puts her case (lack of economic support, overwork, bad interaction with his female relations, his wish to move far from her family, sexual problems, brutality, coercion to agree to the marriage from her father) to the shaykhly women who pass it, along with their comments and advice, onto the shaykh, in her hearing. He mediates between her, the husband, and her father and brothers in terms of honorable behavior; if the husband agrees to a divorce, mediation continues and turns to questions of returning part of the bride price and the future of children, if any. Among shaykhly families, where marriages often have complicated political and economic factors, it is more difficult for a woman to end a marriage.

Customary law holds that anyone fleeing from vengeance has the right to seek protection and that it must be granted. It is the duty of the protector to inform the victim's family's representative of the killer's whereabouts, and initiate the processes toward restitution and compensation. Known killings by women are of their husbands, by accident in a rage, or by intent when consistently refused a divorce by him and their male relatives, and circumstances prevented flight (Lancaster 1981).

Many communities and groups have few honor killings; some, for example parts of mountain Jordan and Palestine, have more. Some groups and individuals regard women as jurally equal and autonomous individuals but men act for them in public arenas; others view women as the jural responsibility of fathers and brothers. Honor killings arise when a woman is thought to have behaved dishonorably by her male relations. Fleeing to take protection was a customary procedure; the shaykhas often gave protection themselves, faced down furious brothers in search of their sister, and mediated a solution through husbands or brothers with the girl's family. A killing within the family can have no vengeance in *ʿurf*. Pregnancy before marriage is known; in some groups the girl is killed, in others, the family make the man responsible marry her. It is said illegitimate children are known in some groups in southern Oman. Married women quietly entertaining lovers when the husband is absent is considered by most to concern only husband and wife.

ʿUrf dispute settlement starts with those closest to the disputants offering advice, calls on precedent, and appeals for reconciliation and compromise. Respected women are consulted and mediate within and between families. Processes are informal until a settlement is near when some formality is seen. The disputants, with the mediator/s, agree to a settlement with witnesses who swear oaths to the agreement, especially if property is involved. Witnesses are summoned and testimony heard, verified by ordeals or sworn oaths; a woman's testimony is worth half that of a man. At this level, the mediator is rarely a woman unless the dispute is between women; even then, many prefer a male mediator, with the women represented by close male relations. Neither side need accept a mediation, and disputes can drag on for years.

Arbitration is binding on the disputants; a few shaykhs mediate but refuse to arbitrate, pushing the responsibility for settlement back on the disputants and their families. A mediated settlement or an arbitration are formal as the shaykh or shaykha "sits," both parties to the dispute are present with witnesses, and the language used is formal.

Customary law functioned through a popular understanding of its rules and procedures and its experts with their specialized knowledge of particular corpuses of law and wide experience. Women had an integral role. Though replaced by national law, *ʿurf* continues; customary law and state law elide or are in conflict (Lancaster and Lancaster 1999, 366–72, 381–2).

Bibliography

M. A. A. al-Abli, al-ʿAlāqa bayn al-jalwa wa-bayn al-tabdīl al-ijtimāʿī fī jamʿiyya badawiyya manzilī, M.A. thesis, Yarmuk University, Jordan 1996.

A. Abu Rabia, *The Negev Bedouin and livestock rearing*, Oxford 1994.

J. L. Burckhardt, *Notes on the Bedouins and Wahabys*, London 1831, repr. London 1967.

A. de Boucheman, *Une petite cité caravanière. Suḫné*, Damascus 1939.

H. R. P. Dickson, *The Arab of the desert*, London 1949.

J. Ginat, Meshamas. The outcast in Bedouin society, in *Nomadic Peoples* 12 (1983), 26–47.

M. J. L. Hardy, *Blood feuds and the payment of blood money in the Middle East*, Beirut 1963.

A. Jaussen, *Coutumes des Arabes au pays de Moab*, Paris 1907, repr. Paris 1947.

——, *Naplouse et son district*, Paris 1927.

A. Jaussen and R. Savignac, Coutumes des Fuqara, supplement to A. Jaussen and R. Savignac, *Mission archeologique en Arabie*, ii, Paris 1914, repr. Paris 1920.

U. M. al-Juhany, The History of Najd prior to the Wahhabis, Ph.D. diss., University of Washington 1983.

W. Lancaster, *The Rwala Bedouin today*, Cambridge 1981, Prospect Heights, Ill. 1997², updated 2000.

W. Lancaster and F. Lancaster, *People, land and water in the Arab Middle East*, Amsterdam 1999.

P. Lienhardt, *Shaikhdoms of eastern Arabia*, ed. A. al-Shahi from Liendhardt's Ph.D. thesis 1957, Houndmills, Basingstoke, Hants 2001.

F. Metral, Elevage et agriculture dans l'oasis de Sukhne (Syrie). Gestion de risques par les commercants-entrepreneurs, in R. Bocco, R. Jaubert, and F. Metral (eds.),

Steppes d'Arabie. Etats, pasteurs, agriculteurs et commercants, Paris 1993, 195–222.
A. Musil, *Arabia Deserta*, New York 1927.
——, *The Manners and customs of the Rwala Bedouins*, New York 1928.

WILLIAM LANCASTER AND FELICITY LANCASTER

Sub-Saharan Africa

How do women use and participate in customary processes of dispute resolution? How do customary and Islamic legal traditions coexist? There is much variation in the position of women and the status of gender relationships vis-à-vis customary law in Sub-Saharan Africa, particularly in Muslim areas where women may also be subject to Islamic law. It is difficult to define what constitutes customary law. In Sub-Saharan Africa, "customary law" has had many meanings: it refers to indigenous African legal institutions, to different kinds of formal and informal social control, and to colonial attempts to restrain subject populations through codification of what they perceived as indigenous law. Law and law-related behaviors are, of course, subject to and dependent upon the cultural, social, and political environments. Law is thus constantly changing and is infinitely variable, and that which is (or should be) considered customary is highly contested.

Women's rights, social status, and access to different forums for dispute resolution vary tremendously across cultures in Sub-Saharan Africa, and they have been subject to significant internal and external changes – particularly with the spread of Islam, the imposition of colonial rule, and later with independence. Although there is much variation in indigenous African legal thought and procedure, some generalities can be addressed concerning the status of women and gender roles. Throughout Africa, much of precolonial law was highly flexible in the sense that it was tailored to meet specific needs in special circumstances – little was codified. In the precolonial era, disputes were often subject to a range of mediation options. In much of Africa, elders have held a great deal of authority in their communities and they often played the lead role in handling disputes. Disputes in the past were most often dealt with at home or in community forums; this is still common in many parts of Africa today, even though most populations are also subject to state law. In Zanzibar, now a semi-autonomous island state of Tanzania, disputes were taken first to the *wazee*, the family elders. While men generally took charge of the proceedings, women's opinions were valued, and a woman could take the lead in resolving a dispute, particularly if she headed a household involved. If the elders failed to resolve the matter, it was taken to the *sheha*, a community leader (almost always male). The final resort was the *kadhi*, in Arabic *qāḍī*, or Islamic judge – also male. This basic course of action is still followed today, although the role of the *sheha* and *kadhi* feature more prominently because they are the state-sanctioned means of handling disputes. While elders remain the first resort, some bemoan the loss of their authority to the state.

THE SPREAD OF ISLAM

The spread of Islam into Sub-Saharan Africa brought with it important changes in legal thought, means of social control, and dispute resolution. Although some scholars argue that Islamic law is not indigenous because it was introduced through the gradual spread of Islam, it has become local in many parts of Africa. Communities and individuals have different ways of interpreting and applying Islamic law and viewing the relationships between customary and Islamic law. Also, women and men can have different ways of framing legal claims and articulating the differences between Islamic and customary law. In some communities of East Africa, for example, Swahili men tend to frame disputes with reference to Islamic law while women are more likely to draw on *mila*, or custom. Despite cross-cultural variation, there are some important general distinctions between Islamic law and customary African legal norms. For example, the acceptance of Islamic law brought with it an increased focus on the rights of the individual over the kinship group. The acceptance of Islamic law also had an important impact on gender relationships because of differences in marriage, inheritance, and land-usage rights. Sometimes women gained rights with Islam and sometimes they lost rights. Thus, the arrival of Islamic law should not be viewed as either progressive or regressive in this regard. In some areas, such as northern Nigeria, women benefited from the acceptance of Islamic legal norms that brought inheritance rights to women that they had not previously enjoyed. In others, such as eighteenth-century Sudan, women lost advantages when the acceptance of Islam influenced inheritance practice and domestic relationships of production by drawing women away from their conventional roles in the productive sector (Spaulding 1984).

THE COLONIAL PERIOD

The colonial period brought significant legal change and affected women's legal practice in important ways. The imperial governments approached the relationship between Islamic and customary law differently in separate areas. In some places, Islamic and customary law were regarded as one and the same, while elsewhere they held different status. In northern Nigeria, Zanzibar, and Sudan, the British kept a separate Islamic legal system in place. Similar recognition was given to Islamic legal authorities in French-held Senegal. In British Tanganyika and Gambia, on the other hand, courts applied both Islamic law and customary law depending on the circumstances of a particular case. In other regions, such as Sierra Leone and Northern Rhodesia, colonial powers equated Islamic law with customary law – and this was the only basis on which Muslims could use Islamic law.

The colonial era had a great impact on how the subject of customary law is addressed. Many scholars agree that what is referred to as "customary" is in fact a creation of colonial governments, which attempted to control their subject populations by codifying customary law. In Tanganyika, for example, the British attempted to identify broad themes in indigenous legal thought and dispute resolution, which were then given the status of "customary" and considered applicable to the indigenous populations. Codifying customary law was not necessarily beneficial to women, and in some cases women lost significant status through the codification process because culturally specific norms involving bridewealth, divorce, and family roles that had privileged women were overlooked. Furthermore, because colonial authorities most often consulted with male elders about norms of customary law, the elders were able to use the opportunity to "create" customary law to attempt to gain greater control over women (Chanock 1982). Similarly, codification sometimes exaggerated the power of chiefs over community disputes to the extent that formerly important roles of diviners and spirit mediums, often women, were diminished. The same could be true for previously autonomous groups such as age sets, women's organizations, and individual households (Mamdani 1996). Women also sometimes suffered an economic loss when customary law was codified: women's traditional roles as property holders were overlooked, and their possessions could be delegated to their husband's ownership.

In many areas, colonialism created additional legal options for resolving disputes; scholars call the existence of such options "legal pluralism." This was of particular importance to women because in the arena of family law – specifically marriage, divorce, child custody, and inheritance – different legal standards were potentially recognized within one territory. This has the potential to benefit women because the introduction of new legal ideas can influence how rights are understood and defined and can change the proportional power of disputants. This may benefit women when the new rights serve to improve their "bargaining power" in social and commercial relationships with men (Merry 1982). However, the reverse can also be true because new laws may undermine previous rights of women. For example, among the Lunda of Zambia, divorce for women was easier to obtain before the colonial government required in 1930 that the Native Court issue a certificate of divorce. In colonial Zanzibar women were able to obtain divorces more easily from Islamic judges than in the British courts.

The postcolonial period

With the dawn of independence in the mid-twentieth century, the status and application of customary law went through important changes. There have been significant differences in the ways in which newly independent states addressed issues surrounding customary and Islamic law, particularly regarding women's status and rights. Interestingly, much of anti-colonial politics of the 1950s both focused on the ideal of a unified legal system for the new states and advocated respect for indigenous law and institutions – this occasionally resulted in a blend of customary and received law in the new states (Mamdani 1994). Some states, such as the former French colonies Mali, Niger, Senegal, and Côte d'Ivoire abolished customary courts altogether, including Islamic courts. Elsewhere, customary law and Islamic courts were preserved, as in Nigeria, where the Islamic courts provided an important means for women to pursue their rights. The official status of Islamic law in Nigeria has been controversial in recent years; this is particularly true since the reintroduction of criminal law in the northern states. In East Africa, Sudan's reforms in the early phases of independence sought to improve women's status under family law by easing judicial divorce in abusive marriage and improving women's rights to maintenance by their husbands. As in Nigeria, the status of Islamic law has also been controversial in later years.

Many new civil codes in the independent states sought to improve women's status through legal means. After liberation from Ethiopia in the early 1990s, Eritrea instituted a civil code with the aim of improving women's status by changing customary marriage and divorce practice. Earlier, Tanzania instituted similar wide reforms by attempting to articulate principles of family law, Islamic, customary, and Christian, in the Marriage Act of 1971. The act set the minimum age of marriage for both girls and boys, and respected customary marriages by acknowledging both monogamous and polygamous marriage. Certain provisions in the act can be read as an attempt by President Nyerere to quell religious controversy in Tanzania by accommodating the needs of a religiously plural population. Although it is part of Tanzania, this act does not affect Zanzibar, where few provisions have been made in either the colonial or independence periods for customary law. Anderson argued that this was because *mila*, which he translates as customary law, was already infused with Shāfiʿī Islamic legal ideas, and thus was not in contradiction with Islamic law and needed no separate recognition (1955). In Zanzibar today, Islamic courts have jurisdiction over all family and personal status law and Islamic law remains essentially uncodified.

Throughout Africa today, women are faced with multiple legal options, some formal and some informal, and they make decisions influenced by family members, the perceived likelihood of a particular outcome in a particular venue, and potential stigma associated with a particular legal option. A woman's socioeconomic status and education affects her litigation strategies, and her social networks influence how she learns about and uses legal forums. The status of customary vis-à-vis other types of law remains an important issue throughout Sub-Saharan Africa, particularly concerning gender and women's rights. A famous Kenyan case that favored customary law illustrates this. In the 1980s, a widow named Wambui Otieno was vying with her deceased husband's clan for the right to bury his body. Because no written law applied, the Kenyan courts decided that customary law must be followed, and the deceased's clan was given the right to bury the body.

The anthropologist S. E. Merry has pointed out that the existence of different fields of law is particularly important to women when there is a resulting variation in the way in which areas of women's rights are defined – as in marriage, divorce, inheritance, property, and child custody (1982). In Zanzibar, many women feel that times have changed for the better because women today have easier access to legal means for resolving disputes.

BIBLIOGRAPHY

J. N. D. Anderson, Customary law and Islamic law in British African territories, in Afrika Instituut (Netherlands), *The future of customary law in Africa. L'Avenir du droit coutumier en Afrique. Symposium-Colloque, Amsterdam, 1955*, Leiden 1956, 70–87.

——, *Islamic law in Africa*, London 1954, repr. 1970.

P. Caplan, "Law" and "custom." Marital disputes on Northern Mafia Island, Tanzania, in P. Caplan (ed.), *Understanding disputes. The politics of argument*, Oxford 1995, 203–21.

M. Chanock, Making customary law. Men, women, and courts in colonial northern Rhodesia, in M. J. Hay and M. Wright (eds.), *African women and the law. Historical perspectives*, Boston 1982, 53–67.

——, *Law, custom and social order. The colonial experience in Malawi and Zambia*, Cambridge 1985.

T. O. Elias, *The nature of African customary law*, Manchester, England 1956.

A. Griffiths, *In the shadow of marriage. Gender and justice in an African community*, Chicago 1997.

M. J. Hay and M. Wright (eds.), *African women and the law. Historical perspectives*, Boston 1982.

J. F. Holleman, *Issues in African law*, The Hague 1972.

M. Mamdani, *Citizen and subject. Contemporary Africa and the legacy of late colonialism*, Princeton, N.J. 1996.

K. Mann and Roberts, *Law in colonial Africa*, Portsmouth, N.H. 1991.

S. E. Merry, The articulation of legal spheres, in M. J. Hay and M. Wright (eds.), *African women and the law. Historical perspectives*, Boston 1982, 68–89.

——, Law and colonialism, in *Law and Society Review* 25:4 (1991), 889–922.

S. F. Moore, *Social facts and fabrications. "Customary law" on Kilimanjaro, 1880–1980*, Cambridge 1986.

J. Spaulding, The misfortunes of some – the advantage of others. Land sales by women in Sinnar, in M. J. Hay and M. Wright (eds.), *African women and the law. Historical perspectives*, Boston 1982, 3–18.

P. Stamp, Burying Otieno. The politics of gender and ethnicity in Kenya, in *Signs. Journal of Women in Culture and Society* 16:41 (Summer 1991), 808–45.

ERIN E. STILES

Turkey

Turkey is unique in the Muslim world with respect to the extent and progressive nature of Family Code reforms affecting women's lives. The founding of the Turkish Republic in 1923 brought an end to the Ottoman Empire's system of parallel laws and established a single, secular, and standardized judicial system adapted from the European system of law. The introduction in 1926 of the Turkish Civil Code, adapted from the Swiss Civil Code, was a major success of the reformists against the conservative forces defending the Islamic Family Code. The new Civil Code abolished polygyny and granted women equal rights in matters of divorce, child custody, and inheritance. However, to this day, customary and religious practices continue to be more influential in the daily lives of millions of women in Turkey than the Civil Code; this is especially the case for women living in eastern Turkey.

The young republic's project of creating a state based on the rule of law was an important development with respect to women. Prior to 1923, laws were based on the religious or customary laws of a particular community, and different laws applied depending on a citizen's religion, gender, occupational status, or sect. Though for Muslim women the Qurʾān was the basic source of family law, particular interpretations and practices depended on the religion, sect, ethnic group, class, and region to which a woman belonged.

Women are those who are generally most disadvantaged in societies where parallel legal systems exist (separate judicial systems for religious or ethnic minorities, or judicial systems whose laws are based on traditions that vary from one region to another), as the laws implemented tend to be the ones with the most negative consequences for women (Shaheed 1994). The new republic's establishment of a modern legal system had two significant advantages for women in Turkey: first, the uniform legal system provided a basis for counteracting or diminishing the harmful impacts of the parallel legal systems on women; second, the new Civil Code undermined the traditional power of religious authorities – including the religious right – over laws pertaining to family, whereas the previous parallel system allowed religious fundamentalists to impose laws in their particular religious communities that were severely discriminatory to women (Ali and Arif 1994, WRAG 1997).

The initial republican reforms aimed at a unified, secular law, and later improvements in the legal domain have signified the end of the official validity of religious and customary laws in Turkey. However, these often continue to shape the daily lives of women, depending on their class, geographical region, and the ethnic and/or religious group to which they belong. The negative impacts of religious/customary practices are generally more severe for women of lower educational and socioeconomic levels; women living in economically disadvantaged regions and women of minority groups are most often unable to benefit from legal reform, as for example is the case for Kurdish women living in eastern Turkey.

Thus, while practices such as early and forced marriages, honor crimes, religious marriages, and polygynous marriages constitute clear violations of either Turkish Civil or Penal Code laws, these all continue to occur. The Turkish constitution and the Civil Code both enshrine the principle of civil marriage, and religious marriages have no validity under Turkish law. Polygamy is forbidden and a religious marriage ceremony cannot be held before a civil one (Articles 130, 143, 145 and 174 of the Turkish Civil Code). Violation of the law regarding civil marriage is a criminal offense for both the couple and the person who conducts such a ceremony (Article 237 of the Turkish Penal Code). However, effective enforcement of these laws is rare. In 2000, 75 years after the enactment of these laws, 7.4 percent of all marriages in Turkey were religious only and lacked a civil marriage contract, and the majority of these (53 percent) occurred in eastern Turkey (DGSPW 2001). Moreover, research shows that one in ten women in eastern Turkey is in a polygynous marriage, despite the ban on polygamy (Ilkkaracan and WWHR 1998).

The higher prevalence of religious and customary practices in eastern Turkey, many in violation of Turkish law, can be attributed in part to socioeconomic conditions, which progressively worsen from west to east; to the dominance of a tribal system among the Kurdish population that constitutes the majority in eastern Turkey; and to legal and non-legal discrimination affecting the Kurdish population as a minority in Turkey. The tribal structures (*aşiret*) dominating the Kurdish population are organized around large, clan-like families with tribal leaders and are based on a feeling of group solidarity involving large numbers of extended family members. The members are deemed to be responsible for upholding customary laws and practices, including early marriage, bride price, and so-called honor crimes, which are based on an ideology that assumes women's bodies are the property of the extended family/tribe/community, and that the honor of the extended family is dependent on the chastity of its women. In addition, Turkish is the only official language of all governmental institutions, including judicial ones, and Kurdish women, who speak little or no Turkish, are left with little recourse to the law for protection.

Research shows a wide range of religious and customary practices are negatively impacting women in eastern Turkey. For example, 16.3 percent of women living in the region were married before the age of 15, the minimum legal age for marriage according to the Civil Code until 2001 (the minimum legal age for marriage was raised to 18 for both sexes in 2001). More than half the women (50.8 percent) were married without their consent, although the consent of both parties is a precondition of marriage according to Turkish law. The percentage of women who thought they would be killed by their husbands and/or families if they committed adultery was 67 percent, although adultery is not even considered to be a crime under Turkish law (Ilkkaracan and WWHR 1998).

The experience of Turkey shows that legal measures alone are not at all enough to prevent the negative impacts of religious and customary practices for women; their prevention requires an effective and holistic women's human rights agenda, integrated with local and national social policies and politics.

Bibliography

S. S. Ali and K. Arif, *Blind justice for all? Parallel judicial systems in Pakistan. Implications and consequences for human rights*, Grabels, France 1994.

DGPSW (Directorate General on the Status and Problems of Women), *Türkiye'de kadin, 2001*, Ankara 2001.

P. Ilkkaracan and WWHR (Women for Women's Human Rights), Exploring the context of sexuality in eastern Turkey, in *Reproductive Health Matters* 6 (1998), 66–75, available at < http://www.wwhr.org/?id=743>.

F. Shaheed, Controlled or autonomous. Identity and the experience of the network, Women Living Under Muslim Laws, in *Signs: Journal of Women in Culture and Society* 19 (1994), 997–1019.

WRAG (Women's Research Action Group), *Women, law and customary practices*, Mumbai 1997.

Pinar Ilkkaracan

ILLUSTRATIONS

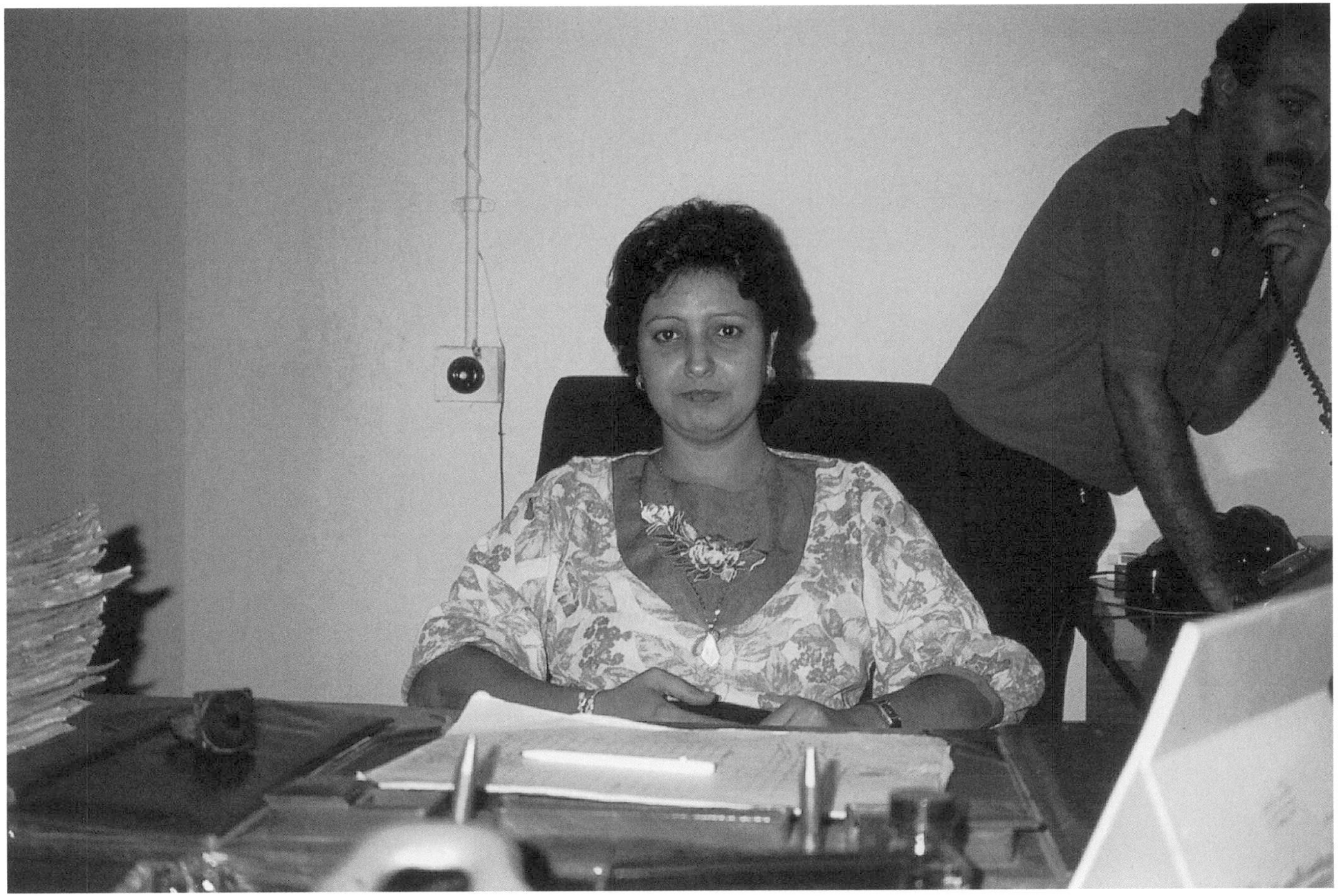

Figure 1. Adeni family court judge in her court with her assistant, early 1990s. After Yemini unification, women were no longer allowed to head a family court or to train as judges. *(Photo: Susanne Dahlgren.)*

Figure 2. Narinjistan, Shiraz. Qājār period building.

Figure 3. Official State Emblem of Iran, early 1970s.

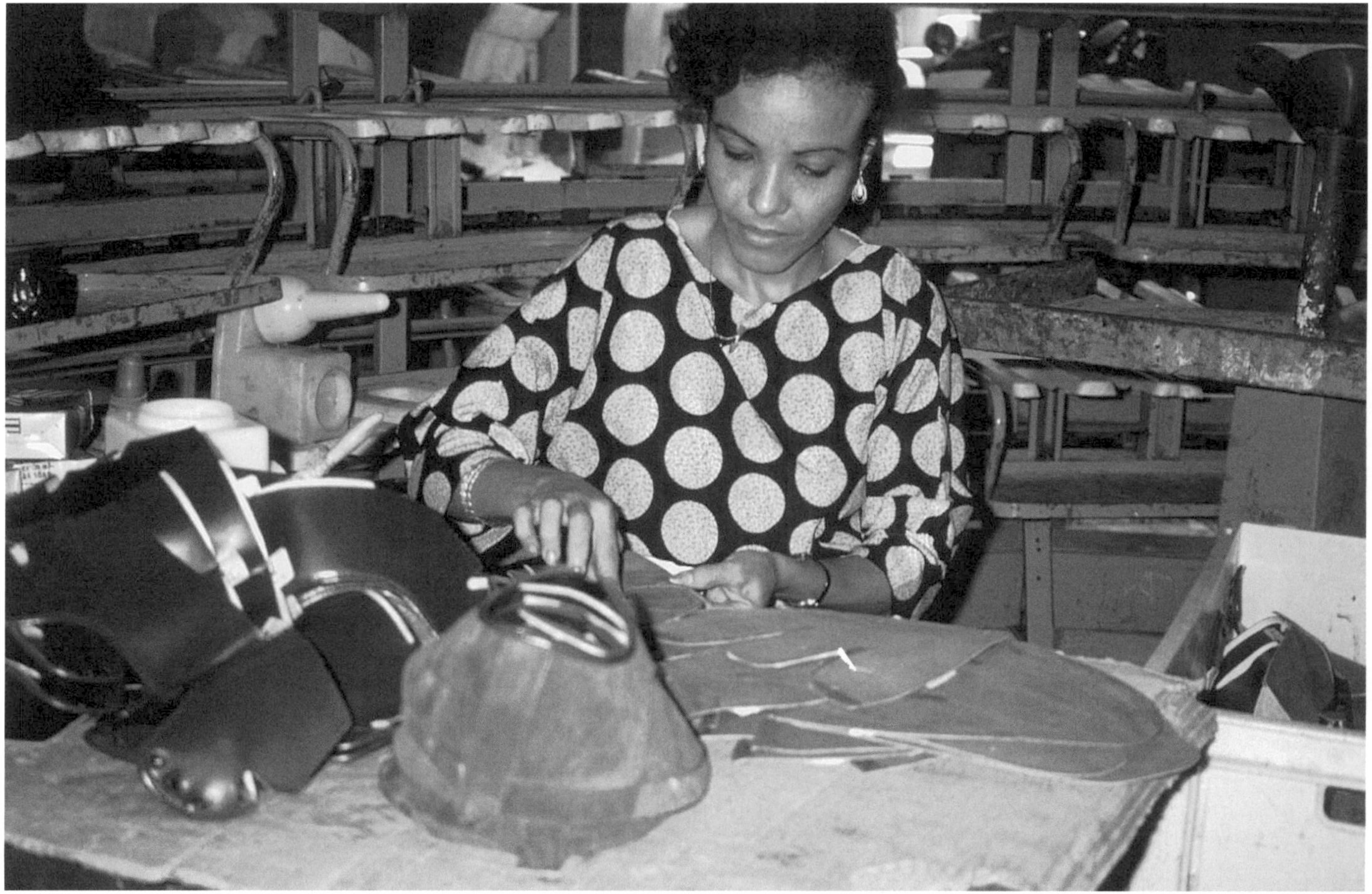

Figure 4. A factory worker in the Leather Shoe Factory, Aden. During the early years of the People's Democratic Republic of Yemen, literacy was a requirement to enter factory work. The photo is from 1989. *(Photo: Susanne Dahlgren.)*

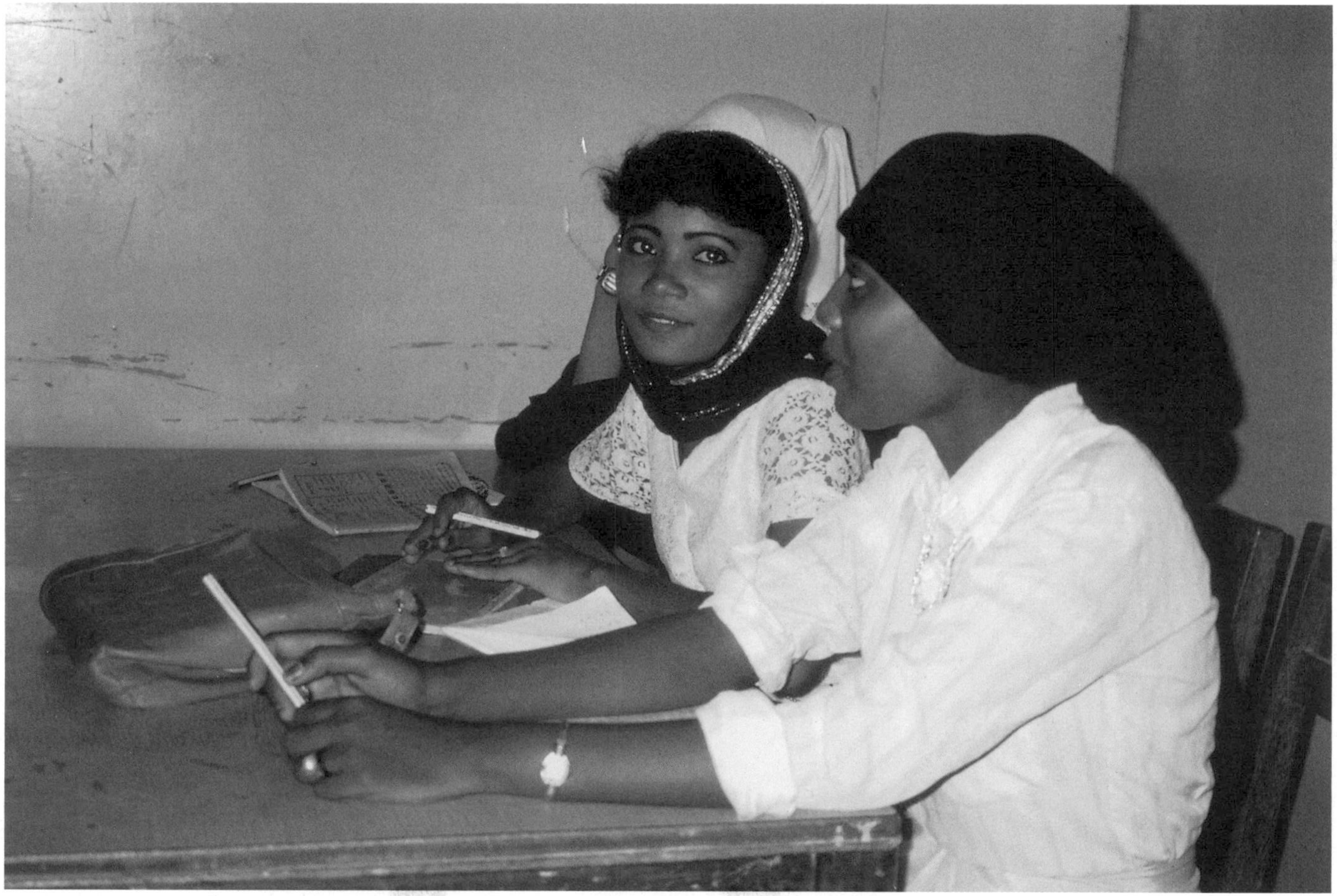

Figure 5. Participants of a literacy class run by a local club of the General Union of Yemeni Women during the late years of the People's Democratic Republic of Yemen. *(Photo: Susanne Dahlgren.)*

Figure 6. *Khayāl al-ẓill* (Cairo: n.d.), vol. 2, no. 62, Sunday, 23 August 1925, p. 16. *(Photo Credit: Near East Collections of the Princeton University Library.)*

Law: Enforcement

East Asia, Southeast Asia, Australia, and the Pacific

The conditions and situations of prisons and prisoners in the region are dependent upon economic growth, the legal system, management or administration, law enforcement, and the political situation. In this context, Islamic culture might have only a little impact. For instance, prison conditions in Brunei Darussalam and Malaysia are different, although both are Islamic countries. In fact, the classic Islamic criminal law is mainly based on *ḥudūd*, such as stoning to death and cutting off of hands, and not on a prison system. This does not mean that the prison system is unjustified. Instead, Islamic criminal law proposes *taʿzīr*, which means that Islamic judges are free to punish the offender in cases of minor felony equivalents (which are not found in the Qur'ān) in almost any fashion, including sending him/her to prison. Whilst *ḥudūd* crimes have fixed punishments, as set down by God, and found in the Qur'ān, and therefore are seen as crimes against God's law, *taʿzīr* crimes are crimes against society (Malekian 1994).

Based on data from 2000, women prisoners constituted 5.1 percent of the total number of all prisoners in the Asia and Pacific region (APCCA 2000). However, there were several countries that had higher than this average proportion: Thailand (17.4 percent), Hong Kong (China) (10.4 percent), Macau (China) (8.7 percent), and Singapore (8.2 percent). By contrast, the proportions were very low in the Pacific island nations of Fiji (1.4 percent), Tonga (1.5 percent), and Kiribati (1.8 percent). All of the other nations in the region had proportions of women prisoners between these figures (APCCA 2000).

One of the possible explanations is that less highly developed nations have lower proportions of women offenders. In other words, nations with a high level of socioeconomic development might generally have higher proportions of women prisoners. Another explanation could be that it is cultural and historical considerations that mark the difference. For instance, in Cambodia there has been no apparent marked increase in women prisoners, while in Kiribati the number of women prisoners is kept very small by the common practice of courts suspending a sentence if the offender is female. In Brunei Darussalam, the total number of women prisoners remained relatively stable between 2000 and 2004, but in most years the majority of female prisoners are foreigners.

Some countries have experienced extreme increases in the numbers of women prisoners, which might be seen as a reason for management concern. In Australia, for example, there have been increases in all jurisdictions except South Australia, while in New Zealand the female prison population increased by 162 percent between June 1986 and June 2000 (APCCA 2000). In Thailand the rate of increase in the female prison population dramatically exceeded the equivalent rate for male prisoners, and this trend is predicted to continue. Even in Japan, where prison populations generally are very stable, there has been an increase in the number of women prisoners of 44 percent between 1998 and 2004. In Malaysia the number of women prisoners has fluctuated over the past decade, but in 2002–4 the numbers have doubled, while in Singapore, since 1993, there has been an increase in female penal offender numbers, but not in numbers of convicted female drug addicts (APCCA 2000).

Regardless of these statistical proportions, women prisoners have special needs, particularly with regard to health care, substance abuse, and family responsibilities. In addition, issues relating to pregnancy, childbirth, contraception, menstruation, and lesbian relationships are of more or less greater relevance in individual cases. In general, arrangements have been made for pregnant women prisoners to deliver their babies in public hospitals rather than in prison. This has ensured that professional obstetric assistance was available and also avoided the stigma of having a prison named as the place of birth on the birth certificate.

There are different approaches, however, as to whether or not mothers in prison should be allowed to keep their babies with them and, if so, for how long. In Japan, mothers are allowed to keep their babies with them for up to one year, while in Kiribati the baby may stay only whilst the mother is lactating. The maximum period in both Singapore and Hong Kong (China) is three years. In Singapore, women prisoners who are young mothers are offered an 8-week parenting course (APCCA 2000).

In New Zealand, facilities are provided for

babies to stay with their mothers in prison. Alternatively, prisoner mothers may be granted early or temporary release. If this is not practicable, arrangements can be made for daily visits to the prison by the baby for breast-feeding, in an appropriate setting. Arrangements can also be made, where necessary, for mothers to express their milk, for delivery to the baby located elsewhere (Kingi 2000). In Korea, it is possible for mothers to keep their babies with them in prison for up to 18 months, while the specified limit in Vietnam is two years. In Thailand, the upper limit is three years. The age limit for children to stay with their mothers is not specified in Cambodia, but the regulations provide for a mother with a baby to receive an extra one half of the adult food ration (APCCA 2000).

In Malaysia, mothers are allowed to keep their babies with them in special units in prison, for a period of up to four years, whereas in Brunei Darussalam the limit is three years, and two years in Indonesia. These Muslim countries follow the Qur'ān: "The mothers shall give suck to their children for two whole years, [that is] for those [parents] who desire to complete the term of suckling, but the father of the child shall bear the cost of the mother's food and clothing, on a reasonable basis" (2: 233).

In Malaysia and Brunei Darussalam, women prisoners may be offered vocational training that has a domestic orientation, and that is not necessarily geared to the needs of the outside labor market, such as beauty treatment, hairdressing, cooking, and secretarial skills. In Japan, training to obtain a license for care/service for the elderly is very popular with women prisoners, and is very useful in obtaining employment after release. Women prisoners in Vietnam may be offered work in tailoring, knitting, handicrafts, fine arts, or weaving (APCCA 2000).

In the majority of the nations of the Asia-Pacific region, a strict policy is pursued, requiring women's prisons, or the women's section of mixed prisons, to be staffed by female officers only. In a small number of nations, however, a policy of cross-gender staffing has been developed, which allows male officers to work in female prisons, and, conversely, female officers to work in male prisons. There are always, however, regulations that ensure that searches, and the supervision of ablutions, is undertaken by same-sex officers.

The majority of countries also follow a policy of strict segregation of male and female prisoners. In Sri Lanka, for example, male and female prisoners are strictly separated and females under 22 years are separated from adult females. There are a few exceptions, however, where contact between male and female prisoners is tolerated, and sometimes even encouraged. In the Australian Capital Territory and in Tasmania, for example, men and women can meet in educational classes. If a husband and wife are both in prison, special visits under supervision can be arranged (APCCA 2000).

In Brunei Darussalam, the law prohibits mistreatment of prisoners, and there have been no reports of such mistreatment. Prison conditions generally meet international standards. There is no overcrowding. However, there is a growing prison population. In mid 2002, there were only 31 women in prison, whereas the number of male prisoners was 423. All prisoners also receive regular medical checkups. The government is generally quick to investigate allegations of abuse and impose fines and punishment, as warranted. For instance, in September 2000, two members of the Royal Brunei Armed Forces were sentenced to four years imprisonment and three strokes of the cane for the attempted molestation and sodomy of a 20-year-old deaf girl. Approaches in female-connected criminal cases are, however, subject to change. In 1999 a photograph of a man accused of stabbing his wife and assaulting one of his children was published in a daily newspaper, a new development in a country in which privacy is generally closely guarded (United States Department of State 2002).

In Malaysia, prison conditions are poor, and prison overcrowding is also a serious problem. There were 1,328 female prisoners in Malaysian prisons in mid-2002, compared to 27,476 male prisoners. In August 2000, prison officials announced that a number of prison rules would be reviewed (United States Department of State 2002), but problems persist. For instance, Irene Xavire was detained under Malaysia's Internal Security Act (ISA), which allows police to detain people without trial indefinitely, as a preventive measure. Since it was enacted in 1960, during Malaysia's colonial era, this act has been used as justification for the arrest of thousands of activists, students, and politicians. Irene Xavire has told of her own experience, being harassed and beaten with a stick during interrogation sessions. "I had to show a policewoman a soiled sanitary pad before I could get sanitary pads and also get to keep my panties on. The police normally demand that you give up all items of clothing in exchange for the Chinese pants and blouse that they give you" (Xavire 2001).

Béatrice Saubin also told her story. In Malaysia, at age 19, she fell in love with Eddy Tan Kim Soo, a handsome, wealthy Chinese man. They planned to meet in Europe and later marry. But at the airport on her way home, her spanking new Samsonite suitcase – a gift from Eddy – was ripped apart by customs officials. Beatrice was horrified to see that it contained several kilos of heroin. Clearly she had been set up by Eddy, who, it turned out, was a member of a powerful drug cartel. Arrested, she languished in prison for two years before she was tried. Her sentence: death by hanging. On appeal, her sentence was reduced to life in prison. Efforts on the part of her grandmother and an impassioned attorney managed to stir up public opinion, finally leading to Beatrice's release after ten years. While in prison, her spirits were never broken: she taught herself Malaysian and Cantonese; she became a model prisoner and a leader as well as a medical supervisor, caring for her fellow inmates (Saubin 1991).

In Singapore, Malaysia, and Brunei Darussalam, criminal law prescribes caning as an additional punishment to imprisonment for those convicted of certain non-violent crimes, such as narcotics possession, criminal breach of trust, and alien smuggling. The caning, which is carried out with a half-inch-thick wooden cane, commonly causes welts, and sometimes causes scarring. However, male criminals age 50 and above, and women, are exempt from caning.

In Indonesia, the Directorate General of Corrections is under the administration of the ministry of justice. The system used by the directorate in carrying out its responsibilities is based on the *pemasyarakatan* system, as stated in Law No. 12 of 1995. This contains the rule that the treatment of offenders is aimed at efforts to manifest social reintegration, that is, the recovery of social relationships, and the unity of the prisoners as individuals, social creatures, and creatures of God.

The directorate currently operates 427 correctional institutions throughout Indonesia. Indonesia has 4 female prisons, whereas 129 units are provided for male prisoners. In mid 2002, there were 2,111 female prisoners, while male prisoners numbered 57,377. However, prison conditions are harsh. Mistreatment, the extortion of inmates by guards, and violence among prisoners is common (United States Department of State 2002). The incidence of mistreatment drops sharply once a prisoner is transferred from police or military custody into the civilian prison system, or into the custody of the attorney general. Nine prisoners died at the Kebon Waru Prison in Bandung, West Java, from untreated illnesses, according to press reports in July 2001. Credible sources report that prisoners in some facilities are beaten routinely and systematically, as punishment for infractions of prison rules and to coerce them into giving information about other prisoners. During an August 2001 raid on Cipinang Prison, in East Jakarta, police seized knives, swords, sickles, machetes, firearms, and hand grenades, which had been smuggled into the prison for the inmates, according to press accounts. It is no secret that prisoners can get better treatment and better conditions by bribing guards.

In relation to overcrowding of prisons in Indonesia, the number of detainees and prisoners increased gradually from 44,344 in 1995 to 48,256 in August 1999. This increase in numbers was likely caused by recent economic, social, and political developments. It was claimed by the office of the Directorate General that numbers were still below the capacity of the Detention Houses and Prisons Branch (APCCA 2000).

In 2003 Scottish academic Lesley McCulloch and her American friend Joy Sadler were accused of violating their tourist visas by carrying out research and cataloguing alleged human rights abuses in Aceh, a province on the northern tip of Sumatra, which had experienced 26-year-long separatist conflict and had been granted by the government the right to institute Sharīʿa law. McCulloch and Sadler revealed the extent to which they were allegedly assaulted, intimidated, harassed, and forced to witness hour-long torture sessions, while being detained in Indonesia. They say, however, that their treatment was luxurious, compared with the regular severe beatings suffered by other inmates, which, the women claimed, often kept them awake at night. This is a clear example of a political situation influencing the conditions of prisons and prisoners (Aglionby 2002).

BIBLIOGRAPHY

J. Aglionby, British woman held in Indonesian prison tells of beatings and torture of inmates, *Guardian*, 25 November 2002, <http://www.guardian.co.uk/indonesia/Story/0,2763,846959,00.html>.

APPCA, Record of the twentieth Asian and Pacific Conference of Correctional Administrators, Report prepared and compiled by D. Biles, N. Morgan, and A. McDonald, Sydney, Australia, 5–10 November 2000.

V. Kingi, The children of women in prison. A New Zealand study, paper presented at the conference on Women in Corrections: Staff and Clients, convened by the Australian Institute of Criminology in conjunction with the Department for Correctional Services SA, Adelaide, 31 October–1 November 2000.

F. Malekian, *The concept of Islamic international criminal law. A comparative study*, London 1994.

B. Saubin, *The ordeal. My ten years in a Malaysian prison*, trans. B. Brister, New York 2001.

United States Department of State, *Country reports on human rights practices for 2001. Prepared by the Bureau of Democracy, Human Rights, and Labor*, Washington, D.C. March 2002.

I. Xavire, My experience with police violence as an ISA detainee, 1 May 2001, <http://dfn.org/voices/malaysia/isatestimony.htm>.

NADIRSYAH HOSEN

Iran and Afghanistan

IRAN

Long-term prisons in Iran were established in the twentieth century. The replacement of corporal punishment with prolonged incarceration was part of the modernization process in which the traditional dual judicial system of Sharīʿa (religious) courts and *ʿurf* (secular) courts was being transformed into a uniform one. Yet some components ascribed to modernity go back to the unique case of Qurrat al-ʿAyn, a woman leader of the Bābī movement in the final phase of medieval judiciary under Nāṣir al-Dīn Shāh (r. 1848–96). She was the only one in the Bābī processes (1264–8/1848–52) to be condemned to lifelong imprisonment. The review procedure in 1268/1852 sentenced her to execution, which was non-public, unlike those of other Bābīs. She was also the first woman executed for "sowing corruption on earth" (there was no death sentence for women in either Sharīʿa or *ʿurf*, except for adultery).

THE CONSTITUTIONAL REVOLUTION 1905–9 AND THE PAHLAVĪ PERIOD (1920–79)

Regular imprisonment of women came into being just before women were granted constitutional rights. The judicial reform by Reza Khan in the early 1920s, however, cut away the power of the Sharīʿa and spared women the death penalty. In some cases women used this advantage to protect their male relatives from the death penalty. They took the blame for murder or drug dealing upon themselves and went to prison with the tacit approval of judges. However, the discrimination against women in the penal code concerning moral issues such as adultery made women vulnerable to sexual abuse by the police and jail staff.

In the most famous modern prison, Qaṣr, built 1920–25, a separate women's section was planned. In actual fact, women's prisons were merely the most underprivileged sections in men's prisons.

With the reforms of Mohammad Reza Shah (r. 1941–79) in the 1960s and 1970s, women were recruited into the police force and trained as wards for women detainees. But this did not lead to a reduction of sexual abuse of female prisoners. The death penalty now also applied to women.

The lack of attention paid to the particular needs of women such as pregnancy care, childcare, and similar matters, often resulted in the demoralization of women. Mothers were also blackmailed for political reasons.

THE ISLAMIC REPUBLIC OF IRAN 1979

The prisons with all-black-veiled inmates are the incarnation of the regime's Islamization program. As supposed "rehabilitation centers" they purport to transform "deviants" into proper human beings (*ādam*). As victims of double persecution female prisoners are forcibly uniformed in black chador in conformity with their female guards and become part of the Islamic media representation, whether they recant or not, whether they are Islamic or laic, Muslim or non-Muslim. "Woman," as defined in the preamble of the constitution of the Islamic Republic, is one of the pillars of the state, a category between army and economy, and is therefore to be converted into the subject of Islamic norm. The Islamization of women became the raison d'être of the *wilāyat-i faqīh* (governance of the religious jurist, the all-embracing system of clerical rule in the Islamic Republic). Islamic justice imposed rigid social, moral, and behavioral codes on women.

From 1980 to 1985, ideological armed forces and numerous paramilitary organizations such as *basīj* arrested masses of women and girls for adultery, prostitution, or simply unlawful contact with men. Revolutionary Islamic courts condemned many to execution and others to physical punishment or imprisonment. As a consequence of the bloody political repression the world public focused on political prisoners but ignored the fate of ordinary prisoners.

After the defeat of the political opposition in Iran, the *ḥijāb* became the main reason for mass persecution. The plan to combat immorality and improper *ḥijāb* (bad *ḥijāb*) of 1990 and the plan for the superior *ḥijāb* (*ṭarḥ-i ḥijāb-i bartar*) of 1994 resulted in massive detentions. In the following years many female street children were imprisoned. Some girls were put in prison for undefined offenses such as running away or wearing boy's attire.

AFGHANISTAN

After British rule ended in 1919, Afghanistan underwent several reform programs: the constitution of 1923 (Amān Allāh Khān); the constitution of 1931 (Muḥammad Nādir Shāh); the modernist reform of 1953 (Muḥammad Dāwūd Khān); and the constitution of 1964 (Ẓahīr Shāh), which sought the way to the modern world. The first "public" arena opened to women and girls during this period was the prison. The imprisonment of female relatives of male opponents was the only constant that cut through the complicated ethno-political conflicts and political changes from monarchy to republic and from republic to Islamic state. The situation of imprisoned women was hidden from public awareness for decades. Gender-based violence such as sexual abuse of women or the virginity test on girls in official detention centers and prisons were only reported after the end of the Taliban regime. Under the rule of the Mujāhidīn groups in the 1990s there was neither a real central power nor a judicial system. Warlords were in charge as Islamic judges and condemned their prisoners arbitrarily.

Under the Taliban (1996–2001) the Islamization of Afghanistan reached its peak. Women were excluded from public life. Sharīʿa courts and the Istakhbārāt (secret service) were established. Taliban militia and the authority for fighting against immorality persecuted women. They arrested, beat, mutilated, imprisoned, killed, kidnapped, and enslaved them with the accusation of immorality or just for being non-Pashtun. Many women were detained and beaten in public for specific offenses such as not wearing a *burqaʿ*, wearing white socks or shoes, or shoes that made a noise when walking, being unaccompanied by a male chaperone in public, or entering a public building through a designated male entrance.

Bibliography

R. Afshari, *Human rights in Iran. The abuse of cultural relativism*, Philadelphia 2001.
J. Ahmadi, Die Justiz der Willkür. Geschlechterideologie als Grundlage der "Rechtsordnung" des Gottesstaates Iran, in Maria Hockstein-Rasch (ed.), *23. Feministischer Juristinnentag. Dokumentation*, Berlin 1997, 61–7.
——, Zur Funktion des Hijab in der Staatsideologie der Islamischen Republik Iran, in *Vorgänge* 150 (2000), 66–70.
A. Amanat, *Resurrection and renewal. The making of the Babi movement in Iran, 1844–1850*, London 1990.
Amnesty International, Afghanistan. Police reconstrution essential to protect human rights, AI Index: ASA 11/003/2003, <http://www.web.amnesty.org/library/index/engasa110032003>.
——, Afghanistan. Re-establishing the rule of law, AI Index: ASA 11/021/2003, <http://news.amnesty.org/library/index/engasa110212003>.
——, Afghanistan. Crumbling prison system desperately in need of repair, AI Index: ASA 11/017/2003, <http://web.amnesty.org/library/Index/ ENGASA110172003?open&of=ENG-AFG>.
Human Rights Watch, We want to live as humans. Repression of women and girls in western Afghanistan, HRW Index: C1411, 2002, <http://www.hrw.org/reports/2002/afghnwmn1202/>.
International Commission of Jurists, Afghanistan's legal system and its compatibility with international human rights standards, final report by M. Lau, 2003, <http://www.icj.org/IMG/pdf/doc-51.pdf>.
H. Nategh, Masa'lah-i zan dar barkhī az mudawwanāt-i chap az nahḍat-i mashrūṭīh tā ʿaṣr-i Riḍa Khān, in *Zamān-i Nu*, 1 (1983), 8–15.
Physicians for Human Rights, *The Taliban's war on women. A health and human rights crisis in Afghanistan*, Boston 1998, <http://www.phrusa.org/research/health_effects/exec.html>.
Provisorisches Frauenkomitee gegen Hinrichtungen im Iran, *Bericht über 83 Gefangene Frauen im Iran*, Berlin 1989.
D. M. Rejali, *Torture and modernity. Self, society, and state in modern Iran*, Boulder, Colo. 1994.
Trapped by tradition. Women and girls in detention in Kabul Welayat, in *Medica Mondiale*, 5 March 2003, <http://www.medicamondiale.de/download/KabulHaft Report_e.pdf>.
United Nations High Commissioner for Human Rights, Integration of the human rights of women and the gender perspective, E/CN.4/2003/134, <http://www.unhchr.ch/Huridocda/Huridoca.nsf/(Symbol)/E.CN.4.2003.134.En?Opendocument>.

Jale Ahmadi

South Asia

This entry covers three countries crafted by violence: India, Pakistan, and Bangladesh. India, with a sizeable Muslim population, is secular by constitution and law; the other two, with majority Muslim populations, have turned from secularism to theocracy.

The Indian subcontinent was structured along tribal and feudal lines during colonial times. The British superimposed upon this a secular common law framework that applied to all areas except personal law, which was left to the discretion of each indigenous community. At the same time, in certain geographical areas, the colonial power accepted the continuation of tribal law through the Frontier Crimes Regulation 1901.

Upon independence in 1947 Pakistan (which at that time included Bangladesh) therefore inherited a secular legal system with a complete hierarchy of courts that had jurisdiction in both civil and criminal matters. In addition, in what were carved out as the Federally and Provincially Administered Tribal Areas (FATA and PATA), the new republic left undisturbed the system of tribal law and tribal courts.

In India, Muslims continue to be governed in matters of personal law by the Muslim Personal Law (Shariat) Application Act 1937. Though this has been amended in some states in India and for some issues (for example, maintenance) the general secular law applies, the Supreme Court of India maintains that its application to Muslims in India is mandatory. Though the institution of the *qazi* (*qāḍī*, Islamic judge) was abolished in British India in 1864, there now exists in some localized areas in India a non-governmental alternative dispute resolution mechanism to decide issues of Muslim personal law. These are called Shariat Courts and are presided over by *qazi*s. The state has often shied away from progressive legislation for Muslim women as it has not wished to create a political issue with Indian Muslims (who have also resisted the idea of integration).

It is, however, important to point out that in India and Bangladesh the applicable criminal law is secular and Islamic laws have not entered into this arena. This is the case even though in Bangladesh the constitution was amended in 1988 to make the religion of the republic Islam, with the rider in the amendment that, "other religions may be practiced in peace and harmony." In Pakistan, the state has taken steps to extend Islamic law outside the sphere of personal law.

Pakistan is a declared religious state and its genesis was the creation of a homeland for Muslims. The legal system has therefore accepted that the state and religion cannot conceptually be separated and that it is the business of the state to ensure that its citizens order their lives according to Islamic ideology. While family law was always included, in 1979 the Hudood Ordinances expanded the scope to criminal laws. In 1980, a Federal Shariat Court was introduced with the power to review all laws (except personal and fiscal laws) and to decide whether these were in consonance with the Qur'ān and *sunna*. Appeal would lie to a special Shariat Appellate Bench of the Supreme Court.

The introduction of Islamic criminal laws had a profound impact on the number of women who were imprisoned and the numbers increased almost threefold over time due to the application of the Adultery Ordinance 1979, which covers the offenses of rape and adultery. In 1989 the number of women imprisoned under the Adultery Ordinance alone was reportedly approximately 6,000.

Adultery, which under the secular British Penal Code was defined as a private offence, was changed under the Adultery Ordinance 1979 and made a public offence (cognizable and non-bailable) for which the state could initiate prosecutions. According to activists in Pakistan, the complainant in an adultery case is often a member of the woman's own family. It is a convenient way for a husband who wants to marry a second time to get rid of his wife; for a father to punish an errant daughter who does not want to follow the family's dictates as to whom she should marry; or an easy strategy to remove a woman if she will inherit property. Further, as the Safia Bibi case and the more recent Zafran Bibi case show, the introduction of adultery as a public offence after 1979 has made a rape victim vulnerable to a counter charge of adultery.

Zafran Bibi had filed a criminal complaint for rape under the Adultery Ordinance 1979. Whilst rape was not proved, on the basis that intercourse had occurred Zafran Bibi was convicted of *zinā* (adultery) under this ordinance and was sentenced to the maximum punishment of death by stoning. The case was taken up by the Human Rights Commission of Pakistan and Zafran Bibi's conviction and sentence were eventually set aside.

Despite intensive lobbying efforts made by human rights groups, even today over 7,000 women and children are imprisoned in the 75 jails of Pakistan, of whom more than 50 percent are women imprisoned under the Adultery Ordinance. Almost all these women come from the poorest sections of society. They are especially vulnerable because of their illiteracy, low economic status, and limited access to legal resources. These women suffer the dual yoke of oppression as state law is superimposed upon the existing tribal structure, which is also protected by Pakistani law. As Nafisa Shah (1998) points out, the imposition of the Hudood Ordinances and the Qisas and Diyat Act 1990 have added tribal characteristics to the Pakistani justice system.

In India and Bangladesh, though women may not be imprisoned for adultery, they are imprisoned as in Pakistan for prostitution or murder (often of their husbands). As in the case of their Pakistani counterparts they come from poverty-stricken backgrounds. In all three jurisdictions these women are kept in overcrowded conditions without access to health or legal aid facilities. Many have young children incarcerated with them as these children have no homes or family to go to. In 2002 the Indian Council of Legal Aid and Advice filed a public interest litigation in the Supreme Court asking that state governments formulate proper guidelines for the protection and welfare of children of women prisoners. In Karachi Central Jail, Pakistan, the children of women prisoners are taught by a teacher whose salary is paid by a local NGO (non-governmental organization), the EDHI Trust, rather than by the government.

The judiciary and the police in the subcontinent have taken an ambivalent view of women's rights. In dealing with the issue of dowry, which is prevalent among Muslims as well as Hindus, activists say that despite the insertion of section 304B in the Indian Penal Code in 1986 convictions are rare and judges are often uninterested. In India it is said that there are about 5,000 dowry deaths annually. In all three jurisdictions allegations are consistently made of custodial rape. A study in Bangladesh by the NGO Odhikar documented that 13 women were raped by members of law enforcement agencies in 2000, the youngest being a girl of six.

Given the strength of patriarchal structures within the subcontinent, the application of "Islamic" criminal law becomes even more complex because of its "moral" connotation. In Pakistan a definite anti-woman bias is evident from the language used by courts to describe a rape victim. Some of the terms used are "loose character," "habitual case of enjoying sexual intercourse," "shady person," "willing party," and "woman of easy virtue." Thus, once women are imprisoned under the Adultery Ordinance 1979 in Pakistan, whether rightly or wrongly, they lose the protection of the family. In the Bangladeshi context, Naila Kabeer (1989) also notes that rehabilitation, whether of prostitutes, jail inmates, or other fallen women, is determined by notions of "purity." As compared to male prisoners, women receive fewer visitors and a larger proportion of women in prison are without legal representation. Their contact with the family is also broken by the fact that in all three countries, there are fewer women's jails than men's jails. Women may therefore be imprisoned away from their hometowns. In the province of Sindh (Pakistan), for example, there is only one woman's jail in Larkana. In Tamil Nadu, India, there are nine central prisons and only two women's jails.

The response of states within the subcontinent has varied. In Bangladesh, a series of laws has been promulgated making kidnapping, trafficking, rape, and acid throwing offenses with a maximum penalty of life imprisonment or death. In India, Muslim women are governed by the secular criminal laws, which have been amended proactively. In 1983 the minimum punishment was increased in cases of custodial rape. To contend with dowry deaths Section 174(2) of the Indian Criminal Procedure Code now requires that in cases of death of a woman within seven years of her marriage the police have to send the body to a civil surgeon for examination. In stark contrast, in Pakistan the state has enacted discriminatory laws in the form of the Hudood Ordinances, which it refuses to repeal on one pretext or another, despite the recommendation of the Pakistan Commission on Inquiry for Women (1997).

In Pakistan, the judicial system also recognizes tribal customary law under which killings of women in furtherance of male honor are condoned. In these cases a lesser sentence is given to the accused because "sudden and grave provocation" is accepted as a mitigating factor. Even in those cases of murder that are prosecuted, under the Qisas and Diyat Law it is possible for the murderer to pay blood money to the heirs of the murder victim and thus, contrary to the principles of human rights, murder has been made a compoundable offence. Ironically, whilst adultery has been categorized as a public offence that is non-compoundable, murder has been reconceptualized as a compoundable private offence against the victim rather than the state.

Judicial acceptance in Pakistan of crimes of honor under the defense of grave and sudden provocation also indicates that the tribal code of justice is not limited to the tribal area (FATA); its principles have a more general application within the Islamic criminal laws and the Indo-British court system. In 2000, the Human Rights Commission of Pakistan reported that over 1,000 honor killings take place in Pakistan every year. These are generally not prosecuted.

In Bangladesh, as the state has begun to sponsor Islamization, activists say that in rural areas women are now increasingly facing trials through the fatwa (religious judgment). Village elders usually form a *salish* or tribunal from which women are excluded, as they are in Pakistan from the tribal *jirga*. Interestingly the tribal *jirga* does not sanctify itself by applying Islamic law, but the Bangladeshi *salish* has meted out "Islamic" punishments in contravention of the Penal Code and some women have been publicly flogged.

Whether finding its justification in religion or tribalism, the ultimate effect of the interplay of tribal laws, customary practices, Islamic law, and Indo-British traditions is to deprive women, and any advantage or opportunity offered by one law or system is cancelled out by the other.

The subordination of women through violence cuts across all cultures and religions within the subcontinent. In Pakistan the situation is starker because of state-enacted Islamic criminal laws that reinforce women's secondary status and are not used for her protection but rather for her policing and punishment. By allowing imprisonment of women in large numbers under the Adultery Ordinance the law has provided an additional tool of oppression for men to wield in Pakistan.

BIBLIOGRAPHY

N. Ahmad, The position of women with reference to the Pakistan criminal justice system, in *Alam-e-Niswan* 1:1 (n.d.), 57.

——, Development in the law of rape, in *The tyranny of rape*, Human Rights Commission of Pakistan, February 1992, 6.
——, The other view point, in Tuesday Review, Rights of Women in Islam, *Dawn* (Pakistan daily) 14–20 November 1995, 88.
S. Ashraf, Behind bars, in *She Magazine* (July 2003), 83.
Bureau Report, *Dawn*, 31 May 2000, <www.dawn.com>.
D. Chanddokhe, Dowry death, <http://www.legalserviceindia.com/helpline/help5.htm>.
Government of Pakistan, *Report of the Pakistan commission on inquiry for women*, Islamabad 1997.
Hinduism today, August 1988, <http://www.hinduonnet.com/thehindu/mag/2003/04/06/stories/2003040600290400.htm>.
N. Kabeer, *The quest for national identity. Women, Islam and the state in Bangladesh*, Institute of Development Studies at the University of Sussex, Discussion Paper No. 268, Brighton, England, October 1989 and in D. Kandiyoti (ed.), *Women, Islam and the State*, Philadelphia 1991, 115–43.
S. Kamal and A. Khan, A study of the interplay of formal and customary laws on women, i, unpublished study by Raasta Development Consultants, Karachi 1997.
D. Kandiyoti, Women and Islam. What are the missing terms? <www.wluml.org/english/pubs/pdf/dossiers5-6.pdf>.
S. Kazi. Muslim women in India, Report of Minority Rights Group International, 1999, <www.minorityrights.org/admin/Download/Pdf/muslimwomenrep.pdf>.
M. A. Khan (ed.), *Constitution of the Islamic Republic of Pakistan 1973*, Karachi 1988.
R. Marcus, Violence against women in Bangladesh, Pakistan, Egypt, Sudan, Senegal and Yemen, March 1993, <http://www.ids.ac.uk/bridge>.
H. Mayell, Thousands of women killed for family "honor," *National Geographic News*, <http://news.nationalgeographic.com/news/2002/02/0212_020212_honorkilling.html>, February 2002.
T. Mehmood, *The Muslim law of India*, Allahabad 2002.
T. M. Murshid, Women, Islam and the state in Bangladesh. Subordination and Resistance, <www.unige.ch/iued/new/information/publications/pdf/yp_creativite_femmes_dev/11-crea_tazeen.pdf>.
M. Pal et al. (eds.), The situation of women in Bangladesh. Study initiated by Asian Development Bank, January 2001, <http://www.adb.org/Documents/Books/Country_Briefing_Papers/Women_in_Bangladesh/default.asp>.
K. Pillai, Women and criminal procedure, <http://www.hsph.harvard.edu/Organizations/healthnet/SAsia/forums/crimes/articles/procedure.html>.
F. Rahman. Female sexuality and Islam, <www.wluml.org/english/pubs/pdf/dossiers5-6.pdf >.
S. Rahman, Women in Bangladesh. Reflections on women and violence in 2000, <http://www.ahrchk.net/hrsolid/mainfile.php/2001vol11no5/67/>.
S. Sardar Ali and K. Arif, Parallel judicial systems in Pakistan and consequences for human rights, in F. Shaheed et al. (eds.), *Shaping women's lives, laws, practices and strategies in Pakistan*, Lahore 1998, 29–60.
N. Shah, Faislo. The informal settlement system and crimes against women in Sindh, in F. Shaheed et al. (eds.), *Shaping women's lives, laws, practices and strategies in Pakistan*, Lahore 1998, 227–52.
Society for the Advancement of Community, Health, Education and Training, study reported in *Dawn*, 20 February 2003. See also Women in jails in miserable state, in *Dawn*, 20 May 2003, <www.dawn.com>.
P. Srinivasan and G. R. Lee, The dowry system in India. Women's attitudes and social change, <www.bgsu.edu/organizations/cfdr/ research/pdf/2002/2002_15.pdf>.
Tamil Nadu, Prison Department, Statistics, <http://www.tn.nic.in/prisons/statistics.htm>.

NAUSHEEN AHMAD

Sub-Saharan Africa

Prisons in Africa are an un-African institution. Nowhere in precolonial African societies were prisons used as a form of punishment; West Africa's measures for crime control were restorative and retributivist justice. European colonialists converted slave forts along the Atlantic coast into gaols or cachots (Bernault 2003). In postcolonial Africa, several notorious prisons were shut down, although a few countries opened separate prisons for women and adolescent males. Prisons turned into "homes" for young, socially displaced, undereducated, unemployed, and poor women.

Certain occupations, such as sex work or domestic work, invite sexual abuse and criminalization. Domestic workers tend to be young, rural, unmarried women who may risk being assaulted or raped by their patron; in countries where abortion is illegal and unaffordable, they may commit infanticide out of despair. In some women's prisons, the majority of prisoners and remanded women are accused – or convicted – of infanticide. The social sanctions for having a child out of wedlock are severe. Amina Lawal, a Nigerian woman who escaped – on appeal – the sentence of stoning in a Sharīʿa court in October 2003, is a case in point. Some women await execution for up to ten years. Unfair and sexist trial procedures put women at further risk; for example, a divorced woman whose baby was stillborn was still charged with murder because her doctor's evidence was not introduced in court (Amnesty International 2004).

In several African countries, the institution of polygamy also has a negative effect, particularly on women who have never received formal education or who dropped out of primary education. A recent Ugandan study (Tibatemwa-Ekirikubinza 1999) actually notes the higher prevalence of female criminality (toward husband, junior co-wife, or the co-wife's child) in rural regions where polygamy prevails. Prisoners, in particular those who were senior wives, note the disparities in asset sharing by their husbands; frequently they justify their offenses by accusing the husband of total economic and emotional abandonment of them and their children.

The threat of sexual violence is intensified in women's prisons, especially where men guard women convicts in women's living quarters. Male prisoners, too, can be a threat to women's well-being. Most African prisons house men, women, and children, and may merely provide separate sleeping facilities. During colonial times, sexual assault and gang rape was particularly prevalent because women were not given separate quarters from men. In Senegal, African women were expected to cook for the entire prison population and sleep in the kitchen or on the porch of the fort or prison compound (Konate 2003). Colonial prisons enforced racial segregation, and European prisoners were housed in the vicinity of the warden's office or compound (Goerg 2003).

Lesbian convicts are particularly vulnerable to attack from heterosexual prisoners and being reported to prison staff (Dirsuweit 1999, Mkhize 1992). Some prisoners also convey fear of guards who are known lesbians and prey on female prisoners (Shawalu 1985).

In many countries, unsentenced detainees held on remand for more than five years comprise over 70 percent of the prison population. What is often deemed "death by natural causes" by prison officials is actually caused by the following factors: lack of sanitation and clean drinking water, dietary deficiency, lack of adequate health care, and overcrowding (an especially dire situation in Rwanda prisons after the recent genocide of Tutsis). Mortality rates increase dramatically during the rainy season. A recent Zimbabwean study illustrates prison conditions that may be generalized for the vast majority of women's prisons in Africa. There is no gender-specific consideration. Men's prisons are the standard and women are housed in sections of men's prisons or – more infrequently – in separate facilities. Women are refused basic sanitary items (Musengezi et al. 2003). South African female common law prisoners were particularly degraded by being denied underwear and cotton from the prison system in the 1970s (Kuzwayo 1985).

Generally, judges do not grant early release to pregnant women, mothers with widow status, or those who have young children. The lack of basic health and dietary needs is particularly grave for pregnant women. In most prisons in Africa, pregnant convicts get minimal or no pre- or perinatal care; child mortality, as a result, is higher in prisons than in civil society. Most prisoners are mothers, and young children often stay with their mothers, in part because the father has abandoned the wife upon her incarceration or because the mother's family is ashamed of her convict status and refuses to take the children. In some prisons, no extra clothing is provided for children, and children suffer from the same poor diet as their mothers; the children are literally punished along with their mothers (Tibatemwa-Ekirikubinza 1999). "Women with babies in prison seem to carry a double punishment of coping themselves and fending for their children" (Musengezi et al. 2003). Measures of rehabilitation are minimal and prison chores are overwhelmingly of a domestic nature, reinforcing a gendered division of labor. Many women are illiterate and have very minimal formal education. Linguistic difficulties may adversely affect ethnic minorities and immigrants, who do not understand the lingua franca of the courts and the prison staff (de Klerk et al. 2001). Amina Lawal did not understand the charge against her, because the Sharīʿa judge used Arabic, rather than her native Hausa, when she was indicted for adultery.

Political prisoners

From the onset of the colonial conquest, the carceral compound was used for political control of Africans. However, after decolonization, many governments continued the practice of incarcerating political opponents (Bernault 2003). Women's political imprisonment is predicated on their participation in liberation struggles during the colonial and apartheid era. Women instigated revolts against poll taxes (Nigeria) and fought with men for national liberation (for example, Mau Mau members in Kenya, pass laws resisters in South Africa). Many women were subjected to sexual assault, rape, and other forms of torture and murder in detention camps and prisons cells (Harlow 1992, wa Wamwere 2002, Konzaye 1985, Tesfagiorgis 1992). Women political leaders also faced house arrest and banishment, which turned the banned person into a self-policing docile body (Ramphele 1995). Winnie Mandela was so acutely aware of her exceptional status in the apartheid regime that she was always prepared to return to prison and had a suitcase ready at all times (Mandela 1985). Gambo Sawaba was similarly prepared; she was incarcerated more than a dozen times for her defiant stance against the Native Authority in northern Nigeria before Nigeria's independence. Often her offenses stemmed from public speaking and consorting with men in public, offenses which also attracted prison terms during the 1960s (Shawalu 1990).

Political detainees and prisoners differentiate themselves from common or social detainees and convicts. They describe serving their sentences with pride and determination, and several prisoners report that their family and community support was essential to endure isolation and torture. They instigate hunger strikes and launch grievances, never coming to terms with the label of prisoner; some refuse to work and all refuse to be "rehabilitated." A few prisoners use violence against guards to resist repression (Makhoere 1988). Some women are erroneously detained for participating in illegal political movements, yet upon release, they actually join the liberation movement to which they were falsely accused of belonging (Tesfagiorgis 1992).

In South Africa under apartheid, women political prisoners attempted to make common cause with common law prisoners, who were condemned to hard labor (Meer 2001). The regime refused acknowledgment of the existence of political prisoners, yet it isolated them from common law prisoners. Sometimes, the warden placed common prisoners with a political prisoner to press them into service to inform on the latter (Makhoere 1988). Northern Nigerian political prisoner Gambo Sawaba counseled women to say they were practicing Christians to evade harsh sanctions of the Sharīʿa court (Shawalu 1990).

But at other times, political prisoners distance themselves from the "unfortunate drunks" and outcasts (First 1989). This hierarchy is reinforced by the warden's "fear of infectious belief": political detainees and political prisoners tend to be totally segregated so that they cannot incite the mass of social prisoners to rise up and organize for better prison conditions or raise their political consciousness. Almost all political prisoners have participated or organized a hunger strike. Caesarina Kona Makhoere reports that her cohort instigated the first strike in South Africa's women's prisons in 1976 – a time of mass arrests and deaths in detention of school children in the aftermath of the Soweto uprising. After 1976, isolation of detainees increased; this method of punishment attacks the soul of the political prisoner and was particularly utilized under the apartheid regime of South Africa (Mashinini 1989, Makhoere 1988, First 1989, Mandela 1985). Sometimes, political prisoners are allowed no literature other than the Bible or the Qurʾān and they use the scriptures in order to make light of their own situation (Makhoere 1988, Meer 2001), in particular when they endure psychological torture, such as prolonged interrogation (First 1989). Despite the severe psychological and physical hardships faced by women prisoners, their situation often is downplayed by male political prisoners and their community while men's political imprisonment is romanticized (Middleton 1998). Yet, women faced torture and death in detention under the apartheid regime; political detainees of both genders faced isolation, often without bedding or thin blankets covering cold, concrete floors. However, the regime sharply discriminated according to the color line; white and colored prisoners did receive better accommodations than black prisoners.

Many former political prisoners complain of heart problems, growth of tumors, and other diseases affecting their health in the long term. Mashinini's account of her six-month solitary detention reveals an intense level of post-traumatic stress disorder. Her isolation was only interrupted by extended interrogations by her tormentors. Yet, all prisoners' testimonials note with pride that they endured persecution, banishment, and prison life and at times even "confess" to their interrogators that "everything I had done I would willingly do again" (First 1989, 90). Fatima Meer, a former president of the Black Women's Federation of South Africa, reports that she would not have wanted to miss the experience of five months detention, despite the fact that she was already a banned person by the time she was detained (Meer 2001, 210). Political prisoners fairly easily reintegrate into their society, thanks to the community support they receive; some leave the country to receive counseling for post-traumatic stress disorder (Mashinini 1989). Common law prisoners, however, face many difficulties post-release. The majority are abandoned by their husbands and even their own families of origin. Long-term prisoners struggle with adjusting to the changes of society, and many face abject poverty, suffering from property loss and even mob justice: a Ugandan ex-prisoner may find her house burnt to the ground and her belongings confiscated (Tibatemwa-Ekirikubinza 1999).

Is there hope for closing prisons all over Africa? A few countries, such as Mali, have closed prisons from the colonial period and have not built new prisons. Yet criminal activities, even committed by women, are a growing concern in many African countries and imprisonment continues to be the choice of punishment, rather than the aberration.

Bibliography

Amnesty International, Nigeria. *The death penalty and women under the Nigerian penal systems*, 2004.

F. Bernault, The politics of enclosure in colonial and post-colonial Africa, in F. Bernault (ed.), J. Roitman (trans.), *History of prison and confinement in Africa*, Portsmouth, N.H. 2003, 1–53.

T. Dirsuweit, Carceral spaces in South Africa. A case of institutional power, sexuality and transgression in women's prison, in *Geoforum* 30:1 (1999), 71–83.

R. First, *117 days*, New York 1989.

O. Goerg, Colonial urbanism and prisons in Africa. Reflections on Conakry and Freetown, 1903–1960, in F. Bernault (ed.), J. Roitman (trans.), *History of prison and confinement in Africa*, Portsmouth 2003, 119–34.

B. Harlow, *Barred. Women, writing, and political detention*, Hanover, N.H. 1992.
V. de Klerk and G. Barkhuizen, Language usage and attitudes in a South African prison. Who calls the shots?, in *International Journal of Social Language* 152 (2001), 97–115.
D. Konate, Ultimate exclusion. Imprisoned women in Senegal, in F. Bernault (ed.), J. Roitman (trans.), *History of prison and confinement in Africa*, Portsmouth, N.H. 2003, 155–63.
E. Kuzwayo, *Call me woman*, San Francisco 1985.
C. K. Makhoere, *No child's play. In prison under apartheid*, London 1988.
W. Mandela, *Part of my soul went with him*, New York 1985.
E. Mashinini, *Strikes have followed me all my life. A South African autobiography*, London 1989.
F. Meer, *Prison diary. One hundred and thirteen days, 1976*, Cape Town 2001.
P. Mkhize, A snake with ice water, in B. Schreiner (ed.), *A snake with ice water. Prison writings by South African women*, Johannesburg 1992, 240–9.
J. Middleton, *Convictions. A woman political prisoner remembers*, Randberg 1998.
T. Modie-Moroka, Vulnerability across a life course. An empirical study. Women and criminality in Botswana prisons, in *Journal of Social Development in Africa* 18 (2003), 145–79.
C. Musengezi and I. Staunton (eds.), *A tragedy of lives. Women in prison in Zimbabwe*, Harare 2003.
M. Nagel, Women, prisons and peacemaking in Mali, in M. Nagel et al. (eds.), *Rethinking prisons. Cross national perspectives*, Rowman and Littlefield (forthcoming).
M. Ramphele, *A life*, Cape Town 1995.
D. Schalkwyk, Writing from prison, in S. Nuttall et al. (eds.), *Senses of culture. South African culture studies*, Oxford 2000, 278–97.
B. Schreiner (ed.), *A snake with ice water. Prison writings by South African women*, Johannesburg 1992.
R. Shawalu, *The story of Gambo Sawaba*, Jos, Plateau State, Nigeria 1990.
A. Tesfagiorgis, *A painful season and a stubborn hope. The odyssey of an Eritrean mother*, Trenton, N.J. 1992.
L. Tibatemwa-Ekirikubinza, *Women's violent crime in Uganda*, Kampala 1999.
K. wa Wamwere, *I refuse to die. My journey for freedom*, New York 2002.
Prisons in Africa, <http://hrw.org/prisons/africa.html>.

MECHTHILD NAGEL

Law: The Four Sunnī Schools of Law

Overview

This entry initially examines the factors that precipitated the rise of the four legal schools in Sunnī Islam, the various methodologies the schools utilized in the derivation of juridical rulings, and the cultural factors that influenced the rulings they issued. These were important considerations in the issuance of rulings on women in Sunnī jurisprudence. Based on the rulings stated in various juridical tracts, the entry also compares and contrasts the treatment of women in these schools.

The establishment of the schools of law (*madhāhib*)

With the establishment of the Umayyad dynasty in the eighth century, Muslims were living under rulers who were not regarded by many as the proper authority to create the Qurʾānic ideal of a just social order. It was at this time that the office of a definitive group of scholars interested in recording traditions took shape. Many Followers (*tābiʿūn*) of the Prophet are also mentioned as having acumen in juridical matters. These experts in the legal field tried to define and expound Islamic legal doctrine especially on issues that pertained to rituals, inheritance, marriage, divorce, and so forth. The early scholars in the legal field formed the provenance of the *fuqahāʾ* – a group of scholarly elite who specialized in the study of Islamic legal science, the Sharīʿa.

Initially, the jurists were private individuals who were keen to discern God's intent on a particular ruling. The goal of the jurists' endeavor was to reach an understanding (*fiqh*) of the Sharīʿa, that is, to comprehend in precise terms the law of God. Guided by a corpus of precepts and laws and their own independent reasoning, the jurists, especially in the ʿAbbāsid period, attempted to construct a legal edifice by developing and elaborating a system of Sharīʿa law binding on all Muslims. They began to interpret and develop Islamic law, invoking various hermeneutical principles such as *maṣlaḥa* (derivation and application of a juridical ruling that is in the public interest), *qiyās* (analogy), *ijtihād* (independent reasoning), *istiḥsān* (preference of a ruling that a jurist deems most appropriate under the circumstances), and other innovative interpretive principles. They aimed to respond to the needs of the times and to go beyond the rulings stated in the revealed texts while at the same time paying respect to the very texts that had empowered them.

Increased legal activities by the *fuqahāʾ* led to the development of ancient schools of law in different parts of the Islamic world. Initially, the schools of law did not imply a definite organization or strict uniformity of teachings within a school. Gradually, the jurists constructed a program for private and public living centered on the Sharīʿa. The Sharīʿa, as articulated by these jurists, became a structured normative praxis and a comprehensive system that governed personal and public demeanor. The schools were named after their founders or prominent jurists in the area.

The jurists of the schools of law

Derivation of legal rulings (*aḥkām*) was contingent on local circumstances and the employment of different sources of law. In Medina the *sunna* (practices of Muḥammad) was informed not only by transmitted reports from the Prophet but also by the transmitted practices of the community. The local character of the traditional practices was partially incorporated in the Medinese concept of Prophetic *sunna*. Preponderance was frequently given to local practice over reports of Prophetic practice since it was argued by the Medinese that contemporary practice could interpret or supplement earlier practice.

In his *al-Muwaṭṭaʾ*, Mālik b. Anas (d. 179/795) often transmits earlier or contemporary Medinese practice on a legal point. He also cites different reports on the practices of the Prophet to vindicate his own legal opinion. He then accepts or rejects these in the light of his own reasoning and based on the practices of Medina. This selective process can be corroborated from his frequent usage of the statement, "This is the opinion that we [the people of Medina] hold." In essence, Mālikī jurisprudence attempted to forge a closer link to practical considerations by attaching greater weight to social customs than did jurists in other areas.

In contrast to the Mālikīs, the jurists of Kufa saw their interpretations based on reasoning (*raʾy*) as an equally authoritative factor in the decision of a point of law. The *raʾy* of a scholar was partially incorporated by Abū Ḥanīfa (d. 150/767) as an important element in jurisprudence. The jurists of Kufa also used *qiyās* (analogy) in the extension of Prophetic practice and often formulated the law on rational grounds as opposed to ruling on the basis of transmitted practice that purportedly reflected Prophetic practice.

Kufan society was very cosmopolitan as it was exposed to different cultures and classes. Its class distinctions were not felt in the closely-knit Arab society of Medina. The school of Medina was conservative and bound to the laws established in Medina, whereas, animated by a spirit of independent thinking and analogy, the school of Kufa was eclectic and receptive to foreign legal systems. The Kufans also incorporated the customs of the divergent cultures that were prevalent there including some Sassanian customs appropriated from Persia.

The views of another prominent jurist of the time, Muḥammad b. Idris al-Shāfiʿī (d. 205/820), differed considerably from those of Medina and Kufa. Shāfiʿī contended that the personal opinion of the jurist must arise within rather than outside of the perimeters of Prophetic *sunna*. If this cannot be demonstrated, he said, then the *sunna* cannot be accepted as it might have arisen from the opinions of local authorities or arbitrary reasoning.

Focusing on the famous Qurʾānic verse "Obey God and His messenger," Shāfiʿī further circumscribed the definition of the *sunna*, restricting it to a textual and transmitted record of Prophetic practice. The Medinese and Kufans would have to base their rulings on a universal standard, the *sunna* as reported in accredited traditions. Although he depended on traditions from the Prophet, Shāfiʿī also allowed limited usage of analogy and a more restricted form of reasoning excluding arbitrary opinions and discretionary decisions. Recognizing the presence of spurious traditions he stipulated strict conditions for the acceptance of traditions. By insisting on the *sunna* of the Prophet, Shāfiʿī nullified the concept of local practices and arbitrary reasoning. Through his efforts, the four schools came to subscribe to a common theory of the sources of law (Qurʾān, tradition, consensus, and analogy).

In contrast to the other schools of law, the main thesis of the *ahl al-ḥadīth* (people of tradition) was that traditions transmitted from the Prophet and his companions superseded local traditions and legal injunctions that were derived independently of revealed sources. They produced traditions to vindicate their views and based their legal system on the Qurʾān and traditions purportedly transmitted from the Prophet. Even though many of these traditions were spurious, the *ahl al-ḥadīth* spurned all forms of reasoning and some jurists, such as Aḥmad b. Ḥanbal (d. 241/855), even claimed that weak traditions were better than human reasoning.

The use of various hermeneutical devices, exposure to diverse cultural influences, and a variegated understanding of the sources, derivation, and contents of the *sunna* were thus important factors that precipitated differences between the schools and influenced the rulings that were issued by them.

It is also important to note that the juridical manuals were composed in the male-dominated centers that excluded female voices in Islamic legal discourse. Women had little say in relation to the laws on marriage, divorce, inheritance, female testimony, and so forth. Consequently women's issues have depended on "representational discourse" conducted by male jurists who interpreted and articulated the rulings related to women. Moreover, patriarchal structures of Arab culture that prevailed in the eighth and ninth centuries were often incorporated in the emerging juridical literature. These were significant factors that influenced how women were treated in the juridical discourse.

The Qurʾān and *ḥadīth* literature on women

Against the background of a tribal society in seventh-century Arabia, the Qurʾān ameliorated the situation of women considerably. It put a stop to female infanticide and prohibited men from inheriting the wives of their fathers (4:19). It also granted women rights of inheritance and permitted them to possess property. Reflecting the patriarchal society of seventh-century Arabia, the Qurʾān also required that men be responsible for the maintenance of women. Muḥammad was asked to accept the pledge of allegiance from women and they were not prevented from participating in public activities.

Many female figures are praised in the Qurʾān. Mary is lauded for her piety and is seen as an example for all righteous people (66:12). Angels visited her and God cast His spirit into her. Similarly the Qurʾān has words of praise for the wife of the Pharaoh for protecting and rearing Moses and commends the Queen of Sheba for her wisdom in accepting Solomon's invitation to submit to God (27:43).

The pro-female tone of the Qurʾān is not replicated in the *ḥadīth* literature. Many traditions incorporated in the *ḥadīth* literature that was compiled in the ninth and tenth centuries denigrated the position of women. The negative cultural evaluation and status of a woman was thus transmitted in some of the *ḥadīth* reports. Some traditions maintain that women were created from a crooked rib; others claim that a woman passing in front of a man who is praying invalidates his prayer. This derogatory tone is also evident in traditions that indicate that most of the inhabitants of hell are women, that women are deficient in intellect, and that a wife's salvation is contingent on keeping her husband happy. A community that is led by women, some traditions assert, cannot prosper. Women are also portrayed as the source of *fitna* or seduction and therefore must be excluded from public participation. Women were therefore encouraged to pray at home rather than in the mosque.

The pejorative stance on women in *ḥadīth* is often reflected in the juridical rulings stated in the four schools of law. For the sake of brevity, the entry focuses on the following women's issues that are discussed in the legal manuals: marriage, divorce, and the rights of inheritance.

Marriage

Emerging in the cosmopolitan and pluralistic milieu of Kufa, Ḥanafī law puts men and women on the same footing with regard to their ability to conclude important transactions, including marriage. In Kufa, a girl who had reached the age of puberty and could manage her own affairs was allowed to marry without the consent of her guardian. Reflecting the patrilineal and more traditional outlook of Medinan society where the male members of a tribe decided on and concluded the marriages of women, Mālik insisted on the need for a guardian to conduct a marriage. The other Sunnī schools of law also require the permission of the guardian to conclude a marriage of a girl unless she is not a virgin. This is a good example of how local circumstances engendered variations in the legal positions adopted by the different schools of law. Under the pressures of reformation in recent times, Tunisia, which follows Mālikī law, adopted the Ḥanafī doctrine in 1957 and allowed an adult woman to choose her spouse independently of the wishes of her guardian.

All four schools allow the drawing of a prenuptial agreement. Due to its extensive employment of the concept of public interest (*maṣlaḥa*), Ḥanbalī *fiqh* is more tolerant and liberal in this ruling. It permits a man to willingly stipulate in a prenuptial contract that he will not marry another wife or, for example, that he will not force his wife to leave her home town. He is bound to honor such conditions and if he violates them then the wife can unilaterally dissolve the marriage. The other three schools regard such conditions as void although the contract is seen as valid. Using the concept of *talfīq* (literally, piecing together), Mālikī wives in Tunisia and Ḥanafī wives in Syria benefit from this liberal Ḥanbalī doctrine relating to provisions in marriage contracts for they are permitted to stipulate such conditions in their marriage contracts.

The marriage contract has to include the mention of bridal gift, called *ṣadāq* or *mahr*. In pre-Islamic Arabia, this was paid to the wife's father. However, the Qur'ān revised this and required that the *mahr* be paid directly to the girl. All the four schools of law maintain that the wife has the right to demand the *mahr* immediately after the marriage has been solemnized and before it is consummated. However, if she willingly accepts the consummation then she loses the right to demand the *mahr* immediately.

The impact of cultural factors is also evident in finding a marital partner who is "equal" (*kafā'a*). Reflecting the different classes of people inhabiting Kufa, the Ḥanafīs had an elaborate system regarding compatibility, maintaining that the occupation of the husband is essential in determining whether he is equal to his spouse. Hence they recognize a detailed hierarchy of professions. Like the Ḥanafīs, the Shāfiʿīs and Ḥanbalīs also require compatibility in religion, social status, profession, and lineage. Reflecting the lack of class differences and social stratification in Medina the occupation of the husband was not deemed to be an important consideration for the Mālikīs. Although the concept of *kafā'a* was later adopted by the Mālikīs, they insist on compatibility of the couple in religious matters only.

Divorce laws

All the legal schools granted a husband the unilateral right to divorce his wife at his discretion, whereas a woman who wished to be separated from her husband had to go through a judicial process where she had to demonstrate good grounds for divorce.

Sunnī law accepted two forms of divorce, the regular form (*ṭalāq al-sunna*) and the reprehensible version of triple divorce called (*ṭalāq al-bidʿa*). The former consists of a single pronouncement of divorce when the wife is not in her menstrual period and without intercourse having taken place since her last period. The husband has the right to take the wife back during the waiting period (*ʿidda*) which lasts for three monthly cycles.

Most sources agree that the triple *ṭalāq* was introduced by the second caliph, ʿUmar b. al-Khaṭṭāb (d. 22/644), to punish some men who had divorced women in jest and had taken it lightly. In this form of divorce the laws of purity are disregarded and the repudiation is made irrevocable by a three-fold pronouncement by the husband in a single meeting. When he says to his wife, "I divorce you" three times she becomes prohibited from him until she remarries and consummates the second marriage. After this second marriage is terminated, she can remarry her first husband once the waiting period has elapsed. The triple *ṭalāq* is irrevocable and thus does not afford the opportunity for reconciliation. Although the *ṭalāq al-bidʿa* is condemned as reprehensible, this form of divorce is accepted by all the four Sunnī schools and is still practiced in many countries.

The perilous position of women in divorce matters can be further discerned from the fact that the Ḥanafīs, Mālikīs, and Shāfiʿīs consider a divorce recited by mistake or in jest or under intoxication to be valid. The Ḥanbalīs, however, do not consider such a divorce valid.

In recent times, reforms have been enacted in various countries to control the husband's unilateral right of repudiation. The Syrian Law of Personal Status of 1953, for example, stipulates that the triple *ṭalāq* is to count as a single repudiation so as to allow the couple an opportunity to reconcile. The law also requires the husband to pay compensation to the wife if the court deems that he divorced her without reasonable cause. Tunisia refuses to recognize any divorce effected outside the judicial process. The Tunisian Law of 1957 also prohibits polygyny, a practice that is endorsed by the Qur'ān provided the wives are treated equally. To prevent abuse of the system, the Iraqi law of 1959 requires a polygamous marriage to be validated by the court.

The impingement of cultural factors engendered significant differences in other juridical opinions that emerged in the different schools. All the schools agree that maintenance is obligatory during the waiting period of a revocable divorce. The schools differed, however, on maintenance during the *ʿidda* (waiting period) of an irrevocable divorce. The Ḥanafīs were more favorable to the women, stating that the rules of maintenance during the *ʿidda* of a revocable divorce were also applicable for an irrevocable divorce. The other schools differentiated based on whether she was pregnant or not. Unless she was pregnant, the wife in Medina was entitled to receive only lodging in her husband's home during the *ʿidda*.

Under Islamic law, the wife has limited options to initiate divorce proceedings. Her right is encapsulated in the *khulʿ* (by the instigation of the wife) form of divorce. Since the Qur'ān recognizes *khulʿ* (2:229), it is accepted by all the legal schools. However, it can be finalized only with the husband's consent. For *khulʿ* to be valid the wife has to petition for divorce and is also required to offer some form of compensation to the husband (such as the return of the *mahr*). *Khulʿ* operates as a single, irrevocable divorce with an *ʿidda* incumbent on the wife. Contrary to Ḥanafī law, the Mālikīs recognized the validity of a *khulʿ* divorce even without the consent of the husband.

Other differences between the schools occur in the laws pertaining to the judicial rights of a woman to seek divorce. Abū Ḥanīfa refused a judicial divorce unless the husband was impotent or had other personal defects. Thus factors such as the failure to provide maintenance, intermittent absence, continuous physical abuse, or life imprisonment do not provide grounds for a judge to dissolve the marriage because divorce is seen as the husband's prerogative.

In this instance, Mālikī law accords more rights to the woman. She can ask for a divorce due to the husband's desertion, failure to maintain her, cruelty, sexual impotence, or chronic disease. Mālikī law also recognized judicial divorce on the grounds of a husband's injurious treatment of his wife. It went further, stating that if the differences were irreconcilable, the court may finalize the divorce even without the husband's consent. The other schools of law allow a woman to demand *ṭalāq* on certain grounds, for example, not providing maintenance, physical abuse, or prolonged imprisonment leading to hardship for the wife. Syria, which normally follows Ḥanafī law, in 1953 adopted the more liberal Mālikī law, which states that the wife may petition for divorce on such grounds as the husband's cruelty, desertion, or failure to maintain her.

Differences between the schools also arose over the question of a missing husband. Mālikī law was more favorable to women in this instance. Mālik held that the wife of a missing husband may seek judicial separation after a four-year waiting period. If he does not reappear within this time, she will observe the *ʿidda* of a widow and is then free to remarry. The Ḥanafīs, Shāfiʿīs, and Ḥanbalīs, in contrast, state that the wife of a missing husband may not remarry as long as he may be considered alive based on the average life span of a person. The Ḥanafīs fix this at 120 years, the Shāfiʿīs and Ḥanbalīs at 90 years. Such laws reflect the patrilineal character and male dominance of eighth- and ninth-century Arabian society when many of the juridical rulings were formulated.

Inheritance laws

In pre-Islamic Arabia, women were not accorded rights of inheritance. This was changed by the Qur'ān, which prescribed that certain inheritance shares be allotted to women since they were now to be counted as heirs of the deceased. The Qur'ān stipulated that men were to provide for and assure the economic stability of the family. Due to this requirement, they were allotted double the share of inheritance of women. Economic independence of the woman was further assured by the fact that no male relative, including the husband, could touch her property. The husband was required to maintain her from his own resources. Moreover, women could and often did initiate their own businesses.

In contrast to the Arabian patrilineal system where agnatic heirs (*ʿasaba*) were the principal heirs before Islam, the Qur'ān did not recognize their rights to inherit. In this the Qur'ān sought to reform the position of female relatives. All legal schools accept the distribution of fixed shares to the Qur'ānic heirs. However, pre-Islamic customary tribal laws prevailed in the Sunnī law of inheritance. All four schools grant distant agnates (*ʿasaba*) the remains of shares after the distribution to heirs that are stipulated by the Qur'ān. These distant agnates thus excluded the rights of the daughters of the deceased. Female heirs would only receive their share if there were no agnate heirs. By recognizing the claims of agnate collaterals, Sunnī law emphasized the tribal concept of an extended family.

Even in the laws of inheritance differences that affected women emerged between the Sunnī schools. When no Qur'ānic heir or agnate relative survived the deceased, the jurists of Kufa allowed non-agnate relatives (daughters and sister's children) to inherit. Such cognate relatives (called *dhawū al-arḥām*) were not allowed to inherit in Medina. In the absence of agnate relatives, the Mālikīs maintained that the public treasury is a "rescue heir," whereas the other three schools allow the cognate relatives such as the children of the deceased's daughter or sister to succeed in the absence of Qur'ānic heirs or agnate relatives. It was the patrilineal society of Medina that denied women such rights of inheritance. In many instances, therefore, the cosmopolitan society and extraneous cultural influences in Kufa led to women enjoying greater rights.

Other miscellaneous differences emerged between the schools with respect to their treatment of women. The view that the Ḥanafīs empower women more than the other schools is supported in their ruling that the voluntary fast of a woman without her husband's consent is reprehensible but not prohibited. In contrast, the other three schools state that it is not permissible for a woman to observe a supererogatory fast without her husband's consent if the fast will interfere with any of his rights over her. Most jurists have held that women cannot lead men in prayers, hold judicial positions, or be political leaders. However, Abū Ḥanīfa asserted that a woman can act as a judge in all commercial and civil cases but not in criminal and personal injury cases. Some Mālikī jurists maintained that a woman can serve as a judge in any case.

The jurists concur on the issue of women's testimony in the courts. Based on the Qur'ānic verse 2:282, which stipulates that when one man is not available to witness a business contract two women should replace him, the jurists of the four schools extended this requirement in all cases of testimony. The verse has also been used to support the alleged inferiority of a woman's evidence as compared to that of a man.

In recent times, courts have departed from the doctrines expounded in the classical legal tracts. Many Muslim countries have enforced the eclectic principle of borrowing from different law schools and have required the involvement of the judicial process so as to ensure a more equitable system and to reform the law to accord with modern contingencies.

Bibliography

K. Abou El Fadl, *Speaking in God's name. Islamic law, authority and women*, Oxford 2001.
N. Abu Zahra, *The pure and powerful. Studies in contemporary Muslim society*, Reading, Berkshire, U.K. 1997.
N. Coulson, *A history of Islamic law*, Edinburgh, 1964, 1978².
——, *Conflicts and tensions in Islamic jurisprudence*, Chicago 1969.
A. Fyzee, *Outlines of Muhammadan law*, Delhi 1972.
Y. Y. Haddad and J. L. Esposito (eds.), *Islam, gender and social change*, New York 1998.
W. Hallaq, *A history of Islamic legal theories*, Cambridge 1999.
——, *Authority, continuity and change in Islamic law*, Cambridge 2001.
W. Madelung, Shiʿi attitudes toward women as reflected in fiqh, in W. Madelung, *Religious schools and sects in medieval Islam*, London 1985, 69–79.
M. Maghniyya, *The five schools of law*, Qum 1995.
F. Mernissi *Beyond the veil. Male-female dynamics in a modern Muslim society*, Cambridge 1975.
——, *Women and Islam. An historical and theological enquiry*, trans. M. J. Lakeland, Oxford 1991.
A. Sachedina, Woman, half-the-man? The crisis of male epistemology in Islamic jurisprudence, in F. Daftary (ed.), *Intellectual traditions in Islam*, London 2000, 160–178.
Joseph Schact, *The origins of Muhammadan jurisprudence*, Oxford 1950.

——, *An introduction to Islamic law*, Oxford 1979.
B. Stowasser, *Women in the Qur'an, traditions, and interpretation*, New York 1994.
A. Wadud, *Qur'an and woman. Rereading the sacred text from a woman's perspective*, New York 1999.
B. Wheeler, *Applying the canon in Islam. The authorization and maintenance of interpretive reasoning in Hanafi scholarship*, Albany, N.Y. 1996.

Liyakat Takim

Law: Other Schools of Family Law

Overview

This entry discusses how women are treated in the twelver Shīʿī (Jaʿfarī) school of law and the factors that shaped the issuance of juridical rulings on women in Shiʿism.

Derivation of legal rulings (*aḥkām*) on women in Shiʿism was contingent on the patriarchal character of Arab culture prevalent in the eighth and ninth centuries. The methodologies that the jurists (*fuqahāʾ*) utilized in the derivation of juridical rulings also affected the rulings on women. Hence before dealing with women's issues, the entry examines the factors that contributed to the rise of the Shīʿī school of law and the hermeneutical devices that the jurists used to deduce rulings.

The formation and crystallization of a Shīʿī school of law coincided with the rise of Sunnī schools of law. The emergence of a distinct Shīʿī school can probably be traced to the time of the fifth Shīʿī imam, Muḥammad al-Bāqir (d. 117/735). Respected by and contemporary to many Sunnī jurists in Medina and Kufa, he is credited with laying the foundations for the establishment of the Jaʿfarī school of law. Al-Bāqir is also the first Shīʿī figure from whom a vast corpus of *ḥadīth* (traditions) literature has been transmitted. His legal formulations were later elaborated by his son, the sixth Shīʿī imam, Jaʿfar al-Ṣādiq (d. 148/765) after whom the school was named. Al-Ṣādiq was a contemporary of prominent Sunnī jurists such as Abū Ḥanīfa (d. 150/767) and Mālik b. Anas (d. 179/795).

Circumstances that led to the rise of the Sunnī schools of law also precipitated a concurrent need for a Shīʿī school. The goal of the jurists' endeavor in the eighth and ninth centuries was to reach an understanding (*fiqh*) of the Sharīʿa, that is, to comprehend in precise terms the law of God. Guided by a corpus of precepts and laws and their own independent reasoning the jurists attempted to construct a legal edifice by developing and elaborating a system of Sharīʿa law. At the same time, the Shīʿī imams began to formulate their own understanding of the law and to establish paradigmatic precedents for the situations they encountered. Knowledge, interpretation, and articulation of the law meant that the imams became the main source of religious authority in Shiʿism.

During the period when the imams were with them, the Shīʿīs accepted their pronouncements as the only valid source of law after the Qurʾān and the *sunna* of the Prophet. The imam was believed to be the final enunciator of the law, occupying the same position as the Prophet himself. Since the imam is also believed in Shiʿism to have inherited the comprehensive authority of the Prophet, the *sunna* of the imam is seen to be as binding as the *sunna* of the Prophet himself. As Shīʿī theology posited the imam to be divinely appointed (*naṣṣ*), endowed with divinely inspired knowledge (*ʿilm*), and infallible (*maʿṣūm*), the authority of the imam supersedes the authority of local practice or speculative reasoning. The emergence of a distinct Shīʿī school of law should thus be viewed as the result of the Shīʿīs' self-understanding of the nature of religious leadership and their limitation of juristic authority to the imams.

Apart from the imams, some of their deputies in places like Kufa reportedly acted as jurists in their communities. In particular, Jābir al-Juʿfī (d. 127/745), Burayd b. Muʿāwiya (d. 150/767), Zurāra b. Aʿyān (d. 150/767), and Muḥammad b. Muslim al-Thaqafī (d. 150/767) are mentioned as some of the *fuqahāʾ* (jurists) of the Shīʿī community. Disciples such as Abān b. Taghlib (d. 142/759) were reportedly authorized by the imams to issue juridical edicts (fatwas) and to respond to legal questions in Medina.

The Shīʿīs were not allowed by the imams to practice *qiyās* (analogy), *raʾy* (opinion), *ijtihād* (independent legal judgment), or other rational methods that were employed in the Sunnī schools. They were required to rely on the Qurʾān and narrations (*riwāyāt*) from the Prophet and the imams in the derivation of juridical rulings. In practice, some of the disciples of the imams, such as Zurāra b. Aʿyān, Muḥammad b. Muslim, and Hishām b. al-Ḥakam, probably influenced by the cosmopolitan and eclectic nature of Kufa, employed many of the speculative methods that were accepted in the Sunnī schools. In addition, after the occultation of the twelfth imam in 940 C.E., Shīʿī jurists had recourse to various hermeneutical devices such as *maṣlaḥa* (enacting a legal point that is most conducive to the welfare of the community) and other interpretive principles to respond to the needs of the times and to go beyond the rulings stated in the revealed texts.

Shiʿism and women

Generally speaking, due to the pivotal roles played by women such as Fāṭima, the daughter of the Prophet, and Zaynab, his granddaughter, women have received better treatment in Shīʿī *ḥadīth* and legal literature than in Sunnī tradition. There are fewer traditions in Shīʿī *ḥadīth* manuals that demean women. Both Fāṭima and Zaynab are portrayed as role models and revered in Shīʿī circles because they resisted injustice and oppression. After the establishment of Shiʿism in Iran in the sixteenth century, women received higher religious education and were even certified to exercise *ijtihād*, although until recently most Shīʿī jurists have barred women from occupying the position of judge. In places such as Iran and Iraq women religious leaders have held a position closer to that of male religious leaders than in most Sunnī countries. In recent times, special religious seminaries have been established and female religious scholars preside over women's religious ceremonies.

Rulings on women in Shīʿī legal manuals are also influenced by what Shīʿīs deem to be anti-female innovations introduced by ʿUmar b. al-Khaṭṭāb. As this entry shows, to refute the legal points introduced by the second caliph, Shīʿī law is opposed to some Sunnī rulings on certain female issues.

As with the Sunnī experience, women's issues in Shīʿī jurisprudence were explored, interpreted, and articulated by male jurists. There is a paucity of female representation in both Sunnī and Shīʿī legal manuals. Women were represented by men who often reflected the male-dominated milieu of eighth-century Arabia when many of the rulings on women were formulated by the imams of the schools.

Although Shīʿī law has its own distinctive character on some points of law, there are many instances where it agrees with one or more of the Sunnī schools. For the sake of brevity, the entry focuses on the following women's issues that are discussed in Shīʿī legal manuals: marriage, divorce, and the rights of inheritance.

Marital laws in Shiʿism

Most Shīʿī scholars agree that a woman who is sane, mature, and can handle her affairs is permitted to contract her own marriage without the consent of a guardian whether she is a virgin or not. This is based on the rational consideration that a human being has the liberty to choose his or her own partner. In this the Shīʿīs tend to agree with the Ḥanafīs who adopted the same ruling on the issue.

The Shīʿīs also state that at the time of marriage, compatibility is required in religious matters only. Reflecting the Medinese origins of the school where class differences and social inequities were largely absent, the Shīʿīs did not consider social status, lineage, or the occupation of the husband to be important factors in choosing a spouse. The Mālikīs, who emerged from the same Medinese environment, held a similar view.

In addition, Shīʿī law also empowers the woman by allowing her to stipulate conditions in a marriage contract that will grant her the right to initiate divorce proceedings should her husband violate the terms of the agreement. She can stipulate, for example, that if her husband abuses her, she has the right to dissolve the marriage. In this way, she can circumvent the judicial process and the cumbersome *khulʿ ṭalāq* (divorce) and can instead recite her own *ṭalāq*. The Shīʿīs predicate this ruling on the principle of *maṣlaḥa*, that is, invoking a law that is conducive to the welfare of the parties concerned.

A distinctive Shīʿī feature concerning marriage is the institution of *mutʿa*, or temporary marriage, which was practiced in the early Muslim community. The Qurʾānic verse: "Those from whom you seek pleasure give them their prescribed dowries" (4:24) is seen as validating this practice. Traditions cited in Muslim's *Ṣaḥīḥ* indicate that the practice was allowed by Muḥammad but later prohibited by ʿUmar. Its acceptance in Shīʿī law is premised on numerous statements from the imams denouncing ʿUmar's proscription of a practice that had been approved by the Prophet. A prominent feature of Shīʿī jurisprudence is its rejection of laws that were introduced by the caliphs, since they are seen as violating Prophetic practices.

Mutʿa differs from permanent marriage in that the duration of the marriage has to be stipulated when it is solemnized. This period can range from a few minutes to many years but it should not exceed the life span of an average person. In addition, like a permanent marriage, *mutʿa* allows for a *mahr* (bridal gift) payable to the woman. However, there is no divorce to be recited when the agreed period expires. The marriage can be renewed or the woman begins a waiting period (*ʿidda*). The waiting period in a *mutʿa* marriage is different from a permanent marriage in that the woman can remarry after observing two (instead of three) menstrual periods.

The institution of *mutʿa* is not favorable to a woman, especially as she is not entitled to any right of maintenance and does not inherit from her husband. The contract may be terminated prematurely either by mutual agreement or by one party unilaterally. The husband is responsible to maintain any children born from a temporary marriage.

Divorce in Shiʿism

Shīʿī laws on divorce treat women more favorably than their Sunnī counterparts. This is because the Shīʿīs do not accept the triple *ṭalāq* that the Sunnīs adopted as a valid form of divorce. The Shīʿīs dismiss the triple *ṭalāq* as an innovation that was introduced by ʿUmar. Shīʿī rejection of this form of divorce is favorable to women since the triple *ṭalāq* allows the husband the right to unilaterally pronounce the divorce in one meeting. The *ṭalāq* bars any further contact between the couple until she is married to another person and terminates the second marriage after consummating it.

Shīʿī law is also stricter than Sunnī law with regard to divorce. It considers as invalid any repudiation during a menstrual period, or when the woman is pure but cohabitation has taken place since her last period. In addition, Shīʿī law also requires the presence of two male Muslim witnesses during the divorce and allows the man to take back his wife during the waiting period (*ʿidda*). Even after the waiting period ends, the couple can get back together by solemnizing a second marriage.

According to Sunnī law, any word indicating repudiation may be used and witnesses are not required for its validity. Shīʿī law confines the husband's power of repudiation to defined limits. It insists on a specific formula and a correct pronouncement of *ṭalāq* is necessary. It is required that the husband states, "You are divorced" or "She is divorced," so that the words recited indicate a clear and unambiguous intention to dissolve the marriage. Any divorce undertaken under duress, in anger, or in jest is not deemed to be valid. The net result of the stricter conditions and the rejection of the triple *ṭalāq* has been a lower divorce rate in many Shīʿī countries.

Since divorce proceedings are normally initiated by the husband, women's rights to seek divorce are more circumscribed. Shīʿī law allows a woman to seek divorce under the *khulʿ* (at the instigation of the wife) form of divorce. *Khulʿ* can be finalized with the husband's consent. For it to be valid, the wife has to petition for divorce and is also required to offer some form of compensation to the husband (such as the return of the *mahr*). *Khulʿ* operates as a single, irrevocable divorce with an *ʿidda* incumbent on the wife.

The wife can also nullify the marriage under certain circumstances without obtaining a formal divorce. Nullification is possible if the husband has no sexual organ, is impotent or insane, or if he has leprosy or leucoderma.

The wife can also obtain divorce if the husband is missing. The ruling on a missing husband is contingent on his financial state. If he has assets from which the wife can be maintained then it is not permissible for her to remarry under any circumstance until she is certain of his death or of his divorcing her. If he does not have enough assets to maintain her then she can obtain a divorce through the judicial process.

Like the ruling of the Mālikī school, the Shīʿī position is favorable to women in this instance. The judge is required to order a four-year waiting period during which time he will initiate a search for the husband. At the end of the period, the judge will pronounce the divorce by using the authority granted to him as the deputed agent of the occult imam. After this divorce the wife will observe an *ʿidda* for four months and ten days, after which she may remarry.

Inheritance laws

The Qurʾān changed aspects of tribal laws that were considered unjust. In pre-Islamic Arabia, women were not accorded rights of inheritance. The Qurʾān ameliorated this situation by allocating certain inheritance shares to women who were now to be counted as heirs of the deceased.

The Shīʿīs refused to recognize any customary law that was not explicitly endorsed by the Qurʾān. Since the Qurʾān does not recognize the preeminence of the male agnate relatives, the Shīʿī law of inheritance rejects the privileged position that Sunnī inheritance rules accord to male blood relatives, the agnates (or *ʿasaba*) of the deceased. Due to this, the Shīʿī law of inheritance is more favorable to women. Shīʿī law states that, regardless of their gender, the closest relatives (*qarāba*) will inherit after the division of Qurʾānic shares. This is in contrast to Sunnī law, which accords distant agnates the remains of the shares after the distribution to heirs that is stipulated by the Qurʾān. The Shīʿīs quote Jaʿfar al-Ṣādiq as saying, "Dust in the jaws of the *ʿasaba*" to justify this exclusion.

The ramifications of the Shīʿī position on female heirs in inheritance become evident from the fact that under Sunnī law, a single surviving daughter was limited to a maximum of half of the inheritance no matter how distant the next eligible male-line relative was. By excluding the agnates, Shīʿī law gave the same daughter the whole inheritance. The inclusion of distant male relatives indicates that the Sunnīs uphold the concept of the extended family, whereas by giving more rights to parents and lineal descendants Shīʿī law stresses the nuclear family.

Shīʿī inheritance laws also stipulate different layers or tiers of inheritance. These are: the lineal descendants and parents of the deceased; brothers and sisters and their issue, and grandparents of the deceased; and uncles and aunts and their issue. The presence of the first category of heirs will exclude the other two from inheriting.

In constructing a typology of male and female relatives based on their relationship with the deceased, Shīʿī law treats male and female relatives equally. It stipulates that any descendant, male or female, in the first category will always exclude the collateral, that is, the second tier (the brothers and sisters of a deceased). Hence the daughter of the deceased will exclude the brother. If she is the only survivor, she will even exclude a distant male agnate such as a cousin from inheritance. Furthermore, the presence of a son's or daughter's daughter will also exclude the siblings of the deceased because a daughter or her offspring belong to the first category of heirs whereas brothers and sisters belong to the second.

Through this principle, female and cognate relatives are integrated within the Shīʿī classes of heirs. Thus the presence of any other relatives in Shīʿī law – child, grandchild, or the mother – precludes the brothers and paternal grandparents from any rights of succession. Reflecting the patriarchal nature of Arab society where men were responsible for the maintenance of women, the Qurʾānic principle that the male relative receives double the share of the female is also enforced in Shīʿī law.

Shīʿīs prefer the nearer relative to the more distant. They say that one who is related through both parents excludes the consanguine (agnate). Hence a full sister excludes a consanguine brother. Sunnī law, on the other hand emphasizes the concept of the family group by recognizing the claims of agnate collaterals.

Political considerations may have influenced the development of the Shīʿī scheme of inheritance. The principle that cognate relationship is a stronger basis for succession than agnate ties and that the claims of collateral are subordinate to those of lineal descendants validate the reported claims of Fāṭima to inherit an estate (called Fadak) from her father, a claim that was rejected by Abū Bakr. The principle of cognate inheritance would also legitimize succession in the female line as all the imams were descendants of the Prophet through Fāṭima.

The Shīʿīs believe that their laws accurately represent the Qurʾānic spirit. Their acceptance of *mutʿa* is based on a Qurʾānic verse that endorses the practice; their rejection of the triple *ṭalāq* and the rights of agnate relatives is premised on the view that these have no Qurʾānic basis. For the Shīʿīs, customary laws could only be implemented if they were explicitly endorsed in the Qurʾān. For the Sunnīs, they could only be repudiated if the Qurʾān explicitly rejected them. This was one major reason for the differences between the Shīʿī and Sunnī legal systems.

Bibliography

N. Abu Zahra, *The pure and powerful. Studies in contemporary Muslim society*, Reading, Berkshire, U.K. 1997.

J. Cole and N. Keddie (eds.), *Shīʿism and social protest*, New Haven, Conn. 1986.

N. Coulson, *Conflicts and tensions in Islamic jurisprudence*, Chicago 1969.

——, *A history of Islamic law*, Edinburgh 1978.

A. Fyzee, *Outlines of Muhammadan Law*, Delhi 1972.

Y. Y. Haddad and J. L. Esposito (eds.), *Islam, gender and social change*, New York 1998.

S. Haeri, *Law of desire. Temporary marriage in Shīʿi Iran*, Syracuse, N.Y. 1989.

W. Hallaq, *Authority, continuity and change in Islamic law*, Cambridge 2001.

W. Madelung, Shiʿi attitudes toward women as reflected in fiqh, in W. Madelung, *Religious schools and sects in medieval Islam*, London 1985, 69–79.

M. Maghniyya, *The five schools of law*, Qum 1995.

F. Mernissi *Beyond the veil. Male-female dynamics in a modern Muslim society*, Cambridge, Mass. 1975.

——, *Women and Islam. An historical and theological enquiry*, trans. M. J. Lakeland, Oxford 1991.

A. Sachedina, *The just ruler (al-sultān al-ʿādil) in Shīʿite Islam. The comprehensive authority of the jurist in Imamite jurisprudence*, Oxford 1988.

——, Woman, half-the-man? The crisis of male epistemology in Islamic jurisprudence, in F. Daftary (ed.), *Intellectual traditions in Islam*, London 2000, 160–78.

J. Schact, *The origins of Muhammadan jurisprudence*, Oxford 1950.

——, *An introduction to Islamic law*, Oxford 1979.

S. Seestani, *Islamic laws*, London 1994.

A. Wadud, *Qurʾan and woman. Rereading the sacred text from a woman's perspective*, New York 1999.

B. Wheeler, *Applying the canon in Islam. The authorization and maintenance of interpretive reasoning in Hanafi scholarship*, Albany, N.Y. 1996.

Liyakat Takim

Law: Family Law, 7th–Late 18th Centuries

Overview

The Development of Islamic Family Law

Classical Islamic family law, like other areas of Islamic law (the Sharīʿa), is based primarily on the texts of the Qurʾān and the *sunna* of the Prophet Muḥammad, and the principles derived and induced from those texts. Both bodies of texts contain specific rulings as well as general principles that form the basis of classical Islamic family law. The foundations for this law were developed over the first three centuries of Islam by scholars who employed various methods of reasoning to interpret the sacred texts. Scholars also developed a doctrine of consensus, the means by which particular interpretations of sacred texts were rendered authoritative (even "orthodox"). Differences in legal theory, as well as cultural differences and various historical developments resulted in scholars forming themselves into "schools" (*madhhabs*) of law. By the fourth/tenth century, there were four main law schools of Sunnī Islam: Mālikī, Ḥanafī, Shāfiʿī, and Ḥanbalī. Among the Shiʿīs, the Twelver (also called Jaʿfarī) and Zaydī schools are the most important.

The formation of a scholarly community developed over time; at the beginning of Islam, it was the Prophet Muḥammad who was the authoritative interpreter of the law. During his lifetime, the Prophet gave rulings on many cases of family law. It is clear that he was determined to provide some regularity to the many diverse customs that governed family life in pre-Islamic Arabia (Hodgson 1974, 340, Stern 1939, 81). Over the next few centuries, the law was developed and systematized by scholars and state officials. Although legal scholars were often reluctant to become involved in the exercise of political power, from early on colleges for religious and legal scholarship (*madrasas*) were often sponsored by political rulers. In most urban areas, judges and other officials who applied the law were drawn from the body of *madrasa* graduates. By the Ottoman period, this was a formalized and centralized system; steps toward codification of the law were taken, and Ottoman officials were usually required to apply Ḥanafī law. At the same time, there were always scholars who did not hold official government positions, yet their opinions were treated as binding by individual followers and communities.

Contributions of Women to the Development of the Law

Understanding the development of a community of orthodox legal scholars and the procedure for selecting judges and other officers of the court is crucial for understanding the development of classical Islamic family law. Many modern scholars have seen the apparent exclusion of women from legal scholarship and institutions to be responsible for the development of a system of family law they perceive to be biased against women. Not all of these perceptions are justified. The content of the law and the nature of its biases is discussed below. With respect to the participation of women in the scholarly discourse, from the beginning of Islam until the end of the classical period, women are included in biographical dictionaries of scholars. Women are especially prominent in the early period as transmitters of Prophetic *ḥadīth* (Roded 1994, 63–89, Stern 1939, 21). On the other hand, it was exceedingly rare for a woman to hold an official political or legal office in medieval Muslim societies. This was primarily due to the widely held sentiment that it was better for women to limit their presence among men in the public sphere in order to maintain a chaste and wholesome society (Fadel 1997, 199). As a result, it is likely that the more scholarship became instititionalized and closely associated with the state, the less opportunity women may have had to participate in the legal discourse.

Throughout the centuries, however, female authorities were never completely absent from the process of law-making and adjudication. Female witnesses were regularly called in paternity cases and in cases that required expertise in some aspect of female physiology or reproduction. Very early in the development of Islamic law, the decisions of some female experts set important precedents that had significant consequences for women and their families for generations. For example, during the time of the Caliph ʿUmar b. al-Khaṭṭāb (r. 634–44 C.E.), a woman who had been widowed gave birth to a fully-developed child, only six months into her second marriage. Naturally, the woman was suspected of having had an illicit relationship before her current marriage. However, a female expert witness called by ʿUmar testified that this was a case of a "sleeping child" (*rāqid*). The woman had been pregnant by her first husband, but when he died, the child, deprived of vital fluids due to the mother's extreme grief, had entered a state of hibernation. When the woman remarried, her new husband's seminal fluid reawakened the child, who completed his development in six months. ʿUmar accepted this explanation by the female expert and the notion of the sleeping child became a part of Islamic law, especially in the Mālikī school. Although not all legal schools accepted this precedent, the law generally relied on female expert witnesses to determine the facts of the case whenever female physiology was involved.

Women also had opportunities to shape the law to the extent that custom was recognized by and incorporated into Islamic law. On matters on which revelation was silent, custom (*ʿurf, ʿāda*) was explicitly recognized as a source of law by the classical jurists. This appropriation of custom into the law was, as Lawrence Rosen has stated, not "an occasional trickle or an idiosyncratic intrusion promoted by a rare commentator." Rather, custom was foundational to all aspects of the law. "Custom is indeed, and always has been, a source of Islamic law – but not in the European sense of source which has been projected onto Islamic law, but as an integral part of the Sharīʿa itself" (Rosen 1989, 96). This is particularly true in family law, where custom is normative in so many areas, particularly in determining maintenance (*nafaqa*), custody, and marital rights. What this means is that women were not simply passive recipients of legal rulings. Rather, where women had any power to shape and articulate community norms (a power that depended on a vast range of sociological and material factors) they had the ability to influence the application of the law. As Rosen has demonstrated for contemporary Islamic courts, for example, the expectations of individuals that the law should produce a "just" result compels jurists to continue to search for principles and values of the law that will support an outcome perceived as just by the community.

Even during the time of the Prophet, as the Qurʾān was being revealed, it seems that Muslim women had expectations that Islamic rulings would do them justice. Islamic literature contains a number of reports of women expressing their conviction that God would affirm their sense of justice by revealing what they considered to be a fair ruling to the Prophet. Thus, ʿĀʾisha received the exoneration she expected when the punishment for the slander of chaste women (*qadhf*) was revealed (24:4). Khawla received the ruling she prayed for when the Qurʾān prohibited men from divorcing their wives by using a pre-Islamic formula known as *ẓihār*, stating "you are to me as the back of my mother" (58:2–4). The Qurʾān refers to Khawla as "the woman who disputed" (*al-mujādila*) and the chapter containing this revelation came to be named after her. This clearly shows the effect of Muslim womens' expectations about Islamic law on the course of revelation itself.

In terms of the *sunna*, women seemed to have had relatively free access to the Prophet, and their support was important in making his mission a success. Women's concerns, complaints, and expectations, therefore, shaped even the primary sources of Islamic law. As Islamic law came to be articulated and formalized over the centuries, women continued to play some part in supporting or discrediting those who claimed to authoritatively represent the law. For example, women could contribute to undermining the authority of scholars by informal social sanctions, like spreading gossip, and they could contribute to the support of those scholars they favored by giving their institutions alms and by sending their children to study with them.

On the other hand, the concerns of men about women's place and authority could also provoke revelation. Thus it is reported that after the Prophet ruled that a woman could physically retaliate against her husband who had hit her, many men complained. The Prophet then conveyed a new revelation that such retaliation was not permitted, that men, as a final measure could use some physical force to discipline their wives, but if that did not work, they must seek arbitration (Qurʾān 4:34). This authority to use force was certainly abused by some men since cases are discussed by the jurists. Muslims jurists developed a standard remarkably similar to the English common law "rule of thumb" in which husbands could not hit their wives with a switch wider than a thumb. In Islamic law, a toothstick (*miswāk*) was the standard. In cases of abuse, some jurists allowed women to sue their husbands for damages if they were injured or visibly hurt by them (Tucker 1998, 66). Other jurists said that any use of physical force could be considered prohibited abuse in cultures where such force was felt to be repulsive. It is likely that any woman seeking protection from an abusive husband needed strong family or community support; legal protection could not be invoked if there were cultural barriers to women accessing such protections.

Guardianship: authority and responsibility

The revelation permitting physical disciplining of wives is one of the justifications jurists gave for granting men in their various capacities certain kinds of legal authority and coercive power over their female relatives. The *sunna* was usually cited to argue that only a male could serve as the guardian (*walī*) of previously unmarried women, and this guardianship was required by most schools of law. What this means is that classical jurists granted men, in certain circumstances, political authority over women within the context of the family. According to jurists, this authority is God-given, for the Qur'ān states that "men are responsible for women (*al-rijāl qawwamūn ʿalā al-nisāʾ*)" (4:34). This authority, however, is functional, and never absolute; it can be taken away by the state if a man abuses or neglects his position (Tucker 1998, 42). For example, a man can lose his right to be his daughter's guardian in contracting her marriage if his motivation is personal gain rather than his daughter's welfare.

Because men have a certain degree of coercive authority over their wives, and because classical jurists did not consider it proper for a non-Muslim to exercise coercive authority over a Muslim, Islamic law forbids the marriage of non-Muslim men to Muslim women, yet permits Muslim men to marry "chaste" women (*al-muḥsānāt*) from the "People of the Book" (Qur'ān 5:5). Another consequence of this principle is that non-Muslim women who convert to Islam can be separated from their non-Muslim husbands; even concubines who convert to Islam can be removed from the ownership of their non-Muslim masters (Mattson 1999, 178).

Any authority that men have over their female relatives is always linked with the responsibility to provide full maintenance (*nafaqa*). Maintenance law is one of the most important areas of Islamic family law, as is evidenced by the early compilation of complete texts devoted to the subject. Fathers are required to provide full support for unmarried daughters, even as adults. A single, divorced, or widowed woman who is in need has the right to support from her male relatives, including her father, brothers, sons, and uncles. Even married women whose husbands are unable to support them can demand support from male relatives; in such cases, however, the support can be considered an obligatory loan to the husband who should reimburse the expenses when he is able.

Given this potential financial and emotional burden male relatives could bear, it was clearly in men's interests to find husbands who were willing and able to support their female relatives for their lives. One instrument for protecting women's interests was the requirement that a previously unmarried woman must have her male guardian consent to her marriage. Among the Sunnīs, only the Ḥanafīs did not require the guardian's approval for the marriage of a female virgin. The Ḥanafīs did protect the family's interests, however, by permitting the family to block the marriage of a female virgin if her mate was not her "equal." Equality (*kafāʾa*) could be considered from many different aspects in the Ḥanafī school, including profession, ethnicity, social status, and religiosity. The other Sunnī schools also recognized the doctine of *kafāʾa*, but they used it to limit marriages arranged by guardians for their dependents. Since guardians are permitted to contract marriages for minor dependents (male and female), the doctrine made it possible for other guardians to object to the contract if they considered the groom unequal to the bride. Among the Shīʿīs, *kafāʾa* was applied to ensure that descendents of the Prophet in particular were not given away in unsuitable marriages.

It would be reductionist to consider guardianship simply an instrument of control that men willfully exercised over women. If this were the case, it would be difficult to explain why a previously married woman (*thayyib*) was permitted to contract her own marriage – especially in an age where second and third marriages were not uncommon. In addition, we cannot reasonably explain guardianship simply as an instrument to protect the financial interests of the family. Rather, the instruments of Islamic family law appear to have more internal consistency if we approach them from the dominant underlying assumption, an assumption that is often explicitly articulated, that the paternalistic protection of male relatives is necessary because women are more vulnerable to poverty, harm, and exploitation than men. The desire to protect both women and their families from predatory outsiders is evident, for example, in an account of a disagreement between the founders of two of the orthodox Sunnī schools of law, Mālik (d. 796) and al-Shāfiʿī (d. 820). Mālik is reported to have waived the requirement that a previously unmarried women had to have the approval of her guardian for marriage if the woman was from one of the lower classes of society whose customs did not include a regular reliance on guardians. Apparently Mālik, who gave significant weight to custom as a source of law, felt that such people, since they had little to lose in the way of wealth or family solidarity in any case, should be permitted to practice their own customs. Al-Shāfiʿī strongly disagreed, arguing that such a woman was even more in need of the protection of a guardian, since she was most vulnerable to deception and exploitation. Such a woman without a male guardian should have one appointed by the state, which, in any case, always retained the ultimate authority to remove or appoint a guardian.

Assuming that most guardians will act in the best interests of their wards, classical Islamic law also grants guardians the power to contract marriages on behalf of minor male and female wards. Such marriages could be consummated at puberty, which is determined physiologically, although a minimum age of nine for girls and twelve for boys is irrefutably presumed (El Alami and Hinchcliffe 1996, 9). At that time, either party can repudiate the marriage, by exercising the "option of puberty." Naturally, custom played an important role in determining the extent to which the option was exercised.

Determining paternity by regulation of sexual relations

Throughout the medieval Islamic world, local customs and beliefs differently affected the way in which women's sexuality was regulated through the law. In some places, previously unmarried women were expected to prove their virginity on their wedding night by bearing an intact hymen. Muslim jurists rejected this customary proof of chastity and the justifications for the harm some men caused to women because of this. As one seventeenth-century Syrian jurist said, "being deflowered does not necessarily mean that illicit intercourse has taken place, for virginity can be lost by jumping, or through menstruation, or with age, and so forth" (Tucker 1998, 1). According to Judith Tucker, classical Muslim jurists "took a clear position here against social customs that assigned fathers, brothers, and husbands the role of enforcer of female sexual behaviour. Men could guard their female relatives, especially minors, against involvement in situations that might lead to improper sexual contact, but an actual instance of sexual intercourse outside of marriage was a crime against religion: rigid rules of procedure and evidence did not allow for any special family role and, furthermore, implicitly condemned any unilateral family move to punish those presumed guilty" (Tucker 1998, 166).

As Tucker notes, however, the family was assigned a dominant role in preventing women from situations that might lead to illicit sexual contact. To this end, customary practices were often given great deference. For example, the fourteenth-century Syrian jurist Ibn Taymiyya permitted female circumcision because it is can limit the "excessive" sexual desire experienced by some women. Astonishingly, Ibn Taymiyya prohibited piercing children's ears because it is physical mutilation. Although the practice of female circumcision was not widespread in the Muslim world, it is significant that Ibn Taymiyya was so convinced of the grave harm that illicit sexual relations would involve that he waived his own clear prohibition against physical mutilation to permit it (Ibn Taymiyya, 18).

In the medieval Islamic discourse, sexuality and sexual relations were generally considered a good thing; at the same time, the desire for sexual fulfillment, like the desire for other worldly pleasures, could be distracting and corrupting. Unregulated, sexuality could lead to injustice in this world and distance from God's presence in the next. Men's sexuality and behaviors were also heavily regulated and controlled by the law and religious discourses. If men engaged in illicit relationships, heterosexual or homosexual, they could be ostracized by society and punished by the law. However, because women are considered to have tangible proof of their virginity, and because sexual intercourse can result in pregnancy, it is much more difficult for a woman to conceal an illicit relationship. A woman could not simply turn to God in repentance for sexual transgressions that harmed her state in the afterlife, she often had to deal with real world consequences of her actions.

In trying to make sense of the medieval jurists' application of the law, we need to consider their understanding of the social and political context in which they lived. In premodern Muslim societies, where security of life and goods was often elusive, where state support and protection of needy individuals was limited, where an official police presence was minimal even in cities, and where highways and rural areas were often subject to attacks by bandits, it was the rare individual who could have a secure life without the support of an extended family. Family solidarity and group interests always limited individual choice, for men and women. Women, however, were considered most in need of protection both because they were deemed more naive and emotional than men, and because it was assumed that there were always men willing to take advantage of vulnerable women. As long as these perceptions about human nature were unchallenged (and as long as women were sheltered from public life they likely remained naive), the authorities seem to have remained convinced that the best way to achieve security for women was to limit their contact with men. The legal principles of "what leads to the prohibited is itself prohibited" and "blocking the means" were invoked, sometimes to a logical extreme, to limit women's presence in the public sphere. Although many Muslim women, urban and rural, needed to work outside the home, in most places unrelated women and men were separated by physical or behavioral barriers to prevent close intermingling. A man could socialize freely with a woman only if he was her husband or *maḥram* – a man permanently prohibited from marrying her. Male relatives, by serving as chaperones or guardians of women, limited the access of unrelated men to those women.

From the standpoint of the law, one of the greatest risks of unregulated sexual behavior was undetermined paternity. If women were considered vulnerable in an insecure world, unprotected children were even more at risk. A consistent underlying principle in Islamic family law is that children have the right to be acknowledged and supported by their biological father. In order to establish this relationship, Islamic law prohibited all sexual activity outside marriage and concubinage. Any child born to a wife is presumptively the offspring of the husband. If a man wishes to deny paternity for his wife's child, he must take an oath that can be rebutted by his wife.

In the case of concubinage, the schools of law were split; the majority did not allow a man to deny paternity of any child his concubine might bear. Concubinage was strictly regulated, so that a man could have sexual relations only with a woman over whom he had full ownership; otherwise he might accuse a business partner of impregnating the slave. All children born to concubines had rights equal to children born of free wives to support and inheritance. A woman who became pregnant by her master acquired the status of *umm al-walad* (mother of a child) and could not be sold or given away for the rest of her life. The *umm al-walad* was freed upon the death of her master. Although the *umm al-walad* did not inherit a fixed share of her master's estate, she could be freely willed up to a third of the estate. Making this kind of provision for concubines seems to have been common; the early jurist al-Shāfiʿī, for example, willed a variety of goods (including a slave of her own) to his concubine (Mattson 1999, 209).

The Ḥanafīs, however, did allow a master to deny paternity of his concubine's child. In areas where Ḥanafī law was applied, the practice of concubinage must have had very different consequences, allowing more abuse of slave women and less control over men's sexuality. Since the Ottomans spread and enforced the Ḥanafī school over many Islamic lands in the later medieval period, this doctrine could have had a significant impact on family relations and the slave trade.

In keeping with the principle that children have a right to their biological lineage, Islamic law forbids fictional adoptions. Caring for foster children or orphans is highly meritorious in Islam, but an adopted child should keep his or her own family name, if it is known. Lineage is also protected by allowing women only one sexual partner at a time – her husband or master – while men can have up to four wives in addition to concubines. After divorce or being widowed, a woman cannot remarry until a certain fixed period has passed (the *ʿidda*) to ensure that she is not carrying her former husband's child. Similarly, a man cannot establish sexual relations with a concubine until she has completed a similar waiting period (the *istibrāʾ*).

Marriage and divorce

With marriage, men assume the responsibility to fully support their wives. Married women have the right to control their own property, and even wealthy women have no legal responsibility to contribute to household expenses or their own daily needs. The level of support provided by the husband depends both on his means and the wife's social status. Both of these principles can be found in the Qurʾān (2:233), where men are ordered to maintain their divorced wives who are nursing their children according to "customary standards of fairness" (*al-maʿrūf*), but that "no one shall have a greater burden placed on them than they can bear," meaning that men should not have to pay greater alimony or maintenance than they can truly afford.

The husband's commitment to the financial support of his wife is symbolized in the *mahr* – the marriage gift pledged at the time of marriage. The *mahr* (also called *ṣadāq*) is typically comprised of cash or other fungible property, although it could be anything of value – for example, the manumission of a slave woman by her master who then marries her (Spectorsky 1993, 121). Typically, the amount of *mahr* is negotiated between the groom and the bride or her family according to individual expectations and cultural norms. The state applies cultural norms in fixing a *mahr* in cases of divorce or dispute if an amount has not been specified in the marriage contract. In such cases, judges normally award a *mahr mithl*, a *mahr* for someone "like her" in terms of social and economic status (Nasir 1986, 90–2). Here again, we see that social customs and individual expectations, including women's expectations, comprised part of the family law that was applied by Muslim jurists.

Islamic law was adamant that the *mahr* was the sole property of the bride; the repeated insistence of jurists on this point in legal texts indicates that it was not unusual for self-interested guardians to take the *mahr* for themselves. Another issue frequently discussed by the jurists is the attempt of some men to avoid paying the *mahr* by agreeing with another family to "exchange" brides between the families, with neither bride getting a *mahr*. This practice, known as *shighār,* was explicitly prohibited by the Prophet, but seems to have continued as a cultural practice among the Beduin in particular (even until modern times, when Beduin women sought the judgment of Sharīʿa courts to secure their Islamic rights over customary practices; see Shaham 1993).

Unlike in many medieval Mediterranean and Asian societies, the family of the bride was not required to pay the husband a dowry. In some societies, however, it was customary for a bride to bring a trousseau (*jahāz*) with her to her husband's home. Consisting normally of bedding, furnishings, jewelry and clothes, the *jahāz* was legally the property of the bride, unless some of it had only been lent to her by her family for a time. Legal texts indicate that some men tried to claim part of their wife's trousseau upon divorce, a claim that was supported by custom in some places, but rejected by Islamic law (Tucker 1998, 54–5).

If a man desired to divorce his wife (*ṭalāq*), he was forbidden to take back the *mahr* or any of the gifts he had given her. It was customary in some communities for couples to split the *mahr* into two amounts: prompt (*muqaddam*) and deferred (*muʾakhkhar*). The prompt *mahr* was paid at the time of marriage, the deferred *mahr* was considered a debt against the husband's estate if he died, or which he had to pay if he divorced his wife. In addition, some scholars, particularly Mālikī scholars, interpreted Qurʾān 2:236 to indicate that the judge could require the husband to pay alimony (*matāʿ*) to his ex-wife.

In classical Islamic law, the husband can exercise his right of divorce without resort to the court. Once the husband utters a statement of divorce, his wife enters a "waiting period" (*ʿidda*) of three months (or menstrual periods), or until delivery of a child if the wife is pregnant. During this time, the couple should live together without having sexual relations. If sexual relations are resumed before the end of the *ʿidda*, or if the husband tells his wife he wants her back as his wife, the marriage is resumed. If no such action is taken during the waiting period, the couple are divorced. If a couple have twice divorced and remarried, a third marriage is forbidden to them unless the woman consummates a marriage with another man. These regulations are intended to deter men from using divorce as a threat and tool of manipulation over women, which seems to have been common in some societies.

Judges have the power to grant a divorce to women for a number of reasons, including abuse, neglect of duty, lack of support, and impotence. Jurists gave a rather wide variety of interpretations of the husband's duties and the wife's rights. For example, some said that the wife had a right to regular sexual intercourse, so that impotence for any extended period was grounds for divorce, while the Ḥanafī school required only that the husband was able to consummate the marriage. With a judicial dissolution of marriage (*faskh*), the wife had the right to retain her full *mahr* and all her marriage gifts, or to receive the remainder of her *mahr* if she had not been fully paid at the time of marriage.

A third means to dissolve a marriage is "divestment" (*khulʿ*) by the wife. In this case, the woman does not claim any neglect or abuse by the husband, but still desires to end the marriage. Some scholars considered this process a kind of divorce, others classified it as "ransoming." The difference is important, because those scholars who consider *khulʿ* to be a divorce conclude that it has legal effect only if accepted by the husband. In contrast, those scholars who consider *khulʿ* a ransom permit the wife to end the marriage without the agreement of the husband, simply by returning to him the *mahr* and any other marriage gifts.

Marriage contracts could be used to provide a woman with stronger legal instruments for securing a divorce against the wishes of her husband. Basic contracts recorded the necessary components of the marriage process, such as the names of the parties, that each consented to the union, and the amount of the *mahr*. In addition, Shīʿī jurists, in contrast to Sunnīs, permitted the contract (written or oral) to limit the duration of the marriage. Sunnī jurists claimed a consensus that "temporary marriage" (*zawāj mutʿa*) had been prohibited by the Prophet Muḥammad.

Marriage contracts seem to have been especially important, however, for recording stipulations made by the bride. The inclusion in early legal texts of sample marriage contracts with a variety of possible stipulations indicates that the practice was relatively widespread. Documentary evidence indicates that stipulations continued to be an important part of marriage contracts throughout the classical period (Abdal-Rehim 1996, 98–103, Spectorsky

1993, 13). Common stipulations included the right of the wife to divorce her husband if he took another wife or a concubine, her right to reside close to her family or in a certain town, her right to a domestic servant, her right to a monthly or yearly allowance beyond her standard maintenance rights, the agreement of the husband to provide support for his wife's children by a previous marriage, and the agreement of the husband not to travel away from his family for long periods of time.

Of course, women's rights to include stipulations in their marriage contracts do not mean that all women had the power to conduct such negotiations. Poverty, low social status, and lack of family support could deprive a women of the power to meaningfully negotiate a contract. Although this is true of people and contracts in general, it is likely that women often had less freedom to freely negotiate contracts than men. Nevertheless, it is significant that by recognizing the validity of stipulations in the marriage contract, classical Islamic law gave women a potential instrument for negotiating the lifestyle they desired with their future husbands, and the legal force to compel their husbands to abandon or adopt certain behaviors, or face punitive measures.

Maintaining family solidarity

The inclusion in marriage contracts of stipulations that a man could not move his wife away from her family is one indication of the importance of family solidarity in premodern Muslim societies. Islamic family law fostered and promoted mutual dependence in a number of ways. The responsibility of men to provide maintenance for female relatives has already been discussed. Minor dependents, male and female, also have the right to complete maintenance from their male guardians. This includes children of divorced men who are in the custody of their mother. Parents and grandparents, if needy, have the right to full support from their adult children and grandchildren.

Apart from financial responsibilities, the law requires guardians to properly care for their children. Babies have the right to be nursed, although some scholars say this is not the legal duty of the mother. If a woman does not want to nurse her child herself, the father must pay a wet-nurse, if he is able. If the parents are divorced, the father must pay support to the mother if she is to nurse the baby. Before age seven, children are considered to need the care of a woman (*ḥaḍāna*). For this reason, most schools of law placed young children in the custody of the mother in case of divorce, but gave the father custody rights for older children, when they were considered in need of the protection and mentoring of a father. Some scholars argued that girls should stay in the custody of the mother until marriage. In all cases, a father could fight the mother's custody if she remarried. Although the step-father became a *maḥram* to his female step-daughters, the girls' male relatives had the right to have them removed from his household. According to most Sunnī scholars, a young child in this situation should be placed in the custody of another female relative; Shīʿīs allow the father to take custody.

Marshall Hodgson has noted that while Islamic law strengthened the nuclear family against the customs of pre-Islamic society, the law also aimed to keep all intimate relationships within the law. Thus, polygamy and concubinage were recognized and legislated. Hodgson says that the "effect of the Shariʿi rules on marriage was to accord to up to four mates absolutely equal rights, which their children also shared in; the kept mistress or the free-born concubine [of the ancient world and Christian Europe] disappeared, in effect, from among the ordinary privileged classes . . . the Christian system sanctified – and under favorable circumstances surely fostered – a solidarity of interest in a couple committed to a single marital union despite the temptations of wealth. The Muslim system sacrificed the primacy of conjugal unity in favour of equality of rights on the part of all concerned" (Hodgson 1974, 341).

To foster the solidarity of the extended family, Islamic law designates fixed inheritance shares for close family members, allowing no disinheritance. In most cases, the Qurʾān allots male relatives double the inheritance of equivalent female relations. This inequality is explained by some scholars as a compensation for the greater responsibility men have to provide maintenance for family members. The Qurʾān lists many categories of relatives who can potentially inherit; the more close relatives there are, the fewer distant relatives will be allotted a fixed share. The Qurʾān does encourage Muslims to leave something for more distant relations from the third of the estate that can be be freely willed to non-Qurʾānic heirs. Relatives who profess a different faith can also receive an inheritance from the third, since they are barred from receiving a fixed share. One of the Prophet's wives used this provision to will a third of her estate to her Jewish nephew (Ibn Saʿd 1990, viii, 102).

Conclusion

Premodern Islamic legal texts display a wide variety of opinions held by classical jurists on almost every issue related to family law. In addition to the diversity of opinion evident in law books, the incorporation of custom into the law meant that Islamic family law often yielded divergent, even contradictory, results in its actual application across the Muslim world. At the same time, the law retained an overall coherence due to the retention of a number of core regulations and underlying premises, some of which have been discussed here. With the coming of colonialism, new world-views and customs challenged many of these premises upon which Islamic family law was built.

Bibliography

Primary Sources

Muhammad Ibn Saʿd. *al-Ṭabaqat al-Kubrā*, 9 vols. Beirut 1990.

Aḥmad b. ʿAbd al-Ḥalīm Ibn Taymiyya, *Fatāwā al-nisāʾ*, eds. Sayyid al-Jamīlī and Aḥmad Sāʾīh, Cairo 1987.

Abū al-Ḥasan ʿAlī b. Muḥammad b. Habīb al-Māwardī, *Kitāb al-nafaqāt*, ed. ʿĀmir Saʿīd al-Zībārī, Beirut 1998.

Abū Muḥammad ʿAbdullāh b. Aḥmād b. Qudāma, *al-Mughnī*, 9 vols., Cairo n.d.

Abū Bakr Aḥmad b. ʿAmr al-Khassāf al-Shaybānī, *Kitāb al-nafaqāt*, Beirut 1984.

Saḥnūn b. Saʿīd al-Tanūkhī, *al-Mudawwana al-kubrā li-al-Imām Mālik ibn Anas*, 6 vols., Beirut 1905.

Secondary Sources

A. A. Abdal-Rehim, The family and gender laws in Egypt during the Ottoman period, in A. E. Sonbol (ed.), *Women, the family and divorce laws in Islamic history*, Syracuse, N.Y. 1996, 96–111.

D. El Alami and D. Hinchcliffe, *Islamic marriage and divorce laws of the Arab world*, London 1996.

M. Fadel, Two women, one man. Knowledge, power, and gender in medieval Sunni legal thought, in *International Journal of Middle East Studies* 29:2 (1997), 185–204.

M. G. S. Hodgson, *The venture of Islam. Conscience and history in a world civilization*, i, *The classical age of Islam*, Chicago 1974.

I. Mattson, A believing slave is better than an unbeliever. Status and community in early Islamic society and law, Ph.D. diss., University of Chicago 1999.

J. J. Nasir, *The Islamic law of personal status*, London 1986.

R. Roded, *Women in Islamic biographical collections. From Ibn Saʿd to Who's Who*, Boulder, Colo. 1994.

L. Rosen. *The Anthropology of justice. Law as culture in Islamic society*, Oxford 1989.

R. Shaham, A woman's place. A confrontation with Bedouin custom in the *Sharīʿa* court, in *Journal of the American Oriental Society* (April–June 1993), 192–7.

W. Robertson Smith, *Kinship and marriage in early Arabia*, London 1903, new ed. 1990.

A. E. Sonbol (ed.), *Women, the family, and divorce laws in Islamic history*, Syracuse, N.Y. 1996.

S. A. Spectorsky, *Chapters on marriage and divorce. Responses of Ibn Hanbal and Ibn Rahwayh*, Austin, Tex. 1993.

G. H. Stern, *Marriage in early Islam*, London 1939.

J. E. Tucker, *In the house of the law. Gender and Islamic law in Ottoman Syria and Palestine*, Berkeley 1998.

Ingrid Mattson

Law: Modern Family Law, 1800–Present

Afghanistan

As a Muslim nation, Afghans consider the Sharīʿa, and specifically Ḥanafī *fiqh*, as the basis of their laws. However, as a tribal society, they have held onto pre-Islamic codes and local customary practices. The line between the two has gradually blurred.

Family law in Afghanistan has developed parallel to the development of the state and political changes. From the inception of the modern Afghan state in 1747, matters pertaining to family law were settled on an ad hoc basis, either in Sharīʿa courts or in tribal assemblies. It was Amīr ʿAbd al-Raḥmān Khān (r. 1880–1901) who first attempted to codify Afghan family law and apply it in a uniform manner throughout the country. He banned child marriage, forced marriage, and exorbitant bride-price. He also declared un-Islamic such practices as bride-price and the giving of girls in marriage to end blood feuds. He also restored to women the right to seek divorce in cases of non-support, and to widows their rights to inheritance. Although these were important first steps, *qāḍī*s in remote areas of the country continued to issue rulings based on traditional practices and on their own interpretation of the Sharīʿa.

Amīr ʿAbd al-Raḥmān Khān's son, Amīr Ḥabīb Allāh Khān (r. 1901–19), continued to emphasize his predecessor's vision and went further in adopting a systematic program of public education on the Sharīʿa. This program, designed by Maḥmūd Ṭarzī, the famous Afghan reformer, consisted of publishing books on the Sharīʿa, including rulings on women's rights, regular appearance of articles in the state-run newspaper, *Sirāj al-akhbār*, and publication of manuals for *qāḍī*s.

King Amān Allāh Khān (r. 1919–29) is considered the champion of modernization and of family law reform. In 1921 he issued a marriage decree in which child marriage was pronounced strictly forbidden and the age of majority was set at 13. In 1924, when he presented the nation with its first constitution, his family law reforms, especially articles related to polygamy, divorce, *mahr* (gift to the bride), and the age of majority came under severe criticism by the conservative *ʿulamāʾ*. In the compromised version of the law, polygamy remained permissible, but an unjust polygamist's wife could go to a Sharīʿa court and seek his punishment. Punishment was also prescribed for husbands who tried to prevent their wives from petitioning against them. Forced marriage between two adults was prohibited. The marriage of minors agreed upon by their fathers or guardians was allowed, but strongly recommended against. In the case of a minor bride, the *ʿaqd* could be contracted, but the marriage could be consummated only upon her reaching puberty, which contrary to the age of 13 that the King had demanded, followed the Ḥanafī norm of age 9. In January 1929 King Amān Allāh was overthrown and achievements dating from the 1880s were reversed.

In 1960 a matrimonial code was adopted, permitting child marriage in principle, meaning that the *nikāḥ* (consummation of marriage) could occur only when the girl reached puberty. Article 2 set the legal age of *nikāḥ* at 15.

The constitution of 1964, introduced by King Ẓāhir (r. 1933–73), stated that "all the people of Afghanistan, without discrimination and privilege before the law, have equal rights and obligations." This provided the legal basis for subsequent petitions and court rulings that were more favorable to women.

The constitution of 1977 explicitly pronounced women legally equal to men. Written and promulgated during President Dāwūd's republican regime, it stipulated that, "all the people of Afghanistan, both women and men, without discrimination and privilege before the law, have equal rights and obligations." This constitution did not name the Ḥanafī school as the official *madhhab* of Afghanistan. Consequently, in the Civil Law of the same year, the Mālikī interpretation of a divorce mechanism using the concepts of *liʿān* and *faskh* was introduced. This allows women to seek divorce by a judicial process and decree. The legal age of majority for females was set at 16 and the law gave adult females the right to enter marriage without their guardian's permission. Among the first legislative acts of the Marxist regime that toppled President Dāwūd in 1978 was the declaration as strictly illegal of marriage of girls under the age of 16; violators became liable to imprisonment of six months to three years. The punitive measures in this decree distinguished it from the earlier law on this matter.

With the outbreak of war against the Soviet invasion of Afghanistan in the 1980s, state institutions, including the judiciary, gradually disintegrated. With it, the practice of family law reverted to the rulings of individual *qāḍī*s based on their own interpretation of the Sharīʿa.

With the coming to power of the Taliban in 1996, a revived attempt was made to implement the law uniformly throughout Afghanistan. The Taliban's understanding of the Sharīʿa was far from the liberal interpretations that had gradually entered the field of family law in Afghanistan before 1978. The Taliban did, however, issue two decrees favorable to women. In September 1998 the Taliban banned the tribal practice of giving a woman in marriage in the settlement of blood feuds, and prohibited the compulsory marriage of a widow to her deceased husband's next of kin.

Throughout all legal reforms, laws on inheritance have remained unchanged and are based on the Sharīʿa. In practice, however, women are often denied their Islamic share of inheritance.

After the fall of the Taliban in December 2001, a presidential decree declared the 1977 family law as valid and applicable.

Bibliography

Primary Sources

A. Y. Ali, *The meaning of the glorious Qur'an. Text, translation and commentary*, Beirut n.d.

Asās al-quḍāt, Kabul 1303/1886.

al-Bukhārī, *Mukhtaṣar Ṣaḥīḥ al-Bukhārī*, Riyadh 1996.

Fatwa-i sharʿī sutr wa-ḥijāb, Kabul, 27 August 1993.

Sultan Mohammad, *The constitution and law of Afghanistan*, London 1900.

F. M. Kātib, *Sirāj al-tavārīkh*, 3 vols., Kabul 1331–3/1913–15.

Matn-i kāmil-i qawanīn-i asāsi-yi Afghānistān (Complete text of Afghan constitutions), Qum, Iran 1995.

Nizāmnāmah-i ʿarūsi. Nikāḥ wa khatna suri, Kabul, 23 August 1925.

Proceedings of the Loya Jirga of 1303 HS, Kabul 1926.

Secondary Sources

A. R. I. Doi, *Woman in Shari'ah (Islamic law)*, London 1989².

J. L. Esposito, *Women in Muslim family law*, Syracuse, N.Y. 1982.

R. Farhādā (ed.), *Maqalāt-i Maḥmūd Tarzī dār sirāj al-akhbār-i Afghāniyya*, Kabul 1977.

H. K. Kakar, *Government and society in Afghanistan. The reign of Amir ʿAbd al-Rahman Khan*, Austin, Tex. 1979.

M. H. Kamali, *Law in Afghanistan*, Leiden 1985.

H. Malikyar, Development of family law in Afghanistan. The roles of the Hanafī Madhhab, customary practices and power politics, in *Central Asian Survey* 16:3 (1997), 389–99.

L. B. Poullada, *Reform and rebellion in Afghanistan, 1919–1929*, Ithaca, N.Y. 1973.

Helena Malikyar

Arab States

The Premodern Era

In order to appreciate the nature of family law reform in the modern era, a cursory reference to rules on the family in the premodern era under Islamic jurisprudence has to be made. The "family," as a unit revolving around the acts of marriage and reproduction, was unknown to premodern Muslim jurists. Rather, they saw marriage as one of several equally important legal relationships that formed in their totality the web of the premodern Islamic medieval household. In this legal household, the man was the financial provider, the head, and the guardian of the household, while the wife (or wives) was the provider of sexual pleasure (obedience) in return for her right to maintenance. Other members of the household (concubines, slaves, children, relatives) also owed the male provider different kinds and degrees of obedience in return for their right to maintenance. The provider had the power to discipline those toward whom he had the duty of maintenance. An important background rule that has survived until modern times is, however, that free women owned property independently from their husbands and had complete freedom to dispense with and administer this property. They had no duty of maintenance to anybody.

The schools of law in the Sunnī world (Mālikī, Shāfiʿī, Ḥanafī, Ḥanbalī) dominated the legal system in the premodern era, in which each school had its own set of jurists who wrote treatises of jurisprudence on various subjects ranging from contract, tort, and crime to marriage, concubinage, and divorce. Each school had a class of muftis who provided legal opinions to the school's constituents. *Qāḍī*s (judges) were affiliated with these schools and interpreted the treatises of their school's main jurists in adjudicating cases. The schools were relatively autonomous and free from the intervention of the ruler in the administration of law.

Transformation of the Legal System in the Early Modern Era

European penetration of the Ottoman Empire (nineteenth century) succeeded by European colonialism (nineteenth and twentieth centuries) triggered a process of substituting the doctrines of the schools with European legal transplants. This process proved unstoppable, especially as it was adopted by local Muslim elites, who saw it as part of an overall modernizing/Europeanizing effort that they themselves embraced and shepherded. The transformation was mediated through the capitulatory regime that brought into existence mixed courts applying European codes in the area of civil and commercial law and extending their jurisdictions not only to foreigners and non-Muslims but also to Ottoman Muslims. Secular national courts eventually replaced the mixed courts while mimicking their structural and textual foundation. By the turn of the twentieth century, Islamic law was left with only the family to regulate.

In the post-Ottoman era (whether under European colonialism or later in the postcolonial period), the nation-state emerged as the central and dominant political unit. The historic autonomy of law that characterized the premodern era was lost, as all law, even God's law, had to be legislated by the state to become official. Courts became part of a centralized legal system dominated by the powers of the state. Courts administering Islamic law came to be distinguished from those that did not, the former known as Sharīʿa courts and the latter as "regular" courts administering transplanted European law. Eventually, most judges were graduates of law schools which taught Islamic jurisprudence as part of an otherwise secular curriculum concentrating on transplanted law; they could adjudicate cases on the family as well as other areas of secular law. Some judges were trained in Sharīʿa faculties (which came to be incorporated within the structure of secular universities) with degrees in Islamic jurisprudence and theology and were only qualified to sit in family courts.

Family law reforms in the Arab world: the first stage

Early reforms of family law, beginning in the first half of the twentieth century and continued in the early part of the second, aimed generally at transforming the legal domestic unit from the "medieval household" of Islamic jurisprudence into the modern "family" of the family code, without radically departing from the premodern schools' conceptual legal structure of gendered reciprocity (husbands maintain and wives obey). The idea behind these early reforms was to chip away at the most cruel aspects of gendered reciprocity by first, limiting the scope of the wife's obedience; second, expanding the scope of the husband's financial duties; and third, limiting the range of powers in the family these financial duties allowed him. Thus, wives' financial rights whether during the marriage or after divorce were increased; new grounds allowing wives to exit from marriage were established; and the husband's right to no fault divorce and to practice polygamy was constrained and limited. Examples include the laws on the family passed in Egypt (1920, 1929), Jordan (1917, 1951, 1976), Syria (1953), Lebanon (1917), Iraq (1959), and Palestine (1919, 1951, 1976). In addition, the state's power to mediate conflicts between husbands and wives was consolidated through the introduction of legal requirements of registration and documentation of marriage and divorce. Early reforms also targeted the law of procedure in Sharīʿa courts to make it less dependent on oral testimony (the rule in the premodern era) and to create an official system of appellate review for the first time in Islamic adjudication (Anderson 1976, Coulson 1964, 163–4, Schacht 1982, 101).

Tunisia is notable in its attempt to realize radical reform through abandonment of the principle of gendered reciprocity. Instead of maintenance for obedience, the Tunisian Majalla (Family Code 1957) advocates reciprocal good treatment by both spouses and shared duty of maintenance (if the wife has money). In exchange for the duty of maintenance, the wife no longer has to obey her husband, and has equal access to divorce, guardianship powers over her children, and the power to consent to a minor child's marriage. For the first time in Islamic history, however, a husband can take his wife to court demanding that she maintains the family if she has money. Husband no longer, per reforms in Tunisia, spares wife's purse. The premodern principle of exempting wife from any duty of maintenance was abandoned.

Methods of reform

To create these doctrinal changes while still basing them on Islamic law, early reformers resorted to acts of *ijtihād* (devising a new rule based on a fresh reading of the Qurʾān and the Prophetic traditions); *ikhtiyār* (choosing among the various opinions of the premodern schools of jurisprudence, even those considered minority schools); *talfīq* (creating a doctrine afresh through combining two rules derived from two different schools); adoption of Shīʿī jurisprudence or opinions of schools long considered "dead"; and finally, the implementation of rules on procedure that make a particular substantive rule ineffective (through legislating statutory limitations or registration requirements) (Hallaq 1997, 210–14). Approaching the doctrines of the schools, alive and dead, Sunnī and Shīʿī, including majority and minority opinions within each, without specific loyalty to the doctrine of any particular school, has created for the first time in Islamic history a kind of supra-*madhhab* legal consciousness that remains prevalent until today among the modern Muslim jurists/reformers/legal commentators (Esposito 2001, 119–26). It should be noted, however, that the doctrines of particular schools remain dominant in certain regions as the historic origin from which departure to alternative doctrines took place (for instance, Mālikī doctrine in North Africa and Ḥanafī in Egypt and the Levant; An-Naʿim 2002, 5–6).

Transformation of the legal treatise on the family

Modern treatises commenting on the modern family code or statute clearly convey the supra-*madhhab* consciousness of their authors. Typically in these treatises, the views of various premodern schools on a particular doctrinal matter are discussed and the rule adopted by the legislature through *ijtihād, ikhtiyār*, or *talfīq* is identified and commented upon. In general, modern treatises share with the reformers the project of transforming the "household" into a "family." Instead of a male provider overseeing a household inhabited by wives, concubines, slaves, children, and relatives, the modern family constructed by these treatises via commentary on the family code is a predominantly monogamous one in which marriage is a matter of offer and acceptance between a man and a woman with the goal of reproduction. Marriage for reproduction in the modern Islamic treatise is a novel construct diverging widely from marriage as a contract between a man and a woman according to which a woman provides sexual pleasure, as was the case in the premodern juristic treatise (Sonbol 2003, 157). However, given that reforms have taken place within the principle of gendered reciprocity without eliminating it altogether, the modern codes and treatises are notable for incorporating rules associated with the premodern household as well as those associated with the monogamous reproductive family unit. The rule on wifely obedience through provision of sexual pleasure to husband (medieval household), as well as the norm of reproduction as the purpose of the marriage contract (modern family) are both present, in tension with each other and each pulling in a different conceptual direction (Badran 1976). A modern innovation of these treatises is the presentation of obedience for maintenance as an element of a long list of reciprocal rights and duties exchanged by the spouses.

Family courts in the modern era

Judges in the contemporary family courts in the various Arab countries, have, in general, used their discretion in interpreting the law to further whittle away at the most detrimental aspects of gendered reciprocity. This is of course not always the case, and depends on how liberal or conservative the judges interpreting the legislation might be. Liberal rulings tend in the direction of increasing the husband's maintenance obligations and of contracting women's obedience obligations; conservative rulings tend in the other direction. Family courts in various states are notorious for delay in settling cases, causing a great deal of hardship for litigants, especially women, rendering their marital status and financial rights uncertain for lengthy periods of time (Hill 1979, 72–101, Sonbol 2003, 180–3).

Debate of family law reform: the second stage

The second stage of family law reform, starting in the early 1980s, brought new actors to the scene and triggered a fresh debate. Unlike the first stage, where reforms took place through an alliance between the secular nationalist elites controlling the state, reforming feminists influenced by Western enlightenment, and modernizing *ʿulamāʾ* (Muslim jurists) seeking to revive Islamic law to challenge the transplantation of European law into the Arab world (Abu-Odeh 2004), the political forces that came to the fore in the second stage look significantly different. The participants in this second stage of debate comprise first, a new generation of Islamicists, including women Islamicists who are offended by the reforms of the first stage and who seek to revive a gendered reciprocity that is unshackled by these reforms. It is noteworthy that women Islamicists might differ from male Islamicists over how to interpret gendered reciprocity with the former seeking to use it to curb male power and the latter seeking to reconsolidate this power. The second party to the new debate is the religious bureaucracy which has played the role after the first stage of reforms of administering Sharīʿa courts and adjudicating family law cases, and which wants to preserve the reforms (reformed gendered reciprocity) while being willing to either minimally advance those reforms or alternatively curb them, depending on its perception of how it is faring in the eyes of the public (in its competition for legitimacy with the new Islamicists). Third, there is a reinvigorated feminism aligned with the international human rights movement which wants to abolish gendered reciprocity altogether in favor of formal equality (both husband and wife share duty of maintenance and treat each other well, no wifely obedience). Fourth, there is a liberal feminism which shares the basic convictions of the human rights feminism but shuns secular discourse and insists on packaging its liberal feminism in the language of a reformed interpretation of Islam. The last participants in the debate are the secular nationalists controlling the state. For them, the stakes are high, as the Islamicists gain popular following among the public, undermining the historic ability of political elites to ally themselves with the feminists to advance micro reforms. Like the Sharīʿa clerics, they engage in push-and-pull support for further reforms depending on the public's reaction, their paramount concern being not the reform but the stability of their control over the state (Moors 2003, Welchman 2003).

The Islamicists in Egypt tried to make their imprint on the debate by arguing before the Supreme Constitutional Court of Egypt (SCC) that certain reforms as they unfolded in Egypt (Law 25 of 1920, Law 25 of 1929, and Law 100 of 1985) violated article 2 of the Egyptian constitution, which establishes that the Sharīʿa is the primary source of legislation. Restricting polygamy, allowing women judicial divorce, and imposing financial duties of maintenance on men retroactively were all rules, the Islamicists argued, that went against the grain of article 2 because they were un-Islamic, or contrary to the Sharīʿa. The SCC developed a judicial test to inspect the Islamicity of the rules which was flexible enough to allow the reforms to survive. The typical approach of the court was to split the difference between the demands of the Islamicists and those of the feminists: polygamy is neither an absolute right of the husband (Islamicists) nor is it to be abolished (feminists) but should survive in a restricted form whereby women can ask for divorce if they prove harm when the husband takes a second wife (Lombardi 1998, El-Morr 1997, Najjar 1988).

The new feminists seem to be demanding a concession from women in the name of formal equality. Women should be willing to waive the rule that protects their wealth from the husband's demands (share in the duty of maintenance of the family) in return for abolishing the rule of wifely obedience. Many feminists treat this as a worthy trade-off and they also argue that it reflects social reality since women do indeed participate in maintaining the family as a matter of fact (CGESWE 1992). This, however, is a contentious strategy of reform given the fact that while rich women tend to go to court to request divorce, poor women for the most part go to court to request maintenance from their husbands (Würth 2003). The trade-off might prove costly to poor women.

Bibliography

L. Abu-Odeh, Egyptian feminism. Trapped in the identity debate, in Y. Y. Haddad and B. F. Stowasser (eds.), *Islamic law and the challenges of modernity*, Walnut Creek, Calif. 2004, 183–212.

——, Modernizing Muslim family law. The case of Egypt, in *Vanderbilt Journal of Transnational Law* and *Oxford Comparative Law Forum* (forthcoming).

N. Anderson, *Law reform in the Muslim world*, London 1976.

A. An-Naʿim (ed.), *Islamic family law in a changing world. A global resource book*, London 2002.

B. A. al-ʿA. Badrān, *Al-fiqh al-muqāran li-al-aḥwāl al-shakhsiyya*, i, Beirut 1976.

J. Y. Brinton, *The Mixed Courts of Egypt*, New Haven, Conn. 1968.

M. M. Charrad, Repudiation versus divorce. Responses to state policy in Tunisia, in E. N. Chow and C. W. Berheide (eds.), *Women, the family, and policy*, Albany, N.Y. 1994, 51–69.

——, *States and women's rights*, Berkeley 2001.

CGESWE (Communication Group for the Enhancement of the Status of Women in Egypt) (ed.), *Legal rights of Egyptian women in theory and practice*, Cairo 1992.

N. J. Coulson, *A history of Islamic law*, Edinburgh 1964, repr. 2003.

D. Crecelius, The course of secularization in modern Egypt, in J. L. Esposito (ed.), *Islam and development. Religion and sociopolitical change*, Syracuse, N.Y. 1980, 49–70.

A. Z. al-Dābṣi, *Kitāb al-nikāḥ min al-asrār*, Cairo 1993

A. al-Dardīr, *Al-sharḥ al-ṣaghir. Taʾlīf Aḥmad al-Dardīr, ʿalā mukhtaṣarihi al-musammā aqrab al-masālik ilā madthhab al-Imām Mālik*, ii, ed. M. al-Ḥamīd, Cairo 1965.

D. S. El Alami and D. Hinchcliffe, *Islamic marriage and divorce laws of the Arab world*, London 1996.

A. M. El-Morr, Judicial sources for supporting the protection of human rights, in E. Cotran and A. O. Sherif (eds.), *The role of the judiciary in the protection of human rights*, Boston 1997, 5–33.

J. L. Esposito, *Islam and politics*, Syracuse, N.Y. 1984, 1998⁴.

——, *Women in Muslim family law*, Syracuse, N.Y. 1982, 2001².

W. B. Hallaq, *A history of Islamic legal theories*, Cambridge 1997, repr. 2002.

E. Hill, *Mahkama! Studies in the Egyptian legal system*, London 1979.

A. Hourani, *A history of the Arab peoples*, Cambridge 1991, repr. New York 1992.

Ibn Qudāma, *Kitāb al-nikāḥ*, ed. M. Khattab and M. al-Sayyid, Cairo 1996.

S. A. Jackson, *Islamic law and the state*, Leiden 1996.

ʿA. R. al-Jazīrī, *Kitāb al-fiqh ʿalā al-madthāhib al-arbaʿa*, iv, Cairo 1990

H. J. Liebesny, *The law of the Near and Middle East*, Albany, N.Y. 1975.

C. B. Lombardi, Islamic law as a source of constitutional law in Egypt. The constitutionalization of the Sharia in a modern Arab state, in *Columbia Journal of Transnational Law* 37 (1998), 81–123.

T. Mahmood, *Statutes of personal law in Islamic countries*, New Delhi 1987, 1995².

G. Makdisi, *Rise of colleges*, Edinburgh 1981.

M. K. Masud et al., *Islamic legal interpretation. Muftis and their fatwas*, London 1996.

A. Moors, Introduction. Public debates on family law reform. Participants, positions, and styles of argumentation in the 1990s, in *Islamic Law and Society* 10 (2003), 1–11.

F. M. Najjar, Egypt's laws of personal status, in *Arab Studies Quarterly* 10 (1988), 319–44.

J. J. Nasir, *The Islamic law of personal status*, The Hague 2002.
J. Schacht, *An introduction to Islamic law*, New York 1982.
A. I. al-Shirazi, *Al-muhadhdhab fī fiqh al-Imām al-Shāfiʿī*, M. Zuhaili (ed.), Damascus 1992.
A. E. Sonbol, *Women of Jordan. Islam, labor and the law*, Syracuse, N.Y. 2003.
M. A. Wani, *The Islamic law on maintenance of women, children, parents and other relatives*, Noonamy, Kashmir 1995.
L. Welchman, *Beyond the code. Muslim family law and the Shari'a judiciary in the Palestinian West Bank*, The Hague 2000.
——, In the interim. Civil society, the Shari'a judiciary and Palestinian personal status law in the transitional period, in *Islamic Law and Society* 10 (2003), 34–69.
A. Würth, Stalled reform. Family law in post-unification Yemen, in *Islamic Law and Society* 10 (2003), 12–33.
F. J. Ziadeh, *Lawyers, the rule of law and liberalism in modern Egypt*, Stanford 1968.

Lama Abu-Odeh

Egypt

Prior to the late nineteenth century family law and family courts, as such, did not exist in Egypt or anywhere else in the Ottoman Empire. Matters pertaining to marriage, divorce, inheritance, and custody, along with criminal and civil matters, were adjudicated through the Sharīʿa courts on the basis of Islamic law or, in the case of Christians and Jews, the *milliyya* (confessional) courts. Administrative cases fell under *qānūn*, or Ottoman executive law. *ʿUrf* (customary law) played a critical role in legal practices, influencing local preferences for particular schools of legal interpretation and strategic choices by plaintiffs about how and where particular sorts of cases were raised. In Egypt, the Shāfiʿī school was favored in the Delta, reflecting the prevalence of the extended family with the father as head of household. In Upper Egypt, the preference was for the Mālikī school, which reflected the prevalence of tribal kinship models, stressing the authority of male members of the wider clan, from father to clan head. Decisions by jurists were interpretive, based on the practice of referencing and interpreting texts, rather than on codes promulgated by the governing authority.

The notion of family relationships as based upon complementary, rather than equal, rights between men and women was foundational to such legal interpretations. The law upheld the authority of men as fathers and husbands with proprietary rights over women and younger family members, based on their status as financial providers to the household. In return for the right to maintenance, a woman owed obedience (*ṭāʿa*) to her husband and father. In practice, however, the fluid nature of adjudication often worked in the interests of women, who used the court system regularly as a way to assert their legal rights. The legal system, therefore, often honored a woman's right to choose a husband, to enter marriage as a propertied person, to demand adequate support for herself and to negotiate a divorce on her own initiative. Such courts, which were authorized to adjudicate the cases of all parties who came before them, were patronized not only by Muslims but also by Christians seeking to gain divorces or register marriages that would then follow the principles of Sharīʿa law.

Egyptian legal reforms of the late nineteenth century drastically altered the terrain of law and adjudication. In 1883, one year after the British had occupied Egypt, a Civil Code based on Napoleonic law was compiled by the colonial administration for the new national (*ahliyya*) courts. These assumed jurisdiction over criminal and commercial matters. Matters related to marriage, divorce, custody, guardianship, and inheritance remained the judicial province of the Sharīʿa and *milliyya* courts. Confining Sharīʿa to domestic matters politicized the family as both a sphere of intimate, affective relations and as a repository of group identity of which religious affiliation was a defining legal and moral characteristic. The politicization of what have come to be known as personal status laws (*aḥwāl shakhṣiyya*) emerged from the intersection of European colonial discourses on domesticity and the primacy of the nuclear family as a hallmark of modernity and anti-colonial nationalist discourses. Egyptian secular nationalist as well as Islamic reformers targeted the family as a site for reforms which aimed both to make Egypt more modern and to preserve a distinctive national culture.

The Muslim personal status laws of 1920, 1923, and 1929 codified and rationalized the rules governing family law. A committee made up of religious leaders incorporated rules from the various *madhāhib* to create a single, unified body of law and procedure, which was then reviewed by the minister of justice and approved by the prime minister. Such reforms institutionalized the authority of religious officials, underpinned by the sanction of secular state institutions, to legally regulate the shape and content of the family.

Legal reforms raised the minimum age of marriage, made state registration of marriage a requirement and rationalized male divorce pronouncements (*ṭalāq*). Amendments laid out provisions for judicial divorce by the wife on the basis of *ḍarar* or harm, making marital discord (*shiqāq*) grounds for divorce. In spite of the very different status of marriage within Coptic law, which recognized marriage as a holy sacrament sanctified by God rather than as a contract between two people, contemporaneous changes in Coptic family law mirrored the general trends toward reform in the Muslim personal status laws. Such reforms were, in part, the result of an intensive campaign by the Egyptian Feminist Union, which had placed modification of the personal status laws at the top of its reform agenda. After an unsuccessful attempt in 1923 to gain voting rights for women, the union turned its attention to improving the status of women within the family. While the campaign was a partial success, the union was unsuccessful in securing the abolition of polygamy and its demand that all divorces be subject to judicial approval.

The codification of family law established the gendered roles of mother and wife and husband and father as a legal basis of personhood (*ashkhāṣ*) and citizenship upon which rights and duties were placed. These rights and duties mirrored not only the position of women in the family but also their status within the nation. Husbands and fathers enjoyed absolute rights to guardianship, divorce, and custody, while wives and mothers had to petition the court to achieve their rights, constituting them as legal dependents of the state. Legally speaking, men, as enfranchised political individuals, could make claims to rights as equal, autonomous individuals. Women, however, had to make claims for rights on the basis that they were mothers of the future generation of Egyptian citizens. This model of maternal citizenship enabled feminists to be partially successful in their calls for changes to family law as well as to successfully claim the right to be educated, but circumscribed the other sorts of demands for rights and inclusion.

While such rights and duties recognized generally prevailing social norms, which viewed men and women as having complementary (and unequal) roles within Egyptian society, the recognition of women as legal individuals with rights that had to be protected was new. Thus, the personal status code laid out the conditions through which women could obtain a divorce, receive support from their husbands, retain custody of their children, and contest marriages concluded by their male guardians without their consent. It was precisely this recognition of rights, however, which constituted women as dependent legal subjects and emphasized male familial authority. As wives and mothers, women were entitled to economic support in exchange for obedience and freedom from *ḍarar*, while unilateral divorce was rigidly enshrined as a male prerogative. At the same time, the legal delineation of the conditions under which both husbands and wives could obtain a divorce privileged new notions of companionate marriage based on the authority of the male breadwinner at the expense of wider male kin and may actually have made divorce more difficult to obtain for both parties. Such a vision of marriage was reflective of relatively new notions of domesticity that favored the bourgeois nuclear family as the linchpin of the Egyptian nation and the foundation of its moral, social, and political order.

These laws remained virtually unchanged until the 1970s despite changes in the structure of the Egyptian court system. In 1955, the Sharīʿa and other confessional courts were abolished by the Nasser regime as a means to bring religious communities more firmly under the control of the state. A new family court was established within the existing national court system. While this may have undermined the control that religious community leaders had exercised over women through the autonomous confessional courts, the preservation of the existing personal status laws meant that the gender inequalities remained.

It is these inequalities that made reform of the personal status laws a particular target of the Egyptian women's organizations, starting in the 1920s. Reform campaigns have achieved some feminist demands (such as raising the age of marriage and raising the age of *ḥaḍāna*, the period in which the mother has rights to custody over her children) but have failed to achieve other chief feminist demands such as abolition of polygamy or restricting male right to divorce by making it subject to a judge's approval. In part, difficulties have stemmed from the monopolization by religious authorities of family law and attempts to preserve the family as a site of cultural authenticity against perceptions of Western encroachment. But difficulties have also derived from the state's attempts to claim sovereignty over women's issues beginning in the 1950s with the Nasser regime's program of state feminism. In 1979, President Anwar Sadat passed a number of reforms to Egypt's family law by executive decree after they failed to be ratified in the Egyptian parliament. Named for Sadat's wife, "Jihan's Law," as it came to be popularly known, gave wives the right to keep the marital home in the event of a divorce and the right to be informed and granted a divorce if their husbands took another wife. The law was widely criticized, not only by Islamists who argued that the changes were contrary to Sharīʿa but by other leftist and secular opposition groups who objected to the authoritarian way the reforms had been enacted. Jihan's Law was struck down on procedural grounds in 1985.

More recent reform campaigns have been more successful. In 2000, the Egyptian parliament passed the Law on the Reorganization of Certain Terms and Procedures of Litigation in Personal Status Matters. Its provision gave women the right to initiate a "no fault" divorce (*khulʿ*) in exchange for giving up her financial claims upon her husband, including the deferred part of her *mahr* (bride money). The legislation was the culmination of a 15-year campaign by a broad coalition of women activists, lawyers, and scholars who used novel organizational strategies to achieve their ends. Unlike in prior attempts at reform, which tended to conceptualize the issue of family law as one of equal rights for women, the protagonists of the most recent campaign focused on increasing women's rights by reinterpreting Islamic tradition. Not only did this allow activists to counter charges that changes to the law were un-Islamic but it also allowed coalition building across the political spectrum. Future attempts to reform law in Egypt are likely to draw on this successful mode of organizing rather than appealing to a discourse of equal rights.

Bibliography

L. Abu-Odeh, *Modernizing Muslim family law. The case of Egypt*, Toronto 2001.

L. Al-Atraqchi, The women's movement and the mobilization for legal change in Egypt. A century of personal status law reform, Ph.D. diss., Concordia University 2003.

M. Afifi, Reflections on the personal status laws of Copts, in A. E. Sonbol (ed.), *Women, the family and divorce laws in Islamic history*, Syracuse, N.Y. 1996, 202–18.

J. N. D. Anderson, Recent developments in Shar'ia law. III. The contract of marriage, in *Muslim World* 41 (1951), 112–26.

——, Recent developments in Shar'ia law. IV. Further points concerning marriage, in *Muslim World* 41 (1951), 187–98.

——, Recent developments in Shar'ia law. V. The dissolution of marriage, in *Muslim World* 41 (1951), 271–88.

M. Hatem, The enduring alliance of nationalism and patriarchy in Muslim personal status laws. The case of modern Egypt, in *Feminist Issues* 6:1 (1986), 19–43.

N. Safran, The abolition of the Sharia courts in Egypt, in *Muslim World* 48 (1958), part 1, 20–8.

R. Shaham, *The family and the courts in modern Egypt*, Leiden 1997.

A. E. Sonbol, Adults and minors in Ottoman *Sharīʿa* courts and modern law, in A. E. Sonbol (ed.), *Women, the family and divorce laws in Islamic history*, Syracuse, N.Y. 1996, 236–56.

——, Law and gender violence in Ottoman and modern Egypt, in M. C. Zilfi (ed.), *Women in the Ottoman Empire. Middle Eastern women in the early modern era*, Leiden 1997, 214–31.

Laura Bier

Gulf, Saudi Arabia, and Yemen

During the last two hundred years, little change has taken place in family legislation in the Arabian Peninsula and the Gulf. These countries still rely on uncodified personal status law with only Kuwait and Yemen as exceptions. While Kuwait was the first country in the Gulf to issue legislation on marital relations – law no. 5 of 1961 on marriages between Kuwaitis and non-Kuwaitis – it introduced a comprehensive family code only in 1984. In Yemen, the first code was promulgated in 1974 in what was at that time the People's Democratic Republic of Yemen.

In marked contrast to other countries in the region, in conservative Gulf states the voice of pressure groups has not been strong enough to force ruling elites to allow reform in family legislation. Introducing women's rights in law has proved difficult. Still, democracy alone is not expected to lead to reforms in Islamic law: women's rights' advocates fear that elections simply bring to power Islamists who do not favor codification.

Prior to the present era, three distinct courses of legal practice were followed: an uncodified version of the Islamic Sharīʿa, often combined with local custom (*ʿurf*) (Saudi Arabia, Kingdom of Yemen, Oman, Aden Protectorates, Gulf Protectorates); Ottoman rule during the latter part of the nineteenth century (Kuwait as part of Basra Province); and British administrative and legal influence (Aden Colony, Kuwait administered from British India). In Aden, with direct British rule, the Anglo-Muhammadan legal practice as developed in India was introduced with British judges applying Sharīʿa for Muslims in matters of personal status.

All the classical schools of Islamic jurisprudence are present in this area. The Ḥanbalī school prevails in Saudi Arabia and Qatar and five of the seven emirates that form the United Arab Emirates (Sharjah, Ajman, Fujayrah, Ras al-Khaymah and Umm al-Qaywayn). Abu Dhabi and Dubai follow the Mālikī school. In Bahrain the population is divided between Mālikīs and Jaʿfarīs with separate courts. Kuwait enacted a family code (Law no. 51 of 1984 concerning Personal Status) 23 years after independence based on Mālikī interpretation. Oman, whose sovereignty Britain acknowledged in 1951, applies Ibāḍī doctrine even though the population includes Shāfiʿīs (Dhofar), Ḥanafīs (al-Batinah), Ḥanbalīs (Jaʿlan), Mālikīs, and Jaʿfarīs.

The majority of Yemenis follow the Shāfiʿī school; the substantial Zaydī population in the north follows the Hadāwī school. Small Shīʿī communities of Jaʿfarīs, Ismāʿīlīs, and Bohras exist in the north and south without the right to follow their own legal school. The present Family Code (Law no. 20 of 1992 concerning Personal Status as amended in 1998 and 1999) draws from all schools of Islamic jurisprudence. When the country was divided, each state applied very different legislation. The Family Law of the Yemen Arab Republic (Law no. 3 of 1978) provided a conservative reading of Islamic law schools and custom (*ʿurf*). The Family Code of the People's Democratic Republic of Yemen (PDRY) (Law no. 1 of 1974 in Connection with the Family), a radical interpretation of the Sharīʿa, was considered one of the most progressive codes in the Islamic world.

The present code provides some improvement for women in the north; for example, in signing the marriage contract the woman's guardian has to be present, while earlier no representative of the bride was needed; the conditions under which polygamy was allowed are tightened, as are provisions regarding the husband's obligation not to cause any material or psychological harm (*ḍarar*) to his wife. In addition, in the event of divorce, the age of children remaining in the custody of the mother was raised. For southern women, all these provisions were clear deteriorations. In the PDRY family code, polygamy was allowed only under special conditions, subject to court decision, and all divorces required litigation.

According to classical jurisprudence, marriage (*nikāḥ*) is a contract between two parties based on an offer and acceptance in the presence of two male witnesses. A woman is represented by her guardian (*walī*) in signing the contract. However, in Ḥanafī and Jaʿfarī law any sane adult can contract marriage on his or her own. The Sunnī schools of *fiqh* agree that a person who is in sound mind is capable of marrying at the onset of puberty. Sunnīs do not specify the age but for Jaʿfarīs this means nine for girls and twelve for boys. The Jaʿfarīs also acknowledge an unlimited number of temporary marriages (*mutʿa*) where the spouses sustain neither mutual obligations nor inherit from each other. Children born in such a union have the same rights as in *nikāḥ*. All classical schools approve polygyny up to four *nikāḥ* unions.

Marriage according to all law schools entails mutual obligations on spouses. The husband is obliged to pay a bridal gift (*mahr*) and provide maintenance and appropriate accommodation. In exchange, the wife is obliged to obey him. What this obedience means in practice is contested among classical jurists. For some it means, besides residing in his house and allowing sexual relations, taking care of the household chores. The majority of Shīʿī and Sunnī jurists agree that a woman who works outside the home without her husband's permission loses her maintenance.

All classical schools grant the husband unilateral right to repudiation (*ṭalāq*). The Ḥanafī school accepts *ṭalāq* pronounced under duress or when drunk. Consequent to *ṭalāq* the wife is obliged to start her *ʿidda*, a waiting period of three menstrual cycles, or delivery if pregnant, before remarriage. During the *ʿidda* the husband is obliged to maintain her. Jaʿfarī law requires two male witnesses and a prescribed formula in Arabic for *ṭalāq*. Classical schools distinguish *ṭalāq al-sunna* (repudiation in accordance with Prophetic *sunna*) and *ṭalāq al-bidʿa* (innovation, irregular *ṭalāq*). In the Kuwaiti code *ṭalāq* should follow oral expressions according to custom or in a case where a person is unable to speak, either in writing or by means of gestures (Article 104). Yemeni law allows both *sunna* and *bidʿa ṭalāq* (Article 62). In a 1998 amendment, women lost the right to compensation in unjustified *ṭalāq*.

Classical schools agree on dissolving marriage by mutual consent (*mubāraʾa*) and on the instigation of the wife (*khulʿ*). Both require the wife to pay compensation to the husband, often the *mahr*, in exchange for divorce. The classical schools see it as reprehensible to ask for more than the *mahr*, but Yemeni law stipulates that the compensation can be either money or service even if it is more than obliged in the contract (Article 72), while in Kuwaiti law the compensation depends on the marriage contract (Article 114). Under Ḥanbalī law, a woman can stipulate in her marriage contract that she has her *ʿiṣma* (bond) in her hand, that is, the freedom to dissolve the marriage. It is reported, however, that Saudi men are reluctant to grant such a clause.

A marriage can also be terminated by annulment (*faskh*) or judicial separation (*tafrīq*). Yemeni law recognizes only *faskh* and grants women a divorce on grounds of the husband's inability to provide maintenance, alcoholism, or prolonged absence (articles 51–3, 55). The classical schools acknowledge also the concept of harm (*ḍarar*) but definitions of injury, physical or mental, vary among jurists. Ḥanafī law is the strictest and allows judicial divorce only on the ground of the husband's impotence. While the Mālikī school is most favorable to woman, Jaʿfarī law is only mildly better than the Ḥanafī and adds insanity, leprosy, and venereal disease to the grounds for divorce. The Kuwaiti law acknowledges *ḍarar* as harm that either spouse has caused the other that makes it impossible for them to live together (Article 126).

According to the Jaʿfarīs, in the event of divorce, the mother loses her children once boys reach age seven and girls age nine. The Ḥanbalīs set the age at seven for both. For Ḥanafīs the mother's custody ends when a boy is able to feed, clothe, and cleanse himself and when a girl attains puberty. Shāfiʿīs require that both sexes reach the age of discretion and are able to make decisions. Mālikīs are the most lenient for mothers and allow a boy stay with his mother until puberty and a girl until she marries. The Yemeni law sets ages nine and twelve unless the judge decides differently (Article 139). However, in cases of charges of immorality, the mother loses her children once they are five (Article 144).

According to the classical schools, the widow is entitled to inherit from her deceased husband after paying funeral expenses, maintenance costs during her *ʿidda*, and debts. All schools agree on the inheritance share allotted to the widow (one fourth), but Sunnīs and Shīʿīs differ on the meaning of a child which reduces that share to one eighth. For Sunnīs, a child must be related to the deceased without a female link while Jaʿfarīs maintain that every child is a descendant. The Yemeni law applies the Sunnī interpretation (Article 307).

Even though it is generally asserted that in the absence of codified law women gaining justice in court depends on the judge, in countries with a code, such as Yemen, the role of the judge is also crucial. Out of the countries discussed here, the PDRY is the only state that has allowed women to act as judges (see Figure 1).

BIBLIOGRAPHY

D. El Alami and D. Hinchcliffe, *Islamic marriage and divorce laws of the Arab world*, London 1996.
S. H. Amin, *Law and justice in contemporary Yemen. People's Democratic Republic and Yemen Arab Republic*, Glasgow 1987.
J. N. D. Anderson, *Islamic law in Africa*, London 1954.
S. Dahlgren, *Contesting realities. Morality, propriety and the public sphere in Aden, Yemen*, Helsinki 2004.
E. A. Doumato, The ambiguity of Shari'a and the politics of "rights" in Saudi Arabia, in M. Afkhami (ed.), *Faith and freedom. Women's human rights in the Muslim world*, Syracuse, N.Y. 1995, 135–60.
M. Fakhro, Gulf women and Islamic law, in M. Yamani (ed.), *Feminism and Islam. Legal and literary perspectives*, Reading, Berkshire, U.K. 1996, 251–62.
E. Hill, Islamic law as a source for the development of a comparative jurisprudence. Theory and practice in the life and work of Sanhūrī, in A. al-Azmeh (ed.), *Islamic law. Social and historical contexts*, London 1989, 146–97.
M. Molyneux, Women's rights and and political contingency. The case of Yemen 1990–1994, in *Middle East Journal* 49 (1995), 418–31.
J. Nasir, *The Islamic law of personal status*, London 1990.
J. Schacht, *An introduction to Islamic law*, Oxford 1964.
L. Welchman, *Islamic family law. Text and practice in Palestine*, Jerusalem 1999.
A. Würth, A Sana'a court. The family and the ability to negotiate, in *Islamic Law and Society* 2:3 (1995), 320–40.

SUSANNE DAHLGREN

Iran

In the domain of modern family law, the changes that have occurred in Iran do not suggest a progressive expansion of women's rights based on a move from tradition to modernity. Rather the changes have fluctuated, at times in opposing directions, depending on the policies and ideological orientations of the men in control of the government.

Although the roots of the modern legislative process in Iran can be traced to the aftermath of the Constitutional Revolution of 1905–11, modern legislation in the area of family law did not materialize until 1967. Before this date, in keeping with the long-standing practices of the Jaʿfarī school of jurisprudence, the position of women within the sphere of family remained precarious. A new Civil Code in 1931 gave women the right to ask for divorce under certain conditions, and the marriage age was raised to 15 years for girls and 18 years for boys. But the Civil Code was secular and family laws remained within the domain of Islamic jurisprudence. For instance, a husband could divorce his wife at will by simply submitting a short letter of intent to be notarized for record. The wife was not required to be present and the husband unilaterally decided on the nature and extent of his financial obligations, if any, after divorce.

Major changes were introduced in the area of family law with the passage of the Family Protection Law of 1967 (significantly amended in 1975). This law did not redress the unequal status of women under Islamic inheritance laws, which continue to be in effect until today. However, it did abolish extra-judicial divorce, and required judicial permission for polygyny and only under limited circumstances after the first wife's consent was given. It also established Special Family Courts for the application of the new personal status legislation. Minimum age of marriage for girls was raised to 18 years old. The establishment of the family courts, in particular, was significant in so far as they created an arena in which judges, lawyers, and interested organizations could see and dwell on the family problems that existed in the society and propose important amendments to the law that came into effect in 1975.

The progressive direction of change in favor of women's rights within the family came to a halt with the 1979 Revolution that ended the Pahlavī dynasty (1925–79) and brought into power a new Islamic leadership. The Supreme Judicial Council issued proclamations directing courts that all un-Islamic legislation was to be suspended. The Special Family Courts established by the Family Protection Act were dissolved. The Special Civil Courts were established in 1979 to adjudicate over matters relating to family law. Once again, the absolute right to divorce for men was instituted, men could register their divorce unilaterally, and marital obedience and maintenance were governed by classical conditions, with obedience squarely resting on the wife's shoulders. Furthermore, specific measures taken to bring polygyny under control and give women more power over questions of child custody, allowing the Special Family Courts to mediate and check the husband's absolute right to the children, were all abolished. The minimum age of marriage was initially set with puberty at 9 years old. In 2002, this minimum age was raised to 13. The marriage of a virgin girl (even after puberty) became dependent on the permission of the father or paternal grandfather, with the proviso that a Special Civil Court may grant permission if the guardian refuses without valid reason. Temporary marriage continued to be permitted.

Despite the complete reversal of the previous gains immediately after the revolution, the status of women within the confines of family law has not remained static. Responding to pressures by women and attempting to resolve major problems that have surfaced with the reinstitution of patently non-egalitarian laws in an increasingly urban and educated society, the Islamic Republic of Iran has been pushed gradually to modify some of the laws that were put into effect immediately after the revolution. However, so far these modifications have occurred within frameworks that continue to insist on the essential inequality of men and women in the sphere of family law.

For instance, a 12-article law on marriage and divorce passed in 1986, while allowing the wife the right to obtain a divorce if the husband marries without her permission or does not treat co-wives equitably in the court's assessment, essentially maintains the husband's absolute right to divorce. A wife may take the matter to court if her husband refuses to pay maintenance and the court will fix a sum and issue a maintenance order. The law also stipulates that arrears of maintenance to the wife have precedence over all other liabilities against the husband. Furthermore, the wife's refusal to have conjugal relations where the husband has contracted venereal disease is no longer deemed as constituting disobedience.

Additional 1992 amendments provide that registration of divorce without a court certificate is illegal. Several other grounds are provided for judicial divorce, including the proven insanity of either spouse, the husband's inability to consummate marriage, the husband's failure to comply with a maintenance order, and where continuation of marriage constitutes proven difficulty or hardship for the wife. Another 1992 amendment law extends the wife's grounds for divorce to the husband's drug addiction constituting a danger to his family, the husband's desertion of the marital home for six months without legitimate cause, and the husband's conviction for a crime bringing dishonor to the family. Yet another reform, also introduced in 1992, extends the divorced wife's financial rights from maintenance during *ʿidda* and her deferred agreed upon sum in case of divorce to the right to sue for payment for household services rendered to her husband during the marriage, although the measure has proved difficult to apply in practice, partly because of the difficulty in assessing wages for housework.

In the area of child custody, the mother's custody now ends at seven years and custody reverts to the father if the mother remarries. The mother may be granted custody in certain cases if the father is proven unfit to care for the child. The increased number of grounds for which women can sue for divorce, seek financial remuneration, and ask for limited custody of their children has in effect led to the return of the family courts, even if the laws remain unequal.

In general, the framework within which changes in family law in favor of women have been approved remains unequal and heavily slanted toward men. In 1997, a prenuptial document to be signed at the time of marriage was approved to bring about more equality. The object was to give women the rights they lacked within the context of Islamic laws. Through this document the future husband can forfeit his rights to polygyny and unconditional divorce. Women can initiate divorce, divide assets, and have joint custody of children and child support. However, all the articles have conditions attached to them. As pointed out by the critics, this is only a voluntary contract, men do not have to sign it and if they do not there are no legal consequences.

Bibliography

H. Afshar, *Islam and feminisms. An Iranian case study*, New York 1998.

S. Haeri, Divorce in contemporary Iran. A male prerogative in self-will, in C. Mallat and J. Connors (eds.), *Islamic family law*, London 1990, 55–67.

M. Kār, *Rafʿ-i tabʿīz az zanān. Muqāyisah-ʾi Kunvānsiyūn Rafʿ-i tabʿīz az zanān bā qavānīn-i dākhilī-i Īrān*, Tehran 1999.

——, *Sākhtār-i ḥuqūqī-i niẓām-i khāvādah dar Īrān*, Tehran 1999.

——, *Pizhūhishī darbārah-ʾi khushūnat ʿalayh-i zanān dar Īrān*, Tehran 2000.

Z. Mir-Hosseini, Women, marriage and the law in post-revolutionary Iran, in H. Afshar (ed.), *Women in the Middle East*, London 1993, 59–84.

S. Pakzad, The legal status of women in the family in Iran, in M. Afkhami and E. Friedl (eds.), *In the eye of the storm. Women in post-revolutionary Iran*, Syracuse, N.Y. 1994, 169–79.

P. Paidar, *Women and the political process in twentieth-century Iran*, Cambridge 1995.

Mehrangiz Kar

South Asia

India (including pre-1947 Pakistan and Bangladesh)

The modern legislative bases for Muslim law in India (and pre-1947 Pakistan and Bangladesh) are the Shariat Act of 1937, which established the inheritance rights of Muslim women, and the Dissolution of Muslim Marriages Act of 1939 (Hidayatullah and Shankardass 1968, 3), which dealt with divorce. These acts modified the Ḥanafī laws, which applied to Muslims in the Indian subcontinent by incorporating the laws of other Muslim jurists to enable Muslim women to have the best available options in divorce and inheritance.

British colonial power in nineteenth-century India limited the political and economic options available to Hindu and Muslim communities. Changes were only possible through communities and social constituencies (including women) working cohesively through political and social organizations. As a result the nineteenth century witnessed the passage of a number of secular laws regarding women's rights, including the Sati Abolition Act of 1829, the Widow Remarriage Act of 1856, the Female Infanticide Act of 1870, and the Child Marriage and Enforced Widowhood Act of 1891.

Family laws pertaining to Hindus and Muslims (including those relating to marriage, divorce, and inheritance), however, were treated as religiously derived and left uncodified partly to stem claims of interference in the rites and rituals of personal law. Due to the administration of all laws through the English court system many existing regional customs and traditions came to be accepted by English courts as Islamic. This Anglicization of Muslim law coincided with the abolition of the advisory post of kazi (*qāḍī*, Muslim judicial adviser) in 1864 (Pearl and Menski 1998, 333–4), depriving many Muslim women of rights to divorce, remarriage, *mahr*, and inheritance. It was not till the heightened political activities of the nationalist movement and the women's movement and the formation of the Jamiat-ul-Ulema-e-Hind in 1919 (Ali 2000, 147) that attention began to focus on Muslim women's rights and the perception that codifying personal laws to restore women's Sharīʿa rights and would unify the community.

Despite common nationalist goals and cross-over membership, the differences between the Hindu and Muslim communities and their political and social goals became increasingly apparent following the formation of organized political parties (the Congress Party in 1885 and the Muslim League in 1906) even when women of both communities were jointly forging a powerful women's movement in the 1920s. The period immediately preceding the passage of the Age of Consent Act of 1929 (which increased the age of marriage of both girls and boys) highlighted the differences between the goals of men and the unity of women of both communities. The extensive evidence gathered by the Age of Consent Committee across the country to promote passage of the legislation brought forth political arguments establishing their differences though both supported the legislation. The passage of the legislation focused attention on the confluence between women's rights and the political agenda of each community, with women's rights representing the area deemed immutable by both sides.

The debates preceding the adoption of the Age of Consent Act presaged those attending the passage of the Shariat Act of 1937 and the Dissolution of Muslim Marriages Act (DMMA) of 1939, both passed in the heightened political and social awareness raised by the activities of the Indian National Congress, the Muslim League, the Indian women's movement (Lateef 1990, 55–73), and Muslim Ullema groups (Narain 2001, 20, Ali 2000, 151–6). Muslim and Hindu women leaders of the All India Women's Conference and the Women's Indian Association supported the legislation. The effect of both acts was to unite the community under one law and provide Muslim women with rights to property, succession, divorce, *mahr*, and remarriage denied them under customary law. From

7 October 1937, the Sharīʿa laws became applicable to all Muslims "notwithstanding any custom or usage to the contrary, in all questions (save questions relating to agricultural land) regarding intestate succession, special property of females, including personal property inherited or obtained under contract gift or any other provision of Personal Law, marriage, dissolution of marriage, including *talaq, ila, zihar, lian, khula* and *Mubaraʾat*, maintenance, dower, guardianship, gifts, trusts and *wakfs*" (Hidayatullah and Shankardass 1968, 3).

In India, custody of children was governed by the Guardians and Wards Act 1890, which distinguished between custody and guardianship: while the custody of children under Ḥanafī rules would allow the mother custody of sons for seven years and daughters for nine years, the guardianship remained with the father. The religious status of the children was considered primary in awarding custody should the mother's religion change due to remarriage (Pearl and Menski 1998, 413–16). In practice secular courts ensure that the best interests of the child are usually considered of primary importance.

In 1986 the Muslim Women (Protection of Rights on Divorce) Act was passed by the Indian Legislature in response to a supreme court judgment with reference to the Mohammad Ahmad v. Shah Bano Begum case for maintenance. The case was filed under section 125 of the 1973 Criminal Procedure Code, which would enable an indigent woman to receive maintenance from her former husband. The supreme court ruled that secular law superseded personal law, a decision in keeping with earlier high court rulings dealing with the same issue. The court ruled that non-payment of maintenance after the prescribed period stipulated by Muslim personal law would be against the intention of the Qurʾān and the *mahr* payment to the wife at marriage could not be regarded as maintenance at divorce and ordered the husband to pay Shah Bano both maintenance and the *mahr* owed her. The chief justice urged the government to pass the Uniform Civil Code specified under article 44 of the Indian constitution (Pearl and Menski 2000, 210–11), which would bring all Indians under secular law.

The Shah Bano case raised fears of assimilation in the conservative and well organized groups of the Muslim community who immediately denounced the judgment and demanded it be repealed. The agitation that ensued led to a hasty effort on the part of the government to undo it through legislation. The resultant Muslim Women's Bill deprived Muslim women of the right to appeal for maintenance using section 125 of the 1973 Criminal Procedure Code but created other provisions for their benefit, which, due to judicial interpretations, have proven more generous to women. Part 2 of the act mandates that a Muslim woman be accorded fair provision and maintenance at the time of her divorce (Pearl and Menski 1998, 212–14). The wife's relatives or the State Waqf Boards, cited in the act as options should the husband fail to provide maintenance, have not been considered as viable or as important as enforcing maintenance and fair provision from the husband. The new law was also immediately challenged as unconstitutional (a hearing is still pending in the supreme court).

PAKISTAN

The Shariat Act of 1937 and the Dissolution of Muslim Marriages Act of 1939 (which had been inherited from India) were modified by the passage of the Muslim Family Law Ordinance of 1961, which was supported by the All Pakistan Women's Association (APWA), an organization that Begum Liaqat Ali Khan established after independence in 1947. The Muslim Personal Law of Shariat of 1948 was the first legislation elaborating on the initiative of the 1937 statute to recognize the right of Muslim women to inherit property from their father's and husband's families (Esposito and DeLong 2001, 85). Pakistani feudal customs including unilateral divorce and unrestricted polygamy accelerated the need for changes in family laws that were designed to go beyond the Shariat Acts of 1937 and 1939. APWA set up five committees to deal with the outstanding issues confronting women: Women and Family Law, Responsibility of Family and Community, Education, Political Rights, and Women in Economic Rights and Facilities. These committees were to lobby government on behalf of women. In the struggle that followed over six years, these groups worked within the framework of established Islamic traditions in order not to raise the ire of the *ʿulamāʾ* establishment of Pakistan who were always ready to challenge women's rights.

The Marriage Commission's Report 1956, a precursor to the ordinance, revealed the differences between Muslim modernists and traditionalists over interpretation of Muslim personal law and the extent to which *ijtihād* or individual reasoning could be exercised by judges rather than religiously trained scholars. The modernists tried to use *ijtihād* as a way of enabling change in the status of women (Haidar 2000, 294, 299), which the traditionalists rejected, seeing it as an encroachment of Western ideas on Islam. The commission used the conservative poet politician Iqbal's criticism of the rigidity that had crept into Islamic legal structures after *ijtihād* had been eliminated in the fourth century to argue in support of *ijtihād*. The commission exercised self-censorship, anticipating a conservative backlash. It conceded that it could not interfere with the Sharīʿa but with real life issues that should not be the monopoly of theologians.

The sole theologian on the commission, Mawlana Haq, objected to its attempts to broaden the scope of *ijtihād* and questioned the validity of equating Islamic scholars with laymen because there is no priesthood to define Islamic concepts. While the Muslim Family Ordinance went some way to redressing the shortcomings of the 1937 and 1939 acts, it tried to avoid taking on the traditionalists by relying on judges to interpret laws liberally. Women were now able to use "incompatibility" that included sexual dissatisfaction and aversion to husband as a basis for divorce if they gave up the right to financial compensation. However, some courts ignored the financial renunciation leaving the husband to sue for it in another court (Haidar 2000, 328, 332–3, 335). On issues of custody Pakistani law follows traditional law and reiterates the mother's subordinate custody to that of the father in accordance with the Guardians and Wards Act (Pearl and Menski 1998, 412). In many recent cases, however, as in Shahzad Muhammad Sidiq v. Shahnaz Farzana (1997) judgment was based on the best interests of the child (Pearl and Menski 1998, 418).

Under General Zia ul-Haq (who seized power in 1977) there was a definite move to bring Pakistan closer to being an Islamic state. A Federal Shariat Court was created to verify the Qur'ānic authenticity of personal law legislation. The Hudood Ordinances outlawed extramarital relations and alcohol, and promoted interest free banking; it also ruled as anti-Islamic the activities of Qadian, Lahori, and Ahmadi groups. The Qanun-e-Shahadat (Law of evidence) 1983–4 differentiated the legal testimony of women to their detriment from that of men and made no distinction between adultery and rape, leaving women to bear the punishment for both (Esposito and DeLong 2001, 90). The Pakistan Dowry and Gifts (Restriction) Act 1976 states that the gifts brought to the marriage by the wife are and remain her property, noting that in Muslim law husband and wife retain their independent legal status, though this is often obstructed by patriarchal social structures.

BANGLADESH

Though Bangladesh inherited Pakistani laws, changes were made, such as the Muslim Marriages and Divorce (Registration) Act 1974 that made registration of all marriages compulsory (though not mandatory). Maintenance rights for divorced women have been liberally interpreted by the Bangladeshi courts with judges re-examining the relevant Qur'ānic passages. Judge Mohammad Gholam Rabbani J. ruled that "every Muslim can and should read and interpret the Qur'ān and it must be in the light of the existing circumstances in changing needs of the world." He further stated: "it is an article of faith of a Muslim that he should follow without questioning what has been revealed in the Qur'ān and disobedience thereof is a sin." On maintenance he ruled that, "a person after divorcing his wife is bound to maintain her on a reasonable scale beyond the period of *iddat* for an indefinite period, that is to say till she loses the status of divorcee by remarrying another person" (Pearl and Menski 1998, 225).

In the case of Mosammat Nur Akhtar v. Abdul Mabud Chowdhury (1996) in which the husband had alleged that his wife had left him voluntarily so no maintenance was due, the wife produced documentation that he had sought permission from the local Union Council to marry another woman. While granting the divorced wife maintenance Judge Rabbani ruled that section 6 of the Muslim Family Law Ordinance of 1961, regarded as permission for polygamy, was against Islamic law and should be deleted from the Ordinance (Pearl and Menski 1998, 226). On the question of custody, Bangladeshi courts have been more conservative and ruled that the mother has custody of her minor daughter till she attains puberty (unless she first marries a person not related within the prohibited degree) as in the case of Akter Jahan Tanzia alias Bab v. state (1986) B.L.D. 281 (Pearl and Menski 1998, 423).

BIBLIOGRAPHY

A. A. Ali, *The emergence of feminism among Indian Muslim women 1920–1947*, Karachi 2000.

J. L. Esposito and N. J. DeLong, *Women in Muslim family law*, Syracuse, N.Y. 2001.

N. Haidar, Islamic legal reform. The case of Pakistan and family law, in *Yale Journal of Law and Feminism* 12 (2000), 328, 332–3, 335.

M. Hidayatullah and R. K. P. Shankardass, *Mulla principles of Mahomedan law*, Bombay 1968.

S. Lateef, *Muslim women in India. Political and private realities 1890–1980s*, New Delhi 1990.

V. Narain, *Gender and community. Muslim women's rights in India*, Toronto 2001.

D. Pearl and W. Menski, *Muslim family law*, London 1998[3].

SHAHIDA LATEEF

Turkey

The Civil Code of the Turkish Republic was passed in 1926, and comprised family law as one of its sub-fields. The new law entailed substantive improvements in the status of women (Starr 1974). Polygamy and repudiation were outlawed while women gained equal rights with men in terms of conditions and initiation of divorce. Custody rights in case of divorce were rearranged so as to bring equal rights to women. Prevailing inequalities in inheritance between male and female children were abrogated. Civil union was recognized as the only legally valid form of marriage, thereby reducing the importance of religious marriage.

The new family law was not recognized as a code in its own right but comprised only a segment of the Civil Code. Nevertheless it was a key element of republican reforms as it rearranged relations between genders and between generations and changed the ways in which household and family were created and dissolved. This was a central part of the republican desire to replace existing Islamic imperial practices and institutions with secular, civic, and so-called "modern" ones. In line with the envisaged civilizational shift of the Turkish Republic from an Islamic culture, perceived as backward, to one based on Western ideals with a progressive ethos, the law made no reference to Islamic law in terms of source or content. The new Turkish Civil Code was mainly a translation and adaptation of the Swiss Civil Code of the time.

Yet, the law cast the husband as head of the household who was to have the ultimate say in matters such as custody of children or domicile. The wife was cast as "assistant and counselor of the husband." In order to work outside the home, married women needed permission from their husbands.

All in all women's rights in terms of family law were meant to sustain the nuclear family by casting women in the roles of enlightened, secular wives and mothers. Women's presence, both public and private, was meant to be primarily for the betterment of the nation and the new republican nuclear family – often conceived in interchangeable forms (Sirman 2000).

In the next seven decades the code remained relatively intact until the 1990s, although efforts to change it had already begun in the 1950s. The 1990s saw the impact of the feminist movement as it publicly problematized the Civil Code in terms of women's rights. Feminists also mobilized the effects of global women's movement such as the Convention on Elimination of All Forms of Discrimination against Women (CEDAW), which Turkey had ratified in 1985. The clause that required the husband's permission for a married woman to be able to work outside the home was annulled in 1994. The Law on the Protection of Family, passed in 1998, enabled women to seek restraining orders in case of physical abuse. In 2001 the constitution was amended to state that: "the family is ... based on the equality of spouses." The new Civil Code, a result of feminist efforts, stipulates equality of spouses within marriage in terms of domicile and custody. The husband is no longer recognized as head of the household; both spouses represent the family. The law sets the age of 18 as the legal minimum age for marriage for both men and women, whereas previously it was 17 for men and 15 for women. Children born out of wedlock have the same rights as the children of married parents and their mothers have primary claim over their custody. The law also allows single parents to adopt children. Moreover, instead of the previous default regime of separate property, it establishes a new matrimonial property regime. In the case of divorce – unless another property regime is selected by the couple – property obtained during the course of marriage is to be divided equally, regardless of whose name it is registered under. Here the law recognizes women's domestic labor in the making of family property. A parliamentary bill, however, limits the application of this law to property acquired only after January 2003, implying the *de facto* exclusion of about 15 million married women from the law's provision. Political and legal contentions around this article continue.

Another important development in terms of family law in Turkey was the establishment of family courts in 2003. The new courts are to apply related sections of the Civil Code together with the Law on the Protection of the Family and are to engage in a deeper examination of the family situation of litigants. The new specialized family courts can potentially facilitate the juridical recognition of disadvantages women face in family life.

Next to the nature of the legal texts, access to law remains another key aspect of gender inequality in family law. There is a significant gender gap in the effect of legal institutions and knowledge on daily life practices. This leaves women vulnerable to customary practices that are themselves reproduced in relation to the weak injunctive power of the law.

Bibliography

I. Ilkkaracan and P. Ilkkaracan, Kuldan yurttaş'a. Kadınlar neresinde?, in A. Unsal (ed.), *75 yilda tebaa'dan yurttaş'a doğru*, Istanbul 1998, 77–90.

D. Kandiyoti, Emancipated but unliberated? Reflections on the Turkish case, in *Feminist Studies* 13:2 (1987), 317–38.
N. Sirman, Writing the usual love story. Fashioning of conjugal and national subjects in Turkey, in V. A. Goddard (ed.) *Gender, agency and change. Anthropological perspectives*, London 2000, 250–73.
J. Starr and J. Pool, The impact of a legal revolution in rural Turkey, in *Law and Society Review* 8:4 (1974), 533–60.

DICLE KOGACIOGLU

The United States

Muslim women in the United States constantly struggle to reconcile the legal requirements and the value system of their faith with the United States system of justice and its system of values. Recent immigrants seeking a divorce, or the enforcement of nuptial agreements obtained in countries where Islamic law is recognized add questions of international law to this struggle as well. Muslim family law is an amalgam of Islamic law and the Mediterranean family structure, which anthropologists characterize as endogamous (practicing marriage largely within one's own group); patrilineal (tracing descent through the male members of the family); patriarchal (empowering the father with the formal and final authority); extended (including three or more generations within the same household); and polygynous (marrying more than one wife). These characteristics, previously restricted mainly to Muslim lands, are today common among Muslims living in Europe and the United States. As for the Islamic elements of the law, these stem largely from the Qurʾān, the practice of the Prophet (*sunna*), the unanimous opinion (*ijmāʿ*) of the learned elders (*ʿulamāʾ*), and the juridical opinions of regional schools of law (*madhāhib*). Family law issues in the United States are based on this classical framework, whereas those stemming from judgments obtained in the Muslim world may also include secular laws unique to individual Muslim countries.

For Muslim women, therefore, painless solutions to marital woes are understandably difficult to procure given the need to comply with the dictates of faith, law in forum, and the protocols of transnational law. Prenuptial agreements, for instance, display strong biases that are clearly Islamic, whereas issues of divorce display equally strong United States juridical biases. Those with marriages solemnized in accordance with Islamic law, in the United States or abroad, may turn to the United States courts to enforce settlements obtained in accordance with Islamic sacred law, or to rescind such settlements. At times the intent is clearly malicious, as in the case of spouses of dual citizenship, who attempt to deprive their partners of a share in the marital estate by obtaining favorable dissolutions only available in a Muslim country, and then enforcing the same through the United States courts. Contrariwise, they may challenge such enforcement efforts by invoking the undue entanglement clause of the First Amendment or public policy arguments. United States courts may also be asked to adjudicate extra-judicial dissolutions, such as a *ṭalāq*, which men generally obtain through the local mosque within the United States, or by mail, through a foreign court that recognizes out-of-court divorces, and which they then present to the United States courts for ratification.

While all such issues hinge to a lesser or greater extent on questions of jurisdiction, domicile, or the undue entanglement clause of the First Amendment, in the case of overseas judgments there is additionally the issue of comity. Whilst not a law as such, the principle of comity is nonetheless a doctrine of reciprocity to which United States courts defer because it ensures the recognition of United States judgments elsewhere. Comity gives due recognition to cases originating in foreign judgments but only if such cases comply with two conditions: first, that the foreign court in question has the required jurisdiction, and second, that its adjudication, in both substance and procedure, does not offend United States public policy. On the question of jurisdiction, the State of New York has refused to recognize unilateral divorce (*ṭalāq*) within the United States because all divorces so obtained, the court ruled, must comply with the laws of the state (Shikoh v. Murff). And on public policy, the courts have ruled that comity will not extend to custody arrangements procured overseas under the influence of Islamic law because the law discriminates against women. That in Islamic law, for example, a child, even while in the physical custody of the mother, remains nonetheless under the guardianship of the father was considered offensive to public policy (Amin v. Bakhaty 2001 WL 1223612 [La.] [2001]). But United States courts also seem to suggest that, whilst structurally indistinguishable from long-established Arab social practice, Muslim family law nonetheless is flexible enough to comply with the public policy of the United States.

Marriages performed by the clergy are recognized by the United States courts, but the same is not true of dissolutions procured outside the jurisdiction of a formal judicial system. The primary instrument for dissolving Muslim marriages, however, is *ṭalāq*, which empowers the male alone to dissolve a marriage unilaterally and extra-judicially. In contrast, the wife has only two options: to dissolve the marriage by way of a delegated *ṭalāq* (*ṭalāq al-tafwīḍ*), which is usually embedded in a prenuptial agreement, or by way of *khulʿ*. In many Muslim countries today, the couple need simply check a box to empower the wife also to unilaterally institute a delegated divorce. Women outside the Islamic world, however, have no legal means to implement such prenuptial clauses and sometimes find themselves in what scholars term a limping marriage. In this case they do obtain civil divorces from a secular court but remain married to husbands who often, out of malice, withhold the *ṭalāq* pronouncements, and deny their otherwise divorced wives the right to remarry according to Islamic rites. This is particularly true of women in countries such as the United States where extra-judicial repudiations are void and where no authority exists to coerce the husband to institute an Islamic *ṭalāq*. Furthermore, *ṭalāq*s obtained overseas have not fared well in United States courts: in a recent ruling the courts deemed such repudiations unenforceable because of irreconcilable differences, both substantive and procedural, between *ṭalāq* and a civil divorce (Seth v. Seth, 694 S.W. 2d 459, 463 [Tex. Ct. App. 1985]). The courts have also refused to enforce financial settlements ensuing from repudiations procured within the United States but through an arbitration process based on Islamic law; this, the court ruled, would be in violation of the First Amendment prohibition against undue entanglement. The wife in classical Islamic law, and under modern legislation in some Muslim countries, has the right to dissolve the marriage through *khulʿ*. In this case she petitions her husband directly, or through the state, or, where no such authority exists, through the local religious authorities, to dissolve the marriage in return for a financial payment, usually equal to her *mahr* payment. Once again, the undue entanglement clause as interpreted currently denies her this relief within the United States. The conversion of spouses to Islam has also created its own set of challenges to Islamic law. According to classical Islamic law Muslim women may not marry, or remain married to, partners who belong to other faiths, which of course means that on conversion the wife's marital relationship is put in jeopardy. Some jurists have now ruled in favor of upholding the marriages of such female converts; but even this small minority has yet to rule in favor of recognizing the civil contracts of Muslim females who marry outside Islam.

In mitigation of the husband's unfettered right to divorce, and the potential cause of financial harm to his wife, Islamic law allows the inclusion of a *mahr* clause in a prenuptial contract. Such clauses routinely split the *mahr* into a cash portion, due immediately, and a deferred portion due on demand, or on dissolution of the marriage. Additional rules govern marriages not consummated and *mahr* not specified: in the first case the *mahr* amount is halved, and in the second, a suitable gift is substituted instead. The United States courts have refused to enforce deferred *mahr*, however, on the basis that a prenuptial clause allowing a spouse to profit from a divorce is contrary to public policy, and thus unenforceable (in re Marriage of Dajani, No. G004356, Court of Appeal of California, Fourth Appellate District, Division Three, 204 Cal. App. 3d 1387; 251 Cal. Rptr. 871; [Cal. Ct. App. 1988]). But they have also considered *mahr* agreements enforceable on the basis that they are property waivers that supersede the laws of alimony or the laws governing the equitable distribution of the marital estate. And the California Courts of Appeal have enforced *mahr* agreements based on the neutral principles of contract law (in re Marriage of Noghrey [1985] 169 Cal.App.3d 326 [215 Cal. Rptr. 153]).

Bibliography

J. L. Esposito, *Women in Muslim family law*, Syracuse, N.Y. 1982.

D. Forte, Islamic law in American courts, in *Suffolk Transnational Law Journal* 7 (1983), 1–33.

A. al-Hibri, Islam, law and custom. Redefining Muslim women's rights, in *American University Journal of International Law and Policy* 12:1 (1997), 15–18.

A. al-Najjār (ed.), *al-Majalla al-ʿilmiyya lī-al-majlis al-Ūrubbī lī-al-iftāʾ wa-al-buḥūth*, Ireland 2003.

J. Nasir, *The status of women under Islamic law and under modern Islamic legislation*, London 1990.

G. Qaisi, Religious marriage contracts. Judicial enforcement of *mahr* agreements in American courts, in *Journal of Law and Religion* 15 (2000–1), 67, 72.

B. Stowasser, Women and citizenship in the Qurʾan, in A. E. Sonbol (ed.), *Women, the family, and divorce laws in Islamic history*, Syracuse, N.Y. 1996, 23–38.

B. Venkatraman, Comment, Islamic states and the United Nations Convention on the Elimination of All Forms of Discrimination against Women. Are the Shariʿa and the Convention compatible?, in *American University Law Review* 44 (1995), 1949, 1970, 1984–5.

Muneer Fareed

Law: Women as Witnesses

Overview

Throughout Islamic history as well as during the contemporary period, Muslim jurists, reformers, and latterly feminists have discussed the concept of women as witnesses in Islamic law, yet the topic has not achieved a prominent status within Islamic legal discourse.

Providing legal evidence is imperative in upholding the Sharīʿa, or divine law in Islam. The three methods through which legal evidence can be provided in the Sharīʿa are confession (*iqrār*), testimony (*shahāda*), and oath (*yamīn*). Testimony is defined as a statement in court concerning the rights of others, which is based on observation, and introduced by the word "*ashhadu*" (I testify) (Peters 1997). The prerequisite for testifying is that the person be *ʿadl*, that is, be of honest, just, and upright character. The person should have reached puberty; be sound in body and mind; must never have been punished or been guilty of a serious offence; and must not have engaged in immoral behavior. One cannot testify for one's immediate family. Testifying is considered a collective obligation, *farḍ ʿalā al-kifāya*, but becomes an individual obligation in cases where it is necessary for a specific person to testify in order to protect the rights of another. This obligation is adhered to in all matters of testifying within the Sharīʿa except when dealing with Islamic criminal law (the *ḥadd* offences), because of the severity of both the crime and the penalty. The act of testifying is an extremely noble act as well as a grave responsibility.

Throughout much of Islamic history the perception and practice has been that witnesses were required to be male for most legal cases. For instance, in the area of the *ḥadd* concerning adultery (*zinā*), the four schools of jurisprudence, namely Ḥanafī, Mālikī, Shāfiʿī and Ḥanbalī, accept only four male witnesses. For *ḥadd* offences other than adultery, such as the law of retaliation for murder (*qiṣāṣ*), theft (*sariqa*), highway robbery or brigandage (*ḥirāba*), and involvement with intoxicants (*khamr*), the four juristic schools require two male witnesses. The Qurʾānic verses utilized to support their claim are 65:2, which describes the number of witnesses required during a divorce, and 5:106, which deals with the writing of a will. In other issues – for example, marriage (*nikāḥ*); divorce (*ṭalāq*); remarriage with one's divorced wife (*rajʿa*); annulment of a marriage after the husband's sworn testimony to have refrained from marital intercourse for a period of at least four months (*īlāʿ*); repudiation (*ẓihār*); relationship by marriage (*nasab*); submission to the will of God (*islām*); apostasy from Islam (*ridda*); declaring witnesses unreliable (*jarḥ*); declaring reliable witnesses (*taʿdīl*); death and poverty (*mawt wa-iʿsār*); appointment of a representative, agent, deputy, proxy or delegation of authority (*wakāla*); guardianship (*wilāya*); and witnessing over another witness (*shahāda ʿalā shahāda*) – the four schools, with the exception of the Ḥanafī, require three male witnesses. The Ḥanafī school accepts two male or one male and two female witnesses for these cases based on Qurʾān 2:282:

> O ye who believe! When ye deal with each other, in transactions involving future obligations in a fixed period of time, reduce them to writing; let a scribe write down faithfully as between the parties; let not the scribe refuse to write: as Allah has taught him, so let him write. The liability dictate, but let him fear His Lord Allah and not diminish aught of what he owes. If the party liable is mentally deficient, or weak, or unable himself to dictate, let his guardian dictate faithfully. And get two witnesses, out of your own men, and if there are not two men, then a man and two women, such as ye choose, for witnesses, so that if one of them errs, the other can remind her. The witnesses should not refuse when they are called on (for evidence) disdain not to reduce to writing (your contract) for a future period. Whether it be small or big: it is juster in the sight of Allah, more suitable as evidence, and more convenient to prevent doubts among yourselves but if it be a transaction which ye carry out on the spot among yourselves there is not blame on you if ye reduce it not to writing. But take witnesses whenever ye make a commercial contract; and let neither scribe nor witness suffer harm. If ye do (such harm), it would be wickedness in you. So fear Allah; for it is Allah that teaches you. And Allah is well acquainted with all things.

Regarding financial transactions, the four schools require two male or one male and two female witnesses based on Qurʾān 2:282. Lastly, in many cases dealing with only women – such as childbirth, stillbirths, and breast-feeding – only female witnesses are allowed. However, jurists differ in the number of female witnesses required taking into account the woman's level of knowledge with respect to the subject matter and *qiyās*, or analogical deduction, based on several verses and *ḥadīth*, especially in relation to Qur'ān 2:282. In summary, the majority opinion amongst the four schools is that for transactions, two males, or one male and two females, are required. In the other areas of law, whether personal or penal, three male witnesses are specified. In situations specific to women, female witnesses are accepted, but the number required varies with the different schools. To a large extent, the four schools of jurisprudence make reference to Qur'an 2:282 as the foundation of their reasoning, followed by the application of *qiyās*.

Other jurists provide contrary opinions to those given by the four main schools. For instance, in the area of the *ḥadd* offences, Ibn Qayyim al-Jawziyya (d. 1350) reported that the testimony of eight women would be sufficient to establish that adultery had been committed, and punishment would follow accordingly. ʿAtā' Ibn Abī Rabāḥ (d. 732) and Ṭawūs Ibn Kaysān (d. 725) reported that womens' testimonies along with those of men are acceptable in any *ḥadd* crime, including *zinā*, where the testimonies of two women and three men can establish the case. Al-Ḥasan al-Baṣri (d. 110) also reported that two women and three men can establish the case. Ibn Ḥazm al-Ẓāhirī (d. 1064) believed that the testimonies of two men, four women, or one man and two women are admissible as proof in *ḥadd* crimes, except in the case of *zinā* where a minimum of four male witnesses is required. Although these jurists differ from the general view and maintain that women can be witnesses in *ḥadd* cases, they are still acting in accordance with Qur'ān 2:282. Another renowned jurist, Abū Ja'far Muḥammad ibn Jarīr al-Ṭabarī (d. 923), maintained that in areas other than commercial and financial matters, he was unable to locate any evidence from the original sources which would exclude women from acting as judges who hear and evaluate the testimony of others. In cases concerning finance and commerce, following Qur'ān 2:282, al-Ṭabarī states that the second female witness may be required to "remind" the first since women are rarely involved in these matters. Prominent jurists such as Taqī al-Dīn Ibn Taymiyya (d. 1327) and Ibn Qayyim al-Jawziyya (d. 1350) concur with al-Ṭabarī's opinion and conclude that testimony cannot be determined by gender, but instead must be established by credibility alone. Thus, when a woman offers credible testimony, the judge must admit it just as he would admit the credible testimony of a man. Therefore, it is evident that renowned jurists differed with the generally held notion regarding women as witnesses.

Regardless of the viewpoints that exist indicating that women may be witnesses in *ḥadd* cases, according to human rights advocates, generally this has not been nor is it currently the practice in the Muslim world. In countries such as Pakistan, Egypt, Nigeria, Sudan, Afghanistan, Malaysia, and Iran, the respective penal codes demand two male witnesses or one male and two female witnesses for cases involving commercial or financial transactions, and do not accept women as witnesses in *ḥadd* related cases. According to human rights activists, the effects of implementing Islamic law in this fashion have been detrimental in certain cases involving women who have been sexually assaulted or raped. However, according to the Sharīʿa, in the case of sexual assault, *bayinna* (evidence) is what is required in order to support a case. None of the aforementioned countries actually implement Sharīʿa in the full sense of the term. Rather, their constitutions are based on a mixture of religious and culturally related enactments.

The notion of accepting women as witnesses is an area of disagreement amongst the jurists and the schools of law, although such disagreement is not an issue in Islamic law. Concepts have been examined and verdicts stated, to the best of the jurists' knowledge, within a specific time frame and within a specific environment. Qur'ān 2:282 pertains to business and commercial transactions which are complicated and ambiguous, even for an expert businessman. It is true that a woman who normally is not involved in such difficult transactions may have neither knowledge nor understanding of the matter and is likely to get confused, especially in the court environment, which is dominated by men. This is also true in recent history where judges, lawyers, litigants, and witnesses are generally men. In no matters other than the transactions referred to in 2:282 does the Qur'ān equate the evidence of two women with one man. On the contrary, in the matter of imprecation where the husband charges his wife with adultery, the testimony of the woman is equal to that of her husband. Thus, the status of women as witnesses in all legal cases, including those involving the *ḥudūd* ordinances, may require further examination by contemporary jurists. Furthermore, according to human rights advocates, in criminal cases such as adultery, it is not possible according to various state constitutions to demand witnesses of a specific gender. The situation is similar in cases of rape and sexual assault, although the Sharīʿa requires evidence to prove or disprove sexual assault. The practice of women serving as witnesses, as well as other rights and freedoms of women in the legal sphere of Islam, are complex matters requiring the accurate comprehension of the original texts. Within the guidelines of Islamic law these issues have been and will continue to be examined.

BIBLIOGRAPHY

A. Y. ʿAli (trans. and comm.), *The Holy Qurʾān*, Beltsville, Md. 1989.

T. J. al-ʿAlwānī, The testimony of women in Islamic law, in *American Journal of Islamic Social Sciences* 13 (1996), 173–96.

M. B. Arbouna, *Islamic law of evidence. The function of official documents in evidence. A comparative study with common law*, Kuala Lumpur 1999.

M. Asad, *The message of the Qurān*, Lahore 1992.

M. Ashraf, *Women's rights in Islam*, Lahore 1991.

J. Badawi, *Gender equity in Islam. Basic principles*, Plainfield, Ind. 1995.

Z. A. Badawi et al., Gender assessment Sudan Interim Strategic Plan, 2003–5, <http://www.usaid.gov/locations/sub-saharan_africa/sudan/sudan_isp_a2.pdf >.

A. E. Brodsky, *With all our strength. The Revolutionary Association of the Women of Afghanistan*, New York 2003.

A. R. Doi, *Sharīʿah. The Islamic law*, London 1984.

——, *Women in the Sharīʿah*, London 1989.

M. Fadel, Two women, one man. Knowledge, power, and gender in medieval Sunni legal thought, in *International Journal of Middle East Studies* 29 (1997), 185–204.

A. Ibn al-Naqīb, *Reliance of the traveller*, ed. and trans. N. H. M. Keller, Evanston, Ill. 1994.

R. Ismail (ed.), *Hudud in Malaysia. The issues at stake*, Kuala Lumpur 1995.

N. E. Jonas, *The role of witnesses in the procedural law of Hudud*, Montreal 1988.

M. Lippman, S. McConville, and M. Yerushalmi, *Islamic criminal law and procedure. An introduction*, Westport, Conn. 1988.

al-Mawsūʿat al-fiqhiyya, Kuwait 1990.

R. Peters, Shāhid, in *Encyclopaedia of Islam* 9 (1997), 208–9.

Y. al-Qaradawi, Islam's stance on women's testimony, 2002, <http:// www.islamonline.net/fatwa/english/FatwaDisplay.asp?hFatwaID=46067>.

M. N. al-Rifāʿī, *Tafsīr Ibn Kathīr*, part 3 (abridged), London 1998.

M. A. A. Sidahmad, *The hudud*, Kuala Lumpur 1995.

A. Taheri, A noble women carries torch for democracy in Iran, in *Wall Street Journal*, 13 October 2003.

G. Webb (ed.), *Windows of faith*, Syracuse, N.Y. 2000.

NADIRA MUSTAPHA

Memory, Women, and Community

Afghanistan

With overall literacy presently estimated at no more than 25 percent and rural female literacy in single digits, Afghanistan has had an oral culture. People maintain everyday information, community historical memory, and entertainment "literature" in memory and share it face to face. Afghan women are vigorous custodians and important icons of memory in the construction of social identity and values.

As agents of memory, women participate in divisions of cultural labor whereby different persons (distinguished by age, gender, class, ethnicity, location, education, work) may specialize in different bodies of knowledge, communicated in different contexts. While much of memory is verbal, some (for example, music, crafts techniques) is communicated primarily by nonverbal performance and imitative practice. Not all performances of memory equip the audience in turn to transmit the specific information communicated. In the women's genre of lament for the dead or in the personal experience narratives women tell each other during their reciprocal *gham-shādī* (Dari, sorrow and celebration) or *tapos* (Pashto, inquiry) visits, women learn by participation the sociolinguistic expectations for listeners and tellers in those social events, then use those verbal forms to claim their own social place and perform their own memories movingly for others on similar occasions (Grima 1992, Kieffer 1975).

Performers and listeners prize accurate memory of specific textual content in proverbs, stories, or songs (notwithstanding narratives' transformations in transmission, Mills 1990). Oral tradition communicates key social ideas, even in fictional entertainment such as folk-tales and romances as well as more serious, believed narratives such as saints' legends, or in didactic proverbs. Female and male performance preferences vary: among Dari (Persian) speakers in Herat City in the 1970s long, multi-episodic romances were predominantly a men's genre, while both women and men would tell folk-tales or *afsānah*, including international tales (for example, Afghan variants of "Cinderella" and "Beauty and the Beast," told mostly by women). While women were about equally likely to tell stories with female and male heroes, men mainly told male-centered tales (Mills 1985). Women and men performed for family members at home; some men did so in more public settings (shrines, bazaars, teahouses). Misogynist stereotypes of hypersexual, greedy, or otherwise disorderly women are widespread in tales and in proverbs, but tellers' and listeners' constructions of female nature could be paradoxical or resistant as well as stereotypical, with particular tellers' views only accessible through interactive, context-sensitive analyses of particular performances (Mills 1991, 2000, 2001).

The ubiquitously popular sung quatrain (Dari *chārbaytī*, Tajik Persian *falak*, Sakata 2002) emphasizes themes of love and separation. Women, besides commanding a repertoire of traditional marriage songs (of separation for the bride's family and triumph for the groom's), enjoyed knowing and singing numerous *chārbaytī* together, accompanied by the *dāyereh* frame drum, at women's wedding parties and in informal home visits. A singer may personalize traditional verses bemoaning separation by naming absent or deceased relatives in the verse, as did returned refugee women recorded in Herat in the 1990s. Separation (of the soul from God) is also a key theme in Sufi mysticism, lending possible mystical-religious implications to verses addressed to an absent love. In Pashto, the similarly popular two-line lyric *laṇḍay*, considered women's poetry but also composed and sung by men, addresses themes including love, loss, honor, and historical events. From the 1950s, female and male performers on the radio (and later on cassettes) added to local people's memorized repertoire and gave women, who rarely attended public musical performances, access to professional singers' repertoires. The Taliban's banning of wedding and entertainment music on religious grounds between 1996 and 2001 may not have much affected the cultural survival of these short songs, performed by women and men in private and often already romantically opposed to public proprieties.

Three decades of warfare and displacement did affect women's status as objects of memory as well as their repertoire and performance occasions. The Marxist regime rallied Afghan women to revolution, invoking female icons of Afghan history (poets and martial heroines), stressing the need for activist women to help right injustice and build a socialist nation. Women's vulnerability to propagandist appropriation and violence, described in personal experience narratives and oral histories, became a rallying theme for the Afghan Islamic resistance after the Soviet occupation in 1979. Protection of women's sexual honor as an icon of national sovereignty was interwoven with ideas of Islamic duty (Dupree 1984). Neither ideology idealized women's self-determination, but rather women's actions and treatment as national (and for Islamists, religious) duty. While Marxists invoked more distant Afghan historical figures, such as Malalay, the Pashtun heroine who fought the British in the battle of Maiwand in 1880, a major anti-Soviet female icon was the Kabul high school student Nahidah, first to call out nationalist slogans against Soviet troops at an Independence Day parade in July, 1980, and shot to death in the ensuing riot. Schoolgirls featured in reports of subsequent anti-government street demonstrations threw their headscarves at Afghan soldiers and police and demanded that they should go home and leave the girls to "defend the motherland" (Dupree 1984, 333). With diffuse resistance coalescing into regional and ideological parties, this fits a larger pattern: female heroes emerge in moments of default of male leadership, thus provoking men to action, but not establishing autonomous female agency.

The anti-Soviet Mujāhidīn resistance (1979–89) and the Taliban movement displacing the warring Mujāhidīn factions after 1995 both removed women from the public sphere, yet explicitly feminist legendry formed, for example around the controversial person of Meena, the assassinated founder of the secular-feminist Revolutionary Association of Women of Afghanistan (RAWA), in RAWA's assiduously maintained oral history (Brodsky 2003). Later, clandestine girls' schools were the least-kept secret of Taliban Afghanistan, widely publicized in the Western media. After the Taliban defeat in 2001, many urban women described participating in this "untold" history of resistance, acting out of nationalist or Islamic commitment to help Afghan women (rejecting the Taliban's gender policies as "un-Afghan" and/or un-Islamic oppression) or from simple need for family income. Time will tell whether the general historical memory of female heroism in Afghanistan will develop from a discourse of sacrifice and devotion and eulogize action for rights and empowerment.

Bibliography

A. E. Brodsky, *With all our strength. The Revolutionary Association of the Women of Afghanistan*, New York 2003.

N. Dupree, Revolutionary rhetoric and Afghan women, in M. Shahrani and R. Canfield (eds.), *Revolutions and rebellions in Afghanistan. Anthropological perspectives*, Berkeley 1984, 306–40.

B. Grima, *The performance of emotion among Paxtun women*, Austin, Tex. 1992.

W. Heston, *Lanḍay*, in M. Mills, P. Claus, and S. Diamond (eds.), *South Asian folklore. An encyclopedia*, New York 2003, 351–2.

C. Kieffer, Les formulas de lamentation funèbre des femmes à Caboul. Áwáz andáxtan-e zaná, in *Mélanges linguistiques offerts à Emile Benveniste*, Paris 1975, 313–23.

M. Mills, Sex role reversals, sex changes and transvestite disguise in the oral tradition of a conservative Muslim community in Afghanistan, in R. Jordan and S. Kalcik (eds.), *Women's folklore, women's culture*, Philadelphia 1985, 187–213.

——, *Oral narrative in Afghanistan. The individual in tradition*, New York 1990.

——, *Rhetorics and politics in Afghan traditional storytelling*, Philadelphia 1991.

——, Seven steps ahead of the devil. A misogynist proverb in context, in P. Enges (ed.), *Telling, remembering, interpreting, guessing. A Festschrift for Prof. Anniki Kaivola-Bregenhøj on her 60th Birthday*, Joensuu, Finland 2000, 449–58.

——, The gender of the trick. Female tricksters and male narrators, in *Asian Folklore Studies* 60:2 (2001), 238–58 (with bibliography).

H. L. Sakata, *Music in the mind*, Washington, D.C. 2002[2].

Margaret A. Mills

The Caucasus and Central Asia

Seven decades of state mandated atheism have not eradicated Muslim identity in Central Asia and the Caucasus because women, who transmit cultural norms and collective identity, are less influenced by cultural diffusion than men. Women, particularly those living outside large urban centers, have been historically less likely than men to have access to secondary education or prolonged exposure to alternative lifestyles than men who are free from social restraints to leave their community in search of work, education, or to fulfill their military obligations. Traditionally, women are not permitted to marry non-Muslims, and commonly remain practicing members of their confession, even if their men are not.

Many girls receive formal religious instruction from female religious specialists – referred to as *otin* or *bibiotun*. Young girls follow the same curriculum as boys attending a *maktab*, and those who wish to become religious specialists will remain with the *otin* for a few additional years for more in-depth study of normative Islam. Their education and the title of *otin*, conferred upon them upon graduation, make them pivotal figures in their communities where they will provide women with access to religious knowledge, assume leadership, and mediate in communal affairs.

The *otin* serves as model for women, who, after decades of Westernization and modernization efforts, first by tsarist Russia and later by the Soviet Union, had been expected to abrogate their "suffocating" and "backward" adherence to tradition and Islam. An *otin* commonly fulfills official religious functions just like female preachers in Iran. She acts as the female equivalent of the mullah and instructs girls in the basics of Islam and the proper way to behave in the given local context. With her students, she introduces women to official Islam mediated by popular rituals and local traditions.

Soviet policies aside, the majority of the peoples inhabiting Central Asia and the Caucasus still adhere to traditional values, because women continued to regale their audiences with stories of their Islamic past. These tales demonstrate God's hand in the affairs of humanity and give hope that faith and proper conduct can overcome all hardships and that good deeds will be rewarded in their own time. Muslim identity was kept alive, albeit surreptitiously, through the stories told by women.

The narratives lean heavily on Sufi literature interwoven with pre-Islamic traditions passed down through the generations. Women such as Fāṭima, the daughter of the Prophet Muḥammad, his wife ʿĀʾisha, and pious local women are held up as models to emulate, or at least to motivate girls to internalize their qualities of piety, to submit to the will of man and God, and to display quiet suffering and self-sacrifice.

These qualities are often embodied by revered saints and are valued even now. Mothers teach them to their daughters by example, through narratives, and by pointing to the *otin* whose authority among women and power in the community can be extensive. Older women debate socioreligious issues and reinforce communal ties by evoking shared values and blood ties – real or imagined – in recounting local history and legends. These stories, laden with moral messages and liberal doses of admonition to miscreants help shape the cultural fabric of the collective. The religious and historical narratives women hear and pass on to others shape their concept of Self and Other within the boundaries of shared Muslim identity.

For women, the opportunity to affirm Muslim identity arises in the context of the ritual meal (*sufra*) held after a shrine visitation (*ziyāra*). This practice is common in the Turco-Iranian cultural zone and predates Islam. During *sufra*, women sit together in honor of the saint whose intercession with God has been sought and apparently been granted. Details of the saint's life are recounted; her/his character is lauded; and readings from the Qurʾān may be offered. The host, who invites relatives, friends, and neighbors, provides a repast consisting of ritual foods commonly associated with the occasion. Histories are exchanged and created during an event that, in traditionally gender segregated societies, solidifies communal ties among women who may not all be related to each other and whose contact is limited by traditions that commonly censure women's social gatherings – unless held under the mantle of religious activity.

Soviet gender policies and mandated atheism did little to change the region's traditional cultures, which had been forged over the centuries, combining animism, shamanism, Zoroastrian tradition, and Islam. Individual and collective identities arose from ties to land, clan membership, belief in common ancestry, and loyalty to a particular leadership figure. The predominantly traditional Muslim societies that today constitute the population of the Caucasus, such as the Chechens, Tatars, and Azerbaijanis, and Central Asia's Kazakhs, Turkmens, and Tajiks, to mention but a few, have relied heavily on women to maintain and communicate Muslim identity.

Construction of identity, collectivity, and the transmission of memory are grounded in popular religious activities that allow women from different social and ethnic backgrounds to meet and exchange experiences and ideas. They tell and retell myths, histories, and legends, emphasizing local ideals and norms, thereby creating a yardstick by which the audience can measure their individual and collective demeanor and adherence to the postulated ideals. They also add something of their own experiences to the blend of narratives. Thus they add their legacy to history and vitalize Islam for the next generation. Islam provides the mirror through which identity – Self and Other – is viewed, crystallized, and reaffirmed.

Note: *ziyāra* and *sufra* are transliterations from the Persian and denote a ritual complex that consists of a "small" pilgrimage – the big one being the *ḥajj* – and a ritual meal that is commonly held in a garden or park in fulfillment of a vow made during a pilgrimage to a shrine or tomb. Persian is used because it is universally understood in the region to convey the religious significance of the event.

Bibliography

N. Abadan-Unat, The impact of legal and educational reforms on Turkish women, in N. R. Keddie and B. Baron (eds.), *Women in Middle Eastern history. Shifting boundaries in sex and gender*, New Haven, Conn. 1991, 195–214.

E. A. Allworth (ed.), *The Tatars of the Crimea. Return to the homeland. Studies and documents*, Durham, N.C. 1998[2].
M. Buckley (ed.), *Post-Soviet women. From the Baltic to Central Asia*, Cambridge 1997.
A. Kefeli, The role of Tatar and Kriashen women in the transmission of Islamic knowledge, 1800–1870, in R. Geraci and M. Khodarkovsky (eds.), *Of religion and empire. Missions, conversions, and tolerance in tsarist Russia*, Ithaca, N.Y. 2001, 250–73.
S. Keller, *To Moscow, not Mecca. The Soviet campaign against Islam in Central Asia, 1917–1941*, Westport, Conn. 2001.
A. Khalid, *The politics of Muslim cultural reform. Jadidism in Central* Asia, Berkeley 1998.
E. J. Lazzerini, Volga Tatars in Central Asia, 18th–20th centuries. From diaspora to hegemony, in B. F. Manz (ed.), *Central Asia in historical perspective*, Boulder, Colo. 1994, 82–102.
S. P. Poliakov, *Everyday Islam. Religion and tradition in rural Central* Asia, trans. A. Olcott, ed. and intro. M. B. Olcott, Armonk, N.Y. 1991.
I. Togan, In search of an approach to the history of women in Central Asia, in K. A. Ertürk (ed.), *Rethinking Central Asia. Non-Eurocentric studies in history, social structure and identity*, Reading, U.K. 1999, 163–93.

ANDREA GIACOMUZZI

Iran

The *Shāhnāma*, a national epic that versifies a mytho-history of Iran, suggests a vital role played by women and the notion of the feminine in general. Omidsalar (2003) argues that feminine symbols, and female figures, appear throughout this epic to "arbitrate all significant instances of transfer of power, be they royal, heroic or magical." The feminine, embodied at times in female literary and historical characters such as Farānak, Barmaya, and the goddess Anāhītā, stands at the birth of "all new orders" and reassuringly watches over moments of transitional trauma.

Reading the periodicals and historical records of the Constitutional Revolution (1905–11) in Iran for the forgotten parliamentary debates that focused on the nation's responsibility for the fate of a large number of Quchani women and girls captured or sold to the Turkmens, Najmabadi (1998) suggests that gender may well be considered a "uniquely structuring category" for the study of similar transitional moments such as Iranian modernity. Though largely forgotten in subsequent renditions of the events of the constitutional period, the debates concerning the "daughters of Quchan" were pivotal to the consolidation of the Iranian parliament and for the constitution of Iran's modern identity. As with the Turkish and the Arabic, the Persian reconfiguration of the term *vatan* defined a nation that was imagined as a community larger than the familial and the immediate and inscribed as a female body. The female body as mother and as beloved became principally the metaphorical, and ultimately the material, battleground for the inscription of the nation and its modernity.

The body of the Bābī poet Ṭāhira Qurrat al-ʿAyn (Fāṭima Baraghānī) is remembered in the chronicle of the nineteenth-century Qājār court historian, Muḥammad Taqī Sipihr, as one such constitutive body. In his *Nāsikh al-tavārīkh*, Sipihr takes pleasure in an exaggerated description of the poet's unveiled body. Her rumored unveiling marks a critical point in the history of Iranian modernity, situating in fact its memorable beginnings. She is represented as the object-cause of national desire, a desire that then is condemned by the force of the law in such a way that the national subject is hailed to destroy it. Reading this and other nineteenth-century narratives hermeneutically, it is impossible to pin down what her particular encroachment on the nation is about. But in the recollection and attachment of the image of this prototypical Bābī, to various local subjectivities in the next eight decades, it is clear that "the Bābī" is indistinguishable from the modern Iranian subject.

Reza Shah's reign is often remembered in association with women's forced unveiling in 1936, an edict that saw the veil as a marker of national backwardness and as a measure of women's social retardation. The enforcement of unveiling sparked new debates about women's education, progress, and women's role in the constitution of the nation. The Bābī as an unveiled female body was recovered again and again in the public and private documents of this era as a threat to the very constitution of the Iranian nation and paradoxically as the marker of its emerging modernity. What is at stake, it would seem, as Najmabadi (1998) also concludes concerning the debates that ensued during the Constitutional era, is the concept of *nāmūs* (honor), "which shifted in this period between the idea of purity of woman (*ʿiṣma*) and integrity of the nation," both subjects of male responsibility and protection.

For a generation of largely upper-class, urban, educated female writers who were born before the establishment of the Islamic Republic of Iran, the body and its compulsory veiling appear in memory as overdetermined sites for the articulation of the sociopolitical tensions that crystallized as aftereffects of the 1979 transition of power and Iran's subsequent war with Iraq. The *ḥijāb* (Islamic dress), which was instituted in the new republic to represent the integrity of the nation and to protect and preserve the purity of its women, is described in the semi-autobiographical texts of Asayesh (1999), Satrapi (2003), and Nafisi (2003), for example, as "stifling" and "unnatural." The Iranian chador (veil) in these texts stands to differentiate the ideological position of the fundamentalist woman from the one who stands in opposition to the Islamic regime. Acts of adornment, polished nails, the wearing of sheer hose, lipstick, or the few purposeful strands of hair that show from under a headscarf appear in these chronicles as embodied principled positions in the war against a perceived repressive theocratic regime. While such notations appear quotidian, superficial, and at times repetitive in the numerous memoirs and biographies that were written within three decades of the revolution, the distinctions, focusing as they do on the agency of women and the honor of men, get to the heart of a question that has dominated Iranian politics in history and memory since the nineteenth century – a question that points up the fault lines of communal belonging, religious identity, class affiliation, and gender dynamics in the constitution of the nation: "Whose country is this?"

Bibliography

G. Asayesh, *Saffron sky. A life between Iran and America*, Boston 1999.

H. E. Chehabi, Staging the emperor's new clothes. Dress codes and nation-building under Reza Shah, in *Iranian Studies* 26:3/4 (1993), 209–33.

Firdawsī, *Shāhnāma*, i–v, ed. D. J. Khaleghi-Motlagh, Costa Mesa 1988–97.

A. Nafisi, *Reading Lolita in Tehran*, New York 2003.

A. Najmabadi, *The story of the daughters of Quchan. Gender and national memory in Iranian history*, New York 1998.

M. Omidsalar, Waters and women, maidens and might. The passage of royal authority in the *Shahnama*, in G. Nashat and L. Beck (eds.), *Women in Iran. From the rise of Islam to 1800*, Chicago 2003, 170–86.

Tāj al-Salṭana, *Crowning anguish. Memoirs of a Persian princess from the harem to modernity, 1884–1914*, ed. A. Amanat, Washington, D.C. 1993.

M. Satrapi, *Persepolis*, New York 2003.

M. T. Sipihr (Lisān al-Mulk), *Nāsikh al-tavārikh*, ed. T. Sirahih and M. B. Bihbūdī, Tehran 1353.

Negar Mottahedeh

Turkey

The relations between memory, gender, and nation-state formation in Turkey can be best captured if their multiplicity is drawn out. This necessarily involves discussing the construction of gendered memories by the early republican elite in comparison with those produced by their "daughters" and looking at contemporary articulations of nostalgia in the identity formulation of different groups.

During the establishment of the Turkish Republic, the state emphasized a qualified Westernization with the aim of undercutting collective loyalties to the Ottoman legacy. This effort was coupled with a unique form of secularism based on a distinction between the "right" and "wrong" Islams – the latter being an umbrella term for any religious activity that had the potential to challenge the legitimacy of the new regime. In creating a collective memory to consolidate and justify the republican pillars, images of women would be indispensable tropes.

Ziya Gökalp, the most significant intellectual of the period, provided the framework of the new Turkish national identity with a pre-Islamic past whereby desired elements of modernization could be Turkified. His theory centralized women as the guardians and transmitters of this pure Turkish civilization, which had characteristics such as gender equality, feminism, and monogamous families (Durakbaşa 1998). As a result, the new collective identity was based on a particular remembrance of the pre-Ottoman past in which gendered subjectivities played a significant role in coalescing the "indigenous" and the "foreign."

Whereas the bigotry of the Ottoman period and heretic religious practices were said to victimize women, the republican ideals and "correct" Islam were seen as sources of moral principles and modesty requirements. Hence, the Woman Question became the pivotal component of the Kemalist project with the image of the modern women symbolizing the break with the past (Kandiyoti 1991). The mainstream historical writing described the enlightened male elites as the pioneers of this change – concealing the suppression of women's autonomous movements (Tekeli 1990). The discourse also distinguished between Istanbul women (among whom such movements had originated) and peasant women. While peasant women's efforts during the war were glorified, "Istanbul women" were seen as betrayers who entertained the enemy (Toska 1998). This gendered differentiation also served the purpose of alienating Istanbul, whose inhabitants were regarded as suspect because of the past political importance of the city.

Another remarkable aspect of this contrast is the way minorities are constructed in popular memory. The close relationship between Turkish nationalism and Turkish ethnicity is reflected in the establishment literature where non-Muslim women were depicted as morally loose, creating an other against which the morality of the "true" Turkish woman could be checked. Reinforcement of ideals of Turkish womanhood vis-à-vis the decreasing visibility of "betraying" women may have also served as a way of erasing the forced and, in many ways, brutal transformation of a heterogeneous society into one that was predominantly Turkish and Muslim. By the same token, the rejection of the Kurds as a minority and their redefinition in terms of religious heresy and regional backwardness find their parallel in literature and memoirs depicting the need to educate women victimized by lack of language skills and modern education (Türkyılmaz 2001).

Until recently, the success of such formulations was reflected in the ways "daughters of the republic" embraced this identity and advocated the nationalist project. Numerous memoirs, biographies, and oral history projects focusing on female witnesses of the early republican era reveal how women from urban, middle- and upper-middle-class families participated in the consolidation of this story (Ilyasoğlu 2000, Tekeli 1988). These elite women tended to narrate their life stories in an epic fashion resembling the historical telling of the founding of the nation, complicating the demarcation between official history and authenticity of life experience. They defined their existential meanings around their biological or spiritual fathers and defended the militarist and elitist tendencies of the republic (Altınay 2000).

Another common thread in these recollections is nostalgia, which is shaped around the contrast between the past and the present. This partly stems from the relatively recent emergence of challenges to the Kemalist visions of these women and from mainstream historical writing (Z. Arat 2000). For instance, in the Islamist construction of the republican history, the equity between modernization and secularization is questioned. At the forefront of this challenge are urban, educated women who enter the public sphere donning the *ḥijāb* (Göle 1996). The new feminist groups also question the thankful attitude of the earlier generations and suggest alternative readings of history and collective memory through which they demand a more comprehensive women's liberation (Y. Arat 2000, Tekeli 1998).

As a result, in Turkey, as in many Third-World nation-state formations, images of women along with the actual participation of particular groups of women in the public sphere have played indispensable parts in shaping and reshaping collective memories.

BIBLIOGRAPHY

A. G. Altınay, Ordu, millet, kadınlar. Dünyanın ilk kadın savaş pilotu: Sabiha Gökçen, in A. G. Altınay (ed.), *Vatan, millet, kadınlar*, Istanbul 2000, 246–79.

Y. Arat, Gender and citizenship in Turkey, in S. Joseph (ed.), *Gender and citizenship in the Middle East*, New York 2000, 275–86.

Z. Arat, Educating the daughters of the republic, in Z. Arat (ed.), *Deconstructing images of "the Turkish woman,"* New York 2000, 157–82.

A. Durakbaşa, Cumhuriyet döneminde modern kadın ve erkek kimliklerinin oluşumu. Kemalist kadın kimliği ve "münevver erkekler," in A. Berktay (ed.), *75 yılda kadınlar ve erkerler*, Istanbul 1998, 28–50.

N. Göle, *The forbidden modern. Civilization and veiling*, Ann Arbor 1996.

A. Ilyasoğlu, Islamist women in Turkey. Their identity and self-image, in Z. Arat (ed.), *Deconstructing images of "the Turkish woman,"* New York 2000, 241–62.

D. Kandiyoti, End of empire. Islam, nationalism and women in Turkey, in D. Kandiyoti (ed.), *Women, Islam, and the state,* Philadelphia 1991, 22–47.

Ş. Tekeli, Birinci ve ikinci dalga feminist hareketlerin karşılaştırmalı incelemesi üzerine bir deneme, in A. Berktay (ed.), *75 yılda kadınlar ve erkerler*, Istanbul 1998, 13–28.

Z. Türkyılmaz, Turkification through girls' education. The case of "mountain flowers" in Elazığ Girls' Institute (1937–1950), unpublished MA thesis, Boğaziçi University 2001.

ÖZLEM ALTAN

Western Europe

This entry deals with women's role in the construction of memory and collective identity in Western Europe. It focuses on migrant Muslim women and the way religious practices are remembered and reconstituted.

MEMORY, GENDER, AND MIGRATION

Studies on memory and remembering are rapidly expanding within the disciplines of the social, historical, and political sciences (Boyarin 1992, Wertsch 2002, Olick and Robbins 1998, Misztal 2003). The same holds true for the notion of identity. This is no coincidence because the two notions are intimately connected. The core meaning of individual or group identity is sustained by remembering and what is remembered is defined by the assumed identity (Gillis 1994, 3).

Memory is influenced by the particular social, cultural, and historical condition in which individuals find themselves. Gender is accordingly an important – but not exclusive – factor in the differentiation of people's memory. Extensive literature points to the importance of women as storekeepers of memory or as custodians of tradition. Boundaries of belonging and constructions of national and collective identities are symbolized by women and the female body (Neubauer and Geyer-Ryan 2000, Anthias and Yuval-Davis 1989, Yuval-Davis 1997, Anthias and Lazaridis 2000).

Connerton (1992) has advanced insights into the importance of ritual celebrations and commemorations for the ways societies remember. He argues that communal memory is shaped by the ritual reenacting of past events. Recollected knowledge of the past is conveyed and sustained by ritual performances. Recollections are at work in two distinct areas of social activity, in commemorative ceremonies and in bodily practices. His major contribution to the study of communal memory consists of connecting commemorative ceremonies and bodily practices. Connerton particularly stresses the incorporated character and habitual practice of memory. In habitual memory the past is sedimented in the body.

Migration entails a radical break with the past. Commemorative ceremonies and bodily practices have to be reproduced in a new context. An important consequence of migration is that "territory is decentred and exploded into multiple settings" (Fortier 2000, 157). That is, in the context of migration, it is no longer the nation that forms the site and frame of memory. A well-documented process for migrants from Muslim backgrounds is the strengthened consciousness of religious identity. This reorientation can take many forms and is the result of internal as well as external factors; in the end, however, most Muslims are forced to deal with religion (Roy 2000, Vertovec and Rogers 1998). Religion thus becomes a central frame of memory and identity formation.

In the new locality, the family also acquires a particularly important role in conveying and sustaining communal memories from one generation to the next. The family displaces the nation as the site of memory (Fortier 2000). This development strengthens women's role in "memory work" within migrant communities (Gillis 1994).

Reproduction of Islamic rituals in Western Europe

It is thus in the religious commemorative rituals within the family and the "mnemonic migrant community" at large that communal memory is reshaped in the context of diaspora. Whereas early in the migration process these commemorations were performed inside private homes or sometimes forgotten, they are increasingly organized by communal associations and mosques and even performed in the streets (Werbner 2002). In the Netherlands, community centers sometimes function as the locus of collective memory for minor celebrations such as Shaʿbān, ʿAshūra, and ʿĪd al-Mawlid for Moroccan migrant women. Recipes for traditional dishes and religious songs are reproduced, meals are shared, and tapes played. Cooking special dishes for commemorative rituals is a central but neglected part of memory work performed by women (Kersher 2002). Spellman (2001) notes a tremendous increase in Iranian social and cultural organizations in London and the reconstitution of religious gatherings (*sufras*) by women. Iranian women use *sufra* gatherings as identity building vehicles, during which cultural constructions of gender are negotiated, contested, and reinforced. The task of sustaining memories and rebuilding communal identities is imbued with current concerns and negotiations.

The Islamic calendar is rich in commemorative rituals such as special days during Ramadan and the concluding feast ʿĪd al-Fiṭr, the Feast of Sacrifice (ʿĪd al-Aḍḥā), Islamic New Year, ʿAshūra, and the Birthday of the Prophet (ʿĪd al-Mawlid). Moroccan migrant women used to prepare in the home country for the month of fasting either through fasting or feasting during the month of Shaʿbān. Women came together and shared a meal of couscous. In the Netherlands, however, many women mention that they tend to "forget" this celebration. Ramadan is important for communal and religious identities and is often referred to as the month of "sharing." This relates to "sharing food," "sharing time," and "sharing with the poor." Fasting is understood as sharing the experience of poverty, and toward the end of the month money is distributed to the poor, practices that are sustained in Europe. The most important difference between Ramadan in Europe and in Muslim countries is the absence of "Ramadan Time" (Armbrust 2000). In many Muslim countries, day and night are turned upside down. Office hours and school schedules are adjusted to Ramadan, television programming is suitable for Ramadan, and the time of breaking the fast is broadcast. In Europe, daily life goes on as usual.

The lack of family and the lack of synchrony of sacred and secular time change the character of most commemorative celebrations in Europe and strongly influence the celebrations for ʿĪd al-Fiṭr and ʿĪd al-Aḍḥā. Schiffauer (1991) observes the experience of emptiness and meaninglessness during religious commemorations among Turkish migrants in Germany. The changing content and meaning is noted particularly with regard to ʿĪd al-Aḍḥā. In the Netherlands, important transformations are occurring in the place and the time of slaughtering. This is also indicated by research in France and Belgium (Brisebarre 1993, 1998, 1999, Dasseto 1998). In Morocco, slaughtering is mostly done inside the home or in the street in front of the house. Selecting and buying the sheep, as well as the sacrifice itself, is a household affair. Because of the transfer to the slaughterhouse in Europe, women are no longer part of the selecting and slaughtering ritual. Many migrants also perceive the temporal reordering of the ritual as a problem. They have to wait at the slaughterhouse and are not able to perform the ritual at the time prescribed by the Mālikī school of law. Moreover, the meat of the sheep should be shared in a ratio of one third for the family, one third for relatives, neighbors, and friends, and one third for the poor. In Morocco meat can easily be distributed to the poor. Most migrants in the Netherlands, however, say that they do not know poor people and eat the entire sheep with relatives and friends. According to them the sacrifice has almost turned into an ordinary meal. Werbner (1990) mentions the changed meaning of the *khatam Qur'ān*, the sealing of the Qur'ān for British Pakistanis. After reading the Qur'ān, an offering of food is made to the guests and a share is put aside for the poor as charity. As "there are no poor people in Manchester," the central meaning of charity is lost and changed into hospitality.

On the 10th of the month of Muḥarram, the first month of the Islamic New Year, ʿAshūra is celebrated. This celebration tends to be forgotten by Moroccan migrant women in the Netherlands because they do not always know when these occasions are celebrated. Not all of them are acquainted with the Arabic calendar and they do not see the tangible signs that would remind them of the approaching commemorations in the country of origin. That is, the sensory aspects of time and habitual aspects of celebrations are absent. During ʿĪd al-Mawlid, some people in Morocco visit a *mawsim*, an annual festival at a saint's shrine, organized by a *zāwiya*, religious brotherhood. The *mawsim* continues for seven days during which people perform *dhikr*s, litanies, and *hadra*s, trance dances. Whereas some migrant women bemoan the disappearance of ʿĪd al-Mawlid, others perceive the way it is sometimes celebrated in Morocco as *bidʿa* (innovation). They regard religious lessons and religious songs as the proper form of commemoration.

Memory work and changing identities

In the process of building new communal identities there are thus diverse and contradictory tendencies. First, new commemorative elements are created, for example in the form of religious classes and lectures on commemorations. Second, migration leads to a process of reconstruction of rituals. Third, it can also lead to a loss of recollected knowledge and erosion of ritual practices.

Celebrations are partly reconstructed in a hybrid and pluralistic fashion that reflects the ongoing process of negotiating identities. There is, for instance, a tendency to organize multicultural *ifṭār* meetings during Ramadan. Especially ʿĪd al-Fiṭr and ʿĪd al-Aḍḥā are occasions for organizing special events with music, singing, and dancing by the younger generation. Other tendencies in addition to secularization and hybridization can also be observed. In the Netherlands, most older women still remember ʿAshūra, if not for the feasting at least for the fasting. The generally observed separation of "culture" or "tradition" from "religion" can be analyzed for religious celebrations as well (Vertovec and Rogers 1998, Roy 2000). Religious aspects tend to become dominant whereas the mixing with cultural traditions is frowned upon.

Minor celebrations tend to be forgotten. Due to migration, bodily and sensory clues for remembering are dislocated and the transmission of societies' memories is no longer performed in habitual spaces. As Dakhlia (2001) claims, however, forgetting is part of the process of remembering since memory erodes at the margins of groups. Forgetting can be conceptualized as a process of reconstruction in which elements that are less relevant for the present context are latent. Explicit reflection is required on the commemorative performances in the new context, which also allows for contest and reconstruction of the way communities remember. Memory is continuously reshaped and the memory work is constantly adapted to new circumstances. As Salih (2000, 2001) observes in her study of Moroccans in Italy, migrants are neither champions of hybridity nor simply reproducing traditional cultures. There are multiple paths through which Muslim migrants in Western Europe renegotiate individual and collective identities within their "mnemonic communities."

Bibliography

F. Anthias and G. Lazaridis (eds.), *Gender and migration in southern Europe. Women on the move*, Oxford 2000.

F. Anthias and N. Yuval-Davis (eds.), *Woman, nation, state*, Houndmills, Basingstoke, U.K. 1989.

W. Armbrust, The riddle of Ramadan. Media, consumer culture and the "Christmas-ization" of a Muslim holiday, paper delivered at the American Anthropological Association, November 2000.

J. Boyarin (ed.), *Remapping memory. The politics of time-space*, Minneapolis 1990.

A. M. Brisebarre, The sacrifice of ʿId al-Kabir. Islam in the French suburbs, in *Anthropology Today* 9:1 (1993): 9–12.

——, *La fête du mouton. Un sacrifice musulman dans l'espace urbain*, Paris 1998.

——, "La fête du sacrifice." Le rituel ibrâhimien dans l'islam contemporain, in P. Bonte et al. (eds.), *Sacrifices*

en islam. Espaces et temps d'un rituel, Paris 1999, 93–122.
P. Connerton, *How societies remember*, Cambridge 1992.
J. Dakhlia, New approaches in the history of memory? A French model, in A. Neuwirth and A. Pflitsch (eds.), *Crises and memory in Islamic societies*, Beirut 2001, 59–74.
F. Dasseto and M. N. Hennart, Belgique. Pratiques et significations de l'Ayd al-kabïr, in A. M. Brisebarre (ed.), *La fête du mouton. Un sacrifice musulman dans l'espace urbain*, Paris 1998, 191–203.
A. M. Fortier, *Migrant belongings. Memory, space, identity*, Oxford 2000.
J. R. Gillis (ed.), *Commemorations. The politics of national identity*, Princeton, N.J. 1994.
A. J. Kersher (ed.), *Food in the migrant experience*, Aldershot, U.K. 2002.
B. A. Misztal, *Theories of social remembering*, Philadelphia 2003.
J. Neubauer and H. Geyer-Ryan (eds.), *Gendered memories*, Amsterdam 2000.
J. K. Olick and J. Robbins, Social memory studies. From "collective memory" to the historical sociology of mnemonic practices," in *Annual Review of Sociology* 4 (1998), 105–40.
O. Roy, Muslims in Europe. From ethnic identity to religious recasting, in *ISIM Newsletter* 5 (2000), 1 and 29.
R. Salih, Shifting boundaries of self and other. Moroccan migrant women in Italy, in *European Journal of Women's Studies* 7 (2000), 309–23.
——, Confronting modernities. Muslim women in Italy, in *ISIM Newsletter* 7 (2001), 1, 32.
W. Schiffauer, *Die Migranten aus Subay. Türken in Deutschland*, Stuttgart 1991.
K. Spellman, Repasts and hopeful futures. Iranian women's religious gatherings in London, in A. Neuwirth and A. Pflitsch (eds.), *Crises and memory in Islamic societies*, Beirut 2001, 347–65.
S. Vertovec and A. Rogers (eds.), *Muslim European youth. Reproducing ethnicity, religion, culture*, Aldershot, U.K. 1998.
P. Werbner, *The migration process. Capital, gifts and offerings among British Pakistanis*, New York 1990.
——, *Imagined diaspora among Manchester Muslims*, Oxford 2002.
J. V. Wertsch, *Voices of collective remembering*, Cambridge 2002.
N. Yuval-Davis, *Gender and nation*, London 1997.

KARIN VAN NIEUWKERK

Military: Women's Participation

Sub-Saharan Africa

Women in Sub-Saharan African countries have had an ambivalent relationship with the militaries of their societies. Since the mid-1990s, African women have become best known for the creation of unprecedented peace networks and movements throughout Africa – a vital response to the rash of post-Cold War armed conflicts there. Although statistics on women and militarism are almost impossible to obtain, the clear involvement of African women with informal militias and informal militaries is disproving Fukuyama's essentialist stereotype (1997) that women are nurturers and not soldiers and causes us to explore Mead's concern with the "unwillingness of most societies to arm women" (1967, 236). The stereotype that Muslim women do not participate in the military is also challenged by the data. In fact, the differential involvement of Sub-Saharan African women with the military is not dependent upon religion, but rather on the nature of ties between the military, culture, the state, and other institutions of the society.

The militaries of most traditional African kingdoms were formed through male conscription, and there was often complementary support given by women of all classes to the process of military conquest by which these traditional states emerged. Few ordinary women were in the military, and neither traditional nor modern African militaries conscripted women.

Under colonialism, African women were excluded from the military. European colonizers shaped the militaries to be institutions that could dominate and subdue African societies, so they conscripted men from marginal areas. These men understood that they were being exploited, but they eventually came to see the military as a job that could guarantee them some economic security.

This relationship of the Sub-Saharan African military dominance over other institutions persisted until recently, manifesting itself in five main trends. The first trend appeared in many Anglophone and Francophone colonies that agitated for independence, and achieved it through elections and negotiations in the 1960s. A decade later, the army was strong enough to take over in states with weak electoral or judicial institutions, or where governments were authoritarian and corrupt. Women became adversaries of the military because of its resistance to elections, abuse of civilians, and assaults on women leaders.

The second trend was the appearance of liberation movements where guerilla armies resisted colonial hegemony in Algeria, Eritrea, Ethiopia, Angola, Mozambique, Namibia, Zimbabwe, Guinea-Bissau, and South Africa. In these cases, both men and women became freedom fighters, and those women who experienced battle on the front lines earned status relatively equal to that of men. However, most women were also a part of the women's wing, the women's auxiliary forces, the nursing unit, or the equipment suppliers and food brigade rather than the heads of regiments. This range of roles still offered women an alternative to male domination in the domestic arena.

As a subset of the above cases, in both Muslim and Christian parts of Sub-Saharan Africa where liberation struggles continued into the 1970s and through the 1980s, women's military involvement depended on the context. In northern Sudan, Muslim women of the National Islamic Front supported their men fighting against the Christian south (Hale 1996), although more pacifism emerged later. In Eritrea, some women resisted religious and cultural conservatism by fighting for liberation from Ethiopia in both single sex and mixed units (Coughlin 2000). Muslim and Christian women participated in a 30-year liberation struggle against Ethiopia until independence was secured in 1993. They formed 35–40 percent of the EPLF freedom fighters, 25 percent of the front line combatants, roughly 20–40 percent of the administrative and industrial occupations, but 50.5 percent of the health fields.

Many women saw the military as a way to alter their subordinate positions within society, whether due to class oppression, or sexism. Many Eritrean women broke out of intolerable marriages by becoming freedom fighters (Leguesse 1994), and some married fellow soldiers. In Eritrea, Tsegga Gaim said: "The gender issue was such a very big part of this struggle for the women fighters . . . I learned in the EPLF not only to fight for independence, but also for equality" (Stephens 2000). But at the end of the early liberation wars, women fighters often paid a high price for the breaking of traditional norms. Most were discharged from the military, but not demobilized and reintegrated as men were. Barth (2002) describes the disappointment of peasant Eritrean female fighters at being neglected by society following the war, remaining unmarried, or being forced to return to unequal domestic situations and rural labor.

A third trend appears in the 1980s and 1990s, where African women entered guerilla armies to help resolve societal injustices and state crises. For example, in Uganda, when the corrupt governments of Idi Amin and Milton Ubote fell through coups, women joined the grassroots National Resistance Army formed by Yoweri Museveni. Ultimately, they were integrated into the Ugandan Defense Force, and today more than 500 Ugandan women serve as captains, administrators, or privates. In South Africa, women joined the African National Congress to resist apartheid, some becoming members of its exiled military leadership, Mkonto we Sizwe. When these women fighters returned at the end of apartheid, they had to force their former comrades and party members to negotiate women's 30 percent representation in political positions within the new South Africa. Ultimately, many ANC women were integrated into the reconstructed South African Defense Forces, joining white women who were already 10 percent of SADF (Cock 1995, 1993). Alternatively, many of these former combatants were elected as parliamentarians on ANC slates throughout the country.

A fourth trend has appeared since the end of the Cold War, where militias or armed forces have waged "wars against the people" (Ferguson 2003). This has involved the captures of girls by rebel groups and formal armies, gang rape, and generalized violence against women in places such as Liberia, Sierra Leone, Sudan, Congo/DRC, and Rwanda during the genocide. In Northern Uganda, the Lord's Resistance Army captured girls as a way of reproducing "rebel families." Elsewhere they were abducted through the killing of their family members, although some entered to escape domestic abuse or through fear of the victimization that could accompany war. The absence of alternatives to fighting may propel them toward joining. Often these girl and women fighters were no less violent than their male counterparts, although ANC women tried to avoid killing people. Overall, the futures of women fighters have tended to be in doubt, since demobilization efforts usually do not include the girl and women fighters (Veale 2003). The exceptions are places such as Sierra Leone, where women's NGOs have taken as their mission the rehabilitation of child fighters and women.

Strong indications of women's opposition to this trend emerged in the 1990s. Women's peace movements were evident all across the continent, especially in Liberia, Sierra Leone, Mali, Nigeria, Kenya, Rwanda, Tanzania, and South Africa (Mikell forthcoming). African women's peace and anti-military themes were evident at the 1995 Beijing Conference and have been carried forward at conferences in Zanzibar, South Africa, and Ghana between 1998 and 2003 that have been distinctly pro-state, antimilitarist, and supportive of civilian control of the military. Women have speculated that in southern Africa, the HIV-AIDS trajectory may be linked to the SADF expansion into frontline states, accounting for the 20–36 percent AIDS prevalence rates in these countries (*Mail and Guardian* 1999). In many of the countries listed here, especially South Africa, Uganda, and Rwanda after the genocide, women became an elected majority within parliament, and were better able to reshape the relationship between state, military, and civil society.

At the same time, a fifth trend is appearing, signaling a new relationship between women and soldiering in those societies undergoing transitions to democracy. Since women are not conscripted in Sub-Saharan Africa, their voluntary entrance into the military indicates their desire for economic mobility as well as their nationalist commitment. Although women are represented in small numbers in these militaries, they are achieving high rank.

Today, women still make up a significant portion of the Ugandan People's Defense Forces. They are now a part of the security bureaucracy and defense ministers for SADF, and they are among the officer corps in international venues such as the Africa Center for Strategic Studies. This trend is likely to increase as Sub-Saharan African countries democratize, and as women demonstrate agency and nationalism by opting for the military because it can offer them career opportunities. One Ugandan woman soldier defended her choice: "You see, in the army your performance will either pull you up or down" (UAF 2001).

Bibliography

A.-O. Agbese, Maintaining power in the face of political, economic and social discrimination. The tale of Nigerian women, in *Women and Language* 26:1 (March 2002), <http://static.highbeam.com/w/womenandlanguage/march222003/maintainingpowerinthefaceofpoliticaleconomicandsoc/>.

E. F. Barth, Peace as disappointment. The reintegration of female soldiers in post-conflict societies. A comparative study from Africa, PRIO Report 3, 2002, <http:// www.prio.no/page/Project_detail/Projects_by_programme_all/9244/37835.html>.

J. Cock, Forging a new army out of old enemies. Women in the South African military, in *Women's Studies Quarterly* 23 (Fall/Winter 1995), 97–111.
——, *Women and war in South Africa*, Cleveland 1993.
Conscription and armies in the world, 2002, <http://www.c3.hu/~farkashe/english/ countries.htm>.
K. M. Coughlin, Women, war and the veil. Muslim women in resistance and combat, in G. J. DeGroot and C. Peniston-Bird (eds.), *A soldier and a woman. Sexual integration in the military*, London 2000, 223–39.
R. B. Ferguson (ed.), *The state, identity, and violence. Political disintegration in the post-Cold War world*, London 2003.
F. Fukuyama, Women and the evolution of world politics, in *Foreign Affairs* 77:5 (September/October 1997), 24–40.
S. Hale, Post-liberation women. The case of Eritrea, in M. R. Walker and J. Rycenga (eds.), *Frontline feminisms. Women, war and resistance*, New York 2000, 349–70.
D. Harman, A woman on trial for Rwanda's massacre, in *Christian Science Monitor*, 7 March 2003.
R. Iyob, *The Eritrean struggle for independence. Domination, resistance, nationalism*, Cambridge 1997.
Y. E. Keairns, *The voices of girl soldiers. Summary report*, Quaker United Nations Office, New York 2002.
A. Leguesse, *Role of women in development. Zula plain baseline study*, Consultancy Report, Appendix 5, Oslo, Norwegian Church Aid 1994.
N. Mba, Kaba and khaki. Women and the militarized state in Nigeria, in J. Parpart and K. Staudt (eds.), *Women and the state in Africa*, London 1989, 69–90.
M. Mead, Epilogue, in M. Fried, M. Harris, and R. Murphy (eds.), *War. The anthropology of armed conflict and aggression*, Garden City, N.Y. 1967, 236.
G. Mikell, Women mobilizing for peace. African-American responses to African crises, in *International Journal on World Peace* 17:1 (2000), 61–84.
——, African women. Globalization and peacebuilding from the bottom up, in *SOULS. A Critical Journal of Black Politics, Culture and Society*, Columbia University Press (forthcoming).
——, African women. Balancing militarism and peace, paper presented at the Invited Session, 102nd Annual Meeting, American Anthropological Association, Chicago, 19–23 November 2003.
A. Nicodemus, Soldiers brought AIDS to SA, in *Mail and Guardian* (South Africa), 3 September 1999, <http://www.q.co.za/news/1999/9909/990902–aids.htm>.
NUEW (National Union of Eritrean Women) *The voice of Eritrean women* (newspaper of NUEW), Asmara 1980, various issues.
M. Nzomo, Governance, gender, and conflicts in Africa, United Nations, Dakar 2002, <http://unpan1.un.org/intradoc/groups/public/documents/CAFRAD/UNPAN008250.pdf>, 7–9.
M. Stephens, Tsegga Gaim. Women and War Project, Eritrea, 2000, <http://www.melaniestephens.com/wwtsegga.htm>.
M. Turshen and C. Twagiramariya (eds.), *What women do in wartime. Gender and conflict in Africa*, New York 1997.
UAF (Uganda Armed Forces), Uganda women in combat. They tell their story, Uganda government homepages, Women of the Uganda Army, <http://web.archive.org/web/20010424124901/http://www.uganda.co.ug/army/>.
S. Urdang, *And still they dance. Women, war, and the struggle for change in Mozambique*, London 1989.
——, *Fighting two colonialisms. Women in Guinea Bissau*, New York 1979.
A. Veale, *From child soldier to ex-fighter. Female fighters, demobilization and reintegration in Ethiopia*, Pretoria 2003.

GWENDOLYN MIKELL

Turkey

One of the foundational myths of Turkish nationalism is that the Turkish nation is a military nation; that "every Turk is born a soldier" (Altınay forthcoming). This entry addresses the implications of this myth for women in terms of military service and citizenship and women's participation in the military as officers.

Military service is compulsory for all males, currently for fifteen months at the age of 21 (six to twelve months for university graduates). The law that regulates this citizenship practice was passed in 1927 after a brief discussion in the parliament. Upon the reading of the first article, which made military service obligatory for all males, one member questioned its implications for women: "If voting and becoming a candidate is a national issue, participating in the country's defense is also a similar right, a similar duty. . . . I would like to ask whether you have taken women's services into consideration, or to what extent" (*TBMM* 1927, 385). The suggestion that women's participation in the military should be considered was not taken seriously by other law-makers in 1927, but it has arisen several times since then. The most recent attempts were in 1996, initiated by the minister of defense (Çalışlar 1996), and in 1999, initiated by a woman member of the parliament (*Hürriyet* 1999). Neither of these proposals went much further, but both sparked heated debate.

"Nationalist projects are simultaneously gender projects" (Walby 1996). The 1927 debate reveals the extent to which the compulsory military service law was as much a part of the state's gender project as it was of its nationalist project. It also reveals that the law-makers were quite aware of this. By bringing male citizens together in the barracks and separating them from female citizens, law-makers were creating a major source of gender difference that was defined and administered by the state. As in many other nation-states, in Turkey masculinity, first-class citizenship, the state, and the military have been interwoven through continuous and compulsory male military service (Enloe 2000, Nagel 1998).

The first woman to serve in the Turkish military after the independence war was Sabiha Gökçen

(1913–2001), one of the adopted daughters of Atatürk and the first woman combat pilot in the world. Gökçen joined the Air Academy in 1936 and participated in a large-scale military operation in Dersim, a Kurdish-Alevi dominated province in southeastern Turkey in 1937. Upon her successful undertaking of combat duties, Gökçen remembers Atatürk telling her: "We are a military nation. From ages 7 to 70, women and men alike, we have been created as soldiers" (Gökçen 1996, 126). For the *New York Times* (19 September 1937), she was "The Flying Amazon of Turkey."

Gökçen remained the only woman to join the military until 1955, when several women won a court case to join the Army College on the grounds that the regulations did not specify gender as a limitation for application. A number of women entered the colleges of the army, navy, and air force in the following years. But in the early 1960s, the entry regulations for military colleges were amended to include "being male" as a requirement for the applicants (Kurtcephe and Balcıoğlu 1991, 172–3). It was only in 1992 that women were, once again, allowed to apply for the military colleges and academies. The 2001 figure for the total number of woman officers in the Turkish armed forces is 918 out of a total force of more than 800,000 (*Year-In-Review 2001*). Turkey has the second largest military in NATO (after the United States), and one of the lowest ratios of female personnel (together with Italy and Poland). The recruitment of women into the military academies after the 1990s may partly have been a result of the pressures coming from NATO, particularly the Committee on Women.

The implications of compulsory military service and becoming a military officer are quite different. While the latter can be seen as the right to choose a military career, the former marks the right of the state to ask for women's service without their consent. In the public debates on both issues, different opinions have been raised by women, ranging from demands to be conscripted to antimilitarist stances critiquing the military establishment altogether. Some women, like Gökçen, have been active in the creation and perpetuation of the myth that the Turkish nation is a military nation. Other women have been critical of this myth altogether (see Emektar 2003, *Cumhuriyet* 1992). In the absence of in-depth research, we know very little about the ideas of the large numbers of women who have not participated in the public debates, but have been essential to the military service system as mothers, wives, girlfriends, and sisters. We also know little about the actual experiences of women officers in the military.

BIBLIOGRAPHY

A. G. Altınay, *The myth of the military-nation. Militarism, gender, and education in Turkey*, Palgrave MacMillan (forthcoming).
A. Arman, Gencim, güzelim, kadınım, denizciyim, in *Hürriyet*, 7 June 1998.
O. Çalışlar, Haydi kızlar askere(!), in *Cumhuriyet*, 21 April 1996.
Cumhuriyet, Aklı başında kadın orduya girmez, 21 June 1992.
G. Emektar, Kadınlar askerlikle özgürleşmeyecek, 15 May 2003, <www.bianet.org>.
C. Enloe, *Maneuvers. The international politics of militarizing women's lives*, Berkeley 2000.
S. Gökçen, *Atatürk'le bir ömür*, prepared by O. Verel, Istanbul 1996[2].
Hürriyet, Kadına 3 ay askerlik, 6 December 1999.
İ. Kurtcephe and M. Balcıoğlu, *Kara harp okulu tarihi*, Ankara 1991.
J. Nagel, Masculinity and nationalism. Gender and sexuality in the making of nations, in *Ethnic and Racial Studies* 21:2 (1998), 242–69.
TBMM Zabıt Ceridesi, Inikat 79, C:1 Devre II, Cilt 33, 21 June 1927.
S. Walby, Woman and nation, in G. Balakrishnan (ed.), *Mapping the nation*, London 1996, 235–54.
Year-in-Review 2001, Committee on Women in the NATO Forces, 25th Anniversary, 2001, <http://www.nato.int/ims/2001/win/00-index.htm>.

AYŞE GÜL ALTINAY

The United States

Women have served on the battlefield as nurses, water bearers, cooks, laundresses, and saboteurs since the revolutionary war. They held no official positions in the military but worked as civilians serving their country's military needs until the establishment of the Army Nurse Corps in 1901 and the Navy Nurse Corps in 1908. During the First World War (1917–18), the first formal military positions were held by 21,480 army nurses and more later served in the Quartermaster's Corps. The Reorganization Act (1920) allowed women to hold "relative rank" from second lieutenant to major (but without rights and privileges).

In 1942, the Army Nurse Corps changed to the Women's Auxillary Army Corps (WAAC) and in 1943 to the Women's Army Corps (WAC), which included the Women's Air force Service Pilots (WASP) who flew as civil service pilots. WASPs flew stateside missions as ferriers, test pilots, and antiaircraft artillery trainers. The navy also recruited women into its Navy Women's Reserve, called Women Accepted for Volunteer Emergency Service (WAVES) (Highlights of Women in the Military). In 1978, the women's corps were terminated and women were integrated with the regular services. The number of women increased from 1.6 percent of the total United States military force in 1973 to 15 percent in 2003 (Manning and Wight 2003, 10). The majority of combat related positions are still off-limits to women, although women are trained to defend themselves and their units. During Desert Storm in 1991, approximately 41,000 women, including Muslims, were integrated in many combat support positions in the theatre of operation in Kuwait and Saudi Arabia. Americans became alarmed about their women supporting the combat forces who were within close proximity of the front lines.

Little information has been collected about Muslim women in the military because their story is still unfolding. There is no reference to them in any books containing information about women in the United States military but more is written about Muslim Women in military services in other countries. The United States military statistics refer to its personnel by gender and ethnic background rather than by religion, which is counted from the perspective of pastoral and religious support. The information for this topic comes primarily from firsthand experience, interviews with women who have served or are serving in the military, and conversations with Muslim chaplains in the military.

It is still uncertain when the first Muslim women joined the United States military. The first evidence found through a survey was of an American Muslim woman born of Lebanese parents from Quincy, Massachusetts who joined the Navy Reserves in 1958, served approximately two years, and later resigned. She joined out of pride because five of her brothers had served in either the Second World War or the Korean War and she felt it was her patriotic duty to do the same. The end of the Vietnam War and the draft opened the way for more women to join the military, most of them African-American, and some immigrants or Americans born of immigrant parents. The statistics available show the largest percentage of the Muslim population in the military now to be African-Americans, followed by South Asians, Arabs, and Caucasians. From the 1970s to the present, the Muslim population increased and gained acceptance and was given space on the military bases to use for worship, Islamic education, and other religious activities. Awareness of Muslim women in the military increased as a result of stories of service women requesting to wear the *ḥijāb* as part of their uniform, and the tragic events of 11 September 2001 with the resulting media exposure of Muslim women in Afghanistan and Arab countries.

Statistics

According to statistics from June 2003 from the Office of the Secretary of Defense (OSD) Manpower Section, there are 1.4 million military personnel on active duty and out of this number there are approximately 4,164 personnel (male and female) or 0.3 percent who have declared Islam as their religion on their personnel records. The American Muslim Armed Forces and Veterans Affairs Council states that there are approximately 15,000 Muslims in the military, which constitutes approximately 1.1 percent of the total force (Barber 2003), of which the female Muslim population is approximately 533 women, or 0.03 percent on active duty.

A number of factors account for the difference in the numbers of Muslims in the military. New recruits at basic training may not state a religious preference out of fear of being singled out or harassed because of their faith, and fail to update their records at a later date. A few women converted to Islam while in the military and did not update their records, and some who say they are Muslim do not want it to be in their records. The record will reflect a "no religious preference" if the records are not updated. The OSD maintains that about 70 percent of military personnel do declare a faith (Akhtar 1998).

The chart below shows the growth of the female Muslim personnel in the active services of the military from 1995 to 2003 and the Reserves in 2003.

Female Muslim Population in the U.S. Military

Service	1995	2003	Reserves	2003
Army	197	257	Army	196
			Air National Guards	16
Air Force	80	132	Air Force	5
Navy	70	117	Naval	9
Marines	23	27	Marines	11
Total	370	533	Total	237

Education

Many Muslim women in the military utilize the education benefits and work on successfully achieving a bachelor's degree. Since the 1970s, women have been required to have a high school diploma (all women's jobs required this) and be in good physical condition to join the military. Their male counterparts were required to have only an eighth-grade education, because of the shortage of men joining the military after the end of the draft, and the assumption that combat positions do not require a high school diploma.

Women were not allowed the free education at the military academies in order to be commissioned as officers until 1976 when Congress changed the rules. There are no records of any Muslim females graduates from the academies. Women were commissioned through other sources, such as the Reserve Officer Training Corps (ROTC) and the Officer Candidate School (OCS) starting in 1972. There are a few Muslim women who were commissioned from these sources. Also, the Equal Rights Amendments of 1972 afforded women the opportunity to have a career within the military with equal pay for equal work.

Why Muslim women join the military, stay in the military, and/or leave the military

From the 1970s until the present, women have been recruited to join the military with benefits of college tuition, military training that could be transferred into a civilian career, travel opportunities, and a paycheck that afforded some single parents the opportunity to put food on the table. Why do they stay in the military? They stay in the military because of job satisfaction and a pension. Part of the job satisfaction is having supervisors and commanders who accommodate their religious needs by allowing them to take time off for prayer and fasting during the month of Ramadan. Some have allowed women to wear their *ḥijāb* while in uniform per the regulation which stipulates that the commander may allow the wearing of the *ḥijāb*. Why do Muslim women leave the military? Many converted to Islam after joining the military and felt that the military was incompatible with their faith because they were not allowed to wear the *ḥijāb*. After completing their contract they left the military. A small number have left because they were harassed by their supervisors who did not allow time off for prayer or leniency with physical fitness during Ramadan and because overall they were not treated well. These women had to make equal opportunity complaints and seek the aid of the chaplains and sometimes legal council to be given their rights to religious accommodations. The main reason why women leave the military, however, is the conflict they have trying to raise their families when they must spend long periods of time away from them.

Roles of Muslim women

Muslim women serve as aviators in the Air Force flying F-16s and in the Army flying helicopters, as doctors working close to the front line in times of combat, as translators (Arabic), intelligence agents, nurses, administrators, military police, chaplains' assistants, food specialists, dentists, mechanics, machinists, and in public relations, logistics, transportation, and many other jobs. Some are placed close to the front lines, as squad leaders, team leaders, platoon leaders, company commanders, and battalion commanders. There are a few examples of Muslim women in the military who have achieved some rank. The highest ranking officer is a lieutenant colonel (0-5) in the Army Medical Corps. She is a white American who converted to Islam after assignment to Tajikistan. A retired African-American lieutenant commander (0-4) in the Navy was the first female Muslim to receive a commission as a line officer in any of the armed services. A major in the Army Reserves applied to become the first female Muslim chaplain, case pending. A captain in the Marines, a public relations officer, and company commander of a public affairs company is following in her father's footsteps, an Arab-American and former Marine. In 1994 many changes were made in terms of occupations that women could hold in the military. Ninety-one percent of the positions in the Army are open to women, 94 percent in the Navy, 92 percent in the Marines, and 99 percent in the Air Force. The restrictions are combat positions or combat related positions (Manning and Wight 2003, 13).

Achievements

The greatest achievement was the appointment of the first Muslim Army chaplain in 1993. The number of Muslims in the military required them to have religious representation, and with the help of outside forces and the exposure of Islam through Desert Storm, the push for acceptance as a Muslim community within the military was inevitable. Joint Forces Commander General Khaled bin Sultan said in his book *Desert Warrior* that there were over 2,000 military personnel who accepted Islam during the first Gulf War while assigned in Kuwait and Saudi Arabia. The Saudi government paid for Muslim military personnel, men and women, to perform the *ḥajj*, giving an international presence to the Muslims in the United States military. Other achievements are access to a pocketsize editions of "The Meaning of the Holy Quran" at military chapels, certified halal Meals-Ready-to-Eat (MREs), and time to perform daily prayers and attend Friday prayers, as well as Ramadan observances. The Chief of Chaplains sends memos to commanders informing them how to accommodate their Muslim personnel. Important goals that are still pending are wearing the *ḥijāb* for female Muslims and possibly the inclusion of female Muslim chaplains to minister to the needs of the Muslim population in the military. The American Muslim Armed Forces and Veterans Affairs Council has been the advocate of many women on bases around the country, especially for wearing the *ḥijāb*. It has ensured that service women are represented and their rights are protected.

Bibliography

H. Akhtar, Islam in the armed forces, in *Nation*, 29 December 1998, <http://www.renaissance.com.pk/febnevi99.html>.

M. Barber, Muslims in the U.S. Military are as loyal as any, chaplain says, *Seattle Post-Intelligencer Reporter*, 2001, <http://seattlepi.nwsource.com/attack/43546_chaplains20.shtml>.

G. J. DeGroot and C. Peniston-Bird (eds.), *A soldier and a woman. Sexual integration in the military*, Harlow, England 2000.

M. C. Harrell and L. Miller, *New opportunities for military women. Effects upon readiness, cohesion, and morale*, Santa Monica, Calif. 1997.

Highlights of Women in the Military, 24 August 2003, <http://womensmemorial.org/Highlights.html>.

Maj. Gen. J. Holm, *Women in the military. An unfinished revolution*, Novato, Calif. 1982, 1992 (rev. ed.).

Capt. L. Manning and V. R. Wight, *Report of women in the military. Where they stand*, Women's Research and Education Institute, Washington, D.C. 2003[4].

B. J. Morden, The Women's Army Corps, 1945–1978, Center of Military History, United States Army, Washington, D.C. 2000, <http://www.army.mil/cmhpg/books/wac/index.htm>.

Women in the Military Service for America Memorial, <http://womensmemorial.org/>.

United States, Department of Defense, Office of the Secretary of Defense, statistics on military personnel, 2003.

Shareda Hosein

Modesty Discourses

Overview

Within the Islamic tradition, a Qur'ānic verse that can be, and frequently has been, drawn upon to authorize discourses of modesty for women is Verse 31 of Sura 24 (Light): "And tell the believing women to lower their gaze and be modest, and display of their adornment only that which is apparent, and to draw their veils over their bosoms, and not to reveal their adornment save to their husbands or fathers or husbands' fathers, or their sons or their husbands' sons, or their brothers or their brothers' sons or sisters' sons, or their women, or their slaves, or male attendants who lack vigor, or children who know naught of women's nakedness."

Across the Muslim world, in a variety of social settings, women's modesty, whether expressed as respectful comportment; the sexual propriety that circumscribes interactions between men and women in public; dress that conceals bodily contours, hair, and sometimes the face; or the emotions of shyness or embarrassment, is a fundamental component of a gendered social morality. Although many aspects of this moral system may be found in non-Muslim societies, especially those of the circum-Mediterranean, what may be distinctive is that the religious source cited above, along with related statements on morality and virtue found in the Qur'ān and the *ḥadīth* (traditions of the Prophet), are available for citation and interpretation. Historically, they have been adapted and adopted to give meaning or authority to local practices and demands. The emphasis has usually been on the importance of modesty for women, the parallel verse (24:30) enjoining men to be modest being less frequently invoked and carrying different connotations.

Approaches to the analysis of modesty

Analysts have taken a number of approaches to understanding the workings of the gendered ideals and discourses of modesty in the social lives of communities across the Muslim world. Many anthropologists who have worked in tribal or rural communities have focused on how the modesty of women is linked to the code of honor that governs social relations in communities organized around kinship. Where the honor and reputation of families, rather than fixed wealth, control over the means of production, or occupation is critical to social ranking, the behavior of individual family members is constrained by the ways in which it might reflect on the family, maintaining, enhancing, or jeopardizing the family's standing or prestige. In many such situations, from societies of the circum-Mediterranean to those of South Asia, the modesty of women – defined by respectful comportment and sexual propriety – is deemed critical to the honor of their families.

Many social functions have been attributed to this moral system, particularly the imperative of women's modesty. Some anthropologists argue that the ideal of modesty for women functions to preserve patrilineal kin groups, restraining women and thus preventing them from disrupting the bonds among brothers and patrilineal kin. Others note that such systems function to preserve patriarchal control by excluding women from interfering in decision-making, whether over property or marriage alliances. Yet others suggest that at the least this system reproduces gender hierarchies since the passions of men for their honor lead them to strictly control the women who might undermine it. This relationship shapes the ties between brothers and sisters.

Those who find unsatisfying these sorts of functionalist arguments about the utility of modesty discourses in preserving social structures favor approaches that place more weight on the honor code as a system of cultural meaning. How do the ideals of modesty, they ask, give value to certain ways of being? For example, Abu-Lughod's analysis (2000) of the Awlād 'Alī Beduin in Egypt questions whether the requirements for women to be modest are patriarchal. She observes that in such social systems both men and women are held to moral ideals; and they are held equally responsible for the maintenance of family and personal honor. She concedes, however, that the ideals are gendered such that men's honor tends to take the form of valor and independence whereas women's honor takes the form of modesty, which can be defined as voluntary deference to social superiors and the sexual propriety that is one aspect of this deference.

Analyzing modesty as part of a system of meaning can lead also to an appreciation of the ways in which discourses of modesty can work to rationalize and reproduce social distinctions among social groups or strata. In deeply hierarchical societies such as that found in Yemen, modest comportment, along with competitive hospitality and consumption, are, as anthropologist Anne Meneley (1996) shows, crucial to the reputations of the socially respected landowning families in at least one city. This moral discourse has the effect, however, of asserting the superiority of this propertied elite group as a whole, in contrast to socially marginal "outcaste" groups. Women from these marginal groups are denigrated by social superiors for lacking modesty and are ridiculed if they try to take on the accoutrements of modesty by veiling. The moral discourse of modesty, in other words, according to Huda Seif, an anthropologist who has studied propertyless and despised social groups in Yemen, should be seen as one of the ideological mechanisms for perpetuating social inequality.

Ethnographers of everyday life in various Muslim communities from Africa to Asia have noted that whatever its functions and meanings, the discourse of modesty is context-sensitive. Expectations about women's modesty come into play only in certain social situations and vary over the life cycle, being dependent especially on age and marital status. The demands for modest comportment are particularly directed at girls and younger women. The restrictions and expectations shift over the life cycle such that morality for older women tends to be less tied to the demands of modesty. In many societies across the Muslim world, older women behave more assertively, are more relaxed in the company of men, and have more public roles. Modesty can also be situational: in many communities that value and insist on the modesty of women, women can be bold, use sexually explicit or coarse language, and be anything but shy and retiring as long as this is within the intimate social contexts of gender-segregated women's spheres. Veiling too can be situational, either being expected only in public or varying by the relative status of the men being encountered. Moreover, in some communities, women have available to them particular forms such as oral poetry in which they can freely express a range of sentiments that, if communicated in ordinary language and in public contexts, would compromise modesty.

Finally, phenomenological approaches to the study of modesty insist, against the functionalists and those interested in interpreting the cultural meaning of modesty, that one must explore how the ideals and discourses of modesty are experienced, learned, or cultivated by women themselves. Some have noted the close relationship between the assertion of modesty as a moral ideal and the feelings of shame or embarrassment that women experience in situations when they find themselves inappropriately dressed, exposed in public, or find their seclusion or separation from unrelated men breached. The critical reports in the early twentieth century of Bengali writer and champion of women's education, Rokeya Sakhawat Husain, on the absurdities of women's lives in purdah (the South Asian term for the seclusion of women) inadvertently reveal the depth to which women have internalized modesty. She recounts an incident in which a young bride, left for hours on her own in her new household, was forced to urinate in a vessel in which she had brought betel nuts because she was too shy to go wandering around the house looking for the bathroom (Rokeya 1988, 27–8). Others have focused on how the dispositions to act modestly and even the sentiments of shyness or embarrassment that underlie them are inculcated in the socialization process. Girls are taught appropriate behaviors, scolded for inappropriate or immodest behaviors, and absorb the ideals of modesty through moving naturally through symbolically loaded everyday worlds constructed in terms of the separation of the sexes.

With the growth and spread of Islamist or piety movements in the last decades of the twentieth century from Egypt to Malaysia, women's modesty has taken on cultural meanings different from the familial core and consequently is experienced differently. Modesty has assumed more explicitly religious meanings. As Saba Mahmood argues, using the case of Egyptian women in the mosque movement in the 1990s, in such contexts modesty or shyness is considered one of the key religious virtues for women. Rather than being linked to the honor of families it is seen as integral to the realization of "closeness to God." Women seek to cultivate modesty and shyness in themselves, many of them sensing that it does not at first come naturally because of their upbringing. Through bodily acts, especially veiling, such women, often from more secular and middle- and lower-middle-class backgrounds, believe that they will be able to imprint on themselves the appropriate attitudes and sentiments of the pious person. If some women complain at first that they feel uncomfortable taking on the *ḥijāb*, the head covering that is part of contemporary Islamic or modest dress, they believe that eventually they will come to feel uncomfortable when they are not wearing it. As Mahmood (2001, 214) concludes, conducting oneself modestly and taking on the veil are treated by these women, as "the *critical markers*, as well as the *ineluctable means* by which one trains oneself to be pious" (emphasis in the original).

The modern politics of modesty

If modesty discourses in the twentieth century have been associated primarily with Muslim piety or with the familial code of honor that is so much a part of rural, tribal, or even conservative urban communities, these are not their only contexts and meanings. Historians and students of the development of nationalism and the nineteenth- and twentieth-century modernizing projects across the Muslim world have observed a pattern whereby women, almost as a condition of their becoming educated and moving into public spaces, have taken on stricter forms of modesty and chastity than those practiced in family-based worlds. It is as if they and their families, or their modernizing rulers, must prove that their moves out of the home and sex-segregated spaces will not threaten the social order or bring about their moral degradation.

Deniz Kandiyoti, for one, has argued that for the Turkish women who benefited from the secularizing reforms of Kemal Atatürk beginning in the late 1920s, being educated and finding public roles in politics and the workplace entailed a desexualization. Cultural emphasis was placed on women's maternal roles or their roles as ungendered citizens. Similarly, historian Afsaneh Najmabadi has argued that as elite and middle-class Iranian women in the early part of the twentieth century unveiled, entered educational institutions, and began to inhabit the "modern" heterosocial space where men and women mingled, they came to strictly control their behavior and language. They lost, she argues, the richly sexual and lively language of the homosocial women's worlds that earlier generations had inhabited. She describes the result as "veiled discourse – unveiled bodies." The secular or nationalist women who emerged out of these projects in Turkey and Iran have been described as "modern-but-modest."

Ideals of women's modesty have also been built into the laws about public morality that have been adopted by many Muslim majority states. Rather than seeing these as vestiges or holdovers from "traditional" values deriving from the honor-based morality of face-to-face communities, analysts such as Ayşe Parla argue that such laws, and the enforcement of sexual modesty represented by such related new practices as state-mandated virginity examinations, must be viewed as new and unprecedented forms of coercion and control over women. Turkish feminists protested at these examinations in the 1980s and 1990s which were conducted mostly on young women in state institutions such as schools or factories when there was suspicion of sexual (immodest) behavior. Carried out by medical doctors and enforced by state agents such as police, principals, and prison guards, these examinations are expressions of new powers the modern state has arrogated for itself. They are fundamentally different from familial controls, even occasionally violent, over the honor and modesty of daughters and sisters. The use of rape, as reported in Turkey, Pakistan, and elsewhere, as part of the torture of political dissidents or intimidation of political rivals is another example of the current exploitation of the cultural ideals of modesty for political purposes in modern states.

The modesty of women, and especially the veiling that is the most visible symbol of it, have also been appropriated and manipulated by modern nation-states in the Muslim world in their bids to declare either their modernity or their cultural authenticity. Although the early twentieth-century debates about veiling in countries such as Egypt or the subsequent laws mandating the removal of the veil and the wearing of "Western" dress in countries such as Iran under Reza Shah illustrate the powerful symbolic value of women's modesty as a sign of national cultural backwardness, the most far-reaching deployment of the discourse of modesty has been that undertaken by the Islamic Republic of Iran under the Shīʿī clergy led by Ayatollah Khomeini in 1979. Immediately, as a sign of the Islamization of society, veiling and the strict separation of the sexes, which some feminist critics call gender apartheid, was imposed. Championed in the name of resistance to the sexual objectification of women associated with the West, and couched in the language of protecting women and respecting them, regulation of women's modesty has sometimes been enforced by self-appointed moral police and zealously promoted by some clerics who express anxiety about the sexual chaos that the free movement of women in public might ignite. Above all, the fact that the modesty and veiling of women have in this case been directly tied to the preservation of a national morality, and to the assertion of an Islamic cultural authenticity that legitimizes this nation-state, distinguishes the state-imposed modesty discourses from family-based ones or even those emerging from grassroots piety movements in nominally secular states.

Islamic prescription in the context of East and West

There are historical precedents for the association of gendered discourses of modesty with Islamic religious virtues, creating a tradition on which those in modern states such as the Islamic Republic of Iran can draw. Religious reformers who have sought to bring their societies into line with what they consider proper Islamic behavior guided by the Sharīʿa have often focused on the modesty of women. In their prescriptive treatises on proper religious, legal, and ethical behavior, Muslim scholars condemn the lax modesty practices of women of their times and assert the importance of restricting women's movements in public as a means to preserve the separation of the sexes. A distinguishing feature of twentieth-century treatises is that the modesty of Muslim women is implicitly or explicitly cast in relationship to the immodesty and immorality of Western or non-Muslim women.

A comparison of treatises on women from different historical periods reveals the shift in the religious signification of modesty. A good example of an early document is the mid-fourteenth-century Egyptian treatise *al-Madkhal* by Ibn al-Ḥājj, analyzed by medievalist scholar Huda Lutfi. This treatise, which criticizes popular social and religious practices of Cairenes of the time, returns again and again to the threats to the social order represented by women's violations of modesty ideals as they dress in their finery to go out in public, mingling with shopkeepers, Sufi adepts, and donkey drivers who take them to visit shrines; as they wear clothing that reveals their bodies and are careless about veiling; and even as they watch processions from behind screened windows.

Five and a half centuries later, at the turn of the twentieth century and on another continent, the Deobandi reformer Maulana Ashraf ʿAlī Thānawī's popular treatise on women called *Bihishti Zewar* (Heavenly ornaments) similarly condemns contemporary women's religious and cultural practices, but in his own region of what is now India. Within his didactic text, Thānawī urges women to be sober and modest, even while advocating, because of the colonial context and Hindu-Muslim rivalry, that they become literate and educated. Because his prescriptive text emphasizes the importance of women's education as part of their fulfillment of religious duties, however, the range of virtues encouraged in women encompasses much more than modesty. Where modesty is explicitly encouraged, as in the reporting of a *ḥadīth* to the effect that "modesty is intrinsic to faith and faith brings one to paradise," the moral commentary that follows warns: "You should never, however, be modest in regard to an act of religion. For example, women often do not perform the prayer during travel or during the days of a wedding. Such modesty is worse than immodesty" (Thānawī 1990, 214).

At the end of the twentieth century, conservative religious authorities such as Egypt's late Shaykh Muḥammad Mutawallī al-Shaʿrāwī, who could disseminate their views through television and pamphlets, articulated the dangers of sexual mixing and urged on women both domesticity and what had since the 1970s come to be referred to as Islamic or modest dress – full length clothing and a new form of veiling that involved either covering the hair or both hair and face, except the eyes. Running through Shaʿrāwī's promotion of a gendered Muslim morality is the negative foil of the West where women are treated as sex objects. To support his views, Shaʿrāwī even alleged that the well-known sex symbol Marilyn Monroe had expressed weariness at the limelight and wished that she had been a housewife (Stowasser 1987, 269). The stereotype of Western consumer society as a place where women are sexualized and exploited is common in Muslim discourses about women. This stereotyping took its most influential form in the revolutionary writings and speeches of the Iranian intellectual Ali Shariati who, in the 1970s, accused local Iranian elite women of being "painted dolls." He warned, in his *Fatima is Fatima*, that women were the weak link in the Western capitalist infiltration and exploitation of the Third World.

These examples show how prescriptive treatises have changed drastically in form and content, even while authoritatively referring to religious sources. The incorporation of modesty discourses into what might be called cultural nationalist arguments, or arguments about the distinction between Islamic society and the West, has given greater weight to calls for changes, often restrictive, in women's freedom of movement and in the conduct of their social lives. These treatises enunciate the dangers of the social chaos that might result or has resulted from failures to enforce women's conformity to ideals of modesty; the latest threat is considered the threat to the integrity of Muslim nations or the Muslim community.

Many Muslim women share these men's concerns about the integrity of their national or religious communities and have proudly embraced the ideals of modesty and the veiling that is associated with it. At the same time, the invigoration of modesty discourse through its bolstering by religious authorities has presented formidable challenges to feminist activists. Those activists who work for an end to punishments of women for sexual infractions, including rape, or who advocate gender equality, more public and professional roles for women, and the non-reduction of women to their sexual identities, find that these goals are not easily reconciled with discourses of women's modesty. Most disturbing is that these goals are now susceptible to delegitimization by being associated with the West.

Conclusion

Women's modesty is a fundamental component of gendered moral systems in many societies across the Muslim world. It has been analyzed using different approaches: tracing textual sources, noting social functions, interpreting cultural meanings, and exploring phenomenologically how it is experienced. Although modesty sometimes finds its authoritative religious justification in the Qurʾān and can be inspired by women's desires to be pious, it cannot in all its daily social practices be derived solely from religious texts. Linked in many societies to a cultural code of honor that determines the respect and reputation of families, it both pressures and motivates women. Such codes are found in non-Muslim as well as Muslim societies, most notably around the Mediterranean. The discourses of modesty have been transformed radically in the twentieth century as they have become integral to piety movements, appropriated and generalized by nationalist movements, and incorporated into modernizing reform movements, secular or Islamic. Some modern nation-states' enforcement through law and the police of women's modest behaviors, whether of sexual propriety and segregation or forms of dress, in the name of protecting public morality and the nation's health or asserting an Islamic identity in contradistinction to the West, has also fundamentally altered its significance as a moral system. It has also generated critiques by feminists within and outside these societies.

Bibliography

L. Abu-Lughod, *Veiled sentiments*, Berkeley 1986, updated with new preface 2000.
H. Afshar, *Islam and feminisms*, New York 1998.
P. Bourdieu, *Outline of a theory of practice*, trans. R. Nice, Cambridge 1977.
D. Kandiyoti, The end of empire. Islam, nationalism and women in Turkey, in D. Kandiyoti (ed.), *Women, Islam and the state*, Philadelphia 1991, 22–47.
H. Lutfi, Manners and customs of fourteenth-century Cairene women, in N. Keddie and B. Baron (eds.), *Women in Middle Eastern history*, New Haven, Conn. 1991, 99–121.
S. Mahmood, Feminist theory, embodiment, and the docile agent, in *Cultural Anthropology* 16 (2001), 202–36.
A. Meneley, *Tournaments of value*, Toronto 1996.
A. Najmabadi, Hazards of modernity and morality, in D. Kandiyoti (ed.), *Women, Islam and the State*, Philadelphia 1991, 48–76.
——, Unveiled bodies – veiled discourses, in *Feminist Studies* 19 (1993), 487–518.
A. Parla, The "honor" of the state, in *Feminist Studies* 27 (2001), 65–88.
Begum Rokeya, *Sultana's dream and selections from The secluded ones*, ed. and trans. R. Jahan, New York 1988.
B. F. Stowasser, Religious ideology, women, and the family. The Islamic paradigm, in B. F. Stowasser (ed.), *The Islamic impulse*, Washington, D.C. 1987, 262–96.
Maulana Ashraf ʿAli Thānawī, *Perfecting women. Maulana Ashraf ʿAli Thanawi's* Bihishti Zewar, trans. B. D. Metcalf, Berkeley 1990.

Lila Abu-Lughod

Central Asia and the Caucasus

"Men can do what they like, and so can Russian women, but not we Muslim women. We have to keep our legs and heads covered. It is a sin for us to expose them in the street. In the past, Muslim women veiled their faces but even today we cannot leave the house without permission and must not be alone with a man except our husbands, whom we must obey in all things." This statement from Tajikistan speaks to the way popular discourse shapes the construction of hierarchical differences between the sexes through the enforcement of female modesty practices.

Historically, details of expected behavior patterns differed considerably over this wide region. Prior to the Russian revolution, some communities, such as the Tatars, allowed women significant mobility, including access to education and jobs, while full seclusion was practiced in others, notably by the Sarts of the Ferghana Valley area, currently divided among Uzbekistan, Tajikistan, and Kyrgyzstan, with women wearing the all-covering cloak (*faranja* or *paranji*) and thick horsehair veil (*chachvon*) if they ventured outside. After the Russian conquest of Turkestan, some young women expressed a wish to be allowed to abandon seclusion, although those who actually did so were mostly lepers, prostitutes, and other social outcasts. The Tatar Jadidist movement and the young Bukharans spearheaded a movement toward modernization, especially of education and, to a certain extent, even of women's position. However, it took the Bolshevik attacks on Islamic traditions in the 1920s to produce real change, although for the following few decades some women continued to veil.

Eventually, Muslim communities adapted to the new situation by changing their definitions of female modesty practices to allow for coeducation and a mixed-sex workforce, thus permitting women to retain their respectability while wearing modern clothes and interacting with males in public. Nevertheless, many families, especially in rural Tajikistan, took their daughters out of school soon after the onset of puberty and never allowed their womenfolk to take a formal job. In Central Asia, a Sovietized form of traditional clothing, usually a dress worn over loose trousers and a small headscarf, came to symbolize modesty for Muslim women. In the most conservative areas, such as Khatlon province in Tajikistan, rural Gharmi women continued to be secluded and cover their faces with a white headscarf in the presence of strangers, right up to the outbreak of the civil war. Today the economic situation has forced them to abandon this. Many now shop in the market and some have even become the family breadwinners.

The struggle by Muslim peoples to retain their cultural identities within the Soviet Union was closely bound up with the construction of difference through gender identities, where female modesty played a major role. Today's endeavors by the newly independent states to devise legitimate national identities are similarly bound up in constructing ideals of national womanhood. Islamic modesty discourses play a significant role here, although the extent to which attempts are made to enforce them varies significantly, depending on social status, class, educational and income levels, and urban or rural residence. For instance, in Kyrgyzstan some young women have adapted their behavior as a response to such influences as soap operas, like *Santa Barbara* from the United States, and make great efforts to procure stylish Western garments. Although many young urban women in Uzbekistan and Tajikistan have begun doing the same, one can also see women there wearing *ḥijāb*.

In fact, Islam enjoins both men and women to observe modesty practices, by keeping their bodies discreetly covered and especially by behaving in such a way as to limit attraction between the sexes. Tajik males, however, rarely regulate their behavior according to such rules. On the contrary, in both urban and rural areas they frequently harass women in the street, often making it difficult for them to face leaving their homes without a male escort. They make particularly free with those wearing modern dress, thus pressuring women into assuming traditional garb. Both during the riots of 1990 and during the power struggles of 1992, young women wearing modern dress were assaulted and raped, supposedly as a way of enforcing Islamic practices. In Kyrgyzstan in the late 1990s, women whose behavior was judged incompatible with such practices were beaten (Handrahan 2001, 477). Since the end of the Soviet Union, similar incidents have occurred in other parts of this region.

Thus, contemporary Islamic discourses, in Central Asia and the Caucasus alike, support the female adoption of explicit practices of modesty expressed both in dress and demeanor. In the most conservative circles, the latter goes beyond promoting the roles of wife and mother to include encouraging women to retire from wage labor, thus allowing men greater access to economic resources in this difficult period. In general, modesty discourses contradict the legal equality expressed in national constitutions, appearing to aim at restoring traditional pre-revolutionary gender identities privileging male domination.

BIBLIOGRAPHY

F. Acar and A. Ayata (eds.), *Gender and identity construction. Women of Central Asia, the Caucasus and Turkey*, Leiden 2000.

L. Handrahan, Gender and ethnicity in the transitional democracy of Kyrgyzstan, in *Central Asian Survey* 20:4 (2001), 467–96.

C. Harris, Women of the sedentary population of Russian Turkestan through the eyes of Western travellers, in *Central Asian Survey* 15:1 (1996), 75–95.

——, Coping with daily life in post-Soviet Tajikistan. The Gharmi villages of Khatlon Province, in *Central Asian Survey* 17:4 (1998), 655–71.

——, *Control and subversion. Gender relations in Tajikistan*, London 2004.

M. Kamp, Unveiling Uzbek women. Liberation, representation, and discourse, 1906–1929, Ph.D. diss., University of Chicago 1998.

G. Massell, *The surrogate proletariat. Muslim women and revolutionary strategies in Soviet Central Asia 1919–1929*, Princeton, N.J. 1974.

N. Tohidi, The intersection of gender, ethnicity and Islam in Soviet and Post-Soviet Azerbaijan, in *Nationalities Papers* 25:1 (1997), 147–67.

M. Tokhtakhodjaeva and E. Turgumbekova, *The daughters of Amazons. Voices from Central Asia*, Lahore 1996.

COLETTE HARRIS

Iran and Afghanistan

In Afghanistan and Iran contemporary Muslim women live under restrictive civil/secular and Islamic Sharīʿa law that regulates their appearance. They struggle to define themselves, their social hierarchy, status, and modesty in economic, political, and religious spheres of influence when and where their appearance is regulated. The two countries share a geographic border and links to a Persian historical and linguistic past. There are seemingly many shared similarities as well as differences that circumscribe Muslim women's daily lives. Consequently, to be female, Muslim, and either Afghan or Iranian is an identity frequently visually essentialized by wearing head coverings (*ḥijāb*) and observing modesty (*ḥayāʾ*).

According to Muslim and non-Muslim scholars, the concept of *ḥijāb* generally in popular Islamic culture is understood in two specific forms. Often, *ḥijāb* is considered as an item of clothing worn as concealment by women as a religious obligation under Islam. More frequently, *ḥijāb* is regarded as various styles of head and/or body coverings adopted within and across cultures where Islam is practiced (Shirazi 2000, 115). However, historically the concept of *ḥijāb* is a much broader concept that refers to the act of covering and the covering practices of both Muslim men and women (El Guindi 1999). The concept of *ḥijāb*, then, is not only an item of dress that has evolved over time as a compulsory practice for Islamization policies but more specifically an item of dress that more often defines women as female.

Ḥayāʾ refers to the concept of modesty that governs both Muslim men's and women's dress (Daly 2000). *Ḥayāʾ* prescriptions vary according to religiosity and personal, social, and cultural contexts. Some of these prescriptions concern the degree of cover or exposure of the body; the area of the body covered; the proximity of the clothing in relation to the body; the opacity or transparency of textile qualities; the public or private nature of a social situation; the prayer versus non-prayer times of day; and the individuals present, their gender, familial relationship, nationality, and religion. An orthodox individual may adhere strictly to these prescriptions and wear a *ḥijāb*. In contrast, the state may impose the wearing of a specific style of *ḥijāb* and how it must be worn. In Iran since the early 1980s the Office of Guidance has imposed on women the compulsory *ḥijāb* (Shirazi 2000, 116). Similarly, during the 1990s under the rule of the Taliban in Afghanistan the most extreme *ḥijāb* restrictions were imposed on women by the Department of Vice and Virtue. Afghan women were denied their human rights based on how they covered or revealed their body when seen in a public social context; wearing or not wearing a head covering, the *chaadaree*, was not a choice (Skaine 2000).

Though many Muslim men and women regardless of culture or ethnic affiliation dress according to an enculturated understanding of *ḥayāʾ*, many Muslims may not actually be cognizant of this Arabic term and merely maintain that "we are dressing as proper Muslims out of respect for our religion and our families." In Islamic states such as Afghanistan and Iran, it is unclear whether modesty is a self-regulated concept or an institutionalized value that governs the modesty of (primarily) women (Nakanishi 1998).

Muslim women's head coverings are not the central focus of most discourses of their lives but in many instances head coverings are implicated in questions about their rights as citizens. Whether historical, religious, generational, political, or gender specific explanations are given, the preoccupation with women's *ḥijāb* and *ḥayāʾ* is more than ambivalence toward their meaning and use in daily and special occasion wear. They have become sites of compliance as well as resistance for women defining their lives.

Afghan women wear two different types of head coverings. Both may be considered *ḥijāb* and both are considered an expression of *ḥayāʾ*. For over a century, Afghan male politicians and religious clerics have debated the form, style, and other aesthetic, social, and moral dimensions of women's head coverings as well as women's rights. The most common are the *chaadar* and the *chaadaree* (Daly 1999). The *chaadar* is a two-dimensional, square or rectangular shaped garment, analogous to the Western notion of a scarf or shawl. Though the style of wearing varies, typically a *chaadar* covers the head including the hair, neck and shoulders of the wearer and protects these parts of the body from view. It is considered a partial head covering, scarf, or shawl worn as part of an ensemble. It is worn in both private and public contexts and it is subject to style variations and personal aesthetic preferences. In contrast, the *chaadaree* is a three dimensional vertically-paneled, seamed, and pleated garment that encompasses and encloses the entire body of the wearer, in order to obscure her from view. It is considered a "full veil" and is worn over a woman's entire ordinary clothing, including a *chaadar*. A rectangular area of open-work embroidery covers the eyes and provides limited vision for the wearer as well as minimal vision by the observer of the wearer. It is worn primarily in public contexts outside the home.

Since the turn of the twentieth century Iranian women's head covering practices and notions of modesty have likewise been regulated by Iranian men. However, proactive Iranian women have manipulated their head coverings to communicate acceptance as well as resistance to political and religious reform movements in Iran (Baker 1997). In Iran, both individual choice and collective consensus have existed simultaneously for decades. But similar to the Afghan women's *chaadar*, an Iranian woman wears "a large scarf that covers the hair, shoulders and neck," the *rusari*, and like the Afghan woman's *chaadaree*, the Iranian *rupush* is "a loose outer garment that flows down the knees and covers the arms" (Shirazi 2001, 1).

Bibliography

P. Baker, Politics of dress. The dress reform laws of 1920/30s Iran, in N. Lindisfarne-Tapper and B. Ingham (eds.), *Languages of dress in the Middle East*, Richmond, Surrey 1997, 178–92.

M. Daly, The paarda expression of hejaab among Afghan

women in a non-Muslim community, in L. B. Arthur (ed.), *Religion, dress and the body*, Oxford 1999, 147–62.
——, The Afghan woman's chaadaree. An evocative religious expression?, in L. B. Arthur (ed.), *Undressing religion. Commitment and conversion from a cross-cultural perspective*, Oxford 2000, 131–46.
F. El Guindi, *Veil. Modesty, privacy and resistance*, Oxford 1999.
N. Lindisfarne-Tapper and B. Ingham (eds.), *Languages of dress in the Middle East*, Richmond, Surrey 1997.
H. Nakanishi, Power, ideology, and women's consciousness in postrevolutionary Iran, in H. Bodman and N. Tohidi (eds.), *Women in Muslim societies*, Boulder, Colo. 1998, 83–100.
F. Shirazi, Islamic religion and women's dress code. The Islamic Republic of Iran, in L. B. Arthur, *Undressing religion. Commitment and conversion from a cross-cultural perspective*, Oxford 2000, 113–30.
——, *The veil unveiled. The hijab in modern culture*, Gainesville, Fla. 2001.
R. Skain, *The women of Afghanistan under the Taliban*, Jefferson, N.C. 2002.

MARY-CATHERINE DALY

The Ottoman Empire

Over the course of its history, the Ottoman Empire incorporated religiously and ethnically diverse populations that held varying beliefs about proper conduct between men and women. This entry focuses largely on official discourse regarding modesty as directed at elite Ottoman women in the fourteenth to the sixteenth centuries, with an emphasis on normative discourse regarding gender segregation and standards of dress. It also emphasizes how expectations of gendered behavior – especially the seclusion and veiling of women – differentially affected women according to status and class.

The Ottoman tribe was one of a number of nomadic pastoralist Turkish tribes that migrated from Central Asia into the lands of the ʿAbbāsid and Byzantine Empires beginning in the twelfth century. Central Asian Turkish tribes included women in positions of political and military power and maintained relatively egalitarian public roles for men and women compared to those in the imperial states of the Near East. Women's involvement in public activities persisted as Turkish tribes gained dominance in Anatolia. The Muslim traveler and chronicler Ibn Baṭṭūta, who visited Ottoman territory during the reign of Orhan I (ca. 1324–62), especially remarked on the fact that in general "among the Turks and the Tatars their wives enjoy a very high position."

As the Ottomans consolidated power in Anatolia and surrounding areas, however, Turkish culture gradually incorporated some of the gender patterns of the sedentary ʿAbbāsids and Byzantines, which emphasized exclusive male succession, and a male administration and military. An ethic that removed elite women from both positions of power and the public sphere gradually became so dominant that by the sixteenth century, women of the Ottoman court were strictly veiled and segregated in the closely guarded imperial harem. Gender segregation was also practiced by the *ʿulamāʾ*, though less formal segregation was the norm among lower status families.

Political discourse about modesty reinforced strict gender segregation as various officials and members of the *ʿulamāʾ* publicly objected to any involvement of royal women in political activities. Various scholars throughout Muslim history cited women's supposedly inferior intellectual or moral capacity as the basis for women's exclusion from politics, while others saw women's political activity as contrary to divine law. In 1599, for example, Mufti Ṣunʿ Allāh issued a written criticism of women's influence in the Ottoman court, claiming that such involvement was an abuse of Sharīʿa. To bolster his argument, Ṣunʿ Allāh drew on a popular *ḥadīth*, in which the Prophet Muḥammad proclaims, "A people who entrusts its affairs to a woman will never know prosperity." While Ṣunʿ Allāh's criticisms of politically active women may have been a play for power in the face of court women who were agitating against him, he was following a long tradition in which questions of female modesty served as a mechanism that kept royal women from becoming overly involved in politics and in general limited women's power. Indeed, Ṣunʿ Allāh's statement about the segregation of the genders echoes earlier pronouncements by religious officials such as the sixteenth-century Mufti Kemalpaşazade, and scholars such as Birgivi Mehmed Efendi (d. 1573) and Ibn al-Ḥajj, all of whom decried the involvement of royal women in politics.

The modesty discourse was directed at the power exercised by royal women, but official statements also called for the exclusion of all women from the public sphere. Ṣunʿ Allāh declared that no women should walk among men in the markets, claiming that such mixing of men and women was a harmful innovation and an abuse of Sharīʿa. Kemalpaşazade likened the socializing of unrelated men and women to cheating in the marketplace and selling alcohol, while the influential *ʿālim* Birgivi Mehmed Efendi devoted a significant portion of his work *Tarikat-ı Muhammediye* to arguments in favor of strict gender segregation as a means of establishing the ideal society.

For these officials and other elites, the control of

women was a metaphor for social order. During periods of rapid social and political change, as occurred in the late sixteenth-century Ottoman Empire, modesty discourse reflected a fear of those changes by focusing on threats to basic social categories (for example, male versus female) and moral norms (gender roles and conduct). A prominent idea among Islamic jurists was that when "proper" gender roles are reconstituted and strictly maintained, society becomes harmonious. As Ottoman historian Leslie Peirce has argued, placing restrictions on subordinate populations, such as women, is certainly an easy way for the government to assert authority in times of anxiety and change. Thus Ṣunʿ Allāh's criticism of the public and political activities of women can also be seen as an expression of concern for what he and others perceived to be an increasingly chaotic society.

The Ottoman government in general had a vested interest in dictating the place and appearance (type of clothing) permitted to women. Indeed, from the sixteenth until the twentieth century, the Ottoman state authorities regularly issued decrees (*firmans*) defining what women may or may not wear, sometimes describing allowable women's clothing in great detail. From the sixteenth to the twentieth century, the Divine Porte frequently issued *firman*s that specified the permissible color and thickness of a woman's coat (*ferece*), the material that could be used for lining a *ferece*, and the acceptable length of veils and scarves. The appearance of the female body was consistently an issue of imperial import.

It would of course be a mistake to assume that modesty discourse calling for restrictions on women's power and movement reflected the actual experiences of women themselves. Women did have the means to exercise influence in politics and society, thus provoking reactions from Mufti Ṣunʿ Allāh and others. For example, the Valide Sultan, the mother of the sultan, exercised a great deal of power over her son's various concubines within the harem, and often had considerable influence over her son's court and politics, especially after the reign of Süleyman the Magnificent (1520–66). Ottoman authorities often recognized that it was the normal role of the Valide Sultan to use political manipulations to assist her son in his ascension to the throne. Furthermore, when a sultan was too young or less than fully competent at the time of ascension (as happened six times during the first half of the seventeenth century), the Valide Sultan could act as virtual regent as long as necessary. Beyond the exercise of power, rules governing gender segregation were suspended under special circumstances, such as during royal pageants or when royal and elite women attended mosque teaching sessions and went to pray at tombs. Finally, seclusion practices became less strict for women past child-bearing age. Ebu's-suʿud Efendi (Abū al-Saʿūd), a jurist and mufti under Süleyman the Magnificent, declared that older women were free to join Friday mosque services from which young women were barred.

While some modesty discourse was directed at all women, most concerned elite women only, since they were the ones who followed the strictest modesty practices. In fact, segregation and veiling were signs of class, so that these practices became more stringent as one moved up the social ladder. Poorer women in both urban and rural settings regularly participated in public life, and were frequently involved in some economic enterprises. For example, agricultural labor among the rural poor required full participation of all able-bodied family members and women regularly worked in fields in the presence of men and without heavy veiling. Lower-class women also worked at certain jobs, such as spinning yarn or preparing dough. Low status women would provide services and goods to elite women sequestered in harems, performing such tasks as acquiring items, ferrying messages, and acting as midwives or entertainers. These poorer women served as a link between the elite women of the harem and the outside world, so that the ability to segregate upper-class women depended on the availability of poorer women who were relatively free to move in public space. Still, gender segregation and modest dress requirements did exist to some extent in the lower classes as well, since women were more restricted in their public activities than men. In periods of social turmoil, officials sometimes attempted to restrict further the public appearance of all women, but only with partial success. At almost all times, non-elite men and women interacted in the public sphere much more than did elite men and women.

In essence, notions of modesty in the Ottoman Empire of the Golden Age (sixteenth century) served not only to define gender roles, but were an idiom through which power and class distinctions were demarcated. The ability – or "luxury" – to segregate women was limited to the ruling and elite classes, so that economic advantage and political power were directly linked to the power to control women.

Bibliography

Primary Sources

Mehmet Birgivi Efendi, *Tarikat-ı Muhammediye*, trans. C. Yıldırım, Istanbul 1981.

O. Bon, *The sultan's seraglio. An intimate portrait of life at the Ottoman court*, trans. R. Withers, London 1996 (first published ca. 1650).
al-Bukhārī, *Ṣaḥīḥ*, N.p., 1378/1958–9, 4:376ff.
M. E. Düzdağ (ed.), *Seyhülislâm Ebusuud Efendi fetvaları ışığında 16. asır Türk hayatı*, Istanbul 1983.
Ibn Baṭṭūta, *The travels of Ibn Baṭṭūṭa, A.D. 1325–1354*, trans. with revisions and notes from the Arabic text edited by C. Defrémery and B. R. Sanguinetti, by H. A. R. Gibb, Cambridge 1962.
Şemseddin Ahmed Kemalpaşazade, *Fetava*, Süleymaniye Library, MS, Dar ul-Mesnevi 118.
Naṣīr al-Dīn Ṭūsī, *The Nasirean ethics*, trans. G. M. Wickens, London 1964.

SECONDARY SOURCES
L. Ahmed, *Women and gender in Islam. Historical roots of the modern debate*, New Haven, Conn. 1992.
M. A. Fay, Women and waqf. Property, power, and the domain of gender in eighteenth-century Egypt, in M. C. Zilfi (ed.), *Women in the Ottoman Empire. Middle Eastern women in the early modern era*, Leiden 1997, 28–47.
G. Goodwin, *The private world of Ottoman women*, London 1997.
H. İnalcık, *The Ottoman Empire. The classical age 1300–1600*, trans. C. Imber and N. Itzkowitz, London 1973.
G. Nashat and J. E. Tucker, *Women in the Middle East and North Africa. Restoring women to history*, Bloomington, Ind. 1999.
L. P. Peirce, *The imperial harem. Women and sovereignty in the Ottoman Empire*, New York 1993.
——, Seniority, sexuality, and social order. The vocabulary of gender in early modern Ottoman society, in M. C. Zilfi (ed.), *Women in the Ottoman Empire. Middle Eastern women in the early modern era*, Leiden 1997, 169–96.
N. Şeni, Fashion and women's clothing in the satirical press of Istanbul at the end of the 19th century, in Ş. Tekeli (ed.), *Women in modern Turkish* society, London 1995, 25–45.
S. J. Shaw, *History of the Ottoman Empire and modern Turkey*, i, *Empire of the Gazis*, Cambridge 1976.
J. E. Tucker, *Gender and Islamic history*, Washington, D.C. 1993.

KIM SHIVELY

South Asia

The material form of Muslim women's modesty in South Asia, appearance, is frequently defined and described politically with respect to powerful cultural Indian and Islamic influences on dress (Tarlo 1996). Though Muslim women living in Bangladesh, India, Kashmir, and Pakistan share a similar regional socioeconomic and geopolitical history their "Muslimness" is often juxtaposed with the Hindu religion, the predominant religion of India. Since the partition of India, Muslim women's identity in nationalist struggles of Bangladesh, Pakistan, and more recently in Kashmir has been a subtle social construction and personification of modesty.

Religion and gender in India are politicized in the public arena to differentiate Muslim and Hindu communities and their power (Shahida 1990). The politicization of Islam and Hinduism is an important issue that circumscribes traditional daily life practices in general and the lives of Muslim women in particular. Muslim women regardless of socioeconomic status and religiosity suffer dual minority status not only as members of the minority Muslim community but also as females who are relegated to minority status, as are other women in India regardless of religious orientation (Lateef 1998). Within this sociopolitical climate, for the purpose of solidarity there is pressure within the Muslim community for both men and women to conform to Islamic standards for gender, dress, modesty, and decorum. Simultaneously, there is also pressure from the Hindu community for minority Muslim women as females to adopt female Indian cultural codes of conduct, including an understanding of modesty and aesthetics.

Like Muslim women elsewhere, South Asian Muslim women's modesty can be understood and socially constructed through the concepts of *ḥijāb*, *ḥayāʾ*, and purdah. Regional, national, and ethnic variations exist cross-culturally but often local customs defer to the Islamic Middle East (El Guindi 1999). In addition, South Asian women's modesty parallels Persian and Afghan women's expressions and practices (Daly 1999). Typically, for Muslim men and women, *ḥijāb* is understood as the act or process of covering specific parts of the body. For women in particular, *ḥijāb* is also an actual covering that conceals varying degrees of the head, shoulders, and upper body. *Ḥijāb* practices are presumed to be governed primarily by the Islamic concept of modesty known as *ḥayāʾ*. Observant Muslims may choose to follow *ḥayāʾ* by wearing an actual garment such as a *ḥijāb* in a local or prescribed cultural regional manner like the Pakistani *dupatta* (head covering, long rectangular thin scarf). Purdah is a multi-dimensional concept of spatial and psychological gender separation that both Muslim and Hindu women may observe (Jeffery 1979, Papanek 1973). A family may designate an actual space within the confines of the domestic environment for purdah, or similar to *ḥijāb*, designate a covering that conceals the female wearer from potential male observers, especially unrelated males. Additional variations, interpretations, and subtleties of these three concepts exist throughout the South Asian subcontinent.

In contrast to Muslim women living in India, the identity of Bangladeshi women has been in part constructed and conflated with issues of nationality, ethnicity, and economics (Kabeer 1994, Hashmi 2000). Since the birth of Bangladesh in 1971, economic development, nationhood, Islamic identity, and gender relations have been intertwined (Siddiqi 1998). Though living in a predominantly Muslim state, women struggle with an increasingly politicized identity, which extends to their public identity in the work environment and their dress. Though "political Islam is conventionally associated with a highly visible code of conduct for women, especially in the realm of dress and comportment and in family relations, . . . the particular conditions under which Islamization has been sponsored by Bangladesh, by an impoverished state confronted with multiple sources of foreign aid and an increasing reliance on women's labor, have ensured that the state leaves untouched issues regarding women's deportment, dress, and working conditions" (Siddiqi 1998, 205–27). Having formerly lived among the Hindu majority in India, Bangladeshi women continue to observe Hindu practices of female seclusion or purdah to safeguard their honor. Bangladeshi women wear head coverings as a comparable and yet portable expression of seclusion while in public, which to a degree circumvents traditional Muslim and cultural customs of the region. Seemingly constrained Bangladeshi Muslim women have redefined former social practices such as purdah with contemporary interpretations of their social reality.

Similar to Indian and Bangladeshi Muslim women, Kashmiri women's identity and modesty continues to be politicized in the pursuit of state sovereignty. India and Pakistan vie for economic and political control of Kashmir and its people. Islamic influence in Kashmir is appreciated in the revival of the material culture and social customs that resonate with the Muslim experience of Afghans, Pakistanis, and Persians. Kashmiri Muslim women's modesty or *ḥayāʾ* as *ḥijāb* and purdah is visually, regionally, and traditionally expressed in the form of the Kashmiri shawl. Though Kashmiri shawls communicate a strong historic and aesthetic weaving and embroidery tradition, more recently the wearing of a shawl expresses religious and political sentiments.

Pakistani women participate in a range of formal and informal educational opportunities and consequently a range of visual appearances are present in private and public contexts. This reflects the varying individual and familial acknowledgment of socioeconomic and religious realities and their experiences. Since the partition of India, Pakistani women participate in the public sphere in demanding positions in political, educational, and economic spheres of influence. Never without their *dupattas*, Pakistani woman appear "unveiled and veiled" in all their permutations, side by side in major cities (Haeri 2002, 8). Haeri reports that "unlike Iranian women, Pakistani women are not mandated by the state to veil." They wear the modest yet beautifully color-coordinated two-piece suit, known as shalwar kameez, which is almost always accompanied by a *duppatta*. In Pakistan, women's attire combines modesty with beauty, while allowing for individual taste and financial resources to improvise upon it.

BIBLIOGRAPHY

H. Bodman and N. Tohidi (eds.), *Women in Muslim societies. Diversity within unity*, Boulder, Colo. 1998.

M. Daly, Pakistani dress, Paper presented at Ars Textrina, Madison, Wis. 1998.

F. El Guindi, *Veil. Modesty, privacy and resistance*, Oxford 1999.

C. F. El-Solh and J. Mabro (eds.), *Muslim women's choices. Religious belief and social reality*, Oxford 1994.

S. Haeri, *No shame for the sun. Lives of professional Pakistani women*, Syracuse, N.Y. 2002.

T. Hashmi, *Women and Islam in Bangladesh. Beyond subjection and tyranny*, New York 2000.

P. Jeffery, *Frogs in a well. Indian women in purdah*, London 1979.

N. Kabeer, Women's labour in the Bangladesh garment industry. Choice and constraints, in C. F. El-Solh and J. Mabro (eds.), *Muslim women's choices. Religious belief and social reality*, Oxford 1994, 164–83.

S. Lateef, Muslim women in India. A minority within a minority, in H. Bodman and N. Tohidi (eds.), *Women in Muslim societies. Diversity within unity*, Boulder, Colo. 1998, 251–73.

H. Papanek, Purdah. Separate worlds and symbolic shelter, in *Comparative Studies in Society and History* 15:3 (June 1973), 289–325.

L. Shahida, *Muslim women in India. Political and private realities*, New Delhi 1990.

D. Siddiqi, Taslima Nasreen and others. The contest over gender in Bangladesh, in H. Bodman and N. Tohidi (eds.), *Women in Muslim societies. Diversity within unity*, Boulder, Colo. 1998, 205–28.

E. Tarlo, *Clothing matters*, Chicago 1996.

MARY-CATHERINE DALY

Sub-Saharan Africa: Somali Society

Somali women's identity, their appearance in general and their modesty in particular, provides a common unifying cultural and religious focus in their life. In Somalia, women's identity is closely linked to patrilineal descent groups, clan, and lineage relationships as well as extended and nuclear family units rather to than a unified Somali national identity (Luling 2002, 223). In part this lack of national identity for both men and women may be attributed to Somalia's recent independence from the United Kingdom and Italy in the early 1960s (Abdullahi 2001). Subsequently, with the collapse of the Somali government, by the 1990s intra- and inter-clan fighting dominated and fragmented the country (Lewis 2002). As a result, many Somali men and women continue to live in disrupted and displaced families within Somalia as well as in diaspora resettlement communities throughout the world (Daly 2002).

Somali women's identity and appearance are closely linked to several Islamic concepts: *ḥayāʾ*, the Islamic concept of modesty and *ḥijāb*, Islamic head coverings and their practices. These concepts are prevalent in several distinctive Somali women's dress choices. Each choice emphasizes a slightly different idealized view of the world: cultural, Islamic, and Western orientations (Daly 2000).

"Somalis were among the first people to become converted to Islam, beginning in about the ninth century of the common era ... Islam is deeply embedded in their culture and is an essential part of their identity" (Luling 2002, 225). During the period prior to independence, geography and trade relationships delineated pastoral rural from urban life experiences of women. Women's dress reflected the indigenous materials available to them or those items acquired through trade (Akou 2001, Loughran et al. 1986). However, stereotypically, traditional Somali women's dress includes a *diric* (dress), *garbarsar* (head covering), and *masar* (scarf). Though one might presume that Somali women dressed modestly according to Islamic prescriptions for *ḥayāʾ* and *ḥijāb*, neither term was significantly used by Somalis until the civil war period of the 1990s. Consequently, Somalis did not distinguish between Somali cultural or Somali Muslim dress or modesty. Although they are Muslim, most Somali women have never worn the face veil (Luling 2002, 225), but do wear head coverings and scarves.

From independence in 1960 until the Djibouti Peace Conference of 2000, civil conflict between clans over scarce resources prevented a unified Somali national identity. Duing the civil war, Somalis witnessed the torture and killing of family members, friends, and others (Aman 1994). In response to these dire circumstances many Somali men and women invoked Islam in both the private and public arenas of life presumably to help solve the economic, political, and social problems of the country. Somali women may have intuitively chosen to dress more modestly to ensure their physical and psychological well-being (Daly 2001). Today, Somali women choose a style of dress that communicates their commitment to Islam and its meaning in everyday life to transcend the cultural politics of nationality. For women, this choice replaces the cultural *garbarsar* and *masar* with the Islamic *khimar* or *jilhabib*, both considered *ḥijāb* head coverings.

Though currently most Somali women would acknowledge that all forms of head coverings are potentially *ḥayāʾ* inspired and forms of *ḥijāb*, the *khimar* and *jilhabib* head covering styles in particular are more modest expressions of *ḥayāʾ* and Islamic wear (Daly 2002). In both Somalia and the diaspora, women report that they began wearing the *jilhabib* when civil war escalated and they fled Somalia to live in interim refugee camps. *Ḥayāʾ*, wearing *ḥijāb*, though ostensibly for religious reasons, also became a political statement. Some Somalis "feel that Islam is the solution to years of political chaos, and have consciously made adjustments to their behavior and dress in hopes of creating a new Somalia" (McGowan 1999, 208).

Like other Muslim women, Somali women's appearance and their modesty is not static but rather a dynamic amalgam of cultural, Islamic, and Western influences. A Somali woman dresses for the occasion emphasizing the personal, social, and cultural values that are appropriate. During weddings, though modesty is a consideration, cultural aesthetics dominate and traditional hand-woven fabrics are used. Throughout Ramadan special attention is given to more modest ensembles, and the most colorful outfits are brought out for the Eid celebrations. Western cut and sewn garments, such as skirts, blouses, dresses, and pants, though seemingly incongruent, do coordinate with *ḥayāʾ* and *ḥijāb* styles and are deemed modest.

Bibliography

M. Abdullahi, *Culture and customs of Somalia*, Westport, Conn. 2001.

H. Akou, Rethinking "fashion." The case of Somali women's dress in Minneapolis-St. Paul as an evaluation of Herbert Blumer's theory on fashion, M.A. thesis, University of Minneapolis 2001.

A. Aman, *Aman. The story of a Somali girl*, New York, N.Y. 1994.

M. Daly, Fouzia Mohamed (affidavit), Minneapolis, Minn. 2000.

——, Dress and legal issues of Somali refugees in Minnesota, paper presented at the Annual Meeting of the International Textile and Apparel Association, Kansas City, Mo. November 2001.

——, Somali, Muslim, American. Women's dress in a diaspora community, paper presented at the 45th Meeting of the African Studies Association, Washington, D.C. 2002.

I. Lewis, *A modern history of the Somali. Nation and state in the Horn of Africa*, Oxford 2002.

K. Loughran, L. Loughran, J. Johnson, and S. Samatar (eds.), *Somalia in word and image*, Washington, D.C. 1986.

V. Luling, The Somali of the Horn of Africa, in R. Hitchcock and J. Osborn (eds.), *Endangered peoples of Africa and the Middle East. Struggles to survive and thrive*, Westport, Conn. 2002, 219–34.
B. McGowan, *Muslims in the diaspora. The Somali communities of London and Toronto*, Toronto 1999.

MARY-CATHERINE DALY

Sub-Saharan Africa: West Africa

Modesty practices are closely related to regionally and historically variable, discursive constructions of propriety and of men and women as embodied sexual beings. Modesty discourses impinge upon and reflect women's and men's respective agentive capacities, capacities that are often class- and age-specific. Most local understandings of modesty refer to the idea that an individual should acquire certain emotional and cognitive capacities to be able spontaneously to distinguish between "shameful" and "decent" acts. Key terms, such as "shame," "restraint," and "patience" are rendered in local vernaculars that sometimes reveal an Arabic origin. Most understandings see modesty as an embodied capacity for self-restraint and control that can be visibly enacted and asserted as a virtue, and that simultaneously constitutes a way of practicing virtue.

Modesty standards, the ways they are defined and negotiated through locally variable notions of respect, honor, and shame, form part of a broader discursive system through which gender relations and other social hierarchies are defined. The latter, based primarily on age and rank difference, feed back into the constructions of moral personhood and reputation. Male modesty practices reveal a concern with the assertion of status among equals and within a hierarchical social order. Gender difference tends to be constructed as a matter of men's and women's differential need for protection. Women are seen as being essentially defined by their bodily constitution. This makes them more vulnerable to moral and physical assault, yet also turns them into a potential threat to the social and moral order associated with men.

Most of the (comparatively scarce) historical and ethnographic documentation on modesty discourses in Muslim West Africa deals with constructions of moral personhood that are related to Sufi orders (*ṭuruq*). In northern Nigeria and Senegal, modesty, as a capacity and an act of virtue, is especially valued in aristocratic women, particularly in the daughters, sisters, and wives of Sufi leaders. Practicing modesty augments the prestige these women enjoy on the basis of their genealogical descent and, occasionally, their scholarly erudition. The scholarly preoccupation with Sufi-based Islam in West Africa has sometimes led to the assumption that Sufi-related modesty practices are representative of constructions of moral and social difference in West African Muslim societies. There is, however, considerable historical and regional variation in the forms and social effects of modesty discourses. The discourses emerge at the shifting intersections between particular regional histories and broader, sometimes global, processes. Modesty practices are interrelated with kinship structures and with the ways these and other social institutions express regionally varying constructions of gender. Historical reconfigurations of modesty standards are often related to political economic transformations which affect women's opportunities for public intervention and their capacities to create themselves as "valuable persons" by means of income generating activities or gift exchange. Contemporary discursive constructions of modesty reveal traces of the changing intertwining of socioeconomic and gender inequalities in nineteenth-century polities and under colonial and postcolonial rule. They mirror the social standing of religious and political authorities who articulate particular readings of Islamic normative systems. The discourses thus expose different historical trajectories of the institutionalization of Islamic moral standards and of their intermingling with non-Islamic notions of propriety.

Late colonial rule witnessed the invigoration of debates on female virtue in many territories of West Africa. These debates revealed that earlier certainties about gender-specific divisions of labor and realms of political intervention were unsettled. Notions of female modesty gained a particular salience insofar as they defined, and were in turn shaped by, the domestic and public activities in which women could legitimately engage. Starting in the mid-1970s, in an atmosphere of widespread disillusionment with the promises of political independence, new debates on cultural authenticity and political autonomy emerged which focused on women's embodied propriety. Since then, female modesty has been of key significance in public controversies over the relationship between national and religious identities and over the normative foundations of the political community. Rather than reflecting a neat divide between secularist and so-called Islamist viewpoints, the controversies reveal an often fierce competition among protagonists of various Islamic viewpoints.

Current modesty discourses highlight ideals of female domesticity; they are closely related to the emergence of stricter dress conventions and practices of female seclusion. In the past, female domesticity occasionally served as a marker of high status (for example, among aristocratic families of the Sokoto Caliphate of Northern Nigeria and, after the 1940s, in Niger, Senegal, Guinea, and Mali among traders with business ties to the Arabic-speaking world). Starting in the 1980s, definitions of female modesty qua domesticity gained currency among broader segments of the urban population, in an economic situation in which lower-class women had to assume greater financial responsibility for the family. To husbands and fathers, keeping a woman at home indicates their ongoing capacity to provide for their family and to maintain control over women and juniors. Thus, the rejuvenation of discourses on female propriety can be understood in the light of recent transformations in domestic economies that are a consequence of neoliberal structural adjustment programs since the mid-1980s. The new ideal of female domesticity contrasts curiously with the significance that protagonists of an Islamic moral reform attribute to women's public appearance. In their view, women's public enactment of modesty is constitutive of the new moral order on which the political community should be based.

Several processes are at the origin of the seemingly contradictory tension between female domesticity as a status marker and the new emphasis on women's public enactment of Islamic virtue. Over the past 20 years, rank and economic differences among women have often been exacerbated, particularly in urban areas. Women of diverse socioeconomic standing reflect on and negotiate their differential capacities for moral self-realization by conveying their often conflicting views on propriety. The fact that women contribute substantively to the discursive construction of female modesty as the cornerstone of different moral and political communities also needs to be related to emergent forms of female mutual support groups, and to the spread of informal educational institutions and activities which often combine old and new paradigms of religious and secular knowledge acquisition. Finally, political liberalization in the late 1980s in some West African countries made possible the emergence of a plural civil society and the proliferation of media technologies which allow for a decentralized appropriation of media products. All these developments made women's public interventions more conceivable and feasible, but also threatened conventional views of women as guardians of family continuity.

The new stress on women's public enactment of propriety needs to be read in the light of this paradoxical development. Proponents of an Islamic revival identify female dress practices as a primary strategy for enacting virtue and for inviting others to follow their call for moral reform. The choice of decent attire entails a set of polysemic, publicly delivered statements about the relationship between political and personal subjectivity, and about the importance of individual virtue to the normative foundations of the political community. In this, current Islamic revivalist trends articulate through their modesty practices a particular vision of why and how the personal is political.

Bibliography

B. Cooper, *Marriage in Maradi. Gender and culture in a Hausa society in Niger, 1900–1989*, Portsmouth, N.H. 1997.

C. Coulon, Women, Islam, and *Baraka*, in D. Cruise O'Brien and C. Coulon (eds.), *Charisma and brotherhood in Africa*, Oxford 1988, 113–34.

E. Evers Rosander, Women and muridism in Senegal. The case of the Mam Diarra Bousso Daira in Mbacké, in K. Ask and M. Tjomsland (eds.), *Women and Islamization. Contemporary dimensions of discourse on gender relations*, Oxford 1998, 147–76.

B. B. Mack and J. Boyd, *One woman's jihad. Nana Asma'u, scholar and scribe*, Bloomington, Ind. 2000.

D. Schulz, Political factions, ideological fictions. The controversy over the reform of family law in democratic Mali, in *Islamic Law and Society* 10 (2003), 132–64.

Dorothea Schulz

Motherhood

Arab States

Mother (*umm*) and motherhood (*umūma*) are highly celebrated in Arab proverbs, poetry, folk-songs, fairy tales, and religious texts. These highlight the central role of the mother in raising children, managing the household, and producing and reproducing families, communities, and nations. They also highlight how mothers are to be loved, honored, and respected by their children. While rarely explored in any explicit way, various studies indicate some interesting variations based on age, gender, and social class in defining motherhood. Still, across all Arab societies, bearing and rearing children are central to notions of femininity and womanhood (Eickelman 1984, Inhorn 1994, Peteet 1997). From an early age, young girls are taught about the centrality of children in a woman's life and girls often actively participate in feeding and taking care of younger siblings. So important is motherhood that most studies take it for granted and rarely go beyond descriptive accounts of the roles of mothers in taking care of their families and children (Rugh 1997, Wikan 1996). Interestingly enough, studies of infertility and women's struggle to conceive a child teach us the most about the emotional value of motherhood and the powerful meanings that society invests in mothering. The equation between motherhood and femininity is clearly manifested in how a woman who cannot conceive and become a mother is viewed as *dhakar* or male (Inhorn 1994).

Bearing children is socially marked and celebrated in almost all Arab societies. A new mother is visited by neighbors and relatives and is usually given gifts (such as jewelry, money, and new clothes for her and the newborn). Special drinks and sweets are offered to the visitors. A new mother is also offered foods rich in protein and is helped by family members and neighbors in doing household chores. She is encouraged verbally and through some taboos (such as restrictions on her movement and leaving the home for up to 40 days after the delivery) to rest and sleep as much as possible. In many Arab countries, the new status of the mother and the importance of a male child are reflected in the custom of addressing a woman after the name of her first-born male child (for example Umm Aḥmad if the name of her first son is Aḥmad).

Unlike common negative images of the "stepmother" (*zawāj al-āb*) and mothers-in-law, many sociological and anthropological studies present a vivid view of the mother as selfless and totally devoted to her children. The strong emotional bonds between mother and child are often contrasted to the more formal relationship that exists between the father and his children. A mother not only nurtures and cares for her children on a daily basis but she also mediates the father's power and works to facilitate the fulfillment of her children's needs and desires when not fully approved by the father (Altorki 1986). She is especially seen as devoted to her male child, who is the source of power, social recognition, and stability in her life as a new wife and the source of emotional and financial support in old age (Rugh 1984, Rassam 1984, Joseph 1999). Studies also refer to the very strong relationship that binds a mother and her daughter and show how women feel sorry for a mother without a female child (Eickelman 1984, Joseph 1999). So strong is the bond between a woman and her children that many women endure difficult marriages and harsh living conditions to avoid the risk of separation from their children (Wikan 1996).

The role of the mother has been central to continuous attempts by governments and various groups to promote family planning, enhance child healthcare, build modern nations, and Islamize society, as well as to define the social, economic, and political rights of women. Many Muslim activists, for example, glorify motherhood and view it as key to a woman's existence and to the construction of the "true" Muslim *umma* (al-Mughni 1993, Sonbol 2003). They emphasize that it is a woman's moral duty to stay at home and raise her children properly. Motherhood becomes the main duty of a woman and must be cherished and embraced. Drawing on various traditions of the Prophet, such as, "Paradise is under the feet of mothers," these activists argue that motherhood is more valuable than any other job outside the home. Other groups see more room for women to work outside but always emphasize the priority of mothering over other activities. Some women's groups place greater value on working outside the home and downplay the role of motherhood. They tend to see women's liberation and empowerment as mainly linked to participation in public life and view motherhood as a tool that has often been used by different groups to restrict women to the domestic sphere.

Motherhood is closely linked with nationalism in various Arabic countries. This is especially true among native populations who fear being outnumbered by foreigners, like the Palestinians (in the context of their struggle for independence) or the Kuwaitis (given the presence of large numbers of foreign migrant workers and their families) (al-Mughni 1993). Accordingly, having children and raising them as Palestinian is seen as an essential part of the Palestinian national struggle. The *umm al-shāhid* (mother of the martyr) is a national Palestinian symbol (inside and outside the West Bank and the Gaza Strip) that is invested with great social and political value (Peteet 1997). She represents cherished notions of sacrifice, resistance, and steadfastness. Despite this strong link between motherhood and nationalism, however, most Arab countries do not grant citizenship to children born to local mothers and foreign fathers. This issue, the custody of children and their support after divorce, and the provision of more facilities which would allow women to combine work and motherhood are some of the key issues that most Arab countries are struggling with.

Bibliography

S. Altorki, *Women in Saudi Arabia. Ideology and behavior among the elite*, New York 1986.

N. Atiya, *Khul-Khaal. Five Egyptian women tell their stories*, Syracuse, N.Y. 1982.

C. Eickelman, *Women and community in Oman*, New York 1984.

M. C. Inhorn, *Quest for conception. Gender, infertility, and Egyptian medical traditions*, Philadelphia 1994.

S. Joseph, My son/myself, my mother/myself, in S. Joseph (ed.), *Intimate selving in Arab families. Gender, self, and identity*, Syracuse, N.Y. 1999, 174–90.

H. al-Mughni, *Women in Kuwait. The politics of gender*, London 1993.

J. Peteet, Icons and militants. Mothering in the danger zone, in *Signs. Journal of Women in Culture and Society* 23:1 (1997), 103–29.

A. Rassam, Towards a theoretical framework for women's studies, in UNESCO, *Social science research and women in the Arab world*, London 1984, 122–38.

A. Rugh, *Family in contemporary Egypt*, Cairo 1984.

——, *Within the circle. Parents and children in an Arab village*, New York 1997.

A. E. Sonbol, *Women of Jordan. Islam, labor, and the law*, Syracuse, N.Y. 2003.

U. Wikan, *Tomorrow, God willing. Self-made destinies in Cairo*, Chicago 1996.

Farha Ghannam

Australia

Introduction

Motherhood is an integral part of a woman's life, but it is culturally constructed (Bernard 1974). The experience of motherhood can be challenging when compounded with migration (Liamputtong and Naksook 2003). This entry discusses the influence of Afghan culture on the ways Afghan women experience motherhood. It also deals with the impact of migration on their mothering roles. It is based on in-depth interviews with Afghan women and participant observations in the Afghan community in Melbourne, Australia.

Afghans in Australia

According to the Australian Bureau of Statistics 2001 Census of Population and Housing, there are 11,296 Afghans living in Australia: 6,776 males and 4,520 females. The first wave of migration dates back to 1859 when Afghan immigrants arrived in Australia as cameleers. The Afghan camel trains provided transport to central Australia and supplied remote sheep and cattle stations as well as new gold mining communities (Wardak 1997). Throughout the history of camel driving in Australia, camel handlers were referred to as Afghans or Ghans. Over the next 40 years, more Afghans arrived in Australia. In the 1901 census, the Afghan population had increased to 394 from only 20 recorded in the 1871 Census. As a result of the Immigration Restriction Act 1901 as well as the introduction of modern transport, the Afghanistan-born community gradually declined (DIMIA 2003). The second wave took place in the 1980s as a result of the Soviet invasion of Afghanistan in 1979 (Wardak 1997, DIMIA 2003). Many Afghans sought refugee status as a result of the civil war in their country of origin. The third wave of immigration to Australia occurred as a result of the brutal Taliban regime from 1995 onwards. There was a decrease, however, in arrivals from Afghanistan due to the introduction of border legislation and the collapse of the Taliban regime. As a result, many Afghans arrived in Australia as illegal immigrants and were sent to detention centers around the country. According to the most recent statistics of the Department of Immigration and Multicultural and Indigenous Affairs (DIMIA), issued on 25 July 2000, the total number of "boat people" arriving in Australia between 1989 and 2000 was 8,289, of whom only 1,141 were Afghans. The Afghans who have arrived in Australia since late 1999 are largely of Hazara background, and came as a result of persecution by the Taliban. Also included are some anti-Taliban Pashtuns or members of other persecuted groups.

Gender roles within Afghan culture

The Afghan immigrants in Australia still strongly adhere to many Afghan traditions. Among these, kinship is the key facet of Afghan life. An Afghan kinship system stretches vertically from nuclear family to the nation as a whole. The system involves a genealogy of ancestry and the "blood aspect permeates the entire fabric, for even the blood feud is inherited" (Dupree 1973, 183). To some degree, the family determines the social rank, marriage partner, religious adherence, and personal standards and manners of its members (Wardak 1997).

Family life is at the core of the psychological well-being of the Afghan people. They tend to socialize exclusively with members of their extended family. Every decision is connected to the family. The typical Afghan family is multigenerational. The senior female supervises and delegates tasks to the other women in the household and directs all female activities (Hemming 1997). The extended family is not only the major social unit but also the major economic unit in society. The family guarantees security for both men and women from the time of birth to the time of death as individual, economic, social, and political rights are found within the family. Gender and age roles are expressed within the household and it is here that young boys and girls learn their place in the world (Hemming 1997).

For all Afghan immigrants, the family functions as the primary social institution. Afghan culture is patriarchal (authority remains in the hands of the elder males), patrilineal (inheritance is through the male line), and patrilocal (the female moves to her husband's place of residence upon marriage) (Dupree 1973, Wilber 1995). However, as Dupree (1973) asserts, "the idealized picture is greatly modified by certain elements which perpetuate matri-influences." As the centrality of the women's roles is pivotal to the well-being of the family, the selection of spouse is important. The preferred marriage for a man is to marry a daughter of his father's brother (Dupree 1973, 191, Wardak 1997). There is a strong matri-core in the Afghan community, which can be seen in intimate aunt-niece relationships and mother-in-law and daughter-in-law closeness (Dupree 1973). Although endogamous marriages are most prevalent among all groups within Afghanistan, inter-ethnic marriages have always occurred, and are increasing due to large populations settling outside the areas of their ancestors, including among those who are in Australia.

The primary obligation for women is to uphold family honor by conforming to the norms of accepted behaviors. Afghan society, with its strong belief in male superiority, gives men the prerogative to make all decisions and few challenge this (Dupree 1998). Afghan women typically have little formal power. However, informally, strength is shown in decision-making in the home and often in economic activities outside the home (Dupree 1973). The traditional conception of the male element is one of strength and the female element is one of weakness (Dziegiêl 1977).

Traditionally, Afghan communities distinguish between two worlds: the world of men and the world of women, which only come together in the home (Dziegiêl 1977). The world of the men is typically the external world, where work outside the home is undertaken. Women are confined to the internal world, dealing with household care and raising children. Traditional ideology favors the subordination of women by men (Dziegiêl 1977, Wilber 1995). This is still prevalent among those who are now living in Australia.

The upbringing of children up to the age of ten years is the domain of the mother who shapes and influences their personalities. This accounts for the high respect that is granted to mothers as well as the acceptance of a "matriarchy," following the death of the father. The widowed mother brings the family together, continuing to live in the household of her adult son (Dziegiêl 1977). The father is in charge of the discipline and punishment of the children. Boys stand in awe of their fathers and the relationship is one of respect and obedience. The mother raises the children from birth and has a strong bond with her children (Wilber 1995). The relationship between mother and daughter in Afghan culture is very close and is extremely warm and affectionate (Hemming 1997). It is the mother that children turn to for support, particularly as her interests are centered around the home (Wilber 1995).

Motherhood: women's voices

The influence of Afghan social structure is clearly mirrored in women's perceptions and lived experiences of being a mother.

The meaning of motherhood

Motherhood is associated with kindness and respect. The mother is responsible for the entire family and she endures many hardships to bring a child into this world. She is acknowledged for this on a daily basis. The virtue of motherhood is metaphorically compared with a "rare" or a "precious" entity.

Islam grants a very high status to motherhood. Hence, many Afghan women marry young, as their primary aim is to become a mother. Motherhood is perceived as the ultimate goal of every woman. The status of a mother is more respected than the status of a father because of the hardships childbirth brings. The high status of the mother is clearly expressed in the religious saying: "Heaven is under the feet of the mother." Motherhood is believed to grant the mother a high status in Heaven.

Islam asserts that parents, particularly mothers, are to be cared for in their old age and treated kindly. Traditionally, children will look after parents in old age. This is the time when mothers are repaid for all their hard work raising children. A mother must always feel that she controls the family and her children should do what she says, particularly in old age. Afghans prefer to have many children so that they will be secure and well taken care of in later life. They believe that more children, especially more sons, will carry the family name and their fathers' traditions.

The mother's responsibility is to raise her children in the best possible way. Religious guidance and moral codes are of utmost importance. Good mothers need to ensure the smooth running of the family and household matters. In addition to taking care of her children, a good mother should ensure that the family life is harmonious. Whether a woman is a good mother or not is usually judged by how the children turn out. However, under the Taliban regime in Afghanistan, some women were denied the opportunity to ensure that their children would be educated.

Living in a new country brings many changes in the women's lives as mothers, particularly their decision to have children. Shabnam, an Afghani immigrant to Australia said: "The way of living was different in Afghanistan than it is in Australia . . . I think that many Afghans are having fewer children. Bringing up children here is harder because their future is uncertain. Parents may fear that they won't be obeyed like they are in our country."

Being a migrant mother

Moving to a new homeland is a significant life change. Moving to another country as a mother is even more difficult. For many women, moving away from Afghanistan is the only option for them to raise their children. Despite difficulties, most women feel positive about being in Australia. They are grateful that their children have escaped from a war-torn country. In Australia, children are free to attend school and enjoy the social environments that Australia has to offer. Many women feel that being a migrant mother in Australia has motivated them to raise their children as good Muslims. They wish to be seen as a person who is a "good migrant." It is a challenge for them.

Many women arrive in Australia as refugees. Their past experiences impel them to see their children succeed. They tolerate hardship as long as they can bring up children to have a better life than theirs. Women anticipate the trials of the future. They fear that their children will want to disconnect from Afghan traditions and follow Australian ways. Many feel that being in Australia creates an extra pressure for them to succeed in raising their children.

Generally, women feel very satisfied with being migrant mothers. As refugees, some women were separated from their husbands and families as they had to escape their countries at different times. Because of this, being together with family is an important factor in their lives. Women realize how lucky their children are to be in Australia, in comparison to those still living in Afghanistan.

Women also hope that their children will become educated in religion and have good moral characters. Some hope that their children will escape the negative influences within Australian society. Women are concerned about the future of their daughters because girls are considered more vulnerable in Afghan culture. A man can always take care of himself but a daughter needs to be taken care of. A concern for many women is that their daughters find good husbands who will treat them well. Good moral character is an important aspect of Afghan culture, particularly for girls. If a young girl is of bad character, this is a reflection upon her mother and sometimes the entire family may be labeled as "bad" and disrespected. Therefore, mothers always try to bring their girls up in the best possible way.

In summary, mothers are held in the highest regard and are granted respect from children and society. Motherhood is thus the ultimate goal of Afghan women. Despite some differences between individual women, collectively, the trend is positive and the women share a view that their new lives in Australia are comparatively better and easier than for those who remain in Afghanistan.

Bibliography

J. Bernard, *The future of motherhood*, New York 1974.
DIMIA (Department of Immigration and Multicultural and Indigenous Affairs), Commonwealth of Australia,

2003, <http://www.immi.gov.au/statistics/infosummary/source.htm>.
L. Dupree, *Afghanistan*, Princeton, N.J. 1973.
N. H. Dupree, Afghan women under the Taliban, in W. Maley (ed.), *Fundamentalism reborn? Afghanistan and the Taliban*, London 1998, 145–66.
L. Dziegiêl, The situations of women in traditional Afghan communities, in *Ethnologia Polona* 3 (1977), 67–71.
R. Hassan, *Faithlines. Muslim conceptions of Islam and society*, Oxford 2002.
I. M. W. Hemming, Gender and Islam, purdah and power. The production and management of Afghan women's health and illness, Ph.D. diss., University of California, Los Angeles 1997.
I. A. Ibrahim, *A brief illustrated guide to understanding Islam*, Houston 1997, <http:// www.islam-guide.com/>.
P. Liamputtong and C. Naksook, Life as mothers in a new land. The experience of motherhood among Thai women in Australia, in *Health Care for Women International* 24 (2003), 650–68.
R. H. Magnus and E. Naby, *Afghanistan. Mullah, Marx, and mujahid*, Boulder, Colo. 2000.
M. Murad, *Islam in brief*, Riyadh 1998.
P. Wardak, *Afghan community profile. A snapshot of Afghans in Victoria*, Melbourne 1997.
D. Wilber, *Afghanistan. Its people, its society, its culture*, New Haven, Conn. 1995.

Pranee Liamputtong and Vicki Tsianakas

The Caucasus

In Caucasian cultures the cult of the mother, which is at the forefront of life, manifests itself at the linguistic level. Many words, such as land, water, and fire in the Vainakh, Daghestan, and Georgian languages begin with the word for "mother," as well as the words denoting sanctity in the Abkhazian language. In these cultures the traditional attitude toward the mother is combined with forms of Christianity and Islam.

Although there are nuclear families in the cities, the extended family predominates in the Caucasus. Islam allows polygyny in both religious and local law, and cases are observed in Azerbaijan, the Caucasian Republic, and Georgia (Pankisi Gorge, mountainous Achara, and Kvemo Kartli, inhabited by the Azeri population).

Female archetypes dictated that a woman's most important function was reproduction. Even today if a married woman does not produce a child, her husband, her relatives and those of her husband, and the woman herself regard it as a tragedy. Traditional ways of combating childlessness are widespread in the Caucasus, such as prayers, baths of holy water, and folk medicine, including sacrifice: *tushol* (Chechnya, Ingushia), *kobilkeri* (Daghestan), and *madimairam* (Ossetia) (Muzhukhov 1989, 52, Chesnov 1993, 60–1). Only after giving birth to a child and the multi-staged ritual of purification that follows is the woman a full member of society. She achieves status only as a mother and, as such, she perpetuates the postulates of patriarchy.

The mother perpetuates the child's gender roles as well. For example, among the Tsezs of Daghestan the boy is referred to as "wolf," "dog," and "lion," the girl as "swallow," "hen," and "bird" (Karpov 2001). In all cultures of the Caucasus the son is the "family defender," responsible for carrying on the status of his family and ancestors. The man's family views the woman as a temporary member, a guest of the family (Karapetian 1967, 40, Gajiev 1985, 110, Kochetova 1991, Smirnova 1968, 113).

In the Caucasian family the notion of fatherhood was often included in the mother's role as parent. The psychologists Nizharadze and Surmanadze call this phenomenon the strength of the "mother line" in the process of child raising. It is firmly established as a tradition. Today, in relation to family and especially to a child, the mother remains an influential figure. She can control the life of her child and she can exert pressure and influence the child's behavior and choice of friends (Surmanidze 1998, 10, Nizharadze 1999, 11).

In many cultures of the Caucasus, the cult of the mother is reflected in the existence of female goddesses: Mother Nature (Nana, symbol of fertility in Georgia, the goddess Ana Hit in Armenia), Mezuzahs (wood housewife in Adige), Jaja (goddess of agriculture), Anana (mother-creator) (Inalipa 1954, 224, Janashia 1960, 22), Tusholi (goddess of spring among the Vainakhs) (Shiling 1934, 107), and Mzekali (goddess of weather and the harvest in Georgia).

As Surmanidze points out, in the mother cult the idealized icon holds a powerful sway over reality. While the idealized icon of mother is far from reality, the mother is often judged by it. It does not leave room for real life development and adaptation, but if the mother does not behave in the stereotyped ways, if she goes beyond the icon's borders, she may incur the disapproval of society (Surmanidze 1998, 10).

However, Soviet policy introduced significant changes and undermined (but did not entirely destroy) many religious dogmas and cultural stereotypes. Despite the fact that the mother may have had an active professional life outside the house as doctor, teacher, or factory worker, her former obligations as the person responsible for domestic life remained paramount. This is the meaning of the woman's "double burden" and lies behind her need to be a "superwoman."

Indeed, for the majority of the population in the Caucasus, the family has continued to be the repository of what was left of tradition and culture. In the post-Soviet period of socioeconomic and political collapse, Caucasian woman have been better able to adapt to the new realities. In the face of great unemployment and pervasive poverty, mothers have the responsibility for children and family survival.

BIBLIOGRAPHY

B. Alimova, *Rites and rituals of childbirth, from the end of the nineteenth to the beginning of the twentieth centuries* [in Russian], Makhachkala 1981.
I. Chesnov, *Archetype of a stone in the Barkar-Karachaev tradition* [in Russian], St. Petersburg 1993.
S. Gajiev, *Family and marriage among the peoples of Daghestan, nineteenth to early twentieth centuries* [in Russian], Moscow 1985.
R. Gamzatov, *My Daghestan*, Makhachkala 1989.
S. Inal-ipa, *Outline of the history of marriage and family among the Abkhazians* [in Russian], Sukhumi 1954.
N. Janashia, *Articles on ethnography of Abkhazia* [in Russian], Sukhumi 1960.
G. O. Karapetian (ed.), *Armenian folklore* [in Russian], Moscow 1967.
U. Karpov, *Woman's place in the cultures of the peoples of the Caucasus* [in Russian], St. Petersburg 2001.
E. Kochetova and U. Karpov, Bringing up children in west Daghestan, in *The world of childhood in traditional cultures of the peoples of the USSR* [in Russian], part 1, Leningrad 1991, 122–40.
M. Muzhukhoev, *Medieval cult monuments in the Central Caucasus* [in Russian], Grozni 1989.
G. Nizharadze, Woman and conflict, in *Alternative to conflicts* (Tbilisi) [in Georgian] 3/4 (1999), 29–33.
E. Shiling, *Tusholi cult among the Ingushians* [in Russian], iv, Orjonikidze 1934^2.
I. Smirnova, *Bringing up a child in Adig. Past and present* [in Russian], viii, *Ethnography*, Maikop 1968.
L. Surmanidze, Georgian attitudes toward women, in *Current gender issues* (brochure) [in Georgian], Tbilisi 1998, 13–14.

FERIDE ZURIKASHVILI

Iran, Afghanistan, and South Asia

In this area, motherhood is at the very center of female identity, activity, and construction. "Paradise lies at the foot of the mother," a *ḥadīth* states. Motherhood brought status to females, and acceptance from parents-in-law. Newly married women were expected to have children as soon as possible. With the birth of her first child, especially if it was a son, a bride began her ascent from the lower end of family position. Her position generally continued to improve with the birth and growing up of more children. Motherhood could bring many rewards and resources. Girls desired motherhood as a mark of becoming an adult woman, and for the ability it gave them to enter into respected social relations. Despite this, motherhood and attitudes toward it were also fraught with danger and difficulty.

Until recent decades, motherhood began early. Parents and relatives arranged marriages for girls at relatively early ages. Even after governments raised the legal age of marriage for females, families found ways of ignoring age requirements. Having children was the main goal of marriage. Becoming a mother outside marriage constituted perhaps the greatest disaster which could befall a female and her family. In some places, an unmarried mother could face severe punishment or even death.

A woman's in-laws, her own parents, and the community expected her to produce a child as soon as possible after nine months of marriage. The mother-in-law watched carefully for signs of pregnancy. For the bride, these early months of marriage might be all the more stressful as she knew her continued position in the household rested on her ability to produce children. If she failed to become pregnant, suffered miscarriages, lost young children, or failed to produce males, she might well be divorced and sent home, or her husband might marry an additional wife. Few husbands tolerated remaining childless.

Because of early marriages, girls often bore children at early ages, which had serious medical consequences, including a relatively high maternal death rate, relatively low birth weight, and high infant mortality. After gestation and childbirth, nursing and caring for an infant also took a heavy toll on immature bodies. Becoming a mother, though necessary to join the community of adult women, also brought a lifetime of hard work caring for the household and children.

Until recent decades, women did not have access to birth control. In any case, husbands generally wanted large families. High child mortality rates also caused women to have many children in order to ensure that a good number would survive. Although hard on the body and health, and requiring a great deal of work, women's status generally rose as they had more children.

Brides and families valued male children far more than females, and for their own status and benefit, women hoped for boys. Young women were prone to feel terribly disappointed, and shamed, upon bearing a daughter. Although male children held authority over their mothers from an easrly age and might disobey and harass them, sons could also be a main source of defense and support for a mother. Because they often had little else as a means to gain power and influence, women catered to their sons.

Although mothers hoped for sons, they also welcomed daughters who, from a young age, could help their mothers. By the time a girl became a young teenager, she might be doing most of the household work. Mothers and daughters often remained close throughout the years.

A young woman was expected to focus her life on her children. Mothers shouldered the responsibilities of raising and training their children. If children did not turn out well, people tended to point to the mother, even suggesting that the children had taken in bad characteristics along with their mother's milk.

A young bride usually faced a mother-in-law who strategized to retain the affection and devotion of her son. Mothers often took a large part in choosing wives for their sons. It was generally assumed that they would look for submissive brides who would obey and work well for them.

Because of their close attachment to her children, women in unhappy or violent marriages were liable to feel trapped and unable to leave. Custody laws favored the father. If a woman remarried, her new husband would not be willing to support children from her previous marriage. Also, a mother would worry about leaving her children under the care of a stepmother. Children could thus become a chain binding mothers in an unhappy and restrictive marital situation.

Given this attachment, the death of a child could also bring down upon mothers the greatest tragedy and unbearable sorrow of loss. During the 1980–8 Iran-Iraq War and the 25 years of war in Afghanistan, mothers suffered terribly on behalf of children injured, frightened, living in privation, or killed. With the death of sons, widowed women, particularly in poverty ridden Afghanistan, lost their means of support and usually became extremely poor.

Although women were expected to bear children starting from nine months after the wedding and then continue to do so, upon reaching the period of life when her children had married, pregnancy often brought embarrassment to a mother because it testified to ongoing sexual relations, deemed unseemly for older females.

Until the last two or three decades, except in very well-off and modernized families, older widowed mothers lived with their children. Homes for the elderly did not exist.

In the 1950s and 1960s, beginning with the more upper-class modernized population – a larger proportion of the population in oil-rich and Westernizing Iran – constructions of motherhood began to change. With more female education, a later age of marriage, birth control, and middle- and upper-class women working in professional positions outside the home, the singular emphasis on marriage and motherhood for women began to weaken. In the period after the Iranian Revolution in 1979, ruling clerics again pressed for women's primary roles as wives and mothers in the home and encouraged high birth rates. However, in the 1990s and into the twenty-first century, the age of marriage and first birth began to rise and the birth rate began to decline drastically. Iranian girls sought education. More females attended universities than males. Even in rural areas, women began to postpone marriage and space and limit their pregnancies. With far fewer children, mothers and fathers began focusing on the emotional, social, educational, and psychological needs of each child. Constructions of mothers and motherhood began to evolve from that of the totally self-sacrificing devoted mother to one of companion and guide. Such changes took place far less often in the other countries of the area. In Afghanistan, in the poverty and disruption of 25 years of war, chaos, and political repression, most females could not attend school or work. Even in the post-Taliban era, conservative gender rules continue to restrict lives of women. This is true among the Afghans and Pakistani Pukhtuns particularly, and also among Muslims in Pakistan and India, although women here are not quite as severely restricted to home-bound roles of wife and mother. However, women who attend university and work outside the home still give priority to their responsibilities of home, husband, and children.

Elderly mothers in Afghanistan continue to live with their children. Nuclearization of the family and grandmothers living separately from their children is not frequent among Muslims in Pakistan and India. However, in Iran, for those widows who are in good enough health to care for themselves, changes are taking place. Although Iranians until recently believed that elderly parents should live with their children and take a central place in their lives, now many, perhaps even most, older widows who are able to care for themselves live in their own homes. The view of mother is changing from that of devoted mother and grandmother to that of rather independent mother and grandmother who decides on her geographical mobility, trips, pilgrimages, and visits. Sometimes these women feel cheated. They had been at the beck and call of a demanding mother-in-law, but now when they have reached the life stage at which they expect to reap the harvest of their acquiescence to a patriarchal system by gaining authority over daughters-in-law and a central position in the extended family, the world has been transformed. Educated and/or working daughters-in-law are not willing to live under the authority of a mother-in-law, sharing the attention and resources of their husbands with her. Most of the time, when mothers decline, their daughters or daughters-in-law care for them. However, both state run and private care facilities for the elderly now exist in Iran. In Afghanistan, Pakistan, and India such changes have taken place far less, if at all.

BIBLIOGRAPHY

S. Ali, *Madras on rainy days*, New York 2004.
V. Doubleday, *Three women of Herat*, Austin, Tex. 1988.
T. Durrani with W. and M. Hoffer, *My feudal lord*, London 1994.
Z. Eglar, *A Punjabi village in Pakistan*, New York 1960.
S. Farman-Farmaian with D. Munker, *Daughter of Persia. A woman's journey from her father's harem through the Islamic Revolution*, New York 1992.
E. Friedl, *Women of Deh Koh. Lives in an Iranian village*, New York 1991.
——, Sources of female power in Iran, in M. Afkhami and E. Friedl (eds.), *In the eye of the storm. Women in post-revolutionary Iran*, Syracuse, N.Y. 1994, 151–67.
B. Grima, *The performance of emotion among Paxtun women*, Austin, Tex. 1992.
S. Guppy, *The blindfold horse. Memories of a Persian childhood*, Boston 1988.
S. Haeri, *No shame for the sun. Lives of professional Pakistani women*, Syracuse, N.Y. 2002.
J. Howard, *Inside Iran. Women's lives*, Washington, D.C. 2002.
P. Jeffery, *Frogs in a well. Indian women in purdah*, London 1989.
M. Kousha, *Voices from Iran*, Syracuse, N.Y. 2002.
S. Lateef, *Muslim women in India. Political and private realities*, New Delhi 1990.
C. Lindholm, *Generosity and jealousy. The Swat Pukhtun of Northern Pakistan*, New York 1982.
N. Lindisfarne (Tapper), *Bartered brides. Politics, gender and marriage in an Afghan tribal society*, Cambridge 1991.
K. Mumtaz and F. Shaheed, *Women of Pakistan. Two steps forward one step back?* London 1987.
A. Nafisi, *Reading Lolita in Tehran*, New York 2003.
P. Omidian, *Aging and family in an Afghan refugee community. Transitions and transformation*, New York 1996.
A. Rauf, Rural women and the family. A study of a Punjabi village in Pakistan, in *Journal of Comparative Family Studies* 18 (1987), 403–15.
Å. Seierstad, *The bookseller of Kabul*, trans. I. Christophersen, London 2003.
A. M. Weiss, *Walls within walls. Life histories of working women in the old city of Lahore*, Boulder, Colo. 1992.

MARY ELAINE HEGLAND

Turkey

The nineteenth and twentieth centuries marked an era of profound change in Turkish society. During the transition from the Ottoman Empire to the Turkish Republic (mid-1800s–1920s), Istanbul experienced the first systematic decline in fertility and reorganization of family life, where gradually the Western ideal of the nuclear family displaced more traditional extended patriarchal family forms (Duben and Behar 1991). The twentieth century witnessed the spread of the nuclear family form to rural areas as well, though in practice the extended family persists as a powerful cultural ideal in both rural and urban areas (White 1994, 35). It is in this context that the social meaning of mothers and motherhood became a focal point for politicians and reformers and mothering came to be seen as an essential aspect of producing and reproducing national identity.

European preoccupation with the politics of population, fueled by the developing sciences of medicine, society, and demography, influenced Ottoman elites in the late nineteenth century and drove social policies created by Turkish national elites after independence in 1923 (Gürsöy 1996). Leaders of the new republic posed population as a key issue in building the nation-state. Linked in rhetoric and policy, early republican leaders promoted population expansion as a means to securing and maintaining state sovereignty and linked population policies directly to Turkish nationalism.

While these leaders worked to elevate the status of women through access to education, suffrage in 1934, and work outside the household (especially in "helping professions" such as nursing and education), they also wanted women to marry, have numerous children, and raise families. Reformers equated notions of biological motherhood with social motherhood in an effort to promote childbirth and "modern" childrearing practices. In the 1930s deputies to the Grand National Assembly (Turkey's parliamentary body) passed several laws to promote marriage and childbirth and declared abortion unlawful (Gürsöy 1996). The extent to which the laws were enforced and effective is questionable, yet these measures signified the importance of marriage, reproduction, and motherhood to the republican nation-building project and demonstrated the intensification of political interest in the everyday social lives of women.

Reformist discourses on motherhood and family in the early republic (1920s–1940s) idealized the fecundity and strength of the Anatolian village mother, promising monetary assistance and tax breaks to women bearing many children. Strong, fertile, and stalwart, Anatolian village mothers were portrayed as true patriots. This idealization coincided with a contradictory impulse to root out aspects of Anatolian culture that were regarded as unhealthy or backward. Educators, social workers, and doctors stressed the need to eliminate many childrearing practices, including swaddling babies, superstition-based customs for protecting children from harm, and beliefs that prevented women from accepting Western biomedical models for childbirth and childrearing. Other elite discourses focused on urban, educated women who married later, practiced birth control or had abortions, challenging their commitment to the call to motherhood in the name of national strength.

Women's associations helped to shape and spread early republican discourses on motherhood and nationhood. Associations such as the Anneler Birliği (Mothers' union) in the 1930s took up philanthropic and educational initiatives, advancing a reformist project that reflected urban, elite social values. Other associations, such as the Women's Union (disbanded by the state in 1935), advanced platforms that promoted women's rights within the family and society as well as broader social justice issues such as peace.

Legal reforms in the 1920s and 1930s offered new rights for women, yet reinforced patriarchal power structures within family and broader kin groups (Kandiyoti 1988). Recent amendments to the constitution and Civil Code (2001–2) have formally introduced equality of men and women within the family. The well-known phrase "The family is the foundation of Turkish society" is now amended with the phrase "and is based on the equality of the spouses." The Civil Code in its first major modifications since the adoption of the Swiss Civil Code in 1926 now recognizes the equality of spouses within the family, has removed the designation of the husband as "head of household," and acknowledges inheritance rights of children born out of wedlock and, importantly, rights to equal shares of property acquired after marriage to all those who married after the law came into effect.

In contemporary Turkish society motherhood remains a dominant cultural ideal and notions of womanhood and femininity are still largely constructed through becoming a wife and mother. Marriage continues to be widely considered biologically and socially necessary – an obligation to one's family and society (White 1994, 41) – especially among rural and working-class women.

In recent decades, despite formal gains made in laws and policies related to women's position within the family and society, the work of parenting remains almost the exclusive province of women (Arat 1996, 30). We cannot assume, however, that this means that mothering takes place exclusively within the nuclear family. Despite the fact that the majority of families in Turkey are nuclear in structure today, the extended family still persists functionally (White 1994, 35, Abadan-Unat 1986, 186). Erel notes that assuming the mother is the primary caregiver is a class-specific, ethnocentric construction, especially if one considers that in rural Turkey women and children participate in agricultural work and child-rearing is the collective labor of mothers, older siblings, aunts, and grandmothers. Erel also points out that in urban areas "housework and childcare often take place in a wider social context of extended-family members and neighbours" (2002, 133; see also EWIC II Household Division of Labor: Turkey and the Caucasus).

Erel's work among Turkish migrant families in Germany points to the need for comprehensive new research on changing forms and ideals of motherhood and family both in Turkey and in diasporic communities (especially in Europe). How does greater integration into Europe shape notions of motherhood? As families temporarily and permanently divide through migration from Turkey to other parts of Europe, how are extended family networks functionally and ideologically maintained? To what extent is the social space for women as subjects outside of motherhood opening up (both within Turkey and Europe)? What new discourses on family, family values, and the meaning of mothers as carriers of the national culture are emerging? And, perhaps most profoundly, what are the long-term effects of a decade of growing poverty rates in Turkey and a weak social safety net on the everyday lives of women and their children? How do economic realities coincide with the social valuation of motherhood and the need for broader systems of familial support for childcare and rearing? These questions call for a renewed focus on the family and constraints facing women in particular in coming years.

Bibliography

N. Abadan-Unat, Social change and Turkish women, in N. Abadan-Unat (ed.), *Women in Turkish society*, Leiden 1981, 5–31.

Y. Arat, On gender and citizenship in Turkey, in *Middle East Report* (January–March 1996), 28–31.

C. Delaney, *The seed and the soil. Gender and cosmology in Turkish village society*, Berkeley 1991.

——, Father state, motherland, and the birth of modern Turkey, in S. Yanagisako and C. Delaney (eds.), *Naturalizing power. Essays in feminist cultural analysis*, London 1995, 201–36.

A. Duben and C. Behar, *Istanbul households. Marriage, family and fertility, 1880–1940*, Cambridge 1991.

U. Erel, Reconceptualizing motherhood. Experiences of migrant women from Turkey living in Germany, in D. Bryceson and U. Vuorela (eds.), *The transnational*

family. New European frontiers and networks, New York 2002, 127–46.
N. Göle, *The forbidden modern. Civilization and veiling*, Ann Arbor 1996.
A. Gürsöy, Abortion in Turkey. A matter of state, family or individual decision, in *Social Science Medicine* 42:2 (1996), 531–42.
D. Kandiyoti, Bargaining with patriarchy, gender and society, in *Feminist Studies* 2:3 (1988), 274–90.
Z. Toprak, The family, feminism, and the state during the Young Turk period, 1908–1918, in E. Eldem (ed.), *Première rencontre internationale sur l'Empire ottoman et la Turquie moderne*, Istanbul 1990, 441–52.
J. B. White, *Money makes us relatives. Women's labor in urban Turkey*, Austin, Tex. 1994.

KATHRYN LIBAL

Nation, Women, and Gender

Overview

In many respects, the study of gender and nationalism in Islamic societies is in its early phase. At the same time, our knowledge about women's experiences in nationalist movements has expanded considerably in the last two decades thanks to micro-level studies conducted by historians and social scientists. With this in mind, the goal of this overview, rather than summarizing an abundance of findings and conclusions, is to point at a major watershed in the study of gender and nation. What is emphasized here, then, is the current methodological shift from questions associated with women's emancipation and political agency to explorations of nations as fundamentally gendered constructs. This conceptual development is a result of recent paradigmatic shifts occurring in both fields of gender studies and the study of nationalism.

Nation and emancipation: fulfilled and unfulfilled promises

Most of the research on the subject of women and nations in Islamic societies has been dedicated to the issues of legal rights and political or cultural emancipation. To be sure, feminist ambitions were part and parcel of nationalist agendas since the earliest manifestations of nationalism in Islamic countries. For many Muslim women in the late nineteenth and early twentieth centuries, participation in nationalist activity offered new channels to the public space. Contrary to the traditional view of Muslim women as utterly confined to the domestic sphere and consequently alienated from everything public or political, women's social agency in public spaces had been exhibited long before nationalism. Women exercised political influence through social networks in imperial courts and households, by applying to judicial courts, and in numerous other forms of daily interaction, not always documented. Nevertheless, one of the new elements introduced by nationalism, which seemed promising at the time in terms of female emancipation, was the factor of mass politics. This was made possible by the press and some new mechanisms of political grouping. For the first time women resorted to nationalist idioms to promote feminist agendas through the press in Egypt, Iran, and the Ottoman Empire of the late nineteenth century, and similarly in Central Asia (especially Tatar women) in early twentieth century. In the first quarter of the twentieth century, the era of mass politics was also marked by the new phenomenon of large-scale demonstrations, wherein women from all social strata took an active part in anti-colonial activities, as was the case in Iran, Egypt, and some of the Ottoman domains.

The early marriage between nation formation and discourses of female liberation was evident throughout the Islamic world. Algeria is a symptomatic case in point. After independence, Algerian female liberating discourse had recourse to women's share in the national struggle. The nation-emancipation linkage was even more conspicuous in the last years of the Ottoman Empire. Subsequent to the 1908 revolution, as soon as women entered the arena of political activism, their claims for rights were expressed in patriotic terms, a trend that was to be continued in the republican period. Female emancipation was a component of nationalist discourses also in Afghanistan, under King Amān Allāh and in Iran under Reza Shah, which looked at the Young Turks, and later Mustafa Kemal's regime, as models to be followed. Correspondingly, the need to liberate women in Central Asian society, embedded in a nationalist discourse, was an integral part of the ideology of Jadidism (the movement for cultural reform in Central Asia at the turn of the twentieth century).

In most of the Islamic countries, the involvement of women in the nationalist discourse suggested a new era of female political and cultural agency. However, more often than not, the post-independence phase marked a setback for feminist movements. The Turkish liberation movement was the only case in which women made their way into the leading core of the nationalist movement (Halide Edib is a salient example), while the general rule for other nationalist movements was that the Woman Question should be postponed until after independence.

It is often argued that throughout the twentieth century women realized that the formulation of "first nation then emancipation" was not to be fulfilled soon. According to the same common wisdom, women participated in nationalist movements with the supposition that the realization of the national goals would bring about their liberation (Fleischmann 1999, 115). Hence, as the promise of emancipation fell short of expectations after independence (Algeria is the most suggestive illustration in this regard), scholars and feminist activists have represented the nation-emancipation linkage as some sort of infringed contract. However, such a "utilitarian" depiction of women's involvement in nationalist struggles, as if it were motivated mainly by feminist aspirations, is somewhat teleological and superficial. It fails to take into account the contingencies of wars and war movements, which are rarely related to any consideration of what will happen after the war ends (Lazreg 1994, 119). Additionally, such a depiction perpetuates the false image of anti-colonial struggles as a masculine affair with women playing only a marginal role, and implies that as far as the nationalist struggle is concerned, women's motivations essentially differed from those of men.

The case of the Palestinian nationalist movement is of particular interest given that it is probably the only ongoing anti-colonial struggle in the Islamic world. The nation-emancipation linkage did not exist in Palestinian nationalist discourse until well into the 1970s, when women joined military operations. Women's partaking in informal communal politics was legitimized by the Palestinian national movement, but the absence of any challenge to patriarchal structures turned aside the emergence of feminist consciousness (Joseph 2000, 37).

"All nationalisms are gendered": from women's agency to gendered nations

Gender as a category of analysis has been absent from the mainstream theorizing about nations and nationalism. This enduring academic oblivion has been explained as an outcome of the male-biased nature of the classical theories of politics (Yuval-Davis 1997, 2). Yet, the dramatic emergence of cultural studies in recent years has inspired a new set of theoretical questions concerning both gender and nationalism. In both fields, foundational concepts have been problematized and deconstructed, and the validity of disciplinary boundaries and definitions has been challenged. While most of the earlier studies of nationalism stressed political and social processes by employing methods from the social sciences, there is a growing contemporary tendency to apply analytic tools developed in poststructuralist and cultural theory, discourse analysis in particular, and explore nationalism as a culturally-constructed phenomenon. By the same token, in the field of gender studies the basic category of "women" as a unitary, homogeneous concept has proven to be methodically misleading together with a series of dichotomies that had previously been taken for granted, including that of male/female. Moreover, it has become evident that if one wants to comprehend social and cultural complexities, one has to ask how gender relations shaped social arrangements and discourses in the most constitutive senses (along with class, ethnicity, and other categories). These conceptual developments are bringing forth what seems to be a major shift in the study of gender and nations, namely, moving from reconstructing women's political position on to looking at nations as historically gendered entities.

The notion that "all nations are gendered," coined by Ann McClintock, has been substantiated since the early 1980s in a good number of studies on gender and nations in various contexts. Nevertheless, as far as Islamic countries are concerned, gender as a critical category of analysis referring to both maleness and femaleness is still missing from most mainstream discussions on nationalism. At best, it is habitually "added" to monographs or anthologies together with other "marginal" social forces (such as minority groups) by way of a standardized lip service, required by the growing appeal of gender studies in the West. Moreover, most of the research about nationalism and women treats the former as a political movement rather than seeing it also as a cultural or discursive project in which ideals of womanhood and manhood, deeply invested in modernist visions, were key elements (Abu-Lughod 1998, 17). While applying the terms "women" and "gender" interchangeably and narrowing the issue of gender to questions of women's rights and political activism, students of nationalism in the Islamic world are, generally speaking, still blind to the significant role of gendered metaphors, constructions of maleness and femaleness, and gender-based discourses in processes of nation formation.

Investigation of nations as culturally-gendered constructs is a new enterprise in the study of Islamic cultures. Most of the questions associated with gender and nation are thus still to be addressed. However, the available research does allow us to presume that in most if not all contexts the gendered nature of nationalism is deeply intertwined with discourses of modernity. There may be little doubt that the production of the woman of modernity, with its various implications, complicates the simple statements about the emancipatory project of modernity (Najmabadi 1998a, 183).

Partha Chatterjee's well-known depiction of Bengali highly gendered anti-colonial discourse appears to be relevant to nationalist formulations in many Islamic cultures. According to Chatterjee, the Bengalis structured a cosmology of modernity and nation intended to sustain the anti-colonial struggle. In this world-view, the Bengalis aspired to become identical to the British colonizer in an outer material domain but preserve difference in an inner spiritual domain as a means of resistance. Middle-class women had a significant role in this formulation of the national project by being the hallmark of the internal spiritual domain, untouched by and protected from the political field within the colonial state. The home was imagined as the realm of the spiritual and accordingly feminine and traditional, in which the "'true identity" existed, whereas the outside world was imagined as material and masculine. Moreover, the idea of the "new woman" was invented and then indoctrinated as a means of formulating an authentic modernity. The new woman was contrasted with modern Western society but at the same time she was distinguished from the "old," namely, traditional woman. Tradition, then, played two conflicting roles in the Bengali nationalist construct: it was a positive marker of the cultural essence but it was also the negative reverse of modernity and thus should be left behind (Chatterjee 1993).

In spite of diverse trajectories of postcolonial states, and running the risk of reductionism, similar imaginations of nationalism are evident in Islamic countries that experienced colonial encounters. In Algeria, for one, the family was represented as a sanctuary of "authentic" values, and the woman as the guardian of traditional values vis-à-vis colonial influences. Akin to the Bengali case, an Algerian convention of the "new woman" emerged as a direct opposite to the one of the "traditional woman," serving as a banner of Algerian anti-colonial nationalism and fueled by the ethos of the heroine *mujāhidāt* (female liberation warriors) (Cherifati-Merabtine 1994). Azerbaijan provides another illustration for the convention of women as repositories of tradition and national identity in the context of confronting colonial domination. Unable to resist Russian cultural domination, the private domain was perceived as the ultimate fortress of identity. In order to avoid the negative label of "Russified," women were assigned the role of bearing "the ethno-nationalist load" (Tohidi 1996). Pakistan may provide an additional case in point, especially with regard to women's education at the turn of the twentieth century, when the confinement of women's education to household chores and religious teaching was perceived as Muslim cultural resistance against colonialism and Hinduism (Jalal 1991, 81). The idea of the family as the bastion of the nation was evident also in Central Asia (Khalid 1998, 226). These illustrations clearly reflect the ambivalence embodied in the notion of the "new woman" in the context of nationalism, a convention symbolizing tradition and its negation at the same time.

In some of the states that did not experience a direct colonial confrontation, however, the idea of modernity as an acute break with the past was promoted by the state more aggressively than in others and lacked the cultivation of the notion of tradition-as-authentic. Such was the case of Kemalist Turkey, which turned its back on the Ottoman past on the grounds of its "traditional" nature. As illustrated by Kandiyoti, the cultural elite, collaborating with the state, promoted a cultural refashioning of not only new idealized femininity but also modernized masculinity. Hence, reformers and novelists represented the Ottoman father and husband as an authoritarian figure who displayed little feeling for his family, while expecting the ideal "new man" of the Turkish nation to be emotionally close to his family and directly involved with his children (Kandiyoti 1998, 281). A comparable project of promoting new wives and mothers for the sake of the nation in accordance with the new totem of modernity occurred also in Iran of the last decades of the nineteenth century and the early decades of the twentieth century, when women were assigned the role of producing the new citizens of the nation (Najmabadi 1998b).

The convention of women as the prosopopeia of the national spirit and honor, associated above all with their marital role while seeing the nation as an extended family, is one of the most profound features of nationalist discourses around the globe. Just as universal is the idealization of masculinity as the foundation of the nation and society, to use Mosse's phraseology (Mosse 1985, 16). This role assigned to the "women of the homeland," highly regarded as it has been, has often been in conflict with interests of women (Yuval-Davis 1997, 67). Family honor has been employed as a means of fortifying patriarchal power by way of controlling female behavior and sexuality. This social trend was not eased by the appearance of nationalism but rather was reinforced and re-presented, now through nationalist idioms. The latter supported the male homosocial nature of nationalist discourses in a way that prevented any significant emancipation after national independence. Egypt at the turn of the twentieth century provides a typical case in point. Popular notions about family honor and female sexual purity were elevated to a national ideal and brought about the construction of a concept of national honor. This development did not imply an invitation to women to take part in the national game. On the contrary, it perpetuated their absence from it as bona fide actors and full partners by reducing their roles to subjects and symbols of a nationalist consciousness monopolized by men (Baron 1993). Hence, in spite of the promise embedded in the mass politics of nationalism to incorporate all members of the nation, male or female, the gendered nature of nationalism actually worked against the inclusion of women. While in many instances early Muslim reformers made efforts to emphasize the inclusiveness of the nation to non-Muslim members of the national community, women were located through the familial metaphor not within the inclusive brotherhood of all men, but as auxiliary to the national fraternity as wives, mothers, or daughters.

According to the conventional modernist narrative, women's progress could be achieved only through state-led modernization and secularization. This founding concept, exhibited in Turkey under Mustafa Kemal and in Iran under Reza Shah, meant that women who were unwilling to come to the public on the state's terms were excluded from the political field of the nation. In fact, some recent versions of the Islamist agenda, well rooted in modernist and nationalist discourses, have meant new options of inclusion for many women. In Iran female illiteracy has been eradicated, in Turkey the growing challenge of the Islamist movement made it possible for religious women to step into the political field on their own terms, and in occupied Palestine the Hamas movement has enabled women to participate in the struggle for liberation and even to acquire the prestigious status of *shāhida* (martyr), a category formerly reserved only for men.

Some of the recent studies on gender and nation in Islamic countries, which treat the nation as a culturally gendered construct, have stressed the male-oppressive nature of the nationalist (and modernist) discourse. This tendency may be partly explained by the critical approach of cultural studies toward the "project of modernity" and partly by historians' awareness that female emancipation is still an unfinished business in most parts of the Islamic world. Nevertheless, the emancipatory potential of nationalist discourses should not be downgraded. Although patronizing and limiting in many ways, it was the modernist visions of Iranian, Turkish, and Central Asian nationalisms under Reza Shah, Mustafa Kemal, and Jadidism respectively that provided for the first time the opportunity for millions of women to enter public spaces on a large scale by virtue of their position as "mothers of the nation." Hence, the cultural refashioning of women's position in Islamic societies in the framework of nationalism was neither totally oppressive nor entirely emancipatory. The "modern educational regimes, deeply gendered from the start" set in motion both emancipatory and disciplinary trends. The former made it possible for women to enjoy a moment of freedom and sharing public spaces with men while the latter contained regulatory practices and concepts that set boundaries to women's participation in public life (Najmabadi 1998b).

In the final analysis, it is important to bear in mind that crucial as they were, the early moments of nationalism in the Islamic world were far from being the last word on the meanings of maleness and femaleness in the never-ending process of inventing the nation. Visions of nation and gender, highly allied from the start, have been constantly negotiated between women and men, governments and citizens. Gendered concepts of nations have been time and again modified to adapt to changing realities and concepts in numerous and conflicting fashions that are still waiting to be studied.

Bibliography

L. Abu-Lughod, Feminist longings and postcolonial conditions, in L. Abu-Lughod (ed.), *Remaking women. Feminism and modernity in the Middle East*, Princeton, N.J. 1998, 3–33.

B. Baron, The construction of national honour in Egypt, in *Gender and History* 5 (1993), 244–55.

S. Berger-Gluck, Palestinian women. Gender, politics and nationalism, in *Journal of Palestine Studies* 24 (1995), 5–15.

M. Booth, Woman in Islam. Men and the "women's press" in turn-of-the-20th-century Egypt, in *International Journal of Middle East Studies* 33:2 (2001), 171–201.

M. Charrad, State and gender in the Maghrib, in *Middle East Report* (March-April 1990), 19–24, reprinted in S. Joseph and S. Slymovics (eds.), *Women and power in the Middle East*, Philadelphia 2000, 61–71.

P. Chatterjee, *The nation and its fragments. Colonial and postcolonial histories*, Princeton, N.J. 1993.

D. Cherifati-Merabtine, Algeria at a crossroads. National liberation, Islamization and women, in V. Moghadam (ed.), *Gender and national identity*, London 1994, 40–62.

E. Fleischmann, The other "Awakening." The emergence of women's movements in the modern Middle East, 1900–1940, in M. L. Meriwether and J. E. Tucker (eds.), *Social history of women and gender in the modern Middle East*, Boulder, Colo. 1999, 89–139.

S. Hale, The women of Sudan's National Islamic Front, in J. Beinin and J. Stork (eds.), *Political Islam. Essays from Middle East Report*, Berkeley 1997, 234–49.

M. Hatem, Modernization, the state, and the family in the Middle East women's studies, in M. L. Meriwether and J. E. Tucker (eds.), *Social history of women and gender in the modern Middle East*, Boulder, Colo. 1999, 63–87.

A. Jalal, The convenience of subservience. Women and the state of Pakistan, in D. Kandiyoti (ed.), *Women, Islam and the state*, Philadelphia 1991, 77–114.

A. Jamal, Engendering state-building. The women's movement and gender-regime in Palestine, in *Middle East Journal* 55 (2001), 256–76.

S. Joseph, Elite strategies for state building. Women, family, religion and the state in Iraq and Lebanon, in D. Kandiyoti (ed.), *Women, Islam and the state*, Philadelphia 1991, 176–200.

——, Women and politics in the Middle East, in S. Joseph and S. Slymovics (eds.), *Women and power in the Middle East*, Philadelphia 2000, 34–40.

D. Kandiyoti, Some awkward questions on women and modernity in Turkey, in L. Abu-Lughod (ed.), *Remaking women. Feminism and modernity in the Middle East*, Princeton, N.J. 1998, 270–87.

A. Khalid, *The politics of Muslim cultural reform*, Berkeley 1998.

M. Lazreg, *The eloquence of silence. Algerian women in question*, New York 1994.

A. McClintock, Family feuds. Gender, nationalism and the family, in *Feminist review* 44 (1993), 61–80.

L. Mosse, *Nationalism and sexuality. Respectability and abnormal sexuality in modern Europe*, New York 1985.

A. Najmabadi, *The story of the daughters of Quchan. Gender and national memory in Iranian history*, Syracuse, N.Y. 1998a.

——, Crafting an educated housewife in Iran, in L. Abu-Lughod (ed.), *Remaking women. Feminism and modernity in the Middle East*, Princeton, N.J. 1998b, 126–70.

N. Othman, Islamization and modernization in Malaysia. Competing cultural reassertions and women's identity in a changing society, in R. Wilford and R. Miller (eds.), *Women, ethnicity and nationalism. The politics of transition*, London 1998, 170–92.

S. Sobhan, National identity, fundamentalism and the women's movement in Bangladesh, in V. Moghadam (ed.), *Gender and national identity*, London 1994, 63–80.

N. Tohidi, Soviet in public, Azeri in private. Gender, Islam, and nationality in Soviet and post-Soviet Azerbaijan, in *Women's Studies International Forum* 19 (1996), 111–23.

N. Yuval-Davis, *Gender and nation*, London 1999.

Avi Rubin

National Insignia, Signs, and Monuments

Arab States

Arab states, like other modern nation-states, produce visual representations of the nation that are often highly gendered; the imagining of nationhood seems to have a great deal to do with the imagining of femininity and masculinity. But representations of gender and nation in Arab countries do not follow a single formula, nor do they remain static over time. In Egypt, where the peasant population was always larger than the urban or nomadic populations, peasants were the chosen symbols of cultural authenticity from the earliest days of nationalist iconography, and the nation was often represented as a peasant woman. In Jordan, where the merchant class was economically dominant from the founding of the state in 1921, tribal men and all women represented tradition in national imagination, while urban males represented the future. The familiar male/female, modern/traditional duality is completely reversed in some Kuwaiti iconography, where "Family Day" commemorative stamps depict the man in full Arab dress as the woman and children, all dressed in Western clothes, sit or play in a circle around him. In addition, when social issues deemed critical to national development are represented (such as education and literacy), women have been used as markers of progress in almost all Arab countries, with the apparent exception of Saudi Arabia, regardless of competing depictions of women as the custodians of tradition (whether peasant or tribal) in most of these same countries.

As the site of one of the earliest nationalist movements in the Arab Middle East, Egypt has a particularly long history of imagining nationhood. After the nationalist leader Muṣṭafā Kāmil died in 1908, a memorial committee created a statue that depicts Kāmil standing erect, delivering a speech. He places his left hand on a bust of the Sphinx, and points down with his right hand. The extended forefinger of his right hand draws us to the pedestal of the statue: a bronze relief shows a seated young peasant woman, with head covered but face unveiled, of slightly smaller dimensions than Kāmil. Entrapped in the square space, she represents Egypt under British occupation. By this time, a consensus had formed in Egyptian nationalist imagination: the nation should be represented as a woman. It had a certain linguistic logic (*Miṣr*, or Egypt, is gendered female in Arabic), and the choice also gave nationalists a rich field for political commentary through sexual innuendo and gendered metaphors. Inspired by the Revolution of 1919, Maḥmūd Mukhtār sculpted a work called *Nahḍat Miṣr* (The awakening of Egypt), which shows a peasant woman lifting her veil from her face with her left arm and placing her right arm on the back of a Sphinx as it rises up on its forelegs. The Sphinx rising suggests a rebirth of Egypt's ancient grandeur; the peasant woman lifting her veil symbolizes the liberation of the modern nation. The statue became the pre-eminent symbol of the national struggle, and the unveiling of women remained a popular metaphor for Egyptian independence.

After 1948, Palestine was often represented by Arab states as a woman in need of rescue. This idea can even be indicated by the absence of women from images. Postage stamps produced by Egypt, Syria, and Jordan since the 1960s portray Palestinian refugees in the form of a man dressed in rags and struggling to carry his children, or as a man and child peering through barbed wire, their landlessness symbolized by the mother's absence. At the same time that Palestine was being imagined as a woman in need of male Arab defenders, however, the very real Palestinian female warrior-martyr was making her way into official national iconography in several Arab states. A 1970 stamp produced by the People's Republic of Southern Yemen depicts silhouetted figures of mixed gender holding guns above their heads as they plant the Palestinian flag in the ground. The same year, Kuwait published a stamp in honor of female "Palestinian commandos"; the image on the stamp depicts a young, unveiled woman brandishing a machine-gun.

While images of Palestine indicate a potential tension between representations of the nation as a woman and representations of women defending the nation, on some levels there may be a continuum from one of these symbols to the other. A 1952 Egyptian postage stamp celebrating the nationalist revolution of that year portrays a female figure in culturally indeterminate dress, broken chains dangling from her raised arms, which are holding a large golden sword in the air, against a crescent background. Such images clearly evoke the use of female figures to symbolize liberty in

Western national iconography, while continuing the well-established tradition of representing the nation as a woman. They also have a resemblance to Arab-Islamic cultural narratives of women who encourage, shame, or even lead men into battle. Shortly after the Iraqi revolution of 1958, the new regime issued a stamp with the image of a woman carrying a torch and followed by two men whose fists are raised in rebellion. The woman clearly represents freedom and leads two main elements of the Iraqi nation – the tribes and the peasantry – into the modern, postcolonial era. But viewed in the context of well-known narratives of resistance in Iraq, in which a single woman is often "the spark that kindles the flame" of revolt, either in the background or as a leader, the image takes on additional resonance.

In a much more grandiose production, the post-revolutionary government commissioned Jawād Salīm to build the "Monument to Liberty," an enormous sculpture in Baghdad's Liberation Square that tells the epic of the revolution. It includes two women representing the Tigris and Euphrates rivers, a female figure symbolizing liberty, mother figures curled around a male martyr and a newborn child, a tribal woman in a wailing pose, her arms raised in grief and/or rage, and two figures of mixed gender representing political demonstrators. The woman demonstrator marches one stride ahead of the man, both fists raised in the air, her face turned toward the monument's viewers; the two seem perfectly matched in physical strength and forward momentum. The female figure was instantly recognized by Iraqi commentators not only as a symbol of the new nation's future but also as a representative of its recent past; women had participated in the rebellions of 1920, 1948, 1952, and 1956, and stories of female leaders and martyrs had developed into local legends. The sculpture shows some of the ways that national imagination can combine local, Western, and Arab gendered iconography, resonating in familiar ways on multiple levels, while also signaling new modes of conceptualizing both gender and nation.

Bibliography

Primary Sources

Arab Postal Union General Secretariat, *Arab postal stamps catalogue*, Cairo 1976.

Ittiḥād al-Shaʿb, Baghdad 1959.

Secondary Sources

B. Baron, *Egypt as a woman. Nationalists, gender and politics*, University of California Press (forthcoming).

S. al-Khalil, *The monument. Art, vulgarity and responsibility in Iraq*, Berkeley 1991.

J. Massad, *Colonial effects. The making of national identity in Jordan*, New York 2001.

L. Wedeen, *Ambiguities of domination. Politics, rhetoric, and symbols in contemporary Syria*, Chicago 1999.

Beth Baron and Sara Pursley

Iran

In Iran the most important iconic sign of modern nation/statehood has been the Lion and Sun emblem. When first adopted in 1836 by Muḥammad Shāh Qājār (r. 1834–48) as the official emblem of the Iranian state, the lion was male, the sun (fe)male, that is, a beautiful face, which in Qājār iconography could be either male or female. Over the following decades the sun burst into a magnificent Qājārī face and the lion became more masculinized (see Figure 2). By the early twentieth century, however, the sun gradually lost hair and distinct facial features. These were permanently erased some time in 1935/6. By the late 1970s, the emblem was fully geometrized (see Figure 3). In the aftermath of the 1979 Revolution, the Lion and Sun, deemed an icon of monarchy, was replaced by a calligraphic depiction of "There is no god but Allah."

The Lion and Sun's genealogy is variously narrated as pre-Islamic (Zoroastrian) or as Central Asian Turkic. It is affiliated with the sign system of astrological tables, and stands for Shīʿī loyalty to ʿAlī through one of his given names, Asadallāh, God's lion. In the Qājār period, the emblem appears on Jewish wedding documents (*ketuba*s), and on Shīʿī banners for Muḥarram processions. This enormous traffic in signs between different sites of representation accounts for the Lion and Sun's unique success as the sign of modern Iranian-ness. It is hard to find any other modern icon of Iranian-ness that belongs to as many domains of signification, bringing together Zoroastrian, Jewish, Shīʿī, Turkish, and Persian symbolics.

The metamorphosis of the Lion and Sun emblem coincided with a period of cultural change in Iran when beauty was feminized. The sun's gender was correspondingly consolidated as female. Its effacement thus makes a paradoxical statement about the gender of modernity. During the very same period in which real women became more publicly visible in Iranian society, the symbolic sun of the national emblem was effaced as it became more identified as female. In fact, Reza Shah's (r. 1926–41) order to erase the sun's facial features occurred within a year of his order for compulsory unveiling of women in public (1936).

To understand this transformation, we need to look at the representational domain to which the sun belonged, the Qājār visual culture. There, the (fe)male face did not represent "real (wo)men," but (wo)men of male artistic, and more particularly male sexual fantasy. S/he fulfilled adult male desire for music, wine, dance, homo/heterosex, or just plain voyeuristic pleasure. S/he illustrated popular romances and classical stories.

For a figure of male fantasy to be the main feature of the national emblem posed a problem. First, the artist's fantasy was denigrated by the reproducibility of an emblem in many media (newspapers, official state signs and stationery, stamps, coins, flags, and so forth). The language of representation increasingly relied on mimicking the camera and attributing authenticity to the photograph. More importantly, the place of artistic representation, the shift from private chambers and books read in private to publicly displayed state signs created an element of conflict between the private nature of fantasies of pleasure and the public nature of its new location. Third, while the purpose of (fe)male representations in the private chambers or even the printed books of the nineteenth century was to provide pleasure to men, public display of the national emblem was a serious matter of national politics and state power. Whether as a medallion to be granted for services to the state, or as a logo printed on the masthead of the official state gazette, on letterheads, stamps, coins and flags, this (fe)male sun was not there for the voyeuristic pleasure of male viewers, but to inspire awe and respect, allegiance and identification. Fourth, the nineteenth century marked a shift in Iranian male sensibilities. The young beautiful male adolescent to whom the adult man was attached had turned from a figure of celebration into one of abjection.

Finally, the incongruity became progressively more pronounced as the project of building a modern Iranian nation increasingly included real women in the public sphere. This latter process brought the modernist embarrassment to a head, becoming a problem by the first decades of the twentieth century as women became readers of gazettes, users of stamps, and viewers of the flag. Public display of (wo)men of male sexual fantasy became a source of modernist anxiety and discomfiture and forced a gradual yet unmistakable eclipse of the sun. The more public the medium, the more the facial features of the sun would fade. We can almost trace the gradual setting of the sun as the century progressed and as the emblem was reproduced on widely circulating artifacts, until its eventual formal effacement.

While the Lion and Sun was eliminated as Iran's official emblem in 1979, it has acquired a deep nostalgic burden among Iranian émigrés.

Bibliography

A. Kasravī, *Tārīkhchah-i shīr va khawrshīd*, in *Armaghān* 11, 7 (1930), 542–54; 8 (1930), 588–98.

M. Mīnuvī Ṭihrānī, *Mansha'-i naqsh-i shīr va khawrshīd*, in *Dinshah Irani memorial volume. Papers on Zoroastrian and Iranian subjects*, Bombay 1948, 85–109.

H. Nayyir Nuri, *Tārīkhchah-i bayraq-i Īrān, va shīr va khawrshīd*, Tehran 1965.

S. Nafīsī, *Darafsh-i Īrān va shīr va khawrshīd*, Tehran 1949.

A. Piemontese, The statutes of the Qajar orders of knighthood, in *East and West* 19:3/4 (1969), 431–73.

Y. Zukā', Tārīkhchah-i taghyīrāt va tahavvulāt-i darafsh va 'alāmāt-i dawlat-i Īrān, in *Hunar va Mardum* 31 (1965), 13-24; 32/3 (1965), 21–38; 34 (1965), 24–40; 35 (1965), 32–7; 36 (1965), 30–7; 38 (1965), 21–9.

Afsaneh Najmabadi

Sub-Saharan Africa

This entry explores what national symbols might mean to women living in Islamic cultures in Sub-Saharan Africa. Little research has been undertaken on this subject so the focus has to be on setting the scene and asking appropriate questions. To do this, it is first necessary to briefly address the question of African nation-building and the processes of gendering of these nations.

Research into nation-building in African countries has been minimal, although specific national discourses have been identified in a few countries (Fosse 1997, Steiner 1997, I. Cusack 1999). The new leaders of independent Africa set about building nations from their multiethnic peoples and used whatever material was at hand to construct a national identity, just as an artist might construct a collage. Thus, religion may or may not contribute to the national culture, although for Islamic states such as Sudan and Mauritania Islam will inevitably be central to the nation-building project. There is a danger of generalizing when writing about Africa because of its ethnic, religious, and historical diversity and the same caveat should be applied to Islamic politics (Eickelman and Piscatori 1996). However, Gwendolyn Mikell argues that "a pattern of gross female exclusion and gender bias emerged as Islam made incursions into sub-Saharan Africa" (1997, 14). Present-day female literacy rates across Africa, comparing countries where Islam is dominant with those where it is not, suggest that this may still be the case.

In addition to nation-specific discourses, nations

generally have a set of symbols and practices that accompany the dominant ideology of nationalism. Thus, when Namibia achieved independence in 1990 the Ministry of Information and Broadcasting produced a folder entitled "Namibian National Symbols" (Fosse 1997, 434). There is a variety of national symbols, some overt, in the form of flags and monuments, and others associated with what Michael Billig has termed "Banal Nationalism" (1995). National cuisine and national dishes are examples of this quiet, everyday, unnoticed nationalism. Thus in Senegal, mention of *le thiéboudienne*, one of the national dishes, will quietly flag the nation. Women, Muslim and otherwise, have been involved in assembling these African national cuisines, for example, by gathering ethnic and regional cuisines into "national" cookery books and thus contributing to the nation-building project (I. Cusack 2003).

Nations can be considered Janus-faced, that is, looking both ways, and providing a past and a future for the retrospective "fictive ethnicity" that is the nation (Balibar and Wallerstein 1991, 102). Women are often the object of the "backward look" that is associated with tradition and ethnic roots. This is particularly so where religion is firmly entrenched, within a nation-state, such as in Ireland after independence in 1922 (T. Cusack 2000). We might therefore ask whether in those countries with a strong Islamic tradition in Sub-Saharan Africa, women are the particular object of this backward look and whether the symbols such as the national flag are seen by women as grounding them in tradition. Alternatively, when comparing the national with ethnic and religious institutions and traditions, do national symbols represent modernity and the possibility of emancipation? Most national symbols such as flags, shields, and emblems, as well as national monuments, are clearly gendered and will typically be associated with male security forces and modernization. National anthems, another overt national symbol, confirm the gendered character of African nations, Islamic and otherwise. Of the 48 Sub-Saharan states, only five anthems mention women in the text while "sons," "men," and "forefathers" appear in many. When women are mentioned they are sometimes marginalized as in Botswana: "O men, awake! And women close beside them" (http://www.thenationalanthems.com.country/Botswana.htm). Likewise, national monuments are often built to commemorate fallen male national "heroes," presumably to encourage others to be willing to sacrifice their lives for the nation. Thus, "Heroes Acre" in Harare, Zimbabwe, contains the tombs of soldiers who fought in the liberation struggle. All except one are men, the exception being President Mugabe's first wife (Werbner 1998, 84).

According to Raymond Firth, the national flag is imbued with "the sacred character of the nation; it is revered by loyal citizens and ritually defiled by those who wish to make a protest" (Billig 1995, 39). Many African flags include the Pan-African colors of green, yellow (gold), and red, the greens sometimes associated with Islam. For instance, the flag of the Islamic Republic of Mauritania is green with a crescent moon and star, in yellow, at the center reflecting the majority Islamic faith. Islam may influence more directly the form of the national flag. Thus, the first Mali flag adopted in April 1959, when Mali was part of a federation with Senegal and French Sudan, had a "kanaga" – a black man-like figure – superimposed on the central yellow band. In 1961 this figure was removed, under pressure from Islamic groups (http://fotw.vexillum.com/flags/ml.html, 2). Marina Warner (1983) has shown how allegorical forms of women representing nations perform functions they would not normally be expected to do – for example, as judges, statesmen, or soldiers; Britannia, Marianne, and "Mother Russia" are such figures (T. Cusack and Bhreathnach-Lynch, 2003). Such allegorical visual representations of women are unlikely to be used as national symbols in the Islamic world.

A turn to Islam in late twentieth-century Sub-Saharan Africa has often had a negative impact on women's rights. In Sudan, the family code of 1991 established Sharīʿa law and limited women's rights; this reached a peak in 1996 when, for example, women in Khartoum were only allowed to work if it was an extension of their domestic duties (Lesch 1998, 133–4). In contrast, women have played an important role in the ruling National Islamic Front (Eickelman and Piscatori, 95). The Sudanese flag, adopted in 1970, uses the pan-Arab colors – red, white, black, and green – perhaps pulling Sudanese identity, and the "sacred character of the nation" more toward the center of the Islamic world and away from Sub-Saharan Africa (http://www.sudan.net/society/flag.shtml).

If we accept the generalization that religious and ethnic traditions are often implicated in the maintenance of masculine dominance (Vail 1989, 14), perhaps the modernizing component of nationalism might be seen as improving the lives of women. In Senegal, a secular republic with a 94 percent Muslim population, the government has used the Islamic Brotherhoods as religious intermediaries between the state and people. It has had a modernizing agenda and has made considerable efforts, for example, to encourage families to educate girls (Gordon and Gordon 2001, 282) and in the 1990s the government appointed a minister for African women's emancipation, Ms. Awa Guéye Kébé. In rural areas women who have taken part in the Tostan ("breaking out of the egg" in the Wolof language) education program have initiated movements to stop the practice of female circumcision (Easton 1998). So despite the still poor literacy levels of women, the Senegalese flag might perhaps be perceived by women as a symbol of the modern face of the nation that allows for their empowerment. Despite the evidence that nations are gendered so as to disadvantage women, the nation-state remains the chief means for economic development and modernization. National symbols are more likely to be associated with bettering the lives of women than grounding them in tradition.

BIBLIOGRAPHY

E. Balibar and I. Wallerstein, *Race, nation, class*, London 1991.
M. Billig, *Banal nationalism*, London 1995.
I. Cusack, Hispanic and Bantu inheritance, trauma, dispersal and return. Some contributions to a sense of national identity in Equatorial Guinea, in *Nations and Nationalism* 5 (1999), 207–36.
——, Pots, pens and "eating out the body." Cuisine and the gendering of African nations, in *Nations and Nationalism* 9 (2003), 277–96.
T. Cusack, Janus and gender. Women and the nation's backward look, in *Nations and Nationalism* 6 (2000), 541–61.
T. Cusack and S. Bhreathnach-Lynch, *Art, nation and gender. Ethnic landscapes, myths and mother-figures*, London 2003.
P. Easton, Senegalese women remake culture, in World Bank, *IK Notes*, 3, 1998, <http://www.worldbank.org/aftdr/ik/default.htm>.
D. F. Eickelman and J. Piscatori, *Muslim politics*, Princeton, N.J. 1996.
L. J. Fosse, Negotiating the nation. Ethnicity, nationalism and nation-building in independent Namibia, in *Nations and Nationalism* 3 (1997), 427–50.
A. A. Gordon and D. L. Gordon, *Understanding contemporary Africa*, Boulder, Colo. 2001[3].
A. M. Lesch, *Sudan. Contested national identities*, Oxford 1998.
G. Mikell (ed.), *African feminism*, Philadelphia 1997.
C. B. Steiner, The invisible face. Masks, ethnicity, and the state in Côte d'Ivoire, in R. R. Grinker and C. B. Steiner (eds.), *Perspectives on Africa*, Oxford 1997, 671–7.
L. Vail, Introduction, in L. Vail (ed.), *The creation of tribalism in southern Africa*, London 1989, 1–19.
M. Warner, *Monuments and maidens. The allegory of the female form*, London 1983.
R. Werbner (ed.), *Memory and the postcolony. African anthropology and the critique of power*, London 1998.

IGOR CUSACK

Networks

North Africa

In North Africa, a person's network consists of a web of social ties with kin, neighbors, friends, and (less commonly for women) co-workers maintained primarily through face to face interactions. Due to Arab-Islamic cultural norms segregating the sexes, men generally socialize with male network members in non-domestic spaces: in cafes, playing board games on street corners, at work, or at public celebrations such as weddings and circumcisions. Likewise, women typically interact with network members in female spaces: paying visits to each other's homes, and taking group female trips to the public baths (*hammams*), local shrines (*marabūt*), and even the beach. While Western ideals of companionship between married couples are reflected today in the increase of mixed-sex socializing at weddings and family events, the majority of men's and women's network interactions continue to be sex-segregated. It is not surprising, therefore, that husbands' and wives' networks are often distinct and separate. There is some evidence to suggest that women's networks may cross-cut the more rigid patronage and political lines of men's networks, creating a more diverse and flexible base of female alliances and loyalties.

Despite women's increasing education and entrance into the workforce (Tunisia leads the region in this regard), women's networks continue to be predominantly kin based. Friends, neighbors, coworkers, and other outsiders form a relatively small portion of the networks of rural and lower-class women's networks. In contrast to prevailing assumptions that the Arab patrilineal family severs women's natal ties, a number of studies demonstrate that after marriage North African women continue to visit and remain close to their natal family, reflecting a female bilateral pattern. This pattern is particularly pronounced among the Berber populations of Morocco and Algeria.

Class, region of origin, and a woman's education all play a role in the composition of networks. After migration to major urban areas, or even internationally, women and their husbands maintain strong ties to their home communities, preferring to interact with, marry, and live near others from the same region and social class. Since membership in a network requires frequent reciprocal exchanges of visits, gifts, and services, networks typically delimit social and class boundaries. A family's social status is defined by its ability to afford to provide the lavish food and hospitality expected by guests in the upper and even middle classes. "Keeping up with the Joneses" (or Abdurahmans in the North African case) is not defined by the size of one's house or car, but by the generosity of one's table and the ability to provide equally valuable social connections and services.

Consequently, visiting networks play a critical role in the economic success and physical survival of a woman and her family. Social networks provide access to goods and services that are difficult to obtain – ranging from foreign electronics to skilled medical care – and provide critical information, whether about jobs, ways to circumvent government regulations, or even the whereabouts of a new shipment of Adidas sneakers in the nearby market. In a region where social welfare programs are limited and poorly implemented, a woman's social network may be her only source of assistance during a serious illness, the death of her husband, or the sudden loss of her father's job.

Although the advent of cars, electronic mail, and cellular phones, and increasing female literacy rates has made communication with network members easier for a small segment of the population, in North Africa hospitality, visiting, and face to face interactions continue to be the primary means of maintaining network ties. Whether daily drop-in visits to a neighbor, or a formal visit at a religious holiday, women's visits are essential in confirming ties to network members. Daily visits to nearby kin and neighbors are generally an informal affair. Visitors may be offered a simple glass of tea, but otherwise are expected to join in the household tasks on hand, whether it be shelling nuts, knitting and sewing, or tending the children. On weekends women and their families make more formal visits, dressing in their finest clothes to pay a call to friends and family not seen during the week. Frequently, weekend visits take on the appearance of large family reunions as relatives from the surrounding area congregate at an older parent's or grandparent's home to eat dinner, drink tea, and watch television together. These visits cultivate intimate ties with a group of close network members who may be counted upon for assistance during life crisis events.

Visits at religious celebrations (ʿayād) and life cycle events (*munāsabāt*) play an important role in reaffirming ties with a larger group of useful connections who can provide information and practical help: obtaining jobs, circumventing government red tape, or locating services such as mechanical repair. Arab tradition requires that friends and relatives visit a woman on the seventh day after the birth of a child. Following a death, a formal visit to bereaved family members is also expected during a seven- to ten-day mourning period. And, depending on the region and local cultural traditions, weddings, engagements, and circumcisions are celebrated over a one- to seven-day period, during which network members visit and attend parties, bearing gifts of food, money, or household items.

Muslim religious holidays also require the exchange of visits and food to maintain network ties. Although there are numerous small religious holidays and special regional saints' days that vary throughout the area, the four primary holidays observed are: Mawlid (the birth of the Prophet Muḥammad), Ramadan (the month of fasting), ʿĪd Ṣaghīr (a two-day holiday following Ramadan), and ʿĪd Kabīr (commemorating the prophet Abraham's sacrifice of Isaac). During each of these holidays, women prepare special dishes and cakes, each region proud of its own unique foods. In most Arab communities in North Africa these dishes and cakes are served during formal holiday visits to as many as several hundred network members. Barring extreme illness or age, failure to visit during these life cycle events and holidays can be sufficient justification for terminating a relationship.

Visiting, exchanging gifts, and maintaining network ties form a central part of Muslim North African women's daily lives and experience. Given the social, practical, and economic importance of women's networks, a woman's daily world of interacting with and visiting female kin, friends, and neighbors, not only provides companionship and joy, but solace and support throughout her life.

BIBLIOGRAPHY

R. Bourqia, M. Charrad, and N. Gallagher (eds.), *Femmes, culture et société au Maghreb*, Casablanca 1996.

S. S. Davis, *Patience and power. Women's lives in a Moroccan village*, Cambridge, Mass. 1983.

E. Fernea. *A street in Marrakech*, New York 1975.

P. Holmes-Eber, *Daughters of Tunis. Women, family and networks in a Muslim city*, Boulder, Colo. 2002.

H. Hoodfar, *Between marriage and the market. Intimate politics and survival in Cairo*, Berkeley 1997.

D. Mahfoudh, *Paysannes de Marnissa. Le difficile accés à la modernité*, Tunis 1993.

D. Singerman, Engaging informality. Women, work and politics in Cairo, in R. Lobban (ed.), *Middle Eastern women and the informal economy*, Gainesville, Fla. 1998, 262–86.

PAULA HOLMES-EBER

The Ottoman Empire

Ottoman women's networks were webs of loose and easily maintained ties that structured the culture of women's worlds, could be mobilized to provide support for families and households, and also functioned to provide access and information between parts of a society. Since the Ottoman Empire spanned seven centuries and included societies from Eastern Europe to Mesopotamia, and since only infrequent glimpses of women's culture are preserved in the historical record, it is impossible to survey the full range of types of women's networks historically or geographically. This entry focuses on women's networks of the Arab Ottoman provinces and practices which, even as they declined through much of the post-imperial era, were remembered by female informants as the way things were done in generations past, but also persisted into the twentieth century because their of their fundamental utility in organizing societies. The ties of female kin, the informal gatherings of neighbors, the formal visits of social self-presentation and marriage scouting, the circulation of midwives and female entertainers through all strata of society, and later the emergence of literary and cultural salons and charitable committees run and frequented by Young Ottoman women provided critical arenas for cultural development, for emotional and material support, and for information about the market and politics.

KINSHIP

The most basic and important form of women's network in Ottoman society was the web of kin relations preserved by religious and legal understandings of the mutual obligations of spouses, parents and children, and siblings and extended families, and reinforced through the devolution of wealth through gift giving, care provision, and inheritance and marriage payments. Maternal and affective webs of kinship were brought to life by the principal of *ṣilāt al-raḥim* (literally, the bonds of the womb). Understood through the secondary meaning of *raḥma* (tenderness), this Arabic term emphasizes the maternal and distant relatives whose ties are not those of juridical obligation but ones of love. The ties of *ṣilāt al-raḥim* were cultivated through festive gatherings of female relatives (mothers, daughters, sisters, aunts, and cousins) as well as through labor sharing and emotional and other types of support in hard times.

Kinship terminology shows that men who would not necessarily belong to the same circles are linked by their relations to women's kin networks. Perceiving the ways in which people are brought together by networks of female relatives adds a dimension to an understanding of juridical paternal kin relations or male dominated religious, guild, or military organizations.

Friendship

The reciprocity that allowed female relatives to exchange visits, time, labor, and even financial support across households provided a template for visits based on physical proximity, namely the custom of the *ṣubḥiyya* (literally, morning event) in which neighbors would regularly get together for conversation, coffee, or refreshments, or seasonal or occasional communal labor after the men had left the house and before the daily routine of housework and food preparation had begun in each home. These neighborly gatherings or visits were marked by informality of dress and manner and access through back doors, over rooftops, or within buildings or compounds. Other neighborly networks were cultivated by the occasional exchange of a plate of cooked food from one house to the next. To return an empty plate would be a breach of etiquette and a lost opportunity to strengthen a bond of proximity and friendship.

The informal morning visits in particular were the locus for the exchange of information ranging from marital politics and advice to discussion of the market, often based on the last evening's discussion with menfolk, and formed a parallel track to what male merchants would discuss in the market and coffeehouse. The neighborly *ṣubḥiyya* may often have served as a financial pool in which periodic contributions were combined and paid out in turn to the members of the pool for emergencies, personal items (such as gold), or even subsidies for male relations' enterprises.

More formal afternoon gatherings took place after the day's work had been done and the day's main meal had been served. These *istiqbāl* or reception visits reinforced broader but more select social groups, and they involved formal dressing, exiting the compound or the neighborhood, and more mannered self-presentation. A hostess might invite her group of friends, neighbors, and relatives to a special occasion to invoke God's blessing for a particular problem or individual in her family. Similar festive gatherings took place in cities' most private public place, the bath or hammam. The musicians who entertained at female gatherings, as well as the midwives who attended to women from all walks of life, circulated between various milieus and provided points of contact between distinct quarter and class social circles.

Patronage, civic associations, and reform

The women's networks that underlay elite Istanbul society provided an important infrastructure for discourses of reform and enlightenment. In the 1870s and 1880s, the female poet Sair Nigar Hanım held a weekly salon on Tuesdays at her mansion in Istanbul attended by intellectuals and reform politicians. Her intellectual-in-residence for these salons was the newspaper woman and novelist Fatma Aliye and the circle included the prominent educator Ayşe Sidika. These women, all members of prominent Istanbul reformist families, used the local tradition of women's sociability as well as a French model of the salon to nurture an Ottoman national reform agenda.

Women's traditional networks were also mobilized at the end of the Ottoman period around charitable work and war relief efforts. Between 40 and 100 women's civic organizations were established between the fall of Sultan Abdülhamid and the founding of the Turkish Republic. These ranged from the Ottoman Ladies' Organization for the Uplifting of the Homeland (officially registered under the Committee of Union and Progress's "Law of Organizations" in 1909), to the Turkish Women Tailor's Cutting Home (registered in 1913), to the Mutual Support Organization of Circassian Women (registered in 1919). The legacy of Ottoman women's formal and informal networks continued to be important well into the national period.

Bibliography

N. Bekiroglu, Ottoman female poets, in K. Çicek et al. (eds.), *The great Ottoman-Turkish civilization*, Ankara 2000, 249–59.

H. Edib, *Memoirs of Halidé Edib*, New York 1926.

H. Gerber, Social and economic position of women in an Ottoman city, Bursa 1600–1700, in *International Journal of Middle East Studies* 12 (1980), 231–44.

L. Hanimefendi, *The imperial harem of the sultans. Daily life at the Çiragan Palace during the nineteenth century*, Istanbul 1995.

K. Kreiser, Women in the Ottoman world. A bibliographical essay, in *Islam and Christian-Muslim Relations* 13:2 (2002), 197–206.

A. Marcus, Men, women and property. Dealers in real estate in eighteenth-century Aleppo, in *Journal of the Economic and Social History of the Orient* 26 (1983), 137–63.

Ş. Mardin, *The genesis of young Ottoman thought. A study in the modernization of Turkish political ideas*, Princeton, N.J. 1962.

M. L. Meriwether, *The kin who count. Family and society in Ottoman Aleppo*, Austin, Tex. 1999.
J. Pardoe, *The city of the sultan, and domestic manners of the Turks in 1836*, Philadelphia 1837.
L. Peirce, Gender and sexual propriety in Ottoman royal women's patronage, in D. F. Ruggles (ed.), *Women, patronage and self-representation in Islamic studies*, Albany, N.Y. 2000, 53–68.
——, *The imperial harem. Women and sovereignty in the Ottoman Empire*, Oxford 1993.
H. Shaʿrāwī, *Harem years. The memoirs of an Egyptian feminist 1879–1924*, trans. M. Badran, London 1986.
A. E. Sonbol (ed.), *Women, the family and divorce laws in Islamic history*, Syracuse, N.Y. 1996.
N. A. N. M. Van Os, Ottoman women's organizations. Sources of the past, sources for the future, in *Islam and Christian-Muslim Relations* 11:3 (2000), 369–83.
M. C. Zilfi (ed.), *Women in the Ottoman Empire. Middle East women in the early modern era*, Leiden 1997.

LEILA HUDSON

South Asia

Visiting each other during the day, when husbands and children are at work and school, is a common practice for housewives of urban upper-middle classes in contemporary South Asia. In fact, this practice dates back many generations, and was prominent amongst the women of the Muslim intelligentsia in pre-partition India as well, as referenced in many women's novels of the time, such as those by Mastoor (1952), Fatima (1993), Shahnawaz (1957) or Chughtai (1995). Here, as in contemporary urban life, such visits serve as a source of bonding for the women, who drop in informally at neighborhood homes for a cup of tea and biscuits around 11 a.m. (before lunch time), as well as an opportunity to exchange neighborhood gossip, particularly on the topics of love, marriage, and childbirth.

Then there are the *mayun* gatherings, when women relatives and friends of prospective brides meet at the home of the bride-to-be every evening for several weeks prior to the wedding ceremony. These informal gatherings are an opportunity to tease and prepare the bride on how to become a proper "wife." They also afford older women with marriageable sons a chance to scout out prospective daughters-in-law from among the unmarried eligible girls participating in the song-and-dance festivities during this *mayun* period – when the bride-to-be is also supposed to be in seclusion from all male relatives and the outside world in general, confined to the home and also restricted to wearing yellow-colored clothing, which she will change only on the day of her wedding.

Coffee mornings are a more formal networking occasion, again for women belonging to the upper or more elite echelons of society. Women do not "drop in" on these occasions, rather, they must be invited by the hostess. The occasion serves as an excuse for high society women to dress up and arrive in their silk shalwar kameezes or latest imported Western fashions. Topics for discussion may be the errant behavior of a husband, or the illness of a mother or grandmother, or laments about the disrespectful behavior of servants, or the latest scandal involving a corrupt politician, or even the extra-marital affair of a friend or acquaintance. Women launching into some business venture, particularly involving the fashion industry, dressmaking, and so forth, may use a coffee morning to showcase some of their merchandise or at the very least advertise their new business. Women involved in social work or other welfare schemes will also use these occasions to discuss upcoming charity functions, and the like, and round up volunteers to help out with these functions, or with collecting donations from their rich husbands or other relatives and friends.

*Milad*s are other social gatherings that have been taking place amongst Sunnī Muslim women in Pakistan since its formation in 1947, and which, of late, have regained their popularity as religious zeal has intensified among the previously more secular upper classes, although women of all social classes have always regularly held these functions at their homes. A *milad* is essentially a prayer-meeting, in the form of a party. These all-female events are held year-round, and a woman will hold a *milad* party if she has a particular favor to ask of God (known as a *manat*) – in return for the granting of which favor she will promise to donate food or money to the poor. Sometimes a *milad* is simply a thanksgiving party, and women gather to sing hymns dedicated to the Prophet Muḥammad (pbuh), asking for his spirit to bless the home of the hostess and the invitees as well. The bulk of the event consists of women reading the Qurʾān collectively, and then, when all 30 sections have been read, dates are passed around, hymns are sung, and the gathering then indulges in rich and tasty foods and desserts and tea or soft drinks, before the party breaks up. These gatherings tend to last several hours and can be either morning or afternoon affairs.

While *milad*s have been common forms of networking for women of the lower middle classes and the urban elite, they have become much more institutionalized and popular over the past decade, taking place in the homes of the very wealthy and privileged women as well. They now often take the form of *dars* parties, that is, Qur'ānic instruction is a regular feature of these gatherings, with sessions often led by a woman who could be described as a female equivalent of a mullah – a learned teacher of the Qur'ān and *ḥadīth*. The educated and wealthy urban women have donated vast sums of money to build or rent spacious halls and buildings in big towns and cities across Pakistan where formal *dars* or instructional classes in Qur'ānic exegesis are held, where women can enroll for short or long courses for a nominal fee. The atmosphere in private homes has also become more religious, and many women choose to hold similar *dars*-type events in their homes that are also occasions for social networking.

A Shīʿī version of a *milad* is known as a *majlis*. These gatherings take place specifically during the Islamic calendar month of Muḥarram, when the Prophet Muḥammad's (pbuh) grandson Ḥusayn was brutally killed during battle in the seventh century C.E. Shīʿī Muslims the world over commemorate his martyrdom to this day by holding mourning meetings every year throughout this month which culminate in a frenzied night of self-flagellation and blood-letting accompanied by intense singing of devotional songs. While the most extreme forms of these practices are reserved for men, Shīʿī women and girls also organize gatherings at their homes and at devotional gathering-places known as "imam baras," in various neighborhoods, and get together to sing mourning dirges, cry, beat their chests, and listen to stories recited by a female religious leader in praise of Ḥusayn's sacrifice for his people, as well as to listen and weep at his sister Zaynab's pure and abiding love for her brother. These occasions serve as a way for the women of this community to reassert their commonality and share their collective pain, and indeed, are cathartic occasions where stories of spiritual miracles pertaining to the martyrdom are exchanged in a spirit of religious bonding. Such occasions also serve the secular function of providing mothers an opportunity to survey the gathering for prospective daughters-in-law.

While *milad* and *majlis* parties do take place in some Muslim households in India, and somewhat more frequently in Bangladesh, these practices are not as widespread there as they seem to be in Pakistan. Indeed, they appear to be more confined to a lower socioeconomic stratum of Muslims. The more educated women of the contemporary Muslim elite in India tend to be more secular-minded, and instead of *milads*, prefer to hold "kitty-parties," a practice which involves several women getting together on a monthly basis after agreeing to contribute a certain pre-agreed amount of money to a kitty. Each month, the sum goes to one of the women in the group. This large sum of money is most often used by the winner of the kitty to purchase big-ticket household items, and occasionally, gold jewelry. Kitty-parties are fairly common practice across South Asia.

There are also potluck lunches held in mixed communities in smaller towns in India such as Benares, which provide educated middle- and upper-class women of both Muslim and Hindu backgrounds to mingle without their menfolk or children present. The women present at these generally informal and often last-minute get-togethers are relatives living in proximity to each other as well as neighborhood women. These religiously mixed or diverse neighborhoods tend to have a similar class composition, whereas Muslim-concentrated neighborhoods or *muḥalla*s tend to be much more class-stratified. In such neighborhoods in Lucknow and Benares, for example, there is not much social intermingling between Muslim women of different classes, save for an occasional conventional greeting exchanged between a woman of a higher socioeconomic class and a woman from a lower class who might be standing at her doorstep while the former walks past. The lower-class woman will usually be illiterate and may visit the upper-class woman's home to have a letter read from her village. Some of the educated women in these neighborhoods start informal schools in their homes to educate the female children of these women, who may also be servants in their homes, and this becomes another means of networking between women of different class backgrounds.

Finally, there is a large and growing network of women's non-governmental organizations (NGOs) across South Asia, which has arisen to fill the gap left by governments that are largely non-responsive to the educational and social welfare needs of their poorest citizens, amongst whom the majority happen to be women. From the "do-good" volunteer model, there are now the professionally run women's organizations, including theater groups that mount educational plays and skits in the most downtrodden communities and neighborhoods, with women and girls comprising the bulk of the audience. Here is an example of a social networking that turns into an opportunity for education and empowerment for social change. Other types of NGOs, such as the Grameen Bank in Bangladesh, provide women with increased financial viability which also encourages new forms of networking, and which in turn leads them to consolidate their sense of empowerment through female solidarity.

BIBLIOGRAPHY

S. Ahmed, The hopes of Bangladeshi women. The social impact of the Micro Credit Program, Dickey fellowship report 2000, <www.alum.dartmouth.org/classes/66/interns>.

I. Chughtai, *The crooked line*, trans. T. Naqai, Oxford 1995.

A. Fatima, *The one who did not ask*, trans. R. Ahmad, Oxford 1993.

R. Ghadially, *Women in Indian society. A reader*, New Delhi 1988.

M. Hydari, Crossing boundaries – Dr. Farhat Hashmi makes her presence felt in UAE, in *Dawn* (Karachi) 2003.

N. S. Khan et al. (eds.), *Aspects of women and development*, Lahore 1995

K. Mastoor, *The inner courtyard*, trans. N. Hussein, Lahore 2000.

F. Shaheed et al. (eds.), *Shaping women's lives*, Lahore 1998.

M. Shahnawaz, *The heart divided*, Lahore 1957.

F. Zafar (ed.), *Finding our way. Readings on women in Pakistan*, Lahore 1991.

FAWZIA AFZAL-KHAN

Turkey

A gendered spatial organization offers women advantages as well as disadvantages. Within societies in which social space is separated according to gender, distinct women's cultures can emerge. Women's visits to each other's homes, to religious sites, and their role in a range of life cycle rituals take on definite social and political significance. One of the effects of the separation of space by gender is that the stricter the boundary between the two domains, the greater the possibility that a certain independence of the female domain will emerge. In such a situation a rich social life and forms of intimacy among women develop. When spatial separation occurs within a society in which men's political patronage networks need to be as wide as possible, women's networks and channels of communication become important to men.

In some regions and societies, restrictions on women's movements through space counter these potentialities, but in Turkey many women have enjoyed considerable autonomy within and between the spaces allocated to them. Under both the imperial society of the Ottoman era (1453–1918) and the secular republic established in the 1920s, Turkish women have a long tradition of visiting and excursions outside the home. Lady Mary Wortley Montagu (Murphy 1988, 111), an early European observer, remarked upon the comparative freedom of the wealthy and powerful women she moved among but later foreign observers sometimes dismissed women's sociality as trivial. These later observers failed to appreciate both the ways in which visiting was integrated into status and power networks and their significance in sustaining women's interests within society more generally.

A number of scholars have described the formalized visiting patterns found among Turkish women (Aswad 1967, Benedict 1974, Dobkin 1974, Fallers and Fallers 1976) and the ways in which women's networks provided both social support and important forums for the circulation of information. Beck and Keddie's important book, *Women in the Muslim World* (1978) brought together the first fruits of the new wave of scholarly interest in the lives of Muslim women and provided a crucial foundation for the work that followed. Kıray (1981) identified four types of visit among women living in the Black Sea town of Ereğli and these forms are found across Turkey. The first was the informal visits of poorer women as they passed their leisure time together. The second was the regular, formal visiting day with formal food and drink held by better off women and from which children are generally excluded. Then there were women's ceremonial visits to households, particularly for the performance of death ceremonies as well as for other life cycle events, leisure excursions to parks, the cinema, or a women-only beach, and visits to the main markets. Women also visit saints' shrines. In the major cities where attendance at visiting days can be difficult, working women may attend afternoon teas held at about five o'clock. Taken together, these patterns of women-only visits and excursions add up to a social life that is far from the lonely seclusion of the Orientalized Western imagination.

Studies emerging under the influence of feminist theory and the women's movement of the 1970s generally adopted some form of structural analysis in developing understandings of the ways in which women's space was established and of how women lived their lives within them. In particular, there was considerable interest in examining the public/private division of space associated with bourgeois modernity as it developed in European states. Many studies considered whether patterns of seclusion should be considered in terms of public and private, whether the private and domestic domain should be given a less subordinate position than it enjoyed in secular, modern societies, and whether religious beliefs could be thought of as causing the seclusion of women. Kıray (1981) argued that visits exchanged between women's homes were equivalent to the ways in which men received visits in coffee shops and that the important role of women in directing the family economy and family relationships saw the emergence of a women-only subculture of mature and responsible personalities (Kıray 1981, 268). Turkish women enjoy the sociality of these visits and they help to develop the independence of mind and personal authority so striking to foreign observers. Kıray's data and interpretation of them remain important in countering Orientalist perceptions of women's lives and in accounting for the personal strength of women who were widely believed to be oppressed, subservient, and silent. They also direct attention to theoretical developments emerging from the work of scholars who have attempted to rethink the public-private dichotomy both from within and from outside existing epistemologies. Marcus (1992, 119), for example, argued that while there is a female domain that is centered on the household, it cannot be described as private or equated to the private domain of Western modernity. Rather, she held, the household is a center for women's public, sociable, and religious lives.

More recently, women scholars writing from within the Middle East and North Africa have developed a number of powerful analytical responses to the concepts of public/private and sex/gender found in universalizing narratives of modernization and aspects of feminist theory as it emerged from the 1960s. For Turkey, the reworking of public and private in the work of Göle (1997, 2002) is of great interest. She points to a very different articulation of gender, space, and modernity in Turkey, one which bears strongly upon debates about the subordination of women, the nature of sexuality, and the lives of women and men in modern Islamist states and societies. Driven by current political events, much recent attention has been given to veiling rather than to segregated space (for example, Yegenoğlu 1998); however the effects of a lessening of gender-segregated activities on women's emotional and political independence and sociality needs further study.

Bibliography

B. Aswad, Key and peripheral roles of noble women in a Middle Eastern plains village, in *Anthropological Quarterly* 40 (1967), 139–52.

——, *Property control and social strategies. Settlers on a Middle Eastern plain*, Cambridge, Mass., 1971.

L. Beck and N. Keddie (eds.), *Women in the Muslim world*, Cambridge, Mass. 1978.

P. Benedict, The *kabul gunu*. Structural visiting in an Anatolian provincial town, in *Anthropological Quarterly* 47:3 (1974), 28–47.

M. Dobkin, Social ranking in the women's world of purdah. A Turkish example, in *Anthropological Quarterly* 40:2 (1974), 65–72.

L. Fallers and M. Fallers, Sex roles in Edremit, in J. Peristiany (ed), *Mediterranean family structures*, Cambridge 1976, 243–61.

N. Göle, The gendered nature of the public sphere, in *Public Culture* 10:1 (1997), 61–81.

——, Islam in public. New visibilities and new imaginaries, in *Public Culture* 14:1 (2002), 173–190.

M.-J. DelVecchio Good, A comparative perspective on women in provincial Iran and Turkey, in L. Beck and N. Keddie (eds.), *Women in the Muslim world*, Cambridge, Mass., 1978, 482–500.

D. Kandiyoti, Sex roles and social change. A comparative appraisal of Turkey's women, in *Signs* 3:1 (1977), 57–73.

M. Kıray, Changing roles of mothers. Intra-family relations in a Turkish town, in J. Peristiany (ed.), *Mediterranean family structures*, Cambridge 1976, 259–74.

——, The women of small towns, in N. Abadan-Unat (ed.), *Women in Turkish society*, Leiden 1981, 259–74.

F. Mansur, *Bodrum. A town in the Aegean*, Leiden 1972.

F. Mansur Coşar, Women in Turkish society, in L. Beck and N. Keddie (eds.), *Women in the Muslim world*, Cambridge, Mass., 1978, 124–140.

J. Marcus, *A world of difference. Islam and gender hierarchy in Turkey*, Sydney 1992.

F. Mernissi, *Beyond the veil. Male-female dynamics in modern Muslim society*, Bloomington, Ind., 1987.

D. Murphy, *Embassy to Constantinople. The travels of Lady Mary Wortley Montagu*, London 1988.

M. Yeğenoğlu, *Colonial fantasies. Towards a feminist reading of Orientalism*, Cambridge 1998

Julie Marcus

Western Europe

Women's Informal Networks and the Interdomestic Domain

Discussions of women's position in Muslim society have repeatedly highlighted the importance of "women's worlds" in contexts of strictly gendered divisions of labor and female seclusion (purdah). In Bosnia, female neighborly networks are formed around coffee morning visiting (Brinja 1995). Intimate circles often articulate counter-hegemonic resistance to male domination (Abu-Lughod 1986). The theoretical point underlying these studies is summed up by Rosaldo's argument that women's position is raised when they can challenge male claims to authority "by creating a sense of rank, order and value in a world of their own" (1974, 36).

The crucial role played by British Pakistani women migrants in creating and controlling the interdomestic domain of sociability between families, neighbors, and friends is developed by Werbner (2002a). In Pakistan, Punjabi women traditionally manage the ritual gift economy known as *lena dena*, practiced during life-course rituals, particularly weddings (Eglar 1960). Werbner shows that the translocation of *lena dena* to Britain was the product of gendered power struggles between married women and their spouses: migrant women fought to recapture this domain, often against the explicit wishes of husbands who regarded ritual gifting as wasteful. In Manchester, women entered the British labor market, often as clothing machinists, to finance their pivotal role as symbolic transactors of gold, cloth, food, and money between households. The scale and cost of celebrations, particularly weddings, is huge.

Writing on recently arrived Moroccans in Italy, Salih found a preference for holding wedding rituals in Morocco, true also of Moroccans in France, Belgium, and Holland, despite lengthy sojourning (2003, 83). Such rituals serve to reintegrate migrants symbolically into their home communties, while enabling them to display their newly acquired wealth and Western lifestyles. Weddings are occasions for family reunions of migrants settled in different European countries.

For Pakistani migrants, the female *mehndi* (henna) pre-wedding ritual is the most elaborate within a complex cycle of rituals. Werbner describes the symbolic transformations occurring during the *mehndi* which, she argues, move bride and groom from a state of culturally constrained "coldness" to framed "heat," in anticipation of the consummation of the marriage. Equivalent female henna rituals known as *kina gecesi, laylat al-ḥinnā'* or *mehndi*, are held by Turkish, Moroccan, and Surinamese Hindustani Muslim migrants in the Netherlands (Dessing 2001). The female dresser, *negaffa*, paints the Moroccan bride with henna and plays an important role in the wedding reception, in which the bride changes her clothes several times, and is carried around the hall amidst singing and ululating. As among Pakistanis, weddings involve elaborate exchange relations.

Importantly, much like in India (Raheja and Gold 1994), the Pakistani *mehndi* is an occasion for bawdy singing, sexual clowning, and masquerade, in what might be termed a resistive or counterhegemonic commentary both on the status of women in Muslim Punjabi society, and of Pakistani migrants within British society. Such clowning is not simply reflexive; it fulfils a symbolic transformational role in the ritual process, occurring at a key liminal moment, before the clown is banished amidst gales of laughter by the women (Werbner 2002a). *Mehndi* rituals allow for inventiveness and cultural hybridity, while revitalizing through aesthetic performance the substances, foods, music, and dance of the homeland. The groom is subjected to hazing, sexual joking, and forced feeding by the female bride receivers, underlining the power and control of Punjabi women over the domestic domain. As Raheja and Gold also argue, such rituals highlight the uninhibited expressive sexuality of South Asian women. Not surprisingly, *mehndis* are disapproved of by Muslim reformists and Islamists.

A key issue concerns the migrants' move from initial isolation to sociability. Saifullah Khan (1977) argued that the supportive world of village women is disrupted when Mirpuri migrant women move to Bradford and are kept isolated in strict purdah in their homes. This is, however, only a stage: the need is to recognize the intersection of the labor migration cycle with the familial life cycle (Werbner 2002a). As families mature, women begin to develop extensive social networks, expanded further as weddings, funerals, and *khatam Qur'ān* multiply.

The movement in purdah can be represented diagramatically (after Werbner 2002a, 150).

DOMESTIC LIFE CYCLE PHASE
Young family

MIGRATION PHASE	*Initial*	*Settled*
Young family	Isolated women	Secluded women, but frequent contact with female kinswomen or friends (sometimes work)
Mature family	Isolated, but for a relatively short period (rarely work)	Extensive women-centered interhousehold network (often work)

Mature family

The centrality of women in "pre-political contexts of everyday life" is one stressed by Ålund in her study of Yugoslav women in Stockholm. She argues that "rather than being passive victims, women who have migrated actively employ the complex cultural symbolism of their histories to challenge contemporary forms of subordination and, in the process, they create new solidarities" (1999, 150–1). As in Bosnia, so too in Sweden women sustain informal networks and foster cross-ethnic local solidarities. Palestinian women asylum seekers in Berlin from Lebanon use streets as intense spaces of sociability and intimacy (Abdulrahim 1996, 62–3). Their networks incorporate Lebanese, Palestinian, Kurdish, and other Arabic speaking women and are instrumental for keeping tabs on husbands and maximizing access to services. Courtyards, parks corners, and squares are used for daily afternoon meetings, although women still suffer isolation, especially during the winter months.

The elaborate preparation of food, a major aspect of all interdomestic relations, is highlighted in a study of middle-class Iranian women migrants in Britain, who lay enormous stress on capturing the flavors and taste of Iranian food (Harbottle 2000). Food is also central to Algerians in South East France, whose rituals follow a set pattern: opening rite, prayers, meal, songs and dances, closing rite (Andezian 1990, 201). The food in such gatherings is blessed, containing *baraka*, and *dhikr* is performed, inducing ecstatic trance (ibid., 202). The female leader, the *muqadma*, presides over the rituals, conducts the supplicatory prayer (*duʿāʾ*), mediates requests to saints, finds solutions to personal afflictions, and accompanies women on Sufi pilgrimage to Algeria. Such invisible neighborhood events, convened in the privacy of homes, link immigrant women of all ages in family, neighborhood, and friendship networks. Like Algerians in France, Pakistani women migrants in the United Kingdom convene domestic communal Qurʾān readings in which food is blessed, to mark death, personal crises, and moments of transition (Werbner 2002a).

Young girls and women figure prominently in Pakistani *mehndi* celebrations. They are the ones who dance, sing, and clown, supporting the bride. Hence networks of second-generation girls and younger women are formed around such interdomestic rituals and celebrations. As they mature, issues of female seclusion and arranged marriage have gained prominence. Quite often, pubescent girls' movements are restricted and they are chaperoned, with family honor or the Islamic edicts regarding modesty repeatedly invoked. Fear of gossip is highly potent in close-knit Pakistani communities in Oxford, England, although illicit love affairs do occur (Shaw 2000, 172–3). Arranged marriages are a source of intergenerational conflict. The rate of Pakistani intercontinental marriages, often with close kin, continues to be high, with rising numbers of divorces and "forced" marriages, in which youngsters are coerced into marriage, sometimes abducted while on overseas visits.

Islamization, Home Study, and Associational Networks

Whether because of global trends toward Islamicization, or the maturation of second-generation migrant women, the spread of the *ḥijāb* (veil) has been marked in Muslim migrant communities across Western Europe, from Norway, Denmark, and Sweden to France, Belgium, the Netherlands, Germany, and the United Kingdom, along with the proliferation of Islamic study groups (*dars*), as noted by Afshar (1998) and Schmidt (2004). These rotate between women's homes or meet in mosques to interpret Qurʾānic verses or learn classical Arabic, often guided by a woman expert in Islamic studies. Some "born again" women belong to national and international networks, such as Al-Huda women's network, which has its headquarters in Pakistan. These networks use electronic mail and the Internet. An increased knowledge of Islam allows young women to resist traditional customs as un-Islamic, and to demand the right to make their own marriage choices (Dwyer 1999, Schmidt 2004).

Countering these conservative trends are more radical networks, such as that of lesbian Muslim and South Asian women in Britain (Kawale 2003). Hence, along with the visible Islamicization there has also been a growth in women's associational networks, whether philanthropic, Islamist, or radically critical of Muslim law and custom.

Turkish and Maghribi women's associations in France differ (Yalçin-Heckman 1997), with Moroccans having stronger and wider contacts with French authorities. Second and third generation Maghribi women are better integrated into the social services and speak good French. Lloyd reports that since 1981, Algerian women in France have founded a vast number of "caring" and cultural associations, some oriented to the homeland (Lloyd 1999).

In the United Kingdom, Werbner (2002b) reports the emergence of a Pakistani women's association that used satirical popular culture and spectacular philanthropic transnational activism to gain recognition. Many federated Muslim associations such as the Young Muslim Association of Britain or the United Kingdom Islamic Mission in Britain have women's sections. Sufi groups allow space for women. The network of Women Living Under Muslim Laws (WLUML), which advocates against infringements of women's human rights in Muslim countries, has its headquarters in London.

Many activist secular associations are multiethnic. In the United Kingdom these include Southall Black Sisters, which advocates against domestic violence, and encompasses South Asian women irrespective of religious origin, and Women Against Fundamentalism, which recently has agitated for women's rights in Algeria (Lloyd 1999). During the autumn of 1998 a *caravane* of Algerian associations, with a very strong representation of women, toured France to raise funds and present information on the growth of civil society in Algeria. Associations joined to defend the rights of asylum seekers (*sanspapiers*) from Algeria and West Africa. In 1996, a protest began of asylum seekers from Mali and Senegal in which women took a leading role. Lloyd (2003) reports that the women were in a stronger position than men to build networked support because they had more contacts with neighborhood structures, such as schools, shops, and local services, and their organizations reached across ethnic and national boundaries. The protest culminated in a march of 100,000 public sector trade unionists. Such alliances have raised consciousness about the plight of asylum seekers in France, many of them from Muslim countries and many of them women.

Conclusion

Muslim migrant women's networks draw on cultural familiars translocated from home into the migration context, enabling migrant women despite their marginality to create new solidarities, to sustain networks for self help, sociability, and study, and, more rarely, to mobilize for political protest.

Bibliography

D. Abdulrahim, Defining gender in a second exile. Palestinian women in West Berlin, in G. Buijs (ed.), *Migrant women. Crossing boundaries and changing identities*, Oxford 1993, 55–81.

L. Abu-Lughod, *Veiled sentiments. Honor and poetry in a Bedouin society*, Berkeley 1986.

H. Afshar, Strategies of resistance among the Muslim minority in West Yorkshire. Impact on women, in N. Charles and H. Hintje (eds.), *Gender, ethnicity and political ideologies*, London 1998, 107–26.

A. Ålund, Feminism, multiculturalism, essentialism, in N. Yuval-Davis and P. Werbner (eds.), *Women, citizenship and difference*, London 1999, 147–61.

S. Andezian, Migrant women in France, in T. Gerholm and Y. G. Lithman (eds.), *The new Islamic presence in Western Europe*, London 1990, 196–204.

T. Brinja, *Being Muslim the Bosnian way*, Princeton, N.J. 1995.

N. M. Dessing, *Rituals of birth, circumcision, marriage, and death among Muslims in the Netherlands*, Leuven 2001.

C. Dwyer, Veiled meanings. Young British Muslim women and the negotiation of difference, in *Gender, Place and Culture* 6:1 (1999), 5–26.

Z. Eglar, *A Punjabi village in Pakistan*, New York 1960.

K. Gardner, *Global migrants, local lives. Travel and transformation in rural Bangladesh*, Oxford 1995.

L. Harbottle, *Food for health, food for wealth. The performance of ethnic and gender identities by Iranian settlers in Britain*, Oxford 2000.

R. Kawale, A kiss is just a kiss . . . or is it? South Asian lesbians and bisexual women and the construction of space, in N. Puwar and P. Raghuram (eds.), *South Asian women in the diaspora*, Oxford 2003, 181–200.

C. Lloyd, Transnational mobilisations in contexts of violent conflict. The case of solidarity with women in Algeria, in *Contemporary Politics* 5:4 (1999), 365–77.

——, Antiracism, racism and asylum seekers in France, in *Patterns of Prejudice* 37 (2003), 3.

G. G. Raheja and A. G. Gold, *Listen to the heron's words. Reimagining gender and kinship in North India*, Berkeley 1994.

M. Z. Rosaldo, Women, culture and society. A theoretical overview, in M. Z. Rosaldo and M. Lamphere (eds.), *Women, culture and society*, Stanford 1974, 17–43.

V. Saifullah-Khan, Pakistanis and social stress. Mirpuris in Bradford, in V. Saifullah-Khan (ed.), *Families in Britain. Support and stress*, London 1979, 35–58.

R. Salih, *Gender in transnationalism. Home, longing and belonging among Moroccan migrant women*, London 2003.

G. Schmidt, Identity formation among young Muslims. The case of Denmark, Sweden, and the United States, in *Journal of Muslim Minority Affairs* 24:1 (2004), 31–46.

A. Shaw, *Kinship and continuity. Pakistani families in Britain*, London 2000.

P. Werbner, *The migration process. Capital, gifts and offerings among British Pakistanis*, Oxford 1990, repr. with new preface 2002a.

——, *Imagined diasporas among Manchester Muslims*, Oxford 2002b.

L. Yalçin-Heckman, The perils of ethnic associational life in Europe. Turkish migrants in Germany and France, in T. Modood and P. Werbner (eds.), *The politics of multiculturalism in the new Europe*, London 1997, 91–110.

Pnina Werbner

Patronage and Clientage

East Asia and Southeast Asia

An impressive amount of research has been conducted on the phenomenon of patronage and clientage. In literature, patronage and clientage are often used synonymously, particularly because anthropological and social science research uses the pattern of patron-client relationships to describe certain forms of dependency and/or loyalty-based interaction in societies. Both expressions refer to a male-oriented concept in ancient Rome, in which the patron (*patronus*) represented the protecting partner in a dyadic relationship. The patron was required to assist the client (*cliens*) in an emergency and defend him in trial. Originally, the client, who always came from a plebeian family, was an obedient servant, a protégé or a dependent slave, attached to a patrician family. Even though the plebeians were obliged to seek a patrician patron, they were free to choose the person they preferred. The client sought the patron's protection and delivered services in return. Later on, in the Caesarian period, the client was usually a poor citizen who served a member of the nobility and received accommodation and other privileges in return.

The early Roman relationship of patron and client implied a reciprocal moral obligation. The patron was morally required to support the client in public and private affairs, whereas the client was expected to display respect and thankfulness for the support he received. The tight personal relationship between the patron and the client (and his household) was initially a clear-cut power relation, but was gradually transformed into a relationship of trust and loyalty. The mutual trust as the core element of the partnership rendered the patron-client relation a lifetime contract, including the hereditary right of the descendants to continue it. As a societal institution, the patron-client relation was normative in moral rather than in legal regard (Weber Pazmiño 1991, 18–19). It was normally men who established the relationship with the client. The fact that the patronage was extended to his household indicates that the women and children were only "attached" to the contract.

Until the late 1960s, research on the topic was mainly conducted by cultural anthropologists. From then on, social scientists joined in to study patron-client relationships first from a sociological and then from a political science perspective. Following the thought pattern of modernization theory, clientelistic relationships were then seen as a feature of premodern societies, which were regarded as underdeveloped. Patronage and clientage were now mentioned in the context of clan structures, tribal culture, and feudal forms of interpersonal relations between the powerful and the powerless. As patronage was predominantly associated with religiously inspired developments in social organization, Catholicism became a focal point for scholars, resulting in extensive case studies focusing mainly on Latin America and Southern Europe. The subsequent extension of the geographical scope of research to Asia, however, challenged the general belief in the disappearance of patronage and clientage once modernization has been set into motion. Theories based on the Western model of development suggested that in industrialized states with complex social structures, the importance of informal institutions, such as patron-client contracts, would gradually be replaced by impersonal, formally legitimated institutions. This proved to be a too hastily generalized theoretical idea, as the case of Japan, one of the most striking cases of non-Western modernization, demonstrated. In Japan, familial ideology played an extraordinary role before the Second World War, when the entire concept of state was based on the principle of the "family state," with the emperor as the godfather of the Japanese race. After the war, familial ideology formed an essential part of Japanese company life. This preservation of traditional values at a time of rapid modernization became crucial for the revision of the classic modernization theory.

For advanced analysis of patronage and clientage, the dynamic character of the phenomenon is relevant. Clientelistic relationships change not only according to their respective societal context; they are also contingent upon the historical setting in which they constitute a structural element of social organization. Irrespective of gender aspects and historical settings, clientelism implies three core elements: first, social inequality and asymmetry in the relation of the partners involved; second, the exchange of goods or services; and third a personal character of the relationship. Gender aspects of patronage and clientage relate to all three elements.

Who enters a clientelistic relationship and why?

In Asia, clientelism is linked ultimately to the forging of loyalty and to family ideology. In societies where descent is of importance, patrons of high-ranking families gather clients around themselves. Until the first half of the twentieth century, clients were not paid for their services with money. The reward for their work and services in paddy fields, in plantations, in orchards, in the house or elsewhere was simply food and accommodation. In modern days, this pattern changed and money began to play a prominent role in patron-client contracts. In Asia's Islamic societies, the patron families often claim a royal lineage – relatives and offspring of a sultan – or trace their family ties back to a *syed* (*sayyid*, of Arab origin). Until the late 1950s (or even later) it was not unusual in some regions for such families to educate and prepare their daughters for their future role as caretaker of the entire entourage of the patron, especially when there was no male family member available to perform this task after the patron passed away. The role of the hereditary caretaker thus became de-gendered to a certain extent.

In insular Southeast Asia, both the dyadic relationship between male patrons and clients and the concept of adopted sons and daughters are still in existence. Today, the patron family becomes the foster family, or *keluarga angkat* in Indonesian/Malay. On their way from one place to another, people can approach the house of a local family, beg for food and shelter and a space to lay down their head. Once they act like a son or daughter – being obedient and loyal to the parents, helping with the housework – they may be adopted by the respective family. While in former times this pattern worked for young people seeking shelter and a place to stay, its role today is more differentiated, ranging from a more or less symbolic expression of liking each other to very pragmatic forms of utilization in the political arena. Another pragmatic motivation for the adoption of a son or daughter is the lack or abundance of female or male children in a household. Since both sexes are assigned gendered roles, their presence is of importance for a family. Therefore, it is common practice to give a child to a related family when there is a need or reason to do so. The concept of *keluarga angkat* is not restricted to Muslims but is a common pattern practiced by families of various ethnic origins and religious orientations.

In Malaysia, adoption has developed into a modern form of a formerly informal, legally non-binding patron-client relationship. Here, the father of the family is even entitled to marry the adopted daughter, which gives the otherwise de-gendered practice a peculiar twist and reveals the dominant position of the male in this practice. Another gender bias is the fact that patron families nowadays have become more reluctant to adopt girls. Current administration requires the registration of adopted children, even if they are nephews or nieces of the same family. Rape and abuse of adopted girls cannot be completely avoided by way of registry, but the adoption is at least legally based, so that any kind of abuse of the relationship can be brought to trial.

It is remarkable that women in many Asian Islamic communities seek advice from an imam, a local shaykh, or an *ʿālim* more often than men in order to cope with personal problems in daily life. The character of such a relationship is not so much shaped by the seeking of shelter or protection but by a mutual arrangement of "advice for money" – concerning matters such as which *sūra* of the Qurʾān should be read in order to ease physical, mental, or emotional pain. The relationship between a client and the provider of spiritual guidance need not last for a lifetime, although it is usually a steady connection. The reason for the higher frequency of female clients seeking help from religious advisors is believed to be the reluctance of men to admit the need for advice. For men, finding solutions for parental and marital problems is facilitated by the possibility of turning to a second, third, or fourth wife, whereas the women who are left behind often struggle to make ends meet, in particular when a regular source of income ceases to exist. The common term for advice from a wise person, and in particular from a religious celebrity, is "spiritual," indicating that humans need more than material security in order to handle the challenges of life. A male bias lies in the fact that the spiritual leaders in these Islamic societies are solely men. There is no *imāma*, *shaykha*, or *ʿālima*.

Patronage and clientage in Northeast Asia, in contrast, inherit elements of Confucian and Buddhist thought. Japan, Korea, and China have preserved these elements until today and have translated them into a modern context (the Japanese company functioning as a "family," for example). Confucian principles relating to seniority and rules of respect within the family (younger brother–elder brother; son–father) do not explicitly refer to women. The status of woman in the hierarchical order, however, is lower than men's. Within the hierarchical order, women assume a respected status only when no suitable male counterpart is available. In rural China, the system of patronage and clientage is ultimately linked to the clan structure, which is deeply embedded in Chinese society. In Japan, specific modes of interaction were cultivated during the seventeenth and eighteenth centuries, resulting in principles such as *giri* (owing somebody something based on moral duties), *oyabu–kobun* (the "parent" partner enjoying the loyalty of the "child" partner) or *sempa–kōhai* (the elder of two colleagues, students, schoolmates, and so forth taking care of the younger and enjoying the latter's loyalty and obedience). In societies where seniority plays an important role, patronage and clientage have strong repercussions in the political and occupational arena. The representation of women in patron functions is rare even today. For most of the women in such societies, breaking through the glass ceiling requires a comprehensive restructuring of the male-dominated organizational arena. Therefore, it is the more remarkable that Northeast, Southeast and South Asia are outstanding examples in terms of the occurrence of female political top leadership. The succession to the posts of minister, prime minister, president or opposition leader by women is extraordinary. The shared element of those women's career pattern is their dynastic background, combined with a traditional clientelistic feature. The obvious importance of dynasties and elite family lineage even in today's political life renders a common theoretical assumption questionable, namely, the assumption of the decreasing importance of patronage and clientage in modern and highly complex societies. Japan and South Korea are cases in point.

In most Asian societies, patronage and clientage mingle with a strong prevalence of paternalism in human interaction. As a general feature of the phenomenon in Asia, the concepts of loyalty and protection bear a strong meaning. Traditionally women have been considered to be in need of protection, which is an argument that also nurtures the frequent understanding among Muslims of the headscarf as a piece of cloth providing protection of women in public life. Men in the role of the patron outnumber the women in such function by far, but there are exceptions to the rule, such as the system of training girls to become the caretaker of extended elite families in Southeast Asia. Patronage does not cease to exist when "modern" principles of social and political organization gain momentum. Conversely, traditional forms, principles, concepts, elements, and mechanisms of clientelism have been translated into a modern context. There is certainly a cultural dimension to the phenomenon, so that the assumption of a connection between Catholicism and clientelism as claimed in earlier research bears some truth. Caution should be employed, however, in ranking the influence of cultural and religious traditions. It is by no means established that Islamic societies display a higher frequency of clientelistic structures than Confucian, Buddhist, Christian, or Hindu societies. The ancient concept of clientelism, with its emphasis on informality in the legal regard, its individual personal relationships, and principal of volunteerism, has widely prevailed until today. Legally registered procedures such as the adoption of a child are an exception to the conventional mechanism. For women, patronage and clientage may imply both privileges and disadvantages in the pursuit of welfare, status, or social position. Women in a clientelistic relation have to cope with different kinds of problems from men, for example when they are urged by the patron to deliver sexual services in exchange for certain privileges. The sanctions for violating the rules of a clientelistic relationship are the same for both sexes: since there is no legal basis, punishment occurs in form of moral degrading such as public exposure, defamation of character, or informal tools of social control such as gossip or ridicule.

BIBLIOGRAPHY

C. Clapham (ed.), *Private patronage and public power. Political clientelism in the modern state*, London 1982.

C. H. Landé, Introduction. The dyadic basis of clientelism, in S. Schmidt, L. Guasti, C. H. Landé, and J. C. Scott (eds.), *Friends, followers, and factions. A reader in political clientelism*, Berkeley 1977, xiii–xxxvii.

R. Lemarchand, Comparative political clientelism. Structure, process and optic, in S. N. Eisenstadt and R. Lemarchand (eds.), *Political clientelism, patronage and development*, Beverly Hills 1981, 7–34.

H.-H. Nolte (ed.), *Patronage und Klientel. Ergebnisse einer polnisch-deutschen Konferenz*, Cologne 1989.

S. Piattoni (ed.), *Clientelism, interests and democratic representation. The European experience in historical and comparative perspective*, Cambridge 2001.

L. Roninger and A. Güneş-Ayata (eds.), *Democracy, clientelism and the civil society*, London 1994.

G. Weber Pazmiño, Klientelismus. Annäherung an ein Konzept, Ph.D. diss., University of Zurich 1991.

CLAUDIA DERICHS

Turkey

Patron-client relationships involve at least two parties and are characterized by enduring, multifaceted exchange over time in stratified societies. While asymmetrical, they are often characterized by personal warmth and affection (Roniger 2001). The relationship can be invoked at any time, and the participants derive from it various forms of security. For example, a patron may acquire from it a reliable workforce, and a client economic and physical security (Platteau 1995). In Turkey women encounter and participate in patronage and clientage in a variety of roles, such as citizens, household members, rural agriculturalists, recent migrants living in cities, and in social and political movements. Patronage and clientage have proven remarkably portable and adaptable during the past century as Turkey has transitioned from a new, mainly rural state in which patronage and clientage existed most classically in the landlord-peasant relationship, to a modernizing, urbanizing state in which they now characterize machine politics and myriad other economic/social relationships (Güneş-Ayata 1994).

The concepts of patronage and clientage, especially as they concern women's lives, have come to be morally laden because they challenge the individualistic, egalitarian ideal articulated by the late modern Turkish state. Studies of Turkish politics and governance, economic development, and civil society (Balci, Burns, and Tongun 2002) and policy papers by multilateral organizations such as the World Bank (2000) often emphasize women's roles in patron-client networks, which the authors regard as related to or synonymous with "corruption."

Patronage and clientage in households

While patronage and clientage are usually associated with male-dominated social arenas, in actuality they may have more everyday relevance in Turkey for women than for men. Adaman and Çarkoğlu, who define corruption in Turkey as the presence of bribery and patronage networks (2001, 2), note that "women, on the average, turn out to have a higher perceived intensity of corruption" of local governments, and speculate that this is due to women's engagement in "ordinary life struggle" such as "shopping, escorting children to and from schools, cleaning houses . . . etc." (ibid. 18). White (1994) characterizes the relationship between a woman and her daughter-in-law in Turkey's patrilineal, patrilocal households as a patronage relationship. Özyeğin (1996) has characterized the relationship between Turkish female employers and domestic workers as based on patronage. Workers received benefits such as loans, educational assistance for their children, and small castoff or new items.

Studies of Turkish peasant communities (Kudat 1975, Sayari 1977) portray communities where patronage and clientage script virtually all social relationships. In such communities, women's activities have provided essential household sustenance. As village economies have been gradually impacted by the market, women's contributions have been devalued as cheap imported goods replace those they once crafted (Delaney 1991, 267).

Millions of households in Turkey have left village life altogether, and more than half of Turkish women now live in urban areas (Hemmasi and Prorok 2002, 399). A major cause of urbanization has been the breakdown of patron-client landlord-peasant relationships due to agricultural mechanization since the 1950s, which has prompted rural families to migrate to towns and cities in Turkey and abroad. Upon arrival, the migrants again "enter into patron-client relationships in terms of work, welfare and political organization" (Akşit, Karanci, Gündüz-Hoşgör 2001, 14).

Patronage and clientage and social movements

Women in Turkey have challenged patronage and clientage through a variety of means. Participants in the 1980s feminist movement among urban elite women implicated patron-client relations by attributing inequality to the networks of gender and production relations (Sosyalist Feminist Kaktüs 1988, cited in Arat 1994, 104). Religious women's organizations, such as the 40 that comprise the Islamist Istanbul Rainbow Women's Platform (Houston 2001, 140) provide an alternative to mainstream patronage and clientage. Since they lack linkages to the powerful business, banking, and media circles, they are able to avoid the rentier and patron-client relationships of the mainstream parties (Balci, Burns, and Tongun 2002, 48). Finally, the separatist Kurdistan Worker's Party, one of the few revolutionary movements in the Islamic world to engage women as combatants, challenged large landowners and other patrons during its violent campaign against the Turkish state from the mid-1980s to 1999.

Conclusion

Although from the start the Kemalist Turkish state granted women significant civil and political rights, it was still patriarchal in most respects and neglected to set up a system that allowed women to exercise these rights. Instead, the system that has prevailed in Turkey is based on patronage and clientage. It is daily invoked and challenged by women in relationships ranging from ideologically diverse public social movements to the most intimate settings of their families and households.

Bibliography

F. Adaman and A. Çarkoğlu, *Engagement in corruptive activities at local and central governments in Turkey. Perceptions of urban settlers*, Marseilles 2001.
Y. Arat, Women's movement of the 1980s in Turkey.

Radical outcome of liberal Kemalism?, in F. M. Göçek and S. Balaghi (eds.), *Reconstructing gender in the Middle East. Tradition, identity, and power*, New York 1994, 100–12.

T. Balci, T. Burns, and L. Tongun, Influence of Turkish Islamist groups on Turkey's candidacy to the European Union, paper presented at the American Political Science Association Annual Meeting, Boston 2002.

C. Delaney, *The seed and the soil. Gender and cosmology in Turkish village society*, Berkeley 1991.

A. Güneş-Ayata, Roots and trends of clientelism in Turkey, in L. Roniger and A. Güneş-Ayata (eds.), *Democracy, clientelism, and civil society*, Boulder, Colo. 1994, 49–63.

M. Hemmasi and C. V. Prorok, Women's migration and quality of life in Turkey, in *Geoforum* 33 (2002), 399–411.

C. Houston, *Islam, Kurds and the Turkish nation state*, Oxford 2000.

A. Kudat, Patron-client relations. The state of the art and research in Eastern Turkey, in E. Akarli and G. Ben-Dor (eds.), *Political participation in Turkey*, Istanbul 1975, 61–8.

G. Özyeğin, Verwandtschaftsnetzwerke, Patronage und Klassenschuld Das Verhaltnis von Hausangestellten und ihren Arbeitgeberinnen in der Turkei, in *Frauen in der einen Welt*, 2 (1996), 9–28.

J. Platteau, A framework for the analysis of evolving patron-client ties in agrarian economies, in *World Development* 23 (1995), 767–86.

L. Roniger, Patron-client relations, anthropology of, in N. Smelser and P. Baltes (eds.), *The international encyclopedia of the social and behavioral sciences*, London 2001, 1118–20.

S. Sayari, Political patronage in Turkey, in E. Gellner and J. Waterbury (eds.), *Patrons and clients in Mediterranean societies*, London 1977, 103–30.

Sosyalist Feminist Kaktüs, Neden dergi çikariyoruz, in *Sosyalist Feminist Kaktüs* 1 (1988), 6.

J. B. White, *Money makes us relatives. Women's labor in urban Turkey*, Austin, Tex. 1994.

World Bank, *Social assessment and agricultural reform in Central Asia and Turkey*, Washington, D.C. 2000.

Diane E. King

Peacekeeping and Conflict Management

Arab States

United Nations peacekeeping and conflict management: historical background

The concepts of peacekeeping and conflict management are primarily classified under the rubrics of political and military categorizations aimed at instilling an impartial military presence in areas of conflict in order to ease political tensions and allow for diplomatic negotiations toward peace to occur. The model for contemporary peacekeeping missions was initiated during the Arab-Israeli war of 1948 following United Nations Security Council Resolution 50, dated 29 May 1948. The mission was called the United Nations Truce Supervision Organization (UNTSO) and is still considered an active mission in the occupied territories of Palestine and Israel. The United Nations has also maintained peacekeeping missions in the Golan Heights (UNDOF) since 1974 and in Lebanon (UNIFIL) since 1978 and has been carrying out missions with the Palestinian Liberation Organization (UNSCO) since 1999 and in Iraq (UNAMI) since 2003. Completed peacekeeping missions in the Arab world include the following:

UN Program	Country	Initiated	Completed
UNEF I	Suez, Egypt	1956	1967
UNIGIL	Lebanon	1958	1958
UNYOM	Yemen	1963	1964
UNEF II	Egypt-Israel	1973	1979
UNIMOG	Iran-Iraq	1988	1991
MINUSRO	Morocco	1991	1991
UNIKOM	Iraq-Kuwait	1991	2003
UNASOG	Chad-Libya	1994	1994

Through the course of development, peacekeeping missions have evolved to incorporate conflict management personnel: these include the traditional "Blue Berets" (the moniker given the international soldiers comprising peacekeeping forces because of their distinctive headgear); civilian police officers; electoral experts and observers; de-miners; human rights monitors; specialists in civil affairs and governance; and experts in communication and public information in order to ease the political and military tensions and to promote the reconciliation and reconstruction process.

Despite the expansion of mission objectives to incorporate aspects of conflict management, peacekeeping issues are primarily analyzed through a strongly militarized perspective of peacekeeping and conflict management activities. This perspective is based on the highly patriarchal conceptualization that the use of force through heavily armed and state centered approaches is the only means available to ensure peace. This ideal has a tendency to perpetuate a cycle of violence that has yet to prove completely effective in ensuring lasting peace and reconciliation, particularly in the Arab world. An essential query that is still not addressed in the peacekeeping and conflict management equation is how these militarized operations have impacted on and affected women.

Until the adoption of Security Council Resolution 1325 on Women, Peace and Security (31 October 2000), the gender variable had not been taken into account; the conduct of peacekeeping and conflict management activities primarily as military operations often resulted in a disproportionate amount of violence and injustice imposed on women. Prior to the adoption of Resolution 1325, women's contributions toward peace-building and conflict resolution were not recognized as significant factors to be incorporated into the organization of peacekeeping missions. Resolution 1325 reaffirms "the important role of women in the prevention and resolution of conflict and in peace-building, and stress[es] the importance of their equal participation and full involvement in all efforts for the maintenance of peace and security, and the need to increase their role in decision-making with regard to conflict prevention and resolution" (UNSCR 2000).

Resolution 1325 called for four main themes to be addressed during peacekeeping operations. The first is the participation of women in decision-making and peace processes: the number of women in institutions and field operations should be increased and women's groups should be consulted and included in actual peace processes. The second theme is the creation of training guidelines and materials to incorporate a gender perspective for all peacekeeping personnel prior to their deployment. The third is the adoption of a gender perspective including measures that protect and respect the human rights of women and girls. The fourth involves gender mainstreaming in United Nations reporting systems and stresses the need to incorporate gender mainstreaming in all aspects of the political decision-making processes among the member states, particularly during the peace-building and post-conflict reconstruction phase (Naraghi-Anderlini 2000).

Gender variable in peacekeeping and conflict management: Arab women

Despite the groundbreaking advances of Resolution 1325, the issues of war, peacekeeping, conflict management, and security are still identified under the patriarchal rubric of political, economic, and military characteristics. These characteristics highlight the pervasive violence against women during conflict, which often persists after armed conflict in the form of domestic violence against women. The most significant factor contributing to the exclusion of women from participating in peacekeeping and conflict management operations is the lack of political opportunities afforded to encourage, and in many cases even allow, the political participation of women in the decision-making process that directly affects their lives.

A study conducted by the United Nations Security Council in October 2002 indicates that first, a mere cessation of hostilities does not bring an end to intra-state conflict. To end conflict, the creation of sustainable peace by means of fundamental societal change is required. Such change includes democracy, good governance, human rights, the rule of law, and gender equality. If half the population – women – are excluded from the equation, these changes simply do not occur. Second, lasting peace must be "home grown" and based on indigenous processes. Local women hold communities together during conflict, organize political movements, manage relief efforts and rebuild societies (United Nations Press Release SC7467).

Based on the findings of the Security Council's report, it may be safely concluded that the highly militarized and patriarchal approaches to peacekeeping missions and conflict management activities must be reconstructed to include a gendered perspective in order to be effective and allow for sustainable peace. Given that the first peacekeeping mission is still in effect 56 years after it was initiated provides enough evidence for the inadequacy of the existing structures.

Bibliography

D. P. Auerswald, *Disarmed democracies. Domestic institutions and the use of force*, Ann Arbor 2000.

G. Cawthra and R. Luckham (eds.), *Governing insecurity. Democratic control of military and security establishments in transitional democracies*, London 2003.

C. Enloe, *Maneuvers. The international politics of militarizing women's lives*, Berkeley 2000.

D. Gioseffi (ed.), *Women on war*, New York 2003.

J. Hagan, Do not send us your weapons. The General Assembly Debates Peace and Security, United Nations Chronicle Online, <http://www.un.org/Pubs/chronicle/2002/issue4/0402p18.html>.

H. Herzog, A space of their own. Social-civil discourses among Palestinian-Israeli women in peace organizations, in *Social Politics* 6:3 (Fall 1999), 344–69.

Independent Commission on Disarmament and Security Issues, *Common security. A blueprint for survival*, New York 1982.

G. E. Irani and N. C. Funk, Rituals of reconciliation. Arab-Islamic perspectives, Columbia International Affairs Online, <http://osiyou.cc.columbia.edu:2226/wps/funo1/funo1.html>.

D. R. Marshall, *Women in war and peace. Grassroots peace-building*, Washington, D.C. 2000.

S. Naraghi-Anderlini, The A-B-C to UN Security Council Resolution 1325 on Women and Peace and Security, 2000, <http://www.peacewomen.org/un/sc/ABC1325.html>.

B. Reardon, *Sexism and the war system*, Syracuse, N.Y. 1996.

I. L. Saqjor (ed.), *Common grounds. Violence against women in war and armed conflict situations*, Quezon City, Philippines 1998.

I. Skjelsbaek, *Gendered battlefields. A gender analysis of peace and conflict*, Oslo 1997.

M. Thee, Militarism and militarization, in E. Lazlo and J. Y. Yoo (eds.), *World encyclopedia of peace*, Oxford 1986, 594–8.

J. Turpin, Many faces. Women confronting war, in L. A. Lorentzen, and J. Turpin (eds.), *The women and war reader*, New York 1998, 3–19.

United Nations Department of Peacekeeping Operations, <www.un.org/Depts/ dpko/dpko/home.shtml>.

United Nations Press Release, <http://www.un.org/News/Press/docs/2002/ sc7467.doc.htm>.

United Nations Security Council Resolution 50, 1948, 1986, <http://www.yale.edu/lawweb/ avalon/un/scres050.htm>.

United Nations Security Council Resolution 1325, 2000, <http://www.un.org/events/ res_1325e.pdf>.

L. M. Woerhle, Silent or silenced?, in L. A. Lorentzen and J. Turpin (eds.), *The women and war reader*, New York 1998, 343–8.

Women's International League for Peace and Freedom. Peace women. UNSC RES 1325 translated, <http://www.peacewomen.org/un/ecosoc/CSW/ELTheme22004>.

Norma T. Nemeh

The Caucasus and Turkey

In the sub-region of the Caucasus and Turkey a variety of recent conflicts have given rise to efforts at peacekeeping and conflict management in which women have played increasingly visible roles. The conflicts have taken place along religious, ethnic, and socioeconomic lines in modernizing states, each of which has a history of empire; these features are all factors in the conflicts and their resolution.

Seven instances of open warfare occurred in the Caucasus in the 1980s and 1990s, and there have been many other cases of the use of armed force against civilians (Hansen 1998, 9). In Turkey, the Partiya Karkerên Kurdistan (PKK, Kurdistan Worker's Party), a Marxist separatist movement, waged an armed campaign against the state during the 1980s and 1990s, and other recent conflicts have occurred on a smaller scale. Domestic violence is also prevalent. A high percentage of women in Turkey report being at least occasionally beaten (Arat 2000). Conflict resolution and peacemaking are thus as applicable to intimate, household levels as to broader geopolitical levels, and local women activists have responded with initiatives aimed at curbing violence of all kinds.

Throughout the sub-region, women have traditionally played an important role in indigenous mediation, often invoking a specific societal role such as motherhood. According to tradition in the Caucasus, a woman could stop a fight by throwing her scarf between the combatants (Garb 1996, 36). In Turkey, the women's activist group "Saturday Mothers" responded with a campaign to unite people from disparate political factions, and assisted Kurdish parents in tracing their imprisoned or "disappeared" children (Anderson 1999, 232).

Women in the sub-region have also built on efforts by their predecessors. Recent attempts to mobilize Azeri and Armenian women for peace in the disputed area of Nagorno-Karabakh have built upon earlier movements dating back to the early twentieth century (Tohidi 2000). Efforts at reducing domestic violence in Azerbaijan date back at least to the 1920s (Heyat 2000).

The vocabularies and institutions of peacemaking, peace-building, peacekeeping, and conflict management in the Caucasus and Turkey have proliferated in recent years as a consequence of the globalization of civic activism. Many recent endeavors at peacemaking, particularly those that specifically involve women, have arisen from collaboration between local activists and international institutions. For example, in 2001 the Center for Global Peace at the American University in Washington, D.C. created a commission to promote peace between Armenians and Turks and between Armenians and Azeris (International Peace and Conflict Resolution 2003). The commission's efforts have engaged women, including a trip by Armenian women to Istanbul and a pilot television show focusing on women's issues designed to reach both Turkish and Armenian viewers.

Local women activists have created local and cross-state peace-promoting linkages both directly and through United Nations agencies and international non-governmental organizations. The Transcaucasus Women's Dialogue, established in 1994, brought together women from Armenia, Azerbaijan, and Georgia to work on such projects as the rehabilitation of child war victims and training in peace- and democracy-building (Reimann 2001, 55). United Nations Security Council Resolution 1325, adopted in 2000, calls for incorporating gender-informed perspectives into disarmament, demobilization, and rehabilitation initiatives in Azerbaijan and has served to sanction the efforts of local activists. Women for Conflict Prevention and Peace Building in the Southern Caucasus, an initiative started by the United Nations Development Fund for Women (UNIFEM) in 2001, addresses the condition of unresolved conflict known as "no-war-no-peace" in Azerbaijan, Georgia, and Armenia. It has engaged in a variety of peace-building activities, such as convening a meeting between women in the Azeri Nakhichevan area; gathering women leaders from among the estimated 1.2 million Internally Displaced People (IDPs) in the South Caucasus for conflict resolution and peace-building workshops; and developing a university curriculum on gender and conflict resolution (UNIFEM 2003).

Peace-promoting vocabularies are transmited through various technologies, of which women activists have recently made creative use. In the late 1990s activist women in Armenia, whose previous strategy had mainly been oral presentation, started using media technologies for peacemaking (McKay and Mazurana 2001, 24). In Turkey, a shift has been taking place in the way the Turkish-Kurdish conflict is talked about. The ban on the public use of the Kurdish language, including on radio and television, has been relaxed, and acknowledgment of Kurdish ethnic difference is now more common in public discourse.

Women are a majority in every state in the sub-region of Turkey and the Caucausus; more women than men are thus affected by conflict. Moreover, in combat zones women are often victimized by rape, displacement, and otherwise to a greater degree than men even though most of the combatants are male. Efforts by women in the region at peacemaking, peace-building, peacekeeping, and conflict resolution demonstrate that women are not content to remain victims, and that they can play a vital role in the struggle for peace.

Bibliography

S. Anderson, Women's many roles in reconciliation, in European Centre for Conflict Prevention (ed.), *People building peace. 35 inspiring stories from around the world*, Utrecht 1999, 230–6.

Y. Arat, Gender and citizenship in Turkey, in S. Joseph (ed.), *Gender and citizenship in the Middle East*, Syracuse, N.Y. 2000, 275–86.

P. Garb, Mediation in the Caucasus, in A. W. Wolfe and H. Yang (eds.), *Anthropological contributions to conflict resolution*, Athens, Ga. 1996, 31–46.

G. Hansen, *Humanitarian action in the Caucasus. A guide for practitioners*, Providence, R.I. 1998.

F. Heyat, Azeri professional women's life strategies, in F. Acar and A. Güneş-Ayata, (eds.), *Gender and identity construction. Women of Central Asia, the Caucasus and Turkey*, Leiden 2000, 177–201.

International Peace and Conflict Resolution (IPCR), Track two project in Turkey and the Caucasus, in *IPCR Newsletter* Winter Issue (2003), 4.

S. McKay and D. Mazurana, *Raising women's voices for peacebuilding. Vision, impact and limitations of media technologies*, London 2001.

C. Reimann, *Towards gender mainstreaming in crisis prevention and conflict management. Guidelines for German technical co-operation*, Eschborn 2001.

N. Tohidi, Gender and national identity in post-Soviet Azerbaijan, in F. Acar and A. Günes-Ayata (eds.), *Gender and identity construction. Women of Central Asia, the Caucasus and Turkey*, Leiden 2000, 249–92.

UNIFEM (United Nations Development Fund for Women), Southern Caucasus Peace Project, *Women for conflict prevention and peace building in the Southern Caucasus*, New York 2003.

DIANE E. KING

South Asia

Women in South Asia have traditionally played an active role in conflict resolution particularly at the grassroots level. They have a history of joining in liberation movements such as the nationalist movements and the Tebhaga and Telengana movements during the late 1940s. However, it was only in the postcolonial period that they consciously organized themselves for conflict resolution. This was as a result of the increasing numbers of intrastate conflicts in South Asia. In the late 1980s conflicts of state versus community were sharply on the rise. In Bangladesh problems over the Chittagong Hill Tracts (CHT) from 1980 led to a series of massacres, plunders, and destruction of villages. In India the 1980s witnessed increasing violence in Kashmir, Punjab, and the Northeast. In Sri Lanka too the post-1983 period was one of growing hostility between the Tamils and the Sinhalese. Again, antagonisms between Sindhis and Mohajirs intensified after the 1985 elections in Pakistan. Although all these conflicts had historical roots they became particularly violent in the late 1980s and 1990s. And in all these movements women played an important role in conflict resolution.

People in the CHT were antagonistic toward the government of Bangladesh from the time the Kaptai dam was built (1957–62) and thousands of people became homeless. In the early 1970s the whole of CHT was brought under military control. The original inhabitants of the CHT were the Jumma (tribal) people. They were aggrieved not just because of the dam but also because the state had undertaken to change the demographic balance of the region through a policy of settling Bengali Muslim people from the plains in the CHT. The protest of the Jumma people brought forth severe counter-insurgency measures leading to extra-judicial killings and massacres by the state. The rebels also formed a military unit called the Shanti Bahani. In all of this the tribal women were targeted; this was dramatically brought to the fore by the abduction of Kalpana Chakma in 1996. While the region was being torn apart the Hill Women's Federation (HWF), a secular women's organization, was formed in 1989 by women students of the Chittagong University. By 1991 it had become extremely popular. One of its main goals was to end Muslim violence against the tribal people. Although secular, it worked with both secular and religious groups such as the Bengali Muslim intelligentsia, human rights groups, and even community-based organizations such as the Tripura Samiti and the Marma Samiti. The main aims of these groups were justice for the tribal people of CHT and an end to violence. They were among the strongest voices for peace with the Bangladesh government in 1997 but once a pact was signed between the people of CHT and the Bangladesh government they were denied any political space.

In India, conflicts between state and community in Kashmir and the Northeast led to women's activism for conflict resolution. In Kashmir, women's popular participation found articulation through organizations such as Duktarane Millat and Muslim Khawateen Markaz. Islamic social reform movements inspired both these organizations. Through these movements women appropriated the democratic space for popular protest in the early 1990s. They mobilized other women and protested against violence directed toward Kashmiri Muslims. They braved the batons of the police and shielded their men. They would run to the security bunker to agitate against unlawful arrest of boys from the neighborhoods. In the early 1990s the *burqaʿ*-clad female protestor was a familiar sight. However, as the movement gained momentum these women became more and more identified with the separatist movements and lost much of their legitimate space for conflict resolution.

In Northeast India, in contrast, some women's groups, particularly the Naga women, have through their activism made spaces for their voices in conflict resolution. The Naga conflict predates Indian independence and began as a movement for autonomy. Soon, however, it converted into a separatist movement leading to increasing violence. In the 1980s the Nagas were fighting not just the Indian state but also a fratricidal war between different Naga groups. It was during this period of extreme violence that women in Nagaland organized themselves into a secular group known as the Naga Mothers Association (NMA). Most of its members were Christians but they did not bring up religion as an issue. They raised their voices against any violent acts and urged the Nagas to work together. They were instrumental in reducing conflict among Naga people and also bringing the Nagas and the Indian state into a political dialogue. They were the first South Asian women's group to sit in a ceasefire negotiation between the government of India and the Nationalist Socialist Council of Nagaland (Isaac-Muivah faction). During the period of ceasefire they have continued their pro-peace activism and have made efforts to improve their relations with people of neighboring Assam and Arunachal Pradesh. One of the main reasons for the success of NMA is that they have legitimized their role in conflict resolution through a non-partisan approach and have been successful in making crucial alliances with other civil society and human rights organizations. Although there is a plethora of women's groups in Northeast India, such as Meira Paibies (Torch bearers) in Manipur, the Kuki Women's Federation, and the Mizo Widows' Union, none of them are as successful in making political interventions as the NMA.

In 1984 the security forces in the Jaffna area detained more than 500 young men who were suspected of being terrorists. It was a time of growing violence in Sri Lanka as the government tried to suffocate the Tamil separatists led by the Liberation Tigers of Tamil Eelam in the east and north of the country. These unlawful detentions triggered a women's movement in Jaffna. The women organized themselves into a Mothers' Front in 1984 and marched with nearly 10,000 participants to protest against the Government Agent. The mothers were able to distinguish themselves as citizens of Sri Lanka and as such different from the rank and file of the liberation movement. The protest march yielded partial and momentary results but effected a permanent impact on the activities of the state, which began to detain Jaffna youths with caution. The Mothers' Front in the north survived for two years and then the women were forced to disperse. There were similar experiments by women in the south but none of these movements lasted for very long. This was because the conflicting sides such as the Sri Lankan government and the Tamil separatists largely opposed women's interventions in conflict resolution. South Asian experiences demonstrate that when both sides in a conflict try to marginalize women very seldom are women able to make any major interventions. Even in conflict resolution women find it extremely difficult at times to transcend their group identities.

The Sindhi Mohajir conflict in Pakistan initially gave women a political space but their own leaders soon took it away from them. The Muttahida Qaumi Movement (MQM) of the Urdu-speaking immigrants from India, who were the voices of the Mohajirs, inspired women to join the movement. In February 1989, 7,500 women enlisted in the MQM in a single day. The MQM was an urban middle-class phenomenon and many of its women participants shunned the veil as they considered themselves to be progressive. But the MQM women soon began to be seen as partisan and militant and their abilities to negotiate politically declined. Even the Sindhiani Tehrik (Sindhi Women's Movement) could make no headway in conflict resolution. This was when a radical women's group known as Women's Action Forum (WAF) stepped in. WAF contacted women from MQM and Sindhiani Tehrik. They held themselves to be a platform for peace and facilitated inter-community dialogues. It was the WAF initiative that made some space for inter-community understanding in Pakistan.

Women's role in conflict management in South Asia has been checkered. Some women's groups such as the NMA or the WAF have made long-term interventions for conflict resolution and others, such as the Mothers' Front in Sri Lanka, have had only immediate success. Most of these women's movements grew out of a necessity to provide alternatives to violence within their society. They are thus always identified with their own communities. They achieve greater success and more political space when they are able to transform their identities from the local to the universal. Most often their activism is rooted in their cultural roles as mothers, wives, and sisters. There is however, a growing recognition among women today that activism based on these roles may be counter-productive. In recent years women have moved away from such identifications and act as women and compatriots rather than as mothers and daughters. After the Gujarat riots against Muslims in 2002 secular women from both the Hindu and Muslim communities came together in an organization called Women for Peace. Even in the conflicts between the state and the Maoists in Nepal women's peace groups have taken such titles as Women's Leadership for Peace. Motherhood traditionally gave women the legitimacy to intervene in conflict management; since it was considered a male domain only mothers, wives, or daughters could raise voices against violence. Recent experiences have led women to make their appeals less as mothers and more as citizens. When women appealed as mothers or wives they were marked as partisan and excluded from political negotiations. In the recent peace talks in Sri Lanka women's groups have represented themselves as citizens and recovered a space for themselves in conflict management. Even in state versus state disagreements women have achieved some success in managing conflicts. Women's groups are increasingly active in civil society initiatives for peace between India and Pakistan. Also, it was the women's movement in Pakistan that condemned the atrocities of its own army and apologized to Bengali women in Bangladesh. However, it is in the intra-state conflicts that women have achieved most in conflict management, particularly when they have been able to feminize the space for peace.

Bibliography

P. Banerjee, Between two armed patriarchies. Women in Assam and Nagaland, in R. Manchanda (ed.), *Women, war and peace in South Asia. Beyond victimhood to agency*, New Delhi 2001, 131–76.

——, Resisting erasure. Women IDPs in South Asia, in P. Banerjee, S. B. Raychowdhury, and S. Das (eds.), *The UN guiding principles and internal displacement in South Asia*, Sage Publications (forthcoming).

A. Basu (ed.), The sacred and the secular. Women's activism and politicized religion in South Asia, New Delhi 1998, 15–32.

K. Bhasin, S. K. Nighat, and R. Menon (eds.), *Against all odds. Essays on women. Religion and development*, New Delhi 1994.

A. M. Chenoy, *Militarism and women in South Asia*, New Delhi 2001.

C. Cockburn, *The space between us. Negotiating gender and national identities in conflict*, London 1998.

R. Coomaraswamy, Report of the Special Rapporteur on violence against women, its causes and consequences, UN Commission on Human Rights E/CN.4/1998/54, 26 January 1998.

——, To bellow like a cow. Women, ethnicity and the discourse of rights, in R. J. Cook (ed.), *Human rights of women. National and internal perspectives*, Philadelphia 1994, 39–57.

M. Guhathakurta, The Bangladesh liberation war. A summons to memory, in A. Kalam (ed.), *Internal dynamics and external linkages*, Dhaka 1996, 19–29.

A. Jehangir, Whither are we?, in *Dawn* (Pakistan), 2 October 2000.

N. de Mel, *Women and the nation's narrative. Gender and nationalism in twentieth century Sri Lanka*, New Delhi 2001.

D. Rahasingham-Senanayake, Ambivalent empowerment midst tragedy of Tamil women in conflict, in R. Manchanda (ed.), *Women, war and peace in South Asia. Beyond victimhood to agency*, New Delhi 2001, 102–30.

T. Sarkar and U. Butalia (eds.), *Women and the Hindu right. A collection of essays*, New Delhi 1995.

Paula Banerjee

Sub-Saharan Africa: The Horn and East Africa

Populations of Muslims extend from the coasts of Eritrea throughout East Africa. Within the Horn of Africa there are diverse Muslim populations living in Eritrea, Ethiopia, Sudan, Somalia, Djibouti, and Kenya. While many of these populations are also related in culture, ideology, and national borders, there are significant regional differences. Muslim women throughout this area have been active in resolving conflicts and disputes, primarily at the household and community level. However, because many of these women are living in societies characterized by long-term, low- and high-level conflict, women have taken an increasingly public role in working for peace in their societies, at a community, national, and international level.

Historically, Muslim women in the Horn and East Africa have played an important role in dispute resolution at the household level. This is facilitated in part by exogamous marriage patterns that ensure women move from their father's households to a neighboring clan or sub-clan when they marry. Women retain the linkages with their familial clan as well as their husband's clan throughout their lifetimes, facilitating communication and dispute resolution between groups. They act as important go-betweens keeping communication between clans flourishing while men are often trapped into a more rigid vertical communication structure within their clan. Women are also assigned the responsibility of ensuring harmony among themselves and their husbands and among their children and their spouses. Muslim women have drawn on notions of purity and religiosity and codes of behavior from the Qurʾān to ensure relationships flow smoothly (Hirsch 1998).

The Horn of Africa has been a site of prolific public peacebuilding efforts by women. Somali populations that reside within Djibouti, Ethiopia, Somalia, and northern Kenya have been active in promoting both conflict and conflict resolution for centuries. Groups of women have taken an increasingly public stance that has challenged gender roles while drawing heavily on notions of Islamic purity and religiosity in order to gain further legitimacy among local, national, and international frameworks. Since the fall of the Siyad Barre regime in 1991, Somalia has functioned without a national government. Somali women came together, both locally and in exile, establishing organizations for peace and reconciliation (Hussein 1995). One of the most prominent organizations is Save Somali Women and Children (SSWC), founded by Asha Hagi Elmi. This group has been instrumental in Somali peace negotiations, demanding a seat at the table at international level peace talks. This organization is open to all Somali women willing to work outside of strict clan alliances and was vital in ensuring women were at the peace talks in Djibouti in 1998. The work of SSWC and other women's organizations has ensured that women will occupy 25 percent of parliamentary seats in the new Somali government. Somali women's organizations have held numerous peace demonstrations and marches throughout Mogadishu and Hargeisa, bringing together warring factions and presenting a united front against war and the continued violence.

Wajir Women for Peace (WWP) began in July 1993 to discuss ways for women to help mitigate the conflicts among women traders in the market place and on a broader clan level throughout the Wajir district in northern Kenya. The organization began because interclan feuding and cattle raiding had become so severe it had spilled into the trade sector, making it impossible for women to bring their goods to market and trade without fighting. However, when these women got together and began to discuss conflict resolution they realized a much broader mandate was required. Mama Fatuma became first chair of WWP. Also leading peace negotiations and establishing grass roots peace initiatives were Mama Halima and Mama Zainab. WWP eventually expanded to include other members of the community including elders, businessmen, religious leaders, and non-governmental organization representatives and renamed itself Wajir Peace Group (WPG). In 1995 WPG became a member of the Kenya Peace and Development Network, linking the local efforts to a national organization.

Delegations of women have been very active in the ongoing peace negotiations between the Afar and the Issa, two ethnic groups living in northwestern Ethiopia. There had been low-level conflict over land and water resources between these two pastoral groups for many generations. Delegations of women from each group visited the opposing communities to establish an initial dialogue for peace. Among the Afar and Issa, if a group of women go and visit an opposing community and are treated well and given good hospitality it indicates the opposing side is serious about peace. If the women are not treated well it indicates the opposing side is not willing to engage in serious dialogue about conflict resolution.

Ethiopian Muslim and Christian women are working together in the eastern highlands to build up conflict resolution skills in their shared communities, promoting increased understanding and stronger community strength across religious lines. In Sudan, women's groups have formed to facilitate communication across religious lines so women from the predominantly Muslim north can maintain dialogue with women from the south. Among these organizations is the Sudan Women's Voice for Peace organization, which seeks to establish peace, democracy, and women's rights in the new Sudan.

Women working for peace in these regions have adopted the position that peace is a collective responsibility and women must take an active role. Women of any age can work in peacemaking roles, but in most cases it is older, respected women who do this work. Respected women peacemakers are seen as wise, broad-minded, and diligent about religion. They are considered truthful and concerned about the welfare of all people, not just their own family or clan. They take the initiative and are able to mobilize others.

Women working in public peacemaking on the Horn and throughout East Africa are committed to ending violence and restoring peace in their society. These groups generally work across clans, and often encounter early hostility from leaders in their society. Many have gradually been accepted and have become important contributors to the ending of conflict in their communities. "Women's peace groups assume that the individual people involved in a conflict situation are responsible for working toward non-violent resolutions of the conflict. Peacebuilding cannot and should not be solely left to the leaders and/or outside interventions" (Elmi et al. 2000, 133).

Bibliography

H. M. Adam, Somalia. A terrible beauty being born? in W. Zartman (ed.), *Collapsed states. The disintegration and restoration of legitimate authority*, Boulder, Colo. 1995, 69–81.

Centre for the Strategic Initiatives of Women, *Women's work in peace. Lessons from training projects in the Horn of Africa*, by H. Osman, Washington D.C. 1999.

A. H. Elmi, D. Ibrahim, and J. Jenner, Women's role in peacemaking in Somali society, in D. L. Hodgson (ed.), *Rethinking pastoralism in Africa. Gender, culture, and the myth of the patriarchal pastoralist*, Oxford 2000, 121–41.

S. F. Hirsch, *Pronouncing and perservering. Gender and the discourses of disputing in an African Islamic court*, Chicago 1998.

M. Michaelson, Afar-Issa conflict management, in *Institute of Current World Affairs Letters*, Hanover, N.H. January 2000.
E. Rehn and E. J. Sirleaf, *Women, war and peace. The independent experts' assessment on the impact of armed conflict on women and women's role in peacebuilding*, New York 2002, <www.unifem.undp.org/resources/assessment>.

EMILY FRANK

Sub-Saharan Africa: West Africa

Women play an important role in the transformation of conflicts in West Africa by becoming active across political, religious, and ethnic affiliations. Theirs is often conflict management at the local level, where Africa's internal wars are increasingly fought, and their efforts can be the first steps toward reconciliation in communities devastated by violence.

At the end of 2000, the United Nations Security Council passed Resolution 1325 to increase the representation of women in peace processes. The issue of women's participation in conflict management, the reconstruction of postwar communities, and the prevention of future conflict are particularly salient in West Africa where women constitute the majority of those adversely affected by armed conflict. Women throughout the region have contributed to the reintegration of combatants and displaced persons, the development of early warning mechanisms, and the formation and management of pressure groups through a cross-section of organizations and civil society networks.

In 2000, women from Liberia, Sierra Leone, and Guinea formed the Mano River Union Women Peace Network (MARWOPNET). The network has taken an active position in pressing for peace in Sierra Leone, but it was the group's initiative to negotiate a meeting between feuding Presidents Charles Taylor of Liberia and Lansana Conté of Guinea in 2001 and convince the leaders to participate in a regional peace summit that illustrated the potential of women's efforts toward conflict resolution in West Africa. Despite its diplomatic success, the effectiveness of MARWOPNET continues to be limited by scarce resources and its exclusion from the formal peace process.

In Liberia, a delegation of six women was organized to make a forced entry into the 1994 Accra Clarifications Conference. Their experience demonstrates that governments and regional bodies may still be gender-biased against women's involvement in the peace process; yet their strategic presence at the conference increased the women's visibility in the media. As a result, the Liberian government supported the appointment of a woman interim president who was instrumental in negotiating a temporary peace.

Women in Senegal have played a prominent role in promoting meetings and rallies in the southern region of Casamance where government forces have struggled to avert an armed insurgency by the rebel Mouvement des forces démocratiques de Casamance (MFDC). In October 2002 over 3,000 women marched in Ziguinchor and solicited new pledges from the regional governor and the MFDC leaders to work toward a settlement.

In Mali, women's associations have been integral to the reconciliation and the restoration of trust between the Northern Tuareg community and the national government.

The National Women Peace Group (NAWOPEG) was founded in Nigeria in 2002 as a grassroots civil society initiative and a peace movement to facilitate the transformation of conflict in Nigeria. The group functions as a network of mediators and a framework for peace through a trained group of women known as Focal Points (FPs), each of whom represents a state in the federation.

Throughout West Africa, women have responded to the urgent demands of managing conflicts and reconstructing societies by breaking boundaries to help build a secure future.

BIBLIOGRAPHY

J. Beilstein, The expanding role of women in United Nations peacekeeping, in L. A. Lorentzen and J. Turpin (eds.), *The women and war reader*, New York 1998, 140–7.
M. Fleshman, African women struggle for a seat at the peace table, in *Africa Recovery* 16:4 (February 2003), 1 and 15–19.
S. Hale, Some thoughts on women and gender in Africa. Listening to the whispers of African women, in *Journal of African Studies* 16:1 (Winter 1998), 21–30.
S. Macdonald, P. Holden, and S. Ardener (eds.), *Images of women in peace and war*, London 1987.
D. R. Marshall, *Women in war and peace. Grassroots peacebuilding*, Washington, D.C. 2000.
L. Olsson, *Gendering UN peacekeeping*, Uppsala 1999.
C. Sylvester, *Feminist theory and international relations in a postmodern era*, Cambridge 1994.
——, *Feminist international relations. An unfinished journey*, Cambridge 2002.
UNESCO, *Women's contribution to a culture of peace, Expert Group Meeting*, Manila 25–28 April 1995.
United Nations Security Council Resolution S/RES/1325, 31 October 2000, <http://www.un.org/events/res_1325e.pdf>.
S. Whitworth, Gender, race and the politics of peacekeeping, in E. Moxon-Browne (ed.), *A future for peacekeeping?*, London 1998, 158–75.

JENNIFER L. DE MAIO

Political Parties and Participation

Afghanistan

The Afghan constitution of 1964 granted universal suffrage; however, political parties were not allowed. Prior to the constitution power was firmly held by the political elite associated with the royal family. Conservative social norms and limited access to education minimized the participation of women. In Kabul, urban women in the education sector and in women's organizations exercised political influence. Women were elected to parliament and in 1965 the first woman cabinet member was appointed.

In 1978 the People's Democratic Party of Afghanistan (PDPA) seized power and implemented radical social reform in which the emancipation of women figured prominently. The communist PDPA welcomed the active participation of women, advocated the equality of the sexes, and sought to integrate women into the government and society at all levels.

Civil war created a large refugee population, primarily in Pakistan and Iran. The resistance organized itself into seven main political parties ranging from conservative Islamic fundamentalists to more moderate and liberal elements. Women played advocacy roles for the resistance and women's rights in a number of these parties but the majority of these groups wished to limit women to traditional roles.

The fall of the communist regime in 1991 resulted in a power struggle that led to continued civil war. In 1996, the reactionary Taliban regime gained power and banned the education of girls and confined women to the home. With the fall of the Taliban, the internationally brokered Bonn agreement in December of 2001 set forth a plan for the re-establishment of a permanent government in Afghanistan. The plan ensured the participation of women in this process. Political parties were legalized in September 2003; however, they remain highly localized and are predominantly Kabul based. The participation of Afghan women in the political process has met resistance but international insistence and support from the Afghan Interim Authority has allowed women election delegates and resulted in women being appointed to key commissions and cabinet positions. At the recent Constitutional Loya Jirga (December 2003), 25 percent of the delegates were women. They protested at their lack of representation in the council's leadership positions and were promptly granted a deputy and two assistants.

Urban Afghan women are deeply committed to participating in politics, while women outside the capital remain marginalized in traditional roles. Whatever the outcome of the unfolding political situation in Afghanistan, women will continue to make their voices heard.

Bibliography

L. Dupree, *Afghanistan*, Princeton, N.J. 1973, 1980[3].

B. R. Rubin, *The fragmentation of Afghanistan. State formation and collapse in the international system*, New Haven, Conn. 1995, 2002[2].

Mark David Luce

Arabian Peninsula

Overview

In the early 2000s, the seven states of the Arabian Peninsula (Bahrain, Kuwait, Oman, Qatar, Saudi Arabia, United Arab Emirates, Yemen) showed different degrees of popular political participation for men and women. Only the Republic of Yemen was equipped with a multi-party system and universal suffrage when it was established in May 1990. Political parties remained banned in all six Gulf monarchies. In five of them, however, the concept of elections have become gradually accepted as part of the political process.

In those four peninsula states where women were allowed to vote and stand for elections (Bahrain, Oman, Qatar, Yemen) they (re-)obtained these rights only in recent decades or even in recent years. However, on election day female candidates could not count on the support of the rising numbers of female voters and were elected to a parliament or a consultative council only in urban coastal centers (Yemen: Aden and Mukalla, Oman: Muscat). While women participated in shaping public opinion to a considerable degree and were prominent in civil society, they remained highly underrepresented in official positions all over the Arabian Peninsula. Even though in some countries women were appointed ministers they did not head ministries of strategic importance. In Yemen Wahība

Faraḥ was appointed minister of state for human rights in 2001, and in Qatar Shaykha bt. Aḥmad al-Maḥmūd became minister of education in 2003. Segregation of the sexes (originating from a mixture of tribal and religious traditions stylizing women as the embodiment of cultural values and identities) kept women out of politics, especially in those states where there were no formal participatory institutions.

The seven peninsular states in detail

In two countries in the peninsula there have not been any elections at all: the United Arab Emirates and the Kingdom of Saudi Arabia. When preparations for local elections in Saudi Arabia were announced in October 2003, women were unlikely to be included in the electorate. A third country, the Emirate of Kuwait, remains the last country in the world where the right to vote only applies to parts of its male population (for example, citizens who have been naturalized less than 20 years ago are excluded). The issue of women's votes has been brought up by the Emir of Kuwait and women activists several times in the past, but was blocked by parliament. This was generally explained by the fact that the Kuwaiti parliament was dominated by Islamist representatives. However, efforts of the Emir to bypass parliament on this issue made female political participation a symbolic bone of contention between parliament and government. This certainly did not serve women's interest. The chances that women might participate in the upcoming local elections looked promising by the end of 2003 and this was likely to be the breakthrough for a further broadening of female political participation in Kuwait.

While the Kingdom of Bahrain saw some kind of local elections in the 1920s, no elections took place on the national level until the early 1970s. From 1973 until 2002 there were no elections at all in Bahrain. Unlike in the 1920s, when women who could prove land ownership were allowed to vote, they could not participate in the elections of the 1970s. In 1992 a formal petition was submitted to the ruler demanding – among other things – a role for women in the political process. While women remained absent from the official scene for another decade, they participated in demonstrations and resistance against the regime, sometimes facing arrest and torture. The year 2001 saw the introduction of universal suffrage, and in 2002 Bahraini women could vote and run for office in the 9 May municipal elections for the first time. As in the 24 October 2002 parliamentary elections, however, they did not win any seats. Women were nevertheless prominent members of civil society and the business community, and some were appointed to highly visible official positions: in 2000 King Ḥamad bin ʿĪsā al-Khalīfa, who took over from his father in 1999, appointed four women to the consultative council, which was turned into the 40-member second chamber of the two-chamber parliament shortly thereafter. The first female ambassador was appointed in 1999 and a number of women have entered the higher echelons of the ministries.

Elections were first introduced to the Emirate of Qatar with local elections in March 1999. Suffrage was universal and male and female candidates ran for office, but none of the six female candidates was elected. Only in the second local election on 7 April 2003 a woman won a seat – after male candidates had withdrawn. Later that month, male and female voters approved a constitution that codified a woman's right to vote and run for office and the first woman cabinet minister was appointed in May 2003. Elections for 30 seats in a 45-member consultative council are planned for 2004.

The Sultanate of Oman held its first elections with limited suffrage in 1991. Suffrage remained limited – the Sultan selected those who could participate – in the 1998 and the 2000 elections when two women were elected to the consultative council. Universal suffrage was only introduced in October 2002, and on 5 October 2003 the 83-member consultative council was elected directly for the first time after the Sultan had given up his right to select from among successful candidates. The two female members of the former council could defend their seats (both in Muscat), but no other women was elected.

In the two predecessor states of the Republic of Yemen female political participation was either not regulated but *de facto* non-existent (in the Yemen Arab Republic) or explicitly encouraged (in the People's Democratic Republic of Yemen). In May 1991 women participated in a referendum that approved the constitution of the newly established Republic of Yemen. Yemen's – and the peninsula's – first fully-fledged multi-party parliament with universal suffrage and male and female candidates was elected on 27 April 1993. As in the 1997 parliamentary elections women won 2 out of 301 seats (in 1993 in Aden and Mukalla, in 1997 both in Aden). On 27 April 2003 only one women was elected (in Aden). The first female minister was appointed in 2001 to oversee the newly established ministry of human rights. One of the major parties still refuses to nominate female candidates in elections.

In most states of the peninsula women's formal and informal political participation has increased over the 1990s. Universal suffrage and the appointment of women to official positions have laid the foundations for a revised perception of women's role in politics.

BIBLIOGRAPHY

S. Joseph and S. Slyomovics (eds.), *Women and power in the Middle East*, Philadelphia 2001.

U. Meinel, Zweifelhafte politische Reformen, in *Informationsprojekt Naher und Mittlerer Osten* 31 (Autumn 2002), 36–8.

D. Nohlen, F. Grotz, and C. Hartmann (eds.), *Elections in Asia and the Pacific. A data handbook*, i, Oxford 2001.

IRIS GLOSEMEYER

The Balkans

The political participation of women is an important aspect of the democratization process. However, in the Balkans there has been a sharp drop in the level of the political representation of women during the transition to democracy. Balkan women have been deeply affected by the social, economic, and political changes in the post-communist era. The political underrepresentation of women was accompanied by increasing unemployment among women and the rise of a neo-conservatism stressing women's maternal and domestic roles (Bracewell 1996).

Although there were tremendous differences among the Balkan countries prior to the establishment of communist systems, in terms of economic development, religion, political heritages, and previous traditions in regard to gender roles, the development of women's roles in communist Balkan countries was similar. Education and employment were the two areas that saw the greatest improvement for women under communist rule. However, this did not mean equality. Women's wages continued to be lower than men's and few women held important decision-making roles in the economy. Although women participated in symbolic political activities such as voting and taking part in mass demonstrations in numbers approximately equal to men, they played a limited role in the exercise of real political power within the Communist Party (Wolchik 1998). Yugoslavia was the only country in Eastern Europe that had a coherent feminist movement (Ramet 1995).

There was a significant decline in the representation of women in political and administrative positions following the multi-party elections in the early 1990s (there are no adequate data on women from different religious groups). Under communist rule, women formed between 20 and 35 percent of the members in the national parliaments of the East European countries. In the parliament of Slovenia, economically the most advanced part of Yugoslavia, women constituted 25 percent of the deputies. However, in the post-communist Slovenian parliament this number fell to 10 percent, while in the Bulgarian parliament it was as low as 3.5 percent. In Albania, there were 73 women out of the 250 deputies in the last communist parliament while in the first post-communist parliament the number of women fell to 9 (Ramet 1995). Though there was some progress in subsequent elections, women are still underrepresented in the parliaments of the Balkan countries (Slovenia 12.22 percent; Romania bicameral 7.86 and 10.72 percent; Serbia and Montenegro 7.94 percent; Croatia 20.53 percent; Bulgaria 26.25 percent; Albania 5.71 percent; Bosnia and Herzegovina bicameral 0.00 and 16.67 percent; Macedonia 18.33 percent). The situation is no different in the Balkan countries with a non-communist background. The percentage of women in the Greek parliament is 8.67 percent while in the Turkish parliament, in a country in which women were granted voting rights as early as 1934, it is just 4.36 percent (Inter-Parliamentary Union).

Transitions to democracy were frequently combined with a new electoral law. The Balkan countries have introduced different variations of proportional and combined electoral laws. Even though there is strong evidence that proportional representation systems tend to benefit women candidates, there is a trend toward the segregation of female and male candidates on party lists (OSCE ODIHR 1998). The long-term effects of the regulations favoring female candidates imposed by the international community, such as the new electoral law in Kosovo, which requires the political parties to reserve a third of their candidate lists for women, remain to be seen.

After the collapse of communism, many of the multi-party elections in the Balkans were held under extraordinary conditions. Particularly, the ethnic tension in socialist Yugoslavia and the disintegration of the country shaped not only the political behavior of men but also of the women living in it. Since the early 1990s the political life of Bosnia-Herzegovina has been to a large extent dominated by nationalist parties formed on ethnic lines. In the first multi-party elections in Bosnia-Herzegovina in 1990, the Muslim party, the Party for Democratic Action (SDA), received an overwhelming majority of the votes in the Bosnian Muslim community (Babuna 1996). This party, which became a center of national resistance under war conditions, was to continue to enjoy the massive support of the Bosnian Muslim men and women until the signing of the Dayton Accord in 1995. In the post-Dayton elections, the SDA had to compete with several other political parties.

In Kosovo, where the ethnic tension was also high, Muslim Albanian women, like the Bosnian women, subordinated women's interests to the national cause and supported the Albanian national leadership in its resistance to Serbian pressure (Mertus 1999). Ibrahim Rugova and his Democratic League of Kosovo continued to enjoy the support of the majority of the Kosovar Albanians after the NATO intervention in Kosovo in 1999. In Bulgaria, the overwhelming majority of the ethnic Turks voted for the Movement for Rights and Freedoms party (MRF). In the elections of 1990 and 1991 the MRF, which became an important political factor in Bulgaria, won the support of over 90 percent of the Turkish minority, 50 percent of the Pomaks (Bulgarian speaking Muslims), and about a third of the Muslim Roma (Eminov 2000). The Muslim and Christian Roma women, who are socially discriminated against, remain largely outside political life in most of the Balkan countries. Furthermore, the Roma political parties rarely cooperate with each other.

In the post-communist period, the nationalist parties in many Balkan countries tried not only to bring about an increase in the birth rates of their respective populations but also to redefine women as primarily biological reproducers of the nation. In Serbia and Croatia, despite the policies of the nationalist regimes, which seem to be in conflict with women's rights and interests, there is only mixed evidence of a gender gap in men's and women's political attitudes and almost none in their voting behavior. Many women supported nationalist parties, even though they remained unwilling to sacrifice their autonomy in reproductive decisions to the nationalist cause (Lilly and Irvine 2002).

BIBLIOGRAPHY

A. Babuna, *Die nationale Entwicklung der bosnischen Muslime. Mit besonderer Berücksichtigung der österreichisch-ungarischen Periode*, Frankfurt 1996.

W. Bracewell, Woman in the transition to democracy in South-Eastern Europe, in M. J. Faber (ed.), *The Balkans. A religious backyard of Europe*, Ravenna 1996, 213–20.

A. Eminov, Turks and Tatars in Bulgaria and the Balkans, in *Nationalities Papers* 28 (2000), 129–46.

Inter-Parliamentary Union (Switzerland), <http://www.ipu.org/parline-e/parlinesearch.asp>.

C. S. Lilly and J. A. Irvine, Negotiating interests. Women and nationalism in Serbia and Croatia, 1990–1997, in *East European Politics and Societies* 16 (2002), 109–46.

J. Mertus, Women in Kosovo: contested terrains. The role of national identity in shaping and challenging gender identity, in S. P. Ramet (ed.), *Gender politics in the Western Balkans. Women and society in Yugoslavia and the Yugoslav successor states*, University Park, Pa. 1999, 171–86.

OSCE/ODIHR (Organization for Security and Development in Europe/Office for Democratic Institutions and Human Rights), *Women and democratization. OSCE Human Dimension Implementation Meeting. Background paper 3*, Warsaw 1998.

S. P. Ramet, *Social currents in Eastern Europe. The sources and consequences of the great transformation*, Durham, N.C. 1995.

S. L. Wolchik, Women and the politics of gender in communist and post-communist Central and Eastern Europe, in S. P. Ramet (ed.), *Eastern Europe. Politics, culture, and society since 1939*, Bloomington, Ind 1998, 285–303.

AYDIN BABUNA

Canada

The story of Muslim women and political parties and participation in Canada is one of beginnings: Muslim women are only just starting to become involved in formal politics in Canada. (This is true also of Muslim men.) As in most other polities, women in general are underrepresented in Canadian legislatures, ranking 35th out of 181 countries according to the Geneva-based Inter-Parliamentary Union (data from IPU December 2002).

In the last ten years, although there has been a remarkable increase in the number of minority women elected to the federal parliament, minority women remain underrepresented in elected bodies (Black 2003, 59). Muslims represent 2 percent of the Canadian population (2001 Census data) but there are no Muslim women elected to the federal parliament and only one (of whom I am aware) elected in a provincial legislature (Fatima Houda-Pepin in Quebec). One Ismāʿīlī woman (Mobin Jaffer) has been appointed to the federal senate, a non-elected body in Canada. Thus, in proportion to the population, Muslim women are clearly underrepresented in elected bodies in Canada at all levels of government – local, provincial, and federal. This is in keeping with Abu-Laban's description of the structure of formal political power in Canada being a "gendered vertical mosaic": majority groups hold more power than minority groups, and within those groups, men hold more power than women (Abu-Laban 2002, 269).

This absence of women from the scene of formal politics raises a host of questions. Is Muslim women's absence due to external factors, such as discrimination, or internal barriers, such as pressures not to be involved in politics? Are there Muslim women who run for office, but who do not get elected? Are Muslim women active in party politics? Unfortunately, these questions cannot be addressed in this brief entry. Though there is a significant body of literature on women's participation in formal politics in Canada, little attention has been paid to the ethnoracial dimensions of women's participation beyond considering the two main groups in Canada, Anglophone and Francophone women (Black 2003, 59, Abu-Laban 2002, 270–5). There is no research on the political participation of Muslim women.

According to Muslim women activists, few Muslim women run for office in Canada. Lila Fahlman, who was born in Canada to a Lebanese father and an American Methodist mother, was the first, running for the Winnipeg nomination of the New Democratic Party (NDP) for the 1971 Federal election (Fahlman 1999, 64). She was not nominated. Natasha Fatah, who was born in Pakistan and moved to Canada when she was almost 10, has been heavily involved in party politics. She joined the Ontario NDP at age 13, and in 1999, at age of 20, was elected co-chair of the Ontario New Democratic Youth. Natasha says that while there are Muslims involved in politics at the youth level, they are not active at the political party level. She was the only Muslim youth (let alone woman) involved in the Ontario NDP.

Scholars have identified several factors that are barriers to women's participation in formal politics. Newman and White (forthcoming) group these barriers into three broad categories: ideational, social, and cultural; organizational; and institutional. Their work, however, deals only with women in general: how they might apply to Muslim women in particular is not explored. It is safe to assume that in addition to facing the kinds of barriers that any woman would face, Muslim women face other barriers unique to them, internal and external. The most important internal barriers facing Muslim women are restrictive interpretations of Islam that say it compromises a Muslim women's modesty to be involved in politics, and that her proper sphere of activity is the home. These opinions are held widely, by both men and women, of all different kinds of ethnic groups.

Of less impact, but still relevant, is an opinion held by some Muslims that Muslims, men or women, should not participate in politics at all. The argument is that since the Canadian polity is not run according to Islamic law, Muslims should not be involved in the making of law, since that would involve them in un-Islamic practices. In the last ten years many Muslim leaders have rejected this view, and are actively encouraging Muslims to be involved in electoral politics in the belief that this is the only way for Muslims to affect positively the communities in which they live (Khan 2002).

The most important external hurdle for Muslim participation in electoral politics, and one that would apply equally to men and women, is the widespread negative perception by the general public of Islam and Muslims. Muslims are cast as "outsiders," often as barbaric "others" who do not hold or respect Canadian values. A Muslim who ran for office would face a challenge in reaching out to the general populace to overcome these negative views. Another important barrier is the systemic racism that applies to all visible minorities. Not all Muslims are from a visible minority, but many are: thus they would face racism as well as Islamophobia, should they run for office.

It is possible (although further empirical research would be necessary to affirm this) that even at the level of the political party, members hold the same, or similar, negative stereotypes of Muslims, thus impeding Muslim involvement at the party political level. Natasha Fatah faced this problem within the NDP. She found that because she was Muslim, she often had trouble getting her perspective on issues properly heard, especially those issues relating to Muslims, like Palestine. Instead of responding to the intellectual issue, people would dismiss her opinion with "you just feel that way because you're a Muslim." There was an assumption that she was inherently biased. The reactions she describes underscore a point made by Jerome Black in his study of ethnoracial minorities in Canadian parliaments: in recent years ethnoracial minorities have concluded that the only way to have their issues addressed at the level of public policy is to have group representation in elected bodies, and not to rely on interest-group based advocacy (Black 2002, 355–6). Group exclusion from the political realm sidelines group issues and concerns (ibid., 369, Newman and White forthcoming). In spite of this, Natasha also believes strongly that none of the barriers were insurmountable to someone who was able to explain herself well, present a strong voice for justice, and was willing to work hard.

An absence in formal politics does not imply that Muslim women are not active in the Canadian polity in other ways. Indeed, as Abu-Laban and other scholars point out, to consider women's involvement in formal politics as the only expression of their political participation is to miss women's activism in informal politics, the arena in which most women activists operate (Abu-Laban 2002, 277). In Canada Muslim women have focused most of their political energies in the area of community activism. Muslim women are found in all kinds of community groups, from social service agencies to media watch groups. Some are activists in mainstream groups, others in Muslim groups with an Islamic focus. Two examples of the latter are directly relevant here. In 1997–8, the Afghan Women's Organization worked with the Federation of Muslim Women (FMW), the Canadian Council of Muslim Women (CCMW), and MediaWatch on a federally funded multi-phase project about Muslim women and the media. The project included focused group discussions with Muslim women about the representation of Muslim women in the Canadian media, with an aim of increasing media literacy and advocacy skills of Muslim women (Jafri and Bullock, 35–40). At their 2003 annual conference, CCMW organized a workshop with the Federation of Canadian Municipalities designed to raise awareness among Muslim women about the non-electoral aspects of municipalities. The extent of Muslim women's involvement in these kinds of informal politics emphasizes that Muslim women in Canada are not politically passive.

Bibliography

Primary Sources

2001 Canadian Census, <http://www12.statcan.ca/english/census01/Products/Analytic/companion/rel/contentscf>.

IPU (Inter-Parliamentary Union), <http://www.ipu.org/wmn-e/classif.htm>.

Natasha Fatah, interview, 10 September 2003.

Secondary Sources

Y. Abu-Laban, Challenging the gendered vertical mosaic. Immigrants, ethnic minorities, gender and political participation, in J. Everitt and B. O'Neill (eds.), *Citizen politics. Research and theory in Canadian political behaviour*, Toronto 2002, 268–82.

J. H. Black, Representation in the parliament of Canada. The case of ethnocracial minorities, in J. Everitt and B. O'Neill (eds.), *Citizen politics. Research and theory in Canadian political behaviour*, Toronto 2002, 355–72.

——, Differences that matter. Minority women MPs, 1993–2000, in M. Tremblay and L. Trimble (eds.), *Women and electoral politics in Canada*, Toronto 2003, 59–74.

K. H. Bullock and G. J. Jafri, Media (mis)representations. Muslim women in the Canadian nation, in *Canadian Woman Studies* 20:2 (2000), 35–40.

L. Fahlman, Lila, in S. Zaman (ed.), *At my mother's feet. Stories of Muslim women*, Kingston, Ont. 1999, 51–69.

M. A. M. Khan, *American Muslims. Bridging faith and freedom*, Beltsville, Md. 2002.

J. Newman and L. White, *Movement and public policy. The political struggles of Canadian women*, Oxford University Press (forthcoming), chapter four.

Katherine Bullock

Iran

Iranian women participated in the events leading to the Constitutional Revolution of 1905/6. Their numbers were few but their involvement signaled a break with the past when women, except occasional women of the court, did not participate in the public life of the country.

Women formed societies (*anjumans*) and women's discussion groups, some of which included men. They founded schools for girls and published magazines both in Tehran and the provinces. These constituted spaces for women's political participation as well. They discussed women's education and health and the problem of veiling. In their writings and their gatherings they drew comparisons between Iranian women and women in more progressive countries. Among the leading women's organizations in the 1920s was the Patriotic Women's League. In the 1930s, a number of women's organizations affiliated themselves to political parties, including the Communist Party and the Revival Party.

Political parties began seriously to recruit and organize women's branches in the 1940s. For example, the Democratic Party of Azerbaijan and the Tudeh (Communist) Party had women's sections. The Tudeh Party even appointed women to its central committee; the Democratic Party founded a women's organization and named one woman to the party's executive committee. A woman served in the leadership of the rightwing Sūmkā Party.

Women were active in the political agitation for nationalization of the British-run Anglo-Iranian Oil Company. They demanded changes in the electoral law to allow women to vote and run for elected office and the revision of sections of the civil law regulating marriage, divorce, and child custody. The Jamʿīyat-i Rāh-i Naw (Society for the new way) and the Jamʿīyat-i Zanān-i Ḥuqūqdān (Society for women lawyers) were at the forefront of these efforts.

In 1963, women were among the founders of the Īrān-i Nuvīn Party, a state-sanctioned organization that became highly influential in Iranian politics. Two women sat on the politburo of the Rastākhīz Party, formed in 1975 when the Shah declared a single party system, and women served on all the party's various committees.

Two underground anti-Shah guerrilla organizations, the Mujāhidīn-i Khalq and the Fidāʾiyīn-i Khalq included women among their rank and file. These organizations acted openly for a brief period after the Islamic Revolution, but were subsequently declared illegal. The Mujāhidīn, who continued their opposition activities from abroad, elected a woman as the head of their organization. Since the Islamic Revolution, women have been members of every political party and political and professional organization, including the clerically-dominated Islamic Republic Party and the reformist Islamic Iran Participation Front.

BIBLIOGRAPHY

J. Afari, *The Iranian Constitutional Revolution, 1906–1911. Grassroots democracy, social democracy and the origins of feminism*, New York 1996.

B. Bāmdād, *From darkness into light. Women's emancipation in Iran*, ed. and trans. F. R. C. Bagley, Hicksville, N.Y. 1977.

G. Nashat (ed.), *Women and revolution in Iran*, Boulder, Colo. 1983.

P. Paidar, *Women and the oolitical process in twentieth-century Iran*, Cambridge 1995.

HALEH ESFANDIARI

North Africa

Considering the role women played in the struggle for liberation, their participation in the political process in post-independence Algeria, Morocco, and Tunisia seemed only natural, as the terms of the first constitutions indicated – even if the modalities of their participation (the right to vote and their access to the public sphere and to political representation) were left undetermined. However, the conditions under which they were associated with the struggle for liberation – they were made to be symbols of the preservation of identity, moral integrity, and authenticity – meant, implicitly, that they would be kept out of the political sphere and that their inferior status would be perpetuated. In all three countries, the question of gender identity combined with that of political participation was to determine the way women – or at least women activists – would go about having their demands taken into account by the political systems put into place during the post-independence period. As we examine that process, a certain number of paradoxes must be considered.

Not counting charities and other benevolent associations established during the colonial era, the first post-independence political organizations and trade unions were created, if not to deny the specificity of women's struggle, at least to underline that their struggle was to be subordinate to the more global struggles in which the nation – the people, the movement for independence, the development forces – was engaged. This was evidenced by the existence of national unions closely supervised by the central governments (the Union nationale des femmes tunisiennes, created in 1958; the Union nationale des femmes algériennes, created in 1963; and the Union nationale des femmes marocaines, created in 1969). There were also women's sections within trade unions (themselves often controlled by the state) as well as within political parties: the Union socialiste des forces populaires and the Istiqlal party in Morocco; and the FLN (Front de libération nationale) in Algeria and the PSD (Parti socialiste destourien) in Tunisia, both single parties. Everywhere, women were asked to choose between identifying themselves as women first and Algerian/Moroccan/Tunisian second, or vice-versa; and between identifying themselves as women first and members of the party or the union second, or vice-versa. Their mission was to mobilize women's energies and potentials toward a common goal rather than to focus on specific demands, which would have left them vulnerable to the criticism of weakening the domestic front. As the 1964 Charter of Algiers indicated, "Algerian women should be able to participate effectively in politics and the building of socialism by joining the ranks of the party and national organizations and acceding to positions of responsibility." All constitutional texts, organic laws, and charters adopted by Algeria, Tunisia, and Morocco since gaining independence have used the same language (minus the mention of socialism), conferring political rights on women in theory when in reality even men themselves are prevented from exercising such rights because of the authoritarianism of the state.

In all three countries, this affirmation in principle of women's political rights had a trade-off in the form of a logic of confinement, which left women with very limited opportunities to become members of parliament, government, or party leaderships – positions to which they had access only through a quota system. As a result, the sole political outlets conceded to women were women's organizations, which were tightly controlled by the state. In Algeria, the only women to be able to claim some political legitimacy were those who were recognized as former *mujāhidāt* – and even they were encouraged to go back home and "rest." And when, on several occasions between 1965 and 1984, women opposed the passing of ever more reactionary family codes, they had to resort to informal or even clandestine means of mobilization and action – petitions, demonstrations, and unauthorized associations – due to the extremely tight control the FLN exercised over the Union nationale des femmes algériennes. Those actions would not be enough to prevent the implementation in 1984 of a particularly retrograde law – "a dramatic regression," to quote Zakya Daoud. In Morocco, the rapid degradation of the relationship between the monarchy and the political parties born out of the national movement meant that the demands for female participation were relegated to the back burner, and the initiative by women militants to have those demands integrated into the platform of the parties they belonged to was deliberately stalled in the name of partisan discipline. As for Tunisia, which had the most advanced legal status for women until the revision of the Moroccan Mudawwana in October 2003, it is without a doubt the country in the Maghrib where the political participation of women is most problematic, as if the "state-backed feminism" instituted by President Bourguiba's regime had rendered ineffective or neutralized the purely political dimension of women's participation in the public sphere – that participation being strictly regimented by the Union nationale des femmes tunisiennes, whose mission is blurred with that of the ministries in charge of social affairs. In the early 1990s, Zinelabidine Ben Ali, Bourguiba's successor, sought to remobilize women and ask for their support in his repression of Islamist movements, only to realize that there were only 7 female members of parliament, that women accounted for only 11 of the 200 members of the RCD (Rassemblement constitutionnel démocratique, the new name for the PSD), and above all that women's – not to mention feminist – magazines had all ceased to exist and that all major newspapers had eliminated their women's sections. Additionally, it must be noted that in all three countries, the political socialization of the feminine vanguard, largely leftist in the 1960s and 1970s, and Islamist since the beginning of the 1980s, contributed to the exacerbation of the political marginalization of those militants, both as women and as sympathizers of political movements that were the constant targets of state repression.

A crucial point to be made here is that the political formula – single party system, as in Tunisia until 1981 or Algeria until 1989, or multiparty system, as in Morocco – does not seem to have any significant influence on the capacity of women to make their presence felt on the political scene, except perhaps in Algeria where, starting in 1989, the proliferation of political parties came with an increase in the number of women in positions of leadership within those parties: 5 women out of 30 members in the political bureau of the Front des forces socialistes (FFS); 10 women among the 42 founding members of the Parti de l'avant-garde socialiste (PAGS); 4 women out of 18 members in the executive bureau of the Rassemblement pour la culture et le développement (RCD); and, with Louisa Hanoune as the secretary general of the Parti des travailleurs, the only women head of a political party in the Arab world. However, what this activism by female militants has shown first and foremost is the limited ability of those organizations to mobilize women, especially when one compares it with the mobilizing power of the Front islamique du salut (FIS), which claimed a million women as members – of a total of three million members – at the time of the legislative elections of December 1991. Moreover, in Algeria as well as in Tunisia, women's rights militants, for whom the state party (the RCD in both cases) is the only vehicle for political participation, run the risk of being perceived as condoning the repressive actions of the two regimes, particularly against Islamist movements, and agreeing with the premise that advances in women's rights might have to be secured to the detriment of human rights. In Morocco, where it was not until 1993 that two women became members of parliament, and until 1998 that a woman was appointed to the position of "minister delegate," the election of 35 women in parliament in the fall of 2002, following the implementation of a gender-based quota system, could primarily be attributed to the king's will – not to the political parties' activism or to women's abilities to have those parties endorse their call for greater female participation in politics.

Looking past the difficulties and obstacles women have to face before they can accede to positions of power within political organizations, be elected as members of parliament, or become ministers, the most insidious form of political marginalization for women continues to be their confinement to women's issues. While no one will dispute the value of having women voice their own concerns and defend their own interests, a female exclusivity on female matters is no more justified than the exclusion of equally competent women from consideration for "general interest" positions of authority, as is almost systematically the case in Algeria and Morocco. In that regard, with three women serving respectively as minister for employment and professional training, minister for the promotion of women and families, and vice-president of the National Assembly; and with women accounting for 21.6 percent of all municipal councils' membership, 24 percent of magistrate positions, and 13 percent of the seats in the Conseil supérieur de la magistrature, Tunisia remains an exception in the Maghrib.

Translation from the French by Matthieu Dalle,
University of Louisville

Bibliography

L. Brand, *Women, the state and the political liberalism. Middle Eastern and North Africa experiences*, New York 1998.

Z. Daoud, *Féminisme et politique au Maghreb. Soixante années de lutte*, Casablanca 1993.

S. Joseph (ed.), *Gender and citizenship in the Middle East*, Syracuse, N.Y. 2000.

Alain Roussillon

South Asia

Introduction

South Asia is home to over 400 million of the world's Muslim population of whom the majority reside in Bangladesh, India, and Pakistan. While Bangladesh and Pakistan have elected women prime ministers, a survey of the national political scene in these three countries indicates limited participation by women in the political process.

In Bangladesh, even though the heads of the two major parties (Awami League and the Bangladesh Nationalist Party, BNP) are women, the 2002 elections led to success for only 6 women candidates (of the 32 fielded). In India, women have a limited presence in the lower house (8.8 percent) and the upper house (10.3 percent) and Muslim women are even less well represented with only one Muslim woman in each house. In Pakistan until the 2002 electoral reforms, which led to reservation of 33 percent of seats for women, there were only 6 female members in the 217-member national assembly and 2 women out of 83 senate members. After the reforms went into effect Pakistani women ended up with 21.6 percent of seats in the lower house and 17 percent of seats in the upper house. These numbers are reflective of the challenges posed by the politicization of religion and the interplay between class and identity politics as Muslim women seek to mobilize and participate in political activities in the South Asian region.

Politicization of religion

The 1980s and 1990s saw dramatic changes in the relationship between states and religious forces in the South Asian region. The Iranian Revolution and the growth of "fundamentalism" in the Middle East, the Salman Rushdie affair, and the Gulf War of 1991 led to heightened polarization along religious lines in Bangladesh, India, and Pakistan.

Bangladesh

In Bangladesh the government of General Ershad made Islam the state religion in 1988. After his departure in1991, the two major political parties, the Awami League led by Sheikh Hasina and the BNP led by Begum Khaleda Zia have had to contend with the growing strength of conservative Islamic forces represented by the Jamaat-e-Islami. The alliance between the BNP and the Jamaat-e-Islami in the 1991 elections pushed the BNP government to arrest a young doctor turned author, Taslima Nasreen, for alleged blasphemy in her novel *Lajja*. The Jamaat for its part used protests and demonstrations to try to get Nasreen executed. In the years that followed the process of Islamization has been pushed even further as the competition between the Awami League and the BNP has intensified with the two parties taking alternate control of the state. In the 2001 elections, the BNP-Jamaat alliance won 215 of the 300 seats in parliament. However despite the presence of a prime minister and an opposition leader who is female, women's participation in national politics and in government is limited.

Pakistan

In Pakistan, the Islamization begun by General Zia ul-Haq was briefly halted by his death in 1988. In the elections that followed, the Pakistan People's Party (PPP) led by Benazir Bhutto came to office. Her tenure was fraught with difficulties because of resistance from the military and religious leadership who were opposed to a woman running an Islamic republic. The PPP government was dismissed after 18 months, plunging Pakistan into a series of short-lived governments until the 1999 military coup led by General Pervez Musharraf who allied himself with Islamic parties represented by the Muttahida Majlis-e-Amal (MMA) in his quest for legitimacy. International and domestic pressure to return Pakistan to a democracy subsided in the wake of the 11 September 2001 attacks as Pakistan became a partner in the United States war on terrorism. In the elections held in 2002, the share of anti-United States and pro-Islamic parties went from 5 to 17 percent of the vote especially in key areas like the North West Frontier Province. However, the Musharaff government did institute the promised 33 percent reservation of seats for women, which has led to the largest ever influx of women politicians into the Pakistani parliament. The fact that these women politicians were not directly elected evoked mixed responses from women's groups who fear that they will do a better job of representing their families than representing the concerns of women.

India

In India, the Congress Party sought to halt its declining public support by pandering to communal forces (Hindu and Muslim). In the 1980s the Shah Bano case led the Congress government to pass the Muslim Women (Protection of Rights on Divorce) Bill. The distinction made between monolithic Hindu and Muslim communities during the debates on the bill fueled the tensions between them and contributed to the success of the Hindu nationalist party, the Bharatiya Janata Party (BJP), which went from 2 seats in parliament in 1984 to 189 seats in the 1999 elections. The BJP also strengthened its position by agitating for the construction of a temple to Lord Ram at Ayodhya on the site of Babri Masjid, a mosque that had been demolished by party supporters in December 1992. The debate over Shah Bano and the destruction of the Babri Masjid led to more involvement by educated, urban Muslim women in the activities of women's organizations such as the Janawadi Mahila Samiti (JMS) and the National Federation of Indian Women. However for most Muslim women, the two events led to a redefinition of Muslim female identity primarily as Muslims and as a minority, and consequently to more constraints on women's rights in the name of Islam.

Class and identity politics

Surveys of women parliamentarians in the South Asian region indicate that most of them come from middle- to upper-class backgrounds, have professional training, have accessed politics through their families, and have few or no links to the women's movements in their countries. Class and kinship ties help these women to defray some of the traditional costs to Muslim women of political involvement. These women are able to afford paid help or have a strong family support system that takes care of household and childcare duties in particular. For women like Benazir Bhutto who were single when they entered politics there is tremendous pressure to conform to traditionally female roles once they marry. The exception to this is political widows like Sheikh Hasina and Begum Zia in Bangladesh who are accorded a special status by virtue of their personal tragedies, which have led them to assume the political mantle of a father (Sheikh Hasina) or husband (Begum Zia). Class can also mediate the influence of religion. In India, Dr. Najma Heptullah, who is the deputy speaker of the Indian Rajya Sabha (upper house) is from an elite class and educational background and has been supported in her career by her family. At the local level, a survey of 20 women ward commissioners from four cities in Bangladesh found a similar nexus between class (as defined by education and income), kinship ties, and political participation. For these women, familial connections to politics provided valuable experiences that later translated into public office and helped smooth their way in a conservative Islamic environment.

Importance of electoral reforms

Most Muslim women in South Asia do not participate in political activity. Women's groups in Bangladesh, India, and Pakistan have been at the forefront of efforts to bring about electoral reforms aimed at giving women access to office in political environments where they are simply not tolerated. While this can be contentious at the national level, governments have been more responsive at the local level. In Bangladesh, during the last local government elections (Union Parishad) more than 12,000 women members were elected directly for reserved seats. In India, the adoption of the 73rd and 74th amendments to the Indian constitution in 1993 led to the reservation of 33 percent of seats for women in elections to local bodies (Panchayati Raj). Over one million women today (some of whom are Muslim) hold office at the local level in India and, more importantly, a third of all chair positions in local bodies are also filled by women. In Pakistan, the Musharraf government reforms led to the election of 120 women in the four provincial assemblies and 36,000 female councilors. The response in Islamic constituencies has been mixed. In some cases there have been efforts by religious leaders to bar women from voting and threaten punishment if they do (North West Frontier Province) and to issue fatwas banning women from appearing on a podium to campaign for election (Mallapuram district in Kerala, India). However, the Islamist MMA in Pakistan fielded 570 candidates in the 2002 elections on a platform focused on women's rights to education, social status, literacy, and protection from violence. The party was able to win 15 seats in the national legislature and a further 20 in the provincial assemblies. The hope is that as more women enter local government they will gain public acceptance for women's role in governance and create a space for new generations of women representatives.

Bibliography

M. Afkham (ed.), *Faith and freedom. Women's human rights in the Muslim world*, Syracuse, N.Y. 1995.

Z. Hasan (ed.), *Forging identities. Gender, communities and the state*, New Delhi 1994.

C. W. Howland (ed.), *Religious fundamentalism and the human rights of women*, New York 1999.

P. Jeffrey and A. Basu (eds.), *Appropriating gender.*

Women's activism and politicized religion in South Asia, New York 1998.
S. Lateef, *Muslim women in India. Political and private realities 1890s–1980s*, New Delhi 1990.
F. Mernissi, *The fundamentalist obsession with women*, Lahore 1975.
——, *Beyond the veil. Male-female dynamics in modern Muslim society*, Bloomington, Ind. 1987.
S. Sutherland (ed.), *Bridging worlds. Studies on women in South Asia*, New Delhi 1992.
UNESCO reports, <www.unescap.org/huset/women/reports>.
S. White, *Arguing with the crocodile. Gender and class in Bangladesh*, Dhaka 1992.

SUDHA RATAN

Sub-Saharan Africa

Women in predominantly Muslim societies in Sub-Saharan Africa have been part of the movements that have shaped the African political landscape from the pre-independence period of the late 1950s and 1960s up until today. Recent developments have shown that Muslim women are assuming political leadership today as they did during the nationalist movements.

In Kenya, for example, Muslim women in the late 1950s were involved through the Muslim Women's Institute and Moslem Women's Cultural Association in a movement to petition the colonial authorities to scrap legislation that did not allow coastal women, who were primarily Muslim, to vote. They argued against the voting policy on the grounds that it was discriminatory because women in other parts of the country were allowed to vote after 1956. Once this victory was won, they initiated campaigns to get women to vote.

In Tanganyika (today Tanzania), Muslim women such as Bibi Titi were leaders of the independence movement from the outset, while others were socialized into political activities through dance groups, networks of food sellers and other self-employed women. Because they were organized as Muslim women into such groups they were considered harmless by the colonial authorities and easily eluded their suspicions. Nevertheless, these women formed the backbone of the nationalist movement and were critical to the success of the Tanganyika African National Union (TANU) and its women's wing that led the country to independence.

In the post-independence period up until the mid-1980s, women throughout Africa were active in the politically motivated and patronage driven women's wings and mass women's organizations that dominated women's mobilization at the national level. They were typically led by female relatives of state and party leaders, and primarily served the ruling party by garnering votes, and serving social functions of dancing, singing, and cooking food for party dignitaries.

In the mid 1980s new movements emerged that were distinct from these earlier women's organizations which had been tied to the single party. The new organizations were autonomous from the ruling party in terms of leadership, funding, and agendas. They took up issues ranging from increasing women's political presence, women's education and literacy, reproductive rights issues, to women's legal rights in areas of inheritance, marriage, divorce, land ownership, and citizenship. Some organizations addressed issues such as violence against women, domestic violence, and sexual harassment. In Senegal, Kenya, Mali, Burkina Faso, and Chad there have been major initiatives to end the practice of female genital mutilation (FGM). Women have sought legislative and constitutional changes to improve the status of women.

In some countries women's organizations addressed the disparaging portrayal of women in the media. In Tanzania, Muslim women were members and leaders of the new generation of women's rights organizations. The very earliest of these new organizations, founded in 1979, the Tanzania Media Women's Association (TAMWA), was formed by Muslim women and had a strong Muslim women's presence in its leadership.

The 1990s also saw the beginnings of a new wave of movements attempting to bring about multipartyism, civilian rule, and democratization in Africa. Women in predominantly Muslim countries were at the forefront of these movements. In Mali, thousands of demonstrating women and children were shot at by forces of President Moussa Traoré in a series of events that led to his downfall in 1991. In Sierra Leone, women were the only group to openly defy soldiers as they demonstrated to demand that free elections be held when rumors began to circulate that the military might postpone the February 1996 elections. In Conakry, Guinea, women organized a sit-in in front of the presidential palace in a support of a 1990 general strike of workers and student demonstrations, and to protest at the economic crisis, which they blamed on the country's leadership. In Niger, several thousand women demonstrated in protest at the exclusion of women representatives from the preparatory commission charged with organizing the national conference in 1991 (only one woman was included out of 68 delegates). In the end, five women were added to the delegate list of the national conference to decide on the country's future.

Muslim women have been actively pursuing strategies to attain political representation in legislatures throughout Africa. Of the ten countries in Africa with the lowest representation of women in the legislature, nine have predominantly or large Muslim populations. It has therefore been in some of these countries that women have sought greater political representation through the introduction of quotas. Already the largely Muslim countries of Senegal, Eritrea, Mali, and Djibouti have begun to meet with success in raising the rates of female representation as a result of such pressures. Even in Somalia, a country that has been torn by civil war based on clan divisions, the Women's Association lobbied the Transnational National Government to make sure they had 25 seats (10 percent) in the transitional assembly.

Those organizations working toward increase in women's political representation are generally linked to organizations that are involved in civic education, leadership training, networking among women to advance women's political awareness and skill, support for women candidates on a non-partisan basis, and media campaigns and other efforts to increase public awareness about the need for women's leadership.

Thus, in Niger, a predominantly Muslim country, women activists have worked to change women's status on a number of fronts simultaneously and they have made a series of gains in a relatively very short period of time. They have succeeded in obtaining major changes in the Family Code that protect women's rights. They achieved the ratification of the Convention on the Elimination of Discrimination against Women in 1999. The following year women activists were able to win a 35 percent quota for women in the legislature in a country where previously only one woman had had a parliamentary seat. In 2001 the government placed heavy penalties on people convicted of practicing FGM.

One issue that has been critical for women has been peace initiatives. Although their role has rarely been acknowledged or publicized, women have been involved in peace movements from Senegal's Casamance region, to Mali, Sudan, Somalia, and Sierra Leone.

With the spread of Islamicist movements in countries such as Niger, Nigeria, Mali, Eritrea, Sudan, Ghana, and elsewhere, some women activists are drawing on alternative traditions within Islam to promote women's rights and/or leadership. Muslim women's organizations have generally taken one of four general approaches. They have worked within Islamic discourses to highlight Islamic traditions that promote women's rights; adopted secular approaches; pursued pragmatic approaches that work either within the framework of Islamic law or by adopting a secular approach depending on the situation; and finally, sought an approach that carves out a niche for women within an Islamicist framework.

For example, the Federation of Muslim Women's Associations of Nigeria (FOMWAN) and Women's Rights in Moslem Law in Nigeria have tried to open up the gender discourse within Islam, pressing for a redefinition of women's rights, including inheritance and custody rights, equality in education, and the full participation of women within the bounds of the Islamic Sharīʿa law that is now followed in twelve Nigerian states.

Some women's organizations within majority Islamic countries have pursued greater secularism as a way of advancing women's rights. By calling for greater gender inclusiveness in politics, Muslim women have become some of the staunchest forces for democratization and a secular state in countries such as Sudan. In the case of Sudan, the regime of General ʿUmar Ḥasan Aḥmad al-Bashīr has undermined the rights of women by imposing increasingly harsh restrictions since he came to power in 1989. These restrictions include dress regulations, banning all political and non-political organizations, restricting travel by women, firing women from top positions, and institutionalizing physical and psychological abuse of women accused of being dissidents. Women's groups such as the Sudanese Women Union have been at the forefront of the movement for a democratic secular state, campaigning against the legal restrictions against women and arguing for an interpretation of the Qurʾān that does not discriminate against women and one that promotes equality, human rights, democracy, and civil liberties. Secular women have also been concerned about the implications of a "pure" and "authentic" Islamic state for the non-Muslim and non-Arab inhabitants of southern Sudan.

Other groups such as BAOBAB in Nigeria seek to advance the rights of women who live under Islamic laws through whatever means women locally deem appropriate, whether it involves taking a secular stance or using arguments based on Islamic law. Nigeria became a focus of international attention in the late 1990s with the expansion of institutionalized Islamic law in the northern part of the country and the imposition of harsh punishments on women charged with violating the laws, including imposing the penalty of stoning to death on individual women singled out and accused of adultery. Women lawyers and organizations like BAOBAB actively appealed against such sentences.

Finally, there are those women's movements that work within the Islamic establishment and are supportive of it, although often with their own interpretations. In Sudan, for example, many leading militant Islamist women of the National Islamic Front (NIF) such as Suʿād al-Fātiḥ al-Badawī and Batūl Mukhtār Muḥammad Ṭāhā were actively involved in interpreting Islam independently and mobilizing supporters for the Islamicist cause in the 1980s.

In addition to these strategies at the national level, there are regional organizations, such as Women Living Under Muslim Laws, which are involved in information sharing, database building, networking, solidarity action, and organizing campaigns throughout Africa and the Middle East. These organizations have allowed women in predominantly Muslim countries to coordinate their activities and learn from one another.

BIBLIOGRAPHY

N. Abdulai, Interview. Dr. Fatima Babiker Mahmoud, in *Africa World Review* (May–October) 1993, 48–50.

B. Callaway and L. Creevey, *The heritage of Islam. Women, religion and politics in West Africa*, Boulder, Colo. 1994.

B. Callaway, Women and political participation in Kano City, in *Comparative Politics* 19:4 (1987), 379–93.

B. M. Cooper, The politics of difference and women's association in Niger. Of "prostitutes," the public and politics, in *Signs* 20:4 (1995), 851–82.

S. Geiger, *TANU women. Gender and culture in the making of Tanganyikan nationalism, 1955–1965*, Portsmouth, N.H. 1997.

S. Hale, *Gender politics in Sudan. Islamism, socialism, and the state*, Boulder, Colo. 1996.

——, Gender politics and Islamization in Sudan, Women Living Under Muslim Laws, Dossier 18, October 1997, <http://www.mluml.org/english/index.shtml>.

F. A. Ibrahim, Sudanese women under repression, and the shortest way to equality, in M. R. Waller and J. Rycenga (eds.), *Frontline feminisms. Women, war, and resistance*, New York 2000, 129–39.

M. Strobel, *Muslim women in Mombasa, 1890–1975*, New Haven, Conn. 1979.

AILI MARI TRIPP

Turkey

In 1934, prior to all Muslim countries and many Western states, Turkish women had full suffrage rights. Following the 1935 elections 4.5 percent of the members of parliament were women; since then this ratio has never been attained.

In the literature few reasons are put forward to explain why Turkish women gained the vote so early. First, and most important, is that female participation in public life was seen as one of the major reflections of the Turkish Republic's project of secularization, Westernization, and modernization. Second, it is argued that the early republican regime was trying to distance itself from the rising fascist regimes in Europe, and granting suffrage rights to women was a show of alliance with democracy in Europe (Tekeli 1982). It has also been argued that demands coming from women's groups, starting in the Ottoman period and including those by the Turkish Women's Association in the 1920s and 1930s, were significant and the republican leaders could not turn a blind eye to them (Çakır 1994). However, we see noticeable decreases in women's representation with the introduction of the multiparty system in 1950, a development that meant that there was no further need to prove democratization of the country.

In 2003 Turkey ranked 110th amongst 173 countries in women's representation in parliament (4.4 percent) and in local government women's representation was less than 2 percent. This low level of participation constitutes a sharp contrast to the relatively high level of participation of women in professions (33.9 percent) and public offices (17 percent) (UNDP 2000). Such low levels of political participation are due to factors that are also common to other parts of the world. Women in general lack assets such as financial resources, organizational capacity, political expertise and experience, as well as a traditional community support base, which are considered essential for political success. Moreover, motherhood, family, and modesty are important values that usually clash with the expected competitive, assertive, argumentative, and extroverted nature of politicians (Güneş-Ayata 1998). Under these circumstances, the majority of the women in political positions are "selected" by the party leadership as tokens to demonstrate egalitarian perspectives of the parties (Yaraman 1999).

Despite this low representation in the political sphere, gender issues and role models have been focal in Turkish politics. Early republican reforms envisaged a woman who was educated, working, and participating equally with men in public life (Durakbaşa 1998). Equality in public life rather than the private sphere was stressed, even though here too there were many advances through the introduction of the Civil Code in 1926, such as equal rights of property inheritance, divorce, and custody.

This model has been challenged since the 1980s from many perspectives. First, feminists from many different ideological standpoints argued that the republican model of equality has been only partly successful because it underestimated the difficulties experienced by women because of family duties, community structures, and conventional role models (Z. Arat 1998). The state was deeply criticized for being gender blind (Kadıoğlu 1998). Low representation of women in politics was considered to be both a cause and outcome of this insensitivity.

Simultaneously, groups who identified more closely with Islam began their criticism. Despite internal variations, in very broad terms, these groups argued that the republican model of women was too insistent on a Westernized public female role model and was intolerant of women with Muslim identities entering public life (Saktanber 2002). In the last decade, women emphasizing a Muslim identity have become increasingly more active, creating non-governmental organizations (NGOs) and charity foundations as well as mobilizing votes (Y. Arat 1999).

The low level of participation of women in politics has been a vocalized concern especially for the secular feminist groups. Women's NGOs have raised this issue and have proposed different methods of improvement. Founded in 1997, Kadın Adayları Destekleme Ve Eğitme Derneği (KADER, Association for the support and training of women candidates), is an organization that specifically aims to promote women in politics.

Two other methods of promotion of women's participation have been through establishment of quotas for women and founding of women's auxiliaries in political parties. At present (2003) four political parties have quotas (Republican Peoples Party 25 percent, People's Democracy Party 25 percent, Freedom and Solidarity Party 30 percent, and True Path Party 10 percent) pertaining to internal elections. While absence of women in electable positions in the lists is uncommon, even the parties that have quotas in their statutes do not apply them to candidacies in local and national elections. Women's auxiliaries in parties have been a controversial issue. Their success has been in vote mobilization and fund-raising rather than in helping women become politicians themselves (Tekeli 1982). The first auxiliary was opened by a left wing party, the Republican People's Party, in 1957 and other political parties soon adopted the idea. Nonetheless, in most center-right and center-left parties the women's auxiliaries remained marginal in the last two decades and women's representation was primarily carried out by feminist NGOs.

Leadership of political parties has never totally neglected women's representation. All have recognized the importance of women's votes – research indicates that about half of women vote independently of their male relatives – and have tried to appeal to them through rhetoric and by appointing a token number of female candidates (Sancar-Üşür 2000).

In the last two decades, with rising sensitivity to gender issues, political parties began to have specific chapters in their programs on gender issues. Two main perspectives are observable here. The political parties of the right (including Islamists and nationalists) have a family centered perspective and propose policies that will facilitate, enhance, and support women in family based roles (Güneş-Ayata 2001). Left and left-of-center parties, however, present a more progressive ideology at least in the rhetoric, where they argue that an egalitarian society can be constructed only with equal participation of women and men in public life. Yet they also avoid a deep questioning of patriarchal systems, and especially problems that pertain to private life and family (Güneş-Ayata and Aslan-Akman 2004).

Feminist groups, with the help of international organizations and media, have persuaded the political decision-making bodies to make gender issues a part of the governmental mechanism. The Directorate General on the Status and Problems of Women was established in 1990 after the ratification of the United Nations Convention on the Elimination of All Forms of Discrimination against Women (CEDAW) as a national mechanism. Even though the directorate has not been very influential in mainstreaming gender issues in policymaking, it has been important in disseminating international norms, supporting gender studies, promoting women's NGOs, and creating wider gender sensitivity.

In conclusion, despite early attempts to encourage women to enter politics, Turkey has a long way to go in gender mainstreaming, the development of a gender sensitive and conscious agenda in policymaking, the adoption of affirmative measures to increase female representation, and the encouragement of women to express their own voices and demands. In short, the empowerment of women through politics will take time.

Bibliography

Y. Arat, *Political Islam in Turkey and women's organizations*, Istanbul 1999.

Z. Arat, Kemalizm ve kadın, in *75 Yılda kadınlar ve erkekler*, Istanbul 1998, 51–70.

S. Çakır, *Osmanlı kadın hareketleri*, Istanbul 1994.

A. Durakbaşa, Cumhuriyet döneminde modern kadın ve erkek kimliklerinin oluşumu. Kemalist kadın kimligi ve münevver erkekler, in *75 Yılda kadınlar ve erkekler*, Istanbul 1998, 29–50.

A. Güneş-Ayata, Laiklik, güç ve katılım üçgeninde Türkiye'de kadın ve siyaset, in *75 Yılda kadınlar ve erkekler*, Istanbul 1998, 237–48.

——, The politics of implementing women's rights in Turkey, in J. H. Bayes and N. Tohidi (eds.), *Globalization, gender and religion. The politics of women's rights in Catholic and Muslim contexts*, New York 2001.

A. Güneş-Ayata and C. Aslan-Akman, Overcoming gender inequalities in political recruitment. Another challenge for democratization in Turkey, in B. Hoecker and G. Fuchs (eds.), *Women's political participation and representation in the states joining the European Union*, Opladen 2004, 259–84.

A. Kadıoğlu, Cinselliğin inkarı. Büyük toplumsal projelerin nesnesi olarak Türk kadını, in *75 Yılda kadınlar ve erkekler*, Istanbul 1998, 89–100.

A. Saktanber, *Living Islam. Women, religion and the politicization of culture in Turkey*, London 2002.

Ş. Tekeli, *Kadınlar ve siyasal toplumsal hayat*, Istanbul 1982.

UNDP, *Human Development Report 2000*, New York 2000.

S. Üşür, *Kadın erkek eşitliğine doğru yürüyüş. Eğitim, çalışma yaşamı ve siyaset*, Istanbul 2000.

A. Yaraman, *Türkiye'de kadınların siyasal temsili*, Istanbul 1999.

AYŞE AYATA

Political Prisoners

Iran and Afghanistan

IRAN

There were female political prisoners in Iran long before women's prisons were established and prior to the modern discourse of the political prisoner, which goes back to the last quarter of the nineteenth century. The imprisonment of women was an important aspect throughout all periods of political suppression.

1840s/1850s. Suppression of the Bābī movement

Qurrat al-ʿAyn, a woman leader of the Bābī movement was until her execution incarcerated (January 1850–October 1852) in a non-official prison, in the upper chamber of the house of Tehran's chief of police, Maḥmūd Khān Kalāntar.

1920s/1930s. Suppression of the socialist movement

In the 1920s, women's associations and newspapers were attacked by the police and groups linked to the mullahs. Some of the prominent feminists were exiled and their journals closed. In Qazvīn alone, 24 members of Anjuman-i Parwarish were incarcerated. In the 1930s, some women linked to the Communist Party were imprisoned.

1950s. Suppression of the National Front and Tudeh Party

Several members of the Iranian Women's Organization linked to the Tudeh Party were imprisoned.

1970s. Suppression of Marxist and Marxist Islamic guerrilla organizations

In the early 1970s, female political prisoners were still seen as an appendix rather than as political opponents and were incarcerated alongside common criminals. Women's suffrage coincided with political suppression in the 1960s. This led to the significant appearance of women in political opposition. Because of the radicalization of political struggles in the 1970s the regime took drastic measures. The Anti-Terrorism Committee, commanded by SAVAK (secret service), brutally tortured prisoners. Women and girls were also victims of sexual torture such as rape. In the maximum security prisons of Qaṣr and Iwīn separate blocks for women were added. Hundreds of women were condemned to imprisonment, many for life. Forty-two were killed, including those killed in armed confrontations and others who committed suicide just before capture. Three were executed by firing squads, three murdered in prison and some died under torture. Under the pressure of protests the regime proclaimed a general amnesty on 26 October 1978.

1979–. Gender-based suppression in the Islamic Republic of Iran

In 1979, Farrukhrū Pārsā, the former female minister of education, was executed for "sowing corruption on earth." Iranian officials announced that she had been "wrapped in a dark sack and machine-gunned." This marked the beginning of gender-specific suppression.

Between 1981 and 1985 the Islamic Revolutionary Committees caused the high-security prisons of Iwīn, Qizil Ḥiṣār, and Guhar Dasht in Tehran and other prisons to be overcrowded with many thousands of female political prisoners, from 10 to over 70 years old, among them members and sympathizers of oppositional groups or mothers helping their children. Closely watched by repenters (*tawābīn*) and female wardens, they were at the mercy of male guards who tortured, raped, married, or executed them.

Sixty died under torture and over 1,500 were executed: 47 were pregnant, 187 were under eighteen, 22 were thirteen to fifteen-years-old, 9 were under thirteen, 2 were over seventy, and the youngest was ten. In addition many Bahāʾī women were executed for refusing to recant.

Ideological courses accompanied the continual torture, which was used not only to obtain information or ideological recantations in public but was also part of everyday life in prison. The goal was to destroy the entire personality. Resistance and disobedience were brutally punished. In 1986, disobedient women were confined in boxes for up to ten months and many went mad.

Some repenters sought an end in (temporary) marriages with eligible guards, others in suicide. In 1988, non-repentant prisoners were executed. Hundreds of women linked to the Mujāhidīn organization were hanged as "armed enemies of God," leftist women were whipped at the five times of prayer for weeks. One woman died after 22 days and three committed suicide. Approximately one hundred women survived the massacre because of the public protests of Iranian women in Berlin in 1989.

In the 1990s and the early 2000s, the female political prisoners were mostly prominent lawyers, journalists, publishers, and others struggling for women's rights.

AFGHANISTAN

Merely for being relatives of male offenders, Afghan women constituted generations of anonymous prisoners, for example women and children belonging to the royal family as well as those belonging to Islamists (1978 and 1979). Women were also imprisoned and tortured as political offenders.

1970s

The first republic (Sardar Dāwūd 1973–8) was based on political repression; one response to this was the foundation of the Revolutionary Association of Women of Afghanistan (RAWA) in Pakistan in 1976.

1980s

Under the Communists and Soviets, the numerous interrogation and torture centers of the secret service, Khidmat-i Iṭilā ʿat-i Dawlatī (KHAD), were opened to women. Numerous women were arrested for taking part in student demonstrations or as members of armed opposition organizations. At the same time, leftist women were condemned by Islamic courts in the regions controlled by Mujāhidīn. There were cases of execution. As prisoners of war, Afghan women and their children were objects of a significant gender-specific victimization.

1990s

Mujāhidīn groups imprisoned, tortured, and raped women and children of ethnic-religious minority groups and those of the rival ethnic groups in official and private prisons. Many were executed and many went missing. In 1993, under President Rabbānī in Kabul, Shīʿī minorities, including women and children, were imprisoned, tortured, and raped. From 1995 to 2001, the Taliban militia kidnapped hundreds of non-Pashtun women and forced them into marriages with Taliban commanders.

Bibliography

J. Ahmadi, Imprisoned women, in *Iran Bulletin* 1997, <http://www.iran-bulletin.org/women/AHMADI.html>.

P. ʿAlīzādah, *Khūb nigāh kunīd, rāstakī ast. Guzārish-i zindān*, Paris 1987.

Amnesty International, *Afghanistan. Leben ohne Menschenrechte*, Bonn 1986.

——, *Women in Afghanistan. A human rights catastrophe*, London 1995

——, *Women in Afghanistan. Pawns in men's power struggle*, AI Index: ASA 11/11/99.

K. Āzarlī, *Maṣlūb. Khāṭirātī az zindānhā-yi Jumhūrī-i Islāmī*, Cologne 2001.

A. Dihqānī, *Ḥamāsah-i muqāvimat*, Beirut 1974.

L. Kelly, *Vision, innovation and professionalism in policing violence against women and children*, Strasbourg 2003.

D. MacEoin, From Shaykhism to Babism. A study in charismatic renewal in Shiʿi Islam, Ph.D. thesis, University of Cambridge 1977.

S. Pārsīʾpūr, *Khāṭirāt-i zindān*, Stockholm 1996.

M. Rahā, *Ḥaqīqat-i sādih. Khāṭirāt-i az zindānhā-yi Jumhūrī-i Islāmī*, 2 vols., Hanover 1992–4.

B. Seel, In diesen Momenten dachte ich, es sei besser, wenn ich stürbe, in *Die Tageszeitung* (Berlin), 27 November 1991, 3.

——, Die Folter diktiert die Sprache der Macht, in *Die Tageszeitung* (Berlin), 12 November 1991, 3.

Jale Ahmadi

Political Regimes

Afghanistan

Gender and women's issues have featured prominently in the political evolution of modern Afghanistan; however, traditional elements have consistently resisted efforts to change Afghan society. King Amān Allāh (r. 1919–29) attempted to transform Afghanistan into a modern state. His modernization campaign produced Afghanistan's first constitution (1924), the secularization of education, and advocated the emancipation of women.

Girls' schools were established in Kabul. Women were encouraged to unveil. Legislation in 1923 gave women the right to marry the man of their choice. Prominent female members of the royal family established the Anjuman-i Ḥimāyat-i Niswān (Women's protective society). Girls were sent abroad for secondary education and coeducation at the primary school level was proposed. Conservative tribal elements decried the emancipation of women as an invasion of privacy, a violation of modesty, and an attack against the chastity of the family.

Rebellion against Amān Allāh's reforms forced his abdication and exile. Nādir Shāh (r. 1930–3) became king and in deference to popular protests, he suspended Amān Allāh's reforms, including female education. After the ascension of King Muḥammad Ẓahīr Shāh (r. 1934–72), female education was gradually reintroduced along with various other reforms. In 1959, a subtle campaign initiated by Prime Minister Dāwūd, successfully unveiled women although purdah prevailed in the rural areas.

The constitution of 1964 granted women the right to vote. Education at the tertiary level was coeducational and women were encouraged to participate in the government and to enter traditionally male dominated professions. In 1965, a woman was appointed as minister of public health. Women were elected to the lower chamber of parliament. By the early 1970s, Afghanistan had trained seven female doctors.

The government discouraged polygamy, child marriages, and domestic violence against women but in the countryside where governmental authority was minimal these practices continued. Many Afghans outside the capital and major cities remained unaware of developments that continued to empower Afghan women. Girls' schools were established in all of the provincial capitals but enrollment remained substantially lower there. University-educated women found it more difficult to find husbands than uneducated women. Many women found employment as teachers. From the 1950s through the 1970s women made steady gains as the government encouraged the integration of women into society, but it was careful not to impose its policies.

The communist regime (1978–91) led by the People's Democratic Party of Afghanistan (PDPA) introduced radical social reform programs reminiscent of Amān Allāh's reign. Compulsory literacy classes for rural women caused an extreme reaction. Coupled with the Soviet occupation a fierce civil war erupted, which tore the country apart. The regime, with its active policy of promoting equality of the sexes, found itself more and more dependent on women as large portions of the population fled into exile. Toward the end of this period, the majority of school children and university students were girls. Women were employed in all sectors, even as bus drivers.

The Taliban regime (1996–2001) took control of the country after a brief unsuccessful Afghan Interim Government (AIG) ended in inter-party civil war. The Taliban interpretation of Islam conformed closely to tribal social norms and essentially espoused no role for women outside the home. This reactionary policy banned female education, prevented women from working outside the home, and forbade them to leave the home without being accompanied by a close male relative.

The December 2001 internationally brokered peace in Afghanistan helped establish a process for the re-establishment of a permanent government in Afghanistan. Women have been included in the process for establishing the interim government and appointed to the cabinet and major commissions. Twenty-five percent of the delegates at the Constitutional Loya Jirga (December 2003) were women. Female education has been reinstituted and women's groups in the larger urban areas have an active voice. A nationwide voter registration campaign has registered large numbers of women for the national elections scheduled for September 2004. While all of these developments are encouraging, the advances made by women in the second half of the twentieth century will only be regained when a stable government and rule of law are reestablished throughout the land.

BIBLIOGRAPHY
L. Dupree, *Afghanistan*, Princeton, N.J. 1973, 1980[3].
L. B. Poullada, *Reform and rebellion in Afghanistan, 1919–1929. King Amanullah's failure to modernize a tribal society*, Ithaca, N.Y. 1973.
B. R. Rubin, *The fragmentation of Afghanistan. State formation and collapse in the international system*, New Haven, Conn. 1995, 2002[2].

MARK DAVID LUCE

Turkey

The late nineteenth and early twentieth centuries were periods of rapid social change in Ottoman society. Confronted with economic pressures, the impact of the West, the reform of education, and especially the demands of conscription during the Balkan War and the First World War, women began moving out of their domestic realm into the public domain of men.

Not surprisingly, this influx of women into the public realm was accompanied by a debate over their rights. The Turkish nationalists, Young Turks, regarded women's emancipation as one of the major requisites of a larger social revolution, but it was not only modernizing male intellectuals who were involved in the debate; women themselves, by organizing in several associations and writing in and even editing daily papers and magazines, actively took part in this debate and thereby contributed to the creation of a civil public space. Feminist voices were even heard asking men to give up their desire to "liberate" women and "leave them to their own devices because women had more subtle ways of defending themselves and their kind" (Çakır 1994, 125).

However, Ottoman and later republican (Muslim) feminists were very aware that Turkish nationalism paved the way for women's citizenship rights, and Turkish feminism in the late nineteenth and early twentieth centuries was dominated by the nationalist ideology. This is obvious in the discourse and practice of women's organizations and in the discourse of prominent female writers such as Sabiha Zekeriya (Sertel). The rationalization she uses for granting political rights to women in 1919 is significant: "We, who have sacrificed most for the life and independence of this country, are the children of this nation too . . . Refusing to include us in general suffrage while granting the right to vote to the minorities who have shown their indifference toward this country is both a sin and a crime" (Toprak 1998). The nascent Kurdish nationalism and Kurdish women's activism of the period also went hand in hand, to a great extent replicating the pattern of the Turkish case (Karakışla 2003).

Women demanded to be full citizens in return for their "sacrifices" in the War of Independence (1919–22). They even applied to establish the "Women's People's Party" as early as 1923, immediately after the proclamation of the Turkish Republic, but were refused authorization on the grounds that women had not yet been given political rights. Instead, they were advised to set up a women's association, illustrating the fact that the stage for the granting of social and political rights for women was set by men as founders of republican Turkey (Arat 1989). One of the most important distinctions between the Ottoman society and the new republic was that now women were visible in the public space, and this constituted an unwanted challenge for men. Although – or perhaps because – this break with the past was so deep as to cause almost a psychological trauma in social life, it was also surrounded by ideological and structural continuities based on patriarchy. This is what some writers term the "replacement of Islamic patriarchy by Western patriarchy" (Z. Arat 1998) and constitutes a telling example of articulation of traditional sexist stereotypes and rules with nationalist, secularist discriminations and new gender roles.

Illustrative of this is that the new Civil Code (1926), which brought the secularization of the family and improved women's social status, also had its own patriarchal biases legally designating the husband the "head" of the family and relegating the wife to being his "helpmate." Explicitly patriarchal clauses of the Civil Code were only amended in 2002 after a long struggle by women. The legal biases reflected a male dominated society that sought to confine women to traditional gender roles while at the same time demanding that they be professionals and good patriots. An explanation of the smoothness with which these biases could find a place in the so-called radically new jurisprudence may be that they were an attempt to cope with the deep fear and challenge men sensed when faced by women's newly gained visibility in the public space and thereby eliminate the patriarchal anxiety prevalent in society.

With the granting of political rights (1934) women were formally accepted as citizens and the public space was now open for their contributions. But the nature of these contributions was to be strictly defined by the male leaders and ideologues of the single party regime who tried to harness the

"New Woman" to the creation and reproduction of a uniform citizenry (Kandiyoti 1991). In 1935 the Turkish Women's Association, obeying the advice of the regime, abolished itself on the ground that it had achieved its end (suffrage). The corporatist ideology of the state denied the existence of class and other sectoral interests in the body politic and controlled not only the women's movement but also the worker's associations, cultural clubs, and so on. However, control of women and their bodies assumed a specific character. A utilitarian approach seeking to mobilize the creative powers of women for the benefit of the whole nation was prevalent and this well served the corporatist/solidarist ideology of the regime. Now that the "overwhelming father," the Ottoman state, who had "long kept the creativity of the Turk under pressure and hindered his coming of age" was no longer there (Bora 1997), the New Man of the republic was obliged to obey the nation-state, whereas the New Woman in her turn was to obey the New Man. This compliance on women's part would, more or less, last until the new feminist movement of the late 1980s when women started to critically evaluate the Turkish experience of modernizing nationalism.

BIBLIOGRAPHY

A. Altınay (ed.), *Vatan, millet, kadınlar*, Istanbul 2000.
Y. Arat, *The patriarchal paradox. Women politicians in Turkey*, Rutherford, N.J. 1989.
Z. Arat, Kemalizm ve Türk kadını, in *75 yılda kadınlar ve erkekler*, Istanbul 1998, 51–70.
F. Berktay, Institutionalization of the Turkish women's movement as an historical experience, in *Institutionalisierung der Frauenbewegung. Chancen und Risiken*, Bonn 1992, 99–106.
——, Doğu ile Batı'nın Birleştiği yer. Kadın imgesinin kurgulanışı, in *Modern Türkiye'de siyasi düşünce*, vol. 3, *Modernleşme ve Batıcılık*, Istanbul 2002, 275–86.
——, Osmanlı'dan Cumhuriyete feminizm, in F. Berktay, *Tarihin Cinsiyeti*, Istanbul 2003, 88–111.
T. Bora, Cumhuriyet'in ilk döneminde milli kimlik, in N. Bilgin (ed.), *Cumhuriyet, demokrasi ve kimlik*, Istanbul 1997, 53–62.
S. Çakır, *Osmanlı kadın hareketi*, Istanbul 1994.
——, Osmanlı kadın dernekleri, in *Toplum ve bilim* 53 (Spring 1991), 139–57.
D. Kandiyoti, *Cariyeler, bacılar, yurttaşlar*, Istanbul 1997.
——, Emancipated but unliberated? Reflections on the Turkish case, in *Feminist Studies* 13:2 (1991), 317–38.
Y. S. Karakışla, Kürt Kadınları Teali Cemiyeti (1919), in *Toplumsal Tarih* 111 (March 2003), 14–25.
Z. Toprak, Sabiha (Zekeriya) Sertel ve Türk feminizmi, in *Toplumsal Tarih* 51 (March 1998), 7–14.

FATMAGÜL BERKTAY

Political-Social Movements: Ethnic and Minority

Iran and Afghanistan

In Afghanistan and Iran markers of group distinction – nationality, ethnicity, religion, language, and race – intertwine in complex ways, and interact with gender, class, and socioeconomic formations such as nomadism, tribalism, and feudalism.

The relative sizes of Afghanistan's ethnic groups have changed in the wake of the internal wars that began in the late 1970s and have turned the country into an international war zone. In the absence of reliable census data, the following are estimates only. By 1978, there were Pashtuns (40 percent, mostly Sunnīs), Tajiks (25 percent, mostly Sunnīs), Hazaras (10 percent, mostly Shīʿī), Uzbeks and Turkmens (13 percent, mostly Sunnī), and smaller communities such as the Aimaqs (Sunnī), Baluches and Brahuis (Sunnī), and Nuristanis. These socio-ethnic formations are diverse in terms of settlement and production relations. Thus, tribalism is more prevalent among the Pashtuns than the Tajiks, while nomadic life is more persistent among the Aimaq. Religious minorities include Shīʿīs, Ismāʿīlīs, Hindus, Sikhs, and Jews (Jawad 1992).

In Iran, there are Persians (50 percent, Shīʿī), Azerbaijani Turks (24 percent, Shīʿī), Kurds (9 percent, mostly Sunnī), Lurs (5 percent, Shīʿī), Baluches (3 percent, Sunnīs), Arabs (2.5 percent mostly Shīʿī), Turkmens (1.5 percent, Sunnī), Qashqayis (1.2 percent, Shīʿī), Armenians (0.71 percent, Christian), Assyrians (0.36 percent, Christian), and Jews (0.25 percent) (data based on government sources cited in Aliyev 1966, 64). While Arabs, Azeri Turks, Baluches, Kurds, and Turkmens live predominantly on their ancestral territories, which extend into neighboring countries, others such as Armenians, Assyrians, and Jews are scattered throughout the country. Religious minorities include, among others, Sunnīs, Bahāʾīs, Christians, Ismāʿīlīs, Zoroastrians, Jews, and Ahl-e Haqq.

Relationships among the groups are marked by inequality, although the minority/majority distinction is not necessarily a question of numerical strength. Thus, while in Afghanistan the Pashtuns are more numerous than the Tajiks and enjoy hegemony in the exercise of state power, their language is overshadowed by the literary and cultural hegemony of Dari, the language of the Tajiks. Afghanistan has therefore been called a "nation of minorities" (Jawad 1992).

Before the twentieth century

These communities lived in harmony and conflict in a feudal regime which tied the majority of the population to agrarian land and did not allow the centralization of state power. The majority were *raʿāyā* (subjects), and lived as peasants or members of tribes, with a very small, though influential, urban population. Allegiance was to kin, tribe, ethnic group, and birthplace, and religion was often ignored when it conflicted with the requirements of nomadic, tribal, and feudal life (Jawad 1992, 7).

While these peoples shared a great deal, from proverbs to songs to tilling techniques, they were aware of their ethnic distinctness, which was often expressed in terms such as Pashtunwali, Kurdewarî, and Baluchmayar (Pashtu, Kurdish, and Baluch way of life). The dominance of the male was one of the markers of ethnic identity (Lafrance 2000, Hassanpour 2001). Women, as bearers of men's honor, carried also the honor of kin, tribe, and people, and were, as such, targets of the enemy in times of war. Ethnicity as a marker of womanhood is articulated in folklore and language, for example, *dukhtar-i tarsā* (Christian girl, Persian) or *kiçe hermenî* (Armenian girl, Kurdish). However, the ethnic particularism of women was dwarfed by the universality of a patriarchal regime that was indispensable for the (re)production of tribal and feudal relations of production.

Nationalism and nation-building

The Constitutional Revolution of Iran (1905–11) aimed at instituting a modern political system distinguished by national sovereignty, citizenship, regime of rights, the rule of law, representative government, and territorial integrity. In Afghanistan, British interest in building a bulwark against Russia, rather than a democratic revolution, initiated the first steps toward the centralization of state power. In both countries, though more so in Iran, the nation-state tended to eliminate the exercise of power by ethnic peoples, and put an end to feudal, tribal, or religious fragmentation of the land and the people. This project, like its Western counterparts, was patriarchal, and moved to control women, who were emerging as a new political force.

Part of the nation-building project was to create an "Iranian woman" and an "Afghan woman," who, as citizens, would be identified by their membership in the nation rather than any particular ethnic group. In both countries, violence was integral to building the state and the nation. Like Western experiments in civic nation-building (see, for example, Nelson 1998), citizenship was, far from being neutral, anchored in the dominant ethnicity. Even in the case of Iran, where Reza Shah changed the ethnic name Persia, "land of Persians," to the less marked name of Iran, "land of Iranians," national womanhood was defined in Persian, cultural, and linguistic terms. Some male Iranian nationalist intellectuals construct Iranianness in opposition to Arabism, and seek the racial, Aryan purity of the nation in the sexual purity of women (Saad 1996, 127–32).

Early twentieth-century attempts to build an Afghan nation-state were "national politics without nation" (Centlivres and Centlivres-Demont 1988, 235). In fact, nationalist consciousness, to the extent that it emerged, lacked a social basis, and the names "Afghan" and "Afghanistan," chosen for citizens and the homeland were used to refer to Pashtuns and their territory. Early efforts to integrate women into the nation through granting them limited rights, especially education, brought one monarch down in 1929. By the 1970s, however, the "Afghan woman" had emerged although limited largely to the capital city of Kabul and the few urban centers, which were dwarfed by the countryside.

In Iran, consciousness of women's rights predated the male-centered "state feminism" of the Pahlavī period. Women's rights debates began in the Persian and Azerbaijani print media in the late nineteenth century. As in the Ottoman Empire, Christian and Jewish women had earlier access to education, and played an active role in the struggle.

Today, almost every ethnic people has developed its own nationalism, often in opposition to state nationalism. Like state nationalisms, they invest in women's rights as part of the nation-building project. Early Kurdish nationalists, for instance, viewed rural women as the bearers of pure Kurdish language and culture untainted by the dominant nation's assimilationist policies. Moreover, as mothers, women were in the best position to instill in the nation's children a pure Kurdish identity.

As early as the beginning of the twentieth century, many nationalists, including Kurds, Persians, and Turks blamed unequal gender relations and especially the oppression of women on Islam and its Arab roots. They construct their pre-Islamic history as an era of gender equality. The evidence, to the extent that it exists, is the old tribal or pastoral society, in which women were the main labor force, and associated, more or less freely, with males. Even in the present, Kurdish nationalists argue that Kurdish women enjoy more freedom than their neighboring Arab, Persian, and Turkish sisters. This claim has been challenged in so far as the cited evidence – mixed dancing, free association of females and males, absence of veiling in rural Kurdistan, as well as the existence of female rulers – is also found among Arabs, Persians, and Turks.

In a similar vein, some followers of pre- and post-Islamic minority religions, for example, Zoroastrians and Bahāʾīs, argue that, compared with Islam, their religions grant women more equality. The coming to power of two Islamic theocracies in Iran and Afghanistan has further invigorated this discourse. The conflict between women and theocracy has contributed to the formation of "Islamic feminisms" and, in contrast, promoted a secular politics of gender relations based on the separation of religion and state, and religion and law. Although Islamists generally argue that their faith is opposed to any division of human beings along the lines of race and ethnicity, and thus that Islam and nationalism are incompatible (Khumaynī 1983), some trends in "political Islam" aim at their fusion, and thus contribute to the ethnicization of Islam along nationalist lines (for example, Arab, Iranian, and Turkish Islamist movements). Another form of nationalist appropriation of religion is the tendency of some Kurdish nationalists to claim either Yezidism (currently a minority religion in Kurdistan and Armenia) or Zoroastrianism (not practiced in Kurdistan) as authentic Kurdish religions, which are said to grant women more freedom.

The ethnicization of women's movements is not, however, a product of Afghan or Iranian experiences. In the context of ongoing transnationalization and globalization, nationalist and religious movements, both minority and majority, everywhere promote a politics of ethnicization, nativization, or indigenization of feminism and women's movements.

Bibliography

S. M. Aliyev, The problem of nationalities in contemporary Persia, in *Central Asian Review* 14:1 (1966), 62–70.

P. Centlivres and M. Centlivres-Demont, *Et si on parlait de l'Afghanistan? Terrains et textes*, Paris 1988.

N. Jawad, *Afghanistan. A nation of minorities*, London 1992.

A. Hassanpour, The (re)production of patriarchy in the Kurdish language, in S. Mojab (ed.), *Women of a non-state nation. The Kurds*, Costa Mesa 2001, 227–63.
R. A. Khumaynī (Ayatollah Khomeini), *Dar justjū-yi rāh az kalām-i imām*, xi, *Millīgirā'ī*, Tehran 1983.
P. Lafrance, La femme et le Pakhtunwali, in Centre d'Etudes et de Recherches Documentaires sur l'Afghanistan, *La femme afghane à travers l'histoire de l'Afghanistan. Actes du Colloque. UNESCO – Paris, 11 décembre 1998*, Paris 2000, 73–9.
D. Nelson, *National manhood. Capitalist citizenship and the imagined fraternity of white men*, Durham, N.C. 1998.
J. B. Saad, *The image of Arabs in modern Persian literature*, Lanham, Md. 1996.

Amir Hassanpour

Iraq, Jordan, Lebanon, Syria

"Mosaic societies": problems of terminology and perception

Iraq, Jordan, Lebanon, and Syria are characterized by a rich ethnic, religious, and cultural diversity that was formed and reconfigured historically through processes of settlement, migration, displacement, war, and state policy. It has long been a cliché to describe the Middle East, and especially the "fertile crescent" region, as constituting a mosaic society (Coon 1958) traditionally characterized by an "ethnic division of labor" (Sussnitski 1917). The easy and misleading premises of these formulations today may be couched in more nuanced language but still often form the basis of scholarly as well as popular and media representations. Assumptions concerning pure identities, impermeable boundaries, and age-old enmities alternately exaggerate or underestimate societal tensions and political mobilizations based on shifting ethnic, linguistic, and confessional identities and do not help in understanding how identities are constructed and reproduced, how they intersect and cross-cut one another, how difference and perceptions of difference are articulated, or why political demands may or may not be made on the basis of ethnic difference or in terms of minority rights.

Adequately understanding how these processes are gendered is even more difficult, given the paucity and the quality of the literature. While, as in any type of collective identity, one can easily see that women and their bodies symbolically operate as markers of difference, that marriage strategies are at the heart of group reproduction as well as inter-group alliance, and that women's participation in political processes are significant, these generalizations cannot easily be substantiated through specific understandings of how they may operate in the case of particular groups, localities, or even states.

States, societies, and nationalisms

Iraq, Jordan, Lebanon, and Syria exhibit significant variation in terms of nation building and state building which creates disparate contexts for political mobilization on the basis of ethnicity or demands in terms of minority rights or national self-determination. It is also important to recognize that groups within these countries have historically always been in interaction with each other and across the borders formed in the twentieth century. Thus the Kurds, but also Turkmens and Assyrians, while constituting a "minority" within particular states (Syria, Iraq, Iran, and Turkey), form large trans-border populations. Others are part of historically constituted diasporas (Jews, Armenians) while all groups are part of contemporary global diasporas as a result of labor and refugee movements. In this diverse landscape, the Kurdish movements are the most salient, and best researched, minority movements and can help illustrate the ways in which religion and gender play into these movements.

It is also important to consider how Syria, Iraq, Jordan and Lebanon (in that order) participate in discourses of Arab nationalism. Syria and Iraq (until the 2003 invasion by the United States and coalition forces) were the most comparable, in terms of the multiple ethnic and minority groups that inhabit their territories, their secular, nationalist, "revolutionary" official rhetoric, and their authoritarian regimes. The ruling groups in these regimes were mostly recruited from communities to which the long-serving presidents belonged ('Alawīs in the case of Syria and Tikrītīs in the case of Iraq) and are thus described by some authors as "minority regimes." Both these states mobilized women through a rhetoric of modernism, nationalism, and state feminism, which privileged the state and broader ideals of the Arab nation over ethnic, religious, or local identifications, as witnessed by the attempts to socialize the "new Iraqi woman" (Joseph 1991).

Jordan participates in the discourse of Arab nationalism through emphasizing the role of the Hashemites in overthrowing Ottoman rule in the 1920s. Equal weight is also given to the monarchy's religious credentials and descent from the lineage of the Prophet Muḥammad. Society and politics is largely fractured on Palestinian/East Bank Jordanian lines as well as through tribal allegiances created by both bottom-up and top-down dynamics. Loyalty to the regime and the monarch is the basis for privileging groups. In this context the minority groups, such as Circassians, Chechens, Christians (both Palestinian and East Bank), and Armenians, have not formed movements on a minority basis although they do make political claims on this basis. Circassians and Christians (as well as Beduin tribes) have allotments in parliamentary seats through quotas in certain electoral districts. Furthermore, ethnicity and religion certainly play important roles even in the absence of formal movements. For example, Circassians and Chechens mobilized to extend aid and medical relief during the Abkhasian-Georgian war of 1992–3, as well as for the ongoing Chechen-Russian conflict, in the latter case finding common ground with Jordanian Islamist groups.

The experience of Tūjān al-Fayṣal, the only woman thus far elected (in 1993) to the Jordanian parliament (there are women appointed to the senate) is also instructive. Although Tūjān al-Fayṣal did not campaign on ethnic issues, she did run for the Circassian seat in her electoral district thus enabling her to win with significantly fewer votes than she would have needed for a majority seat. As a member of parliament, her progressive politics were not based on lobbying for her ethnic community but when she became the target of Islamists and conservatives in parliament and eventually of the government (she was taken to court for apostasy by the former and charged and imprisoned for slander by the latter), the Circassian community leadership rallied around her and interceded on her behalf with the king. In this way, ethnicity plays a political role even in the absence of movements as such.

Lebanon is the most anomalous state in the group, constituted (in the French mandate formulation) as "a nation of minorities – where the largest minority rules," with the Maronite Christians having been designated the largest minority. The Maronites' collective sense of identity is tied to the church (an Eastern Christian church later Romanized) and was forged historically through territorial and political conflicts (for example, the Maronite-Druze "civil war" of 1860). An ethnic dimension is added to this identity through asserting descent from the Phoenicians and distance from Arabs and Muslims. This identity was continually mobilized, as were Sunnī, Druze, and Shīʿī identities, due to the sectarian basis of the Lebanese state, reinforced by such practices as the lack of civil marriage and the relegation of all personal status matters to religious authorities (Joseph 1991). The language of political competition and conflict is that of sectarianism and confessionalism rather than minority politics. In spite of the Maronite "defeat" with the end of the civil war in 1990–1, and shifts in balance, such as the emergence of the Shīʿīs as a powerful political force, Lebanese politics is not about majorities and minorities but consists of shifting alliances among the 17 "sects" which are officially designated as comprising the Lebanese polity.

Kurdish politics in Iraq: religion, women, and rights

It should be stated clearly that Kurdish movements are more properly described as national movements espousing the goal of national self-determination (the term Kurdistan first appeared in the fourteenth century.) However, given that the Kurdish population exists as "minorities" within four contiguous states (Iran, Iraq, Syria, and Turkey), as well as in various diasporic communities, the form in which political struggles have taken place has been that of minority and ethnic movements and bargaining with the central state for certain forms of political and cultural expression and autonomy. The remainder of this entry offers a brief discussion of how these politics unfolded in the context of the Iraqi state, where Kurds form between 15 and 20 percent of the population, with the recognition that this only addresses one part, albeit an important one, of the Kurdish situation. Iraqi Kurdish society is characterized by religious, linguistic, and tribal diversity. Most Kurds are Sunnī Muslim with a small percentage of Shīʿīs. Some Kurds also adhere to Islamic heterodox and pre-Islamic religions (such as Yezidism) and there are also Kurdish-speaking Jews.

In 1925, the League of Nations awarded the Ottoman vilayet of Mosul to Iraq rather than Turkey, but the area was supposed to remain under League Mandate for 25 years and the Iraqi state was to guarantee Kurdish autonomy. This did not come to pass and the long history of clashes and negotiations between various Kurdish political parties and movements and the central government in Baghdad is one of promises not kept and hopes dashed. For example, when the Baʿth party first took power in Iraq in 1963, the Kurdish Democratic Party (KDP) requested autonomy in Kurdistan over everything except foreign affairs, finance, and national defense, but this was not accepted. In 1970 a peace accord with the regime outlined a 15-point program which included Kurdish language education, respect for culture, economic support, land reform, self government, and the freedom to establish student, youth, women's, and teachers' organizations (McDowall 1996). Despite the importance of this formal recognition, the plan was not implemented, setting the stage for the next conflict. The unilateral 1974 Autonomy Law promulgated by Baghdad foundered over oil and Kirkuk, which Mustafa Barzani claimed as the Kurdish autonomous capital and the state refused to cede. This led to the 1974–5 war between government and Kurdish forces, which was followed by a policy of forced resettlement of Kurds to other areas of Iraq, redrawing of administrative boundaries, and Arabization, which included "financial rewards to Arabs who took Kurdish wives, a deliberate encouragement of ethnic assimilation . . . and the Arabizing of some place names" (McDowall 1996, 340).

It is important to add, however, that Kurds and non-Kurds have long cooperated in forming political platforms. For example, the KDP, formed in August 1946, changed its name to the Kurdistan Democratic Party in 1953 so as to include non-Kurds, while up to 35 percent of the members of the Iraqi Communist Party, established in 1934, were Kurdish. More recently, the Kurdistan Front in 1985 was formed of the five major parties, Kurdish and non-Kurdish, including the Assyrian Democratic Movement, reflecting the fact that Iraqi Kurdistan comprises a number of groups, most notably Turkmens and Assyrians.

Things changed with 1988 and the notorious Anfāl operations, which killed approximately between 150 and 200 thousand villagers in Kurdistan. Some elderly and women and children survivors were sent to a concentration camp in southwest Iraq, and most women where taken to a camp near Kirkuk where thousands died. In several of the Anfāl operations men were singled out for execution, while in southern Kurdistan women and children were also executed. The post 1990–1 Gulf War period has seen the designation of northern Iraq as a safe haven, and no-fly zone, with a high degree of self-determination in politics and economy. At the same time, the region saw the growth of extremist Islamist movements such as Anṣār al-Islām which, among other things, have tried to impose the veiling of women's faces and bodies and the banning of girls' education and women's work outside the home. As this volume goes to press, the final status of this region, and indeed of Iraq itself, is yet to be determined. Whatever the outcome, it will have a momentous impact on Kurdish politics and populations in neighboring countries, especially Turkey.

The gender dimensions of these political vagaries obviously extend beyond the mention of women as victims of violence and ethnic cleansing. While cautioning against exaggeration, several authors emphasize the important role of women in Kurdish politics and public life, including activism, participation in elections, women's publications, and the formation of women's organizations within the main Kurdish parties. In the 1992 elections in the Kurdish autonomous zone, six women were elected to parliament out of 105 seats. These female deputies and women activists lobbied (albeit unsuccessfully) for legal reform and the rescinding of the personal status and penal laws of the Iraqi government that discriminated against women. Women also organized a 200 kilometer peace march to protest against the war between the two major parties, the Patriotic Union of Kurdistan (PUK) and the KDP, in 1994.

In spite of this progress, the general consensus of most feminist authors is that national liberation has overshadowed women's emancipation. Still, nationalist and popular discourses promote a representation of Kurdish women as traditionally enjoying high status, relative freedom, and equality as compared to women in Arab, Turkish, and Persian societies. In a familiar twist, these same images are deployed by outsiders to accuse Kurdish women of promiscuity especially in the context of the religious practices of heterodox groups. Historical studies reveal that Kurdish women played leading roles in religious lodges and movements as well as in political and military leadership. There are several accounts of Kurdish women leading tribal groupings and confederations, usually after the death of their husbands, and in some cases of their fathers. The participation of women in the military continues today in Kurdistan, as nearly all Kurdish political parties (except the Islamist ones) include guerrilla women fighters in their militias.

Bibliography

M. van Bruinessen, *Agha, shaikh and state. The social and political structures of Kurdistan*, London 1992.

C. Coon, *Caravan. The story of the Middle East*, New York 1958.

A. Hourani, *Minorities in the Arab world*, Oxford 1947.

S. Joseph, Elite strategies for state-building. Women, family, religion and state in Iraq and Lebanon in D. Kandiyoti (ed.), *Women, Islam and the state*, Philadelphia 1991, 176–200.

D. McDowall, *A modern history of the Kurds*, London 1996.

S. Mojab (ed.), *Women of a non-state nation. The Kurds*, Costa Mesa 2001.

M. Rubin, Are Kurds a pariah minority? in *Social Research* 70:1 (2003), 295–330.

A. J. Sussnitzki, Zur Gliederung wirtschaftslicher Arbeit nach Nationalitaten in der Turkei, in *Archiv fur Wirtschaftsforschung im Orient* 2 (1917), 382–407.

Seteney Shami

North Africa

The Berber cultural movement is the most significant minority sociopolitical movement to emerge from North Africa's rich racial, ethnic, and religious landscape. Berberophones constitute approximately 25 percent of the population of Algeria and 40 percent of Morocco. With roots stretching back to the 1920s, the contemporary movement consists of a diffuse network of activists organized into cultural associations and political parties primarily located in Algeria (especially Kabylia), Morocco, and the North African diaspora in Europe and North America. The movement claims the indigenousness of Berbers (or *imazighen*, free men, in activist discourse) to North Africa and contests the "minority" label imposed on them by North African states with official Arab nationalist ideologies. Berber activists advocate the recognition of Berber language (Tamazight) as an official and national language of Algeria and Morocco equal to Arabic in the public sphere (education, media, government). Although generally marginalized from leadership roles, women play significant roles in the movement as salient symbols and outspoken militants.

Berber activists underline the cultural distinctiveness of *imazighen* from the Arab populations of North Africa. The elaboration of an Arab/Berber ethnic divide derives to a great extent from the efforts of French military and colonial administration to extensively document Berber legal codes and oral poetry. Their divide-and-rule policies targeted Berber populations for potential assimilation due to their perceived sedentary nature, laboring qualities, republican social organization, and lack of visible religiosity (as indicated primarily by the non-veiling of women) (Lorcin 1995). Such strategies resulted in the 1930 so-called "Berber Dahir" (decree) that created separate juridical systems for Arab and Berber populations in Morocco.

Reacting to these policies, early articulations of nationalism advocated the multicultural (Arab and Berber) identity of Algeria and Morocco. In the 1960s, these were gradually replaced by an ideology of Arab nationalism and policies of linguistic Arabization by the ruling National Liberation Front and Istiqlal parties. In response, Berber activists founded the Berber Academy and the Berber Study Group in Paris, and the Moroccan Association for Cultural Research and Exchange in Rabat, to standardize Tamazight, develop a Berber script, and publish Berber poetry.

These efforts developed into a widespread social movement after the Kabyle student uprisings of April 1980, known internationally as the "Berber Spring." The events provoked the founding of an umbrella political organization, the Berber Cultural Movement, as well as hundreds of cultural associations throughout North Africa and the diaspora that sponsor courses in Tamazight and Berber history and serve as loci for cultural expression. Since 1989, the advocacy of Berber cultural and linguistic rights has been further taken up by Kabylia-based political parties: the Socialist Forces Front and the Algerian Rally for Culture and Democracy (RCD). A World Amazigh Congress was founded in 1995, coordinating the efforts of Berber associations across the globe. Through electioneering, school strikes, and petitioning supranational human rights bodies, the movement has succeeded in garnering the official recognition of "Berberity" as a constituent part of Algerian and Moroccan identity, as well as the tentative introduction of Tamazight in the media and education systems. However, struggles continue, with violent encounters between Kabyle youth and the Algerian military in July 1998 and April 2001 (Maddy-Weitzman 2001, Silverstein 2003).

Within this multi-stranded movement, women have played an important, if often marginalized, role. The movement has appropriated a number of women from history into its pantheon of cultural heroes, including Kahina, Kheïra, and Fathma n'Soumer – women Berber leaders who fought against the Arab and French invasions of the seventh and nineteenth centuries (Ferrah 1997). Their images adorn Berber cultural productions and meeting halls, and songs memorializing their achievements galvanize association meetings. These historical women also function as an imagined genealogy for contemporary female Berber militants, such as Khalida Messaoudi and Djura Abouda, who look to them for inspiration (Messaoudi 1995, 1998, 27–8, Djura 1993, 116–25).

Women's participation in Berber militancy has generally been relegated, however, to the sidelines of direct confrontation, as the mourning sisters to their fallen brothers. One of the strongest voices from the Kabyle diaspora, Malika Matoub, remains known primarily as the sister of the militant folk-singer Lounès Matoub, having led rallies after his 1998 assassination and written a biography memorializing his life (Matoub 1999). Women have often been leaders and founders of cultural associations, but their role in the political movement, particularly in Morocco and Algeria, has been primarily limited to participation in organized actions. Messaoudi, elected to the Algerian parliament in 1997 on the RCD ticket, perhaps represents an exception to this general trend. However, her alliance with the RCD is largely situational; while an advocate for the recognition of Berber culture and language, her primary activism has revolved around the repeal of the 1984 Family Code (Messaoudi 1995).

Such feminism underlines another space for women's participation in the Berber cultural movement: artistic performance. Female singers – including Hanifa, Chérifa Ouardia, and Taos Amrouche – were particularly prevalent in the Kabyle immigrant scene of the 1950s and 1960s, melding a Berber cultural revival with an early feminist politics. Taos became a star of international folk festivals by collecting and recording the oral poetry of her mother Fadhma, whose autobiography she later edited (Amrouche 1968). Considered too proximate to Berber ethnonationalism, she was barred from representing Algeria at the first PanAfrican Cultural Festival in 1969 (Goodman 2002, 97).

Male musicians and songwriters of the militant "new Kabyle song" style of the 1970s and 1980s similarly deployed and reworked maternal genres and images, creating idealized visions of Berber village domesticity and culture (Mahfoufi 1994). In this process, however, they have often silenced the women whose songs they appropriate (Goodman 1996). Contemporary female singers – such as the group Djurdjura, Malika Domrane, Nouara, Houria Aichi (Aurès region), and Fatima Tabaamrant (Morocco) – have attempted to recapture the genre, using it not only to celebrate Berber culture and language, but also to critique the patriarchal structures of Berber society and the misogynist violence of their fathers and brothers (Djura 1991, 1993). In their songs and performances, they inject a critical feminist counterpoint to the cultural movement as a whole.

BIBLIOGRAPHY

F. Amrouche, *Histoire de ma vie*, Paris 1968.

S. Chaker, *Berbères aujourd'hui. Berbères dans le Maghreb contemporain*, Paris 1998[2] (rev. ed).

Djura, *Le voile du silence*, Paris 1991.

——, *La saison des narcisses*, Paris 1993.

A. Ferrah, *Kahina*, Algiers 1997.

J. Goodman, Dancing towards "la mixité." Berber associations and cultural change in Algeria, in *Middle East Report* 200 (1996), 16–20.

——, Writing empire, underwriting nation. Discursive histories of Kabyle Berber oral texts, in *American Ethnologist* 29:1 (2002), 86–122.

C. Lacoste-Dujardin, Femmes kabyles. De la rigueur patriarcale à l'innovation, in *Hommes et Migrations* 1179 (1994), 19–24.

P. Lorcin, *Imperial identities. Stereotyping, prejudice and race in colonial Algeria*, London 1995.

B. Maddy-Weitzman, Contested identities. Berbers, "Berberism" and the state in North Africa, in *Journal of North African Studies* 6:3 (2001), 23–47.

M. Mahfoufi, La chanson kabyle en immigration. Une retrospective, in *Hommes et migrations* 1179 (1994), 32–9.

M. Matoub, *Matoub Lounès, mon frère*, Paris 1999.

K. Messaoudi, *Une Algérienne debout. Entretiens avec Elisabeth Schemla*, Paris 1995, trans. A. C. Vila, *Unbowed*, Philadelphia 1998.

P. Silverstein, Martyrs and patriots. Ethnic, national, and transnational dimensions of Kabyle politics, in *Journal of North African Studies* 8:1 (2003), 87–111.

T. Yacine, La revendication berbère, in *Intersignes* 10 (1995), 95–106.

PAUL A. SILVERSTEIN

Sub-Saharan Africa: South Africa

This entry examines the situation of Muslim women in South Africa. They are a heterogeneous group who manifest diverse attitudes and tendencies but are beginning to assert their rights and challenge "traditional" modes of thought and patterns of behavior. They are doing this within the context of being minorities three times over: first, they are Muslims, a religious minority of just over half a million out of South Africa's total population of 41 million; second, they represent a number of ethnic groups originally from Asia and the Arabian Peninsula as well as other parts of Sub-Saharan Africa; and third, they are women. Accordingly, their involvement in South African political and social movements has been multifaceted and draws on a number of ideological discourses. The two most important loci of these, from the mid-twentieth century to the present time, have been the struggle against the old South African regime's policy of racial discrimination against non-whites – with whom most Muslims were included – and contemporary activism for women's rights.

BACKGROUND: ASSIMILATION, ISOLATION, AND INTEGRATION

Traditionalist values remain important in some sectors of South Africa's Muslim population and among these women adopt a minimalist approach to involvement with the state or with the broader community. Any interaction or cooperation with either tends to be on the basis of necessity, not motivated by a sense of identity with national goals. Their concerns are expressed in such areas as the recognition of Muslim Personal Law, including provisions of the Muslim Marriage Bill. In contrast, some Muslim women have become full participants in South Africa's emerging "rainbow nation." They identify with national rather than Muslim-specific interests. The new South African Bill of Rights and the constitution provide the basis for their decisions and continued activism. Some of these Muslim women played key roles in the long struggle against apartheid and the subsequent envisioning of a new, multicultural nation.

Located between these two positions is the pragmatism that characterizes the majority of Muslim women in South Africa who seek a balanced assimilation, fearing the loss of their identity yet also rejecting isolationism as self-defeating. Thus, while they maintain constructive engagement with various levels of government and civil society, they continue to proclaim their Islamic identity.

Political leadership

Cissy Gool (d. 1963) is one of the trail blazers for women in the field of politics. The daughter of the famous Dr. Abdullah Abdul Rahman, the first "Black" South African to graduate as a medical practitioner, she served as a city councilor in Cape Town for many years and was an instrumental role model for other Muslim women.

Beginning in the mid-twentieth century, Muslim women played a prominent role in national politics. Leaders included Amina Cachalia and her older sister, Zaynab Asvat, and Fatima Meer, all of whom were actively involved in resistance politics. Amina Cachalia, wife of the veteran freedom fighter Molvi Cachalia, was active in the Transvaal Indian Congress, and became treasurer of the Federation of South African Women which spearheaded the Defiance Campaign, culminating in the famous march by 20,000 women to the Union Buildings in Pretoria to protest against the pass laws in 1956.

The sociologist Fatima Meer (born 1928), author of Nelson Mandela's biography, *Higher Than Hope*, and of over 40 other books and numerous articles, is among the best-known anti-apartheid activists. A disciple of Mahatma Gandhi's philosophy of passive resistance, she endured banning, detention, and death threats with calm resolve. A close friend of both Nelson and Winnie Mandela, she is now one of the key figures in the anti-globalization movement in South Africa. She supported Steve Biko's (murdered 1975) Black Consciousness Movement and established the Institute of Black Studies at the University of Natal.

In the 1970s and 1980s young and old Muslim women marched through the streets of major cities demanding an end to apartheid. Scores were arrested and detained, some were tortured. One of these women, Zubeida Jaffer, a journalist by profession, has recently published an autobiographical account of her involvement in resistance politics during the heyday of the United Democratic Front entitled *Our Generation*.

Today, several Muslim women occupy key positions in government ministries such as education, and four currently serve as members of the national parliament: Naledi Pandor, Fatima Chohan, Farida Mohamed, and Fatima Hujaig.

For traditionalist women, involvement in national level politics is to be avoided because they believe that the secular policies of the South African nation conflict with their religious beliefs. For example, many avoid political participation because the state supports rights such as abortion on demand, gambling, and homosexual unions. They are unlikely to vote in elections because they do not wish to be involved in a system which they perceive to be essentially immoral.

Social welfare and women's organizations

Muslim women have long been active in social welfare and development in their communities and form the majority of the staff of virtually every organization dealing with social welfare issues. The Islamic Social and Welfare association is one of the larger and better-known groups in the Cape Province. In the northern city of Johannesburg, Soraya Hassim of the Islamic Relief Agency has been carrying out important work among the destitute for decades, a contemporary expression of *zakāt*. The Women's Cultural Group in Durban, Kwa Zulu-Natal, under the guidance of Zuleikha Mayet, has been providing financial assistance to needy university students for decades and is a strong example of Muslim women's ongoing commitment to educational excellence. Involvement in social welfare groups is not only important in and of itself but also provides a public and therefore political voice for women. Likewise, there is a long history of women's organizations active in the country. The *Directory of Muslim Institutions and Mosques in South Africa* provides a list of 20 women's organizations. The activities of these groups include education, social relief, propagation of Islam, promotion of culture, and participation in politics.

Political activism in mosques and theological councils

Most mosques in South Africa still prohibit women from attending prayers. The Cape Province, historically the earliest home to South African Muslims, has a more liberal tradition and women there not only join the congregation in the mosque but also visit the cemetery. Interestingly, land for the first mosque to be established at the Cape was donated by a woman, Saartijie van de Kaap in 1794, at the end of the period of Dutch occupation.

Women have started a campaign to be admitted in all mosques. With the support of male champions of women's rights, they have also started the family *ʿīd* congregation in several major centers, much to the chagrin of those who believe that they are violating a sacred tradition.

The exclusively male theological councils' decisions are now being questioned by women, especially in the realm of family law, for example, issues of divorce and custody, which they believe to reveal a male bias. Challenges have been made to other aspects of Islamic law that are perceived as discriminatory as well. One crucial area has been in the realm of inheritance, traditionally weighed in favor of men. Muslim activists are demanding that inheritance should be shared equally between men and women and that divorced women should be provided with maintenance even after the end of *ʿidda*, the three-month waiting period for Muslim widows, after which they are allowed to remarry. Women also demanded and succeeded in obtaining the right to have input in the drafting of the Muslim Marriage Bill. An interesting related development is the recent employment of women counselors by theological councils to advise families experiencing marital problems.

Conclusion

A distinctive ethnic and cultural minority, South Africa's Muslim women bring the strengths of their past struggles as Muslims, as Asian and African immigrants, and as women to the challenges of nation building in the new South Africa.

Bibliography

L. Ahmed, *Women and gender in Islam*, London 1992.
S. E. Dangor, Historical perspective, current literature and an opinion survey among Muslim women in contemporary South Africa. A case study, in *Journal of Muslim Minority Affairs* 21:1 (2001), 109–29.
M. Davids (comp.), *Directory of Muslim institutions and mosques in South Africa*, Maraisburg 1996.
E. Everett, Zainussia [Cissie Gool] [1897–1963]. A bibliography, B.A. hons. paper, University of Cape Town 1978.
Z. Hasan (ed.), *Forging identities. Gender, communities and the state*, New Delhi 1994.
R. A. Hill, The role of Muslim women in Cape Town, B.A. hons. paper, University of Cape Town 1977.
Z. Jaffer, *Our generation*, Cape Town 2003.
D. Kandiyoti, *Identity and its discontents. Women and nation*, Women Living Under Muslim Laws Dossier 20, July 1998.
R. Ridd, Separate but more than equal. Muslim women at the Cape, in C. F. El-Solh and J. Mabro (eds.), *Muslim women's choices. Religious beliefs and social practice*, Oxford 1993.
F. Seedat, Women and activism. Indian Muslim women's responses to apartheid South Africa, M.A. thesis, University of Cape Town 2003.
Straight Path (South African-based Islamic magazine) ed. F. Asmal.
C. Waddy, *Women in Muslim history*, London 1980.
Women's Cultural Group, brochure commemorating 35 years of community service 1954–1989, Durban 1989.
R. F. Woodsmall, *Moslem women enter a new world*, New York 1975 (reprint of the 1936 ed.).

Suleman E. Dangor

Turkey

At the start of the twenty-first century, Turkey's state institutions are increasingly unable to keep up with the complex changing structure, needs, and demands of a heterogeneous Turkish society. Despite strong centrifugal tendencies along ethnic, religious, and national lines among the population, Turkish nationalism or its more recent version, the so-called Turkish-Islamic synthesis, is still promoted as a unifying force (Bozarslan 1996). In its practical functioning the state has been forced to take some steps in the field of religious, ethnic, and women's rights. Yet attempts by the state and military establishment to control opposition movements such as political Islam and Kurdish nationalist politics, both movements with a large female constituency, continue to be sources of serious crises and violence (Çaha 2000, Cizre 1999). In particular, ethnic minority women in Turkey are confronted with multi-layered forms of oppression and violence.

At the root of Turkey's problems lies the process of nation building. Republican Turkey is a typical example of a state forging a nation from above. The founding of the Turkish Republic in 1923 and its official ideology, Kemalism, which prescribed ethnonationalism, etatism, and secularism as main pillars of the political system, represented an important break with the Ottoman multi-ethnicity. As part of the broader project of nation building, the status of women was made into the barometer of Turkish modernization. Turkish nationalism, however, contained contradictory elements from the very beginning. On the one hand, Turkish citizenship was defined as an all-embracing concept encompassing all citizens, regardless of ethnic origin or gender, granting them equal rights and obligations. On the other hand, every citizen in republican Turkey, which according to Andrews (1989) counts at least 47 distinct ethnic groups, was by official definition declared to be a "Turk." The concept of minority in a juridical sense was limited to non-Muslim and thus religious minorities (Greek-Orthodox, Jews, and Armenians).

From early on subsequent governments had recourse to forced assimilation, and preferred mass deportations as a means of Turkification. This applied in particular to the Kurds, Turkey's largest ethnic minority who make up around 15 percent of the population. Kurdish resistance movements during the 1920s and 1930s, typically male dominated movements with ethnic and religious elements, were violently oppressed (Bruinessen 1992). Compulsory education, state controlled media in Turkish, and general conscription, proved relatively effective for integrating Kurdish men into "national" politics. Kurdish women were much less affected by assimilation policies. Modernizing and emancipating reforms such as obligatory primary education for girls or rights guaranteed by legal marriage, such as inheritance and child custody, also had very little impact on their lives. In particular the lives of Kurdish women in eastern and southeastern Turkey, which is often characterized as a semi-feudal society relying on traditional and agricultural economy, continued to be ruled by customary and religious laws and traditional gender patterns.

Turkey suffered three military coups (1960, 1971, and 1980), of which the last had the most pervasive effect on politics and society, inciting both majority and minority women to activism in the public sphere. Paradoxically, the period of depoliticization of society after 1980 provided a space for the development of a feminist movement that questioned constructions of Turkish identity and women's "liberation" (Tekeli 1993, Sirman 1979). Gender related issues and notions of the "ideal woman" also became part of an ideological terrain on which issues of national, ethnic, and religious identities were being debated, as exemplified by debates on the covering of women and the Kurdish women fighters. The 1980s turned out to be a watershed. Questions of identity and diversity forged a process of fragmentation in society, for example, Turks-Kurds, secularists-Islamists, Alevis-Sunnīs and nationalists-leftists. Stress on Sunnī Islam in official constructions of Turkish identity further alienated the Alevis, a heterodox religious minority consisting of both Turks and Kurds. Political Islam, which locally has an important Kurdish element too, emerged as a mass movement and an important political force, gaining absolute majority in the parliamentary elections in 2002.

A major development in the 1980s and 1990s was the rise of a Kurdish national movement in Turkey and in Western Europe, headed by Abdullah Öcalan's Partiya Karkerên Kurdistan (PKK). From 1984 until 1999, the PKK fought a guerrilla war against the Turkish state, which led to its partial success but also caused massive destruction and displacement in the Kurdish areas. The Kurdish national movement drew considerable public attention owing to the high number of women militants among PKK ranks (20 percent) and the prominence of the so-called Woman Question in its political discourse (Yalçın-Heckmann and Gelder 2000). Stress on women's emancipation and gender equality incited Kurdish women to become politically active: Leyla Zana became first woman member of parliament with a distinct Kurdish identity in 1991. For the majority of women in the Kurdish area, however, decades of war and economic crisis had grave consequences. The armed conflict merely strengthened the male-dominated structure of the community through the increase of cooperation between the military and Kurdish tribal leaders and through the rise of militaristic values in society. Incidence of gendered violence in the predominantly Kurdish areas is relatively high (Gökçeçiçek-Yurdakul 2001). Yet, apart from literacy courses by the state-run adult education centers (for example, ÇATOM), no rehabilitation program for women has been undertaken.

During the 1990s there was a significant degree of liberalization of state policies. Legal constraints remained, however, and liberalization coincided with an unprecedented decline in standards of human rights, exemplified by increased violence against women during detention (Amnesty 2003). Kurds, Alevis, and some smaller ethnic groups such as the Laz and Circassians started cultural publications and organizations, and pro-Kurdish political parties were established. Also Kurdish women's groups in the large urban centers began publishing their own magazines (for example, *Roza, Jujin, Jin û Jiyan*, and *Özgür Kadın*), addressing the position of Kurdish and other minority women from various points of view, ranging from feminist to nationalist. Debates on differences (ethnicity, class, religion) are nowadays common among women's movements in Turkey, inciting literary and scientific production on multiple gendered identities (Altınay 2000).

Bibliography

A. Altınay, Giriş. Milliyetçilik, toplumsal ginsiyet ve feminizm, in A. Altınay (ed.), *Vatan, millet, kadınlar*, Istanbul 2000, 11–29.

Amnesty International, *Turkey. End sexual violence against women in custody*, London 2003.

P. Andrews, *Ethnic groups in the Republic of Turkey*, Wiesbaden 1989.
H. Bozarslan, Political crisis and the Kurdish issue in Turkey, in R. Olson (ed.), *The Kurdish nationalist movement in the 1990s. Its impact on Turkey and the Middle East*, Lexington, Ky. 1996, 135–53.
M. van Bruinessen. *Agha, shaikh and state. The social and political structures of Kurdistan*, London 1992.
Ö. Çaha, *Aşkın devletten, sivil topluma*, Istanbul 2000.
Ü. Cizre, *Muktedirlerin siyaseti. Merkez Sağ-Ordu-İslâmcılık*, Istanbul 1999.
A. Gökçeçiçek-Yurdakul, Culture of honor, culture of change. A feminist analysis of honor killings in rural Turkey, in *Violence against Women* 7:9 (September 2001), 964–98.
D. Kandiyoti, End of empire. Islam, nationalism and women in Turkey, in D. Kandiyoti (ed.), *Women, Islam and the state*, London 1991, 237–60.
N. Sirman, Feminism in Turkey. A short history, in *New Perspectives on Turkey* 3:1 (1989), 1–34.
Ş. Tekeli (ed.), *1980'ler Türkiye'sinde kadın bakış açısından kadınlar*, Istanbul 1990, 1993².
L. Yalçın-Heckmann and P. van Gelder, Das Bild der Kurdinnen im Wandel des politischen Diskurses in der Türkei der 1990er Jahre – einige kritische Bemerkungen, in E. Savelsberg et al. (eds.), *Kurdische Frauen und das Bild der kurdischen Frau*, Münster 2000, 77–104.

Pauline van Gelder

Political-Social Movements: Feminist

Afghanistan

Much of the documented information in English about women's rights in early twentieth-century Afghanistan emphasizes state-imposed changes to women's legal and social status in Afghan society. Most of these reforms were initiated between 1919 and 1929, during the reign of King Amān Allāh: the constitution was changed to guarantee equal rights for women and men; female students were sent to pursue higher education in Turkey; and the Anjuman-i Ḥimāyat-i-Niswān (Association for the protection of women's rights) was established. Most shocking, perhaps, for the clergy was the public unveiling of Queen Ṣurayyā and other female members of the royal family. King Amān Allāh was overthrown in 1929.

It took approximately another 30 years for the ruling government to address women's rights in Afghanistan. In 1959, under Muḥammad Ẓahīr Shāh, policies were put in place to enable women to unveil voluntarily, to attend university, and to find employment outside the home. By 1964, women gained the right to vote, and became increasingly vocal, forming organizations that actively worked to redress gender inequality in Afghanistan.

The Democratic Organization of Afghan Women (DOAW) was formed in 1965; its main objectives were promoting women's literacy and banning forced marriages for women. In 1986, however, the DOAW was renamed the All-Afghan Women's Council, and became less forceful in its demands for gender equality, providing instead legal and social assistance to poor Afghan women. In 1977, Mīna Kishwār Kamāl (Meena) founded the Revolutionary Association of the Women of Afghanistan (RAWA), an independent political organization of Afghan women fighting for women's rights and social justice in Afghanistan. In 1981, RAWA launched a bilingual magazine, *Payām-i-Zan* (Woman's message) in Persian (Dari) and Pashto. After the Soviet occupation of Afghanistan in December 1979, RAWA became directly involved in resistance movements. Meena was assassinated in Quetta, Pakistan in February 1987 by Islamists supported by the KGB. RAWA's original objective was to gain equal rights for Afghan women, and continues its work today, establishing schools and orphanages in Pakistan's refugee camps, and providing health services for women.

Recent Afghan feminist organizations include: Shuhada, a non-governmental organization which worked against the Taliban to provide Afghan women access to health care and education; Shirkat Gah, an organization operating out of Pakistan that works with refugee Afghan women to teach them about the Islamic laws under which they are living; Women for Afghan Women, established in spring 2001, a diasporic group whose target membership is Afghan women in New York and Afghanistan; and Negar-SAFA (Soutien aux femmes d'Afghanistan), based in Paris and founded by Afghan and French women, which works for the betterment of Afghan women's lives, promoting women's education and employment. The organization describes its conception as a response to Afghan women's call of distress under the Taliban. During Taliban rule in Afghanistan, Negar enabled Afghan women's groups to make contact with each other and with diasporic Afghan women's organizations.

BIBLIOGRAPHY

A. E. Brodsky, With all our strength. The Revolutionary Association of the Women of Afghanistan, New York 1998.

S. Mehta (ed.), *Women for Afghan women. Shattering myths and claiming the future*, New York 2002.

V. Moghadam, Reform, revolution, and reaction. The trajectory of the "Woman Question" in Afghanistan, in V. Moghadam (ed.), *Gender and national identity. Women and politics in Muslim societies*, London 1994, 81–109.

——, Revolution, religion, and gender politics. Iran and Afghanistan, in *Journal of Women's History* 10:4 (Winter 1999), 172–96.

NIMA NAGHIBI

Arab States

The 22 Arab states, with a population of over 280 million, range from Morocco in North Africa to Iraq in West Asia. These states share many similarities in terms of culture, religion, and historical evolution, while also differing widely in their respective socioeconomic dynamics and political experiences. All states share particular regional challenges, themselves a function of international relations and politics, and while some have hugely developed oil-rich economies, others have little or no natural resources. Some of these states boast relatively modernized polities, while others verge on the politically semi-feudal. Religion has enormous social, political, and cultural impact, particularly as the region is the historical meeting place of the three monotheistic world religions, but the region as a whole is predominantly Islamic.

It is too common a refrain, indeed a cliché, to assume that Islam determines the debate around women and women's rights. The complex reality is that religion (whether Islam, Christianity, or any other faith tradition in this fertile religious landscape) plays an important role as an identity marker, a phenomenon which increased significantly toward the latter part of the twentieth century. This heightened role and awareness of religion has entailed a redefinition of the role of the state, civil society, and economy, and within that framework, of women's specificities. Whether Muslim or Christian, Arab women have become increasingly conscious of the fact that no matter how qualified and capable they are, there is a glass ceiling that – barring one or two cases – prevents women from occupying important decision-making positions in the political (for example, as presidents or prime ministers), judicial (as judges), or religious realms (for example, as a mufti). This is blamed not on any one religion per se (because this would not explain the fact that other non-Arab Muslim countries often have very different sets of conditions (for example, women occupy important decision-making positions).

Women form nearly 60 percent of the population of these states and, in some countries, they form also approximately 60 percent of the student body at various levels. The first feminist movement was fashioned in the shadow of the colonial era and manifested itself in Egypt in the late 1800s, later traveling to all corners of the Arab world, such that by the 1960s many of the seeds of contemporary feminist organizations had taken root. Anti-colonial struggles moulded much of the discourse supportive of feminist rhetoric, as well as that opposed to it. To this day, feminist movements are regarded with suspicion, and are seen as either a harbinger or a manifestation of Western imperialist encroachment. After the events of 11 September 2001 and subsequent United States military action in Afghanistan, followed closely by the invasion of Iraq and its unfolding dynamics, women activists find themselves facing the same challenges today that they faced earler: to speak of women's rights when the Muslim world is facing its toughest challenge since colonial times is to support "the enemies of Islam."

Definition and terminology

But what do feminism or gender mean in the Arab context? To many, feminism, in so far as it is an attempt to struggle for more rights for women (whether the right to vote, to equal pay, or to divorce and custody of children without the legal harassment currently in store for many women), has been a permanent feature of the social, cultural, and political landscape. Although the first modern feminist movements (as opposed to feminist discourse, which was attributed to men in Egypt and Tunisia) are often spoken of as appearing in the late nineteenth and early twentieth centuries, students of religious history (whether that of Islam or Christianity) are quick to unearth examples of much earlier champions of women's rights. Claiming back this history (or "herstory") is in fact slowly gaining credibility as a legitimate scientific enterprise in Arab academia, and is supported by several activists in the non-governmental sphere as well.

Feminism as a term, however, is far from widespread. With no equivalent in the Arabic language, the word contributes to the misperception of the entire movement as foreign. Few women activists feel comfortable with the term, and those who do are not necessarily consistently vocal about it as a self-definition. It is not uncommon to find researchers referring to feminism – or to certain activists as feminists – while the activists themselves baulk at the reference. At the same time, however, an alternative mode of reference to these women and men has yet to appear. Some have toyed with the Arabic terms *niswiyya* or *nisā'iyya* (which act as a translation of the word feminism) but such terminology has simply not become popular.

The term gender also has no Arabic translation, but is more often used by feminist groups and sometimes social scientists as a descriptive or analytical category. Gender is still seen as synonymous with "women" and a widespread or popular appreciation of the nuances of the term – whether semantic or actual or both – remains lacking in the Arab world. At the same time, the social construction of masculine and feminine roles and identities is central to an understanding of the social oppression and the cultural constructions of violence that affect women in the Arab world.

The continuum of feminism

For the sake of clarity in this entry, a broad definition of the term feminism is used with two key components: a consciousness that women are oppressed in many ways, and actual attempts to rectify or deal with this reality (Karam 1998). This working definition is inspired by the extensive research carried out by Arab women researchers such as Leila Ahmed, Mervat Hatem, Evelyne Accad, Souad Dajani, Fatima Mernissi, Suad Joseph, Lila Abu-Lughod, Soraya Altorki, Yvonne Haddad, and Nadje Al-Ali – to mention but a few. Arab women are probably amongst the most written and researched about women in the world, and several non-Arab women researchers have also presented landmark and seminal studies over the years such as Judith Tucker, Beth Baron, Elizabeth Fernea, Nikkie Keddie, Sondra Hale, Barbara Stowasser, Susan S. Davis, Cynthia Nelson, Margot Badran, and many others. Together, these works continue to inform and transform feminist consciousness and practice in the Arab world.

With the above definition, it is possible to identify three main feminist streams in the Arab world that fall firmly within a continuum: secular (herein understood as non-religious discourse); religious (largely, but not only, couched in Islamic terms); and Islamist (framed within and advocating for political Islam). None of these streams is by any means homogeneous or generic; each category is full of diversity (and ambiguity) and often the barriers delineating one form of discourse from another are tenuous, hence the importance of imagining a continuum of discursive practice.

Secular feminists on the whole tend to shun faith-based discourse. This does not mean that they disrespect religion or are themselves non-religious. On the contrary, some of them can be devout (and are keen to describe themselves as such) in their personal lives. When it comes to framing their discourse on women's rights publicly, many secular feminists will skirt around religious issues or argue that to bring in religion is to risk endangering women's rights – either because of the dominance of conservative religious establishments, or because they fear creating a rift amongst their own ranks (since they will not all share the same faith tradition). Secular feminists are generally comfortable with the term "feminist" and many have strong connections with their feminist sisters from other countries, working for the implementation of all international legal human rights instruments and against all forms of discrimination, such as CEDAW (Convention for the Elimination of All Forms of Discrimination against Women), the Beijing Platform for Action, and others.

Some secular feminists can be openly antagonistic about and toward religion, maintaining that religion itself is the cause of much of the oppression women suffer, and are thus unwilling to engage with their more religious sisters, seeing them as laboring under a false consciousness. The more religious the message of the social or political activists, the more suspicious the secular feminists tend to be – often for good reason. Rarely in the Arab world is there any praise from religious circles for those who promote women's rights outside religious frameworks. Similarly, wherever there is an active Islamist movement (for example, in Algeria, Egypt, Yemen, Jordan, and Lebanon) some of the strongest opposition will be from secular feminists, believing that women's rights will be the first casualty of any Islamist regime, and citing Afghanistan, Iran, and Saudi Arabia as examples.

On the opposite side of the continuum, Islamist feminists – to many, a contradiction in terms – have an important role to play. In the same way that not all secular women are feminists, not all women members of Islamist movements (which themselves exist right across the Arab world) are feminists by any means. On the contrary, some of the most vociferous critiques of feminists and feminism emanates from Islamist circles – men and women. So who are Islamist feminists? These are the activists within the movement who advocate political Islam and who subscribe to the working definition of feminism used above. In other words, these are the women who acknowledge that women are oppressed and see the Islamist reality as an option to bring about a better world for both men and women.

For Islamist feminists, broadly speaking, the reasons for women's oppression are often explained in terms of society's lack of adherence to Islam (or to God) and the adjuncts of that faith in general. It is because Arabs are not following God's laws (which can only be just), runs the argument, that we confront the social, political, and structural problems we have today. A society dominated by (an enlightened interpretation) of the Sharīʿa, or Islamic law, is one that, in these women's opinion, will guarantee justice for women and thus improve Muslim women's condition. Islamism, seen as favoring a more just society, is also perceived as the means to achieve this end. Islamist feminists share one thing in common with their secular counterparts: a sense of unease, or even outright suspicion vis-à-vis each other. They argue that international legal instruments are at best redundant, and at worst, problematic and foreign, since all Muslims need are the Qurʾān, the *sunna*, and the *ḥadīth*.

Religious feminists fall somewhere in the middle of the continuum. They are to be distinguished from Islamists in that they do not support any one political philosophy or ideology and, in fact, many of them can be uncomfortable with what they perceive as the homogenizing tendency of Islamist feminists and their dogmatism with respect to interpretation and understanding of the Sharīʿa. With a healthy respect for the role of faith in empowering and liberating women and men, religious feminists are nevertheless keen on emphasizing new and evolving interpretations of doctrine, and advocate for the meeting point between international legal instruments (for example, CEDAW) and the essence of all faith traditions.

Religious feminists stand apart from their secular counterparts by maintaining that no discourse of women's rights that rejects religion can achieve its objectives in contexts where such a religion is the pervasive lingua franca of the masses and the politicians. Religious feminists are vociferous in urging caution with blind espousal of a religio-political cause (without a distinct women's rights agenda). They are equally cautious about any outright rejection of religion as a framework for reference. For many of them, faith traditions (in this case mostly Islam) guarantee a context of infinite justice for women – but the way the religion is preached, interpreted, and manipulated (politically) is highly problematic. In order to counter this manipulation, many religious feminists are keen on learning or advocate a rereading of religious and non-religious history and religious texts and traditions. Familiarity with, if not mastery of, the religious language is seen as one of the strongest tools for rejecting religious dogmatism, political obfuscation, and manipulation of religious rhetoric against women, as well as the formation of constituencies that can engender social transformation.

As indicated earlier, women activists are not glued to or within these feminist categories. In fact, on some women's rights issues, such as abolishing female circumcision, changing family (and/or civil) laws, and with certain political dynamics, such as support for the Palestinian cause and calls for democratization, there is often an overlap of interests and a commonality of agendas amongst the otherwise different streams.

Regardless of their position on the continuum, many of today's feminist organizations had some of their roots in charity work in the late 1800s and early 1900s. By the middle of the twentieth century, charity work gave way to activities that ranged from promoting women's electoral participation and running for political office, to organizing and providing small grants to rural development projects, micro-financing and income generation initiatives, organizing and lobbying politicians, and producing some seminal academic research.

Some organizations that started out combining a feminist agenda with anti-colonial opposition, such as Bint al-Arḍ (Daughter of the earth) in Egypt or the more radical women's work committees in the West Bank, which called for women's issues to be worked on during the nationalist struggle (as opposed to waiting for national liberation to actually happen), have more or less disbanded. This is an indication of both a shift in feminist discourse over the years (where one could argue that locating women's emancipation within national liberation may have been limiting and was ultimately unsuccessful), and of the changing political realities. Other groups, locating their discourse in broader social development language, such as the Palestinian Inʿāsh al-Usra (Family rejuvenation society), the Rābiṭat al-Nisāʾ al-Sūdāniyyāt (League of Sudanese women), or the Women's Cultural and Social Society of Kuwait continue to exist in various guises, though in a much less prominent fashion. More recently however, in the mid-1990s and particularly in the lead-up to the United Nations International Conference on Population and Development in 1994 and the Fourth United Nations World Women's Conference in Beijing in 1995, a number of groups have become far more vocal with agendas that openly – and courageously – deal with political participation, violence against women (particularly rape and clitoridectomy), and reproductive rights issues (abortion and contraception), many of which are still largely considered social taboos. Such organizations include the Al-Marʾa al-Jadīda (The new woman) in Egypt, which, at different times, also included women from Sudan and neighboring North African countries; al-Nadim Center (also in Egypt); and the Collectif 95 Maghreb Egalité, which brought together women (and feminist groups) from Tunisia, Algeria, and Morocco.

In addition to these, women's committees have formed and are extremely active in academic contexts in universities in Arab capitals such as Cairo, Khartoum, Beirut, Algiers, and Rabat, boasting a body of work on women that is both extensive and intensive, and publications (including books and a rich variety of journals, and research papers) that are impossible to quantify. Women's committees in national non-governmental umbrella organizations and/or syndicates (such as human rights organizations, lawyers and teachers' unions), and within regional Arab bodies (such as the Arab Lawyers'

Union and the Arab Organization for Human Rights) have also amassed a legacy of impressive work on, with, and for women's rights issues. Tied to and separate from these, some Arab regional women's only organizations have also emerged with varying degrees of success, with agendas that focus on common challenges (particularly political participation, economic empowerment, and cultural – especially educational – development issues), such as the Arab Women's League based in Cairo. All of these are separate from other women's organizations that are formed under the aegis of certain governments, and often headed by the first ladies of countries such as Tunisia, Egypt, Lebanon, and Jordan. These are in many ways offshoots of what Mervat Hatem referred to as "state feminism" or the kind of women's rights discourse that is acceptable to, if not promoted by, governments. It is worth noting that in Iraq until the collapse of the Saddam regime, state-sponsored women's unions were, in the limiting framework of Baʿth party politics, able to mobilize women on the national and provincial levels, a situation similar to that in some Eastern European states until the collapse of communism. Needless to say, whereas all these groups face a huge challenge in the form of resource mobilization and funding in particular, state-sponsored feminism, depending on the time, location, and sociopolitical context, fares comparatively better.

The issue of resources, however, can be crippling to a great many of these organizations, and can significantly limit the diversity of issues and initiatives dealt with. Not only that, but feminist discourse is enriched by the activities that unfold in the field, such that a limitation of these activities can and does impact on the development of the discourses themselves. On the brighter side, however, the lack of resources, coupled with the imperatives of changing political contexts (globally and locally) may also forge issue-based alliances (for example, over changes in family laws) that significantly enhance feminist praxis in the Arab world. This is not simply a matter of optimistic assessment, but realistic feasibility.

Bibliography

M. Afkhami and E. Friedl (eds.), *Muslim women and the politics of participation. Implementing the Beijing Platform*, Syracuse, N.Y. 1997.
L. Ahmed, *Women and gender in Islam*, New Haven, Conn. 1992.
N. Al-Ali, *Secularism, gender and the state in the Middle East. The Egyptian women's movement*, Cambridge 2000.
S. Altorki and C. F. El-Solh (eds.), *Arab women in the field. Studying your own society*, Syracuse, N.Y. 1988.
M. Badran, *Feminists, Islam, and nation. Gender and the making of modern Egypt*, Princeton, N.J. 1995.
H. Bodman and N. Tohidi (eds.), *Women in Muslim societies. Diversity within unity*, London 1998.
C. F. El-Solh and J. Mabro (eds.), *Muslim women's choices. Religious belief and social reality*, Providence, R.I. 1994.
N. Ḥasan (ed.), *al-Marʾa al-ʿArabiyya wa-al-ḥayāh al-ʿāmma*, Cairo 1997.
M. Hatem, Gender and Islamism in the 1990s, in *Middle East Report* 222 (2002), 44–8.
D. Kandiyoti (ed.), *Women, Islam and the state*, London 1991.
A. Karam, *Women, Islamisms and the state. Contemporary feminisms in Egypt*, London 1998.
—— (ed.), *A woman's place. Religious women as public actors*, New York 2001.
N. Keddie and B. Baron (eds.), *Women in Middle Eastern history. Shifting boundaries in sex and gender*, New Haven, Conn. 1991.
S. al-Khayyat, *Honor and shame. Women in modern Iraq*, London 1990.
F. Mernissi, *Beyond the veil. Male-female dynamics in Muslim society*, London 1985.
G. Nashat and J. E. Tucker, *Women in the Middle East and North Africa. Restoring women to history*, Bloomington, Ind. 1999.
New Woman Research Center, *Al-haraka al-nisāʾiyya al-ʿArabiyya. Mudhākhalāt min Tūnis, Falastīn, Miṣr wa-al-Sūdān*, Cairo 1995.
B. Shaaban, *Both right and left handed. Arab women talk about their lives*, Bloomington, Ind. 1991.
S. Shami et al., *Women in Arab society. Work patterns and gender relations in Egypt, Jordan, and Sudan*, Providence, R.I. 1990.
H. Sharabi, *Neopatriarchy. A theory of distorted change in Arab society*, Oxford 1988.
E. Sullivan, *Women in Egyptian public life*, Syracuse, N.Y. 1986.
J. E. Tucker, *Arab women. Old boundaries, new frontiers*, Bloomington, Ind. 1993.

Azza M. Karam

The Caucasus

Caucasian peoples tend to enjoy a collectivist type of culture. Hence, unlike the feminist movements of the West, women's rights activism has not taken the shape of movements centered on women's individual rights.

During the Soviet period equality between women and men was advocated by the official ideology and legislation. The highest management body, the Supreme Soviet, had quotas of between 38 and 40 percent for women deputies. In 1948 the only official women's organization, the Women's Council, was founded, with centralized administrative and network structure. All levels of education, and all professions and careers were equally accessible for men and women. Yet women's integration into political life was incomplete since women were not appointed to positions where actual political decisions were made (Chubinidze 2000, Tsereteli 2000).

From 1991, after the dismantling of the Soviet Union, the first women's non-governmental organizations started to appear in the Caucasus. By the end of the twentieth century women's organizations in Caucasian countries were powerfully developed, with between 150 and 170 active organizations. Permanently operating special women's state committees were also set up. In the higher educational institutions courses covering various aspects of gender are available. There are also scientific research centers on gender and women's rights. From 2002 to 2004 the speaker of the parliament of Georgia, and the interim president, was a woman, N. Burdjanaze.

Modern Caucasian women are actively involved in community life, but decision-making positions are less accessible to them. The average membership of women in parliaments in the Caucasian countries is 12 percent (Babayan 1999, Tsintsadze 2003).

BIBLIOGRAPHY

S. Babayan, Gender realities and the prospects of the society in transformation, in Association of Women with University Education, *Proceedings of the 3rd international conference. Woman and society. Gender equality in the perspective of democratic development* [in Armenian], Tsakhtadzor, Armenia 1999, summary in English, p. 174.

N. Chubinidze, Discussion of women's economical and political status issues, in N. Devdariani et al. (eds.), *Women in political and social life* [in Georgian], Tblisi 1998, 75–86.

Y. Y. Karpov, Caucasian woman. World vision premises of the public status [in Russian], in *Etnograficheskoe Obozrenie* (Moscow) 4 (2000).

M. Tsereteli, *Women's rights in the light of their motivation values* [in Georgian], Tblisi 2000.

MZIA TSERETELI

Central Asia

In the Muslim regions of the Russian Empire, the Woman Question was initially dealt with mostly at the beginning of the twentieth century and particularly after the revolution of 1905, or rather when the reforming Muslim Jadidist movement included the Woman Question in its political and social program. In these regions, the Muslim press contributed a great deal to the implementation of the question. The Central Asian intellectual Jadidists participated in the reform movement, but because they were excluded from the political realm their program remained only a theory. Even before the October Revolution of 1917, the Central Asian Jadidists proposed to ban the *parandzha* (clothing that covered women from head to foot) and the *chachvan* (horse-hair veil) by decree, but the proposal lacked a following. Contrary to the Jadidists, the Qadimists (the traditionalist clerics) defended the veil and the seclusion of women. The debate between Muslim reformism and conservatism continued after 1917.

The Woman Question acquired fundamental importance after the October Revolution. Women's emancipation was one of the main objectives of the Bolshevik government. For this purpose, in 1919 it instituted the Zhenotdel, the women's department of the Communist Party. While in European Russia the Zhenotdel immediately became active amongst women, in Central Asia its real activity did not begin until 1923–4. The issues that the Soviet government had to fight against to emancipate Central Asian women were linked to Muslim traditions and institutions: polygyny, *kalym* (bride-price), the forced marriage of underage children, the seclusion of women, and the veil. The Soviets were committed to struggle against traditions considered backward in the name of modernization and secularization of the country. More, they intended to use women to destroy the Muslim patriarchal family and consequently to break the blood and tribal ties that were at the base of society and to establish new social bonds on a socialist basis. Female emancipation was essentially directed at promoting social change and undermining Muslim religious identity. In Central Asia, woman was considered the vehicle of change, the "surrogate of the proletariat" (Massell 1974), considering the almost total absence of a working class. For this aim, the Zhenotdel created institutions to inform women of their rights, ratified by Soviet legislation, and to furnish medical, legal, and professional help that was almost completely absent before 1917. In 1926, the Soviet government planned an attack against the former everyday life and against Muslim tradition: the *khudzhum* (attack, Uzbek) was effectively launched in 1927, promoting mass unveilings (mostly in Uzbekistan and Tajikistan) on dates such as 8 March, 1 May, and the anniversary of the October Revolution. The Jadidists supported the policy of mass unveilings. During 1927, thousands of women took off their veils, but most of them came back to the veil following the reprisals carried out by their families, by some of the more conservative fractions of the populace, and by most Muslim religious leaders. Many women were killed or suffered physical and moral violence. In 1930, the Zhenotdel was disbanded, but in Central Asia some cells continued to operate.

During the Soviet period, the emancipation of Central Asian women was extolled as accomplished: this discourse was subjected to criticism during the Gorbachev era. The official data claimed that the quotas of representation within government and party organs reserved for women had been achieved (in the 1970s, in Uzbekistan, women constituted about 47 percent of employees in the government and party apparatus); female illiteracy had been almost eradicated (the percentage of literate women aged between 9 and 49 had risen from 2 percent before the revolution to 99 percent in 1970); and all professional careers and all levels of education were open to women. Nevertheless, women were far from having reached full equality with men: discrimination against them persisted in all fields. Women, especially indigenous women, were concentrated in manual, lower-skilled, and lower-paid jobs; there was no increase of female employment during the last decades of the Soviet Union; in the 1970s, women did not occupy prestigious posts in the high spheres of industry or in crucial sectors of the economy. There was evident inequality between women of the indigenous nationalities and the Russians, who obtained the best posts. In the republics of Central Asia, feminist movements were not present because of the peculiarity of the system. The Woman Question was an affair of state that controlled and eventually financially supported women's associations. The Soviet establishment claimed that since the emancipation of women had been completely accomplished, there was no necessity for any feminist movement.

After the collapse of the Soviet Union and the gaining of independence by the Central Asian republics, the Woman Question started to assume a new importance. After 1991, some international women's conferences were held in Alma-Ata, Kazakhstan. In this context it is not possible to speak about "feminism" in its traditional meaning: Central Asian feminists criticize Western feminism, which, in their opinion, does not take into consideration the issues relating to women with different experiences. Central Asian women, as bearers of values of the national cultural identity, feel their role is to defend these values rather than to sustain feminist values: the Woman Question has entered a second stage as regards the issues of national and cultural identities. There are some feminist movements in Kazakhstan (such as WLCI, the Women's League of Creative Initiative, founded in 1994, one of whose primary goals is to "study and spread the ideas of feminism") and in Uzbekistan, but the debate is still at an initial stage. Indeed, the feminist movements started to emerge at the same time as the revival of traditional society which is supported in part by Central Asian states and governments. In Tajikistan and in Kyrgyzstan, some women's non-governmental organizations have formed with different aims and constitutions, but it is very difficult to speak about organizations with a declared and marked feminist outlook; they are mostly associations and foundations directed to the improvement of women's conditions in different fields. The Women's Resource Center in Tashkent, established in 1994, is a center that supports women: one of its aims is the provision of information on legal rights. In Uzbekistan, some female councils and committees which act at all levels of public life have been established by state organs, but they seem still to be weak. Some Turkmen women reckon that in their country a feminist movement cannot develop because of the strong traditions of the society.

With the collapse of the Soviet Union and the emergence of poverty, inflation, unemployment, and economic crisis, Central Asian women are involved in the daily struggle to survive. Probably the Woman Question and feminist movements will receive a greater impulse during the next few years, when the transition from a state planned economy to a market economy has been concluded. Central Asian republics will be more settled and women will be freer to think how to locate themselves within the new society and the women's movements.

BIBLIOGRAPHY

S. Akiner, Between tradition and modernity. The dilemma facing contemporary Central Asian women, in M. Buckley (ed.), *Post-Soviet women. From the Baltic to Central Asia*, Cambridge 1997, 261–304.

J. Baker, The position of women in Kazakhstan in the interwar years, in *Central Asian Survey* 4:1 (1985), 75–114.

L. M. Handrahan, Gender and ethnicity in the "transitional democracy" of Kyrgyzstan, in *Central Asian Survey* 20:4 (2001), 467–96.

C. Harris, The changing identity of women in Tajikistan in the post-Soviet period, in F. Acar and A. Güneş-Ayata (eds.), *Gender and identity construction. Women of Central Asia, the Caucasus and Turkey*, Leiden 2000, 205–28.

D. M. Heer and N. Youssef, Female status among Soviet Central Asian nationalities. The melding of Islam and Marxism and its implications for population increase, in *Population Studies* 31:1 (1977), 155–73.

D. Kandiyoti, Identity and its discontents. Women and the nation, in *Millennium. Journal of International Studies* 20:3 (1991), 429–43.

N. Lubin, Women in Soviet Central Asia. Progress and contradictions, in *Soviet Studies* 33:2 (1981), 182–203.

G. J. Massell, *The surrogate proletariat. Moslem women and revolutionary strategies in Soviet Central Asia. 1919–1929*, Princeton, N.J. 1974.

P. A. Michaels, Kazak women. Living the heritage of a unique past, in H. L. Bodman and N. Tohidi (eds.),

Women in Muslim societies. Diversity within unity, Boulder, Colo. 1998, 187–202.
D. Northrop, *Veiled empire. Gender and power in Stalinist Central Asia*, New York 2004.
A. Samiuddin and R. Khanam (eds.), *Muslim feminism and feminist movement. Central Asia*, Delhi 2002.
S. Tadjbakhsh, Between Lenin and Allah. Women and ideology in Tajikistan, in H. L. Bodman and N. Tohidi (eds.), *Women in Muslim societies. Diversity within unity*, Boulder, Colo. 1998, 163–85.
M. Tokhtakhodjaeva and E. Turgumbekova, *The daughters of Amazons. Voices from Central Asia*, Lahore 1996.
Women Living Under Muslim Laws, *Assertions of self. The nascent women's movement in Central Asia*, Lahore 1995.

Chiara De Santi

Iran

There were a significant number of active feminist organizations from the beginning of the twentieth-century to the 1960s in Iran. These included the Women's Freedom Society, founded in 1906 by a group of male and female intellectuals who gathered in secret to discuss the status of women. In 1910, the Anjuman-i Mukhadirāt-i Vatan (National ladies' society) was formed. Its members were active in promoting women's education, and encouraging the use of Iranian-made rather than imported goods. As such, the organization was active in promoting the economic independence of Iran. In 1922, the Anjuman-i Nisvān-i Vaṭankhvāh-i Īrān (Patriotic women's league of Iran), launched a magazine called *Patriotic Women*, which emphasized women's rights, including women's education and women's right to marry later in life. In 1927, Zandukht Shirazi founded the Association of Revolutionary Women in Shiraz. The organization worked for women's unveiling and gender parity. Zandukht began a newspaper entitled *Daughters of Iran* in 1931–2. It printed news about international feminist efforts, literary articles, and Zandukht's radical poems and editorials.

The Kānūn-u Bānuvān (Ladies' center) was formed in 1935; its goals included improving the morality of women, training women in modern domestic chores, and opening charity centers for poor mothers and orphans. According to some scholars, the establishment of the Kānūn-u Bānuvān marked the transformation of twentieth-century Iranian feminist activism into a state-sanctioned and contained feminism, since the organization was overseen by Reza Shah's daughters, Ashraf and Shams Pahlavī, and received significant government funding. Recent scholarship demonstrates, however, that there was a variety of Iranian feminists and groups who pursued feminist goals autonomously. State-legislated policies such as the 1936 Unveiling Act, for instance, were preceded by women's heated debates on the subject of unveiling and women's employment.

In 1961, however, the High Council of Iranian Women was established with Ashraf Pahlavī as the honorary head; at this point, all women's organizations were encouraged to join the High Council in order to gain legitimacy. In 1966, the state replaced the High Council with a larger bureaucratic organization, the Sāzman-i Zanān-i Īrān (Women's organization of Iran). This state-sponsored organization professed to work for the social, political, and economic advancement of all women, but during the revolutionary years the organization came under attack for its perceived inattention to the needs of working-class and rural women.

Women's activism peaked during the 1978–9 revolutionary period, as women demonstrated against the Shah and what they understood to be the regime's imperialist policies. At the same time, they demonstrated against the restrictive policies regarding women's dress and mobility that the nascent Islamic Republic was beginning to promote. Because of the perception of a state-sanctioned Westernized feminism under the Pahlavīs, anti-imperialist nationalists denounced feminists as imperialists and counter-revolutionaries.

A decade and a half later, there was a resurgence of diverse and forceful Iranian feminist voices in the public arena. Women's magazines and journals have provided an important public forum for debates between secular and religious feminists in contemporary Iran. Although most of these magazines are published by religious feminists, secular feminists have been welcomed to contribute to them. Some of the more outspoken and influential of these feminists include: Shirin Ebadi, lawyer, human rights activist and winner of the 2003 Nobel Peace Prize; Mehrangiz Kar, human rights lawyer and secular feminist activist who has published extensively on the legal rights of Iranian women; Shahla Lahiji, founder of the first women's publishing house in Iran; Shahla Sherkat, editor of the religious feminist magazine, *Zanān* (Women); and Faezeh Hashemi, editor of the daily *Zan* (Woman, banned at the time of writing). The current state of the media in Iran is such that while magazines are regularly forced to cease publication, other magazines soon emerge to take their place. In feminist debates in Iran, a multitude of voices is participating and attempting to shape the future of an indigenous Iranian feminism.

BIBLIOGRAPHY

A. Najmabadi, Hazards of modernity and morality. Women, state and ideology in contemporary Iran, in D. Kandiyoti (ed.), *Women, Islam and the state*, Philadelphia 1992, 663–87.

——, Feminisms in an Islamic republic, in J. Scott, C. Kaplan, and D. Keates (eds.), *Transitions, environments, translations. Feminisms in international politics*, New York 1997, 390–9.

——, Authority and agency. Re-visiting women's activism during Riza Shah's period, in T. Atabaki (ed.), *The triumphs and travails of authoritarian modernisation in Turkey and Iran. Twentieth-Century Turkish and Iranian histories from below*, Routledge Curzon (forthcoming).

M. Poya, *Women, work and Islamism. Ideology and resistance in Iran*, London 1999.

E. Sanasarian, *The women's rights movement in Iran. Mutiny, appeasement and repression from 1900 to Khomeini*, New York 1981.

NIMA NAGHIBI

Israel

The lives of Israeli women, a nationally, ethnically, and religiously diverse category, reflect a complex of opportunities and barriers. Of 6,439,000 citizens in 2001, there were 77 percent Jews, 15 percent Muslims, 2 percent Christians, and 1.6 percent Druzes (Israel 2002, table 2.1). Nominally, women of all groups enjoy basic liberal civil rights, including the right to vote and be elected to political office, and the right to free, universal education, health services, and legal defense. However, the application of these to the lives of women varies considerably. The lack of separation between state and religion produces discrimination against women, since family matters fall under the jurisdiction of the religious courts. During the 1990s, women's struggles registered some significant gains in this regard, with the establishment of a civil court for family affairs, which decides property and child custody settlements, although it cannot grant the divorce itself. A second locus of discrimination is the exclusion of women from formal politics. In 2003 women comprised only 14 percent of members of parliament. All of them were Jewish, and only two women, also Jewish, were heads of local municipalities. In the work arena, women's earnings fall far below those of men. The rate of labor-force participation among Jewish women (53 percent) is similar to that of women in many industrial countries, while that of Arab women (15 percent) is lower than in some neighboring Arab countries, which bears direct implications for poverty. For Arab women, particularly, gender discrimination is amplified through articulation with national exclusion, and often also with class marginalization.

Organized feminism in the region, in both national communities, dates to the early decades of the twentieth century. In Israel impressive achievements were registered at the stage of state formation in establishing extensive state-provided services for working women, especially those relating to maternity and childcare. The oldest women's organizations, most identified with these achievements, have become well-established. Funded by state or party agencies, with branches spread throughout the country, they provide mostly legal and social support services. On the grassroots level, feminist activism resumed in the 1970s and has remained lively, with some significant changes. The 1970s wave was led by upper-middle-class Jewish women of European and American descents (Ashkenazi). Their major focuses were consciousness-raising groups on the one hand and fighting male domestic violence on the other. Achievements included the establishment of rape-crisis centers, hot lines, and shelters for battered women, and breaking the silence that surrounded the problem. Parallel to that, feminists continued to lobby for women's work, domestic wages, and civil rights. Many of these activities have increasingly come to rely on state support.

From the 1980s, and more so through the 1990s, many feminists became involved in peace activism, calling for a two-state solution to the Israeli-Palestinian conflict. This development politicized local feminism, creating complex effects. From the perspective of Jewish women from marginalized groups, mostly Mizrahi (Jews of North African and Middle Eastern origin) and lower-class, it marked Israeli feminism as elitist, as it oriented itself outwardly, toward Palestinians, instead of addressing the class and ethnic cleavages within the Jewish society. This led to a second wave of politicization, mostly throughout the 1990s, in which mainstream Jewish feminists were challenged from within. It culminated in institutionalizing the quarters policy, a declared commitment to equal self-representation of Ashkenazis, Mizrahis, Palestinians, and lesbians in shared feminist activities.

In separate settings, Mizrahi feminists have concentrated their efforts in the educational system, empowering mothers to fight the tracking system that discriminated against their children. Later they also engaged in fighting for the labor rights of working-class and poor women. Arab feminists concentrated their efforts on education, creating progressive curricula and empowering teachers, on anti-violence measures, and on creating a discourse of sexual liberation. Religious Jewish and Muslim feminists addressed, separately, scriptural and spiritual issues. Most Arab feminists have also been closely involved in male-dominated circles supporting Palestinian nationalism. In terms of its institutional basis, the second wave feminism yielded an array of non-governmental organizations, funded by external donors, which are more radical than the older organizations, and consequently also more marginalized. Notably, despite their separate identities, the various groups also form coalitions and share many of their members.

The 1990s witnessed a proliferation of women's studies in academia, which in the early 2000s have yielded several programs and even some departments of women and gender studies. Into the first decade of the twenty-first century, with heightened political hostilities, an ongoing economic recession, and a rapid retreat of the welfare state, Israeli feminism is orienting itself increasingly toward the economic empowerment of women, through skills training, workers' organizations, and microcredit programs. Notwithstanding the creativity, foresight, and commitment of the feminists, the majority of Israeli women of all groups remain reserved regarding the title "feminist." While they tend to endorse the discourse of women's rights, the mainstreaming of a gender perspective on society and politics remains far outside local popular discourses.

Bibliography

D. Amir, S. Fogiel-Bijaoui, R. Giora, and E. Shadmi (eds.), Feminist theory and research. Israeli institutions and society, in *Israel Social Science Research* (special issue) 12 (1997), 1–2.

A. Ilany, The Israel report, in US/Israel Women to Women, *20th anniversary learning and strategic planning initiative*, New York 2001, 29–53.

Israel, Central Bureau of Statistics, *Statistical abstract of Israel*, no. 53, [Jerusalem] 2002.

D. Izraeli, A. Friedman, H. Dahan-Kalev, S. Fogiel-Bijaoui, H. Herzog, M. Hasan, and H. Neveh (eds.), *Sex, gender, politics* [in Hebrew], Tel Aviv 1999.

R. A. Kanaaneh, *Birthing the nation. Strategies of Palestinian women in Israel*, California 2002.

P. Motzafi-Haller, Scholarship, identity, and power. Mizrahi women in Israel, in *Signs* 26:3 (Spring 2001), 697–734.

T. Rapoport and T. El-Or (eds.), Cultures of womanhood in Israel, in *Women's Studies International Forum* (special issue) 20 (1997), 5–6.

H. Stier and A. Lewin, Does women's employment reduce poverty? Evidence from Israel, in *Work, Employment and Society* 16:2 (2002), 211–30.

Amalia Sa'ar

South Asia

Women in South Asia have participated in many movements. For example, historical records speak of women as revolutionaries in the early colonial period. The nationalist struggle saw many women as leaders and participants, and in the postcolonial period women have initiated and achieved many goals. However, whether the women's movement and the feminist movement are the one and the same thing is a contentious issue.

There is a prevalent tendency to define feminism as a phenomenon that originated in Europe and was informed by the self-conscious concerns of women as women. Women in South Asia exist in the context of religious divisions and, to a large extent, of sexual segregation. These women's interests span much more than issues of gender hierarchies. After initial resistance feminist analysts are now beginning to accept the multiplicity of differences that inform our experiences of gender hierarchy. Keeping with this understanding of feminism this entry uses the concept of feminist movements to include all mobilizations of women. This is also consonant with the description of feminism as a new social movement.

In South Asia women's participation in the public sphere can be usefully divided into three phases: the early colonial period, the nationalist struggle, and the postcolonial period.

Early colonial period

Women in this historical period feature as revolutionaries resisting the British efforts at colonization. Although most accounts of resistance to foreign powers by women describe them as wives or mothers of political rulers it is important to emphasize that these women were mostly uneducated and belonged to a social milieu that valorized seclusion for women, whether or not that was the social reality. For them to take up arms when their menfolk were not able to do so was revolutionary in the most radical sense. The most prominent names are those of Rani of Jhansi and Begum Hazrat Mahal, both of whom actually stepped in to direct and lead armed struggle against the British colonists.

Women in the nationalist struggle

Many social reformers seeking to change undesirable aspects of Indian society preceded the nationalist movement. Both Hindu and Muslim reformers identified women's condition as the target of reform. For a number of Hindu reformers widow remarriage, age of consent, and child marriage were the glaring injustices to be rectified. Muslim reformers were in a more difficult situation as they invoked the minority Muslim identity against the dominant Hindus and the English colonists. For them to identify the disadvantages of their tradition was not politically viable in this context.

Lack of education for women became a major concern in India partly because the colonial rulers constructed the Woman Question in such a manner that it came to signify their moral superiority over the colonized (Ray 2002). In slightly different ways both Hindu and Muslim reformers sought to construct ideas about the modern woman that drew upon the Victorian ideal of womanhood but also depended on a glorified golden past of their own traditions. The reformers were, however, less focused on education as enhancing women's development and more concerned to make them better partners and mothers. This manifested as valorization of motherhood in the nationalist discourse. There is evidence in women's writings in the contemporary journals that seems to indicate that most educated women accepted these ideas and emphasized the nurturing roles of wives and mothers.

Muslim community leaders also tried to address the problem of non-education for Muslim girls and women especially since the dictates of purdah (seclusion) made it more difficult for them to access public institutions of education. Muslim male leaders were divided about the need and use of education for Muslim girls. The most contentious issue turned out to be whether Muslim girls should be tutored at home or in schools. Many individual Muslim women supported girls' education by endowing schools. Rokeya Sakhawat Husain is one of the better-known women who started a school for girls and ran it successfully. Unlike many men, Rokeya saw education as the means for enabling women to fend for themselves and live with dignity.

The availability of formal education for women led to the emergence of a group of women with a desire for organized action to improve the position of women (Kasturi and Mazumdar 1994). A number of associations were formed in the early nineteenth century. Invariably the members of these associations were from reformist middle-class families. Such associations faced much opposition in the early part of the century but in the latter part the resistance decreased as the revivalist ideology provided an alternative rationale for improving the position of women. By the end of the century a nascent women's movement was under way.

The newly educated younger women thus found themselves in the throes of nationalist struggle. However, the religious divide between Hindus and Muslims complicated matters. Although the main leaders of the nationalist movement declared time and again that theirs was a secular struggle on behalf of all Indians, Muslims nevertheless found themselves in another camp. Many Muslim women continued to be part of the women's and nationalist political organizations but others felt compelled to join Muslim-only associations. The All India Muslim Ladies Conference was founded in 1914 (Minault 1981).

There is considerable disagreement among scholars about the exact effect of the nationalist movement on the women's movement. One stream of thought suggests that issues of reform and in particular the women's issue, were subsumed within nationalism (Natarajan 1959). Another suggests that the politics of nationalism fostered conservatism in social beliefs and practices as it glorified India's past and tended to defend everything traditional (Ghulam 1983). Another view is that nationalism resolved the Woman Question by relying on the ideological framework of the home-world dichotomy and giving women the responsibility to maintain the cohesiveness of the family and kin group to which men could not give much attention (Chaterjee 1989).

Kasturi and Mazumdar (1994) disagree with all these analyses as they all seem to look for a linear connection between the nineteenth century reform movements and the growth of nationalism in the twentieth century and the roles prescribed for or played by women in Indian nationalism. Moreover, these analyses totally ignore the way women themselves responded to the challenges of colonialism. There is ample evidence that once mobilized, women moved on their own, acquiring new confidence and articulating new priorities. A number of scholars (Forbes 1982, Minault 1982) have separately analyzed Gandhi's role in mobilizing women in the nationalist struggle as one dependent on the ideology of a self-sacrificing paragon of virtue. However, Kasturi and Mazumdar (1994) see Gandhi's success in his perceptiveness that the plight of women was a direct consequence of the economic depredation of colonialism. He preached gender equality in economic rewards and political decision-making and women responded in great numbers to Gandhi's call for khadi (spinning and weaving of thin cotton fabric) because it represented a method of employment generation for the masses.

Women in postcolonial states of South Asia

In the independent states of India, Pakistan, and Bangladesh women have struggled for diverse rights.

India

In India much feminist effort has been directed at the state to reform laws. Criminal law relating to rape was reformed as a consequence of the women's movement organizing protests at the inept handling of the complaint of rape of a woman in police custody. Laws relating to dowry, *sati*, and selective abortion of female fetuses are some of the other notable achievements of the women's movement.

However, efforts of women are not only directed at the state. SEWA (Self Employed Women's Association) represents the best known example of grassroots mobilization of women. Ela Bhatt has been instrumental in organizing self-employed women and empowering them to generate incomes and manage available resources (Crowell 2003).

Communal schism in the Indian women's movement happened after the government capitulated to the demands of Muslim fundamentalists and enacted the Muslim Women's Act 1986 (Agnihotri and Mazumdar 1995). Muslim women were divided over the question of maintenance for divorced Muslim wives and it became difficult for Hindu women to argue against the measure when some of the Muslim women demanded it (Agnes 1999).

Pakistan

In Pakistan, women's organizations were primarily constituted by middle-class women who oriented their work toward improving the conditions for women from lower socioeconomic strata (Alvi and Rause 2002). It was in 1980s that the feminist movement became active in opposing the efforts at Islamization of some parts of the laws (Weiss 1986, Kennedy 1988). In 1981 the Women's Action Forum was formed and subsequently endorsed by seven women's groups (Ahsam 2002). Although started by professional women, WAF has widened its base by cooperating with other women's organizations.

Bangladesh

Women in Bangladesh had to experience the turmoil of nationalist struggle first against the British and then against the state of Pakistan. In the struggle for independence from Pakistan women of Bangladesh had to bear the indignities of mass rape by the Pakistani army, yet the new government marginalized them. The nascent feminist movement did not work actively to mobilize support for them either (Hossain and Hossain 2002). Subsequently the feminist movement has directed its attention to dealing with escalating violence against women. It has successfully lobbied the government to enact the Prohibition of Dowry Act, 1980. However, an effort to modify the Muslim Family Law Ordinance of 1961 has not produced any change. This ordinance, enacted in the early days of Pakistan's existence, gave Muslim women some legal protection but in Bangladesh the state has to juggle the demands of feminists with those of the religious fundamentalists.

Bibliography

F. Agnes, *Law and gender inequality. The politics of women's rights in India*, Oxford 1999.

I. Agnihotri and V. Mazumdar, Changing terms of political discourse. Women's movement in India, 1970s–1990s, in *Economic and Political Weekly* 30:29 (1995), 1869–78.

A. Ahsam, Fundamentalist ideology and feminist resistance, in A. Samiuddin and R. Khanam (eds.), *Muslim feminism and feminist movement. South Asia*, ii, *Pakistan*, Delhi 2002, 53–70.

H. Alvi and S. Rause, Pakistani feminism and feminist movement, in A. Samiuddin and R. Khanam (eds.), *Muslim feminism and feminist movement. South Asia*, ii, *Pakistan*, Delhi 2002, 1–52.

P. Chatterjee, The nationalist resolution of the women's question, in K. Sangri and S. Vaid (eds.), *Recasting women. Essays in colonial history*, New Delhi 1989, 233–54.

D. Crowell, *The SEWA movement and rural development*, New Delhi 2003.

G. Forbes, From purdah to politics. The social feminism of the All India Women's Organization, in H. Papanek and G. Minault (eds.), *Separate worlds. Studies of purdah in South Asia*, Delhi 1982, 219–44.

M. Ghulam, *Reluctant debutante. Responses of Bengali women to modernization, 1849–1905*, Rajshahi 1983.

S. Hossain and R. Hossain, Feminism and feminist movement in Bangladesh, in A. Samiuddin and R. Khanam (eds.), *Muslim feminism and feminist movement. South Asia*, iii, *Bangladesh*, Delhi 2002, 1–62.

L. Kasturi and V. Mazumdar, Introduction, in L. Kasturi and V. Mazumdar (eds.), *Women and Indian nationalism*, New Delhi 1994, xxv–lxvii.

C. Kennedy, Islamization in Pakistan. Implementation of the Hudood Ordinances, in *Asian Survey* 28:3 (1988), 307–16.

G. Minault, Sisterhood or separatism? The All-India Muslim Ladies Conference and the nationalist movement, in G. Minault (ed.), *The extended family. Women and political participation in India and Pakistan*, Delhi 1981, 83–108.

——, Purdah politics. The role of Muslim women in Indian nationalism, in H. Papanek and G. Minault (eds.), *Separate worlds. Studies of purdah in South Asia*, Delhi 1982, 245–61.

H. Moghissi, *Feminism and Islamic fundamentalism. The limits of postmodern analysis*, London 1999.

S. Natarajan, *A century of social reform in India*, Bombay 1959.

H. Papanek and G. Minault (eds.), *Separate worlds. Studies of purdah in South Asia*, Delhi 1982.
B. Ray, *Early feminists of colonial India. Sarla Devi Chaudhurani and Rokeya Sakhawat Hossain*, Delhi 2002.
A. Samiuddin and R. Khanam (eds.), *Muslim feminism and feminist movement. South Asia*, ii, *Pakistan*, Delhi 2002.
A. M. Weiss, Implications of the Islamization program for women, in A. M. Weiss (ed.), *Islamic reassertion in Pakistan*, Syracuse, N.Y. 1986, 97–113.

Archana Parashar

Sub-Saharan Africa

For this entry, the authors have adopted Valentine Moghadem's definition of feminism: "feminism is a theoretical perspective, and a practice that criticizes social and gender inequalities, aims at women's empowerment, and seeks to transform knowledge – and in some interpretations, to transform socio-economic structures, political power and international relations" (Moghadam 2002, 45). Defined in this way, feminism may have different specific objectives depending on the social, economic, and political context in which it is functioning. In Muslim West Africa Islamic beliefs and practices are not uniform, even in those countries where more than 85 percent of the population is Muslim. In this context, feminism wears many faces. West African feminists define their own goals in regard to what features of their society or polity must be changed to give women a fair and just place, and these goals differ depending on the context, time, and circumstance. The following examples are indicative of the extremes of the range of goals and activities of Islamic West African feminist groups.

Since January 2000, twelve states in northern Nigeria have adopted Sharīʿa law and Sharīʿa-based penal codes under the leadership of fundamentalist Muslim leaders. Married women are therefore secluded during their child-bearing years, and women do not go out alone. When they do go out, they are covered from head to toe. In October 2001, Safiya Yakubu Hussaini was sentenced to death by stoning after having been found guilty of adultery by the Sharīʿa court in Sokoto, Nigeria. Since that time, although Safiya Hussaini has been acquitted by the Sharīʿa Court of Appeal, the cases of two other women sentenced to death by stoning by two other Sharīʿa courts in northern Nigeria (one for conceiving a child out of wedlock and the other for adultery) are wending their way through the courts.

Muslim women leaders in Nigeria, working in concert with the International Solidarity Network of Women Living Under Muslim Laws, have begun to challenge aggressively the interpretations of Islamic law that have sanctioned the imposition of harsh sentences against women while the male perpetrators of these crimes are not punished. In this work, they stand on the ground first laid by Nana Asmaʾu, daughter of the legendary Usman don Fodio, leader of the Islamic Jihad in northern Nigeria in the mid-nineteenth century. Nana Asmaʾu (1793–1864) remains to this day much revered as a pious woman, as an important leader in the Jihad, and indeed as the ultimate role model for a Muslim woman (Mack and Boyd 1995). Educated by her father in classic Islamic scholarship, Asmaʾu was designated by him, when she was only 20 years old, as the "leader of women." She immediately began to teach the Qurʾān to women whom she then sent throughout the Caliphate to spread that teaching, and, of more importance to contemporary Islamic feminists, to teach women about their rights under Islam. Nana Asmaʾu did not challenge the fundamental principles of her teachers or their understandings of the secondary position of women in Islam. But she did create the space for women to seek education and to be respected for their learning and revered in their own right as learned Muslims. It is into this space that present day Islamic feminist activists are stepping, challenging the interpretation and application of Muslim law by the Sharīʿa courts against women in northern Nigeria.

In contrast to northern Nigeria, political power in Senegal is not held by Muslim fundamentalists. Both politics and policy are dominated by Western-educated technocrats who have traditionally turned to conservative rural Muslim leaders for electoral support. Unlike the case in northern Nigeria, women in Senegal are not veiled and not secluded, but move about freely and fully participate in the economy. They do not have the same access as do men to economic, social, and political power, however. Women are less likely to be educated, less able to get higher paying jobs, and distinctly less likely to hold political office or manipulate political power than are Senegalese men (Callaway and Creevey 1994, Creevey 1996).

In this context it is not surprising that Senegalese feminism was represented in the 1990s by groups that argued directly for governmental and societal reform to allow social changes that would empower women (Sow 1997a, 54, 1997b, 1973, 1985). Yewwu Yewwi (a Wolof term meaning "raise consciousness for liberation") is one group that has embodied this liberal feminist approach. Led by educated Muslim Senegalese women, this group headed the opposition to the 1974 Family Code. Yewwu Yewwi leaders did not hesitate to conduct public forums, to write articles for Senegalese newspapers and to publish their own newsletters. They also networked, using family and friends and political connections. The code was finally revised in 1989, and most of the changes were favorable for women (Creevey 1996, 299–301, Callaway and Creevey 1994, 176–81). Yewwu Yewwi and its successor, Réseau Siggil Jiggeen (Network of women rising), continued to agitate for further improvements in the code throughout the 1990s. In 2000, they were rewarded when a new constitution that made further reforms was introduced.

Conditions are always changing throughout Muslim West Africa. Women's definitions of what is important to them will also change. In Senegal, the replacement of Yewwu Yewwi by Siggil Jiggeen in the late 1990s signaled a tactical move by Senegalese feminists away from identification with the Western feminist confrontational emphasis on equality and toward the more widely accepted goal of achieving economic power and independence for women. Nonetheless, they continued to struggle for governmental reform and broadened their activities in many ways. Fatou Sow, a feminist leader and distinguished scholar, has even started her own radio station, Sokna FM (*sokna* is a honorific title for a woman), which deals solely with issues and concerns of women. In Nigeria, Ayesha Imam, also a noted scholar and feminist leader, and other Muslim feminists have established "action research" teams composed of women's rights activists, *ʿulamāʾ* (scholars of Islam), lawyers, historians, and Arabic linguists to research Muslim jurisprudence, the history of Islamic law in Nigeria, and Sharīʿa court decisions in order to challenge the interpretations of Islamic law by fundamentalist judges in the Sharīʿa courts.

Many West African women, of course, belong to a wide variety of groups that are not included in this discussion because of our definition of "feminist." Many more Senegalese women in rural areas belong to women's associations, which have limited social and/or economic objectives, than to Siggil Jiggeen. These groups empower women in their businesses and lives and may ultimately result in increased demand for specifically feminist objectives among a wider population (Creevey 2004). However, women's perceived goals can also become limited rather than expanded. A good example is the transition in Sudan in the late 1980s and early 1990s when educated women brought into the National Islamic Front (NIF) moved from supporting social reform to aspiring to "ideal" Muslim womanhood (Hale 1995, 185–218). In northern Nigeria, women working to reinterpret Muslim law are working within a specific Islamic framework and do not challenge its underlying gender conservatism. Sudanese and Nigerian women are responding to the growing wave of fundamentalist power and trying to see it in a positive way, as did Nana Asma'u many years ago. Perhaps there is a danger that acknowledging such limited movements and labeling them as "Islamic feminism" will undercut support for those Muslim women who are both unwilling to compromise with conservative religious teachings and trying to change the social and political structure of their society to fully empower women (Moghissi 1999). In the real world of Islamic West Africa, however, the context defines what is possible. Feminists here are responding realistically to their specific conditions and will continue to do so.

Bibliography

B. Callaway and L. Creevey, *The heritage of Islam. Women, religion and politics in West Africa*, Boulder, Colo. 1994.

L. Creevey, Islam, women and the role of the state in Senegal, in *Journal of Religion in Africa* 26:3 (1996), 268–307.

——, Impacts of changing patterns of women's association membership in Senegal, in B. Purkayastha and M. Subramaniam (eds.), *The power of informal networks. Lessons from South Asia and West Africa*, Lanham, Md. 2004, 61–74.

S. Hale, *Gender politics in Sudan. Islamism, socialism, and the state*, Boulder, Colo. 1996.

B. B. Mack and J. Boyd, *One woman's jihad. Nana Asmaʾu, scholar and scribe*, Bloomington, Ind. 2000.

V. Moghadam, Islamic feminism and its discontents. Towards a resolution of the debate, in T. Saliba, C. Allen, and J. A Howard (eds.), *Gender, politics, and Islam*, Chicago 2002, 15–51.

H. Moghissi, *Feminism and Islamic fundamentalism*, London 1999.

F. Sow, Dépendance et développement. Le statut de la femme en Afrique moderne, in *Notes africaines* 130 (July 1973), 256–65.

——, Muslim families in contemporary Black Africa, in *Current Anthropology* 26:5 (December 1985), 566.

——, The social sciences in Africa and gender analysis, in A. M. Imam, A. Mama, and F. Sow (eds.), *Engendering African social sciences*, London 1997a, 31–60.

——, Gender relations in the African environment, in A. M. Imam, A. Mama, and F. Sow (eds.), *Engendering African social sciences*, London 1997b, 251–70.

Barbara Callaway and Lucy Creevey

Turkey

The history of the Woman Question in Turkey goes back to the second half of the nineteenth century, a period marked by far-reaching Westernizing reforms that aimed at reinvigorating the declining Ottoman Empire. Women's issues emerged as the foremost battlefield for debates between modernizers and conservatives of the era, the former identifying women as the loci of Ottoman backwardness, and the latter condemning any major reforms in this arena as foreign encroachments on the cultural essence of Ottoman society. Initially it was a group of male reformers who began criticizing practices such as arranged marriages and polygamy, and emphasized the importance of women's education as a prerequisite for progress. Scattered women's voices soon joined the debate, a development fostered by the emergence of a women's press toward the end of the century. In general the women's discourse was similarly one of progress and education, rarely challenging the identity of women as wives and mothers. While Islam maintained its prominence as a point of reference for many reformists, misguided traditions were often blamed for Muslim women's oppression.

The Second Constitutional Period, ushered in with the 1908 Young Turk Revolution, was a turning point in the treatment of the Woman Question. The terms of the debate were modified with the emergence of a Turkist movement that idealized pre-Islamic Turkish history for its record of women's rights, thereby creating a new reference of authenticity and thus relegating traditions oppressive to women to some undesirable, foreign influence. This was also the time when the women's press and women's organizations flourished in numbers and diversity, and *feminizm* (feminism) became a central signifier in debates surrounding women's issues. The modest improvements in women's educational opportunities that began in the nineteenth century, moreover, continued at a faster pace during this era, with women gaining access to higher education for the first time in the 1910s.

During the War of Independence following the First World War, many women voluntarily involved themselves in the nationalist struggle, and some filled the posts emptied by men going off to war. Nationalist activities of women not only legitimized their public presence, but also provided them with a new image, that of asexual sister-in-arms and patriotic citizen. This image was best personified, as well as created in writing, by Halide Edip Adıvar, one of the well-known novelists of the early republican era, who was distinguished both by her defense of women's rights and by her patriotism. Many radical reforms regarding women followed the declaration of the Turkish Republic in 1923, making Turkey a pioneer in woman's rights, especially among Muslim countries. Between 1924 and 1926, women were granted equal rights with men in the field of education, a new Civil Code based on the Swiss model was passed, replacing Muslim family law, and religious restrictions on women's dress were lifted. Finally, by 1934, women were fully enfranchised. These reforms facilitated the emergence of a substantial group of middle-class female professionals, represented in impressive numbers within a few decades in fields such as academia, law, and medicine, who in turn became the leading symbols of the secular and democratic nature of the republic. Ironically, however, soon after the achievement of full political rights, the single most important women's organization of the time, Türk Kadınlar Birliği (Turkish women's union) disbanded, deeming itself no longer necessary.

From the 1930s until the 1980s, there was a virtually dormant period in Turkey in terms of an autonomous women's movement, a situation commonly linked to the prevalence of the nationalist/modernizing discourse among educated middle-class women, and to the domination of left-wing ideologies in oppositional circles. The former typically assumed incomplete modernization as the root cause of women's continued subordination despite the achievement of formal legal equality, while the latter treated women's oppression as only secondary compared to class oppression and, similar to the former, idealized the image of a desexualized comrade-woman. The new women's movement of the 1980s, influenced by the second-wave feminist ideas coming from the West, challenged the adequacy of formal legal equality achieved as a result of republican reforms, which many criticized as "state feminism," while at the same time asserting its independence, or at least distinctiveness, from other social causes. The new feminists insisted on the political nature of the personal sphere, and emphasized the importance of reclaiming female sexuality. Emerging against the backdrop of the depoliticized atmosphere following the 1980 coup, the new feminist movement germinated in small, informal groups that came together for consciousness-raising sessions and panels in a few metropolitan centers, and carried out ideological debates in certain non-mainstream periodicals. Toward the end of the decade, starting with the 1987 march against domestic violence and continuing with the 1989 campaign against sexual harassment in the streets, the new feminist message eventually succeeded in reaching beyond the bounds of small intellectual circles, and attracted the attention of a larger public.

The new feminist wave passed on to the 1990s with increased internal diversity, greater emphasis on institutionalization and issue-oriented activism. From the few metropolitan centers, it expanded into smaller cities, and the intellectual monopoly of secular, left leaning circles over the subject was to some extent challenged with the rise of a women's rights discourse among Islamist women, and among women active in the Kurdish nationalist movement. Collaborations between women's groups and the government, especially at the local level, produced new institutions such as shelters for battered women and a women's studies library in Istanbul. As a combined effect of Turkey's ratification of the United Nations Convention on the Elimination of All Forms of Discrimination against Women (CEDAW) in 1985 and pressure coming from feminist groups for its full implementation, the 1990s and 2000s also witnessed modifications in the Civil Code and criminal law toward greater legal equality of men and women. Parallel to increased feminist activism, moreover, there has been an increase in the number of literary works by women raising issues such as female sexuality, as well as a visible upsurge in scholarly publications on women's studies and history, which, among other things, recovered for contemporary feminists in Turkey their long forgotten predecessors of the late Ottoman era.

BIBLIOGRAPHY

N. Abadan-Unat (ed.) *Women in Turkish society*, Leiden 1981.

Y. Arat, Women's studies in Turkey. From Kemalism to feminism, in *New Perspectives on Turkey* 9 (Fall 1993), 119–35.

A. Bora and A. Günal (eds.), *90'larda Türkiye'de feminizm*, Istanbul 2002.

S. Çakır, *Osmanlı kadın hareketi*, Istanbul 1994.

A. Durakbaşa, *Halide Edib. Türk modernleşmesi ve feminizm*, Istanbul 2000, 2002[2].

N. Göle, *The forbidden modern. Civilization and veiling*, Ann Arbor 1996.

A. İlyasoğlu and N. Akgökçe, *Yerli bir feminizme doğru*, Istanbul 2001.

D. Kandiyoti, Women and the Turkish state. Political actors or symbolic pawns?, in N. Yuval-Davis and F. Anthias (eds.), *Women-nation-state*, Houndmills, Basingstoke, Hampshire 1989, 126–49.

——, End of empire. Islam, nationalism, and women in Turkey, in D. Kandiyoti (ed.), *Women, Islam, and the state*, Philadelphia 1991, 22–47.

A. Karakaya-Stump, Debating progress in a "serious newspaper for Muslim women." The periodical *Kadın* of the post-revolutionary Salonica, 1908–1909, in *British Journal of Middle Eastern Studies* 30:2 (November 2003), 155–81.

A. Parla, The "honor" of the state. Virginity examinations in Turkey, in *Feminist Studies* 27 (Spring 2001), 65–88.

N. Sirman, Feminism in Turkey. A short history, in *New Perspectives on Turkey* 3 (Fall 1989), 1–34.

Ş. Tekeli, *1980'ler Türkiye'sinde kadın bakiş açısından kadınlar*, Istanbul 1990, 1995[3].

AYFER KARAKAYA-STUMP

The United States

The multiple challenges and issues confronting Muslim women in their own communities, as well as in their relations and interactions with mainstream American society, have facilitated a spirit of activism and engagement in public life. Across the United States a number of community-based and national Muslim women's organizations and initiatives have formed, prompted by efforts to advance Muslim women's education and women's rights, to address women's social and economic concerns and to promote scholarship and activism on issues of jurisprudence, theory, and hermeneutics (Webb 2000). Although many of these initiatives relate to and have engaged in national and international feminist campaigns and discussions, strategic alliances and efforts at coalition building between American Muslim women and the broader feminist movement have remained limited.

According to Fernea (1998) the word "feminism" to many Muslim women in the United States evokes an exclusively Western, almost imperialist movement that does not affirm or validate faith-centered identities and realities. A vast majority of Muslim women have largely disengaged from the feminist movement because they feel not only that their diverse narratives and experiences as Muslim women are silenced, but that the movement typically directs, defines, and prioritizes needs and issues on behalf of Muslim women (Fernea 1998, Haddad and Smith 1996, Webb 2000, Ahmed 1992). Ahmed (1992) points to a neocolonial legacy embedded within the dominant feminist movement that seeks to rescue the typical downtrodden oppressed Muslim woman. Contemporary feminist campaigns in the United States addressing the "Muslim woman" issue, notably the campaign to end gender apartheid in Afghanistan, echo this critique. As Chishti (2003) indicates, the highly visible and politically charged campaign to "emancipate" Afghan women successfully influenced United States foreign policy toward Afghanistan. The political campaign alienated many American Muslim women not in terms of the actual goals, but because of the dichotomized simplicity of pitting secularism against religion and Western liberal freedom against "backward" Islamic tradition. In doing so, the feminist campaign not only heightened

Islamophobia and reinforced stereotypes of Islam and Muslim women in the United States, but simultaneously undermined the complex historical, political, and economic factors that contributed to the conditions of women in Afghanistan.

Despite these challenges, a growing number of Muslim women's initiatives in the United States emerged or were cemented preceding the 1995 United Nations World Conference on Women. Organizations such as the Muslim Women's League, based in California, drafted position papers on the United Nations Platform for Action, and a number of discussions took place across the country gearing up for the conference among Muslim women scholars, activists, and lawyers (Webb 2000). In particular, the 1994 conference in Washington on "Religion, Culture and Women's Human Rights in the Muslim World," co-sponsored by the Sisterhood is Global Institute (SIGI), brought to light the work of existing research and activist Muslim women's organizations in the United States such as Karamah: Muslim Women Lawyers for Human Rights, founded by Azizah al-Hibri, and the North American Council for Muslim Women (NACMW) founded by Sharifa Alkhateeb. The latter organization, in addition to the Muslim Women's Georgetown Study Project, worked extensively on analyzing the connections between CEDAW (Convention on the Elimination of All Forms of Discrimination against Women) and the Qur'ān and *ḥadīth*, leading to their participation on five panel discussions at the World Conference in Beijing (Abu Gideiri 2001). The national advocacy work of Karamah and NACMW continues, as both organizations actively address the issues and concerns of Muslim women and the American Muslim communities nationwide, particularly at the White House and on Capitol Hill. NACMW has been encouraging the greater involvement of Muslim women in public life and addressing key social justice issues, such as violence against women, loans for economic ventures, health care, and female genital mutilation. Similar national efforts by Karamah include acting as consultants in legal cases (such as divorce) to American courts on issues related to women and Muslim Sharīʿa law. As a networking organization, Karamah engages in writing and education on numerous issues such as domestic violence, women's rights in Islam, and legal education. These two organizations in particular have paved new roads for the scholarly and activist contributions of American Muslim women at the national and international level.

The majority of Muslim women's community-based organizations across the United States are working for women's rights and education and addressing the social, economic, and political concerns of American Muslim women. Muslim women's organizations have formed or have increased their public activities to address the needs of Muslim women, largely bypassed by both mainstream feminist organizations and mainstream Muslim organizations. The former typically do not recognize the complexity of the American Muslim women's experience and the latter exclude women from senior decision-making bodies and are largely informed by patriarchal attitudes and practices (Ali 2003, Abu Gideiri 2001). In this regard, Abu Gideiri writes, "Muslim women are sustaining, resisting, adjusting or changing their historical roles within contemporary American circles" (2001, 1). Dozens of national Muslim women's organizations have been formed in the United States, a great majority of them promoting women's empowerment through education. The Muslim Women's League, the United States chapter of Sisters in Islam and the International Union of Muslim Women are some examples of national organizations that promote comprehensive and critical Islamic education for women, alongside addressing misconceptions and common misunderstanding of gender in Islam in the broader community. In researching the challenges faced by American Muslim women, Haddad and Smith (2003) comment that Muslim women in America have a history of activism, helping to create institutions, social structures, and support groups across the country. Although they have suffered a setback due to the backlash and profiling as a result of 11 September 2001, there is a new kind of activism emerging among American Muslim women, mainly to reach out to mainstream society in efforts to inform the public about Islam and dispel popular myths and stereotypes, particularly about Muslim women.

There is undoubtedly a growing community of Muslim women activists and organizations in the United States addressing critical concerns faced by American Muslim women. Although few Muslim women's organizations identify themselves as feminist, their work is addressing the immediate and strategic needs and concerns of Muslim American women and their families. Thus many Muslim women activists, scholars, and organizations are increasingly finding themselves engaged in feminist discussions and interacting with the broader feminist movement (Haddad and Smith 1996, Webb 2000). In her study of Muslim women's identity in North America, Khan (2000) identifies the critical need for Muslim women living in North America to engage in feminist discourse in order to explore how gender, capitalism, and patriarchy implicate their lived realities at various levels, and to carve their own niche in feminist organizing, which she argues is vital for progressive alternatives and collective strategies. Coalition building among Muslim women and the larger feminist movement in the United States holds great potential, not only to build an inclusive movement but also to promote collective analyses and work toward achieving mutually defined goals.

Bibliography

H. Abu Gideiri, The renewed woman of American Islam. Shifting lenses toward gender jihad?, in *Muslim World* 91:1/2 (2001), 1–18.

L. Ahmed, *Women and gender in Islam*, New Haven, Conn. 1992.

S. Ali, Building a movement. A woman's work, in *Islamic Horizons* (May/June 1424/2003), 16–24.

M. Chishti, The international women's movement and the politics of participation for Muslim women, in *American Journal of Islamic Social Sciences* 19:4 (2002), 80–99.

E. W. Fernea, *In search of Islamic feminism*, New York 1998.

Y. Y. Haddad and J. I. Smith, Islamic values among American Muslims, in B. Aswad and B. Bilge (eds.), *Family and gender among American Muslims*, Philadelphia 1996, 19–40.

——, Adjusting the tie that binds. Challenges facing Muslim women in America, in H. Jawad and T. Benn (eds.), *Muslim women in the United Kingdom and beyond*, Leiden 2003, 39–64.

S. Khan, *Muslim women. Crafting a North American identity*, Gainseville, Fla. 2000.

G. Webb (ed.), *Windows of faith. Muslim women scholar-activists in North America*, Syracuse, N.Y. 2000.

Maliha Chishti

Political-Social Movements: Islamist Movements and Discourses

The Caucasus and Central Asia

Introduction

We define Islamist movements very broadly, referring to political movements that either adopt Islam as a principle ideology or include it as a main constituent of their ideology or ideologies. There has been very little research on the role of women in shaping Islamist movements and discourses in the Caucasus and Central Asia. Nevertheless, from what we do know, women have played a significant historical role in the struggles against Russian presence in the region. Informally, women also struggle to define varying aspects of their Muslim and ethnic identities against the backdrop of Islamist discourse and nationalist resistance.

Historical Background

The Russian invasions of the Caucasus and Central Asia in the eighteenth and nineteenth centuries ignited several cycles of resistance that were initially successful, but finally defeated. Beginning in 1783 with Shaykh Manṣūr's multiethnic Caucasian resistance and continuing until the establishment of the North Caucasian state in 1918 and the Soviet invasion of that nascent state in 1921, the Caucasus barely enjoyed a peaceful period during the Tsarist era. The Tsarist era also witnessed the 30-year Caucasian wars (1829–59) involving the legendary Imām Shāmil, whose wife was a central figure in his resistance campaign. Similarly, in Central Asia, the resistance was losing ground to the Russian advance, with Tashkent falling to Tsarist Russia in 1865, Samarkand and Bukhara in 1868, and the Turkmen regions in 1883–4 (Haghayeghi 1996, 93). The same cities fell to the Soviets again in the 1920s after short periods of independence.

One of the reactions to losing the battle against the Russians was the birth of the reformist Jadid movement. Established in 1883 by Ismail Bey Gaspıralı (1851–1914), the movement advocated a modern interpretation of Islam, spreading education and allowing greater freedom for Muslim women as methods of combating Russian imperialism. The Jadid movement "not only included the 'women question' in their political and social agenda but transformed it into a 'cause célèbre'" (Rorlich 2002, 247). Gaspıralı declared, "Whoever loves his own people and wishes them a [bright] future must concern himself with the enlightenment and education of women, restore to them [their] freedom and independence and give wide scope to the development of their minds' capabilities" (Rorlich 2002, 249).

Confronted with the 1917 developments and upheavals, the Jadidists were divided between several strategic choices, ranging from full cooperation with the new "progressive" Soviets to militarily resisting the "new invaders." Factionalized and fractured, the movement was easily suppressed by Lenin and later crushed by Stalin. The demise of the Jadid movement ended the "reform from within" attempt and it became the exclusive task of the Soviets to "emancipate" the Muslim women of the Caucasus and Central Asia.

Termed the "surrogate proletariat," Muslim women were targeted exclusively as a way to simultaneously weaken traditional Central Asian identities and impose a uniform socialist, "modern," Russian model of society. This program focused on incorporating women more visibly into the public sphere, emphasizing their labor participation, educational opportunities, and equality before the law (Akiner 1997, 262). In addition, symbols of their Islamic identity, such as the veil, were systematically targeted. In 1955, under Khrushchev, veil burning ceremonies were given widespread publicity and in 1959, the "end of the era of the veil was officially announced with a ceremonial burning of the last veil in Bukhara" (Rashid 1994, 34). This forced Soviet "emancipation" was not completely successful. Although many women benefited from the educational and work opportunities offered to them, not all necessarily subscribed to the ideological components of the Soviet program.

Another Soviet policy that affected Muslim women was the suppression of Islam in the public sphere. As a result, Islamic belief and rituals were mainly preserved in the private sphere, the realm of the family and community. As primary caregivers in the family, women could engage in private religious practice and maintain rituals and customs that reflected both their Islamic and ethnic heritages, without state intrusion (Akiner 1997, 274). They were therefore key actors in preserving their Islamic and traditional Central Asian identities, individually and collectively, under Soviet rule, even as they were the "objects of emancipation" in the public sphere.

Post-independence era

The process of defining women's roles, socially and politically, is part of the general resurgence of Islamist and ethnonationalist identities, both of which serve as contrast to Soviet imperialism. One manifestation of this sociopolitical dynamic is the focus on women's dress as a marker of traditional, ethnic, and Islamic identities (Tadjbaksh 1998, 175). In Tajikistan, for example, between 1990 and 1992, when nationalist sentiments were at their peak, the veil and traditional dress (*atlas*) were declared a national dress by both Muslim men and women (Tadjbaksh 1998, 175).

More generally, competing ideals of womanhood have come to dominate social Islamist discourse in post-independence Central Asian society. As part of the backlash against the Soviets, there is a positive view of the "traditional, Muslim, Central Asian woman" and a negative perception of the "emancipated, modern, Russian woman." In reality, most Central Asian women do not fall easily into either category. The majority seek to balance the two, rather than to replace the latter with the former in a reversal of the Soviet female emancipation campaign (Akiner 1997, 263). For example, at a conference on "Islam and the Role of Women" in September 1992, Central Asian women favored the domestic role of traditional women in the education and upbringing of their children, while assessing the difficulties for modern women to juggle their professional and domestic responsibilities (Tadjbaksh 1998, 177).

Women's responses to Islamist and nationalist pressures are expressed predominantly in informal ways, and not exclusively through organized, political involvement. For example, Muslim women's organizations have not been very successful so far, partially due to lack of sufficient funding, and there is not much evidence of a specifically feminist component to Islamist movements (Akiner 1997, 294). In social practice, although many women are inclined to view Islam favorably, not many choose to express it by adopting the veil. Most women see it as a matter of personal commitment and not a political statement of their identity (Akiner 268). Many Tajik women continue to work outside the home, if and when they can find work in the midst of political insecurity, due to financial necessity, and do not practice female seclusion as part of the ideal for traditional women (Tadjbaksh 1998, 180).

Yet many Central Asian and Caucasian women support Islamist-oriented and nationalist political movements. In Central Asia, during the Tajik civil war, a significant percentage of Tajik women supported the United Tajikistani Opposition (UTO), whose backbone was the Islamic Renaissance Party (IRP). In 1992, Nazarudin Zuberdulla, commander of the UTO's military wing, declared that the UTO's women supporters were selling their jewelry to buy arms (Rashid 1994, 180). In the Caucasus, a study conducted by the Union of Women of the Don Region (UWDR 1999) about Chechen women's attitudes toward making Chechnya an Islamic state showed that a significant percentage favored the idea. Two out of three women looked favorably upon the prospect of establishing an Islamic state in Chechnya, while one in four respondents favored the Sharīʿa courts, which were re-established in Chechnya from 1997 to 1999 (UWDR 1999). This is in addition to Chechen women's participation in the war for "independence" as well as in field-commanding resistance units (Chechen women 1999).

Bibliography

Primary Sources

UWDR (Union Women of the Don Region), Chechen women's attitude towards making Chechnya an Islamic state, 1999, <http://home.novoch.ru/~donwomen/Report_ChechWom&War _09.htm>.

Secondary Sources

S. Akiner, Between tradition and modernity. The dilemma facing contemporary Central Asian women, in M. Buckley (ed.), *Post-Soviet women. From the Baltic to Central Asia*, Cambridge 1997, 261–304.

Chechen women during war, 1999, <www.amina.com/article/chech_wom.html>.

M. Haghaygehi, *Islam and politics in Central Asia*, New York 1995.

A. Rashid, *The resurgence in Central Asia. Islam or nationalism?* London 1994.

A. Rorlich, Muslim feminism and nationalism. Crimea, Middle Volga and Caucasus, in A. Samiuddin and R. Khanam (eds.), *Muslim feminism and feminist movements*, Delhi 2002, 245–67.

S. Tadjbaksh, Between Lenin and Allah. Women and ideology in Tajikistan, in H. L. Bodman and N. Tohidi (eds.), *Women in Muslim societies*, Boulder, Colo. 1998, 163–85.

Omar Ashour and Uzma Jamil

Indonesia

Indonesian women activists have been involved in women's issues since the beginning of the twentieth century. Dewi Sartika (1884–1947), a Sundanese noblewoman in West Java who founded a school in 1904, was influenced by the ideas of Princess Raden Adjeng Kartini (1879–1904). In West Sumatra, Rahmah El-Yunusiah was concerned with women's education and Rasuna Said with politics and journalism.

Born in a strongly Islamic background on 20 December 1900, El-Yunusiah pioneered an Islamic school dedicated exclusively to women. She believed that women in many respects lagged behind men and this induced her to build the Madrasah Diniyah Puteri (Islamic School for Women). This school inspired other women activists to open similar schools in other parts of the country. El-Yunusiah successfully wedded Islamism with the women's emancipation movement in Indonesia; she was labeled by some the "Kartini of Islamic Schools" (Burhanudin 2001).

Said built political consciousness among young women in West Sumatra. Initially she was involved in education and taught on the staff at El-Yunusiah's school for some years. Later on she turned to politics and journalism. She left El-Yunusiah and began to develop her career as an activist. On many occasions she attempted to argue that women's roles in liberating the country were as important as those of men. As a result, she was indicted by the Dutch colonial administration and spent some years in jail.

Another prominent women is Roehanna Koeddoes, who published a magazine, *Soenting Melajoe*, dedicated to the progress of women. Through this magazine, Koeddoes disseminated not only the ideas of women's emancipation and women's skills, but also of gender equality. Although it survived for only a short period of time (1912–21), it succeeded in raising women's consciousness of several issues, for example, their roles in education, politics, and social life.

Emancipation as part of modernization

The struggles of El-Yunusiah and Said to improve the conditions of women cannot be separated from the waves of Islamic modernization movements in West Sumatra in particular and in Indonesia in general at the beginning of the twentieth century. A number of Islamic organizations were founded with the aim of modernizing Indonesian Muslims. Muhammadiyah, the locomotive of the Islamic modernization movement in Indonesia, laid a strong emphasis on education, including women's education.

Muhammadiyah chose education and social activities as its most important agendas. As a modern organization, Muhammadiyah believed that women should be included in the modernization processes. This meant that women's education became the highest priority in its activities. Nyai Ahmad Dahlan, the wife of Ahmad Dahlan, the founder of Muhammadiyah, founded Sopo Tresno in 1914, a study circle dedicated to women which became the means for the dissemination of a progressive spirit among women, especially those involved in the Muhammadiyah. In 1917, it was transformed into a larger organization called Aisyiyah, a women's sub-organization within Muhammadiyah which remains active until today.

Another modernist Muslim organization, Persis (The unity of Islam), established Persistri as a sub-organization concerned with women. It oriented its activities toward giving religious guidance to its members. Nahdlatul Ulama (NU) established a sub-organization concerned with women, Muslimat. Like Aisyiyah, Persistri and Muslimat provide skills and knowledge for their members, founding branches of their organizations all over the country to support their activities.

Despite the consciousness of progressive ideas among Indonesian women in terms of education and emancipation, certain other problems, including polygamy, were not addressed. A number of women opposed polygamy since it conflicts with the principle of equality between men and women. But many Muslim women still considered polygamy to be a part of religious obligation as it is mentioned in the Holy Qur'ān. Polygamy became a crucial issue in modern Indonesian history. Despite women's severe criticism of it, they could not ignore religious stipulations which clearly support it. Aisyiyah, for instance, at the Bukit Tinggi congress in 1930, stated that polygamy is a part of Islamic teaching. In contrast, Aisyiyah criticized some practices imported from the West, for example, female workers and male–female relationships, which did not fit with religious teachings. These were considered to be un-Islamic, and not perceived as progressive.

Indonesian women activists at the beginning of the twentieth century understood women's movements largely in terms of women's education. This can be seen in the work of El-Yunusiah and Nyai Ahmad Dahlan for whom women's education, more precisely Islamic education, was the main prerequisite for women's emancipation. This understanding seems logical, given that at the time schools remained closed to women. Only a small number of women from the privileged groups, such as Kartini, could enjoy education.

Some women activists had a slightly different understanding concerning women's emancipation: Rasuna Said stressed the importance of women's political consciousness as part of women's emancipation. It can even be said that she was the first woman activist who believed that women cannot be separated from politics. Rasimah Ismail, Said's successor, emphasized her belief that women should contribute to Indonesia's independence movement.

Women's political consciousness became more apparent in 1928 when the first national women's congress was held in Jakarta. At this congress the women addressed the issue of the improvement of women's education, and also supported the independence movement. A year later, at their second congress, also in Jakarta, they restated political agendas including their support for independence and their rejection of provincialism and regionalism.

From emancipation to gender

By the late 1980s, there was a shift of paradigm among women activists concerning women's discourses. Emancipation had been achieved and the issue of gender came to the fore. A number of Muslim intellectuals introduced gender discourse to Indonesian Muslims, along with the issues of democracy, human rights, and environment. Prominent figures concerned here are, among others, the late Mansour Fakih, a representative of a nongovernmental organization who attempted to explain gender from a sociological point of view and Masdar F. Mas'udi, who explained it through examination of Islamic classical texts (*fiqh*).

Gender discourse raised contrary opinions among Muslims. Conservative Muslim groups believe that gender ideas have been influenced by Western liberal principles which undermine religious teachings. They argue that Muslims should be aware that not all Western concepts, including that of gender, align with the teachings of Islam. For this reason, they rejected gender discourse as being un-Islamic. Rejection of gender discourse comes mostly from the so-called Islamist groups who believe that since Islam is a complete religion, there is no need for Muslims to seek other principles and models for their life.

In contrast, a number of young Muslim intellectuals hold that the principles of gender equality should be disseminated among Muslims because there are still certain practices in the community which are undermining of women. Some Muslim gender activists believe that certain Qur'ānic verses and the *ḥadīth* of the Prophet Muḥammad were biased by the social structure of the Muslim community, which supported patriarchal cultures. This problem, they believe, can only be solved by deconstructing the principles of Islam. Some gender activists even say that it is time to demasculinize the paradigm.

Among various intellectuals who examine Islam vis-à-vis gender from different perspectives is Nasaruddin Umar, who uses hermeneutical methods in understanding the gender verses in the Qur'ān. Umar finds that the Qur'ān was revealed in a language highly influenced by patriarchal cultures and is therefore gender-biased. Another gender activist, Badriyah Fayumi, examines a number of *ḥadīth* that are supposed to be biased by gender issues. She finds that gender biases in the *ḥadīth* are influenced by historical and sociological contexts which infiltrated the body of Islam.

Another prominent figure is Husein Muhammad. From a deeply Islamic background, Muhammad approaches Islam and gender through classical Islamic textbooks (*fiqh*). According to him, *fiqh* actually gives a huge perspective on women, ranging from conservative to liberal. Gender inequalities emerged when conservative precepts dominated *fiqh* and appeared to be the only *fiqh* available for Muslims; this took place as a result of attempts made by certain groups in the Muslim community to maintain the status quo within the community.

Attempts such as those made by Masdar F. Mas'udi have succeeded in improving gender understandings within the members of the NU, the largest Islamic organization in Indonesia, frequently labeled as representing "traditionalist Islam." Mas'udi is now a member of the top executive board of the NU. During the late 1970s, he founded P3M, the Center for Research and Development of the Pesantren [Islamic boarding school] and Society, and attempted to disseminate gender ideologies among the members of the NU community.

Many Muslim gender activists in Indonesia come from traditionalist Muslim backgrounds. Rahima, one of the most important NGOs in Indonesia working on gender issues, was founded by NU intellectuals, including Husein Muhammad. The Modernist Muhammadiyah also works on gender. Siti Ruhaini Dzuhayatin, a gender activist from Yogyakarta with a Muhammadiyah background, established Rifka Annisa, an NGO working on women and gender issues.

Works of international Muslim feminists also exert an influence. By the late 1980s, Fatima Mernissi, Riffat Hassan, Nawal Sadawi, Ashgar Ali

Engineer, and Amina Wadud Muhsin had stimulated Indonesian Muslims to think more deeply about women's issues, leading to new understandings of gender. This was supported by *Ulumul Qur'an*, a new Indonesian journal dedicated exclusively to the discussion of various issues concerning Islam, including gender. In 1989, it published an article by Yvonne Haddad on the image of Eve in the Qur'ān. This article was received positively by its readers. A year later, it published an article by Riffat Hassan on women's theology in Islamic tradition which also evoked positive responses. This is the period when Indonesian Muslims came into contact for the first time with the concept of gender in a very broad sense. More female and male intellectuals realized that gender equality was the most important aim to be realized. They held various discussions and seminars, and undertook research and training concerning this issue. The number of Muslim students exploring gender as their research project grew significantly in Muslim campuses in the country. Some of them went on to become women or gender activists.

A number of key figures, among them Lies Marcoes-Natsir and Farha Ciciek, have played a great role in socializing and disseminating gender and women's issues to a wider Muslim community, especially students. They represent the first generation of Indonesian Muslim women who are seeking rationalization of gender from religious perspectives. Despite challenges from conservative Muslim groups, they dedicate their lives to the issues surrounding gender and are positively reinforced by younger fellow Muslims. Among young Muslim intellectuals emerging from the 1990s are Nurul Agustina, Ratna Batara Munti, Ala'i Najib, Syafiq Hasyim, Ratna Megawangi, and Badriyah Fayumi. They flourish as the second generation and, like their predecessors, are committed to the dissemination of the gender discourse in Indonesia.

Bibliography

Primary Sources (all in Indonesian)

N. Agustina, Islamic traditionalism and feminism, in *Ulumul Qur'an* (fifth year special edition) 5:5/6 (1994).

A. Arani (ed.), *Body, sexuality, and women's sovereignty, anthology of young* 'ulamā's' *thoughts*, Yogyakarta 2002.

F. Ciciek, *Attempts to overcome domestic violence. Learning from the life of the Prophet Muḥammad p.h.b.u.*, Jakarta 1999.

M. Chalil, *Women's dignity*, Bandung-Jakarta 1954.

Z. Daradjat, *An accountable marriage*, Jakarta 1975.

A. A. Engineer, *Women's rights in Islam*, Yogyakarta 1994.

M. Fakih, *Gender analysis and social transformation*, Yogyakarta 1996.

—— et al., *Discussing feminism. Gender discourses in Islamic perspectives*, Surabaya 1996.

B. Fayumi and A. Najib, The creature who receives the most attention from the Prophet. Women in Prophetic narratives, in A. Munhanif (ed.), *The hidden pearl. Women in classical Islamic literatures*, Jakarta 2002.

Fitriyani, *Roehana Koeddoes. A West Sumatran woman*, Jakarta 2001.

F. Mernissi and R. Hassan, *Equal before God. Writings of Riffat Hassan and Fatima Mernissi (translated into Bahasa Indonesia)*, Yogyakarta 1995.

L. M. Marcoes-Natsir and J. H. Meuleman (eds.), *Muslim women in textual and contextual studies*, Jakarta 1993.

S. Wieringa, *A scented malicious supernatural being. Women's organizations in post- 1950s Indonesia*, Jakarta 1998.

Secondary Sources

I. Abdullah, *The origins of gender*, Yogyakarta 1997.

L. Ahmed, *Women and gender in Islam. Historical roots of a modern debate*, New Haven, Conn. 1992, trans. into Indonesian, *Wanita dan gender dalam Islam*, Jakarta 2000.

E. Amalia, Muslim women's aspirations and their political roles during the New Order concerning women's empowerment. Gender relations in Islam, undergraduate thesis, IAIN Syarif Hidayatullah, Jakarta 1999.

J. Badawi, *Gender equity in Islam. Basic principles*, Plainfield, Ind. 1995.

K. Bhasin, *Understanding gender*, Jakarta 2002.

J. Burhanudin (ed.), *Indonesian women 'ulamā'*, Jakarta 2001.

B. S. Dewantara, *Nyi Hajar Dewantara in myth and reality*, Jakarta 1979.

Jajang Jahroni

Iran and Afghanistan

Massive participation of Iranian women in the 1979 Islamic Revolution and women's support for political Islam in the 1980s have led specialists to inquire into the reasons behind women's participation in Islamist movements whose aim, it is argued, is to limit women's rights and their political, economic, and social choice. Given the limitation of existing research and published material on Afghanistan this entry focuses on Iran.

In the name of religion some Islamists with a positivist approach to nature essentialize gender inequality, which they consider to be natural and to originate in the divine will. They confine women to domesticity where natural hierarchy limits the equality between men and women. Sayyid Javād Muṣṭafavī, an Iranian cleric and the author of a widely read book on the family (1995), argues, "God has created women to do the housework, child-bearing and child-rearing. God has created men for activities outside the home, for confronting the hardships of life." Likewise, in Afghanistan, the Taliban denied women their basic rights and secluded them from public life.

Islamists are not unanimous in limiting the role of

women to that of mother and wife. Some endorse women's active presence in the public sphere but are opposed to egalitarian gender relations and women's autonomy. In the aftermath of the Iranian Revolution Ayatollah Khomeini encouraged Islamist women's activities in the public sphere and criticized the traditionalist clergy, saying, "God is satisfied with women's great service. It is a sin to sabotage this [women's activity in the public sphere]." In Afghanistan, some members of the Northern Alliance, especially Aḥmad Shāh Masʿūd, who fought against the Taliban from 1996 onwards, shared more or less the same view.

Reasons that lead to women's participation in Islamist movements are manifold. Some women who valorize the centrality of women's role in the family, and disapprove of individualism, which, they think, is provoked by Western sociocultural influence, are attracted to Islamist discourse. For these women Islamic values can and should be preserved through maternity. Maryam Bihrūzī, a member of the first to fourth Islamic Majlis (assembly) who was a preacher prior to the revolution and leads the conservative Zaynab Association, is among this category. She declared that "according to Islam men are protectors of women" and that "the home is the most suitable place for women because children need their mother's presence" (1983).

Some lower-class women who suffer from their social condition and demand social justice are drawn to Islamist organizations and associations because of their charitable activities rather than their Islamist political discourse. In the absence of social institutions Islamists assist the needy through their solidarity networks thereby winning the loyalty of poor or impoverished women. In Iran, prior to the unfolding of the revolution, revolutionary clergy and their *bāzāri* (merchant) allies gained the support of poor urban women and women rural migrants thanks to religious charitable activities before mobilizing them to participate in the revolution. They became the main pillars of the Islamic regime. The increasing gap between the rich and the poor in post-revolutionary Iran and the persistence of poverty, however, have led to the disillusionment of these women. The wife of a man wounded at war (*jānbāz*) who lives in a poor suburb of Tehran declares: "We are even more disinherited than before the revolution. The Islamic state did not keep its promise. My husband went to the war as a volunteer (*basījī*) and was severely wounded. What did he obtain in return? Just a wheelchair" (personal interview, Khak-i Sefid 1996).

Young and educated women from religious lower- or middle-class backgrounds who are not subordinated to traditional religious views and aspire to social participation join Islamist movements in order to enhance their active presence in the public sphere. Their aspiration to autonomy, their efforts to reappropriate modernity and to provide new interpretations of religious laws and traditions in order to promote women's status, however, are disapproved of by their male counterparts who consider moves toward women's autonomy and emancipation to be a Western plot against Islam. In post-revolutionary Iran, the implementation of the Sharīʿa (Islamic law) and the excessive privileges granted to men gradually led to the disillusionment of some young Islamist women, contributing to the emergence of gender sensitivity among them and ultimately to their mobilization against sex discrimination. According to an Iranian Islamist activist: "I realized that revolutionary social activity was meaningless when women were losing their rights and started to defend women's rights" (personal interview, Tehran 1994).

Some radical religious women with a political agenda join Islamist movements to promote their political stands. A'ẓam Ṭaliqānī, daughter of the radical cleric Ayatollah Maḥmud Ṭaliqānī and the editor of the magazine *Payām-i Hājar* is an example. Her work for the cause of the disinherited brought her into contact with the plight of women, especially the poor: "Poverty and polygamy are the only things that poor women have obtained from the revolution" (1990). *Payām-i Hājar* was the first women's magazine to advocate the reinterpretation of Qurʾānic verses, especially *al-Nisāʾ* (Women) and to refute the legalization of polygamy.

The institutionalization of gender inequality in the aftermath of the Iranian Revolution has provoked general discontent among women, including many former Islamists, and triggered their mobilization against segregation laws and institutions. These women reject divine justifications for gender inequality through a new reading of Islam that accommodates the equality of rights between men and women. Shahlā Shirkat (1996) the editor-in-chief of the influential women's magazine *Zanān* (Women) argues: "Radical legal changes are needed to solve women's problems. Because many articles of the Civil Code are based on the Sharīʿa, its reinterpretation proves necessary and women should be involved in this undertaking." Likewise, Zeiba Shorish-Shamley (2001), an Afghan activist, argues that "men and women have equal status in Islam. However, in practice these rights have been violated."

Faced with these intellectual endeavors and women's social struggle for equal rights, a new perspective has emerged among reformist clerics. They now oppose the official and rigid interpretations of Islam that essentialize gender inequalities, and present an evolutionist perspective that attempts to adapt Islam to women's modern demands. Muḥammad Mujtahid-Shabistarī (2000) argues, "The Qurʾān and traditions should be understood and interpreted in the framework of a historical and social approach. The Prophet modified a number of rights and regulations that he considered to be unjust vis-à-vis women. He changed flagrant inequalities that adversely affected women according to the understanding of justice that existed in his time. The main message is that other inequalities imposed on women throughout history should also be abolished."

BIBLIOGRAPHY

M. ʿAbbāsqulīzādah and M. Ibtikār, personal interview, Tehran, July 1996.

M. Bihrūzī, Ṭarḥ-i kumīsyūn-i vizhieh-i umūr-i zanān dar majlis, in *Zan-i Rūz* 26 (February 1993), 11–12.

——, Interview, *Ettalaat*, 22 February 1983, 6, 11.

R. Khumaynī (Ayatollah Khomeini), sermon on 19 September 1979, in *Ṣaḥīfh-yi nūr*, ix, Tehran 1989, 136.

——, declaration issued on 12 March 1982, in *Ṣaḥīfah-yi nūr*, xvii, Tehran 1989, 211.

A. Kian-Thiébaut, From Islamization to the individualization of women in post-revolutionary Iran, in S. Ansari and V. Martin (eds.), *Women, religion and culture in Iran*, Richmond, Surrey 2002, 127–42.

M. Mujtahid-Shabistarī, *Naqdī bar qirāʾat-i rasmī az dīn*, Tehran 2000, 503–4, 509.

S. J. Muṣṭafavī, *Bihisht-i khānavādah*, i, Tehran 1995, 118.

J. Nachtwey and M. Tessler, Explaining women's support for political Islam. Contributions from feminist theory, in M. Tessler (ed.), *Area studies and social science. Strategies for understanding Middle East politics*, Bloomington, Ind. 1999, 49.

S. Shirkat, personal interview, Tehran, July 1996.

Z. Shorish-Shamley, Women's position, role, and rights in Islam, <http//www.afghan-web.com, April 2001>.

A. Ṭāliqānī, interview, in *Ettalaat*, 3 March 1990, 4

——, personal interview, Tehran, February 1996.

AZADEH KIAN-THIÉBAUT

Mashriq, Egypt, and North Africa

Just as there are differences within any political ideology and movement, Islamism also embodies various competing streams of thought and modalities of engagement. Although all these share the ultimate objective of Islamizing (rendering more Islamic through the application of Sharīʿa law) both the state institutions and legislation, as well as the society as a whole, they differ radically as to the methods they employ.

Fundamentalism and rising religious extremism are not one and the same phenomenon. Originally, "fundamentalism" was coined to define a Christian movement which was literal in its interpretation of Christian texts in the Western world, and particular to a certain era. While the literal interpretation of texts (be they religious or even non-faith based documents such as legislation) remains an important aspect of fundamentalism, the movements today understood as "religious fundamentalist" vary widely in their composition, objectives, organization, and mode of operation.

Muslim, or Islamic, fundamentalism, is thus a problematic concept – unless used to apply narrowly to those who espouse very literal understandings of the Qurʾān, *sunna*, and *ḥadīth* in their lives and outlook. Primarily, fundamentalists may follow a relatively strict interpretation of their religious tradition in their own personal lives. There is, therefore, a substantial difference between Islamic fundamentalists and Islamists. Whereas Islamists organize and distinguish themselves as political parties with an agenda to compete for political and state power (for example, the Muslim Brotherhood in Egypt, Jordan, and Syria, and more extreme, that is, armed, groups such as Jihad in Egypt, Hamas in Palestine, and Hizballah in Lebanon), many fundamentalists abhor political engagement, believing that the entire process of politics is impure at best and corrupting at worst. Some fundamentalists may also be Islamists (that is, belong to Islamic political organizations), but many Islamists are not even well-versed in the religious doctrine per se, and are not literal in their interpretation and practice. In fact, some leading Islamist ideologues, such as Sayyid Quṭb, are credited with being creative and often innovative in their interpretation of text and tradition to adjust to contemporary political discourses.

Religious extremism, in contrast, should be distinguished from both fundamentalism and religio-political movements. Religious extremism exists within all religious traditions and definitions of it vary depending on the vantage point of the researcher or institution. It is present in both the private (personal and family) sphere as well as the larger public (state and society) sphere. At its base, it can be understood as the use of religious discourse to validate violence, in a Machiavellian sense, as a means to a political end. Not all Islamist or fundamentalist movements are extremist since most of them are based on principles that condemn all violence and are committed to investing in and serving society and educating people about religion. Moderate Islamists are known to set up social institutions which perform important social services (health care, shelter provision, education, and the like) and to participate peacefully in electoral politics.

On the political continuum of Islamism the differences in methods veer from the moderate to the extreme. At one end, the moderates believe in gradual Islamic education and awareness raising amongst peoples; active, legal, and peaceful political participation; condemnation of violence as a means to achieving an end; and the importance of actively participating in the social sector (through donations of various forms of resources – personal, financial, or other – to education, health care, welfare services, and so forth). The moderates tend to believe in political participation, democratization, and respect for human rights as principles and standards which are advocated by Islam itself, and will seek to create alliances across the political spectrum.

At the opposite end of the continuum are the radicals, or extremists, many of whom condone the use of violence as a legitimate means to the sanctified objective of spreading the word of God. Most radicals eschew existing political arenas as fundamentally corrupt and opt out of participation, or at worst decide to wage war against the political regime and the society. Some radicals also believe in contributing to social work, but very often such contributions are made available only to a limited circle of partisans.

Some Islamists, therefore, have undertaken to bear arms in a struggle specifically tailored to wreak mass havoc and destruction in order to bring about a more religious (and in their eyes, just) political order, or to consolidate an existing one – such as the Taliban in Afghanistan, and modern day al-Qāʿida (al-Qaeda). Although they are a minority amongst Islamists, and certainly on the wider political spectrum, such extremists are also heard the most and known the best. Partly because many radicals initially tended to embrace a moderate version of political conviction, and later (due to a variety of reasons) veered toward a more radical stance, and because all Islamists ultimately champion the implementation of Sharīʿa, secular politicians tend to be deeply suspicious of the democratic credentials of Islamists. This is despite the fact that many Islamists assert democratic values of consultation, consensus, and justice.

Women are active members of all these groups: fundamentalists, Islamists, and religious extremists. When the first Islamic political party in the twentieth century – the Ikhwān al-Muslimīn (Muslim Brotherhood) of Egypt – was nearly annihilated by the then president and Arab nationalist leader Gamal Abdel Nasser, it was single-handedly kept alive – despite great odds – by one woman, Zaynab al-Ghazālī. Al-Ghazālī was instrumental in maintaining the infrastructure, and even the ethos of the movement, and eventually went on to become a strong proponent of women's activism within Islamist movements around the Arab and Muslim world.

From India to the United States, women are actively recruiting other women (and men) into fundamentalist movements. As spokespersons for the ideology, as the motors of organizations, and often as ideologues of the need to make women focus on their primary responsibility as mothers and wives, women play an important role in recruiting and mobilizing others within these movements.

As for religious extremists, research into members of Egyptian Jihad and Lebanese Hizballah has shown that there were women, fully and diversely veiled, who were prominent not only during the executive meetings of the movements, but also in undertaking activities which could – and in some cases, did – imperil their lives. Whether discussing strategies of confronting state repression, or carrying arms from one location to another, highly educated and eloquent women were often crucial actors and partners within such extremist movements. In other words, not only are women not absent from religious extremism, but they can be critical to the success of such movements.

Secular women activists in the Arab world claim such participation to be "false consciousness." Unable to fathom why women would be part of movements which limit women's public roles, secular women activists often regard their female counterparts in Islamist and extremist movements as being either brainwashed or downright unintelligent. Islamist women activists – and to a large extent the women members of extremist movements – in turn, see their secular counterparts in much the same terms: indoctrinated by Western values and agents of corruption. It might be said that no movement is as polarized as the women's movement between the religious and more secular activists.

What must be borne in mind, however, is that the women members of Islamist movements differ widely in and amongst themselves, more so perhaps than their sisters in extremist religious organizations. Indeed, some women Islamists see their engagement within such movements as an empowering reality, and apply this discourse to argue for women's equity and the religious imperative behind women's social, economic, and political advancement in

Muslim societies. Whereas secular women activists see the United Nations conventions and civil laws as the means to an enhanced women's status, Islamist women – some of whom are equally keen on the same improvement to women's positions – see the Qur'ān (and a more enlightened practice of "the real Islam" more broadly) as the only (and far more powerful) vehicle to achieving this aim.

Even though many Islamist women prioritize women's roles as mothers and wives, some of them argue that, far from limiting women's active participation in the public arena, these roles can also be strategic forms of public engagement. By performing these roles, the proponents argue, women learn and practice important skills that strengthen the family unit (the most important nucleus of any society), which is critical for propagating certain ways of thought and eventually building a powerful national infrastructure that services both *dīn wa-dawla* (religion and nation). In other words, there is such a thing as "political motherhood." Thus, in an ironic twist on feminist language ("the personal is political"), some Islamist women activists interpret the political to be broader than the traditionally defined public space, and inclusive of the (previously) private domain of family. Hence the family is conceived of as a mini-state, and women, as leaders of that, become important political actors.

Not all Islamist women think along these lines. Nevertheless, it is significant that some of the most vocal political opposition in many parts of the Arab world today – the Islamists – have women leaders who uphold versions of such a philosophy. In so doing, these women are simultaneously being respectful of their religious tradition – as well as very protective of it – and advocating for women's active public service.

There remains a group of women and men, active within fundamentalist and Islamist extremist groups, who openly oppose women occupying any public roles whatsoever and, indeed, feel that many of the rights granted to women in legislation (whether, for example, pay equal to that of men in labor contexts and/or equal access to divorce in some personal status situations) are contrary to the spirit and letter of religious advocacy. Some of the loudest voices in the religious communities in Arab countries today uphold such views, and the cacophony that ensues is fueled by factors which are often not even related to religion. From the point of view of the woman or man on the Arab streets, there is a vacuum where grand mobilizing ideologies such as Nasserism and Arab socialism used to be. Liberalism appears to have failed in everything except increasing the divide between rich and poor, and the democratic deficit. In addition, various governments and regimes, hampered by debt and structural adjustment – thus crippling their ability to provide necessary social services to the most vulnerable constituencies – also appear increasingly emasculated in a foreign policy context that has led to a virtual loss of one land (Palestine) and a recolonization of another (Iraq).

Into this vacuum and seeming chaos, the relative certainty of the unchanging religious texts (and those who speak in its name) is alluring. Where governments offer no mobilizing collective ideology and appear remote from people's needs and wants, religious spokespersons elucidate the justice and inherent communal welfare of the never changing Qur'ān. Where governments fail to provide basic social services, Islamists run schools and donate their expertise and time to clinics and hospitals that care for the poor and even provide stipends, pensions, and much more. And where governments appear undermined in political and military conflicts, religious extremists uphold the sanctity of martyrdom in the name of nobler causes. The fact that many Arab governments have also begun to use religious rhetoric means that religious discourse has become a normative form of social and political engagement.

In such a situation, women (and particularly women's bodies) become charged political and cultural symbols. In much the same way that the colors and placement of flags are meant to symbolize various issues, women's bodies also become symbolic of larger issues. In turbulent times, control over women, as the upholders of the honor and integrity of the community and the nation, stands as a potent signifier for political control.

Activists for women's rights in the Muslim world, together with those intellectuals arguing for both moderate Islamic and secular political dynamics, are always attempting to ward off criticisms from two sides: the religious right in their own countries (for whom they are never "authentic" or "Islamic" enough) on the one hand, and the Western right (seeing much of what takes place in the Muslim world as principally anti-Western) on the other. In this situation, a possible third way of thinking politically, socially, culturally, and economically in the Muslim world and amongst Muslim communities, is muted.

Religious discourse has an important role in Arab society. That is not, per se, problematic. Serious challenges are presented, however, in the shape of the abuse of the religious terrain as a result of local democratic deficits, global economic trends, and the subsequent utilization of women as a vehicle to express supremacy in turbulent times. An additional challenge is the inability of many political actors to distinguish between the various forms of religious engagement in the contemporary polity. Were such distinctions as those mentioned earlier made, and if the assumption that fundamentalist movements invariably result in the restriction of women's rights be questioned, there would be important opportunities for strategic alliances to be formed which could address pressing social, political, and economic concerns, while empowering significant sectors of the population.

Success stories have emerged through the realization by some activists that, regardless of their own personal convictions and/or feelings about religion, it continues to play an important role in the average person's life. One of the critiques most frequently leveled against secular women activists is their lack of knowledge of the religious texts, which can be a major hindrance in the process of arguing for certain kinds of social change. Qualified women scholars and activists now form a significant element of the women's movements, providing important advice and argumentation when necessary.

It is also becoming increasingly more evident (even palatable) to many women activists that to bring about social change, it is important to involve all actors in society, including men, but especially religious leaders. The experiences of Egyptian mothers married to non-Egyptian men, and those of Moroccan women in favorably amending their personal status/family laws, point to the importance of mobilizing the male constituency, both secular and – most importantly – religious.

BIBLIOGRAPHY

M. Afkhami and E. Friedl (eds.), *In the eye of the storm. Women in post-revolutionary Iran*, New York 1994.

H. Afshar, *Islam and Feminisms. An Iranian case study*, Houndmills, Basingstoke, U.K. 1998.

——, *Women and politics in the Third World*, London 1996.

D. Kandiyoti (ed.), *Women, Islam and the state*, London 1991.

A. Karam, *Women, Islamisms and state. Contemporary feminisms in Egypt*, New York 1998.

—— (ed.), *Transnational political Islam. Religion, ideology and power*, London 2004.

—— (ed.), *A Woman's place. Religious women as public actors*, New York 2001.

V. Moghadam, *Gender and national identity. Women and politics in Muslim societies*, London 1994.

M. Poya, *Women, work and Islamism. Ideology and resistance in Iran*, London 2000.

A. Saad-Ghorayeb, *Hizbullah. Politics and religion*, London 2003.

B. Winter, Fundamental misunderstandings. Issues in feminist approaches to Islamism, in *Journal of Women's History* 13:1 (2001), 9–41.

AZZA M. KARAM

Pakistan

Pakistan is part of a region where the sense of the spiritual is palpably present in ordinary people's lives. Islam is the shared identity of an otherwise heterogeneous, multiethnic, and multilingual country. Islam provides community, ethics, morality, and rituals, understood and practiced in myriad ways, not all of which are accepted by high, scripturalist Islam. Islam is a living oral spiritual tradition, an essential part of women's lives; they understand it in ways that help them make sense of their lives. In this context, a small minority of literate, urban, and relatively privileged women participate in or oppose the Islamist movement.

Islam as personal faith of the literate and the non-literate, Islam as a movement in opposition to oppressive regimes, and Islam as an oppressive theocracy are three distinct phenomena. While the last two in particular are male defined enterprises, Islam as faith may have the least confining or the most liberating potential for women. This potential fast declines in Islamist opposition movements and tends toward gross oppression in theocratic Islamist governments. Pakistan's government has vacillated between military dictatorship and civilian rule or a combination of the two. Ayub Khan (1958–69) liberalized family laws to make them slightly more equitable for women. Zia ul-Haq (1977–88) disenfranchised women to an alarming degree under the pretext of Islamization. The current military ruler, Pervez Musharraf, seems inclined toward undoing Zia ul-Haq's Hudood Ordinances but faces strong opposition from the Islamists within and outside the parliament. The Islamist movement and Islamist elements within the government generate a discourse of "liberation" of women from "Western ignorance." In a Muslim country with a colonial past and with deep sympathies for countries like Afghanistan, Iraq, and Palestine, anti-Western sentiment serves the Islamists well as women's liberation/feminism is presented as a ploy to further destroy the fabric of Muslim life.

Islamist activity revolves around two main axes, personal reform and political ascendancy. Personal reform is carried out through preaching (*daʿwa*) and creation of Islamized space entailing segregation, prayer, fasting, and veiling of women. It does not necessarily ask urban women to return to their homes but endeavors to separate them in public. Women are increasingly engaged in religious, cultural, and social life outside the private realm, but this has not led to a new model of womanhood. Conventional female virtues like modesty, obedience, and self-sacrifice in relation to children and family are still upheld even when women actively engage in public life in ways that were previously inaccessible to them. Political ascendancy entails will to gain political power based on the belief that Islam is the only true religion and that it requires governance according to God given and unchangeable laws. These laws mostly uphold male and Muslim supremacy, surveillance and control of Muslim women's lives, disenfranchisement of religious minorities, and criminalization of sexual minorities. Leadership in the name of God is the prerogative of Muslim men although women are not prohibited from participation at the lower levels.

The thrust of most Islamist movements is to keep women in a subordinate place even after they have gained access to means of self empowerment such as education and paid work in the public sector. Escape from freedom and escape from materialism are given as two reasons for women's willing participation in Islamist movements.

Women continue to be the object and primary victim of Islamist discourse in Pakistan. The so-called Islamization during Zia ul-Haq's military regime and now of the North West Frontier province focuses on reclaiming traditional male privilege, which may seem to be slipping away with the modernization and education of women.

In the vacuum created by a politically stifling and at times treacherous environment, which seriously curtails the possibility of free exchange of ideas between women of various persuasions, secular and religious, Muslim and non-Muslim, it is movements such as al-Huda, led by Dr. Farhat Hashmi, an Islamist female scholar/preacher, that take hold. Dr. Hashmi's organization has gained some following amongst the literate urban women in the major cities of Pakistan. She advocates *ḥijāb* and calls women to study the text of the Qur'ān for themselves. She makes the familiar claim that it is the male interpretations of the word of God which have subjugated and oppressed women, and that as women study the Qur'ān themselves they will be liberated. The study of Qur'ān in her centers is limited to a preliminary study of the meaning of the Arabic text in Urdu. Relative to the circumstances of the individual woman Hashmi's message may have some liberating elements. Hashmi's schools have provided a safe haven for modern educated and elite women who are seeking to hold onto a respectable traditional identity while integrating into a male workforce or enjoying the lifestyle of the privileged housewife.

The United States based Pakistani theologian Dr. Riffat Hassan has pointed out that Hashmi does not engage with any real issues of social and economic justice. According to Hassan this is a betrayal of a religion that takes egalitarianism and social justice very seriously. Hashmi, an Islamist and Hassan, a liberation theologian, both rally Muslim women back to an interpretation of a Qur'ān affected by their geographical and ideological location. Neither of them has formulated a cogent theological response to contemporary developments in historical critical studies of Islam.

The work of secular women activists and lawyers is another important context for discussing women and Islamist discourse in Pakistan. According to Hassan the shortcoming of the human rights activism and discourse is its anti-religious stance, which cannot gain root in a religious society like Pakistan. Hassan makes a distinction between a secularism that respects the individual's freedom of choice in matters religious and a secularism that is anti-religious. She considers the work of human rights activists and lawyers, such as Asma Jehangir, to be socially and politically irrelevant in Pakistan because of their "anti-religious" stance. In her critique of Jehangir, Hassan seems to confuse Islam as personal faith with Islam as a theocratic imposition. Hassan proposes that Jehangir assume an American-style religion-friendly secularism in a theocratic state like Pakistan and that she respect "freedom of religion" in a political context where there is very little freedom of religion. Since the almost theocratic Pakistan is a signatory to United Nations documents, in advocating for individuals' rights vis-à-vis the state, having recourse to international standards of human rights (as upheld in documents generated and endorsed by the United Nations) is a valid strategy especially when very few other options are available. On the other hand, discourses that draw on the liberating and empowering elements of the people's own heritage and beliefs may be most relevant and effective as means of empowerment at the grassroots level. However, these may not accord with Hassan's understanding of "ethical-normative" Islam, which she sees as the option that would bring desperately needed positive social change in Pakistan. Hassan's International Network for the Rights of Female Victims of Violence in Pakistan (established 1999), which maintains a chronicle of violence against Pakistani women, is secular and is not used by her as a vehicle for her feminist liberation theology.

The issue may not be how to convince ordinary Pakistani women that they deserve respect and fair treatment. They may already be convinced of it without any reference to either the Qur'ān or a United Nations document. The issue may be the question of how they empower themselves vis-à-vis the state and society.

Bibliography

Primary sources

K. Bhasin, R. Menon, and N. S. Khan (eds.), *Against all odds. Essays on women, religion, and development from India and Pakistan*, New Delhi 1994.

Z. Hasan, *Forging identities. Community, state and Muslim women*, Karachi 1996.

R. Hassan, *Woman and the Qur'an*, Utrecht, The Netherlands, 2001.

——, Islam and human rights in Pakistan. A critical analysis of the positions of three contemporary women, in *Canadian Foreign Policy* 9:2 (Winter 2002), 131–56, reprinted in *Dawn Review Magazine* (Karachi), 7 and 14 November 2002.

A. Jehangir and H. Jilani, *The Hudood Ordinances. A divine sanction? A research study of the Hudood Ordinances and their effect on the disadvantaged sections of Pakistan society*, Lahore 1990.

M. K. Masud, H. D. Shakeel, and H. Jaffery (eds.), *International conference on Islamic laws and women in the modern world*, Islamabad 1996.

K. Mumtaz and Y. Mitha, *Pakistan, tradition and change*, Oxford 1996.

A. Samiuddin and R. Khanam (eds.), *Muslim feminism and feminist Movement. South Asia*, ii, *Pakistan*, Delhi 2002

Secondary sources

K. Abou El Fadl, *Speaking in God's name. Islamic law, authority and women*, Oxford 2001.

Ibn Warraq (ed.), *What the Koran really says. Language, text, and commentary*, New York 2002.

——, *The quest for the historical Muhammad*, New York 2000.

H. Moghissi, *Feminism and Islamic fundamentalism. The limits of post-modern analysis*, London 1999.

L. Ziring, *Pakistan at the crosscurrent of history*, Oxford 2003

Ghazala Anwar

Sub-Saharan Africa

Islamism appeals to millions of women worldwide. The same is true in Sub-Saharan Africa, although expressions and content as well as reasons for adherence vary considerably. Islamist discourse in general finds itself in opposition to aspects of what is perceived and denounced as "Western" modernity. This modernity is characterized by social ills such as loose morality, materialism, substance abuse, alienation, and crime. Islamist discourse and action are directed against these ills: Islamists want to replace the corrupt modern order with an Islamic one, based on the revelation of God. The resistance to Western modernity is but one aspect of Islamism. In Sub-Saharan Africa in particular, Islamist reaction against "traditional" Islam makes for a second religious-ideological pillar. Sufi mysticism – the Islam of the majority of African Muslims – and the practice of saint worship, a widespread "traditional" Islamic practice, are considered as illegitimate innovations and in principle are heavily condemned by Islamists. The Islamist actions and discourse, however, must be contextualized in their particular local settings. Islamist leaders, groups, and individuals – men and women – operate in a given sociopolitical context that informs their actions. These are not everywhere the same. For example, African Islamists do not all hold the same position on the issue of women going out in public. Women will not necessarily join Islamist movements for the same reasons, nor do they always give their membership the same meaning or content. Women and men develop various strategies for negotiating space and power within a given society. Islam and Islamism are, like other institutions or ideologies, instrumental in this process of constant renegotiation.

Islamism has been credited for widening the scope of the participation of women in public life, religiously as well as intellectually. Mosque attendance, not common for women in Sub-Saharan Africa, is not an exclusively male practice any more. This is beginning to become noticeable in the architectural set-up of Islamist mosques throughout Africa, which explicitly provide space for women to pray. Old, traditional mosques only had a small space for elderly women; younger women stayed at home and prayed there (Cantone 2002). Islamist movements have been very active in the field of modern Islamic education, aimed at men and women. The Senegalese Islamist association, Jamaatu Ibadu Rahmane, successfully runs a number of primary and secondary schools in various parts of the country. These schools provide an innovative kind of Islamic education: they teach Islamic sciences, but also recognize the importance of "marketable skills," such as mathematics, computer science, and language education. About half of the pupils in the primary schools are girls. Through this Islamic education, acceptable even to more "traditional" Muslims who have not been particularly concerned with female education, girls are given independent Islamic knowledge as well as worldly skills they can usefully employ in later life

(Renders 2003). The result of the Islamist initiative in Senegal was that "traditional" Muslims, notably the potent Sufi brotherhoods, followed their example and started their own programs accessible to both boys and girls. In Nigeria, the late 1970s saw the start of the campaign for new Islamic education of the Islamist organizationYan Izala. A major reason for success of Yan Izala in Nigeria was their efforts to start schools and to advocate women's education. The same phenomenon can be seen in Eastern Africa (Loimeier 1997).

The most significant contribution of Islamism in comparison to traditional Sufi Islam seems to be the possibility for both Muslim men and Muslim women to gather and master religious knowledge independently. Women are enabled to participate more actively in the public sphere as Muslims in their own right. A woman submits herself directly to God, as a Muslim individual. She does not need an intermediary such as her father or her husband. In principle, she is an independent, thinking human being with direct access to religious knowledge. Islamist organizations organize Arabic classes for women, who will be able to study original sources independently. Sometimes religious material is provided in the local language, written or on audiotape, which makes the effort easier for women without formal schooling. Whereas in the traditional practice the Qurʾānic school laid the basis for the women's – very elementary – religious education, which was completed by her husband, now young girls can go to Islamic institutes before marriage (Taguem Fah 2002). An Islamist woman is by no means in all instances secluded – she is often able to lead an active social life and become a member of the Islamist associations. However, this does not mean that women have an actual role in the decision-making process of Islamist movements, which are invariably led by men. Women's authority in religious matters is also not valued equally with men's. Yet women's access to Islamic knowledge could potentially change the context in which sociopolitical interaction takes place.

Islamist women often have their own subgroups and associations, such as the Muslim Sisters Organization in Nigeria, the female branch of the Muslim Students Society (MSS). The MSS also participated in the formation of the Federation of Muslim Women's Association of Nigeria (Barkindo 1993). In the northwest of the now imploded Somali Republic, Islamist women have organized religious study groups. The members come together once a week, for example on Thursday night at the beginning of the weekend, to listen to a lecture by a shaykh, to watch a film or to read a book, and to discuss their findings and questions. Participants in the sessions are well-to-do and well educated, businesswomen, or even university graduates who have had an international experience. They are critical of traditional Somali Sufism, not so much in the theological sense, but rather in its social implications, notably the widespread male consumption of *qāt*, a mild narcotic leaf imported from Ethiopia. They argue that according to real Islam one has to be useful to society and denounce the men who sit down all day to chew *qāt* claiming it is "something religious" (Ali 2002).

In the process of political and social positioning of Islamist organizations, moral issues are often very prominent in the discourse. Women's issues are considered of paramount importance in the proper exercise of Islamic morality. Therefore, the Muslim woman and her perceived role and duties as a daughter, spouse, and mother are hotly debated issues. In fact, they have never before been so central to the discussions and controversies between different Islamic groups as well as between Islamist groups and the secular state. Family planning in particular is a bone of contention for Islamist movements. The 1994 United Nations conference on population and development held in Cairo provoked passionate reactions. A number of Muslim organizations chose at the instigation of the Senegalese government to participate in Réseau islam et population, an organization working to promote means of family planning – notably birth spacing – acceptable to Islamic scholars and the religious leaders of the Sufi brotherhoods. The Réseau caused a major stir-up, even within the organization itself, when they took the initiative of promoting the use of condoms in an AIDS awareness campaign. The actions of the Réseau are abhorred by the Islamists. To them, the only acceptable protection against AIDS is abstinence. In the case of married couples, birth control is not acceptable under any circumstance. The Islamist Jamaatu Ibadu Rahmane accused the government and the Sufi Muslim organizations of immorality and of collaboration with the vicious strategy of Western neo-Malthusianism. The "satanic programme geared at the depopulation of the planet" was attributed to Western fears of "new barbarian invasions" and "the pressure of feminist movements wanting to cause women to revolt by allowing them to decide by themselves about issues of procreation" (*Le Musulman* 1994, 4–5).

Yet, concerning other issues, the position of the Islamists is progressive compared to the opinions of other Muslim individuals and organizations. Female genital mutilation (FGM) is a widely accepted practice in the whole of Eastern Africa. Social pressure to perform the operation is very strong. In Somalia, where the prevalence of FGM approaches nearly 98 percent, it is Islamist organizations such as al-Ittihad and al-Islah who strongly condemn the practice and actively work against it. The Somalis practice the "pharaonic" variety of FGM (infibulation) resulting in serious risks for girls' and women's health. The Somali Islamists consider it forbidden in Islam to harm one's own body. Al-Ittihad women move around in public wearing a *burqaʿ*-like attire, with only a small space for the eyes. Sometimes they even wear stockings and gloves in the often extremely hot desert climate. But the girls do not have to undergo FGM. In Somalia, as elsewhere in Sub-Saharan Africa, it is this non-traditional attire of the women that distinguishes them visibly as members of Islamist groups. The practice of fully covering the head and body is in most instances a recent phenomenon, imported by the Islamists. Although in many Sub-Saharan regions Islam has been present for many centuries, the women did not usually cover their hair, except for prayer.

Where and under what circumstances a woman's honor – and therefore the honor of her male relatives – is considered to be in jeopardy is not univocally determinable. In some instances, mixing of men and women in public is problematic in the view of African Islamists. In others it is not: "Islamic" dress is viewed as sufficient to guarantee the prevention of vice. The prevailing approach varies and is likely to depend on a particular sociopolitical situation and context. In the case of Nigeria, in 1983 a number of Muslim politicians, including the leader of the Islamist Yan Izala, Abubakar Gumi, started a campaign for wider participation of women in Nigerian politics. This move was informed by the hope that a Muslim candidate would win the presidential election. Abubakar Gumi appealed to Muslim men to allow their wives and daughters to register for the election and to go out and cast their votes, for as Gumi phrased it: "politics is more important than prayer." His position was condemned by a number of his opponents as outright heresy. Yet Gumi took matters even further when he stated that the election was to be considered a jihad. Muslims had to protect their religion: if Muslim women did not vote, a non-Muslim would win. Eventually, a Muslim did win the election due to the mobilization of the Muslim women's vote. The same arguments were used again in the next local government election. On that occasion, the leader of Yan Izala in Kaduna declared that Muslim women could leave their houses without any problem, as long as they dressed properly. Men preventing their wives from registering for the vote would feel sorry afterwards, "because the wrong people would be voted to power" (Loimeier 1997).

In some cases Islamist movements have stimulated social emancipation among Muslim women. This emancipation is not really driven by Islamist ideology per se. On the one hand, women are recognized as Muslims able to acquire religious knowledge independently. On the other hand, the issue of morality in the Islamist discourse puts the greatest burden on women. It seems that the sociopolitical context and the power relations in a given situation are of paramount importance in determining Islamist discourse concerning gender issues. Women in Islamist movements also have to act within an existing context. Relations between men and women as well as among the women themselves within an Islamist organization is a matter of day-to-day negotiation. It is not unthinkable that Islamism in female branches of Islamist movements will ultimately develop its own dynamic. But this depends on what is possible in a given context and on the agency of the relevant actors – men and women – themselves.

Bibliography

Primary sources

Amran Ali, businesswoman, interview with the author, Hargeysa, 3 June 2002.

Le Musulman (journal of the Jamaatu Ibadu Rahmane) 47 (1994).

Secondary sources

B. M. Barkindo, Growing Islamism in Kano city since 1970. Causes, form and implications, in L. Brenner (ed.), *Muslim identity and social change in Sub-Saharan Africa*, London 1993, 91–105.

C. Cantone, Radicalisme au féminin? Les filles voilées et l'appropriation de l'espace dans les mosquées à Dakar, paper presented at conference on L'islam politique en Afrique Subsaharienne d'hier à aujourd'hui. Discours, trajectoires et réseaux, Université Paris VII Denis Diderot, 28–9 October 2002.

R. Loimeier, Islamic reform and political change. The example of Abubakar Gumi and the Yan Izala movement in northern Nigeria, in D. Westerlund and E. Evers Rosander (eds.), *African Islam and Islam in Africa. Encounters between Sufis and Islamists*, London 1997, 286–307.

M. Renders, Muslim organisations and the discourse of "development" in Senegal, in *Journal of Religion in Africa* 32:1 (2003), 61–81.

G. Taguem Fah, Pouvoir du savoir. Renouveau islamique et luttes politiques au Cameroun, paper presented at conference on L'islam politique en Afrique Subsaharienne d'hier à aujourd'hui. Discours, trajectoires et réseaux, Université Paris VII Denis Diderot, 28–9 October 2002.

Marleen Renders

Sudan

With a legacy of Sufi-inspired Mahdism in the nineteenth century and with Sufi-organized political sectarianism dominating northern Sudanese politics from that century on, Sudan's middle-class, modernist Islamist revolution of 1989, promulgated through a military coup d'état, can, in a number of ways, be seen as a model of an attempt to build a Sunnī republic. Significant aspects of its modernist character have been the mobilization of public consciousness of citizenship in an Islamic state and the conspicuous gendering of the processes involved.

Islamist women activists have been among the most politically active women in Sudan's history and were instrumental in the gaining of power by the Islamist regime. The National Islamic Front (NIF), the initial guiding party of the revolution, is an off-shoot of the Muslim Brotherhood (Ikhwān); women began their activism early within both of these movements.

In building an Islamic nation particular hegemonic strategies were developed. Among northern Muslims (Muslims comprising perhaps two-thirds of the population and unarguably being politically dominant) women have both been constructed and have constructed themselves as the woman citizen – Muslim, mother, teacher, student, socializer of Islamic values, political organizer, and militia member. State hegemonic strategies have involved the manipulation of gender and other identities, especially as these are manifested in the fashioning of this "new Muslim woman." Women have been fashioned through the media (especially television); the schools (where palpable changes in the curriculum have been made to accommodate the religious ideology of the state); the legal apparatuses (through the enforcement of particular aspects of Sharīʿa); and through community organizations, which were working to develop an "authentic" Sudanese culture, one based on Islamic identity that was to supersede Arab identity. In this way women could see themselves as oppressed in the past by Arab patriarchy but potentially liberated by Islam. Women's complicity in and resistance to these constructions are among the dynamics of contemporary northern Sudan.

The discourse that framed women within the Islamist movement was generated by both men and women and was contested, leading to societal debates about the roles of women. The leading ideologue of the NIF, Ḥasan al-Turābī, took a modernist and liberal approach to the role of women, arguing that the Islamic movement in Sudan had developed its own version of equality for women and was not reliant on the West for its ideas. He claimed that the Islamist movement presented no obstacles to women advancing or holding a position anywhere in society (Lowie 1993, 46–7). Women ideologues of the NIF, while also disavowing Western influence, nonetheless coopted some of the discourse of Western feminism. In framing women within Islamist discourse, activist Suʿād al-Fātiḥ al-Badawī distanced herself from the idea of separatist roles for men and women and opted for a complementarity approach, namely, that "men and women complete and perfect each other." Al-Badawī stressed the responsibility educated women have to raise the consciousness of others (al-Badawī 1986).

Of enormous interest to the Islamist regime was the gender division of labor, which ideologues and state officials were attempting to transform. In the post-independence period (after 1956) women had begun to move into most economic spheres and occupations. Because girls soon began to compete with and often outscore boys in the Sudan School Certificate examination, they were channeled into the most prestigious university faculties. By the 1980s conservative Islamists saw a distortion of a healthy gender division of labor that promoted Islamic values. When the NIF began its rise to power, the gender division of labor was re-evaluated and changes made. Women's activism within political Islam had first been in the schools as teachers of Islamic principles, as organizers and teachers within nursery schools set up in mosques, in neighborhood medical clinics, and in various Islamic charity organizations. Politicized religious women also permeated the ranks of various lower and middle-rung civil service jobs, taking over these jobs from dismissed non-*ḥijāb*-wearing liberal and leftist women. Once the NIF took power, Islamist women continued to move into the universities in large numbers, but were admitted into the fields sanctioned by the movement rather than other fields of study deemed inappropriate for women. Within the faculty of medicine, for example, women were encouraged to study general medicine and eschew such lucrative fields as surgery or even obstetrics.

The Islamist movement in Sudan, although a modernity project, fostered tight control over women's sexuality (for example, monitoring relations with men, controlling dress and public "moral" behavior, regulating birth control, forcing group weddings, and encouraging female circumcision) and positioned women in ways that served the regime. Women, for their part, both struggled against these assignments and collaborated in their creation.

BIBLIOGRAPHY
S. F. al-Badawī, article in *al-Ṣaḥāfa* (Khartoum), 3 May 1986, 10.
M. Badran, Khartoum's answer to Beijing, in *Al-Ahram Weekly*, 5–11 September 1996a.
S. Hale, *Gender politics in Sudan. Islamism, socialism, and the state*, Boulder, Colo. 1996.
——, "The new Muslim woman." Sudan's National Islamic Front and the invention of identity, in *Muslim World* 86:2 (1996b), 177–200.
A. L. Lowie (ed.), *Islam, democracy, the state and the West. A round table wth Dr. Hasan Turabi*, Tampa 1993.

SONDRA HALE

Turkey

Turkey is one of those countries where reaction against the ambivalent consequences of modernization assumed the form of identity politics, and where an Islamist movement pushed the Muslim woman's "covered identity" to the center of the debates surrounding secularism, modernization, and Westernization.

In the mid-1980s when civil society began to flourish in Turkey, Islamist women's groups also took their place among the numerous civil initiatives. Although part of a general Islamist movement that was an outlet to express political dissatisfaction caused by the sharp social, economic, and politico-cultural cleavages in the Turkish system, the Islamist women's groups had their own specificities. They organized primarily in defense of their right to wear headscarves, especially in the universities, and to promote an Islamic way of life in general. Women, supported by men, engaged in public demonstrations and boycotts, and the battle given in defense of the headscarf was interpreted as an act of protest by the general public against the secular state. The 1990s witnessed a new yet vigorous activism by these women who organized in the Ladies' Commissions of the (Islamist) Welfare Party. They contributed considerably to the electoral victories of this party both at the local (1994) and national (1995) levels by registering almost one million members to its ranks in six years. However, to their disappointment, women were pushed backstage immediately after the elections.

The activism of Islamist women was echoed in various publications, pamphlets, and books, which led to a heated debate over women's issues among themselves. It also drew the attention of non-Islamist women academicians and feminists resulting in a proliferation of academic work on Islamist women. Although very careful about not calling themselves "Muslim feminists" and always keeping their distance from feminism, which they claimed to be a Western import corrupting especially women, Islamist women nevertheless tried from within an Islamic framework to develop emancipatory agendas for women. Both female and male Islamist writers tried to steer a middle course between interpretations of sociopolitical and cultural realities (veiling and segregation, for example) of Islam and the universal human rights discourse. In their effort to assert that there is complete gender equality in Islam they pointed to the chasm between the message of the Qur'ān (egalitarianism) and the manner in which it is historically interpreted, and argued that it is "tradition tainted by Judaism" and not Islam as such that has oppressed women; thus a return to the sources – the Qur'ān and the *sunna* – was to be sought (Aktaş 1991, Akdemir 1991, Kırbaşoğlu 1991).

Islamist women's activism provided an opportunity for marginalized women to seek empowerment (Arat 1999, 89), yet it also demonstrated the limits of an identity politics based on religiously sanctioned biological essentialism of bodily difference. According to Islamist writers, gender roles were God given, therefore fixed and unchangeable; anyone attempting to change them or blur the boundaries between them was in rebellion against God and showed a "pathological *nafs* situation" (Hatemi 1991, 329). In the process of modernization, doubly burdened with wage work and family responsibilites, women had lost their identity as women and the only solution lay in reinforcing traditional gender roles. Therefore it was complementarity and not equality that women should demand. A prominent Islamist woman writer, Cihan Aktaş, argued that the feminist movement, in seeking equality with men and ignoring "women's *fitrat*," failed to acknowledge the importance of women's roles as mothers and homemakers; Islam had given woman the position of helpmate to man, not his enemy. Aktaş, while demanding a more active life for women and their right to enter the public domain, at the same time endorsed the concept of women's *fitna* (the destructive effects of woman's potential for creating discord in the community): "If women will be shut in the home, then what is the rationale for veiling and covering? Is this [covering] not the way to ensure women's participation in the social arena without her giving way to *fitna*?" (Aktaş 1991, 255).

Islamist women's struggle to question the fairness of republican secularism that excluded them from the public domain is part of women's general critique and contestation of the republican project of modernity, which failed to ensure full equal rights and responsibilities of citizenship for them. However, it was the view of the women's movement that gender inequality was not only due to the failure of the "liberal contract" but also to the deeply patriarchal religio-cultural context of the country. It was here that the Islamist and secular women parted ways. Islamist women stopped short of challenging the dominant patriarchal order, and moreover, "otherized" all women reluctant to accept an Islamic lifestyle. The body of the covered woman was declared "sacred" whereas that of the secular woman a "sexual object," and she was seen as an accomplice of the secular "lowly moral order" (Aktaş 1984, Gülnaz 1996, Çaha 1996).

Bibliography

F. Acar, Women in the ideology of Islamic revivalism in Turkey. Three Islamic women's journals, in R. L. Tapper (ed.), *Islam in modern Turkey. Religion, politics and literature in a secular state*, London 1991, 280–303.

S. Akdemir, Tarih boyunca ve Kuran-ı Kerim'de kadın, in *Journal of Islamic Research* 4 (1991), 260–70.

C. Aktaş, *Sömürü odağında kadın*, Istanbul 1984.

——, Kadının toplumsallaşması ve fitne, in *Journal of Islamic Research* 4 (1991), 51–9.

——, *Tesettür ve toplum*, Istanbul 1991.

Y. Arat, *Political Islam in Turkey and women's organizations*, Istanbul 1999.

——, Group-differentiated rights and the liberal democratic state. Rethinking the headscarf controversy in Turkey, in *New Perspectives on Turkey* 25 (Fall 2001), 31–46.

F. Berktay, Grenzen der Identitatspolitik und Islamistische Frauenidentitat, in B. Pusch (ed.), *Die neue muslimische Frau*, Würzburg 2001, 67–87.

——, Islamic concept of gender equality, in N. Arat (ed.), *Mediterranean women and democracy*, Istanbul 2002, 107–21.

A. Bulaç, İnsan, örtü ve medeniyet, in *İzlenim* (July–August 1995), 4–6.

Ö. Çaha, *Sivil kadın*, Ankara 1996.

R. Çakır, *Direniş ve itaat*, Istanbul 2000.

N. Göle, *The forbidden modern*, Ann Arbor 1996.

M. Gülnaz, Suyu tersine akıtanlar, in *Birikim* 91 (1996), 66–9.

H. Hatemi, İslamın kadına bakışı, in *Journal of Islamic Research* 4 (1991), 328–31.

A. İlyasoğlu, *Örtülü kimlik*, Istanbul 1994.

M. H. Kırbaşoğlu, Kadın konusunda Kuran'a yöneltilen başlıca eleştiriler, in *Journal of Islamic Research* 4 (1991), 271–83.

N. Narlı, Modernization, political Islam and women, in N. Arat (ed.), *Mediterranean women and democracy*, Istanbul 2002, 91–96.

A. Saktanber, Becoming the "other" as a Muslim in Turkey. Turkish women vs Islamist women, in *New Perspectives on Turkey* 11 (1994), 99–134.

Fatmagül Berktay

Political-Social Movements: Islamist Movements and Discourses and Religious Associations

Canada

The role of women in the rise and development of Islamic organizations in Canada is one of extraordinary and unique efforts owing to the wide diversity of people, cultures, races, languages, and ethnicities within the Muslim Canadian community and the Canadian mosaic at large.

The Islamic organization is the primary venue in which Muslims express and safeguard their identity. In 1963, Muslim university students founded the Muslim Students Association of the United States and Canada (MSA), consisting of 13 chapters across the United States. In 1967, the MSA encompassed 36 chapters across North America and by 1970 the number had risen to 68. The establishment of the MSA took place almost one century after Muslims first arrived in Canada. History records the first Muslim presence in Canada as Agnes and James Love, a Scottish couple who gave birth to the first Canadian Muslim child in 1854. The first wave of Muslim immigration began in 1880, and a second wave arrived following the First World War. The third and major wave of Muslim immigration came to Canada following the Second World War.

The multicultural nation-state par excellence fully welcomed the new waves of refugees and immigrants fleeing from repressive governments or simply seeking an opportunity for an enhanced life. Educational pursuits were swiftly fulfilled, jobs obtained, and Muslims contributed economically to the multicultural society. From a mere 13 Muslims in 1871 to 98,165 in 1981, and 579,640 in 2001, organizational bodies sprouted up across Canada revealing the Canadian Muslim presence, of which the first was the MSA.

In the initial stages of development of the MSA, most of the Muslim university students, predominantly international students, were men. (In Canada the MSA membership included, in addition to students, those immigrants who had already established themselves in the workplace). Consequently the executive committee was comprised of only men. Eventually, wives of the male MSA members became involved as members of the MSA in their own right. Most of the menial tasks in the MSA fell to women; these included assisting in the typing and editing of the first MSA publication, *al-Ittihad*, and organizing and founding numerous structured fundraising projects, such as the bazaar at each MSA Convention. Consequently, most of the financial resources of the MSA can be attributed to the efforts of its female members. The financial contribution in addition to other behind-the-scenes work of women formed the backbone of the historical movement.

In 1968, the MSA created a women's subcommittee as a means for female members to voice their opinions as well as to initiate projects within the organization. In 1972, Khadija Haffajee, of South African descent, was the first woman to lecture from an MSA platform. Subsequently, she rose to the position of Canadian Zonal MSA Representative for women in 1978, a position she held until 1986. During this period, she was the only woman present at the MSA National meetings in Canada. Furthermore, Haffajee was the first Canadian woman to become chairperson of the Women's Committee for MSA Continental in 1982. This position involved overseeing projects conducted mainly by women, which included developing educational literature and hosting religious learning circles and camps. These endeavors fostered some of the most prominent contemporary women activists in North America.

In MSA chapters that were dominated by foreign attitudes and/or cultural paradigms, women were not publicly or visibly involved. Nonetheless, in other chapters, women easily occupied advisory and/or executive positions, including that of president. This phenomenon is widely observed commencing in the 1990s when the children of those who came to North America in the 1960s and 1970s (the generation which initiated the MSA) entered university or college and became a predominant part of the MSA themselves (as first generation Canadians/Americans). Currently, in 2003, the Continental MSA Executive, which at one point was all male, consists of five women and three men, while a female president heads at least 25 percent of the MSA-affiliated chapters. However, maintaining a presidency position does not determine the extent and/or level of women's activism within the MSA since some women implement an equally strategic and active position by assuming a behind-the-scenes role.

As an increasing number of MSA members graduated to become professionals in their communities, it became apparent that a different type of organization was required. Thus the Islamic Society of North America (ISNA) was formed in 1983. From the onset, the organizational structure included a women's committee to oversee women-related issues through which female members participated in initiatives similar to those they were involved in within the MSA sphere. Haffajee became the first ISNA Canadian Zonal Representative of the women's committee from the beginning of ISNA's existence. In 1997, 13 years after ISNA's inception, Haffajee was elected as the first and only woman on the Majlis al-Shura, ISNA's highest decision-making body. Currently another woman, Dr. Ingrid Mattson, who is also a Canadian but resides in the United States, holds the position of ISNA Vice-President (USA).

The next stepping stone after the establishment of ISNA was the Muslim Youth of North America (MYNA), founded for the children of those in ISNA. This group, dedicated to youth in junior and senior high school, originated in 1985, partially as an initiative by the youth themselves. Females and males hold the positions of continental president or zonal representatives and thus travel to annual meetings and mobilize their respective regions, maintain executive positions, give lectures, and chair meetings. MYNA, similar to the MSA, falls under the umbrella of ISNA.

As a result of MSA's continued success and fortitude, numerous organizations evolved throughout the United States and Canada. In 1971, a handful of MSA members developed a study circle in order to intensify their Islamic education. Eventually, this study circle labeled itself the Islamic Circle of North America (ICNA). The founding members were both men and women with separate yet parallel executive bodies. The ICNA Ladies' Wing organizes activities for Muslim women across North America, such as Qurʾān and *ḥadīth*-based study circles, training camps, and programs to teach non-Muslims about Islam.

In 1997, an organization was founded with objectives and an organizational structure similar to that of ICNA, but dedicated solely to Canada: the Muslim Association of Canada (MAC). Currently women host separate executives but liaise at certain junctures with corresponding male members. However, women participate at almost every level of the association, such as maintaining positions in the National Convention and on the Board of Trustees, which are the association's highest bodies, as well as spearheading youth committees in which they are responsible for coordinating youth activities for both men and women.

As the Muslim community in Canada continued to grow, several Islamic organizations formed in order to present a more accurate portrayal of Islam and Muslims in Canada. The Council of American Islamic Relations (CAIR) was founded in the United States in 1994, with the launching of the CAIR-Canada chapter in 2000. Some of CAIR-Canada's tasks are to monitor local and national media in order to challenge stereotypes, work for human rights causes, host information seminars and workshops, distribute action alerts, and advance intercommunity relations. Dr. Sheema Khan, a woman activist, is the founder and current chairperson of CAIR-Canada and is thus responsible for overseeing all endeavors. The Canadian Islamic Congress (CIC) was formed in 1998 with constructive objectives such as to educate Canadians about Islam and Muslims, and to network with all levels of government, academia, and non-governmental organizations (NGOs). Wahida Chishti Valiante, a family counselor, is one of the founding members and vice president of CIC. While overseeing the various CIC initiatives, she lectures regularly at both national and international conferences, and is a published author of major research papers related to media and social work. CAIR and CIC executive members and members-at-large consist of men and women who may fulfill parallel roles within media-related organizations.

The contribution of Muslim women in the development of the *masjid* – a place for worship, education, community functions, and recreation – has varied across Canada since the establishment of the first mosque in Canada on 12 December 1938, founded and for which funds were raised by pioneer Canadian Muslim women, until the present day. This is primarily due to the diversity of people, cultures, races, and ethnicities within Islam and the Muslim community. In some mosques women maintain executive positions, chair meetings, organize events, and deliver lectures, whereas in other mosques these roles are uncommon. The imam, the governing council of the mosque, and/or cultural differences play a major factor in determining how a woman may contribute within the mosque.

Canadian-based Muslim women's organizations such as the Canadian Council of Muslim Women (CCMW 1982) and the Federation of Muslim Women (FMW 1997) serve as catalysts for Muslim women to attain a voice within the larger Islamic movement and the Canadian community as a whole. These organizations mirror identical objectives and maintain a similar role to the MSA and ISNA women's subcommittees that presided in the early years of the two organizations.

The role of Muslim women in the development of the Islamic organizations in Canada is one of remarkable and diverse endeavors. Women have assisted in building a dynamic Islamic Canadian community with over 650,000 Muslims. It represents the history of a people who wish to maintain a proper decorum between men and women yet simultaneously align with the community at large. Despite the challenges created by numerous cultures, languages, races, and over 60 ethnicities within the Muslim community, Islam provides a democratic environment for a multiplicity of views to be thoroughly discussed. Canada, a country propagating multiculturalism, is a genuine land of opportunity in which to practice Islam in its purest form.

In conjunction with the chosen mandates of each organization and mosque, Muslim women on mosque executive committees and within core Canadian Islamic organizations utilize the Qur'ān and the *sunna* as their model for activism. This influential and formidable activism mirrors outstanding and influential women at the time of the Prophet who participated in the rise and development of every dimension of the Prophet's society.

Bibliography

O. B. Abdullah, Springboard to a reality, in *Horizons* (May/June 2003), 43–53.

O. Alam, Women in MSA. From leaders on campuses to leaders in communities, unpublished paper.

S. Ali, Birthing a movement, in *Horizons* (May/June 2003), 18–19.

——, The founding mothers, in *Horizons* (May/June 2003), 20–1.

S. Azmi, Canadian social service provision and the Muslim community in metropolitan Toronto, in *Journal of Muslim Minority Affairs* 17 (1997), 153–66.

J. Badawi, *Gender equity in Islam. Basic principles*, Plainfield, Ind. 1995.

A. Bewley, *Islam. The empowering of women*, London 1999.

R. Bothwell and J. L. Granatstein, *Our century. The Canadian journey*, Toronto 2000.

M. D. Bryant, Some notes on Muslims in Canada and the USA, in *Hamdard Islamicus* 24 (2001), 7–10.

K. Bullock, *Rethinking Muslim women and the veil*, Herndon, Va. 2002.

Y. Y. Haddad, *A century of Islam in America*, Muslim World Today Occasional Paper No. 4, Washington, D.C. 1986, reprinted in *Hamdard Islamicus* 21:4 (1997), 1–12.

Y. Y. Haddad and J. I. Smith (eds.), *Muslim communities in North America*, Albany, N.Y. 1994.

D. H. Hamdani, Muslims and Christian life in Canada, in *Journal Institute of Muslim Minority Affairs* 1 (1979), 51–9.

——, Muslims in the Canadian mosaic, in *Journal Institute of Muslim Minority Affairs* 5 (1984), 7–16.

——, Canada's Muslims. An unnoticed part of our history, in *Hamdard Islamicus* 20 (1997), 97–100.

——, Canadian Muslims on the eve of the twenty-first century, in *Journal of Muslim Minority Affairs* 21 (1999), 197–209.

——, A century of Islam in Canada, in *Horizons* (May-June 2002), 18–22.

——, Muslims and Islam in Canada, in M. M'Bow and A. Kettani (eds.), *Islam and Muslims in the American Continent*, Beirut 2001. See also <http://muslim canada. org/cdnmuslm.htm>.

A. Kettani, *Muslim minorities in the world today*, London 1986.

A. W. Lorenz, Canada's pioneer mosque, in *Aramco World* 49 (1998), 28–31.

A. Lotfi, Creating Muslim space in the USA. Masājid and Islamic centers, in *Islam and Christian-Muslim Relations* 12 (2001), 235–54.

Y. al-Qaraḍāwī, *Markaz al-mara' fī al-ḥayā al-Islāmiyya*, Amman 1996.

Nadira Mustapha

Political-Social Movements: Millenarian

South Asia

Islam, as a religion of revelation, began as an apocalyptic movement anticipating the Day of Judgment, and retains apocalyptic and millennial elements to this day, especially in Shia theology, but also in many forms of popular religiosity. In particular, the *mujaddid* tradition, that foresees a "renewer" at every century turn (A.H.), appears to constitute – before the century has turned – a form of apocalyptic messianic expectation in the coming of the hidden Mahdī. South Asian Islam, however, in comparison with other parts of the world, has not been particularly renowned for the presence of millenarian movements. This absence of significant millenarian tendencies in South Asia can be linked, on the one hand, to the strong Sufi and syncretic traditions that have flourished for much of the period since Islam was introduced to the subcontinent in the early eighth century C.E. On the other hand, South Asian Islam has also encompassed a tradition of reform movements, which have sometimes acted as powerful vehicles for Islamic renewal and resurgence. It is, therefore, in the context of these kinds of reforming impulses that millenarian-style trends have periodically surfaced.

The millenarian idea that divine or supernatural intervention will bring about a reversal of worldly expectations resulting in an earthly paradise tends to appeal to those who are dispossessed both culturally and economically. This has been the case in South Asia where such movements have arisen during periods of great social or political uncertainty, or during crises of one sort or another. However, unlike other parts of the so-called Muslim world, these millenarian impulses did not necessarily revolve around a central Mahdī figure. All the same, they were usually associated with charismatic male leaders, whose leadership skills proved essential to the dynamics of the movement, as reflected in the title of *mujaddidi-i* (renewer of the faith) by which they often came to be known. The millenarian movements that made the greatest impact in South Asia emerged from the eighteenth century onwards, and were often linked with the concept of jihad (holy war), thus involving some degree of popular uprising directed at the overthrow of infidel power, which was regarded as essential if the Islamic community were going to be able to renew its strength and vigor. Inevitably perhaps, bearing in mind the gender norms associated with South Asian Muslims during this period, it is virtually impossible to find concrete evidence of female involvement in such movements, but, as with any populist uprising, it is possible that female sympathizers backed their male relatives' participation by looking after affairs at home while the men carried on the struggle elsewhere. The problem is to identify such activity in the patchy source material that is available.

Early Mahdist movements, with millenarian associations, were connected with the completion of the first one thousand years of the Muslim era. In South Asia, they took definite form through the teachings of Mīr Sayyid Muḥammad of Jaunpur in the later fifteenth century C.E., who claimed that a voice from heaven had whispered to him "Thou art the Mahdī." Other Mahdīs emerged during this period in different parts of the subcontinent, but, on the whole, they were educated men who possessed great oratorical power as preachers, tended to be hostile to established elites at court and within the ranks of the *ʿulamāʾ*, and claimed to be renovators of Islam, that is *mujaddidūn*. Perhaps the best known example of this millenarian tendency was Shaykh Aḥmad Sirhindī (1564–1624), given the honorific title of Mujaddid-i alf-i thānī (Renewer of the second millennium). As a young man he learned the fundamentals of Sufism from his father. Later he was initiated into the Naqshbandī order. Toward the end of his life, his reputation as "renewer of the faith" was established when he was viewed by his followers as the renovator expected to arrive at the beginning of the second millennium after Muḥammad on account of his efforts to purify Islam and restore its traditional orthodoxy. His stand against what he perceived as anti-Islamic practices in India helped to bring about a religious renaissance. To counteract the forces of heresy, which he believed had been encouraged by the religious innovations associated with the Mughal Emperor Akbar, he sent trained disciples out to towns and cities across the subcontinent in order to propagate what he regarded as the true spirit of Islam. How far his ideas penetrated the world of Muslim women remains impossible to quantify, though it is known that he married a woman belonging to a noble family and that it was through personal links and correspondence with noblemen and courtiers that he was able to bring some pressure to bear on the court of Akbar's successor, Jahāngīr.

The shaykh fought for the suppression of all innovation (*bidʿa*) introduced into Islamic culture, but, on the whole, his exhortations to this effect were general and rarely attacked specific deviations. However, in one letter, addressed unusually to an anonymous Sufi woman, he did elaborate on the innovations peculiar to Muslims in India, and attributed many of them to the greater tendency of women than men to perform blameworthy actions. Utter stupidity on their part, he claimed, meant that women prayed to stones and idols and asked for their help to such an extent, especially at such times of crisis as when smallpox struck, that virtually all Indian Muslim women were involved in polytheistic practices of one sort or another. Likewise, their celebration of Hindu festivals such as Diwali, and their insistence on sacrificing animals at the tombs of Sufi saints, meant that they had violated the conditions upon which the Prophet Muḥammad had accepted the "pledge of the women" (*bayʿat al-nisāʾ*). As was the case with many Islamic reformers of this and subsequent periods, lapses in correct behavior on the part of Muslim women were held responsible for much of what was perceived to be wrong with existing Muslim society.

By the middle of the eighteenth century, mounting pressure on Muslim interests in South Asia helped to produce a further round of millenarian-style movements. During this period, the might of the Mughal Empire was steadily eroded by the rise of various indigenous successor states and the encroachment of European influence. Faced with crisis on a massive scale, Muslim intellectuals in centers of Muslim power such as Delhi grappled with ways of responding. In Delhi, Shāh Walī Allāh (1703–62), like Shaykh Aḥmad Sirhindī, believed himself to be a *mujaddid*, charged with purifying Islam from the accretions that he believed were responsible for its political weakness. Again, like his predecessors, while he came from a Sufi tradition and had been initiated into the Naqshbandī, Chishtī, and Qādirī orders, Shāh Walī Allāh was highly critical of tomb worship and the veneration of saints. Since Muslim women remained closely associated with these populist forms of Islamic practice, it can be deduced that such thinking must have played a large part in marginalizing and undermining central aspects of their spiritual lives, devaluing to a great extent the authority that they could exercise in relation to the rhythms and nature of religious practice within their families and communities.

While Shāh Walī Allāh's thinking had an enormous impact on intellectual developments within north Indian Islam and influenced a wide range of later reformers, it was his "successors" in the nineteenth century who translated this thought into action in the shape of a number of millenarian-style protest movements. Again, however, the evidence for how these movements affected women's lives is very sparse, and the conclusions that can be drawn are largely conjectural. The best known nineteenth-century movement was that associated with Sayyid Aḥmad Shahīd of Rae Bareilly (1786–1831) who studied for a period of time in Delhi under the guidance of Shāh Walī Allāh's son, ʿAbd al-ʿAzīz Dihlawī. A charismatic personality, he acquired influential supporters who were attracted to his emphasis on pure *tawḥīd* (monotheism) as well as to his opposition to "saint worship" and social customs such as excessive expenditure on marriages and the Hindu-like taboo against widow remarriage that had developed among many Indian Muslims. Here again, it was on aspects of women's lives in particular that the spotlight of reform was turned, though, as yet, there has been no academic study undertaken to explore the specific consequences of this movement from either a female or a gender perspective. It is, however, now well established that reform movements across the spectrum at this time focused much of their effort on making Muslim women into "better" Muslims, since they were regarded by many reformers as holding the key to community renewal.

Upon his return from performing pilgrimage (*ḥajj*) to Mecca in 1821, the Sayyid began to prepare for a jihad, which was launched in 1827, against the Sikhs in northwestern India. His defeat and death at Balakot in 1831, however, did not put an end to his Mujāhidīn movement, which persisted for decades against the British presence, with his followers often known as Wahhābis on account of alleged connections with the Arabian movement of the same name. British perceptions that Wahhābis played a key role in the Mutiny of 1857 intensified efforts to control the movement, and two major Wahhābi trials were held in Amballa and Patna in 1864 and 1870 respectively. Meanwhile, the related Farāʾidi movement led by Ḥājjī Sharīʿat Allāh (1781–1840) developed in Bengal during the same period with similar priorities of fighting against rites and rituals influenced by Hindu customs. Sharīʿat Allāh declared British India to be a *dār al-ḥarb* (land of war) and, therefore, permitted no community prayers either on Fridays or on the occasion of religious festivals. How far this particular proscription would have influenced women's lives, however, is debatable since the vast majority of Muslim women in South Asia have rarely prayed outside their homes. His son Dūdū Miyān (1819–62) organized his father's movement further by sending out agents into the Bengali countryside, where their protest frequently merged with resentment against richer landowners who tended to be Hindus, endowing it with an element of class conflict. All the same, these reformers laid special emphasis on eradicating particular rituals, such as forbidding drums and dancing girls at the marriages of villagers' daughters. Likewise, a short-lived rebellion in Bengal in the early 1830s, led by Tītū Mīr, who may have been a disciple of Sayyid Aḥmad Shahīd, targeted landowners who, to restrain his activities, had imposed a tax on the beards of his followers, a distinguishing mark among Muslims and hence a very provocative move. In the official court records that document the trial of Tītū Mīr's followers in 1832–3, there is no evidence of active involvement on the part of women, though the imprisonment and exile of male family members must undoubtedly have had had a significant effect on their lives.

One further development that exhibited millenarian-style affinities in South Asia was the Aḥmadī movement, which emerged at the end of the nineteenth century. While it is generally accepted that it arose as a protest against the success of Christian proselytization, as well as in response to the perceived decadence of prevailing Islamic mores, its founder, Mīrzā Ghulām Aḥmad (1839–1908) claimed to have received a revelation at the start of the fourteenth century A.H. authorizing him to receive allegiance as the promised Messiah and Imām Mahdī, that is, the apocalyptic savior who according to Muslim tradition will appear at the Day of Judgment. His claims earned the persistent enmity of the general Muslim community, which branded him a heretic and labeled members of the Aḥmadī movement as non-Muslims. However, the involvement of middle-class urban supporters, who formed the nucleus of the so-called Lahore branch when the movement split around 1914, meant that this section became noted for its liberal, modernizing tendencies. This was reflected in the emphasis that was placed on educating women and setting up schools for girls, constituting a fairly radical move in the context of early twentieth-century Muslim South Asia. On the other hand, the so-called Qadian section remained more traditional, strictly enforcing purdah and encouraging polygamy. The Aḥmadī movement remains, to this day, characterized by these apparently contradictory trends with respect to the lives of its female members.

BIBLIOGRAPHY

A. Ahmad, The political and religious ideas of Shah Waliullah of Delhi, in *Muslim World* 52 (1962), 22–30.

Q. Ahmad, *The Wahabi movement in India*, Calcutta 1955.

Y. Friedmann, *Shaykh Ahmad Sirhindi. An outline of his thought and a study of his image in the eyes of posterity*, Montreal 1971.

——, *Prophecy continuous. Aspects of Ahmadi religious thought and its medieval background*, Berkeley 1989.

P. Hardy, *The Muslims of British India*, Cambridge 1972.

K. W. Jones, *Socio-religious reform movements in British India*, Cambridge 1990.

M. A. Khan, *History of the Fara'idi movement in Bengal (1818–1906)*, Karachi 1965.

——, *Titu Mir and his followers in British Indian records (1831–1833 AD)*, Dacca 1980.

D. N. MacLean, La sociologie et l'engagement politique. Le Mahdawiya indien et l'état, in *Revue des mondes musulman et de la Mediterranée* 91–94, *Mahdisme et millenarisme en islam*, ed. M. Garcia-Arenal, Paris 2002, 239–56.

B. D. Metcalf, *Islamic revival in British India. Deoband, 1860–1900*, Princeton, N.J. 1982.

——, *Perfecting Women. Maulana Ashraf ʿAli Thanawi's* Bihishti Zewar, Berkeley 1990.

A. Powell, Duties of Ahmadi women. Educative processes in the early stages of the Ahmadiyya movement, in A. Copley (ed.), *Gurus and their followers. New religious reform movements in colonial India*, New Delhi 2000, 128–56.

A. Schimmel, *Islam in the Indian subcontinent*, Leiden 1980.

W. C. Smith, *Modern Islam in India*, Lahore 1963.

M. T. Titus, *Islam in India and Pakistan*, Serampore 1959[2].

B. Wilson, Millenialism in the comparative perspective, in *Comparative Studies in Society and History* 6 (1963), 93–114.

SARAH ANSARI

Turkey

The concept of the millennium was transformed in the Islamic world under the influence of remnants of Central Eastern and Judeo-Christian mythology into a type of Messianism known as Mahdism.

In Turkish history, from the thirteenth to the twentieth centuries, there were a number of Mahdist uprisings, two of which, the Bābāʾī revolt in 1240 in the Seljuk period and the Shaykh Badr al-Dīn revolt in 1416 in the Ottoman period, were of particular importance as regards both their immediate and subsequent effects. Apart from these two revolts there were also other Mahdist uprisings on a smaller scale. The Timurtash revolt in 1321 during the Seljuk period, the growth of underground opposition to the Ottoman government among the Bayramī Melāmīs in the sixteenth century, the Shahqulu (1511), Nur ʿAlī Khalīfa (1512), Bozoklu Djalāl or Shāh Walī (1520), and Shāh Qalandar (1527) revolts, some of which had links with the

Safavid State, as well as the armed Qizilbash Turkmen rebellion, the Sakarya Shaykh, and the Urmiye Shaykh in the time of Murad IV (seventeenth century), and finally the Sayyid ʿAbd Allāh (1668) revolts were all in the Mahdist tradition.

As for the republican period, the Menemen incident in 1930 might be regarded as another example, but as this incident was somewhat different in character and was closely associated with the domestic political opposition of the day, it is rather doubtful whether it can be classed as a truly Mahdist revolt.

Apart from the Shaykh Badr al-Dīn revolt, almost all the Mahdist uprisings during the Ottoman period were in the nature of rebellions waged by the nomadic Turkmen tribes against the central government's policy of the enforced adoption of a settled lifestyle and subjection to taxation. In Turkish history, Messianism has always acted as the ideological motivation for revolts against the central political government based on the social and economic discontent felt by the periphery. The local administrators sent by the central government had a significant share in the causes of these rebellions. Indeed, they could be said to have provoked the revolts by their refusal to recognize the people's beliefs, customs, and traditions and by the dislike or even contempt they displayed for their ways of life. An individual would emerge – usually from among the Turkmen *baba*s who were their religious leaders – proclaim himself as the Mahdī and summon the people to revolt, whereupon the Turkmen, with their great devotion toward these religious leaders, who were sometimes also heads of the tribes, would have no hesitation in joining in the rebellion. As a result of the hard way of life to which they were exposed in the steppes of Asia Minor, the Turkmens who took part in these movements represented a group in which women played as important a part as men in everyday life. Thus it was that these Mahdist uprisings, composed mainly of nomadic Turkmens, were afforded very great support by the participation of women at every level. Anatolian epics such as *Kitāb-i Dede Korkut* and *Dānishmend-nāma* contain episodes illustrating the heroic deeds of the nomadic Turkmen women. These episodes show that some of these women enjoyed a high social status in the tribes to which they belonged.

It is well known that in Central Asia in the eleventh and twelfth centuries, the followers of Aḥmad-ı Yasawı included a large number of women and that, although it is not regarded as generally acceptable in Islam, these women performed religious rites together with men. Moreover, Baba Ilyās-i Khorasānī (d. 1240), a Wafāʾiyya shaykh in Anatolia in the thirtheenth century who took a leading part in the Bābāʾī revolt, is known to have performed rites with a congregation composed of both men and women. Ottoman archival documents reveal that in mystical circles Turkmen women could even act as *tekke* shaykhs. Turkmen women belonging to these circles, some of whom may well have taken part in the Mahdist uprisings, are known to have formed a recognized group referred to in one of the early Ottoman chronicles (*Âshikpashazâda tarîkhi*) as Bajiyān-i Rūm (Anatolian sisters). Although we have very little detailed information regarding the nature of these groups, Ottoman archival records prove that there is no doubt of their existence. In these records we find mention of women sheikhs with the title *bājī* or *khātun*, such as Fāṭima Khātun, Bülbül Khātun, Hajjī Fāṭima, Bājī Ana, Fāṭima Ana, and Akhī Fātima. Hagiographic sources also attest to the existence in mystical circles in Anatolia of a group of women of this kind. A very good example of this is Fāṭima Bājī, who was close to Bektāsh-i Walī, the eponymous founder of the Bektāshī religious order. Fāṭima was given the title *bājī* because of her position as a female *awliyya*, greatly honored in Bektāshī tradition. The view proposed by some scholars that these *bājī*s were the wives of members of two very important mystical groups referred to in Ottoman records as *Akhīyān-i Rūm* and *Abdālān-i Rūm* may well contain a great deal of truth.

Bibliography

Ö. L. Barkan, Kolonizatör Türk dervişleri, in *Vakıflar Dergisi* 2 (1942), 279–304.
U. Firdevsî, *Velâyetnâme-i hacı Bektaş-ı velî*, Istanbul 1953.
Kitāb-ı Dede Korkut, ed. M. Ergin, Ankara 1964.
F. Köprülü, *Türk edebiyatinda ilk mutasavvıflar*, ed. O. Köprülü, Ankara 2003⁹.
I. Melikoff, *La geste de Melik Danişmend. Etude critique du Danişmendname*, 2 vols., Paris 1960.
İ. Mevlânâ, Jāmiʿ al-meknūnāt, Istanbul University Library, İbnü'l-Emin, MS no. 3263, vv. 49b–50b.
Müneccimbaşı, *Sahāʾif al-akhbār*, iii, Istanbul 1285, 436–8.
J. Muṣṭafā (Qoja Nishanji), *Tabaqāt al-Mamālik wa darajāt al-masālik*, ed. P. Kappert, Wiesbaden 1981, 384b.
A. Y. Ocak, XVI yüzyıl Osmanlı Anadolu'sunda mesiyanik hareketlerin bir tahlil denemesi, in *V. Milletlerarasi Turkiye Sosyal ve Iktisat Tarihi Kongresi Bildirileri*, Ankara 1989, 817–26.
Â. Paşazâde, *Osmanoğulari'nın tarihi*, ed. K. Yavuz and M. A. Y. Saraç, Istanbul 2003, 298.
İ. Peçevî, *Tārīkh-i peçevī*, i, Istanbul 1283, 120–2.
A. Refik, Osmanlı devrinde Râfızîlik ve Bektaşîlik, in *Istanbul Universitesi Edebiyat Fakultesi Mecmuasi* 9 (1932), 21–59.
Khwāja Saʿd al-Dīn, *Tāj al-tawārīkh*, iii, Istanbul 1280, 162–81.

Silahdar Mehmed Pasha, *Tārīkh-i Silahdār*, i, Istanbul 1928, 334–5.
H. Sohrweide, Der Sieg der Safaviden in Persien und seine Rijckwirkungen auf die Schiiten Anatoliens, in *Der Islam* 15 (1965), 145–86.
A. Tchelebi, *Menākıbu'l-qudsiyye. Baba İlyas-ı Horasanī ve sülalesinin menkabev tarihi*, ed. I. E. Erünsal and A. Y. Ocak, Ankara 1995.
Ş. Tekindağ, Şahkulu Baba Tekeli isyanı, in *Belgelerle Türk Tarihi Dergisi* 3 (December 1967), 34–9 and 4 (January 1968), 54–9.

Ahmet Yaşar Ocak

Political-Social Movements: Peace Movements

Central Asia

This entry is about women, gender, and the peace movements in Central Asia. Women have made substantial contributions to peacebuilding and conflict resolution in the five Central Asian states of Kazakhstan, Kyrgyzstan, Turkmenistan, Tajikistan, and Uzbekistan as they have worldwide. International recognition of women's peacebuilding role is a recent phenomenon (Marshall 2000), and much of the recent global attention paid to it has focused on the post-Soviet republics because of their numerous and varied conflict zones. This has been concomitant with the tremendous focus by global development organizations and local non-governmental organizations (NGOs) on "civil society" in the region.

During Soviet times, women political actors were virtually by definition part of state institutions such as the Soviet Women's Committee (Reardon 1993, 123). While Soviet communist ideals were egalitarian and called for women's participation in government, the women who did assume leadership roles were generally not allowed to address concerns, including peacebuilding, that might threaten the state.

Women's post-Soviet peacebuilding contributions have taken place in the context of the transition from centralized Soviet to republican state control and from a stridently socialist political system to new state structures to varying degrees both socialist and capitalist. In this new milieu, the percentage of women participating in government has decreased in many categories. At the same time, a "third sector" NGO culture has flourished in which women have assumed active leadership roles.

That women are "naturally" associated with peace and men with war has long been seen as self-evident both in Western society and globally, and this is still accepted unquestioningly by some feminists (for example, Reardon 1993). But opponents of this view call it unnecessary essentializing (for example, Smith 2001). In Central Asia, the importance of women in non-governmental activism seemed curious to a Western observer given the strong traditions of patriarchy in the region, who then noted that such avenues allowed women leadership opportunities not available to them elsewhere in the society (Klose 2000). Structures of governance that exclude women, then, may do as much to encourage them to promote peace through NGOs as local ideas about proper gender roles discourage them from entering government institutions.

Many Central Asian NGOs focus on conflict prevention, conflict resolution, and peacebuilding either exclusively or as part of a broader platform. In a few cases women's opportunities for activism lie within organizations that predate independence but that operate with new leeway. For example the Women's Association of Tajikistan, founded during the final years of the Soviet Union, has been active in post-conflict efforts focused on identifying needs and coordinating government assistance following the 1992–7 civil war (Schoerberlein-Engel 1997, 225). For the most part, however, the post-Soviet NGOs represent a new kind of women's activism, much of it endeavoring to promote peace outside state channels at a grassroots level, and often with funds from international donors.

There have been only two major conflicts in the post-Soviet Central Asian republics in contrast to the adjacent Caucasus, in which several major conflicts have taken place. Islamism has played a role in both cases, pitting Muslims against other Muslims. In the civil war in Tajikistan, "neo-communists" and "Islamists" sparred, and in Uzbekistan the Islamic Movement of Uzbekistan waged a campaign against the government in 1999 and 2000 in an attempt to create an Islamic state (Roy 2002). Both movements have now been curtailed, especially since the United States began its "war on terrorism" and removed the Islamist Taliban in neighboring Afghanistan from power.

While major conflict has been rare, many areas of small-scale and potential conflict exist in Central Asia. Most are ethnically delineated. In Uzbekistan, for example, the state aspires to mono-ethnicity and has vigorously promoted Uzbek identity to the consternation of its non-Uzbek population, which includes ethnic Tajiks and Russians (Liu 1997). In the Ferghana Valley, divided awkwardly between Uzbekistan, Kyrgyzstan, and Tajikistan, complex border disputes, many with histories rooted in the early twentieth century, are ongoing (International Crisis Group 2002). Extra-regional state actors are also highly influential; Iran, Turkey, and Russia all vie for influence, as do mainly Western multinational corporations seeking to exploit the region's rich oil and gas reserves (Olson 2001).

Contributions by women acting through NGOs have included local activism inspired by international conflict resolution methods, such as in the case of a rural women's group in Kyrgyzstan that participated in advocacy training, which it used to appeal to the local land commission to change a land redistribution system it regarded as unjust (Estes 2000). In Kazakhstan, an NGO called the Centre for Effective Gender Policy conducted a needs assessment and found violence and sexual harassment to be the most common problems young women face (International Federation of University Women 2001); in identifying these problems, the NGO addressed aspects of violence that since the 1980s have been recognized by the United Nations as part of the definition of "peace" (Gierycz 2001, 15–16). Work on discrimination and violence toward women has also been carried out by the Almaty Women's Information Center in Kazakhstan (Center for Civil Society International 1998). Such activity is a vital starting point in efforts toward peace of all kinds in societies with high rates of gendered violence; one study found that in Tajikistan, 67 percent of women were "regularly exposed to some form of violence in the home" (United Nations Development Fund for Women 2003).

The Kyrgyz NGO Foundation for Tolerance International, which was founded and is headed by a woman, works toward the prevention and resolution of inter-ethnic conflicts in cross-border areas. It monitors conflict situations, organizes mediation processes, and conducts training exercises (Joan B. Kroc Institute for Peace and Justice 2003).

At the United Nations-sponsored Commonwealth of Independent States Regional Workshop in Almaty in 1999, participants recognized a "shared responsibility for the peacefulness and prosperous future" of the region in response to "the senseless horrors and tragedies of war" (Karat Coalition 2003). Across Central Asia, women are rising to this challenge and taking responsibility for the peace and prosperity of their societies.

BIBLIOGRAPHY

Center for Civil Society International, *Almaty women's information center*, Seattle 1998, <http://www.civilsoc.org/nisorgs/kazak/awic.htm>.

V. Estes, Lessons in transition. Gender issues in civil society development, in E. K. Klose (ed.), *Give and take. A journal on civil society in Eurasia*, Washington, D.C. 2000, 5–6.

D. Gierycz, Women, peace and the United Nations. Beyond Beijing, in I. Skjelsbaek and D. Smith (eds.), *Gender, peace and conflict*, Thousand Oaks 2001, 14–31.

International Crisis Group, *Central Asia. Border disputes and conflict potential*, Osh/Brussels 2002.

International Federation of University Women, UNIFEM uses the technology to support women in LDCs, *Global Perspective* (Geneva) 8:2 (May/June 2001), <http://www.ifuw.org/gs-0601.htm>.

Karat Coalition, *The priority of women from Central and Eastern Europe and the Commonwealth of Independent States*, Warsaw 2003, <http://www.karat.org/achievements/beijing_statements1.html>.

E. K. Klose, The third sector. A place of opportunity for women, in E. K. Klose (ed.), *Give and take. A journal on civil society in Eurasia*, Washington, D.C. 2000, 3.

Joan B. Kroc Institute for Peace and Justice, *Women PeaceMakers program. 2003 Women PeaceMakers biographical abstracts*, San Diego, Calif. 2003.

M. Liu, The perils of nationalism in independent Uzbekistan, in *Journal of the International Institute* (Ann Arbor, Mich.) 4:2 (Winter 1997), <http://www.umich.edu/~iinet/journal/vol4no2/uzbek.html.

D. R. Marshall, *Women in war and peace. Grassroots peacebuilding*, Washington, D.C. 2000.

R. Olson, *Turkey's relations with Iran, Syria, Israel, and Russia, 1991–2000. The Kurdish and Islamist questions*, Costa Mesa 2001.

B. Reardon, *Women and peace. Feminist visions of global security*, Albany, N.Y. 1993.

O. Roy, Islamic militancy. Religion and conflict in Central Asia, in M. Mekenkamp, P. Van Tongeren, H. Van De Veen, and G. R. Tinterow (eds.), *Searching for peace in Central and South Asia. An overview of conflict prevention and peacebuilding activities*, Boulder, Colo. 2002, 97–108.

J. S. Schoerberlein-Engel, Overcoming the ravages of Tajikistan's civil war, in M. M. Cernea and A. Kudat (eds.), *Social assessments for better development. Case studies in Russia and Central Asia*, Washington, D.C. 1997, 199–225.

D. Smith, The problem of essentialism, in I. Skjelsbaek and D. Smith (eds.), *Gender, peace and conflict*, Thousand Oaks 2001, 32–46.

United Nations Development Fund for Women (UNIFEM), New York 2003, *Tajikistan quick facts*, <http://www.womenwarpeace.org/tajikistan/tajikistan.htm>.

DIANE E. KING

South Asia

The role of women in peace movements in South Asia began with women's participation in national liberation movements from the early twentieth century. Two developments of the nineteenth century particularly helped Indian women's entry into the formal political space. These were the social reform movements fostered by men such as Ram Mohan Roy and Iswar Chandra Vidyasagar, and the growing popularity of movements that challenged British imperialism. Women participated in the "Extremist Movements" in the late nineteenth and early twentieth centuries and took part in acts of extreme violence. It was Mohandas Karamchand Gandhi who perceived a direct and peaceful political role for women in large numbers.

Gandhi launched his massive non-violent non-cooperation movement in 1919 and encouraged the participation of women in it. Thousands of women responded to his call. Gandhi urged women to be peaceful in their demonstrations as they were the repositories of "moral force." However, Gandhi never challenged the essentially patriarchal structure on which Indian society was built. He also used Hindu symbols to encourage women to participate in the movement, thereby furthering the polarization of politics on the basis of religion. Female leaders such as Sarojini Naidu emphasized harmony and comradely cooperation between men and women in the struggle for freedom from British rule. Apart from Gandhi, the communist movement also brought women into mass politics. Women from the Communist Party including Manikuntala Sen, Renu Chakravarty, and Ela Reid actively participated in humanitarian activities during the infamous Bengal famine of 1942. They espoused the view that humanitarian work and political work were one and same.

After India, Pakistan, Bangladesh, and Sri Lanka became independent, women made claims on the formal political space. Although some of them assumed leadership roles that in no way feminized the political space. The protracted Tamil and Singhala conflict in Sri Lanka, the Sindhi Mohajir (Muslims who came from India during partition) problems in Pakistan, the Indian state's conflict with Muslims in the Kashmir valley and with indigenous people in Northeast India, and the Bangladesh government's conflict with the Jumma (tribal) people in the Chittagong Hill Tracts (CHT) brought women to the forefront of activities for conflict resolution and peace. Mothers' associations epitomized women's peacemaking roles in South Asia. In the Sri Lankan conflict there were at least four mothers' associations at different times. Even in the Indian context there were the Naga Mothers who made remarkable progress in their movement for peace.

The mothers' associations in South Asia appeared mainly in the 1980s. Both the Naga Mothers Association (NMA) and the first Mothers' Front in Sri Lanka were started in 1984. These were the result of women's spontaneous peaceful protest against protracted violence in their own societies. None of these women's groups were created to intervene in peace politics. The NMA had its birth in women's social protest against alcohol abuse and the Mothers' Front was created to protest against disappearances in the region. Both these groups appropriated gender roles to make space for their entrance into mass politics. They appealed as mothers to warring factions to stop violence. Motherhood allowed them to speak for peace with authority in a situation of tremendous aggression. One of the first pamphlets published by the NMA was entitled *Shed No More Blood*. Although the NMA has survived till today the Mothers' Front disappeared after a few years. One of the main reasons for the disappearance of the Mothers' Front in Sri Lanka was that its members could not get support from either the state or the rebels. The NMA survived because both the warring factions considered its survival to be crucial to the politics of peace in the region.

In the CHT the Hill Women's Federation (HWF) took up the mantle of peace. They protested against abuse of the Jumma people including illegal arrests, kidnapping, killing, and rape. The HWF found a platform in the emerging women's movement in Bangladesh and came together with it over the disappearance of Kalpana Chakma, a leader of the HWF. The government of Bangladesh signed an accord with the Jumma people in 1997. With the growing strength of Islamic political parties in Bangladesh women's peace initiatives of both Bengali and tribal women are now under severe threat.

Women's peace movements in South Asia have traditionally utilized the gendered roles of womanhood. Appeals made on the basis of gendered roles such as motherhood have often led to positive results for women in peace politics in South Asia. It is true that none of the women involved in peace movements challenged the patriarchal social structure. But unlike the Mothers' Front in Sri Lanka, the NMA retained their relevance in politics through a number of radical activities. They tried actively to negotiate for peace not just between the state and the Naga communities but also between different tribal groups. They actively campaigned for women's rights to inherit landed property. They also tried to build bridges between communities. Unlike the Mothers' Front, the NMA resisted efforts by political parties in conflict to subsume their agenda. For their efforts in peacemaking they enjoyed the honor of being the first South Asian women's group to sit on a ceasefire negotiation.

Among women's groups for peace in the urban areas in South Asia are Women in Peace in South Asia (WIPSA), and Women in Security, Conflict Management and Peace (WISCOMP). Although these groups make appeals for peace on the basis of their femininity, they do not espouse gendered roles such as motherhood. They consciously distance themselves from being identified with any particular ethnic or religious communities. These groups concern themselves more with interstate conflicts, such as that between India and Pakistan, rather than intra-state conflicts. They are also vociferous critics of the nuclear program of India and Pakistan. In Sri Lanka a few such women's groups campaigned successfully for women's participation in ceasefire negotiations.

Women's peace movements are largely issue-based in much of South Asia. Different women's groups for peace come together on the same platform in moments of crisis. The one common aim of these groups is to fight against the marginalization of women through adherence to personal law. The Shah Bano case in India brought women's groups together to protest against Muslim personal law. Women's peace movements were losing much of their fervor when the riots against the Muslim population in Gujarat brought them together once again. There was widespread protest against growing fundamentalism in the region and an effort was made to build up a regional women's movement for peace on the platform of opposing all anti-feminist laws and ordinances such as the Hudood and blasphemy laws in Pakistan and the growing popularity of Hindutva in India. The greatest challenge to such movements is delivered by women's groups belonging to the extreme right, such as women in the Jamaat-e-Islam in Pakistan and Bangladesh and the Sangh Parivar in India.

One of the main contributions of South Asian women's peace movements is that they define peace in much larger terms than merely the end of war. Many of these groups, both secular and religious, speak of peace with equitable distribution of resources among all segments of the population. They are severely critical of the growing militarization of the region. However, a major defect in South Asian women's peace movements, both rural and urban, is that they are unable to disassociate themselves from their communities. Peace movements across communities, such as women's groups within the Pakistan India People's Forum for Peace and Democracy, often have a socialist orientation. These are the movements that are fighting against fundamentalism and radical nationalisms in the region. They are making an effort to build bridges across communities but their efforts are as yet in the nascent stage.

BIBLIOGRAPHY

P. Banerjee, Peace initiatives of Naga women, in *Canadian Women's Studies* 19 (Winter 2000), 137–42.

M. Burguières, Feminist approaches to peace. Another step for peace studies, in *Millennium. Journal of International Studies* 19:1 (1990), 1–18.

U. Butalia, *The other side of silence. Voices from the partition of India*, New Delhi 1998.

CIDA (Canadian International Development Agency), *Gender equality and peacebuilding. A draft operational framework*, Ottawa 1998.

R. Manchanda (ed.), *Women, war and peace in South Asia. Beyond victimhood to agency* New Delhi 2001.

G. Shangkham, Naga women and the peace process, in *Kohima News Letter*, 8 June 2000, 1–8.

Women's Coalition for Peace, Statement I and II in *Nivedini* 6:1 (1998), 195–9.

Women's Initiative, *The green of the valley is khaki. Women's testimonies from Kashmir. A report by Women's Initiative*, Bombay 1994.

WSRC (Women's Studies Research Centre, Guwahati University), *Women in the North East. Challenges and opportunities in the 21st century*, Guwahati 2002.

PAULA BANERJEE

Turkey and the Caucasus

This entry is about women, gender, and the peace movement in Turkey and the Caucasus, where women peace activists are responding to conflicts that have disrupted the lives of millions and killed thousands of people. Armenia and Azerbaijan have sparred over Nagorno-Karabakh. In Georgia, several separatist movements and boundary disputes flared in the 1990s. Chechens, aided by non-Chechen Muslim fighters from a diverse array of countries, have been fighting a war against Russia that is both separatist and Islamist. In Turkey, Kurdish separatists have fought government forces in a secularist, Marxist bid for autonomy, and Turkey has strained relations with several of its neighboring states. These and the histories of other conflicts, of the grievances of their participants, and prospects for peace are diverse. Exacerbating factors include ethnic, nationalist, and territorial assertions, religion, and designs by both local and international entities on the rich oil and gas reserves in the region.

Despite this diversity and complexity, peace movements by women have emerged that cut across ethnic, religious, and political categories. Non-governmental organizations (NGOs) and government agencies focus on mobilizing people for peace, and a significant proportion of these have been initiated and are headed by women. One observer claims that approximately 60 to 70 percent of Azerbaijani NGOs, many of which promote peace, are headed by women (Bickley 2000). Women's NGO participation is highly visible in the surrounding states as well. It is likely that the conflicts in the Caucasus and Turkey have attracted more female than male protest. For example the Conflict Research Center, an independent organization in Baku headed by a woman, promotes civil society (Davis 2000). In

Georgia, the Tiblisi-based Caucasus Women's Research and Consulting Network (CWN) educates people about gender inequalities and socialization. Most of its representatives are minority women (Reimann 2001, 41).

Global/local peace activism

Most facets of the peace movement of women in Turkey and the Caucasus involve practical efforts such as the networking of activists, the promotion and implementation of community development programs, and political lobbying. They also, although less frequently, take on the form of public protest, as exemplified by the activities of 100 Chechen women who blocked the main highway between Grozny and Ingushetia to draw attention to Russian aggression (Islam Online 2002), or anti-war protests in Turkey during the weeks leading to the coalition war against Iraq in March 2003 during which activists, many of them women, held marches, rallies and other anti-war events in Turkish cities to protest at the entry of the Turkish military into the war (Altınay 2003).

International concern for democratization and the promotion of civil society has prompted support for grassroots peace efforts by women from the United Nations, international NGOs, and Western government agencies. Local women activists who succeed at the local level are frequently offered support that enables them to ramp up previously small-scale efforts and to initiate new ones. For example, the Regional Bureau for Europe and the Commonwealth of Independent States (RBEC), a division of the United Nations Development Programme (UNDP), initiated the Regional Programme in Support of Gender in Development in Central Asia, the Caucasus and Turkey. This has provided an umbrella for regional meetings such as "Women's Rights are Human Rights: Women in Conflict," which brought together peace activists from 13 countries in 1998 (UNDP 1998). Similarly, the Women Peacemakers Program of the International Fellowship of Reconciliation (IFOR) holds training sessions for women peacemakers; in 2003 it convened workshops in Armenia and Azerbaijan (IFOR 2004).

Historicizing the peace movement in the Caucasus and Turkey

In the three autonomous Caucasus states of Georgia, Armenia, and Azerbaijan as well as the independent northern Caucasus republics of the Russian Federation, the legacy of former control by the Soviet Union is profoundly influential. Kemalist ideology wields influence of a similar magnitude in Turkey. These historical forces strongly affect current peace movements by women and have yielded a number of ironies. For example, gender inequity and gendered violence are prevalent throughout the Caucasus and Turkey despite strong emphasis throughout most of the twentieth century by the governments of both Turkey and the Soviet Union on equality for women. Women activists thus are faced with overcoming profound social barriers to their leadership, but can simultaneously appeal to egalitarian discourses already familiar to their hearers. Similarly, the Soviet system, which yielded an increase in women's literacy from 10 percent in 1926 to around 100 percent in the 1960s (Akiner 2000, 124), gave women in the Caucasus the educational background they would later need for organizing in new political environments that are in large part more tolerant of grassroots activism than were the Soviets. However, without the lifting of centralized, imposed Soviet control, many of the current conflicts against which peace activists campaign might not have occurred in the first place (Cornell 1997).

While many of the conflicts in Turkey and the Caucasus have taken on a new character during the past two decades, in nearly every case the etiology of hostilities can be traced to at least the early twentieth century. For example the Turkish state's aspirations to mono-ethnicity, which belie the ethnic diversity found in it (Andrews 1989), have been strong since its founder Mustafa Kemal Atatürk espoused them. Ethnic conflicts in Turkey and its Ottoman predecessor state have taken place on a variety of scales, the grandest being between Turks and Armenians during the late nineteenth and early twentieth centuries, and the state and the PKK (Partiya Karkerên Kurdistan, Kurdistan Workers' Party), a Kurdish rebel movement that carried out a violent campaign against the state during the 1980s and 1990s. Women in Turkey have consistently stepped forward to oppose violence as a solution. Peace Mothers Initiative was founded during the PKK war by mothers of PKK fighters. Its members called upon both parties to end the conflict (İstanbul Sosyal Forumu 2004); some have reportedly endured torture (Amnesty International 2000). The Turkish Mothers Association, an association founded in 1959 which focuses on the advancement of women and children (Turkish Mothers Association 1998), also called for an end to the PKK conflict.

Enmity between Turkic and Armenian peoples has a long history in the Caucasus as well as in Turkey itself. A major clash took place in Baku in

1905 (Fraser et al., 655) and hostilities continued into the First World War. This was followed by several decades of relative quiet under Soviet control. From 1988 to 1994, the two sides engaged in open warfare over Nagorno-Karabakh, and although a cease-fire has been in place since 1994, the conflict remains largely unresolved. Women on both sides have responded with peace efforts. For example, in 1999 a group of women from Azerbaijan and Armenia, both of which had a history of activism at the local level, were involved in founding the Women Waging Peace initiative with backing from a United States foundation that has sponsored similar initiatives elsewhere. Azeri and Armenian members of Women Waging Peace have worked to promote peace over Nagorno-Karabakh both locally and in national and international forums (Women Waging Peace 2004).

The dilemma of the naturalized association of women with peace

A longstanding association of women with peace and men with conflict persists in the popular discourse of diverse societies and among activists and analysts of peace movements. This portrayal and the dilemma that it presents have been the subject of numerous recent articles on the subject of peace movements and conflict resolution by academicians and activists. Tickner (2001, 21) offers this summary of the dangers: "Besides the obviously problematic slide into distinctions such as good women/bad men, the association of women with maternal qualities and peacemaking has the effect of disempowering both women and peace and further delegitimating women's voices in matters of international politics."

In an article in which she touts women's strength in conflict resolution due to their "already existing roles" but also points out some of the dangers associated with such generalizations, Anderson (1999) cites several examples from the Caucasus and Turkey, including the "practical" work of the IDP Women's Association of Georgia in bringing Georgian, Abkhazian, and Ossetian children together at summer camps, and the revival in the 1990s of an old custom whereby women waved white scarves to intervene in the Armenian-Azerbaijani conflict. Among women peace campaigners in the Caucasus and Turkey, the deployment of women's "traditional" roles and already-existing networks seems to have more legitimizing than marginalizing power. A Turkish woman leader in the peace movement in Cyprus noted this, pointing out that when bi-communal peace groups started to grow in the 1990s and were eventually shut down by government authorities, they targeted the women's peace groups first. She theorized that the women's groups were more threatening to the authorities than mixed-gender groups (Uludağ 1999).

Whether they continue to use the social capital uniquely afforded to them by their gender, or decide to downplay "tradition" in favor of less gender-bound expressions, ongoing conflicts ensure that women peace activists in Turkey and the Caucasus have plenty of work yet to do.

Bibliography

S. Akiner, Emerging political order in the new Caspian states. Azerbaijan, Kazakstan and Turkmenistan, in G. K. Bertsch, C. Craft, S. A. Jones, and M. D. Beck (eds.), *Crossroads and conflict. Security and foreign policy in the Caucasus and Central Asia*, New York 2000, 90–128.

A. G. Altınay, What will the Turkish government remember as it votes on the war this week?, New York 2003, <http://www.peace-initiative-turkey.net/AAltinay.doc>.

Amnesty International, Public AI index. EUR 44/55/00. UA 319/00 Torture/ill-treatment 19 October 2000, Library. Online documentation archive, <http://web.amnesty.org/library/Index/ENGEUR440552000?open& of=ENG-IRQ, London 2000>.

S. Anderson, Women's many roles in reconciliation, in European Centre for Conflict Prevention (ed.), *People building peace. 35 inspiring stories from around the world*, Utrecht 1999, 230–6.

P. A. Andrews, *Ethnic groups in the Republic of Turkey*, Wiesbaden 1989.

C. Bickley, Gyulyum. Azeri college friends found NGO, find new opportunities, Initiative for Social Action and Renewal in Eurasia (ISAR), Washington, D.C. 2000, <http://www.isar.org/isar/archive/GT/GT8irada.html>.

S. E. Cornell, Conflicting identities in the Caucasus, in *Peace Review* 9 (1997), 453–9.

S. Davis, *Eurasia insight. Women waging peace in the Caucasus*, New York 2000, <http://www.reliefweb.int/w/rwb.nsf/0/ed0fc625c73644588525687b006ba5da?OpenDocument>.

N. Fraser, K. W. Hipel, J. Jaworsky, and R. Zuljan, A conflict analysis of the Armenian-Azerbaijani dispute, in *Journal of Conflict Resolution* 34 (1990), 652–77.

IFOR (International Fellowship of Reconciliation), Women Peacemakers Program, in WPP home, Alkmaar 2004, <http://www.ifor.org/WPP/>.

Islam Online, Chechen women block highway to protest arrests by Russian army, News, 2002, <http://www.islamonline.net/English/News/2002-07/18/article04.shtml>.

İstanbul Sosyal Forumu, Proposal to the ESF, Istanbul 2004, <http://www.sosyalforum.com/English/proposal.htm>.

C. Reimann, *Towards gender mainstreaming in crisis prevention and conflict management. Guidelines for German technical co-operation*, Eschborn 2001.

J. A. Tickner, *Gendering world politics. Issues and approaches in the post-Cold War era*, New York 2001.

Turkish Mothers Association, About T.M.A, Ankara 1998, <http://www.geocities.com/ turkander/>.

S. Uludağ, Strategies for women in peace-building, in Women and armed conflict list archive, 1999, <http:// www.sdnp.undp.org/ww/women-armdconf/msg00071.html>.

UNDP (United Nations Development Programme), Summary of the sub-regional conference. Women's rights are human rights. Women in conflict, Baku 1998, <http://www.undp.uz/GID/eng/AZERBAIJAN/SEMINARS/report.html>.

Women Waging Peace, Armenia/Azerbaijan, Women waging peace, Cambridge, Mass. 2004, <http://womenwagingpeace.net/content/conflict_areas/armenazer.asp>.

DIANE E. KING

Political-Social Movements: Protest Movements

The Balkans

This entry describes the participation of Muslim women in two different protest movements, each of which, in its own way, affects the social and political behavior of women in the Balkans. The entry focuses primarily on Bosnia-Herzegovina but includes, in a broader context, Serbia, Montenegro, Macedonia, and Kosovo. The first protest movement is the controversy surrounding the unveiling of women – the removal of the *zar* and *feredža*, as the traditional women's costume in the region is called. The second, more recent, is the public protest by the women of Srebrenica who are calling for the truth about their menfolk who have been missing since the mass murders at the United Nations safe area of Srebrenica in 1995. The removal of the *zar* and *feredža* encourages Muslim women to participate in public and economic life. The protest of the women of Srebrenica is indicative of changes in the way Muslim women react to the problems they face and the way these problems are articulated in public. This is all the more significant since it is happening among poorly educated rural women brought up in the traditional manner.

Unveiling

The unveiling of Muslim women in the Balkans was a long and contentious process, the early signs of which were to be seen when the issue of the emancipation of Muslim women was first raised. At various times, different groups were involved: male Muslim intellectuals, men and women associated with the Communist Party and its agenda, and members of the legislature, who concluded the matter by passing a law banning the wearing of the *zar* and *feredža*. The process that had begun with the debates of 1878 ended with the enactment of the law in September 1950. It was accompanied by public polemics, propaganda, and actions in support of the unveiling of women, but also by resistance by both women and men – traumatic experiences that left their mark in the memories of women and in unrecounted history.

The first stage of this dynamic process extended from 1878 to 1918, and was characterized for Muslims by the encounter with different cultural and civilizational values and with capitalism at the start of Austro-Hungarian rule. Changes to their way of life put the spotlight on the position of Muslim women. The traditional way of life, the view of gender roles, and the understanding of religion prevented Muslim women from taking an active part in the new social and economic trends. Arguments over the status of women, the education of Muslim women, their manner of dressing, and the response to new challenges were largely conducted by men, Muslim intellectuals whose views met with condemnation from conservative circles.

The second stage lasted from 1918 to 1941. With the end of the First World War, the debate over the status of Muslim women took on a sharper edge. The open confrontation of two opposing views continued: one advocating the unveiling of women, education for girls and women, and women's involvement in public and social life, and the other rooted in traditional, conservative views of the status of Muslim women which kept them home- and tradition-bound. The debate was accompanied by the publication of works interpreting Islamic teachings as posing no obstacle to the education of women and their participation in public life, and calling for the emancipation of Muslim women in line with the demands of modern life. This standpoint was upheld by Rāʾis al-ʿUlamāʾ Čaušević, whose understanding was that religious precepts were not contrary to the unveiling of women and who was openly of the opinion that Muslim women could be seen in the streets with their faces unveiled. Typically, at that time the issue was reduced to the veiling or unveiling of women and public debate between men.

In the final stage, 1941 to 1950, women began taking an active part in the process, which was now conducted within the ideological matrix of communism and the equality of the sexes in the process of class liberation and equality of rights. The activities of Muslim women cannot be considered in isolation from the women's movement as a whole in Bosnia-Herzegovina and Yugoslavia at the time. Women were actively engaged in every aspect of the war of national liberation, and were also active in urging Muslim women to become involved in changing their own position by attending literacy classes and forming various associations and groups. Organized action to unveil women began in 1947 and used propaganda involving both women and men. This propaganda presented the *zar* and *feredža* as symbols of backwardness, lack of education, and inequality. The actions led to the passing of the law banning the wearing of the *zar* and *feredža*.

Studies dealing with women's experience of unveiling have drawn attention to the culture shock experienced by women. The abrupt shift from one form of outward appearance to another was accompanied by adverse feelings, including confusion, disorientation, and the sense of being exposed to external pressure – these were particularly marked among the uneducated rural female population.

In conclusion, it can be said that the *zar* and *feredža* were the symbols on which appeals for changes to the rights and status of Muslim women in society were focused. Although it was not primarily a women's protest, from the very outset it altered the way of life of Muslim women in the region, and met with resistance from both women and men. Among men, resistance took the form of attempting to retain the traditional, male-dominated society. Among women, it was an expression of their disorientation and confusion when confronted with changes to their way of life. The outcome was that women emerged from the private sphere, becoming involved in the economic domain and education, and made themselves heard in public.

The mothers of Srebrenica

The movement launched by the mothers of Srebrenica began following the fall of the United Nations safe area of Srebrenica and the mass killings of men and boys in 1995. It brought together Muslim women, mainly from rural areas and with little education, in their efforts to find out the truth about the atrocities committed in Srebrenica and the fate of their missing family members. This women's organization should be viewed not only through the lens of the reasons for their coming together and protesting, but also as a new political phenomenon. It was not part of Muslim tradition in this part of the world for women to come together and protest openly, in public. Just as their unveiling was seen, in its day, as showing themselves in public contrary to their culture and tradition, so their public protest and revelation of their feelings were forms of expression inappropriate to the cultural tradition of Muslim women. Brought together by shared tragedy, they went beyond the traditional reaction to tragedy – a dignified silence, in the home, with the least possible outward manifestations – and came out on the streets with placards calling for the truth and accountability. By making their presence felt and constantly reminding the public of what had happened, they made sure that the tragedy of Srebrenica was not relegated to the sidelines.

Compared with women in the early years of the twentieth century, who had no right to speak out in public and political life, the women of today (with all their limitations in regard to political and public experience, level of education, and civic participation) have become a political factor. They are calling for local and international politicians to be held to account, and showing themselves willing and able to become actively involved in matters that affect their own lives. These activities have been supported by other women's and human rights groups in the region.

Bibliography

Primary Sources

M. Begović, *On the position and responsibilities of Muslim women with regard to Islamic teachings and the spirit of the times* [in Bosnian], Sarajevo 1931.

S. Penava, Sources and references for problems concerning the emancipation of Muslim women in Bosnia-Herzegovina [in Croatian], in *Prilozi* 18 (Sarajevo 1981), 273–84.

Secondary Sources

V. Bogičević, *Literacy in Bosnia-Herzegovina from the origins of Slav literacy to the end of Austro-Hungarian rule in 1918* [in Bosnian], Sarajevo 1975.

For or against unveiling [in Serbo-Croatian], in *Reforma*, a periodical launched by young people in early 1928 which campaigned for the unveiling and emancipation of women.

O. N. Hadžić, *The Muslim issue in Bosnia-Herzegovina* [in Serbo-Croatian], part 1, repr. from *Obzor*, Zagreb 1902.

A. Hotić, *Causes of the decline of the Islamic peoples* [in Serbo-Croatian], Bos. Novi 1913.

S. Kačar, *Women's narratives* [in Serbian], Podgorica 2000.

A. Studnička, *What do the Muslims of Bosnia-Herzegovina need to secure a better future?* [in Bosnian], Sarajevo 1906.

——, *Record of Islamic educational survey* [in Bosnian], Sarajevo 1911.

Đ. beg Sulejmanpačić, *A proposal for the resolution of the question of our Muslim women* [in Bosnian], Sarajevo 1918.

Newspapers

Novo doba (published by the Muslim Central Committee), *Nova žena* (published by the Antifascist Front of the Women of Bosnia-Herzegovina), *Sarajevski dnevnik*, *Oslobođenje*, *Borba*, *Ženski svijet*.

Jasna Bakšić Muftić

The Caucasus and Central Asia

Women's protests in Central Asia and the Caucasus are embedded in the context of history, socioeconomics, politics, and gender. In spite of women's participation in the political and economic development of Central Asia and the Caucasus, gender roles still place women in the domestic arena. Within current contexts, women protestors utilize their gender roles as mothers to confront regional regimes. This produces new cultural frames for viewing local women as public women, protectors of men.

Central Asia is a cultural and geographic area of five countries situated in close proximity: Kazakhstan, Tajikistan, Uzbekistan, Turkmenistan, and Kyrgyzstan. They are linguistically similar (except Tajikistan), share Islamic religious beliefs and practices, a common history, and internal ethnic diversity. Prior to the nineteenth-century Russian conquest all were a part of Turkestan, and then between 1920 and 1990 a part of the Soviet Union until independence in 1991. All these countries experience local economic decline and vast unemployment. They share quasi-democratic, totalitarian regimes, which persecute political and Islamic opposition. Uzbekistan has enacted harsh laws against religious and secular opposition. Currently, 7,000 detainees are charged with religious and antigovernment activities in the country (HRWWR 2002). Fearing imprisonment, local men are reluctant to protest in the streets. Hoping that they will not be dealt with as harshly as men, local women become publicly active as a way of protecting their male relatives (UDD 2002).

The Caucasus, another cultural and geographic area, includes Armenia; Azerbaijan and Nagorno-Karabakh; Georgia and its three "entities" of Abkhazia, Ajara, and South Ossetia; and the Checheno-Ingush Republic (Chechnya). Although religio-cultural diversity characterizes the region, these administrative entities are united by close proximity to each other and a common historical and sociopolitical background. Conquered by Russia by the nineteenth century, these areas became a part of the Soviet Union. While some republics (Georgia) became independent at the end of the twentieth century, others (Chechnya) are still disputing their administrative relationships with Russia. Politically, these areas are "anocracies," transitional between autocracies and democracies (Marshall 2003, 17). Unlike Central Asian states, the Caucasus has an active opposition, a relatively free press, and a vibrant political life (for example, Azerbaijan). At the beginning of the twenty-first century, the Caucasus suffered from socioeconomic and political instability, due in part to the influx of thousands of refugees, and infrastructural damage resulting from unresolved regional conflicts. Chechnya, a predominantly Muslim republic, has been in armed conflict with Russia for a decade (1994–6 and 1999–2003). During this conflict, Chechen civilians continued to "disappear" while in the custody of Russian Federal troops (HRW 2002). Often left as the sole heads of their families, women in these areas take to the streets to prevent further persecution of their male relatives.

Historically, albeit inconspicuously, women participated in the sociopolitical life of Central Asia and the Caucasus as a separate force or united with men. Women's social positions were transformed by these protests, which were staged by groups as diverse as Soviet ideologues and nativist movements. The regions' oral traditions include stories about women's protests against political and personal subjugation. In the epic "Forty Maidens," Central Asian women warriors physically resisted foreign intrusions and shared the same rights and responsibilities as men (Chatterjee 1997). The oral tradition of the Caucasus describes the foremothers of local women as Amazons. Late nineteenth-century travel accounts report that local women, like Amazons, fiercely resisted Russian conquests. During the siege of the town of Ahloulgo, 400 women threw themselves from the walls of the fortress as a sign of protest (Golovin 1854, 94). Some women, like the Georgian Queen Tamara, assumed state leadership in their societies. In fact, Georgia's power and influence reached its peak during her reign in the twelfth to thirteenth centuries.

At the beginning of the Soviet era, women of these regions took an active part in the transformation of their social positions. In Turkestan in 1916, "Ruzvan-bibi Akhmedzhanova, Zukhra-bibi Musaeva and other women, while protesting against sending their sons to war, were shot dead by [Russian] soldiers" (Alimova). In Turkestan, women's protests against the veil, *khudzhum* (assault), began on International Women's Day, 1927. Organized by the Sredazburo's (Central Asian Bureau) Zhenotdel (Women's Section) under the direction of Serafima Lubimova and her deputies, these protests triggered social changes, which came at a terrible price for local women (Keller 1998). Inspired by Soviet emancipation rhetoric local women tore off and burned their veils in public. In conjunction with other aspects of the liberation campaign, these public protests inspired thousands of regional women to burn their veils on the spot (Massell 1974). At the same time, this public unveiling drastically increased violence against unveiled women and cost tens of thousands of lives. In 1928 alone, about 300 women were killed either by their close relatives or by *basmachi* (local guerilla movements) (Popov 1938).

There was no information about regional women's protests during the Soviet period. Some examples were discovered after the disintegration of the Soviet Union, while others were reported outside the country. Under Soviet rule, women were active participants in nationalist movements in the Caucasus. In a popular nationalist protest in 1989, 20 Georgians, most of them women, were killed and hundreds injured when Soviet troops attacked a demonstration in Tbilisi.

Contemporary women's protests underscore political/religious persecution and power abuses by existing regimes. In Uzbekistan on 2 July 2001, an Uzbek militia rounded up about 50 women and their children in Tashkent and 30 in Andijan. These women were protesting against the detention and harsh treatment of their male relatives, alleged members of banned religious groups. Protestors were trying to present a petition addressed to the Uzbek president, which accused the interior ministry's staff of torture and physical pressure against the detainees. Chechen women also protested against the detention, ill-treatment, and disappearance of local males during the Russian federal troops' cleansing operations in Chechnya (HRWWR 2003b). On 15 March 2001, federal troops carried out a punitive operation in the settlement of Novogroznenskii, killing several civilians. In response, several hundred local women blocked traffic on one of the main roads in Chechnya. For three days, they chanted "No to murders, cleansings, robbery and camps! Where are you, leaders of Chechnya? Where are you, muftis? Where are you, judges? They are killing us with your agreement!" (MHRC 2001) Some of these protests are documented either by regional mass media (Chechnya) or on the Internet (Uzbekistan, Chechnya).

Women's protests expose political problems by constructing a sociopolitical critique of the existing regimes around women's roles as mothers and wives, thus becoming a strong political voice and a source of opposition to the local governments. On 21 March 2001, about 300 female protestors in Andijan (Uzbekistan) demanded the release of their male relatives, imprisoned for their religious practices. The signs that women carried read: "2001: Year of the Widow and Orphan," a hollow echo of the Uzbek president's declaration of the year of 2001 as the "Year of the Mother and Child." The demonstration was dispersed by local militia forces (HRWWR 2002). Similarly, in Chechnya on 8 March 2001, International Women's Day, about a hundred women, whose male relatives had disappeared after being arrested by federal troops, gathered in the center of Grozny. They had signs in their hands that read "Russia, return our children!" and "Let our children go!" (PRIMA News Agency 2001).

The regional governments' persecution of female protesters shows that local regimes perceive women's actions as a direct political threat (HRWWR 2003a). In spite of growing harassment, local women challenge the regimes' treatment of civilians by globally publicizing the abuse of power. As a result, the Uzbek government has finally allowed international observers access into some of the country's prisons (HRWWR 2002). Russian authorities also introduced two decrees requiring the presence of local officials during the arrest of civilians in Chechnya, as well as some degree of infrastructure to address grievances. They also began an investigation into disappearances (HRW 2002, HRWWR 2003b).

Although governmental concessions seem to be small and illusory, women's protests persist in publicly confronting existing power relations in the regions by producing a social critique that uses their gender roles as mothers and wives (HRW 2003). Thus, women's protests have become "one of the major channels of public voice" in both Central Asia and the Caucasus at the beginning of the twenty-first century (Norris et al. 2002, 19).

Bibliography

D. Alimova, Women's issue in Uzbekistan. Lessons of the history and today's objectives, <http://www.undp.uz/GID/eng/UZBEKISTAN/PUBLICATIONS/uz_bul3_7.html>.

S. Chatterjee, M. Mazumdar, and A. Sengupta, Unveiling stereotypes. Transitional politics and gender in Central Asia, in R. Samaddar (ed.), *Women in Asia. Work, culture, and politics in South and Central Asia*, Dehli 1997, 101–21.

I. Golovin, *The Caucasus*, London 1854.

HRW (Human Rights Watch), Russia. Chechen "disappearances" continue, New York 2002, http://www.hrw.org/press/2002/04/chechnya041502.htm>.

——, *Uzbekistan. Progress on paper only. Analysis of the U.S. state department's certification of Uzbekistan*, New York 2003, <http://www.hrw.org/europe/uzbekistan.php>.

HRWWR (Human Rights Watch World Report), *Uzbekistan*, New York 2002, <http://www.hrw.org/wr2k2/europe22.html >.

——, *Uzbekistan*, New York 2003a, <http://www.hrw.org/wr2k3/europe16.html>.

——, *Russian Federation*, New York 2003b, <http://www.hrw.org/wr2k3/europe11.html>.

S. Keller, Trapped between state and society. Women's liberation and Islam in Soviet Uzbekistan, 1926–1941, in *Journal of Women's History* 10:1 (Spring 1998), 27–36.

M. Marshall, Global trends in democratization, in M. Marshall and T. R. Gurr (eds.), *Peace and conflict 2003*, College Park, Md. 2003, 17–23.

G. Massell, *The surrogate proletariat. Moslem women and revolutionary strategies in Soviet Central Asia, 1919–1929*, Princeton, N.J. 1974.

Memorial Human Rights Center (MHRC), Peaceful mass protests in Chechnya 2001. Human Rights Center "Memorial," <http://www.memo.ru/eng/memhrc/texts/protests.shtml>.

P. Norris, S. Walgrave, and P. Van Aelst, Who demonstrates? Anti-state rebels, conventional participants or everyone?, draft, 25 October 2002, forthcoming in *Comparative Politics*, <http://ksghome.harvard.edu/~.pnorris.shorenstein.ksg/ACROBAT/ Who%20demon strates.pdf>.

F. Popov, Work among women in Uzbekistan [in Russian], in *Antireligioznik* 12 (1938), 14.

PRIMA News Agency, Women of Chechnya spend International Women's Day fighting for their children, 9 March 2001, <http://www.primanews.ru/eng/news/news/ 2001/3/9/19004.html>.

Uzbekistan Daily Digest (UDD), Uzbek women beaten up, threatened with rape in detention, Voice of the Islamic Republic of Iran, Mashhad [in Uzbek] 2002, <http://www.eurasianet.org/resource/uzbekistan/hypermail/200205/0016.shtml>.

Svetlana Peshkova

Indonesia

Since the beginning of the twentieth century Indonesian women have been voicing their protest at conditions they considered oppressive. Indonesia is the country with the largest Muslim population in the world: 90 percent of its 210 million inhabitants adhere to Islam, so much of women's protest was articulated in terms of Islamic teachings and practices. This multiethnic country has many local traditions in which male dominance is entrenched. As well as Islam, which entered the archipelago in the thirteenth century, Dutch colonialism and postcolonial nationalism are the other major forces that affect women's subordination. Patriarchal structures are most strongly encountered in family relations. The struggle against polygyny has been one of the central elements in the Indonesian women's movement.

Historical overview

In various regions women wielded considerable political, social, and economic power. The Muslim realms of the Moluccas and Aceh were once ruled by queens. Women also led in wars or served as soldiers. When, by the beginning of the seventeenth century, the Dutch consolidated their colonial presence, they strengthened patriarchal and feudal structures. Only the titled and other elite males had access to political and economic power (Onghokham 2003). Racial politics were also introduced. The Muslim population fell under patriarchal Islamic laws, while customary law was applied to the non-Muslim native population. This legal dualism was perpetuated after independence in 1945. At that time there was some support for the idea of using Islamic law as the foundation of the nation, but for the sake of pluralism this was rejected; however, some groups still favor it.

The first Indonesian modern feminist was Princess Raden Adjeng Kartini, who died during childbirth in 1904. Her passionate and brilliant letters became an inspiration for women all over Indonesia as well as abroad. She struggled against polygyny, forced marriages, feudal customs oppressive to women, and colonial injustice and also advocated women's education. In the pre-independence period, women's struggles concentrated on these areas, as well as trafficking of women and children, the rights of women laborers, and political rights (Suryochondro 1984, Wieringa 2002). The first women's schools were set up in the first decades of the century by such prominent leaders as Dewi Sartika in Bandung and Rahmah El Yunusiah in Western Sumatra. The Muslim women's organization Aisyiyah also set up schools for girls in this period. By 1930 the colonial government prohibited schools set up outside its jurisdiction, as it feared such schools might instill nationalist sentiments. Women were very active in the protest movement that followed.

In 1938 the colonial government granted white women both active and passive political rights, but Indonesian women only passive rights. The Indonesian women's organizations strongly resisted, arguing that in several regions in precolonial times they had also been able to stand for election. Women played an active role both in the armed resistance against the Dutch in colonial times, and in the war for national independence after the Japanese defeat of 1945.

During the Old Order period (1945–65) of Indonesia's first president, Sukarno, the Indonesian women's movement was at its strongest. The most prominent women's organization at that time was the communist-oriented Gerwani, which fought for women's social and political rights, for instance for women's land rights. This militant organization was associated with sexual perversions by the military who, under the leadership of General Suharto, took over from President Sukarno after one of the most bloody massacres of modern history (Wieringa 2002). The New Order regime (1967–98) was characterized by the muting of all democratic forces, including women fighting for their rights. Right-wing women's organizations, including Christian and Muslim groups, rallied against their socialist counterparts. Muslim women's organizations even took over the school that had been set up by Gerwani (Baidlowi 1993). The military regime set up its own women's organizations in which women no longer struggled for their own rights, but were mobilized for the maintenance of military power and for national development as obedient wives and dutiful mothers. The marriage law adopted in 1974 entrenched this process.

This process of depoliticization and domestication of women by the state (Suryakusuma 1987) led to the erosion of women's economic and political rights. Defined as dependent housewives they were exploited as cheap laborers. The colonial policy of denying women subject status before the law was maintained, so that women did not have, for instance, independent access to credit provided by banks.

In the New Order period women did not demonstrate for their own rights, but many women joined other protest movements, such as the human rights or student movements. Women were also in the forefront of the struggles for labor and land rights. In a strongly patriarchal culture such as that of North Sumatra women might bare their breasts in their struggles to prevent their land being taken away from them.

In February 1998 women staged major protests against the high cost of living, particularly of baby milk. By mobilizing the perception of women as mothers with a major responsibility for their children's welfare, the failure of the military New Order was demonstrated. The organization Suara Ibu Peduli (Voices of concerned mothers) brought together women of all social classes. When mass protests followed and major riots broke out (in which many women, particularly of Chinese descent, were raped and killed), President Suharto was forced to step down.

The Reformation Era (after 1998) made it possible for women again to set up mass organizations fighting for women's rights, such as the Indonesian Women's Coalition for Justice and Democracy. One issue that attracted much attention was women's political leadership. Certain Islamic parties declared that Megawati Sukarnoputri (the daughter of former President Sukarno), the leader of the party that had won the 1999 elections, could not become the president of the country. Other Islamic groups and many women's groups contested this. Only in 2002 could she take up the presidency.

Since 1998 many women's groups have emerged or have become more active. Critical issues they are fighting against include the influence of the military and continued human rights violations as well as sexual violence against women. Amid rampant corruption the living conditions of the majority of the people have not improved so that women again take to the streets, protesting at the return of the army to the center of power and at the neoliberal economic policies.

The decentralization policy of the government poses new problems for women. The identities of the newly defined autonomous provinces or regions are constructed along concepts of women's behavior and control over their bodies, often based on particular Islamic interpretations that, for instance, prescribe the veil or restrict their movements. In Aceh several women had their heads shaved for not wearing the veil. Women's groups are divided between those who support the introduction of Islamic law and those who oppose it.

Marriage law

One of the issues that have haunted the Indonesian women's movement from its beginning, and which still has not been solved satisfactorily, is that of equal marriage rights for women. While the Indonesian women's movement has been able to unite on many issues, it has continuously been split on the struggle against polygyny. Secular and Christian women's organizations have fought for its abolition while Muslim women's groups have defended it as an essential part of Islamic teaching. Yet individually many Muslim women have taken part in actions to abolish this practice, which demonstrates how Muslim women are controlled by male-dominated Islamic organizations.

After Kartini had first written about the pain polygynous husbands caused their wives, referring to it as a great evil supported by customary law and Islam, the newly formed women's organizations started discussing it. The first all-Indonesian Women's Congress in 1928 proposed to fight for a marriage law that would guarantee women's rights. In 1937 the colonial government proposed a draft marriage law that stipulated monogamy and equal rights for women in divorce. Islamic groups, including women's organizations, strongly opposed it, and the Women's Congress could not support it, in order to preserve its own unity, and also in the face of preserving national unity in the struggle against the Dutch colonial power.

After independence in 1945 the issue was not resolved. In 1952 a government decree guaranteed the widows of polygynous men twice the amount the widow of a monogamous husband would get. Nineteen women's organizations strongly opposed this *de facto* legalization of polygyny, which also amounted to the state subsidy of the practice. In 1953 women took to the streets, in the first demonstration for women's rights after independence. Muslim women joined individually, not as members of their organizations. Indonesia has two large Islamic women's organizations. Aisyiyah was set up in 1917, as the women's wing of the Muhammadiyah movement. One of their major contributions was the demand to install female judges in the courts dealing with marriage issues. This demand was met in the 1950s. The other Islamic mass women's organization is the women's wing of the Nahdlatul Ulama, the Muslimat Nahdlatul Ulama, which was set up in 1946.

President Sukarno's polygynous marriage in 1954 evoked major protests from women's organizations. Again the major Muslim women's organizations kept silent, as did Gerwani. They aspired to become a mass organization and followed the directive of the Communist Party to always support the national hero, Sukarno. Many individual members deplored this, for Gerwani had always been in the forefront of the struggle for equal marriage rights. In 1958 two draft marriage laws were discussed in parliament, one proposed by the government, and a more radical one proposed by a feminist member of parliament. The discussions were stalled because of opposition from Islamic organizations.

In 1973 again a draft marriage law was proposed that stipulated monogamy and civil marriage. Islamic groups and parties strongly opposed it, both on the streets and in parliament. A compromise was agreed which stipulated that monogamous marriage was the rule, but which allowed polygyny when a woman did not have children, was not able to fulfil her marital duties, or had an incurable illness. Interreligious marriages were prohibited (Saptaningrun 2000).

The fact that polygyny is still allowed provokes much debate. The rules affecting the military and civil servants have been tightened. Men of other groups feel they are free to contact polygamous marriages, even without the consent of the court, which is stipulated in the law. They see it as a deed sanctioned by Islam. Pro-polygyny groups even organized a contest for a Polygamy Award in July 2003. This provoked strong protests from women's groups, including many Muslim women. A group of veiled women wanted to climb onto the stage where the award was being given, claiming that they as women belonging to polygynous groups had the right to be heard. They were prevented from reading their protest statement by security forces. At the time the mass media trumpeted around that the four wives of the men who received the award were happy with him. Yet the first wife openly stated that she was sick at heart at his behavior. Interestingly both pro- and anti-polygamy groups based their arguments on particular interpretations of the Qur'ān and used Islamic symbols, such as the veil. This testifies to the plurality of views on Islam, its practices and teachings, in Indonesia. This plurality has become more manifest since the 1990s, when gender issues were widely discussed for the first time within Islamic organizations.

Conclusion

Interests of the state or of Islamic groups have often been superimposed on women's interests, even if these had been formulated since the beginning of the women's movement. This has been possible because the major Muslim women's organizations, as well as the largest socialist women's organization, Gerwani, were formed as women's wings of male-dominated parties or organizations, even if they were independent in name. Independent Muslim women's groups have been better able to fight for women's rights. Only since the 1990s have women both within Islamic organizations and outside them touched on areas that had previously been considered male monopolies. Gender analysis and feminist interpretations of Islam have gained wide currency with the translation of many books on such topics into Indonesian. Feminist debates also have a great influence on the general discourse in Indonesia, which is still very much male-oriented. Indonesian feminist interpretations also serve to stem the influence of the Middle Eastern culture that has been promoted by fundamentalist groups who have become stronger since the fall of Suharto.

Bibliography

N. Anderson, *Law reform in the Muslim world*, London 1976.

A. H. Baidlowi, The profile of an Indonesian women's organization. A case study of the Muslimat Nahdlatul Ulama, in L. Marcoes-Natsir and J. Meuleman (eds.), *Indonesian Muslim women in textual and contextual studies* [in Indonesian], Jakarta 1993.

R. A. Kartini, *Letters to Mrs. Abendanon-Mandri and her husband*, trans. S. Sutrisno, Djambatan, Jakarta 1987.

Onghokham, *The thugs, the curtain thief and the sugar lord. Power, politics and culture in colonial*, Jakarta 2003.

I. D. Saptaningrum, The history of law no. 1/1974 on marriage and gender stereotyping [in Indonesian], mimeo 2000.

J. Suryakusuma, State Ibuism. The social construction of womanhood in the Indonesian New Order, M.A. thesis, The Hague 1987.

S. Suryocondro, *A portrait of the Indonesian women's movement* [in Indonesian], Jakarta 1984.

S. Wieringa, *Sexual politics in Indonesia*, Houndmills, Basingstoke, Hampshire 2002.

Nursyahbani Katjasungkana

Iran

Despite historical blindness to women's participation in various social and political movements in Iran, scattered accounts show women's involvement in local and national protests, such as riots against bread scarcity, rising prices, and tax increases. Since at least the mid-nineteenth century, women have made enormous contributions to efforts for social change in Iran.

The development of gender consciousness and the women's rights struggle were hindered by sexual segregation and restrictive moral codes, which deprived women of access to literacy, paid work outside the home, and the right to a public presence. Yet there were always exceptional women, such as Ṭāhirah Qurrat al-ʿAyn (1815–51) and Bībī Khānum Astārābādī (1858–1921), who openly exposed and opposed male supremacy and the patriarchal values and practices that barred women from the acquisition of knowledge and access to the country's social and economic resources (Nāṭiq 1358/1980, Nāṭiq and Ādamiyat 1368/1989).

By participating in wider social and political movements of the period, such as the Tobacco Protest of 1891–2, and particularly, the Constitutional Revolution of 1905–11, women gained a new political maturity and began to forge an independent political identity. Thus empowered, activists crossed gendered boundaries and social norms. For example, women disguised in men's clothing joined military actions in the civil war that followed ratification of the constitution (Nāhīd 1360/1981); in support of pro-constitution clergymen, others built strongholds on the rooftop of a religious shrine near Tehran, throwing stones at the attacking army.

Disappointment at the consolidation of their legal and social inferiority in the first Iranian constitution subsequent to the victory of the Constitutional Revolution increased activist women's gender consciousness and self-image, giving rise to the Iranian women's movement. In 1906, a group of women marched in the streets of Tehran, took off their veils, and demanded recognition of their rights. Outraged, prominent Constitutionalists called them prostitutes hired by "reactionaries" to discredit the revolution (Bayat-Philip 1978).

Women's protests against the injustices to which they were subjected were expressed in remarkably diverse forms. Some sought radical short-term goals while others pursued more lasting, fundamental changes in women's status. These efforts sometimes evoked a violent response. A group of women in Shiraz became targets for mob attacks when they changed their black chador to brown ones, in protest at veiling (Sanasarian 1983, 14). But the women persisted. Activists burned in public a pamphlet written by a clergyman opposed to women's rights (Bāmdād 1977, 63). Adult literacy classes and girls' schools were established at enormous costs to the pioneers of women's rights. Many groups and associations were formed. Over 20 women's periodicals were published between 1910 and 1930.

However, one contradictory result of the evolution of the modern Iranian state under the two Pahlavī Shahs (1925–79), including structural and legal changes in society and economy, was increasing police repression and the creeping extension of autocratic state control over civil society. While some changes benefited women, they also had a damning effect on the burgeoning women's movement (Najmabadi 1991, 56–8). Cooptation of women activists, and the appropriation of the feminist agenda by the state, circumscribed and discredited women's militant efforts, and put a stop to indigenous, radical, and independent forms of protest for over 50 years, to be revived only after the 1979 Revolution, ironically, under the rule of Islamic clergy.

Only a few weeks through the revolution, following Ayatollah Khomeini's decree for the reveiling of women (8 March 1979), Iran saw a chain of women's powerful, spontaneous protest marches, sit-ins, and work stoppages in ministries, hospitals, and girls' high schools (Moghissi 1994). This marked the rebirth of an independent, powerful, and effective women's movement for change. The consolidation of the power of the Islamic state and the political repression and ousting of organized opposition a year later also dismantled many secular women's associations and groups that proliferated immediately after the revolution. Yet political repression has failed to silence women.

Signs of women's resistance to gender barriers and their resistance to legal restrictions and gendered social and moral codes imposed by the new state have been observable throughout the country since the revolution. These have included secular women's defiance of the *ḥijāb* code; their remarkable resilience and skill in reclaiming educational and employment spaces they lost after the revolution; the voices of discontent and protest coming from Muslim women activists against gendered values promoted by the media and the education system; and the astute and skillful use of national and international days for protests such as antiwar marches and, more recently, the re-emergence of International Women's Day celebration (*Faṣl-i*

Zanān 1382/2003) to voice women's urgent concerns and demands. All these speak, eloquently, to the presence of women as a highly potent political force for social change in contemporary Iran.

BIBLIOGRAPHY

B. Bāmdād, *From darkness into light. Woman's emancipation in Iran*, ed. and trans. F. R. C. Bagley, Hicksville, N.Y. 1997.

M. Bayat-Philip, Women and revolution in Iran, in L. Beck and N. Keddie (eds.), *Women in the Muslim world*, Cambridge, Mass. 1978, 301–2.

Y. Dawlatābādī, *Ḥayāt-i Yaḥyā*, Tehran n.d.

Faṣl-i zanān, Tehran 1382/2003.

K. Millett, *Going to Iran*, New York 1982.

H. Moghissi, *Populism and feminism in Iran. Women's struggle in a male-defined revolutionary movement*, New York 1994.

ʿA. A. Nāhīd, *Zanān-i Īrān dar junbish-i mashrūṭa*, Tabriz 1360/1981.

A. Najmabadi, Hazards of modernity and morality. Women, state and ideology in contemporary Iran, in D. Kandiyoti (ed.), *Women, Islam and the state*, Philadelphia 1991, 48–76.

H. Nāṭiq, Nigāhī bih barkhī nivistihhā va mubarazat-i zanān dar dūra mashrūṭa, in *Kitāb-i Jumʿa* 30 (1358/1980).

H. Naṭiq and F. Ādamiyat, *Afkār-i ijtimāʿi, va siyāsī va iqtiṣādī dar āsār-i muntashir nashudah-i dawrān-i Qājār*, Saarbrücken 1368/1989.

E. Sanasarian, *The women's rights movement in Iran. Mutiny, appeasement and repression from 1900 to Khomeini*, New York 1983.

HAIDEH MOGHISSI

North Africa

Beyond the Mediterranean tradition of patriarchy, whose mechanisms have been uncovered by Germaine Tillon (1996), does it make sense to examine the trajectories of women's struggles in the Maghrib's three main countries (Tunisia, Algeria, and Morocco) as part of a single movement? In Tunisia, Bourguiba instituted a system of state-backed feminism, whose preservation nowadays is, for some, one of the last valid reasons to support the regime of Bourguiba's successor against the threat of "Islamist regression." In Algeria, in the period that followed independence from France, the collusion of the Front de libération nationale (FLN) and conservative religious forces to send women back into the home, paved the way for a true "civil war within the civil war" dating back to the early 1990s, in which gender relations are at stake, and that is at least equal in violence to the war between the military and Islamists. Finally, in Morocco, subtle adjustments to the Mālikī tradition, supported by the monarchy, have barely weakened masculine domination, but have given some degree of liberty to elite urban women on the economic, political, and intellectual fronts. In the meantime, ordinary women continue to share with ordinary men the unfavorable fate cast upon the underprivileged by the Sharifian kingdom. These significant differences notwithstanding, the three countries present several common traits forming a system of constraints that determine the way women will organize their struggle in relation to the global societal evolutions of each country, and are indicative of obstacles or even regressions recorded in those societies.

In Tunisia, Algeria, and Morocco, resistance to colonization turned the family structure and the preservation of women's honor into the last bastion of a distinctive identity as well as symbols of maintained integrity. As a result, a contradiction emerged between the role of women in the resistance – which was important, particularly in Algeria and Morocco – and women's ability to articulate autonomous demands. An additional possible consequence was the continued subjugation of women. In contexts where the aim for reform constituted the modality of both the interactions and the confrontation with the colonial power and its "civilizing mission," the first "feminists" in the Maghrib were men: Tahar Haddad and Bourguiba in Tunisia; Ben Badis and Ferhat Abbas in Algeria; and Sultan Mohamed Ben Youssef and Allal al-Fassi in Morocco. They preached the renovation of the feminine condition by the resurrection of the models of pious ancestors. But as soon as women took it upon themselves to articulate their own demands, they faced the recurring accusation of Westernization, notably on the issues of the veil, polygamy, and *ṭalāq* (repudiation).

Once independence was obtained, the one-party systems in place in Algeria and Tunisia, and the monarchy in the case of Morocco, did not deem it necessary to address the question of the place of women in society as a specific issue: as long as the state promised improvements in the condition of women – and delivered them in the sectors of education, health, and employment – women were strongly discouraged from raising the question of their status, in spite of the fact that the constitutions of all three countries stated that they should enjoy the same rights and responsibilities as men. A long period of latency followed, during which women's demands could only be expressed – cautiously – through organizations created by and under the control of the state or the single party – the Union nationale des femmes tunisiennes, created by Bourguiba in 1958; the Union nationale des femmes algériennes, created in 1963 under the supervision of the FLN; and the Union nationale des femmes marocaines, created in 1969 by the monarchy and headed by the sister of King Hassan II – or within the framework of the trade unions.

In all three countries, new forms of protest, specifically feminist in their nature, have arisen through the realization that improvements – very real in Tunisia and Algeria; less so, or at least limited to certain sectors, in Morocco – did not translate into a transformation of women's status, or worse, were used as a justification for the consolidation of the patriarchal order. These new forms of protest explicitly challenge the nature of gender relations and question the reformist framework within which women's rights and status have been discussed up to this moment. Still in question, in terms that are specific to each country, is the possibility for feminine demands and modes of action to move toward an increased degree of autonomy. Without delving into the details of mobilizations taking place in each of the three countries, a number of common characteristics can be identified.

One is the focus on the question of personal status, particularly in Algeria and in Morocco, where feminist demands have centered around the reexamination of the Family Code enacted by the Assemblée nationale populaire in 1984 in Algeria, and of the Mudawwana (code of personal status) promulgated by Mohamed V in 1957 in Morocco. Both codes adhere to the Muslim Sharīʿa on issues such as polygamy, repudiation, matrimonial guardianship, and inheritance. In both countries, protest is voiced through press releases, petitions, and, less frequently, marches and demonstrations organized by groups of women often comprised of intellectuals and scholars, who have difficulties relating to women from lower classes, especially rural women. At the core of the argument formulated by feminists in Algeria and Morocco is the denunciation of the codes as unconstitutional insofar as they contradict the principle of equality of all citizens affirmed in each country's constitution, and are incompatible with international conventions signed by both countries. In Algeria, no notable results have been achieved: the regime's promises to reexamine the Family Code are regularly forgotten as soon as the electoral campaigns have ended, as was the case in 1999 when Abdelaziz Bouteflika was elected president, and after the May 2002 legislative elections. More substantial progress has been attained in Morocco, where in October 2003, King Mohamed VI implemented profound changes to the Mudawwana, which fulfilled some of the most fundamental demands by militant members of the women's movement – in particular the abolition of matrimonial guardianship (*wilāya*), the restriction of polygamy, and the institution of legal divorce in place of *ṭalāq*. In Tunisia, feminist protest tends to align itself with a more general movement that favors human rights against the authoritarian regime of Zinelabidine Ben Ali – though some women willingly accept token positions in government. In a country whose personal status code is considered the most progressive in the region, women's resistance since the 1980s has been based on the denunciation of the dichotomy that exists between the law and promises made by politicians, which outline tangible benefits for women that must be defended, and the reality of masculine domination, which, for intellectuals in feminist circles, appears to have been only superficially challenged.

In Algeria, Morocco, and Tunisia alike, the question of women's participation in the political process tests the ability of feminist militants to put in place autonomous organizational structures in a fundamentally hostile environment: since they have not succeeded in influencing single parties or parties that hold some sort of monopoly on political legitimacy, such as the FLN, the Neo-Destour, or the Union socialiste des forces populaires (USFP), which they cannot afford to leave, feminist militants tend to rely on two fall-back strategies as they organize themselves. First, they work within the realm of civil society by creating an increasing number of associations specializing in problems that affect women (literacy, single mother assistance, domestic violence, and so forth) as well as general interest non-governmental organizations, which operate independently of "official" feminist groups – the Association démocratique des femmes du Maroc and the Union de l'action féminine in Morocco; Egalité, emancipation et promotion and the Association pour le triomphe du droit des femmes in Algeria; Club Tahar Haddad, the Association des femmes universitaires, and the Association tunisienne des femmes démocrates in Tunisia – and whose objective is to put pressure on the political establishment. Second, they concentrate on the regional and international arenas, where they work through human rights organizations, the United Nations system, European and North American feminist organizations, and foundations for development assistance. This strategy has yielded some positive results in recent years: for instance, the World Bank's technical and financial assistance in the preparation of the "Plan d'intégration des femmes au développement" drafted by a group of Moroccan feminists and later embraced by the new government. Another achievement was the collaboration of feminists from Algeria, Morocco, and Tunisia, who started the Collectif 95 Maghreb-Egalité in order to be represented at the fourth United Nations World Conference on Women in Beijing in 1995. Consider also that the support for the Palestinian intifada between 1987 and 1989 and since 2000, or for the Iraqi people during the Gulf war of 1990–1 and since the beginning of the American occupation in 2003 have provided ideal opportunities for feminists in the Maghrib to unite and minimize their differences.

In all three countries, feminist demands regarding women's personal status provide a central argument and a powerful lever for mobilization to Islamists and all kinds of conservatives who denounce the collusion of feminists with the Western world and with corrupt regimes as they conspire against Islam. In Algeria, the support of some feminists for repression of the Islamic movement has given credence to these accusations. In Tunisia and Morocco, especially since the 1990s, feminists have also come up against the emergence of what can only be called "Islamist feminism," whose proponents – some, if not all – have adopted most feminist demands in terms of education, employment, and participation in the political process, while still calling for the enforcement of the Sharīʿa as it applies to personal status. In countries where Western models are discredited more than ever before, the ability of Islamist feminists to reach milieus that secularist feminism is unable to access appears to be one of the key factors in the struggle of women in the contemporary Maghrib.

Translation from the French by Matthieu Dalle, University of Louisville

Bibliography
Z. Daoud, *Féminisme et politique au Maghreb*, Casablanca 1993.
G. Tillion, *Le haram et les cousins*, Paris 1966.

Alain Roussillon

Palestine

Over the past century, Palestinian women's political protest has been anchored in nationalist responses to colonialism, dispossession, and military occupation. Despite a tumultuous history marked by serial crises, social fragmentation, and statelessness, women's forms and focuses of protest have been remarkably enduring.

A defining moment in the history of women's organized protest was the 1929 gathering of 200 elite Muslim and Christian women in Jerusalem to found the Arab Women's Congress; resolutions against Zionist colonization were delivered to the British High Commissioner and a demonstration of women in a honking car cavalcade wound around Jerusalem. Resolutions and demonstrations represent two consistent features of Palestinian women's protest: the first, appeals to justice or, more prosaically, public relations, and the second, public protest that both breaks and uses gender boundaries. The unveiling of women at the congress also highlighted aspects of modernity that were to become contested issues in Palestinian women's activism. Articles in the Arabic press (often by women) during British rule (1917–47) contained both a modernizing discourse of "women's awakening" and a more traditional call for women to defend men, home, and family (Fleischmann 2003). Both discourses resonate throughout the century.

Most Palestinian women, including the 70 percent of peasant women living in villages, were not represented at the congress. While elite-popular divisions have characterized other women's movements in the Arab region, the Palestinian situation is distinguished by the role of peasants, and particularly peasant women, as national signifiers, and by the sustained and multiple roles of peasant women in maintaining resistance whether in the 1936–39 Great Revolt, in exile in refugee camps, or under Israeli military occupation. Peasant women's repertoire of protest has included aid to militants, intervention in arrests, silence and misidentification of militants, manipulating their "inferior" status to smuggle weapons (Swedenburg 1995, 180), comfort to the injured and families of the martyrs, as well as casting responsibilities of care and socialization in terms of nationalist resistance. Older and married women have served as expressive voices for the community: cursing soldiers, praising courage, and mourning the dead. More organized protest activities have centered on prisoners, including sit-ins and demonstrations, sometimes bringing women together across socioeconomic divides. Elite and later middle-class women have made varied efforts to link with rural and poor refugee women, most successfully in the first Palestinian intifada (1987–93). Student activism has also been a bridge between classes and social groups, particularly with the sharp rise in female education commencing in the 1960s, when many young women and men were the first in their families to enter secondary or post-secondary education.

In the wake of mass dispossession and the fragmentation of Palestinian society in 1948, elite women turned largely to charitable or service activities to meet the needs of the refugee population as well as continuing in appeals to the international community. Women in refugee camps engaged in scattered protests, participating in demonstrations, sometimes against the United Nations Relief and Works Agency (UNRWA), the agency in charge of Palestinian refugees, sometimes against the state regime. Statelessness, where any "rights" granted by prevailing powers were both difficult to acquire and could be withdrawn arbitrarily, also increased women's role as mediators and strategists for the travel documents, food rations, and security approval needed for family and individual survival and mobility, a role that turned easily to protest. Older women might use their status to defy officials whether by simply jumping queues or by haranguing a soldier to see a detained son. Although Palestinian female students joined in the widespread Nasserist protests of the day in Jordan and Lebanon, there were not substantial numbers of female prisoners until the period of Israeli occupation.

The June 1967 war and the founding of the Palestinian resistance opened up new arenas and possibilities for women's protest, and at the same time the military occupation of the West Bank and Gaza imposed new restrictions. In the latter context, practices of daily life became reinterpreted as *ṣumūd* (steadfastness) and often acts of resistance. Tilling the land, picking wild thyme, contacting a relative in Lebanon, or even going to school, could be illegal acts. In Jordan and Lebanon, the armed resistance brought women into its ranks (to some extent) and made refugee camps sites of mobilization where new roles of women as militant cadre (usually the young and unmarried) joined the more familiar informal roles of women assisting fighters and undertaking neighborhood-based actions when their camps were under siege (Peteet 1991). These activities continued even after the departure of the organized Palestinian resistance: in the wake of the 1982 Sabra and Shatila massacre in Lebanon, women spontaneously organized a commemorative march despite the high risk (Sayigh 1991).

The widespread and visible participation of Palestinian women in the intifada that erupted in the West Bank and Gaza in December 1987 against Israeli military occupation took place in the context of the earlier rise of mass-based women's, students', and community voluntary work associations (Taraki 1990). From 1978, women's committees, led by former student activists, were linked to clandestine political movements, but had considerable independence of action. Their leadership consciously broke from the charitable mode of women's activism and aimed to link with rural and refugee camp women. Although formal membership in these committees was limited, they provided a framework at the local level for women's protest where even informal activities, like visiting families of the martyred, injured, or detained, were charged with an "organized" aspect. The first year of the intifada saw weekly women's marches from churches and mosques and women were particularly active in the educational committees that taught children (illegally) when schools were closed by military order (Jad 1999). A series of emblematic Women's Day's demonstrations on 8 March 1988 showed the women's movement at full force, with participation across classes and locales. A leaflet issued by "the Palestinian women's movement" proclaimed a dominant theme: "Let each women consider the wounded and imprisoned her own children." Women's extension of their mothering and domestic roles to include the community (Giacaman and Johnson 1988, Peteet 1997) was a noted feature of the first intifada. A remarkable level of women's participation was confirmed in a 1995 survey of 6,024 married women where nearly half the women had protected someone, usually a young man, from arrest by the Israeli army, over a third had marched in a demonstration, and over a quarter had thrown stones. On average, women had engaged in these activities at least ten times (Huntington et al. 2001, 10). Another significant feature of the intifada period was growing links with Israeli and international women's peace groups.

While some analysts saw women's public participation as drawing them away from the isolation and repression of domestic life (Strum 1992) others identified the home and family as sites of protest and transformation, whether women were defending their home against invasion, mobilizing family and kin networks for protest, or mothers were using narrative strategies and social support to constitute the heroic self of an imprisoned son (Jean-Klein 2000). Women's protest also encountered backlash in the form of a campaign to impose the *ḥijāb* (headscarf) on women in Gaza. Coupled with the male political hierarchy failing to recognize women's leadership in the intifada, social and gender issues (the terms were often conflated) became a new focus of women's protest, particularly in the interim period of nascent state-building (1996–2000). Women's protest had a dual focus in the interim period: first, for equality as "citizens" in legislation and governance under the Palestinian Authority and second, against continued Israeli occupation, with a particular emphasis on prisoners, land and Israeli settlements, and Israel's closure of the Palestinian territory.

The second intifada, which erupted in September 2000, has been sharply contrasted with the first in terms of participation by both women and civil society as a whole (Johnson and Kuttab 2001). Aside from the distinct features of the second intifada, including Israel's excessive force, the consequent extreme risk of public protest, and the Palestinian turn to militarism, the demobilization of the interim period and the profound crisis in Palestinian nationalism in the wake of the Oslo accords weakened abilities to mobilize and organize (Hammami and Johnson 1999). Although scattered candlelight marches and other peaceful protests occurred, usually sponsored by women's organizations, women's main avenue of protest lay in neighborhood and community activities such as participation in funeral marches and visiting families of the dead and wounded. If in the first intifada previous practices of steadfastness ripened into organized resistance, *ṣumūd* and organized resistance in the second intifada seem sharply divided, with women, and most civilians, in an increasingly difficult struggle to maintain the rudiments of daily life. The separation of communities through Israeli policies of closure and siege also weakened political organization, while borders and crossing points – and the building of the separation wall – became sites of both women's formal and informal protest, side by side with rites of humiliation and repression.

Bibliography

E. Fleischmann, *The nation and its "new" women. The Palestinian women's movement, 1920–1948*, Berkeley, 2003.

R. Giacaman and P. Johnson, Palestinian women. Building barricades and breaking barriers, in Z. Lockman and J. Beinin (eds.), *Intifada. The Palestinian uprising against Israeli occupation*, Boston 1990, 155–69.

R. Hammami and P. Johnson, Equality with a difference. Gender and citizenship in transitional Palestine, in *Social Politics* 6 (Fall 1999), 314–43.

R. Huntington, B. C. Fronk, and B. Chadwick, Family roles of contemporary Palestinian women, in *Journal of Contemporary Family Studies* 32:1 (Winter 2001), 1–19.

I. Jad, From salons to the popular committees. Palestinian women 1919–89, in I. Pappé (ed.), *The Israel/Palestine question. Rewriting histories*, London 1999, 249–68.

I. Jean-Klein, Mothering, statecraft and subjectivity in the Palestinian intifada, in *American Ethnologist* 27:1 (2000), 100–27.

P. Johnson and E. Kuttab, Where have all the women (and men) gone? Reflections on gender and the second Palestinian intifada, in *Feminist Review* 69:1 (Winter 2001), 21–43.

A. Kawar, *Daughters of Palestine. Leading women of the Palestinian national movement*, Albany, N.Y. 1996.

J. Peteet, *Gender in crisis. Women and the Palestinian resistance movement*, New York 1991.

——, Icons and militants. Mothering in the danger zone, in *Signs* 23:1 (1997), 103–29.

R. Sayigh, Palestinian women and politics in Lebanon, in J. E. Tucker (ed.), *Arab women. Old boundaries, new frontiers*, Washington, D.C. 1993, 175–94.

P. Strum, *The women are marching. The second sex and the Palestinian revolution*, Chicago 1992.

T. Swedenburg, *Memories of revolt. The 1936–39 rebellion and the Palestinian national past*, Minneapolis, Minn. 1995.

L. Taraki, The development of Palestinian political consciousness, in J. Nassar and R. Heacock (eds.), *Intifada. Palestine at the crossroads*, New York 1990, 53–72.

Penny Johnson

Purdah in South Asia

The issue of purdah (literally "curtain," limiting interaction between men and women outside well defined categories, see Papanek 1982, 194) became central to the effort of the women's movement in India in the early twentieth century. It was viewed as the one custom most responsible for confining Hindu and Muslim women to their traditional domestic roles. Women's protest against purdah provided a commonality of interests that appeared to supersede communal differences and furthered cooperation on political and economic issues. The Indian women's movement was the culmination of efforts by women leaders, both Hindu and Muslim, to move away from the shadow of male reformers of the nineteenth century and to become directly involved in women's education and their social and economic independence, the very issues that had traditionally held them back.

The sanction for purdah or seclusion of Muslim women is ascribed to an injunction in the Qurʾān urging modesty for men and women: "Say to the believers, that they cast down their eyes. . . . And say to believing women, that they cast down their eyes . . . and reveal not their adornments save such as outward, and let them cast their veils over their bosoms" (Arberry 1973, 49). Among the Hindus the custom had been institutionalized into the social structure, for which justification was found in the Puranas, Mahabharata, and the Ramayana (Stuers 1968, 79, Gordon 1968, 7). Muslim purdah in the early twentieth century was characterized by the wearing of an over garment or *burqaʿ*. This was considered an advance, since it enabled mobility outside the house while still maintaining seclusion (Amin 1996, 130).

Purdah, along with semi-religious social taboos, became identified with child marriages and the inability of child widows to be independent, as Hindu reformers in the nineteenth century turned their attention to the situation of women. The custom of purdah had led to the closing of options available to women outside marriage compounded by lack of inheritance rights and if widowed, no prospect of remarriage. Their lives, from birth onwards, were entirely controlled by the father or by the husband's family. Though Hindu purdah is observed within the family between male and female members and Muslim purdah is from the outside world (Papanek 1982, 194), and despite regional variations in patriarchal structures, the purdah mentality existed in all regions. While child marriage and lack of widow remarriage were not specifically associated with Islam, the pervasiveness of cultural and regional customs tended to influence both communities and to supersede specific Muslim laws pertaining to women (Lateef 1990, 62–4), depriving them of the right to education, inheritance, and remarriage.

Muslim reformers did not immediately join their Hindu counterparts in condemning such customs. However, as the debate on the position of women evolved, the lack of education and early marriage became inextricably linked to the custom of purdah. In the nineteenth century Muslim reformers focused on purdah and argued that the rigidity with which it was enforced exceeded the original intent of the Qur'ān. A distinction was drawn between customary purdah and the Qur'ānic requirement of modesty (Ali 2000, 10). Reformist teaching, emanating from the Dar-ul-Ulum at Deoband urged Muslim women to absorb a mixture of Islamic and Western education and impart it to the family and the community in order to protect Muslim society from colonial influences (Ali 2000, 11, 12). By 1899, Bengali intellectuals were urging Western education for Muslim women though not the total abandonment of purdah (Amin 1996, 198). Neither Hindu nor Muslim reformers wanted to alienate conservative societies of the time. However, even Muslim conservatives had difficulty justifying the custom on the basis of Qur'ānic injunctions (Rahman 1982, 291).

Since girls' education was considered the most important factor in reducing the incidence of purdah and raising age at marriage, the Mohammadan Educational Conference, established in 1886 to promote English education in the community, passed the first resolution urging the education of women in 1888. By 1896 a separate segment was devoted to women's education and in 1903 women began to participate in the activities of the conference (Nehru n.d., 23).

The pace of change and social support for women varied between regions (including united Bengal and Punjab, currently Bangladesh and Pakistan) depending upon the extent of purdah and the activities of reform groups. In Bengal the activities of Hindu reformers were reflected in Muslim women's writing (Amin 1996, xiii). The political ferment in the Muslim community in India and abroad mobilized the community and encouraged women to organize politically. This was strengthened by the setting up of purdah clubs, which increased the interaction between women of the Western educated Muslim community. They became venues for discussion of contemporary issues, for exchanging information and experiences outside the confines of the family. The Anjuman-i-Khawatin-i-Islam (Muslim Ladies' Association or Conference) was set up in Hyderabad in 1901 (Zaidi 1937, 107), in Aligarh in 1905 (Mirza 1969, 13), in Lahore in 1907 (Shahnawaz 1971, 25), and in Calcutta in 1913 (ibid., 94). The leadership of these organizations was drawn from prominent families already involved in political and educational activities. Polygamy, education, and the constraints imposed by purdah on the exercising of rights in the Sharī'a were their main concerns.

With the proliferation of women's organizations, it was inevitable that non-partisan national organizations would be created to cater to the broader needs of women. The establishment of the Women's Indian Association in Madras in 1917 and the All India Women's Conference (AIWC) in 1928 drew many women of ability across the religious spectrum. The work of these organizations went beyond social issues such as purdah and widow remarriage to political participation. To most women leaders, both Hindu and Muslim, purdah and its restrictions were to be cast aside so that women could participate in social and political policymaking that directly affected them.

The women's movement benefited from the momentum of the nascent national movement. The imprisonment of male leaders enabled women to set aside purdah and their restrictive familial roles to step forward in their place. The activities of Abadi Banu Begum and Bi Amman were just such an example. Bi Amman, the mother of prominent Muslim politicians Shaukat Ali and Muhammad Ali, active in the 1920s–1930s, acted as a bridge between the women's and the political movements. At meetings to encourage women's participation, Bi Amman was propelled into the political limelight. In 1917, she appeared in a *burqa'* and spoke at the Muslim League and Congress meetings alongside Hindu women leaders. Her activities, commitment to the political aspirations of the Muslim community, nationalist credentials, and her effort to recruit women to both movements, provided the women in purdah a connection to the national movement. This was demonstrated at a public meeting in Punjab. When arguing that the whole audience was after all part of her family, she lifted the veil of her *burqaʿ* and came out of purdah (Minault 1982, 252–4).

The formation of non-partisan women's groups enabled Muslim and Hindu women to fight together for their rights and to steadily recognize the irrelevance of purdah. Sultan Jahan Begum, the politically active ruler of Bhopal, shifted from a position of support for purdah to its renunciation. Early in her rule she opposed coeducational institutions because of the prevalence of purdah. In 1922 she reportedly wrote that "to expect Muslim girls to go to schools and colleges with open faces or with veils on with boys to obtain instruction . . . is tantamount to the death of their finer sentiments, morality and religion" (*Roshini* 1946, 11, 92). Several years later, in a report of the AIWC, she is quoted as having said: "The present strictness of *purdah* system among Muslims does not form part of their religious obligations. The Mussalmans should coolly and calmly decide whether by respecting a mere custom should they keep their women in a state of suspended animation" (Kaur 1968, 26). It was only in 1929, when she presided over the AIWC session, that she publicly and symbolically removed her purdah. At that session a resolution against purdah was passed (Caton 1930, 123).

Though purdah had already been identified as the chief impediment to the progress of women in the nineteenth century, it was not till the formation of the women's movement in the twentieth century that women leaders belonging to politically active families were able to render purdah irrelevant and to center women's issues within the goals of the national movement. In turn, the national movement with its broad alliance of communities provided women leaders with a platform that gave no importance to their traditional roles or purdah but instead supported them in promoting issues that increased their social and political participation and created links between communities and regions across the subcontinent, even when political aspirations of male leaders and political parties diverged (Lateef 1990, 85).

Bibliography

A. A. Ali, *The emergence of feminism among Indian Muslim women*, 1920–1947, Oxford 2000.

S. N. Amin, *The world of Muslim women in colonial Bengal, 1876–1939*, Leiden 1996.

A. J. Arberry, *The Koran interpreted*, New York 1973.

A. R. Caton, *The key of progress*, Oxford 1930.

D. Gordon, *Women of Algeria. An essay on change*, Cambridge, Mass. 1968.

M. Kaur, *Role of women in the freedom movement*, Delhi 1968.

S. Lateef, *Muslim women in India. Political and private realities 1890s–1980s*, New Delhi 1990.

G. Minault, Purdah politics. The role of Muslim women in Indian nationalism, 1911–1924, in H. Papanek and G. Minault (eds.), *Separate worlds. Studies of purdah in South Asia*, Delhi 1982, 245–61.

S. H. Mirza, *Muslim women's role in the Pakistan movement*, Lahore 1969.

S. K. Nehru (ed.), *Our cause*, Allahabad n.d.

M. A. Nuhuman, Ethnic identity, religious fundamentalism and Muslim women in Sri Lanka, in Muslim Women's Research and Action Forum, *Alternative perspectives. A collection of essays on contemporary Muslim society*, Colombo 1997, 11, 12; also in Women Living under Muslim Laws, Dossier 21 (September 1998), 89–111.

F. Rahman, The status of women in Islam. A modernist interpretation, in H. Papanek and G. Minault (eds.), *Separate worlds. Studies of purdah in South Asia*, Delhi 1982, 285–310.

Roshini, publication of the All India Women's Conference, 11 (February 1946).

J. Shahnawaz, *Father and daughter*, Lahore 1971.

C. Vreede-de Stuers, *Parda. A study of Muslim women's life in northern India*, New York 1968.

S. M. H. Zaidi, *Muslim womanhood in revolution*, Calcutta 1937.

Shahida Lateef

Political-Social Movements: Revolutionary

Egypt

Women have played a prominent role in Egyptian revolutionary movements over the last century. The three major revolutionary movements have mirrored the three broad, overlapping political trends that have shaped Egyptian politics in the twentieth century: nationalist, leftist, and Islamist.

The participation of women in the 1919 Revolution has been enshrined in Egyptian nationalist historiography as the beginning of Egyptian women's public participation in the nation. The events of 1919 were touched off in March by the deportation of Saʿd Zaghlūl, leader of the nationalist Wafd (delegation) party, by the British colonial authorities. As news of the deportation spread, cities and towns erupted in mass strikes and demonstrations against British rule. Modes of women's participation in anti-colonial activism tended to be class specific. Elite women formed the Wafdist Woman's Central Committee, participated in organized strikes and provided support to the efforts of the Wafd's Central Committee. Lower-class women participated in spontaneous street demonstrations; some were killed by British troops and honored as martyrs to the Egyptian nationalist cause. In the countryside, rural women provided food and assistance to activists charged with sabotaging the rail lines.

Although Egyptian nationalist accounts have come to stress women's militant participation in demonstrations and their martyrdom at the hands of British troops, the iconography of the revolution itself relied heavily on familial imagery which stressed the maternal roles women had to play in revolution. Saʿd Zaghlūl's wife Ṣafiyya played a prominent political role during the unrest of 1919, making speeches to crowds who gathered in front of her home, which was popularly known as Bayt al-Umma (House of the nation), and writing articles in support of political action. Her actions, however, were conceptualized as part of her duties as Zaghlūl's wife and her role as Umm al-Miṣriyyīn (Mother of the Egyptians) rather than as radical political acts in their own right. Ṣafiyya's role as a symbol of the proper Egyptian woman, sacrificing for nation and family, served to justify the new sorts of political activities women were undertaking even as it circumscribed more radical claims that women could make on the basis of those activities. When Egypt was granted independence in 1922 and the 1923 constitution recognized the principle of universal male suffrage, feminist demands for the vote on the basis of revolutionary participation were ignored.

The immediate post-Second World War period witnessed a second wave of revolutionary activity brought on by the political deadlock produced by the struggle for control between the monarchy, the Wafd, and the British and the emergence of new social and political movements. Leftist organizations which rose to prominence during this period, including communist, socialist, and labor groups maintained a broad, ideological commitment to women's rights as part of their general programs aimed at securing wider social, political, and economic rights for the lower and middle classes and included women in leadership positions. The student movement in particular saw active women's participation and leadership, among them Sayza Nabarāwī, Laṭīfa Zayyāt, Widād Mitrī, and Injī Aflāṭūn. For the most part, however, the platforms of such organizations de-emphasized specific feminist struggle, subsuming the issue of women's liberation into the broader struggle for the liberation of the Egyptian masses. Nonetheless, the general atmosphere of radical political activism encouraged the formation of ad hoc groups and committees (such as the League of Women Students and Graduates of the University and Egyptian Institutes, the Committee of Young Women, and the Women's Committee for Popular Resistance), which organized specifically around women's issues and mobilization, providing a forum for new articulations of the relationship between class, nation, and feminism.

The other major revolutionary movement during the post-Second World War period was the Muslim Brotherhood, which advocated the end of British and Western influence in Egypt and the institution of a government based upon Islamic principles. A fundamental part of their program was the return to what they argued as more Islamically "traditional" roles for women, valorizing women's roles as mothers and wives whose religiously ordained place was in the home. The Muslim Brotherhood was an exclusively male organization, but it often coordinated activities with another Islamist group, the Muslim Sisters, led by Zaynab al-Ghazālī. Like the Muslim Brotherhood, the Muslim Sisters defined women primarily as mothers, calling on them to take up their duty to raise the next generation of Muslim believers.

The 1952 "Revolution" was actually a military coup led by Gamal Abdel Nasser who claimed to embody the popular and revolutionary will of the Egyptian people. As part of its avowed task to make Egypt into a modern, independent nation by mobilizing previously disenfranchised groups and achieving social justice, the Nasser regime granted women the right to vote and hold public office, the right to work, and the right to obtain an education on the same level as men. Although women gained recognition as enfranchised citizens, however, like other groups they lost political autonomy. In 1954, political parties were abolished in favor of a series of single party organizations. Many women who were active in revolutionary organizations in the 1940s, such as Zaynab al-Ghazālī and Injī Aflaṭūn were jailed, as were other Islamists and communists.

In the post-Infitāḥ period, political Islam has become the main framework of revolutionary opposition to the Egyptian regime. Revolutionary Islamist groups such as Takfīr wa-Hijra, Jihād, and the Jamiʿat al-Islāmiyya trace their roots back to the Muslim Brotherhood. What distinguishes these radical groups from the majority of Islamist organizations (which are reformist in nature) is that they advocate the violent overthrow of the Egyptian state. What revolutionary Islamist groups share with reformist groups is a common conception of women's primary roles as mothers and spouses. Within the context of Islamist struggle, however, these are viewed as fundamentally political, not social, roles. There has been significantly more scholarship on the participation of women in the project of Islamic reform (as opposed to Islamic revolution). What information exists suggests that women's activities vary from organization to organization. Female members of Jihād have often been used to carry explosives and messages between cells as well as forge links with other revolutionary groups. For the most part, however, women in revolutionary Islamist organizations have been primarily charged with "reproducing" the female ranks of the organization, by identifying wives for male organization members and spreading *daʿwa* (the call) through prayer meetings and study groups.

BIBLIOGRAPHY

S. Botman, The experience of women in the Communist movement, in *Women's Studies International Forum* 11:2 (1988), 117–26.

Z. al-Ghazālī, *Ayyām min ḥayātī*, Cairo n.d.

A. Karam, *Women, Islamisms and the state*, New York 1998.

A. Khater and C. Nelson, Al-harakah al-nisā'iyyah. The women's movement and political participation in modern Egypt, in *Women's Studies International Forum* 11:2 (1988), 465–83.

A. L. al-Sayyid Marsot, The "revolutionary gentlewomen" in Egypt, in L. Beck and N. Keddie (eds.), *Women and the Muslim world*, Cambridge, Mass. 1978, 261–76.

L. Zayyat, *The search. Personal papers*, trans. S. Bennet, London 1992.

LAURA BIER

Indonesia

In 1942 colonial rule over Indonesia ended with the defeat of the Dutch by the Japanese. When the imperial army was conquered in 1945 Indonesia declared its independence. A national liberation war of four years followed. Women's participation in the nationalist and revolutionary movement was considerable. Until 1965 Indonesia's first president, Sukarno, steered Indonesia on a nationalist and socialist course. The Communist Party, the PKI, gained considerable influence and became the third largest communist party in the world. Islamic and right-wing military forces resented this development. A bloody putsch by left-wing colonels in 1965 was followed by a massacre of socialist groups, spurred on by military-instigated accusations of sexual perversions allegedly committed by young communist women. This led ultimately to the establishment of a right-wing military regime under general Suharto. Women played critical roles in these developments. The women's wing of the PKI, Gerwani, became a women's mass organization until it was banned in 1966. Right-wing women took to the streets after the putsch and demanded the banning of Gerwani.

NATIONAL LIBERATION

By the beginning of the twentieth century the newly-educated indigenous elite of Indonesia began to harbor nationalist sentiments. Inspired by the brilliant letters of the young Javanese princess Kartini (Kartini 1987), women began to chart their own course, which combined demands for their own rights, notably that of education with national liberation. The first women's organization was set up in 1912. In the following years many more organizations were formed, particularly in Java and the Minangkabau, a region in Sumatra that is characterized both by matrilineal customary law and a strict adherence to Islam. Both religious (Muslim and Catholic) and socialist women organized themselves. A major Islamic organization, Aisyiyah, was set up in 1917 mainly to give women religious instruction. They opposed a major demand of non-Islamic women's organizations, monogamy in marriage. Socialist women organized under the banner of a male-dominated socialist Islamic organization, the Sarekat Rakyat (People's league). In those years socialist and Islamic views were not so much perceived to clash as they would be in later years. The PKI, established in 1924, counted several women among its members. Some of them were also involved in the 1925–6 communist uprising, which was quickly crushed by the colonial government.

In 1928 the first all-Indonesian women's congress was held. Until the Japanese occupation, the unity of the women's movement was continuously threatened by the opposition between Islamic and non-Islamic groups over the issue of marriage reforms. Gradually the women's movement rallied behind the nationalist movement. Their leaders maintained that Indonesian women could only be emancipated after national liberation was won. Sukarno spoke of women as being the "second wheel of the chariot" of national liberation (Sukarno 1963, 255).

Women joined the guerilla war against the Dutch who refused to accept Indonesia's independence and tried to regain control of the region. Some young, radical women joined the Laswi, women's army units, and engaged in active combat. Others were engaged as messengers. Many more were involved in public kitchens to feed the fighters and in hospitals to care for the wounded soldiers.

Several national women's meetings were held during the years the national liberation struggle lasted. This period culminated in a major national women's congress held in August 1949, which was attended by 82 groups from all religions. Major women's interests were formulated, such as equal rights for women, protection for women workers, and education. The unity achieved at this congress was geared toward the achievement of national unity but left two major issues unresolved – the extent of the marriage reforms discussed (Suwondo 1981), and the struggle for socialist emancipation.

Women and socialist nationalism

The reign of Indonesia's first president, Sukarno, lasted until 1965. This was a period of nation building in which women and men were swept up in nationalist rhetoric, which became increasingly socialist. The new constitution of the republic guaranteed women equal rights, but the marriage issue remained unsolved. Now that the struggle for national independence was won, non-socialist women retreated to the domestic realm and left the political arena to men. Particularly religious (both Muslim and Christian) women increasingly returned to the "kodrat wanita," an essentialist, supposedly divinely-ordained code of women's conduct, which stipulates women's obedience to men. Gerwani was founded in 1950. Many of its members had been actively engaged in the guerilla struggle against the Dutch. In the first years they focused on building a small group of dedicated women. After 1954 they followed an instruction from the PKI, and started building a mass movement of revolutionary women. The PKI saw itself as the head of an Indonesian "communist family" in which Gerwani was assigned the role of the "mother." After 1959, when Sukarno established his authoritarian rule called "Guided Democracy," Gerwani also became radicalized. It was the only women's organization that refused to leave the national political arena to men. The organization's "militant mothers" (Wieringa 2002) concentrated less on gender concerns than they had in their first years but increasingly voiced national concerns. This led to tensions with non-socialist women's groups, particularly the Islamic mass women's organizations. Gerwani never officially became the PKI's women's wing. They had a weekly corner in the communist daily, and for many years published a magazine called *Api Kartini* (Kartini fire).

On 30 September 1965 leftist colonels abducted the nation's top generals, except General Suharto, and murdered them on a field on which young communist women were being trained for a nationalist campaign of Sukarno against the formation of Malaysia. Later the military accused these women of having castrated the generals. This greatly antagonized conservative groups in society and particularly Islamic youth groups were mobilized. Ultimately over a million socialist women and men were massacred and tens of thousands detained for many years. Muslim and Catholic women were in the forefront of the demonstrations and joined in demonizing Gerwani members as "whores" and "perverse women." General Suharto replaced President Sukarno and restored an order built on women's domestication. During his reign women's political agency was associated with sexual and moral disorder (Wieringa 2002). Initially Islamic women's groups experienced relief; later they realized that they too were no longer able to implement the social programs they had formerly harbored.

Bibliography

R. A. Kartini, *Brieven aan Mevrouw R.M. Abendanon-Mandri en haar Echtgenoot met andere Documenten*, ed. F. G. P. Jaquet, 1912, Dordrecht 1987.

Sukarno, *Sarinah. The duty of women in the struggle of the Indonesian Republic* [in Indonesian], Jakarta 1947, 1963.
N. Suwondo, *The position of Indonesian women in law and society* [in Indonesian], Jakarta 1981.
S. Wieringa, *Sexual politics in Indonesia*, Houndmills, Basingstoke, Hampshire 2002.

Saskia E. Wieringa

Iran and Afghanistan

IRAN

Women's emancipation as a component of social progress surfaced before the emergence of Iran's constitutional movement (1905–11). In the 1840s, the Bābī movement projected equality between the sexes in many domains of social life (Cole 1998). The Constitutionalists supported female education and increased social participation. Women contributed to the revolution, but the Majlis, influenced by religious leaders, denied women enfranchisement, categorizing them with the mentally handicapped and criminals (Afary 1996).

In the early 1900s, advocates of women's education included women with socialist sympathies. Socialists saw women's rights as a prerequisite to social progress and opposed state and clerical suppression (Shahidian 2002a).

Reza Shah's ascendancy signaled the demise of activism by leftists and women (Sanasarian 1982). Neither movement resurfaced until the Shah's abdication in 1941.

In 1943, the Organization of Iranian Women, affiliated to the Tudeh (Communist) Party demanded legal transformations regarding women in the family and workplace. In 1945, the short-lived autonomous governments of Azerbaijan and Kurdistan approved women's enfranchisement. Before it was outlawed in 1949, the Tudeh Party introduced legislation for enfranchisement and improved conditions. Clerics and conservatives rejected the bill (Abrahamian 1982).

The 1953 coup brought widespread arrests. Only state-approved organizations existed for the next 25 years. Women participated in student movements and semi-clandestine circles. Activists discussed land reform and infiltrating the working class, rarely addressing women's issues.

In the 1970s, the People's Mujāhidīn Organization of Iran and the Organization of Iranian People's Fedaii Guerrillas offered opportunities for expressing women's dissent. The former, radical religious activists, relied on Marxist political economy, the latter on Marxism-Leninism (Abrahamian 1989). Initially, women participated in neither group; it took time for the Mujāhidīn to recognize them (Najāt Ḥusaynī 2001). Marxists attracted more women than religious organizations; their membership drew on colleges, urban intellectuals, and liberal-minded professionals (Abrahamian 1982).

Though female leftists loomed significantly in the 1979 Revolution and most maintained independence from Islamists, the left disregarded feminist autonomy. Many leftist women's organizations functioned primarily as recruiters (Moghissi 1994, Shahidian 2002a). Women participated on the left, opposing the Islamic Republic of Iran's assault on rights (Tabari and Yeganeh 1982, Moghissi 1994, Hajebi Tabrizi 2000).

After 1981, leftists and women activists were imprisoned or exiled. Exiled women organized, some affiliating with political organizations, others advocating autonomy. They recounted their tribulations, especially prison experiences (Barādarān 1992). Discussions have reassessed culture and politics through a gender lens; an autonomous women's movement has gradually taken root. Women's involvement in community activism includes establishing libraries and family crisis centers; providing services for expatriates; and broadcasting (Shahidian 1996, Ghorashi 2002).

Those in Iran established study groups and engaged in writing and publishing. Veterans and newcomers have revisited leftist approaches to gender. Secular women concentrated on the emerging – albeit amorphous – women's movement, rallying for rights, participating in conferences, organizing celebrations of 8 March. Some wrote for reformist journals; others cooperated with reformists but maintained independence. Their writings were later published as books and anthologies (Shahidian 2002b).

AFGHANISTAN

Women's rights have also been an ingredient of modernization in Afghanistan, dating from the early 1900s. Yet weak central governments, tribal factionalism, reforms from above, and conservative reactions have retarded gender reforms (Dupree 1980).

Not until the 1964 constitutional debate did women publicly voice concerns over rights (Dupree 1984). Organized movements soon emerged. Liberals advocated eliminating sex discrimination and increasing government participation. Socialists proposed changing the material bases of women's oppression by eradicating semi-feudalism and capitalism (Emadi 2002).

Under Dāwūd's presidency, strong student movements developed in the 1970s. Nationalist and leftist women participated in protests to promote student demands and gender equality.

A small group, led by Meena (1957–87), established in 1977 the first independent feminist organization: the Revolutionary Association of the Women of Afghanistan (RAWA), partly in response to the marginalization of women's issues in existing organizations. RAWA emphasized clandestine, grassroots activism and empowerment (Brodsky 2003).

Established in 1965, the pro-Soviet Democratic Party of the People of Afghanistan (PDPA) soon split into two factions: Khalq (Masses) and Parcham (Banner). The Parcham formed the Women's Democratic Organization of Afghanistan (WDOA). Each faction organized clandestine cells that infiltrated governmental and educational institutions and youth groups. When their party ruled, women from each faction gained prominence. Their impact was limited since the public could not relate to well-known female politicians (Emadi 2002).

Various PDPA governments initiated gender reforms, emphasizing kindergarten expansion, literacy, education, job security, and health services. Decree No. 7 aimed to change marriage customs, but retained laws on custody, divorce, polygyny, and abuse (Dupree 1984).

Under the PDPA, the state assumed protection for women instead of welcoming women's grassroots activism. Women were heralded in stereotypical supportive roles. Autocratic reforms provoked resentment, especially in villages (Dupree 1984). The PDPA responded by slowing reform and reinstating Islamic family law. Party followers purportedly retained PDPA initiatives (Moghadam 1992). There were, nonetheless, reports of abuse of power by party members. Many female members were obliged to allow their parents to choose their mates (Emadi 2002).

Particularly in Kabul, women and youth initially supported leftist rule. Yet factional conflicts heightened, and promises of reforms failed to materialize. Disillusionment turned into feelings of betrayal after the invasion by the Soviet Union. Women's resistance emerged in informal gatherings, but when information exchange about imprisoned loved ones proved ineffective, collective protests formed (Emadi 2002).

Invasion created educational and employment opportunities for some women; for many it meant loss of family, and captivity in Soviet and Mujāhidīn jails. Women played key roles in grassroots opposition and experienced enhanced community status and empowerment by learning new organizational and military skills (Ellis 2000). Many joined the resistance following the imprisonment or death of sons and husbands. Though military participation was not extensive, women took part especially in identifying and executing collaborators (Dupree 1984, Emadi 2002).

Invasion shifted emphases of the movement from gender struggle to community services at refugee camps and support for male Mujāhidīn whose vision of an independent Afghanistan did not include gender equality (Brodsky 2003, Emadi 2002). Various organizations in camps were involved in activities such as health services, education, and creating revenues for women. Fundamentalists in camps and the Pakistani police often harassed activists. Many organizations learned to act within limits set by fundamentalists who wielded tremendous power (Dupree 2001). RAWA alone simultaneously opposed Soviets and fundamentalists (Brodsky 2003).

Far from emancipation, the Taliban's demise restored the Northern Alliance, Mujāhidīn who earlier inflicted wounds on Afghan women: "The oppression of Afghanistan and particularly Afghan women did not start with the Taliban nor has it ended with its defeat" (RAWA, in Brodsky 2003, ix).

Sociopolitical change in Iran and Afghanistan intertwines with concern for women's rights. Women symbolize modernity for governments and parties, a condition that may advance status but costs women's movements autonomy. Iranian women emerged as an active group earlier than Afghani women, but revolutionaries in both countries showed reluctance toward feminist autonomy. One factor for this resistance was a common ideological source: Soviet Marxism. Upheavals in the late 1970s effected divergent results. In Iran, the Islamic Republic assaulted women's rights; in Afghanistan, a paternalist Marxist regime dubbed autonomous activism counter-revolutionary. Afghani women have also had to ward off Islamist denial of women's rights, even after resisting Soviet occupation. Exiled Afghani and Iranian women defended women's rights in the homeland and experienced new forms of activism and community involvement.

Bibliography

E. Abrahamian, *Iran between two revolutions*, Princeton, N.J. 1982.

——, *The Iranian mojahedin*, New Haven, Conn. 1989.

J. Afary, *The Iranian Constitutional Revolution, 1906–1911. Grassroots democracy, social democracy, and the origin of feminism*, New York 1996.

M. Barādarān (M. Rahā), *Ḥaqīqat-i sādah*, Hanover, Germany 1992.

A. E. Brodsky, *With all our strength. The Revolutionary Association of the Women of Afghanistan*, New York 2003.

J. Cole, *Modernity and the millennium*, New York 1998.
L. Dupree, *Afghanistan*, Princeton, N.J. 1980.
N. H. Dupree, Revolutionary rhetoric and Afghan women, in M. N. Shahrani and R. L. Canfield (eds.), *Revolution and rebellion in Afghanistan. Anthropological perspectives*, Berkeley 1984, 306–40.
——, Afghan women under the Taliban, in W. Maley (ed.), *Fundamentalism reborn? Afghanistan and the Taliban*, New York 2001, 145–66.
D. Ellis, *Women of the Afghan war*, Westport, Conn. 2000.
H. Emadi, *Repression, resistance, and women in Afghanistan*, Westport, Conn. 2002.
H. Ghorashi, *Ways to survive, battles to win. Iranian women exiles in the Netherlands and the United States*, New York 2002.
V. M. Moghadam, Revolution, Islam and women. Sexual politics in Iran and Afghanistan, in A. Parker et al. (eds.), *Nationalisms and sexualities*, New York 1992, 424–45.
H. Moghissi, *Populism and feminism in Iran. Women's struggle in a male-defined revolutionary movement*, New York 1994.
M. Najāt Ḥusaynī, *Bar farāz-i khalīj*, Tehran 2001[2].
E. Sanasarian, *The women's rights movement in Iran. Mutiny, appeasement, and repression from 1900 to Khomeini*, New York 1982.
H. Shahidian, Women and clandestine politics in Iran. 1970–1985, in *Feminist Studies* 23:1 (1997), 7–42.
——, *Women in Iran. Gender politics in the Islamic Republic*, Westport, Conn. 2002a.
——, *Women in Iran. Emerging voices in the women's movement*, Westport, Conn. 2002b.
A. Tabari and N. Yeganeh (eds.), *In the shadow of Islam. The women's movement in Iran*, London 1982.

HAMMED SHAHIDIAN

Iraq

Shortly after the Iraqi Revolution of 14 July 1958, which toppled the British-backed Hashemite monarchy, the new republic commissioned Jawād Salīm to build "The Monument to Liberty," an enormous sculpture in Baghdad's Liberation Square that tells the epic of the revolution. Among its more famous images are two political demonstrators of mixed gender. The woman marches one stride ahead of the man, both fists raised in the air, her face turned directly toward the monument's viewers; the two seem perfectly matched in physical strength and forward momentum. Salīm's powerful depiction of a woman in protest was immediately recognized by Iraqi commentators not only as a symbol of the nation's future but also as a representative of its recent past.

The participation of Iraqi women in revolutionary uprisings during the first half of the twentieth century is well established, and their roles in the rebellions of 1920, 1948, 1952, and 1956 even developed into national legends. Women were active in Arab and Kurdish uprisings, in urban and rural demonstrations, and in underground revolutionary parties. This participation often took an unorganized form, as women spontaneously entered the streets en masse with men. Well-known cultural legends, as well as numerous accounts by historians, also illuminate a recurrent theme in Iraq's narratives of resistance, in which a single woman leads a group of men or of mixed gender in revolt. In one such legend, a woman named Danuka is said to have led a demonstration of male workers to the house of Prime Minister Ṣādir during the Wathba (Leap) rebellion of 1948, and then addressed him in front the crowd, waving a revolver in each hand. This story resembles a number of well-documented incidents in Arab as well as Kurdish regions of Iraq. In October 1956, for example, a woman was shot and killed by Iraqi police as she led the funeral procession of Shaykh Maḥmūd of the Barzanjī Kurds into an attack on the local jail, which was holding one of the shaykh's sons. The monarchy announced in its defense that the woman was a "communist sympathizer," but she would become known in national legend as "the martyr Akhtar."

In addition to spontaneous participation in uprisings, women were involved in Iraq's underground revolutionary movements in more organized ways. The Iraqi Communist Party (ICP), the country's most significant revolutionary organization from the Second World War through 1958, actively recruited women for demonstrations, for example by bringing truckloads of rural women into Baghdad for nationalist marches, as well as for long-term mobilization. Women's cells were established in the ICP during the 1940s, as was the position of *mas'ūl*, the comrade in charge of organizing and recruiting communist women. In 1952, female members of the party founded its women's auxiliary, the League for the Defense of Women's Rights, which distributed clandestine literature promoting sexual equality and organized women to participate in the 1952, 1954, and 1956 rebellions. It also attracted a number of the best-known female artists, poets, and intellectuals of Iraq's artistic and political underground.

After the 1958 Revolution, the public visibility of women at political meetings and street demonstrations, while in many ways consistent with the historical participation of Iraqi women in rebellion, may have also gone beyond the earlier paradigms as women organized their own mass demonstrations, went door-to-door educating people in Marxist ideology, and took up arms in the new republic's civilian militia, the People's Resistance Forces. While women were represented in many of the grassroots organizations that emerged after the revolution, they were particularly active in the Peace Partisans, the Federation of Democratic Youth, the Iraqi Teachers' Union, and, above all, the League for the Defense of Women's Rights.

The league achieved some substantial victories during its two years of active public life. In 1959, it won its legal campaigns to outlaw honor killings and to implement the personal status law, which stipulated a minimum age of 18 years for marriage and expanded women's protection against arbitrary divorce; most controversially, female descendants were accorded equal rights with males in matters of intestate succession. Also in 1959, Prime Minister Qāsim appointed a founder of the league, Nazīha Dulaymī, as his minister of municipalities, making her the first woman and the first member of the Communist Party to serve in the Iraqi cabinet. Dulaymī claimed in her opening speech at the league's second conference, on 8 March 1960, that league membership had grown from 20,000 to 42,000 in a single year, and that thousands of additional women were receiving literacy training and medical services at league branches throughout the country. An Iraqi women's art exhibit was opened at the Institute of Modern Art in Baghdad in conjunction with the conference; it contained works "depicting the Iraqi woman's struggle in the eradicated regime and her gains and efforts in the flourishing era of the Revolution" (*Iraq Times*, 3 August 1960).

In 1960, Qāsim's regime began suppressing the country's revolutionary organizations, including the League for the Defense of Women's Rights, and the first Baʿth coup of 1963 dealt the final death blow to a public, autonomous women's movement in twentieth-century Iraq. One of the new regime's first policy acts was to repeal the clause of the personal status law that guaranteed equality between male and female heirs. The second Baʿth government, which ruled Iraq from 1963 to 2003, was more progressive on women's issues, and strove to integrate women more fully into the national labor force and educational system. It was also fond of using such achievements as evidence that a state-directed approach to women's rights was more effective than one led by an autonomous feminist movement. But the Baʿth Party's success in this area rested at least partly on its ability to contain and control gender challenges and women's rights discourses that emerged before and during the revolutionary years of 1958–60. Baʿth leaders adopted the popular if highly contested rhetoric of women's equality produced by the League for the Defense of Women's Rights and other revolutionary groups, while effectively containing their more radical implications and possibilities.

Bibliography

Primary Sources

Iraq Times, 1958–60.

Ittiḥād al-shaʿb, 1958–9.

United States Department of Commerce Joint Publications Research Service, *The communist movement in Iraq*, parts I and II, Washington, D.C. 1967.

Secondary Sources

H. Batatu, *The old social classes and the revolutionary movements of Iraq*, Princeton, N.J. 1978.

J. Ismael and S. Ismael, Gender and state in Iraq, in S. Joseph (ed.), *Gender and citizenship in the Middle East*, Syracuse, N.Y. 2000, 107–36.

Sara Pursley

North Africa

Although largely ignored in the official recorded histories of the Maghrib, women have greatly contributed to the political and social construction of the modern countries of this region of the world. They fought for independence, militated in political parties, initiated activism and civil society, infiltrated academia, and boldly combated religious fanaticism. Throughout the period that extends from pre-colonization, colonization, independence, and state-building to the era of democratization, women have always been active in private and public spaces. Their movements started as political, focusing on education and legal rights, and moved to include civil society and academia as well. The strategies used by women to counter the inequities they protest against have been shaped by specific historical, social, political, economic, and linguistic environments where reformism, colonization, leftist political parties, civil society, multilingualism, academia, and Islamism played a significant role.

The history of women's movements in the Maghrib goes back to the pre-colonization and the colonization periods during which male leaders of the Islah (reform) movement such as Allal al-Fassi (Morocco), Ibn Badis (Algeria), and Tahar Haddad (Tunisia) argued for women's emancipation within the cultural/religious value systems of Maghribian societies. These leaders linked social development and modernization with women's education. This instigated many women of the 1930s and 1940s to start claiming their rights through pioneer women's organizations such as Akhawāt al-Ṣafāʾ (Sisters of purity) in Morocco, the Association of Muslim Women in Algeria, and the Union of Tunisian Women. These associations were created and led by educated urban elite women who had connections with the larger national liberation movements.

Women such as Malika El-Fassi (Morocco), Djamila Debeche (Algeria), and Bchira M'rad (Tunisia) are examples. The first women's organizations did not problematize women's status because women believed that independence would bring about their emancipation; their aim was to make women aware of their social importance and train them in the public organization of their demands. These pioneer women used strategies such as press articles, public speeches, and private or public gatherings where they explained the importance of women's education and participation in the struggle for independence. As a result of these actions, women participated in revolutionary movements by combating the enemy, hiding male members of their families, and smuggling weapons.

Following the independence of Morocco (1956), Tunisia (1956), and Algeria (1962), the new ruling elites sought to re-establish Islam in their sociolegal institutions through family laws based on the Sharīʿa (Islamic law). However, it was only in Tunisia that the family law was progressive. In spite of unfair legal treatment, women's lifestyle on the eve of independence was different from that of their mothers. They took advantage of improved health standards, massive access to schooling in urban areas, generalized paid work, and an increasing participation in the labor force, all of which were needed for the economic development of the newly independent countries to broaden their horizons beyond the domestic sphere.

These benefits allowed women academics to become aware of the fact that the shift from the ideology of liberation to that of state-building marginalized women. Fatima Mernissi and Leila Abouzeid (Morocco), Assia Djebbar and Fadma Amrouche (Algeria), and Souad Guellouz and Emna Belhaj Yahya (Tunisia) are examples. In Morocco and Algeria, these voices were particularly fueled by the bitter realization that the family laws turned out to be a betrayal in relegating women to home and hearth and distancing them from public spheres. From then on, women's struggle was concentrated on the revision of family law in these two countries. Only in Tunisia did family law give women basic rights.

In addition to academics, many women activists started organizing themselves politically by creating women's sections within leftist parties. Representative names of prominent women in this respect are Nouzha Skalli and Rabéa Naciri (Morocco), Louisa Hanoun and Khalida Messaoudi (Algeria), and Bochra Belhaj Hamida and Sihem Ben Sidrine (Tunisia). They used this space to challenge the "reactionary" establishment and called for more social equity and human rights. In the mid-1980s, women's role in development surfaced in the countries of the Maghrib with more acuity, because of four major factors: literacy, the law of the job-market, democratic political values, and international pressure. These factors were heavily exploited by the leftist socialist movements. Women's voices within these movements became louder and two trends emerged: women who pushed for social equity through party line and women who, although partisans of social movements, stressed the gender issue and the singularity of women's demands. It is the latter type of women who largely contributed to the emergence of a strong civil society in the Maghrib.

Pioneer activist associations such as the Association marocaine des femmes démocrates, the Association pour le triomphe des droits des femmes, and the Association tunisienne des femmes démocrates were a prominent part of an overall social movement which, backed by calls for more human rights, launched the era of civil society that is still thriving. In capitalizing on civil society, women were a prominent part of the overall progressive and human rights promotion movement of the mid-1980s onwards. The area of family law remained the focus of women's demands either in political parties or in civil society in contexts where Islamism resists any amendment of family law. In Morocco, Algeria, and also Tunisia, women struggled for the revision of family law. Tunisian family law was amended in 1965, 1966, and 1981, and the Moroccan in 1993 and 2004. The Algerian family law was amended in 1984 and demands to introduce more amendments are becoming ever louder. In Morocco and Algeria, demands for women's rights are being accompanied by demands for cultural and linguistic rights.

An important aspect of women's movements in the Maghrib is their great impact on the democratization processes in their countries, the lifting of the sacredness that surrounded religious texts, and on mentalities. More and more female voices such as Farida Bennani, Zainab Maadi, and Latifa Jbabdi are advocating a reinterpretation of the sacred texts (the Qurʾān and the Prophet's sayings) from a feminist perspective. It is such endeavors that partly led to the recent revision of Moroccan family law.

From the mid-1990s onwards, women's movements in the Maghrib have been greatly enhanced by the creation of centers and groups for academic research on gender or women's studies such as the Center for Studies and Research on Women in Fes and various university women's groups. These movements have also been consolidated by the pioneer creation of university graduate units such as one for women's studies in Rabat and another for gender studies in Fes. These graduate units have produced the first cohorts of masters and doctorate holders in women's and gender studies in Morocco. University centers and graduate units have significantly contributed to bridging the gap between the university and civil society as students often carry out fieldwork with women's non-governmental organizations. They have also been very instrumental in democratizing higher education. More national and international colloquia are devoted to women's issues and more books by and on women are introduced in the university curricula. The current move in Maghribian women's movements is from a predominantly political discourse to more academic discussions, building-up of scholarship and fieldwork, bridging gaps between academia and activist civil society, and, most importantly, preparing students who will ensure continuity. Gender is more and more used as an analytical tool for understanding men, women, and society in this part of the world.

The great headway obtained by women in the Maghrib highlights the fact that women's experiences, interpretations, and understandings of issues and events were unique and often differed from men's. These endeavors brought about the issues of health, enterprise, jobs, and other similar influences, as relating to women for the first time. Women's voices began to be taken seriously by the decision-makers. Women's movements in the three countries of the Maghrib share some aspects and differ in others. On the one hand, these movements crystallize around continuous demands for the revision of the family laws, they denounce the sexist practices of their heavily patriarchal sociocultural environment, they want more political and legal rights, and they capitalize on education as women's empowerment. On the other hand, women's movements are deeply affected by the political leadership of each country: while the king in Morocco as the highest political and religious authority is in favor of women's promotion, no such support is found in Algeria or Tunisia. In Algeria, women rely more on political parties, and in Tunisia, the secured rights may be jeopardized by increasing restrictions on human rights.

All in all, the role of women in the revolutionary movements of the Maghrib has become nowadays one of the pillars of the general development and democratization. Through their movements, women in this region have succeeded in creating and maintaining opportunities for women by providing education, health care, legal assistance, and economic opportunities. Their achievements are remarkable in a social order based on heavy patriarchy.

Bibliography

Primary Sources

D. Amrane, *Les femmes algériennes dans la guerre*, Paris 1991.

A. Belarbi, Mouvements de femmes au Maroc, in *Annuaire de l'Afrique du nord* 28 (1989), 455–65.

F. Bennani and Z. Maadi, *Sélection de textes sacrés sur les droits humains de la femme en islam*, Rabat 2000.

R. Bourquia (ed.), *Etudes féminines*, Rabat 1997.

Z. Daoud, *Féminisme et politique au Maghreb. 60 ans de lutte*, Casablanca 1993.

G. El Khayat, *Le Maghreb des femmes*, Casablanca 1992.

S. Ferchiou, Féminisme d'état en Tunisie. Idéologie dominante et résistance féminine, in R. Bourquia, N. Charrad, and N. Gallagher (eds.), *Femmes, culture et société au Maghreb*, Casablanca 1996, 134–8.

G. Halimi, *La cause des femmes*, Paris 1992.

R. Naciri, Genre, pouvoir et prise de la décision au Maroc, in Nations Unis, Commission Economique pour l'Afrique, *Disparité entre femmes et hommes et culture en Afrique du Nord*, 2001, 25–40, <http://www.uneca-na.org/francais/un/ PUBLICATIONS%20 DU%20CENTRE/DISPARITES%20ENTRE%20 FEMMES%20ET%20HOMMES%20ET%20CULTURE 20E.PDF>.

F. Sadiqi, *Women, gender and language in Morocco*, Leiden 2003.

——, Women and politics in Morocco, in International Feminist Journal of Politics. E-Journal, Routledge (forthcoming).

Secondary Sources

Collectif 95 Maghreb Egalité, *Women in the Maghreb. Change and resistance*, Brussels 1995.

——, *Les maghrébines entre violences symboliques et violences physiques (Algérie, Maroc, Tunisie)*, Brussels 1999.

Fatima Sadiqi

Palestine

Palestinian women have been part of the resistance against Israeli colonialism throughout the history of the conflict. They have often been mobilized via their domestic roles and kinship ties as mothers and wives, but also as militants, politicians, and grassroots organizers.

During the Arab Revolt (1936–9), a sustained strike against the British Mandate and Zionist incursions in Palestine, women hid and prepared food for fighters and acted as couriers for men who had less freedom of movement (Sayigh 1993, 188). Through their involvement, some women gained political consciousness and awareness of social problems, and their families encouraged their participation because it supported the national cause (Antonius 1979, 36). These themes would reappear in future phases of the struggle for national liberation: politicization of women's domestic roles; the influence of kin relations; exploitation of the adversary's gender prejudices; and the impact of political work on women's empowerment.

When it was located in Lebanon the secularly based resistance involved women's broad, and active, participation. It motivated a degree of structural and ideological transformation in gender-based social relations, and women leaders consciously sought to exploit the malleability of social structures and values that can accompany war (Peteet 1991). Some women were mobilized via extensions of their domestic roles, while others challenged gender boundaries even further by fighting. During this period when nationalist values and valor were prioritized, in many cases activism was tolerated and encouraged by women's families and the society.

The nationalist inspiration of domestic activities was also central to the first intifada (uprising) in the Occupied Territories (1987–93). Not only did women shelter activists hiding from occupation authorities, they also actively confronted Israeli soldiers. A typical image from that period was that of a Palestinian woman, wielding a pot threateningly in one hand while wrenching some young man free of the grips of an Israeli soldier trying to arrest him. "All the boys are my sons," became a saying which, calling on traditional kinship relations, both explained and justified such courageous acts.

Through the promotion of national products and the local economy, women's popular committees, active since the 1980s, likewise extended women's traditional domestic activities into forms that helped sustain the first intifada. The committees' members, recruited from all social strata, encouraged home gardening and ran sewing or canning cooperatives as part of a strategy of "steadfastness," thus enabling women to help support their families during a time of economic hardship when many male bread-winners were imprisoned or otherwise unable to work (Hiltermann 1991). Although the committees were designed to raise both national and gender consciousness through widening women's participation in the economic and political spheres, societal expectations that women would prioritize the demands of raising families sometimes superseded their political commitments, curtailing women's involvement after marriage.

Women's political and militant activities have often been facilitated by Israeli gender biases. During the first intifada, the Israeli military did not shut down offices of the women's committees with the same frequency as they did other political offices. Women did not, however, escape imprisonment, beatings, and other reprisals, punishments which are often sexualized. Israeli interrogators use rape, sexual threats, and threats against children as forms of intimidation and torture against female prisoners. Some have asserted that withstanding such sexual harassment was transformed into a nationalist badge of courage, and that men sought women who had been political prisoners as marriage partners in order to defy the Occupation authorities (Thornhill 1992). Despite their brave and sustained participation and sacrifices for the sake of the nation, however, women's activism has not yielded a revolution in their social and political position. Not every family has accepted their daughters' political participation, and former female prisoners are not always seen as being desirable wives.

Another example of the exploitation of Israeli gender prejudice appeared during the second intifada, which began in 2000, when female suicide bombers slipped past Israeli security because they did not fit the typical profile of the male religious devotee. The wave of female suicide bombers attracted shocked curiosity in a Western press used to characterizing the perpetrators of such acts as young, fanatical men seduced into jihad by the promise of doe-eyed virgins in heaven. Women's involvement in what many Palestinians refer to as "martyrdom operations" served first, to counter orientalist stereotypes of the lascivious and religiously fanatical male "Arab terrorist," and second, to reassert the political message of these acts: that Palestinian women, men, and children are suffering from Israeli occupation.

The more militarized and less popular nature of the second intifada has created a starker distinction between the battlefront and home front, minimizing both men's and women's roles in direct resistance to the occupation. Women's participation has been largely confined to support roles, hiding and supplying food to fighters, for example. Mothers of martyrs continue to be a primary symbol of resistance, thereby heightening the significance of women as bearers of fighters (Johnson and Kuttab 2001, 31). While combat and imprisonment are not exclusively men's experiences, they are more central to the construction of male gender ideals. Beatings and detention have been described as rites of passage that transform young men into resistant subjects endowed with social prestige (Peteet 1994, 31).

The growth of the Islamist movement began to cause a restrictive conflation of women with national honor during the first intifada, when a campaign was waged in Gaza to impose the *ḥijāb* on women. The headscarf was re-encoded as a sign of women's political commitment, and women who did not wear it were defined as insufficiently nationalist. One analyst interpreted the "intifada *ḥijāb*" as signifying not modesty or respect; it was, rather, an indication of "the power of religious groups to impose themselves by attacking secularism and nationalism at their most vulnerable points: over issues of women's liberation" (Hammami 1990, 26). In part as a response to growing Islamism in Palestine, women activists reasserted the link between the struggle for an independent state with democratization and women's rights, as exemplified in the discussion of personal status law during the 1998 Model Parliament. Some Islamists tried to justify their rejection of the women activists' demands in nationalist terms by accusing them of being tools of imperialism and Zionism (Moghadam 2003, 179–80). Since women's military participation in the resistance in the 1970s, a dominant discourse has been that women's liberation would come through participation in the nationalist struggle and that a focus on specifically women's social issues was a distraction from the national struggle. And while leftist parties have mouthed support for women's issues, the dominant party, Fatah, has never had an articulated ideology concerning women, and their rhetoric reasserts women's primary role as "the mainstay of the family and the vessel of Palestinian culture" (Gluck 1995).

BIBLIOGRAPHY

S. Antonius, Fighting on two fronts. Conversations with Palestinian women, in *Journal of Palestine Studies* 8:3 (Spring 1979), 26–45.

R. Giacaman, I. Jad, and P. Johnson, For the common good? Gender and social citizenship in Palestine, in *Middle East Report* 198 (January–March 1996), 11–16.

S. Gluck, Palestinian women. Gender, politics and nationalism, in *Journal of Palestine Studies* 24:3 (Spring 1995), 5–15.

R. Hammami, Women, the *hijab*, and the *intifada*, in *Middle East Report* 164/5 (August–May 1990), 24–8.

J. Hiltermann, *Behind the intifada. Labor and women's movements in the Occupied Territories*, Princeton, N.J. 1991.

P. Johnson and E. Kuttab, Where have all the women (and men) gone? Reflections on gender and the second Palestinian intifada in *Feminist Review* 69 (Winter 2001), 21–43.

J. Peteet, *Gender in crisis. Women and the Palestinian resistance movement*, New York 1991.

——, Male gender rituals of resistance in the Palestinian *intifada*. A cultural politics of violence, in *American Ethnologist* 21:1 (1994), 31–49.

——, Icons and militants. Mothering in the danger zone, in *Signs. Journal of Women in Culture and Society* 23:1 (1997), 103–29.

R. Sayigh, Palestinian women and politics in Lebanon, in J. E. Tucker (ed.), *Arab women. Old boundaries, new frontiers*, Bloomington, Ind. 1993, 175–92.

T. Thornhill, *Making women talk. The interrogation of Palestinian women security detainees by the Israeli General Security Services*, London 1992.

LORI A. ALLEN

South Yemen and Dhofar

During the latter part of the twentieth century, the southern part of the Arabian Peninsula gave birth to revolutionary movements which fully engaged women but which left them with different outcomes. While in southern Yemen women can still enjoy most of the revolution's fruits, in Dhofar, the western province of Oman, the revolutionary movement was crushed, leaving few accomplishments.

In South Yemen, demands for reforms for women were raised first in Aden in the 1940s in pamphlets issued among cultural circles comprised of men from intellectual and commercial families. Aden formed part of British India until 1937. After Indian independence there were demands for freedom, the significant source of influence in Aden coming from centers of Arab radicalism such as Cairo and Beirut. Another influence was North Yemeni resistance to the rule of the imams driven by Arab nationalists, and the presence of exiles from this movement in Aden.

Radicalism in Aden followed different roads. A haven for labor migration from all over the peninsula, Aden harbored a strong trade union movement and radical political parties. Women's right to education, their legal rights, and the freedom to discard the *ḥijāb* were on the agenda of the radical wing of the independence movement. News and inspiration came through Ṣawt al-ʿArab radio in Cairo and the BBC Arabic service. At an early stage of the revolution, the National Liberation Front in its National Charter demanded women's emancipation from traditional roles and their subjugation to men.

Women's societies began in 1951 when the British founded the Aden Women's Club, a charity that later became radical and, with local leaders, was renamed the Arab Women's Club. By the 1960s, the Arab Women's Club and its rival, the Aden Women's Association, each had 300 members. By independence in 1967, women's associations were united in the General Union of Yemeni Women (see Figure 5).

The revolution in South Yemen began in 1963 with the uprising in Radfān, a mountainous area north of Aden. Women participated in the armed struggle and two women became famous fighters, Khadīja al-Ḥawshabī, a member of the ruling family and martyred in the fight, and Da'ra. Other rural women carried food and messages to fighters. In Aden, women's role was merely political. They led demonstrations, initiated strikes in schools, took care of the wounded, and carried arms and hand grenades under their cloaks. In the women's societies, activists confronted the British and recruited more participants to the struggle.

After independence in 1967, women's issues only came to the fore after a radical leadership in the National Liberation Front gained power in 1969. Women were now called to join the labor force, educate themselves, and use the newly available health services. A committee formed of pro-revolutionary religious scholars, juridical experts, and women's activists began drafting a family code that would reflect the spirit of the 1970 constitution which gave women rights equal to men. The Family Law (law no 1 of 1974) deviated from the Sharīʿa in placing the obligation to support the family on both men and women, limiting polygamy to cases of the wife's barrenness or incurable illness (subject to court hearing) and prohibiting unilateral divorce. The law was in congruence with classical Sharīʿa law on marriage payment (*mahr*) and the wife's waiting period after divorce or widowhood (*ʿidda*).

In line with the constitution, the law declared marriage to be a contract between a man and a woman equal in rights and duties, and outlawed child marriages and marriage of a woman below 35 years to a man 20 years older. Saudi Arabia and conservative Yemeni circles targeted the law as un-Islamic. Ordinary women saw it as allowing them free-choice marriage and giving them rights for the first time.

In Aden during the 1980s and 1990s women reached high positions in working life, even supervising large factories (see Figure 4), while in the countryside achievements were smaller and women activists had to struggle to get local women to visit health clinics. In Aden girls' enrollment in secondary education was high; in some rural areas families did not allow daughters to finish primary school. In leaders' speeches, misogynism was attacked and men were taught to treat every woman as if she were his sister. Working women in Aden remained critical of the lack of public childcare and the fact that they worked a double shift at home, but at the same time responded positively to the state policy of women's liberation (*taḥrīr al-marʾa*). Few women reached high positions in the state hierarchy and women remained the minority in the ruling party apparatus. After the unification of Yemen in 1990, northern traditionalists who held that women had too many rights demanded adjustment, and this was echoed by some southern leaders. The Personal Status Law (law no 20 of 1992) accomplished this in relation to family affairs; but while women lost most of their earlier legal rights, progressive judges in family courts continued defending vulnerable women. After unification, the nomination of the first ever female full cabinet member has remained one of the few accomplishments.

In Dhofar, guerilla movement against the despotic Sultan Saʿid bin Taymūr and the British military started in 1965, quickly developing into a people's struggle with women fighting alongside men. The Dhofar Liberation Front was established in 1964 by exiled Omanis with Nasserist and radical Arab nationalist ideas, with women leaders who had become politically active while studying in Beirut. The organization soon incorporated activists from other Gulf countries and adopted the name Popular Front for the Liberation of Occupied Arab Gulf. In 1968, the front launched an educational campaign to spread socialist ideas among the population to complement its literacy campaigns. Females aged twelve and upwards participated in camps with political and military training.

Slavery was abolished in the liberated areas and women engaged in the dual front of armed struggle and the fight against backwardness. Women were seen to face double oppression, that of a repressive social system and as victims of men. Young country women were reported to have developed consciousness of the role reactionary men have had in alienating Islam from its progressive message. Guerilla actions continued until 1981 when they were finally defeated by the new ruler, Qabūs, son of Sultan Saʿid bin Taymūr, with the aid of foreign troops. Dhofar was showered with development money from neighboring countries and schools, clinics, and roads were built. However, reforms were carried out in order to strengthen the traditional social structure where a woman's place is at home.

Bibliography

L. Ahmed, Feminism and feminist movements in the Middle East, a preliminary exploration. Turkey, Egypt, Algeria, People's Democratic Republic of Yemen, in *Women's Studies International* 5 (1982), 153–68.

D. Chatty, Women working in Oman. Individual choice and cultural constraints, in *International Journal of Middle East Studies* 32 (2000), 241–54.

S. Dahlgren, Yemen, in B. Sherif-Trask (ed.), *The Greenwood encyclopedia of women's issues worldwide. The Middle East and North Africa*, Westport, Conn. 2003, 437–66.

F. Halliday, *Arabia without sultans*, Harmondsworth 1979.

H. Lackner, *PDR Yemen. Outpost of socialist development in Arabia*, London 1985.

M. Molyneux, Women and revolution in the People's

Democratic Republic of Yemen, in *Feminist Review* 1 (1979), 4–19.
——, Women's rights and and political contingency. The case of Yemen 1990–1994, in *Middle East Journal* 49:3 (1995), 418–31.
M. Paluch, *Yemeni voices. Women tell their stories*, Sana'a 2001.

SUSANNE DAHLGREN

Sub-Saharan Africa: Eritrea

Women played a central role in Eritrea's 30-year war for independence from Ethiopia, which annexed the former Italian colony in the 1960s, but their post-independence participation in public life presents a mixed record. By the nationalist victory in 1991, they made up nearly a third of the 95,000-strong Eritrean People's Liberation Front (EPLF) and 13 percent of the frontline fighters in what had been the longest-running conflict in modern African history – a conflict characterized by remarkably successful efforts to unify the diverse society of four million people, half Muslim and half Christian, from nine ethnic groups while promoting egalitarian social relations across both gender and class.

Women served in many non-combat capacities – as teachers, paramedics, political organizers, technicians, garage mechanics, drivers and more – while thousands of women civilians organized to support the war effort. This positioned them to challenge traditionally submissive roles in the strictly patriarchal society and to demand equal participation in the economy and the country's post-independence political life. But there has been significant slippage in their wartime gains.

Women activists were drawn into important but time-consuming political projects: writing a new constitution, revising the Civil Code, developing legislation, restructuring the civil service, demobilizing former fighters, forwarding recommendations for economic development, and drafting other new policy initiatives. This represented a sharp break with the grassroots-level work to change gender relations with which they had been engaged. Meanwhile, women fighters saw a spike in the divorce rate as male comrades opted for more subservient partners. Men in some communities also formed clandestine committees – later exposed and dismantled – to prevent women from participating in postwar land reform.

These social struggles took place against the backdrop of a complex process of state building. The decades-long independence war had left Eritrea in ruins. At the close of the fighting, water and sewage systems in the towns barely functioned; the few asphalt roads had been torn up; port facilities were badly damaged; the rail system was entirely dismantled; and the whole country had a generating capacity of only 22 megawatts, barely enough to keep the lights burning in the major towns. The World Bank estimated the country's per capita income at less than US $150, compared to US $330 for the rest of Sub-Saharan Africa. Nor was there a political infrastructure to take over and transform – it, too, had to be built from scratch.

The starting point was decidedly weighted against women's participation. In a mixed Muslim and Christian society where close to 80 percent of the people relied on agrarian-related activities, women were uniformly denied the right to own or inherit land. Women had been specifically denied the right to vote in the 1950 constitution which governed Eritrea's early relationship with Ethiopia, and in all but one minority community (the Kunama, whose people practice a traditional faith), women were excluded from village and clan self-governance.

In both Muslim and Christian communities, girls were routinely married at puberty under contracts arranged at birth. A bride might be as young as nine, though she continued to live at home until menstruation. Female genital mutilation (FGM) was widely carried out and girls frequently contracted serious infections during these crude operations. Death in childbirth was extremely common, due to the chronic malnutrition and anemia. At the end of the protracted conflict, Eritrean women had a life expectancy of barely 40 years; by 2001, it had risen to 54 years.

In 1994 the new government nationalized urban and rural land and allocated use-rights to all Eritrean women and men. The government also decreed a national service campaign that required women and men over 18 to undergo six months of military training and spend a year on reconstruction projects. This was partially intended to weld together the multicultural society, while placing women and men in a condition of relative gender equality, much as service in the liberation front had done.

However, measures such as land reform, national service, the enforcement of laws against sex discrimination by a woman minister of justice, the appointment of a near majority of women to the Constitution Commission, and the reservation of 30 percent of the seats for women in newly-elected regional and national People's Assemblies were not enough to counter the resurgence of patriarchal values in the deeply conservative society. In addition to struggles over land and spiraling divorce rates, there were sharp rises in child marriage and other formerly banned practices, such as humiliating "virginity testing" for prospective brides.

The National Union of Eritrean Women (NUEW), with 200,000 members in 2004, was the largest of three sectoral associations (along with those of workers and youth) that spun off from the liberation movement and was the main institutional vehicle for women's interests in postwar Eritrea. Founded in 1979 by the EPLF, the NUEW retains strong links with the liberation movement (renamed the People's Front for Democracy and Justice [PFDJ] in 1994), which controls both the program and the composition of the NUEW's leadership. Its current head, Luul Gebreab, is a former platoon commander in the EPLF who now sits on the central council of the PFDJ.

The union manages skills training, literacy, and self-improvement programs, as well as rural credit schemes and other development projects, each of which is accompanied by consciousness-raising seminars, and it advises other bodies on legislation, trade union contracts, and policies that affect women. However, the ruling party does not tolerate rival non-governmental organizations (NGOs), and it discourages program initiatives outside the union's mandate, so there is no women's organizing or advocacy outside the NUEW framework except for that among youth.

Another party-controlled mass organization, the National Union of Eritrean Youth and Students (NUEYS), runs education and training programs and cultural and recreational activities for young women and men aged 16 to 35 in both Christian and Muslim communities. Unlike the NUEW, the youth movement, with an estimated 120,000 members in 2004, makes the issue of combating "harmful traditions" a centerpiece of its advocacy work and campaigns against FGM in Christian and Muslim communities with considerable success. Female NUEYS members target young women, and male members target young men in three-day educational programs held in villages and poor urban neighborhoods around the country to end the practice.

One alternative attempt at women's self-organizing came in 1995 when former guerrilla fighters established the Eritrean Women War Veterans Association, BANA. Members pooled demobilization payouts to set up a share company. Later, they registered as an NGO to solicit foreign funds. In one year, membership grew to 1,000. They established a fish market, a bakery, a training program for commercial drivers, and other projects aimed at economic self-sufficiency. However, in 1996 the government shut down the NGO, forbidding BANA to raise foreign funds but permitting it to operate as a private enterprise.

The Tesfa Association, formed by ex-female fighters in 1994 to address the lack of childcare facilities for working mothers, was another failed NGO experiment. Tesfa established a kindergarten and ran public fundraising campaigns in Asmara. Soon, however, it too began to attract foreign funds, as its leaders looked to replicate their success. In 1996, shortly after BANA was stripped of its NGO status, Tesfa was closed down without explanation. Its projects and resources were given to the NUEW.

The government's early hostility to independent civil society organizing intensified after the renewal of conflict with Ethiopia in 1998–2000 over unresolved border issues. Since then, it has also shut down the country's private press, detained leading critics and stifled policy-oriented public debate. Thus there are no public forums in 2004 – in or out of government – where women can contest law or policy.

Despite these stark limitations, the NUEW provides a base for women to struggle at the local level with "traditional" power, and it functions as a discrete lobby with government and within the ruling party. In the early 1990s, the NUEW successfully spearheaded a number of reforms in the inherited Ethiopia Civil Code (*Eritrea Profile*, 20 August 1994). These include the following provisions: marriage contracts must have the full consent of both parties; the eligible age for marriage is raised from 15 to 18 for women, the same as that of men; both mothers and fathers are recognized as heads of the family; there is to be no discrimination between men and women in divorce cases (grounds for which are adultery, desertion for two years, venereal disease, and impotence); paid maternity leave is extended from 45 to 60 days; abortion is now legal in cases where the mother's mental or physical health is threatened and in instances of rape or incest; and the sentence for rape is extended to 15 years.

The country's new constitution, ratified by the National Assembly in 1997 but not yet implemented by the president, prohibits discrimination based on race, ethnic origin, color, and gender and mandates the National Assembly to legislate measures designed to eliminate such inequality. The government has also declared International Women's Day an official holiday and signed the Convention for the Rights of the Child and ratified the Convention on the Elimination of All Forms of Discrimination against Women (CEDAW).

A number of prominent women influence public policy. In 2004, three women, two of whom are Muslims, held ministerial portfolios: justice (Fozia Hashim), tourism (Amna Nur Husayn), and labor and social affairs (former NUEW chair Askalu Menkerios). The same three women sat on the PFDJ's 19-member Executive Council, chosen at the party's last congress in 1994, and women held 22 percent of the seats in the National Assembly and 11 percent of ambassadorial posts. In no-party elections held throughout the country in 2002 for village administrators and deputy administrators in both Muslim and Christian communities, women won more than a fifth of the posts.

However, gender-related changes in the public sphere are not woman-led. Eritrean women have access to the top, but they lack organized representation in the president's inner circle, where most policy is determined. More importantly, women lack a genuinely autonomous and activist social movement to push the state (and the party) from the outside.

Bibliography

D. Connell, *Against all odds. A chronicle of the Eritrean revolution*, Trenton, N.J. 1997.

——, *Rethinking revolution. New strategies for democracy and social justice. The experiences of Eritrea, South Africa, Palestine and Nicaragua*, Trenton, N.J. 2002.

R. Iyob, *The Eritrean struggle of independence. Domination, resistance, nationalism 1941–1993*, Cambridge 1995.

NUEW, NUEW and gender issues in Eritrea (1991–2001). A self-assessment, in *The proceedings of the 20th anniversary conference of the National Union of Eritrean Women. November 27–29, 1999*, Asmara 2002, 127–35.

T. Tekle, Women's access to land and property rights in Eritrea, in United Nations Development Fund for Women (UNIFEM), *Women's land and property rights in situations of conflict and reconstruction*, New York 1998, 104–12.

UNDP (United Nations Development Programme), *Human development report*, Geneva 2003.

United States Department of State, Senior Coordinator for International Women's Issues, *Eritrea. Report on female genital mutilation (FGM) or female genital cutting (FGC)*, Washington, D.C. 2001.

A. Wilson, *The challenge road. Women and the Eritrean revolution*, Trenton, N.J. 1991.

Dan Connell

Sudan

Sudan has experienced a number of revolutionary movements: for example, the Mahdist messianic movement of the nineteenth century, freeing the area for a time from the British and building its own society and administration; the nationalist movement of the first half of the twentieth century, culminating in independence from the British in 1956; the guerilla war that spanned the second half of the twentieth century and extended into the twenty-first century, pitting the southern region against the northern region, and led primarily by the Sudan People's Liberation Movement/Army (SPLM/SPLA), a revolutionary organization that aimed for a united socialist Sudan; the Islamist revolution (1989) that transformed the society into one guided by Sharīʿa and Islamic principles; and various socialist, progressive, and "minority" liberation movements and fronts in the late twentieth and early twenty-first centuries. Especially since the "Islamic Trend" emerged in the 1980s and Islamists took power in 1989, imposing Islamization projects, different regions of the country have engaged in uprisings that are broader than identity or minority politics (for example, in eastern Sudan the Beja People's Party; in the west the Nuba Mountains resistance, and in the west an uprising in Darfur). Like all sociopolitical movements, these have been gendered. Women have played greater and lesser roles in terms of the armed/military struggles, but have played essential support roles as well as engaging in political activity and some leadership roles. Furthermore, each of these revolutionary or proto- and quasi-revolutionary movements has altered the gender division of labor and gender relations in significant, if not revolutionary, ways.

The only enduring progressive revolutionary party to develop in Sudan in the twentieth century was the Marxist-Leninist Sudanese Communist Party (SCP). Although an offshoot of the Egyptian communist party and having strong ties to the Soviet Union, it was still very much a "national" party. As Sudan's main leftist party, the SCP has been persecuted, driven underground and into exile, and has been beheaded (with the 1971 execution of Secretary-General ʿAbd al-Khāliq Maḥjūb). The SCP has fought for social revolution via paths mostly eschewing armed struggle, the failed 1971 coup d'état being one of the exceptions. A full-scale revolutionary process in the Marxist sense has not occurred in Sudan – in fact has seen a severe setback since the 1989 Islamist coup d'état.

Despite impediments within the context of a conservative, religious sectarian, Muslim society, the SCP was strong in its organizing in various spheres: the tenant farmers, the trade unions, and especially among railroad workers, youth, the intelligentsia, and women. Even some strong influence in the all-powerful military occasionally emerged.

However, foremost among the organizing achievements of the SCP was its foundation of an affiliated Sudanese Women's Union (SWU), at one time one of the strongest women's organizations on the African continent or in the Middle East. The SWU was founded in 1952, was active during the late nationalist period (1952–6), and reached its zenith in 1965, with branches opened throughout the country and liberal gains in women's rights such as suffrage, equal pay, and maternity leave.

Despite this achievement, however, the patriarchal ideology, paternalism toward the SWU, and the structure of the SCP and the gender strategies it has followed have greatly diminished its effectiveness as an agent of socialist gender transformation. Most cadres have not had an adequate understanding of the subjectivity of oppression and of the connections between personal relations and public political organization, nor have they understood issues of sexuality, let alone directly addressed them. With these omissions, it is unlikely that the SCP could have done more than politicize the conventional roles of Sudanese women. While it would be wrong to say the SCP did not consider the role of women in building the revolution or did not imagine the place of women in a liberated Sudan, it did not advocate or engage in, even within its own organization, transformative gender practices aimed at a revolutionary transformation.

Bibliography

Z. B. El-Bakri and El-W. M. Kameir, Aspects of women's participation in Sudan, in *International Social Science Journal* 35:4 (1983), 605–23.

A. Gresh, The Free Officers and the Comrades. The Sudanese Communist Party and Nimeiri face-to-face, in *International Journal of Middle East Studies* 21 (1989), 393–409.

S. Hale, The wing of the patriarch. Sudanese women and revolutionary parties, in *Middle East Report* 16:1 (1986), 25–30.

——, *Gender politics in Sudan. Islamism, socialism, and the state*, Boulder, Colo. 1996.

F. A. Ibrāhīm, *Ṭarīqnā ilā al-tuharrur*, Khartoum n.d.

F. B. Mahmoud, The role of the Sudanese women's movement in Sudanese politics, M.A. diss., University of Khartoum 1971.

G. Warburg, *Islam, nationalism, and communism in a traditional society. The case of Sudan*, London 1978.

Sondra Hale

Syria

Revolutionary movements in twentieth-century Syria have been a platform for women's demands for emancipation and access to political power. However, even when they have captured control of government, these movements have not revolutionized women's legal, economic, or social status, primarily because of the weaknesses of the Syrian state and economy, and the strength of conservative opposition movements.

The 1908 Constitutional Revolution fostered a new politics of citizenship in Syria and across the late Ottoman Empire. Elite urban women mobilized as citizens to promote social reforms, especially in family life, girls' education, and public hygiene, through the formation of charity groups and through the newly uncensored press. Most important was Mārī ʿAjamī's magazine *al-ʿArūs* (Bride), founded in 1910 in Damascus, which portrayed its female readers as agents of a social renaissance. The Young Turk government supported Syrian women's efforts to feed the poor and to educate girls during the First World War. It also decreed the Family Law of 1917, which limited the authority of religion in matters of marriage and divorce. After the Ottomans' defeat in 1918, Syrian women activists supported constitutionalism and advocated women's suffrage under Faysal's short-lived Arab regime (1918–20). Their leader, Nāzik ʿĀbid, published a reformist journal, *Nūr al-Fayḥāʾ* (Light of Damascus), and headed a nurses' battalion in the fight against French occupation.

The French, who ruled Syria from 1920 to 1946, did not promote reform of women's legal or social status. Women instead pursued reform through alliances with the nationalist opposition to French rule. Adīl Bayhum al-Jazāʾirlī, who headed the Syrian Women's Union for decades after its 1928 founding, cooperated with the National Bloc. Their alliance was based on shared commitments to liberalism and nationalism (Sakākīnī 1950) among the landowning and rising middle classes. Jazāʾirlī led women in campaigns for education and personal status reform, as well as campaigns for Arabist causes, especially in defense of Palestinians. Thurayā Ḥāfiẓ also emerged as a leader in public demonstrations for women's political rights and against veiling (Shaaban 1998, 47–51). Women supported nationalists in armed revolt against the French in 1925–8 and again in May 1945. But willingness to fight for their country did not win women immediate rights. Leaders of the National Bloc, who inherited rule from the French, expanded women's access to education after 1946, but they were not politically strong enough to promote substantive legal reform in face of opposition from the Muslim Brotherhood. It was only with Ḥusnī al-Zaʿīm's military coup against the nationalist elite in 1949 that women attained partial suffrage (Razzaz 1975, 151–60). Another dictator, Adīb al-Shīshaklī, awarded women full suffrage in 1953.

After independence, women turned to leftist movements to advocate for their reforms, but they too were limited by religious opposition. In contrast to the segregated movements of nationalist liberals, communist women like Amīna ʿĀrif al-Jarrāḥ attended meetings and public demonstrations unveiled in the 1940s and 1950s. Maqbūla Shalaq, a leader of the Communist Party's women's wing, promoted women's right to work against the maternalist agendas of other parties and the dominant Women's Union (Thompson 2000, 241). But even as many female students joined the communists, the party backpedaled on its commitment to women's equality. In response to directives of the Soviet Comintern and to rival recruitment by Islamic populists, party leaders openly opposed reform of women's personal status laws in 1939, claiming that it would inflame sectarian divisions and weaken working-class solidarity (Thompson 2000, 161). The Muslim Brotherhood advanced a counter-revolutionary platform that rejected Ottoman-era restrictions on religious law and favored the status quo in women's confinement to the domestic sphere. The extent of women's support for the Brotherhood remains unclear. While some Islamist women campaigned against women like Thurayā Ḥāfiz, most urban women discarded their veils after independence in 1946.

The emergent Baʿth Party reasserted a commitment to integrating women fully into public and national life (Razzaz 1975, Jamāl al-Dīn and al-Khūri 1976). Promoting an Arab socialism, the party became an important political force in the 1950s. Some women, mostly university students, also joined the party. The Baʿthists took power in a 1963 coup and have ruled Syria since. The party has explicitly promoted general social reforms, especially in education, that aimed to raise women's status. It worked not just through the Women's Union, which was incorporated into the party apparatus in 1968 as the General Federation of Women, but also through its peasant, workers, and youth organizations. These were corporatist entities designed as much to control constituent groups as to mobilize them. Nonetheless, by 1990 the regime had begun enforcing equal pay laws, had raised women's literacy significantly, and had appointed a female minister. Thirteen women had served as members of parliament (Shaaban 1988, 51, 56). Women's use of contraception rose, and the fertility rate fell from 7.4 to 3.6 births per woman between 1980 and 2000. But in other areas women's progress was stalled. In 2000, women represented little more than a quarter of the labor force and their literacy rate had reached only 60 percent (World Bank GenderStats).

Lack of social progress coincided with a lack of legal and political reform. While the 1964 Syrian constitution mirrored much of the party's founding constitution, it omitted the party's earlier language that had explicitly guaranteed women's equality with men. The 1964 document referred only to educational, health, labor, and legal rights that belong to "all citizens" (Abu Jaber 1966, 127, 170, 176–7). Only a few women, mainly party members, advanced to higher positions in government and the professions. And while all women enjoyed the right to vote under the Baʿth, elections had been rendered empty exercises. Scholars and observers blame the failure to improve women's economic status on the fact that the Syrian economy, stagnant since 1980, could not absorb women into the workforce. It also reflected state preferences for male employment that date to the French era: upon coming to power in 1970, President Ḥāfiẓ al-Asad awarded family bonuses only to male employees (Perthes 1995, 24–9).

The economic and political exclusion of women also reflects continued pressure from religious opposition. By the late 1970s an Islamic Front emerged in the provinces to contest Asad's hold on power. The Front's 1980 manifesto adopted the language of gender equality that Syrians had been using since Faysal's day, but explicitly limited that equality within bounds set by Islamic law on women's duty toward her home, husband, and children (Abd-Allah 1983, 247–8). The Front also explicitly advocated women's veiling as a political symbol of dissent (Abd-Allah 1983, 189). After brutally defeating the Front in 1982, the Baʿth trod lightly on women's issues. The General Federation of Women shrank from advocating women's rights in conservative villages so as not to antagonize religious men (Hinnebusch 1990, 234, 250, 272). And the regime promoted a patriarchal cult of Ḥāfiẓ al-Asad that demanded women's sacrifice to their father-leader and their nation (Wedeen 1999, 49–65). In the 1990s, many Syrian women took up the veil again, as a visible sign of opposition to the Baʿth regime that had long proclaimed women's liberation as its goal. The taboo on personal status reform since the Ottoman era reflects the ongoing tension between revolutionaries and conservatives who seek to retain the status quo of male privilege and male guardianship over women.

BIBLIOGRAPHY

U. F. Abd-Allah, *The Islamic struggle in Syria*, Berkeley 1983.

K. S. Abu Jaber, *The Arab Baʿth Socialist Party. History, ideology, and organization*, Syracuse, N.Y. 1966.

R. A. Hinnebusch, *Authoritarian power and state formation in Baʿthist Syria*, Boulder, Colo. 1990.

D. Hopwood, *Syria 1945–1986. Politics and society*, London 1988.

N. Jamāl al-Dīn and S. al-Khūri, *Ḥawla al-marʾa*, Damascus 1976[2].

A. ʿA. al-Jarāḥ, *Ayyāmī kānat ghaniyya*, Damascus 1985.

V. Perthes, *The political economy of Syria under Asad*, London 1995.

N. al-Razzāz, *Mushārakat al-marʾa fī al-ḥayat al-ʿāmma fī Sūrīya mundhu al-istiqlāl 1945 wa ḥatt*, Damascus 1975.

W. Sakākīnī, *Inṣāf al-marʾa*, Damascus 1950.

B. Shaaban, Syria. Guaranteed rights for all, except at home, in B. Shaaban, *Both right and left handed. Arab women talk about their lives*, Bloomington, Ind. 1988, 28–80.

E. Thompson, *Colonial citizens. Republican rights, paternal privilege, and gender in French Syria and Lebanon*, New York 2000.

L. Wedeen, *Ambiguities of domination. Politics, rhetoric and symbols in contemporary Syria*, Chicago 1999.

World Bank Group, GenderStats database of Gender Statistics, <http:// devdata.worldbank.org/genderstats/ home.asp>.

ELIZABETH F. THOMPSON

Turkey

The revolutionary movements in Turkey can be traced back to the late Ottoman period, to the Young Turks (Hanioğlu 1995) who eventually came to power in the Second Constitutional Period (1908), and to other groups, some of them socialist, which were active but never dominant within the state structure. Prior to the Turkish Republic, modernizing movements sought to accomplish social transformation in the Ottoman state. The influence of Islam in cultural, spatial, and social spheres was viewed as responsible for the exclusion of women from most parts of public life. The legal codifications of 1839 and the constitutional reform movements of 1876 and 1908 brought about change in this structure toward centralization, secularization, and freedom, directly affecting women's claims for individual rights and independence against the constraints of traditional gender roles. The political discourse of prevailing intellectual trends, namely Ottomanism, Westernism, and Turkism, always included the theme of women's emancipation; hence, the first protagonists of the Woman Question were modernist men. However, the debate over this issue was not confined solely to men; women themselves were actively involved in it too. These pioneering women wrote in women's journals, such as *Aile* (Family), *Hanımlara Mahsus Gazete* (Journal for women), *Genç Kadın* (Young woman), *Demet* (Bunch), *Kadın* (Woman), *Süs* (Ornamentation), *Kadınlar Dünyası* (Women's world) and *İnci* (Pearl), of which there were altogether 40. These activities can be defined as the "Ottoman women's movement," for the number of journals and organizations run by women at the time deserves such a characterization (Çakır 1993).

The Osmanlı Müdafaa-i Hukuk-u Nisvan Cemiyeti (Association for the defense of the rights of Ottoman women) founded by Ulviye Mevlan, and its publication *Kadınlar Dünyası*, problematized women's status in Ottoman society and struggled against traditional gender inequalities as Ulviye Mevlan's words witness: "Women shall not any more rely on male writers' deceitful remarks that women are men's life-long comrades and companions. These are all lies. However, although we know they are lies, they lure our feelings. This is why we cannot defend our rights" (Çakır 1994, 125).

The revolutionary nature of the Turkish Republic is evident in the abolition of the Caliphate (1924), the secularization of education by the enactment of the Tevhid-i Tedrisat Kanunu (Law of union of education, 1924) and the adoption of the new Civil Code (1926), which opened the way for women's citizenship. The modernization project of the republic aimed at national mobilization of both genders, and important steps toward the inclusion of women into the public sphere were achieved. The "new man" of modern Turkey tried to define and promote the "new woman," equipping her with certain rights of citizenship and professional roles in the public realm. But the Turkish Republic was based on the fraternity of male citizens (Durakbaşa 1998) and women were not regarded as parties in the social contract until 1934 when they acquired full citizenship rights.

Politically eminent women such as Halide Edip (Durakbaşa 2000) and Nezihe Muhittin protested against the terms of emancipation defined by the male protagonists of Turkish modernization, arguing for the political rights of women against the idea that the republic was not mature enough to grant women the right to vote. Nezihe Muhittin founded the Kadınlar Halk Fırkası (Women's people's party, 1923) to defend the participation of women in politics. She became the founder of Türk Kadınlar Birliği (Turkish women's association) when this party was not legally authorized.

As the republic established itself ideologically and institutionally the revolutionary character of the modernization project weakened until the 1960s when major republican values were reawakened. A socialist party, Türkiye İşçi Partisi (Labor Party of Turkey, LPT) was represented in the parliament for the first time and became the major locus of revolutionary projects and political opposition. Behice Boran, the leader of the party, is an important symbol of the socialist movement, with a life that extended from the university to the parliament, surviving many trials and prison terms because of her political career and beliefs until her death in 1987 (Berktay 2002).

The socialist movement (Tunçay 1991) was not confined to the leadership of the LPT; a number of socialist parties, notably the Turkish Communist Party (TCP) whose origin can be traced back to the 1920s, were present in the late Ottoman period; and the TCP remained illegal until the elections of 2002. The 1970s were the years when the leftist political organizations, parties, and youth movements, also under the influence of 1968 student activism in the West, determined the political agenda until the 1980 military coup. Many women supported these groups who saw the solution to the Woman Question as lying within class struggle. Women in leftist politics were usually excluded from decision-making mechanisms, an experience they shared with women in nationalist or Islamist political frameworks (Berktay 1995). In 1975, under the influence of the TCP a semi-independent women's association, İlerici Kadınlar Derneği (Progressive women's association) was set up with a mass membership of 15,000. Still, their main target was to recruit women to the socialist cause. It was only after 1980 that women realized the significance of autonomous women's organizations in the struggle against male dominance and patriarchy, and that women's liberation could not be reduced to socialist revolution.

The post-1980 leaders of the feminist movement were mostly disillusioned women who had learned from their experience in left-wing political circles. These women, academics and students among them, preferred to define themselves as feminists and advocated an independent women's movement challenging the patriarchal structures in society. Their major accomplishments were: feminist consciousness-raising groups; a campaign against violence against women (Say No to Wife-Beating Campaign); publication activities; campaigns to amend the articles that discriminate against women in the Civil Code and the Penal Code; the founding of the women's library in Istanbul and women's research centers in the universities; women's shelters; and the recent amendment of the Civil Code in 2002.

The 1980s also saw the politicization of the Kurdish movement, which equally affected the Kurdish women's cause. Although caught between national and feminist identities, Kurdish women created publications and organizations that problematized issues such as polygamy, violence against women, adult education, and honor killings, and searched for possible solutions. In contrast, the Islamist women's movement focused on the attempt to demonstrate that prevailing oppressive Islamic practices concerning women had their origins not in the Qur'ān but in the "implementation" dominated by patriarchal traditions.

Bibliography

F. Berktay, Has anything changed in the outlook of the Turkish left on women?, in Ş. Tekeli (ed.), *Women in modern Turkish society*, London 1995, 250–62.

——, Olagandisi bir kadın. Behice Boran, in *Tarihin cinsiyeti*, Istanbul 2003, 192–204.

S. Çakır, Die historische Entwicklung der Frauenbewegungen in der Turkei vom Osmanishen Reich bis zur Türkischen Republik, in A. Kaputanoğlu et al. (eds.), *Die türkische Frauenbewegung*, Karlsruhe 1993, 47–56.

——, *Osmanlı kadın haraketi*, Istanbul 1994, 125.

A. Durakbaşa, Kemalism as identity politics in Turkey, in Z. Arat (ed.), *Deconstructing images of "the Turkish woman,"* New York 1998, 139–57.

——, *Halide Edib. Türk moderleşmesi ve feminizm*, Istanbul 2000.

Ş. Hanioğlu, *The Young Turks in opposition*, New York 1995.

M. Tunçay, *Türkiye'de sol akımlar*, Istanbul 1991.

Serpİl Çakır

Political-Social Movements: Unions and Workers' Movements

Arab States (excepting North Africa and the Gulf)

National constitutions in Egypt, Iraq, Jordan, Lebanon, Syria, and Palestine identify the equality of citizens of both sexes before the law; Egypt, Iraq, Jordan, and Lebanon ratified the Convention on the Elimination of Discrimination against Women (CEDAW). This suggests uneven patterns of worldwide protection, meaning some Arab women enjoy law-based health benefits, employment safeguards, and paid maternity leave, while others are left unprotected. In general, working women enjoy differential work protection on account of their sector of employment; the predominance of women employed in education and civil service in the central Arab states prohibits them from either joining labor unions or participating in collective bargaining.

Sovereign central Arab states are party to the International Labour Organization Forced Labour Convention 1930 (ILO C. 29); the Right to Organize and Collective Bargaining Convention 1949 (98); the Equal Remuneration Convention 1951 (100); the Abolition of Forced Labour Convention 1957 (105); and the Discrimination (Employment and Occupation) Convention 1958 (111). Yet in all six states, public demonstrations require the authorities' prior approval; in Egypt, Syria, and Iraq, labor issues are or recently have been the purview of a state-based trade union federation. Of the ILO "core conventions," Iraq, Jordan, and Lebanon have not ratified the Freedom of Association and Protection of the Right to Organize Convention, 1948 (No. 87), as discussed below. All states' trade unions are affiliated to the International Confederation of Arab Trade Unions (ICATU).

Egypt's state has taken responsibility for the interests of those women who work even though at present the unemployment rate is 19 percent among women and 5 percent among men (Farah 2002, 1). Egypt's constitution of 1956, and as amended two years later, guarantees women's equality with men before the law. The 1971 constitution adds: "The state is responsible for striking a balance between woman's family duties and her work in society and standing on equal footing with men in political, social, cultural and economic domains." Laws 47 and 48 of 1978 regulate Egyptian women working in the public sector. Three times during their working lives, such women have the right to a three-month paid maternity leave and two-year unpaid childcare leaves. Women working part-time have the right to half salary and half-holidays. Law 137 for 1981 extended ILO benefits – working women and men are equal before the labor law; women are forbidden from night work, immoral, or unhealthy work – to the private sector; the law went on to require that private firms also offer paid maternity leave, lactation breaks, and unpaid childcare leaves, as well as requiring employers of more than 100 women to provide childcare.

If Egypt's state has taken responsibility for working women's interests, this legal framework is not necessarily to all workers' benefit. While Egyptian workers may join trade unions, the law does not require them to do so; it is notable that most union members (approximately a quarter of the labor force) work in state-owned enterprises. The government sets wages, benefits, and job classifications by law, so few issues are open to negotiation. A 1985 ILO report notes that, in contravention to ILO C. 87 to which Egypt is signatory, the Egyptian Trade Union Federation is the named central organization of a legally-proscribed single trade-union system. Workers' right to strike is not guaranteed by law; the public prosecutor may call for a trade union employee's removal from office should that employee call for abandonment of work or be deliberately absent from public service (Upham 1991, 132). While existing labor laws are prejudiced against collective bargaining, the new Unified Labor currently under discussion in the parliament would provide the right to strike and statutory authorization for collective bargaining (United States Department of State 1998). However, activists on behalf of working women complain that the new law would represent a step backward from the present levels of working mothers' entitlements.

Iraq's 1970 constitution granted women equal access to education, property, the franchise, and public office (article 19). Iraq's labor law no. 151 (1970), its provisions renewed by law no. 81 (1987), established women's right to equal opportunities in the civil service and equal pay; the 1971 maternal law provided for six months' paid maternity leave, with the right to an additional six months' unpaid leave. The General Federation of Iraqi Women (GFIW), based in law 139 (1972) provided women with literacy classes, vocational training, and childcare (Farouk-Sluglett 1993; data refer to 1980). By 1986, women were said to be 40 percent of public sector employees, although Iraq does not register women's labor force participation with the ILO.

The labor code also established a single trade union structure, the General Federation of Trade Unions (GFTU), with 1,250,000 members (Upham 1991, 233). The GFTU excluded civil servants, and any demonstrations required prior approval from the ministry of the interior. Labor conscription was introduced in 1980, at the beginning of the war with Iran. Decree 150 (1987) left public sector employees rights of association. In 1991, Kuwaiti labor activists complained to the ILO that Iraqi occupation authorities banned trade unions, destroyed their offices, and deported, imprisoned, or killed Kuwaiti trade union leaders.

Iraqis currently live and work under military occupation. Coalition Provisional Authority Order I (16 May 2003) disestablishes Iraq's Baʿth Party "by eliminating the party's structures" such as the GFIW and GFTU. CPA Order 1 may contravene the International Covenant on Economic, Social, and Cultural Rights (ICESCR), which "includes the right of everyone to the opportunity to gain his [sic] living by work which he [sic] freely chooses or accepts" (AI I 2003). "Elimination of the party's structures" also results in an inability to maintain civil order, and Iraqi women's experience with violence keeps them from work and activism.

Jordan's 1952 constitution grants citizens the right to work (requiring special conditions for women's employment) and to form trade unions "within the limits of the law" (article 23). Jordan reports employment indicators to the ILO; of those employed in Jordan, 14.2 percent were women. Of employed women, 48.9 percent in 2000 worked outside the home (Jordan 2000, cited in Ghosheh 2002); of those, half work for the government, 15 percent were self-employed, and about 10 percent employed by family members (1997). In addition to education, in which women are 42.1 percent of all employees, Jordanian women work in health and social services (13.9 percent), domestic labor (0.6 percent), and non-governmental organizations (0.5 percent).

Unlike in Egypt and Iraq, only Jordanian medical professionals and teachers working in the private sector have the right to join unions. While unions are not required to affiliate with the Jordanian Federation of Trade Unions (JFTU), all do, as in Egypt and Iraq. The JFTU reported 200,000 members in 1994, with 17 unions representing 30 percent of Jordanian workers (Upham 1991, 239). The labor law no. 8 (1996) excludes public servants (including women who work as teachers, municipal and agricultural workers, and non-nationals) from its protections. The one million foreigners working in Jordan are barred from trade union membership. Permission is required to strike, and is granted only if the ministry of labor fails to initiate arbitration. Furthermore, recent emergency decrees (laws of 2 October 2001) criminalize a number of vaguely defined offenses, including unauthorized public meetings (AI I 2002).

Lebanon's constitution (1926, including 1990 amendments) guarantees equality of citizens before the law (article 7). In 1994, 12.9 percent of Lebanon's female population was economically active. Two years later, 26.8 percent of formally employed women were teachers, 14 percent worked in commerce and maintenance, 13.8 percent in industry, 9.8 percent in health and social work, and 8 percent in domestic service. While Lebanese labor law guarantees equal remuneration for similar positions for men and women, agriculture lies beyond the reach of national legislation (Lebanon 1996, cited in Nauphal 1997). A considerable percentage of rural women work as seasonal daily paid laborers, and survey results suggest even women with skills receive half men's remuneration, particularly in rural areas. Likewise, while the labor law regulates women's maternity leave, such protections do not cover women working in agriculture or family businesses.

Women and youth participate in unions to represent their interests. Strikes in the private sector were suppressed by armed forces between 1975 and 1990. Given that young Lebanese workers associate political parties with militia rule, the Confederation générale des travailleurs libanais (CGTL) acts as a political party. The CGTL, with approximately 77,100 members (1990) advocates policies on poverty, social inequality, and civil rights. While women – the majority married and over 40 years of age – form about half of union members, their representation in leadership positions is significantly less (Lebanese Centre for Policy Studies 1993, *al-Nahar* 1996, Moghaizel 1987, all cited in Nauphal 1997). During 1992, Lebanon witnessed the most significant labor mobilization since 1975, with a nationwide strike protesting at the collapse of living standards.

Palestinians live and work under military occupation, which means that Palestinians experience both high unemployment and severe restrictions on movement. Palestine's women's labor force participation was 11.3 percent, with 4.2 percent of women employed as technicians, experts, and clerks, and 3.3 percent in agricultural labor (UNDP 2000).

Even with the establishment of the Palestinian National Authority (PNA) in 1996, different labor laws govern Palestinians. The West Bank and Gaza are governed by a combination of Jordanian law and PNA decisions, while residents of Jerusalem are subject to Israeli labor law. Palestine's labor law (2000) prohibits gender discrimination in the labor market, stresses non-discrimination in wages, forbids women's employment in risky and arduous jobs, on night shifts and during pregnancy, and grants maternity and lactation leaves. The PNA civil service law also provides for women's maternity leave.

Even though Palestinian women compose about 7.6 percent of trade union membership, their activities indicate the limits military occupation imposes on workers and union officers' movement. The General Federation of Palestinian Trade Unions reported 100,000 members and the Gaza Federation of Trade Unions an additional 25,000 (1993). Palestinians' access to permits to work in Israel or to travel remains a leading issue. According to the BBC, Israeli authorities prevented activist Amīna al-Rīmāwī from speaking on Palestinian working women's status at the 31st Arab Labor Conference meeting in Damascus during February 2004.

Syria reports economic activity rates to the ILO, and the International Confederation of Arab Trade Unions (ICATU) has its headquarters in Damascus. Women were 19.8 percent of Syria's workforce in 2000: 58.7 percent of agricultural laborers, 22.2 percent of crafts persons/technicians, and 8.3 percent of executives/clerks (SAR 2000a). Many Syrian women find employment in state sponsored-education, where they are 65.7 percent of primary teachers, 48.2 percent of secondary school instructors, and 23.1 percent of university faculty (SAR 2000b). Syrian women are least represented in manufacturing (5.7 percent) (SAR censuses, SAR 2000a, cited in SAR unpublished).

Syria's citizens are equal before the law, according to the 1973 constitution (article 25). Syria's labor law grants women the right to employment in both the private and public sectors. Even though Syria has not ratified the CEDAW, the labor law emphasizes that both sexes must receive equal wages for equal work. Since 1968, the ministry of social affairs and labor sets minimum wages, establishes occupational safety specifications, pays social security premiums, and controls the right of association. Syria's workers have been represented by a single trade union structure, which restricts the rights of foreign and non-Arab workers. State of emergency legislation in force since 8 March 1963 constrains men and women from extending their rights through collective action (AI I 2004).

Bibliography

Primary Sources

AI I (Amnesty International Index), MDE 12/176/2003, 4 December 2003, Iraq. Memorandum on concerns related to legislation introduced by the Coalition Provisional Authority, <http:// web.amnesty.org/library/Index/ENGMDE141762003?open&of=ENG-2MD>.

——, MDE 16/007/2002, 19 March 2002, Jordan. Freedom of expression at risk, <http:// www.hrea.org/lists/hr-media/markup/msg00004.html>.

——, MDE 24/016/2004, Syria. 41 years of the state of emergency. Amnesty International reiterates its concerns over a catalogue of human rights violations, 8 March 2004, <http:// web.amnesty.org/library/Index/ENGMDE240162004>.

N. R. Farah, Egypt. Gender Indicators, National Council for Women, NCW/R/02/006/E, February 2002, unpublished.

Jordan, Department of Statistics, Percentage of Jordanian workers aged 15 and above according to employment status, in *Annual report of employment and unemployment in Jordan*, Amman 2000.

Lebanese Centre for Policy Studies, *A study of the needs and opportunities for skilled workers in Lebanon*, 1993, <http://www.lcps-lebanon.org/resc/eco/9294/workers 93.html>.

Lebanon, Ministry of Social Affairs, *The population and housing database*, Beirut 1996.

SAR (Syrian Arab Republic), General Union of Women, External Relations Office/UNIFEM (2001), The gender indicators required for monitoring and following post-Beijing activities in the Syrian Arab Republic, unpublished.

——, Central Bureau of Statistics, *Internal migration survey*, Damascus 2000a.

——, Central Bureau of Statistics, *Statistical abstract*, Damascus 2000b.

——, Central Bureau of Statistics, *Census*, Damascus 1970, 1981, 1994.

UNDP, *Palestine human development report 2000*, New York 2000.

United States Department of State, *1998 country report on economic policy and trade practices. Egypt*, Washington, D.C.

Secondary Sources

M. Farouk-Sluglett, Liberation or repression? Pan-Arab nationalism and the women's movement in Iraq, in D. Hopwood et al. (eds.), *Iraq. Power and society*, Oxford 1993, 51–73.

H. Ghosheh, Mainstreaming gender in the Jordanian national economic and social development plan. A case study 1999–2003, report commissioned by the United Nations Interagency Gender Task Force with the Jordanian National Commission for Women, 15 April 2002.

L. Moghaizel, Participation politique des femmes pendant la guerre, in Actes du colloque, *La femme libanaise témoin de la guerrre*, Paris 1987.

al-Nahar, poll, September 1996.

N. Nauphal, Post war Lebanon. Women and other war affected groups, ILO action programme on skills and entrepreneurship training for countries emerging from armed conflict 1997, <http://www.ilo.org/public/english/employment/skills/training/publ/pub9.htm>.
M. Upham, *Trade unions of the world*, Harlow, Essex 1991.

Elizabeth Bishop

Iran

The labor movement and trade unions in Iran began in the early twentieth century. They have not been homogeneous institutions; some have had grassroots support and some have been agents of the state. They survived long periods of authoritarian regimes. At different historical periods their actions have confirmed a profound reactivation of civil society (Bayat 1987, Ladjevardi 1985). However, they remained male dominated organizations. In 2003, 30 percent of formal sector workers in state enterprises and 6 percent of formal sector workers in private enterprises were women. Notions of masculinity and femininity locate women in unskilled and low paid work; they pay higher taxes and receive lower levels of bonuses and other entitlements. There are large numbers of women unpaid workers and even paid workers in the agriculture and the informal sector in rural and urban areas whose issues are not addressed by the male dominated trade unions (Poya 1999, 83–98).

Historically women played important roles within the labor movement. In 1930, a leading member of the oil workers' strike committee, which organized the first strike against the Anglo-Persian Oil Company, was a woman called Zahrā; other details about her are not available. In the 1930s, women workers won their specific demands: maternity leave and the right of mothers of newborn babies to have paid time off to breast-feed their babies in the factory during working hours. In 1944, women workers established the Union of Women Workers, alongside the United Central Council of Workers Unions. In 1947, Raziyya Shaʿbānī, a trade union activist, was arrested as the first woman political prisoner from the labor movement (Partuvi 2002).

In 1951, the oil workers' strike led to the victory of Muṣaddiq's nationalist government and oil nationalization. This period ended with the 1953 CIA coup. In the 1960s and 1970s the dictatorial regime controlled the trade union movement and changed the term "trade unions" to "syndicates." Nevertheless, many workers remained militant and class conscious. Women workers' strikes have been significant in the history of labor movement in Iran: at the Shahnaz Factory in 1960 and 1962; the Ziba Factory in 1971; the Pars Electric and Milli Shoe Factories in 1974; and the Shahi Textile Factory in 1976 (Partuvī 2002). In February 1979, a growing revolutionary movement and a general strike resulted in the collapse of the monarchy and the establishment of the Islamic state.

Before 1979, cultural restrictions affected women's mobility and many families did not allow their daughters and female members of their families to join trade unions. But during and after the 1979 Revolution more women became active members of *shawrā*s, workers' councils, which replaced the syndicates of the pre-1979 period. Many women workers in pharmaceutical, food, and textile industries were involved in the *shawrās*. They were struggling to set up workplace nurseries, literacy classes for women workers, and better health and safety conditions at work. In this period women's activities raised gender consciousness. Women were engaged in trade union activities as women. This was significant in a number of ways. The *shawrās* were under attack by the autocratic Islamic state and both female and male workers were struggling to save the *shawrās*. But male workers were against female representation; they believed that women should leave these activities to men. For their part, women believed that they should be represented in the *shawrās* as women workers because they had specific demands. These experiences, together with the imposition of *ḥijāb*, Islamic dress code, and sex segregation, originally designed to marginalize women in the public sphere of life, ironically opened up opportunities for many women workers to participate in trade unions. In the early 1990s, for the first time in Iran, Afsarmulūk Yasan, a woman activist, was elected as the leader of the hairdressers' *shawrā* (Poya 1999, 125–130).

However, studies on gender and trade unions in Iran demonstrate that despite increase in women workers' activities in trade unions since the 1980s, they have remained in a minority and have very little voice at any of the decision-making levels. There has been a continuing resistance by male trade unionists to women's participation in trade unions. In most *shawrā*s a woman serves as treasurer, but their participation is limited when important decisions are taken (Āqājānī 2000, Ardalān 1999, Lāhījī 1999).

Since the 1990s, a growing women's movement has challenged the patriarchal institutional domains of the Islamic state. Women workers reacted to male dominated trade unions by forming women's trade associations: for example, there are trade associations for women publishers, teachers, nurses, and lawyers (Rostami Povey 2001, 44–71). In 1998, Jamīla Kadīvār, a journalist and a member of parliament (2000–4) established the Women Journalists' Trade Association and in 2002 published *Ṣid-yi zan* (Woman's voice). In the first edition of this publication, Laylī Farhādpūr, a journalist and a member of the association, discussed gender wage differentiation amongst the media workers, women's long hours of work, their absence at the management level, and the impact of the closure of the media in 2000–2 on women's employment (Farhādpūr 2002). On 8 August 2003, this association together with two other media unions – the Journalists' Trade Union and the In Defence of Freedom of Media Association – organized a successful strike of all media workers in support of the democracy movement and to protest at the death of Zahra Kazemi, an Iranian-Canadian journalist who died in custody in Iran during the pro-democracy movement in the summer of 2003.

The establishment of women's trade associations from the late 1990s demonstrates that Iranian women workers find it difficult to create conditions that furnish their democratic rights within existing unions. So in their own way they are challenging the male dominated trade unions. This may lead to the formation of more women's trade unions or women workers may force male dominated institutions to recognize women's full participation in trade unions. In the meantime, some women's non-governmental organizations are providing an array of support groups available to women outside the formal workplace (Rostami Povey 2004). They are not replacing the trade unions and they do not organize women as workers. Nevertheless, despite their limited activities, they function as an alternative civil society organization, finding it easier to construct democratic rights through women's institutions.

Bibliography

F. Āqājānī, Ṣandūq-i hamyar-i dar karkhana ma, in *Jins-i duvvum. Majmūʿa-i maqālāt* 5 (2000), 91–2.
P. Ardala-n, Aya dar itihadiyah-i sinfi zanān bi shahrvandī shinākhta mishavand?, in *Jins-i duvvum. Majmūʿa-i maqālāt* 4 (1999), 43–8.
A. Bayat, *Workers and revolution in Iran*, London 1987.
L. Farhādpūr, Aya zanān-i rūznāma nakār iḥtiyāj bi yik tashakul-i sinfi khas darand?, in *Ṣida-yi zan. Nashrīya anjoman-i rūznāma nakār zan-i Īrān* 1 (2002), 2.
S. Lāhījī, Sih tajruba va yik ārzū, in *Jins-i duvvum. Majmūʿa-i maqālāt* 1 (1999), 37–44.
H. Ladjevardi, *Labor union and autocracy in Iran*, New York 1985.
M. Partuvī, Jāyigāh-i zanān dar tabaqa kārkar, in *Faṣl-i zanān. Majmūʿa-i ārāʾ va dīdgāʿhā-yi fimīnīstī* 2:2 (2002), 149–153.
M. Poya, *Women, work and Islamism. Ideology and resistance in Iran*, London 1999.
E. Rostami Povey, Feminist contestations of the institutional domains, in *Feminist Review Collective* 69 (2001), 44–72.
——, Trade unions and women's non-governmental organizations. Diverse civil society organizations in Iran, in A. Leather (ed.), *Development in practice* 14:1/2 (2004), 254–66.

Elaheh Rostami Povey

Turkey

Turkish women enjoyed a wide range of civil and political rights and were granted new opportunities by the republican regime as early as the 1920s. Even though much progress was made compared to the Ottoman period, the new regime proved to be limited in the full realization of women's liberation. The inferior position of women in organized labor both in numbers and influence demonstrates their prevailing subordination in Turkish society. The membership of females in labor unions today is variously estimated to be between 6 and 10 percent of total unionized workers. Their position in the union administrative bodies, on the other hand, is one of outrageous underrepresentation, far below the numbers proportionate to their membership. Despite the fact that recent years have marked a certain level of progress in terms of integration of women members into the unions, their involvement is still largely confined to the women's committees, bureaus, and workplace representation.

The story of women workers' experience with workers' organizations in Turkey is by and large an unexplored topic. Although the establishment of the first workers' organizations comparable to labor unions goes back to the early twentieth century, women's position in the union movement attracted scholarly attention and became an issue only after the 1980s with the rise of the feminist movement in Turkey. Apart from the very small amount of research conducted in the 1970s, memoirs and works on the history of strikes and on the working class in general are the major sources of evidence for women's status in organized labor during the pre-1980 period. The limited statistical data and research, however, show that women have played a minor role in the union movement in Turkey with the exception of a few "heroines," and these exceptions were mostly masculinized activists concerned with general problems of workers rather than women-specific issues.

Along with the low level of industrialization, and the structural weakness of workers' movements and unionism, the low union membership rate among women workers, as well as their restricted representation among the administrative cadres, are mainly attributable to the pre-eminence of traditional values in Turkish society. While women have access to the public sphere as citizens equal with men in modern Turkey, the private sphere is still held to be the appropriate place for women, since their roles as mothers and wives are prioritized by the prevailing patriarchal mentality. This has strong implications for the marginalization of women in the labor market, which reinforces labor union discrimination against women, and hence reproduces the gendered ideology in the labor market. The female labor force participation rate, 24.3 percent of the total female population above the age of twelve, as well as the dominance of unpaid family labor as the major type of female economic participation, 51.9 percent of the total female labor force, are crucial factors in explaining the exclusion of a large proportion of women from union membership in Turkey. Moreover, urban women working in the marginal service sector, such as cleaning on a daily or monthly pay basis, women engaged in home production, and most of the women working in small-size enterprises are deprived of both social security rights and union membership.

Even though the low unionization rate among women workers partly highlights their limited representation in the union decision-making process, as well as the low rate of participation in union activities, the correlation between numbers and influence is mostly misleading. In fact, women's secondary status within the unions continues to be the case where the female membership is relatively high. This is essentially related to the reflection of sexual division of labor at the organizational level, as has been the case in most of the other political and economic organizations in Turkey. Women workers' passive stance in the unions is largely linked with the double burden caused by the separate roles that they have to perform at home and at work. Women workers generally do not have the opportunity to engage in any other activity, even if they would prefer to do so. In addition, the deep-rooted preconception concerning the masculinity of politics at large has its negative repercussions on the socialization of women members in unions. Within the context of the traditional distinction between women's and men's jobs, most women either are habitually apathetic or do not perceive themselves as potential decision-makers or as being capable of undertaking union activities. The lack of sufficient information concerning the functions of labor unions further aggravates the alienation of women within the unions. Most women perceive unions as organizations solely responsible for defending their economic interests and thus their expectations from the unions are very limited. Besides the scarcity of educational facilities, this perception is highly related to the profile of unionism in Turkey, which is largely confined to the collective bargaining process. Women who do have labor union consciousness remain aloof to the unions when faced with their indifferent stance toward their special needs and demands, such as childcare support, reduction of working hours, and improvement of working conditions.

The post-1980 period has seen the advancement of certain policies for the encouragement of women's participation at all levels and the management of women-specific problems. The establishment of the Bureau of Women Workers under the Confederation of Trade Unions of Turkey in 1982 with the support of the International Confederation of Free Trade Unions represents a significant step in this respect. Similar initiatives followed, accompanying the rise of the feminist movement. The steps taken so far are nevertheless far from effective in undermining male domination. Today, the number of unions that have acknowledged the significance of the Woman Question still remains very limited.

BIBLIOGRAPHY

Devlet İstatistik Enstitüsü, *Türkiye istatistik yıllığı 2002*, Ankara 2003.

Y. Ecevit, Shop floor control. The ideological construction of Turkish women factory workers, in N. Redclift and M. T. Sinclair (eds.), *Working women. International perspectives on labour and gender ideology*, London 1991, 56–68.

S. Erdoğdu, Kadın işçiler ve sendikalar, in O. Baydar and G. Dinçel (eds.), *75 yılda çarkları döndürenler*, Istanbul 1999, 271–80.

M. Koray, *Çalışma yaşamında kadın gerçekleri*, Ankara 1993.

A. Öğün and A. Özman, *Türkiye'de kadın-sendika ilişkisi. Sendikalılaşma ve örgüt içi temsil*, Ankara 1998.

G. Toksöz, Kadın çalışanlar ve sendikal katılım, in *A.Ü. Siyasal Bilgiler Fakültesi Dergisi* 49:3/4 (1995), 439–54.

G. Toksöz and S. Erdoğdu, *Sendikacı kadın kimliği*, Ankara 1998.

AYLİN ÖZMAN

Postcolonial Dissent

Malaysia and Indonesia

Dissent that is postcolonial in orientation requires a double move. It must be critically aware of the discourses, categories, and power structures of both colonialism and nationalism. This form of dissent requires a sustained analysis of the ways in which social and political structures as well as language itself perpetuate colonial structures that entrap women and other unrepresented groups even when they seem to be liberating in their overall intent. The analytical framework on which this type of dissent is based was first articulated by a group of mostly diasporic scholars in universities in the United States and United Kingdom who identified their work as "postcolonial criticism" and "colonial discourse theory" in the 1980s and 1990s. With the benefits of both experience in and distance from their homelands, these postcolonial critics have worked to disentangle an array of colonial, national, and as well as neocolonial and neonationalist forces that constrain thought and language and justify inequalities. Postcolonial critics are particularly attentive to the ways in which nationalists struggling to gain political and cultural independence were caught in a series of oppositions: between the notions of "East" versus "West"; the "civilized" versus the "uncivilized"; the elite versus masses, urban versus agricultural; those who followed indigenous traditions versus those who followed the so-called "book" religions (those with written sacred texts), among other issues. Those who practice postcolonial dissent in Malaysia and Indonesia focus attention on the ways in which these divisions continue to be exploited in the development and maintenance of local, regional, and national power.

Prior to the 1990s, it was difficult to develop and maintain an active practice of postcolonial dissent in Malaysia and Indonesia, where governments as well as local leaders called upon the discourse of nationalism to rally responses against threats to sovereignty and self-determination. During the decade of the 1990s, however, this situation was transformed as a convergence of events occurred. The central themes and points of analysis of postcolonial criticism were translated into the languages and contexts of Indonesia and Malaysia, and connections were established between local or indigenous knowledges and the insights of a growing number of global social justice activists and scholars. These groups began to advocate for a stronger and more unified response to problems related to economic globalization, military and governmental oppression, environmental justice, and the rights of women and indigenous peoples. Systems for national, regional, and transnational networking constructed by non-governmental organizations (NGOs) and the United Nations system created opportunities for activists and scholars to exchange ideas at such conferences as the Rio Summit on the environment in 1992 and the Beijing Women's Conference in 1995. Each of these major events was preceded by significant preparatory activity at the regional and local levels, in which activists met to collect information and develop platforms for action, leading to productive discussion and interaction among various communities of activists and stakeholders. The follow-up conferences, including "Beijing+5" and "Rio+10" have created structures that motivate participants to maintain a high level of activity on their issues of concern, and to intensify their cross-issue networking to prepare for specific major events. The activity of those conferences has been sustained and increased with the development of the annual World Social Forum, an alternative to the major United Nations conference venue, where grassroots organizing was the main focus. The result of this activity has been the normalizing of the idea of interconnectedness across national boundaries, and the increase of large-scale coalition building and networking activity.

In 2002, for example, Indonesian activists created a broadly integrated coalition in response to their government's efforts to prepare for the World Summit on Sustainable Development (WSSD) in Johannesburg, South Africa. The coalition consisted of groups concerned specifically with environmental issues such as climate change and biodiversity in forestry and marine life, as well as those overseeing human, labor, and environmental issues in the areas of mining and agribusiness, and human rights activists focused on children, women, and indigenous peoples. This kind of coalition-building, also known as "civil society" action results in part from the dissemination of ideas produced through postcolonial critique that see beyond the conventional disciplinary and issue-area boundaries and categories.

Developments in postcolonial dissent have emerged in part out of particular urgencies brought on by the economic and political crises that hit both countries in 1997–9, including mass riots and the overthrow of the 30-year Suharto regime in Indonesia and the jailing of the progressive Deputy Prime Minister Ibrahim Anwar in Malaysia on specious charges of corruption and sodomy. One of Anwar's major contributions to political activism was his popularization of the term *masyarakat madani*, Malay for "civil society," which he promoted as a "path for a Malaysian-style Islamic modernity and civilization (Othman 2003, 126). In contrast to other Malaysian leaders, Anwar argued that *masyarakat madani* required "a political climate which accepts dissent, critical judgment, and pluralistic views as part of the democratic process of governance" (ibid., 127); these views inspired the group of supporters who demonstrated against his incarceration in 1998.

As these crises have unfolded, activists have been increasingly ready to respond, because of widespread awareness of how national governments, like their colonial predecessors, use ethnic, religious, and class- and gender-based "divide and conquer" techniques to distract the populace. As Ariel Heryanto and Sumit Mandal explain in their recent book *Challenging Authoritarianism in Southeast Asia: Comparing Indonesia and Malaysia*, the term *reformasi* (reform) traveled across the border in 1998 from Indonesia to Malaysia, along with the idea of "*reformasi* activism" (Heryanto and Mandal 2003, 7). Reformers in both nations are currently in the process of comparing the structures of "othering" that occur between ethnic groups, particularly concerning Chinese populations (ibid., 8–11), and indigenous peoples. Similar cross-border activity is evident among Muslim feminists, as evidenced in regional workshops sponsored by the Malaysian group Sisters in Islam.

Challenges to postcolonial dissent

Postcolonial dissent in the diasporic arena differs from that practiced within the "excolonized nations" such as Malaysia and Indonesia in two ways. First, activists from these nations experience a greater degree of danger and sacrifice in their efforts; they have been vulnerable to imprisonment without trial, torture, and other forms of silencing. Second, political and religious leaders in both Malaysia and Indonesia are adept in presenting critiques of the West that coincide with the intentionality of postcolonial dissent even as they maintain the hierarchical structuring of "East versus West" of the colonial period. Malaysia's Prime Minister Dr. Mahathir Mohamad has been instrumental in promoting the idea of "Asian values," in response to threats to Malaysia's sovereignty by the international human rights regime together with the regimes of economic globalization (interventions by the International Monetary Fund and more recently, the World Trade Organization). While the concept of "Asian values" is meant to empower Asian nations, it does so at the expense of popular sovereignty within Malaysia, as it promotes communal and patriarchal values for the purposes of maintaining a strict socioeconomic order. Similarly, the denunciation by Muslim leaders of "Western" practices in an effort to create a sense of Islamic unity and dignity has in some instances led to a loss of women's rights. While women have increasingly donned the *jilbab* (head covering) in part to promote Islamic empowerment, changes in Malaysian family law have restricted their rights in marriage and divorce (Othman 2003, 139). In Indonesia, Muslim leaders presented readings of Islamic texts to argue that a woman could not take the role of the presidency. In both cases, the rhetoric of postcolonial dissent was utilized to negate its fundamental spirit by reversing efforts to dismantle hierarchical and exclusive power structures to the benefit of the underrepresented and subaltern.

Responses to the "Asian values" debate

One dissenting voice in the "Asian values" debate has come from Malaysian human rights organization SUARAM (Suara Rakyat Malaysia, People's voice of Malaysia). Speaking for the group, Kua Kia Soong has argued that Asian society and culture encompass more than the narrowly defined model Dr. Mohamad put forth. Asian values may also include the philosophies of Hindu, Buddhist, and Taoist philosophies (represented by Malaysia's Indian and Chinese populations) as well as animist beliefs held by indigenous peoples of the region, and as such, a respect for human life, social equity, and "ecological harmony" (Kua Kia Soong 2001, 10). With this approach, SUARAM has worked with other human rights and environmental justice activists to reframe struggles against Malaysia's economic development policies in terms of popular rather than national sovereignty and human security as opposed to national security. SUARAM focuses on struggles for popular sovereignty – the rights of peoples whose lands have been targeted for development by the central government to determine how their land will be developed and how profits from that development will be distributed. In this work, SUARAM has formed coalitions with such organizations as SIRD (Strategy Info Research Development) to draw attention to issues of urbanization, indigenous people's rights, and environmental justice in Malaysia, concentrating in particular on the Sungai Selangor Dam project and its displacement of the Temuan peoples from their native villages. The movement to protect land and culture from development projects intersects with SUARAM's central focus, the protest against Malaysia's ISA (Internal Security Act) which was recently invoked against demonstrators supporting Ibrahim Anwar and numerous other activists since that time.

In Indonesia, activists offer another alternative to the "Asian values" paradigm through their focus on developing processes for "transitional justice" based on the model of South Africa's Truth and Reconciliation programs. Efforts toward truth and reconciliation are linked to aspects of postcolonial dissent, in that they seek intersections between the binarized narratives of victim and perpetrator, and cultivate relationships between people from a variety of ethnic and religious backgrounds to draw out broad, liberating truths. These efforts expand upon postcolonial theory in their advocation of a hybrid form of justice that draws from multiple legal systems and results not in punishment but accountability and healing. Many activists in Indonesia at present are committed to this approach as perhaps the only means of facing the future in the wake of 40 years of severe violence and oppression that is yet unabated.

Efforts toward "truth seeking" came to the fore with the work of TRK (Tim Relawan Kemanusiaan, Volunteers for humanity), an assemblage of rights workers from a variety of NGOs and other organizations, and multiple religious and ethnic backgrounds that targets its efforts at major flashpoints of ethnic and gender violence in Indonesia. TRK began its work by supporting the efforts of student and other demonstrators at the height of the struggle against the Suharto regime. After the riots of 1998, the TRKP (the Violence against women division of the TRK) collected data on the victims of the mass rapes against Chinese women in several Indonesian cities, and publicized the events in an effort to force the accountability of the Indonesian military. Using the discourse of the international women's movement, the TRKP argued that the rapes were "crimes against humanity," not just "anti-Chinese" violence (Budianta 2003, 163). TRK's efforts led to the establishment of the Komnas Perempuan (National commission on violence against women), which is currently involved in an initiative to map and document violence against women throughout Indonesia (Farid and Simarmatra 2004, 24). Recently, TRK has set up field offices in Aceh, Maluku, and East Timor (Timor Larosae) and works to distribute medicines and help displaced peoples while collecting information for investigations of human rights violations. Along with TRK, several organizations have been working on the collection of testimonies and oral histories from the 1965–6 violence that brought ex-president Suharto (1966–98) to power, including JKB (Jaringan Kerja Budaya, Cultural network) and ELSAM (Lembaga Studi dan Advokasi Masyarakat, Institute for policy research and advocacy). Despite the government's slow progress in the establishment of a truth and reconciliation commission in Indonesia, the activists at these organizations are continuing to prepare for the opportunity to revisit past injustices in order to "forgive but not forget."

Postcolonial dissent and Muslim feminism

In response to the "Islamization" of social and legal systems through increased influence of Islamic law over civil law, women in Malaysia formed the organization known as Sisters In Islam. Since its inception in 1998, Sisters in Islam has taken an inclusive approach to its discussions of the relationship between mosque and state, incorporating the views of Muslim scholars and members of Islamic organizations with or without political affiliations, as well as lawyers schooled in civil law, journalists, academics, and activists. The organization's inception was transnational in scope, incorporating many of the ideas in circulation throughout the Islamic world, including those of African American theologian Amina Wadud, who was at that time teaching at the International Islamic University in Kuala Lumpur. A group of interested women scholars studied Wadud's concept of Islamic hermeneutics, which distinguish those elements that "are universal and eternal" from those that refer to "the cultural and historical specificities of seventh-century Arabia" (Anwar 2001, 229). Since that time, co-founders Zainah Anwar and Norani Othman have written for Malaysian and international audiences about their organization's efforts to include all of the *umma* or Islamic community (men and women) in "female inclusive" readings of Islamic texts, drawing upon insights developed by Muslim feminists working in national and international contexts, including Pakistani American writer Riffat

Hassan, Morrocan feminist Fatima Mernissi, and Wadud (Anwar 2001, Othman 1994, 2003). Othman and others call for the reclaiming of *ijtihād* (individual interpretation of scripture) for women, and the transformation of this process to a more "dialogical or communitarian" approach (Othman 1994, 153).

The exchange of ideas and strategies at international as well as regional women's conferences has been instrumental in the work of Sisters in Islam, as has increased access to print media and the use of the Internet. The organization, working with other groups, used the opportunity of the 1995 Beijing Conference for women to collect data on the conditions of women in Malaysia. The group has also employed CEDAW (the Convention on the Elimination of Discrimination against Women, which Malaysia ratified in 1995) as a rallying point to make transparent some of the unspoken arguments for misogynistic practices. Men were forced to publicly argue, for example, that they had a right to beat their wives (Anwar 2001, 236) and that laws prohibiting domestic violence in Malaysia (in response to the CEDAW) should thus be applicable only to non-Muslim men. Using several modes of interpretation and argument sanctioned under Islam, women counter-argued that surely, wife-beating was not in the spirit or world-view of the Qur'ān. Malaysian women then worked through the legal system to pass new legislation known as the Domestic Violence Act in such a way as to include Muslims within its jurisdiction.

Similar activity has occurred in Indonesia, led by the initial efforts of Wardah Hafidz, one of the first Indonesian women to speak to a Muslim audience about the "misogynist" aspects of "Islamic fundamentalism" in the magazine *Ulumul Qur'an*. Citing Pakistan as an example, she argued that "women are the first targets of Islamization," to the degree that regressive steps concerning women are taken as a means of demonstrating progress in the "Islamizing" of society (Hafidz 1993a, 39). Muslim feminism is now widely represented in Indonesia through print journalism and on television, as well as through the Internet on such sites as islamlib.com, homepage of the Indonesian organization Liberal Islam, and rahima.or.id, website of the Islamic women's organization Center for Training and Information on Islam. The recent opening of dialog and public expression in Indonesia appears to be positively affecting the dissemination of ideas associated with Muslim feminism, at least among elite women with access to newspapers and the Internet. Several prominent female activists have helped in this process. Through her position as a senior researcher at the Ministry of Islamic Affairs, Musdah Mulia has had a prominent voice in the current movement, as has Indonesian sociologist Dr. Siti Ruhaini Dzuhayatin. The Muslim feminist movement in Indonesia was given greater visibility and influence through the participation of former First Lady Sinta Nuriyah. In 2001, she established a 13-member panel of experts to examine the "yellow books," the Islamic texts taught in most religious schools in Indonesia, for examples of discriminatory interpretations of the sacred texts. As in Malaysia, the purpose is to draw together scholars from a variety of disciplines, including experts in the Islamic legal code and in the interpretation and exegesis of Islamic texts, as well as anthropologists, linguists, and scholars of gender studies, to invoke a communitarian response to the role and treatment of women in Islamic society.

Conclusion

Postcolonial dissent was once marginalized in Malaysia and Indonesia, along with writers, artists, and academics who employed this mode of critical analysis. This form of dissent is becoming the basis for participation in national, regional, and transnational activism on a variety of interconnected topics centered around human rights, human security, and popular sovereignty. Increased dialog between Malaysia and Indonesia has given strength to movements in both countries as they have formed webs and networks that enable communing, strategizing, and the sharing of information. Despite the prominence of these movements in the international arena and in academic research, they are still challenged by powerful national governance systems that display limited openness to democratic reforms and transitional justice processes. However, participants in these movements continue to build on strong theoretical and practical foundations, increased awareness and normalization of human rights discourse in the media and populace, and transnational support from activists in other nations working toward the same ends.

Bibliography

H. Abugidieri, A historical model for gender jihad, in Y. H. Haddad et al. (eds.), *Daughters of Abraham. Feminist thought in Judaism, Christianity, and Islam*, Gainesville, Fla. 2001, 81–107.

Z. Anwar, What Islam, Whose Islam? Sisters in Islam and the struggle for women's rights, in R. Hefner (ed.), *The politics of multiculturalism. Pluralism and citizenship in Malaysia, Singapore, and Indonesia*, Honolulu 2001, 227–52.

A. Appadurai, Disjuncture and difference in the global cultural economy, in *Public Culture* 2:2 (1990), 1–24.

—— (ed.), *Globalization*, Durham, N.C. 2001.

K. A. Appiah, Is the post- in postmodernism the post- in

postcolonial?, in *Critical Inquiry* 17 (Winter 1991), 336–57.

H. Bhabha, *The location of culture*, New York 1994.

M. Budianta, The blessed tragedy. The making of women's activism during the *reformasi* years, in A. Heryanto and S. Mandal (eds.), *Challenging authoritarianism in Southeast Asia. Comparing Indonesia and Malaysia*, New York 2003, 145–77.

A. Chayes and M. Minow (eds.), *Imagine coexistence. Restoring humanity after violent ethnic conflict*, San Francisco 2003.

N. van Doorn-Harder, Interview. Sinta Nuriyah Abdurrachman Wahid. A Muslim feminist stirs Indonesia's waters, in *Christian Science Monitor*, 17 May 2001.

J. L. Esposito (ed.), *The Iranian Revolution. Its global impact*, Miami 1990.

H. Farid and R. Simarmatra, The struggle for truth and justice. A survey of transitional justice initiatives throughout Indonesia, International Center for Transitional Justice Occasional Paper Series, 2004, <http://www.ictj.org/indo.asp>.

W. Hafidz, Misogyny and fundamentalism in Islam [in Indonesian], in *Ulumul Qur'an*, 1993a.

——, Islamic women's organizations and the direction of their development, in L. M. Marcoes et al. (eds.), *Muslim women of Indonesia in textual and contextual studies* [in Indonesian], Jakarta 1993b.

R. Hassan, Feminism in Islam, in A. Sharma et al. (eds.), *Feminism in world religions*, Albany, N.Y. 1999, 248–78.

P. Hayner, *Unspeakable truths. Confronting state terror and atrocity*, New York 2001.

A. Heryanto and S. Mandal (eds.), *Challenging authoritarianism in Southeast Asia. Comparing Indonesia and Malaysia*, New York 2003.

M. Kick and K. Sikkink, *Activists beyond borders. Advocacy networks in international politics*, Ithaca, N.Y. 1998.

Kua Kia Soong (ed.), *People before profits. The rights of Malaysian communities in development*, Kuala Lumpur 2001.

F. Mernissi, *The veil and the male elite. A feminist interpretation of women's rights in Islam*, trans. M. J. Lakeland, Reading, Mass. 1991.

S. Nuriyah, Many religious interpretations discriminate against women, in *Tempo*, 16–21 January 2001.

N. Othman, Hudud law or Islamic modernity?, in N. Othman (ed.), *Shari'a law and the modern nation-state. A Malaysian symposium*, Kuala Lumpur 1994, 147–53.

——, Islamization and democratization in Malaysia in regional and global contexts, in A. Hernanto et al. (eds.), *Challenging authoritarianism in Southeast Asia. Comparing Indonesia and Malaysia*, New York 2003, 117–44.

N. Peluso and M. Watts (eds.), *Violent environments*, Ithaca, N.Y. 2001.

R. Radhakrishnan, Postmodernism and the rest of the world, in F. Afzal-Khan and K. Seshadri-Crooks (eds.), *The pre-occupation of postcolonial studies*, Durham, N.C. 2000, 37–70.

B. Stowasser, Gender issues and contemporary Quranic interpretation, in Y. Y. Haddad and J. L. Esposito (eds.), *Islam, gender and social change*, New York 1998, 30–44.

SUARAM (Suara Rakyat Malaysia), <http://www.suaram.org/home.htm>.

TRK (Tim Relawan Kemanusiaan), <http://trk.sekitarkita.com/siapakami/sk.htm>.

A. Wadud, *Qur'an and woman. Rereading the sacred text from a woman's perspective*, New York 1999.

JULIE SHACKFORD-BRADLEY

Public Office

Afghanistan

For the vast majority of Afghan women, the family functions as the paramount social institution. Thus women's participation in public office remains conspicuous by its absence.

King Amīr Amān Allāh (1919–29) tried to liberate women but his programs met with tribal backlash and led to his overthrow. During the premiership of Muḥammad Dāwūd (1953–63) an attempt at public unveiling occurred on the second day of Jeshn (24–30 August 1959). Other bold steps were also taken; for example, a delegation of Afghan women participated in a conference on Asian women in Ceylon in 1957 and a women delegate was sent to the United Nations in 1958.

King Ẓāhir Shāh (1933–73) inaugurated a liberal era in 1959 when he formally announced the voluntary end of female seclusion. During the constitutional period (1963–73) a liberal constitution accorded significant rights to women, including the right to vote and the right to education. The Constitutional Advisory Commission included two women appointed by the king. The Loya Jirga (Grand Assembly) also included four women. A distinctive feature of the election of 1965 was the election of four women. Miss Kubra Nurzai, minister for public health, was the first female minister in Afghanistan. Mrs. Shafiqa Ziayee was another woman minister who remained without portfolio in Etemadi's second cabinet (1969–71). Women were enfranchised by the constitution and they voted in the urban centers.

During the 1980s, after the communist government (1978–92) came to power, a central feature of government policy was the emphasis on education and vocational training, including women's education. The educational policy of the communists saw the dispatch of children, including hundreds of girls, from urban areas to the Soviet Union. It was estimated that by the end of this period, women were to be found in all major government departments, in addition to the police force, the army, business, and industry. Women taught, studied, and acted as judges in the family courts. They worked as scientists and pharmacists in government laboratories and comprised over 75 percent of teachers, 40 percent of medical doctors, and approximately 50 percent of civil servants, almost all of them city based (Human Rights Watch 2001).

The social policies of the Taliban led to a drastic curtailment of women's freedom. Girls and women were denied the opportunity to receive education or employment (other than in the health sector) and forbidden to leave their homes unless completely veiled and accompanied by a male relative. Following strong protests by the international community over the wholesale dismissal of female government employees after the Taliban took power in 1996, it was agreed that they could continue to draw their salaries without being allowed to perform their work functions. However, in 1999 a report of the United Nations Secretary-General noted the widespread dismissal of female civil servants in a move to cut government spending (United Nations 2003).

One of the major political achievements of the Bonn process (December 2001), which occurred after the fall of the Taliban, was the effort to make Afghan women an increasingly active political force. The independent commission for the convening of the Emergency Loya Jirga (February 2002) included 3 women out of 21 commissioners, including one vice-chair of the commission. Women from all segments of society, across ethnic and religious communities, accounted for 200 delegates to the Loya Jirga, or 12.5 percent. One woman was elected vice-chair of the Loya Jirga, and another, Massouda Jalal, received the second largest number of ballots for the position of president. The Emergency Loya Jirga endorsed the cabinet of the Transitional Administration, which includes three women: Habiba Sorabi, minister of women's affairs, Suhaila Siddiq, minister of public health, and Mahbooba Hoquqmal, minister of state for women's affairs. The minister of state for women's affairs provides policy advice for gender mainstreaming, legal issues, and political participation. Despite this success, women continue to face enormous challenges in the public sphere.

Bibliography

Primary Source

United Nations Commission on the Status of Women, *The situation of women and girls in Afghanistan, Report of the Secretary-General*, E/CN.6/2003/4, Forty-seventh session, 3–14 March 2003.

Secondary Sources
L. Dupree, *Afghanistan*, Princeton, N.J. 1980.
N. H. Dupree, Afghan women under the Taliban, in W. Maley (ed.), *Fundamentalism reborn? Afghanistan and the Taliban*, London 1988, 145–66.

Arpita Basuroy

Arab States

Women in the Arab world today enjoy the smallest share of parliamentary seats worldwide. They occupy only 5.7 percent of all parliamentary seats in the region, as compared to 15 percent in Sub-Saharan Africa and 12.9 percent in Latin America and the Caribbean countries. Women hold 3 out of 128 (2.3 percent) seats in Lebanon; 6 out of 110 (5.4 percent) in the lower house and 7 out of 55 (12.7 percent) in the upper house in Jordan; 11 out of 454 (2.4 percent) in the lower house in Egypt; 24 out of 389 (6.2 percent) seats of the lower house in Algeria; 30 out of 325 (9.2 percent) in Morocco; and 30 out of 250 (12 percent) in Syria. Most of the Gulf countries do not hold elections, and Kuwait does not allow women the right to vote.

Some Arab countries have adopted legislation to increase the representation of women in key positions, but these laws are sometimes not enforced or not adequate to ensure women significant representation. Recently, Arab countries such as Morocco and Jordan have adopted quotas that guarantee the representation of women. Both Morocco and Jordan have reserved parliamentary seats specifically for women; Morocco has set aside 30 of a total 325 parliamentary seats and Jordan 6 out of 110. The number of female politicians elected at the communal level in Morocco's 2003 elections rose from 84 to 127, but this is out of a total of 22,944 elected officials. Lebanese women hold fewer than 1 percent of all seats at the municipal level. The King of Morocco has recently appointed the first female royal counselor, Zoulikha Nasri. Egypt has instituted different forms of quotas, but none are currently in effect. At the ministerial levels, Arab states employ a larger concentration of women in key public offices (these may include women serving as ministers and vice ministers and women holding other ministerial positions, including parliamentary secretaries). In fact, Lebanon ranks fourth in the world, while Jordan is eighth. Egypt employs women as prominent judges in the Female Shūra Assembly.

Although women are underrepresented in elected or appointed positions, their employment in key government offices is on the rise. For instance, women occupy prominent positions in the United Arab Emirate's ministry of education. The UAE ministry of planning reported that there were more female than male employees in the more than 25 federal ministries; in 2001, 16,223 workers were women and only 9,518 men (Gulf News 2002).

The limited presence of women in parliament has raised considerable concern among observers and policymakers. Egypt's ʿAmr Mūsa, for instance, has suggested that women's status in the Arab world will improve only when they hold prominent decision-making positions. In Morocco, women's parliamentary participation hastened the adoption of the family code provisions of 2004. Yet, a recent examination of the last four Egyptian parliaments seems to imply that female presence has had no direct effect on the levels of gender issues raised in parliamentary sessions.

Arab women active in political life are not content with the current status quo. They often find themselves having to secure the male and female vote. To secure the male vote female candidates discuss national issues, and issues regarding gender become secondary. As a result, and further complicating matters, most women do not see the formal legislative process as a viable means to improve their condition. Of Arab women MPs, 68 percent are dissatisfied with the current level of women's political participation and 80 percent of women active in public life claimed that they could accomplish their goals without having to participate in formal state institutions.

Certain political, material, social, and cultural conditions continue to stifle women's ability to attain their goals. Political parties remain weak and ineffectual, thereby reducing their impact on policy. The rule of law, too, is weak in the Arab world, and though a few laws guaranteeing women's participation in the public sphere exist, they need to be enforced as well. The dearth of legislation promoting women's presence in parliament also explains their continued marginalization. Reactionary forces seek to exclude women from the public and political spheres, and many current political regimes promote these conservative elements. Prior to unification, half of the judges in South Yemen were women, but subsequently conservative forces have reappointed these women to clerical positions. In fact, the patriarchal political environment does not favor equal participation in the political sphere. Other factors, including the lack of political party support for and backing of female candidates, have hindered women's formal participation. A disjunction between women's civil organizations and current women MPs who are often less concerned with gendered causes encumbers the advancement of women's issues in legislative processes. Familial dynamics also promote male, rather than female, political participation. Finally, the dismal state of Arab economies structures women's access to the public sphere. As standards of living decline and unemployment rates rise, women are becoming unable to afford the education necessary to enhance their human capital.

The impediments to meaningful gender representation are thus located in the political, economic, and cultural realities of the region.

BIBLIOGRAPHY

L. Brand, *Women, the state and political liberalization. Middle Eastern and North African women*, New York 1998.

M. Charrad, State and gender in the Maghrib, in *Middle East Report* (March–April 1990), 19–24, updated and reprinted in S. Joseph and S. Slyomovics (eds.), *Women and power in the Middle East*, Philadelphia 2001, 62–71.

Gulf News online edition, 16 December 2002, <http://www.gulf-news.com/Articles/ news.asp?ArticleID=71228>.

M. Hatem, Economic and political liberalization in Egypt and the demise of state feminism, in *International Journal of Middle East Studies* 24:2 (1992) 231–51, reprinted in S. Sabbagh (ed.), *Arab women. Between defiance and restraint*, New York 1996, 171–93.

IDEA <http://www.idea.int/women/parl/studies1a.htm>.

S. Joseph, Gender and family in the Arab world, in S. Sabbagh (ed.), *Arab women. Between defiance and restraint*, New York 1996, 194–202.

R. Khalidi and J. E. Tucker, Women's rights in the Arab world, in S. Sabbagh (ed.), *Arab women. Between defiance and restraint*, New York 1996, 9–18.

NationMaster.com, <www.nationmaster.com.>

D. Singerman, Where has all the power gone? Women and politics in popular quarters of Cairo, in F. M. Gocek and S. Balaghi (eds.), *Reconstructing gender in the Middle East. Tradition, identity and* power, New York 1994, 174–200.

United Nations Development Programme, Programme on governance in the Arab region, Yemen. Women in public life, 2003, <http://www.pogar.org/countries/yemen/gender.html>.

Women in national parliaments, 2003, <http://www.ipu.org/wmn-e/world.htm>.

S. Zuhur, Women and empowerment in the Arab world, in *Arab Studies Quarterly* 25:4 (Fall 2003), 17–38.

AMANEY JAMAL

The Caucasus and Central Asia

From the early days of its establishment (1917), the Soviet state pursued policies that would emancipate women and give them equal rights with men, as an important part of the overall strategy to build a new society. The first Soviet constitution (1918) and a series of subsequent decrees granted women equal political rights that gave them access to civil service. In implementing these policies, which were advanced for their time, the Bolshevik government made special provisions to ensure that Muslim women of ex-colonial Russian territories were involved in the process. Before that, participation of women in public office was not possible, especially in the highly traditional and segregated societies of the ex-colonial Muslim territories of the Russian Empire.

The policies of the Bolshevik government during its first decade resulted in the first women being elected to local and central governing bodies (soviets). However, this representation remained low until the end of the 1930s. In 1922, in spite of invitations from the Bolsheviks, women made up 11 percent of deputies of city councils and 1 percent of village councils (Khasbulatova 2001). In Turkestan, fewer than half the elected female delegates in 1926 represented the Muslim population (Khairullaev 1990). In light of this, starting from 1925, the Soviets accelerated their work toward the emancipation of Muslim women of the Caucasian and Central Asian republics by publishing the appeal of the Central Executive Committee of the USSR, "On the rights of the working women of the Soviet East and necessity to combat all forms of their enslavement in economic and family areas" (Khairullaev 1990). This called for more active measures in involving Muslim women (or as they were called at that time "women of the Orient") to participate at all levels of public and political life. This important political document was discussed at numerous meetings organized by local soviet bodies, women's councils (*zhenotdel*), and youth communist organizations (*comsomol*) and was followed by concrete steps taken by the Communist Party that included measures to create an environment enabling Muslim women to be active in public life. One of the principal requirements of these policies was increasing women's representation in public office, as well as their membership in the only political force of the time – the Communist Party. As a result of these policies, within two years, in 1927–8, with the initiation of the "Khudjum" campaign, the representation of local women in elected bodies doubled (Khairullaev 1990). In addition to that, from 1937, the Communist Party started to integrate quotas for women in elected bodies of power at all levels. At that time, the quota for the Supreme Soviet (equivalent to parliament) of the Soviet Union was 30 percent, and locally elected bodies up to 40 percent. In 1960, the proportion of women in representative bodies of power fluctuated from 27 percent in the Supreme Soviet, up to 41 percent in the district councils of the people's deputies (soviets).

This proportion was maintained until 1989 (Khasbulatova 2001).

The Soviet state was not persistent in implementing its declared policies to promote the participation of women in governing the state. Except in a few cases, women were not appointed to top decision-making positions in the government. Throughout Soviet history, only two women were appointed (at all-union level) to the position of minister (culture and health). Periodically, a few more women headed the presidiums of the Supreme Soviet at the republican level (equivalent to a speaker of parliament). The Communist Party controlled the process of involvement of women in executive powers through giving them secondary positions, whether in councils of ministers, line ministries, or party committees at territorial levels. Only once, a woman from a Muslim republic, Yadgar Nasretddinova, was able to achieve the highest levels of power in the Soviet system from the 1940s to the 1970s, occupying at various times the positions of Chair of the Supreme Soviet in the Uzbek SSR and Chair of the Upper Chamber of the Supreme Soviet of the USSR.

The substance of the seemingly progressive objective of increasing access and participation of Muslim (and all other) women in public office was distorted by the Soviets because a top-down approach was predominant in the process of its implementation. The demands for promoting female candidates came from central to local bodies (quotas). The practices of the Soviet period demonstrated that actual capabilities and talents of women, including their educational and professional abilities, were least required by the state and society. What really mattered was the social origin of those being promoted, or their conformity to and compliance with the general aims. This was one of the major principals for the formation of the echelon of delegates and deputies of the Soviet ruling elite. Such realities often resulted in non-professional women and men being promoted to positions of power; women patronized by the government occupied a visible but often decorative place in public office. The impact was dubious as the public mentality for many decades captured the image of a female politician negatively, often seeing them as incapable of meaningful decision-making.

However, the overall impact of Sovietization was that Muslim society was changed and gender segregation was in principal liquidated. The farewell to the past was not an easy one given the victims of the Khudjum campaign but it was still a step forward. At the same time, actual equality was never achieved as there was no social base for a wider and real women's movement in Muslim republics. Instead, Sovietization brought new challenges. The lives of Muslim women during Soviet times were regulated by the state and family, with numerous invisible and hidden barriers women had to overcome themselves.

The quota system for women so widely practiced by the Soviet regime was abolished in 1989. This resulted in an immediate and sharp decline in the proportion of women involved at all levels of local and central governmental bodies. In the post-Soviet republics, a comparatively higher level of women in public office is observed so far only in Turkmenistan with 26 percent of members of parliament being women (the highest in the Commonwealth of Independent States). The representation of women in administrative and managerial posts is 36 percent and in senior posts approximately 16 percent. In other Muslim republics these figures are lower. For instance, in Uzbekistan, women have a representation in the parliament of only 9.9 percent. The percentage of women in supreme organs of government stood at the beginning of 2002 at only 13.7 (Uzbekistan 2002). In Tajikistan, after the election of 2000, the percentage of elected women in parliament was about 14.9, and in administrative and managerial posts 15.5 percent.

The Soviet policies were not consistent in promoting women in public office but the current situation gives even more reasons for concern. Growing poverty and unprecedented revival of customs and traditional attitudes pose the danger of losing the gains achieved in the past at huge costs.

The national governments made international commitments after the Caucasian and Central Asian republics gained independence in 1991, in terms of protecting and promoting gender equality. In compliance with them they established institutional mechanisms and are working toward further improvement of national legal frameworks. In the majority of Muslim countries of Central Asia, equal rights and opportunities laws have been drafted and in Kyrgyzstan were approved by the parliament in early 2003. However, the traditional patriarchal attitudes that replaced communist ideology prevail and women remain associated with "social" or just "women and family" issues in public office, usually stranded in secondary positions.

The quota system practiced in Soviet times discredited itself as an avenue for letting non-professionalism and conformism dominate decision-making; therefore despite international commitments for soft quotas, even some women's non-governmental organizations in post-Soviet Caucasian and Central Asian republics are reluctant to promote this concept.

The issue of participation of women in public office remains marginalized and its links to democratic and people-centered development remain outside general public discourse. Unless proper attention is given to these issues at the highest level and comprehensive national programs are designed and implemented, there is a potential danger of losing the momentum to rectify the initial drawbacks that occurred at the early stages of independence and making the process, at least in some of the countries, irreversible.

BIBLIOGRAPHY

S. Akiner, Between tradition and modernity. The dilemma facing contemporary Central Asian women, in M. Buckley (ed.), *Post-Soviet women. From the Baltic to Central Asia*, Cambridge 1997, 261–304.

D. Alimova, *Women's issues in Central Asia. A history of studies and current problems*, Tashkent 1991.

M. M. Khairullaev (ed.), *Islam and women of the Orient. History and present day* [in Russian], Tashkent 1990.

O. A. Khasbulatova, Russian state policies toward women (1900–2000), in *Theory and methodology of gender studies* [in Russian], Moscow 2001.

M. B. Olcott, Women and society in Central Asia, in W. Fierman (ed.), *Soviet Central Asia. The failed transformation*, Boulder, Colo. 1991, 235–56.

S. Tadjbakhsh, Between Lenin and Allah. Women and ideology, in H. L. Bodman and N. Tohidi (eds.), *Women in Muslim society. Diversity within unity*, Boulder, Colo. 1998. 163–87.

M. Tokhtakhodjaeva, *Between the slogans of communism and the laws of Islam*, Lahore 1995.

UNDP (R. Ibrahimbekova coordinator), *The report on the status of women of Azerbaijan Republic* (available in English and Azeri), Baku 1999.

Uzbekistan, Ministry of Macroeconomics and Statistics, *Women and men in Uzbekistan. Collection of statistics* [in Russian], Tashkent 2001.

DONO ABDURAZAKOVA

Iran

Women participated actively in the Constitutional Revolution of 1905/6. The constitution recognized all citizens as equal before the law, but the electoral law of 1906 barred women from voting and being elected to parliament.

Proposals for revision of the electoral law were advanced on a number of occasions in the five decades between the ratification of the 1906 constitution and the extension of suffrage to women in 1963. The issue of female suffrage was raised by a single deputy in the Majlis (parliament) in 1911 and debated on the floor of the legislature in 1944. In the early 1950s, Premier Muḥammad Muṣaddiq considered enfranchising women, but abandoned the idea. Throughout this period, the clerical leaders opposed the extension of the vote to women, declaring such a step incompatible with Islamic teachings and a source of corruption among women.

Iranian women voted for the first time in the 1963 referendum on the White Revolution – a program of reform introduced by Mohammad Reza Shah. The government did not sanction women's participation in the referendum but at the same time did not prevent women from setting up their own ballot boxes, casting votes, and announcing the results. Newly enfranchised women voted in the September 1963 parliamentary elections. For the first time, six women were elected to parliament. The Shah appointed two other women to the senate. In subsequent parliamentary elections the number of women deputies increased. In 1978, on the eve of the Islamic Revolution, 22 women sat in parliament.

Women retained the right to vote after the Islamic Revolution and four women were elected to the first parliament under the Islamic Republic. In the 2000 Majlis elections, 13 women were elected to parliament. A number of women tried to run for the presidency in the elections of 1997 and 2001 but were disqualified. The Iranian constitution is vague concerning the gender of the president. Women also successfully competed for seats in pre- and post-revolution local council elections.

Two women were appointed to the cabinet in the 1960s and 1970s: Farrukhrū Pārsā as minister of education and Mahnāz Afkhamī as minister of state for women's affairs. The position of minister of state for women's affairs was abolished in 1978 to appease the unfolding Islamist movement.

Immediately prior to the Islamic Revolution in 1979 women were employed in significant numbers in both the private and public sectors and held numerous decision-making positions. Despite the significant participation of women in the protests leading to the revolution and the overthrow of the monarchy, women in decision-making positions were purged or given early retirement. Female judges were dismissed.

But women gradually inched their way back into the public sphere. In 1997, Maʿṣūmeh Ibtikār became the first woman vice president for environmental affairs. By 2004, women were serving as members of parliament, deputy ministers, and directors-general of government ministries. Most cabinet ministers and provincial governors appointed advisers for women's affairs. Women were permitted to serve as advisors to some courts, even if they continued to be barred as judges.

BIBLIOGRAPHY

J. Afari, *The Iranian Constitutional Revolution, 1906–1911. Grassroots democracy, social democracy, and the origins of feminism*, New York 1996.

M. Afkhamī, *Jāmiʿah, dawlat va junbish-i zanān-i Īrān, 1357–1342. Muṣāḥbah bā Mahnāz Afkhamī*, ed. G. R. Afkhamī, Bethesda, Md. 2003.

B. Bāmdād, *From darkness into light. Women's emancipation in Iran*, trans. F. R. C. Bagley, Hicksville, N.Y. 1977.

M. Dowlatshahi, *Women, state, and society in Iran 1941–1978*, Washington, D.C. 2002.

H. Esfandiari, *Reconstructed lives. Women and Iran's Islamic Revolution*, Washington, D.C. 1997.

P. Paidar, *Women and the political process in twentieth-century Iran*, Cambridge 1995.

A. Tabari et al. (eds.), *In the shadow of Islam. The women's movement of Iran*, London 1982.

HALEH ESFANDIARI

Turkey

In Turkey, women's formal political participation began with the rise of the Turkish Republic. Although the governing party of the Ottoman Empire's last decade, the Union and Progress, had defined itself as the "party of the male and female Ottomans" (Çavdar 1991, 17) the issue of the political rights of women never appeared on its agenda. After the foundation of the Turkish Republic, a group of women attempted to establish a women's party. This was not allowed by the single-party authorities. The changes in the legal status of women promoted by the state between 1920 and 1935 have been defined as one of the foremost examples of state feminism in history (Tekeli 1990, 152). With great support from Atatürk, Turkish women were granted political rights much earlier than women in many Islamic or European countries. They were enfranchised for local elections in 1930 and subsequently for national elections in 1934.

From 1930 until 1946, there was overwhelming support by single party leaders for increased women's participation in both local government councils and the national assembly, with the adoption of an informal quota system. In the 1935 national elections, 18 women (4.6 percent) were elected to the parliament. With the advent of the multi-party regime, however, a sharp decline in the participation of women was observed. Until 1984, the percentage of women parliamentarians ranged between 0.61 and 1.76 (KSSGM 2001, 104). After 1984, a slight increase occurred, though the percentage did not surpass that of 1935. Although the number of women taking an active role in politics has increased in recent years, in the last general election (2002), of 550 deputies elected into the parliament, 24 were women (4.5 percent). Of 365 deputies of the governing Justice and Development Party (AKP), which holds a moderate Islamic position and has recast itself as conservative-democratic, 13 are women. The Social Democratic People's Republican Party (CHP), the opposition party, has 11 women deputies out of 177.

Between the years 1935 and 2004, only 126 women became members of parliament and nearly half of them (48.9 percent) did not have the opportunity for a second term. Therefore, out of a total 8,517 seats women occupied only 183 (2.1 percent). Women have mostly been elected from the lists of majority parties.

Studies show that men play a critical role in drawing women into politics. Women elected to political office have been introduced to politics by men. Party leaders have recruited daughters of eminent "political families" because of their family names. However, another pattern is that of apolitical women, with no previous political interest and experience. These apolitical women have been drawn into politics because of their high social or professional standing (Arat-Pamuk 1990, 30–3; Talaslı 1996, 206). Women parliamentarians have been better educated and are more professional than their male colleagues (Kovanlıkaya 2001, 425). With the rise of religious political parties, a new counter-elite of women who dress according to Islamic traditions has emerged. They participate in the public domain and politics and are also composed of urban, well-educated, and professional women.

WOMEN IN GOVERNMENT

In spite of their educational and occupational superiority, women parliamentarians have been underrepresented in government or in ministerial posts. Since 1971, only 14 women have taken part in 16 cabinets occupying 28 ministerial posts. Women ministers have been mainly concentrated in social areas such as women's affairs, culture, and tourism (78.6 percent) compared to legal (3.6 percent), economic (10.7 percent), foreign affairs (3.6 percent), and internal affairs (3.6 percent). In 1993, a woman (though hardly a feminist), Tansu Çiller, the leader of the True Path Party (DYP), became the first female prime minister in Turkey and served till June 1996. Presently, in the AKP's 23-member cabinet there is only one woman minister of state responsible for women and family affairs.

The causes of underrepresentation of women in parliament and cabinets are:

1. In general, women's patterns of political participation reflect their disadvantageous position in society. The majority of women lack political resources such as education, occupation, and wealth. This limits their political participation and representation. Besides, a kind of self-imposed limitation interrupts women's participation in politics (Koray 1991, 125).

2. The legal rights of women are sometimes ignored in favor of more traditional provisions of Islam in relatively closed provincial communities. Women in most small towns and villages are still socially secluded. The success of legal reforms in changing women's conditions has been limited largely because Islamic beliefs and traditions concerning gender roles continue to be socially valid (Toprak 1990, 43). It is commonly believed that participation of women in social life will be destructive of the functions of the family. Social and political activities of women are controlled and limited by their husbands, their families, and social/political actors (TUSİAD 2001, 208).

3. The political parties have never considered gender equality as an issue of democracy. It is still a rhetorical subject only to be remembered during election campaigns. It can be easily asserted that political parties have used women only as a symbol of Westernization and modernity. Furthermore, it is claimed that the political parties in Turkey have been the reproducer and the supporter of sexist ideology (Çakır 2001, 401). It is thus not surprising that there is insufficient support, such as quotas or short lists for female candidates, to increase women's chances of being elected. As a result women still tend to be nominated in limited numbers and for marginal seats.

4. Lastly, the instability of the Turkish party system has a negative effect on women's participation and representation in politics.

Women in public administration

Turkish women began to work in public administration in the 1880s as teachers and nurses. After the foundation of the Turkish Republic, the number of women officials increased due to the proliferation of bodies and functions of public administration. Especially in the early years of the Turkish Republic successful, professional, avant-garde women were presented to the public as model pioneers on the path of new, Western inspired civilized society by the single-party leaders (Abadan-Unat 1981, 102). During the multi-party period, while the political parties seem not truly interested in promoting women's situation in public administration, such factors as economic necessity, the rising educational level, changes in the family structure, and decline in birth rate have encouraged women to go to work. In other words, the growing participation of Turkish women in public administration is essentially the result of economic and social change, rather than specific egalitarian political policies. In this sense, it is largely a "spontaneous development" (Çitçi 1998, 575).

The statistical data on women working in public administration show that their total number has increased at a faster rate than that of their male colleagues. Between 1938 and 2003 the total number of women in the public service increased sixty-fold, while the total number of male public officials has increased thirteen-fold. According to the 2003 statistics women constitute percent 31.8 of public officials (T. C. Emekli Sandığı 2003). As in politics, they are much more educated than their male counterparts. However, it should be noted that they tend to be concentrated in areas associated with women's traditional societal roles in, for example, education and health. At the senior level of civil service, while 10.5 percent of high administrative officers are women, at present there is no female permanent secretary or provincial governor. Moreover, women constitute only 2.1 percent of sub-governors, 3.7 percent of chiefs of police, and 4.3 percent of ambassadors. Nonetheless, it could be said that women in public administration are in a much better position than those in politics.

Conclusion

Turkish society is characterized by the contrasts and combinations of East and West, by a confluence of modernity, traditionalism, and Islamism. Varied subcultures, classes, and values shape educational, occupational, and political opportunities for women in Turkey today. Educated women from urban, middle, and upper classes have been able to take advantage of participating in bureaucracy and politics. Since women are particularly weak in electoral politics, their parliamentary performance has not actually increased female representation or women's participation in the decision-making process.

Bibliography

N. Abadan-Unat, Women in government as policy-makers and bureaucrats, in M. Rendel (ed.), *Women, power and political systems*, London 1981, 94–115.

Y. Arat-Pamuk, From the private to the political realm. Female parliamentarians in Turkey, in F. Özbay (ed.), *Women, family and social change in Turkey*, Bangkok 1990, 28–38.

S. Çakır, Bir'in nostaljisinden kurtulmak. Siyaset teorisine ve pratigine cinsiyet açısından bakış, in A. İlyasoğlu and N. Akgökçe (eds.), *Yerli bir feminizme doğru*, Istanbul 2001, 385–422.
T. Çavdar, *Ittihat ve terakki*, Istanbul 1991.
O. Çitçi, Son söz yerine. 20. yüzyılın sonunda kadınlar ve gelecek, in Oya Çitçi (ed.), *20. yüzyılın sonunda kadınlar ve gelecek*, Ankara 1998, 571–82.
A. Güneş-Ayata, Türkiye'de kadının siyasete katılımı, in Ş. Tekeli (ed.), *Kadın bakış açısından kadınlar*, Istanbul 1993, 293–312.
KSSGM (Kadının Statüsü ve Sorunları Genel Müdürlügü), *Türkiye'de kadın 2001*, Ankara 2001.
M. Koray, Günümüzdeki yaklaşımlar ışıgında kadın ve siyaset, in Ş. Tekeli and M. Koray, *Devlet-kadın-siyaset*, Istanbul 1991, 81–153.
Ç. Kovanlıkaya, Erkek parlamentonun kadın siyasetçileri, in A. İlyasoğlu and N. Akgökçe, (eds.), *Yerli bir feminizme doğru*, Istanbul 2001, 423–53.
G. Talaslı, *Siyaset çıkmazında kadın*, Ankara 1996.
T. C. Emekli Sandığı, 1 July 2003 <www.emekli.gov.tr>.
Ş. Tekeli, The meaning and limits of feminist ideology in Turkey, in F. Özbay (ed.), *Women, family and social change in Turkey*, Bangkok 1990, 139–59.
B. Toprak, Emancipated but unliberated women in Turkey. The impact of Islam, in F. Özbay (ed.), *Women, family and social change in Turkey*, Bangkok 1990, 317–38.
TUSİAD, *Kadın-erkek eşitligine doğru yürüyüş Egitim, çalışma yaşamı ve siyaset*, Istanbul 2000.

Oya Çitçi

Public/Private Dichotomy

Overview

Gender distinctions in Muslim societies have often been approached through a clear dichotomy between the public (equated with men) and the private (equated with women) domains. Corresponding to this split is a whole set of oppositions such as male/female, honor/shame, outside/inside, active/passive, powerful/powerless, superior/inferior, and visible/invisible. While these oppositions have been especially common in the study of the Middle East, they have also directly and indirectly informed the study of Muslim communities in other parts of the globe. From Saudi Arabia, Egypt, and Morocco to Azerbaijan, the Philippines, and Indonesia, in the literature an emphasis on spatial and symbolic distinctions that structure interaction between men and women is frequently encountered. Different (Muslim and non-Muslim) writers have seen this opposition as central to the construction of Muslim femininities and masculinities.

Public/private and the question of power

Since the late 1960s, several studies have questioned the public/private dichotomy and its value in understanding power and gender inequalities. This critique has focused on two aspects. An earlier set of studies aimed to show how the dichotomy fails to capture the active role women play in social life and the significant power they exercise in running the affairs of their families (Nelson 1974, Altorki 1986, Rassam 1984). In an article published in 1974, Cynthia Nelson provided a powerful critique of this split, linking it to Western categories that inform discussions of power, privacy, and publicness. In contrast to the sharp dichotomy and the great emphasis most (mainly male) researchers placed on the power that men exercised in the public domain, Nelson drew on various ethnographic studies (mainly conducted by women) to show the complex interplay between the public and private spheres. She demonstrated that despite the segregation of men and women, the latter still had the ability to influence men and exercise more power than had been assumed in earlier studies. Through sorcery, witchcraft, and healing, women exercise considerable influence over men and their decisions. In short, women's networks always cross the boundaries between inside and outside and function to link the concerns of men and women. Authors such as Soraya Altorki (1986), Asma Afsaruddin (1999), and William Lancaster (1997) have revealed the political implications of the roles of mothers, sisters, and other female relatives in arranging marriages. Other studies have shifted the attention to the symbolic and political significance of the private domain and documented how the house unit may become fundamental to the resistance of domination, marginalization, and colonization as well as to the assertion of ethnic/national identities. When Azerbaijan was part of the Soviet Union, for instance, anti-religious policies pushed Islam to the private domain of the family. Within this context, women and their ritual practices acquired central significance in resisting Soviet domination and in asserting Azeri national and religious identity (Tohidi 1998). Similarly, the house, its decoration, and women's religious practices are important markers of the differences between Bosnian Muslims and their Christian neighbors (Bringa 1995). While these conditions increase the symbolic power invested in the private domain, they may also facilitate and legitimize the possibility of imposing restrictions on women and their access to various public spaces.

Public/private as contested domains

A second and more recent set of studies question the meaning of "publicness" and "privacy," emphasizing the shifting and unstable meanings of these two concepts (Afsaruddin 1999, Bringa 1995, Ghannam 2002, Meneley 1996). In particular, these studies have been critical of the male-based definition of the "public" common in the literature. While many researchers tended to view men's activities and spaces as part of the public domain, they usually saw women's practices (even when conducted outside the immediate domain of the household) as "privatizing" public spaces. In contrast to this view, recent anthropological research has demonstrated how women have their own "publics." Anne Meneley, for example, illustrates how Yemeni women through visiting and networking are active in enhancing their families' honor and status. While the domains of their visits are separate from men, as dictated by prevailing social tradition and Islamic norms, they nevertheless formulate publics invested with power and social value. Honor is not limited to men; women are also active in boosting the prestige and good reputation of their families. Rather than assuming fixed notions of public and private and equating them with one group or another, Ghannam (2002) argues that it is crucial to always question who is defining these two concepts and how the distinctions between them are negotiated by gender and age groups in different contexts. Various actors ranging from family members (a brother, a husband, or a mother) and local men and women (a neighbor or a friend), to government officials (a police officer or a judge) and religious figures all struggle to define and redefine the social spaces that are accessible to men and women. Women's access to the mosque, for example, has shifted. Studies show that during the Prophet's lifetime, women were allowed free access to the mosque (Ahmed 1992). Over time, various rulers and religious figures have facilitated or restricted women's access to the mosque. Currently, women have free access to it in most Muslim countries. In Egypt, the government and most religious groups do not prevent women from attending the mosque. In fact, there are many religious figures and activists who strongly advocate women's attendance of weekly lessons, Friday sermons, and daily prayers at local mosques. Other groups, motivated by a specific understanding of Islam or by social norms of shame and honor (as is the case in some parts of Upper Egypt), make strong arguments against women's participation in mosque-related activities and emphasize that it is more religiously sanctioned for women to pray at home.

Islam and the public/private split

Several scholars see the public/private opposition as inherently Islamic (Mernissi 1987, Abu-Lughod 1987). They argue that the fundamental differences Islam envisioned between men and women have been translated into spatial distinctions between the domains allocated to each side in the housing unit and the community at large. This argument is perhaps best exemplified in the common discussions of seclusion and veiling (or more accurately, the *ḥijāb*, which refers to different styles of covering specific parts of the female body, most frequently the hair but sometimes also the face and hands), both of which have historically attracted the attention of Western travelers, writers, colonial authorities, and policymakers.

Some authors argue that before the arrival of Islam women were not segregated from men but enjoyed sexual freedom and played an active role in public life (Mernissi 1987). The arrival of Islam introduced new restrictions on women's movement, marriage choices, and participation in public activities. Because Islam conceptualizes female sexuality as powerful and potentially destructive, it instituted seclusion and veiling as strategies to control and manage these threats. Fatima Mernissi argues that to be able to cross the boundaries that separate the public from the private, Islam urges women to prevent any potential social disorder (*fitna*) by veiling themselves. Veiling in this context desexualizes the woman and renders her invisible in the street, the domain of men (Mernissi 1987, 143).

Various studies have added complexity to this sole emphasis on Islam by looking at the continuities between pre-Islamic and Islamic traditions. Leila Ahmed (1992), for example, shows how veiling was a tradition that predated Islam and that marked social divisions. Elite women donned the veil before the arrival of Islam to distinguish themselves from slaves and "improper" women. Other scholars examine factors such as class and tribal structures that shape the distinction between the public and the private in contemporary Muslim societies. Seclusion and veiling, for instance, were mainly practiced by upper-class Muslim families while peasants and the urban poor could not afford to conform to such ideals (Tucker 1993, Altorki 1986, Cooper 1998, Abu-Lughod 1987). Studies also show that notions such as purdah (segregation) in Pakistan are more informed by specific regional cultural norms (such as shame and honor) that are shared by other religious groups and that cannot be explained mainly by Islamic values (Weiss 1998). At the same time, Muslim women are a heterogeneous group and may give diverse meanings to the same practice. For example, they may cover their hair in different ways and for a variety of reasons. Some see the veil as part of their religious duties. Others see it primarily as an obligatory social tradition or as a practical tool for allowing them to go out to work while maintaining their honor and respectability. In contexts where Muslims are a minority and may feel excluded from the dominant culture (as is the case in France), veiling may be highlighted as a signifier of the religious and ethnic collective identities that Muslims aspire to maintain. All of this makes Islam one powerful factor among several in the construction of gender distinctions and the making of public and private spaces.

Current debates

The meanings of public and private and the boundaries that differentiate the spaces allocated to men from those allocated to women are contested and struggled over. Currently, this contestation is best manifested in attempts to expand or restrict women's access to education, political participation, and wage employment. Various groups and activists believe that women should not be limited to the domestic domain but should be active in public life. Behind this view is a strong belief that education and work outside the home will empower women and transform inequalities in family relationships (Al-Ali 2000). Other groups draw on Islamic traditions and values to argue that, rather than reflecting inequality, the public/private distinction shows that men and women complement each other. Men, they argue, should be the providers and protectors while women should be the mothers, the home-makers, and care givers (Karam 1998). Working outside the home is a form of oppression because it contradicts the "natural role" that God granted women. Female Islamist advocates in particular are actively defining the proper role of women as wives and mothers and working to communicate this to other women through various means such as informal networks, visits to homes, and weekly lessons in local mosques. Some scholars and activists are rereading religious scriptures to provide alternative interpretations that allow women to play more active economic and political roles. They argue that it is the interpretations of Islamic scriptures, done mainly by men, and not the scriptures themselves that support male domination and exclude women from various public spaces.

Muslim women belong to different nations, regions, classes, ethnicities, and age groups. They often live in heterogeneous communities where different religions and cultural systems coexist. Accordingly, Islamic texts and discourses are interpreted in many contexts and by different actors. All of these factors complicate any simple generalizations about the public/private dichotomy. Muslim women in countries such as Tunisia, Indonesia, and Turkey, for instance, tend to have more rights than women in Saudi Arabia, Pakistan, and Afghanistan when it comes to voting, the legal age of marriage, divorce, child custody, and work outside the home. Women's various public spaces and activities are shaped not only by Islam and social norms but also by economic and political forces. For example, unemployment is high in several Muslim countries for both men and women. In Egypt, where women were usually employed in the public sector, recent structural adjustment programs have reduced the opportunities open for them in the public sector without expanding their access to the private sector (Karam 1998). Many women find their only option to be "informal" employment, which grants them little employment security. At the same time, global changes such as the development of new means of communication (including satellite television and the Internet) and new systems of transportation are challenging conventional spatial distinctions between public and private spaces. Therefore, the shifting meanings of private/public and women's access to paid work, education, health services, and the legal system are all shaped by the complex interplay between global forces and local/national religious, social, political, and economic factors.

Bibliography

J. Abu-Lughod, The Islamic city. Historic myth, Islamic essence, and contemporary relevance, in *International Journal of Middle East Studies* 19:1 (1987), 155–76.

A. Afsaruddin, *Hermeneutics and honor. Negotiating female "public" space in Islamic/ate societies*, Cambridge, Mass. 1999.

L. Ahmed, *Women and gender in Islam*, Cairo 1992.

N. Al-Ali, *Secularism, gender and the state in the Middle East. The Egyptian women's movement*, Cambridge 2000.

S. Altorki, *Women in Saudi Arabia. Ideology and behavior among the elite*, New York 1986.

T. Bringa, *Being Muslim the Bosnian way. Identity and community in a central Bosnian village*, Princeton, N.J. 1995.

B. Cooper, Gender and religion in Hausaland. Variations in Islamic practice in Niger and Nigeria, in H. Bodman and N. Tohidi (eds.), *Women in Muslim societies. Diversity within unity*, Boulder, Colo. 1998, 21–38.

F. Ghannam, *Remaking the modern. Space, relocation, and the politics of identity in a global Cairo*, Berkeley 2002.

S. Joseph, The public/private. The imagined boundary in the imagined nation/state/community. The Lebanese case, in *Feminist Issues* 57 (Autumn 1997), 73–92.

A. Karam, *Women, Islamisms, and the state. Contemporary feminisms in Egypt*, Houndmills, Basingstoke, Hants. 1998.

W. Lancaster, *The Rwala Bedouin today*, Cambridge 1981, Prospect Heights, Ill. 1997^2.

A. Meneley, *Tournaments of value. Sociability and hierarchy in a Yemeni town*, Toronto 1996.

F. Mernissi, *Beyond the veil. Male-female dynamics in modern Muslim society*, Bloomington, Ind. 1987.

C. Nelson, Public and private politics. Women in the Middle Eastern world, in *American Ethnologist* 1:3 (1974), 551–63.

A. Rassam, Towards a theoretical framework for women's studies, in UNESCO, *Social science research and women in the Arab world*, London 1984, 122–38.

N. Tohidi, "Guardians of the Nation." Women, Islam, and the Soviet legacy of modernization in Azerbaijan, in H. Bodman and N. Tohidi (eds.), *Women in Muslim societies. Diversity within unity*, Boulder, Colo. 1998, 137–63.

J. E. Tucker, Women and the state in 19th century Egypt. Insurrectionary women, in *Middle East Report* (January–February 1986), 9–13.

—— (ed.) *Arab women. Old boundaries, new frontiers*, Bloomington, Ind. 1993.

A. Weiss, The slow yet steady path to women's empowerment in Pakistan, in Y. Y. Haddad and J. L. Esposito (eds.), *Islam, gender, and social change*, New York 1998, 124–43.

Farha Ghannam

Race, Gender, and Difference

Egypt and Sudan

Our investigation of the lived experience of women in Egypt and Sudan acknowledges the importance of viewing race and gender as variables within an interlocking system of domination and oppression that includes class, age, sex, ethnicity, and religion (Collins 2000). Within this framework, difference is constructed within a matrix of domination where distinctive systems of oppression, such as racism, sexism, and patriarchy, are interconnected and have similar ideological explanations for the subordination of individuals and groups within a society. Difference in these countries is experienced by women as a complex set of fluid and inter-discursive processes shaped by Islam, patriarchy, colonialism, slavery, and the several nationalisms (for example, Egyptian nationalism, Arab nationalism) that have arisen in the Nile Valley region.

In the Nile Valley, race has long been more of a social than a biological construct, including in its definition cultural, religious, linguistic, and historical elements that in many cases overshadow the genetic. The Nile Valley region contains a multitude of ethnic groups, including Egyptians of Arab/European/African ancestry, Nubians, Copts, Berbers, northern Sudanese of Arab/African ancestry, Dinka, Nuer, Nuba, and the nomadic and semi-nomadic Rashaida, Baggara, and Bishari pastoralists, as well as Armenians, Greeks, Italians, and French. Most of these groups have experienced genetic intermixture with members of other ethnicities.

Many of those who write about the relationships between the various ethnic groups in Sudan charge that racism is a defining characteristic of these relationships (Deng 1995, Jok 2001, Hale 2003). In Egypt, on the contrary, this subject remains a source of great debate (Powell 2000, Fluehr-Lobban and Rhodes forthcoming). Whereas racism in the past has been defined as the construction of categories of "others" that have immutable boundaries (most often genetic in nature) in order to exclude, inferiorize, and/or exploit them, this definition is changing. There is a growing acceptance that the old biological basis of racism is giving way to the justification of bigotry through the invocation of cultural difference (Silverman and Yuval-Davis 1999, Blaut 1992, Back and Solomos 2000, Smedley 1998, Stam 1997), and even a "racism without races" (Balibar 1991). The criteria for prejudice in cultural racism are ethnic group traditions, practices, and cultural heritage rather than biological makeup. Yet, the commonality between cultural and biological racisms is the fact that they are, above all, social relations rooted in material structures and historical relations of power. It is in light of this emerging definition of racism that we may interpret the attitudes of the ethnic groups of Sudan and Egypt toward each other.

A greater understanding of attitudes about race in Egypt and Sudan necessitates an examination of Islam. Islam has a well-earned reputation as a religion of tolerance, welcoming people of all ethnic heritages and viewing them all as equal in Islam. Passages in the Qurʾān reflect an awareness of difference among people, but express no racial or color prejudice; in fact, the message is that piety is more important than birth. However, in social thought and practice, there has been a hierarchy based upon skin color and ethnicity (Drake 1987, Lewis 1971).

Scholars have linked notions of race and color in the Nile Valley with Arab culture, Islam, and the institution of slavery (Marmon 1999, Hunwick and Powell 2002). In the literature of ancient Arabia, color terms were used to describe human skin tones and sometimes ethnic groups, but in a relative rather than an absolute sense. After the Islamic conquests of Africa and Asia, however, color terms were applied to humans. Although in pre-Islamic times, "blackness" was not invariably negative, it became more so as time went on, until finally by the time of the Umayyad caliphs, it was nothing but an insult. The African slave trade influenced Arab attitudes toward dark-skinned people by reinforcing the association of blackness with slavery, low-status positions, and demeaning occupations. Although there were white slaves, it seems that they tended to fill higher administrative positions and once freed, could rise to any level. This was not the case for Blacks, perhaps because their color made them more visible in Arab society (Drake 1987, Lewis 1971, Segal 2001). This indicates the beginning of the salience of whiteness and blackness in the formation of class positioning in Nile Valley cultures. Moreover, it highlights how the invisibility of whiteness allows the assertion of racelessness in these societies.

Islam did not consider owning slaves sinful, although there were strictures against owning fellow Muslims. Even here, Blacks were at risk, as history shows that the law was not always strictly enforced to protect African Muslims from slave raids. Slaves historically were exported from Sennar, Kordofan, Darfur, and Nubia to northern Sudan and Egypt, as well as to many countries in the Middle East.

Overlapping this color/race hierarchy was a gender hierarchy: female slaves outnumbered male slaves in Sudan by two to one, and by three to one in Egypt. They not only provided domestic help but were also a large part of the harems of wealthy men. Islam did not forbid a slave master to have sex with his slaves, and many slave women became concubines (Baer 1967, Collins 1992, Cunnison 1966, Segal 2001, Lewis 1971, Marmon 1999, Willis 1985), as it was openly acknowledged that the sexuality of all enslaved women was a primary aspect of their productive labor. A hierarchy existed among the female slaves, with whites being valued above their darker counterparts. This distinction between white and black women has shaped the sociocultural landscape, as evidenced by the interstitial position white women still occupy as individuals who are simultaneously racially privileged and sexually marginalized.

Moreover, the association of African women with concubinage, a status lower than that of wife, remains and has fed into stereotypes about them. Children born of an enslaved mother and a free Arab father were considered members of their father's lineage and ideally, therefore, free Muslim Arabs. In reality however, there were degrees of Arabness, and this attitude showed itself most clearly when the slave mother was of African origin. The many negative proverbs, anecdotes, and stereotypes about Africans, slaves, black skin, and Black slaves bears this out: "son of a Negress" is still a customary pejorative epithet in many areas of the Arab world (al-Afif Mukhtar forthcoming, Drake 1987, Lewis 1971). The impact of the race/color hierarchization, therefore, is reflected in the institution of marriage, whereby some families may be reluctant to align themselves with those that obviously possess Sub-Saharan African ancestry, and by the over-accentuation of particular white ethnic heritages such as Turkish.

In addition to nineteenth-century slavery, notions of race and ethnicity in the Egyptian context have been greatly influenced by the colonial aspirations of Egyptians. Egypt's leading scholars in the nineteenth century initially viewed humankind in terms of social evolutionary thought propounded by its British colonizers. But by the end of the nineteenth century, this perspective was overshadowed by their desire to colonize Sudan. Egypt attempted to demonstrate the legitimacy of its claims to Sudanese territory by asserting that the Sudanese were its kinsmen rather than racially distinct people. Although during his presidency Gamal Abdel Nasser often extolled pan-African unity in his speeches, reminding his fellow Egyptians that they were Africans as well as Arabs, the more persistent construction was of the Sudanese as inferior and "in need of Egyptian guidance" (Powell 1995, 29). In contemporary times, remnants of this ideology can be found in discourses about Sudanese-Egyptian relations within Sudanese communities in Cairo, and in popular culture (Armbrust 1996, Fabos 1999, Morsy 1994, Powell 2000, 2001). In Egypt the Sudanese number as many as four million, due to their migrations north throughout the twentieth century. They live in rural and urban centers there, and have an ambiguous relationship with the rest of the society. Legally granted full rights, including the right to own land, the Sudanese are not classified as refugees. However, they are often unable to obtain legal authorization to work and housing, and are subject to intense discrimination and abuse at the hands of the Egyptian authorities.

Arab nationalism, which claims that all members of the society could be unified through a common ancestry that was based primarily on Islam, but also upon a sense of shared history, language, and culture, underscores conceptualizations of race and ethnicity in Egypt. This ideology disregards ethnic, religious, and linguistic differences, and at key historical moments, calls for cultural assimilation (for example, the inundation of ancient Nubia due to the raising of the Aswan High Dam). This desire to deny and purge difference in Egyptian culture can be viewed as "an insidious albeit unsystematic racism" (Harrison 1995, 55).

As non-Egyptian segments of Egyptian society (from Palestine, Sudan, Somalia, Eritrea, and Ethiopia) continue to grow as they seek political asylum in Cairo, scholars are beginning to carry out more in-depth analyses of the cultural construction of race and racism. A review of newspaper articles and journals suggests that the Sudanese are subject to harassment and bodily harm, as evidenced by the Sakakini Riot in 2000, which was sparked by the reported harassment of southern Sudanese women by Egyptians on the streets of Cairo (Apiku 2000a, 2000b, Fabos 2000).

In Sudan, to be an "Arab" is to embody a composite of ethnicity, language, skin color, and culture (Deng 1995). Although there are over 500 different ethnic groups in Sudan, most research has been concentrated upon the "Arabs" of northern Sudan, the Dinka of the Bahr al-Ghazal area, and the Nuba of southern Kordofan. These groups have been genetically intermixed for centuries, yet they continue to define each other as members of separate races, some of whom are superior to others (Deng 1995, Jok 2001).

The "Arabs" of the north, a mixture of Arab and African peoples, are politically dominant although in the minority numerically. They defined, until recently, Sudanese nationality as Arab and Muslim, effectively disenfranchising the inhabitants of the south and west, who define themselves as "African" (although there is some Arab admixture), and non-Muslim. Because the southerners have resisted governmental attempts to impose Sharīʿa law upon them, they have been subjected to military action against them for at least 47 years. Since 1956, each successive government has pursued a policy of the Arabization and Islamization of the country, using negative stereotypes of Africans as backward, primitive, and pagan as justification for this, and thereby encouraging what has become in effect ethnic cleansing and cultural genocide (Spaulding and Beswick 2000).

The southern Sudanese, many of whom are now refugees in the north, are stereotyped as unfit for anything but menial labor, in fact as "naturally slaves" (Jok 2001). Since they are not legally recognized as citizens of Sudan, southerners have no recourse to police protection. Indeed, they are subject to police profiling, arrest, and incarceration in jails where they may be beaten and raped. Women and children from the south and west, primarily Dinka and Nuba, who were captured in raids on their villages, work mainly in northern households as domestics and nannies. It has been argued that they are, in fact, enslaved. The women and girls are especially vulnerable to sexual abuse by the male members of the families they work for as they are thought to be sexually wanton: the stereotype of Africans as primitive, along with the history of enslaved African women as concubines, encourages this belief. Domestic workers are given Muslim names and forbidden to speak their own language; this is used as an indication of a family's ability to "convert" a southern woman, an action which is highly regarded among northerners. A women who converts may have a clitoridectomy (Gruenbaum 2001, Hale forthcoming, Jok 2001, van Achterberg 1998).

Although there are surely women among the population of northern Sudanese who do not ascribe to the prevailing beliefs discussed here, it appears that most do. Many are complicit in the oppression of southern women because they provide cheap household labor: the ailing economy has forced many northern women to seek work outside the home, and household help has enabled them to continue to fulfill their domestic duties as well. Many deny that the oppression of ethnic groups goes on, arguing that the reports of raiding and enslavement by government-funded militias are lies told by the United States and Europe. Others believe that they are helping the southern Sudanese by raising them from their primitive state: "One influential woman leader in the Islamist movement suggested that a solution to the 'southern problem' was for Muslim men to take non-Muslim Dinka women as second wives or concubines, assuming that their children would be raised as Muslims" (Gruenbaum 2001, 119).

Hale (forthcoming) reports that Sudan is now in the process of reinventing its national identity, decentering its "Arab" identity and centering "Islam," as a way of furthering political goals. Islamist northern women have been most instrumental in this, as they have very negative feelings about "Arab" patriarchal culture. Southern and western non-Muslim women share these feelings, but they are also quite resistant to Islamization. They charge that the Muslims with whom they interact every day are racist, pointing to the history of slavery among their people by these very Islamists, to their casual use of racial epithets, to their prejudice against dark skin, as well as to their own experiences while working in "Arab" households, to support these charges. But they also have their prejudices, and may be heard to refer derogatorily to families with "Arab blood," implying an impurity in their Dinka or Nuba gene pools (Deng 1995). In addition, younger northern Sudanese scholars have begun to ask why they must deny their African heritage in order to be considered Sudanese. Al-Afif Mukhtar concludes: "Northerners believe that they are descendents of an Arab father and an African mother, and they identify with the father and reject the mother. To the average Northerner, the mother symbolizes the Southerner within, and unless Northerners accept their mother and identify with her, they will not accept Southerners as their equals" (forthcoming, 43).

Bibliography

Primary Sources

A. van Achterberg (ed.), *Out of the shadows. The first African indigenous women's conference (FAIWC)*, Amsterdam 1998.

A. al-Afif Mukhtar, The crisis of identity in northern Sudan. A dilemma of a Black people with a White culture,

in C. Fluehr-Lobban and K. Rhodes (eds.), *Race and identity in the Nile valley. Ancient and modern perspectives*, Africa World Press (forthcoming).
S. Apiku, Sudanese rounded up in Cairo, in *Middle East Times*, 20 May 2000, <http://www. metimes.com/2K/issue2000-20/eg/sudanese_rounded_up.htm>.
——, Sons of the Nile slug it out on Abbasiyya's Ahmed Said Street, in *Middle East Times*, 31 July 2000, <http://www.metimes.com/2K/issue2000-31/eg/sons_of_the.htm>.
W. Armbrust, *Mass culture and modernism in Egypt*, Cambridge 1996.
L. Back and J. Solomos (eds.), *Theories of race and racism. A reader*, London 2000.
G. Baer, Slavery in 19th century Egypt, in *Journal of African History*, 3 (1967), 417–41.
E. Balibar, Is there a "neo-racism?" in E. Balibar and I. Wallerstein (eds.) *Race, nation, class. Ambiguous identities*, London 1991, 17–27.
J. Blaut, The theory of cultural racism, in *Antipode. A Radical Journal of Geography* 23 (1992), 289–99.
P. Collins, *Black feminist thought. Knowledge, consciousness and the politics of empowerment*, Boston 1990, 2000 (rev. ed.).
R. O. Collins, The Nilotic slave trade. Past and present, in *Slavery and Abolition* 13:1 (April 1992), 140–61.
F. Deng, *War of visions. Conflict of identities in the Sudan*, Washington, D.C. 1995.
S. Drake, *Black folk here and there. An essay in history and anthropology*, ii, Los Angeles 1987.
A. Fabos, Ambiguous ethnicity. Propriety (*adab*) as a situational boundary marker for the northern Sudanese in Cairo, Ph.D. diss., Boston University 1999.
——, Cosmopolitan racism? Nationalism, refugees, and integration, <http://www.evensfoundation.be/Common lang/Fabos.pdf>.
E. Fernea and R. Fernea, *The Arab world. Personal encounters*, New York 1985, 1991[2].
C. Fluehr-Lobban and K. Rhodes (eds.), *Race and identity in the Nile valley. Ancient and modern perspectives*, Africa World Press (forthcoming).
E. Gruenbaum, Sudanese women and the Islamist state, in S. Joseph and S. Slyomovics (eds.), *Women and power in the Middle East*, Philadelphia 2001, 116–25.
S. Hale, Nationalism, "race," and class. Sudan's gender and culture agenda in the 21st century, in C. Fluehr-Lobban and K. Rhodes (eds.), *Race and identity in the Nile valley. Ancient and modern perspectives*, Africa World Press (forthcoming), chap. 11.
F. Harrison, The persistent power of "race" in the cultural and political economy of racism, in *Annual Review of Anthropology* 24 (1995), 47–54.
——, Introduction. Expanding the discourse on "race," in *American Anthropologist* 100:3 (1998), 609–31.
J. Hunwick and E. T. Powell (eds.), *The African diaspora in the Mediterranean lands of Islam*, Princeton, N.J. 2002.
M. Jok, *War and slavery in Sudan*, Philadelphia 1995, 2001[2].
B. Lewis, *Race and color in Islam*, New York 1971.
S. Marmon (ed.), *Slavery in the Islamic Middle East*, Princeton, N.J. 1999.
S. Morsy, Beyond the honorary "white" classification of Egyptians. Societal identity in historical context, in S. Gregory and R. Sanjek (eds.), *Race*, New Brunswick, N.J. 1994, 175–98.
E. T. Powell, Egyptians in blackface. Nationalism and the representation of the Sudan in Egypt 1919, in *Harvard Middle East and Islamic Review* 2 (1995), 27–45.
——, Brothers along the Nile. Egyptian concepts of race and ethnicity, 1895–1910, in H. Erlich and I. Gershoni (eds.), *The Nile. Histories, cultures, myths*, Boulder, Colo. 2000, 171–81.
——, Burnt-cork nationalism. Race and identity in the theater of ʿAli al-Kassar, in S. Zuhur (ed.), *Colors of enchantment. Theater, dance, music, and the visual arts of the Middle East*, Cairo 2001, 27–38.
R. Segal, *Islam's Black slaves. The other Black diaspora*, New York 2001.
M. Silverman and N. Yuval-Davis, Jews, Arabs and the theorization of racism in Britain and France, in A. Brah, M. Hickman, and M. Mac an Ghaill (eds.), *Thinking identities. Ethnicity, racism and culture*, London 1999, 25–48.
A. Smedley, "Race" and the construction of human identity, in *American Anthropologist* 100:3 (1998), 690–702.
J. Spaulding and S. Beswick (eds.), *White Nile, Black blood. War, leadership, and ethnicity from Khartoum to Kampala*, Lawrenceville, N.J. 2000.
R. Stam, *Tropical multiculturalism. A comparative history of race in Brazilian cinema and culture*, Durham, N.C. 1997.
J. Willis, *Slaves and slavery in Muslim Africa*, 2 vols., London 1985.

SECONDARY SOURCES
M. Anderson and P. Collins (eds.), *Race, class, and gender. An anthology*, Belmont, Calif. 1992.
J. Cole, Commonalities and differences, in J. Cole (ed.), *All-American women. Lines that divide, ties that bind*, New York 1986, 1–30.
K. Dugger, Changing the subject. Race and gender in feminist discourse, in B. P. Bowser (ed.), *Racism and anti-racism in world perspective*, Thousand Oaks 1995, 138–53.
J. Jok, Militarization and gender violence in south Sudan, in *Journal of Asian and African Studies* 34 (1999), 427–42.
J. Lado, Women as refugees. Change through displacement among southern Sudanese women in Cairo, M.A. thesis, American University in Cairo 1996.
K. Saks, Toward a unified theory of class, race, and gender, in *American Ethnologist* 16:3 (1989), 534–50.

ANNE M. JENNINGS AND MAURITA POOLE

The Ottoman Empire

The Ottoman Empire was a territorial aggregation of ethnicities and races which practiced variations of policies emphasizing integration rather than exclusion. Ottoman officials asserted, for instance, that the empire's population shared a supranational identity, the *Osmanlı milleti* (Ottoman nationality). This formulation, adopted by Ahmet Cevdet Pasha (1823–95), the Ottoman Empire's premier historian and advisor to three sultans, highlights the many ways state and subject generally succeeded in navigating the empire's diversity for six hundred years.

The role of women proves central to understanding this process. Women effected through marriage or inheritance the commercial and cultural fusion of the Balkans and Eastern Mediterranean worlds and linked otherwise racially and ethnically incongruent components to an Ottoman society. The very origins of the Ottoman dynasty reflect the function of marriage in bridging racial and ethnic divides. Sultan Osman's Turkic-speaking contemporaries in the late fourteenth century forged relationships with other culturally hybrid peoples throughout the Anatolian and Balkan regions through marriage. These marriages constituted political and economic alliances that ignored religious or ethnic differences, assuring in the process a harmonious transition of newly conquered territories to Ottoman rule.

Over time, the empire affirmed these methods of distributing power by way of a uniquely structured military apparatus. The Janissaries, for example, represented a confluence of the empire's ethnic diversity, integrating marginal communities through the *devşirme* (recruitment of Janissaries) into the mainstream of imperial power. Formerly "Christian boys," Africans and mountain villagers from the Caucasus trained as loyal extensions of the empire, representing a system that linked Istanbul with subject societies in North Africa, the Arab-speaking territories, and the Balkans. While representing distinct, often self-identifying units embedded in occupied regions, Janissaries usually integrated with the local community by marrying women from prominent local families.

The Harem-i Hümayun (Imperial harem) and the harems of prominent officials in the provinces also served this integrative function at the highest level of imperial politics. The harem was a virtual melting pot of the world's racial and ethnic diversity as the politics of reproduction assured integration of much of the empire's peoples. Race and ethnicity did matter in the empire's harems to the extent that chief eunuchs of African origin were highly prized, creating a lucrative market in captured slaves. While slavery was practiced in many corners of the empire, there are many cases in Ottoman history of African men wielding considerable power. The sultan's palace as a whole served as a microcosm of imperial diversity in which Albanians, Arabs, Slavs, Ethiopians, Nubians, Kurds, and Turks all specialized in specific duties. These servants, much like the harem's eunuchs, operated within networks that linked people through common origin. These regionally based networks explain how certain groups in Ottoman society monopolized particular trades, a source of the periodic outbreaks of ethnic or sectarian violence that resulted in the breakdown of the empire's stewardship of its diversity.

Women played the symbolic as well as practical role of preserving the integrity of the communities out of which the diversity in imperial circles came. This is clear in how local traditions (*örf* or *yasa*) evolved during Ottoman history to prescribe specific productive roles for women in societies throughout the Balkans, Middle East, and Anatolia. The Kanun of Luk Dukagjin found in Northern Albania, for example, went to great lengths to outline the Albanian woman's role in the larger context of how the community interacted with the Ottoman state. These traditional systems, found from Bosnia to the Caucasus to Yemen, reflected an undercurrent of tension in which women would serve as markers of the community's self-perceived boundaries, separating the local from a heterogeneous empire that often used marriage to integrate these otherwise isolated communities.

In many documented cases, women were able to utilize the institutions erected by the state to secure greater individual rights, often at the expense of these local misogynistic traditions. Scholarship has shown that women who had access to Ottoman courts in cities, Damascus and Jerusalem for instance, sometimes challenged indigenous legal codes, liberating them from strategic marriages as well as securing their personal fortunes. Ultimately, the Ottoman state's capacity to shape the lives of individual women by way of its institutions helped affirm the integrative principles at work among the empire's elite. Many powerful local women used the state's administrative mechanism to catapult them beyond their immediate, at times repressive, environment and assure them a prominent place in the larger world.

Of course, the empire's heterogeneous character left it vulnerable to periodic conflict among various communities. This is particularly true in the nineteenth century when the significance of racial, ethnic, and religious differences took on new weight in the face of Christian Europe. One consequence of this was the economic changes induced by greater European influence. These changes systematically extricated large numbers of Ottoman woman from their traditional roles in local communities. Cases in Lebanon, for instance, demonstrate how European capitalists and missionaries targeted rural women, tying them to small-scale factory labor schemes that, coupled with increasing violence instigated by members of self-identified ethnic-national communities protected by outside powers, often resulted in the increased importance of using ethnicity or religion to disaggregate Ottoman society. Calls from various Christian communities for greater autonomy or even outright independence from the Ottoman state helped reformulate the self-perceptions of the Ottoman elite, resulting in the transformation of the *Osmanlı milleti* into a more rigid and ultimately self-defeating definition of Ottoman identity that relied on shared religious and, later, linguistic associations to determine an individual's affiliation to community.

BIBLIOGRAPHY

A. Cohen, A tale of two women. Facets of Jewish life in nineteenth-century Jerusalem as seen through the Muslim court records, in A. Levy (ed.), *Jews, Turks, Ottomans. A shared history, fifteenth through the twentieth century*, New York 2003, 119–27.

A. Duben and C. Behar, *Istanbul households. Marriage, family and fertility, 1880–1940*, Cambridge 1991.

J. Hathaway, Marriage alliances among the military households of Ottoman Egypt, in *Annales islamologiques* 29 (1995), 133–49.

A. Khair, "House" to "Goddess of the House." Gender, class and silk in 19th century Mt. Lebanon, in *International Journal of Middle East Studies* 28:3 (1996), 325–48.

M. Mundy, Women's inheritance of land in highland Yemen, in *Arabian Studies* 5 (1979), 161–87.

L. Peirce, *The imperial harem. Women and sovereignty in the Ottoman Empire*, New York 1993.

T. Shuval, The Ottoman Algerian elite and its ideology, in *International Journal of Middle East Studies* 32:3 (2000), 323–44.

J. E. Tucker, *In the house of law. Gender and Islamic law in Ottoman Syria and Palestine*, Berkeley 1998.

M. C. Zilfi (ed.), *Women in the Ottoman Empire. Middle Eastern women in the early modern era*, Leiden 1997.

ISA BLUMI

Turkey

The intersection of race and gender in Turkey can best be understood in the context of Turkey's ethnic diversity, the paradoxical construction of Turkish nationalism, and the state's official denial of non-Turkish identities within its borders. A well-known Turkish saying holds that "there are seventy-two-and-a-half peoples in Turkey." The category "Turkish" thus masks a wide range of ethnic heritages, encompassing many people of Balkan, Anatolian, Caucasian, and Asian origin. In the context of this diversity, the Turkish state has promoted a contradictory formulation of national identity, first articulated during Ottoman times in the writings of Ziya Gökalp (1876–1924). "Turkishness" came to refer at once to a civic identity (all those who are citizens of the Turkish state, regardless of ancestry) and to an exalted ethnic group, the Turkic people of Anatolia (Kadıoğlu 1996). Since the early years of the Turkish Republic (founded in 1923), gendered ideologies of nationalism have both valorized rural women as the workers and mothers of the Turkish nation, and, at the same time, glorified the ideal of the "modern" Turkish woman who would take her place beside men in the Westernized public sphere of the nascent state (Kandiyoti 1987, Göle 1996). Turkish national identity has thus been configured through contested and sometimes contradictory representations of women and the social-spatial enactment of gender roles.

From the Laz of the Black Sea region to the Kurds of the southeast and the Arabs of the southern border regions, the boundaries of Turkey thus encircle many different groups that can claim non-Turkic ethnic identities; Peter Andrews (1989) catalogues 47. While Arabic is spoken as the mother tongue of about 2 percent of the population, the Kurds are Turkey's largest linguistic minority, comprising approximately 15 percent of the population and speaking two different dialects of Kurdish (Kurmanji and Zaza). The everyday circumstances of ethnically marked women in Turkey are linked to larger patterns of material inequality. Among Turkey's linguistic minorities, almost a quarter of women (compared to 1 percent of men) do not speak Turkish. Kurdish and Arabic speaking women in Turkey have notably lower rates of literacy and educational access than do other women, although these differences decline in the urban areas (Gündüz-Hoşgör and Smits 2001). The predominantly Kurdish and Arab provinces of the southeast comprise the poorest region of the country and these ethnic minorities are relatively worse off compared to the country as a whole (Içduygu et al. 1999). However, for women of all backgrounds, educational opportunities and economic conditions are also shaped by social values, patriarchal structures, and levels of family control (Gündüz-Hoşgör and Smits 2001, Cindoğlu and Sirkeci 2001).

Like Turkish national identity, Kurdish identity has also been articulated in part through representations of women and ideologies of gender. The idea that Kurdish society is notably egalitarian has been promulgated by both Western Orientalists and Kurdish nationalists, whose modernist political ideology encouraged the ideal, if not the reality, of gender equality. The claim that Kurdish culture has historically afforded women relative strength and power is often staked on the prominence of individual women leaders in Kurdish history. More recently, scholars have begun to challenge these narratives and to look more closely at the patriarchal structures that pervade rural Turkey (Mirzeler

2000, Mojab 2001. Finally, the diversity of Kurdish culture calls into question any attempt to generalize the situation of "Kurdish women." Not only do women's lives differ across class and rural-urban environments, but Alevism, a Muslim religion practiced by 30 percent of Kurds in Turkey, plays a critical role in shaping attitudes and practices regarding gender relations and women's education among Kurdish communities in Turkey (Wedel 2001).

There are few published accounts of gender relations or women's lives among Turkey's ethnic minorities. Only a small number of survey-based and ethnographic studies have attempted to portray the lives and social relations of Kurdish and Arab women in Turkey. Ethnographic work with Kurdish women migrants in Istanbul has given voice to women's experiences of migration and urban life (Wedel 2001, Secor 2004). For many Kurdish, Arab, and other women in Turkey, the armed struggle between the militant PKK (Kurdish Worker's Party) and the Turkish state reconfigured the conditions of their lives in the 1990s. While Kurds had long been among those migrating to Turkish cities in search of economic and educational opportunities, this decade saw these numbers swell to include thousands of refugees. Many migrant Kurdish women describe encountering discrimination in urban neighborhoods, workplaces, and schools. At the same time, the city opens new channels for women's education, economic independence, and political participation. For example, the 8 March World Women's Day demonstrations in Istanbul have been an important site for Kurdish women's political mobilization. Finally, like other ethnic minorities in Turkey, Kurdish women find themselves struggling with questions of assimilation, solidarity, and identity in a context of ongoing uncertainty as to what it means to be an ethnically marked citizen of the Turkish Republic.

BIBLIOGRAPHY

P. A. Andrews (ed.), *Ethnic groups in the Republic of Turkey*, Wiesbaden 1989.

D. Cindoğlu and I. Sirkeci, Variables that explain variation in prenatal care in Turkey. Social class, education and ethnicity revisited, in *Journal of Biosocial Science* 33 (2001), 261–70.

N. Göle, *The forbidden modern. Civilization and veiling*, Ann Arbor, Mich. 1996.

A. Gündüz-Hoşgör and J. Smits, Linguistic capital. Language as a socio-economic resource among ethnic women in Turkey, paper presented at the meeting of the ISA Research Committee on Social Stratification and Mobility (RC28) in Mannheim, Germany 26–28 April 2001.

A. Içduygu, D. Romano, and I. Sirkeci, The ethnic question in an environment of insecurity. The Kurds in Turkey, in *Ethnic and Racial Studies* 22 (1999), 991–1010.

A. Kadıoğlu, The paradox of Turkish nationalism and the construction of official identity, in *Middle Eastern Studies* 3 (1996), 177–94.

D. Kandiyoti, Emancipated but unliberated? Reflections on the Turkish case, in *Feminist Studies* 3 (1987), 317–38.

M. K. Mirzeler, The formation of male identity and the roots of violence against women. The case of Kurdish songs, stories and storytellers, in *Journal of Muslim Minority Affairs* 20 (2000), 261–9.

S. Mojab (ed.), *Women of a non-state nation*, Costa Mesa 2001.

A. J. Secor, "There is an Istanbul that belongs to me." Citizenship, space, and identity in the city, in *Annals of the Association of American Geographers* 94:2 (2004), 352–68.

H. Wedel, *Siyaset ve cinsiyet. İstanbul gecekondularında kadınların siyasal katılımı*, Istanbul 2001.

ANNA J. SECOR

Western Europe

INTRODUCTION

Muslim women of immigrant origin have had a particular experience in Europe as the interplay between gender and their ethnic and religious backgrounds has presented obstacles from both external society and from within the Muslim family structure itself.

Research about Muslim identity in Europe suggests that younger generations of Muslim women might increasingly be drawing on Islam as a positive means of differentiating themselves from others. Thus, how they express their religion differs from the way in which Islam has been practiced by their parents in the transplanted context.

MUSLIM WOMEN AS IMMIGRANTS

Many women who accompanied their immigrant husbands to Europe had little choice in the matter. In some ways, these women were the most visible immigrants in their new societies, seen around communities as they performed their daily tasks of shopping and taking their children to school. It was through them that many Europeans had their first contact with Muslims.

This high degree of visibility and the obvious differences in appearance sometimes gave rise to racial prejudice and discrimination, be it due to their religion, clothing, or their color, combined with the fact that they were women.

Some of the prejudice and discrimination was, in part, linked to the way in which Muslim women have been seen by non-Muslims. What is often seen as a religious difference and attributed to Islam is actually a product of cultural or national differences. Indeed, for the immigrant women themselves, cultural and religious elements of customs often overlap. They know religion as part of their everyday lives in their countries of origin, where most people around them were also from the same culture and religion. Thus, the boundaries between that which is religious and that which is cultural have often been blurred.

It was noted in a recent British study that the daughters of original immigrants are expected to behave modestly and are subject to stricter parental control than are their brothers. This is culturally common across the Indian subcontinent, particularly with Muslim and Sikh girls (Henninck, Diamond, and Cooper 1999). Moreover, girls of all religious affiliations from the Indian subcontinent are more influenced by their cultural traditions and their religions than are their European peers.

For many young Muslim women, the discrepancies between the customs of European society and the expectations of their parents and communities are significant. The internal family expectation, on the one hand, and general trends in youth behavior in the broader social environment, on the other, can create an imbalance, more so for young Muslim females than for Muslim males. A young woman's sense of "self" in external society and within her internal domestic realm can be very different (Keaton 1999, 50) and this requires that she constantly negotiate between them in order for her to achieve a balanced psychological state (Hashmi 2003b).

In this way, Muslim women of all ages face a dual discrimination as a racial minority in the majority society and as women within their internal family and community structures. As noted in reference to Britain, "Sexism is intertwined with racism; one reinforces the other, as far as Asian girls are concerned" (Brooks and Singh 1978 cited in Brah and Shaw 1992, 2).

Multiple discrimination

Muslim women living in Europe experience a two-fold discrimination (Hashmi 2000b). Being Muslim in a non-Muslim society has led to some difficulties, raising issues such as wearing the headscarf in school (for example, in France) or at work, fitting prayer times into a work timetable, obtaining halal meat or, since 11 September 2001, being subject to the broad political discourse of terrorism that is now associated with Islam.

While in religious terms women are supposedly equal to men (apart from when acting as witnesses or in the Islamic law of inheritance), in reality their positions are often far less fair. Within many Muslim families, a woman's primary cultural role is that of mother and a wife. However, this is frequently oversimplified by observers from Western viewpoints, and results in Muslim women being seen as subordinate to Muslim men because their careers and educations are not prioritized and their opinions and sexual freedoms are suppressed. While many Muslim women do face this two-tier discrimination, there is recent evidence of change.

In research conducted in the late 1990s, young Muslim women born and educated in France and Britain felt that negative perceptions of Muslim women were inaccurate and that they did not in fact feel disadvantaged because of their gender in religious contexts (Hashmi 2003b). The fact that these young women were participating in higher education was clearly a factor contributing to these opinions. Being in an external liberal environment gave them the freedom to express themselves personally and academically and opportunities to mix more freely with a wider range of people – including males of similar Muslim backgrounds who might become prospective marriage partners. It also indicates how education for females of this generation is no longer stigmatized; only a narrow segment of extremely traditional Muslims view university education as jeopardizing their daughters' marital opportunities. Indeed, many Muslim parents in Europe realize that having an education is an important safety net for young women, should a marriage fail (Ahmed 2001). However, the very fact that education can be viewed as merely a safety net indicates the view of many that marriage is still the most important goal for their daughters.

New generations and the expression of "difference"

For young Muslims, Islam is learned from their immigrant parents. Yet, in the transplanted context of European Christian or secular society, it can take on a more direct and personal meaning than the customs of their parents' country of origin. In its purest form, Islam has more defined boundaries than ethnicity or culture (Jacobson 1999, Hashmi 2000a) and thus can become a locus of identity that acknowledges and incorporates their perceived "differences" (Hashmi 2003b).

In the 1950s and 1960s, Muslims often wanted to remain inconspicuous in order to fit into European society. Nowadays, Muslim children are much more visible in their local communities, in places such as restaurants, shops, and the workplace.

This is epitomized in the wearing of the headscarf (*ḥijāb*) by Muslim women in Europe (Gaspard and Khosrokavar 1995). Although European women historically have covered their heads as well, nowadays, for many non-Muslims, the headscarf symbolizes the oppressive patriarchy that they believe Islam to be. When women are forced to wear *ḥijāb*, this argument stands. However, research indicates that many young Muslims choose to wear the *ḥijāb*, even though their mothers do not and their fathers do not insist upon it (Hashmi 2003b, 195).

The wearing of the *ḥijāb* infuriates some Muslim women who feel that to wear it simply acknowledges Muslim female inequality and negates what the Western world has granted them: treatment as equals outside their communities and families, allowing them to question the patriarchal values underlying certain traditions, and re-educating and empowering them without criticism or alienation from their religious communities.

The wearing of the headscarf is just one indication of the reinvention of Islam in Europe that must be distinguished from the Islam of their immigrant parents. Young Muslims are more confident in expressing their religious identities and of being accepted as women, Muslims, and ethnic minorities. This trend has been aided by recent developments in European Union anti-discrimination legislation that now protects women, racial minorities, and the practice of religion (Bell 2002).

Recently, the issue of forced marriage has typified the negative aspects of what young Muslim women must endure from their families. The idea of an unmarried girl or woman bringing shame on her family as a result of liaisons she might have with males (whether sexual or not, Muslim or non-Muslim) is also viewed as archaic and indicative of a cultural interpretation of Islam that is both sexist and hypocritical. British cases of fathers killing their daughters (known as "honor killings") because of this shame have exacerbated the view that Islamic domestic life continues to be a domain of female servitude, even though this practice is mainly cultural. Forced marriages are a similar concern, where daughters (although also sons) are sent overseas to marry against their will. This problem is largely confined to families where the parents are less educated immigrants from rural areas of the Indian subcontinent who live within insular communities in Britain, where the predominant interpretation of Islam is based on a cultural patriarchal misinterpretation.

Research has shown that it is these daughters who are questioning their place as Muslim women (Hashmi 2003b). It is perhaps on this basis, and with optimism, that future generations of female European Muslims may be less subject to these internal levels of cultural discrimination. Moreover, as young women become more open in discussing their religion with non-Muslims, they may help form new perceptions and realities for and about Muslim women externally in contemporary European societies.

Bibliography

F. Ahmed, Modern traditions? British Muslim women and academic achievement, in *Gender and Education* 13:2 (2001), 137–52.

K. Armstrong, *The battle for God. Fundamentalism in Judaism, Christianity and Islam*, London 2000.

M. Bell, *Anti-discrimination law in the European Union*, Oxford 2002.

A. Brah and S. Shaw, *Working choices. South Asian young Muslim women and the labour market*, London 1992.

D. Brooks and K. Singh, *Aspirations versus opportunities for Asian and white school leavers in the Midlands*, London 1978.

F. Gaspard and F. Khosrokavar, *Le foulard et la République*, Paris 1995.

N. Hashmi, Immigrant children in Europe. Constructing a transnational identity, in A. Höfert and A. Salvatore (eds.), *Between Europe and Islam. Shaping modernity in a transcultural space*, Brussels 2000a, 163–74.

——, *Gender and discrimination. Muslim women living in Europe*, London 2000b, <www.epic.ac.uk>.

——, *A Muslim school in Bristol? An overview of the current debate and Muslim school children's views*, Bristol 2003a.

——, *From ethnicity to religion. The shifting identities of young Muslims in Britain and France*, Florence 2003b.

M. Hennick, I. Diamond, and P. Cooper, Young Asian women and relationships. Traditional or transitional?, in *Ethnic and Racial Studies* 22:5 (1999), 867–92.

J. Jacobson, *Islam in transition. Religion and identity among British Pakistani youth*, London 1999.

T. D. Keaton, Muslim girls and the other France. An examination of identity construction, in *Social Identities* 5:5 (1999), 47–64.

M. Pickthall (trans.), *The meaning of the glorious Koran*, New York 1991.

Nadia Hashmi

Rape

Overview

In Islamic law, rape is placed under the category of *ḥadd* (pl. *ḥudūd*) crimes, which are offenses with specific punishments ordained by God. *Ḥadd* crimes include offenses such as apostasy, drinking, theft, *zinā* (sexual indiscretion), and false accusation of *zinā* (*qadhf*), and are crimes warranting some of the harshest punishments in Islamic law including the death penalty. Rape is defined as a *zinā* crime in juridical writings. Unlike Western legal traditions, Islamic law does not consider rape a separate legal category, but places it together with other sex acts outside of the marriage contract, such as fornication, adultery, incest, homosexuality, prostitution, procurement of prostitution, and bestiality. The inclusion of rape in the catch-all classification of *zinā* has led some authors to question whether the concept of rape exists at all in Islamic law. Historical sources clearly do recognize rape as a social reality, and it is usually described in Islamic sources as forced *zinā* and, as such, a crime subject to prosecution.

Rape in history

Although rape is not discussed in the Qur'ān, it is mentioned in *ḥadīth* sources. One *ḥadīth* transmitted by Ṣafiyya bt. ʿUbayd describes how rape cases were treated: "A state-owned slave had sexual intercourse with a girl from among the war booty (*khumus*). He had coerced her until he raped her. Therefore, ʿUmar flogged him according to the *ḥadd* and banished him, but he did not flog the girl because she was forced" (al-Bukhari 1985, ix, 67). This is one of the earliest documented cases of rape in Islamic history and demonstrates the difference between willing and coerced *zinā*. It draws an important distinction between rapist and victim. *Ḥadīth*s were used to set legal precedents in the early Islamic community, and in this case the *ḥadīth* advocated flogging and banishment as punishment for rape. As Islamic law developed, rape was considered bodily harm and was subject to the payment of blood money (*diya*). As a result, juridical writings often suggested monetary payment for reparations in rape cases.

Rape is discussed in several Islamic sources such as *fiqh* (Islamic jurisprudence), fatwas (legal opinions), and Sharīʿa court records. In these sources rape is described as "forced *zinā*." Coercion to commit *zinā*ʾ, whether forced prostitution or rape, is viewed as the worst form of *zinā* in Islamic law. Abū Ḥanīfa argued that if anyone forced another to commit *zinā* he was subject to punishment. This is why several sources discuss the punishment of procurers and not the punishment of prostitutes, since prostitutes were viewed as being subject to coercion.

Islamic law passed through another significant phase of development in the early Ottoman period. As a consequence there are several sixteenth-century sources for Ottoman law that include the *kanūn-nāme*s (Ottoman imperial codes) and thousands of fatwas issued by Ebu's-suʿud (Abū al-Saʿūd Muḥammad b. Muḥammad, 1492/3–1574/5), Ottoman jurist and Shaykh al-Islām, who was the supreme religious counselor under Sultan Süleymān (r. 1520–66). One fatwa written by Ebu's-suʿud demands that a man who raped a boy was to be executed if force were proven by bodily damage, namely a ruptured anus. According to the *kanūn-nāmes* if a man abducted a boy, he was to be punished by castration or payment of 24 gold pieces. The *kanūn-nāme*s contain several codes on the abduction of girls, boys, and women. Abduction was a crime viewed as rape since it was often performed for that purpose. Throughout the sixteenth century raids by tribesmen and disgruntled irregular troops in Anatolia often included the abduction of girls and boys. The *kanūn-nāme*s reflect an attempt to curb this activity by prescribing severe punishments for abduction. The punishment of castration was also applied in cases of the abduction of women from private homes.

The *kanūn-nāme*s advocate severe flogging and a fine of one *akçe* per stroke in cases of molestation or "kissing" of women, both terms connoting rape. The *kanūn-nāme*s discuss rape euphemistically, for example: "If a person enters a woman's house or approaches her on her way and cuts off her hair or takes away her garment or kerchief, [thus] offering [her] a gross indignity, the cadi shall, after [the offense] has been proved, chastise [him]; he shall have [him] imprisoned" (Heyd 1973, 100).

Ebu's-suʿud advocates a woman's right to self-defense during rape stating that she has the right to defend herself to the point of killing her attacker with an ax without suffering punishment. Ebu's-suʿud states that a woman who defends herself in this way has committed an act of jihad. Jihad in this case is a matter of self-defense and illuminates the meaning of jihad as more than a defense of Islam against attack.

Evidence requirements for rape in Islamic law fall into two categories, eyewitness accounts and oath taking. If eyewitness evidence is available, four male eyewitnesses must appear and must have seen the act of penetration itself "as a rope in a collyrium jar" or "like a well-rope in a well." The evidence requirements are extremely rigid in these cases making it difficult if not impossible to prove cases of *zinā* particularly, since rape often took place in private and secluded spaces. Even in cases where potential witnesses were in close proximity, rape was difficult to prove. In a case found in Sharīʿa court records from Aleppo one rapist stuffed a handkerchief into the mouth of his victim to keep her from screaming according to the victim's testimony. This prevented a call for aid or the arrival of witnesses at the scene of the crime. Oath taking, however, was an option for powerful testimony in the court and on occasion rape victims would use the oath for recourse. Oaths were taken very seriously in premodern Islamic courts: a witness swore by God in front of a judge that an event had or had not occurred. In the early modern period professional midwives would appear in court as expert witnesses to attest to the condition of the rape victim offering testimony of forced entry.

Often the sources advocate punishment without specifying its form. The Ottoman imperial codes advocate imprisonment for rapists, but if the crime is combined with other crimes, such as breaking and entering and abduction, the severity of the punishment increases to castration. In the court records compensation was the standard punishment for rape offenses in an amount to be paid to the victim. Compensation was a variation on customary payments (*diya*) for bodily damage found in Islamic law.

Missing in the *kanūn-nāmes* is a specific category or language for rape. Euphemisms are used to describe cases of rape (as well as other cases of *zinā*) in the *kanūn-nāmes* and court records. The *kanun-names* use terms such as "abduction by force" (*çikup cebr ile*) and "forceable marriage" (*nikâh itdiduruna cebr ile*) to describe issues of gender violence. Ottoman sources also use the familiar term "forced *zinā*" (*zina cebr ile*) to describe rape. This euphemistic approach to a delicate subject can cloud the real issue at law: that in cases of abduction, forced marriage, and forced *zinā*, the victim is unwilling and therefore a victim of rape. In the Ottoman and Arabic legal codes the term "force" (*cebr, jabr*) conveys the meaning of a non-consensual act and cannot be ignored. It is not until the nineteenth century that a new word appears in the Arabic vocabulary to describe rape cases. *Ighṭisāb*, a term that literally means illegal appropriation, becomes the standard term to describe this crime. The evolution and development of the word evokes the patriarchal values of the ancient Mesopotamian world in which rape was viewed as a crime against property. In the ancient code of Hammurabi, rape was seen as a usurpation of a husband or father's property depending on the marriage status of the victim. In turn, a rapist was to be punished in accordance with theft laws in ancient Mesopotamia and not for sexual assault. Jewish law, on the other hand, recognized rape as a criminal offense of the same type as physical assault and murder. Under the category of *zinā* criminal offences, Islamic law treats rape as both a sexual offense and an attack on property. Another concept that becomes attached to the meaning of rape in the modern period is that of honor. The application of the term *hatk al-ʿirḍ*, literally meaning to "violate the honor" of a person, can also be patriarchal. The question hangs – whose honor has been violated, the woman's or her patriarch's – be it her father, husband or brother. As Islamic law developed specific legal categories for rape, premodern patriarchal values were conveyed through the concept of *ighṭisāb* and *hatk al-ʿirḍ*.

Rape in the Islamic world today

Rape has increasingly become an issue of debate as modern codes of law have offered legal loopholes for rapists to evade punishment. One major change is the way in which rapists are punished. In the early modern period, the laws advocated punishments such as castration and imprisonment, yet most often the offender was given a fine and paid "compensation" to the victim. In the modern period laws have made it more difficult for women to prosecute their attackers and even encourage rape victims to marry their attackers. This practice, common in Egypt, was fostered to discourage abductions of young women.

Today, a common legal device used by rape offenders is the moral profiling of women who are "asking for it." Cases in Pakistan show that working women, in particular women who work at night, are often profiled as "loose" women and targets of rape. Often the *modus operandi* of rapists is a gang attack, in which several rapists unite against a single woman. One explanation proposed as to why gang rape is prevalent today is the economic conditions of most Muslim countries. Problems of unemployment have made it difficult for men to produce dowries and strict moral standards make it impossible to be with a woman outside of marriage. Therefore, rape is viewed as the only way for a man to "know a woman" outside of marriage. Gang rape has become a common trend for another reason; it is used since the legal system has allowed rapists to become witnesses in court to testify against the rape victim. Often the testimony of rapists includes the accusation that the woman was a prostitute. This spin on Islamic law is an interpretation of the Sharīʿa that holds that there must be four male eyewitnesses to *zinā* as proof of the crime. The jurists never intended the crime of *zinā* to apply only to women and be used in this way, but under modern interpretations, punishment is reserved for women alone, many of whom sit in Pakistani jails today.

In the 1990s, working and "Westernized" women were profiled as "prostitutes" in Algeria by Islamic militants belonging to a number of militias including the GIA (Armed Islamic Group). Rape and throat slashing were often the methods used to punish these women. Women profiled as "prostitutes" were often those who wore blue jeans, smoked cigarettes, and were employed outside the home. Not only were Westernized or professional women targeted but also women who dared to go out in public unchaperoned. One of the most disturbing cases of rape in recent years is the 1992 gang rape of a young Egyptian woman in a crowded bus station in Cairo. Despite the great number of witnesses the case was dismissed for lack of evidence. The Egyptian media commented that the girl deserved to be raped since she should not have been allowed to leave home unattended. As a reaction to this case, a law was proposed by the Egyptian National Assembly that blamed the families of rape victims for allowing their daughters out of the home. The law did not pass. The clearer identification of what constitutes rape should have resulted in a fairer treatment of women under Islamic legal systems. Two issues, however, have hindered the prosecution of rape in several Muslim countries in the recent past. First, the notion that women are the torch bearers of public morality and as such are in a great way responsible for breaches of morality such as rape – the victim becomes the perpetrator; second, conditional on the first, a gendered interpretation of *zinā* law in which only women are subject to punishment. This brand of moral fundamentalism prevalent in the Islamic world today contorts the law in support of a particularly perverse aspect of patriarchy.

Bibliography

Primary Sources

Muḥammad b. Ismāʿīl al-Bukhārī, *Ṣaḥīḥ al-Bukhārī*, Islamic University, Beirut 1985.

M. E. Düzdağ (ed.), *Şeyhülislâm Ebussuud Efendi fetvaları ışığında 16 asır Türk hayatı*, Istanbul 1972.

U. Heyd, *Studies in old Ottoman criminal law*, ed. V. L. Menage, New York 1973.

ʿAlī b. Abī Bakr al-Marghinānī, *The Hedaya, or guide. A commentary on the Mussulman laws*, trans. C. Hamilton, 4 vols., London 1791, 1870[2].

Secondary Sources

C. Imber, Zina in Ottoman law, in Ö. L. Barkan et al., *Contributions à l'histoire économique et sociale de l'Empire ottoman*, Leuven 1983, 59–91.

E. Semerdjian, Gender, violence and intent in Ottoman law. A view of the imperial kanunnames and fatwas of the sixteenth century, in A. E. Sonbol and J. O. Voll (eds.), *A history of her own. Deconstructing women in Islamic societies*, Syracuse University Press (forthcoming).

A. E. Sonbol, Law and gender violence in Ottoman and modern Egypt, in A. E. Sonbol (ed.), *Women, the family, and divorce laws in Islamic history*, Syracuse, N.Y. 1996, 277–89.

——, Rape and law in Ottoman and modern Egypt, in M. C. Zilfi (ed.), *Women in the Ottoman Empire. Middle Eastern women in the early modern era*, Leiden 1997, 214–32.

Elyse Semerdjian

The Ottoman Empire

As elsewhere in the premodern world, rape was a common occurrence in the lands governed by the Ottoman sultans. Because of the tenacious habit of abduction, it was probably more common in rural than in urban areas. Rape was clearly viewed as a criminal offence by both the Islamic law (Sharīʿa) enforced by the sultans and their own statutes (*kanun*) (al-Marghinani 1791, al-Halabi 1891, Düzdag 1983, Heyd 1973). As a legal problem, rape was treated under the broad rubric of *zinā*, illicit sexual relations; the usual term for rape in Ottoman Turkish was *cebran zinā*, *zinā* by force. As a social phenomenon, rape was intertwined with a number of concerns, including personal honor, lineage, property, and the sometimes difficult process of making marriages. A noteworthy feature of rape in the premodern Ottoman context is the willingness of victims to speak out in demanding the punishment of rapists.

Who were the victims of rape and its perpetrators? State documents tended to view those at risk to be married women and boys, and the threat of rape to stem from young male adults, unmarried and unsocialized (Heyd 1973). But young girls too were raped and/or abducted, and rapists included men of varied ages and social standing. There was often a social gap between rapist and victim, the latter's lesser status sometimes exacerbating the difficulty of making an accusation stick. With boys and young men, rape was not necessarily homosexual in the modern understanding of the term, since it was sometimes an aspect of establishing heterosexual male hierarchies. In normative legal discourses, the typical rape scenario envisioned breaking into a house, but actual accusations against rapists suggest that they found their victims equally on the streets and in open spaces on the perimeters of villages, towns, and cities. As for the domestic rape of household servants and slaves, it is difficult to estimate the extent of this hidden phenomenon.

If we define rape to include instances more complex than the isolated act of an individual, then rape scenarios proliferate. Prostitution operations where pimps (female as well as male) coerced individuals into sexual commerce were sometimes taxed (and thus quasi-sanctioned) by the state (Imber 1983). More common, forced sex was institutionalized through the practice of slavery: a female slave owned by a male was by legal definition sexually licit to him. Although the law prescribed harsh penalities for habitual sodomists and pederasts, it did not formally regulate a man's sexual use of a male slave (paternity not being an issue). Finally, the frequent wars fought by the Ottomans furnished opportunities for rape and the enslavement of captives. Evliya Çelebi, Ottoman courtier and traveler, noted the outbreak of pregnancies among the women of Ferdenvar after Ottoman forces attacked in 1661 (Dankoff 2004). The Ḥanafī school of Islamic law, adopted by the Ottoman sultans (but not necessarily by their Muslim subjects), tacitly sanctioned wartime rape by permitting the suspension of Sharīʿa for Muslims outside "the domain of Islam" (in contrast, the Mālikī and Shāfiʿī schools required Muslims to follow Sharīʿa – and thus avoid *zinā* – wherever they found themselves) (Sonbol 1997).

Despite the recognition of rape as a serious criminal offense, punishment of rapists was difficult to accomplish. Even though the Sharīʿa requirement of four witnesses to the act of penetration was routinely recognized as unrealistic (as it was in the legal handbook of the Ḥanafī jurist, al-Marghīnānī, popular among the early-modern Ottomans) (al-Marghīnānī 1791), this strict standard influenced prosecution of rape. When there *were* witnesses, they typically chose to remain silent because a defect in the testimony of one brought punishment on all four (Peirce 2003). When the accuser could not provide proof, the alleged rapist could be acquitted by providing character witnesses, unless he had a previous reputation for loose behavior. This was a common phenomenon throughout the empire. In 1621, witnesses for a Cairene man accused of rape testified that the accuser herself was immoral, with the result that she was banished from her city quarter (Sonbol 1997). In 1681, five men on the Aegean island of Samos testified to the innocence of another when a woman accused him of raping her in her house (all were Christians) (Laiou forthcoming). Moreover, if an accusation could not be substantiated, the accuser was likely to be punished for slander (*qadhf*). Finally, under the legal doctrine of *shubha* (resemblance), rapists were sometimes pardoned by claiming belief that their act was permissible, if it resembled licit sexual behavior, for example, assuming (erroneously) that they had a valid marriage contract with the raped woman or that sex with the female slave of another household member was lawful (Tucker 1998). In such instances, legal practice was soft on rapists, but it should be noted that this attitude was in keeping with a long tradition in Muslim-ruled states of avoiding routine use of corporal or capital punishment (the Sharīʿa punishment for a married freeborn Muslim adulterer or rapist was death by stoning).

However, the frequency of rape accusations dealt with by the empire's judges and muftis demonstrates that such legal obstacles could be overcome. Circumstantial evidence of various kinds was accepted in lieu of the testimony of four witnesses, for example, physical examination by midwives, bystanders testifying to the victim's distress even if they did not witness the rape itself, or the believability and/or social prominence of the accuser. If punishment was hard to bring about, compromise solutions were not, although they varied according to local legal customs. Marriage of a virgin to her rapist (with her consent) was one; it is hard to know how often rape was a ploy to precipitate a marriage otherwise difficult to contract (desired at least by the rapist). Compensation of the victim (*diya*) was another compromise solution; for example, a man pleading a mistaken belief that he had a valid marriage contract with a virgin had to pay her the "fair dower" amount in compensation. Here, rape was seen as a violation or theft of a person's rights over his or her body (Sonbol 1997, Tucker 1998). Finally, the numbers of patently unprovable rape accusations made around the empire make it hard to avoid the conclusion that even if a person had to pay the slander penalty, publicly accusing a rapist was an avenue to recovering some honor from a morally fraught situation (Peirce 2003).

Why were rape victims willing to speak out? A variety of reasons suggest themselves. First, because *zinā* was considered a crime against God (thus against the community at large), it fell to the ruling authority to prosecute and punish sexual crime, so accusations against rapists were not always voluntary. Moreover, the Ottoman preference for imposing fines rather than physical punishment meant that state officials who received such fines as part of their stipends had an incentive to bring rape out into the open. Second, the acute sense of personal honor prevalent among Ottoman subjects compelled individuals to speak out about a whole array of assaults on the person (verbal harrassment, yanking beards and hair, touching, and so forth); this encouragement to publicize dishonor to one's body lowered the threshold of courage required to speak out about rape. Third, victimization by rape was not gender specific, so that males and females were both expected to speak out. Lastly, there was a widespread culture of slander and accusationism, with women not infrequently making baseless accusations of harrassment and rape (and being punished for doing so). In short, talk of rape was neither hushed nor necessarily damaging in the premodern Ottoman world.

The question of rape as a social problem in the premodern Ottoman period can be studied through a variety of legal sources, including works of Islamic jurisprudence, fatwas, sultanic *kanun*, and the large numbers of court records that survive from the late fifteenth century onward. Chronicles and other narrative sources occasionally provide insights, as in the example of Evliya Çelebi. However, only a small fraction of these materials has been studied as yet, so it is difficult at present to know if and how attitudes toward rape and its legal treatment may have changed over time.

Bibliography

R. Dankoff, *The world of Evliya Çelebi*, Leiden 2004.

M. E. Düzdağ (ed.), *Şeyhülislam Ebussuud Efendi fetvaları ışığında 16. asır Türk hayatı*, Istanbul 1983.

Ibrāhīm ibn Muḥammad al-Ḥalabī, *Multaqā al-abḥur*, Istanbul, 1309/1891 or 1892.

U. Heyd, *Studies in old Ottoman criminal law*, ed. V. Menage, Oxford 1973.

C. Imber, *Zina* in Ottoman Law, in J.-L. Bacqué-Gramont and P. Dumont (eds.), *Contributions à l'histoire économique et sociale de l'Empire ottoman*, Leuven, Belgium 1983, 59–92.

S. Laiou, Christian women in an Ottoman world. Interpersonal and family relations brought before the Ottoman judicial courts, 17th–18th centuries, in M. Buturović and I. Schick (eds.), *Women in the Ottoman Balkans* (forthcoming).

ʿAlī ibn Abī Bakr al-Marghīnānī, *The Hedaya, or guide. A commentary on the Mussulman laws*, trans. C. Hamilton, 2 vols., London 1791.

L. Peirce, *Morality tales. Law and gender in the Ottoman court of Aintab*, Berkeley 2003.

A. E. Sonbol, Rape and law in Ottoman and modern Egypt, in M. C. Zilfi (ed.), *Women in the Ottoman Empire. Middle Eastern women in the early modern era*, Leiden 1997, 214–31.

J. E. Tucker, *In the house of the law. Gender and Islamic law in Ottoman Syria and Palestine*, Berkeley 1998.

Leslie Peirce

South Asia

In South Asian societies, rape has been used against women from minority communities and from economically deprived social groups to intimidate women in particular and the targeted community/groups in general. This entry examines the specific connections between rape and minoritism in India, Pakistan, and Bangladesh and state and community responses to rape in these countries.

Rape and minoritism

The connection between rape and male power has been noted by South Asian feminists (Gandhi and Shah 1989) who have also pointed to the conjunction of factors that increase the vulnerability of some women such as minority women and working-class women. Communalization and the social and economic marginalization of Muslims in post-independence India has resulted in sexual assaults perpetuated on Muslim women, as was apparent in the anti-Muslim pogrom in Gujarat in 2002 (Hameed et al. 2002). Similarly, Christian women in Pakistan have suffered sexual assault following the invasion of Iraq by American forces in 2003 (Duin 2003, Shakir 2003) and Hindu women have been raped in Bangladesh during communal riots following the demolition of the Babri Masjid in Ayodhya, India by Hindu fundamentalists in 1992 (Nasrin 1994). In all these cases of sexual violence, women are seen as repositories of community honor. Thus rape is experienced as something more than violence against individual women; members of the communities of both the perpetuators and the victims experience the rape of minority women as symbolic dishonor of the community. However, in the case of the Gujarat riots, it has been persuasively argued that the nature of violence against minority women – stripping, beating, throwing acid, raping, burning, killing of pregnant women, and killing of children before their parents' eyes –

went beyond collective dishonoring. It was meant to destroy or punish the fertile Muslim female body and to destroy future generations (Sarkar 2002).

Social activists and commentators have noted the culpability of the nation-state in cases of sexual assault during communal riots. A report by women's organizations after the 2002 Gujarat riots states: "There is evidence of State and Police complicity in perpetuating crimes against women. No effort was made to protect women. No Mahila (women) Police was deployed. State and Police complicity in these crimes is continuing, as women survivors continue to be denied the right to file FIRs (First Information Reports). There is no existing institutional mechanism in Gujarat through which women can seek justice" (Hameed et al. 2002, 1).

Social commentators and activists in Bangladesh and Pakistan have similarly noted state silence and complicity in cases of violence against minority women during and following communal riots, including failure to intervene in time or at all, failure to register cases of assault, and a complete denial of the problem by state representatives (Nasrin 1994, Duin 2003, Shakir 2003). This leads to a silencing of the experiences of minority women. Social activists in all these countries have also found that their families and their communities further silence women because the articulation of the experience of rape is seen as further dishonoring the community. In situations where minority women experience sexual or physical violence in non-riot situations, their experience of communalism and communal violence can contribute to their silencing. For instance, following the communal riots in 1992–3 in Mumbai, India, an activist pointed out: "The reality of being Muslim in this city cannot be wished away . . . After the riots, women feel that their problems multiply after going to the police" (Hasina Sheikh, cited in Gangoli 2000, 212).

Rape, honor, and social status

The perception of women as repositories of family and community prestige is not confined to situations of communal tension and riots. In 2002, members of the tribal council of the Mastoi tribe in Meerwala, Pakistan passed a decree ordering the gang rape of a women as punishment for a crime allegedly committed by her brother. Three members of the Mastoi tribe aged between 11 and 14 raped her younger brother and when he protested he was accused of raping an adult woman. The police did not help the family and the tribal council ordered that the sister be raped by four men as revenge (Sarwar 2002). In cases such as these, the complacency of the rapists derives not only from the culpability of the state, but also from the inequities within the social system. The family of the raped woman in Meerwala were poor and socially marginalized and hence not in a position to influence opinion or to persuade the police to assist them. There are recorded instances of similar cases where poor and socially marginalized women have failed to get justice from the legal system in Bangladesh and India; and traditional forms of justice, including village mediation systems, work against the interests of women (Gangoli 2000).

Legal systems

There is some degree of variation within the law on sexual assault and rape in South Asia. However, to some extent, the legal concern with defining rape as an offence in South Asia is with regulating the sexuality of the woman, rather than with protecting her bodily integrity. To varying degrees, rape laws in South Asia are based on, and legitimize, patriarchal presumptions and attitudes regarding male and female sexuality. While purporting to provide justice to raped women, the laws in actuality reinforce patterns of heterosexual dominance in which women are seen as inferior, sexually passive, and, within marriage, the sexual property of their husbands.

Bangladesh has laws protecting women's right to life and safety. These include articles in the Penal Code relating to rape. The Women and Children Repression (Special Provisions) Act 2000 provides stringent punishment for offenders. Marital rape is criminalized in Bangladesh. However, the implementation of laws is very poor and convictions for rape are rarely made, because women are unaware of their rights and the legal system is misogynist (Marcus 1993).

Pakistan is governed by the Hudood Ordinance, which was passed in 1977 under President Zia ul-Haq, ostensibly to bring the laws of the country into conformity with "the injunctions of Islam" (Quraishi 1997). Under this law, rape is termed *zinā bi-al-jabr* and is based on the principle of non-consensual penile penetration into the vagina; it carries a penalty for the perpetrator of 25 years imprisonment. However, this offers little support to women as under this law, the proof required for *zinā bi-al-jabr* is either a confession by the accused or witness statements by four Muslim adult men. If a *zinā bi-al-jabr* case fails for lack of witnesses or a confession, the legal system concludes that the intercourse was consensual and the rape victim is charged with *zinā* (adultery), which is a criminal offence. Following the Hudood Ordinance, there has been a rise in the incidence of rape as men are more confident of escaping detection, while fear of imprisonment for *zinā* dissuades women from making accusations of rape (Marcus 1993). Within the rape law in Pakistan, marital rape is not criminalized, giving husbands hegemonic rights over the bodies of their wives.

In India, rape is legally defined as penile penetration into the vagina. Amendments to the rape law made in the 1980s introduced a new category of rape, namely, rape by members of the police within their official jurisdiction, by public servants, by superintendents or managers of jails, remand homes, hospitals, of women under their custody, including gang rape. Within this category of rape the onus of proof was shifted from the defendant to the accused, which reversed the generally applicable legal principle of innocence until proven guilty. As in Pakistan, the rape law does not recognize marital rape as a legal category under Section 375 of the Indian Penal Code.

Civil society responses

While the reality of rape and sexual assault for women in South Asia can seem daunting the responses of civil society are extremely heartening. In Bangladesh, many women's organizations exist that work toward responding to specific cases, legal awareness, and consciousness raising. These include autonomous groups such as Ain o Salish Kendra and Nari Pokkho, party-linked organizations such as Bangladesh Mahila Parishad, and state agencies such as the government of Bangladesh's Women's Affairs Directorate.

In Pakistan, women's organizations in Pakistan include the Women's Action Forum, which was formed in response to a judgment on *zinā*. Women Against Rape works specifically with rape victims. Simorgh Collective documents media coverage of rape (Marcus 1993).

In India, the first major campaign of the fledgling women's movement was in the early 1980s around the gang rape of a tribal girl, Mathura, by a group of policemen in a police station and the role and complicity of the judiciary in condoning it. The anti-rape campaign took off in different cities around the country almost simultaneously. Some of the autonomous groups that emerged at this point were the Forum Against Rape (later Forum Against Oppression of Women), Saheli, Stree Sangharsh, Asmita, and Vimochana (Vibhuti et al. 1983). Responses to sexual violence against minority women have been an integral part of the agenda of these organizations, articulated in reports on the Gujarat riots by women's organizations (Hameed et al. 2002).

Bibliography

J. Duin, Christians beseiged in Pakistan, in *Washington Times*, 28 June 2003, <http:// www.washingtontimes.com/world/20030627-092413-5203r.htm>.

N. Gandhi and N. Shah, *The issues at stake. Theory and practice in the contemporary women's movement in India*, New Delhi 1989.

G. Gangoli, Law, patriarchy and the feminist movements in Bombay, 1975–1993, Ph.D. diss., University of Delhi, 2000.

S. Hameed et al., *How has the Gujarat massacre affected minority women? The survivors speak*, Ahmedabad 2003.

R. Marcus, Violence against women in Bangladesh, Pakistan, Egypt, Sudan, Senegal and Yemen, Bridge Report no. 10, Brighton 1993, <http://www.ids.ac.uk/bridge/Reports/re10c.pdf>.

T. Nasrin, *Shame*, trans. K. Datta, New Delhi 1994.

A. Quraishi, Her honor. An Islamic critique of the rape laws of Pakistan from a women-sensitive perspective, in *Michigan Journal of International Law* 18 (1997), 287.

T. Sarkar, Ethnic cleansing in Gujarat. An analysis of a few aspects, in *Akhbar* 3 (2002), 2.

N. Shakir, Women, minorities and Hudood law in Pakistan, in *Asian Human Rights Commission* 5:31 (2003), 4.

P. Vibhuti et al., The anti rape movement in India, in M. Davis, *Third World, second sex. Women's struggles and national liberation*, London 1983, 180–6.

Geetanjali Gangoli

Religious Associations

Central Asia

Women's religious associations and gatherings in Central Asia are closely connected with the historical, political, economic, ethnic, and social evolutions of the region. Their larger presence was noticed during the last decades of the twentieth century and they have become still more evident since the collapse of the Soviet Union, when the Central Asian republics gained their independence and Islam was recognized as an important element of ethnic-religious identity.

Until the Russian conquest of Central Asia in the second half of the nineteenth century, state power and religious authority were closely intertwined. During the centuries that followed the introduction of Islam to Central Asia, the female presence within Muslim religious institutions was almost nonexistent: while the public sphere was reserved for men, women were restricted to the private sphere (women's gatherings took place mostly within the home). This opposition between the public and private persisted throughout the twentieth century.

After the tsarist conquest, most Islamic institutions such as mosques, religious schools, and courts were placed under the control of the Russian government, while others, such as *waqf* endowment and alms giving (*zakāt*) were banned. Despite the close control and prohibitions imposed by the Russians, Islam continued to expand. During the period of the tsarist government, as before, Muslim women played an almost insignificant role within official Islam. Some of them, wives of mullahs, gave private lessons to girls belonging to the richer families. These women clerics (in Uzbek, *otins*) became more evident in the religious world of Central Asia during the twentieth century. At the end of the nineteenth century, with the birth of the Jadidist reform movement in the Muslim regions of the tsarist empire, an interest in the Woman Question emerged in the Islamic Russian world. Whilst remaining within the framework of Muslim values, the reformists wished essentially to modernize the education system. In their program, which remained at a theoretical level, the Jadidists supported the unveiling of women and their education. Central Asia was influenced by this attempt at modernization, even if it did not represent the cultural center of the movement, which was strongest in Crimea, the Middle Volga, and the Caucasus.

With the October Revolution, power relationships in Central Asia underwent important changes. Islam as a religious and social system was placed under attack from the Bolsheviks. The Soviet government adopted different religious policies during its existence. After 1917, religious schools and courts were prohibited, and the *waqf* lands were confiscated. After 1922, with the introduction of the New Economic Policy, these restrictions were eased. From 1925, following the regionalization of Central Asia, the Soviet government took up a more intransigent and authoritarian position toward religion; strong anti-Islamic campaigns were implemented during the 1930s. After the Second World War, an increase in religious activity and an impulse to the faith, due in part to the new spirit of cooperation of the government with the religious institutions, were registered; this revival again fell into abeyance during the Khrushchev era (1957–64) with his campaign of religious persecution. During the 1970s, a new détente developed: the pressure on believers was slackened, even though atheistic propaganda was still disseminated. During the 1970s and 1980s, there was a resurgence of Islam in Central Asia.

Between 1917 and 1991, most of the pre-revolutionary Islamic traditions survived and in some cases were strengthened. During these decades, Central Asian people lived in two dimensions: one public and Sovietized, the other private and Islamized. In this way, the official Muslim religion coexisted side by side with the more popular, underground, and familiar religion, where women have always predominated. The prevalence of beliefs in female spirits and the female reliance on Muslim clergy, amulets, and pilgrimages to the shrines of the saints gave the perception of a "women's religion" in Central Asia. Women's gatherings had a private dimension, where the official religion and the state could not enter.

After 1991 and the collapse of the Soviet Union, the Islamic resurgence became more marked. Islam became a fundamental part of the religious-cultural identity of the Central Asian people. The presence of Muslim women in society increased. In Uzbekistan, some religious schools exclusively for women were opened and some male schools started to accept female students. In Kyrgyzstan, departments for female students were established within important Islamic institutions. Women started to attend the mosques – which until then had been an exclusive male prerogative – and to wear the veil again. In Uzbekistan, the state established women's committees at the level of the *maḥalla* (neighborhood community): the primary task of the committees is to inform and to support families on all issues, such as finding jobs or providing financial help. Religious activity within the *maḥalla* is continuously increasing. Girls still receive an elementary religious education from the *otin*s, the female equivalent of the mullahs: they have a rudimentary knowledge of the Qurʾānic precepts, but they are unable to decipher the Arabic script. The *otin*s prepare girls for marriage and motherhood and provide basic religious instruction; they are in charge of prayers and important celebrations within the community such as weddings and births. Every *maḥalla* has its *otin*, but sometimes one *otin* is shared by two or three *maḥalla*s. Within the *maḥalla*, women meet generally every Saturday to pray in a room reserved for them and to receive advice about the Qurʾān, about the fundamental rules of the Sharīʿa, and about correct Islamic behavior. Women who attend these meetings are often over 50 years old. After the religious part of the meeting, women drink tea, eat previously prepared food, and chat. Many women, mostly in rural areas, where the level of education is lower, are attracted by religious groups which preach the return to authentic Islamic values and to the traditional family. Soon after the independence of the Central Asian republics, some organized groups of Islamic women emerged: they are national nongovernmental organizations acting on the territory of groups generally incorporated in political parties with an Islamic matrix.

Bibliography

S. Akiner, Islam, the state and ethnicity in Central Asia in historical perspective, in *Religion, State and Society* 24:2/3 (1996), 91–132.

——, Between tradition and modernity. The dilemma facing contemporary Central Asian women, in M. Buckley (ed.), *Post-Soviet women. From the Baltic to Central Asia*, Cambridge 1997, 261–304.

D. Alimova and N. Azimova, Women's position in Uzbekistan before and after independence, in F. Acar and A. Güneş-Ayata (eds.), *Gender and identity construction. Women of Central Asia, the Caucasus and Turkey*, Leiden 2000, 293–304.

M. Brill Olcott, Women and society in Central Asia, in W. Fierman (ed.), *Soviet Central Asia. The failed transformation*, Boulder, Colo. 1991, 235–54.

H. Fathi, Otins. The unknown women clerics of Central Asian Islam, in *Central Asian Survey* 16:1 (1997), 27–43.

O. V. Gorshunova, The otin [in Russian], in *Etnograficheskoe Obozrenie* 3 (2001), 135–7.

P. A. Michaels, Kazak women. Living the heritage of a unique past, in H. L. Bodman and N. Tohidi (eds.), *Women in Muslim societies. Diversity within unity*, Boulder, Colo. 1998, 187–202.

S. P. Poliakov, *Everyday Islam. Religion and tradition in rural Central Asia*, New York 1992.

A. Saktanber and A. Özataş-Baykal, Homeland within homeland. Women and the formation of Uzbek national identity, in F. Acar and A. Güneş-Ayata (eds.), *Gender and identity construction. Women of Central Asia, the Caucasus and Turkey*, Leiden 2000, 229–48.

A. Samiuddin and R. Khanam (eds.), *Muslim feminism and feminist movement. Central Asia*, Delhi 2002.

S. Tadjbakhsh, Between Lenin and Allah. Women and ideology in Tajikistan, in H. L. Bodman and N. Tohidi (eds.), *Women in Muslim societies. Diversity within unity*, Boulder, Colo. 1998, 163–85.

M. Tokhtakhodjaeva, *Between the slogans of communism and the laws of Islam. The women of Uzbekistan*, Lahore 1995.

M. A. Tolmacheva, The Muslim woman in Soviet Central Asia, in *Central Asian Survey* 12:4 (1993), 531–48.

Women Living Under Muslim Laws, *Assertions of self. The nascent women's movement in Central Asia*, Lahore 1995.

Chiara De Santi

Iran and Afghanistan

This entry introduces the historical and contemporary developments of women's religious gatherings and associations in Iran and Afghanistan. It presents the ways in which national and Islamic state led projects and movements, at different historical moments, have shaped voluntary associational life in both locations. While considering the unintended consequences of state led approaches to associational life, attention is also paid to the interrelationship and levels of cooperation between informal, seemingly private religious women's gatherings and grassroots religious associations in the public domain. It demonstrates how religious gatherings and associations have been vehicles that both reinforced and challenged national and Islamist movements with their strictly delineated gendered norms of behavior. They have also served as pathways to participation in public matters and have enlarged women's scope of action to tackle harsh social, political, and economic realities. Women's religious associations are heterogeneous and must be considered in relation to the interplay between specific national and regional contexts, as well as women's socioeconomic, religious, ethnic, and political orientations. Particular consideration should be given to the increasing exchanges and linkages with global movements, international associations, and human rights groups around the world.

It has been customary in Iran and Afghanistan for Muslims to gather together in gender-specific groups for religious instruction and practices. Whereas men's religious events are usually held at mosques or local shrines, women's religious activities, such as *sufra*s and *jalasa*s, are usually held privately in women's homes or in front of mosques in order to provide food and welfare for the disadvantaged. Social service activities stemming from religious traditions, which have a long history in Iran and Afghanistan, reveal the interchange between religious commitment and civic participation. While women's religious associations vary greatly in terms of their specific agendas and priorities, their entrance into public space at the beginning of the twentieth century signified a new sense of public presence that altered the distinction between the public domain of employment, governance, and culture – reserved for men – and the private domain of the family, reserved for women.

In Iran, middle- and upper-class women from Tehran and the provinces started to form a number of *anjuman*s (grassroots associations) during the period around the Constitutional Revolution of 1905/6. The few women who emerged onto the political stage turned their informal religious and social gatherings into political meetings. A number of independent associations, which were influenced by different nationalist and religious ideologies, actively promoted women's political advancement and made concerted efforts to raise funds for schools, health clinics, and orphanages.

In Afghanistan, the foundation for associational activities were laid in the late 1920s when King Amān Allāh and his wife Queen Ṣurayyā introduced new reforms for women to express their grievances (ibid.). However, tribal and religious opposition to the reforms led to the overthrow of the king in 1929 – and it was not until the reign of Ẓahīr Shāh (1933–73) that moves toward women's advancement in the public domain were observed. Even so, women continued to exercise political and social influence through informal and less visible community support networks.

In Iran the newly formed women's associations were appropriated by Reza Khan (1925–41) as a result of his ambitious program of modernization. Women's appearance and involvement in public life – seen as signifiers of national identity – were also shaped by Western norms and Atatürk's model of reform. During the rule of Mohammad Reza Shah Pahlavī the state continued to institutionalize women's issues and address them as social welfare concerns. Under strict state control, however, independent associations were largely silenced and did not have the freedom to assemble their own agendas.

During the late 1960s and 1970s a coalition of Iranian opposition groupings, comprised of men and women with sundry Islamist, nationalist, and Marxist leanings, challenged the Pahlavīs' monopoly over political activity. Women spread political information through informal religious networks stemming from mosques, bazaars, and women-only religious gatherings, *jalasa*s and *sufra*s. Women activists, endorsing diverse religious and political platforms, joined forces and played an important role in overthrowing the Pahlavī dynasty in 1979.

In Afghanistan the period between the 1950s and the Soviet invasion of 1979 saw the formation of a number of secular women's groupings, consisting mainly of urban-based, educated women who aimed to advance the human rights of women. Women's independent activities were, however, restricted by the rise of the People's Democratic Party of Afghanistan and the Soviet invasion in 1979.

In Iran, after two years of revolutionary transition, Ayatollah Khomeini and Islamic forces eradicated political opposition and dominated the revolutionary process and its outcome.

The 1980s witnessed the development of "official" women's Islamist religious associations. However, many women who were not involved in the official religious associations have organized themselves through women-only religious gatherings, co-operatives, grassroots religious charities, mosque networks, and the growing number of service-oriented non-governmental organizations (NGOs). Paradoxically, the governmental policies controlling dress codes and gendered access to public space made it possible for women, particularly those from families that customarily isolate women from public activity, to work and learn in the public arena. Inadvertently, women's public involvement shed light on the impracticality of many governmental policies.

Religious gatherings and novel NGOs have become platforms for secular and religious feminists to debate and negotiate legal status and social positions of women. Many associations, including those that actively question the dominant role of Islam in public life, have acquired religious overtones in order to frame their grievances in the public sphere. Feminist debates extend to and are informed by women's associations that are organized by women who live outside Iran. Religious gatherings and associations – often linked to mosques, schools, and charity foundations – are a few of the many spaces where some women living in the diaspora become involved in welfare concerns and political matters.

In Afghanistan in the latter part of the 1990s the theocratic dictatorship known as the Taliban came to power and instituted a severe gender regime that prohibited women's freedom to work and be educated. Under brutal conditions, some Afghans exercised their informal religious and social networks and organized underground schools and health services for women. The world learned about the dire conditions of Afghan women largely through communication links forged between refugee and diasporic networks, the Internet, and women's associations. Through these levels of cooperation women and men have successfully linked with feminist and human rights groups across nation-state borders and invoked international attention.

To conclude, this entry has surveyed the linkages and barriers between women's informal and seemingly private religious activities and associational opportunities for women in public life. Local and global women's religious voluntary associations – in a range of political and religious shades – have multiplied in Iran and Afghanistan in the beginning years of the twenty-first century. While both Iranian and Afghan local and nationally-based women's religious associations are increasingly linked to international women's associations, the political and economic situation in Afghanistan has generated greater involvement of international associations.

Bibliography

F. Adelkhah, *Being modern in Iran*, New York 2000.
J. Afary, Steering between Scylla and Charybdis. Shifting gender roles in twentieth century Iran, in *National Women Studies Association* 8:1 (1996), 28–49.
——, *The Iranian Constitutional Revolution, 1906–1911. Grassroots, democracy, social democracy, and the origins of feminism*, New York 1996.
H. Ahmed-Ghosh, A history of women in Afghanistan. Lessons learnt for the future, in *Journal of International Women's Studies* 4:3 (2003), 1–14.
B. Bāmdād, *From darkness into light. Women's emancipation in Iran*, trans. F. R. C. Bagley, New York 1977.
S. Barakat and G. Wardell, Exploited by whom? An alternative perspective on humanitarian assistance to Afghan women, in *Third World Quarterly* 23:5 (2002), 909–30.
N. H. Dupree, *Women of Afghanistan*, Bonn 1986.
H. Hoodfar, *The women's movement in Iran. Women at the crossroads of secularisation and Islamization*, Women Living Under Muslim Laws 1999, <http://www.iranchamber.com/podium/history/020312_women_secularization_islamization1.php>.
Islamic Republic of Iran, Constitution, <www.unesco.org>.
Z. Mir-Hosseini, *Islam and gender. The religious debate in contemporary Iran*, Princeton, N.J. 1999.
V. Moghadam, *Modernizing women. Gender and social change in the Middle East*, Boulder, Colo. 1993.
——, Revolution, religion, and gender politics. Iran and Afghanistan compared, in *Journal of Women's History* 10 (1999), 172–95.
A. Najmabadi, Feminism in an Islamic republic. Years of hardship, years of growth, in Y. Y. Haddad and J. L. Esposito (eds.), *Islam, Gender, and Social Change*, London 1998, 59–84.
B. Namazi, Summary of study on Iranian NGOs, November 1999.
P. Paidar, *Gender of democracy. The encounter between feminism and reformism in contemporary Iran*, United Nations Research Institute for Social Development, October 2001.
K. Spellman, *Religion and nation. Iranian local and transnational networks in London*, Berghahn Books, Oxford (forthcoming).
A. Torab, Piety as gendered agency. A study of *jalaseh* ritual discourse in an urban neighbourhood in Iran, in *Journal of the Royal Anthropological Institute N.S.* 2:2 (1996), 235–52.

Kathryn Spellman

Malaysia and Indonesia

Introduction

Much has been written about gender and Islam in recent decades. The upsurge of interest in this topic is influenced by people's attempt to understand the position of men and women in Islam and their interrelations, which have become the subject of repeated controversy. One view is that Islam guarantees equality of the sexes in all matters of vital concern (Qurʾān 33:35) and endorses harmonious relationships between men and women (Qurʾān 30:21). The second view is that Islam promotes the devaluation of women and the social domination of men, and this is reproduced and maintained in the social system deliberately and purposely (see also Metcalf 1998, 108).

The rise of Islamic movements and associations in Muslim countries has reinforced the stereotypes of Islam's inferior treatment of women. It is therefore imperative to examine how gender is constructed in these movements in the light of the members' interpretation of Islam. This entry examines the gender ideology of Jamaat Tabligh in Malaysia, and the Nahdlatul Ulama (NU) and Muhammadiyah, the two largest Islamic organizations in Indonesia. NU has two women's organizations, Muslimat and Fatayat. Muhammadiyah has one women's organization known as Aisyiyah.

These organizations occupy an important and potentially powerful position in Indonesia (Marcoes 2002, 188).

The historical background

Jamaat Tabligh

The breakup of the global system of Muslim empires caused by religious and political rivalry in the Muslim world and the expansion of European colonial powers during the eighteenth and nineteenth centuries influenced the emergence of reformist, revivalist, and scripturalist movements in the Muslim world (Ali 2003, 108). The emergence of the Jamaat Tabligh (Society for the propagation of the faith) was part of the Muslims' response to the broad historical forces that swept the Muslim world. It is a quietist, apolitical, and spiritual movement founded by Maulana Muhammad Ilyas in 1927 in Mewat, south of Delhi in India (Ali 2003, 175).

Since the the partition of India and Pakistan in 1947, Jamaat Tabligh has developed into a transnational movement aimed at educating Muslims in Islamic values and practices (Ali 2003, 175). The movement is bound by six principles: *kalima*, the declaration of faith that there is no God but Allah and Muhammad is His Messenger; *ṣalāt*, the performance of the five daily prayers; *ʿilm* and *dhikr*, knowledge and remembrance of Allah; *ikhlās al-niyya*, the purity of intention and sincerity as most pleasing Allah; *ikrām al-Muslimīn*, the respect and honor that Muslims should demonstrate toward fellow-believers; and *tafrīʿ al-waqt*, sparing time for self-reformation and missions for proselytization to the movement (Ali 2003, 176).

Nahdlatul Ulama (NU)

The Nahdlatul Ulama (Revival of religious scholars) was established by Javanese religious scholars in 1926 to strengthen traditional Islam in Indonesia and to counterbalance the religious appeals of modernist Muhammadiyah (Candland and Nurjanah 2004, 2). Since NU was composed of *ʿulamāʾ* who were exclusively male, the wives of the scholars formed Muslimat and Fatayat to promote the well-being and status of women (Tristiawati and Munir 1995). Muslimat was founded in December 1940 in Surabaya, East Java for NU women above the age of 40. Fatayat was established in Surabaya, East Java, in April 1950, for women between the ages of 20 and 40. Structurally, Muslimat and Fatayat are linked to thousands of villages and millions of women in the country (Candland and Nurjanah 2004, 5).

Muhammadiyah

The Muhammadiyah (followers of Muhammad) is a reformist socioreligious movement set up in Jogjakarta in 1912 by a modernist Muslim, Ahmad Dahlan (Alfian 1969, 244–5). Its aim was to bring Muslims to the true teachings of Islam as enshrined in the Qurʾān and *ḥadīth*. To achieve this objective, Ahmad Dahlan laid down the major activities to be undertaken by the movement. These activities consisted of *tablīgh* (religious propagation), education, Aisyiyah (the sister organization of the movement), social welfare, boy scouts, enterprise, publications, libraries, and a few other activities (Alfian 1969, 263). Unlike NU affiliated women's organizations, Aisyiyah was initiated not by women members but by the founder himself (Alfian 1969, 245). Concerned with the backward social status of women, he established Aisyiyah in order to improve their position in society (ibid., 246–7). Until today, Muhammadiyah has continued to undertake activities similar to those identified by Ahmad Dahlan. The participation of women is encouraged. Aisyiyah, however, concentrates on religious, education, and health activities.

Gender relations

Generally, societies in the developed countries believe that men and women have equal rights and responsibilities in every aspect and activity in life. Rather than merely copying the Western model, the Islamic movements and associations in Muslim countries offer a distinct understanding of what it means to be a woman and a man in society. The Jamaat Tabligh is a case in point. In its ideological construction of gender, both men and women are enjoined to share responsibility for family and *daʿwa* (propaganda) work. Indeed, men and women in this group engage in what some societies would label as masculine or feminine roles, yet they do it to create a moral order which they believe to be Islamic in character and founded on the *sunna* of the Prophet.

When they set out on a *daʿwa* mission, men are exposed to different roles regardless of their socioeconomic status. These roles vary from teacher, to nurse, cook, or cleaner. Through this, they learn progressively how to perform the roles that are traditionally associated with femininity and they apply this not only during the mission but also when they are at home. While men are on a mission, or otherwise absorbed in the *tablīgh* movement, the women also learn how to be the only breadwinner and the head of the family in order to sustain the household. These roles are associated by some traditional societies with men. In the *tablīghī* view, parenting and housework are an integral part of everyone's obligations to the family and they are part of *ʿibāda* (worship).

To facilitate women's involvement in *daʿwa*, men provide full support and assume responsibilities for housework and childcare (Metcalf 1998). It is the task of the movement to remove all hindrances for both sexes from playing its full part in family life and *daʿwa* work. Therefore, the cultural ideal of separate spheres, which suggests that women belong to the private/home sphere and men belong to the public/work sphere, appears questionable from the perspective of this movement. As a result, the *tablīgh* movement creates a unique family type where the husband and wife run the household, bring up the children, and participate in the movement together. In performing their dual obligations, both sexes are required to emulate the ideal patterns of behavior exemplified by the Prophet. They are expected to cultivate the virtues of humility, sincerity, gentleness, perseverance, meticulous observance of prayer, and commitment to the service of others. These virtues are inculcated in members through practical experience and translated into practice in their daily undertakings both at home and during the mission tours.

However, while women are recognized as part of the life-force of the movement, their freedom of expression is regulated by men. During meetings, each *tablīghī* woman is given only 15 minutes to discuss matters related to the six fundamental principles of the movement. In contrast, Islam enjoins equal rights for men and women including the expression of emotions and opinions (Qurʾān 9:71). In addition, the movement promotes complete segregation of sexes. Women are not only separated by the veil, but also by the absence of social interaction. In Islam, there is no complete segregation between men and women. The most important aspect that should be observed by them is related to their behavior and manner in dealing with both sexes (Qurʾān 24:31).

Despite some restrictions imposed on them, women argue that the movement offers them an opportunity to live as true Muslims who conform to the teachings of Islam. In other societies women are treated as commodities and inferiors, but the *tablīghī* women claim that they are accorded respect and dignity, and they are given the same rights, responsibilities, and opportunities as men. In their view, there is no need for them to join any feminist movements fighting for equal rights because they are already liberated by the movement from oppression, seclusion, and subordination.

While it is true that women's *daʿwa* activities are confined to women only, they also contribute to the development of the society. In the view of *tablīghī* women, they play different roles in society, and through their performance of these roles they are able to transmit Islamic culture and traditions to other groups in society. To outsiders, the veil symbolizes female oppression, seclusion, and subordination to the male sex. The *tablīghī* women, however, disagree with this notion. Like other revivalist women's groups (Afshar 1996), they argue that the veil is a symbol of Islamization, and that it is a liberating rather than an oppressive force. With the veil, they are able to participate in public life, while at the same time preserving their modesty and chastity.

Women's organizations affiliated to NU and Muhammadiyah

Like *tablīghī* women, members of women's organizations affiliated to NU and Muhammadiyah are encouraged to lead a dynamic public life without sacrificing their domestic responsibilities or their modesty. Although their participation in politics is rather limited, and their activities are confined to women only, they run their own organizations, initiate religious and educational activities, and implement government-sponsored programs. Unlike the *tablīghī* women, however, they are not required to put on the veil and observe uniformity of dress.

In Muslimat, women are involved in three ways (Candland and Nurjanah 2004, 5): first, as women of the NU community, with religious affinity toward, but no official status in, the association; second, as registered members (*anggota*) of the association; and third, as elected members of various committees (*pengurus*) of Muslimat. Fatayat initiates different programs: organization and management; leadership and education; economic and cooperative activities; health and sports; *daʿwa* and information; advocacy and legal affairs; social, artistic, and cultural activities; research and development; and foreign connections (Candland and Nurjanah 2004, 5). Since its funding is limited, it has collaborated with international bodies such as UNICEF, Asia Foundation, and the Ford Foundation to implement its programs.

Likewise, Aisyiyah undertakes various development activities for women such as building women's mosques, kindergartens, and women's

Islamic schools. It also promotes women's participation in the public sphere in religious, educational, and health activities. It has established an extensive network of family planning and maternity clinics. Through this network it provides health, nutrition, and family education and assistance to women. The government's family planning program is based on Aisyiyah's concept of ideal family (*keluarga sakinak*) (Candland and Nurjanah 2004, 6).

Division of labor based on gender is manifest in both NU and Muhammadiyah. The activities of Muslimat, Fatayat, and Aisyiyah are women-centered and less political. However, these roles are chosen and defined by women themselves. The members we interviewed argue that in Islam, politics is inseparable from other dimensions of social life. Therefore, when female members have chosen to work for women only, they also contribute to the political life of NU and Muhammadiyah, and to the development of their families and the Indonesian society at large. In both organizations, members claimed that men and women do not compete for power, but rather complement each other in their roles.

Bibliography

H. Afshar, Islam and feminism. An analysis of political strategies, in M. Yamani (ed.), with additional editorial assistance from A. Allen, *Feminism and Islam. Legal and literary perspectives*, New York 1996, 197–216.

Alfian, Islamic modernism in Indonesian politics. The Muhammadiyah movement during the Dutch colonial period (1912–1942), Ph.D. diss., University of Wisconsin, Madison 1969.

A. Y. Ali, *The meaning of the Holy Qur'an*, Beltsville, Md. 1999[10].

J. Ali, Islamic revivalism. The case of the Tablighi Jamaat, in *Journal of Muslim Minority Affairs* 23:1 (April 2003), 173–81.

C. Candland and S. Nurjanah, Women's empowerment through Islamic organizations. The role of Indonesia's *Nahdlatul Ulama* in transforming the government's birth control program into a family welfare programme, a case study prepared for the World Faith Development Dialogue Workshop in New Delhi, India, 9–11 February 2004.

L. Marcoes, Women's grassroots movements in Indonesia. A case study of the PKK and Islamic women's organizations, in K. Robinson and S. Bessell (eds.), *Women in Indonesia. Gender, equity and development*, Singapore 2002, 187–97.

B. D. Metcalf, Women and men in a contemporary pietist movement. The case of the Tablighi Jamaʿat, in P. Jeffery and A. Basu (eds.), *Appropriating gender. Women's activitism and politicized religion in South Asia*, New York 1998, 107–21.

S. Tristiawati and R. Munir, The Nahdlatul Ulama, mimeograph, 1995.

Pute Rahimah Makol-Abdul and
Saodah Abdul Rahman

North Africa

Women's associations meet to perform religious rituals on a regular or occasional basis throughout North Africa. These associations are autonomous, attached neither to each other, nor to parallel men's associations, although some associations recognize distant or former affiliation with Sufi (Islamic mystical) orders. They are usually loosely structured with membership based on ritual participation. Their rituals may take the form of the *dhikr*, or Sufi remembrance ritual, a spirit possession ceremony called *ḥaḍra* or *līla*, or a combination. Some are held exclusively for women, whereas men affiliated with Sufi orders may be present at others to play instruments, chant, slaughter sacrificial animals, or observe. The rituals provide the women with an opportunity for social contact and a communal worship experience of their own design.

Documentation of women's associations holding spirit possession rituals exists for Tunisia, Algeria, and Morocco. In the case of Tunisia, the association's rituals are held in the tombs of holy figures. A woman healer orchestrates the ritual and treatment of women participants afflicted with spirit possession. The few men present watch or play drums and castanets and chant to summon the spirits. The spirits inhabit the afflicted causing them to move rhythmically and to fall into trance. While in trance, they are encouraged by the healer to articulate their personal dilemmas and formulate solutions (Ferchiou 1991). Women's associations holding similar rituals exist in urban centers in Algeria (Jansen 1987) and Morocco (Fernea 1979, 1988, Maher 1984, Rausch 2000, Reysoo 1998). The healers directing the ritual, who are often freelance seers, may claim affiliation with the male musicians' Sufi order. However, the female participants consider themselves bound to each other and the ritual leader. The rituals are usually held in private homes, sometimes during rites of passage celebration such as weddings (Jansen 1984) or circumcisions (Maher 1984). They allow the participants to process gender-related conflicts.

Two differing examples of women's associations performing *dhikr*-like rituals exist in Algeria. Despite distant affiliation with the Qādirī Sufi order, both function autonomously. The female leader of the first association orchestrates rituals held on Friday afternoon in the tomb of a holy figure. The rituals consist of prayers and litanies praising the Prophet, followed by the expression of requests by individual women for the resolution of personal problems transmitted to the holy figure by the leader who requests intercession. Then current daily dilemmas related to gender issues are discussed, followed by closing prayers (Andezian 2001). The second association is more structured, with the leader in charge of scheduling the rituals and admitting new members. The *dhikr*-like ritual is held in holy figures' tombs or private homes at the request of those needing assistance with infertility, illness, and other afflictions. After guiding the participants in multiple repetitions of Arabic phrases praising Allah, the leader gives a lesson on religious matters and leads the chanting of poetic verses, which may vary according to the context. Rhythmic movements to induce trance may accompany the chanting. The ritual includes the sacrifice of an animal provided by the afflicted. The members are usually older, and widowed or divorced and view their participation as an expression of piety in preparation for Judgment Day (Jansen 1987).

Based on unpublished fieldwork data, two types of associations holding rituals resembling the *dhikr* exist among Berber women in the Souss region of southwestern Morocco today. The first association is located in the village of Agard Udad near Tafraout in the Anti-Atlas Mountains. The association meets daily between the afternoon and sunset prayers in a meeting room in a centuries-old mosque on an embankment which overlooks the village. The mosque also contains a kitchen where the women prepare ritual meals when a villager donates an animal for sacrifice to acquire special blessing. Membership is based on attendance and open to all women. Many of the regular participants are advanced in age. The women chant multiple repetitions of a series of Arabic phrases as well as long age-old Berber poems praising Allah, with intermittent Arabic and Berber prayers. Halfway through the ritual, the women pause to drink traditional Moroccan sweet green tea with mint. The ritual content is unique to this location. The association leader, an older woman, introduces the chants, prayers, and poems. Besides the entire ritual, she, like the older participants, preserves in her memory the legendary history of the mosque in rhymed Berber prose. Former leaders also instructed the women in religious matters on separate occasions (Qasim 1991).

The second type of association can be found in variant forms throughout the Souss region of southwestern Morocco. Three associations exist in the Atlantic coastal town of Tiznit and two in Bounaaman, a village in the foothills ten kilometers due south of Tiznit. In Tiznit, the ritual gatherings are held in the tomb complexes of holy figures. In Bounaaman, they take place in a tomb complex and a private home. In all five locations, the ritual consists primarily of Berber couplets chanted multiple times, sometimes accompanied by drumming or clapping, and intermittent Arabic prayers. In Tiznit, the women occasionally chant long age-old Berber poems as a group or with one woman chanting the poem and the others the refrain. The couplets and poems express veneration of and longing for the Prophet and call on local holy figures to intercede in times of need. All five associations are loosely structured with membership based on open ritual attendance. The participants vary in age, but the majority in Tiznit are older, whereas middle-aged women are common among participants in Bounaaman. Unlike those in Tiznit, the associations in Bounaaman have no officially designated leaders. The leaders in Tiznit give sermon/lessons periodically throughout the ritual on religious topics. One association leader prefers to speak about pertinent daily life issues such as local girls' changing dress styles, growing materialism, and abortion. Lively discussions ensue. The rituals occur between the afternoon and sunset prayers, daily or weekly. Midway through the ritual, sweet green tea with mint and bread, purchased with participants' donations, are served. Local inhabitants occasionally bring a meal for the women to share to ensure the salvation of a family member who has died.

BIBLIOGRAPHY

S. Andezian, *Expérience du divin dans l'Algérie contemporaine. Adeptes des saints dans la région de Tlemcen*, Paris 2001.

S. Ferchiou, La possession. Forme de marginalité féminine, in *Annuaire de l'Afrique du Nord* 30 (1991), 191–200.

E. W. Fernea, *Saints and spirits. Religious expression in Morocco. A guide to the film*, Austin, Tex. 1979.

——, *A street in Marrakech*, Prospect Heights, Ill. 1988.

W. Jansen, *Women without men. Gender and marginality in an Algerian town*, Leiden 1987.

V. Maher, Mutterschaft und Moralität. Zum Widerspruch der Frauenrollen in Marokko, in D. W. Sabean and H. Medick (eds.), *Emotionen und materielle Interessen. Sozialanthropologische und historische Beitraege*, Goettingen 1984, 143–78.

H. Qāsim, *The mosque up above* [in Tashilhit Berber], Casablanca 1991.

M. J. Rausch, *Bodies, boundaries and spirit possession. Moroccan women and the revision of tradition*, Bielefeld 2000.

F. Reysoo, *Pèlerinages au Maroc. Fête, politique et échange dans l'islam populaire*, Paris 1991.

MARGARET J. RAUSCH

Turkey

From the earliest days of acceptance of Islam by Turks women have played an important role in the formation and development of religious associations, particularly of Sufi orders, though few are known by name. Turkmen tribes first came to Anatolia at the end of the eleventh century. During the twelfth and thirteenth centuries, with increased Turkmen migration, Islam spread throughout tribal society, mainly through dervishes, who were dedicated, humble male believers. In the formative years of Ottoman society dervishes also took part in the conquest of Thrace and the Balkans and became *gazi*s, Islamic war heroes. They received land in the conquered territories and built their dervish lodges, which often became centers of Turkic cultures and religious teaching (Barkan 1942).

The Bektaşi order was prominent, especially in rural Anatolia, and its dervishes led a sedentary life in organized lodges in contrast to the anarchical dervish groups who later on formed the heterodox groups in Turkey called Alevis. Both Alevis and Bektaşis refer to a popular saint called Hacı Bektaş (d. 1270) who belonged to Turkmen tribes and became the symbol of Anatolian Islam. Unlike his contemporary, Mevlana Celaleddin Rumi (1207–73), he did not study in the *medreses*. Bektaş was not a theologian but a mystic, and throughout his life he remained close to people and did not give up the shamanism customary in Central Asia (Mélikoff 1998). In both Bektashism and Alevism women took part in religious gatherings together with men, and some women *veli*s (friends of God), addressed as *bacı* (sister), were as highly regarded as their male counterparts (Çamuroğlu 1992, Ocak 2000). In Bektashism the chief of the *tekke* is *baba* (father) and in Alevism *dede* (grandfather) is the spiritual chief of the community, but according to a fifteenth-century Ottoman historian, Aşıkpaşazade, the Bektaşi order was founded after the death of Bektaş by a woman called Kadıncık Ana (*ana* means "mama/mother," *kadıncık* "little woman"). Kadıncık Ana, either the adoptive daughter of Bektaş, according to Aşıkpaşazade, or his spiritual wife, according to the *Vilâyetnâme*, Bektaş's hagiography, saved his life during the Babāʾī revolts (1241–3) and also founded the order with the help of his disciple Abdal Musa (Mélikoff 1998, 2).

In medieval Anatolia giving women a socially recognized place in the public sphere by addressing them as sisters or mothers was not peculiar to religious associations. During the Seljuk period, a semi-mystical organization and forerunner of the trade guilds, the Ahi brotherhood, had a branch, said to be established by Fatma Bacı, whose members were women engaged in weaving and related occupations and which was known as Bacıyân-i Rûm (Bayram 1994).

Many women followed the path of Sufism opened by Mevlana Celaleddin Rumi, a path which advocates unlimited tolerance regardless of religious background. Some women, not necessarily his descendants, became the representatives of the order in the Mevlevi *mukabele* (*sema* or whirling ceremony), were appointed as shaykha, wore traditional *hırka* and *sikke*, whirled with men, took responsibility for both men and women on the Sufi path, and had numerous murids (Helminski 2003). They are still known as the female saints of Anatolia and their tombs and shrines have been visited throughout the centuries, especially by women (Araz 1966). However, following the empowerment of the *medreses* in Ottoman society, including in the Mevlevi order, in many religious orders women and men were segregated and only in Bektaşi and Alevi circles could women regularly continue to participate in religious gatherings with men (Gölpınarlı 1969, 147).

Owing to this time-honored tradition, the relegation of women to women-only gatherings and keeping their saintly presence publicly under low profile became salient characteristics of many religious associations in modern Turkey as well. For example, in the provincial towns of eastern and southeastern Anatolia, and in the conservative religious orders of the large cities, wives or daughters of shaykhs are usually considered to be responsible for maintaining the communication between the shaykhs and their female followers; hence women function as the female representatives of those particular orders, yet they do not actually hold office. In modern Turkey women continue to be active participants of religious associations, whether in newly established non-governmental organizations or branches of various traditional religious orders, but because of the orthodox Islamic modesty codes which entail the seclusion of women, they stay one step behind men. This does not reflect either their spiritual or mental capacities, but the gender biases prevalent in those associations.

Bibliography

N. Araz, *Anadolu evliyaları*, Istanbul 1966.

Ö. L. Barkan, Osmanlı İmparatorluğunda bir iskan ve kolonizasyon metodu olarak vakıflar ve temlikler I. İstila devirlerinin kolonizatör Türk dervişleri ve zaviyeleri, in *Vakıf Degisi* 5 (1942), 279–386.

M. Bayram, *Fatma Bacı ve Bacıyân-i Rûm*, Konya 1994.

R. Çamuroğlu, *Tarih, heterodoksi ve babailer*, Istanbul 1992.

A. Gölpınarlı, *100 soruda tasavvuf*, Istanbul 1969.

C. A. Helminski, *Women of Sufism. A hidden treasure*, Boston 2003.

I. Mélikoff, Bektashi/Kızılbaş. Historical bipartition and its consequences, in T. Olsson, E. Özdalga, and C. Raudvere (eds.), *Alevi identity. Cultural, religious and social perspectives*, Istanbul 1998, 1–8.

A. Y. Ocak, *Alevi ve Bektaşi inançlarının İslam öncesi temelleri*, Istanbul, 2000.

Ayşe Saktanber

The United States

Methodical research on the social and political conditions of American Muslim women is almost non-existent. There is little reliable information that would allow observers to draw an accurate portrait of the facts and perceptions of the involvement of women in communal and public life. However, the pool of Muslim women in the American public sphere is growing, as they are increasingly joining the ranks of upper middle-class professionals and community activists.

There are a few Muslim women leaders who have run for public office, such as Representative Yaphett El-Amin, a democrat who represents the 57th district in the Missouri House. She worked as a counselor to young men in trouble before she became the first ward Democratic committeewoman in 1997. She is public about her faith and receives support from her husband in her involvement in politics. She has established her political career through the Democratic Party apparatus. However, little is known about her involvement in Muslim women's issues.

Muslim leaders, women included, have engaged in the polemical discourse on the status of contemporary Muslim women. This activism represents the hallmark of such groups as the Muslim Women's League, which is headed by a Los Angeles pediatrician, and Muslim Women Lawyers for Human Rights, which is headed by a law professor in Richmond, Virginia. These groups and others profess interest in reclaiming the status of women as free, equal, and vital contributors to society. As they implement educational programs designed to achieve this objective, they stand in sharp contrast to the stereotypical images of Muslim women as an oppressed, helpless segment of the Muslim community.

There is also the International League of Muslim Women, an organ affiliated with the W. D. Mohammed Ministry, founded by the mainline African American Muslim leader. This women's group was established in 1984 and now has 33 chapters, 3 of which are located in the West African countries of Togo and Ghana. To many Muslims, these Muslim women stand as a good example of how American citizens in the age of globalism see the whole world as a natural domain for Islamic sisterhood and for cultural and religious connectivity.

A new trend in Muslim women's activism focuses on the human experience of women rather than the politically charged dialogue on the status of Muslim women. A number of groups have begun to identify areas of need by women that do not offend the sensibilities of the various sides of the ideological debate. Some have organized to provide services to women, beginning predictably in the area of education.

American Muslim organizations continue to struggle to define the role of women in public life. Although there are no religious objections to this type of involvement, men are less interested in such prospects than women. In Muslim community forums, these women have begun to make the case for inclusion. *Azizah*, a magazine founded by two women in 2001, which accepts contributions only from women, works to encourage Muslim women to forge their own identity in community and public arenas. The founders of the magazine have decided that it is essential to include the various experiences of women, whether they are immigrant or indigenous, wear the *ḥijāb* or not, and whether they choose to pursue careers outside the house or are satisfied with their roles as mothers and homemakers. As a result, the magazine's articles cover a range of topics, including fashion, ethnic cuisines, the opportunities and challenges facing women in the workplace, marriage, and the role of women in their communities.

Muslim households in the United States usually lack the extended family support system that is strong in Muslim countries. Community is the family's secure bridge to the outside world. Similar to trends in Christian and Jewish congregations, Muslim places of worship represent hubs of activity for women, who usually form auxiliary committees running programs for mosque participants. They also teach children the value of volunteerism and supporting their mosque through a variety of fundraising activities, including bake sales. Women usually take on these tasks merely as members of the community doing their part to meet their collective needs. Additionally, women's committees at mosques organize speaking events and discussion groups focusing on women's concerns.

Islamic centers with adequate facilities have offered women's fitness programs. Others have arranged for all-female sports events, including swimming, in outside facilities. In most mosques women are usually allowed to serve on the board of directors, although this actually occurs in only a small number of congregations. In 2001, Cherrefe Kadri, a resourceful lawyer, became a chairperson for the Islamic Center of Greater Toledo in Perrysburg,

Ohio. She has taught and served as a director of the center's weekend school, organized youth summer programs, edited the center's bimonthly magazine, and served as secretary and vice president of the society's executive committee.

Women staff several other community organizations. Islamic schools in particular provide several thousand jobs, which are largely occupied by women who teach and perform administrative functions. Women also work as reporters in community media outlets and spokespersons in a number of public affairs agencies. Indeed, groups like the Council on American-Islamic Relations, which is heavily staffed by women, often measure progress in the status of Muslim civil rights in the United States by improvements in the treatment of Muslim women.

National community development groups have increasingly recognized the importance of women's involvement in community life. Some have opted for organizational structures for women parallel to those led by men. An example of such a tendency is the Sister's Wing of the Islamic Circle of North America (ICNA), which was established in 1979. Its website notes that the women's department was developed "to enable ourselves, the sisters, to work on the establishment of the Deen [faith] freely and within our own circle." The group's heightened recognition of the social problems that face the community has led it to establish Muslim Family Services, an agency that aims to help families become self-sufficient. According to the organization, the divorce rate among American Muslim couples is intolerably high and represents a serious threat to Muslim family life. The group has supported the construction of women's shelters and initiated a matchmaking program.

In addition to the faith-based organizations, there are several women's groups that identify themselves with a certain ancestry; few of these groups, which are mainly Palestinian and Lebanese, have organized for the sake of gender and ethnic awareness. For example, the Palestinian-American Women's Association has worked to highlight the suffering of Palestinian women under Israeli occupation. There is also the Lebanese Women's Awakening in North America, a feminist discussion forum on the web. But ethnic women's groups tend also to be social service oriented, offering programs directed at beneficiaries in their local areas.

In regions with a significant Muslim population, social service centers have paid special attention to issues affecting the lives of women, such as domestic abuse. In Wood Dale, Illinois, the Hamdard Center for Health and Human Services has provided medical and counseling services since 1994. The center's crisis hotline is staffed by multilingual workers who are able to communicate with recent immigrants from the Middle East and South Asia. The center's shelter assists women and child victims of domestic abuse. Hamdard also provides court-ordered assessments in divorce and child-abuse cases, and serves as a facilitator for publicly funded social service programs. When the agency started, it was completely dependent on community support. While the demand for services grew over time, donations lagged. The agency continued to grow, but it has become increasingly dependent on public funding.

Muslim women's organizations have clearly contributed to the welfare of women and society. These groups have offered replicable models for Muslim women's involvement outside family circles. Departing from earlier periods in the development of Muslim communities, when the discussion of women's issues was only a matter of intellectual interest, Muslim women's groups are paying more attention to the practical needs of women and their families and communities. This pragmatic tendency is taking hold not only in shaping internal community communications, but also in defining women's needs and the ways to mobilize resources to meet them.

BIBLIOGRAPHY

Y. Y. Haddad and J. I. Smith. *Muslim communities in North America*, Albany, N.Y. 1994.

Islamic Circle of North America (ICNA), <http://www.icna.org/ sisterswing/ 20_years.htm>.

Karamah, Muslim Women Lawyers for Human Rights, <http://www.karamah.org>.

Muslim Women's League, <http://www.mwlusa.org>.

M. Nimer, *The North American Muslim resource guide. Muslim community life in the United States and Canada*, New York 2002.

Pakistan Link, Crossing the Rubicon in Toledo, Ohio, <http://pakistanlink.com/sah/01-12-2001.html>.

J. I. Smith, *Islam in America*, New York 1999.

MOHAMED NIMER

Western Europe

Associations based on gender and Islam in Western Europe can be divided broadly into three, not necessarily mutually exclusive, categories: (1) informal women's groups with grassroots membership or affiliation, linked to local mosques; (2) associations run by women as the female branch of an international male-dominated association, most often with headquarters in the Muslim world, or of a male-dominated, European-based association, responding to the needs of Muslims in Europe; and (3) autonomous associations organized by women and bringing together Muslim women from different ethnic, national, linguistic or ideological backgrounds to serve women's particular needs and interests or to promote needs of the the broader Muslim community.

Informal women's groups

The local mosque is most often the natural arena for women's activities, and in many cases it has taken on a new importance in a Western context. The mosque has become the place where women can meet regularly with others who share the same faith, language, and culture. Increasingly, mosque activities seem to reflect a recent, slowly growing trend toward solidifying a collective Muslim identity in the public domain, and often the mosque has become the main center for community functions as well as for religious instruction for men, women, and children. Teaching activities in the local mosques usually include Qurʾān classes for girls; such classes are quite often, at least on the basic level, organized and carried out by women. However, some mosques – like a few South-Asian Deobandi and most Tabligh-oriented mosques – are still closed to women; women belonging to these circles have, to some extent, recourse to other arenas for organized religious and social activities.

This first category primarily includes informal women's groups linked by gender-segregated participation in annual religious festivals and rituals that previously took place in private homes. These groups meet regularly through the year, providing *ifṭār* for women during Ramadan, arranging *mawlid* (Prophet's birthday) celebrations in the women's section of the mosques, and sometimes organizing women's *ḥajj* groups. When needed, they perform particular rituals, such as *ʿaqīqa* celebrations for a newborn child or the recitation of the whole Qurʾān during Ramadan or on the occasion of a death, as is often the case in South Asian Brelwi mosques. In the Shīʿī community, women's groups meet on a regular basis in private homes for *majlis-i ʿazā* (mourning assemblies) during the month of Muḥarram. Muḥarram activities in the women's section of the *ḥusayniyya* (mosque) are often extensive and include recitation of religious poetry and preaching by the women themselves. All these groups, which organize traditional ritual activities, have had to take into account their new setting and the long distance traveled to reach it; women have thus developed social networks and new organizing skills in order to fulfill their wish to participate and perform. First-generation immigrants seem to be the most faithful participants in these informal groups.

Local mosques may also make room for women's groups that initiate social and cultural activities or even new ritual activities. To give one example: the largest Arab mosque in Oslo (1,700 members in 2004) had four women's groups in 2003. Three were responsible for courses for women and girls: one class for *tajwīd* (recitation of the Qurʾān), one for *tafsīr* (explanation of the Qurʾān), and one art class (painting, embroidery). The fourth group organized lectures on topics of religious and cultural interest, open to mixed audiences (men and women as well as Muslims and non-Muslims). Such activities, when well organized, also attract women from mosques of different ideological and ethnic affiliations, and may help build bridges between different communities. These groups occasionally initiate and encourage ritual participation in new ways. Since 1990, in the same Arab mosque in Oslo, women participate in the men's ʿĪd prayer (although in a separate room), and this particular ceremony also draws women from other mosques – Turkish, Pakistani, or African.

Converts to Islam often play a central role in women's organized mosque-related activities. Probably a majority of European converts to Islam are women, and some of them also bring organizational skills into the community and encourage born Muslims to engage in new activities. These local activities can easily be combined with membership in women's associations outside a particular mosque, and active women often become members of autonomous women's associations.

Women's branches of male-dominated associations

A number of mosques are affiliated to specific Islamic movements or international organizations. Some of them find a base for women's activities in private homes (such as members of Jamaat Tabligh), in mosques with women's quarters (such as the Pakistani Idara Minhaj ul-Qurʾān or the Turkish Milli Görüs), or have mosques reserved for women (as is often the case among the Turkish Süleymanlis, namely members of the Avrupa Islam Kültür Merkezleri Birligi).

The Jamaat Tabligh, founded in British India in the late 1920s, recruits mainly from South Asian and Arab communities (particularly Moroccan), and has established preaching networks and mosques throughout the world. Although women are expected to conform to strict rules of modesty and seclusion, those married to active Tabligh members are often encouraged to engage in *daʿwa* activities as long as they do not mix with unrelated men. In Norway, women's *jamaʿāt* gather in small preaching groups (two to four women), addressing themselves to Muslim women in their neighborhood. Wives of active members of the Tabligh may travel with their husbands, organizing parallel gatherings for women. As the Tabligh movement mainly focuses on devotional practice, "an arena where women and men are, fundamentally, on the same ground" (Metcalf 2003, 56), the Tablighis remain open, at least to a certain degree, to organized women's activities.

Several associations are linked to one particular ethnic or linguistic community. The Pakistani Idara Minhaj ul-Qur'ān, founded in the 1980s with headquarters in Lahore, Pakistan, has established branches in several European countries; the founder and leader runs a political-religious party in Pakistan. Idara has succeeded in recruiting a number of followers from the Pakistani communities, particularly in Denmark and Norway. The mosque-related activities of Idara's women's groups are centered on devotional activities as well as on regular gatherings where social, legal, or medical instruction is given by educated female members of the movement (medical doctors, teachers, and so forth). The Turkish Milli Görüs, as well as the Süleymanlis, have women's branches that organize both religious education and devotional activities; they also provide, at least to some extent, social aid to Turkish women and to families in need. The Milli Görüs federation has around 791 local branches in Western Europe and of these, 445 have an active women's section. The Süleymanlis offer an interesting example of a traditional, hierarchical, and Sufi-oriented organization with an active female branch, led by a hierarchy of women linked to gender-segregated teaching activities. Their teaching program also includes more advanced religious studies (in Turkey) for those who aspire to the title *hoca hanum*, "madam imam" (a parallel to *hoca efendi*). At their headquarters in Cologne, Germany, the women's house is spacious and well kept, receiving girls for religious instruction from the Turkish community at weekends. The girls also participate in devotional activities, mainly *dhikr* meetings twice a day, and receive spiritual guidance from their female teachers. These women's centers are now established in numerous cities and smaller towns in Western Europe. The female teachers also function as preachers; the most talented are sent on preaching tours during Ramadan. In 1999, the young woman (24 years of age) who was preaching in two of the Süleymanli mosques in Norway (that is, the mosques permanently reserved for women in Oslo and Drammen) had the previous year been on a preaching tour to Sydney and Melbourne. This second category also includes Sufi networks where women organize *dhikr* gatherings or participate in the men's *dhikr*. Of a different character are the relatively small number of male-dominated religio-political associations or parties that also recruit women for their female sections, like Hizb ut-Tahrir. This militant party, which in Western Europe is mainly active in Great Britain and Denmark, runs a women's section in Denmark, and recent numbers indicate around 100 female recruits (Grøndahl et al. 2003, 35); no woman, however, is accepted in the leadership of the party.

A small number of associations anchored in the Muslim world are controlled or strongly influenced by Muslim governments; the most explicit example is the Turkish Diyanet (Diyanet İşerli Türk İslam Birliği). In these mosques women's groups are encouraged to take care of basic religious and ritual activities for women and children and of certain social events, such as national day celebrations.

Associations based in the Muslim world – however greatly they might differ among themselves – are founded on an ideology of segregation, and women have little or nothing to say in the leadership. This state of affairs is repeated by most of the new and influential, European based, male-dominated associations.

Since the 1980s, a number of new associations have been established, some of them with a female branch or a parallel organization taking care of women's concerns. For example, women have been, at least to some extent, included in the two large French organizations, the influential Union des organisations islamiques de France (UIOF), founded in 1983, and the Féderation nationale des musulmans de France (FNMF), established in 1985. Parallel women's associations also exist, like the nationwide Ligue française de la femme musulmane (LFFM); this association was created in 1995 to encourage social contacts between Muslim women and "to coordinate local women's associations and to support and help female initiatives pertaining to social questions" (LFFM web page). LFFM, linked to UOIF, is responsible for gatherings and colloquia, for example, on themes such as violence in the home or violence against women in society (two examples from 2003).

A new trend among the recent male initiated

associations in Western Europe should also be mentioned: some accept gender cooperation, like the Union de la jeunesse musulmane in France, established at the end of the 1980s, and Présence musulmane from the 1990s.

Autonomous women's associations

This grouping includes autonomous associations organized by women; this trend can be traced back to the mid-1980s and became clearly visible during the 1990s. Although many – in particular Turkish, Moroccan, and Pakistani Muslims – interact almost exclusively with Muslims of the same ethnic origin, an increasing number of Muslim women's associations are crossing or superseding ethnic, national, or linguistic barriers. Such associations, most often based on the initiative of an individual person or of a small group, are promoted by a new generation interested in communicating in European languages, committing themselves to local women's concerns, and cooperating with non-Muslim authorities and contacts with European society at large. These groups offer counseling and address social problems of the Muslim community. They may offer remedial classes for young girls or obtain space for sporting activities. Some sell, and sometimes publish Islamic books, or they organize telephone helplines for women.

Well known are the activities of An-Nisa Society, founded in 1985, with headquarters in London and related groups in Bradford and Birmingham. An-Nisa Society provides a range of services not provided by the larger society or by male-dominated Muslim associations or mosque groups. Their activities include social work (counseling, information concerning the rights of women, and so forth); at the same time they also promote cultural activities such as art exhibitions, and encourage women's creative and artistic abilities.

In several European countries similar associations have been developed. Examples are the women's group of the Islamic Information Centre in the Hague and the Foundation for Muslim Women, also in the Netherlands. Autonomous associations have existed in France since the early 1990s, when the Union des soeurs musulmanes of Lyon was established as a support group for young women who had been excluded from the educational system for insisting on wearing headscarves. The association Femmes actives et sportives has promoted participation in sports for women, and the Ecole Lamalif offers courses in classical Arabic, tutoring for schools and literacy classes, and plans to open the first Muslim female chaplaincy in France, in the women's prison at Nanterre (Maréchal 2003, 106). The London-based Muslim Women's Helpline, established in 1989, offers counseling for women with family problems, for elderly and isolated women, and the like.

Although not all of them are long-lived, these associations can be seen as an important sign of vitality and of the will and motivation to ameliorate Muslim women's living conditions. In Norway, the Oslo-based Islamic Women Norway, established in 1991, rapidly became one of the largest Muslim associations in the country, with 3,500 active members (in 2000) and with branches in three Norwegian cities; the aim of the leadership is to encourage sporting activities, mainly swimming, and to encourage women and young girls to take social responsibility by learning how to organize such activities, to collect membership fees as well as to receive their own modest wages, to fill out their own tax returns, and so forth. Sporting activities, for those interested, are combined with counseling or Norwegian language courses. Because of the swimming lessons, the association recruits members who otherwise rarely engage in activities outside their homes, and who are not easily reached by non-Muslim social services. Male members of the Muslim community in many cases encourage their wives or daughters to participate, but have also expressed concern that women could develop non-Islamic attitudes or that an activity which is not *ḥaram* (forbidden) in itself could eventually lead to one that is.

Conclusion

Since the mid-1980s, different categories of women's associations have become increasingly visible, not only among Muslims themselves but also in the larger society. The status of women has become the symbol of an Islamic way of life in front of the Western majority, and the importance of the position of women is growing. Social problems of the Muslim community are constantly in focus in European societies. These include forced marriages, Islamic divorce practices, and polygamous marriages and have prompted some Muslim women to become more active in the public sphere and to establish groups or associations to support and represent Muslim women. One of the more contentious issues is, of course, the Islamic dress code, especially the headscarf. Since the mid-1990s, exclusion of women and girls from schools or jobs, mainly in France, has led to the organization of support groups. The handling of the *ḥijāb* question – an issue symbolically important both outside the Muslim community and inside the associative milieus – will most probably remain a long-lived cause for organized efforts.

Although it is obvious that Muslim women are still far behind Muslim men in organizational activities, numerous small-scale activities are carried out by almost anonymous Muslim women's groups. These groups are still based on segregation and traditional values, and most emphasize ritual and moral obligations. However, as traditional mosques in the countries of origin often had no place for women, their present inclusion in most mosques can be seen as an accommodation to changing circumstances.

As members of male-dominated religious associations, women are definitely not as active as male members; they often remain restricted to specifically female issues, with limited influence on decision making, and with no, or very limited, place in the leadership.

Until now, the most vital and original contributions to women's organizational life are the new European associations based on gender cooperation (such as Présence musulmane) and the autonomous female associations. Together with informal groups and networks, they represent organizational training fields for women; they attract members and followers from different ethnic and linguistic backgrounds, thus counteracting the present fragmentation and lack of cooperation present in local Muslim mosque communities. Such associations, even if few in number, can be seen as another sign of how political, social, and cultural priorities, both of the Muslim community and probably also of their European interlocutors, are beginning to produce new types of Muslim organization. The founding members of women's groups and associations are not blind to shortcomings of male-biased mosque leadership or male-dominated associations; until now, however, such criticisms have been articulated in guarded terms. In general, women's associations are more centered on social issues than on ideology.

Increasing literacy as well as economic independence have given at least some women more autonomy and greater courage to affirm their rights, to take responsibility and to encourage female leadership. Consequently, women are gradually becoming more active in associations based on gender cooperation and as participants in debates concerning what kind of visible roles they are to play in the community's organizational life. Several trends are thus at work, but the fact remains that women are still playing a secondary role in the organizational development of the European Muslim community as a whole.

Bibliography

L. Babès, *L'islam positif. La religion des jeunes muslmans de France*, Paris 1997.

M. Grøndahl et al., *Hizb ut-Tahrir in Denmark* [in Danish], Aarhus 2003.

Y. Y. Haddad and J. I. Smith, *Muslim minoritites in the West. Visible and invisible*, Oxford 2002.

S. T. Hunter, *Islam, Europe's second religion. The new social, cultural, and political landscape*, London 2002.

F. Khosrokhavar, *L'islam des jeunes*, Paris 1997.

B. Maréchal, Mosques, organisations and leadership, in B. Maréchal et al., *Muslims in the enlarged Europe. Religion and society*, Leiden 2003, 79–150.

B. D. Metcalf, Tablighi Jamaʿat and women, in M. K. Masud, (ed.), *Travellers in faith. Studies in the Tablighi Jamaʿat as a transnational Islamic movement for faith renewal*, Leiden 2000, 44–58.

—— (ed.), *Making Muslim space in North America and Europe*, Berkeley 1996.

T. Modood and P. Werbner (eds.), *The politics of multiculturalism in the new Europe*, London 1997.

A. S. Roald, Eve's other face. Muslim women's activities, in I. Svanberg and D. Westerlund (eds.), *Blue-yellow Islam. Muslims in Sweden* [in Swedish], Nora 1999, 123–39.

O. Roy, *Vers un islam européen*, Paris 1999.

S. Vertovec and C. Peach, *Islam in Europe. The politics of religion and community*, Houndmills, Basingstoke, Hampshire 1997.

K. Vogt, *Islam in Norway. Mosques and Islamic organizations* [in Norwegian], Oslo 2000.

——, Integration through Islam? Muslims in Norway, in Y. Y. Haddad (ed.), *Muslims in the West. From sojourners to citizens*, Oxford 2002, 88–100.

Kari Vogt

Sectarianism and Confessionalism

Egypt

Coptic Christians are Egypt's largest religious minority. Today, the exact number of Copts is unknown, with estimates ranging from six to ten million. Most Copts follow the Coptic Orthodox faith, although a small number identify with the Roman Catholic and Anglican Churches. Because of their visible status, a discussion of sectarianism and gender in Egypt is ultimately a discussion of Coptic women. Within this context, it should be noted that Coptic women have historically lived "doubly marginal" lives, under the authority of patriarchal rules, which have often repressed them as women and, due to sporadic sectarian strife in Egypt, as members of a minority group.

In the 1980s and 1990s, the debate over the issue of sectarianism in Egypt resurfaced with great intensity. At the heart of this discussion is whether or not Coptic Christians constitute a minority or even a sect in Egypt. Since the late nineteenth century, at the time when the Egyptian nationalist identity was being formulated, the prevailing argument was that Copts are Egyptians who, aside from their religious affiliation, are ethnically identical to their Muslim counterparts. Then and now, this viewpoint has generally disregarded the idea that a Coptic socioreligious experience might be distinct from a Muslim experience. The inattention to Egypt's multi-sectarian social composition, which once included a visible number of Greeks, Armenians, and Jews, comes at a time when Egyptian society is increasingly being defined as "Islamic." The pervasive focus on constructing a homogeneous nationalist identity seems to override the distinctiveness of the Coptic experience. The role of women in this discussion has received little scholarly attention, most likely because Coptic women constitute a marginalized group within a minority community.

There are two predominant factors that shape the lives of Coptic women today: the laws and rules governing Muslim Egyptian society at large and the rules internal to the Coptic community itself, mostly as dictated by the Coptic Church.

Many of Egypt's laws draw on the Sharīʿa, or Islamic law, and according to a 1995 law, the application of family law is based on an individual's religion. In regard to matters of divorce, then, Coptic women are more restricted in their rights than their Muslim counterparts since the Coptic Church forbids divorce with few exceptions. The 2000 Personal Status Law made it easier for Muslim women to obtain divorce without a husband's consent, but the application of this law among Christian women has been practically unachievable. In contrast, because inheritance laws for all Egyptian citizens are based on Sharīʿa, both Muslim and Christian female heirs receive half the amount of a male heir's inheritance. Occasionally, on a case by case basis, the Coptic Church has exerted informal pressure to win more favorable inheritance rights for Coptic women, but the enforcement of this matter has been inconsistent.

In broader society, during the 1980s, using a tone similar to that used to characterize the position of Muslim women, fundamentalist groups such as the Egyptian Islamic Jihad maintained that "the imposition of Muslim law on Copts will be beneficial to them (e.g., strict regulations in matters of feminine dress that enhance virtue)" (Sivan 1985, 148). While this statement represents a viewpoint probably uncommon among Muslims, since the 1970s the growing Islamist tide has exacerbated tensions between Egyptian Muslims and Christians as sectarian violence has erupted sporadically throughout Egypt. In the context of gender relations, this tension is particularly evident in the issue of the veil or *ḥijāb*. Historically, both Coptic and Muslim women wore the veil until the turn of the twentieth century when unveiling came to symbolize a woman's advancement. Scholars have noted that in the past decades, many Muslim women have chosen to reveil; their reasons range from protecting their modesty to publicly asserting their religious identity (Macleod 1991, Rugh 1986). This phenomenon, however, has forced the issue of gender, minority status, and public religious expression to the fore in the lives of most Coptic women. Although the Christian religion does not articulate the need for women to wear a veil, Coptic women in urban centers have commonly adopted a modest style of dress. They have been careful to avoid offending the moral standards upheld by conservative Islamic teachings and by their own church, so they wear, in general, longer skirts, they cover their arms, and in some cases they don headscarves. However, in a situation where most Muslim women are veiled and most unveiled women are Copts, it is easy to single out Coptic women in the public arena. While Coptic men dress similarly to their Muslim counterparts and therefore blend in more easily, Coptic women consistently complain of daily harassment and discrimination, particularly in densely populated urban centers such as Cairo, Alexandria, and Asyut. As there are increasingly fewer Muslim women going about unveiled, Coptic women are harassed because they are perceived as being "immodest" and because, as Christians, they are acting against Islamic prescripts on gender roles.

The second facet affecting Coptic women is shaped by their role within the church. In general, the day-to-day problems of Copts and Muslims in Egypt are similar. In the face of economic hardships and burdensome societal demands, both communities have turned to religion to find answers and communal support. As a consequence of their minority status and because society does not wholly condone their public expression of Christianity, women have found new roles in the confines of the Coptic Church. Today, Coptic women are active as Sunday school teachers, religious mentors, and volunteers (*khuddām*). However, the religious conservatism that has affected the Muslim community at large has similarly shaped the teachings of current Coptic clerical leaders in ways that have hampered the role of Coptic women. Within the church, a plethora of books, pamphlets, articles, and sermons address women on the codes for proper and improper behavior within the community and offer role models in the form of "virgin-saints" or idealized married women. For years, the Coptic Church has tied the role of "wife-mother" to the advancement and survival of the Coptic minority. Policing young women and instructing them on how to raise loyal members of the community has become a central duty of Coptic priests. Some women have rejected marriage and the perceived loss of their independence, resorting instead to Coptic convents where they serve as nuns. But there are groups of women who have sought another alternative: these women have realized, as one scholar writes, that "education, access to paid work, and especially the possibilities of being active in the church, constitute alternatives for self realization" (Thorbjørnsrud 1997, 187). This situation has created a dilemma for Coptic church leaders: while the church relies upon the community service provided by unmarried female *khuddām*, it also sees itself as the institution that has the power to sustain the Coptic minority's reproductive future – a future increasingly threatened by sectarian tensions – by influencing women in their marriage decisions and in their family lives.

Bibliography

Anon., *Al-marʾa wa-tanmiyatihā ḥiṣād al-sinīn*, Cairo 1998.

F. Armanios, "The virtuous woman." Images of gender in modern Coptic society, in *Middle Eastern Studies* 38 (2002), 110–30.

——, Coptic Christians in Ottoman Egypt. Religious worldview and communal beliefs, Ph.D. diss., Ohio State University 2003.

A. Ayalon, Egypt's Coptic Pandora's Box, in O. Bengio and G. Ben-Dor (eds.), *Minorities and the state in the Arab world*, London 1999, 53–71.

P. van Doorn-Harder, *Contemporary Coptic nuns*, Columbia, S.C. 1995.

M. ʿIrjāwī, *Qawānīn aḥkām al-usra ʿindā ghayr al-Muslimīn min al-Miṣriyyīn*, Cairo 1986.

A. Macleod, *Accommodating protest. Working women, the new veiling, and change in Cairo*, New York 1991.

M. Purcell, A place for the Copts. Imagined territory and spatial conflict in Egypt, in *Ecumene* 5 (1998), 432–51.

A. Rugh, *Reveal and conceal. Dress in contemporary Egypt*, Syracuse, N.Y. 1986.

E. Sivan, *Radical Islam. Medieval theology and modern politics*, New Haven, Conn. 1985.

B. Thorbjørnsrud, Born in the wrong age. Coptic women in a changing society, in N. van Doorn-Harder and K. Vogt (eds.), *Between desert and city. The Coptic Orthodox Church today*, Oslo 1997, 167–89.

ʿA. Zaki, *Al-marʾa fī al-kanīsa al-Miṣriyya*, Cairo 1995.

Febe Armanios

The United States

Women from among the roughly six million Muslims living in the United States represent diverse sectarian, ethnic, cultural, educational and class backgrounds. Thus it is difficult to generalize about one gender structure in Islamic communities, or what constitutes normative roles for women, informing their self-image, religious beliefs and practices, and their relations with men. It is important to distinguish among members of any of the branches or sectarian groups of Islam between those who are self consciously practicing Muslim women, either in mosques or other institutions, and those who are secular and generally non-practicing. Sometimes secular Muslim women of diverse sectarian backgrounds are actually more active and collaborative in professional circles or groups as a way of networking than are those who are more religiously observant. This entry highlights some sociological and historical features pertaining mainly to religiously observant women.

Under the rubric "Muslim" and "Islamic" lie numerous diverse and at times antagonistic groups and sects. Differences in religious consciousness and what is considered the right approach to Islam have varied from one wave of immigrants to another. South Asians Muslims in a locale such as New York or California differ from Arabs in Michigan or Ohio in the way women shape their identity and the level at which they participate in Islamic associations. With Black American Muslims the picture becomes even more complex. While Black women traditionally associated with the Nation of Islam have put great emphasis on the racial and national implications of the movement, other African Americans, such as those of the Ḥanafī *madhhab*, for example, are more concerned with following what they understand to be orthodox Sunnī beliefs and practices.

Much of the Islamic literature in the United States today tries to reduce this multivocal and heterogeneous mix of American Islam and to point to the reality of Muslim women as one uniform body. The political dynamics of life in a secular society dominated by a still white protestant middle-class ethos has helped create a uniform and non-gendered image of American Islam, which does not match reality. Both in academic scholarship and in journalistic representations, the "Muslim woman" – either a convert or one born and raised in the American context – is seen as the "other," someone with somehow false or inferior claims to American Western culture. This neo-Orientalist discourse functions to clinically remove the Islamic experience from its natural historical habitat, the American West, and identifies it anachronistically with a Third World whose qualities seem more appropriate for Islam. This artificial removal of the Islamic from the West is internalized by Muslim women and men themselves, in their defense of their religion, and upheld as a definitive trait of their identity and history. American Muslim women across sectarian lines have used a fixed binarism of Islam versus the West to describe ethos, religion, and even behavioral patterns in their communities.

Within and across the various groups that make up Islam in the United States – Sunnī, Shīʿī, Sufi, and heterodox movements – there are important differences in ritual, doctrine, and interpretation of Qurʾān and *ḥadīth* that have direct bearing on women's status, self-image, and gender relations. Around one fifth of American Muslims are Shīʿīs of Twelver, Ismāʿīlī, and Zaydī branches. In urban areas these groups maintain their separate mosques and centers, but in smaller towns Twelvers and Zaydīs often participate in Sunnī places of worship. Sunnī and Shīʿī women generally differ in terms of female role models and spiritual guides. Sunnīs tend to identify with the "mother of the faithful" image found in the Prophet Muḥammad's wives, particularly Khadīja and ʿĀʾisha. Khadīja is depicted as an assertive and able businesswoman, and ʿĀʾisha as a political activist and an important source of some of the *ḥadīth* and law pertaining to women. Sunnī women have embellished the lives and feats of the Prophet's wives to confirm Islam's support of female leadership and educational and professional ambitions.

Twelver Shīʿī women emphasize the role and position of the Prophet's daughter Fāṭima, tracing the imamate through her and her husband ʿAlī. Fāṭima's centrality to the early imamate tradition historically has given Shīʿī women a superior spiritual and social position as compared with Sunnī women, particularly with respect to inheritance and leadership in public religious activities. Ismāʿīlī women especially tend to underscore the esoteric and symbolic nature of Islamic rituals such as prayer, fasting, pilgrimage, and testimony, arguing that inner faith is more important than outward, exoteric manifestations of worship or verbal adherence to Islam. Ismāʿīlīs today debate the possibility that the Agha Khan's daughter may become the leader of the movement, since he seems to have favored her over his sons. The Druze branch of the Ismāʿīlīs, often referred to as "Unitarian," make up a small minority of American Muslims. They consider mainstream Muslims to have diverted from the true spirit of monotheism. Depending on geographical region and class, Druze women may favor a greater association and even marriage with Christians over Muslims. In general, however, marriage outside the sect is discouraged.

Sufi movements such as those of Ḥaẓrat Ināyāt Khān and Idries Shah have competed with mainstream Islam in attracting women converts from Christianity and Judaism. Among Sufi groups that embrace puritanical or traditionalist restrictions on social life, women's roles and experiences have differed little from those manifest in major Sunnī and Shīʿī groups. In a few cases, female Sufi groups have succeeded in transcending gender inequality and seem to have been empowered by an escape from a Sharīʿa-based regulation of their activities. In *Angels in the Making*, Laleh Bakhtiar discusses the lives of women who joined the Sufi movement in the United States, showing that Islamic mysticism can be therapeutic and helpful in preserving the mental health of (especially young) Muslim women. It functions as an alternative to Western psychoanalysis for a range of psychological disorders.

American Muslim women generally believe that Islam affords equal rights and opportunities for both genders, but that roles for men and women are complementary rather than identical. The economic burdens facing working- and middle-class Muslim families, both native and immigrant, and the apparent need for the income of wives as wage earners, have reconfigured gender relations in a manner that has encouraged decision-making and certain social freedoms for women within an Islamic frame of reference. Meanwhile, many Muslim groups in the United States are fearful of these changes, and continue to argue that the man is the natural family provider with female labor outside the house devalued. In this context, several legal injunctions issued by clerics and muftis encourage Muslim men across sectarian lines to participate in housework and childrearing activities. Muslim women in all sects and denominations may find themselves torn in these discussions. Often as a result of American discrimination and social marginalization, they have tried to preserve a united front with their male counterparts in defining what constitutes proper female behavior in Islam. Some consent to male paternalism and gender inequality, reject premarital sexual relations, and submit to spousal control as a confirmation of their Islamic identity in the face of delegitimization. It is not surprising that many Muslim women describe veiling, in any of its various manifestations, as liberating in ways hard for Western feminists to comprehend. The extensive legal and informal debates on the veil confirm not its normative appearance in Islam, but rather the challenges Islam faces as well as the fluidity of sectarian translations of Islamic ritual, attire, and sexual modesty.

Both Sunnī and Shīʿī Muslim women put great emphasis on making their marriages work, accommodating differences with their spouses and resorting to divorce only when all communal and familial reconciliatory approaches fail. Marrying outside the faith is discouraged, but it occurs often enough to be a source of concern for American Muslims. Among the thorny issues facing Muslim families of various sects and social classes is validating female virginity, prohibiting premarital relations, and controlling the extent of socialization among young Muslim women and non-Muslim men. Illustrative of the experiences of many American Muslims, Maryam Qudrat Aseel (2003), of Sunnī Afghani background, notes that in her culture the struggle with familial authority is much more intense in the case of young girls. Boys are free to do as they please, with no accountability, while girls are not. Aseel confirms the strong sectarian character of her Islamic upbringing in which girls are expected to marry not only a Sunnī Muslim, but one who is Tajik or Pashtun Afghani.

The practice of polygamy, itself banned by United States law, is found in very small numbers of American Muslim families, especially among some members of the Nation of Islam and other African American sectarian movements. Some Shīʿīs practice *mutʿa* (temporary marriage), though it is generally discouraged. On the whole, an increasing number of Muslim women want greater control over the conditions of their marital contracts, with the resulting increase in detailed premarital agreements. The rights accorded to women under American civil law seem to have made less urgent the call raised in many countries for reforming Islamic law on marriage, polygyny, and divorce.

American Muslim women of all sects and classes, mainstream and heterodox, continue to struggle over access to and manipulation of public space. Many feminist Muslims support gender commingling in religious congregations, whether in the mosque or Sufi circles, during prayer or in other religious performances. Sunnī, Twelver Shīʿī and Ismāʿīlī women have sought leadership roles within their American communities and religious circles, invoking Qurʾānic verses, traditions from the *ḥadīth*, and/or the sayings of imams and other religious leaders. But there are limits to the goals and scope of female leadership in any classical religious establishment, including the various branches of Islam. A select number of women from all the main branches of Islam in America have embraced a feminist approach to the textual sources of Islam and advocated reforming positions in relation to women's status and gender relations. This approach has contested male-dominant views of women's rights in Islam, emphasizing female education and political leadership. Feminist Islam attempts a hermeneutical manipulation of religious texts to empower women not through open protest or dismissal of the foundational scriptures, but rather by reinterpretation of the verses and the law. Sunnī and Shīʿī women, immigrants and American-born, are struggling to be responsive to the traditions that have formed them and their communities. At the same time they are learning how to work together to challenge the bias that pits Islam against the West and to find their place and their voice as American Muslims.

Bibliography

C. L. Anway, *Daughters of another path. Experiences of American women choosing Islam*, Lees Summit, Mo. 1996.

M. Q. Aseel, *Torn between two cultures*, Sterling, Va. 2003.

L. Bakhtiyar, *Angels in the making*, Chicago 1996.

Y. Y. Haddad (ed.), *The Muslims of America*, New York 1991.

Y. Y. Haddad and J. L. Esposito (eds.), *Muslims on the Americanization path?*, New York 2000.
Y. Y. Haddad and A. T. Lummis, *Islamic values in the United States. A comparative study*, New York 1987.
Y. Y. Haddad and J. I. Smith, *Mission to America. Five Islamic sectarian communities in North America*, Gainesville, Fla. 1993.
—— (eds.), *Muslim minorities in the West. Visible and invisible*, Walnut Creek 2002.
A. G. Hasan, *American Muslims. The new generation*, New York 2001.
R. Hassan, Women in the context of change and confrontation within Muslim communities, in V. R. Mollenkott (ed.), *Women of faith in dialogue*, New York 1987, 96–109, repr. in World Council of Churches, *The challenge of pluralism*, Geneva 1988, 17–26.
A. Lebor, *A heart turned east. Among the Muslims of Europe and America*, New York 1997.
M. F. Lee, *The Nation of Islam. An American millenarian movement*, Syracuse, N.Y. 1996.
A. B. McCloud, *African American Islam*, New York 1995.
C. E. Marsh, *From Black Muslims to Muslims. The transition from separatism to Islam, 1930–1980*, Metuchen, N.J. 1984.
B. D. Metcalf (ed.), *Making Muslim space in North America and Europe*, Berkeley 1996.
A. Mohammad-Arif, *Salaam America. South Asian Muslims in New York*, trans. S. Patey, London 2000.
D. Ribadeneira, Questions on the Koran. Some Islamic women challenge interpretations they say have hurt their gender, in *Boston Globe*, 15 January 1997, A1.
J. I. Smith, *Islam in America*, New York 1999.

Rula Abisaab

Secularism

Arab States (excepting North Africa and the Gulf)

If secularism is regarded as a political ideology the aim of which is to remove religion from public political life, then secularism does not fare well in the Arab countries in the early twenty-first century. Political parties and movements, which only a few decades ago publicly advocated a firm separation between religion and state, *dīn* and *dawla*, now keep a low profile in such matters, or have lost their political influence. But if secularism is understood as the process by which "religion" is perceived as separate and different from "non-religion," then secularism prevails in Arab states and has done so for a long time.

In order to understand how gender intersects with secularism it is crucial to delineate the relationship between secularism as ideology and secularism as a historical process. One obvious link is the legal reforms of the Tanzimat period in the late nineteenth century whereby administrative law (*qānūn*) in various fields was separated from religious law (Sharīʿa). This continues through the break-up of the Ottoman Empire, the mandate period, and the establishment of independent states. During this period what became Syria, Lebanon, Iraq, and Jordan were secularized. The body politic came to be regarded as independent of the will of God. Educational institutions were set up outside religious institutions, and education was gradually seen to be relevant for other than religious purposes. In most countries men of religion became servants of the state. In this historical process secularism as an ideology was subservient to ideas of national rebirth or development. Women became symbols of the backward nation: just as the nation needed to be liberated, so did women. Religion as such was not attacked but only the effects of "backward" practices or "backward" religion. And, as has been amply shown, legal reform of family law was commonly influenced by European patriarchal notions as espoused in the Code Napoleon, for example. The very concept of personal status law is a direct import from France.

In the 1970s the aim of the Palestine Liberation Organization (PLO) was to establish a secular state in all of Palestine. At the turn of the twenty-first century the Palestinians in occupied territories are at loggerheads in defining the role of religion in a new constitution. This development can be seen as typical of political change in the Middle East where the last decades have marked a move away from secularism toward the increased influence of religion. But is such a characterization really true?

In the post-independence period the nationalist discourse overshadowed all other political discourses in these states. In such a discourse all citizens – men and women – have a holy duty to their country or to the Arab nation. It has been noted that expressions of nationalist movements in many parts of the world are infused with religious vocabularies stressing sacrifice and submission. While class interests were recognized by various socialist and communist parties, the needs of the nation were still the most important. While some parties, notably the communist parties in various countries, claimed that Arab women were downtrodden and exploited, their liberation could come only with the true liberation of the nation. Women therefore had to wait patiently for their rights to be realized, or in the case of the Palestinians, had to obediently serve the resistance. Such misogynist ideas were, of course, not invented in the Arab world, but have been part and parcel of modern nationalist and revolutionary movements everywhere. The secular vernacular of the PLO in the 1970s, it can be said, was part of a Zeitgeist, just as the religious vernacular today is an essential part of contemporary politics. It is also noteworthy that the religious vernacular of today has been shaped by decades of nationalist secular rhetoric.

Thus we need to look beyond the simple dichotomy of secular/religious. We should first of all ask: what are the perceptions of gender in secular nationalist and in religious ideologies? Second, we should seek to understand the relationship between perceptions of gender and gendered policies.

In most Arab states the modern constitution based on secular nationalist ideologies grants women and men equal rights and obligations. Women and men are perceived to be essentially similar. In the religious ideologies of some states and religious opposition movements women and men are regarded as different and dissimilar. While women and men are equal before God they have different rights and duties in society. Hence from an ideological point of view there is a vast difference between secular and religious ideologies. Yet the gendered policies are not simple reflections of these ideologies. Take Syria as an example of a secular state with a nationalist ideology. State employees have the same salary regardless of gender and entry to the university is based on grades and unrelated to gender (thus favoring women). But within the family a Syrian women is still not equal to a man. Family law is fairly complicated with special provisions for religious minorities. Christians apply the rules of the various churches for marriage and divorce and Druzes have no recourse to polygamy. There is no civil marriage in Syria, and a marriage between a Christian man and a Muslim woman is not legally recognized. Although there have been debates in Syria, just as in Lebanon, about the need to secularize family law, both the Sunnī majority and the various minorities have been staunchly opposed to this.

Leading Christians have voiced a fear over the demise of their congregations and for many of the Sunnī majority the secularization of family law is seen as the work of the ethnic and religious minorities. Due to this sensitivity, the Syrian regime, which is perceived as dominated by non-Sunnī interests, has been reluctant to push for reforms in family law. In 2003, however, more than ten thousand Syrians from all walks of life petitioned to increase the custody rights of mothers. The petition was presented as a bill in parliament, but instead the issue was settled by a presidential decree whereby custody rights were extended but not as far as the bill had suggested. In this way Syrian political leaders could show the world their support for women's rights while avoiding a sensitive public debate in parliament and preventing the conservative opposition from using the bill to make a religious statement. Hence Syria can be said to be a secular state but one in which religion plays a very important role in the gendering of polices.

Bibliography

T. Asad, *Formations of the secular. Christianity, Islam, modernism*, Stanford 2003.

D. Kandiyoti (ed.), *Women, Islam, and the state*, Philadelphia 1991.

M. L. Meriwether and J. E. Tucker (eds.), *Social history of women and gender in the modern Middle East*, Boulder, Colo. 1999.

J. M. Peteet, *Gender in crisis. Women and the Palestinian resistance movement*, New York 1991.

M. Yamani (ed.), *Feminism and Islam. Legal and literary perspectives*, Berkshire, U.K. 1996.

Annika Rabo

India

In India secularism has never been based on the idea of a wall of separation. Since independence in 1947, almost all discussions of secularism have been based on the idea of equal respect for all religions, a concept propounded by Mahatma Gandhi. This approach to secularism requires an equal respect for all religions within both the public and private spheres.

The meaning given to this concept of secularism depends in large part on the meaning given to equality. If equality is understood in a formal sense – treating likes alike – then secularism will insist on treating India's various religious communities alike. By contrast, if equality is understood in a more substantive sense – of addressing disadvantage – then secularism will allow for an accommodation of difference between religious groups, and the protection of the rights of religious minorities.

Indian secularism has been based on a substantive approach to the equal respect for all religions, which has allowed for the protection of religious minority rights primarily through temporary special measures. This includes the right of a religious minority to be governed by its personal laws. Women are governed by customary laws that are seen to infringe on their rights to gender equality. The progressive groups and the Hindu right (who are intent on setting up a Hindu state in India) have called for the adoption of a secular Uniform Civil Code (UCC) to be applicable to all communities in the same way. Muslim women fear that such a code would be based on the norms and values of the majority community, the Hindus. If the code is based on a formal notion of equality, then Muslim women will have to surrender their distinct religious practices in favor of equality. This forces a choice between religion and equality, which does not recognize that women from the minority community are not just women, or Muslims, they are Muslim women. Formal equality emphasizes sameness in treatment. The Hindu right uses its support for the UCC to argue that all women must be treated the same, which means Muslim women must be treated in the same way as Hindu women. Any recognition of difference is seen to constitute a violation of secularism. Any recognition of difference between women in different religious communities is seen to violate the constitutional guarantees of equality, which, the Hindu right states, require formal equal treatment. There are a few voices urging that any adoption of a UCC must be based on a substantive understanding of equality and intersectionality, that is, the recognition that Muslim women have suffered historical disadvantage based on both their gender and religious identity.

BIBLIOGRAPHY
T. Basu and T. Sarkar, *Khaki shorts, saffron flags. A critique of the Hindu right*, London 1993.
R. Bhargava (ed.), *Secularism and its critics*, Delhi 1998.
R. L. Chaudhari, *The concept of secularism in the Indian constitution*, New Delhi 1987.
B. Cossman and R. Kapur, *Secularism's last sigh? Hindutva and the (mis)rule of law*, New Delhi 2001.
M. S. Gowalkar, *Bunch of thoughts*, Bangalore 1966.
R. C. Heredia and E. Mathias (eds.), *Secularism and liberation. Perspectives and strategies for India today*, New Delhi 1995.
Z. Pathak and R. S. Rajan, Shah Bano, in *Signs. Journal of Women in Culture and Society* 14:3 (1989), 558–82.
T. Sarkar, *Hindu wife, Hindu nation. Community, religion and cultural nationalism*, London 2002.
T. Sarkar and U. Butalia (eds.), *Women and the Hindu right*, New Delhi 1995.
V. D. Savarkar, *Hindutva. Who is Hindu?* Pune, India 1929.

RATNA KAPUR

Iran

Gender has worked as a key category in defining the secularism of Iranian modernity. Iranian politics of modernity, since the mid-nineteenth century, has been marked by the emergence of a spectrum of nationalist and Islamist discourses. Within that spectrum, one notion of Iranian modernity took Europe as its model of progress and civilization (*taraqqī va tamaddun*) – the two central terms of that discourse – and increasingly combined that urge with recovery of pre-Islamic Iranianism. Other trends sought to combine their nationalism with Islam, by projecting Shiʿism as Iranianization of Islam in its early centuries (Tavakoli-Targhi 2001). Later twentieth-century developments largely led to ejection/abandonment of what may be called an Islamist nationalist trend from the complex hybridity of Iranian modernity – until its re-emergence in new configurations from the late 1980s. Until recently, it had become a commonly accepted notion that Iranian politics is and has been a battleground, since the nineteenth century, between modernity and tradition, with Islam always in the latter camp. Similarly, the beginning of Iranian feminism was not marked by a boundary, setting Islam to its beyond. Women's rights activists made rhetorical use of any available position to invent a female-friendly discourse.

Though there were debates among women on certain issues, these differences were not consolidated as incompatible and contradictory positions. Nor was Islam viewed as inherently anti-women. While anti-Constitutionalist forces grounded their political opposition to the constitution (1906–9) and to the reforms advocated by modernists, such as women's education, in their interpretations of Islamic precepts, the advocates of these reforms also drew from the same sources to argue their case.

The conflation of modernist with non-Islamic and Islamic with tradition and anti-modern took shape in the course of the twentieth century through a series of gendered conflicts.

A critical period was the reign of Reza Shah Pahlavī (1926–41), and more specifically the unveiling campaign initiated in winter 1936. As Tavakoli-Targhi has argued, in the nineteenth century European and Iranian/Islamic women (perceived as radically different) emerged as "terrain[s] of political and cultural contestations" (1990, 74). These contestations "resulted in the valorization of the veil (*ḥijāb*) as a visible marker of the self and the other" (2001, 54). Despite this mid-nineteenth-century preoccupation, during the early decades of the twentieth century unveiling was not on the agenda of reformers, who were more concerned with women's education and reform of family laws. A changing social context later in the twentieth century, however, began to bring the issue to the fore. Women began to be more visibly part of the social scene, through their participation in Constitutionalist activities, forming associations and holding meetings, establishing schools and holding public graduation ceremonies for students, and writing in the press and publishing women's journals. They also began to circulate more openly in the streets. Urban middle- and upper-class women began to slowly challenge and expand their very restrictive gender spaces – a space much more restricted than that of lower middle- and working-class women who had a claim to streets and moving around the city.

By the early 1920s, in certain neighborhoods, mostly "north" Tehran, women had begun to go out on the street without a face veil. Some women began to venture out without the chador, replacing it with loose long tunics. From the very beginning, unlike issues such as women's education or reform of family laws, unveiling was a contested issue among reforming women themselves (Hoodfar 1997, Najmabadi 2000).

After the official ban on the chador was imposed in 1936, state violence entered into the picture and an unbridgeable chasm opened up among women themselves. Girls were withdrawn from schools and kept at home. Women teachers who did not want to unveil resigned from their jobs or were dismissed. Girls' schools that had been the site for women's public togetherness, with women acting not only as students and teachers but also as citizens, now became the site of a division. The unveiling campaign as enforced by the government now expelled some from this common site. As with other measures taken by Reza Shah's government, increasingly modernization became conflated with only that modernity in which becoming modern was disaffiliated from Islam and made to coincide with pre-Islamic Iranianism. Those who had sought to combine their quest for modernity with a reconfiguration of Islam were unmistakably marked as traditional and anti-modern – an identification that has only in recent decades been reshaped. This process changed the meaning of modernity, Iranianism, and Islam. Iranian modernity took increasingly a non-Islamic (though not necessarily anti-Islamic) meaning. Iranian secularism and nationalism were critically reshaped through the expulsion of a different kind of modernity, one that had attempted to produce a different hybrid made of grafting Iranian nationalism onto Shiʿism.

In the 1960s, the contests over women's suffrage (1963) and the introduction of the Family Protection Act (1967) similarly consolidated secularism of modernity with the modernization program of the Pahlavī state which was opposed by the clerical establishment. Once again women's rights issues served as a marker of the Islamic and the secular. Perhaps more than any other sociopolitical and cultural issue of contention, women's rights issues became markers of secularism of modernity. This historical legacy lies behind the current fears of contamination of secularism and feminism by religion.

The emergence of a vocal feminist position from within the ranks of the Islamist movement over the past decades in Iran constitutes an important break from the past positioning of all Islam to the beyond of the modern and the secular. By opening up the domain of Islamic interpretation to non-believers and non-Muslims, by insisting on the equality of women and men in all areas, by disconnecting the presumed natural or God-given differences between women and men from the cultural and social constructions of gender, these currents have opened up a space for dialogue and alliance between Islamist women activists and secular feminists, reversing a 60-year-old rift in which each treated the other as antagonist.

Bibliography

F. Adelkhah, *Being modern in Iran*, trans. J. Derrick, London 1999.

H. Hoodfar, The veil in their minds and on our heads. Veiling practices and Muslim women, in L. Lowe and D. Lloyd (eds.), *The politics of culture in the shadow of capital*, Durham, N.C. 1997, 248–79.

A. Najmabadi, (Un)veiling feminism, in *Social Text* 64 (2000), 29–45.

P. Paidar, *Gender of democracy. The encounter between feminism and reformism in contemporary Iran*, Geneva 2001.

M. Tavakoli-Targhi, Imagining Western women. Occidentalism and Euro-eroticism, in *Radical America* 24:3 (1990), 73–87.

——, *Refashioning Iran. Orientalism, occidentalism and historiography*, New York 2001.

N. Tohidi, *Fiminīzm, dimukrāsī va islāmgarayī*, Los Angeles 1996.

Afsaneh Najmabadi

Pakistan

As in other parts of South Asia, the Woman Question in Pakistan has long been mired in a communitarian mode of analysis that privileges religion over other forms of collective identity. This is in no small part the legacy of a colonial sociology of knowledge that treated Indian society as an aggregation of religious communities, and created notions of majority and minority communities that ignored internal differentiations along lines of gender as well as class, caste, region, and language. Because Pakistan came to justify its creation on the basis of Islam, an emphasis on religion as the organizing principle of society has been a leitmotif of state policies in the postcolonial period as well. The fracturing of gender by religion has allowed the Pakistani state to continue to skirt the specific problems of its female citizens, the vast majority of whom live in conditions of abject poverty and disease.

Although extending control over virtually every aspect of life, the colonial state vowed not to interfere in the religion and culture of Indians. This policy was accomplished by removing the personal law of India's main religious communities from the purview of British colonial law. Sharīʿa law was shorn of public content – civil and criminal – and privatized to apply only to issues of marriage, divorce, and inheritance; cases pertaining to Muslim personal law, however, were heard in British law courts, an important appendage of the public sphere. Customary practices were allowed to overrule the personal laws of religious communities in regions that today constitute Pakistan.

The policy of non-interference in religion created an artificial separation between a political public and a religious and culturally informed private sphere. Far from emptying politics from the realms of religion or culture, and vice versa, the colonial state did much to bring these spheres closer together and reshape them in the process. Instead of being relegated to the private sphere, religious and cultural differences were orchestrated in the public arena by social groups competing for government patronage.

Women were central to this orchestration, in particular to the redefinition of a Muslim male middle- to upper-class identity. Concerned with projecting and preserving their distinctive religiously informed cultural identity, the Muslim *ashraf* (literally, "respectable") classes were anxious to protect their women from the "evil" influences of the colonial "public." This anxiety was shared by Muslims who were products of theological seminaries as well as so-called reformers ready to incorporate aspects of modernity in order to engage more effectively with Western colonialism. The cherished model of womanhood was that of the literate but domesticated, wise but chaste, intelligent but submissive wife, a conception that stood in stark contrast to the other major image of woman – the prostitute who lured respectable men into temptation and ruined them, financially, morally, and psychologically. The shattering experience of partition in 1947 only hardened the Muslim *ashraf* classes in their opinion that an unprotected woman was the source of immorality, irreligiosity, and social degradation.

A few gestures were made to prove the Islamic bona fides of the new state. The West Punjab Muslim Personal Law (Shariat) Application Act of 1948 superseded custom by conferring inheritance rights on women, including agricultural land. Apart from legal loopholes that allowed families to circumvent the law, giving women the right to inherit landed property, this was a class rather than a gender concession. Adopting the colonial state's restricted view of the Sharīʿa, the managers of Pakistan were prepared to consider social legislation on behalf of women dealing with marriage, divorce, and the guardianship of children. Middle- and upper-class women at the vanguard of the movement to secure women's rights used this opening to good advantage. The crowning achievement of women's rights activists was the Family Law Ordinance of 1961, which granted women rights in marriage, divorce, and guardianship. It was a fitting conclusion to a debate that had concentrated on issues of personal law at the expense of broader social and economic entitlements in the public sphere.

The Family Law Ordinance became one of the main targets of attack by the anti-women's rights lobby, threatening as it did the personal autonomy of Muslim men by bringing the protected space of the home under the direct scrutiny of the state. While opposing the rights of women as equal citizens, this lobby had no qualms about appropriating another key legacy of Western colonialism – the modern nation-state. For Pakistani women the problem has been worsened by authoritarian rulers looking for legitimacy by making women the focal point of state-sponsored Islamization. In the late 1970s and early 1980s, the military regime of General Zia ul-Haq introduced wildly discriminatory legal measures against women. This period in Pakistan's history marked a departure from the colonial pattern of confining the legal discourses of Islam to the personal domain. The Hudood Ordinance made rape and adultery indistinguishable. Along with the law of evidence, which reduced the worth of a woman's testimony to half that of a man, Zia's Islamization program created parallel systems of law, complicating the already inadequate mechanisms of assuring civil and criminal justice. In a sense, while the crusaders for democratic and women's rights like the Women Action Forum (WAF) were engaged in rearguard action to defend the small gains made since the 1960s in the area of personal law, a military ruler under the banner of Islam colonized a significant part of the public space where the battle for equal political, social, and economic rights ought to have been fought in the first place.

Successive governments have continued to invoke an Islamic national identity that overrides all differences. Together with the prolonged denial of democratic rights, the state's ideological posture has prevented a resolution of the nexus between gender and class and gender and community as well as between gender and nation – a failure exacerbated by the fact that in Pakistan, as in other parts of the world, it is largely the class origins of those at the vanguard of the "feminist movement" that have shaped the articulation of women's issues at the level of the state. Concerned more with rights denied them than the economic entitlements of their less privileged sisters, women belonging to the upper and middle strata have done a better job of defending their class interests than they have those of their gender. Educated, urban, middle- and upper-class in the main, these women have for the most part worked within the state's restricted definition of the women's question as one pertaining to issues of personal law – marriage, divorce, guardianship, and inheritance – and have thus largely ignored the social, economic, and political entitlements of women cutting across class and community, with grave implications for women's rights as equal citizens of the state.

Women in Pakistan are now debating the terrain on which their struggle for equal citizenship rights can be most effectively waged. A first step in that direction is a forceful rejection of the false dichotomy between the colonial public and communitarian private, which has provided the foundation for a military-bureaucratic public and a male-defined private sphere in Pakistan. Such a system affords protection of a sort to domesticated middle- to upper-class women while leaving women facing both class and gender oppression outside the purview of the discourse on rights. Violence against women has become a defining feature of an imploding authoritarian state and an exploding anarchic society. Tinkering with minor improvements in personal law leaves the entire field of political, economic, and social rights open to manipulation by the self-appointed guardians of an Islamic moral order.

Bibliography

D. S. Ahmad, *Masculinity, rationality and religion. A Feminist perspective*, Lahore 2001.

——, Hysterics, harems and houris. Cultural and psychological reflections on women, sexuality and Islam, in D. S. Ahmad, *Women and religion*, iv, Lahore 2000, 167-207.

R. Ahmad (trans.), *Beyond belief. Contemporary feminist Urdu poetry*, Lahore n.d.

S. S. Ikramullah, *From purdah to parliament*, New York 1998.

——, *Behind the veil. Ceremonies, customs and colour*, New York 1992.

A. Jalal, Convenience of subservience. Women and the State of Pakistan, in Deniz Kandiyoti (ed.), *Women, Islam and the state*, London 1991.

——, *Self and sovereignty. Individual and community in South Asian Islam*, London 2000, especially chapter 2.

B. Metcalf, Reading and writing about Muslim women in British India, in Z. Hasan (ed.), *Forging identities. Gender, communities, and the state in India*, Boulder, Colo. 1994.

G. Minault, *Secluded scholars. Women's education and Muslim social reform in colonial India*, Delhi 1998.

H. Papanek and G. Minault (eds.), *Separate worlds. Studies of purdah in South Asia*, Columbia, Mo. 1982.

D. Saiyid, *Muslim women of the British Punjab. From seclusion to politics*, New York 1998.

F. Shaheed and K. Mumtaz (eds.), *Women of Pakistan. Two steps forward, one step back*, London 1987.

A. Weiss, *Walls within walls. Life histories of working women in the Old City of Lahore*, Boulder, Colo. 1992.

Ayesha Jalal

Turkey

Secularism in Turkey has been closely intertwined with discourses and practices of Westernization, modernity, and nationalism. Secularization efforts date back to the nineteenth century, when the Ottoman state granted complete equality before the law to all subjects regardless of their religious creed. The subsequent modernization reforms gradually contributed to the emergence of Turkish protonationalisms at the end of the century. Although the nationalists had different stands on the degree and the role of religion in public life (Hanioğlu 1995), they generally agreed on the urgent need to modernize the state as well as the society for the sake of imperial survival. Eventually, the collapse of the empire in the First World War (1914–18) and the consequent victory in the War of Independence (1919–22) led to the crystallization and hegemony of Kemalist nationalism.

Kemalist nationalism constituted the radicalization of previous secularization attempts, primarily because it aimed at eradicating the legacy of the Ottoman practices that were partly legitimized by the Islamic Caliphate. Shortly after the proclamation of the Turkish Republic (1923), the Kemalists abolished the Caliphate (1924), closed down the Islamic brotherhoods (1925), adopted a modified version of the Swiss Civil Code (1926), and changed the script from Arabic to Latin (1928). It is apparent from the scope of the reforms that they aimed not only to transform the political structure, but also to rearrange social relations. The reforms did not, however, intend to directly challenge people's identification with Islam but to secularize everyday conduct with minimum popular resistance from the predominantly Muslim citizenry. More specifically, the Kemalists, like the late nineteenth-century modernizers, aimed at making religion subservient to the state's interests (Turhan 1991, Deringil 1998). They redefined the proper forms of religious practices in relation to their secularist ideals, frequently appealing to these novel concepts in consolidating their nationalist agenda, and strictly prohibited other groups from autonomously employing religious signs at state institutions. Islam was therefore confined to the private sphere and its entry to the public realm was determined by the secular nationalist standards (Tarhanlı 1993, Yavuz 2000, Keskin-Kozat 2003).

The nationalist co-optation of religion is best illustrated in the case of women's rights and the regulations concerning veiling. Women actively participated in the nationalist struggle by raising significant popular and financial support for the Kemalist forces. After the War of Independence, Kemalists attempted to incorporate women's autonomous activism into the nationalist framework so that they could both secure an important vanguard group for their secularization reforms and assimilate a strong rival that might easily mobilize resources against them (Çaha 1996, 115–16). They therefore granted women equal rights in educational, social, and political spheres. Various scholars took issue with the content and the limits of these reforms, asserting that although they provided women with unprecedented opportunities, they preserved the predominant patriarchal structures and failed primarily in rural areas (Tekeli 1990, Kandiyoti 1991, Arat 1994). Building upon such arguments, this entry explores how in the specific case of veiling women's emancipation in Turkey is significantly contingent on their compliance with the nationalist regulations of Islam.

Kemalists did not initially ban but informally discouraged women's veiling, arguing that it symbolized social backwardness and religious obscurantism. It was implicitly assumed in the early twentieth century that female civil servants, parliamentarians, and students should not wear headscarves. Nevertheless, the relative relaxation of state controls over religion in the 1950s and the resurgence of religious activism in the 1960s compelled the Kemalist elite to take more austere measures. In the 1970s, a considerable number of veiled university students were dismissed from school because of their improper attire. In 1983, the Higher Education Council introduced the first nationwide ban on the wearing of the veil on university campuses. The ban was severely contested by the Islamist groups and later by the members of the Motherland Party, then in power. The Turkish Constitutional Court put an end to the legal aspect of the debate in 1988, stipulating that the veil was a political rather than a religious symbol and hence it should not be worn at universities (Özdalga 1998, 41–6).

It is important to dwell upon the consequences of the ban on veiled women's socioeconomic and political status. While the court's decision does not prohibit women from wearing headscarves in public spaces, veiling is prohibited in educational institutions, which provide individuals with the formal training and qualifications necessary for attaining future success. The decision also serves as the primary legal justification for denying veiled women employment in the state sector, a crucial source of employment in contemporary Turkey. Women's participation in national politics is also restricted by the internal ordinances of the parliament, which endorse that women should not wear headscarves within the General Assembly. In 1991, two veiled women, Neslin Ünal of the Nationalist Action Party and Merve Kavakçı of the Virtue Party, were elected to the parliament for the first time in the history of the republic. Whereas the former took off her veil and served her term, the latter faced vehement protest from secularists for having come to the oath-taking ceremony with her veil on. Kavakçı had to leave the chambers without being sworn in and later lost her parliamentary seat on another technicality (Göçek 2000).

The legal restrictions on veiling are usually coupled with a general endorsement from secularist social groups that "women may wear headscarves at their homes but doing so as a civil servant or student should be considered as a sign of religious fundamentalism" (Oran 2000). Such exclusions of veiled women from the nationalist public sphere have accelerated their involvement in the Islamist circles, which also curtailed their autonomous demands. Considering the Woman Question secondary to other macro-political issues (Karabıyık-Barbarosoğlu 2000), Islamist elites granted them inadequate representation in the party mechanisms (Saktanber 2002), supervised their publications to the degree of purging them (Göle 1996, 121–6), and denied employment in order to foster a "modern" company image (Özbilgin 2000). Hence, at the beginning of the twenty-first century, secularism and Islamist mobilization in Turkey both enable and constrain women's struggle for greater rights in different ways.

Bibliography

Z. Arat, Turkish women and the republican reconstruction of tradition, in F. M. Göçek and S. Balaghi (eds.), *Reconstructing gender in the Middle East. Power, Identity, and tradition*, New York 1994, 57–78.

Ö. Çaha, *Sivil Kadın. Türkiye'de sivil toplum ve kadın*, Ankara 1996.

S. Deringil, *The well-protected domains. Ideology and the legitimation of power in the Ottoman Empire, 1876–1909*, London 1998.

F. M. Göçek, To veil or not to veil? The contested location of gender in contemporary Turkey, in *Interventions* 1:4 (2000), 521–35.

N. Göle, *The forbidden modern. Civilization and veiling*, Ann Arbor 1996.

Ş. M. Hanioğlu, *Young Turks in opposition*, New York 1995.

D. Kandiyoti, End of the empire. Islam, nationalism and women in Turkey, in D. Kandiyoti (ed.), *Women, Islam and state*, Philadelphia 1991, 1–21.

F. Karabıyık-Barbarosoğlu, Kendisi Olmaktan Vazgeçmiş İslamcı Kadınlar, in *Yeni Şafak*, 10 March 2000.

B. Keskin-Kozat, Entangled in secular nationalism, Islamism and feminism. The life of Konca Kuriş, in *Cultural Dynamics* 15:2 (2003), 183–212.
B. Oran, İç politikada nafile sorunumuz. Türban, in *Agos*, 6 October 2000.
M. F. Özbilgin, Is the practice of equal opportunities management keeping pace with theory? Management of sex equality in the financial services sector in Britain and Turkey, in *Human Resource Development International* 3:1 (2000), 43–67.
E. Özdalga, *The veiling issue, official secularism, and popular Islam in modern Turkey*, Richmond, Surrey 1998.
A. Saktanber, Whose virtue is this? The Virtue Party and women in Islamist politics in Turkey, in P. Bacchetta and M. Powers (eds.), *Right-wing women. From conservatives to extremists around the world*, New York 2002, 71–84.
İ. B. Tarhanlı, *Müslüman toplum, "laik" devlet. Türkiye'de Diyanet İşleri Başkanlığı*, Istanbul 1993.
Ş. Tekeli, The meaning and limits of feminist ideology in Turkey, in F. Özbay (ed.), *Women, family and social change in Turkey*, Amsterdam 1990, 139–59.
İ. Turan, Islam and nationalism as political ideology, in R. Tapper (ed.), *Islam in modern Turkey. Religion, politics, and literature in a secular state*, New York 1991, 40–56.
H. M. Yavuz, Cleansing Islam from the public sphere, *Journal of International Affairs* 54:1 (2000), 21–42.

BURÇAK KESKIN-KOZAT

Western Europe

The Western notion of secularism in the context of law means the withdrawal or dismissal of properties, people, or things from the churches' observance or power (Lübbe 1965, 23). In a more general sense secularism refers to theories of modernization which assumed, up until the late 1970s, that religion had lost its relevance and meaning in society. Today sociologists of religion describe secularism as a typical development in modern times that only aims at changing the shape of religion in modern societies (Casanova 1996). This is shown, for instance, by the differentiation of subsystems in society, which also means the separation of religion and state, and the individualization of religion. Secularism is analyzed by stripping off religious meanings in regard to religious symbols, practices, and ideas while keeping it a profane tradition or social structure (Weber 1920).

The Western historical and sociological concepts of secularism are not entirely transferable to Islam. Nevertheless in the context of immigration to Europe and the confrontation with Western Christian secularism, they are helpful heuristic paradigms for the understanding of some of the developments of Islam in Western Europe.

SECULARISM AS DIFFERENTIATION OF RELIGION AND STATE

Muslims in Western Europe have not yet shaped a church-like organization. The special circumstances they must acknowledge in their new situation, however, involve particular methods of accommodation. Since second generation immigrants are more oriented to Europe, they have built mosque associations in a more Western style. These mosque associations still substitute the missing cultural institutions of their homelands. Thus in many cases the mosque is used, for example, to celebrate religious ceremonies that would not take place in or around the mosque in most parts of the Muslim world, in particular weddings, rites of circumcision, or funeral ceremonies (Shadid and Koningsveld 1995, 25). Customs that in another context were seen to be located between the realm of religion and culture are now defined as religiously bounded. The imam, who traditionally had only the function of prayer leader, has various "religious" tasks in Europe and consequently has become a more religious authority. Mosque associations also offer cultural and social activities and courses along with religious services. A differentiation is made between members and non-members of mosques, again differing from what pertains in most of the Muslim world. The pluralistic situation in which Muslims find themselves sets many of them in a more distant and perhaps more service-oriented relation to the mosque (Shadid and Koningsveld 1995).

At the same time, a female second generation has moved into the mosques and aspired to participate, since the mosques are the only public places in which, for most Muslims, it is socially acceptable for women to be present. Even though the boards of directors of the mosque associations have mostly been filled by men, women continue to gain more influence in the mosques. Today no mosques are built without rooms for female believers. The women provide religious and non-religious activities, including instructional courses, in these rooms. Women have also formed their own associations in the fields of consulting and education (for example, Klinkhammer 2000, Jonker 2001). This autonomous empowerment of Muslim women, which is observable in all Western European countries, is supported by some associations. One of the larger German associations has established a permanent women's representative. In France, Belgium, and other countries the state representatives demand the participation of women when they begin to negotiate on their behalf.

Beyond these structural developments, which implicitly accept the separation of state and religion, there are also public statements of individuals and mosque associations. The most recent and most widely discussed statements are the German Islamic Charta (2002), which declares in 21 points the loyal relationship of Islam to the secular democratic society, and the books of Tariq Ramadan (1994, 1998), who also argues that Muslims can live in harmony as religious people in a secular state.

Secularism as individualization of religion

The individualization of religion can be based on the possibility of selecting one's own way of religious life. For example, Muslims in Europe choose between different forms of Islamic associations – those concerning religion, ethnicity, or other matters. Individualization of religion can also refer to the way and content of religious life. This form of individualization seems to be more characteristic of the better educated second generation Muslim women and men.

Muslims generally express the desire to experience Islam and the Islamic beliefs in their life, although many Muslims disapprove of formal authorities like muftis. They often read the Qurʾān on their own and interpret it in light of their own personal experiences. Some of them are interested in spiritually-oriented and experience-oriented forms of Islam such as *dhikr*.

Some empirical studies have shown that certain practices of Muslim women, such as wearing a headscarf, automatically mean falling back into old traditional tracks. For many women, however, it is very important to affirm that this behavior is not based on a traditional understanding of relationships, personality, and Islam. These women, who are mostly well educated, insist that they have chosen to wear the covering on their own initiative. They feel accountable to neither a man nor their parents in their decision, but affirm themselves personally bounded to Allah, who is the center of their religion. They interpret the religion of Islam from their own experience and their claim to freedom and independence in private and public spheres. Of course this interpretation is also connected to the respect that is thereby accorded to them by other Muslims, both men and women. As they understand it, the decision to accept the headscarf as an expression of their personal religiosity is made exclusively through this possibility of individual freedom of action (Klinkhammer 2003, Karakaşoğlu 1998).

Secularization of religious celebrations and ideas

Genuine secularization of Islamic ideas and practices is rare in Western Europe, although there is almost no research in this field. While great attention has been given to the increasing identification of Muslim migrants with Islam in the last 20 years, the question of a decreasing relevance of Islamic norms and practices has not yet been examined.

Certain realities, however, can be noted. It is observable that secular but not atheistic Muslims in Europe celebrate the last days of Ramadan. Ramadan Bayram, a feast for all Muslims, has been transformed into a family celebration similar to Christmas in Christian-secular culture. It may well be that certain Muslim concepts, such as *tawḥīd* (unity), may also be taken over and adapted to a secular Muslim mind. In this sense, secularism points to some principles or models of cultural behavior that have already been stabilized by religion. However, most of the time Muslim migrants adapt to Western secular culture concepts and modes of behavior such as individualism. At the same time some Muslims have started to celebrate secular feasts that are common in Western societies, for example birthdays and the New Year (Yalzin-Heckman 1994).

Thus in spite of the increasing influence of modernization on the religion of Islam in Western Europe, secularism in terms of a decrease of meaning or of the relevance of religion is not apparent. Islam has become an important issue in the politics of personal and collective identity in the context of migration. Many Muslims in Western Europe differentiate their community structures from those of the general cultural in which they are now located, even though it is clear that they are affected by the trend of individualization. The individualization of Muslim women actually seems to bring about the opposite of a decrease in the relevance of religion insofar as it makes Islam visible in the public sphere through women's decision to wear a headscarf. These developments confirm recent analyses of modernization, which have shown that secularism generates changes in the face of the religion, but does not necessarily bring about its dissolution.

Bibliography

J. Casanova, *Public religions in the modern world*, Chicago 1994.

G. Jonker, Religiosität und Partizipation der zweiten Generation. Frauen in Berliner Moscheen, in R. Klein-Hessling, S. Nökel, and K. Werner (eds.), *Der neue Islam der Frauen. Weibliche Lebenspraxis in der globalisierten Moderne. Fallstudien aus Afrika, Asien und Europa*, Bielefeld 1999, 106–23.

Y. Karakaşoğolu, "Kopftuchstudentinne" turkischer Herkunft an deutschen Universitaten. Impliziter Islamicmusvorwurf und Diskriminierungserfahrungen, in H. Bijlefeld and W. Hetimeyer (eds.), *Politisierte Religion*, Frankfurt 1998, 450–93.

G. Klinkhammer, *Moderne Formen islamischer Lebensführung. Eine qualitative Untersuchung zur Religiosität sunnitisch geprägter Türkinnen der zweiten Generation in Deutschland*, Marburg 2000.

——, Modern constructions of Islamic identities. The case of second generation Muslim women in Germany, in *Marburg Journal of Religion* 8:1 (2003), http://www.uni-marburg.de/religionswissenschaft/journal/mjr/current.html>.

J. M. van der Lans and M. Rooijackers, Types of religious belief and unbelief among second generation Turkish migrants, in W. A. Shadid and P. S. Koningsveld (eds.), *Islam in Dutch society. Current developments and future prospects*, Kampen, The Netherlands 1992, 56–65.

C. Leggewie, Der Islam im Westen. Zwischen Neo-Fundamentalismus und Euroislam, in J. Bergmann, A. Hahn, and T. Luckmann (eds.), *Religion und Kultur*, special issue of *Kölner Zeitschrift für Soziologie und Sozialpsychologie* (Opladen) 33 (1993), 271–91.

H. Lübbe, *Säkularisierung. Geschichte eines ideenpolitischen Begriffs*, Munich 1965.

T. Ramadan, *Les musulmans dans la laïcité. Responsabilités et droits des musulmans dans les sociétés occidentales*, Lyon 1994.

——, *To be a European Muslim*, Lyon 1998.

W. A. Shadid and P. S. Koningsveld, Blaming the system or blaming the victim? Structural barriers facing Muslims in Western Europe, in W. A. Shadid and P. S. Koningsveld (eds.), *The integration of Islam and Hinduism in Western Europe*, Kampen 1991, 2–21.

——, Integration and change. Some future prospects, in W. A. Shadid and P. S. Koningsveld (eds.), *The integration of Islam and Hinduism in Western Europe*, Kampen 1991, 228–39.

——, *Religious freedom and the position of Islam in Western Europe. Opportunities and obstacles in the acquisition of equal rights*, Kampen 1995.

N. Tietze, *Jeunes musulmans de France et d'Allemagne. Les constructions subjectives de l'identité*, Paris 2002.

M. Weber, *Gesammelte Aufsätze zur Religionssoziologie*, i, Tübingen 1920.

L. Yalzin-Heckmann, Are fireworks Islamic? Towards an understanding of Turkish migrants and Islam in Germany, in C. Steward and R. Shaw (eds.), *Syncretism/anti-syncretism. The politics of religious synthesis*, New York 1994, 178–95.

GRITT KLINKHAMMER

Sexual Abuse: Children

The Balkans

This entry reviews sexual abuse of children in central Balkan countries and territories (Slovenia, Croatia, Bosnia-Herzegovina, Serbia, Kosovo, Montenegro, Macedonia, and Vojvodina), where different Muslim ethnic groups live as a majority or a minority, and mostly as indigenous peoples (Roma, Bosniaks, Albanians, Turks, and others).

At the end of Ottoman rule, Sharīʿa courts were transformed from courts of general jurisdiction into special courts whose jurisdiction was reduced to the issues of family and succession law, and issues related to endowments. The Austro-Hungarian Empire took over these courts and the establishment of the Kingdom of Serbs, Croats, and Slovenes did not change the position of Sharīʿa courts significantly. After the Second World War, a law was passed disbanding Sharīʿa courts in the People's Republic of Bosnia-Herzegovina. That was the end of Sharīʿa law as part of the applicable law, but its norms had a major influence on the morals and customs of Muslims in Bosnia-Herzegovina.

According to the Qurʾān and the traditions of the Prophet, incest and other forms of sexual abuse are mortal sins. They threaten all three levels of human dignity: soul (God inspired human being with His spirit); body (human beings are created in the most beautiful uprightness); and sociability (a general alliance of all human beings with God). This attitude, based on spiritual tradition, pervades Muslim culture. However, the only comprehensive legal sanctioning against such crimes has been achieved with the current application of secular criminal laws.

Incomplete research on sexual abuse in Macedonia, Serbia, Montenegro, Croatia, Kosovo, Vojvodina, and Bosnia-Herzegovina, while they were federal units of the former Yugoslavia, confirms that this issue was mainly absent from courts. The phenomenon was, as a rule, considered taboo, and both victims and witnesses avoided reporting them to the police and courts. Although crimes of sexual abuse were considered the worst violations of individual and collective dignity, publicizing them would permanently stigmatize the victim and his or her family. Records of Sharīʿa courts in Bosnia-Herzegovina cover various crimes, but a sample of records revealed no court case regarding sexual abuse of children between the sixteenth and nineteenth centuries. New legislation concerning sexual abuse of children has had broad popular support.

Sexual abuse is defined in the criminal legislation of Bosnia-Herzegovina (in the Criminal Codes of the Federation of Bosnia-Herzegovina and the Republic of Srpska), Serbia, Montenegro, and Croatia. Crimes of sexual abuse of children were included in those laws in the first years of the twenty-first century as a result of a worldwide debate on these issues. Description of the crime of sexual abuse is now more detailed than was the case in legislation after the Second World War and earlier. The criminal legislation of Bosnia-Herzegovina includes sexual abuse of children in the group of crimes against sexual freedom and morality. Sexual abuse of children includes rape, sexual intercourse by abuse of office, sexual intercourse with a child, fornication, sexual act in front of a child or a minor, forcible prostitution, using a child or minor for pornographic purposes, introducing a child to pornography, and incest. There are no significant differences in the crimes defined as sexual violence in the criminal legislation of Bosnia-Herzegovina, Serbia, Montenegro, and Croatia.

According to statistical data of the ministry of the interior in Bosnia-Herzegovina, 208 criminal reports on sexual abuse of children were filed between 1997 and 2002. Perpetrators were 15 to 85 years of age. Victims of violence were, as a rule, girls aged 3 to 18. According to the Helsinki Committee for Human Rights in Bosnia-Herzegovina, 16 percent of all abuse is sexual abuse. These data include all ethnic communities in Bosnia-Herzegovina (Serbs/Orthodox Christians, Croats/Roman Catholics, Bosnians/Muslims, and others). There are no data regarding distribution of these crimes among different ethnic populations. During the systematic rape of Bosnian Muslim women in the 1992–6 war against Bosnia-Herzegovina, many cases of rape of underage girls were recorded. In some Serb prisons, such as Foča, Muslim girls were kept and systematically raped.

According to public sources, 100 cases of sexual abuse of children were registered in Croatia between 1996 and 1999. Fifty percent of the cases happened within the home, and 35 percent of perpetrators were family members. According to the statistics of the Serbian ministry of the interior, 892 criminal reports of sexual abuse of children were filed between 1998 and 2002. According to the data of the nongovernmental organization (NGO) Incest Trauma Center in Serbia, the number of reported cases of child sexual abuse has increased since 2000; currently, some 50 new cases are reported every week. Data on sexual abuse of children in Slovenia, Kosovo, Macedonia, and Montenegro were not available.

After the war against Bosnia-Herzegovina (1992–6), numerous NGOs for human rights and related issues were established in the country and in the region. These organizations work on raising awareness regarding women's issues, gender, and sexual abuse of children in accordance with general European standing on these matters. There are public demands all over the region to improve the existing documents by precisely defining sexual abuse of children. There are also more and more requests to develop legislative, executive, and judicial powers in order to efficiently register, prosecute, and veto these crimes. These issues are presented in public debates and in the media, particularly in women's and feminist organizations, but so far no general position on them has been reached. There are no unified and developed procedures for registering sexual abuse of children in any of these countries, which is why the existing statistics are inconsistent. In some countries there is an obvious increase of the number of cases of sexual abuse of children that is not visible in others. It is reasonable to assume that the magnitude of sexual abuse of children in all the countries concerned is similar.

Bibliography

Primary Sources

CID, *I begged them to kill me* [in Bosnian], Sarajevo 1999.

Commission for Gathering Facts on War Crime, *The sin of silence. Risk of speech* [in Bosnian], Sarajevo 1999.

F. Karčić, *Studies of Sharīʿa law* [in Bosnian], Sarajevo 1997.

M. Milosavljević, *Child sexual abuse* [in Bosnian], Sarajevo 2002.

Z. Mršević, *Incest between myth and reality* [in Serbian], Beograd 1997.

Secondary Sources

M. Singer, *Criminal-judicial responsibility and protection of youth* [in Croatian], Zagreb 1998.

V. Nikolić, *Domestic violence in Serbia* [in Serbian], Beograd 2002.

Džamna Duman

The Caucasus and Turkey

All countries of the southern Caucasus region – Armenia, Azerbaijan, and Georgia – as well as neighboring Turkey, have signed the United Nations Convention on the Rights of the Child (CRC). This stipulates that a child is any human being under 18 unless they have attained legal majority earlier. The particular articles of the CRC that apply to child sexual abuse and exploitation are numbers 19 and 34, 35, and 39. Only the two majority Islamic countries – Turkey and Azerbaijan – have additionally signed the Optional Protocol on the Rights of the Child on the Sale of Children, Child Prostitution and Child Pornography.

Age limits for sexual activity remain controversial in the Caucasus. Girls in both majority Islamic and Christian countries of the Caucasus region and Turkey, living in rural areas especially, can marry "voluntarily" as early as age 12 or 13. Younger brides marry older adolescents or young adult men, and almost certainly drop out of the education system without completing minimum schooling. Definitions of abuse, however, imply a lack of consent for sexual contact between a child and an adult or someone at least 5 years older. Some Western European countries have set the legal age for consent to sexual relations at 12 or 14. National legislations in the Caucasus lack precise legal age prescriptions on this issue, though an initiative in the Georgian parliament in 2003 requests that this limit now be set at 16.

Abuse within the family and the commercial sexual exploitation of children, both boys and girls, exist universally to some degree. However, a lack of serious research in the Caucasus is actually contributing to and covering the growing problems.

In Turkey there is cause for alarm because of the lack of investigations into cases of abused children. Cases are increasingly reported, but inadequate follow-ups mean that the children continue to be abused, or have even been known to be killed when abuse was reported.

Rape has the clearest legislative consequences in all countries concerned. In Georgia, the criminal code specifies details of the act and the ages, as well as length of imprisonment; for example, raping a person younger than 14 is punishable by imprisonment from 10 to 20 years. In Azerbaijan, the criminal code mentions the rape of infants as well as of juveniles, acts which engender imprisonment from 8 to 15 years.

Child prostitution in the Caucasus

Georgian law does not define prostitution in general or child prostitution in particular. Prices for an underage prostitute in Georgia range from around $5 for 2 hours in small rooms in beerhouses, to luxury hotel prices at $200 per night. None of the countries concerned, however, have gathered real statistical data concerning child prostitution. In 1997 the Georgian Ministry of Internal Affairs had registered 50 minors who worked as prostitutes in Tbilisi. A study by the United Nations Children's Fund (UNICEF) and the Center for Intercultural and Social Studies in Tbilisi showed that 112 prostitutes aged between 12 and 16 were known, with an average age of 13, most of whom were encouraged, assisted, or forced into the activity by their parents or families. The activity often grows out of other street activities such as begging, though in some cases girls from rural families come to the capital for prostitution without their families' knowledge. Child prostitution in Georgia is a well-organized business, with the ensuing financial interests of certain circles, including the very government services that would be expected to enforce legislation; instead they control most prostitution establishments, albeit inconspicuously. Also, expatriates have been accused of increasing the market, and a 2003 report on expatriate patrons of a beer bar in Tbilisi caused a well-respected international peace-keeping agency to reorganize itself and discreetly dismiss certain ranking employees.

Trafficking

The Caucasus countries are under-informed on most issues of child abuse and exploitation, and none have fully investigated trafficking. The prostitution of women and minor Georgian girls in Turkey has been largely documented, both by scientific research and on Internet "sex tourism" sites. The baseline for the issue on trafficking is the Stockholm Declaration on Commercial Sexual Exploitation of Children. Although Turkey has ratified the latter, none of the southern Caucasus countries have.

A Georgian minister of internal affairs stated that "no kind of trafficking exists," while "the UN, OSCE, IMO, Interpol, Europol, US State Dept, European Commission, and other agencies unanimously rate Georgia as the leader in Caucasus countries and Central Asia" (UNICEF 2001). Jean-Christophe Peuch, of Radio Liberty, Prague, reported on 27 July 2001 that "deteriorating economic conditions, corruption and a high rate of unemployment are factors that have contributed to the growing phenomenon of trafficking women and girls from the three Caucasus states of Armenia, Azerbaijan and Georgia." Azeri and Armenian women are trafficked to Turkey and the United Arab Emirates while the destinations of Georgians are more diverse. An End Child Prostitution, Child Pornography and Trafficking of Children (ECPAT) report of 2000 states that "Georgia holds the leading position" in the increase of commercial sexual exploitation of children (CSEC) in the Central Asia and Caucasus regions. Georgia heads the three categories of child prostitution, child pornography, and trafficking in children in Central Asia and the Caucasus, although at the same time attempts are being made to combat the problems through non-governmental organization work and with UNICEF. However, Azerbaijan has serious problems in child prostitution and trafficking, yet CSEC in that country is not regarded as a problem that warrants measures to be taken. Armenia has an important trafficking problem but, again, no measures are being taken.

The increased trafficking through Turkey reported by IOM includes trafficked migrants exposed to labor exploitation, but children are particularly vulnerable to these smugglers who commit human rights violations "in the form of rape, physical and mental abuse, food deprivation, abandonment and even death" (IOM 2000).

Bibliography

ECPAT (End Child Prostitution, Child Pornography and Trafficking of Children), < http:// www.ecpat.net/eng/index.asp>.

IOM (International Organization for Migration), *Report on irregular migration in Turkey*, 2003.

Parliament of Georgia, Independent Board of Advisors, *Legal mechanisms against commercial sexual exploitation of children*, Tbilisi 2001.

UNICEF (United Nations Children's Fund), The general situation of children's rights and commercial sexual exploitation of children in Georgia, in *Situation analysis of women and children in Georgia*, Tbilisi 2000.

UNOCHA (United Nations Office for the Coordination of Humanitarian Assistance to Afghanistan) Tbilisi, *Georgia humanitarian situation and strategy 2003*, Tbilisi 2003.

World Congress against Commercial Sexual Exploitation of Children, *Declaration and Agenda for action*, Stockholm 1996.

Women for Future, *The problem of women's trafficking in Georgia*, Tbilisi 2002

Mary Ellen Chatwin

Iran

A review of Iranian newspapers and magazines reveals that child sexual abuse is a problem and there is a need for laws protecting victims when sexual abuse happens inside the family. Among constraints that have hindered the preparation of a national plan of action is cultural resistance to addressing the problem because the subject is largely taboo. Often the issue is dealt with more generally under headings such as "violence" and "trauma" (UNICEF 2003). Sexual violence and abuse within the family is rarely reported and children themselves are largely silent on this issue. Laws make reporting by children unlikely. Article 220 of the Iranian Penal Code recognizes only a light sentence and fine for a father who kills his child in the course of administering "educational" punishment. Early marriage with the permission of the guardian is valid provided that the interests of the ward are duly observed. According to ʿUlyā-i Zand (2002), this could also potentially be a form of female sexual abuse.

Despite the cultural resistance and the taboo nature of the subject, there has been a recent interest in this issue due to the problem with runaway youths. Investigations show that a large number of girls run away from home because they are mistreated by their parents (Shīkhāvand 2003). Many suffer sexual abuse from their father, or brothers, and out of fear of being beaten they do not dare to speak about it. Many boys between the ages of 11 and 15 are victims of pedophilia, a subject also largely taboo in this society (Shīkhāvand 2003).

ʿUlyā-i Zand (2002), a prominent researcher who has done extensive work concerning prostitution in Iran, found that in a sample of 147 women prostitutes, 22.5 percent of them had been sexually abused as a child by their father, brother, step-father, friend, or neighbors. In the latest report by the Iranian Surgeon General, out of 324 reported cases of child sexual abuse, 237 were females under 15 with ages ranging from 0 to 13 (83 percent were between 11 and 13). ʿUlyā-i Zand (2002) cites children as "the most innocent victims of sexual assault" in the society. She adds, "speaking concerning sexual abuse of children is quite hard, but keeping mum on the issue is unjust." She also claims that studies of 99 percent of underage children who had been sexually assaulted indicate the phenomenon is more common among "lax and despotic families." Among those interviewed, mothers had knowledge of the assault in 48 percent of child abuse cases but refused to disclose it for fear of the "despotic father's" reaction (ʿUlyā-i Zand 2001).

In another important study by Ibrāhīmī-Qavām (1991), 39 girls and 11 boys between ages 10 and 18 who reported sexual abuse to their school officials were compared with 200 adolescents with comparable socioeconomic status who had not suffered from sexual abuse. Out of these 50 adolescents, 18 had been abused by father, 7 by brother, 9 by neighbor, 4 by stranger, 5 by cousin, 1 by brother-in-law, and 4 by someone unknown. The ages at the time of abuse ranged from 4 to 15. The result indicates a significantly higher level of disturbance with respect to anxiety symptoms, social avoidance, fear of negative evaluation, physiological and psychological disturbances, and self esteem among victims of sexual abuse, especially female victims.

These scattered pieces of research indicate that there have been some attempts on the part of female scholars and advocates to discuss the issue in depth with the hope of creating laws to protect children from sexual abuse and breaking the taboo that surrounds it so that children can feel safe to report the abuse.

Bibliography

150 Children end up in Iran court daily for harassment, in *Ḥayāt-i naw* (Tehran daily), 20 November 2001.

S. Ibrāhīmī-Qavām, Study on the level of anxiety and self esteem among victims of sexual abuse, unpublished manuscript, Tehran 1991.

Shīkhāvand, interview in *Hambastigī* (Tehran daily), 20 November 2001, 11.

S. ʿUlyā-i Zand, Unsuitable marriage. A fundamental ground for prostitution, in *Journal of Scientific Research on Social Welfare* 5:2 (2002), 119–41.

UNICEF, *Commercial sexual exploitation of children. The situation in the Middle East/North Africa region*, Second World Congress against Commercial Sexual Exploitation of Children, 20 October 2003, <http://www.unicef.org/events/yokohama /backgound8.html>.

Manijeh Daneshpour

South Asia

In South Asia, sexuality remains a taboo topic in public discourse and, consequently, little research has been conducted on sexual abuse of adults or children. In the 1990s, three surveys conducted in Delhi and Mumbai by Sakshi, RAHI, and the Tata Institute of Social Sciences indicate that over 40 percent of young girls in India might be victims of sexual abuse. The majority of abusers are kin to their young victims and trusted individuals such as servants and family friends. Of the 800 cases of rape reported in Pakistan in 1994, 50 percent of victims were minors and only a fraction of the perpetrators were outside the girls' families.

In South Asian Islamic cultures, chastity is considered to be a woman's crowning glory and without it, she is worth nothing to her family and society. This dictum extends even to young girls. For a "good" girl, sexual awakening is permitted only after marriage and by her husband. Girls and women fervently internalize the social message that a virtuous female is sexually naive. This may place young girls in a difficult bind, not only in terms of defending themselves against sexual assault, but also speaking openly when such abuse occurs.

Since every sex act is considered to be a carnal deed even when coerced, a girl/woman is considered to be indirectly, if not directly, complicit in her own victimization. While Sharīʿa confers adulthood on boys at 18, girls become adults at menarche. Thus, underage female rape victims in Pakistan are often charged with *zinā*. Regardless of age, a girl is "damaged goods" if sexually violated and can almost never reclaim her former right to moral integrity and decency. Once a girl's "sexual ruin" becomes public knowledge, she may be perceived as an open target for men within and outside her family as it is assumed that she is now valueless. A girl's safety often rests on the impeccability of her social reputation. Many rape victims in Pakistan have been murdered to restore family honor. Consequently, parents seldom report the rape or sexual abuse of their daughters to legal authorities. Instead, mention of such violence is routinely suppressed and kept secret even from close relatives. Parallel attitudes toward and consequences for men, even perpetrators, do not seem to exist.

While perpetrators of child sexual assault could be of any class, in South Asian Islamic communities, assault might be less common among girls of middle- and upper-class families as they are rarely allowed out unescorted. Thus, class privilege provides some protection to girls against assault by strangers. Girls from poor families, who may work as maids or laborers, are exceptionally vulnerable to sexual assault by their employers or acquaintances, as they have no significant family protection to depend on.

A few other social structural conditions affect child sexual abuse in all South Asian societies. First, although the two sexes are strictly separated to ensure girls' safety, the extended family configuration allows many men, related and unrelated, access to the family/women's quarters. While older women stringently supervise activities of adolescent females, younger girls are given more latitude of action and movement under the assumption that their age makes them immune to unwanted sexual attention. Such relative freedom renders young girls vulnerable to abuse by acquaintances and relatives.

Since children are brought up in strict sex-segregation, even siblings and cousins who grow up in the same household scarcely get an opportunity to develop mutual friendship and companionable affection. Thus they may deem sexual relationship as the only feasible option between opposite genders. In a society where girls and women are almost universally out of reach, adolescent boys and men of all ages may be inclined to sexually exploit vulnerable young girls, whom they can control through threats and coercion.

Second, in the Islamic household the father is the leader and, although ideally both parents ought to share power, it is the father who has the ultimate authority. Accordingly, the patriarch and older men in the family expect complete respect and loyalty from all family members, especially women and girls. South Asian children are taught absolute obedience to age-superiors, which makes it difficult to defy demands from elders, especially when accompanied by threats and coercion. Compliant victims might easily be commanded to submit to sexual abuse and intimidated into silence.

Lastly, most South Asian societies vigorously deny the existence of child sexual abuse in their midst. In Islamic communities, incest takes two forms: child sexual abuse and sex in forbidden relationships such as between father-in-law and daughter-in law. Even when mothers and other women realize that sexual abuse is occurring within the family, they may feel helpless and unable to ameliorate the situation. Economic dependence on men and the fear of social reprobation effectively gag women and keep them from supporting victims.

Regarding legal recourse for sexual violence, most South Asian nations implement a mixture of Sharīʿa laws and uniform legal codes for Islamic communities. Although a number of civil codes guiding marriage, divorce, and property rights follow Sharīʿa directives, sexual assault including rape and incest falls within the purview of the criminal legal systems. In Islamic countries such as Pakistan and Bangladesh, local community administrations frequently attempt to employ religious laws for *zinā* transgressions; but these have been recurrently overturned by the court systems.

Regardless of legal efficacy, social attitudes and belief systems dominate the conduct of Islamic societies in South Asia. Correspondingly, a number of social obstacles prevent girls and women from seeking legal redress for sexual violation. For instance, codes of family honor overwhelmingly prevent individuals from lodging complaints against members of their own family. The potential loss of the victim's reputation acts as further discouragement from seeking outside help. Even when victims overcome these difficulties and lodge complaints with law enforcement agencies, other extralegal obstructions arise.

The police in South Asia have been determinedly reluctant to register grievances of gender violence such as domestic violence, sexual assault, and incest. Notoriety regarding police brutality and custody rape also inhibits individuals from pursuing legal remedies. The dire lack of well trained medical personnel, appropriate facilities, and technology further impedes rigorous prosecution of sexual assault cases. The length of time taken to bring each case to trial, the insensitivity of judges and court personnel, and the enormous burden on victims to produce proof, effectively thwart efforts to bring abusers to justice.

Bibliography

Primary Sources

Amnesty International, *Women in Pakistan. Disadvantaged and denied their rights*, New York 1995.

——, *Pakistan. Violence against women in the name of honor*, New York 1999.

H. Begum, Violence in Islamic texts and its relevance to practice, in I. Mukhopadhyay (ed.), *Violence against women*, Kolkata, India 2002.

A. Bouhdiba, *Sexuality in Islam*, trans. A. Sheridan, London 1998.

Breaking the Silence Group, *Non-commercial sexual abuse of children in Bangladesh. A case study based report*, Dhaka 1997.

A. A. Engineer, *The rights of women in Islam*, New York 1992.

J. Goodwin, *Price of honor. Muslim women lift the veil of silence on the Islamic world*, New York 2003.

M. A. Khan, Two case studies from a Muslim mohalla. Bigamy and incest, in *Islamic Voice* 14-07:163 (July 2000), <www.islamicvoice. com/july2000/law.htm>.

U. Mazhar, Rape and incest. Islamic perspective, in *Crescentlife* 2002, <www. crescentlife.com/articles/rape_and_incest_islamic_perspective.htm>.

R. Menon, Sexual abuse of children. Hidden peril, in *India Today*, 31 October 1992, 69–73.

S. Moitra (ed.), *Women, heritage, and violence*, Calcutta 1996.

G. Poore, *The children we sacrifice. A resource book*, Silver Spring, Md. 2000.

RAHI Findings, *Voices from the silent zone: Women's experiences of incest and childhood sexual abuse*, New Delhi 1999, <rahisupp@del2.vsnl.net.in>.

Rahima, Centre for Training and Information on Islam and Women's Rights Issue, The problem of incestuous rape is no longer a private problem!, interview with Husein Muhammad (n.d.), <www.rahima.or.id/English/interviews_8b.htm>.

Rape. When victim is seen as villain, in *India Abroad*, 10 July 1998, 1, 30–4.

S. Sood (ed.), *Violence against women*, Jaipur 1990.

Secondary Sources

Sakshi Violence Intervention Centre, Report on a survey of 350 school children in New Delhi, India 1997, as cited in G. Poore, *The children we sacrifice. A resource book*, Silver Spring, Md. 2000.

Tata Institute of Social Sciences, Report on a 1994–1995 survey of 150 school children in Mumbai, India, as cited in G. Poore, *The children we sacrifice. A resource book*, Silver Spring, MD 2000.

Shamita Das Dasgupta

Shah Bano Affair

Overview

In a landmark judgment delivered in April 1985, India's Supreme Court granted a small maintenance allowance to Shah Bano, a seventy-three-year-old Muslim divorcee, to be paid by her husband under the Criminal Code. Shah Bano had been married to Mohammed Ahmed Khan since 1932. Ahmed Khan married again in 1946, and in 1975, on account of property-related disputes between the two wives, Shah Bano and her children moved out from their family home; in 1978 she filed a maintenance suit against her husband in the Judicial Magistrate's Court in Indore, appealed to Section 125 of the Criminal Procedure Code, and pleaded for Rs. 500 as monthly maintenance. To avoid maintenance under this section, Khan divorced Shah Bano by irrevocable triple *ṭalāq*. In August 1979, the local magistrate ordered that Ahmed Khan pay her maintenance of Rs. 25 per month, which was later revised on her appeal to Rs. 179 by the Madhya Pradesh High Court. In an appeal to the Supreme Court, Ahmed Khan argued that since he had fulfilled his obligations under religious personal laws, Islamic law placed no further maintenance liability upon him; rather Section 125 conflicted with his rights under personal law.

The Supreme Court, headed by Chief Justice Chandachud, dismissed the appeal and confirmed the judgment of the Madhya Pradesh High Court. The Apex Court was asked to pronounce on the relationship between these sections of the Criminal Procedure Code of 1973 and religious personal law. The Court ruled that Section 125, as part of criminal rather than civil law, overrides all personal law and is uniformly applicable to all women, including Muslim women. The judgment was supported by detailed citations from the Qur'ān, to show that a husband is obliged to provide maintenance for his divorced wife if the wife is unable to provide for herself. It also raised the question of a uniform civil code, arguing that if the constitution was to have meaning, the aspiration contained in Article 44 must be realized.

The judgment sparked off a major political uproar. Outraged by the judgment, the religious leadership, including the Jamaat-e-Islami, the Jamiat-al-Ulema and the All India Muslim Personal Law Board, spearheaded an agitation to repeal it. There was a spate of meetings, marches, and conferences all over the country to protest against the danger it posed to Muslim minority identity. The central issue in the agitation was the sanctity of religious personal law. As against this, the campaign in favor of the judgment, dominated by champions of women's rights and liberal Muslims who considered the reform of personal laws desirable, was much smaller.

To understand this controversy one has to look at the context in which it arose. The past two decades have witnessed a steep rise in communal violence and identity politics in the larger political arena. The Shah Bano affair and the unlocking of the gates of the Babri Masjid in Ayodhya in 1986 saw the growth of a massive Rama temple movement, resulting in the rapid escalation of political violence and support for the Hindu nationalist Bharatiya Janata Party (which leads the National Democratic Alliance that has ruled India since 1998). The lack of any noticeable opposition among Hindus to the countrywide violence unleashed in the wake of the temple movement, compared to the outrage against the Muslim Women's (Protection of Rights on Divorce) Act (MWA) of 1986, left large sections of the Muslim population feeling vulnerable. For its part, the Congress government showed no concern for Muslim feelings about the campaign against the Babri mosque, which culminated in its eventual demolition in December 1992, in contrast to the extraordinary concern for the Muslim position on the Shah Bano case.

Prime Minister Rajiv Gandhi sought to placate the disquiet of the religious leadership and their perception of threat to Muslim identity by enacting the MWA to override the judgment and unequivocally exclude Muslim women from the purview of the Criminal Code, to which all citizens otherwise had recourse. The principal objective of the legislation in the context of the Shah Bano controversy was: "to specify the rights which a Muslim divorced woman is entitled to at the time of her divorce and to protect her interests." Under the MWA a divorced Muslim woman is entitled to, (a) "a reasonable and fair provision of maintenance" within the period of *ʿidda*; (b) two years' maintenance for her children; (c) her dowry and all other properties given to her by her relatives, husband,

and husband's relatives. If the woman is unable to maintain herself after the ʿ*idda* period, the magistrate can order those relatives who are entitled to inherit her property to maintain her in proportion to their share of the inheritance in accordance with Islamic law. If the woman has no such relatives, the magistrate is to ask the State Wakf Board to pay maintenance. Several rulings in the state high courts have interpreted the act so as to provide Muslim women with a higher maintenance amount than was given under Section 125 and, more importantly, lump sum payments for the future security of women.

The critics of the judgment ignored the crucial question of women's rights, which remained confined to feminists and left-wing parties. The Muslim leadership focused on issues that linked women and family life to Islamic legal identity. The government defended the new legislation on the ground that it conformed to the wishes of the Muslim community and should be supported irrespective of the opinion of large sections of Muslim women, or other communities, or society at large.

Several individuals and groups challenged the constitutionality of the MWA in the Supreme Court, its violation of several articles on fundamental rights, and its discriminatory character vis-à-vis Muslim women. The verdict of the five-judge Constitutional Bench in the *Latifi* case delivered in 2001 confined itself to the constitutionality of the MWA, which limits Muslim women's right to maintenance to the ʿ*idda*. The court ruled that a divorced woman is entitled to a "reasonable and fair provision of maintenance" to be made and paid to her within the ʿ*idda* period by her husband. Significantly, this includes future needs. The word "provision" indicates provision in advance for meeting future needs and "reasonable and fair provision" may include provision for her residence, her food, her clothes, and other articles. The *Latifi* judgment is important as it provides some relief to divorced Muslim women by expanding the notion of "a reasonable and fair provision for maintenance" to include their future needs.

Two issues are central to the reform of personal laws in India. First the relationship of personal law to the state, and second, the appropriate institutions through which reform of personal laws could be organized and carried outside the arena of the state. Personal laws are discriminatory; they run counter to Article 14's guarantee of the equal protection of the laws, Article 15's prohibition of discrimination on grounds of sex and also discrimination on grounds of religion, and Article 21 interpreted by the court as involving a life with human dignity. The constitution included a provision to recognize pre-constitutional laws only if they conformed to fundamental rights. Even so, all such laws were recognized and continued after the constitution came into effect and thus the courts have allowed women to be governed by the law of religion without subjecting such laws to the test of constitutionality.

Based on the principle of separation of public and private domains, the Indian state has tacitly accepted that it cannot intervene and initiate change in religious personal laws, namely, the private sphere of Muslims. There are two questions here. One is the relationship of Muslim personal law with the state. Two factors are important in analyzing this relationship: the development of Islamic jurisprudence and its role within the state. More specifically, although those engaging in the current debate over personal law cite the Qurʾān in their arguments for and against reform – whether state induced or community based – what gets ignored is the fact that Islamic jurisprudence is a separate entity from the Qurʾān, and is so not only because of its own relationship with the state, but also because its historical development has actually made it such. Furthermore, when combined with the power of the modern nation-state, the degree of change is limited because the moral and legal framework on which it is based is itself immutable. State initiated reform within personal law poses a problem because of the contradictory nature of Islamic law. It is also problematic not just because of who the state decides to listen to, but also because India is not a Muslim state but a secular state in which Muslims are a sizeable minority. In this situation, Muslim personal law is seen as representative of all Muslim sentiment. This diminishes its diversity and contradictoriness and perpetuates the myth of a single Muslim personal law, and considers changes in personal law in other Muslim countries as irrelevant. It becomes clear then that Indian Muslims see themselves and are seen as Muslims of a particular demographic and historical setting, and it follows that Muslim personal law does not involve Muslims per se, but specifically Muslims in India.

The second and more complicated question is whether the Indian state, through its courts and parliament, can initiate social reform in the same way as these institutions had intervened to change Hindu family laws. The Muslim leadership has not spurned state intervention altogether. Indeed state intervention was desired to encode and enforce restrictive and repressive laws; it was equally favored as the agency for legal reform of personal laws. Ashraf ʿAlī Thānawī, a leading Islamic scholar/reformer in the 1930s worked with Muslim converts in Punjab and Central India to eradicate non-Islamic and pre-Islamic practices, which subsequently led to the Shariat Act of 1937. He engaged in the same political and legislative activity to find Islamic precedent for Muslim women to seek divorce, which subsequently led to the Dissolution of Muslim Marriages Act, 1939. While Thānawī was sharply critical of the "state's" treatment of Muslim personal law, it was this institution that he approached first to rectify its legal misperceptions. The critics of the Shah Bano judgment approached the state in the same way. Even though the state is often blamed for interpreting and misinterpreting religious laws, its critics have invariably appealed to it. Religious and political leaders are not completely opposed to state intervention when it is advantageous to them. These laws become off-limits only when they concern judicial scrutiny and reform in favor of women's rights.

For a long time after independence, the standard liberal-modernist and feminist narratives demanded the abolition of personal laws and the institution of a uniform civil code on liberal grounds of equal rights for women. This argument called for reforms from above on the initiative of the state much the same way as reforms were introduced within Hinduism in the mid-1950s. Pitted against them were the conservative communitarians who demanded strict maintenance of separate personal laws for each religious group. However, the modernist and feminist positions have changed in part because of their appropriation by Hindu nationalists and also because of the Muslim perception of external threat to their religious identity and culture prompted by the dramatic growth of the Hindu right and its ambition to establish a singular citizenship through an eradication of the legal recognition of community differences. This has meant a less secure environment for minorities, especially Muslims. But, more importantly, the assertion of Hindu identity is taking place through a renewed emphasis on Muslim identity as obscurantist and fundamentalist. Given that Hindu nationalism has now become a powerful political force, many feminists feel rather uncomfortable with the demand for state-initiated personal law reform, considering that the call for uniform laws could turn into a device to attack minorities. In view of this, a reformist position in which personal laws need internal reform, not outright rejection, has gathered support since the early 1990s.

Ideally, the initiative for change of personal laws should come from within the community, which can better define the scope, institutional location, and justification for reform. However, the basic problem is the absence of authoritative institutional structures within the Muslim community that can undertake this difficult project. In the last few years women's groups, principally Muslim women's organizations, have mobilized in favor of the internal reform project. They have addressed their reformist appeal to the *ʿulamāʾ* and at the same time made efforts to influence public opinion. In October 2000 and April 2001 the Muslim Personal Law Board, a male-dominated body of over 150 Muslim clerics held meetings in Bangalore and New Delhi concerning the problems of Muslim women in the light of the Sharīʿa. For the first time Muslim women and religious clerics shared a common platform to discuss issues of Muslim personal laws. Both meetings witnessed Muslim women raising their voice in favor of change and the religious clerics dodging the issue by blaming unjust religious practices on the distortions in Muslim *samaj* or society, which needs reform, rather than personal laws as such.

Yet all these initiatives have not had the effect of promoting reform because the conditions for meaningful dialogue are wanting. This is due mainly to the multiplicity and heterogeneity of the community, which makes the emergence of a resolute leadership of the entire community very difficult. The Muslim community is diverse, heterogeneous, and hierarchical, with no identifiable institution and agencies with the requisite power and legitimacy to interpret and undertake reform. What counts as the leadership of the community is an artifact of power. Governmental policy in the Shah Bano case played right into the hands of powerful religious leaders who do not consult women. It bolstered the existing power structure of the community and accepted the clergy as the sole spokesmen and allowed them to define any potential change in the Muslim community's practices as a distortion of religiously sanctioned practices. Moreover, the external environment is not conducive to modernization owing to the insecurity in which most Muslims live. The majority within the Muslim community, which most likely supports reform, is unable to overcome its defensiveness toward external and internal pressures on the community.

In this situation the *Latifi* judgment is a step forward in the road to equality between the sexes because it provides a predominantly social, rather than religious, grounding for maintenance provisions. By interpreting the provisions of the MWA in a manner that enhances rights of women by taking into account gender disparities and social conditions, the court adopted a socially based reading that can further constitutional goals and can bring personal laws in line with equality and justice.

BIBLIOGRAPHY
R. Baird, *Religion and law in independent India*, New Delhi 1993.
Z. Hasan (ed.), *Forging identities. Gender, communities and the state*, New Delhi 1994.
P. Jeffery and A. Basu, *Appropriating gender. Women's activism and politicized religion in South Asia*, New York 1999.
R. Kapur (ed.), *Feminist terrains in legal domains. Interdisciplinary essays on women and law in India*, New Delhi 1996.
A. Parasher, *Women and family law reform in India. Uniform civil code and gender equality*, New Delhi 1992.
Women's Action and Resource Unit, *Muslim women speak. Testimonies of women*, Ahmedabad, 2000.

ZOYA HASAN

Social Hierarchies: Modern

East Asia, Southeast Asia, Australia, and the Pacific

Introduction

A multi-faceted web of classes, states, ethnicities, social statuses, property rights, ranks (seniority), and kinship hierarchy shapes, to varying degrees, the construction of gender and women's lives throughout the developing world. Added to this complexity are worldwide forces such as globalization, feminism, the Charter of the United Nations, and Islamization. The combination of these local and global forces has generated a new image of women as progressive, modern, and industrial, and yet confined by the persistence of traditional and local cultures. In view of these changes, this entry describes the competing powers of local institutions and global forces that mold the constitution of gender and the construction of modern social hierarchies and examines their impact on women's experiences in East Asia, Southeast Asia, Australia, and the Pacific Islands.

Women and gender in East Asia

Although women's lives and experience in East Asia are far from unitary, the resilience of Confucianism and the underlying construction of social, political, and daily practices shape Chinese, Korean, Taiwanese and Hong Kong women's choices, opportunities and lives. Similarly, the industrializing economics, social change, and political transformation do not set women free from the unshackled patriarchal demands of family obligations, the bearing of male children, and the support of the men in the family. At the same time, women also struggle with their own personal choices (Chiang 2000, 243, Hampson 2000, 170, Tang et al. 2000, 189). In the Chinese post-Mao era and with the escalating unemployment, state ideology shifted into a discourse of the ideal modern "Eastern woman" (*dongfang funü*) – as distinct from the ideal Western woman whose merit lies in her career – who is professional, while still remaining a "virtuous wife and good mother" (*xiangi liangmu*) (Hooper, 187–9). Like their sisters, Japanese women have never fully abandoned the patriarchal view of the ideal "good wife, wise mother" (*ryosai kenbo*) that persists from the days of Meiji state ideology. The fundamental concept of women as nurturers and reproducers both in the domestic and public spheres continues to persist because of numerous factors, such as gendered upbringing, education, corporate structure, state ideology, media and consumer culture (Tipton 2000, 210, 225).

The same is true for Muslim women in East Asian society, forced as they are to diversify their strategies in order to achieve the ideal of balancing their role as good wives and caretakers of the household and their reality as members of a minority (Pillsbury 1978, 657–65, Jaschock and Shui 2000, 28). East Asian Muslims are not nearly as concerned about producing male offspring as they are about giving the children a good education and bringing them up as Muslims. Women are usually in charge taking care of the household, educating the children, and providing *ḥalāl* (licit and clean) foods, whereas men are breadwinners and the heads of the families. While Chinese Muslim women's full commitment to become good wives and mothers limits their full participation in the public realm, except in women' mosques and social organizations, their sisters in Taiwan find the need to contribute to the family finance (Pillsbury 1978, 666). Both, however, face a restricted mobility, not because of seclusion or strict veiling practices, but due to the fact that they are members of a minority group.

Women and gender in Southeast Asia

Southeast Asian culture appears to attribute greater equality to men and women (Errington 1990, 3). The high status that women generally enjoy is largely due to a social organization based on bilateral kinship, making for no apparent preference for male over female (Robinson 2000, 143). Ideally, a family is happy to have both a son and a daughter; daughters alone are, however, equally welcome. As parents grow older, they usually allow the daughters to stay with them or inherit the house. This arrangement is possible within bilateral kinship and its variations are found in Java, Sunda, South Sulawesi, the matrilineal society of Minangkabau in Sumatra, and Thailand (Dube 1997, 7, Robinson 2000, 143, Limanonda 2000, 248–61, Puntarigvivat 2001, 233). In other societies, especially in the greater part of Sumatra, Bali, Vietnam, and Singapore, the kinship relation is more patriarchal in that wives usually move in with their husbands' families, prior to renting or owning their own houses.

However, the bilateral, matrilineal, and uxorilocal mechanism does not directly bestow equality in the sense that men and women are equal in every respect. The cultural construction of gender in most of Southeast Asia is still rooted in *dapu[r]* (kitchen), *sumu[r]* (well), and *kasu[r]* (bed); even if women enjoy greater financial autonomy, careers, education, inheritance, and mobility, they are still burdened with the task of maintaining the household in their parents' house and later in their husband's household. The ideal of a woman's total devotion to family is also echoed in the state regulations. The Malaysian, Indonesian, and Singaporean governments emphasize the model of the ideal harmonious Asian family where the man is head of the family and the woman head of the household (Stivens 1998a, 103, Robinson 2000, 141). Thai culture even encourages the daughter's devotion to the family. Since women have no religious role, they must perform "filial piety" by relieving the parents of their household tasks or economic needs, even by means of prostitution (Puntarigvivat 2001, 229). The image of ideal wife and mother also emerged in Vietnam during the renovation (*dong moi*) era, especially in the 1980s and 1990s, when women were forced back into the domestic sphere (Fahey 1998, 244).

The unequal status existing between men and women clearly shows that the cultural construction of power and privilege in societies is not equally distributed. Unlike the Western construction of power, which lies in economic control and coercive power, the Southeast Asian construction depends on "spiritual power and effective potency" (Errington 1990, 5). Apart from this tangible measure, kinship relations, seniority, nobility, education, wealth, occupation, and social standing affect a person's status in the society (Brenner 2000, 139). A woman's control over economic resources by means of managing the husband's wealth, inheritance, or personal earnings and their power over the household does not lend her any higher status. However, a woman's blood or spousal relation to powerful men with cultural refinement, spiritual potency, or respected political status can indirectly lead to plenty of privileges being granted to her.

The inequality between men and women in Southeast Asia is often religiously derived. In a predominantly Buddhist country such as Thailand, the notion of the dutiful and virtuous wife originates in the *Anguttara Nikaya*, where Buddha equates women's power to her ability to manage household along with other virtues, such as confidence, charity, and wisdom (Puntarigvivat 2001, 219). In countries where Confucianism is widespread, such as Singapore and Vietnam, the good wife is seen as keeping the society upright. Similarly, the traditional role of a woman, that is, to be obedient to her parents and later to her husband and to be responsible for the household and caring for the family, finds its justification in predominantly Muslim countries (such as Malaysia, Indonesia, and Brunei) in the Qurʾān (4:34). The higher status enjoyed by men over women is derived from the view that men are the primary and women the secondary creation and that men receive more privileges with respect to matters of inheritance and divorce.

Muslim feminists, womanists, and male advocates for women's rights object to the subordination of women through the institution of sexist religious doctrines. They urge Muslims to reinterpret the Qurʾān and understand it within the context of the mission of human beings as God's vicegerents, who will receive either reward or punishment depending on their good deeds in this world, and from the perspective of Islam as a complete system for both men and women. However, the very notion of Islam as a complete system itself generates heated debate in the forum of Islamic revivalism, which regards an Islamic state based on the Sharīʿa as the ideal solution to all such problems – a view current among minorities in Indonesia, Malaysia, Thailand, and the Philippines.

Women and gender in Australia

Although Australia is a melting pot of the diverse Aboriginal cultures and the white English-speaking and non-English-speaking immigrants, it is primarily dominated by Anglo-Celtic, post-European culture. On gaining commonwealth status in 1901 as a federation of the former British colonies, the new state committed itself to the "White Australia Policy," which excluded non-Europeans, including early Afghan Muslim settlers, from citizenship (Johns and Saeed 2002, 198). When Australia grew more open to Muslim immigration, it applied an assimilationist policy to integrate the immigrants into Anglo-Celtic Australia (Bulbeck 1998, 193). However, with the abolition of the policy in the 1970s and a boom in immigration from non-European and non-Christian countries, Australia introduced a new policy called multiculturalism, which recognized the immigrant heritage while adjusting to a new culture and environment.

Given the multicultural background of Australian citizens, the construction of gender varies depending on the society to which a woman belongs. Among the predominantly Anglo-Celtic Australian feminists, a liberal attitude prevails in ensuring women's freedom from violence in the private sphere and their access to the public sphere (Bulbeck 1998, 8). These feminists often apply the same yardstick to Australian women of non-English speaking background, insisting that they too should be speaking, autonomous, authoritative subjects in both the private and public spheres.

Women's authority within non-English speaking communities, however, operates somewhat differently from that of Anglo-Celtic Australian women. Among Aborigines, for example, a woman's authority increases as she ages, even though this authority is never fully equal to that of a man (White 1974, 37). While women's authority in many aspects of life (such as economic matters, the betrothal ceremony, and religious ritual) is never formally acknowledged or equal by Western standards, women do take a role in influencing and supporting male decisions. The only aspects over which women take full in charge are those linked to major life events, such as menstruation, pregnancy, and childbirth, which is performed in secrecy and without male attendance. Women's authority is thus more informal, and it increases or decreases depending on age, the husband-wife relation, the parent-child relation, kinship, and economic power (Berndt 1974, 67–70).

Many non-Anglo-Celtic Australians are Muslim women who migrated to Australia along with their families or were born in Australia. As their immigration status is closely related to that of the family, gender-based definitions operate within that unit, especially among married women who choose to maintain the household and take care of the children in order to educate them properly (Yasmeen 2002, 220–1). Women's full engagement with the family, the division of labor within the family, their lack of education, the language barrier, the wearing of the *ḥijāb*, and stereotypical images of Muslim women among Anglo-Celtic Australians as subordinate all restrict Muslim women's participation in the public sphere (Yasmeen 2002, 224–7, Rozario 1998, 654). This limited participation, however, like their marginal status as immigrants, is not restricted to Muslim women, but is common among women with a non-English speaking backgrounds as well.

Women and gender in the Pacific Islands

As in Australia, the social hierarchies that shape the construction of gender and women's lives in the Pacific Islands are far from homogeneous. Colonization, self-government, the flow of urbanization, employment, and the demand for cash cropping are the contending issues that alter realities in the Pacific Islands and women's lives in general (Marsh 1998, 666). Despite the changes that these have entailed, indigenous cultures still have an effect on women's lives. Among the Anganen of the Southern Highlands Province of Papua New Guinea, for instance, men enjoy a higher status than women. Male territoriality, patrilocality, patrilineality, virilocality, and clanship support a social order in which wives provide the bride-price for their exchange, are separated from their natal kinfolk and are totally absorbed into their husbands' clans (Merrett-Balkos 1998, 233). By contrast, in societies where there are few differences between matrilineality and patrilineality, such as in the Solomon Islands, the status of women as "breeders and feeders" increases their self-reliance (Bulbeck 1998, 124). In short, the hierarchical social system affects the way men and women relate in their daily lives, ritual practice, public roles, and access to opportunities.

Conclusion

While the social hierarchies that shape women and gender in East Asia, Southeast Asia, Australia, and the Pacific are far from unitary given the vast geographical extent of this region, their diverse cultures, and the varying degree of external pressures, they share one thing in common: traditional norms that preserve the prevailing image of women as reproducers and nurturers and maintain the entrenched notion of the sexual division of labor. Yet while these traditions will continue to exert their influence on women, progress toward gender equality will continue to flourish, as more women become involved in policy-making that affects women's choices and national development.

Bibliography

C. H. Berndt, Digging sticks and spears, or the two-sex model, in F. Gale (ed.), *Women's role in Aboriginal society*, Canberra 1974, 64–84.

S. A Brenner, Why women rule the roost. Rethinking Javanese ideologies of gender and self control, in C. B. Brettell and C. F. Sargent (eds.), *Gender in cross-cultural perspective*, Upper Saddle River, N.J. 2000, 135–56.

C. Bulbeck, *Re-orienting Western feminism*, Cambridge 1998.

L. N. Chiang, Women in Taiwan. Linking economic prosperity and women's progress, in L. Edwards and M. Roces (eds.), *Women in Asia. Tradition, modernity, and globalization*, Ann Arbor 2000, 229–46.

Confucius, *The analects* (*Lun yü*), trans. and intro. D. C. Lau, New York 1979.

L. Dube, *Women and kinship. Perspectives on gender in South and South-East Asia*, Tokyo 1997.
L. Edwards, Women in the People's Republic of China. New challenges to the grand gender narrative, in L. Edwards and M. Roces (eds.), *Women in Asia. Tradition, modernity, and globalization*, Ann Arbor 2000, 59–84.
S. Fahey, Vietnam's women in the renovation era, in K. Shen and M. Stivens (eds.), *Gender and power in affluent Asia*, London 1998, 222–49.
M. Ferguson, *Women and religion*, Englewood Cliffs, N.J. 1995.
S. Hampson, Rhetoric or reality? Contesting definitions of women in Korea, in L. Edwards and M. Roces (eds.), *Women in Asia. Tradition, modernity, and globalization*, Ann Arbor 2000, 170–87.
B. Hooper, Flower vase and the housewife. Women and consumerism in post-Mao China, in K. Shen and M. Stivens (eds.), *Gender and power in affluent Asia*, London 1998, 167–93.
M. Jaschock and Shui, J. J., *The history of women's mosques in Chinese Islam. A mosque of their own*, London 2000.
A. H. Johns and A. Saeed, Muslims in Australia. The building of a community, in Y. Y. Haddad and J. I. Smith (eds.), *Muslim minorities in the West. Visible and invisible*, New York 2002, 195–216.
B. Limanonda, Exploring women's status in contemporary Thailand, in L. Edwards and M. Roces (eds.), *Women in Asia. Tradition, modernity, and globalization*, Ann Arbor 2000, 247–64.
S. T. Marsh, Migrating feminisms. Maligned overstayer or model citizen, in *Women's Studies International Forum* 21:6 (1998), 665–80.
L. Merrett-Balkos, Just add water. Remaking women through childbirth, Anganen, Southern Highlands, Papua New Guinea, in K. Ram and M. Jolly (eds.), *Maternities and modernities. Colonial and postcolonial experiences in Asia and the Pacific*, Cambridge 1998, 213–38.
B. L. K. Pillsbury, Being female in a Muslim minority in China, in L. Beck and N. Keddie (eds.), *Muslim women in the Muslim world*, Cambridge 1978, 651–73.
T. Puntarigvivat, A Thai Buddhist perspective, in J. C. Raines and D. C. Maguire (eds.), *What men owe to women*, Albany, N.Y. 2001, 211–37.
K. Robinson, Indonesian women. From *Orde Baru* to *Reformasi*, in L. Edwards and M. Roces (eds.), *Women in Asia. Tradition, modernity, and globalization*, Ann Arbor 2000, 139–69.
S. Rozario, On being Australian and Muslim. Muslim women as defenders of Islamic heritage, in *Women's Studies International Forum* 21:6 (1998), 649–61.
M. Stivens, Sex, gender and the making of the new Malay middle class, in K. Shen and M. Stivens (eds.), *Gender and power in affluent Asia*, London 1998a, 89–126.
——, Theorizing gender, power, and modernity in affluent Asia, in K. Shen and M. Stivens (eds.), *Gender and power in affluent Asia*, London 1998b, 1–32.
C. Tang, W. T. Au, Y. P. Chung, and N. Y. Ngo, Breaking the patriarchal paradigm. Chinese women in Hong Kong, in L. Edwards and M. Roces (eds.), *Women in Asia. Tradition, modernity, and globalization*, Ann Arbor 2000, 188–207.
E. K. Tipton, Being women in Japan, 1970–2000, in L. Edwards and M. Roces (eds.), *Women in Asia. Tradition, modernity, and globalization*, Ann Arbor 2000, 208–28.
I. M. White, Aboriginal women's status. A paradox resolved, in F. Gale (ed.), *Women's role in Aboriginal society*, Canberra 1974, 36–46.
S. Yasmin, Muslim women as citizens in Australia. Perth as a case study, in Y. Y. Haddad and J. I. Smith (eds.), *Muslim minorities in the West. Visible and invisible*, New York 2002, 217–32.

Etin Anwar

The Gulf and Yemen

The oil economies of many of the Gulf emirates and states have undoubtedly had an impact on social hierarchies. The shifts in social hierarchies, however, should not be seen as simply transforming from "traditional" to "modern." Indeed, local practices and social organization, such as tribal affiliation, have both accommodated and been remobilized by new state bureaucratic systems. Nevertheless, the dramatic transformation in the region's economy – from subsistence agriculture and pastoralism to rentier – has certainly affected how hierarchies are both produced and maintained. Similarly, it should be noted that while some of the Gulf emirates and states, such as Abu Dhabi and Kuwait, have substantially more oil than others, the others, such as Yemen and Bahrain – especially through trade and remittances – are not exempt from the dramatic transformations wrought by oil, forming what some scholars have argued to be an integrated regional economy (Owen 1985). Oil revenues and the structure of the oil market, however, have not affected social hierarchies on their own: notions of "tradition" as well as national education systems, enabled by oil revenues, are also seen to have transformed social and gendered hierarchies (al-Falah 1991).

Although what might be understood as traditional and modern hierarchies might not necessarily correspond to the shifts in how certain identities have come to matter in the post-oil era, there have, nevertheless, been changes in how hierarchies are produced and reproduced. To understand the ways hierarchies have transformed, it is important to examine hierarchies in the early days of oil and the establishment of the modern states. In Bahrain, for example, hierarchies in the late 1960s, at least, were reproduced primarily through profession or craft (Serjeant 1968), sometimes intersecting with tribal affiliations. As in a caste system, certain professions (such as butcher, tailor, barber, carpenter, office worker, agricultural worker, poultry dealer, pearl diver) were relegated to the lower strata of society while other professions were preserved for the upper strata (Bujra 1971). This division of professions was and is important for men as well as women. At the same time, according to Serjeant, the main social cleavage in Bahraini society was between what were considered the "Arabs of tribal descent," who are Sunnīs, and the Shīʿī Baḥārna, while in Southwest Arabia – in Oman and Yemen (although also mentioned in Kuwaiti literature) – a distinction might be found between a variety of ethnic identities as well as the tribal, Arab, or Bayasira (Wilkinson 1974).

Lienhardt (1972) who wrote of the Trucial States in the 1960s suggests that the strict sex segregation of the society accounts for the lower status of women. Nevertheless, he wrote, men were not as dominant in society as they claimed to be and one of the reasons for their limited dominance, especially in the practices of divorce, was that the Trucial States are influenced by Beduin rather than peasant society, the mobile rather than settled. Lienhardt's description of the status of women in the early days of development and oil, however, also suggests that although women maintained the honor of the family and often had its support and protection, they had – as they intersected with the statuses of their "ethnic" or "caste" positions – less access to wealth, power, and prestige.

In contrast, it has been argued that the oil economies of the region have enabled the expansion of national education systems which, in turn, have produced greater equality between men and women in the professional labor market, countering the practices of "traditional patriarchal societies" (al-Falah 1991). However, the transformation of the economies, bureaucratic regimes, and education systems has also produced new gendered hierarchies, based not only on new class formations, but also on national and ethnic identities and stratifications. Indeed, despite the formal "modern" education of Gulf populations, relatively few women enter the labor market, leaving most positions to Arabs of other nationalities or to Europeans, Iranians, and Indians (Longva 1993, Seikaly 1994). And, while some of the Gulf emirates and states have promoted the hiring of local populations, other policies that encourage women to be good housewives seem to discourage local women's entrance to the labor market. Thus, although greater wealth has given women in the Gulf a fair amount of independence, many – sometimes in the name of "tradition" – have not entered the labor market, leaving both government and private employment to men as well as a hierarchy of expatriate workers. Similarly, while it seems as though the new hierarchies are more based on wealth rather than profession and patrilineal descent, marriage between members of historically professionally and ethnically distinct groups remains limited.

Finally, it should be noted that town and village social networks among women, often across different status groups, continue to remain strong. And, as men move to capital areas and the city-states of the Gulf, women generally remain in the towns and villages, sometimes complementing their remittance incomes with small-scale trade. However, as men in unstable labor markets lose their jobs, they return to the towns and villages, sometimes creating tensions with the women who have remained.

Bibliography

A. Bujra, *The politics of stratification. A study of political change in a South Arabian town*, Oxford 1971.

N. al-Falah, Power and representation. Social change, gender relations, and the education of women in Kuwait, in E. Davis and N. Gavrielides (eds.), *Statecraft in the Middle East*, Miami 1991, 149–75.

P. A. Lienhardt, The position of women in the society of the Trucial Coast, in D. Hopwood (ed.), *The Arabian Peninsula*, London 1972, 219–30.

A. N. Longva, Kuwaiti women at a crossroads. Privileged development and the constraints of ethnic stratification, in *International Journal of Middle East Studies* 25:3 (1993), 443–56.

R. Owen, The Arab oil economy. Present structure and future prospects, in S. K. Farsoun (ed.), *Arab society. Continuity and change*, London 1985, 16–33.

M. Seikaly, Women and social change in Bahrain, in *International Journal of Middle East Studies* 26:3 (May 1994), 415–26.

R. B. Serjeant, Fisher-folk and fish traps in al-Bahrain, in *Bulletin of the School of Oriental and African Studies* 31:3 (1968), 486–514.

J. C. Wilkinson, Bayasirah and bayadir, in *Arabian Studies* 1 (1974), 75–85.

Mandana Limbert

North Africa

The hierarchies that characterize the social landscape of North Africa today are the outcome of profound changes triggered by colonial institutions beginning in the early nineteenth century. Since 1830, when the French first entered Algeria, North African social organization and stratification have been modified by new roles and functions open to women. However, before discussion of how the present reality slowly emerged, it is important to place it in its larger cultural and historical context.

The three nation-states (Tunisia, Algeria, and Morocco) that constitute the geographical area of North Africa share a number of characteristics making the claim of a single cultural area possible. They have in common, for example, the following elements: an ethnic-linguistic component in the form of Berber and Arab populations as well as mixed Berber/Arab groups; the experience of Islam as one religion and the adoption of the Sunnī rite, with its own interpretation and legislation of reality; and, later, the French colonial experience with its linguistic, organizational, and institutional characteristics.

Although these strong connections illustrate a shared imaginary and role attribution according to gender and age, there are still limitations that complicate the description of these three nation-states as a unified culture. First, there exist within each nation-state extremely varied communities: urban, semi-urban, rural, and other (tribal nomads, for example, though to a lesser extent in Tunisia). These each have their own internal hierarchies and predispositions/resistance to accepting change to their social structures. Second, the political model each country adopted after its independence from France differs from the others in many ways. In 1956 Morocco laid claim to an institutional monarchy, while Tunisia adopted a liberal economic regime headed by the then-maverick Bourguiba. Then in 1961 Algeria adopted a socialist regime based on a single party model (Front de libération nationale).

The post-independence political management of existing social and economic structures in these three countries consequently wrought different changes. The remainder of this entry focuses on two elements as start points for a discussion of these changes: first, it examines the common imaginary structures in premodern North Africa; second, it looks at the formal, official structures of the post-independence era.

In premodern North Africa, women rarely stood as individuals or possessed an independent status; rather, they were always defined relationally. As we know through historical treatises and early colonial ethnographies, women were invested with symbolic values that made them, more often than not, objects of the culture rather than its subjects. In any given social setting, the social standing of a woman was defined by four determining elements: the larger net of kinship with whom and by which she is identified (namely, her consanguineous kin, those of simulated kinship, and those built through marriage); property or possession of goods (even if the woman does not lay actual claim to the property proper because she is married outside her kin group); her fertility and especially her capacity for bearing sons; and finally, for lack of a proper expression, the "cultural capital" stemming from her own general behavior and her group's ascribed status of social importance, honor, and/or religiosity.

"Cultural capital" means the political role or leadership position from which a woman may originate that gives her a distinguished social status, as in the example of *sharīf* families, descendants of the Prophet who have strongly influenced the history of North Africa. Women lived with and evolved within vertical links of dependence, whether of their kin group, their in-laws, or both. The modes of relationships were largely predetermined by these external elements and only rarely were there women who could effectively, though positively, separate themselves from these traditional structures. A woman's status could only be defined by and via her kinship relations, and not through her being an individual in her own right, as exemplified by women prostitutes who had forsaken (or were forced to break from) the dominant social structures in a negative way – as morality would define it.

An important number of elements played rather positively in the emergence of what is identified today as modern social hierarchy, a term that implies social mobility: a relatively more progressive understanding of social regulations; the consideration of merit as a criterion of social mobility; and, generally, a stratification that differs both in scale and function from the older one. These elements may be separated into two clusters: one set that is conjectural but has a profound bearing on the structural level, and a set that is more internal and inevitable. The latter stems from a cultural logic and patterns of accommodation to external pressures necessary for the survival of any group under a centralized political power.

Concerning the conjectural cluster of effects, three factors should be stressed: the birth and spread of nationalist ideology, which recognized, in some sense, a woman's "subject-hood"; high population growth due to medical progress that led to mass migration and, to varying degrees, a break with traditional ways; and the development (slow especially in the case of Tunisia and Morocco) of an industrial infrastructure that gave rise to important population movements and social reorganization that both indirectly and, at times, directly challenged traditional statuses and roles. An important result of these changes was the emergence of social classes (and especially the middle class).

Throughout the formative years following political independence, these social classes would become a dominant principle in understanding North African social organizations and political institutions. The remaining internal processes, such as education, access to salaried labor, and "a possibility of corporeal freedom," have also played extremely decisive roles in engendering new social roles and statuses for North African women.

Historical processes distributed political and economic power unevenly throughout the North

African region under consideration; however, thanks to mass education and access to wage labor, women (either as active agents or as agents unconsciously drawn into this overwhelming current) contributed to the erosion of the traditional cultural definition that they were only relational beings. All three countries adopted an open and free-of-charge schooling system, a democratic institution par excellence, that offered the same education to girls and boys alike. Although the number of illiterate women is still relatively high in all three countries, especially in rural, southern, or mountainous areas, an important number of women who studied in schools, universities, and institutes were able to change the professional profile of their countries and, therefore, be defined by their professions and their individual achievements. Though this route of education was first paved, and often appropriated, by elite urban women, women of migrant origin or of "lower" social status were later able to reap the benefits of education. This effect is seen especially in the case of Algeria during its heyday of socialism and state services.

A notably more important number of women have had access to wage labor which has turned them into productive agents within their immediate environments. By contributing to and benefiting from this market economy, women today are able to accumulate and consume goods, activities that have ostensibly altered their ascribed status as primarily consumers (though they were always also producers, but in ways society considered natural). The values and characteristics attributed to women have therefore changed. When entering into marital alliances, for instance, in all three urban cultures attention was given not only to the women's cultural capital but also to their financial contributions and the commodities they were able to harness.

Although women's rank and standings have changed from a relational and largely passive role definition to a more active model in economic and sociopolitical terms, such a transformation does not mean that the entire structure of cultural meaning has changed. This quasi-autonomy of women, the spread of consumer culture, and the more recent revisions of family laws (in Morocco and those proposed for Algeria) have had the ill-fated effect of whetting the conservative, if not rigid, societal patterns that embrace the idea of male supremacy under the pretense of religious authenticity. What started as a political contestation by the Islamist movement during the early 1980s in North Africa has practically permeated all social segments and realities. Women's access to public space, to salaried labor, and to political representation, all of which were instrumental in opening a new era for women in the aftermath of independence, are nowadays in dispute.

As often illustrated in the case of Tunisia, where women have more legal rights even while they are socially and culturally disfavored, the same pattern of two divergent perspectives prevails in North Africa: that is, a discursive and official one that sees women's contribution to society as a motor of development and equity, and a more reality-oriented view that is increasingly pulled toward a conservative trend that imprisons women in their biological role. This reigning mentality, which the women themselves uphold, and the effects of the immediate history of women's contribution to the public space, reflect the beleaguered values that define North African social spaces today.

BIBLIOGRAPHY

M. Charrad, *The state and women's rights. The making of postcolonial Tunisia, Algeria and Morocco*, Berkeley 2001.

J. Clancy-Smith (ed.), *North Africa, Islam and the Mediterranean world. From the Almoravids to the Algerian war*, Portland, Oreg. 2001.

S. Ferchiou (ed.), *Hasab wa nasab. Parenté, alliance et patrimoine en Tunisie*, pref. F. Héritier-Augé, Paris 1992.

P. Knauss, *The persistence of patriarchy. Class, gender, ideology in twentieth-century Algeria*, New York 1987.

V. Maher, *Women and property in Morocco*, New York 1974.

JAMILA BARGACH

Stereotypes

Afghanistan

Afghan women remain at the crossroads of different kinds of stereotyping. The sex/gender system practiced exemplifies "ineluctable patriarchy" and necessitates that young girls marry into large families, gain respect primarily by bearing sons, and later in life obtain power as mothers-in-law. Seclusion of women from all males excepting the *maḥārim* (acceptable male guardians) through a system of purdah (seclusion) is widely practiced while most women are required to wear a *burqaʿ* (veil) in public. This kind of seclusion is regarded as crucial to the family's honor and pride. Afghan society regards women as the perpetuators of the ideals of the society, symbolizing honor of the family, community, and the nation. Scholars have attributed Afghan patriarchy to the mode of production based on nomadic pastoralism and settled agriculture, all constituted patrilineally (Riphenburg 2003). Women and children are often incorporated into the idea of property belonging to a single male. This is especially true of the Pashtuns (the largest ethnic group) whose tribal code is masculine.

It is also widely believed that women must be controlled and protected so as to maintain moral purity. A large section of conservatives also consider women socially immature with less moral control and physical restraint than men, and hence untrustworthy. Such attitudes lead to "generic" stereotyping – not specifically related to Islam – that Afghan women are alienated, incapable of decision-making, subjugated, and inferior to their male counterpart. Other characteristics that are directly related to Islamic tenets, such as the Prophet's wives' behavior as representing the ideal, subordinate, and domestic roles for women, upholding of polygamy for men, and marriage and motherhood being the only opportunities for women, lead to "sectorial" stereotypes. This kind of stereotype relies on essential and cultural views of Islam and harps on generalizations that Muslim women have more children, are ignorant, and do not have access to the outside world because they belong to a particular culture.

Discourses on Afghan women have also stressed the centrality of women in Afghan society. This contradicts the stereotype of Afghan women living lives of unremitting labor, valued by men solely for sexual and reproductive services. Many stress respect for women as an important value that cannot be undermined. There is also a fine line of difference with regard to private and public roles of women. Some claim that there is a noticeable sharing of ideas and responsibilities in many households and sometimes individual charisma and strength of character surmount conventional subordinate roles. Public image is very important, requiring urban women to be models of reticence and rural women to be properly submissive. Any digression from prescribed roles can lead to moral condemnation and social ostracism. Elphinstone's accounts (1815) indicate that although women did not have a large role to play outside their homes, they had an important position within their homes and did have a right to socialize. However they had to cover themselves when in public to maintain chastity and modesty. This hardly produced any feeling of confinement.

Among the rural, nomadic, and some ethnic groups, such as the Nuristani, digressions from the stereotypical role are often found. They do not observe purdah. Rural women often participate in agricultural activities and also specialize in handicrafts such as carpet- and felt-making. In contrast, Nuristani women plow the fields while men herd the flocks and process dairy products. Nomadic women take care of their cattle and prepare dairy products. Felt- and rug-making are also part of female activity. Urban women joined the workforce in large numbers during the Communist period (from 1978) and the majority of them were professionals; technicians and administrators employed by the government provided appropriate support. Health and education were the two sectors where they participated most, probably because they were extensions of the traditional roles of women. However some also worked for the police, army, and airlines and also in government and private industries.

The way the West perceives Afghan women is largely dependent on international political developments. This leads to a mixture of misperceptions and flawed judgments. They are classified as women belonging to members of a particular group (Afghan as well as Muslim) and hence stereotypical inferences are drawn, resulting in faulty generalizations. During the Taliban regime Afghan women were stereotyped as alienated and subjugated with no rights. Although primarily true, what the West chose to ignore was the atrocities committed on women by the previous regime and also the lack of security in the post-Taliban Karzai regime. The perception of Afghan women in the Karzai period is significantly that of a liberated and publicly active group. Such conclusions stem from lack of knowledge about Afghan social norms and problems of transitional countries.

BIBLIOGRAPHY

PRIMARY SOURCES

Amnesty International, Women in Afghanistan. A human rights catastrophe, 1995, <http://www.amnesty.org/ailib/intcam/afgan/afgtoc.htm>.

United Nations, Economic and Social Council, Report of the Secretary-General on the situation of women and girls in Afghanistan, 21 July 2000, E/CN.4/Sub.2/2000/18, < http://www.unhchr.ch/Huridocda/Huridoca.nsf/ 0/4f3b6f16c0088a70c125694d0053823a?Open document>.

SECONDARY SOURCES

M. Elphinstone, *An account of the kingdom of Caubul and its dependencies in Persia, Tartary and India*, London 1815, Karachi 1972[3].

J. L. Esposito, Introduction. Women in Islam and Muslim societies, in Y. Y. Haddad and J. L. Esposito (eds.), *Islam, gender and social change*, Oxford 1998, ix–xxviii.

C. J. Riphenburg, Gender relations and development in a weak state, in *Central Asian Survey* 22:2/3 (June–September 2003), 187–207.

ARPITA BASUROY

Canada

Ethnically and socially diverse, Canadian Muslims enjoy legal equality regarding citizenship, religious practice, and institution building, yet experience prejudice and religious intolerance that is rooted in twentieth-century racially structured immigration policy, reinforced by Canadian and American media portrayals, and centered on images of male violence (particularly to Muslim women) that legitimize Western political motives.

The extent to which Muslim Canadians differ in their informal identification and formal affiliation with coreligionists makes it problematic to speak of a single Canadian Muslim community. Canada's 2001 national census revealed that roughly 580,000 Canadians, nearly 2 percent of the population, are Muslim. It is essential to acknowledge the diversity of this population so as to recognize the multiple forms of bias and prejudice against Muslims: religious intolerance, racism, and xenophobia. In fact, 86 percent of Canadian Muslims identify as members of visible minority groups, and 72 percent indicate that they were born outside Canada. Of the total Canadian Muslim population, 46 percent immigrated to Canada between 1991 and 2001, including 30 percent who immigrated between 1996 and 2001. The largest ethnic groups are South Asian (37 percent) and Arab (21 percent).

Quotas imposed on non-European immigrants between 1891 and 1962 demonstrate structural racial prejudice that affected Muslim populations; immigrant-sending countries were arranged hierarchically according to desirability, with Syria (Canada's primary sender of Muslim immigrants) ranked next to last (Kelly 1998, 86). Yet, notwithstanding varying degrees of religious intolerance and racial prejudice (particularly associated with skin color), many Muslim women who immigrated to Canada during this period integrated into mainstream society to a greater extent than recent immigrants, and experienced economic and social mobility (Husaini 1999, 17). Class and education have been significant but not sufficient factors in overcoming societal barriers to mobility; as a group, Muslims are characterized by higher educational levels and lower incomes than the Canadian average.

Despite having its own domestic news and entertainment industry, Canadian society is pervaded by media images, including images of Muslims, produced in the neighboring United States. Portrayals of fictional terrorists as Muslim, as in the feature film *Executive Decision* which depicts a terrorist praying to Allah, and in another scene, a man holding a Qur'ān while committing a terrorist act, have been condemned by Canadian Muslims. News reporting is another medium in which Islam is represented as a religion that promotes violence. While archival video footage of Muslims prostrate in prayer and sound files of the call to prayer have been used in Canadian television and radio to accompany reporting on violence committed by Muslims, by contrast, communal rituals and religious symbols of Christians and Jews are not featured during news accounts of political violence by members of these faiths.

Increases in bias and prejudice against Muslims in the news media have corresponded to international political events. Since 1979, when Iranian students stormed the American Embassy in Tehran and held 66 Americans hostage for up to 444 days, images of Muslims (especially Iranians and Arabs) in popular culture have emphasized tropes of violence, irrationality, and female oppression more than exoticism (Khan 2002, 4–5). Like the American media, Canadian news sources immediately speculated that the 1995 bombing of a United States government building in Oklahoma City was committed by Middle Eastern terrorists; juries later convicted two Americans, both fundamentalist Christians, of the act. Widespread condemnation of the media for its coverage of this event, in particular, was instrumental in decreasing (though not eradicating) bias against Muslims in Canadian news reporting. In a headline that appeared in 2000, a major metropolitan newspaper characterized as an "Islamic bomb" a nuclear weapon possibly under development by Osama bin Laden. Following public criticism, the newspaper later issued a retraction, and stated that the association of the suspected plot with Islam was gratuitous and unjustified.

The theme of violence and discrimination against women in Muslim societies was a prominent aspect of the Canadian media's coverage of the 11 September 2001 attacks by al-Qāʿida (al-Qaeda) on American targets. In this message, also promoted by the French in the early twentieth century to justify their colonization of North Africa, the West depicts itself as the welcomed liberator of Muslim women. Nonetheless, the Canadian media have provided for divergent voices of Muslims, male and female, which are accorded legitimate space for engagement of these issues in national newspapers, radio, and television.

Canadian Muslims have addressed stereotypes and biases in several ways. Some families, a minority, have organized and supported full-time Muslim schools where children are isolated from a vilification of Islam and Muslims that parents view on television and suspect is present at school as well (Kelly 1999, 211–12). According to these parents, Muslim schools offer children, as Muslims and as immigrants, the opportunity to be part of a majority group and develop psychological strength that they would not otherwise acquire.

Several voluntary associations have been formed. The goals and activities of the Canadian Council of Muslim Women, founded in 1982, include helping Muslim women integrate into broader society, educating Canadians about Islam and Muslim cultures, and monitoring the portrayal of Islam in public schools (McDonough and Alvi 2002, 79, 85). Through letters and articles published in Canada's national papers, CAIR-CAN, the Council on American-Islamic Relations Canada, has frequently drawn the attention of Muslims and the wider public to negative and inaccurate media representations of Islam and Muslims. Electronic mail, the Internet, and fax machines have been used effectively by CAIR-CAN as tools for acquiring and disseminating information about instances of misrepresentation and biased reporting, and for organizing response.

Prejudice and bias against Canadian Muslims affect women, in particular, when they wear distinctive dress such as the *ḥijāb* and jellaba (a minority practice among Canadian Muslim women). In many contexts, these garments are associated with a political and social stance that is thought to be incompatible with mainstream secular democratic Canadian values, particularly among the French-speaking majority in the province of Quebec. In several instances since 1994, girls have been expelled from Quebec schools for wearing the *ḥijāb*; in each case, school administrators have said the *ḥijāb* contravenes their secular ethos. Public debate on this question has been marked by statements from Quebec nationalists and feminists that prohibiting it in the classroom will free young Muslim girls from patriarchal oppression.

Experience of bias and prejudice is entwined with Canadian women's decisions to wear *ḥijāb*. Feelings of exclusion from mainstream society have influenced the choice of some young Canadian-born Muslim women to identify more closely with their heritage, construed in both religious and ethnic terms. Wearing *ḥijāb*, a choice that is valued in some religious communities, is considered by some to be a proactive strategy through which women assert and define their identity to mainstream society and within the diasporic Muslim community. Expressing their decision both in terms of religious freedom valued by mainstream society and as a personal choice that reflects commitment to communal religious ideals, young women who wear *ḥijāb* often experience greater authority and freedom (particularly relating to mobility) within the family.

Discussion among feminist Canadian Muslim scholars of *ḥijāb* and women's legal and social status in Muslim societies has often been moderated by the desire not to reinforce the dominant stereotype of Muslim men's cruelty toward women. The vigor with which Canadian media, feminist groups, and society at large have discussed and defended the legal and social position of Muslim women and girls in Canada, and more generally "women in Islam," has been attributed by these scholars to a subtle racism that elides ethnicity, class, and place of origin in a general condemnation of Muslim men/civilization (Hoodfar 1993, Jamal 1994, Khan 2002). Future research by and about Muslim women in Canada must address both how negative stereotypes influence individuals' social strategies, and how variables such as class, ethnicity, marital status, age, place of birth, and personal narratives as refugees and immigrants intersect with experiences of, and strategies to combat, bias and prejudice within dominant Canadian society.

Bibliography

S. Alvi, H. Hoodfar, and S. McDonough (eds.), *The Muslim veil in North America. Issues and debates*, Toronto 2003.

H. Hoodfar, The veil in their minds and on our heads. The persistence of colonial images of Muslim women, in *Resources for Feminist Research/Documentation sur la recherche féministe* 22:3/4 (1993), 5–18.

Z. Husaini, Historical background, in S. Zaman, *At my mother's feet. Stories of Muslim women*, Kingston, Ont. 1999, 13–19.

A. Jamal, Identity, community and the post-colonial experience of migrancy, in *Resources for Feminist Research/Documentation sur la recherche féministe* 23:4 (1994), 35-41.

Z. Kashmeri, *The gulf within. Canadian Arabs, racism, and the Gulf War*, Toronto 1991.

P. Kelly, Muslim Canadians. Immigration policy and community development in the 1991 census, in *Islam and Christian-Muslim relations* 9:1 (1998), 83–102.

——, Integration and identity in Muslim schools, in *Islam and Christian-Muslim relations* 10:2 (1999), 197–217.

S. Khan, *Aversion and desire. Negotiating female identity in the diaspora*, Toronto 2002.

S. McDonough and S. Alvi, The Canadian Council of Muslim Women. A chapter in the history of Muslim women in Canada, in *Muslim World* 92:1/2 (2002), 79-97.

A. Rashid, *The Muslim Canadians. A profile*, Ottawa 1985.

S. Zaman, *At my mother's feet. Stories of Muslim women*, Kingston, Ont. 1999.

Patricia L. Kelly Spurles

South Asia

Stereotypes either depict Muslim women as exotic, oppressed, and almost totally enslaved by men in Islam, or as defending the virtues of Islam and the status and rights accorded to women. Both these stereotyped approaches must be avoided as they are apologetic and hardly take into account contemporary problems in society or women's position from a gender perspective within a historical context. Women's position is determined more by sociocultural practices, political interests, and current realities of each area than by Islamic principles, for instance, the global interpretation and application of personal laws.

The defenders of Islam argue that Islam has showered women with ample rights and that therefore there is no need to launch a campaign or movement to reform Islamic principles. Historically, it is certainly true that Islam was one of the earliest organized religions to have accorded certain rights to women. With this in mind, many Muslims refuse to acknowledge the changes that have taken place both historically and politically the world over. The social and political diversity that exists in the Muslim world is considerable. Consequently, Muslim women are not a homogeneous group with a single identity. Their ideas, knowledge, and status vary with culture, class, education, and their access to power and resources in society. The intersection of religion with local culture, politics, economics, gender relations, and gender norms shapes the lives of women.

Muslim women in South Asia, particularly in India, suffer from various stereotypes of backwardness; their status is attributed to the prevalence of purdah, polygamy, divorce, and large family size. This entry examines first the gaps between the stereotypes and the reality of Muslim women's lives, and second how the stereotypes of Muslim women are imbibed and promoted by the general population, the academy, and the media. The stereotypes and the real situation of women are guided by the prevailing power relations but often justified in the name of religion.

In spite of the emphasis on education and earning a living in Islam, most Indians, including many Muslims, subscribe to the view that Islam prohibits women from acquiring education and taking up employment. The overall educational level and the representation of Muslims in the organized sector as a whole, particularly in government, is low, and that of Muslim women even lower. The proportion of Muslim women in higher education in India is only 3.56 percent (Muslim Women's Survey 2002). The average work participation rate for Muslim women is 14 percent lower than that of scheduled caste women (37 per cent) This stereotypical perception of education and employment of Muslim women to a large extent overlooks the historical context of their backwardness and the overall socioeconomic position of the community, their minority status, and the political climate of the country (Hussain 1998) and disregards discrimination in education, employment, and gender norms.

Personal law is often seen as a symbol of identity and any discussion of it becomes political. Women are sacrificed on the altar of Muslim identity on the pretext of preserving it. At the application level these laws are influenced by their gendered interpretations and the local culture. For example, a woman is entitled to an inheritance worth half that of her brother, but in practice the impact of local culture and its application indirectly debar her from inheriting anything. This practice is justified by various arguments: the family will spend on her marriage; after marriage she will receive hospitality from her brothers whenever she visits her natal family; and asking for her share will spoil her relationship with her brothers and bring disrespect to the family honor (Hussain 1998). Thus, the gendered practices and the local culture determine what women's behavior should be and bind them to the role of guardians of the threatened identity.

In the area of marriage and divorce, once again, the practice of Islam overrides scriptural Islam because of prevailing local culture. For example, the consent of a girl to marriage is rarely sought and registration of marriage (*nikāḥnāma*) is hardly practiced. Personal choice of marriage partner is considered to be disrespectful of family honor. Divorced women are left with very little or no support from family, community, or the Wakf Board. The interests of dominant political and conservative groups restrict women's options. For example, the Muslim Women's Protection of the Right to Divorce Act 1986 and the judgment of the Supreme Court of India in 2001 prevented Muslim women from claiming maintenance as Indian citizens. Thus, both the gendered practices and interpretations of personal laws and the interest of particular groups from within or outside the community must be taken into account in explaining the stereotypes of Muslim women.

In the sphere of sexuality and reproduction, Islamic provisions are overruled or misinterpreted by the *maulana*s, senior religious leaders, resulting in various misconceptions about the fertility pattern of Indian Muslims. These misconceptions and misinterpretations both within the community and outside it further bolster the stereotypical image of Muslim women and give the impression that marriage and motherhood are the only opportunities for them. Women are often held responsible for the birth of female children and for infertility, thus providing the rationale for a man to divorce or marry a second wife because the family needs a male heir to carry the family name (Hussain 2001). Such interpretations are gendered and rooted in, and reinforced by, the cultural and ideological systems of multiple patriarchies rather than mere religious prescriptions.

The public stereotypical views of Muslim women, including in the media, hold that a woman can be divorced any time for no given reason and can easily remarry (as shown in many television serials and films) and that every Muslim man has four wives. These two views have most often been cited and visualized by the general public as the main reasons for the miserable and subordinate status of Muslim women. But the fact is that the possibility of remarriage for a divorced woman is almost absent because of the stigma, shame, and disrespect related to divorce and the problems of dowry. It is easier for a divorced man to remarry even if he has grown children (Hussain 2003). The legal provision for four wives is often used to explain the miserable condition of Muslim women and is considered a reason for the growth of the Muslim population in India. This stereotype is negated by various reports that show Muslims as the least polygamous community compared to other religious communities (India 1975). The supposed backwardness of Muslim women in India is not a result of this provision; rather it is due to a combination of various factors. Growth and decline of population is dependent on other socioeconomic and political factors, as is evident from the population decline of other Muslim countries, particularly Bangladesh.

Academic writings also create stereotypes of Muslim women and relate their backwardness to religion, ignoring the power and gender dynamics of the wider social structure: "Muslim women are miserable creatures without any rights whatsoever in respect of marriage, succession, guardianship or birth control. Islam has accorded the right to a man to have four wives. The most abominable is the system of purdah. In Muslim society a double standard of morality is prevailing" (Subbama 1998, 3).

The prevalence of stereotypes and the observance of gendered practices show that patriarchal norms and hegemonic ideologies use a selective interpretation of religion and culture. These ideologies support social, economic, and political practices that sustain the dominance of certain groups; religion is often used to justify existing social relations in the society. It is these that are the root cause of gender inequality and gender discrimination. It seems that differentiations within the community in terms of class and money, power, and privilege are often used as powerful and unifying forces in a "cultural articulation of patriarchy" (Shaheed 1997). The rigid cultural strictures and the prevailing stereotypes override the religious prescriptions and skew the rights of women (Hussain 2003).

Bibliography

S. Hussain, *The changing half. A study of Muslim women in India*, Delhi 1998.

——, Inter-generational mobility among Muslim women in India. Report, Indian Council for Social Science Research, Ministry of Human Resource Development, Delhi 1999.

——, Do women really have a voice in reproductive matters?, in *Asian Journal of Women Studies* 7:4 (2001), 29–69.

——, Male privilege female anguish. Divorce and remar-

riage among Muslims of Bihar, in I. Ahmad (ed.), *Divorce and remarriage among Muslims in India*, New Delhi 2003, 263–90.
M.-A. Hélie-Lucas, The preferential symbol for Islamic identity. Women and Muslim personal law, in V. Moghadam (ed.), *Identity politics and women*, Boulder, Colo. 1994, 399.
India. Committee on the Status of Women in India, *Towards equality. Report of the committee on the status of women in India*, New Delhi 1975.
K. Mason, Conceptualizing and measuring women's status. Paper presented at Population Association of America Meeting, Miami, Fla., 5–8 May 1994.
ORG-Marg Muslim Women's Survey 2001–2002, <www.infochangeindia.org/bookandreportsst_A1jsp>.
F. Shaheed, The interface of culture, custom and law. Implications for women and activism law in legal education and practices in Pakistan. North South co-operation, in R. Mehdi and F. Shaheed (eds.), *Women's law in legal education and practice in Pakistan. North South cooperation*, Copenhagen 1997, 151–64.
Women facing Muslim personal laws as the preferential symbol for Islamic identity, first draft, paper prepared for the WIDER Round Table on Identity Politics, 8–10 October 1990, Helsinki.

Sabiha J. Hussain

The United States: Arab Muslim Women as Portrayed in Film

Motion pictures are one of the most powerful teaching tools ever created. "There exists today no means of influencing the masses more potent than the media" (Pope Pius XI). "The cinema must and shall become the foremost cultural weapon of the proletariat" (Nikolai Lenin). This entry examines how image-makers have presented the Arab Muslim woman in film. History reveals that since the beginning of cinema, in fact for more than a century, Hollywood's movies have humiliated, demonized, and eroticized the Muslim woman. Obviously, filmmakers did not create these images, but inherited and embellished Europe's pre-existing Arab stereotypes. In the eighteenth and nineteenth centuries European artists and writers offered fictional renditions of women as swathed and submissive exotic "objects." The stereotype that came to be accepted as valid, becoming an indelible part of European popular culture, has been transferred into American filmmaking.

I began my research on Arab Muslim women as portrayed by Hollywood in 1960. By locating, viewing, and studying more than 60 movies, I discovered many portraits that are dangerous and destructive and should be taken seriously, as well as others that are less offensive. In films ranging from yesteryear's foreign legion thrillers up to and including contemporary political dramas, producers associate the Arab Muslim woman with violence, sex, and oppression. Locked into a cycle of predictable character-types, she has appeared in every sort of film imaginable: sword-and-sandal soaps, musical comedies, magic carpet fantasies, historical tales, movie serials, and terrorist shoot-'m-ups. In films that feature any image of an Arab Muslim woman, stereotypical idiosyncrasies abound that can be seen as rigid and repetitive.

It all began with two silent shorts – one censored, the other uncensored – *Fatima* (1897) and *Fatima's Dance* (1907). Both feature Fatima, the star of Chicago's 1896 World's Fair, as a veiled bosomy belly dancer. To see Arab belly dancers appearing in early films is not surprising. At the turn of the century, in vaudeville and burlesque circles, the dancers were familiar fare. Hollywood simply emulated this image. In Arabian Nights fantasy films such as *The Sheik* (1921), *Slave Girl* (1947), and *John Goldfarb, Please Come Home* (1964), Arab women appear leering out from diaphanous veils, or as unsatisfied, disposable "knick-knacks" lounging on ornate cushions, or scantily-clad harem maidens with bare midriffs, all closeted in the women's quarters of the palace and/or on display in slave markets. The phantasm of the harem still persists. In Disney's remake of *Around the World in Eighty Days* (2004), for example, Arnold Schwarzenegger portrays Prince Hapi, a Middle Eastern shaykh with "one hundred or so wives."

Many films feature Arab women in far less alluring images. In features such as *My Favorite Spy* (1959), *Shark* (1969), and *Deception* (1992) women lurk in the background as unattractive, covetous beasts of burden carrying jugs on their heads; others lie as they rob Westerners; still others are portrayed as obese and revolting. Films like *Protocol* (1984) and *The Sheltering Sky* (1990) feature Muslim women as a cackling horde of crows, and as shapeless black bundles of covered, ululating women, trekking behind their unshaven mates.

The portrayal of Arab women as black magic vamps began in 1917, with Fox's silent *Cleopatra*, starring Theda Bara. Studios promoted them as "serpents" and "vampires," as a result of which the word "vamp" was added to English dictionaries. Movies such as *Saadia* (1953) and *Beast of Morocco* (1966) feature Arab women as enchantresses in cahoots with and possessed of devils.

A very different image of Arab women is projected in films that portray them as active agents of warfare, most specifically as bombers. Perhaps the most overlooked portrait of the Arab woman is the bomber image. The Arab woman as bomber began with Republic's movie serial, *Federal Agents vs. the Underworld Inc.* (1948). Since then, Hollywood has released six feature films showing Palestinians, Moroccans, and other Arab women not as exotic, bumbling and subservient maidens, but as terrorists invading the United States and killing American civilians. *Federal Agents* displays Nila, Hollywood's first-ever Arab terrorist. Described as an "alien threat," this Egyptian "female fanatic" and her Arab cohorts move to bring down United States federal agents. Nila tries to eradicate the agents by administering a deadly "rare oriental herb," firing a pistol, and tossing a bomb at the American "infidels." But she's no match for the Western protagonists. In the end, a huge statue crushes her. Nila gasps her last as the hero quips, "Seeking to destroy others, Nila succeeded in destroying herself."

Not until some 30 years later, in *Black Sunday* (1977), did Hollywood aggressively show another Arab terrorist. Like books, movies last a very long time. Thanks to network and cable systems, at least once a year, usually days before the annual Super Bowl game, generations of viewers have witnessed Dahlia, a Palestinian, trying to blow up the Super Bowl and everyone in it. In *Black Sunday* Dahlia arrives in the United States, acquires a bomb, then seduces a former Vietnam prisoner of war and enlists his aid. She proceeds to help gun down American citizens "where it hurts": in Los Angeles, Washington D.C., and Miami. Final frames show Dahlia and the veteran steering a blimp over Miami's Super Bowl stadium, intending to detonate a cluster bomb that would massacre 80,000 spectators, including the American President. In time, an Israeli officer, not an American agent, terminates them.

Four years later Shakka, a dangerous Moroccan terrorist, surfaced in the 1981 drama, *Nighthawks*. Aware that Shakka is in New York City, the city's security chief warns his colleagues to be wary of her: she was "born in Tangiers, of wealthy parents; a spoiled broad who kills without provocation." His profile proves correct – moments later Shakka shoots him dead. In the end, Shakka and her cohort, a German assassin named Wulfgar, hold the families of United Nations officials hostage in a cable car dangling 250 feet above the East River. As expected, the Western protagonists save the day and the terrorists are shot dead.

Wrong Is Right (1982) portrays hateful Arab students as terrorists. Clad in robes and checkered headscarves the students march on Times Square and tussle with New York policemen, shouting "Death to America." One young Arab woman fastens a plastic bomb onto her body, blowing up herself and injuring onlookers. In the James Bond thriller, *Never Say Never Again* (1983), Fatima, a nuclear terrorist working with SPECTRE, attempts to detonate two nuclear bombs in the West. She fails, terminated by James Bond.

The greater Los Angeles area is the setting for *Wanted: Dead Or Alive* (1987). Here, Palestinian and homegrown Arab Americans go on a killing spree, blowing up more than 200 men, women, and even children. Just outside the city, the camera reveals an Arab-American terrorist factory. Inside the plant are more than 50 chemical weapons that are about to be released into the atmosphere, intended to kill millions. When Malak, the primary villain, and Jamilla, his loyal sidekick, find out the powerful explosions could also kill them as well as their fellow conspirators, Malak cancels the mission. The angry Jamilla protests. Determined to launch the weapons, she is willing to die for the cause. Malak shoots her dead. *True Lies* (1994) presents Juno, a female Palestinian terrorist, who with her fellow Palestinians, members of the "Crimson Jihad," move to launch nuclear missiles over American cities. Final frames show the movie's hero and the Marines kicking "Arab ass."

The message contained in all seven of these films showing Arab women as terrorists, and especially in the four that portray her as a nuclear terrorist, is that Arab Muslim women are capable of the most malicious actions and that the solution is to rid the United States of their presence. In contrast, only a handful of old-fashioned, out-of-date movies – such as *The Return of Chandu* (1934), *Princess Tam Tam* (1935), *Baghdad* (1949), *Flame of Araby* (1951), and *Princess of the Nile* (1954) – present the Arab woman as characterized by intelligence, courage, and beauty. Admirable Egyptian queens appear in the 1934 and 1963 versions of *Cleopatra*, and in *Caesar and Cleopatra* (1946). When, on rare occasions, the dark-complexioned, heroic Arab woman tries to woo a Western protagonist, she is inevitably disappointed. Films such as *Outpost in Morocco* (1949) and *Secondhand Lions* (2003) assume that an Arab woman in love with an American protagonist must die.

In most Hollywood films, then, the portrayal of Arab Muslim women is as exotic, violent, and distinctly other. Arab women are seldom projected to look and behave like most of the viewers. Producers never show them at home with family, or functioning in the workplace as professionals. Instead of revealing a common humanity, Hollywood movies from the beginning have fostered xenophobia and prejudice by their assumption that women under Islam are in a pathetic state, thus helping alienate the Arab woman from her international sisters, and vice versa.

BIBLIOGRAPHY
M. Alloula, *The colonial harem*, Minneapolis, Minn. 1986.
W. Buonaventura, *Serpent of the Nile. Women and dance in the Arab world*, Northampton, Mass. 1998.
L. Jacobs, *The rise of the American film*, New York 1961.
A. Naff, *The Arab Americans*, New York 1988.
J. G. Shaheen, *The TV Arab*, Bowling Green, Ohio 1984.
——, *Reel bad Arabs. How Hollywood vilifies a people*, Northampton, Mass. 2001.
W. Zinsser, In search of Lawrence of Arabia, in *Esquire*, June 1961.

JACK G. SHAHEEN

Western Europe

The hallmark of stereotypes is the lack of individual distinguishing marks giving birth to standardized and oversimplied mental pictures. What are the specific expectations and stereotypes as far as Muslim women in Europe are concerned?

The way Western Europeans consider and perceive Muslim women is hard to measure because it varies over time. It is more a complex mixture of misperceptions, quick judgments, and even racism than a precise feeling limited to certain attitudes. Moreover, inadequate or selected knowledge makes it very difficult for people to view individuals as unique and complex persons and encourages them to rely on stereotypes articulating a selection of social or physical traits such as race, sex, or religion. Certainly the media, in particular television but also newspapers and magazines, have very much helped this process of stereotyping Muslim women by systematizing the association of specific images – the most internationally admitted one being that of a woman wearing a black headscarf – with the journalistic coverage of issues such as political Islam in Europe, terrorism and religion, the failure of integration, and so forth. This is the case with all weekly magazines published in Western Europe, some being more or less the champions of that type of photo-discourse association (*Der Spiegel, Focus, Le nouvel observateur*).

Muslim women living in Europe are at the crossroads of many kinds of stereotypes, some related to gender, others to religion. Some gender stereotypes implicitly recall more classical ones (not specifically related to Islam): women are unstable, irrational, and vulnerable when they are not protected by men. We would call these stereotypes "generic" as they refer to a general picture of women at large as alienated and submitted to male authority, not capable of any autonomous decision. The categorization of persons on the basis of gender implies the existence of gender related characteristics consistent with this classification. Other stereotypes are directly related to what is seen in Europe as the intangible main characteristics of Islam (for instance polygamy, the behavior of the wives of the Prophet Muḥammad, Islamic law, inequality between men and women, the subordinate role attributed to women within marriage, and motherhood being the only opportunities for them). We would call these "sectorial stereotypes" as they explicitly rely on an essentialist and cultural view of Islam (Muslim women have more children than others, they are ignorant, they do not have access to external society because of their specific "culture"). Islam appears as the key to explain and justify differences between us and them. To some extent, these two main lines of stereotypes interact more or less strongly according to the national context in which they emerge. Independently from Islam, gender stereotypes vary from one European country to another. The national shape taken by the public debates around gender equality clearly demonstrated this variance some years ago when it came to be introduced as a central principle at the European level. Explicitly looking at Muslim women in Western Europe, there is, however, one main issue that seems to represent a common focus for the specific stereotypes of which these women may be the objects: the headscarf. The public representations that come out in such debates vary over time and place and help us to question the changing parameters of the stereotyping processes at stake.

The veil is widely considered to be what makes a Muslim woman visible as a believer and embeds hers in specific inter-gender relationships (men dominating women). By extension, it gives rise to specific views on sexuality of Muslim women. However, when it comes to headscarf controversies – obviously with varying resonance in the Western European countries, from indifference in the United Kingdom to the polemic national crisis that started in the late 1980s in France – the time dimension appears central. Indeed, the Muslim women who were at the core of the first discussions at the end of the 1980s do not have the same social and economic profile as the contemporary girls and women who claim the right to wear the veil while studying or working. This difference of profile is reflected by the types of argument used by politicians and opinion makers to explain why it should be strictly forbidden to wear a headscarf in public places. Twenty years ago, the dominant argument dealt with male domination over women in Muslim societies at large and by proxy in the Western European countries. Nowadays, new elements are incorporated such as the individual right to choose how to express religious affiliation and the potential emancipatory function of this religious sign (this taken from the literature analyzing the political commitment of women in Muslim societies such as Iran and Turkey). It is now commonly admitted that if in some cases the veil comes from a top-down imposition (from father, brothers, a religious authority, and so forth), it may also be a rational choice strategy to wear it as it opens margins of movement that otherwise would not be available.

Public stereotypes of Muslim women basically moved from the image of the non-educated peasants who constituted the majority of the first waves of migration to Europe and hardly spoke European languages, to the one of the educated and smart young women who have engaged in a radical political movement. Interestingly, this perception of the generational changes gave also birth to "positive" stereotypes such as the idea that Muslim girls would be more successful at school than Muslim boys. These kinds of generalized opinions have recently been revised to form a more differentiated picture including variables such as the educational arena in which boys and girls are trained, the level of education they receive, and access to employment. Western European societies in general have learned a great deal during the last 40 years. The debate over female genital mutilation (FGM) is a relevant illustration of how societies incorporate new forms of knowledge: it is now generally admitted that FGM is not an Islamic practice but rather a local historical tradition in places such as Sub-Saharan Africa or Egypt. It is, however, important to consider that stereotypes surrounding Muslim women settled in Western Europe also stem from Muslim populations living in the same contexts, both men and women. Most of the criticism comes from a reading of Islamic traditions that stick to the original text without elaborating on the changing contexts and eventual new interpretations, such as those of the reformists. Muslim women in Europe are either perceived by their peers as too close to or too far from the original message and its essential values. More and more social studies are trying to focus on the gender issues among Muslim populations not only through the lens of family or political commitment, but also by working on specific topics such as emerging female religious authorities.

The stereotyping process that shapes the public images of Muslim women in Western Europe is more and more dependent on international political developments, and thus constantly evolving. There is no doubt about the intimate tie binding the perception of Islam in Europe with the representation of Islam out of Europe: the common representation of Muslim women in Europe is very much linked with the perception of women's life in Muslim societies. The Western European reliance on stereotypes follows the path of salient international events (for instance at the beginning of the 1980s, the surprising role of women in revolutionary processes and their ambiguous social and political position in the following years, or, during the 1990s, the rise and fall of the Taliban regime in Afghanistan with its consequences for women).

Stereotypes concerning Muslim women in Western Europe depend upon time and place but still constitute forms of categorization of others attributing certain patterns of attitude (negatively connoted) to ethnic and religious identity. By classifying women as members of a group (Muslims), stereotypes draw inferences about them stemming from their perception of the group itself. This often leads to abusive generalizations and even types of discrimination that may lead to further exclusion as expressed in the report of the French Haut conseil à l'integration (HCI 2001, 98–9).

Bibliography

V. Amiraux, Discours voilés sur les musulmanes en Europe. Comment les musulmans sont-ils devenus des musulmanes? in *Social Compass* 50:1 (2002/3), 85–96

HCI (Haut conseil à l'intégration) *L'Islam dans la république*, Paris 2001.

L. Reina, *Gendering Orientalism. Race, feminity and representation*, London 1996.

Valérie Amiraux

Sufi Orders and Movements

The Balkans

The presence of Sufi orders in the Balkans is closely linked to Ottoman rule over this ethnically mixed peninsula between the fourteenth and early twentieth centuries. The diversity and number of Sufi orders indicate that most of the peninsula provided receptive grounds for the dissemination of Sufi ideas and practices. Indeed, it would be impossible to imagine the high conversion rate to Islam in many areas without an active Sufi presence. Balkan Islam, then, has been neither fully defined by Sufi ideas or practices, nor has it been influenced by a single Sufi way. While a number of orders that set foot in the region subsequently lost their initial importance and membership, others endured in one or several Balkan regions until the present. Among the most important orders are the Halvetī, Naqshbandī, and Bektāshī, while less prevalent ones include the Qādirī, Rifāʿī, Mevlevī, Bayrāmī, Melāmi, and Bedevī. Overall, Sufi orders infused Balkan Islam with new vigor in both belief and practice. While some were highly syncrectic and therefore enjoyed popular appeal (for example, the Bektāshī), others were more attractive to intellectual and literate circles (for example, the Halvetī).

As regards Muslim women, their access to and participation in Sufi life is difficult to assess due to the lack of adequate and consistent sources. However, the Sufi inclinations of many Muslim women were recorded sporadically. For example, the presence of the "Sisters of Rum" (Bacıyân-i Rûm), a mystical organization of women with roots in Asia Minor, is mentioned in fragmentary references across Bosnia and Greece. Thus, a nineteenth-century English travelogue mentions one Derviş Hanım in Thessaloniki, and another woman who replaced her dead husband as the shaykh of the Sisters of Rum's lodge in Kavala, Greece. In Bosnia, they were locally known as Badžijanije, and anecdotes about their lives in hagiographical literature date to the seventeenth century. Badžijanije are spoken of as spiritual masters, educators, influential ladies, even eccentrics. As late as the mid-twentieth century, a prayer to "Seven Sisters" who were part of this movement was included in the mourning ceremony in some parts of Bosnia. Among these "Seven Sisters" was the wife of the Qādirī Shaykh Hasan Kaimi in Sarajevo of the seventeenth century. She worked as the shaykh of Kaimi's auxiliary lodge which was later instituted as specifically women's.

Other women left their own works testifying to Sufi links and experiences. Worthy of mention is the seventeenth-century Asiye Hatun of Skopje, Macedonia, who left a log of her dreams which she had recorded and discussed with her Halvetī shaykh. Both the dreams and the shaykh's commentary reflect the richness of Asiye Hatun's Sufi knowledge. Likewise, the nineteenth-century Bosnian Habiba Stoćević Rizvanbegović wrote love poetry, in Ottoman Turkish, which reveals typical Mevlevī motifs. Her biography mentions that she left Bosnia for Konya to join the Mevlevī order, to which she dedicated the rest of her life. But while their membership in most Sufi orders continues today, women's experiences are by and large relegated to private space as they are commonly not allowed to participate in *dhikr* ceremonies or engage in other rituals and practices side by side with men. If they do come to *dhikr* on special occasions, they are usually placed in a separate room. Perhaps the most notable exception to such segregation at rituals is the Bektāshī order.

Long associated with the Ottoman military establishment, Bektāshī activity spread throughout the Balkans, as evidenced by the remains of their *tekke*s (lodges) and *türbe*s (tombs) in Greece, Macedonia, Bosnia, Bulgaria, and Albania. Shīʿī in orientation and organized around a shaykh referred to as *baba*, the Bektāshīs intertwine Islamic teachings with local customs and folklore, making the order popular especially in rural areas. The most enduring presence of the Bektāshī is to be found in Albania. Despite heavy persecution by Enver Hoxha's atheist regime in the 1970s and 1980s, the Albanian Bektāshī managed to regroup once the state relaxed its religious policies, instituting themselves in 1993 as a community separate from Sunnī Muslims. This has enabled the Bektāshīs to augment their membership and restore some of the *tekkes* and *türbes* that had been confiscated or destroyed. As regards gender relations, the Bektāshīs proudly maintain that women are granted equal opportunities in all matters of belief and practice. Indeed, Bektāshī women undergo the same initiation ceremony, participate side by side with men in all rituals, and are equally involved in the tradition of composing sacred songs, as evidenced by a collection of spiritual songs entitled *Gül Deste* (Bouquet of roses). This level of gender intermixing and equality is certainly not the case with other Sufi orders in the region, and has been used by certain Sunnīs to slander Bektāshī morality.

Despite the lack of direct participation in other Sufi orders, however, women have adopted and adapted to Sufi teachings in a variety of ways. One interesting development linked to Sufi influence is the ritual of *tevhid* (Arabic *tawḥīd*) practiced by women in Bosnia-Herzegovina. *Tevhid* is primarily the ritual of mourning, performed on several occasions: the day of the burial (*dženaza*), the seventh day, the fortieth day after death, and subsequently six months and one year after death. *Tevhid* is led by professional *bula*s, the women educated in the religious school for women (*ženska medresa*) that has operated in Sarajevo with interruptions since 1940. Among their various responsibilities is to attend ceremonies and family rituals, but their most central duty lies with the *tevhid* and *mevlud* (Arabic *mawlid*, a festive occasion). When the *medresa* was closed down between 1949 and 1978, the *tevhid* ritual underwent a crisis as a new generation of women had to be trained either by older *bula*s or by their husbands who worked as Islamic teachers and community leaders. *Tevhid*s are attended by the female relatives, neighbors, and friends of the deceased, and are commonly held at his/her home, though they can take place in a mosque. The *bula*s lead the prayers, recite appropriate verses from the Qurʾān, and appoint other women to carry on the recitation. Every recital is followed by a collective prayer and the mention of the deceased, as well as of other dead relatives, who thereby receive "gifts" in the afterlife. During the final prayer, women collectively recall the names of God and the Prophet Muḥammad. Ritually, *tevhid* is likened to the Sufi *dhikr* in that it emulates some of its aspects, including, in some cases, the use of large rosaries (*tespih*) similar to those used in Sufi *tekke*s, and a rhythmic swaying of the body. One theory holds that in Ottoman times Sufi masters were invited to perform mourning rituals at the house of the deceased. While the men attended the burial, the women who stayed at home followed the Sufi way of ritual mourning and gradually adopted it as their own practice. Nowadays, *tevhid* is certainly the most common ritual in Bosnia and one that bears an important witness to the influence of Sufi practices on women's religious life.

BIBLIOGRAPHY

J. K. Birge, *The Bektashi order of dervishes*, London 1956.

T. Bringa, *Being Muslim the Bosnian way*, Princeton, N.J. 1995.

N. Clayer, Islam, state and society in post-communist Albania, in H. Pulton and S. Taji-Farouki (eds.), *Muslim identity and the Balkan state*, New York 1997, 115–38.

L. Garnett, *Mysticism and magic in Turkey*, London 1912.

M. Hadžijahić, The Badžijanije in Sarajevo and Bosnia, in *The Annals of the Gazi Husrev Beg Library* [in Bosnian] 7/8 (1982), 109–33

A. Hatun, *Rüya mektuplari*, ed. and intro. C. Kafadar, Istanbul 1994.

F. Nametak, *Bosniak diwan literature* [in Bosnian], Sarajevo 1997.

H. T. Norris, *Islam in the Balkans*, Columbia, S.C. 1993.

A. Popovic, The contemporary situation of the Muslim mystic orders in Yugoslavia, in E. Gellner (ed.), *Islamic dilemmas. Reformers, nationalists and industralization*, Berlin 1985, 240–54.

A. Softić, *Tevhids in Sarajevo* [in Bosnian] Sarajevo 1984.

AMILA BUTUROVIC

Egypt

Medieval historians were uninterested in recording women's participation in Sufi orders which must be inferred from incidental references to shaykhs in Mamluk and Ottoman Egypt who catered to women and admitted them into their orders – controversial topics among Sufi men – and from denunciations of women's participation in *dhikr*, the ritual "remembrance" of God through repeated chanting of some of His Names. There are rare notations of women who became *shaykha*s, such as Zaynab Fāṭima bt. al-ʿAbbās (d. 1394), head of a women's retreat house in Cairo founded in 1285 by Princess Tadhkaray for Zaynab bt. Abū al-Barakāt "al-Baghdādiyya" and her women. Most of these women were widows or divorcees. Some men's Sufi retreat houses may have included women; the historian Maqrīzī mentions that one of them had a separate bathroom for women.

Traditional male disregard for women's participation in Sufism continues in the official denial by the government-sponsored Supreme Council of Sufi Orders that any women are members in the more than 70 registered Sufi orders. In reality, women participate in the orders, and a few women are *de facto* shaykhs of orders, though officially unrecognized. The policies of individual orders toward women vary a great deal; some orders exclude them altogether, while others create space for them. Some shaykhs instruct their disciples primarily through visions, and this may be particularly important for women, whom social conventions often bar from direct interaction with a shaykh.

Women in Cairo and the Delta are much more visible, vocal, and assertive than women in Upper Egypt, where it is sometimes still considered appropriate to seclude girls when they reach puberty. Many shaykhs in Upper Egypt have only male disciples. One woman who frequented a shaykh was shot by her father for dishonoring the family. She survived and fled to Cairo, where she was free to pursue the Sufi life. In Upper Egypt women do not participate in the *dhikr* rituals held at *mawlid*s (saint's day celebrations), although they visit the saints' tombs and sometimes observe the *dhikr*.

In the Delta and in Cairo, women participate more visibly in the Sufi orders, including *dhikr* and other *mawlid* activities. During the "great night" of the *mawlid* of Aḥmad al-Badawī in Tanta, the floor of the mosque is covered with men, women, and children, without any gender segregation. Economic transactions, secular entertainment, and games are more evident at *mawlid*s in Cairo and the Delta.

Dhikr is held weekly, in both afternoon and evening, at some saint's shrines or within certain Sufi groups. Women are more likely to participate in the afternoon than at night. Some shrines attract more women's participation than others. Not all shrines are equally holy, and those with less sanctity (accorded by undefined popular consensus) are more accessible to women. Women are barred from the shrines of Ḥusayn and Sayyida Zaynab after sunset, although they sit outside the gates. In contrast, the visitors to the shrine of Abū Suʿūd are nearly all women. Women are less likely to rise to join the *dhikr* rows in a mosque, although they may watch in large numbers. Women who participate in *dhikr* often remain where they are in a seated position, drawing a thin veil over the face to avoid being watched while in trance. Women are more likely to participate if *dhikr* takes place in the street or in a square outside the mosque, although men always outnumber them. If men break into a folk-dance during *dhikr*, this is usually tolerated as a spontaneous expression of joy, but if a woman does this, it is usually seen as provocative.

Sufism in Egypt is largely associated with rural areas and the lower urban classes, although participation of well-educated and wealthy urbanites is not uncommon, as Sufi rituals and festivals, respect for Sufi shaykhs, and veneration of Sufi saints are well integrated into Egyptian religious life, often without being identified as "Sufi." Women's participation crosses categories of age and social class and is often connected with their family's involvement with a particular order, but other women are led into Sufism through life crises, spiritual impulses, or visions that lead them to a particular spiritual guide. Certain orders cater specifically to the middle and upper classes. The Jāzūliyya Ḥusayniyya Shādhiliyya, a mainly middle-class order, employs popular musical styles rather than traditional Sufi music, to attract educated youth. Women's participation is unusually equal to that of men: they sit on one side of the shaykh, while men sit on the other, and everyone performs *dhikr* in a seated position.

In Egypt Sufi women do not generally meet separately from the men. The only order with a separate section for women is al-Sharʿiyya al-Muḥammadiyya, the order of Muḥammad's Sharīʿa, a name that deflects criticism from those who feel Sufism contradicts the Sharīʿa. The *dhikr* of these women, all upper-class, is solemn and dignified, lacking music, motion, or ecstatic expression. Upper-class women do not speak loudly or express emotion in public, although such behaviors are typical of lower-class women in Cairo.

Women prepare food at *mawlid*s, where Sufis offer food and drink to passers-by. They may be hidden from sight or actively involved with the guests. Some women as well as men devote much of their life to traveling the circuit of the *mawlid*s to honor the saints, camp by the shrines, and offer hospitality.

Women who are leaders in the Sufi orders are usually called "mother," not *shaykha*, just as disciples are the "sons" and "daughters" of a shaykh. Sufi "mothers" have "sons" as well as "daughters." They have recognized spiritual virtues, especially visions and miraculous knowledge, but a brother or son is appointed official shaykh of the order. Although women are generally perceived as spiritually weaker than men, some women attain very high spiritual rank.

Some Sufis feel that gender concerns are inappropriate among those who have passed beyond the domain of the flesh. They claim not to be subject to sexual passions, and freely interact with Sufis of the opposite sex. One Sufi "mother" lives with two unrelated "sons." Ḥāgga Zakiyya ʿAbd al-Muṭṭalib Badawī, an older woman, allowed a young man to rest his head on her lap, calling him her "daughter," to indicate transcendence of normal gender distinctions. On the other hand, some Sufis feel observance of strict segregation is imperative when outsiders are present, out of respect for their weakness.

Bibliography

A. ʿAbd al-Rāziq, *Al-marʾa fī Miṣr al-Mamlūkiyya*, Cairo 1975.

V. J. Hoffman, *Sufism, mystics, and saints in Modern Egypt*, Columbia, S.C. 1995.
C. Mayeur-Jaouen, *Al-Sayyid al-Badawi. Un grand saint de l'islam égyptien*, Cairo 1994.
E. B. Reeves, *The hidden government. Ritual, clientelism and legitimation in northern Egypt*, Salt Lake City 1990.
M. Winter, *Society and religion in early Ottoman Egypt. Studies in the writings of ʿAbd al-Wahhab al-Shaʿrani*, New Brunswick, N.J. 1982.

Valerie J. Hoffman

North Africa

Women have been active in Sufi orders in North Africa throughout history. They participated in separate women's *dhikr*s (Sufi remembrance rituals), and served as *muqaddamāt* (circle leaders). *Muqaddamāt* acted as liaisons between the men's and women's groups, led the women's *dhikr*, initiated new women members, and taught Sufi doctrine and practices to women members. Some women took charge of the internal administration of the *zāwiya*s (Sufi lodges) in which they lived and worshipped. The primary sources for these roles and practices include Arabic historical works and treatises, anthropological studies, travel literature, and reports written by the French colonial administrators. Although their objectives and male authorship limited the details on women, considerable insight can nonetheless be gained from them into Sufi women's practices.

Today, women are active in Sufi orders of two types based on ritual content. The first ritual type, the *dhikr*, involves multiple repetitions of Arabic poems, phrases, or words in praise of Allah or the Prophet Muḥammad to induce an ecstatic state or divine union. The second, the *ḥaḍra* or *līla*, is a therapeutic spirit possession ceremony, in which rhythmic music accompanied by chants is performed to summon supernatural beings which inhabit participants causing them to move rhythmically and fall into trance. Despite some decline in Sufi activities due to oppositional efforts by Islamic reformists over the past century, scholarly interest in exploring women's participation in the surviving orders is growing.

Whether they were local creations or pan- or trans-regional institutions, many orders had parallel forms of women's participation. An investigation in 1917 revealed that 18 women members of the Tijāniyya in the Tunis region held *muqaddama* certificates (Clancy-Smith 1992). The details of Libyan women's roles in the Sanūsiyya remain limited, but its founder, who was raised by his aunt, an active teacher and preacher, was criticized for allowing gender-mixed gatherings. His wife was known for the extreme demands she placed on the male members' piety (Vikør 1995).

Algerian women's participation in Sufi orders has been documented for two time periods: the early nineteenth to the early twentieth century and 1983 to 1999. At the end of the nineteenth century, there were 27,000 women members of Sufi orders in Algeria, mainly in the Qādiriyya, Raḥmāniyya, and Tijāniyya (Jansen 1984). There were 4,000 women Raḥmānī members in the commune of Akbou. In 1913, there were three times as many female as male Raḥmānī members in a *zāwiya* in the Tkout region. *Muqaddamāt* presided over women's *dhikr*s and initiated women adepts using men's procedures. Furthermore, special procedures were developed when men initiated women, in order to avoid direct physical and eye contact (Clancy-Smith 1992).

While no specifics are available on women's groups' educational and ritual practices, some details exist on women's headship of *zāwiya*s. One example is Lālla Khadīja who directed a Raḥmānī *zāwiya* in Kabylia after her husband's death, from 1837 to 1842. Her daughter, who married her mother's successor, also had a leadership role. Moreover, she is reported to have been the first woman to initiate women members and authorize *muqaddamāt*. In the 1890s, the co-wives of the deceased *zāwiya* leader at Laghouat and the Kanadsa *zāwiya* leader's mother, who was both feared and venerated, were in charge of the administration of their respective *zāwiya*s. The ages and backgrounds of these women leaders are unknown (Clancy-Smith 1992).

Another example is Lālla Zaynab, who directed the Raḥmānī *zāwiya* in al-Ḥāmil from her father's death in 1897 until she died in 1904 at about age 50. She fought an intense legal battle against her male cousin to acquire this position. Educated by her father, intimately involved with the functioning of the *zāwiya* all her life, and saintly in status, she was better suited to take on responsibility for the education and social welfare of its members. During her tenure, she initiated both men and women into the order. A large number of women of varying ages and backgrounds lived in the lodge during her and her father's tenure (Clancy-Smith 1992, 1994).

Today, women are active members of the ʿĪsāwiyya, both in Algeria and France. Men dominate the order structurally, but ʿĪsāwī women's groups hold separate, self-styled weekly *jamaʿ* rituals. These rituals consist of a *dhikr* of litanies expressing intense love for the Prophet with percussion accompaniment, followed by individual women divulging their personal problems to the *muqaddama* before the group. A *līla* may also follow. Furthermore, the women attend the annual four-day pilgrimage festival, where they observe men's spirit possession rituals, which culminate in such feats as slashing themselves with swords and consuming poisonous snakes. On the fourth day, the women perform a self-designed theatrical ritual, donning costumes and re-enacting daily events exemplifying gender conflicts in the relationships among members. The ritual serves to process these conflicts. Algerian ʿĪsāwī women in France have initiated the weekly performance of *dhikr* and *līla* in two locations (Andezian 2001).

Moroccan women's historical participation in Sufism has received little scholarly attention. When the early sixteenth-century head of the Jāzūliyya, al-Ghazwānī, called for reform of urban and rural religious education and women's integration into religious life as measures to remedy the moral deterioration of Moroccan society, the number of educated Sufi women increased. Several distinguished themselves as authorities on Sufism including ʿĀʾisha al-Idrīsiyya. Al-Ghazwānī's two most important disciples, al-Habṭī and al-Tlīdī, maintained separate women's *zāwiyas*, identical to the men's, with *muqaddamāt* trained in jurisprudence. Al-Habṭī's wife, Amīna bint Khajjū, a fully trained legist, presided over a women's *zāwiya*, where she taught Islamic and Sufi fundamentals (Cornell 1998).

Some eighteenth- and nineteenth-century Moroccan branches of the Tijāniyya appointed *muqaddamāt* to lead women's *dhikrs* and initiate new women members. The *muqaddama* Ḥajja Khadīja wrote a treatise on Sufi doctrine (al-Ḥajja n.d.), traced her ancestry back to the Prophet, and initiated men into the order (El Adnani 2001). The Darqāwiyya encouraged women's participation, claiming eight *muqaddamāt* in 1942 (Trimingham 1971), and allowed gender-mixed gatherings (Vikør 1995).

The scholarly studies of three orders holding spirit possession ceremonies, the Ḥamādsha (Crapanzano 1973), Raḥḥāliyya (Naamouni 1995), and Gnāwa (Welte 1990), discuss women's participation tangentially. Women are not included in the orders' hierarchies, but actively participate in their therapeutic spirit possession practices. Their needs and experience of trance are recognized as differing from those of men.

As for orders performing *dhikr*, in and around the town of Taroudant, Nāṣiri, Jillālī and Darqāwī women's groups separately perform *dhikr* in local holy figures' tombs. Nāṣirī and Jillālī women choose their group leaders, whereas male leaders appoint them in the Darqāwiyya (Dwyer 1978).

Based on fieldwork observations, Nāṣirī women perform *dhikr* every afternoon in the order's main *zāwiya* in Tamegrut. Likewise, in the Khalūfī tomb complex in Oujda, women hold a *dhikr* every Friday afternoon in one of the two *zāwiyas*. Until 30 years ago, 30 to 40 Tijānī women gathered daily to perform *dhikr* in a separate room in the *zāwiya* in Tiznit. The age and socioeconomic background of these women vary broadly, but older women tend to make up the largest age group.

Fieldwork observations have revealed that women throughout Morocco actively participate in the Būdshīshiyya, a branch of the Qādiriyya established in northeastern Morocco in the early twentieth century with a developed national and international recruitment program. Girls and young unmarried women (aged 14 to 30) from all over the country participate in the annual one-month summer training camp at the main *zāwiya* in Birkan. In Tiznit, the women's group consists solely of Ishilhin (Berbers) from a wide range of socioeconomic backgrounds. About half are unmarried high school students or graduates who are fluent in Moroccan and Modern Standard Arabic and attend the annual Būdshīshiyya training camp. The other half are mostly illiterate, middle-aged to elderly women with very limited knowledge of Arabic. On Sundays and Wednesdays, they all gather in the *zāwiya* to perform the Arabic *dhikr* led by the younger members or the *muqaddama*, who initiates new members and links the group to the men's group through contact with the local shaykh. Midway through the *dhikr*, two young women, trained at Birkan, give lessons in *ḥadith* and *fiqh* in Tashilhit, and the group chants an age-old Tashilhit religious poem in unison.

Bibliography

S. Andezian, *Expérience du divin dans l'Algérie contemporaine. Adeptes des saints dans la région de Tlemcen*, Paris 2001.

J. A. Clancy-Smith, The house of Zainab. Female authority and saintly succession in colonial Algeria, 1850–1904, in N. R. Keddie and B. Baron (eds.), *Women in Middle Eastern history. Shifting boundaries in sex and gender*, New Haven, Conn. 1992, 254–74.

——, *Rebel and saint. Muslim notables, populist protest, colonial encounters (Algeria and Tunisia, 1800–1904)*, Berkeley 1994.

V. J. Cornell, *Realm of the saint. Power and authority in Moroccan Sufism*, Austin, Tex. 1998.

D. H. Dwyer, Women, Sufism and decision-making in Moroccan Islam, in L. Beck and N. R. Keddie (eds.), *Women in the Muslim world*, Cambridge 1978, 584–98.

J. El Adnani, Entre hagiographie et histoire. Les origines d'une confrérie musulmane maghrébine. La Tijāniyya (1781–1881), book manuscript 2001.

al-Ḥajja Khadīja bint Aḥmad (Qari'at al-Maghrib), *al-Sayf al-Yamānī*, Cairo n.d.
W. Jansen, *Women without men. Gender and marginality in an Algerian town*, Leiden 1987.
K. Naamouni, *Le culte de Bouya Omar*, Casablanca 1995.
J. S. Trimingham, *The Sufi orders in Islam*, Oxford 1971.
K. S. Vikør, *Sufi and scholar on the desert edge. Muḥammad b. ʿAlī al-Sanūsī and his brotherhood*, Evanston, Ill. 1995.
F. M. Welte, *Der Gnāwa-Kult*, Frankfurt 1990.

MARGARET J. RAUSCH

Turkey, South Asia, Central Asia, Afghanistan, Iran, the Caucasus, and the Arab East

Many contemporary scholars have noted that the mystical or Sufi interpretation and practice of Islam is an arena that provides scope for female participation and women's leadership. Others (Murata, Ahmed) have understood Sufism as providing a counter or alternative philosophical strand within Islamic traditions that allows for greater expression of feminine spirituality.

The fact that many manifestations of Sufism take place outside of the mosque relieves female participants of the strict imposition of certain formal ritual restrictions such as gender segregation. However, the mixing of males and females in these environments may become a target of criticism for opponents of Sufism. Whether in some cases the incorporation of pre-Islamic popular practices and concepts by Sufis gives greater opportunity for women to participate is open to debate.

History and theory

The understanding that Sufism arises from a mystical philosophy embedded in the Qur'ān permits the expression of the feminine or receptive aspect of the ultimate reality represented by divine attributes such as the Merciful, the Inner, and so forth. In the other main source of religious authority, the Prophet's *sunna*, his "beautiful" (*jamālī*) qualities such as gentleness and forbearance may be seen as supporting a feminine ideal.

The Qur'ānic figure most associated with concepts of female sanctity is Mary, mother of Jesus. Her attitude of acceptance and her state of purity and receptivity to divine revelation sets a pattern for female sainthood in Islam that is similar to her role in Christian piety. Later Sufi-influenced poets have expanded the Qur'ānic account of Yūsuf and Zulaykha into an allegory of spiritual transformation in which the female's lust for this handsome youth is transformed through suffering into mature spiritual love.

Among the Prophet's family, his most saintly female relative is his daughter, Fāṭima, who is elevated to a special spiritual status in the Shīʿī tradition. Here she embodies the archetype of the suffering mother whose sons will ultimately be martyred, as well as the pure virgin (*bātūl*) who is beyond the lusts and defilements of the physical body. Other descendants of the Prophet such as Sayyidnā Nafīsa (824), a descendant of Ḥasan, his grandson, and Sayyidnā Zaynab, the Prophet's granddaughter, are venerated in Cairo as female saints and their shrines are important pilgrimage sites for both men and women.

Female ascetics

The Sufi tradition's most prominent female is Rābiʿa al-ʿAdawiyya of Basra (d. ca. 801). Her story is an appealing legend of a slave girl whose piety won her freedom after which she became a lifelong ascetic. The anecdotes of her reported by ʿAṭṭār (d. 1230) in the *Tadhkirat al-awliyā'* contrast her to the male ascetic, Ḥasan of Basra, whose spiritual states and insights she is able to best through her pragmatic wisdom and more developed miraculous powers. ʿAṭṭār termed her a "man," a common way of appreciating the achievements of Sufi females. For example, Jāmī (d. 1492) in his *Nafaḥāt al-uns* entitled the section of biographical anecdotes of 33 women, "those who have achieved the stations of men." According to Baldick, later legends of Rābiʿa conflate two historical persons. In this case, "the pair of the penitent courtesan and the sexually abstinent wife form a pattern that continues in Sufi biographies" (1989, 30).

The wife of the Sufi al-Ḥākim Tirmidhī (d. ca. 932) is said to have achieved the same spiritual status as her husband and her dreams are reported in his spiritual autobiography. Other notable Sufi women include Fāṭima of Nishapur (d. 849), admired by famous male Sufis Biṣṭāmī and Junayd. Given the social conditions of earlier times many female saints are reported as "anonymous" in the biographical compendia.

While the literary tradition may under-report their existence, at the popular level the evidence of shrines to female saints remains, for example the shrines of Lalla Sittī in Tlemcen, Lalla ʿĀ'isha al-Mannubiyya in Tunis, and Bībījān Pāk Dāmanān in Pakistan. Sūlamī (d. 1021) and many other early hagiographers devoted separate sections to biographies of pious and ascetic females. Sūlāmī's notices present to us pre-*ṭarīqa* female Sufis who embody ascetic and world-denying qualities. As is the case with female scholars in Islam, the number of female saints proportionate to males who are reported seems to decrease over time. Besides the early ascetics, other female Sufis for whom we have information tended to come from the elite classes such as the Mughal princess Jihān Ārā Begum (d. 1680). She is said to have composed a biography of the Sufi master, Muʿīnuddīn Chishtī as well as her own mystical poetry. In addition she was a patroness of architecture.

Sufi theory of the feminine

Ibn al-ʿArabī (d. 1240) mentions several females who were his spiritual guides including Fāṭima of Cordoba (1971). His writings reveal a spiritual egalitarianism in which his characterization of male and female gendering is "accidental" rather than essential to human nature. He asserts that women can be spiritually perfected and that there is "no spiritual qualification conferred on men which is denied to women." It is reported that a number of female disciples received the *khirqa* or cloak of spiritual transmission from him.

The Sufi theorist al-Ghazālī (d. 1111) articulated a more negative opinion of females, seeing their attractiveness as a distraction on the path to spiritual submission. In fact, the image of the feminine in the Islamic tradition and for male Sufis is often ambivalent. Females may represent for some male writers worldly temptation or the lower soul (*nafs*). A *ḥadīth* represents women as deficient in religion and reason and the "affliction" of menstruation was perceived as reflecting women's inability to participate in formal ritual and spiritual practices at certain times.

Practice: popular and high tradition

Sufi shrines are more accessible to females than many mosques because of the lack of formal regulations and the spontaneous nature of ritual expression. Visits to shrines may provide sanctioned outings for women that are undertaken for healing and other benefits beyond religious edification. Common disorders addressed by visiting shrines are infertility, mental disturbance, and marital problems. While women of all social classes may perform shrine visits, they provide in particular an outlet for poorer women to picnic, visit, and relax.

In South Asia many of the saints' tombs are internally gender segregated so that females cannot approach the actual burial site of a male saint and vice versa. In Central Asia, shrines or *mazār*s of female saints are pilgrimage sites of their own. Throughout the Muslim world females are the majority of visitors to shrines and may perform rituals such as lighting candles (North Africa) or tying strings on the grilles or trees surrounding the tomb as a symbol of the binding nature of ritual vows. Certain aspects of popular Sufism and the cult of the saints are particularly accessible to females, for example, their participation in the preparation of special foods or meals for distribution, known in South Asia as *langar*. The anniversaries of the deaths of South Asian saints and *ʿarūs* (marriage) days, may require the preparation of special sweet dishes involving further female expertise. For example, some families commemorate the Sufi saint, ʿAbd al-Qādir Gīlānī (d. 1166) in a household ritual, held on the eleventh day of every lunar month in which a series of devotional food offerings are prepared according to rules that stress ritual purity.

The celebration of the Prophet's birthday in *mawlid/mevlid* ceremonies that may occur throughout the year provides further occasions for female gatherings. While not exclusively confined to practicing Sufis, *mawlid*s usually involve Muslims who believe in the saints and continued access to the Prophet as intercessor.

The extent to which women participate in ritual aspects of formal Sufism varies with the Sufi order and region. In the Turkish Bektāshī Order women are said to participate equally in ritual. In many parts of the Muslim world, however, women are not encouraged to become practicing Sufis. Most traditional scholars hold that the permission of a husband or guardian is required for a woman to take initiation in a Sufi order, presumably since this might challenge the husband's authority. Initiation of females may consist of putting the hand in a bowl of water or holding onto a piece of cloth held by the male shaykh in order to avoid direct physical contact, based on the practice of the Prophet when accepting the allegiance of females. Some Sufi authors such as ʿAbd al-Wahhāb Shaʿrānī (d. 1565) see the relationship between a male shaykh and female disciples as being problematic. This highlights the difficulty of women receiving personal guidance and achieving the requisite intimacy with a teacher within a gender segregated social system. Some female Sufis circumvent barriers on gender mixing by receiving their spiritual instruction from the shaykh in dreams and visions.

At Sufi ceremonies the women are often gathered in a separate room or space or behind a screen or curtain where the sense of participation in the ritual *ḥadrat* or *dhikr* is limited. Children and uninterested females may also be present in the female space, further detracting from the experience. In Sufi ritual women may be discouraged from pronouncing the sacred formulas aloud, from standing, or from performing vigorous bodily movements due to taboos on males hearing the female voice and perceptions that women might become excessively emotional or ecstatic and violate rules of decorum. In Egypt, however, women may on occasion celebrate the *dhikr* standing, swaying to the rhythms in lines or spaces separate from males or on special days assigned to them. For example, at the shrine of Sīdī ʿAlī Zayn al-ʿĀbidīn in the City of the Dead area of Cairo, women attend at a special time and weave to music performed by male performers (*munshidūn*), some going into trance-like states. Female participants often draw their veils over their faces, symbolically demarcating private space.

In the Iranian Niʿmatullāhī Order women are initiates but have never been shaykhs. Among the women's circles a female may serve as a *pir dalīl* (guide for female novices) or as a tea master/mistress, but they listen to the poetry and music sung in the men's section conveyed by a loud speaker. One report of a Qādirī Order meeting for women in Kermanshah has the female Sufis meeting separately and drumming and chanting for their own sessions.

In general, women's dress at Sufi ritual events is less likely than that of males to bear special emblems of authority. In some Sufi orders, however, women don white robes over their usual clothing during more formal *dhikr* sessions.

In societies such as Egypt, Sudan, and Somalia a popular female religious practice that may be associated with Sufism is the *zār*, a sort of dance that evokes cathartic and healing powers. Sometimes female musical troupes perform at *zār*s. Hoffman (1995) notes that in mixed Sufi performance gatherings female performers face the problem that if they sing songs of love, they may become the objects of romantic imagination on the part of males in the audience.

Music and performance traditions associated with Sufism may provide scope for women's participation. For example in Oujda, Morocco Aissawa women convene their own gatherings on Friday afternoons, involving music and trance states. In South Asian mystical poetry, the longing spiritual aspirant is usually given the female gender in mystical romance. Thus the female voice becomes the dominant one, at least theoretically, while some evidence for female performance in limited contexts can be found in the South Asian context. For example, the well-known Pakistani artist, Abida Parveen, specializes in Sufi songs of Punjabi saints while affecting masculine dress and mannerisms in her public performances of this material.

In addition, wealthy women are known to have supported particular Sufi masters and institutions. Separate convents or refuges for Sufi women have been sponsored by female patrons at various epochs of Muslim history. For example, *rabat*s or shelters for women were constructed in premodern Cairo, Aleppo, and Baghdad. Their functions may have overlapped spiritual retreat with charitable shelter.

Female leadership

It has been reported that charisma is passed down in female lineages in certain Moroccan Sufi orders. Tombs of females associated with saints as mothers, wives, and daughters may be visited or venerated on their own, reflecting these womens' residual charismatic powers.

The question of whether a female could be appointed as an initiating master (*murshida*) or even a spiritual successor (*khalīfa*) within Sufi lineages receives various responses. Some writings deny the possibility whereas others record instances of such female leadership while expressing concern as to whether a female *shaykha* could guide male disciples. For example, Mu'inūddīn Chishtī of India (d. 1236) is said to have designated his daughter, Bībī Jamāl, as a *khalīfa*. In contrast, a later Chishtī saint, Bābā Farīd (d. 1265), said that his daughter, Bībī Sharīfa, would have been appointed a *khalīfa* except that this role was not available to women. The twentieth-century Chishtī, Khwāja Ḥasan Niẓāmī (d. 1955) of Delhi, is known to have appointed some female *khalīfa*s. Clancy-Smith (1992) documents the case of a nineteenth-century female Sufi leader in Algeria, Lalla Zaynab of the Raḥmāniyya. Due to the restrictions on the public role of women, their leadership in Sufi orders was usually transmitted through female networks and female ritual leadership generally takes place within exclusively female gatherings.

Contemporary developments

Islamist movements have tended to discourage Sufi interpretations of Islam and popular practices such as the veneration of saints and shrine visitation. At the same time, elements of asceticism and self-fashioning, together with a renewed interest in the traditional sciences of the Unseen, enable a particular strain of Islamist piety accessible to both males and females that is close to the mood of early Sufism.

In other developments female members of American Sufi movements have agitated for greater gender equality, for example, female Mevlevis have introduced training in the *sema* (whirling ceremony) for women and have even performed the ceremony publicly in Turkey. In Algeria, the government-sponsored council of *zāwiya*s is contemplating giving more recognition and encouragement to female participation and such trends seem likely to increase with shifting concepts of gender roles in the public space, whether emerging from Islamist or modernist interpretations of Islam.

Elite women from the Muslim world might join one of the modern urban *ṭarīqa*s that offer more individualistic concepts of spiritual growth, for example, the Dhawqī Shāh branch of the Chishtī Ṣābirī Order based in Karachi, Pakistan. Research on urban elite women of Damascus documents how they constitute their own Sufi circles within the Naqshbandī movement, led by Mufti Aḥmad Kaftārū, under the direction of his daughter, Shaykha Wafā'. Böttcher (1998) reports attendance of between one and two thousand women at *dhikr* sessions sponsored by this group in the Abū al-Nūr mosque in Damascus. Sub-groups of women of this movement sponsor more "select" *dhikr*s for initiates in private homes. This form of Sufi teaching stresses Islamic knowledge and piety and is encouraged as part of a Syrian state-sponsored Sunnī re-Islamization in which Sufism is a preferred alternative to political activism. Other groups of Syrian Sufi women are necessarily less overt in their activities. Contemporary transnational Sufi movements such as the Naqshbandī Ḥaqqānis of Shaykh Nāẓim draw participation from Muslim elites in Malaysia and Egypt, including many women.

The current situation of female Sufis in Iran must be viewed in the context of Sufism in general. While intellectual Sufism representing a cultural heritage of art and poetry is supported by the Islamic Republic, a fairly systematic repression of practical Sufism has occurred, including the persecution and surveillance of known Sufis and the closure and confiscation of Sufi centers, thereby restricting the involvement of both men and women.

In Uzbekistan's Ferghana valley, Sultanova (1999) finds females known as the Otin-oy (*otin*s), usually the relatives of male religious leaders, sustaining a "domestic" or "reflected" Sufism that includes poetry, chanting, *dhikrs*, and even a Qādiriyya dance. These sessions, in general, celebrate life cycle rituals and religious holidays, rather than being specifically *ṭarīqa*-based practices. Her observation is that the importance of such female religious activity was enhanced under communist rule since it was less susceptible to persecution than more usual forms of Sufism. Its fate in the post-Soviet context remains to be seen.

In modern Turkey neo-Sufi movements such as the Sait Nursi and Gülen communities draw inspiration from some aspects of Sufism and attract large numbers of female members. In these movements the philosophical elements of Sufism and an activist agenda have replaced traditional forms of initiation, *ṭarīqa* identity, and charismatic transmission; female leadership, however, is not yet significant.

The fact that much of our information about contemporary Sufi practice comes from studies written by Western or Western trained researchers leads to the translation of "inner" experiences of Sufi women into modern psychological or anthropological systems. For example psychologist Michaela Özelsel (1996) documents her 40-day Sufi retreat under a Turkish shaykh in diary form, ultimately invoking Jungian theory as an interpretive framework. Anthropologists have analyzed the dynamics of the intersection of emotion and embodiment in contemporary South Asian females affected in varying ways by Sufism (Werbner 1998). Female public intellectuals such as Ayşe Sasa in Turkey and Karīmān Ḥamza in Egypt represent cases of secularized Muslim women turning to Sufism in a quest for emotional stability and religio-cultural authenticity.

These literary and theoretical developments provide material that was absent or difficult to access in more traditional Sufi writings, and in some cases an entry into specifically female Sufi experience.

> Rābiʿa al-ʿAdawiyya (d. ca. 801) also known as Rābiʿa of Basra is one of the best-known early Sufis, largely because of her biography in *Tadhkirat al-awliyā'*, by Farīd al-Dīn ʿAṭṭār (d. 1230). Her inclusion among the "ranks of men" represents a state of mystical unity that transcends any class or gender distinctions. She is also portrayed as besting male saints and authorities of her time through her sincerity, spiritual insight, and level of intimacy with the divine beloved. Among famous anecdotes concerning Rābiʿa are the Kaʿba's coming out to meet her and her desire to burn paradise and extinguish hell so that love for God would be sincere, removed from extrinsic fears and expectations of punishments or rewards.

BIBLIOGRAPHY

S. B. Abbas, *The female voice in Sufi ritual. Devotional practices of Pakistan and India*, Austin, Tex. 2002.

L. Ahmed, *Women in Muslim history*, New Haven, Conn. 1992.

Ibn al-ʿArabī, *Sufis of Andalusia. The "Rūh al-Quds" and "al-Durrat al-fākhirah" of Ibn ʿArabī*, trans. and intro. R. W. J. Austin, foreword M. Lings, London 1971.

J. Baldick, *Mystical Islam. An introduction to Sufism*, New York 1989.
A. Böttcher, L'élite féminine kurde de la Kaftariyya. Une confrérie Naqshbandi damascene, in *Les annales de l'autre islam* 5 (1998), 125–39.
M. Chodkiewicz, Female sainthood in Islam, in *Sufi* (Spring 1994), 12–19.
J. Clancy-Smith, The house of Zainab. Female authority and saintly succession in colonial Algeria, in N. R. Keddie and B. Baron (eds.), *Women in Middle Eastern history. Shifting boundaries in sex and gender*, New Haven, Conn. 1992, 254–74.
——, The shaykh and his daughter. Coping in colonial Algeria, in E. Burke III (ed.), *Struggle and survival in the modern Middle East*, Berkeley 1993, 145–63.
R. E. Cornell (ed. and trans.), *Early Sufi women. Dhikr an-Niswa al-Mutaʿabbitdāt aṣ-Ṣūfiyyāt by Abū ʿAbd ar-Raḥmān as-Sulamī*, Louisville, Ky. 1999.
A. Dialmy, *Féminisme, islamisme, soufisme*, Paris 1997.
D. H. Dwyer, Women, Sufism and decision-making in Moroccan Islam, in L. Beck and N. R. Keddie (eds.), *Women in the Muslim world*, Cambridge, Mass. 1978, 585–98.
J. Elias, Female and feminine in Islamic mysticism, in *Muslim World* 78 (1988), 209–24.
al-Ghazālī, *Marriage and sexuality in Islam*, trans. M. Farah, Salt Lake City 1984.
Habiba. A Sufi saint from Uzbekistan, video film directed by C. Allione, Mystic Fire Video 1996.
V. Hoffman, *Sufism, mystics, and saints in modern Egypt*, Columbia, S.C. 1995.
P. Jeffery, *Frogs in a well. Indian women in purdah*, London 1979.
F. Malti-Douglas, *A woman and her Sufis*, Washington, D.C. 1995.
F. Mernissi, Women, saints, and sanctuaries, in *Signs* 3 (1977), 101–12.
S. Murata, *The Tao of Islam. A sourcebook on gender relationships in Islamic thought*, Albany, N.Y. 1992.
Mystic Iran. The unseen world, film directed by A. Farshad, 2002.
M. Özelsel, *Forty days. The diary of a traditional Sufi solitary retreat*, Brattleboro, Vt. 1996.
C. Raudvere, *The book and the roses. Sufi women, visibility and the Zikir in contemporary Istanbul*, Istanbul 2002.
S. Reinhertz, *Women called to the path of Rumi. The way of the whirling dervish*, Prescott, Ariz. 2001.
Saints and spirits (Morocco), film directed by M. Llewelyn-Davies, produced by E. Fernea, 1979.
A. Schimmel, *My soul is a woman. The feminine in Islam*, New York 1997.
M. Smith, *Rabīʿa and her fellow saints in Islam*, Cambridge 1924.
R. Sultanova, Uzbekistan. Female rites as a musical phenomenon, 1999 <http://www.santacecilia.it/ italiano/archivi/ etnomusicologico/ESEM99/musicspace/papers/sultanova/ sultanova.htm> (includes video of female *dhikr*).
P. Werbner and H. Basu, *Embodying charisma. Modernity, locality, and performance of emotion in Sufi cults*, New York 1998.

Marcia Hermansen

The United States

In the United States Sufi orders range from universal or New Age movements whose membership is largely Euro-American to transplanted communities of recent Muslim immigrants. Other American Sufi orders are hybrids of traditional Islamic and modern Western attitudes, practices, and individuals.

To the degree that Sharīʿa-based rituals are incorporated by a particular Sufi order, gender distinctions become visibly operative in its functioning in America. In the more strictly Islamic Sufi movements such as the Naqshbandī-Ḥaqqānī order led in the United States by Shaykh Hishām Kabbānī, deputy and son-in-law of Shaykh Nāẓim, women participate in the gender segregated rituals but are not accorded formal leadership roles. Female members of the leaders' families are viewed as role models for women disciples.

In the case of many American Sufi women, gender segregation and other restrictions on female participation are likely to provoke some discomfort. This leads to a subversive quality in these women's reflections on Sufism in which they challenge normative Islamic concepts and cultural expectations regarding maleness and femininity and gender-specific roles. It is noteworthy that when Western women visit Sufi teachers in the Muslim world they are often accorded privileges of the shaykh's company and occupying male spaces denied to local females. The symbolic masculinization of Sufi women in American orders may include the adoption of symbols of affiliation and authority that were traditionally unique to men such as wearing special caps or robes.

It is said that Sufism was first brought to the United States in 1912 by the Indian Chishtī teacher, Ḥaẓrat Ināyāt Khān. His teachings evolved into a universalist interpretation of the unity behind all Prophetic revelations inspired by the same spirit of guidance. After Khān's untimely death in 1926 his movement was revived by his son, Pīr Vilāyat Khān, in the 1970s and joined for a time by disciples of an American Sufi, Murshid Samuel Lewis (1971). Eventually Lewis's disciples broke off to form their own movement, the Sufi Islamia Ruhaniat Society, now an international movement including practitioners of the Dances of Universal Peace developed by Lewis. Ināyāt Khān initiated a number of Western women as Sufi teachers (*murshida*s) and himself married an American. Today his grandson, Ziā Ināyāt Khan, directs the movement in the United States.

American Sufi movements of Turkish origin, the Halvetī-Jerrāḥīs and Mevlevīs, are particularly interesting in terms of the extent of their female participation and leadership. The Halvetī-Jerrāḥī order was brought to America by Shaykh Muzaffer Ozak

(1993) of Istanbul who first came to the United States in 1980. Branches of this *ṭarīqa* developed in New York under the leadership of Tosun Bayrak and Shaykh Nūr (Lex Hixon), and in the San Francisco Bay Area under Ragip (Robert) Frager. After the death of Shaykh Muzaffer, the American order branched into two movements. Ultimately one branch of the American Jerrāḥīs, known as the Ashkijerrāḥīs, drawn mainly from Lex Hixon's followers, evolved separately, under a female teacher, Shaykha Farīḥa Fāṭima al-Jerrāḥī. The biographical notice of Shaykha Farīḥa notes that she was made a female leader or shaykha by Muzaffer Ozak in 1985 and is the first female leader in the Jerrāḥī order in over 300 years. The leader of this movement in Mexico is also a woman.

In the case of the Turkish Mevlevī order (often referred to as whirling dervishes), American initiates may learn the traditional practice of "turning." Among these disciples are American women who are set on breaking the barrier to female participation in the *dhikr* (form of Sufi meditation). Traditional shaykhs from Turkey may be pleased that Americans are becoming dervishes, but are unsettled to be asked to give permission for females to whirl, at least publicly. In another branch of the American Mevlevī movement, Camille Helminski joins her husband, Kabīr, in writing and teaching activities.

Among the challenges to traditional norms that have been raised by converted American Sufi women is activism. In the same way that third wave or cultural feminists try to avoid the past mistakes of white middle-class feminists in attempting to impose their agenda on women of color, female participants in Western Sufi movements feel the need to negotiate their understandings of gender roles so as to reflect both traditional authenticity and justice.

Webb's edited volume (2000) on Muslim women's activism in America includes articles by two women associated with Sufi movements. These women exemplify the active roles played by many Sufi women in American Muslim life today. Rabia Terri Harris is a member of the Halvetī-Jerrāḥī Sufi order. Harris has university degrees in Middle Eastern Languages and Cultures and has contributed translations of Arabic texts by the classical Sufi writer al-Qushayrī (d. 1072). She is involved in peace and justice movements and lectures on progressive Islam.

Gwendolyn Zohara Simmons is a member of the Sheikh Muhammad Raheem Bawa Muhaiyaddeen Mosque and Fellowship in Philadelphia. Guru Bawa Muhaiyaddeen (d. 1986), a Sufi teacher from Sri Lanka, settled in Philadelphia in 1972, and attracted many American followers. The community has evolved at present into two branches, one more focused on Bawa as a spiritual teacher in a non-denominational orientation and the other more Islamic Sharīʿa-oriented. In her writings Simmons, an African-American, directly confronts the oppression of women in some Muslim contexts, including among some American Muslim communities, in the light of her personal experiences in the American Civil Rights movement. According to Simmons, the Sufi master Guru Bawa taught that women manifest the feminine qualities of Allah, and gave special recognition to women's participation and leadership.

The directness of some female Sufis is sometimes seen by male Sufi leaders as rebelling against conventional gender expectations. In an incident at an International Association of Sufism Conference in the San Francisco Bay Area in 1994, a Rifāʿī Sufi shaykh from Kuwait was leading a collective *dhikr*, in which a succession of universal and Sharīʿa-oriented teachers took turns directing the audience in Islamic chants. The shaykh commented that since some female participants were not covering their hair during the practices, the angels could not be present at the gathering. Some American Sufi women were outraged at this comment and protested by walking out, in a few cases provocatively tossing their heads to flaunt their cascading tresses in defiance.

In summary, it is clear that female members of Western Sufi movements take positions about gender along some sort of continuum from subversion and activism directed to challenging and reforming traditional Muslim practices to acceptance of the rationale for "gender complementarity."

In fact, the concept that maleness and femaleness function as distinct energies is expressed not only by Sharīʿa-oriented movements, but also in certain teachings of universalist groups such as the Islamia Ruhaniat International. Members of these groups cultivate specific movements, dances, or practices as part of "attuning" to essentially different gender frequencies.

Several Shīʿī Sufi orders are present in the United States. Dr. Nahid Angha, daughter of the Sufi teacher Shāh Maghsoud (d. 1980), whose shrine is located in Novato, California, is the leader of the International Association of Sufism. In her movement a woman friendly approach is taken. Initiatives of this group include trying to foster cooperation and communication across all Sufi movements. In addition, in 1993 they established a global networking movement for female Sufis, the Sufi Women Organization.

The son of Shāh Maghsoud, Saleheddin Ali Nader Angha, heads a separate organization known as the MTO (Maktab Tarighat Oveyssi) or the Shahmaghsoudi School of Islamic Sufism with over 39 centers in North America. The membership is drawn from both the Persian émigré and American convert Muslim communities. Women have a high degree of leadership within the movement and run a number of the local centers, giving lessons and teaching Sufi practices. Rituals (the *dhikr*) of the MTO are performed with males and females seated separately but in the same space. Head covering is not required although both genders generally wear white clothing for the ceremonies. A number of the female members of the movement have published works related to Sufism, including California psychologist Dr. Lynn Wilcox, Linda O'Riordan, Barbara Larsen, Soraya Behbehani, Farnaz Khoromi, Melvina Noel, and Avideh Shashaani.

Another prominent American Sufi woman is Dr. Laleh Bakhtiar of Chicago, who has been affiliated with several Sufi orders. She is a writer in the fields of Sufi thought and psychology and edits and translates classical Sufi and Islamic sources.

Gray Henry is an American woman who was initiated into the Shādhilī order. Through the publishing houses Islamic Texts Society and Fons Vitae, which she founded, Henry makes available scholarly translations of works on Islamic spirituality for both the serious seeker and the academic classroom.

In the African American Muslim community Sufism has not played a very large role. African American Muslims usually join Sharīʿa-oriented movements such as the Bawa Muhaiyadeen Foundation and the Naqshbandī-Haqqānī order. In African-based immigrant movements such as the Tijāniyya, the Burḥāniyya, and the Murīdiyya the leadership is largely drawn from African immigrants, and therefore women's leadership roles have not been prominent.

BIBLIOGRAPHY

N. Angha, *Principles of Sufism*, Fremont, Calif. 1991.
L. Bakhtiar, *Sufi women of America. Angels in the making*, Chicago 1997.
L. Banner, *Finding Fran. History and memory in the lives of two women*, New York 1998.
C. Helminski, *Women of Sufism. A hidden treasure*, Boulder, Colo. 2003.
M. Hermansen, What's American about American Sufi movements?, in David Westerlund (ed.), *Sufism in Europe and North America*, New York 2004, 36–62.
S. Reinhertz, *Women called to the path of Rumi. The way of the whirling dervish*, Prescott, Ariz. 2001.
G. Webb (ed.), *Windows of faith. Muslim women scholar activists in North America*, Syracuse, N.Y. 2000.
L. Wilcox, *Women and the Holy Quran. A Sufi perspective*, Riverside, Calif. 1998.
Sufi Women Organization, *Sufi women. The journey towards the beloved*, Novato, Calif. 1998.

MARCIA HERMANSEN

Western Europe

THE RECEPTION OF SUFISM

When European research about the "Orient" began in the eighteenth and nineteenth centuries, the poet Johann Wolfgang von Goethe (1749–1832) included Islamic and especially Sufi motifs in many of his poems, serving to introduce some of the ideas of Islamic mysticism in the West. Founders of European Islamic studies such as Ignaz Goldziher, Carl Heinrich Becker, and Christiaan Snouck Hurgronje saw Sufism as functioning to close the gaps between Islamic law, theology, and individual piety, and Sufism was labeled as secondary to the dominant development of orthodox Islam. Not until the middle of the twentieth century did Sufism come to be understood by European scholars as an integral part of the cultural heritage of Islam and as a widely influential power in the development of the religion. In recent years, Sufism has also been transformed into a medium for dealing with East-West philosophy and cultural globalization by Western researchers and believers.

THE ESTABLISHMENT OF SUFI GROUPS AND ORDERS

Sufism in Western Europe has developed in three primary types. First is that developed by Westerners in the early twentieth century looking for sources of religious and spiritual truth outside the Christian church. Second, since the 1960s Muslim labor migrants have brought traditional Sufi orders and practices to the West. Third, today there are Western Sufi orders which are mixtures of the first two types.

WESTERNIZED SUFI GROUPS

Some extraordinary forms of Sufi practices attracted Western intellectuals and travelers. One of the first travelers to be initiated into a Sufi order was a woman, the Russian Isabelle Eberhardt (1877–1904). In 1900 she became a member of the Qadiri order in Tunisia, but she died four years later. The initiation of the Swiss Fritjof Schuon (1907–98) in 1932, and more especially of Georges Ivanovitch Gurdjieff (1866–1949), had a serious impact on the spread of Sufism. Gurdjieff was a central figure for various Sufi orders in Western Europe and the United States who were attracted to his Sufi music and dance performances.

One of the first Sufi groups to be established in the West was that of Ḥaẓrat Ināyāt Khān (1882–1927), an Indian Pīr of the Chishtiyya order who traveled to the United States, England, and Germany in 1910. During his travels he attracted a number of Western disciples. He started publishing books in English about Sufism in 1914, and two years later he settled in London and founded the first Sufi order in Western Europe. Also important for the development of this Westernized Sufism were the writings of such dominant figures as Idries Shah (an Indian with a Scottish mother), who published *The Sufis* in 1964, and Reshad Feild, who wrote *The Last Barrier* in 1976. These books became very popular and were translated into other Western languages. Although the authors were influential and famous in the arena of Westernized Sufism, they were almost never leaders of Sufi orders. Westernized Sufism was generally presented as something that can be separated from Islam. The followers were almost always non-Muslim Westerners who understood Sufism more as a kind of philosophy or universal religion than as a religious practice of Islam, although it was often combined with forms of music, dance, and meditation.

Today the best-known and most widespread association of trans-Islamic Sufism is the Western Sufi movement founded by Pīr Ḥaẓrat Ināyat Khān. The group has branches in France, Germany, the Netherlands, the United States, and several other countries. Today the association is led by the Pīr's son, Vilāyāt Ināyāt Khān. Followers believe in the wisdom of uniting different religious forms of mystical expression and in the mystical relationship between God, man, and creation. Within the Sufi movement, special techniques and steps of mystical learning, spiritual healing, and spiritual symbology exist (Jironet 2002).

Sufi orders in the West

With the immigration of workers from Muslim countries starting in the 1960s, Islam became established in Western European countries. Sufi orders were built by labor migrants from Morocco, India, Sudan, and other countries. In the beginning, they were not noticed much by Westerners because the existence of something other than orthodox Islamic practice was not known. Today these orders are ethnically closed groups which do not differ in any significant aspect from their counterparts in the Islamic world or in non-Muslim countries outside the West. A Punjabi immigrant in Britain, for example, may belong to a British branch of the same order that his family belongs to in the Punjab. The Punjabi order supports the expatriate in Britain with spiritual guidance and material assistance. The Punjabi shaykh or his *khalīfa* (Arabic, successor, here the second in the hierarchy) travels to Britain often, and the British immigrant goes regularly on a pilgrimage to his shaykh or his shrine. Often the children of immigrants are sent by their parents to the order in their country of origin for a traditional education. Attempts to establish independent branches of such ethnic traditional Sufi orders have often failed because of the power of different groups in the country of origin (Geaves 2000).

Traditional Sufi orders are found especially in Britain and France where workers emigrated from countries with vivid Sufi traditions. All followers share the same ethnic background and special devotional practices of their order such as the *dhikr* ceremony and pilgrimage to the shrine of a dead shaykh. Many orders also celebrate the birthday of the Prophet Muḥammad with a procession in the streets in some European cities. In Germany such Sufi groups are rare because the majority of immigrants come from Turkey where Sufi orders have been forbidden since 1925. But today there are so-called laic Sufi orders (for example, Süleymanciler) without a living shaykh but with ceremonial practices, such as *dhikr* and recitation of the *silsila*, of the founder of the group.

Western Sufi Orders

There are also Sufi orders that are trans-ethnic and Islamic. Two groups are worth mentioning because they are widespread in Western Europe. One of the most prominent Western Sufi orders is the Naqshbandī order of the Cypriot Shaykh Muḥammad Nāẓim ʿĀdil al-Qubruṣī al-Ḥaqqānī. Shaykh Nāẓim made his first visit to Europe in 1974. Twenty years later more than three thousand people attended the London mosque each night where he led prayers during Ramadan. Today he has followers all over the Islamic world and in the West. Although the practices of the order do not differ much from other Naqshbandī orders, the Western followers of Nāẓim differ from other traditional Sufi orders because the majority are women and from the spiritual left. The Western order is ethnically mixed, so Muslim-born and converts pray together. The order has established an independent identity in the West. The weekly *dhikr* and the visits from Shaykh Nāẓim, who travels throughout the world, are the center of the social activities of the order.

The other important Western Sufi order is the Sudanese Burhāniyya, a branch of the Shadhiliyya founded by Shaykh ʿUthmān (d. 1983). His son, the present Shaykh Ibrāhīm, resides in Khartoum and visits Germany annually. At first the Western non-Muslim Burhānīs were spiritually oriented seekers who only practiced Sufi *dhikr*, but today they claim to be orthodox Muslims. Sudanese advisers have been acting as teachers of the Western converts. The order does not differ from traditional Islamic Sufi orders. Only the trans-ethnic spread in Western Europe and the central role of Western women in the Western branches are unusual.

In general it can be said that female Western murids (pupils) are in the majority in Westernized and Western Sufi orders in Europe. The separation of the sexes is not as strict as is usual in Sufi groups in Islamic countries. Nevertheless, *khalīfa*s are almost always men. One exception is Irina Tweedie, who has followed the Indian Naqshbandī way and today has many murids in the West. All the Westernized and Western Sufi groups focus on ritual, mostly with music and dance. Members practice no silent *dhikr* in the Westernized Naqshbandī tradition and only a minority of them perform the five Islamic ritual prayers. Western shaykhs seldom practice spiritual healing.

Bibliography

T. Atay, The significance of the other in Islam. Reflections on the discourse of a Naqshbandi circle of Turkish origin in London, in *Muslim World* 89:3/4 (1999), 455–77.

M. Dressler, Sufismus in Deutschland, in *Handbuch der Religionen* 4:2 (1997), 1–10.

K. Duran, Muslim diaspora. The Sufis in Western Europe, in *Islamic Studies* 30:4 (1991), 463–83.

S. Galip, Un gourou Nakshibendi. Sheyh Nazim Kibrisi, in M. Gabrieau, A. Popovic, and T. Zarcone (eds.), *Naqshbandis. Historical developments and present situation of a Muslim mystical order*, Istanbul 1990, 437–40.

R. Geaves, *The Sufis of Britain. An exploration of Muslim identity*, Cardiff 2000.

K. Jironet, *The image of spiritual liberty in the Western Sufi movement following Hazrat Inayat Khan*, Leuven 2002.

M. H. Kabbani, *The Naqshbandi Sufi way. History and guidebook of the saints of the Golden Chain*, Chicago 1996.

A. Rawlinson, A history of Western Sufism, in *Diskus* 1:1 (1993), 45–83.

L. Schlesann, *Sufismus in Deutschland. Deutsche auf dem Weg des mystischen Islam*, Cologne 2003.

S. Sviri, Documentation and experiences of a modern Naqshbandi Sufi, in E. Puttick and P. B. Clarke (eds.), *Women as teachers and disciples in traditional and new religions*, Lewiston, N.Y. 1993, 77–89.

L. F. Williams (ed.), *Sufi studies. East and West. A symposium in honor of Idries Shah's services to Sufi studies by twenty-four contributors marking the 700th anniversary of the death of Jalaluddin Rumi* (A.D. 1207–1273), New York 1973.

Gritt Klinkhammer

Umma

Overview

The term *umma* designates one of the most fundamental concepts in Islam. Often translated as the "Muslim community" of men and women, the term has assumed different meanings in evolving historical circumstances. Conceptually, the meaning of the term *umma* underwent significant transformations in three main contexts: the early, formative use of the term in the Qurʾān and *ḥadīth*; the elaboration of the concept in Islamic legal and political thought; and finally, the extension of the use of the term to denote national communities and the concept of a nation. The sources for the study of the concept of *umma* in the first phase are both relatively limited and equivocal. In the second and third phases of its development, a wealth of historical information and a vast and diverse literature both refine and complicate the understanding of the concept in its different settings and contexts.

The foundational source for the study of the Islamic concept of *umma* is, naturally, the Qurʾān. The term *umma* appears 64 times in the Qurʾān; in Qurʾānic usage, it usually designates a people to whom God sends a prophet, or a people who are objects of a divine plan of salvation. In both cases, the term *umma*, and the communities identified in its various uses, equally refer to and are made up of men and women. According to most studies of the Qurʾānic concept, the term *umma* refers to a single group sharing some sort of common religious orientation. In Qurʾānic usage, however, the connotations of community and religion do not always converge.

The word *umma* has multiple and diverse meanings in the Qurʾān. In several instances it refers to an unspecified group of people (for example, "And when he [Moses] came to the water of Madyan, he found on it a group of men [*umma min al-nās*] watering," 28:23). The term can also mean a specific religion or the beliefs of a group of people (for example, "they say: We found our fathers following a certain *umma*, and we are guided by their footprints," 43:22), or an exemplar or model of faith, as in the reference to Abraham as an "*umma*, obedient to God" (16:120). *Umma* also refers to the followers of prophets (for example, "For every *umma* there is an apostle," 10:47); to a group of people adhering to a specific religion (for example, "To each one of you We have appointed a law and a pattern of life. If God had pleased He could surely have made you all a single *umma*," 5:48); to a smaller group within the larger community of adherents (for example, "They are not all alike; among the people of the Book is an upright *umma*," 3:113); to the followers of Muḥammad who are charged with a special responsibility (for example, "And thus We have made you a medium *umma* that you may be the bearers of witness to the people and that the Apostle may be a bearer of witness to you," 2:143); or to a subgroup of these followers (for example, "So let there be an *umma* among you who may call to good, enjoin what is right and forbid the wrong, and these it is that shall be successful," 3:104).

Umma also often denotes a misguided group of people (for example, "Were it not that all people would be a single *umma*, We would certainly have allocated to those who disbelieve in the Beneficent God [to make] of silver the roofs of their houses and the stairs by which they ascend," 43:33), or a misguided party from among the followers of a prophet (for example, "And on the day when We will gather from every *umma* a party from among those who rejected Our communications, then they shall be formed into groups," 27:83, or "Then We sent Our apostles one after the other; whenever there came to an *umma* their apostle, they called him a liar, so We made one follow the other [to its dooms], and We turned them into bygone tales," 23:44). *Umma* could mean a period of time ("And if We hold back from them the punishment until a stated *umma*/period of time, they will say," 11:8); it can also mean an order of being ("And there is no animal that walks upon the earth nor a bird that flies with its two wings but they are an *umma* like yourself," 6:38).

With the vast majority of Qurʾānic injunctions addressed jointly and explicitly to men and women (*al-muʾminīna wa-al-muʾmināt*), and lacking any textual evidence for a gender specific use of the term *umma*, the community in the Qurʾānic conception of *umma* encompasses men and women alike. This inclusive use of the term is corroborated in the events of the formative period and, to a great extent, in the *ḥadīth* literature where the communal sense of the term is clearly articulated. Although it is hard to come up with precise estimates, it is likely that in the Meccan period of Muḥammad's prophethood, a majority of the converts to Islam were women. In fact, the first person to accept Muḥammad's call to Islam was his wife Khadīja who played an instrumental role in supporting Muḥammad and reassuring him in times of doubt and hardship. Women converts to Islam also played a central role in spreading the teachings of the new religion, gaining new converts, and protecting the young and vulnerable community of Muslims. For example, the early sources provide accounts of the role Muslim women played in subverting, and eventually lifting a Meccan siege and boycott of the Banū Hāshim (Muḥammad's clan) quarter of Mecca. Thus, women were not just included in the new Muslim community, but they played a vital role in constituting this community and securing its survival.

The dichotomy between the communal and religious notions of *umma* in the Qurʾānic use of the term has parallels in *ḥadīth* literature. In several traditions attributed to Muḥammad, the term "my *umma*" is used to refer to his kinship group and not to those related to him by religion. Nonetheless, *ḥadīth* literature provides the concept of *umma* with its precise and focused meaning. Besides the Qurʾān, the earliest extant source of Islamic provenance is a set of documents written by Muḥammad shortly after his arrival at Medina. These documents, commonly referred to in modern scholarship as the "constitution of Medina," comprise several practical provisions designed to regulate social and political life in Medina under Islam. The main purport of the "constitution" is political and not religious. It defines treaty relations between the different groups living in Medina and its environs, including the Muslim tribes of Medina, Muslims who emigrated from Mecca, and Jews. The constitution starts with the pronouncement that all these groups constitute "one distinct community (*umma*) apart from other people." In the 47 clauses of the constitution, the term *umma* appears only in one other instance when the Jews of Banū ʿAwf are said to constitute "an *umma* with the believers." The same clause goes on to state that the Jews have their religion and the Muslims have theirs. The meaning of the term *umma* in the constitution is clearly not synonymous with religion. The constitution also delineates relations of mutual aid between the different constituent tribal groups, actions to be taken against those who violate the terms of the agreement, and actions to be taken against criminals belonging to the incipient community in Medina. Rather than supplanting or abolishing the tribal bonds, the constitution regulates the relations within tribes, and between them and the outside world, on the basis of the higher order of *umma*. *Umma* here is a concept of daily life that also stands for a certain kind of identity and defines a social unit.

While the "constitution of Medina" sanctions diversity within the Islamic *umma*, the Qurʾān further sanctions differentiation between various *ummas* as a norm decreed by God. Sūra 10:19 reads, "People were once a single *umma*; but they differed (and followed different ways). Had it not been for the word proclaimed by your lord before, their differences would have been resolved" (see also 2:213, 5:48, 11:118, 16:93, and 42:8). To some extent, therefore, the Qurʾānic concept of *umma* refers to an ideal collective order, an original all-encompassing unity which is always invoked, but never completely recovered. This rudimentary concept of the *umma*, however, is complemented by the narrower concept of the *umma* of believers. This is the "medium *umma*" (2:143) which is further qualified in the Qurʾān as: "the best *umma* evolved for mankind, enjoining what is good, forbidding what is wrong, and believing in God" (3:110; see also 4:41 and 16:89). This specific *umma*, or the followers of Muḥammad, is further differentiated from the followers of earlier messengers and prophets; whereas the latter's sphere of influence is restricted to particular peoples, the former's scope is all of humanity. When referring to prophets before Muḥammad, the Qurʾān says, "To every *umma* We have sent an apostle [saying:] Worship God" (16:36; see also 10:47); in reference to Muḥammad, however, the Qurʾān adds: "Say: O people, I am verily the apostle of God to you all" (7:158). The universality of Muḥammad's mission was thereby asserted, and the "medium *umma*" played the central role in the fulfillment of this mission after him. Once again, this medium *umma* is not specified along gender lines, and no differentiation is made between men and women in its constitution.

The concept of *umma* underwent substantial developments immediately after Muḥammad's death. Different circumstances accompanied the selection of each of the first four caliphs after Muḥammad, yet in each of these cases the appointment was conferred by the majority of the *umma*, thereby investing ultimate political authority in the *umma* and its consensus. Other developments sharpened the conceptions of *umma* and its theoretical authority. For example, many early leaders and religious authorities argued that, to preserve its unity, the *umma* needs a leadership unified in the person of one imam. According to this view, therefore, the interests of the *umma* provided the justification for the authority invested in the office of the imam or caliph, and as such, the *umma* served as the ultimate source of political authority. The second caliph, ʿUmar, relinquished the distribution of conquered land to Muslim conquerors, and considered it public property, the property of the whole *umma*. In addition to its social and political ramifications, ʿUmar's action effectively treated the *umma* as a corporate legal entity. To be sure, in subsequent periods of Islamic history, the ideals of the formative period were often violated; yet the tension between these ideals – the unity of the *umma* and its role as the ultimate source of political authority – and the political and social realities of Muslim societies continued to inform Islamic legal and political theory and practice throughout history.

Under Umayyad rule, the need for a unified political authority was overemphasized, and was used to justify an exclusive Arab dynastic rule at the expense of the ideal of the unity of the *umma*. Under the ʿAbbāsids, the inclusive Qurʾānic notion of the *umma* was revived, and the political dominance of the ʿAbbāsid family did not preclude the participation of other ethnic groups. This participation, however, led to the gradual loosening of political centralization. As the ʿAbbāsid caliphs wielded less control over an increasingly decentralized state, they continued to function as symbols for the unity of its *umma*. This unity was also corroborated by an Islamic cultural tradition which was well developed by the end of the second century of Islam.

Traditionalists and *ḥadīth* scholars argued that Islam can only be preserved by safeguarding the unity of the *umma*. The standard legal formulations of the classical period defined the *umma* as a spiritual, non-territorial community that is distinguished on the basis of the shared beliefs of its members. The literature of the classical period also viewed the *umma* as a socioreligious reality with legal and political import. There were no formal conditions or ritual requirements for joining the *umma* aside from being born to Muslim parents or freely choosing to become a Muslim. Membership in this *umma* can thus be viewed as a sort of citizenship which guarantees the equal-ity of all Muslims. Yet although this equality extended in the Qurʾānic formulations to both genders, in the lived experiences of Muslim societies women were often excluded from the exercise of political authority. For example, while most legal scholars recognized the intellectual authority of women scholars and their right to issue legal rulings (*fatwa*s), they also argued that women cannot occupy executive office, thus restricting the effective participation of women within the collective order of the *umma*.

Tensions between various ethnic groups in Muslim societies also compromised the ideal of a unified *umma*. Beginning with the third century after the *hijra*, Islamic literature conferred a distinguished status to the Arabs within the larger *umma* of Muslims. This literature emphasized the centrality of the Arabs and their language to Islam in response to the *shuʿūbiyya* movement, which denigrated the Arabs in favor of other ethnic identities. Al-Shāfiʿī (d. 820), for example, lists in his *Risāla* the Qurʾānic references to Arabic and its prominence, while Aḥmad ibn Ḥanbal (d. 855) collects numerous *ḥadīth*s which enumerate the virtues of Arabs and reprimand their foes. In different genres of writing, including jurisprudence, philosophy, history, poetry, and prose, the Arabs are said to be privileged with the language of the Qurʾān and of Paradise, and by being the core community to whom Muḥammad was sent. As the political hegemony of the Arabs receded, so did the cultural tensions between them and other ethnic groups. The initial reactive defenses of Arabs and Arabic gave way to independent self-conscious reflections on Arabness as a cultural identity, and on its unique and organic link to the religious, political, and social identity of the Islamic *umma*.

The social reality of the unified *umma*, and the related concept of the abode of Islam (*dār al-Islām*), were not undermined by political decentralization in the Islamic world. However, under the pressure of European colonial encroachment on Muslim domains, this social identity was seriously challenged. Attempts to defend and redeem Muslim unity by reviving the idea of the *umma* included popular Islamic resistance movements as well as the officially-sponsored pan-Islamic policies of the Ottoman Sulṭān ʿAbd al-Ḥamīd the Second (1878–1909). Equally significant was the call by Jamāl al-Dīn al-Afghānī (1839–97) for Islamic solidarity to reinvigorate the *umma* in the face of European aggression. The European colonial challenge, however, had an intellectual dimension: European ideas of the secular nation-state and of reforming social and gender relations had some appeal among Muslim elites. Nonetheless, the earliest forms of nationalism in the Islamic world conceived of Islam as a central component of the nationalist project, and appropriated the Islamic concept of *umma*. While nationalist movements in the guise of Islamic reform often disrupted the actual political unity of the *umma*, they did not challenge the theoretical authority of its idea. The secularization of nationalism came at a later stage, and with it the sharpening of the conflict between loyalties to the sovereign, secular nation-state, and the religious *umma*. These competing loyalties eventually led to a larger separation between Islam and nationalism.

Women participated in the nationalist movements and were also symbolically invoked in the emerging nationalist discourses. Generally, however, nationalist movements and discourses did not provide effective solutions for problems of gender inequality, and the nationalist project remained heavily dominated by men. When, in the second half of the twentieth century, some nationalists began to speak out in favor of a complete separation of religious and national identities, many Islamists responded by arguing that loyalty to the Islamic *umma* negates any other loyalty to ethnic, linguistic, or geographical entities. To a greater extent than their nationalist counterparts, women participated in the Islamist movements and here too were symbolically invoked in the Islamic critiques of nationalism. Nonetheless, the idea of an Islamic *umma*, as it is used in contemporary political discourse, carries the imprints of the nation-state with which it is competing. Similarly, the challenges facing women within the context of the nationalist movements, whether secular or Islamic, are intertwined. And despite substantial limitations on political and legal expressions of the idea of the *umma*, it remains a significant source of social identity for many Muslim men and women throughout the world.

Bibliography

A. Al-Ahsan, *Ummah or nation? Identity crisis in contemporary Muslim society*, Leicester, U.K. 1992.

N. Berkes, *The development of secularism in Turkey*, Montreal 1964.

W. R. Darrow, Ummah, in *The encyclopedia of religion*, xv, New York 1987, 123–5.

F. M. Denny, The meaning of *ummah* in the Qur'ān, in *History of religions* 15 (1975), 34–70.

——, *Ummah* in the Constitution of Medina, in *Journal of Near Eastern Studies* 36:1 (1977), 39–47.

E. Giannakis, The concept of *ummah*, in *Graeco-Arabica* 2 (1983), 99–111.

H. A. R. Gibb, The Islamic congress at Jerusalem in December 1931, in A. J. Toynbee (ed.), *A survey of international affairs*, London 1935, 99–109.

——, The community in Islamic history, in *Proceedings of the American Philosophical Society* 107:2 (1963), 173–6.

G. E. von Grunebaum, Nationalism and cultural trends in the Arab Near East, in *Studia Islamica* 14 (1961), 121–53.

——, *Modern Islam. The search for cultural identity*, Berkeley, 1962.

Muḥammad Ḥamadallāh al-Ḥaydarabādī, *Majmūʿat al-wathāʾiq al-siyāsiyya li-al-ʿahd al-nabawī wa-al-khilāfa al-rāshida*, Cairo 1956. Includes the Arabic text of the "Constitution of Medina," 15–21.

A. Hourani, *Arabic thought in the liberal age, 1798–1939*, Cambridge 1983.

M. Kramer, *Islam assembled. The advent of the Muslim Congress*, New York 1986.

H. Kruse, The development of the concept of nationality in Islam, in *Studies in Islam* 2:1 (1965), 7–16.

L. Massignon, L'*umma* et ses synonymes. Notion de "communauté sociale" en islam, in *Revue des études islamiques, 1941–1946*, Paris 1959, 151–7.

N. Nassar, *Mafhūm al-umma bayn al-dīn wa-al-tārīkh*, Beirut 1978.

——, *Taṣawūrāt al-umma al-muʿāṣira*, Kuwait 1986.

C. A. O. von Nieuwenhuijze, The *ummah*. An analytic approach, in *Studia Islamica* 10 (1959), 5–22.

R. Paret, *Umma*, in *The Encyclopedia of Islam*, new ed., iv, Leiden, 1960–, 1015–16.

I. H. Qureshi, *The struggle for Pakistan*, Karachi 1969.

F. Rahman, The principle of *shura* and the role of the *umma* in Islam, in *American Journal of Islamic Studies* 1:1 (1984), 1–9.

U. Rubin, The "Constitution of Medina." Some notes, in *Studia Islamica* 62 (1985), 5–23.

R. al-Sayyid, *Al-umma wa-al-jamāʿa wa-al-sulṭa. Dirāsāt fī al-fikr al-siyāsī al-ʿarabī al-Islāmī*, Beirut 1984.

——, Dār al-Islām wa-l-niẓām al-duwalī wa-al-umma al-ʿArabiyya, in *Mustaqbal al-ʿalam al-Islāmī* 1:1 (1991), 37–70.

——, *Mafāhīm al-jamāʿāt fī al-Islām*. Beirut 1993.

R. B. Serjeant, The Constitution of Medina, in *Islamic quarterly* 8 (1964), 3–16.

A. D. al-ʿUmari, *Al-mujtamaʿ al-madanī fī ʿahd al-nubūwa*, Medina 1983, 107–36.

W. M. Watt, *Muhammad at Medina*, Oxford 1956.

Ahmad Dallal

Women's Rights: Male Advocacy

Overview

THE NINETEENTH AND TWENTIETH CENTURIES

The Woman Question early on became a key component of state actors' attempts to mobilize all available resources to fend off encroachment by European powers looking to colonize or simply render usable (to them) the geostrategic assets of the Middle East, North Africa, and other traditionally Muslim territories. Beginning in the early nineteenth century, reformers in the Ottoman Empire and the Egyptian khedival state started to expand the roles of women in society as a distinct category of modern state-building efforts. Mehmet Ali (Muḥammad ʿAlī) (r. 1803–48), as governor of Egypt when it was a semi-autonomous province of the Ottoman Empire, identified women as part of a reproductive formula to create the strong and healthy population he needed to build his military and economic strength. Ironically, his reforms led to famine and ill health through the loss of much subsistence agriculture. Mehmet Ali implemented reforms to reduce infant mortality and improve female reproductive health, including founding a state school of midwifery. The first classes of midwives to graduate were African slave women, but the school recruited more widely as it expanded. Midwife graduates were married to medical school graduates before being sent out to set up public health services in the countryside. Such reforms, driven by state necessity to create new roles for women, were repeated throughout the remainder of the nineteenth and twentieth centuries, and continue today.

Beginning in the 1850s, Ottoman intellectuals started to debate the implications of these policies. The prominent intellectual and journalist Namık Kemal argued in 1867 that Ottoman women had become weak and wasteful in the nineteenth century from aping Western bourgeois mores, while at the same time becoming woefully ignorant, leaving them unable to conceive of alternatives to what was presented to them by local Europeans and by the European press as new, chic, and appropriate. Namık Kemal attempted to remedy this with the first Ottoman publication for women, a supplement to his own gazette, in which he argued for a distinctly Ottoman and Muslim vision of modern women through discussions of education, public comportment, educated motherhood, and patriotic shopping as part of managing a household's finances. In 1882, another prominent Ottoman intellectual tied the nation's progress to its treatment of women, in a formula that was to become characteristic of modern Muslim intellectuals. Şemseddin Sâmi's pocket paperback entitled *Kadınlar* (Women) became a bestseller, and was reissued in 1895, but he was forced by censors to cut out a section on veiling as a condition of being allowed to publish it. Our only indication of what this section argued is a photograph of himself and his wife, both dressed in Western style, and she without *charshaf* (unveiled). Like Namık Kemal, Şemseddin Sâmi saw education as the key to progress not simply for women but through women, for Muslim societies and states in general.

At roughly the same time in Egypt, Qāsim Amīn published in Arabic very similar arguments for changes in the status of modern Muslim women. In the 1880s, women began to enter these debates on their own behalf, and to challenge, adapt, and manipulate state reform agendas to expand women's roles. In the Ottoman center of Istanbul and the main port cities of the empire, the Woman Question arose at the same time that newspapers and other cheap print media began to spread from state-sponsored gazettes to more private and corporate productions, and as public education was vastly expanded and modernized. Here again, state imperatives opened doors for women, and female journalists, teachers, and entrepreneurs began to achieve prominence under the protection of male publishers and bureaucrats. By 1900, the Woman Question had taken the form it has held mainly to this day among Muslim thinkers ranging from conservative to radical: delineating the place of women in society and the role of education in allowing them to fulfill their societal duties; providing a history of women's rights in other eras and concurrently in other countries; and describing the place of women according to any given writer's understanding of Islam. Among these three writers, Şemseddin Sâmi seems to have been the most radical, and the only one to argue consistently that women's education would not simply benefit the health and well-being of their families, but could also allow women into the workplace. From the

1870s onwards, most of the empire was devastated by continuous warfare on the frontiers, with two key results for our purposes here: massive refugee flows into the empire from lost provinces, and conscription of men of all ages into the army, leaving women as *de facto* heads of households. These demographic facts gave weight to arguments of Şemseddin Sâmi that women needed to be educated for work outside the home, and women were actively recruited by state actors into the new high tech sectors of telegraphy and telephony, as well as into teaching and writing for publication. By the end of the First World War, women in the workplace had become familiar to urbanites in the Mediterranean basin from Cairo to Istanbul, and out to the borders of Iraq. The situation in Iran, in majority-Muslim colonies in south and east Asia, and in North Africa was somewhat different.

Interwar era

After the First World War, much of the Muslim world was under the rule or "tutelage" of European and east Asian powers. In the 1920s and 1930s, local notables were deeply invested in proving their fitness to rule, which included the display of modern attitudes toward women. Nonetheless, women in this region underwent a similar pressure to return home and leave jobs to the male survivors of the First World War. An example of how European attitudes were used to criticize and at the same time subvert local authorities is the odd character of Lord Cromer, consul-general of Egypt. When at home in England, Lord Cromer was an active member of a club aiming to suppress efforts by British women to gain the vote. In Egypt, though, he was a trenchant critic of veiling and other local practices that he portrayed as oppressive of Muslim women, arguing that their piteous state was evidence of Muslims' inability to rule themselves. Though his intentions were not aimed in the end at expanding women's rights, his rhetoric nonetheless opened doors to heightened debate about the potential and necessity of educating women and allowing them more public roles in modernizing Islamic societies and states. Qāsim Amīn's arguments were given an extra boost, for example, and Egyptian and Syrian women took the changed public atmosphere as their opportunity to found women's magazines promoting a variety of feminist agendas. During the British Protectorate of Egypt and the mandate system in the Arab heartlands, male bureaucrats saw to it that women's education expanded along with general education throughout the region as a way of mobilizing human resources for independence. Nation-states required local leadership with local loyalties at the ruling level, but equally essential were loyal citizens, conscious of their democratic rights and responsibilities and capable of fulfilling their new roles. For this reason, women were activated as educated housewives and mothers, having the primary responsibility for raising children to become the new patriotic and hardworking citizens of modern nation-states.

In the mandate territory of Palestine, this project was complicated by a continual flow of Jewish immigrants into and out of Palestine. Jews of European origin arrived with a civilizing mission in mind, and many of them also arrived with socialist and communist ideals they pursued, including absolute equality (outside the home) for women. The kibbutzim and moshavim (collective communities) of early Palestine were active areas of experimentation in such radical ideas as collective childcare and women's equal participation in the workforce in areas not traditionally associated with women. Some of these early collectives attempted to establish peaceful coexistence with Arab populations, incorporating them into their collective projects of improving the land. The effect of this radical stream of European thought has been diluted by the continuing marginalization of Jewish Zionists arguing for peaceful coexistence and other alternative social visions in the twentieth and twenty-first centuries, as well as the State of Israel's need to develop a vibrant capital sector in order to support its military expenditures. Nonetheless, the ideas of Marx and Engels, along with those of Fourier and other European radicals of the late nineteenth and early twentieth centuries, put these men, and their followers in the region, in the camp of men supporting expansion of women's rights and responsibilities to support state-building projects.

In North Africa, women were extremely active in the bloody struggle for independence from France throughout the 1960s and still echoing in Algerian politics today. In post-revolutionary states and postcolonial states, the new rulers were often either military men wedded to meritocratic ideas that some applied and some did not apply to women along with men. Another variant was a new or modernizing monarchy as in Morocco or Afghanistan, where kings moved rapidly to pull women into educational and work environments, and even into active political life as elected and appointed officials of the state. In Dutch colonies in southeast Asia, as well as the former British colony of India, Muslim women became objects of reform, as well as activists in anti-colonial struggles. Male Muslim scholars and activists participated directly in the formative debates of Arab-Muslim modernity and liberation struggles, achieving fame and a wide readership in the Muslim world at large, as they forwarded arguments debating possible roles for women. Many had recognizably feminist agendas; many made traditional arguments for women's participation in the workforce and public life after their children were school-age or older; many argued for a preservation of local ethnic traditions that defied Qur'ānic injunctions for women's rights in family and property laws.

Colonial and postcolonial struggles

While men were the leaders of most anti-colonial struggles at the beginning of the twentieth century, women rose to prominence as heroes of the resistance and protectors of guerrilla fighters throughout the century. Their fame was sharply curtailed, however, by traditional attitudes compounded of Greco-Roman and Mesopotamian imperial cultures with a broad variety of tribal cultures that privileged men's roles in warfare and resistance over that of women. An early exception was Mustafa Kemal Atatürk, founder of modern Turkey, who instituted universal public education and female suffrage in the 1920s and 1930s, arguing that giving women equal rights was a way of paying off the debt Turkey owed them for their heroic service during the First World War and the war for Turkish independence (see Figure 6).

While Iran was not formally colonized, it had been an intense focus of Anglo-Russian conflict since the nineteenth century, with England attempting to protect its south Asian colonies, and Russia pushing toward Iran's rich reserves of manpower, wealth, and natural resources. Most activist intellectuals focused intensely on preserving or regaining Iran's economic independence from these struggles even as the ruling dynasty and local governors traded resources for cash at a stunning rate, leaving much of Iran's economic potential in the hands of foreigners. After the Constitutional Revolution of 1905–11, boycotts of colonized sectors of the economy, and the establishment of the Pahlavī regime in the 1920s, Iranian elites took the newly discovered resources of oil to fuel rapid modernization of state institutions, economic sectors, and the peoples of Iran. In a highly controversial move, the first Pahlavī Shah of Iran banned the veil from public life, compelling observant Muslim women to remove this ritually significant means of preserving modesty from their daily practice. Despite his dictatorial policies that, in the end, stripped women and men alike of civil rights, some women were able to take the terms of Iranian modernity as presented to them, and manipulate those terms to expand the possibilities of their public roles. Still further to the East, Muslim scholars in British India and Dutch Indonesia drew on debates from Iran and the Ottoman Empire as they developed their own anti-colonial struggles, and as they negotiated their own terms of modernity.

Starting at the end of the nineteenth century, the long-time trickle of emigrants from Muslim regions to the United States and Europe took on the force of streams and then rivers, with enough Christian Syrians and Armenians in Boston, for example, to found their own papers and build neighborhoods that replicated socioeconomic patterns in their countries of origin. Starting at the end of the twentieth and beginning of the twenty-first century, Muslim emigrants began to outnumber Christian and Jewish emigrants from the Middle East to the United States and Europe, and as a result, new debates over Muslim identity in concert with new national identities – German, Canadian, American – forced new formulations of male-female legal and social issues. These fast-paced debates and adaptations played out in diaspora at the same time that Muslims were coming to equally rapid, some would say forced, terms with new national identities in what has been traditionally recognized as the Muslim world in Eurasia, Africa, South Asia, and Southeast Asia.

The nation-state era

From the middle of the twentieth century, and earlier in Iran and South Asia, European radical ideas had been adapted to the purposes of anti-European colonial struggles, and then into the project of building former colonies and mandate territories into modern nation-states. The first generation of Arab revolutionaries of non-elite origins, such as Gamal Abdel-Nasser in the 1950s, were socialist and secularist military men. They saw all elements of their populations as resources to be developed (and in many cases exploited) in order to build their territories into strong, economically and politically independent nation-states. Most signally in socialist Iraq of the late 1960s and 1970s, women were sent to school by state edict, trained in modern professions, and given jobs ranging from factory worker to trained surgeon and engineer. These programs were resisted, in turn, by religious Muslims who saw the turn toward secular states as a danger and a betrayal of Muslim tradition. Like the thinkers of the late nineteenth century in the Ottoman Empire and Egypt, they rehabilitated Islam and argued that Muslim women had traditonal rights, privileges, and protections that they had lost under secularist regimes. They argued that unveiled women in the workplace were vulnerable to sexual harrassment, and that a woman living under Muslim law had more property rights, civil rights with respect to marriage, and public respect than did the "new women" of secular Iran, Egypt, or Turkey in their Western suits and Western jobs. The Muslim Brotherhood supported the formation of a women's auxiliary, the Muslim Sisterhood, and women rose to political prominence through the organization. Women's rights have been entangled in this struggle for decades now, and can be seen in varying forms in Muslim-majority societies as different as post-revolutionary Iran, the Kingdom of Morocco, and wartorn Indonesia.

Important developments have taken place in Southeast Asia or in formerly low-visibility groups that have a dramatic impact via the Internet, cheap recorded media such as cassettes and compact disks, and ease of travel. One figure who has risen to new prominence comes out of a tradition, Sufism, with terms of sociopolitical engagement very different from those discussed so far. A Naqshbandī shaykh originally from Beirut, Muhammad Hisham Kabbani, has continued the tradition of writing biographies of the Prophet's female companions, and is a strong advocate of women's rights under Sharīʿa. He has also argued for adaptation of Islamic social and legal traditions to changing terms of a new era and new settings for Islam. He founded an organization, Kamilat, to advocate for women's rights and give guidance to modern Muslim women in matters large and small, and appointed his wife, Hajja Naziha Adil, as executive co-chair. The current executive director of this organization, Hajja Taliba Jilani, is an American convert to Islam. Women play prominent roles as writers, correspondents, and objects of discussion in Kamilat, and like many new Muslim organizations, Kamilat has established a strong presence on the Internet at <www.kamilat.org>, but is also under constant attack from more mainstream and right-wing Muslim organizations. At the same time, Muslim men and women of all denominations are under fire from secularists in the countries to which they have emigrated, including those where freedom of religion is enshrined as a founding value of the state. Muslim women are, perhaps, finding new variants of patriarchal support for their rights in new state settings in a world-wide diaspora. It remains to be seen how this will play out in terms of individual rights within Muslim communities, and within various political regimes.

From the nineteenth century, then, male politicians, activists, and intellectuals have attempted to change the status of Muslim women, and to delimit or expand their public roles, as key elements of strategies of modernization, anti-colonial resistance, state-building, and internal reform. The Turkish feminist Şirin Tekeli put this dynamic in a wry formulation, asking "how is it that we are emancipated, but not liberated?" – by which she meant that Turkish women were emancipated from above for the purposes of the state, but that they did not set the terms of their own liberation through struggle and demands from below. Turkey is the most stark example of this dynamic, but it has variations throughout the Muslim and non-Muslim world. Even as male state actors have seen uses for women in public life, they have been less concerned with improving the actual conditions of women's (or other citizens') daily lives, so that most Muslim women in most national and diasporic settings, like their sisters elsewhere, continue to carry the burden of housework and child rearing while also pursuing a career outside the home. The continuing inequalities in professional, political, and home life leave the question of male advocacy of women's rights vexed by two questions. First, why do men advocate an expansion of women's roles in their societies? And second, what happens to male advocacy when women advocate for themselves and demand more than their male "advocates" are willing to grant them?

BIBLIOGRAPHY

L. Abu-Lughod, *Remaking women. Feminism and modernity in the Middle East*, Princeton, N.J. 1998.

L. Ahmed, *Women and gender in Islam. Historical roots of a modern debate*, New Haven, Conn. 1992.

C. M. Amin, *The making of the modern Iranian woman. Gender, state policy, and popular culture, 1865–1946*, Gainesville, Fla. 2002.

E. Frierson, Unimagined communities. Educational reform and civic identity among late-Ottoman women, in *Critical Matrix* 9:2 (Fall 1995), 57–92.

M. Ghoussoub and E. Sinclair-Webb (eds.), *Imagined masculinities. Changing patterns of identity for Middle Eastern men*, London 1999.

Y. Y. Haddad and J. L. Esposito (eds.), *Islam, gender, and social change*, Oxford 1998.

D. Kandiyoti (ed.), *Gendering the Middle East. Emerging perspectives*, New York 1996.

A. Najmabadi, *The story of the daughters of Quchan. Gender and national memory in Iranian history*, New York 1998.

Ş. Tekeli, Emergence of the new feminist movement in Turkey, in D. Dahlerup, (ed.), *The new women's movement*, Beverly Hills 1986, 179–99.

E. Thompson, *Colonial citizens. Republican rights, paternal privilege, and gender in French Syria and Lebanon*, New York 2000.

United Nations. Economic and Social Commission for Asia and the Pacific, *Women in Indonesia. A country profile*, New York 1998.

ELIZABETH FRIERSON

Women's Studies Programs in Muslim Countries

The Caucasus and Turkey

TURKEY

The development of women's studies in Turkey in academic units at universities in the 1990s owes much to the changes in social and cultural politics in the country which were accelerated in the 1970s and 1980s. In this period, activist women aimed at eliminating the androcentric biases and the unbalanced gender dynamics of epistemology in social sciences (Kandiyoti 1996, 2–3, Abadan-Unat 1995, 15). The 1980 coup d'état created a political vacuum in which several women's groups formed a movement and expressed a secular response to the rising Islamic fundamentalism (Y. Arat 1995, 80, Doltaş 1995, 61).

The 1980s mark the initial efforts of mapping histories and preparing translations of feminist research that developed outside Turkey. Women's journals and non-governmental organizations (NGOs) focused on issues such as domestic violence, women's rights, and political participation. A group of women established the journal *Somut* (Concrete) in 1983. Several publications followed this initial attempt (Y. Arat 1995, 80), including *feminist* (sic), and the socialist feminist journal *Kaktüs* (Cactus). The Womens' Solidarity Association was established in 1989. The Women's Library in Istanbul, established in 1991, is the first and only documentation center that houses information on women in many languages.

After these developments outside academia, the institutionalization of academic women's studies in Turkey developed in the early 1990s in two distinctive structures: in research centers with interdisciplinary research teams and in departments with courses in graduate and undergraduate programs. The development and institutionalization of women's and gender studies in Europe and the United States influenced Turkish academia. For example, the 1991 meeting organized by Frauen Anstiftung in Bonn made scholars think about institutionalization and its effects (Akkent 1994).

Marmara University Research and Implementation Center for the Employment of Women was established in 1992. Istanbul University Women's Research and Education Center launched its classes in the academic year 1991/2, and the Women's Studies Department opened in 1993 with an interdisciplinary curriculum for graduate students.

Ankara University Women's Studies Center (KASAUM) was established in 1993 with an interdisciplinary perspective for feminist research, education, and networking with women's organizations and NGOs. The Department of Women's Studies was established in 1996, offering courses on theories and methodology of social sciences and women's studies, history of feminist thought, and the women's movement.

The Middle East Technical University (METU) Gender and Women Studies Center organizes seminars and activities on women's issues, publishes articles and research, provides gender training, and maintains close links with women's NGOs. Gender and Women's Studies at METU is an interdisciplinary program, established in 1994 as a part of the Graduate School of Social Sciences. The Gender and Women's Studies Graduate Program is the only program in Turkey that carries the word "gender" in its title, offering both thesis and non-thesis alternatives.

Mersin University Women Studies Center (MERKAM) was established in 1997 with different working groups, mostly using volunteer efforts of the academic personnel and NGOs. They focus on forming and maintaining databases and publications, networking with NGOs, organizing seminars and meetings, and offering vocational training for women.

Çankaya University Women's Research Center and Van Yüzüncü Yıl University's Women's Research Center (YUKAM) were both established in 1998. Ege University Women's Studies Research Center conducts research on women's issues. Established in 2000, Ege University Women's Studies Graduate Program offers classes on gender and the history of the women's movement.

Other centers for women's studies include Atılım University (Ankara), Çukurova University (Adana), Eskişehir Anadolu University (Eskişehir), Gazi University (Ankara), and Hacettepe University (Ankara).

Gender courses are also integrated into the curricula of other academic establishments, mostly in the departments of sociology, anthropology, and literature. There is a debate as to whether women's studies is a discipline in and of itself or an interdisciplinary area. Questions relate to pedagogical and methodological issues. Curricula for women's and gender studies programs are not yet fully expanded to include issues such as queer theory, race, and ethnicity. There seems to be a discrepancy in communication and activities between urban centers and those that are less urban, not to mention the weakness of links between women within and outside academia. Particular issues related to Turkey need to be developed rather than borrowing paradigms from abroad. The boom in enrollment in women's studies centers and programs faces a decline since there are limited work options after graduation.

AZERBAIJAN

In Azerbaijan, the establishment of women's studies aimed to explain why women have always been degraded by men in the economic, social, decision-making, and human development spheres. A sub-regional conference entitled "Women's Rights are Human Rights: Women and Military Conflict" was held in Baku with the participation of governmental and non-governmental representatives from Azerbaijan, Armenia, Georgia, Iran, Kazakhstan, Kyrgyzstan, Moldova, Russia, Tajikistan, Turkey, Turkmenistan, Ukraine, and Uzbekistan on 18–20 May 1998 (Mustafayev 2001, 8). The Gender and Human Rights Research Unit (GIHAB) began its activities with the United Nations Development Programme (UNDP) Gender Project in 1998 with a conference on gender issues, mainly on education, human rights, and women's refugee problems (GIHAB 2002, 5).

Issues related to gender education were initiated by the UNDP Gender Project and, at the end of 1998, activities were implemented in this direction as mentioned in the plan for action of the project's second phase. At the same time, the Open Society Institute-Soros Foundation and the Central European University based in Budapest started certain projects in higher educational institutions in Azerbaijan concerned with gender education.

There are 42 state and 19 private higher educational institutions in the Azerbaijan Republic. Western University, Azerbaijan Public Administration Academy, Baku State University, Khazar University, and Baku Slavic Languages University offer courses on gender.

Gender courses on political science, philosophy, psychology, sociology, culture, legal aspects, Azeri history, and economics are open to all departments of the Western University. In addition to developing syllabi, the Gender Studies Center has also directed academic activities of teachers and masters and bachelors program students, and made proposals regarding the incorporation of gender and peace-related topics in course and diploma theses. Special focus was placed on development of materials for the national scientific conference organized on 23 December 2000, "Integration of Gender Theory into Social and Humanitarian Sciences," where 50 scholars, researchers, teachers, masters students, and leaders and specialists from gender centers participated.

At the Baku State University, gender courses are given in the psychology, sociology, and philosophy departments and are integrated into different subjects, such as ancient history, international relations, and English. Baku Slavic Languages University places more emphasis on eliminating the gender stereotypes apparent in textbooks and aims to develop focused gender pedagogy.

The Women's Studies Center at Khazar University was established in 1991, aiming at protecting and promoting women's rights. It maintains close collaboration with Purdue University and implements joint programs. It is a member of the Global Sisterhood Institute. In 1997, the center set broader goals and reinforced studies on women's issues. It has invited scholars from the United States, Western Europe, Turkey, Pakistan, Israel, and Norway who run sessions on gender. Students at the Women's Studies Center have maintained close relationships with women refugees and internationally displaced persons, and encouraged them to support the peace-building process in Southern Caucasus (Khazar University 2001–3, 125).

KYRGYZSTAN

The Department of Equal Rights in Kyrgyz-Russian Slavonic University has a special gender studies course, taught for the past five years. Kyrgyz National University, Bishkek Humanitarian University, Osh State University, and Kyrgyz Pedagogical University have special courses on gender within the sociology, history, and pedagogy departments.

Before proposing the new gender studies program for implementation in 2003/4, the National Council on Gender Development in cooperation with UNDP, UNFPA (United Nations Population Fund), and SFK (Soros Foundation Kyrgyzstan) representatives provided two round tables on gender studies perspectives in Kyrgyzstan. Although gender courses have been taught in various departments, the necessity for professional development by increasing knowledge about gender theory and methodology was stressed. Participants at educational events will receive the opportunity to prepare the syllabus and approve it in their universities (Shishkereva 2003).

BIBLIOGRAPHY

N. Abadan-Unat (ed.), *Türk toplumunda kadın*, Istanbul 1979.

——, Kadın araştırmalarında neden. Amaç ve kapsam, in N. Arat (ed.), *Türkiye'de kadın olgusu. Kadın gerçeğine yeni yaklaşımlar*, Istanbul 1995, 15–50.
A. Abasov, Gender research in Azerbaijan, in R. Mirzəzade (ed.), *Gender research in Azerbaijan* [in Azeri], Baku 2002, 9–18.
M. Akkent (trans.), *Kadın hareketinin kurumlaşması. Fırsatlar ve rizikolar*, Istanbul 1994.
N. Arat (ed.), *Türkiye'de kadın olgusu. Kadın gerçeğine yeni yaklaşımlar*, Istanbul 1995.
Y. Arat, 1980'ler Türkiyesi'nde kadın hareketi. Liberal Kemalizmin radikal uzantısı, in N. Arat (ed.), *Türkiye'de kadın olgusu. Kadın gerçeğine yeni yaklaşımlar*, Istanbul 1995, 71–92.
A. Asedov, Special course programs on gender education, in R. Mirzəzade (ed.), *Gender research in Azerbaijan* [in Azeri], Baku 2002, 62–79.
F. Berktay, Women's studies in Turkey 1980–1990, in *Women's memory. Proceedings of the International Symposium of Women's Libraries*, 8–10 October 1991, Istanbul 1991, 271–5.
H. Birkalan, Türkiye'de feminist etnografya yeri ve zamanı?, paper presented at the First Conference of Turkish Cultural Studies Meeting in Van, Turkey, 3–6 September 2003.
N. Çilingiroğlu, Türkiye'de akademik düzeyde kadına yönelik kurumsallaşma, in *Hacettepe Toplum Hekimliği Bülteni* 22:2 (2001), 4–6.
D. Doltaş, Batıdaki feminist kuramlar ve 1980 sonrası Türk feminizmi, in N. Arat (ed.), *Türkiye'de kadın olgusu. Kadın gerçeğine yeni yaklaşımlar*, Istanbul 1995, 51–71.
R. İbrahimbeyova, Gender aspects of education, in R. Mirzəzade (ed.), Gender research in Azerbaijan [in Azeri], Baku 2002, 48–52.
D. Kandiyoti, Contemporary feminist scholarship and Middle Eastern studies, in D. Kandiyoti (ed.), *Gendering the Middle East. Emerging perspectives*, New York 1996, 1–27.
Khazar University 2001–2003 Catalogue, Baku 2001.
F. D. Mammedova (ed.), *On gender education in higher education institutions* [in Azeri], Baku 2001.
R. Mirzəzade (ed.), *Gender research in Azerbaijan* [in Azeri], Baku 2002.
F. Özbay (ed.), *Study of women in Turkey. An anthology*, Istanbul 1986.
Qerb Universiteti, Gender research center [in Azeri], pamphlet, Baku 2002.
Z. Quluzadi, On gender education in Azerbaijan, in R. Mirzəzade (ed.), *Gender research in Azerbaijan* [in Azeri], Baku 2002, 44–8.
E. Shishkereva, personal communication 2003.
A. Veyselova, Learning gender relations in Azerbaijan, in R. Mirzəzade (ed.), *Gender research in Azerbaijan* [in Azeri], Baku 2002, 177–8.

HANDE A. BIRKALAN-GEDIK

Central Asia

TAJIKISTAN

In Tajikistan, gender studies were launched in 1996. For the first time sociological research focused on gender roles within the family and the sources of gender inequality. Studies have looked at women's participation in entrepreneurship and women's legal status and local legislation on gender equality have been examined. The results of sociological research were published in a series of brochures called *Women in Transition in Tajikistan*. A statistical and analytical study of modern gender statistics was conducted and published in the collection *Gender Statistics in the Republic of Tajikistan*, in addition to the statistical collections on *Women and Men in Tajikistan* and *Family and Children in the Republic of Uzbekistan*. In 1999, *Gender and Culture*, a textbook, was published for high school students through the activities of non-governmental organizations (NGOs). The government approved a program entitled "The Direction of Government Policy on Equal Rights and Equal Opportunities for Women and Men, 2001–2010."

TURKMENISTAN

The issues of gender development in Turkmenistan have become integral to government policy. A National Action Plan on the Advancement of Woman was drafted with the United Nations as follow-up to the Fourth World Conference on the Advancement of Woman (Beijing 1995) and the results of its implementation are detailed in the *Report on Implementation of the National Action Plan 2000*. Also in 2000 the National Statistical Institute of Turkmenistan (NTISF) prepared a *Review of the National System of Collection, Analysis, and Distribution of Data on Population and Reproductive Health*. In 2001 NTISF published *Gender Aspects of Socioeconomic Indicators*. Materials from the seminar "Gender Equality in Compliance with Turkmenistan's Constitutions and Legislation" were published in 2002. Among the materials from the International Summer School ("Gender Studies in Central Asia") was a course on "Gender in the Economy." This course was designed by the faculty members of the Turkmenistan State University and the Women's Resource Center. According to the brochure "Gender Studies and Gender Awareness in Turkmenistan: Problems of Higher Education" the university students of law and business and management attended a special 14-hour course on "Gender and Economics."

KYRGYZSTAN

In Kyrgyzstan the international environment stimulated public awareness of the concept of gender in the second half of the 1990s. Ideas about gender appear in all government programs. Among them are "Development Strategy for the Kyrgyz Republic to 2010"; "National Plan for the Development of Education in the Kyrgyz Republic to

2015"; and the "National Plan for Achieving Gender Equality in the Kyrgyz Republic, 2002–2006." In March 2003 a law outlining government guarantees for the provision of gender equality was approved. There is ongoing preparation of a 36-hour course on "Basic Theories of Gender Equality," which will be obligatory for all students. Since 2002 Kyrgyzstan has been attempting to integrate gender awareness into the ministries and other governmental bodies.

UZBEKISTAN

Uzbekistan was one of the first Central Asian countries to take measures to provide equal rights for men and women. In 1995 Uzbekistan ratified the Convention on the Elimination of All Forms of Discrimination against Women (CEDAW), intending to include these protections in national legislation. In 1996 the UNDP initiated introductory workshops on gender awareness. The term "gender" became known and was included in government vocabulary. However, gender awareness among NGOs is much better developed, and since 1996 NGOs have been conducting sociological research in gender studies. Research has been undertaken on rural women, on gender in basic textbooks, and on violence against women. A new course on "Basics of Gender: Theory and Practice" and a textbook for high school students was designed. The ministry of education approved the course and the textbook and they will be incorporated into the humanities curriculum in national universities.

Bibliography

Asian Development Bank/Global Security and Cooperation, *Gender expertise of basic education textbooks in Uzbekistan* [in English and Russian], (forthcoming).

Association of Businesswomen in Tajikistan, *Women in transition in Tajikistan*, i, *Women and entrepreneurship*, ii, *Women's health problems*, iii, *Women and the law*, iv, *Violence against women* [in Russian], Khujant 1998.

Family and children in the Republic of Tajikistan. A statistical collection [in Russian], Dushanbe 2002.

Gender and culture. Textbook [in Russian], Dushanbe 1999.

Men and women in the Republic of Tajikistan. Statistical collection [in Russian], Dushanbe 2002.

UNDP, *Human development report. Uzbekistan* [in English, Russian, and Uzbek], Tashkent 1999.

Status of rural women in transition, in *Collected materials UNDP/INTAS/WRC/SABR* [in English, Russian, and Uzbek], Samarkand 2000.

Women in Development, *Gender Statistics in the Republic of Tajikistan* [in Russian], Khujant 1998.

Dinara Alimdjanova

Iran

Women's studies programs in Iran are of very recent vintage, developed through a process mostly guided from above and without effective input from individuals with expertise in women's studies or groups and institutions that have been instrumental in pursuing feminist causes. The initial idea for the establishment of women's studies programs was put forth by the Center for Women's Studies and Research, which was established in 1986 as "non-governmental" and yet affiliated to the Ministry of Sciences, Research, and Technology to enhance the integration of women in the state-guided process of economic development. The proposed programs were initially relatively broad in scope and breadth and included study of feminism and women's movements and issues in all its dimensions throughout the world.

In January 2000, the Supreme Council for Planning at the Ministry of Sciences, Research, and Technology approved the plan for a master of arts program in women's studies but only allowed for three specializations within the program: woman and family, women's rights in Islam, and women's history. The limited scope of the approved subjects places various universities in the difficult position of attempting to start programs with state-imposed guidelines, which many of the interested faculty do not accept as useful or sufficiently comprehensive. Given this predicament, the women's studies programs in several public universities, three of which began accepting students for the first time in the 2002/3 academic year, are bound to be evolving as various faculties within these institutions attempt to adapt guidelines developed elsewhere to their own particular needs, resources, and constituency.

Public universities have dealt with the tension between imposed specializations and their own resources and needs in different ways. For example, the College of Humanities at Tarbiat Modarres University, a teacher training college, has mostly followed the three main specializations approved by the Ministry of Sciences, Research and Technology, only replacing the specialization in women's history with women in development and politics. The women's studies program at ʿAllāmah Tabātabāʾi University, on the other hand, is housed in the social sciences faculty and has only accepted woman and family as a specialization. It has also removed Arabic as a requirement and added courses such as introductions to women's studies and women's movements to its curriculum. Al-Zahrā University, a women's college, while accepting students, has not assented to any of the proposed specializations and has instead focused on prerequisites and a few main courses, delaying the decision about better-suited specializations within its program until later. The same holds for the College of Social Sciences at Tehran University, which is to begin accepting students in women's studies in 2003/4 without specifying any specialization within the program. The publicly stated intent at Tehran University is to develop the program either without specialization or introduce specializations different from those approved.

So far none of the private or semi-private universities have shown interest in the development of women's studies programs, and chances of them showing interest are slim given the lack of a strong demand for the establishment of such programs. However, now that several programs have been established at public universities, the likely trend will be an increasing attempt on the part of various civil society forces interested in women's issues, particularly as represented in the vibrant women's press, to shape the evolution of these programs in directions that will take them beyond the existing state-imposed limits. Already critics have pointed out the lack of qualified instructors as well as the oddity of having a master of arts degree in women's studies without the existence of the prerequisite women's studies courses at the bachelor level. They have also questioned the top-down, male-dominated process that led to the creation of what some worry will become mere "for show" women's studies programs developed by the Ministry of Sciences, Research, and Technology.

BIBLIOGRAPHY

P. Ardalān, *Majira-hayah ta'sis-i rishti-yi muṭāliʿāt-i zanān*, in *Zanān* 81 (2001), 36–40.

N. Moti', *Rishti-yi muṭāliʿāt-i zanān. Ta'liq-i vaqiʿiat ya ta'in-i muqiʿiat-i zanān-i Īrān?*, in *Zanān* 80 (2001), 36–7.

FARIDEH FARHI

Women's Unions and National Organizations

Afghanistan

Women's organizations in Afghanistan have been profoundly affected by power struggles surrounding government-sponsored modernization projects expressed through liberal or leftist discourses, and resistance to such social upheaval expressed through Islamist discourses, both resulting in coercively undemocratic practices. Women's organizations have moved toward and away from state institutional affiliation according to regime changes and the changing orientations of leading activists.

The Anjuman-i Ḥimāyat-i Niswān (Association for the Protection of Women) was established in 1928 by Sirāj al-Banāt and Queen Ṣurayyā to encourage women to demand the rights provided by King Amān Allāh's reforms of marriage customs and restrictive social practices, and advocacy of women's education (Moghadam 1993, 218–20).

The Mu'assasa-i Khayriyya-i Zanān (Women's Welfare Association, WWA), established by the monarchial state in 1946, was founded by Zaynab ʿInāyat Sirāj and Bibī Jān, both members of the royal family. Its members consisted of liberal upper- and middle-class activists. Although it tried to encourage unveiling, the emphasis of WWA was to encourage income-generating activities and to modernize women by providing literacy, family planning, and vocational classes. In 1953 it established the journal *Mirman*. In 1975 WWA became institutionally independent and changed its name to the Women's Institute (WI). The WI had branch offices in ten provincial cities and grew to 8,000 members. Kubra Noorzai, the institute's director, was elected to the National Assembly under President Dāwūd, and the organization began to promote gender equality through the state's modernization policies (Emadi 2002, 91–2, 97, Ellis 2000, 164–6).

The Sāzmān-i Demokratik-i Zanān-i Afghanistān (Women's Democratic Organization of Afghanistan, WDOA) was created by the Parcham faction of the socialist People's Democratic Party of Afghanistan (PDPA). The leading activists of the WDOA, such as Anahita Ratibzad and Ṣurayyā, fought for women's rights in marriage, education, and suffrage (Moghadam 1993, 225, Emadi 2002, 95). After the PDPA came to power, WDOA (temporarily renamed Khalq Organization of Afghan Women), led an aggressive, coercive, and unpopular national literacy and marriage reform campaign and was staunchly pro-Soviet. In 1987 WDOA, now claiming almost 95,000 mostly urban members, was renamed the Afghan Women's Council under the non-PDPA leadership of Masuma Asmati Wardak, who adopted a less confrontational approach (Emadi 2002, 107, Moghadam 1993, 228–36, Dupree 1984).

The Jāmʿiyat-i Inqilābi-i Zanān-i Afghanistān (Revolutionary Association of Women of Afghanistan, RAWA) was founded in 1977 by Meena. RAWA opposed the repressive tactics of the PDPA and organized women and girls in factories and schools to fight against the Soviet invasion through armed struggle, strikes, demonstrations and distribution of night communiqués (*shabnāmas*). RAWA's goal of women's equality within a socialist democratic Islamic republic was framed as inseparable from their goal of national liberation and overrode criticisms of the Mujāhdīn in importance (Emadi 2002, 108–11). The Mujāhidīn regime and later the Taliban caused RAWA to denounce Islamism and armed struggle and call for a secular state. RAWA clandestinely provides basic healthcare, education, and income-generating activities in Afghanistan and refugee camps in Pakistan and strives to draw international attention to the situation of Afghan women (RAWA 2002).

Limited reforms have been hampered by a of lack public security resulting from the transitional government's weakness, local unrest, and resistance to continued American occupation and the deleterious local rule of former Mujāhidīn leaders. The Afghan Women's Network, a coalition of 24 non-governmental organizations founded in 1996, has taken a conciliatory approach toward the transitional government, framing suggestions to expand women's rights in the constitution within an Islamist framework. RAWA is critical, viewing the constitution as an unacceptable concession to the detriment of Afghan women (Human Rights Watch 2002, Afghan Women's Network, RAWA).

Bibliography

Primary Sources

Afghan Women's Network, <http://www.afghanwomensnetwork.org/>.

Nationwide Conference of the Women of Afghanistan,

Text of speeches in the nation-wide conference of the women of Afghanistan, held in Kabul from Nov. 28–30, 1980, Kabul 1980.
RAWA, <www.rawa.org>.
RAWA, Shoulder to shoulder, hand in hand. Resistance under the iron fist in Afghanistan, in *Radical History Review* 82 (2002), 131–40.

Secondary Sources
N. H. Dupree, Revolutionary rhetoric and Afghan women, in M. Shahrani and R. L. Canfield (eds.), *Revolutions and rebellions in Afghanistan. Anthropological perspectives*, Berkeley 1984, 306–40.
D. Ellis, *Women of the Afghan war*, Westport, Conn. 2000.
H. Emadi, *Repression, resistance, and women in Afghanistan*, Westport, Conn. 2002.
Human Rights Watch, "We want to live as humans." Repression of women and girls in western Afghanistan, *Human Rights Watch Report* 14:11 (December 2002), <http://www.hrw.org/reports/2002/afghnwmn1202/>.
V. Moghadam, Women and social change in Afghanistan, in V. Moghadam, *Modernizing women. Gender and social change in the Middle East*, Boulder, Colo. 1993, 207–48.

Mana Kia

Iran

Women's organizations in Iran have primarily been concerned with educating women, bettering their rights within the family and asserting their rights to excel in the public sphere. Many organizations have published newspapers and journals to voice their views and raise awareness. Predominantly nationalist and secular in nature, their rhetoric, rather than directly attacking Islam, has criticized elements of Iranian society seen to have warped Islam, which in its "true" form supports the women's rights being sought. Institutionally autonomous during times when the state has been weak, women's organizations have been subsumed within the state during periods of centralization. Following the 1979 revolution, national women's organizations have become overtly Islamist in nature, though no less modernizing and feminist.

The Jāmʿiyat-i Nisvān-i Vaṭankhvāh (Society of Patriotic Women, SPW) was formed in 1922 and was led by strong activists, such as Muḥtaram Iskandarī, Mastūrī Afshār, and Ṣadīqa Dawlatābādī, who had differing priorities with regard to women's rights. SPW's activities included rallies, meetings, demonstrations and petition campaigns. The SPW disbanded when deep divisions over veiling and "how to relate to the increasingly autocratic government of Riza Shah" came to a head at the Second Congress of Women of the East in 1932. In 1935 the state established the Kanūn-i Bānuvān (Women's Center) to support its gender policies, particularly unveiling, through education and awareness raising activities. Many former members of the SPW were amongst its leading activists (Najmabadi 2000, 36–9, Sanasarian 1982, 55).

With the weakening of the central state between 1941 and 1953, women's organizations once again multiplied. These included the Jāmʿiyat-i Zanān-i Īrān (Iranian Women's League); the Hizb-i Zanān-i Īrān (Party of Iranian Women) led by Ṣaffiya Fīrūz and Fāṭima Sayyāḥ, later the National Council of Women; and the Tudeh affiliated Tashkīlāt-i Zanān-i Īrān (Organization of Iranian Women), later the Society of Democratic Women (Sanasarian 1982, 72–3, Amin 2002, 226–7, 234–8).

After the 1953 coup d'état, smaller women's organizations began to reappear. By 1959 14 of these groups coalesced into the Federation of Women's Organizations, a loose body designed to foster greater effectiveness and cooperation amongst its component organizations.

The Shawrā-yi ʿĀlī-yi Jāmʿiyāt-i Zanān (High Council of Women's Societies) was created in 1961, consisting of 18 women's associations. Although international activities were under government control, member organizations enjoyed a fair degree of autonomy to conduct their domestic work and enjoyed the benefit of state resources (Sanasarian 1982, 80–1, Dolatshahi 1984, 14–16).

In 1966 the Sāzmān-i Zanān-i Īrān (Women's Organization of Iran, WOI) was established under the leadership of Ashraf Pahlavī. It was a centralized, nationwide women's organization consisting of 33 smaller organizations. Individual societies in the provinces were replaced with WOI branches, and Mahnāz Afkhamī served as secretary-general from 1970 to 1979 (Dolatshahi 1984, 22–3, Afkhami 1984, 337). The WOI was more integrated into the state apparatus and less democratic than its previous forms – although officers were elected from each branch, Pahlavī had the power to appoint the majority of the organization's eleven-member central council (Sanasarian 1982, 83–5). Activists within the WOI had to realign their political demands and socioeconomic projects to fit with those of the state.

Since the 1990s, secular feminists have been in dialogue with Muslim feminists, who challenge clerical religious interpretations by drawing from the Qurʾān and reinterpreting Islam to critique the state and call for women's rights. Some post-revolutionary Islamist women's organizations are: Women's Society of Islamic Revolution; the Iranian Islamic Women's Institute; the Ḥaẓrat-i Khadīja Association; the Women's Solidarity Association; and the Social-Cultural Council of Women. Secular feminists, such as Mehrangiz Kar, are active in the women's periodical press, as legal advocates, and in promoting feminist education and awareness. Roshangaran, the first independent publisher of mostly women writers, was founded by Shahla Lahiji, who also established a research institute devoted to women's studies.

BIBLIOGRAPHY

PRIMARY SOURCES

B. Bāmdād, *From darkness into light. Women's emancipation in Iran*, trans. F. R. C. Bagley, Hicksville, N.Y. 1977.

M. Dolatshahi, Interview recorded by Shahrokh Meskoob, 15 May 1984, Paris, tape no. 4, Iranian Oral History Collection, Harvard University.

Women's Organization of Iran and International Institute for Adult Literacy Methods, *The design of educational programs for the social and economic promotion of rural women. An international seminar 19–24 April 1975*, Tehran 1975.

SECONDARY SOURCES

M. Afkhami, Iran. A future in the past – the "prerevolutionary" women's movement, in R. Morgan (ed.), *Sisterhood is global*, Garden City, N.Y. 1984, 330–38.

M. Amin, *The making of the modern Iranian woman. Gender, state policy and popular culture, 1865–1946*, Gainesville, Fla. 2002.

A. Kian-Thiébaut, From Islamization to the individualization of women in post-revolutionary Iran, in S. Ansari and V. Martin (eds.), *Women, religion and culture in Iran*, Richmond, Surrey 2002, 127–42.

A. Najmabadi, (Un)veiling feminism, in *Social Text* 18:3 (2000), 29–45.

G. Nashat, Women in pre-revolutionary Iran. A historical overview, in G. Nashat (ed.), *Women and revolution in Iran*, Boulder, Colo. 1983, 5–35.

E. Sanasarian, *The women's rights movement in Iran. Mutiny, appeasement, and repression from 1900 to Khomeini*, New York 1982.

MANA KIA

Turkey

The history of women's issues in Turkey goes back to the nineteenth-century Ottoman period, but more organized women's movements emerged in the context of the atmosphere of relative freedom created by the revolution of 1908. Following this revolution women were permitted to found associations pertaining to their own interests. The most outstanding of these was the Ottoman Association for Defense of Women's Rights, established in 1913. It sought to reform existing family law with the aim of creating an egalitarian family and to encourage women to take part in public life (Çakır 1996).

At the beginning of the republican regime (1923), those women who joined the feminist movement defined enfranchisement as their basic demand. Serving this aim, they established the first political party in republican Turkey, the Kadınlar Halk Fırkası (Women's People Party) in 1923 as soon as the republican regime was declared. Since the party was officially not allowed, members of the party established the Türk Kadınlar Birliği (Union of Turkish Women) in 1924, which struggled for voting rights until 1935.

The founder of the Turkish Republic, Mustafa Kemal Atatürk, and his associates advocated that women should have equal rights with men in every respect. They made substantial reforms toward promoting women's status. Women were given rights in three main areas: new rights that came with the adoption of the Swiss Civil Code in 1926; education for females alongside males; and enfranchisement in 1934. Polygamy was forbidden and women gained equal status in legal and political areas. In the election of 1934, the first election in which women participated, 18 women (4.5 percent) were elected to the parliament.

Having gained these rights, the leaders of the women's movement decided that there was no longer any need for a women's movement. In 1935, some leaders of the Union of Turkish Women, particularly those who were in sympathy with the regime, abolished the union. Thus from 1935 onward, women came to serve as the vanguard of the Kemalist regime rather than to seek to improve their status (Göle 1992). This continued at least until the 1980s.

From 1980, the women's movement was revived in Turkey as a direct consequence of the liberal policies pursued by civilian governments. Women who sought prestige under the banner of official ideology started to shift their attention to struggle for self-realization in the public sphere. Feminist women started to raise their voice first in *Somut* (Concrete), a weekly magazine, in 1983 and then in many other feminist journals through the 1990s and 2000s. Different women's groups have brought to light local problems by means of these journals and have taken many actions. They have mainly concentrated on such issues as the right to abortion, divorce on demand, equality in family life, elimination of legal norms detrimental to women, and elimination of assault on women in the public sphere (Tekeli 1990).

Under the influence of the women's movement women's issues are among the hottest topics discussed in the media, in cinema, and in politics since the 1980s. Women's issues have continued to occupy the agenda of different social groups ranging from ethnic to traditional and modern (Çaha 1995).

Some of the prominent nationwide voluntary associations established by these groups are Ayrımcılığa Karşı Kadın Derneği (Women's Association for struggling against discrimination), Çagdaş Yaşamı Destekleme Derneği (Association for the support of contemporary life), and Kadın Adayları Destekleme ve Eğitme Derneği (KADER, Association for the support and training of female candidates for parliament).

In addition to these voluntary organizations there are two important official national associations. The first one is Başbakanlık Aile Araştırma Kurumu (Prime ministry family research institution), established in 1989. The basic aim of this organization is to protect the family and any value associated with the family. The integration of different generations in the family, the protection of family as an institution, and the protection of the rights of family members figures prominently in the work of this organization. It sees women as members of the family and deals with their problems within that perspective. Beyond women's problems, the organization addresses the issue of how the Turkish family can be strengthened. This is the reason why this association has been strongly criticized by feminist groups.

The second official national women's organization is Başbakanlık Kadının Statüsü ve Sorunları Genel Müdürlüğü (Prime ministry directorate for women's problems and status), established in 1990. Its aim is substantially different from the previous one; it has cooperated with other women's organizations to solve women's problems. It mainly searches for grounds to obtain equality of opportunity for women and many feminist women have participated in its projects. It has struggled particularly against Turkish laws which discriminate against women, and demands that women and politicians work to eliminate such norms.

Bibliography

Y. Arat, *The patriarchal paradox. Women politicians in Turkey*, London 1989.

Ö. Çaha, *Sivil kadın. Türkiye' de sivil toplum ve kadın*, Ankara 1995.

S. Çakır, *Osmanlı kadın hareketi*, Istanbul 1996.

N. Göle, *Modern mahrem. Medeniyet ve örtünme*, Istanbul 1992, translated as *The forbidden modern. Civilization and veiling*, Ann Arbor 1996.

Ş. Kurnaz, *Cumhuriyet öncesinde Türk kadını 839–1923*, Ankara 1991.

T. Taşkıran, *Cumhuriyetin ellinci yılında Türk kadın hakları*, Ankara1973.

Ş. Tekeli (ed.), *Kadın bakışaçısından 1980'ler Türkiye'sinde kadın*, Istanbul 1990.

Ömer Çaha

Youth Culture and Movements

Iran

Although Iranian youth have been the subject of state development policies for several decades, the fully-fledged arrival of what can be and has been identified in the Iranian public discourse as a youth culture and movement must be traced to the post-revolutionary era, particularly in the mid to late 1990s. In the 1960s and 1970s various attempts were made to organize and create public spaces – for example, the Kākh-i Javānān (Palace of Youth) or summer and athletic camps – for the youth of both sexes to encourage their congregation and engagement in social and cultural activities. However, it is in the later period that the immediate post-revolutionary population boom of the early 1980s confronts the Iranian Islamist state with difficult youth related issues to manage. Figures ranging from 60 to 70 percent have been reported regarding the percentage of the Iranian population that is young, depending on the cut-off age used. According to the Iran Statistical Yearbook 1378/1999, which is based on the 1996 census, approximately 60 percent of the Iranian population in 1996 was under the age of 24. This population bulge is expected to continue until the latter part of the current decade, when it will begin to taper off owing to the implementation of population control policies in the late 1980s.

The increasing number of youth coupled with the Islamist state's harsh policies toward many forms of social and public activities, ranging from enforced Islamic dress codes (mostly for women but also for men) to public inhibitions or outright ban on certain types of social interaction among men and women, as well as on many cultural activities such as concerts and other forms of entertainment, have made Iranian youth increasingly restless since the 1990s. While not articulated in an organized social movement, the demands and needs associated with Iranian youth have loosely but clearly manifested themselves in the Iranian fledgling press; student demonstrations for increased political, social, and cultural freedom; unorganized but nevertheless systematic disobedience of publicly enforced Islamic dress codes and guidelines for proper Islamic behavior in public; electoral behavior; and clandestine cultural activities in music and the arts. These disparate political, social, and cultural activities have become so prominent and troublesome for the Islamic Republic that the social category of "youth" and what to do about their needs, demands, and problems have become an integral part of the Iranian public discourse.

In this public discourse, however, the nature of the relationship between gender related issues and the loosely knit youth movement is not yet clear. In fact, the categories of "youth" and "women" are generally discussed as though they are completely separate entities, with distinct problems and issues. At the same time, there seems to be an unstated assumption that the problems of young men and women are largely the same: the existence of an autocratic and moralistic state that treats both with disdain; imposes rigid guidelines on their public and even private behavior; inhibits their political participation; is incapable of creating suitable employment opportunities for their increasing numbers; and is unable to deal forthrightly with severe social problems such as prostitution and drug abuse among youth. As such, the particular problems gender related issues pose for Iranian youth within and beyond the dictates of the Islamic theocracy are not yet adequately conceptualized. There are discussions of important social issues, such as the rise in number of young female prostitutes or runaway girls (some of whom trans-dress as boys in order to survive in the streets), in Iran's women's press and the press directed at youth. But there has been little systematic discussion of how gender dynamics make the lives of youth in the confines of the Islamic Republic differentiated and varied. Similarly, until recently there has been very little critique of the continued dominance of young men in the more organized parts of the youth movement such as the student movement. This is despite the fact that young Iranian women through a variety of activities, ranging from their continued defiance of the Islamic dress code, to their now higher acceptance rate at the universities, to their strong voice in arts and literature, have been critical contributors to the emergence and sustenance of the youth movement and culture. However, the situation is rapidly changing. The increasing presence of younger women in the Iranian press, the creation of feminist Internet sites such as <www.womeniniran.org> run by a younger generation of women activists, and the explosion of young Iranian web bloggers, many of whom are women, are bound to significantly affect the way gender issues are discussed in the Iranian youth culture and movement.

BIBLIOGRAPHY
F. Adelkhah, *Being modern in Iran*, New York 2000.
Statistical Centre of Iran, *Iran statistical yearbook 1378/1999*, Tehran 2001.
B. Yaghmaian, *Social change in Iran. An eyewitness account of dissent, defiance, and new movements for rights*, Albany, N.Y. 2002.

FARIDEH FARHI

North Africa (including Egypt)

The period extending from the 1940s to the 1980s witnessed a demographic explosion in greater North Africa which had the significant side effect of producing a large youth population between the ages of 15 and 24 whose various needs (education, health, leisure) demanded attention and heavy state investment. The 2000 census in Egypt reported a high percentage (20.5) of youth out of a population of 67 million; Libya registered a significant 24.1 percent out of a population of little over 5 million; Tunisia 20.9 percent out of 9 million; Algeria 21.7 percent out of 30 million; and finally Morocco 21.2 percent out of 29 million (United Nations 2002). These percentages denote the extent to which youth continues to be the center of gravity for all these nation-states. While the historical legacy of each country differs to varying degrees from its neighbors concerning programs, political mobilization, and other cultural activities involving youth, this entry focuses on the underlying assumptions that govern the youth movements and their main commonalities.

Youth remains at the heart of the social and political debate in all of the Arab world today as it did during and following the achievement of political independence in these countries. This is because of the demographic weight of youth and because the future of any nation-state rests on its shoulders. Hence, there is an obligation to provide a well-rounded education and grooming for various forms of responsibility. The creation of youth organizations for education, culture, sports, and leisure were important historical moments that were meant to symbolize the overarching promise that youth represent in general: the capacity of work, dedication, promise, and hope for a bright future. Though the ideologies that nourished their activities differed widely, youth organizations as distinct as scout movements or neighborhood local associations contributed to the preparation and the mainstreaming of their adherents into a normative ideology. Associations of course possessed varying statuses: from those that were aligned with political parties, as is the case with Nasserist Egypt or socialist Algeria and Libya, to others that claimed an apolitical character and were more interested in cultural activities such as theatre, painting, sports, group-games, and similar activities. Despite these differences there was, nevertheless, a current of politization underlying cultural events such as popular theatre or anti-illiteracy programs. An example of this ideological substratum is the Arab Scout Conference; the first was held in Syria in 1954 at the height of Arabic nationalism (*qawmiyya*) and it continued its aim of pan-Arabism even as late as its 23rd meeting in 2001 in Saudi Arabia. Associations were often used for ideological purposes, but they were also seen and as a means for fostering respect for difference and for learning the values of democracy. Their educational role as models of democratic institutions, on the one hand, and as places for talent and initiative to find their expression, on the other, attracted all sorts of youth. More specifically, in the case of Morocco, Algeria, Tunisia, and Libya, during the immediate post-independence period and thanks to the euphoria of nationalistic feelings, highly important projects were realized thanks to the collective efforts of youth. Building roads, constructing schools, or contributing to large-scale afforestion were among such programs.

During the research for this entry, the notorious and rather heartbreaking absence of specific programs or discussions concerning young women in youth culture(s) became obvious. While young women benefited from summer camps and contributed largely to the making of the youth movements in all their facets, it is more their age group, their status as being young, that was of importance rather than their gender. It seems from the scant sources available that active realization and consciousness of young women's issues were either lacking or considered secondary during the process of nation-building throughout the mid-twentieth century. While the socialist regimes espoused a Marxist inspired model of economic exploitation as the basis of injustice and therefore saw no need to be gender specific, other regimes paid only lip service to issues relating to women when they actually addressed them consciously. Following turbulent decades in the contemporary history of the Arab world in the wake of continuous wars with Israel, the disillusionment with pan-Arabism, internal conflicts between Arab countries, especially the three Gulf wars, the polarization of politics, and the lessening of job opportunities for massive numbers of youth, the realities of the youth movement today are totally different from the spirit that characterized its birth during the 1940s and institutionalization in the 1950s. Throughout North Africa and Egypt, the infrastructures put in place for youth sensitization and participation are experiencing, to varying degrees, serious shortages, if not outright failure, as in Algeria and Morocco. This gloomy spectrum ranges from the meager subsidies they receive, the extremely limited numbers of educators who create and watch over programs and projects, to the bankruptcy of the belief-systems that nourish them. The weight of Islamist movements and the spread of various non-governmental organizations (NGOs) specializing in artistic movements are the two, though quite polarized, ingredients that have somewhat slowed down the apathy and alienation vis-à-vis public affairs that have suffused youth movements in these countries – though such apathy exists to a much lesser extent in Libya due to the repressive political regime. Women educators and younger women beneficiaries are active participants and actors within youth movements in these countries today.

Examples of modern organizations in Egypt are AIESEC Egypt, the Arab Office of Youth and Environment (AOYE), and the Egyptian Girl Guides Association (EGGA). In Libya organizations include the Secretariat of Youth and Sport of the Masses and and an NGO, the General Union of Great Jamahiriya Students (GUGJS). In Tunisia there is a ministry of youth (Ministère de la jeunesse et de l'enfance), and an important NGO is the Union of Tunisian Youth Organizations (UTOJ). In Algeria, there is the Algeria National Union of Algerian Youth (UNJA) and the famous Conseil supérieur de la jeunesse (CSJ). In Morocco there is also a ministry and a number of other NGOs such as AIESEC Morocco, Chantiers jeunes Maroc (CJM), and the Fédération nationale de scoutisme marocain (FNSM). Though there is no longer the euphoria of youth movements that existed in the mid-twentieth century, the current programs of these associations and NGOs have not only created a new dynamic of societal relations but have also opened up the public space for youth for various forms of expression. They aim at fostering self-esteem and group solidarities that exemplify, in the end, the underlying philosophy that has always nourished the culture of youth movements since its inception with socialist ideologies.

Bibliography

Arab Scout Conference, <http://www.arabscout.org/About Us/Organizational_Body.htm percentArabScoutConference>.

N. Bancel, D. Denis, et al. (eds.), *De l'Indochine à l'Algérie. La jeunesse en mouvements des deux côtés du miroir colonial, 1940–1962*, Paris 2003.

R. Meijer (ed.), *Alienation or integration of Arab youth. Between family, state and street*, Richmond, Surrey 2000.

NITLE (National Institute for Technology and Liberal Education) Arab World Project, <http://arabworld.nitle.org/main_menu.php>.

M. Tessler, Morocco's next political generation, in *Journal of North African Studies* 5:1 (Spring 2000), 1–26.

United Nations, Youth Profiles Online research reference, 2002, <http://www.un.org/ esa/socdev/unyin/wywatch/country.htm>.

Jamila Bargach

Turkey

The study of youth culture and movements in Turkey is relatively new. Kinship terminology and the use of a term to denote the period between puberty and marriage suggest that age, and the distinction between juniors and seniors, play a central role in the construction of personhood in Turkish society. Historically, it was preferable, for reasons of social control, to keep the period between puberty and marriage as short as possible. In Ottoman society, young men formed the backbone of revolts from the sixteenth century. "Wild blood" (*delikanlı*, the term used to refer to youth) was to be channeled along tracks acceptable to adult society, such as the military, apprenticeship, agricultural/pastoral labor, and early marriage. The threat of nonconforming behavior on the part of young women required even more stringent and internalized systems of domination.

The period of reforms known as the Tanzimat (1839–76) ushered in a new conception of youth. It is no coincidence that the main social movements of the late Ottoman period were known as the Young Ottoman movement and the Young Turk movement. In the late nineteenth century, educated young Ottomans (mostly men) were called upon to save the institutions of empire. The emphasis on the modernizing role of educated youth culminated in the 1920s in a veritable cult of youth initiated by the new Turkish state to build a national consciousness and a modern nation-state. The phrase "children of the republic" refers to this new youth. Up until the present, it would be young women's bodies in particular that would come to symbolically represent the nation.

In 1960, the Democratic Party, which had ruled the country since the first multi-party elections, was removed from power by a military coup. University students played a role in protests against the regime. In the late 1960s, under a liberal constitution, the growing student movement, increasingly disillusioned with the status quo, influenced by youth movements in Europe and elsewhere in 1968, spurred on by various forces with much to gain from the rise of extremism, moved outside the legal terrain, culminating in increased violence followed by brutal repression subsequent to the military coup of 1971 (and again in 1980). Youth, who embodied the new nation in the early republican period, were now reconstructed in the public discourse as a threat to the national interest. Youth themselves, in contrast, claimed it was the government itself that was illegitimate. Despite their differences, the early republican and youth of the late 1960s shared a modernist construction of youth. Men tended to dominate the student movement; a history of women in the politics of this period remains to be written. The feminist movement of the 1980s arose as much out of the experience of 1968 as from a critique of it.

The 1980 military coup was an important watershed in Turkish politics. A new constitution that restricted civil liberties was put into effect, and young people born in the 1980s were raised in a relatively depoliticized environment. In the 1980s and 1990s, in addition to Islamist and Kurdish nationalist movements, a variety of subcultures including environmentalists, human rights activists, feminists, gays, and others entered the public sphere. Just as it symbolizes a break in Turkish political culture, the post-1980 period constitutes a rupture with modernist constructions of youth. Today, constructions of youth circulate through the media, where young people are increasingly represented. For youth who reject the way they are depicted, existing categories do not seem to fit. Their individualism, denigrated by previous generations, stems from a hesitancy in linking their subjective identities and lifestyles to a single collective project. The feminist movement had an influence on this subjective turn. Young people are increasingly challenging their construction in public discourse, the established hierarchy between elders and juniors, and the mission imposed on them by adult society. This suggests that the construction of youth (and of age) in Turkish society may be changing.

Today, one half of Turkish society is under the age of 25; these young people are mostly urban. The rise in educational attendance and age at marriage, coupled with high unemployment, have led to the extension of youth as a life stage – without, however, reducing the economic dependence of young people on the older generation. Growing economic inequalities threaten to disenfranchise a youthful population from the rights of citizenship. The development of a more participatory public sphere is predicated upon the restructuring of a political system that amounts to a gerontocracy. Young people in Turkey are caught between disillusionment with the promises of the nation-state and the hope of greater participation in what has become a transnational public sphere requiring new definitions of citizenship as well as of adulthood and youth. The issue for young people today is how to achieve (or maintain) the promises of modernity within conditions of neo-liberal globalization.

BIBLIOGRAPHY

F. Berktay, Has anything changed in the outlook of the Turkish left on women?, in Ş. Tekeli (ed.), *Women in modern Turkish society. A reader*, Atlantic Highlands, N.J. 1994, 250–62.

A. Kaya, Ethnic group discourses and German-Turkish youth, in G. G. Özdoğan and G. Tokay (eds.), *Redefining the nation state and citizen*, Istanbul 2000, 233–51.

Ş. Mardin, Youth and violence in Turkey, in *International Journal of Social Science* 29:2 (1977), 251–89.

——, The mobilization of youth. Western and Eastern, in J. Kcuzynski et al. (eds.), *Perspectives on contemporary youth*, Tokyo 1988, 235–48.

L. Neyzi, Object or subject? The paradox of "youth" in Turkey, in *International Journal of Middle East Studies*, 33:3 (August 2001), 411–32.

L. Peirce, Seniority, sexuality, and social order, in M. C. Zilfi (ed.), *Women in the Ottoman Empire. The vocabulary of gender in early modern Ottoman society*, Leiden 1997, 169–96.

LEYLA NEYZI

The United States

Youth cultures are distinct in that peer groups dominate social relationships. Of notable significance to Muslim youth is how interpretations of Islam influence the socialization of women. However, much of what is deemed appropriate behavior for girls in the name of religion stems from select interpretations of religious teachings in particular cultural settings. Interpretations of Islam, and the range of its application to youth behaviors in the United States, constitute the focus of this entry. While the topics covered are not necessarily exhaustive, they illustrate key issues regarding women and gender among Muslim youth in the United States, including the matters of dating, youth movements, and parent-child relations.

DATING

Youth culture in the United States centers on relations between boys and girls, with dating often the theme of movie plots, music, and school activities (for example, dances). Whether the Muslim family is liberal in its interpretations of Islam or heavily involved in organized religion, the main objection to dating by Muslim parents stems from the link it has to premarital sex, particularly for girls. Parents are likely to state their dislike of dating in general, but stress specifically their concern for daughters, upon whom restrictions are often more intensely enforced (Ajrouch 1999, Mohammad-Arif 2000). The tendency to apply strict religious teachings to a girl's behavior, predominantly her sexuality, stems from the patrilineal organization of the family, where obligation and group membership derive from identifying a child's father. It is also necessary to consider, however, that notions of "good girl" behavior do not apply exclusively to Muslim youth. As many groups based either on religious affiliation or national origins struggle to maintain an identity and produce a sense of belonging, socialization advocating "good girl" behavior weighs heavily in that effort. While similarities exist between Muslim youth and other ethnic groups in the United States, those parallels often go unrecognized due to a tendency to view Muslims as the cultural "other."

Applications of Islam to boy-girl relationships in the United States often include parents looking the other way when it concerns their sons' dating behaviors. A study focusing on children of Lebanese Muslim immigrants living in Dearborn, Michigan found that although girls' social activities are strictly monitored in Dearborn, boys frequently act under less supervision, and are given more freedom and autonomy to make choices about dating (Ajrouch 2000). This double standard links to beliefs that boys have little to lose should they engage in premarital sex (they cannot become pregnant), but is lodged in religious mandates about modesty.

Youth sometimes proactively seek out Islamic teachings because of this double standard, learning that the religion advocates similar standards and expectations for both boys and girls. This knowledge may influence Muslim youth in the United States to embrace a religious identity as a strategy to counter parental rules based on cultural traditions (Schmidt 2002). As such, some young Muslim women in the United States choose to wear *ḥijāb* (head covering) in the search for a Muslim identity (Naber 2002, Mohammad-Arif 2000, Shakir 1997). Those who make that choice often describe feeling protected, respected, and safe from unwanted male advances. The work of Nadine Naber (2002) illustrates how girls from Arab Muslim families adopt a "Muslim first, Arab second" approach to identity in order to challenge parental restrictions on public interactions and marriage choices.

The response among young women toward the United States norm of dating ranges from dating without their parents' consent or knowledge to organizing gender specific activities. For instance, a group of Muslim high school students in San Francisco, California organized a "Muslim Prom," where Muslim high school senior girls joined together, without boys, for an evening of dressing up, dancing, and eating, stopping only for evening prayers (Brown 2003). Also, a Muslim version of dating sometimes emerges in which a boy and girl may rendezvous, but time spent together always includes an adult chaperone, and the intent of dating involves plans to eventually marry. Dating for the simple pleasure of enjoying the company of the opposite sex is generally unacceptable (Haddad and Smith 1996).

Youth movements

The importance of gender relations to youth culture is also evident in youth movements. While movements based on Islam among youth whose parents or grandparents emigrated from an Islamic country are rare in the United States, youth organizations do emerge within religious institutions in an effort to increase interactions among Muslim youth. Depending on the institution, activities range from conservative events such as religious lectures to more liberal associations such as picnics and dances.

One persistent youth organization, founded in 1963, is the Muslim Student Association. It was established at University of Illinois Urbana-Champaign by a group of foreign Muslim graduate students who organized as a means to foster support for one another (Mohammad-Arif 2000). Forty years later, this organization exists on college campuses across the United States, now mainly comprised of United States born and/or raised Muslim youth wishing to carry out Islamic programs and projects. Campus activism frequently involves coordinating to fight for justice and reform in the United States political system (Schmidt 2002). Muslim youth also often organize on college campuses to protest against United States foreign policy (Naber 2002).

Observers of youth movements on college campuses note the tendency to build a religious affiliation into an ethnic identity (Schmidt 2002). In other words, an Islamic identity emerges, void of culture, distancing Muslim youth from both mainstream American culture and the culture of their immigrant parents (Hermansen 2003). Hermansen highlights disquieting trends within Muslim youth movements including a lack of intellectual analysis of their situation, promulgation of rigid norms (for example, *ḥijāb* for women, beards for men), and discouragement from studying the humanities or pursuing social science careers. Gender relations figure prominently in such movements, particularly the tendency for Muslim youth to announce their difference from American youth by ensuring gender segregation at campus events. Separating young men from young women allows Muslim youth not only to differentiate themselves from their non-Muslim American peers, but also to claim moral superiority in that they adhere to religious teaching about modesty and protect themselves from potential sexually charged situations. Hermansen suggests that such tendencies may result from adolescent anxieties.

Islam has also inspired youth movements among African American adolescents. One such movement, for example, called Five Percenters, emerged in the 1960s in Harlem, New York as a splinter group from the Nation of Islam (Nuruddin 1994). Adherents believe that they are the 5 percent of humanity who understand true Islam and are dedicated to living a righteous life. They view Islam as a natural way of life as opposed to viewing it as a religion. A focus on the young black male is central. While this movement has been applauded for the self-esteem it nurtures among adolescent males, representing a subculture that speaks directly to disenchanted youth, it builds in part on an explicit ideology that men are superior to women. This ideology is found in official declarations such as the belief that only men can attain perfection, and that the highest level women may reach is one step below perfection. Women are also viewed as dangerous in that while they may use their "magnetic" qualities for good, that is, to bear a child, they also may use those qualities for sexual promiscuity. Interestingly, African American youth often outgrow the Five Percenter ideology, in search of "mature" outlets for political and spiritual energies. Many of those who were Five Percenters in the mid 1960s and 1970s became mainstream Muslims as adults (Nuruddin 1994).

Parent-child relations

Youth culture generally encompasses young people between the ages of 12 and 20.

While many youths are relatively compliant, youth cultures among Muslims in the United States are notable for the tensions that exist in relationships with parents and with dominant cultural norms. For instance, among South Asian Muslim youth in the United States, tensions between immigrant parents and United States born children often result in a double identity for youth (Mohammad-Arif 2000). As South Asian Muslims in the United States often live in upper middle-class suburbs, youth respond to pressure from their American peers, sometimes engaging in activities about which parents do not know, such as meeting friends of the opposite sex, or listening to rap music. They retain a desire to please parents, but they also acquire "American" traits such as independence and autonomy. Interestingly, once South Asian Muslim youth attend university, they often shed the need to fit in in favor of a quest to get back to their roots. Contrary to trends in the homeland or in Europe, South Asian Muslim parents in the United States value a university education for both daughters and sons. While restrictions on social activities and a stated desire for arranged marriages is prevalent among South Asian Muslim parents, they express a determination to ensure that their daughters receive the same opportunities for university education as do their sons (Mohammad-Arif 2000). However, the preferred areas of study include those where children may be assured of economic success. Children often enter the parentally sanctioned fields initially (for example, medicine), but then later switch to the areas they find most personally satisfying, much to the dismay of their parents.

Those young women who learn to navigate the two cultures, that of their parents and that of the dominant culture, will undoubtedly benefit from both worlds. However, the situation may arise where they embrace one culture over the other. Muslim girls occupy a unique position in that conforming to parental values constitutes a deviation from dominant cultural norms yet conforming to dominant cultural norms likely challenges parental values. Girls from Muslim families living in the United States must negotiate between two worlds, and two sets of cultural values that often seem incompatible. Whether a person is a child of immigrants, third generation, or a member of a family that converted to Islam, the influence of religion on gender roles, however indirect, permeates the youth experience.

As a final note, it is difficult to speak of Muslim youth in the United States as one monolithic category. National origins range from the Middle East, to Southeastern Asia, to Africa, to converts within the United States. The interplay between religion, culture, and race produces a myriad of situations such that it is impossible to posit a universal Muslim youth culture.

Bibliography

K. J. Ajrouch, Family and ethnic identity in an Arab American Community, in M. Suleiman (ed.), *Arabs in America. Toward a new future*, Philadelphia 1999, 129–39.

——, Place, age, and culture. Community living and ethnic identity among Lebanese American adolescents, in *Small Group Research* 31 (2000), 447–69.

P. L. Brown, At Muslim Prom, it's a girls-only night out, in *New York Times*, 9 June 2003, A20.

Y. Y. Haddad and J. I. Smith, Islamic values among American Muslims, in B. C. Aswad and B. Bilgé (eds.), *Family and gender among American Muslims*, Philadelphia 1996, 19–40.

M. Hermansen, How to put the genie back in the bottle? "Identity" Islam and Muslim youth cultures in America, in O. Safid (ed.), *Progressive Muslims*, Oxford 2003, 306–19.

A. Mohammad-Arif, A masala identity. Young South Asian Muslims in the U.S., in *Comparative Studies of South Asia, Africa, and the Middle East* 20 (2000), 67–87.

N. Naber, Arab San Francisco. On gender, cultural citizenship and belonging, Ph.D. diss., Department of Anthropology, University of California, Davis 2002.

Y. Nuruddin, The Five Percenters. A teenage nation of gods and earths, in Y. Y. Haddad and J. I. Smith (eds.), *Muslim communities in North America*, New York 1994, 109–32.

G. Schmidt, Dialectics of authenticity. Examples of ethnification of Islam among young Muslims in Sweden and the United States, in *Muslim World* 92 (2002), 1–17.

E. Shakir, *Bint Arab. Arab and Arab American women in the United States*, Westport, Conn. 1997.

Kristine Ajrouch

Western Europe

Muslim youth in Western Europe do not belong to one monolitic category. A variety of conditions must be taken into consideration including the sociopolitical context of each country, the differing social position and cultural origin of their families, and the fact that both natives and immigrants are included in this classification. This entry deals with changes in the understanding of Islamic beliefs and practices among young Muslim women born or raised since early childhood in Europe. The key issues for these current changes are the individualization of the faith, the empowerment of young Muslim women through education, the growing importance of youth associations, and the use of diversity as a resource for participation.

Individualization of the faith

For youth who live in Europe, being Muslim is a question of personal choice. In contrast to their parents, they feel that they have become Muslims after undergoing an individual quest which has led them to emphasize the ethical and spiritual dimensions of Islam rather than the normative aspects (Babès 1997, Moreno Alvarez 2001). As with other young people, religiousness is one subjective resource among many others with which to construct a personal identity that is always changing and complex (Tietze 2002). Young Muslim women actively reinterpret the religious traditions of their parents, selecting some aspects and deciding against others in such a way as to create a sense of meaning in their lives. They criticize patriarchal customs by distinguishing religion from local traditions that have been confused with Islam by their parents (Saint-Blancat 2003). For example, they generally refuse an arranged marriage and wish to choose their husband even if his national origins differ from that of their parents The important issue for many is that he should be a "true Muslim" and not simply a Muslim by tradition.

All these elements show a process of individualization of the Islamic faith, which does not mean that religion is enclosed in a private space, as we will see in the next key issues.

Empowerment through education

Young Muslim women have increased their autonomy by becoming engaged in professional or academic preparation (Amiraux 2000). Their studies bring changes in power relationships inside the family, with traditional gender roles being questioned. A wider access to Islamic knowledge and recourse to produce it on their own is of notable significance to Muslim girls. As in other religions, male experts have been the sole possessors of religious authority for a long time, but now a generation of Muslim women experts is emerging. They are developing an innovative theological commentary that enables them to defend their human rights in a religious perspective and to assume a key position between the Muslim communities and society as a whole (Jonker 2003).

Youth associations

Many girls join Muslim associations for family reasons: parents or brothers already take part in them. By choosing a Muslim youth association they are more easily able to meet peers, and to develop and discuss their religious knowledge in a protected social environment as it has been understood by their parents. A common result of those encounters is that Muslim girls are silently gaining autonomy (Amiraux 2000). As it happens these associations become an environment in which they meet peers, and in which religion is merely a possible topic of common interest. Trips and visits to the cinema and other sources of entertainment are provided, with the spiritual dimension of the association not always evident. In this way many Muslim girls are learning to participate in civil society. In some European countries Muslim youth associations are connected with other youth organizations (not only religious ones) and they are working on common themes (for example peace or human rights). In 1995 the JMF (Jeunes musulmans de France), the YMUK (Young Muslims UK), and the SUM (Sveriges Unga Muslimer) first promoted a network of youth associations. Since 1996 several Muslim youth organizations from different European countries have created the FEMYSO (Forum of European Muslim Youth and Student Organizations), which is now a well-known INGO (international non-governmental organization) composed of 37 associations. FEMYSO is a member of the European Youth Forum.

Diversity as a resource for participation

In the present historical and political context of global war and Islamophobia, Islam is often construed negatively and thus stigmatized by others. European Muslim youth identities are forged in reaction to negative and essentialist representations of both Islam and immigrants (Vertovec and Rogers 1998). Some scholars have underscored the exclusion and the social marginalization of these youths (Khosrokahvar 1997) and interpreted the proclaiming of their religious diversity as a reversal of the stigma, as a sort of withdrawal to the community, and as a social rebellion against the social majority. Recent studies have indicated the social and political involvement of those young Muslims who clearly express a desire to contribute to the development of the European society to which they feel they belong (Lathion 2002, Bouzar and Kada 2003). For these youths, religious identification with Islam becomes a resource for participation in civil society. This is expecially true for the girls who wear the *ḥijāb* and feel they are victims of an overt stigmatization due to their high level of visibility. This level of recognition often leads to a sense of responsibility for the girls who are ever more frequently called upon by the society in which they live to act as intercultural mediators and social brokers, and to daily reconstruct new social bonds.

It is not only a question of demanding recognition of the right to diversity. It is also a request to be considered as equals and to take part in the public sphere in the development of social and political projects in common with other citizens.

The information presented here is not intended to be exhaustive, but rather to illustrate key issues of the main social and cultural changes regarding European Muslim girls. As with all changes there are obstacles to be overcome in terms of the European society, the families, and the religious communities to which these youths belong.

Bibliography

V. Amiraux, *Jeunes musulmanes turques d'Allemagne. Voix et voies de l'individuation*, in F. Dassetto (ed.), *Paroles d'islam. Individus, sociétés et discours dans l'islam européen contemporain*, Paris 2000.
L. Babès, *L'islam positif*, Paris 1997.
D. Bouzar and S. Kada, *L'une voilée, l'autre pas*, Paris 2003.
G. Jonker, Islamic knowledge through a woman's lens. Education, power and belief, in *Social Compass* 50:1 (2003), 35–46.
F. Khosrokhavar, *L'islam des jeunes*, Paris 1997.
S. Lathion, *La jeunesse européenne vers une identité commune?*, in *Cahiers d'études sur la Méditerranée orientale et le monde turco-iranien* 33 (January–June 2002), 109–25.
L. F. Moreno Alvarez, *El islam positivo. La religión de los jóvenes musulmanes en España*, in *Migraciones* (Madrid) 10 (2001), 249–94.
C. Saint-Blancat, La transmission de l'islam auprès des nouvelles générations de la diaspora, in Social Compass 51:2 (2004), 235–47.
N. Tietze, *Jeunes musulmans de France et d'Allemagne. Les constructions subjectives de l'identité*, Paris 2002.
S. Vertovec and A. Rogers, *Muslim European youth. Reproducing ethnicity, religion, culture*, Aldershot, England 1998.

Annalisa Frisina

Zoroastrian Women

Overview

The history of Zoroastrian women stretches back at least two thousand years. The focus of this entry is on Zoroastrian women living in Iran, a society that became Muslim in its majority. Today there are possibly twenty thousand Zoroastrians in Iran. It examines their situation from ancient times to the present, with special consideration of women's role in religious ceremonies.

Historical evidence

Until the end of the second millenium B.C.E. and the beginning of the first millenium B.C.E., in what is today Iran, conditions for women were relatively superior compared to subsequent developments. There is written evidence from the ancient province of Ilam (which includes today's Khuzistan) and the love stories of *Shāhnāma* (Book of Kings) also suggest the favorable position of women (Mazdāpūr, 1975).

In Gāhān, the oldest and most authentic section of the Avista (Avesta, the central scripture of Zoroastrianism), versified by Zoroaster himself, women and men are invited to perform religious and social duties together and the promise of salvation extends to both sexes. In other sections, Avista addresses both women and men (Yasnā 35, 6). The book salutes and prays for both men and women. Nonetheless, the patriarchal structure of social institutions is clearly expressed in Avista and other ancient Iranian writings. The frequency with which Avista addresses men and the heavier duties ascribed to them makes apparent men's pre-eminence in the social hierarchy. By studying ancient texts and graphic archeological remains, we can trace through history this male superiority, which reached its zenith after the establishment of Islam in Iran.

The title *dēnak* places the grandmother as the head of the dynasty in the Sasanian tablets. The names of queens and goddesses are also mentioned here and there. We know of the female royal titles *dukhshī* and *wis-dukht* (Benveniste 1966, 24–50, Brosius 1998, 183–4) and other noble and religious titles in the Soghdian language as well. Sasanian lay women had signets that testified to their economic activity. Royal women had their own assistants and property. Nevertheless, these indications of female high status gradually give way to male values.

The Sasanian family, or *dūdag*, has an intricate structure, from the extended family in antiquity to the modern nuclear family. At the head of the family was *dūdag-sālār*, invariably a male. Women and children were in his custody. He represented the family to the outside world and society to his household. Existing manuscripts present him as the owner of properties and even of family members whom he had the right to sell. This contradicts the rights of women and children to property mentioned by some sources. Either the laws were not consistent or refer to special circumstances. From Vandīdād (Fargard 15:11, 13, 15), it appears that a woman was sometimes in the custody of her father, husband, brother, or son, and sometimes free, or *khawd-sālār*. A *khawd-sālār* woman could appear before a court of law as a witness or serve as a judge (Mazdāpūr 1990, 80–1).

In Sasanian society there were many kinds of marriage, for example, *pādikhshā zanīh*, *stūr zanīh*, *ayōkēn zanīh*, and *chakar zanīh*. In *pādikhshā zanīh*, the consent of the woman and the family head are required. Her *sālār* is her husband or his father. She could, under certain conditions, become her husband's absolute equal – *hanbāaz*. Such a marriage was sexual, economic, and ceremonial. It was considered eternal. *Stūr zanīh* (and a particular type of it, *ayōkēn zanīh*) was strictly ceremonial with an economic component. When a girl with this kind of nominal marriage married, her real marriage was called *chakar zanīh*. A woman's second marriage was also called *chakar zanīh*, but had no economic implications. She was still eternally wed to her first husband, and her actual husband could adopt one or several of her children. A boy who was born from a *pādikhshā zanīh* or *stūr zanīh* marriage, or was a *padīriftag* (stepson), could reach *dūdag sālārī* at the age of 15. If a *pādikhshāyīh* wife remarried after her husband's death, the man in the second marriage was not called her husband unless the authorities agreed to it and allowed him to be the *sālār* of the family.

These intricate relationships needed explanation even in the Pahlavī texts from the ninth century C.E., for example, *Ravāyat-i umīd ashawahishtān*, where their ambiguity subjected them to inquiry. This evolving trend has resulted in the modern nuclear family in the Zoroastrian community.

Choosing the head of the household and the dividing the inheritance among the living members was the duty of the father and the head of the family (Mazdāpūr 1990, 80, 86), even though the *kadagbānūg* (housewife) could choose the *dūdagsālār* after the death of her husband.

The contemporary Zoroastrian family is monogamous and children take the father's surname. The Zoroastrian wife, like other Iranian women, usually continues to carry her father's name after marriage. There are special marriage and divorce registries for Zoroastrians in Tehran, Yazd, Kirman, and Ardakan.

A wife could not be divorced without her consent according to Pahlavī texts. In modern times, and before the 1967 Family Protection Law, there was no official divorce in the traditional Zoroastrian community. Subsequently, divorce became common, with a sudden increase recently, and no *mahr* (or *kābīn*) for women.

The *pādikhshāyīh* wife's inheritance from her husband was equal to that of the *pādikhshāyīh*'s son from his father. Her husband could not nullify her inheritance in his will. The *mahr* was considered the husband's debt and had to be paid from his estate before all other payments. A daughter's inheritance from the father was half that of a brother. The economic relationship of the *chakar* wives was based on an agreement. At various points in time *chakar* children took from half the *pādikhshāyīh* children's inheritance to none at all. Today, a daughter's inheritance is equal to that of a son but may be altered by agreement. It is not customary to distribute the inheritance while one of the parents is alive, unless all inheritors agree. Of course, contemporary Zoroastrians can also use the state laws. According to the Iranian Islamic Inheritance Law (Article 881), if there is a Muslim in the family, non-Muslims cannot inherit. There is evidence that many Zoroastrians in the past converted to Islam to take advantage of this distinction.

A good part of the extant jurisprudential ancient texts deal with female-related taboos, such as menstruation and impurities associated with pregnancy, and their attendant purification. During menstruation and after childbirth, women were banned from participating in social and religious ceremonies. Therefore women could not be priests or achieve other official religious positions. They were also prohibited from holding positions that required attendance every day. Such prohibitions and purifications are no longer followed except in religious ceremonies.

Although there is no formal evidence, Zoroastrian women are believed on average to enjoy better health and more comforts of modern living than other women in Iran. Higher educational levels, the establishment of Zoroastrian hospitals, and the availability of trained obstetricians gradually altered the practice of home birth, especially in cities. Even though rural women are still largely deprived of proper medical care, they have had access to services for the past 60 years.

Zoroastrian women today

The Islamic community's measures to convert others to Islam put pressure on the Zoroastrian community (Boyce 2001, 145–215). This weighed heavier on Zoroastrian women. When the powerful Zoroastrian community of the Sasanian period submitted to laws that were unfavorable to them, the role of Zoroastrian women was greatly transformed. It was left to Zoroastrian women to raise their children to cleave to the ancestral religion under difficult circumstances and tolerate deprivations to protect their ancient way of life. At the same time, Zoroastrians were able to establish, albeit with some distance, a friendly relationship with a majority that considered them impure and imposed the *jizya* (poll tax) on them.

When the *jizya* was abolished in 1882, the Zoroastrian community moved closer to equality with other Iranians and achieved better living conditions. With the forced unveiling of women (1936), Zoroastrian women often abandoned their traditional colorful clothing whose details and adornments were different from the clothing of Muslims. Even though many women remained faithful to their way of life, there are few visible differences between Zoroastrian and non-Zoroastrian women today.

Modernity and new research into the Zoroastrian religion and customs have changed the general public's perception of Zoroastrians. Iranian Muslims have long considered Zoroastrians to be a sincere and honest community. It is even possible currently to detect a kind of nostalgia for the ancient past. Although in Iranian society today a Zoroastrian woman is first an Iranian, she is still subject to discrimination on the basis of her religion. The biggest injustice was the unequal *diya* (compensation) allotted to non-Muslims, especially women. Recently, a law abolished this inequity. There is ample evidence that until recent times, Zoroastrians, especially young girls, were forced to convert to Islam. They were denied employment or education, often when their merits qualified them.

In modern Iranian society, Zoroastrian women are largely like other women and often benefit from the prevailing laws and state facilities, except in certain circumstances. Zoroastrian women no longer dress in distinctive clothing and avoid other limitations to activity; with certain restrictions, they can enter various educational fields and occupations – from medicine, teaching, and state employment to menial work. Often, their lives are indistinguishable from the lives of other Iranian women. True, the small Zoroastrian population and its scattered situation, resulting from migrations, creates certain problems, especially for women at the age of marriage. But in general, the doors to better lives are not closed to Zoroastrian women and girls, and within the old structures, most can cope with current conditions.

Education

From the distant past, the education of Zoroastrian girls has been acceptable. Knowledgeable and experienced women in the neighborhood conducted private instruction. They taught various kinds of housework, from washing dishes, sewing patterns, and knitting, to taking care of sheep, and sometimes even reading and writing. This tradition can perhaps be attributed to the emphasis that Pahlavī texts placed on girls' education (Navvābī 1976, 474, Mazdāpūr 1990, 104). Illustrations of female education are also found in early books, such as *Mādāyan-ī Hazār Dādistān*. They indicate that women were familiar with difficult court rulings and were well versed in the law (Mazdāpūr 1990, 105).

Beginning in the nineteenth century, Zoroastrian girls attended Christian missionary and American girls' schools and later girls' schools were established in Yazd, Kirman, and Tehran. The first such school was established in Kirman in 1892. The percentages of literate Zoroastrian girls at the end of the Qājār period is noteworthy (Amini, 210–11). Today, the number of illiterate Zoroastrian women is negligible.

The oldest Zoroastrian girls' schools, which are still in existence, were founded in 1908. The most famous is in Tehran (Anūshīravān Dādgar, established in 1936). Today, of the approximately 50 Zoroastrian schools, 20 are girls' schools. From the beginning, the staff and students in these schools were often composed of both Zoroastrians and non-Zoroastrians.

Employment

Teaching and school administration in Tehran and other big cities as well as in rural areas with more traditional schools were the first forms of employment for women in the modern period. Next were midwifery and nursing, and a wide array of other vocations including university-level teaching, state employment, journalism, medicine, painting, and commerce. There was also the maintenance and cleaning of other Zoroastrian homes and the fire altars and other tasks linked with religious ceremonies, which have always been customary among Zoroastrians.

In former times, women performed what today would be considered masculine work, such as the grafting of trees and animal husbandry. There are reports of Zoroastrian women midwives and *hakīms* (healers) who practiced medicine and orthopedics. In the absence of men who had to pay their *jizya* with their labor or who went searching for income-producing labor, women were forced to run household and farm and to manage the household expenses after the payment of *jizya*. Once they completed the arduous farm work and household tasks, they turned to their traditional duties, such as weaving fabrics or textiles, making shirts and wool clothing, and sewing and stitching.

Women no longer sew old, intricate patterns on clothes. Traditional domestic weaving looms can no longer compete with factory-produced fabrics. Zoroastrian woven products required skill and were different from those of the Muslims. They varied according to the fabric and the use for which they were intended. Nowadays, there are only a handful of looms in operation. While the spinning of cotton has been abandoned, spinning wool is still practiced and women still knit wool clothing. Formerly, to save fuel and heat, girls and young women gathered in the winter and work together in a designated place.

The gender division of labor was rooted in the Pahlavī text, *Ardā-Wirāf Nāmag*, which attributes man's sins generally to his labor and employment, while the woman's are fixed in her sexuality and her relationship with her children (Mazdāpūr 1990, 108). While the text lauds the role of woman in farming and animal husbandry, it disapproves vocations thought to encourage impurity or sinful behavior. Thus, wet-nursing is prohibited because of the possibility that a mother might inflict damage on her own child. Prostitution is an absolute sin. In Pahlavī texts, the source of a female prostitute's sinfulness lies in the mixing of men's sperm (*shuhr gumīzishnīh*) inside a woman's womb. Any man who has unsanctioned sex with a woman will acquire all her sins and she all his spiritual reward. The Zoroastrian community, at least in the modern age, lacks women prostitutes.

Aside from royalty, women are not mentioned in Zoroastrian history. A woman who played a determining role in changes in Iranian society is Gulistān Bānū from Kirman. She emigrated to India in 1795 and influenced Indian Zoroastrians to come to the aid of their fellow Zoroastrians in Iran. The Gulistān Dakhmah (Tower of Silence) in Kirman and another in Yazd are named after her. The Zoroastrian cemetery in Tehran (Qaṣr-i Firūza) is named after the wife of its founder, Arbāb Kaykhusraw Shahrūkh. Today, two Zoroastrian women are acknowledged: Bānū-yi Khādim-i Pīr-i Sabz (d. 1987), and Farangīs Shahrūkh (Yeganegi) (b. 1916). The late Bānū-yi Khādim-i, whose ancestors served the Pīr-i Sabz sanctuary, or Chakchak, for seven generations, stayed in the sanctuary by herself or with another person for 21 years. She lived on an isolated mountain to perform her service. Her strength and solitude bestowed upon her a magnificent and unique status in the Zoroastrian community. In a way, Bānū has become a spiritual figure. Farangīs Khānum is the face of the modern Zoroastrian woman. She worked to introduce Zoroastrian women to modern culture. Thanks to her efforts, Iranian handicrafts revived and flourished. She founded Zoroastrian women's associations and helped shape the coeducational Center for Zoroastrian University Students in Tehran (1967). The Ancient Iranian Cultural Society, established in Tehran in 1961, was also the result of her initiative. Currently, there are many professional Zoroastrian women both in Iran and among Iranian immigrants abroad.

The Zoroastrian Women's Organizations in Tehran (founded 1950) and Yazd are both presently active. These organizations engage in charity work and provide many kinds of assistance. Women are also members of the Society of Zoroastrians of Tehran and other cities.

Female figures in religious rituals

Although Zoroastrian women cannot become priests because of entrenched taboos related to impurities associated with childbirth and menstruation, female family members of priests sometimes participate in activities that have religious significance, such as sewing the *kushtī*, the sacred belt of the Zoroastrians. Sometimes they participate in religious ablutions as well. Such tasks, as well as serving ceremonial foods, are mainly performed by postmenopausal women. Women's main role in religious events, however, is to observe the traditional everyday religious customs and prepare ceremonial foods. Sometimes this responsibility translated into a woman's profession. Although men also cooked for guests, the preparation of ceremonial foods was women's special domain.

In Gāhān, the name Pūrūchīstā (holder of much knowledge, Yasnā 53, 2), the youngest daughter of Zoroaster, is mentioned. The prophet expects her to use her own wisdom and select a husband who embodies wisdom. In the non-Gāhān Avista (Younger Avista), several women are mentioned, especially in Farvardīn-yasht, where respect is paid to those who have passed away. Some of these women were real historical figures, but they are mentioned less often than men. In *Bundahish*, which is written in the Pahlavī language, there is a mention of 15 immortal women and 15 men. None of the women's names have survived.

As in the Semitic religions, the Zoroastrians speak of angels, male and female. Upon closer examination, it becomes clear that the sex distinctions were rooted in the grammatical structure of the language. In Gāhān, out of six Ameshaspentas, who are equal to esteemed angels, three are male and three are female. Also, in the complete Gāhān, we find the names of Daēnā (Pahlavī, Dēn, conscience) and Ashī (the reward of good deeds), who in the Younger Avista are both identified as goddesses. In the Younger Avista, numerous female gods are also mentioned, most prominent among them Anāhītā. Her name is in the epigraphs of the second period of Achaemenid kings. It is generally accepted that the growth of the religion of Anāhītā or Nāhīd is owed to the influence of Mesopotamian goddesses, namely the Sumerian Inanna, the Akkadian Ishtar, and possibly the indigenous Nana. Anāhītā is the most famous Zoroastrian goddess and is better known than Spəntā ārmaitī or Sepandārmaz, the superior Gāhānic goddess.

Today well-known shrines play a major role in Zoroastrian rituals: Chakchak or Pīr-i Sabz, Pīr-i Nāraki, Pīr-i Bānū-yi Pars, Pīr-i Hrisht, Seti Pīr, and Pīr-i Naristāna. According to the prayer books (*ziyāratnāma*), these sacred sites served as hiding places for Zoroastrians. When a foreign enemy was closing in and the possibility of capture was at its greatest, the mountains and earth hid them. Other than Pīr-i Naristāna and another sacred site, far from Yazd, these shrines are all named for women and girls.

Finally, female figures play a role in various sacred Zoroastrian banquets. In recent years, these banquets have become very important and although they contain no particular religious element and priests are not in attendance, people have fervently turned to them. They consist of the banquet of the daughter of Shāh-i Parian (the ruler of fairies), the banquet of Bībī Si'Shanbah, the banquet of Nukhūd-i Mushgil'gosha (which eases and resolves difficulties), and the banquet of Bahman Amishaspand. Among these, the banquets of the daughter of Shāh-i Parian and Bībī Si'Shanbah are named after women, and in the story of the other two, women play important roles. Women are responsible for carrying out the detailed ceremonies of all four banquets.

BIBLIOGRAPHY

T. Amīnī, *Asnādī az Zartushtiyān-i muʿāṣir-i Īrān (1258–1338 Sh.)*, Tehran 2001.

C. Bartholomae, *Uber ein sasanidisches Reshtsbuch*, Heidelberg 1910.

E. Benveniste, *Titres et noms propres en iranien ancien*, Paris 1966.

M. Boyce, *Zoroastrians. Their religious beliefs and practices*, New York 2001.

M. Brosius, *Women in ancient Persia (559–331 BC)*, New York 1998.

K. H. Gould, Outside the discipline, inside the experience. Women in Zoroastrianism, in A. Sharma (ed.), *Religion and women*, Albany, N.Y. 1994, 139–82.

K. Mazdāpūr, Nishān-ha-yi zan-sarvārī dar chand izdivāj-i dāstāni-i Shāhnāmah, in *Farhang va zindagī* 19:20 (1975), 94–120.

——, Zan dar ʿa'in-e Zartushtī, in Mārkiz-i Farangī-Sīnimāyī, *Ḥayāt-i ijtimāʿī-i zan dar tārīkh-i Īrān*, Tehran 1990, 42–111.

M. Navvābī, *Andarz-i āzurbud mārsipindān*, Tehran 1976.

A. Perkhanian, *The book of a thousand judgements (A Sassanian law-book)*, trans. N. Gasoian, Costa Mesa 1997.

M. Shaki, The Sassanian matrimonial relations, in *Archiv Orientalni* 39 (1971), 322–45.

K. Shārukh, *Yāddāshthā-yi Kaykhusraw Shāhrukh. The memoirs of Keikhosrow Shahrokh*, ed. and trans. S. Shahrokh and R. Writer, Lewiston, N.Y. 1994.

G. Ushīdarī, *Tārīkh-i Pahlavī va Zartushtīyān*, Tehran 1976.

KATAYUN MAZDAPOUR

Name Index

Subject Index